PSYCHOLOGY

FIRST CANADIAN EDITION

JOHN W. SANTROCK

University of Texas at Dallas

JOHN O. MITTERER

Brock University

 **McGraw-Hill Ryerson**

Toronto Montréal Burr Ridge, IL Dubuque, IA Madison, WI New York San Francisco St. Louis
Bangkok Beijing Bogotá Caracas Kuala Lumpur Lisbon London Madrid Mexico City Milan
New Delhi Santiago Seoul Singapore Sydney Taipei

McGraw-Hill
Ryerson Limited
A Subsidiary of The **McGraw·Hill** *Companies*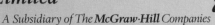

PSYCHOLOGY
First Canadian Edition

ISBN: 0-07-087132-9

2 3 4 5 6 7 8 9 10   TCP   0 9 8 7 6 5 4 3 2

Printed and bound in Canada

Vice President and Editorial Director: *Pat Ferrier*
Senior Sponsoring Editor: *Veronica Visentin*
Associate Sponsoring Editor: *Marianne Minaker*
Marketing Manager: *Ralph Courtney*
Supervising Editor: *Julie van Veen*
Copy Editor: *Gillian Scobie*
Production Coordinator: *Brad Madill*
Compositor: *Bookman Typesetting Co.*
Cover Design: *Dianna Little*
Interior Design: *Diane Beasley*
Cover Image Courtesy of Kinsman Robinson Galleries, Toronto. Copyright Norval Morrisseau.
Printer: *Transcontinental Printing*

Canadian Cataloguing in Publication Data

Santrock, John W.
  Psychology

1st Canadian ed.
Includes bibliographical references and index.
ISBN 0-07-087132-9

1. Psychology.   I. Mitterer, John Otto, 1950–   .   II. Title.

BF121.S267 2000   150   C00-930512-2

With special appreciation
to my wife Mary Jo
—John Santrock

For Elizabeth and Otto,
my mother and father, and for
Heather, my spiritual partner
—John Mitterer

About the Authors

John W. Santrock

John Santrock received his Ph.D. from the University of Minnesota in 1973. He taught at the University of Charleston and the University of Georgia before joining the psychology department at the University of Texas at Dallas. He was recently a member of the editorial board of *Developmental Psychology.* His research on father custody is widely cited and used in expert witness testimony to promote flexibility and alternative considerations in custody disputes. John has also authored these exceptional McGraw-Hill texts: *Child Development,* Eighth Edition, *Life-Span Development,* Seventh Edition, *Children,* Fifth Edition, and *Adolescence,* Seventh Edition. He is co-author, with Jane Halonen, of *Psychology, the Contexts of Behavior,* Third Edition.

John O. Mitterer

John Mitterer was awarded his B.A. from the University of Calgary in 1974 and his Ph.D. from McMaster University in 1981. His primary research focus has been the application of technology in education. He has carried out and published basic research and consulted with numerous companies. He makes extensive use of multimedia in his lectures and has been invited to talk about his approach to lecturing at many conferences. John's research and teaching foci have converged in his multimedia work. He has produced several videodiscs and CD-ROMs for first-year introductory psychology courses, and has been a Webmaster for the Brock University Psychology Department.

John Santrock has been teaching introductory psychology since the 1960s and continues to teach a range of undergraduate psychology courses.

Introductory psychology has been John Mitterer's primary teaching focus for almost 20 years. He also currently teaches a course on the psychology of men.

Brief Contents

CHAPTER

1 What Is Psychology? 2

2 Psychology's Scientific Methods 32

3 Biological Foundations and Neuroscience 64

4 Sensation and Perception 100

5 States of Consciousness 148

6 Learning 184

7 Memory 216

8 Thinking and Language 252

9 Intelligence 284

10 Human Development 318

11 Motivation and Emotion 366

12 Personality 410

13 Abnormal Psychology 446

14 Therapies 478

15 Health Psychology 514

16 Social Psychology 548

Contents

SUMMARY TABLES xv
PREFACE xvii

CHAPTER

1

What Is Psychology? 2

- IMAGES OF PSYCHOLOGY AND LIFE
  Why Youth Kill 3
Exploring Psychology 4
  Defining Psychology 5
  The Beginnings of Psychology as a Science 6
  Early and Contemporary Approaches to
    Psychology 7
- THINKING ABOUT PSYCHOLOGY AND LIFE
  Saddam Hussein and Mother Teresa 14
Psychology and Life: What Matters 17
  Biological Processes Matter 17
  Environmental Processes Matter 17
  Mental Processes Matter 18
  The Social World Matters 19
  Culture Matters 19
  Individual Variations Matter 20
  Science Matters 20
  Conceptual Diversity Matters 21
  Controversies Matter 21
  Critical Thinking Matters 22
Psychology's Careers and Areas
  of Specialization 22
- EXPLORATIONS IN PSYCHOLOGY
  From Horoscopes to the Sex Lives of Tigers 23
  Careers in Psychology 24
  Areas of Specialization in Psychology 24
- THINKING ABOUT PSYCHOLOGY AND LIFE
  *Which Areas of Psychology Interest You
  the Most?* 27

CHAPTER

2

Psychology's Scientific Methods 32

- IMAGES OF PSYCHOLOGY AND LIFE
  Scientific Research and You 33
Scientific Research and the Scientific Method 34
  Exploring the Science Side of Psychology 34
  The Scientific Method and Its Steps 35
- THINKING ABOUT PSYCHOLOGY AND LIFE
  *Participating in Psychological Experiments on the
  Net* 35
Who Will the Participants Be? 37
Research Methods 40
  Observation 40
- EXPLORATIONS IN PSYCHOLOGY
  Hans, the Clever Horse 41
  Interviews and Questionnaires 43
  Case Studies 43
  Standardized Tests 44
  Physiological Research 44
  Correlational Research 45
  Experimental Research 46
- THINKING ABOUT PSYCHOLOGY AND LIFE
  Isn't Everyone a Psychologist? 47
- THINKING ABOUT PSYCHOLOGY AND LIFE
  No Magic Bullet 49
  Multiple Research Methods 49
Research Challenges 51
  Ethics and Values 51
- EXPLORATIONS IN PSYCHOLOGY
  Psychology and Values 54
  Gender, Culture, and Ethnicity 54
  Reading and Understanding Research Journals 56
  Being a Wise Consumer of Information
    About Psychology 57

3 Biological Foundations and Neuroscience 64

- IMAGES OF PSYCHOLOGY AND LIFE
  - *The Jim and Jim Twins* 65

Biological Foundations 66
  - Heredity 66
  - The Evolutionary Perspective 68
  - Nature and Nurture 69

- THINKING ABOUT PSYCHOLOGY AND LIFE
  - *Nature, Nurture, and Politics* 69

The Field of Neuroscience, the Nervous System, and Neurons 70
  - The Field of Neuroscience 70
  - The Organization of the Nervous System 71
  - Neurons 72
  - Glial Cells 78

Brain Structure and Function 79
  - Embryological Development and Levels in the Brain 80
  - Neocortex 84
  - The Cerebral Hemispheres and Split-Brain Research 87

- THINKING ABOUT PSYCHOLOGY AND LIFE
  - *Your Brain and Your Behavior* 87
  - Integration of Function in the Brain 88

- EXPLORATIONS IN PSYCHOLOGY
  - *Left-Brain, Right-Brain Myths* 89

Exploring the Brain 91
  - Brain Damage, Plasticity, and Repair 91

- EXPLORATIONS IN PSYCHOLOGY
  - *The Brains of the Mankato Nuns* 92
  - Techniques for Studying the Brain 93
  - The Brain and the Endocrine System 95

4 Sensation and Perception 100

- IMAGES OF PSYCHOLOGY AND LIFE
  - *To Feel or Not to Feel?* 101

Detecting and Perceiving the World 102
  - Defining Sensation and Perception 102
  - Thresholds 102

- EXPLORATIONS IN PSYCHOLOGY
  - *Analyzing Subliminal Perception* 104
  - Signal Detection Theory 105

The Visual System 106
  - The Visual Stimulus and the Eye 106
  - From Eye to Brain and Neural-Visual Processing 110
  - Sensory Adaptation 110
  - Color Vision 111

The Auditory System 116
  - The Nature of Sound and How We Experience It 116
  - Structures and Functions of the Ear 118
  - Theories of Hearing 118
  - Neural-Auditory Processing 120

Other Senses 120
  - The Skin Senses 120
  - The Chemical Senses 122
  - The Kinesthetic and Vestibular Senses 125

Perception 128
  - Attention 128

- THINKING ABOUT PSYCHOLOGY AND LIFE
  - *Counting Aces of Spades* 129
  - Principles of Perception 129

- THINKING ABOUT PSYCHOLOGY AND LIFE
  - *Examining Art for Perceptual Cues and Organization* 131

- EXPLORATIONS IN PSYCHOLOGY
  - *The Perceptual Worlds in Art* 134
  - Illusions 137

■ THINKING ABOUT PSYCHOLOGY AND LIFE

Inventing a Video Game   139

Issues in Perception   139

■ EXPLORATIONS IN PSYCHOLOGY

Debunking Psychics' Claims   143

CHAPTER

5

States of Consciousness   148

▣ IMAGES OF PSYCHOLOGY AND LIFE

Colin Kemp's Tragic Night Terror   149

What Is Consciousness?   150

▣ EXPLORATIONS IN PSYCHOLOGY

Altered States of Consciousness and the

World's Great Religions   153

Sleep   154

Why Do We Sleep?   154

Sleep and Circadian Rhythms   154

Sleep Deprivation and Sleep Needs   156

Stages of Sleep   156

▣ THINKING ABOUT PSYCHOLOGY AND LIFE

The Neural Basis of Sleep   159

Sleep Disorders   159

▣ EXPLORATIONS IN PSYCHOLOGY

Can We Learn While We Are Asleep?   160

▣ THINKING ABOUT PSYCHOLOGY AND LIFE

Do You Get Enough Sleep   161

Dreams   164

The Interpretation of Dreams   164

More About Dreams   166

Hypnosis   167

Definition and History   167

The Hypnotic State: Features and Individual

Differences   168

Theories of Hypnosis   168

▣ EXPLORATIONS IN PSYCHOLOGY

Is Hypnosis a Window to Forgotten Events?   169

Applications of Hypnosis   170

Psychoactive Drugs   170

The Uses of Psychoactive Drugs   170

Types of Psychoactive Drugs   172

■ THINKING ABOUT PSYCHOLOGY AND LIFE

Do You Abuse Drugs?   173

Exploring Addiction and Drug Abuse   175

CHAPTER

6

Learning   184

⌐ IMAGES OF PSYCHOLOGY AND LIFE

Learning to Die   185

What Is Learning?   186

Classical Conditioning   186

Pavlovian Conditioning   187

Temporal Contiguity and Contingency   188

Extinction, Generalization,

and Discrimination   188

How Classical Conditioning Works: Pavlov

and the Contemporary Perspective   191

Classical Conditioning in Humans   191

▣ THINKING ABOUT PSYCHOLOGY AND LIFE

Classical Conditioning and Beer Ads   192

Evaluating Classical Conditioning   193

Operant Conditioning   194

What Operant Conditioning Is   194

Thorndike's Law of Effect   195

Skinner's Operant Conditioning   196

▣ EXPLORATIONS IN PSYCHOLOGY

The Role of Immediate and Delayed Consequences

in Developing Self-Control   200

Applications of Operant Conditioning   203

▣ EXPLORATIONS IN PSYCHOLOGY

Using Behavior Modification

to Improve Self-Control   205

Observational Learning   207

▢ THINKING ABOUT PSYCHOLOGY AND LIFE

Models and Mentors in My Life   208

Cognitive Factors in Learning   208

Expectations and Cognitive Maps   208

Insight Learning   209

Biological and Cultural Factors in Learning   209

Biological Factors   209

Cultural Factors   211

CHAPTER

7

Memory   216

▪ IMAGES OF PSYCHOLOGY AND LIFE
   M. K. and the Russian, S.   217
The Nature of Memory   218
   What Is Memory?   218
   Exploring Memory   218
Memory Encoding   219
   Rehearsal   219
   Deep Processing   220
   Elaboration   220
   Imagery   221
   Organization   222
Memory Storage   223
   Memory's Time Frames   223
   Memory's Contents   227
   Representing Memory   229
▪ THINKING ABOUT PSYCHOLOGY AND LIFE
   Evaluating People's Memories in the Courtroom   231
▪ EXPLORATIONS IN PSYCHOLOGY
   Memory Construction and Eyewitness Testimony   232
   The Neurobiological Basis of Memory   233
▪ EXPLORATIONS IN PSYCHOLOGY
   Cognitive Neuroscience: Watching Brain Activity
   During Memory Encoding   236
Memory Retrieval and Forgetting   236
   Retrieval from Long-Term Memory   236
▪ THINKING ABOUT PSYCHOLOGY AND LIFE
   Generating Retrieval Cues   238
   Autobiographical Memory   239
   Emotional Memories   240
▪ EXPLORATIONS IN PSYCHOLOGY
   Repressed Memories, Child Abuse,
   and Reality   242
   Forgetting   243
Memory and Study Strategies   246
   Effective Strategies   246
   Taking Good Notes   247

▪ THINKING ABOUT PSYCHOLOGY AND LIFE
   Memory and Study Strategies   247
   The PQ4R Method   248

CHAPTER

8

Thinking and Language   252

▪ IMAGES OF PSYCHOLOGY AND LIFE
   The Human Versus Big Blue, Cog, and CYC   253
The Cognitive Revolution in Psychology   254
Thinking   256
   What Is Thinking?   256
   Forming Concepts   256
   Solving Problems   258
▪ THINKING ABOUT PSYCHOLOGY AND LIFE
   The Candle, Nine-Dot, and Six-Matchstick
   Problems   260
   Thinking Critically, Reasoning,
   and Making Decisions   262
▪ THINKING ABOUT PSYCHOLOGY AND LIFE
   Seeking Multiple Explanations   263
Language   268
   What Is Language?   268
   Biological and Environmental Influences   269
▪ EXPLORATIONS IN PSYCHOLOGY
   How to Talk with Babies and Toddlers   270
   How Language Develops   272
   Can Animals Use Language
   to Express Thought?   275
   Language, Culture, and Cognition   277
▪ EXPLORATIONS IN PSYCHOLOGY
   In Pursuit of Language in Animals:
   Observations of Ake and Phoenix   278
   Language and Cognition   278

CHAPTER

9

Intelligence   284

▪ IMAGES OF PSYCHOLOGY AND LIFE
   Being Creative in "X"   285

The Nature of Intelligence and Early History
    of Assessment   286
        What Is Intelligence?   286
        Early History of Assessment   286
Intelligence Tests   288
        How Tests Are Constructed and Evaluated   288
        The Binet Tests and the Wechsler Scales   291
        Group Tests   292
■ THINKING ABOUT PSYCHOLOGY AND LIFE
        Should Parents Be Testing Their Own Child's IQ?   294
        Aptitude and Achievement Tests   294
Do We Have a Single Intelligence
    or Multiple Intelligences?   295
        Early Views   295
        Contemporary Approaches   295
■ EXPLORATIONS IN PSYCHOLOGY
        Project Spectrum   297
■ THINKING ABOUT PSYCHOLOGY AND LIFE
        Evaluating Your Multiple Intelligences   298
Controversies and Issues in Intelligence   299
        The Heredity-Environment Controversy   299
■ EXPLORATIONS IN PSYCHOLOGY
        The Repository for Germinal Choice   302
■ THINKING ABOUT PSYCHOLOGY AND LIFE
        Can Intelligence Be Increased?   303
        Culture and Ethnicity   304
        The Use and Misuse of Intelligence Tests   306
The Extremes of Intelligence and Creativity   307
        Mental Retardation   308
        Giftedness   309
        Creativity   310
■ THINKING ABOUT PSYCHOLOGY AND LIFE
        Evaluating Your Creative Thinking   313

Biological, Cognitive, and Socioemotional
        Processes   320
        Periods of Development   321
■ THINKING ABOUT PSYCHOLOGY AND LIFE
        Is There a Best Age to Be?   323
        Developmental Issues   323
Child Development   324
        Prenatal Development and Birth   324
■ EXPLORATIONS IN PSYCHOLOGY
        The Power of Touch and Massage in Development   327
        Physical Development   328
        Cognitive Development   331
        Socioemotional Development   336
■ THINKING ABOUT PSYCHOLOGY AND LIFE
        Why Do People Want to Have Children?   341
■ EXPLORATIONS IN PSYCHOLOGY
        Child Care in North America   343
Adolescence   345
        Historical Beginnings and the
            Nature of Adolescence   345
        Physical Development   346
        Cognitive Development   346
        Socioemotional Development   349
Adult Development and Aging   352
        Physical Development   352
■ THINKING ABOUT PSYCHOLOGY AND LIFE
        How Long Would You Like to Live?   354
        Cognitive Development   354
        Socioemotional Development   356
■ THINKING ABOUT PSYCHOLOGY AND LIFE
        Exploring Personal Life Investment   359
        Successful Aging   360
Death and Dying   361

CHAPTER

10 Human Development   318

■ IMAGES OF PSYCHOLOGY AND LIFE
        Jessica Dubroff, Child Pilot   319
What Is Development?   320

CHAPTER

11 Motivation and Emotion   366

■ IMAGES OF PSYCHOLOGY AND LIFE
        Terry Fox's Marathon Run   367

Some Ideas About the "Whys" of Behavior   368
    Defining Motivation   368
    Biological Influences   368
    ▢ THINKING ABOUT PSYCHOLOGY AND LIFE
        Are You a Sensation Seeker?   369
    Cognitive Influences   370
    Behavioral/Social/Cultural Influences   370
    The Hierarchy of Motives   371
    Issues in Motivation   372
Hunger   372
    Biological Factors   373
    External and Cognitive Factors   375
    Eating and Weight   376
Sexuality   379
    Biological, Cognitive, Sensory/Perceptual,
        and Cultural Factors   379
    The Human Sexual Response Cycle   382
    Psychosexual Dysfunctions   383
    Heterosexuality and Homosexuality   384
    ▢ EXPLORATIONS IN PSYCHOLOGY
        North America's Sexual Landscape and Its Myths   386
Achievement Motivation   387
    Need for Achievement   388
    Person/Cognitive Factors   388
    ▢ THINKING ABOUT PSYCHOLOGY AND LIFE
        How Goal-Directed Are You?   390
    Cultural, Ethnic, and Socioeconomic Variations
        in Achievement   390
    ▢ EXPLORATIONS IN PSYCHOLOGY
        *Comparing Math Achievement in Asian
        and North American Cultures*   391
Emotion   393
    Defining Emotion   393
    Biological Dimensions   393
    ▢ EXPLORATIONS IN PSYCHOLOGY
        Evaluating Lie Detectors   395
    Cognitive Dimensions   397
    Behavioral Dimensions   398
    Sociocultural Dimensions   400
    Classifying Emotions   402
    ▢ THINKING ABOUT PSYCHOLOGY AND LIFE
        Pursuing the Good Life   404

CHAPTER

12 Personality   410

■ IMAGES OF PSYCHOLOGY AND LIFE
    Everyday Descriptions of Personality   411
What Is Personality?   412
Perspectives on Personality   413
    Psychoanalytic Perspectives   413
■ EXPLORATIONS IN PSYCHOLOGY
    Freud, da Vinci, and Dali   414
■ THINKING ABOUT PSYCHOLOGY AND LIFE
    Your Defense Mechanisms   415
■ EXPLORATIONS IN PSYCHOLOGY
    *Freud's Oedipus Complex: Cultural
    and Gender Biases*   418
    Behavioral and Social Cognitive Perspectives   423
    Humanistic Perspectives   425
■ THINKING ABOUT PSYCHOLOGY AND LIFE
    Evaluating Who's Among the Self-Actualized   427
    Trait Perspectives   429
■ THINKING ABOUT PSYCHOLOGY AND LIFE
    Are You Introverted or Extraverted?   432
Personality Assessment   433
    Some Themes in Personality Assessment   434
    Projective Tests   435
    Self-Report Tests   436
■ EXPLORATIONS IN PSYCHOLOGY
    Being Skeptical About Graphology   437
    Behavioral and Cognitive Assessment   439
Comparing Perspectives on Personality   439

CHAPTER

13 Abnormal Psychology   446

■ IMAGES OF PSYCHOLOGY AND LIFE
    The World of Jenny Z.   447
Understanding Abnormal Behavior   448
    Defining Abnormal Behavior   448

Legal Aspects of Mental Disorders   449

■ EXPLORATIONS IN PSYCHOLOGY

Some Famous Insanity Plea Cases   450

The Causes of Abnormal Behavior   450

Rates of Disorders   452

Classifying Abnormal Behavior   452

Categories of Mental Disorders   455

Anxiety Disorders   455

Somatoform Disorders   459

Dissociative Disorders   460

Mood Disorders   463

■ THINKING ABOUT PSYCHOLOGY AND LIFE

Evaluating Whether You Are Depressed   464

■ EXPLORATIONS IN PSYCHOLOGY

Suicide   465

Schizophrenia   467

■ EXPLORATIONS IN PSYCHOLOGY

NIMH—Nora, Iris, Myra, and Hester, the

Schizophrenic Genain Quadruplets   471

Personality Disorders   472

CHAPTER

14

Therapies   478

■ IMAGES OF PSYCHOLOGY AND LIFE

Our Native Peoples Heal Themselves   479

The Nature and History of Psychotherapy   480

What Is Psychotherapy?   480

The History of Psychotherapy   480

Mental Health Professionals   483

Connections with Personality Theories   484

Approaches to Psychotherapy   484

Psychodynamic Therapies   484

■ EXPLORATIONS IN PSYCHOLOGY

Penetrating Mrs. A. H.'s Thoughts   488

Humanistic Therapies   489

Behavior Therapies   491

Cognitive Therapies   494

■ EXPLORATIONS IN PSYCHOLOGY

Contemporary Behavior Therapy and the Treatment

of Depression—the Lewinsohn Approach   495

■ EXPLORATIONS IN PSYCHOLOGY

"My Work Is Boring and I Resent It"   496

Group Therapies   497

Is Psychotherapy Effective?   501

■ THINKING ABOUT PSYCHOLOGY AND LIFE

Designing a Study to Evaluate the Effectiveness

of Psychotherapy   501

■ THINKING ABOUT PSYCHOLOGY AND LIFE

Evaluating Whether to Seek Psychotherapy   502

■ EXPLORATIONS IN PSYCHOLOGY

Guidelines for Seeking Professional Help   503

Biomedical Therapies   504

Drug Therapy   504

Electroconvulsive Therapy   506

Psychosurgery   507

Therapy Integrations   508

CHAPTER

15

Health Psychology   514

■ IMAGES OF PSYCHOLOGY AND LIFE

Mort, Overwhelmed with Stress   515

The Scope of Health Psychology   516

Stress   517

Biological Factors   518

Personality Factors   521

Cognitive Factors   522

Environmental Factors   523

■ THINKING ABOUT PSYCHOLOGY AND LIFE

Evaluating Life Events in Your Life   524

Sociocultural Factors   525

■ EXPLORATIONS IN PSYCHOLOGY

Jen and Nick: Faces of Welfare Poverty in Canada   527

Coping   527

Problem-Focused Coping and Emotion-Focused

Coping   527

■ THINKING ABOUT PSYCHOLOGY AND LIFE
　　Opening Up　529
　　Optimism and Positive Thinking　529
　　Self-Efficacy　532
　　Social Support　532
■ EXPLORATIONS IN PSYCHOLOGY
　　Using Optimistic Thinking to Go from Sausage Stuffer
　　to Supersalesman　533
　　Assertive Behavior　533
■ THINKING ABOUT PSYCHOLOGY AND LIFE
　　Dealing with Conflict　534
　　Stress Management　534
■ THINKING ABOUT PSYCHOLOGY AND LIFE
　　Coping with Failure　535
　　Multiple Coping Strategies　536

Promoting Health　537
　　Regular Exercise　537
　　Proper Nutrition　539
　　Not Smoking　540
　　Sound Sexual Decision-Making　542
■ THINKING ABOUT PSYCHOLOGY AND LIFE
　　Sexual Myths and Realities　542

CHAPTER

16 Social Psychology　548

■ IMAGES OF PSYCHOLOGY AND LIFE
　　The Reverend James Jones' Dark Side　549

Social Thinking　550
　　Attribution　550
　　Social Perception　552
■ EXPLORATIONS IN PSYCHOLOGY
　　Impression Management and Job Interviewing　555
■ THINKING ABOUT PSYCHOLOGY AND LIFE
　　Self-Monitoring　556
　　Attitudes　556

Social Influence　559
　　Conformity and Obedience　559
　　Group Influence　565
　　Cultural and Ethnic Influences　569
■ THINKING ABOUT PSYCHOLOGY AND LIFE
　　Prejudice and Reconstructive Memory　570
■ THINKING ABOUT PSYCHOLOGY AND LIFE
　　Seeking Common Ground　574

Social Interaction and Relationships　576
　　Aggression　576
　　Altruism　580
　　Attraction, Love, and Relationships　584
■ THINKING ABOUT PSYCHOLOGY AND LIFE
　　The Types of Love You Have　587

APPENDIX　A-1
GLOSSARY　G-1
REFERENCES　R-1
CREDITS　C-1
NAME INDEX　NI-1
SUBJECT INDEX　SI-1

Summary Tables

CHAPTER 1

Exploring Psychology   16

Psychology and Life: What Matters; Psychology's Careers
    and Areas of Specialization   28

CHAPTER 2

Scientific Research and the Scientific Method;
    Who Will the Participants Be?   39

Research Methods   50

Research Challenges   60

CHAPTER 3

Biological Foundations   70

The Field of Neuroscience, the Nervous System,
    and Neurons   79

Brain Structure and Function   90

Exploring the Brain   96

CHAPTER 4

Detecting and Perceiving the World   106

The Visual System   115

The Auditory System and Other Senses   127

Perception   144

CHAPTER 5

States of Consciousness and Sleep   163

Dreams   167

Hypnosis   171

Psychoactive Drugs   180

CHAPTER 6

The Nature of Learning and Classical Conditioning   194

Operant Conditioning   206

Observational Learning, Cognitive Factors, and Biological
    and Cultural Factors in Learning   212

CHAPTER 7

The Nature of Memory and Encoding   223

Memory Storage   235

Memory Retrieval and Forgetting   245

Memory and Study Strategies   248

CHAPTER 8

The Cognitive Revolution in Psychology, and Thinking   262

Thinking Critically, Reasoning, and Making Decisions   267

Language: Its Nature, and Biological and Environmental
    Influences   271

How Language Develops, Whether Animals Can Use Language to
    Express Thought, and Language, Culture, and Cognition   280

CHAPTER 9

The Nature of Intelligence and Early History of Assessment;
    Intelligence Tests; and Whether We Have a Single Intelligence
    or Multiple Intelligences   300

Controversies and Issues in Intelligence   307

The Extremes of Intelligence and Creativity   314

CHAPTER 10

What Development Is; Prenatal Development and Birth   328

Children's Physical, Cognitive, and Socioemotional
    Development   344

Adolescence   351

Adult Development and Aging; Death and Dying   362

CHAPTER 11

Some Ideas About the "Whys" of Behavior   373

Hunger   379

Sexuality   387

Achievement   392

Emotion   406

CHAPTER 12

The Nature of Personality, and Psychoanalytic Perspectives   422

The Behavioral and Social Cognitive Perspectives,
    and the Humanistic Perspectives   430

Trait Perspectives   434

Personality Assessment and Comparing Perspectives
    on Personality   442

CHAPTER 13

Understanding Abnormal Behavior   454

The Anxiety, Somatoform, and Dissociative Disorders   462

Mood Disorders, Schizophrenia, and Personality Disorders   474

CHAPTER 14

The Nature and History of Psychotherapy   485

The Psychodynamic and Humanistic Therapies   490

The Behavior and Cognitive Therapies   497

Group Therapies; Effectiveness of Psychotherapies; and
    Biomedical Therapies   510

CHAPTER 15

Health Psychology and Stress   528

Coping   538

Promoting Health   544

CHAPTER 16

Social Thinking   560

Social Influence   575

Social Interaction and Relationships   590

Preface

I have been teaching introductory psychology at Brock University in St. Catharines since 1981. When I first saw John Santrock's *Psychology,* Sixth Edition, I liked the book and immediately knew that John was a psychologist I could work with. It turns out that John, who has been teaching introductory psychology since 1967, and I both share a deep motivation and love for imparting psychology as a relevant science—one that is empirically sound yet meaningful for people's lives. In no other discipline (we are admittedly biased) will you find so many opportunities to better understand yourself and the people around you than in the discipline of psychology. This belief has not only been a foundation of our teaching introductory psychology for so long, but is also the heart of this book. When I was asked to undertake a First Canadian Edition, I leapt at the chance.

New or Revised?

When an introductory textbook reaches past its fifth edition to a sixth edition and a First Canadian Edition, it typically generates three reactions from instructors. First, many instructors may believe the book must be successful to have lasted this long in such a highly competitive and, most would say, overpublished market. Second, some instructors may believe they are already sufficiently aware of the book's content and approach, because they have either used or evaluated a previous edition. Third, some instructors may wonder why a First Canadian Edition is needed at all.

John Santrock deserves tremendous credit for the accuracy of the first impression—over 300,000 students have used his previous editions. To the instructors who have the second frame of mind: with a new theme based on extensive marketing research, the inclusion of many new topics, the deletion of others, a new illustration program, more than 400 new citations from 1998–2000 alone, new learning and study aids, new design, and line-by-line revision of existing material, this edition more closely resembles a new rather than a revised edition. For those with the third frame of mind, students and instructors identified relevance in relating psychology to their own lives and experiences as most important in a textbook. I undertook the creation of this First Canadian Edition with this theme in mind. I am pleased with the result and optimistically challenge you to put it to the test. I think you will agree that this adaptation subtly but importantly increases the relevance of psychology to your Canadian students. You will, for example, find that about 380 Canadian citations have been added. I am confident that the closer you look, the more you will be surprised and impressed by the changes.

What Did We Learn?

What do most instructors and students really want from an introductory psychology text? In preparation for these revisions, John Santrock and the publisher were determined to obtain a concrete answer to this question. To accomplish this, the publisher solicited and received, through reviews and focus groups, more feedback from instructors and students than for all of the previous editions combined.

What was learned? At the top of both instructors' and students' lists was their desire for a text that presents psychology as a relevant science. In this research, the majority of students gave their texts low grades for relevance and many believed their courses failed to satisfy the goals they had in taking them. When asked to say how the subject matter could be presented in more relevant terms, students most commonly replied that the author must succeed in relating it to their own lives and experiences. Our panel of instructors agreed that the principal goal of the course is to present psychology as a science that students understand from an applied and personal perspective.

Psychology: The Relevant Science

As many instructors (and authors) know, it is quite a challenge to perceive what is needed to fulfill students' expectations, and then to fulfill them. How can we ensure that every page of a textbook has relevance? As we revise each sentence and each feature in the book, we must constantly ask ourselves: Why is this important? Is this a meaningful issue for today's students?

Like its American counterpart, *Psychology,* First Canadian Edition, has been infused with content, exercises, and resources that focus on psychology as a relevant science. The discipline of psychology is ideally suited to address some of the most important aspects of our lives. We don't have the answers to all of life's questions, but psychology can tell us much about matters like these:

- How our biological heritage affects our behavior
- How, and to what extent, our environmental experiences can change our lives
- How we perceive, remember, solve problems, and can become more creative
- How the social worlds of people and relationships affect the way we behave
- How the culture we live in influences us
- How we are similar to and different from others
- How science can provide us with more objective information about many aspects of life
- How to draw on conceptually diverse ideas in thinking about problems and issues

- How to understand controversies about mind and behavior
- How to think critically about many aspects of mind and behavior

The above ten areas are featured in a new section in Chapter 1 called "Psychology and Life: What Matters." They also are woven through the remainder of the text where appropriate. In addition, as you will see shortly, some of the book's main features emphasize psychology's relevance.

Every chapter of the book includes these "Psychology of Life" features:

Images of Psychology and Life
This section appears at the beginning of each chapter and introduces students to some aspect of the chapter in an interesting way. Examples of topics include: "Why Youth Kill" (Chapter 1), "The Human Versus Big Blue, Cog, and CYC" (Chapter 8), and "The World of Jenny Z." (Chapter 13).

Explorations in Psychology
These boxes, seamlessly interwoven with the text, provide an expanded look at many fascinating ideas and issues related to the content at that particular point in the chapter. Examples of topics include: "From Horoscopes to the Sex Lives of Tigers" (Chapter 1), "The Brains of the Mankato Nuns" (Chapter 3), and "Jen and Nick: Faces of Welfare Poverty in Canada" (Chapter 15).

Thinking About Psychology and Life
These boxes appear several times in each chapter and encourage students to think critically or evaluate themselves in regard to content in that part of the chapter. Examples of topics include: "Nature, Nurture, and Politics" (Chapter 3), "Evaluating Your Creative Thinking" (Chapter 9), and "Are You Introverted or Extroverted?" (Chapter 12).

Resources for Psychology and Life
This section appears at the end of each chapter and lists books, agencies, phone numbers and Web sites, research journals, and psychological organizations. These extensive resources enlarge the scope of the chapter to help students learn more about research and practical matters in psychology and life.

Development

As we have emphasized, the content of *Psychology* was extensively overhauled and fine-tuned. Two types of consultants went over every sentence and section with a fine-tooth comb, making countless recommendations for what to add, subtract, revise, update, and rephrase.

Expert Research Consultants. A number of leading research experts in psychology evaluated individual chapters in their areas of expertise. Their detailed recommendations significantly improved the currency and accuracy of the text's research content.

Expert Teaching Consultants. As previously mentioned, these editions of *Psychology* underwent a more thorough review by individuals who teach introductory psychology than all of its first five editions combined. Their overall "big picture" view and detailed, line-by-line comments about what should go into an introductory psychology text and how it should be said have substantially reshaped this book in very positive ways.

Student Reviews and Focus Groups

For the first time in a formal context, we involved students in almost every facet of this revision. After all, they are the ultimate consumers of its content, and based on what we learned and the changes and improvements that were made as a result, we only wish we had obtained more of their input on earlier editions.

In addition to their part in determining the "relevance" theme for this edition, they told us (in focus groups) which elements worked and did not work for them in the various texts they used. They reacted to and advised us regarding several ideas we had developed for new substantive as well as pedagogical features. They critiqued the illustration program and gave numerous suggestions that helped guide the new format and design you see featured in this edition. All in all, their preferences are evident throughout the book.

∾ *"I really enjoy the layout of the book. I think the design, graphics are the most appealing part of this book. They make it interesting and they make it easier to turn the page."*

"This is definitely a student-friendly book, and it is not too intimidating, so it's accessible. I think [Explorations in Psychology] is a very interesting section in the book. It is aesthetically pleasing, it adds a little bit of more interesting info among pages of technical info. It offers more ease of reading."

Heather Shafer, Student

∾ *"Pretty student friendly and accessible. It's an attractive, inviting book. [Through the Eyes of a Psychologist] . . . is aesthetically pleasing, with good interesting quotes."*

Srin Chakravorty, Student

∾ *"I like how the authors are writing on a personal level. It's easy to read . . . [the text is] . . . well laid out, easy for eyes to move through the book, adds to the overall effect quite positively. . . ."*

Kelly Murphy, Student

∾ *"[The text is] very easy to comprehend. It is coherent . . . box titles are very attention-grabbing . . . good explanations. [The design] is the best part. The art is really cool, attention getting and visually appealing."*

Erica Mezi, Student

Adapting the Book for Canada

With the completion of this major revision of *Psychology*, I then adapted the text for use by Canadian students, with the help of Canadian reviewers. Two major principles guided my adaptation. The first was the "relevance" theme discussed above. Without forgetting that Canadians and Americans share much in common, in a number of cases American examples and statistics were replaced with Canadian ones. Canadian statistics from Statistics Canada, Canadian examples of creative and prominent people, as well as hypothetical scenarios relevant to Canadians serve to unobtrusively sharpen relevant Canadian perspectives without creating an overly Canadian focus.

The second guiding principle was to draw attention to Canadian research in psychology. This was achieved by including more than 300 Canadian references not in the U.S. sixth edition. Work by influential Canadian researchers like Endel Tulving, John Berry, Robert Ladouceur, Sandra Witelson, Robert Hare, Douglas Wahlsten, Norman Endler, Donald Saklofske, and many others has been woven into John Santrock's already strong manuscript. Again, however, this adaptation does not parade Canadian psychology at the expense of coverage of American and European psychology. With careful rewriting and editing, I did not have to cut any of the existing references or sections of the book. In this regard, the First Canadian Edition reads at a bit higher level than does the U.S. edition.

Fewer Chapters

The standard text for the Fifth Edition had 17 chapters. Because most instructors continue to ask for less encyclopedic texts, we reduced the number of basic chapters to 16 by combining the two social psychology chapters into one. However, based on extensive reviewing, we are confident that you will find the combined social psychology chapter complete without being encyclopedic.

We have significantly updated and improved the content in *Psychology*, First Canadian Edition. Much of this updating and improvement is based on input from the research and teaching experts. Following is a chapter-by-chapter overview of the new content in *Psychology*, First Canadian Edition, relative to *Psychology*, Fifth Edition:

CHAPTER 1 What Is Psychology?

Images of Psychology and Life: Why Youth Kill

Psychology's Beginnings: Merging Ideas from Philosophy and the Natural Sciences

Revision of Wundt's, Titchener's, and James' ideas

Updating of Bandura's social cognitive theory

Updating of the behavioral neuroscience approach, including mention of D.O. Hebb as the founder of the neuroscience approach

Expansion and updating of the evolutionary psychology approach

An eclectic approach

Thinking About Psychology and Life: Saddam Hussein and Mother Teresa

Extensive new section: Psychology and Life: What Matters

Explorations in Psychology: From Horoscopes to the Sex Lives of Tigers

Expanded and updated coverage of careers in psychology

Some job possibilities for students with an undergraduate degree in psychology

Thinking About Psychology and Life: Which Areas of Psychology Interest You the Most?

CHAPTER 2 Psychology's Scientific Methods

New section: Exploring the Science of Psychology

Thinking About Psychology and Life: Participating in Psychological Experiments on the Internet

Substantial revision of the discussion of the scientific method with Bandura's classic research on observational learning and aggression as a theme

Operational definition

Who Will the Participants Be?

Extensive revision and updating of research methods with examples of aggression research carried through as a common theme

Recent research on physiological underpinnings of spousal abuse

Experimental Research Cautions: Experimenter Bias and Research Participant Bias

Thinking About Psychology and Life: No Magic Bullet

Multiple Research Methods

Thinking About Psychology and Life: Isn't Everyone a Psychologist?

Revision and updating of CPA ethics guidelines

Revision of Explorations in Psychology box: Psychology and Values

Updating of treatment of CPA guidelines for nonsexist research

Revision and updating of the research challenges involved in gender, culture, and ethnicity

Reading and Understanding Research Journals

CHAPTER 3 Biological Foundations and Neuroscience

New chapter title that includes neuroscience

Dynamic photographs and drawings of the brain's structures

Genotype and phenotype

The Human Genome Project

The new view of heredity-environment interaction

Thinking About Psychology and Life: Nature, Nurture, and Politics

New section: The Field of Neuroscience

Updated and expanded discussion of neurotransmitters

Agonists and antagonists

Wernicke-Geschwind model

Sandra Witelson and the notion of bihemispheric representation of functions

Brandi Binder's case, which provides evidence of hemispheric flexibility

Thinking About Psychology and Life: Your Brain and Your Behavior

CHAPTER 4 Sensation and Perception

Dynamic drawings and photographs

Psychophysics

Revised discussion of absolute thresholds

Explorations in Psychology: Analyzing Subliminal Perception—Work by Philip Merikle and Meredith Daneman

Revised discussion of signal direction theory

Updated coverage of feature detectors

Comparison of trichromatic and opponent-process theories

Different types of pain receptors

Thinking About Psychology and Life: Counting Aces of Spades

The Stroop Effect

Thinking About Psychology and Life: Examining Art for
Perceptual Cues and Organization

Attention

Approaches to perception including comparison of
information-processing and ecological theories

Thinking About Psychology and Life: Inventing a Video Game

James Alcock on extrasensory perception

CHAPTER 5 States of Consciousness

Larry Jacoby on controlled vs. automatic processes

The range of sleep in animals

Circadian rhythms, shift workers, and seasonal affective disorder
in Canada

Revised and expanded discussion of sleep deprivation and needs

Thinking About Psychology and Life: Do You Get Enough
Sleep?

Sleep across the human life span

Expanded discussion of sleep disorders including strategies for
reducing insomnia

Revised discussion of interpretation of dreams

Do males and females dream about different things?

Thinking About Psychology and Life: Lucid Dreaming

Revised discussion of theories of hypnosis, Including Nicholas
Spano's nonstate theory

Updated coverage of trends in drug use

The hazards of binge drinking in university

Thinking About Psychology and Life: Do You Abuse Drugs?

Caffeine

Expanded coverage of alcoholism and prevention/treatment of
drug abuse

CHAPTER 6 Learning

Images of Psychology and Life: Learning to Die—Shepard
Siegel's work on the role of classical conditioning in drug
overdoses

Diagram of Pavlov's classical conditioning

Contingency in classical conditioning

Thinking About Psychology and Life:

Classical Conditioning and Beer Ads

Ethics of conditioning a phobia in Little Albert

Associative learning including figure that compares associative
learning aspects of classical and operant conditioning

Diagrams that compare positive reinforcement and negative
reinforcement

Revised and expanded coverage of punishment, including
positive and negative punishment

Figure that compares positive reinforcement, negative
reinforcement, positive punishment, and negative
punishment

Recent Canadian research on spanking and antisocial behavior

Thinking About Psychology and Life: Models and Mentors in
My Life

CHAPTER 7 Memory

Substantial overhaul of chapter organization with this new
sequence: The Nature of Memory, Memory Encoding,
Memory Storage, Memory Retrieval and Forgetting, and
Memory and Study Strategies

Exploring memory with an emphasis on Endel Tulving's ideas
on the remarkable capabilities of memory as well as its
imperfections

Dynamic diagrams of memory processes

Thinking About Psychology and Life: Evaluating People's
Memories in the Courtroom

Explorations in Psychology: Cognitive Neuroscience: Watching
Brain Activity During Memory Encoding

Remembering faces: Ted Kaczynski

Thinking About Psychology and Life: Generating Retrieval Cues

Revised discussion of priming

The three-level hierarchical structure of autobiographical
memory

New main section: Emotional Memories

Memory and personal trauma

Revised and updated discussion of repressed memories

Significantly revised and expanded coverage of memory and
study strategies

Thinking About Psychology and Life: Memory and Study
Strategies

CHAPTER 8 THINKING AND LANGUAGE

Images of Psychology: The Human Versus Big Blue,
Cog, and CYC

New sequential organization of thinking: What Is Thinking?;
Forming Concepts; Solving Problems; Thinking Critically,
Reasoning, and Making Decisions

The concept of schools of art

Revised discussion of finding and framing problems

New section on obstacles to solving problems that focuses on
becoming fixated and lacking motivation and persistence

Thinking About Psychology and Life: The Candle, Nine-Dot,
and Six-Matchstick Problems

Revised and updated discussion of critical thinking

Thinking About Psychology and Life: Seeking Multiple
Explanations

Ellen Langer's ideas about mindless behavior

Confirmation bias

Belief perseverance

Overconfidence bias

Hindsight bias

Research on language environments of children in poverty

Explorations in Psychology: How to Talk with Babies and
Toddlers

Revision and updating of bilingual education in Canada

Ellen Bialystok's ideas about metalinguistic awareness

CHAPTER 9 Intelligence

Images of Psychology: Being Creative in "X"
Reorganization with the construction/evaluation of intelligence
    tests now discussed early in the chapter
Links between reliability and validity
Thinking About Psychology and Life: Should Parents Be Testing
    Their Own Child's IQ?
Explorations in Psychology: Project Spectrum
Thinking About Psychology and Life: Evaluating Your Multiple
    Intelligences
Sternberg's triarchic intelligence and schools
Evaluating the multiple intelligences approach
Douglas Wahlsten's critique of the notion of heritability as
    applied to human intelligence
Explorations in Psychology: The Repository for Germinal
    Choice
Thinking About Psychology and Life: Can Intelligence Be
    Increased?
Extensive revision and expansion of discussion of creativity
Thinking About Psychology and Life: Evaluating Your Creative
    Thinking

CHAPTER 10 Human Development

Sequential reorganization of chapter so that major theories,
    such as Piaget's and Erikson's, are now presented intact
    rather than in separate locations
Discussion of gender removed and placed in Chapter 16,
    "Social Psychology"
Images of Psychology: Jessica Dubroff, Child Pilot
Thinking About Psychology and Life: Is There a Best Age
    to Be?
Early-later experience issue
Conclusions about developmental issues
New research on mothers who smoke
Canadian work on physical development
Balanced evaluation of Piaget's Theory
Evaluation of Erikson's Theory
Temperament
Explorations in Psychology: Child Care in North America
The mother's and father's roles
Why do people want to have children?
Revised discussion of Kohlberg's theory
Thinking About Psychology and Life: How Long Would You
    Like to Live?
Contemporary discussion of estrogen replacement therapy
Revised and expanded coverage of biological theories of aging
Alzheimer's disease
Revised and updated coverage of cognition and aging including
    discussion of Jane Dywan's work on declines in controlled
    processing
Skills that employers want job candidates to have
McArthur (1999) study of midlife development
Successful aging
Thinking About Psychology and Life: Exploring Personal Life
    Investment

CHAPTER 11 Motivation and Emotion

Images of Psychology: Terry Fox's Marathon Run
Reorganization of some ideas about the "whys" of behavior
Revised discussion of drive reduction theory
Thinking About Psychology and Life: Are You a Sensation
    Seeker?
Janet Polivy's ideas on eating
Revised and updated discussion of obesity
Moved discussion of dieting to this chapter from health
    psychology chapter
Moved discussion of anorexia nervosa and bulimia to this
    chapter from health psychology chapter
Pheromones and aphrodisiacs
Viagra
Explorations in Psychology: North America's Sexual Landscape
    and Its Myths
Goal-setting, planning, and monitoring
Thinking About Psychology and Life: How Goal-Directed Are
    You?
Explorations in Psychology: Comparing Math Achievement in
    Asian and North American Cultures
Reorganization of discussion of emotions. New sequence:
    Defining Emotion; Biological Dimensions; Cognitive
    Dimensions; Behavioral Dimensions; Sociocultural
    Dimensions; and Classifying Emotions
Explorations in Psychology: Evaluating Lie Detectors—Michael
    Bradley's work on the Guilty Knowledge Test
Expanded discussion of the autonomic nervous system
New section on neural circuits and neurotransmitters
More dynamic diagrams of emotion topics
The Facial Feedback Hypothesis
Thinking About Psychology and Life: Pursuing the Good Life

CHAPTER 12 Personality

New summary figure on defense mechanisms
Thinking About Psychology and Life: Your Defense Mechanisms
Change of social learning theory to more contemporary social
    cognitive theory
Thinking About Psychology and Life: Evaluating Who's Among
    the Self-Actualized
Self-esteem research
Revision of Allport's view of traits
Thinking About Psychology and Life: Are You Introverted or
    Extraverted?
New figure on the Big Five factors of personality
Research on the Big Five factors including the Jackson
    Personality Inventory
Updated research on the MMPI-2

CHAPTER 13 Abnormal Psychology

Restructured chapter headings and subheadings
Images of Psychology: The World of Jenny Z.
Revised discussion of defining abnormal behavior and improved
    examples
Some myths and misconceptions about abnormal behavior

Legal aspects of mental disorders moved to earlier in chapter
    with expanded, revised content
Explorations in Psychology: Some Famous Insanity Plea Cases
Figure 13.4: Some Prominent Categories of Mental Disorders
    in DSM-IV
Revised and updated discussion of panic disorder and agoraphobia
Social phobia
Dr. Howard Lim and Jack Nicholson
Dissociative identity disorder
Thinking About Psychology and Life:
Evaluating Whether You Are Depressed
More on manic episodes
Explorations in Psychology: Suicide
Sandy Charles, Andre Dallaire, and schizophrenia
Revised discussion of personality disorders with expanded
    description of clusters
Robert Hare's work on psychopaths

CHAPTER 14 Therapies

New, less complex organization
Images of Psychology: Our Native Peoples Heal Themselves
Revised and updated discussion of mental hospitals and
    deinstitutionalization in the U.S. and Canada
Recent developments, including managed care in the U.S.
Licensing and certification
Connections with personality theories
More case study examples
Figure 14.5: Overview of Main Psychotherapy Approaches
Revised discussion of person-centered therapy, including new
    therapist-client exchange
Figure 14.9: Classical Conditioning: The Backbone of Aversive
    Conditioning
Donald Meichenbaum's cognitive behavior therapy
Revised and expanded discussion of Beck's cognitive therapy
Comparison of Ellis' and Beck's therapies
Revised, updated discussion of self-help support groups
Thinking About Psychology and Life: Designing a Study to
    Evaluate the Effectiveness of Psychotherapy
Revised, expanded, updated discussion of research on the
    effectiveness of psychotherapy
Thinking About Psychology and Life: Evaluating Whether to
    Seek Psychotherapy
Revised, updated discussion of gender/ethnicity and therapy
Updated, revised discussion of drug therapy
Figure 14.12: Drug Therapy for Mental Disorders
Revised, expanded Figure 14.13: Therapy Comparisons
New final section for chapter: Therapy Integrations

CHAPTER 15 Health Psychology

Reorganization of chapter with stress and coping now coming
    prior to promoting health
Revised, updated, expanded introduction to the scope of health
    psychology
Two biological pathways to stress
Updated, revised discussion of psychoneuroimmunology
    including recent research

Revised discussion of Lazarus' ideas on stress
Thinking About Psychology and Life:
Evaluating Life Events in Your Life
John Berry's ideas on acculturative stress
Explorations in Psychology: Jen and Nick: Faces of Welfare
    Poverty in Canada
Thinking About Psychology and Life: Opening Up
Explorations in Psychology: Using Optimistic Thinking to Go
    from Sausage Stuffer to Optimistic Supersalesman
Recent research on social support and coping with stress
Updated, revised discussion of assertive behavior
Thinking About Psychology and Life: Dealing with Conflict
Thinking About Psychology and Life: Coping with Failure
Revised discussion of proper nutrition
Updated and expanded discussion of not smoking
Sound Sexual Decision Making (new section for this edition)
Thinking About Psychology and Life: Sexual Myths and
    Realities

CHAPTER 16 Social Psychology

This edition has an integrated single chapter on social
    psychology (the Fifth Edition had two separate chapters)
Images of Psychology and Life: The Reverend James Jones' Dark
    Side with Marshall Applewhite and Luc Jouret
Substantial reorganization of chapter. Attribution now is the
    first main topic discussed
Expanded, updated coverage of attribution
Self-serving bias
Revised and updated discussion of attitudes and behavior
Social influence is now a major heading with subheadings of
    Conformity and Obedience, Group Influence, and Cultural
    and Ethnic Influences
Normative social influence and informational social influence
Revised, updated discussion of groupthink, with a Canadian
    example
Revised discussion of cultural/ethnic influences
Thinking About Psychology and Life: Prejudice and
    Reconstructive Memory
Mark Zanna's theory of prejudice
Thinking About Psychology and Life: Seeking Common Ground
New section on aggression
Gender now discussed at appropriate places in this chapter
    rather than in Chapter 10, "Human Development."
Updated discussion of freshman life goals
Thinking About Psychology and Life: The Type of Love You
    Have
Strategies for overcoming loneliness
Ellen Berscheid's (1999) ideas about environmental demands
    and close relationships

Optional Chapters

In addition to the main 16 chapters that are standard in many
introductory psychology texts, the optional bundle for *Psychology*, First Canadian Edition, consists of four chapters that can
be packaged with the main book:

Evolution and Heredity
Gender and Sexuality
Applied Psychology
The Psychology of Religion

These four chapters were chosen by instructors as the most popular ones to add to a standard introductory psychology text. Each chapter is accompanied by a full Web-based ancillary package including Student Study Guide, Instructor's Manual, and Test Bank.

CHAPTER 17 Evolution and Heredity

More streamlined and easier to read discussion of evolution
Thinking About Psychology and Life:
The "Nobel Prize Sperm Bank"
New research on sperm sorting for selection of the offspring's sex
Expanded and updated coverage of genetic counseling
Incorporated material on identical twins reared apart into body of text
Contemporary section on conclusions about heredity-environment interaction
Thinking About Psychology and Life:
Nature, Nurture, and Politics

CHAPTER 18 Gender and Sexuality

Improved discussion and definitions of estrogens and androgens
New coverage of evolutionary psychology view of gender
New discussion of social roles view of gender
Thinking About Psychology and Life: Rethinking the Words We Use in Gender Worlds
New section on gender in contexts
Extensively revised and updated discussion of men's issues
Expanded coverage of the human sexual response pattern
New material on Viagra
Expanded discussion of heterosexual attitudes and behavior
Revised and updated coverage of forcible sexual behavior and harassment
New section on sound sexual decision making
Thinking About Psychology and Life: Sexual Myths and Realities
New discussion of strategies for protecting against AIDS and other sexually transmitted diseases

CHAPTER 19 Applied Psychology

This is virtually a completely new chapter for *Psychology*, Sixth Edition and First Canadian Edition
Thinking About Psychology and Life: Knock 'Em Dead in an Interview
New discussion of research on the Big Five factors and predicting job success
New section on leadership in the world of work
Human factors psychology no longer is discussed under I/O psychology but now has its own section
New research on human factors by the FAA
New research on human factors involved in touch
New description of environmental psychologist Roberta Feldman and her work

Thinking About Psychology and Life: Analyzing the Built Environment in Which You Live
New main section: Forensic Psychology
Explorations in Psychology: Psychological Profiling
New main section: Sport Psychology
New main section: Educational Psychology
Explorations in Psychology and Life: Schools for Thought

CHAPTER 20 The Psychology of Religion

Includes recent survey on religious interest in North America
New discussion of controversy involving what religion is and what spirituality is
Thinking About Psychology and Life: Spiritual Well-Being
New discussion of positive and negative aspects of religion
Deletion of section on fundamentalism and right-winged authoritarianism
New section on religion and physical health
Much expanded and updated coverage of religion and mental health
Recent research on religious coping styles
Recent research on religion and sexuality
Recent research on gender and religion
Recent research on religiousness and generosity toward the poor
Thinking About Psychology and Life: Religion, Spirituality, and Cults
New section on religion and cults
Significantly updated research citations

Acknowledgments from John Santrock

I owe debts to many people who worked to substantially improve the Sixth Edition of *Psychology*, but three individuals deserve special thanks. Joseph Terry, Psychology Editor, was especially influential in supporting and shaping the book. Jim Rozsa, Senior Marketing Manager in Psychology, played a key role in conceptualizing the book's many changes and themes. I also benefited enormously from Glenn Turner's extensive, detailed analysis and recommendations. I value not only the extraordinary, competent professional input of these three individuals, but also their friendship.

In both the Fifth Edition and U.S. Sixth Edition of *Psychology*, a number of leading experts in different subfields of psychology have provided me with invaluable advice about their areas of expertise.

Chapter 1: What Is Psychology: Ludy Benjamin, Texas A&M, Charles Brewer, Clemson University; Chapter 2: Psychology's Scientific Methods: Keith E. Stanovich, University of Toronto; Chapter 3: Biological Foundations and the Brain: Jackson Beatty, UCLA; Chapter 4: Sensation and Perception: Alice O'Toole, University of Texas at Dallas; Chapter 5: States of Consciousness: G. William Domhoff; Chapter 6: Learning: Michelle Perry, U. of Illinois at Urbana, Champaign; Chapter 7: Memory: James Bartlett, University of Texas at Dallas; Daniel Schacter, Harvard University, Steven Smith, Texas A&M; Chapter 8: Thinking and Language: Karen A. Luh; Jean Berko Gleason;

Chapter 9: Intelligence: Mihalyi Csiksentmihalyi, University of Chicago; Chapter 10: Human Development: Illene Noppe, University of Wisconsin—Green Bay; Chapter 11: Motivation and Emotion: Laura King, SMU; Chapter 12: Personality: N.C. Higgins, University of Northern British Columbia; Chapter 13: Abnormal Psychology: Lillian Comas-Diaz, Transcultural Institute; Chapter 14: Therapies: Richard P. Halgin, University of Massachusetts, Amherst; Chapter 15: Health Psychology: David Mostofsy, Boston University; James Pennebaker, University of Texas; Chapter 16: Social Psychology: Stanley Gaines, Pomona College; James Jones, U. of Delaware; John Harvey, U. of Iowa, Richard Brislin, East-West Center; Chapter 17: Evolution and Heredity: David Buss, University of Texas; Chapter 18: Gender and Sexuality: Florence Denmark, Pace University; Seth Kalichman, Georgia State U.; Chapter 19: Applied Psychology: Robert Gifford, University of Victoria; Chapter 20: The Psychology of Religion: Raymond Paloutzian, Westmont College

In addition, many instructors who teach introductory psychology made special efforts to provide detailed feedback, in many cases on a line-by-line basis, about *Psychology*, Sixth Edition. They were:

Valerie Ahl, *University of Wisconsin—Madison*
Susan Amato, *Boise State University*
Jim Backlund, *Kirtland Community College*
John Best, *Eastern Illinois University*
Michelle Boyer-Pennington, *Middle Tennessee State University*
James Calhoun, *University of Georgia*
Ellen Dennehy, *University of Texas—Dallas*
Kim Dielmann, *University of Central Arkansas*
James Francis, *San Jacinto College*
James Greer, *Louisiana State University*
Jean Berko Gleason, *Boston University*
James J. Johnson, *Illinois State University*
Paul R. Kleinginna, *Georgia Southern University*
Linda Kline, *California State University—Chico*
Karen Kopera-Frye, *The University of Akron*
Phil Kraemer, *University of Kentucky*
Eric Landrum, *Boise State University*
Gary D. Laver, *California Polytechnic, San Luis Obispo*
Marta Losonczy, *Salisbury State University*
Karen E. Luh, *University of Wisconsin—Madison*
Jerry Marshall, *University of Central Florida*
Vicki Mays, *University of California—Los Angeles*
Carol Nemeroff, *Arizona State University*
Cindy Nordstrom, *Illinois State University*
David Penn, *Louisiana State University*
Jeffrey Pedroza, *Lansing Community College*
Lawrence A. Pervin, *Rutgers University*
Vincent Punzo, *Earlham College*
Ed Raymaker, *Eastern Main Technical College*
Judith A. Sheiman, *Kutztown University*
Paula Shear, *University of Cincinnati*
Cynthia Sifonis, *University of Illinois*
Charles M. Slem, *California Polytech University*
Jutta M. Street, *Wake Technical Community College*
Roger M. Tarpy, Jr,. *Bucknell University*
Christopher Taylor, *University of Arizona*
Leonard Williams, *Rowan University*
Michael Zickar, *Bowling Green State*

Another group of psychologists also deserve thanks. They wrote material for individual chapters in previous editions and some of this material served as a base for the development of chapters in the Sixth Edition. In this regard, thanks go to:

Alice O'Toole, *U. of Texas—Dallas (Research in Psychology; Sensation and Perception)*
James Bartlett, *U. of Texas—Dallas (Memory; Thinking and Language)*
Laura King, *Southern Methodist University (Motivation and Emotion)*
David Neufeldt, *Hutchinson Community College (Applied Psychology)*
Robert Gifford, *U. of Victoria (Applied Psychology)*
Raymond Paloutzian, *Westmont College (Psychology of Religion)*
Morton Harmatz, *U. of Massachusetts (Therapies)*
Barry Stein, *Tennessee Technological U. (Thinking and Language)*

Acknowledgments from John Mitterer

The extensive work of updating and revising *Psychology*, Sixth Edition formed the basis of the First Canadian Edition. Veronica Visentin, Senior Sponsoring Editor, Ralph Courtney, Marketing Manager, and Marianne Minaker, Associate Sponsoring Editor, of McGraw-Hill Ryerson brought their considerable expertise to bear on the details of this Canadian adaptation.

Thoughtful reviews of the Sixth Edition by the following psychologists were also invaluable:

Robert Moore, *University of Regina*
Kathy Denton, *Douglas College*
Richard Maddigan, *Memorial University*
Douglas Needham, *Redeemer College*
Gary Bonczak, *Sir Sandford Fleming College*

Roisin O'Connor, Randall Barkwell, Joanne Boekestyn, Linda Pidduck, and Brenda Correy of Brock University helped with preparations. Many colleagues at Brock were patient with their expert advice, including Jack Adams-Webber, Michael Ashton, Kathy Belicki, John Benjafield, Stefan Brudzynski, Nancy DeCourville, David DiBattista, Jane Dywan, Dawn Good, Carolyn Hafer, Harry Hunt, Darla MacLean, Zopito Marini, Robert Nadon, Robert Ogilvie, Edward Pomeroy, Joan Preston, Linda Rose-Krasnor, Stan Sadava, Sidney J. Segalowitz, Paul Tyson, William Webster, and Teena Willoughby.

Many other Canadians were warmly supportive of my efforts to create *Psychology*, First Canadian Edition. Canadian psychology has much to be proud of and I thank the following people for their gracious assistance:

James Alcock, *York University*
Robert Altemeyer, *University of Manitoba*
John Berry, *Queen's University*
Ellen Bialystok, *York University*
Joanna Boehnert, *University of Guelph*
Michael Bradley, *University of New Brunswick Saint John*
Roger Broughton, *University of Ottawa*
Heidi Burgess, *McGill University*
Fergus Craik, *University of Toronto*
Martin Daly, *McMaster University*
Meredyth Daneman, *University of Toronto*
Caroline Davis, *York University*
Joseph De Koninck, *University of Ottawa*
Beverly Devins, *Sleep/Wake Disorders Canada*
Kenneth Dion, *University of Toronto*
Cheryl Driskell, *Anxiety Disorders of Ontario*
Joan Durrant, *University of Manitoba*
Norman Endler, *York University*

Raymond Fancher, *York University*
Ronald Holden, *Queens University*
Michaela Hynie, *York University*
Joy Ikelman
Douglas Jackson, *University of Western Ontario*
Larry Jacoby, *McMaster University*
Donald Jamieson, *University of Western Ontario*
Herbert Jenkins, *McMaster University*
Gary Johns, *Concordia University*
Julie Johnson, *First Call: BC Child and Youth Advocacy Coalition*
Doreen Kimura, *Simon Fraser University*
Barbara Kisilevsky, *Queen's University*
Bryan Kolb, *University of Lethbridge*
Albert Kozma, *Memorial University of Newfoundland*
Debbie Krulicki, *Alzheimer Society of Canada*
Robert Ladouceur, *Université Laval*
Herbert Lefcourt, *University of Waterloo*
Robert Lockhart, *University of Toronto*
Roberta MacDonald, *Anxiety Disorders Association of Manitoba*
Rod Martin, *University of Western Ontario*
Alex McKay, *The Sex Information and Education Council of Canada*
Donald Meichenbaum, *University of Waterloo*
Ronald Melzack, *McGill University*
Phillip Merikle, *University of Waterloo*
Debbie Moskowitz, *McGill University*
David Olson, *Ontario Institute for Studies in Education*
Ivan Parisien, *Canadian Psychological Association*
Linda Parker, *Wilfrid Laurier University*

Sampo Paunonen, *University of Waterloo*
Marie-Christine Pearson, *Canadian Psychological Association*
John Pinel, *University of British Columbia*
Patricia Pliner, *University of Toronto*
Janet Polivy, *University of Toronto*
Sandra Pyke, *York University*
William Roberts, *University of Western Ontario*
Donald Saklofske, *University of Saskatchewan*
Chip Scialfa, *University of Calgary*
Peter Seraganian, *Concordia University*
Shepard Siegel, *McMaster University*
Richard Sorrentino, *University of Western Ontario*
Cannie Stark-Adamec, *University of Regina*
Barbara Steele, *Heart and Stroke Foundation of Canada*
Michael Stones, *Lakehead University*
Endel Tulving, *University of Toronto*
Anne-Marie Wall, *York University*
Douglas Wahlsten, *University of Alberta*
Jerry Wiggins, *York University*
Margo Wilson, *McMaster University*
Sandra Witelson, *McMaster University*
Mark Zanna, *University of Waterloo*

John Mitterer
Brock University
March, 2000

For the Student

ONLINE QUIZZING

Do you understand the material? You'll know after taking an Online Quiz! Try the Multiple Choice and True/False questions for each chapter. They're auto-graded with feedback and the option to send results directly to faculty.

WEB LINKS

This section references various Web sites including all company Web sites linked from the text.

MICROSOFT® POWERPOINT® PRESENTATIONS

View and download presentations created for each text. Great for pre-class preparation and post-class review.

INTERNET APPLICATION QUESTIONS

Go online to learn how companies use the Internet in their day-to-day activities. Answer questions based on current organization Web sites and strategies.

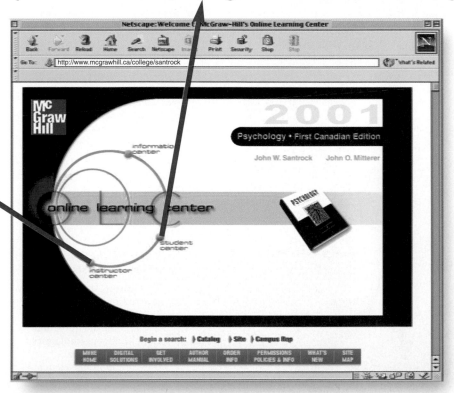

Your Internet companion to the most exciting educational tools on the Web!

The Online Learning Centre can be found at:
www.mcgrawhill.ca/college/santrock

Student-Driven Pedagogy

Students not only should be challenged to study hard and think more deeply and productively about psychology, they should also be provided with an extensive pedagogical framework to help them learn. Each of the learning and study aids that follow, some of which are unique to this text, have been tested and endorsed by the majority of students attending our focus groups. As a consequence, we are more confident than ever before that your students will find this edition of *Psychology* to be very student friendly.

Images of Psychology and Life

Opens each chapter with an imaginative, high-interest discussion that focuses on a topic related to the chapter content.

Chapter Outline

Shows the organization of topics by heading levels.

NEW!
Mini Cognitive Maps

These mini-maps appear three to five times per chapter and provide students with a more detailed, visual look at the organization of the chapter.

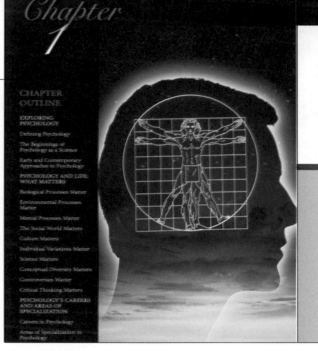

Preview

A brief look at what the chapter is about, including a series of questions that will be explored.

NEW!
Through the Eyes of Psychologists

This feature, appearing several times throughout each chapter, includes a photograph and quotation from leading psychologists to stimulate further thinking about the content.

Cartoons

Students like cartoons—perhaps because learning works best when the learner is in a good mood. To that end, cartoons appear several times in each chapter.

Summary Tables

These within-the-chapter reviews are coordinated with, and have the same headings as, the within-the-chapter cognitive maps. They give students a handle on information before they reach the end of the chapter.

Explorations in Psychology

This feature addresses many controversial issues in psychology and science, asking the student to think critically and evaluate their own stance on these issues.

NEW! Key Terms

These are boldfaced in the text and their definition is italicized.

NEW! Cross-Linkage

This system, unique to this text and new in this edition, refers students to the primary discussion of all key concepts. A specific page reference appears in the text with a backward pointing arrow each time a key concept occurs in a chapter subsequent to its initial coverage.

NEW! McGraw-Hill Website

A Web site icon appearing in the margin next to content guides student to the *Psychology*, First Canadian Edition Web site where they will find connecting Internet links that provide them with additional information. The label for each Web icon corresponds to the same label on the Santrock Web site.

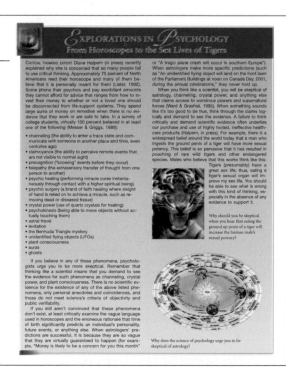

Thinking About Psychology and Life

This feature emphasizes the relevance of psychology to a student's everyday life through use of surveys and illustrative problems.

Overview

This consists of 2 parts: (1) an overall cognitive map of the entire chapter, and (2) a brief summary of the chapter.

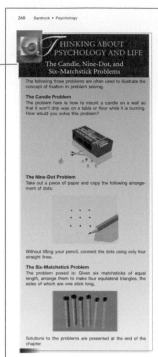

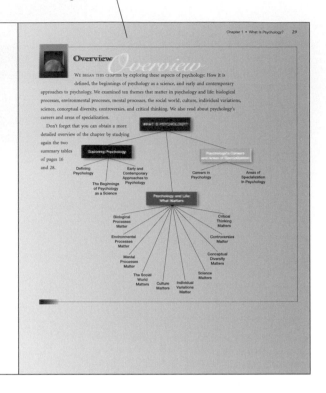

End of Chapter Key Terms

The key terms are listed and page-referenced to the chapter in addition to a comprehensive glossary at the end of the book.

NEW! Key People

The most important theorists and researchers in the chapter are listed and page-referenced.

NEW! Psychology Checklist

This checklist provides students with an opportunity to check their knowledge and understanding of the chapter's content.

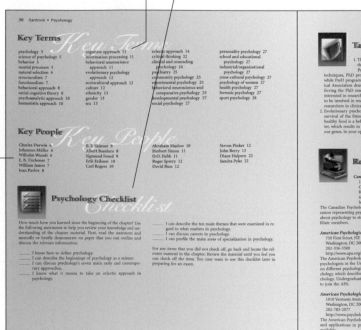

NEW! Taking It To The Net

Students are presented with questions to explore on the Internet, related to the chapter. From the *Psychology,* First Canadian Edition Web site under Taking It To The Net, students will find links to other Websites providing information that will help them to think more deeply about the questions posed.

Resources for Psychology and Life

Here, students will find information about both academic and practical resources, including books, phone numbers, agencies, research journals, and psychological organizations.

Illustration Program

The illustrations in introductory psychology texts have, in theory, always been important—but as almost any student will tell you, it is rare that the majority of photographs and figures are consistently relevant in a pedagogical context. This is usually because the authors and publishers place a far greater emphasis on the narrative content. However as more and more students become visual learners, the illustrative half of this equation must be accorded more attention. Failure to do so will result in texts that are unnecessarily more difficult for some students.

In this edition, we worked hard to give the illustration manuscript more relevance than the usual facelift would produce. Each photograph and figure was carefully selected and/or developed for its pedagogical significance, including those that open each chapter. Virtually every two-page spread contains one or more illustrations, providing visual interest and reinforcement for all key concepts. Many of the photo captions now contain critical thinking questions designed to encourage students to think more thoroughly about and apply the topic of the illustration to their own lives or related events.

Critical Thinking Questions

Many of the photos are now accompanied by critical thinking questions, designed to encourage students to think more thoroughly about topics and apply the material to their own lives.

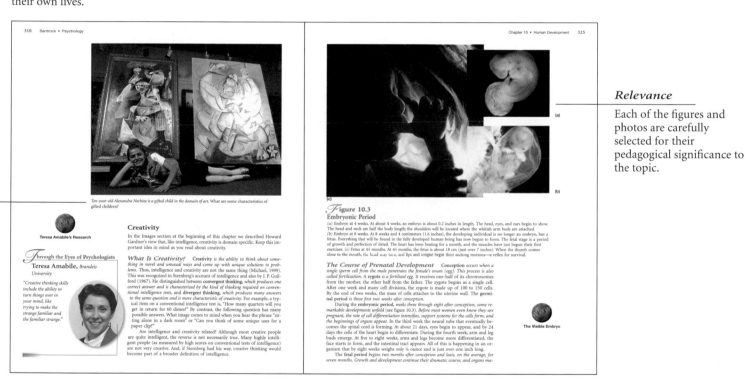

Relevance

Each of the figures and photos are carefully selected for their pedagogical significance to the topic.

FOR THE STUDENT

Student Study Guide (as prepared by John Mitterer, Brock University)

All answers and explanations provided

The Big Picture

Invitation to and brief overview of the main chapter points.

Learning Objectives

Identical to those that appear in the IM and TIF.

Chapter 1 - What is Psychology?

The Big Picture: Chapter Overview

Psychologists define their field as the scientific study of behavior and mental processes and rely upon systematic methods to observe, describe, predict, and explain behavior. The history of psychology is rooted in philosophy, biology, and physiology. The first scientific psychology laboratory was developed by Wundt in 1879. Working in his laboratory in Germany, Wundt studied consciousness with Titchener expanding Wundt's work. Their approach, which emphasized the importance of conscious thought and classification of the mind's structures, was called structuralism. William James, the first psychologist in the United States, emphasized the functions of the mind in adapting to a changing world; his approach was called functionalism.

There are seven main contemporary approaches in psychology. The behavioral approach focuses on using science to study how the environment influences behavior. In the social cognitive theory, behavior is seen as determined by environmental conditions and how thoughts affect the impact of those conditions on behavior. The unconscious mind, conflict between biological instincts and society's demands, and early family experiences characterize the psychoanalytic approach. In the humanistic approach, people are seen as having the capacity for personal growth, freedom to choose their own destiny, and as possessing positive qualities. The cognitive approach focuses on mental processes such as attention, perception, memory, thinking, and problem-solving. The brain and nervous system and their relationship to behavior, thought, and emotion are the areas of interest in the behavioral neuroscience approach. The evolutionary psychology approach argues for the importance of adaptation, reproduction, and survival of the fittest in explaining behavior. The newest perspective, the sociocultural approach, emphasizes that culture, ethnicity, and gender are necessary to understanding behavior, thought, and emotion. Most psychologists take an eclectic approach, selecting and using the best in each approach. There are several principles and themes that exert great influence on our lives and on psychology. Biological processes, like those of the brain, have powerful influences on behavior. Repeated experiences acting as environment processes can wire or rewire the brain. Mental processes matter since they allow us to remember, make decisions, plan, set goals, and be creative. Other people and our relationships to them matter in the social world.

Learning Objectives

When you have studied the material in this chapter, you should be able to:

1. define psychology.
2. identify the two disciplines from which psychology emerged.
3. distinguish among the following early psychologists and their approaches to psychology: Wundt and Titchener (structuralism) and William James (functionalism).
4. distinguish among the seven contemporary approaches to psychology and identify contributions to each approach:
   - behavioral
   - psychoanalytic
   - humanistic
   - cognitive
   - neurobiological
   - evolutionary
   - sociocultural
5. explain what is meant by an eclectic approach.

1

Guided Review

Fill-in-the-blanks chapter review.

Guided Review

Exploring Psychology

Psychology is the ________ of behavior and mental processes. The term ________ refers to everything that we do that can be directly ________. Mental processes refer to the thoughts, feelings, and motives that are not directly observable. Because psychology is a _______, it uses systematic methods to observe, describe, predict, and explain behavior. Influenced by the field of _______, psychology emerged as a science in the nineteenth century. Darwin developed the concept of ________.

In 1879, __________ developed the first scientific laboratory in psychology. His work was popularized in the United States by ________. Their approach emphasized the importance of conscious thoughts and a classification of the mind's structure and become known as ________. William James, meanwhile, examined the mind's ability to adapt to the environment, in an approach called ________. Pavlov and Watson emphasized measuring overt behavior as they rejected inferences about the conscious mind in the approach called ________ approach. In this approach, behavior is influenced by the ________ determinants. Social cognitive theory stresses that ______ modifies the impact of the environment on behavior. According to this perspective, ________ is an important process by which we learn about the world.

Freud believed that the key to understanding mind and behavior rested in the _______ part of the mind. Freud's approach is known as the ________ approach. In explaining behavior, Freud argued that people were heavily influenced by ________ and _________ instincts. These instincts conflicted with the demands of ________. Contemporary psychoanalytic theories place more emphasis on ________ experiences. Another approach in contemporary psychology stresses a person's capacity for personal growth, freedom of choice and the positive qualities of people, which is called ________ approach. These psychologists believe individuals ________their own lives. Two psychologists who influenced this approach are ________ and ________.

In the ________ approach, there is an emphasis on mental processes involved in knowing. This type of psychologist views the mind as a(n) _____ and aware problem-solving system. Within this approach, there is a perspective that studies how individuals ________ information. It compares the human mind with a _______. An approach that gives the brain the central nervous system primary roles in understanding behavior, thoughts, and emotions is called behavioral _________.

_________ approach examines the conditions that allow individuals to survive or to fail. According to this approach, the mind has ________ in such a way to increase the chance of survival. The ________ approach to psychology stresses the importance of culture, ethnicity, and gender. The term ________ refers to the behavior

scientific study - p. 5
behavior - p. 5
observed - p. 5
science - p. 5
philosophy - p. 6
natural selection - p. 6
Wundt - p. 6
Titchener - p. 7
structuralism - p. 7
functionalism - p. 7
behavioral - p. 8
environmental - p. 8
thinking - p. 8
imitation - p. 8
unconscious - p. 9
psychoanalytic - p. 10
sexual - p. 10
aggressive - p. 10
society - p. 10
cultural - p. 10
humanistic - p. 10
choose - p. 10
Rogers/Maslow - p. 10
cognitive - p. 11
active - p. 11
process - p. 11
computer - p. 11
neuroscience - p. 11
Evolutionary - p. 12
evolved - p. 12
sociocultural - p. 12
culture - p. 13

2

Correcting the Incorrect
(15–20 per chapter)

Identify the factual error and correct accordingly.

In Your Own Words
(5–10 per chapter)

Students are promoted to paraphrase what they've learned in the chapter, fostering independent thinking rather than memorization of details.

In Your Own Words

To respond to the questions and exercises presented in this section, please write your thoughts, perspectives, and reactions on a separate piece of paper.

Critical Thinking Exercises

- ✓ Put the definition of psychology into your own words.
- ✓ What are some examples of mental processes that you have experienced in the last 10 minutes?
- ✓ List some things about you that have been influenced by the culture in which you live. (Hint: Don't overlook the obvious.)
- ✓ Thinking about how individual variations matter, list some things about you that are unique.
- ✓ Based on your experiences and what you've learned so far in this course, what about people fascinates you the most?
- ✓ Imagine that you work for an advertising agency. Your team is creating television commercials for each of the perspectives. Your part of the project is to write a catchy jingle or slogan for each perspective.
- ✓ Make up a title of a fictitious book that could have been written by Wundt, James, Freud, Skinner, Simon, and Sperry. Try writing a book title for a book on clinical psychology, developmental psychology, forensic psychology, and the psychology of women. The title should reflect the perspective or specialization. Be creative!
- ✓ Chapter One discusses several specializations of psychology. Which one sounds most appealing to you? If you could create a new specialization in psychology, what would it be?

Correcting the Incorrect

Carefully read each statement. Determine if the statement is correct or incorrect. If the statement is incorrect, make the necessary changes to correct it. Then look directly under the statement for the correct statement and page reference in the textbook.

1. Psychology is the scientific study of people's psychological problems and how to help those people.
   - ❑ *Psychology is the scientific study of behavior and mental processes. (p. 5)*
2. Mental processes include thoughts, feelings, and motives that cannot be observed directly.
   - ❑ *Mental processes include thoughts, feelings, and motives that cannot be observed directly. (p. 5)*
3. Since mental processes are not directly observable, they are actually not real.
   - ❑ *Mental processes are not directly observable, but they are nonetheless real. (p. 5)*
4. As a philosophy, psychology uses systematic methods to observe, describe, predict, and explain behavior.
   - ❑ *As a science, psychology uses systematic methods to observe, describe, predict, and explain behavior. (p. 5)*
5. Charles Darwin established the first psychological laboratory.
   - ❑ *(p. 6)*
6. Wundt and Titchener developed an approach called functionalism.
   - ❑ *Wundt and Titchener developed an approach called structualism. (p. 7)*
7. The first psychologist in the Germany was William James.
   - ❑ *The first psychologist in the United States was William James. (p. 7)*
8. Behaviorists, like Freud and Rogers, would say that the environment determines behavior.
   - ❑ *Behaviorists, like Watson and Skinner, would say that the environment determines behavior. (p. 8)*
9. Social cognitive theory focuses on unconscious motives.
   - ❑ *Social cognitive theory focuses on how thoughts modify the impact of environment on behavior.(p. 8).*
10. B. F. Skinner suggested psychology should study the mind.
    - ❑ *B. F. Skinner suggested psychology should not study the mind. (p. 8)*

3

Explorations in Psychology: From Horoscopes to the Sex Lives of Tigers

- What does the word "skepticism" mean to you? Does it have a bad connotation to you?
- Have you ever had an experience with one of the phenomenon listed in this section?
- If so, how might a person who practices skepticism explain your experience.
- What does a belief in horoscopes give people?
- What would you say to a person who has totally bought into one of the phenomena listed in this section?

Practice Test

1. Psychology is best defined as the
   - a. study of perception and memory.
   - b. investigation of the human psyche.
   - c. scientific study of conscious and unconscious processes.
   - d. scientific study of behavior and mental processes.

> a. no; psychology is more than the study of just perception and memory
> b. sorry this is not the best definition
> c. even though psychology does study conscious and unconscious processes, this is not the best answer
> d. THAT'S CORRECT; psychology is best defined as the scientific study of behavior and mental processes

2. As you read the definition of psychology you begin to think about examples. Of the following, which one is the best example of behavior?
   - a. planning your weekend activities
   - b. adding two numbers in your head
   - c. a two-year-old boy coloring a picture
   - d. thinking about this question

> a. planning is an example of a mental process since it cannot be directly observed
> b. adding is an example of a mental process since it cannot be directly observed
> c. CORRECT; coloring a picture is behavior since it can be directly observed
> d. thinking is an example of a mental process since it cannot be directly observed

3. A team of researchers wants to study aggressive behavior in adolescents. The researchers plan to use observations to describe, make predictions about, and explain adolescents' aggressive behavior. Which of the following best describes what these researchers are doing?
   - a. They are trying to define mental processes.
   - b. They are identifying environmental determinants of behavior.
   - c. They are studying peer pressure.
   - d. They are following the scientific method.

> a. aggression is behavior, not a mental process
> b. no, observations in description, predictions, and explanation are part of the scientific method
> c. the researchers might be studying peer pressure, but this is not the best answer
> d. CORRECT; this option best describes what the researchers are doing

4. The definition of psychology is made up of several parts. Which part refers to "thoughts, feelings, and motives"?
   - a. scientific study
   - b. behavior

1

Explorations in Psychology
(4–6 per chapter)

Thought-provoking questions related to chapter features.

Practice Tests

15–20 composed by author; 15 selected from TIF. Multiple-choice items followed by immediate feedback and explanations.

FOR THE INSTRUCTOR

Instructor's Manual (as prepared by John Mitterer, Brock University)

Teaching Objectives

Objectives are page-referenced and identical to the TIF objectives and the SSG learning objectives.

Chapter Overview

Brief summary of chapter highlights.

Chapter One: What Is Psychology

- **Chapter Overview**
- **Teaching Objectives**
- **Teaching the Chapter**
  - Lecture Outlines by Section
  - Lecture/Discussion Suggestions by Section
- **Explorations in Psychology**
  - Critical Thinking Questions
- **Thinking About Psychology in Everyday Life**
  - Student Activities
- **Learning Style Activities**
- **Connections**
  - Suggested Articles from Annual Editions
  - Suggested Articles from Sources: Notable Selections in Psychology
  - Film Suggestions
  - Suggestions for Additional Reading

Chapter Overview

Images of Psychology and Life: Why Youth Kill: By opening the chapter with this feature, Santrock illustrates one of psychology's most important constructs: the psychology of any human being is a complex system of thoughts and behaviors constructed from and influenced by multiple determinants. Because multiple determinants require multiple approaches, psychology studies the complexity of human nature from a multitude of perspectives—each designed to address very different aspects of what makes us human.
Defining Psychology: Psychology is defined as the science of behavior and mental processes. A science seeks to observe, describe, predict and explain events. Psychology uses systematic methods to observe, describe, predict and explain behavior and mental processes.
From Myth to Philosophy to Psychology: Psychology emerges from two distinct lines of inquiry: philosophy and the natural sciences of biology and physiology. The first recognition of psychology as a separate and distinct science begins with Wilhelm Wundt and his early attempts to systematically study consciousness.
Early Contributors: An introduction to Tichener is followed by a traditional discussion of the early competing schools of thought: structuralism, with its emphasis on conscious thought and classification of the mind's structures and functionalism, with its emphasis on the functions of the mind in adapting to the environment.
Early and Contemporary Approaches: As he moves into the contemporary approaches, Santrock notes that new approaches continue to evolve. The contemporary approaches begin with a brief introduction to the work of Pavlov and his use of careful observation to study overt behavior. While an emphasis on observable behavior and environmental determinants is characteristic of all behavioral views today, different forms of behaviorism have stemmed from the work of Skinner and Bandura. In particular, Bandura's social cognitive theory has broadened the scope of behaviorism to include the ways in which information about the environment is cognitively processed. In the psychoanalytic approach, Freud emphasized the influence of unconscious aspects of mind, the conflict between instincts and society's demands, and the importance of early family experiences. Contemporary psychoanalysis is illustrated by the revisionist work of Erickson, who developed the concept that personality develops in stages over the course of the life span. The humanistic approach, with its emphasis on the capacity for personal growth and freedom to choose, offers a

1

Teaching Objectives

When students have studied the material in this chapter, they should be able to:

1. define psychology.
2. identify the two disciplines from which psychology emerged.
3. distinguish among the following early psychologists and their approaches to psychology: Wundt and Tichener (structuralism) and William James (functionalism).
4. distinguish among the seven contemporary approaches to psychology and identify contributors to each approach:
   - behavioral
   - pychoanalytic
   - humanistic
   - cognitive
   - neurobiological
   - evolutionary
   - sociocultural
5. explain what is meant by an eclectic approach.
6. discuss why biology, environment, mental processes, social world, culture, and individual variations all matter in the study of psychology.
7. discuss the importance of systematic methods in the study of psychology.
8. explain why conceptual diversity, paradox, and controversy help to advance the study of psychology.
9. list five thinking strategies essential to good critical thinking.
10. summarize and relate the material from *Explorations in Psychology: From Horoscopes to the Sex Lives of Tigers*, to the material on critical thinking.
11. identify the various areas of specialization in psychology.

Teaching the Chapter

I. What Is Psychology

A. Images of Psychology and Life: Why Youth Kill
1. Predicting if a youth turns violent is a complex task.
2. Multiple factors can influence the development of violence.
   a. feelings of powerlessness
   b. urban poverty
   c. inadequate parenting and supervision
3. Studies attempt to approach the question from many different angles.

B. Exploring Psychology
1. Defining Psychology
   a. Psychology is the science of behavior and mental processes.
   b. Psychology uses systematic methods to observe, describe, predict, and explain.
   c. A behavior is anything we do that can be observed.
   d. Mental processes are the thoughts, feelings and motives we experience privately that cannot be observed directly.

Lecture/Discussion Suggestions

What Is Psychology: Prior to beginning your lecture on the definition of psychology, you can have students volunteer their own definitions. Ask students to respond individually or break them into small groups to write an agreed upon "group" definition. Some of the definitions will be simplistic and some amazingly complex. Many will include the terms: thinking, mind, brain, abnormal, and emotion. Terms

2

Teaching the Chapter

Lecture outlines by chapter; lecture/discussion suggestions by section.

Learning Style Activities

Additional student activities also accompanied by handouts.

Explorations in Psychology

Critical thinking questions and exercises.

Explorations in Psychology: Critical Thinking

From Horoscopes to the Sex lives of Tigers: In this feature, students are presented with evidence that many persons do not use critical thinking in their everyday life. The failure to think critically leads people to purchase products that are virtually ineffective and to believe in phenomena that are clearly unsupported by scientific evidence. If critical thinking asks us to "think like a scientist" then we must be skeptical of anything that sounds "too good to be true" and demand to see the evidence.

1. **Classroom Activity: Evaluating the Infomercial:** Tape or have students tape a ten-minute segment from any infomercial on TV. Excellent examples are those guaranteeing 'instant results' ("weight loss with no effort," "healing with magnetic bracelets," "a six-figure income in your spare time"). View the segment together and ask students to answer the following questions:
   a. What am I being asked to believe or accept?
   b. What evidence is available to support the advertiser's claim?
   c. In reviewing the evidence presented, are their alternative ways to interpret that evidence?
   d. What additional evidence is needed to support the advertiser's claim?
   e. Given only the evidence presented by the advertiser, what conclusions are most reasonable?

   As an alternative to using infomercials, ask students to bring a variety of advertising claims to class. Choose several and have students evaluate the claims using the questions provided.
2. **Prisoners of Silence:** If you can spare fifty minutes of class, this film is a powerful example of what can happen when scientists and the public *want* to believe. Frontline tells the story of facilitated communication and the belief that it would open the doors into the silent world of autism. It is a disheartening story that details widespread acceptance of the technique by psychologists, parents and schools before validity was ever determined. The film is a remarkable demonstration of the need for scientific validation and the harm that results when claims are not thoroughly investigated.

   Frontline: Prisoners of Silence (1992). Available from PBS Video, a division of the Public Broadcasting Service.

Learning Style Activities

(AE) Active Experimentation: Doing

1. Goal: To gather material that demonstrates what various subgroups of a general population believe psychology to be.
2. Task: Develop a brief audio and/or visual presentation.
3. Instructions: Develop a list of several questions pertaining to the nature of psychology. For example: Can you tell me what psychology is? Choose several populations of persons and interview a sample of the population. Your populations might be hospital personnel, faculty at your school, friends, or even family members. Once you have asked the questions and recorded the answers, you will need to develop some way to organize the responses. You might make different categories for the responses, color-code them according to sample, and present a summary of the answers on a posterboard. You might wish to videotape your interviews and carefully edit responses representative of each population. Several students could combine results.

(RO) Reflective Observation: Watching

1. Goal: To illustrate popular portrayals of psychology.
2. Task: Observe behavior on two different daytime soap operas for three consecutive days.
3. Instructions: Videotape two different daytime soap operas for three consecutive days. Watch the tapes and try to map out a data recording sheet that would apply to both shows. For example, you might divide your sheet and have columns headed "Males" and "Females." As you watch the tapes, try to

3

Thinking About Psychology and Life

Student activities accompanied by handouts and correlated with features in the texts.

Activity Handout 1.4

Elza: The Impact of Changing Contexts

Instructions: Read the following case study and answer the questions that follow.

"The year is 1998. Elza is a 60-year-old female who has been widowed for two years. Her husband was a well-educated man who left her with a comfortable income when he died. Currently she is healthy though she does have some arthritis developing in her knees. She is active as a hospital volunteer and a member of the quilting circle at her church. Ellen is college graduate but has never worked outside the home. She has two daughters and five grandchildren. Both daughters live about fifty miles from her home."

After reading Elza's story, you will be asked to change one context in her life and to imagine the impact that change would have on the other contexts. As one context changes, write a description of how it might affect the other circumstances of Elza's life.

1. Change the historical context from 1998 to 1890.

2. Change the economic context from a comfortable income to social security only.

3. Change the biological context from relatively healthy to chronic heart disease.

4. Change the educational context from a college graduate to illiterate.

Connections

Suggested Articles from Annual Editions Publications

- From *Psychology 98/99* (Twenty-eighth edition)

Article 1: The Origin of Psychological Species: History of the Beginnings of the American Psychological Association Divisions. Ludy T. Benjamin Jr., *American Psychologist*, July 1997.

Article 2: The Benefits and Ethics of Animal Research. Andrew N. Rowan, *Scientific American*, February, 1997.

Suggested Articles from Sources: Notable Selections in Psychology, 2e

1.1 William James, from The Principles of Psychology.
1.2 John B. Watson, from "Psychology as the Behaviorist Views It," *Psychological Review.*
1.3 Gordon H. Bower, from "The Fragmentation of Psychology," *American Psychologist.*
2.1 Roger W. Sperry, from "Hemisphere Deconnection and Unity in Conscious Awareness," *American Psychologist.*
6.2 B. F. Skinner, from *Science and Human Behavior.*
6.4 Albert Bandura, Dorothea Ross, and Sheila A. Ross, from "Imitation of Film-Mediated Aggressive Models," *Journal of Abnormal and Social Psychology.*

Suggested Films and Videocasettes

1. *Discovering Psychology 1: Past, Present, and Promise.* (Annenberg/CBP Project, 1990, 30 minutes)
   Introduces psychology and shows its relationship to different fields of knowledge.
2. *Aspects of Behavior.* (CRM/McGraw-Hill, 1971, 26 minutes)
   Introduces psychology and experiments. Interviews with noted figures such as Stanley Milgram and Abraham Maslow.
3. *The Mind: Part 1, Search for Mind.* (WNET/New York, 1988, 58 minutes.

4

Connections

Suggested articles from annual editions; suggested articles from Sources: Notable Selections in Psychology; film suggestions; suggestions for additional readings.

FOR THE INSTRUCTOR

TEST ITEM FILE (as prepared by
John Mitterer, Brock University)

True/False Items

15–20 per chapter

Fill-In-The-Blanks

20 per chapter

Teaching Objectives

Objectives are page-referenced and identical to the TIF objectives and the SSG learning objectives.

Teaching Objectives

When students have studied the material in this chapter, they should be able to:

1. define psychology.
2. identify the two disciplines from which psychology emerged.
3. distinguish among the following early psychologists and their approaches to psychology:
   Wundt and Tichener (structuralism) and William James (functionalism).
4. distinguish among the seven contemporary approaches to psychology and identify contributors to each approach:
   - behavioral
   - pychoanalytic
   - humanistic
   - cognitive
   - neurobiological
   - evolutionary
   - sociocultural

Chapter 1: What Is Psychology?

Multiple-Choice Questions

*1. Psychology is **best** defined as the
   a. study of perception and memory.
   b. investigation of the human psyche.
   c. scientific study of conscious and unconscious processes.
   d. scientific study of behavior and mental processes.
   Ans.: d   LO: 1   Page: 5   QT: F

2. Which of the following is **not** one of the three primary aspects of the definition of psychology?
   a. science
   b. behavior
   c. analysis
   d. mental processes
   Ans.: c   LO: 1   Page: 5   QT: F

3. The basic goals of any science are to
   a. think, feel, remember, and analyze.
   b. analyze, speculate, hypothesize, and control.
   c. observe, describe, predict, and explain.
   d. speculate, think, control, and predict.
   Ans.: c   LO: 1   Page: 5   QT: F

4. In everyday interactions, we often make observations about the behavior of other people. What is the **main** difference between this type of casual observation and that conducted by a research psychologist?
   a. A psychologist would observe the other people for a longer period of time.
   b. A psychologist would use systematic methods to observe the behavior.
   c. A psychologist would tell people that they are going to be observed.
   d. A psychologist would predict the behavior before observing it.
   Ans.: b   LO: 1   Page: 5   QT: C

Chapter 1   Page 1

---

*True/False Questions

___ 1. The science of psychology concerns itself only with the study of observable behavior.
___ 2. One goal of the science of psychology is to predict behavior.
___ 3. The discipline of philosophy represents one of the roots of psychology.
___ 4. Wilhelm Wundt founded the school of functionalism.
___ 5. William James was the first psychologist in the United States.

Answer Key for True/False Questions:

1. Ans.: F   LO: 1   Page: 5
2. Ans.: T   LO: 1   Page: 5
3. Ans.: T   LO: 2   Page: 7
4. Ans.: F   LO: 3   Page: 8
5. Ans.: T   LO: 3   Page: 9

Fill-in-the-Blank Questions

1. Psychology is the scientific study of _____ and mental processes.
2. The four goals of psychology are to observe, describe, predict, and _____ behavior.
3. Remembering your best friend's phone number is a _____ process.
4. The roots of psychology can be found in _____, biology, and physiology.

Answer Key for Fill-in-the-Blank Questions

1. Ans.: behavior   LO: 1 Page: 5
2. Ans.: explain   LO: 1 Page: 5
3. Ans.: mental   LO: 1 Page: 6
4. Ans.: philosophy   LO: 2 Page: 7

Matching Questions

___ 1. not directly observable   A. psychoanalytic approach
___ 2. philosophy   B. critical thinker
___ 3. structuralism   C. promoting the research and study of women
___ 4. Ivan Pavlov   D. community psychology

Answer Key for Matching Questions

1. Ans.: F   LO: 1   Page: 6
2. Ans.: L   LO: 2   Page: 6
3. Ans.: T   LO: 3   Page: 8
4. Ans.: O   LO: 4   Page: 10

Essay Questions

1. Compare and contrast the psychological approaches of Wilhelm Wundt, Edward Titchener, and William James. What beliefs did they hold in common? How did their beliefs differ? (LO: 3)

   Answer Guidelines: Possible options include mentioning Wundt and structures of the mind; Titchener and structuralism and introspection; and James and functionalism. Common focus on conscious experience. Different view on how this experience should be studied (subjective introspection versus real-life experiences).

Chapter 1   Page 2

Multiple-Choice Questions

Approximately 100–125 per chapter

Matching Items

15 per chapter

Essay Questions

5 per chapter

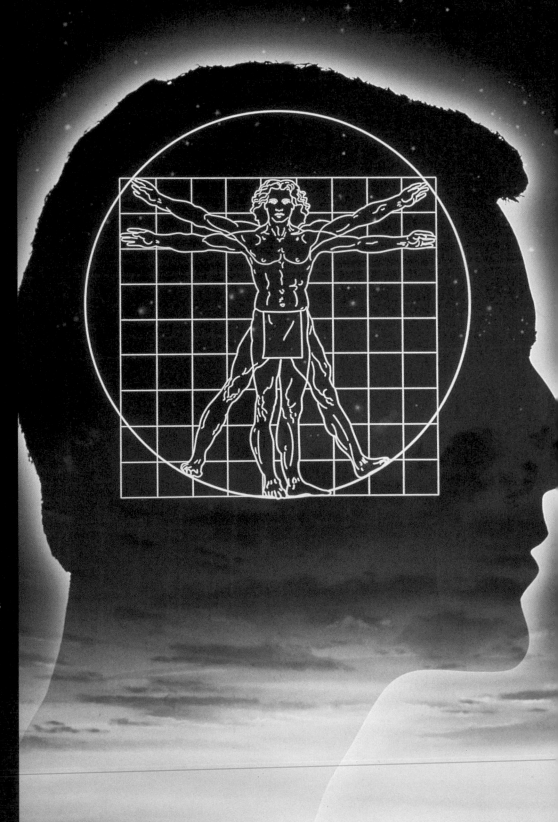

Chapter 1

CHAPTER OUTLINE

EXPLORING PSYCHOLOGY

Defining Psychology

The Beginnings of Psychology as a Science

Early and Contemporary Approaches to Psychology

PSYCHOLOGY AND LIFE: WHAT MATTERS

Biological Processes Matter

Environmental Processes Matter

Mental Processes Matter

The Social World Matters

Culture Matters

Individual Variations Matter

Science Matters

Conceptual Diversity Matters

Controversies Matter

Critical Thinking Matters

PSYCHOLOGY'S CAREERS AND AREAS OF SPECIALIZATION

Careers in Psychology

Areas of Specialization in Psychology

What Is Psychology?

Images of Psychology and Life
Why Youth Kill

*"M*y friend . . . care for your psyche, and . . . make it as good as possible. . . . Know thyself, for once we know ourselves, we may learn how to care for ourselves, but otherwise we never shall.*"*

Socrates
Greek Philosopher, 5th Century B.C.

Preview

PSYCHOLOGY IS A FASCINATING FIELD that contains some of the most interesting inquiries you will encounter in any area you study in college. In the following Images of Psychology section we will introduce you to one of those interesting areas of inquiry: Why do youth kill? Some of the other intriguing questions we will explore in this chapter are these:
• How did psychology come into being?
• What matters in psychology and life?
• How does our brain influence what we do?
• How can children be taught to think critically?
• How did David Suzuki grow up to become a world-famous scientist?

ON APRIL 20, 1999, AT Columbine High School in Littleton, CO, Eric Harris, 18, and Dylan Klebold, 17, members of an outcast clique called the "Trenchcoat Mafia," killed 12 students and a teacher, planted bombs and then committed suicide. Harris had a Web page on which he had bragged of making four pipe bombs more than a year earlier but apparently no one took it seriously, an unfortunately common response (Cornell, 1998).

Canadians had eight days to tell themselves it couldn't happen here before a 14-year old Alberta youth entered W.R. Myers High School in Taber, killed one student and wounded another. According to his mother, the youth, whose identity is protected by the Young Offenders Act, was a lonely, depressed social reject obsessed by the news from Columbine.

Females are increasingly involved in violence. On November 14, 1997, 14-year-old Reena Virk was assaulted and left to drown in Saanich, BC. Eight teenagers aged 14 to 16—seven of them female—were charged in Reena's death. She was kicked and beaten so viciously that her arms, neck and back were fractured. A sister of one of the assaulters says Reena begged, "Help me, I love you," as she neared death.

Students from Columbine High School in Littleton, Colorado, leave the school after two classmates went on a shooting rampage in April, 1999.

Students from Taber clutch programs from a memorial service for shot student Jason Lang. What are some of the possible reasons youth can be moved to commit brutal acts of violence?

3

Can psychologists predict whether a youth will turn violent? It's a complex task but they have pieced together some clues (Cowley, 1998). Young violent males are driven by feelings of powerlessness. Violence seems to infuse these youth with a sense of power (Garabino, 1999). According to Sybil Artz, director of the University of Victoria's School of Child and Youth Care (Artz, 1998), young violent females also respond to social pressures to be popular, sexy and powerful. When they fail to achieve those goals with traditional means, more and more females mimic what they see in males by turning to violence.

While it is difficult to predict whether a youth will actually act on his or her anger and sense of powerlessness with violence, various risk factors have been identified (Artz, 1998; Garabino, 1999). The more risk factors a youth has been exposed to, the greater becomes the risk of a violent response in the future.

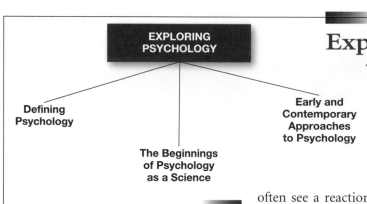

EXPLORING PSYCHOLOGY

Defining Psychology

The Beginnings of Psychology as a Science

Early and Contemporary Approaches to Psychology

Exploring Psychology

Trying to figure out what motivates some teenagers to commit murder is one of the many things psychologists do. What else do psychologists do?

Imagine that you are seated at dinner next to someone you have never met and learn that she is a psychologist. What comes to mind when you find out she is a psychologist? To many people, it means that she analyzes people's problems. When either of us meets people, and they find out we are psychologists, we often see a reaction like, "Uh oh, I'd better be on my guard because they are going to psychoanalyze me and find out what I'm really like."

Many psychologists do analyze people's problems and try to help them cope with them. However, many psychologists are researchers, not therapists. No single image encompasses psychologists' varied activities. Consider the following descriptions of some contemporary psychologists at work:

- A research psychologist trained in cognitive psychology painstakingly constructs the thousands of steps of a computer program that, presented with hundreds of sentences, will learn language as an infant does.
- Another research psychologist trained in physiological psychology and neuroscience injects epinephrine into a rat that has learned a maze, to determine how the hormone affects its memory.
- A clinical psychologist probes a depressed client's thoughts for clues about the cause of the depression and thinks about ways to help the client cope more effectively.
- A school psychologist with a background in linguistics and bilingualism might design a program to immerse English-speaking children in French for much of their early childhood education in Ontario, or vice-versa in Quebec.
- A psychologist interested in gender and women's issues teaches at a university and works with her university and the community to eliminate sexual harassment.
- An organizational psychologist has a consulting firm that advises corporations on ways to improve communication and work productivity.

PEANUTS reprinted by permission of United Feature Syndicate, Inc.

These are but a few of the many different portraits of psychologists. As you read this book, you will discover that psychology is a diverse field and psychologists have heterogeneous interests. Let's now see how psychologists define their field.

Defining Psychology

To some extent, psychology's findings may strike you as being simple common sense, but studies often turn up the unexpected in human behavior. For example, it may seem obvious that couples who live together before marriage have a better chance of making the marriage last. After all, practice makes perfect, doesn't it? But researchers have found a higher success rate for couples who marry before living together (Teachman & Polonko, 1990). It might also seem obvious that we would experience more stress and be less happy if we had to function in many different roles than if we only functioned in a single role. However, women who engage in multiple roles (such as wife, mother, and career woman) report more satisfaction with their lives than do women who engage in a single or fewer roles (such as wife or wife and mother) (Cozby, 1991). As you can see, psychology doesn't accept assumptions about human nature at face value, however reasonable they may sound. It is a rigorous discipline that tests assumptions.

Psychology *is the scientific study of behavior and mental processes.* There are three aspects to this definition: science, behavior, and mental processes.

As a **science**, *psychology uses systematic methods to observe, describe, predict, and explain behavior.* Psychology's methods are not casual. They are carefully and precisely planned and conducted. They are often verified by checking to see if they *describe* the behavior of many different people. For example, researchers might construct a questionnaire on sexual attitudes and give it to 500 individuals. They might spend considerable time devising the questions and determining the background of the people who are chosen to participate in the survey. The researchers may try to *predict* the sexual activity of university students based on their liberal or conservative religious attitudes, or on their sexual knowledge, for example. After the psychologists analyze their data, they will also want to *explain* what they *observe.* If the researchers discover from their survey that university students are less sexually active than they were a decade ago, they seek to explain why this change has occurred. They might ask, Is it because of increased fear of sexually transmitted diseases? As can be seen, psychology is recognized as a scientific discipline.

Let's now examine what behavior and mental processes are. **Behavior** *is everything we do that can be directly observed*—two people kissing, a baby crying, a university student riding a motorcycle.

Mental processes *are trickier to define than behavior; they are the thoughts, feelings, and motives that each of us experiences privately but that cannot be observed directly.* Though we cannot directly see thoughts and feelings, they are nonetheless real. They include *thinking* about kissing someone, a baby's *feelings* when its mother

The Canadian Psychological Association
APA PsycNET
The American Psychological Society

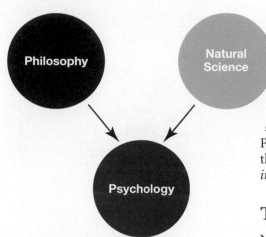

$\mathcal{F}$igure 1.1
Psychology's Beginnings

Psychology's seeds were sown in the nineteenth century by merging ideas from philosophy and natural sciences such as biology and physiology. Why did psychology emerge as a hybrid offspring from these areas?

History and Philosophy of Psychology
History of Psychology
Exploring the History of Psychology

Wilhelm Wundt (1832–1920), a philosopher-physician, who founded the first psychology laboratory at the University of Leipzig in Germany in 1879. Psychology Archives–University of Akron

leaves the room, and a university student's *memory* of a motorcycle episode. Psychology is not a cure-all for every knotty problem, and it doesn't tell us the meaning of life. It does, however, contribute enormously to our knowledge about why people are the way they are, why they think and act the way they do, and how they can cope more effectively with their lives. Many of life's problems today are psychological problems: death caused by unhealthy lifestyles (such as lack of exercise, poor eating habits, and inability to cope with stress), pollution, violence, racism, and employment in a changing information age. Psychologists are enthusiastic about psychology's potential to improve our lives in these and many other areas as we move into the twenty-first century. *It is an exciting time of discovery in the field of psychology* (Dobson, 1995).

The Beginnings of Psychology as a Science

Now that we have defined psychology, let's explore the development and evolution of the field of psychology. How did a field so varied as psychology emerge? Who were its earliest contributors?

From Myth to Philosophy to Psychology
Ever since our ancestors first gathered around a fire to create and embellish myths, we've been trying to explain why things are the way they are. Myths attributed most events to the pleasure or displeasure of the gods: When a volcano erupted, the gods were angry; if two people fell in love, they were the target of Cupid's arrows. As we became more sophisticated, myths gave way to *philosophy,* the rational investigation of the underlying principles of being and knowledge.

For centuries, philosophers enjoyed arguing and debating (and still do today) questions like these: Do we acquire knowledge? Does information come to us through our senses and our experiences with the environment, or is it inborn? Although such speculation fuels a great deal of intellectual passion, psychologists always have searched for more concrete evidence than philosophers. Philosophers think about thinking and discuss thinking. So do psychologists, but psychologists also do something else. They systematically obtain and interpret evidence about thinking.

Philosophy was not the only discipline out of which psychology emerged. Psychology's roots are also in the natural sciences of biology and physiology (Benjamin, 1999). The intellectual atmosphere when psychology emerged as a science was heavily flavored by the work of British naturalist Charles Darwin. He developed the concept of **natural selection,** *that the organisms that are best adapted to their world are the most likely to survive, reproduce, and pass on their characteristics to their offspring.* Later in this chapter and in subsequent chapters, you will see that psychology has recently rediscovered Darwin's evolutionary approach. In addition to Darwin's influence on psychology's emergence, physiologists in the middle of the 19th century, such as the German Johannes Müller, were already proposing that the brain's role is to associate incoming sensory information with appropriate motor responses.

Thus, by the late nineteenth century, conditions were ripe for psychology to emerge as a scientific discipline, a hybrid offspring of philosophy and natural science (Leahey, 1997; Benjafield, 1996) (see figure 1.1). Indeed, as we will see shortly, it was a philosopher-physician who put the pieces of the philosophy-natural science puzzle together to create the academic discipline of psychology.

Early Contributors
What was the first psychology lab like? What conceptual orientation did psychology's earliest contributors have?

Wundt's Laboratory   Imagine a room in Leipzig, Germany, in the year 1879, where a bearded man with a wrinkled forehead and pensive expression is sitting on a chair. He turns his head toward a soft sound coming from the far side of the room. After several seconds, he turns his head again, this time toward a loud sound. The activity is repeated with sounds of varying intensity. The man is Wilhelm Wundt, a philosopher-physician, who is credited with developing the first scientific laboratory in psychology. By systematically varying his experiences and then recording his reactions, Wundt was studying awareness of immediate experience, or what psychologists call *consciousness.*

Titchener and Structuralism   Students trained by Wundt formed the first generation of North American psychologists. James Mark Baldwin, trained in the Wundtian tradition, established the first psychological laboratory at the University of Toronto in 1889. Four years later he left Canada for Princeton. The most influential of Wundt's students was E.B. Titchener, an Englishman, who put his own spin on Wundt's psychology of consciousness after he immigrated to the United States to teach psychology at Cornell University in Ithaca, New York. Titchener attempted to classify the structures of the mind, not unlike the way a chemist breaks down chemicals into their component parts—water into hydrogen and oxygen, for example. Thus, for Titchener, just as hydrogen and oxygen were structures, so were sensations and thoughts. He conceived of hydrogen and oxygen as structures of a chemical compound, and of sensations and thoughts as structures of the mind. This approach became known as **structuralism,** *an early theory of psychology developed by Wundt and Titchener that emphasized the importance of conscious thought and classification of the mind's structures* (Benjafield, 1996).

James and Functionalism   The first psychologist in the United States was not Titchener, but William James. James (1890/1950) did not believe in the existence of the elementary, rigid structures of the mind for which Titchener searched. James argued that our minds are characterized by a continuous flow of information about our experiences rather than by discrete components. Following in the steps of Darwin, James emphasized the mind's ability to continuously evolve as it adapts to information about the environment. James's view shifted attention away from the mind's content to the mind's functions. James especially believed that the function of choosing was important in adapting to a changing world (Leahey, 1997). This approach became known as **functionalism,** *William James' theory that psychology's role is to study the functions of the mind and behavior in adapting to the environment.*

Edward Titchener (1876–1927), in the long, flowing black gown that he liked to wear when he lectured at Cornell University. When Titchener immigrated to the United States, he developed his own brand of psychology. What was Titchener's psychology like? *Psychology Archives–University of Akron*

William James

Early and Contemporary Approaches to Psychology

The two approaches we just discussed—structuralism and functionalism—are no longer listed among psychology's main approaches, although most psychologists today continue to stress functionalism's emphasis on the importance of mind and behavior in adapting to the environment. Currently, seven main approaches compete in trying to explain psychology's subject matter: behavioral, psychoanalytic, humanistic, cognitive, behavioral neuroscience, evolutionary psychology, and sociocultural. Some of these approaches (behavioral, psychoanalytic) emerged very early in the twentieth century, others (evolutionary and sociocultural) are of very recent vintage. We will briefly study each of the seven approaches here, then return to them in greater depth later in this book.

The Behavioral Approach

The year is 1898. You are ushered into a room, where you see a dog salivating profusely, and you wonder what is going on. A gentleman in a white laboratory coat walks over and quietly informs you that an experiment on learning is taking place. He explains that it is a very simple form of learning, in this case documented by the dog's salivation in anticipation of being fed. The man is Ivan Pavlov, who shows you that if he puts the dog's tray down or allows the dog to catch a glimpse of the attendant who fed him the previous day, the dog will begin to salivate.

Pavlov's experiments emphasized careful observation of overt behavior following precise manipulation of the environment. The observations were very different from the information collected through Wundt's introspection, which emphasized inferences about the conscious mind. Pavlov's interest in the overt behavior of organisms and the precise manner in which he observed behavior impressed a young American psychologist by the name of John B. Watson. Watson believed that conscious thought and mental processes had no place in psychology—they lacked objectivity and could not be measured, he said. The view of Pavlov and Watson is called the **behavioral approach,** *which emphasizes the scientific study of behavior and its environmental determinants* (Mills, 1998). According to behaviorists, we do well in school because of the rewards we experience; we behave in a well-mannered fashion for our parents because of the controls they place on us; and we work hard at our jobs because of the money we receive for our effort. We don't do these things, according to behaviorists, because of an inborn motivation to be a competent person or because a reward makes us feel better about ourselves. We do them because of the environmental conditions we have experienced and are continuing to experience.

Although an emphasis on observable behavior and environmental determinants is characteristic of all behavioral views today, different forms of behaviorism have developed. One form is close to the beliefs of Watson and is best represented by the well-known behaviorist B. F. Skinner (1938). Like Watson, Skinner argued that looking into the mind for the determinants of behavior detracts the investigator from the true cause of behavior—the external environment. Behaviorists who follow Skinner's approach modify and rearrange environmental experiences to determine their effects on an organism, whether rat, pigeon, or human. A father complains that his son misbehaves at home. Careful observation reveals that the father rarely rewards his son, even though his son gets good grades in school, is well liked by his peers, and does a number of chores around the house. The behaviorist calls the father's attention to this pattern of behavior and instructs him to tell the child how pleased he is whenever the child behaves positively, such as when the child does a chore. In this example, the behaviorist is not interested in what the father or the son is thinking or feeling. The behaviorist is only interested in their behavior, which can be directly observed.

Contemporary behaviorism also emphasizes the importance of observing behavior to understand an individual, and the rigorous methods for obtaining information about behavior advocated by Pavlov and Watson remain a cornerstone of the behavioral approach (Martin & Pear, 1999). Contemporary behaviorists continue to stress the importance of environmental determinants of behavior as well (Pierce & Epling, 1999).

Not every behaviorist accepts Skinner's rejection of thought processes. **Social cognitive theory,** *as proposed by Albert Bandura (1986, 1998), stresses that behavior is determined not only by its controlling environmental conditions but also by how thoughts modify the impact of environment on behavior.* Perhaps the son in our example has observed and remembers other children misbehaving. The son might imitate their behavior, especially if the children are popular with peers. Bandura believes that imitation is one of the main ways we learn about our world. To reproduce a model's behavior, we must code and store the information in memory, which is a mental, or

Bandura's Theory

B. F. Skinner was a tinkerer who liked to make new gadgets. The younger of his two daughters, Deborah, was raised in Skinner's enclosed Air-Crib. Some critics accused Skinner of monstrous experimentation with his children; however, the early controlled environment has not had any noticeable harmful effects. Debbie, shown here as a child with her parents, is currently a successful artist, is married, and lives in London. Where do you stand on the ethics involved in Skinner's use of the enclosed Air-Crib to rear his infant daughter?

cognitive, process. Thus, social cognitive theorists broadened the scope of behaviorism to include not only observed behavior but also the ways in which information about the environment is cognitively processed.

The Psychoanalytic Approach

You are lying on an incredibly comfortable couch in an office in Vienna, Austria. A gentleman with a stern look on his face walks in and sits down near you. He asks you to close your eyes. After several minutes of silence, he inquires about your childhood experiences. The man asking the questions is Sigmund Freud and the year is 1904.

Unlike many pioneer psychologists, Freud was intrigued by the abnormal aspects of people's lives. Others were interested in either the conscious aspects of mind or in directly observable (overt) behavior. For Freud, the key to understanding mind and behavior rested in the unconscious aspects of mind—the aspects of which we are unaware. Freud compared the human mind to an iceberg. The conscious mind is only the tip of the iceberg, the portion above water; the unconscious mind is the huge bulk of the iceberg, the portion under water.

Freud (1917) believed that unlearned biological instincts influence the way individuals think, feel, and behave. These instincts, especially sexual and aggressive impulses, often conflict with the demands of society. Among other things, in Freud's view, a child inherits the tendency to act aggressively. The aggressive instinct is located in the child's unconscious mind; it is responsible, for example, for the aggressive energy a boy shows in destroying a friend's sand castle, in punching his brother in the nose, or in running wildly through a neighbor's flower garden. The aggressive instinct conflicts with acceptable social behavior, so the child must learn to adapt.

Although Freud saw much of psychological development as instinctually based, he argued that our early relationships with parents were the chief environmental contribution to our personality. That is why he asked you about your childhood as you relaxed on the couch. By getting you to talk about your early family life, Freud

The Psychoanalytic Approach

hoped you would unconsciously reveal clues about the conflicts causing your problems. The **psychoanalytic approach,** then, *emphasizes the unconscious aspects of the mind, conflict between biological instincts and society's demands, and early family experiences.*

The psychoanalytic approach has survived, although its form has changed somewhat from Freud's original theory. Many contemporary psychoanalytic theorists place less emphasis on sexual instincts and more emphasis on cultural experiences as determinants of personality. Unconscious thought remains a central theme, but contemporary psychoanalytic theorists believe conscious thought makes up more of the iceberg than Freud did.

Erik Erikson (1968) is an important revisionist of Freud's views. Erikson believed we progress through a series of personality stages over the human life span, unlike Freud, who thought personality was virtually etched in stone by 5 years of age. Erikson believed Freud shortchanged the role of culture in personality. Consider, for example, the adolescent years. In Erikson's approach, the key developmental task to be achieved during adolescence is identity, a search for who one is, what one is all about, and where one is going in life. For Freud, adolescents were primarily sexual beings, not wrapped, as Erikson believed, in an exploration of many different roles, some sexual but also some vocational, ideological, religious, lifestyle, and gender. Erikson believed that, by exploring alternatives in many different roles, an adolescent moves toward an identity. Erikson's view fits with our achievement-oriented culture, where exploration of alternative career options is a salient part of finding out who one is and where one is headed in life.

The Humanistic Approach

The Humanistic Approach
Some psychologists are not satisfied with either the behavioral approach, with its emphasis on environmental determinants of behavior, or the psychoanalytic approach, with its focus on instincts, abnormality, and unconscious thoughts. The **humanistic approach** *stresses a person's capacity for personal growth, freedom to choose his or her destiny, and positive qualities.* Humanistic psychologists take particular opposition to behaviorists, saying that individuals have the ability to control their lives rather than be manipulated by the environment. Humanists stress that our subjective, personal perception of ourselves and the world is more important than behavior itself. Humanists believe we have a tremendous potential for self-understanding. They also think we can help others achieve this self-understanding by providing a nurturant, warm social climate—in other words, by being supportive.

Carl Rogers (1961) and Abraham Maslow (1971) were the main architects of the humanistic approach. Rogers placed special emphasis on improving an individual's self-conception by providing a warm, supportive therapeutic environment. Maslow stressed the importance of achieving our potential, which he thinks is virtually limitless. Maslow called humanistic psychology the "third force" in psychology, believing it deserved the attention accorded the first two forces, behaviorism and psychoanalytic theory. The humanistic approach is a more recent view than behaviorism and psychoanalytic theory, so its staying power in psychology is yet to be determined. Critics call the humanistic approach unscientific, but it has been applauded for helping us reach our human potential and cope more effectively with our problems.

Humanists believe that we have a natural tendency to be loving toward each other and that each of us has the capacity to be a loving person if we would recognize it.

The Cognitive Approach   For many contemporary psychologists, the cognitive approach is an extremely important force in psychology. The **cognitive approach** *emphasizes the mental processes involved in knowing*: how we direct our attention, how we perceive, how we remember, how we think and how we solve problems. For example, cognitive psychologists want to know how we solve algebraic equations, why we remember some things only for a short time but remember others for a lifetime, and how we can use imagery to plan for the future.

A cognitive psychologist views the mind as an active and aware problem-solving system (Baddeley, 1998; Haberlandt, 1999; Simon, 1996; Benjafield, 1997). This positive view contrasts with the pessimism of the psychoanalytic approach, which sees the individual as controlled by instincts, and the behavioral view, which portrays behavior as controlled by external environmental forces. In the cognitive view, an individual's mental processes control behavior. The use of memories, perceptions, images, and thinking allows greater cognitive control over behavior than is envisioned in either the psychoanalytic or the behavioral approach. In the humanistic approach, emotions play a much stronger role than in the cognitive approach, and the humanistic approach does not emphasize the scientific study of mental processes, as the cognitive approach does.

Information processing *is the most widely adopted cognitive approach. Information-processing psychologists study how individuals process information—how they attend to information, how they perceive it, how they store it, how they think about it, and how they retrieve it for further use.* Computers played an important role in the development of the information-processing perspective. Essentially, computers are high-speed information-processing systems. In the 1950s, it was discovered that if computers were programmed appropriately, they could perform tasks that previously only humans could perform, such as playing chess or computing the answers to complex math problems. Computers provide a logical and concrete, though perhaps oversimplified, model of how information is processed in the mind.

Herbert Simon (1969) was among the pioneers of the information-processing approach. He reasoned that the human mind is best understood by comparing it to a computer processing information. In this model, the sensory and perceptual systems provide an "input channel," similar to data being entered into a computer. As information (input) comes into the mind, mental processes, or operations, act on it, just as the computer's software program acts on data. The transformed input generates information that remains in memory much in the way a computer stores what it has worked on. Finally, the information is retrieved from memory and put to use in the form of an overt response that can be observed, not unlike a computer searching for, finding, and printing out information.

The Behavioral Neuroscience Approach   According to the **behavioral neuroscience approach**, *the brain and nervous system are central to understanding behavior, thought, and emotion.* Neurobiologists believe that thoughts have a physical basis in the brain (Jausovec, 1999; Kolb & Whishaw, 1999). The human brain and nervous system constitute the most complex, intricate, and elegant system imaginable. The human brain is only a 3-pound lump of matter, but in this lump are more than 100 billion interconnected nerve cells. Electrical impulses zoom throughout our brain cells, and chemical substances are released as we think, feel, and act.

Behavioral neuroscience originated with the 1949 publication of *The Organization of Behavior,* by McGill psychologist D.O. Hebb. Hebb stressed the need for an interdisciplinary approach to brain and behavior, emphasized the central problem of internal mental processes, critiqued then-current theories of learning and perception, and proposed a broad and imaginative theory of his own (Klein, 1980; Fentress, 1999).

Neuroscientists have studied the memory of the sea slug, a tiny snail with only about 10,000 nerve cells. How did they investigate the sea slug's memory?

The Cognitive Approach

The Behavioral Science Approach

Calvin and Hobbes

by Bill Watterson

CALVIN AND HOBBES © 1991 Watterson. Reprinted with permission of UNIVERSAL PRESS SYNDICATE. All rights reserved.

The Evolutionary Psychology Approach

Roger Sperry (1964) made some of the most exciting discoveries in neuroscience by observing patients in whom the corpus callosum, the main communication link between the hemispheres, had been severed as a therapy for otherwise intractable epilepsy. His results revealed that some aspects of our behavior are controlled more by one side of the brain than by the other. Our own gift for human speech, for example, primarily involves the left side of our brain.

Behavioral neuroscientists also study simpler nervous systems (Changeux & Chavillion, 1995; Wicks, Roehrig, and Rankin, 1996) such as that of the sea slug, a tiny snail with only about 10,000 nerve cells. If given an electric shock to its tail, the sea slug withdraws its tail quickly. It withdraws the tail even faster if it was previously shocked. Shocking the sea slug's tail releases a chemical called a neurotransmitter that basically provides a reminder that the tail was shocked and informs the nerve cells to retract the tail the next time it is touched (Kandel & Schwartz, 1982). Since nature builds complexity out of simplicity, the mechanism used by the sea slug seems to work in the human brain as well.

The Evolutionary Psychology Approach

Although Darwin introduced the theory of evolution by natural selection in 1859, his ideas about evolution have only recently emerged as a popular framework for explaining behavior. Psychology's newest approach, the **evolutionary psychology approach,** *emphasizes the importance of adaptation, reproduction, and "survival of the fittest" in explaining behavior.* Evolutionary psychology's emphasis on adaptation reflects the earlier views of functionalism. Evolution favors organisms that are best adapted to survive and reproduce in a particular environment (Buss & Greiling, 1999). The evolutionary psychology approach focuses on conditions that allow individuals to survive or to fail. In this view, the evolutionary process of natural selection favors behaviors that increase organisms' reproductive success and their ability to pass their genes to the next generation (Daly & Wilson, 1983).

David Buss' (1995, 1999) ideas on evolutionary psychology have ushered in a whole new wave of interest in how evolution is involved in explaining human behavior. He believes that just as evolution shapes our physical features, such as body shape and height, it also pervasively influences how we make decisions, how aggressive we are, our fears, and our mating patterns.

Steven Pinker (1997) recently argued that "how the mind works" can be summarized by three main points: (1) The mind computes, (2) the mind was designed to compute by evolution, and (3) these computations are performed by specialized brain systems that natural selection has designed to achieve specific kinds of goals, such as survival. Thus, in Pinker's view, the mind analyzes sensory input in ways that would have benefited the hunters and gatherers of human prehistory. Minds that understood causes and effects, built tools, set traps, and avoided poisonous mushrooms had the best chance of surviving and having offspring that would someday be able to invent mathematics and make movies about robots.

Through the Eyes of Psychologists

Steven Pinker, MIT

"The mind is a system of organs of computation that allowed our ancestors to outsmart plants and animals."

The Sociocultural Approach

The **sociocultural approach** *emphasizes that culture, ethnicity, and gender are essential to understanding behavior, thought, and emotion.* **Culture** *is the behavior patterns, beliefs, and other*

In Xinjiang, China, a woman prepares for horseback courtship. Her suitor must chase her, kiss her, and evade her riding crop—all on the gallop. A new marriage law took effect in China in 1981. The law sets a minimum age for marriage—22 years for males, 20 years for females. Late marriage and late childbirth are critical efforts in China's attempt to control population growth. What do you think about such laws?

The tapestry of Canadian culture has changed with the increasing ethnic diversity of Canada's citizens. According to Statistics Canada, by 1996 only 20% of Canadians had their origins in the British Isles and France. The rest have come from around the globe, with visible minorities making up the fastest-growing group. Two of psychology's challenges are to become more sensitive to race and ethnic origin and to provide improved services to ethnic minority individuals. What might these communication strategies be like?

products of a particular group of people, such as values, work patterns, music, dress, diet, and ceremonies, that are passed on from generation to generation. A cultural group can be as large and complex as Canada, or it can be as small as an African hunter-gatherer tribe, but whatever its size, the group's culture influences the identity, learning, and social behavior of its members (Matsumoto, 1996; Triandis, 1994).

Ethnicity *(the word* ethnic *comes from the Greek word for "nation") is based on cultural heritage, nationality characteristics, race, religion, and language.* Ethnicity involves descent from common ancestors, usually in a specifiable part of the world. Given descent from common ancestors, people often make inferences about someone's ethnicity based on physical features believed to be typical of an ethnic group. For example, one of the downed Coalition flyers in the Gulf War had features that would be considered "Arab." He was treated worse than the other prisoners of war, who had non-Arab features. This reminds us that ethnicity is a category that is often applied to people even if they don't want to be categorized that way and feel the inferences are unfair (Brislin, 1990).

Canadian culture is becoming more diverse by including more people from disparate cultures. These demographic changes promise not only the richness that diversity produces but also difficult challenges in extending fuller opportunities to all ethnic minority individuals (Berry, 1999; McLoyd, 1998, 1999). Queen's cross-cultural psychologist John Berry (1993) suggests that our low population density, cultural, social and linguistic dualism (French and English), and growing cultural pluralism require a uniquely Canadian response (e.g., Pruegger & Rogers, 1993).

So far we have discussed two aspects of sociocultural influences—culture and ethnicity. A third important aspect is **gender,** *the sociocultural dimension of being female or male.* **Sex** *is the biological dimension of being female or male.* Few aspects of our existence are more central to our identity and to our social

Cross-Cultural Psychology
Diversity Resources
Women Pioneers

relationships than our sex and gender (Bonvillian, 1998). Our gender attitudes and behavior are changing, but how much? Is there a limit to how much society can determine what is appropriate behavior for females and males? A special concern on the part of many feminist writers is that in much of its history psychology has portrayed human behavior with a "male-dominant theme" (Pyke, 1997; Doyle & Paludi, 1998; Yoder, 1999).

The sociocultural approach is one of psychology's newest lenses for examining behavior and mental processes. As the future brings increasing contact between people from quite different backgrounds, the sociocultural approach will help to expand psychology's role as a relevant discipline in the twenty-first century.

Which Approach Is Best?

All of these approaches to psychology are in a sense correct. They are all valid ways of looking at human behavior, just as blueprints, floor plans, and photographs are all valid ways of looking at a house. Some approaches are better for some purposes. A floor plan, for instance, is more useful than a photograph for deciding how much lumber to buy, just as the neurobiological approach is more useful than the sociocultural approach for explaining how cells in the brain communicate with each other. And, in turn, the sociocultural approach is more useful than the neurobiological approach for understanding how to reduce prejudice and discrimination. But no single approach is "right" or "wrong."

Some psychologists adopt a particular approach, such as cognitive or behavioral or sociocultural; many others take a more eclectic approach. An **eclectic approach** *does not follow any one conceptual approach, but rather selects and uses whatever is considered best in each approach.* No single approach is infallible or capable of explaining all of psychology's rich and varied subject matter. Thus, the behavioral neuroscience approach informs us about the detailed workings of the brain and how they influence behavior, the cognitive approach provides guidance in how people make decisions, and the sociocultural approach describes strategies for communicating more effectively across cultures.

In our coverage of early and contemporary approaches, we have examined a number of approaches and individuals who were pioneers in various areas of psychology. For a glimpse of some of the main theorists and pioneers in psychology's history, see figure 1.2.

At this point we have explored many ideas about psychology, including its definition, the beginnings of psychology as a science, and early and contemporary approaches. An overview of these ideas is presented in summary table 1.1. In presenting psychology's seven main approaches, we have encountered various themes that characterize the field of psychology. Next, we systematically explore these themes.

THINKING ABOUT PSYCHOLOGY AND LIFE

Saddam Hussein and Mother Teresa

WE HAVE EXAMINED seven different approaches in psychology. As a check on your understanding of these approaches and to stretch your thinking, explain how the seven approaches would differ in accounting for Iraqian leader Saddam Hussein's inhumane behavior and Indian religious leader Mother Teresa's humanitarian efforts.

Saddam Hussein has repeatedly embarked on campaigns of violence against people in his own country and other Middle Eastern nations.

Mother Teresa of Calcutta, a Catholic nun, was a pillar of altruism in helping people in poverty, not just in India but around the world.

Psychology's Early Approaches

Wilhelm Wundt (1832–1920) William James (1842–1910)

Alfred Binet (1857–1911) Ivan Pavlov (1849–1936)

John Clark Murray (1836–1917) B. F. Skinner (1904–1990)

Erik Erikson (1902–1994) Abraham Maslow (1908–1970)

Carl Rogers (1902–1987) Albert Bandura (1925–)

Sandra Bem (1944–) D.O. Hebb (1904–1985)

1879: Wilhelm Wundt develops the first psychology laboratory at the University of Leipzig.

1885: McGill professor John Clark Murray publishes *A Handbook of Psychology,* one of the first psychology textbooks.

1889: James Mark Baldwin founds the first psychology laboratory in Canada at the University of Toronto.

1890: William James publishes *Principles of Psychology,* which promotes functionalism.

1891: Mary Calkins establishes a laboratory for psychology at Wellesley.

1892: E. B. Titchener popularizes structuralism in the United States. G. Stanley Hall founds the American Psychological Association at Clark University.

1894: Margaret Washburn becomes the first woman to receive a Ph.D. in psychology.

1900: Sigmund Freud publishes *The Interpretation of Dreams,* reflecting his psychoanalytic view.

1905: Alfred Binet (with Theodore Simon) develops the first valid intelligence test to assess French schoolchildren.

1906: The Russian Ivan Pavlov publishes the results of his learning experiments with dogs.

1913: John Watson publishes his book on behaviorism, promoting the importance of environmental influences.

1938: B. F. Skinner publishes *The Behavior of Organisms,* expanding the view of behaviorism.

1945: Karen Horney criticizes Freud's psychoanalytic theory as male-biased and presents her sociocultural approach.

1949: McGill psychologist Donald O. Hebb publishes *The Organization of Behavior,* influencing the work of a generation of neuroscientists.

1950: Erik Erikson publishes *Childhood and Society,* a psychoanalytic revision of Freud's views.

1954: Abraham Maslow presents the humanistic view, emphasizing the positive potential of the individual.

1954: Gordon Allport writes his now classic book, *The Nature of Prejudice.*

1958: Herbert Simon presents his information-processing view.

1961: Carl Rogers publishes *On Becoming a Person,* highlighting the humanistic approach.

1961: Albert Bandura presents ideas about social learning theory, emphasizing the importance of imitation.

1964: Roger Sperry publishes his split-brain research, showing the importance of the brain hemispheres in behavior.

1969: John Berry, a Canadian psychologist, presents his ideas on the importance of cross-cultural research in the International Journal of Psychology.

1969: Neil Agnew and Sandra Pyke finish the first of six editions of *The Science Game.* Sandra Pyke goes on to champion women's issues in Canadian psychology.

1974: Sandra Bem and Janet Spence develop tests to assess androgyny and promote the competence of females.

Mary Calkins (1863–1930) G. Stanley Hall (1844–1924)

Margaret Washburn (1871–1939) John B. Watson (1878–1958)

James Mark Baldwin (1861–1934) Karen Horney (1885–1952)

Gordon Allport (1897–1967) Sigmund Freud (1856–1939)

Roger Sperry (1913–1994) John Berry (1939–)

Sandra Pyke (1937–) Herbert Simon (1916–)

Figure 1.2
Important Pioneers and Theorists in Psychology's History

SUMMARY TABLE 1.1
Exploring Psychology

Concept	Processes/ Related Ideas	Characteristics/Description
Defining Psychology	Its Nature	Psychology is the scientific study of behavior and mental processes. Behavior is everything people do that can be directly observed. Mental processes are thoughts, feelings, and motives that each individual experiences. As a science, psychology uses systematic methods to observe, describe, predict, and explain behavior.
The Beginnings of Psychology as a Science	From Myth to Philosophy to Psychology	Myths gave way to the rational logic of philosophy, but the intellectual debate of philosophers did not yield much in the way of concrete, empirical answers.
	Early Contributors	Wilhelm Wundt developed the first scientific laboratory of psychology in 1879 in Leipzig, Germany. James Baldwin established the first psychological laboratory in Canada. E.B. Titchener, a student of Wundt's, developed structuralism, an early theory of psychology that emphasized the importance of conscious thought and classification of the mind's structures. William James, the first psychologist in the United States, emphasized the functions of the mind in adapting to the environment. His view was called functionalism.
Early and Contemporary Approaches	Behavioral	This approach emphasizes the scientific study of behavior and its environmental determinants. Pavlov and Skinner developed important behavioral approaches. Social cognitive theory argues that thought processes modify environment-behavior connections.
	Psychoanalytic	This approach stresses the unconscious aspects of mind, conflict between biological instincts and society's demands, and early childhood experiences. Freud was the main architect of psychoanalytic theory. Erikson presented an important revision of psychoanalytic theory.
	Humanistic	This approach emphasizes a person's capacity for personal growth, freedom to choose one's destiny, and positive qualities. Rogers and Maslow were the main developers of the humanistic approach.
	Cognitive	This approach places a premium on cognitive, or thought, processes. Simon viewed a person's mind as an active, aware problem-solving system. Information processing is the most widely adopted cognitive approach.
	Behavioral Neuroscience	This approach stresses that the brain and nervous system play important roles in understanding behavior and mental processes. Hebb founded the behavioral neuroscience approach. Sperry conducted important research on the brain's two hemispheres.
	Evolutionary Psychology	This approach emphasizes the importance of adaptation, reproduction, and "survival of the fittest" in explaining behavior. Buss' ideas have ushered in a whole new wave of interest in evolution's role in explaining behavior.
	Sociocultural	This approach emphasizes that culture, ethnicity, and gender are essential to understanding behavior, thought, and emotion. Berry studied how immigrants acculturate and the psychological preconditions for living together in culturally diverse societies.
	Which Approach Is Best?	No single theory offers all the answers; each contributes to the science of psychology. Some psychologists adopt a particular approach; others take a more eclectic approach.

Psychology and Life: What Matters

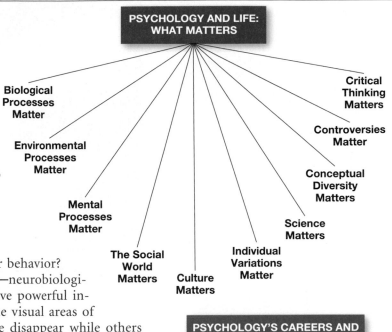

What matters in psychology and life? There are few bigger questions we can tackle. We are going to describe ten things that do matter in psychology and life. These ten principles and themes are also woven through *Psychology,* sixth edition. You will discover that these principles and themes have relevance for understanding the academic discipline that studies mind and behavior (psychology) but also have applications to the real lives of people.

Biological Processes Matter

How strongly does your biological makeup influence your behavior? According to two of the approaches we discussed earlier—neurobiological and evolutionary psychology—biological processes have powerful influences on behavior. And they do. For example, when the visual areas of the brain are damaged, some aspects of visual experience disappear while others remain intact (Pinker, 1997, 1999). Individuals with such brain damage might see a complete world but pay attention only to half of it—they might eat food from the right side of the plate, shave only their right cheek, and draw a clock with all 12 numbers placed on the right half. Others lose their sensation of color but do not see the world as an artsy monochromatic film. Rather, surfaces appear as grimy and rat-colored, dulling their world. Yet others see changes in objects' positions but cannot see the objects move. The steam from a teapot does not flow but looks like an icicle. The cup does not gradually fill with tea. It is empty and then suddenly full. Others don't recognize the objects they see. They might copy a drawing of a tiger faithfully but identify it as a car. When they try to weed the garden, they pull out the roses. These faulty interpretations of the world are caused by an injury or a stroke that affects one or more of the thirty brain areas that make up the primate visual system. Some areas of this system specialize in form and color, others in where an object is, and yet others in how it moves. When you gaze at the world, you don't fathom all of the complex, inner workings of brain systems that are needed to perform behaviors you take for granted, like copying a drawing, perceiving an object as moving, and weeding a garden. The brain, after all, does nothing visible to you. But when injury and disease assault the brain, its powerful role in influencing behavior becomes apparent (Stoler & Mill, 1998; Melzack, 1989). In psychology and life, *biological processes matter.*

Environmental Processes Matter

According to the behavioral approach we discussed earlier, environmental processes have powerful influences on behavior. Might the experiences you had when you were growing up have influenced the development of your brain and your behavior? Environmental experiences can contribute to a wiring, or rewiring, of the brain (Greenough, 1999; Nash, 1997; Mitchell, 1989). Repeated experiences especially contribute to this wiring or rewiring. For example, each time a baby tries to touch an attractive object or gazes intently at a face, tiny bursts of electricity shoot through the baby's brain, knitting together brain cells into circuits. And when Mark Rosenzweig (1969) randomly assigned animals to different environments to determine whether early experiences might alter the course of the brain's development, he found that they did. Animals in an enriched early envi-

In neuroscientist Mark Rosenzweig's research, an "enriched" environment rewired the brains of rats by dramatically increasing their neural connections and neurochemical activity. In psychology and life, both biological and environmental processes matter. Can you think of other ways scientists might study how "enriched" environments might influence behavior?

ronment lived in cages that offered stimulating experiences. They rotated wheels, climbed steps, pressed levers, and manipulated toys. The results were stunning. The brains of the "enriched" animals weighed more, had thicker layers, had more neural connections, and had higher levels of neurochemical activity than those of animals raised in standard cages or barren, isolated conditions. In psychology and life, *environmental experiences matter.*

Mental Processes Matter

How important is your mind in all that you do? We are not only biological and environmental beings, we are also mental beings. This concept is at the center of the cognitive approach we discussed earlier in the chapter. The universe inside your skull consists not only of a brain, but also of a mind whose mental processes allow you to remember, make decisions, plan, set goals, and be creative (Runko & Pritzker, 1999). Just as we take for granted the marvels of the brain's intricate workings, we also tend to gloss over the mind's remarkable adaptive and generative capacities that we use every day of our lives. Think about the following two mental feats that you are capable of (Hunt, 1982):

- *What is Sir John A. Macdonald, Canada's first Prime Minister's phone number?* . . . You likely were quick to recognize that this question is absurd. But how did you know it was absurd without even considering the matter? Did you mentally search your memory phone book in a millisecond? Did you consult the encyclopedia of history in your mind? Whatever you did, it was a fine mental performance!
- *ACORN is to OAK as INFANT is to* _____. . . . Unless your mind was not focusing well, you knew at once that the blank should read *ADULT.* But how did you know? In brief, you compared the attributes of the first two capitalized words, inferred a rule that reflected their connection, and applied the rule to the third capitalized word *(INFANT).* Then you extrapolated to come up with the missing fourth word *(ADULT).*

To perform these two tasks, you had to use your memory and you had to think. As you read this section you thought about your mind and how it works. Twentieth-century French philosopher Albert Camus said that an intellectual is someone whose mind watches itself, but this is true of all human beings, more or less. An important dimension of psychology is the rigorous effort expended by many scientists to explore the inner workings of the human mind. In psychology and life, *mental processes matter.*

The Social World Matters

Take away people and what would your life be like? Imagine it. No one to talk with. No one to comfort you. Challenge you. Smile and cry with you. We are social beings who need other people to satisfy our wants and desires. Parents, teachers, peers, friends, and partners in close relationships play important roles in our socially connected lives (Collins & Laursen, 1999). How we treat others and they us, whether caring or hurting, stirs our minds and hearts. Most of us search for closeness, intimacy, and love. Some find these treasures, others discover they are elusive.

Consider the social merits of David Suzuki, one of Canada's most famous and popular scientists. Like many Japanese-Canadians, his parents expected him to work hard to become successful in the world, and had a great respect for education. They wanted him to devote himself fully to whatever he did and to excel in school. By the age of four he was going fishing with his father, and he began learning about nature by learning the names of trees, fish and birds. He overcame early feelings of not belonging and went on to have many friends throughout his school life, participate in and win public speaking contests and become the president of his high school class.

On a scholarship to university in the United States, he completed his studies quickly, played lacrosse, participated in the civil rights movement and married. He eventually returned to Canada, where he taught at the University of Alberta and UBC. His fame as a geneticist grew and he was honored with many awards, including being named the best young research scientist in Canada three years in a row. His popularity in Canada soared when the CBC began broadcasting his programs, such as *Quirks and Quarks* and *The Nature of Things.* Today he is one of the best-recognized and most-loved Canadians. David Suzuki's values, forged in his family and his Japanese-Canadian culture, have enabled him to become a part of, and then go on to influence, his social environment throughout his life. In psychology and life, *the social world matters.*

Dr. David Suzuki has been sustained throughout his life by a strong sense of values which he learned from his family and Japanese-Canadian culture. These values allowed him to rise above the pain inflicted on him when his family was interned along with other Japanese-Canadians in World War II and by racial discrimination to become one of the best-recognized and most-loved Canadians.

Culture Matters

How important for you is the culture in which you grew up, and the culture in which you now live your life? Earlier we indicated that one of psychology's newest approaches is the sociocultural approach, which has brought an increasing examination of culture's role in behavior. A change in cultural values and social policy took place in Zimbabwe in 1980 (Konner, 1991). At that time, fewer than 20 percent of the nation's children were enrolled in school and only a third had completed the seventh grade. Within 5 years, every child—2.3 million—was starting school and three of four had completed the 7-year course. The changing cultural values in Zimbabwe led to spending on education rising to 22 percent of the national budget, more than the defense and health care budgets combined. Instead of working in the fields, Zimbabwe children now study science, mathematics, and the language arts. In a school at Tafara, children dug a fishpond in the shape of a world map and proceeded to study topics ranging from fish farming to geography to the control of water-borne diseases. They have no Cuisiniere rods or calculators; the children count with stones. There are no art supplies, but the children exercise their creative thinking by making compositions from mud and leaves.

Religion is also an important cultural area of study in psychology (Emmons, in press; Paloutzian, 2000; Hunsberger, 1991). As nineteenth-century clergyman Henry Newman commented, religion can enlighten, terrify, and subdue. It can give faith,

With such a high divorce rate in the United States, psychologists are intrigued by what makes a successful marriage. In the recent study by John Gottman and his colleagues (1998), what were the best predictors of a successful marriage?

inspire resolutions, and stir up wars (Peterson, 1999). Religion can also inflame devotion, as it did in the 1990s when Branch Davidian leader David Koresh and Order of the Solar Temple leader Luc Jouret used religion to gain unwavering conformity in their followers. In adolescents, those with religious convictions are less likely to engage in sex than their less-religious counterparts (Thornton & Camburn, 1989). But when religious adolescents do have sex, they are less likely to use contraceptives. In psychology and life, *culture matters*.

Individual Variations Matter

How important is it to recognize that people are different from each other? Individuals play out their lives in different ways. No two people are exactly alike. Anyone who has lived with or been around another person for even a brief period of time knows this important principle. Roommates, parents and children, teachers and students, and friends and lovers soon find out that they are different from each other. One of psychology's important agendas is to chart not only the commonalities that we share with all others but also the unique ways we use our minds and the individual twists we put on our behavior (Stanovich, 1999). Your mix of genes and experiences cannot be duplicated. Even in these days of animal cloning and the potential for human cloning, unique experiences imprint every person's life.

If we observed a group of seven people, we might find that each has a different set of skills, interests, and experiences (Gardner, 1993). One person excels at solving verbal problems and likes to do crossword puzzles, one loves math and reads computer magazines, one is good at creating mental maps of physical space and likes to draw buildings, one has great hand-eye coordination and excels at racquetball, one plays a musical instrument and likes to go to concerts, one has good self-evaluation skills and likes to write in a journal, and one is competent at "reading" other people and likes to help friends with their problems. Do you know anyone who is good at all of these things? At none of these things? Probably not. Our biological and experiential legacies interact to produce a unique composite of mind and behavior. In psychology and life, *individual variations matter*.

Science Matters

Does science matter in psychology and life? It is sometimes said that experience is the most important teacher. However, much of the knowledge we get from personal experience is based on our individual observations and interpretations. How do we know if these are accurate? Sometimes we make errors in sight, hearing, or perception. Chances are you can think of hundreds of situations in which you thought that other people read you the wrong way, just as they may have felt that you misread them. We bring our biases to situations and sometimes see only what we want to see. When we rely only on our own personal experiences, we aren't always totally objective because we sometimes base our judgments on a desire to protect our ego and self-esteem (McMillan, 2000).

As you read earlier in the chapter, psychology is a science. As a science, psychology can provide you with knowledge and understanding that is more objective than your personal interpretations. When asked about his personal thoughts on what it takes to make a good marriage, one man said "a wife who is attentive and listens to me." But in a recent scientific study of 130 newlywed couples over 6 years, John Gottman and his colleagues (1998) found that successful marriages are characterized by husbands who are flexible and often give in to what their wives want.* The

*The inclusion of this research was encouraged by author John Santrock's wife, Mary Jo

autocratic husbands who failed to listen to their wives' complaints, greeting them with stonewalling, contempt, and belligerence, were doomed to have a failed marriage. However, wives were not completely off the hook in contributing to a successful marriage. When they couched their complaints in a gentle, soothing, sometimes even humorous, manner, their marriages were more successful than when they were belligerent. Gottman says that his research suggests there has to be a kind of gentleness in the way conflict is managed for marriages to work. Men have to be more accepting of a woman's position, and women have to be more sensitive in opening discussions. Scientific studies such as Gottman's can help correct our personal misinterpretations. In psychology and life, *science matters*.

Conceptual Diversity Matters

How varied are psychology's approaches? Earlier in this chapter we presented seven different approaches to psychology and concluded that all seven had some validity for examining and explaining behavior. Psychology is a field with considerable conceptual diversity. All of the seven grand approaches described in this chapter have made important contributions to psychology.

The diversity of approaches makes understanding psychology a challenging undertaking. Just when you think one approach provides the best explanation of behavior, another approach will crop up and make you rethink your earlier conclusion. To avoid frustration, remember that mind and behavior are very complex, and no single approach has been able to entirely explain them. Together, the varied conceptual approaches stimulate us to think about the complex landscape of mind and behavior and to search for more accurate understanding of it.

Psychology is characterized not only by grand approaches (like behavioral, cognitive, and behavioral neuroscience), but also by many "local" or "micro" approaches. Within the global cognitive approach are many specific approaches to studying memory, thinking, and creativity. For example, cognitive psychologists have proposed a number of competing theories about how people represent information in their memory, which we will discuss in chapter 7. This "micro" approach focuses on a specific aspect of mind and behavior, seeking precise explanations (Kuhn, 1998). As you read this book, you will come across many of these more focused views. Together the macro and micro approaches produce a more complete portrait of mind and behavior. In psychology and life, *conceptual diversity matters*.

Controversies Matter

How might psychology benefit from controversies? Psychology has advanced as a field because it does not accept simple explanations and because everyone does not agree with each other about why mind and behavior work the way they do. Rather, we have reached a more accurate understanding of mind and behavior because psychology is a field characterized by controversies.

What are some of psychology's controversies? In the area of gender, evolutionary psychologists argue that sex differences are large and biologically based. By contrast, sociocultural psychologists stress that sex differences are small or nonexistent in most areas and that when differences occur they are based on experience. Here is a brief sampling of other controversies in psychology:

- Whether memories of sexual abuse are real or imagined
- Whether intelligence can be increased
- Whether alcoholism is a biologically based disease or a learned behavior
- Whether it is best to treat depression with drugs or psychotherapy

As you read the remaining chapters of the book, you will come across many more controversies. In psychology and life, *controversies matter*.

Being Skeptical

Critical Thinking Matters

Are you a critical thinker? What does it mean to be a critical thinker? Understanding the complex nature of mind and behavior requires **critical thinking**, *which involves thinking reflectively and productively, and evaluating the evidence.* Thinking critically means asking yourself how you know something. Too often we have a tendency to recite, define, describe, state, and list rather than analyze, infer, connect, synthesize, criticize, create, evaluate, think, and rethink (Brooks & Brooks, 1993). Following is a brief sampling of some thinking strategies that can stimulate you to think reflectively and productively:

- *Be open-minded.* This involves exploring options and avoiding narrow thinking.
- *Be intellectually curious.* This includes wondering, probing, questioning, and inquiring, as well as recognizing problems and inconsistencies.
- *Be intellectually careful.* This consists of checking for inaccuracies and errors, being precise, and being organized.
- *Look for multiple determinants of behavior.* People have a tendency to explain things as having a single cause. After all, that's a lot easier than having to analyze the complexity of, say, mind and behavior and come up with multiple explanations. However, one of psychology's important lessons is that mind and behavior have multiple determinants. For example, if someone asked what causes a person to be a good critical thinker, the person might respond, "Being open-minded." However, that is really not a cause, but rather one of critical thinking's multiple dimensions. When another person is asked what causes critical thinking, that individual might respond, "Practice." Yet another person might say, "An inquiring, critical thinking mentor. Someone else might say, "A lifetime of education that stimulates wondering and probing." And someone might mention "good genes."
- *Think like a scientist.* A glimpse of how scientists think appeared earlier in this section. We said that science urges us to keep in mind that personal experiences and interpretations can be filled with errors and biases. Scientific thinkers examine what evidence is available about some aspect of mind and behavior, evaluate how strongly the data (information) supports their hunches, analyze disconfirming evidence, and carefully consider whether they have explored all of the possible factors and explanations (Agnew & Pyke, 1993). Similarly, Halpern (1996) underscores the importance of looking for biases in the way people think and behave. Neil Agnew and Sandra Pyke (1993) stress that thinking like a scientist about human minds and behaviors can be learned. In the next chapter, in our discussion of the scientific method, we will explore more systematically how to think like a scientist.

To read about some other areas in which people often fail to think critically, ranging from taking advice based on horoscopes to believing that eating a ground-up version of a tiger's sexual organ will increase the human male's sexual potency, see the Explorations in Psychology box. Also, because thinking critically is such an important aspect of psychology, several times in each chapter of this book you will be encouraged to think critically in Thinking About Psychology and Life boxes. In psychology and life, *thinking critically matters.*

Psychology's Careers and Areas of Specialization

Psychologists don't spend all of their time in a laboratory, white-smocked with clipboard in hand, observing rats and crunching numbers. Some psychologists spend their days seeing people with problems, others teach at universities and conduct research.

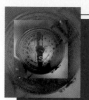

CRITICAL THINKING EXPERT Diane Halpern (in press) recently explained why she is concerned that so many people fail to use critical thinking. Approximately 75 percent of North Americans read their horoscope and many of them believe that it is personally meant for them (Lister, 1992). Some phone their psychics and pay exorbitant amounts they cannot afford for advice that ranges from how to invest their money to whether or not a loved one should be disconnected from life-support systems. They spend large sums of money on remedies when there is no evidence that they work or are safe to take. In a survey of college students, virtually 100 percent believed in at least one of the following (Messer & Griggs, 1989):

- channeling (the ability to enter a trace state and communicate with someone in another place and time, even centuries ago)
- clairvoyance (the ability to perceive remote events that are not visible to normal sight)
- precognition ("knowing" events before they occur)
- telepathy (the extrasensory transfer of thought from one person to another)
- psychic healing (performing miracle cures instantaneously through contact with a higher spiritual being)
- psychic surgery (a brand of faith healing where sleight of hand is relied on to achieve a miracle, such as removing dead or diseased tissue)
- crystal power (use of quartz crystals for healing)
- psychokinesis (being able to move objects without actually touching them)
- astral travel
- levitation
- the Bermuda Triangle mystery
- unidentified flying objects (UFOs)
- plant consciousness
- auras
- ghosts

If you believe in any of these phenomena, psychologists urge you to be more skeptical. Remember that thinking like a scientist means that you demand to see the evidence for such phenomena as channeling, crystal power, and plant consciousness. There is no scientific evidence for the existence of any of the above listed phenomena, only personal anecdotes and coincidences, and those do not meet science's criteria of objectivity and public verifiability.

If you still aren't convinced that these phenomena don't exist, at least critically examine the vague language used in horoscopes and the erroneous rationale that time of birth significantly predicts an individual's personality, future events, or anything else. When astrologers' predictions are successful, it is because they are so vague that they are virtually guaranteed to happen (for example, "Money is likely to be a concern for you this month"

or "A tragic plane crash will occur in southern Europe"). When astrologers make more specific predictions (such as "An unidentified flying object will land on the front lawn of the Parliament Buildings at noon on Canada Day, 2001, during the annual celebrations," they never hold up.

When you think like a scientist, you will be skeptical of astrology, channeling, crystal power, and anything else that claims access to wondrous powers and supernatural forces (Ward & Grashial, 1995). When something sounds like it's too good to be true, think through the claims logically and demand to see the evidence. A failure to think critically and demand scientific evidence often underlies our purchase and use of highly touted, ineffective health-care products (Halpern, in press). For example, there is a widespread belief around the world today that a man who ingests the ground penis of a tiger will have more sexual potency. This belief is so pervasive that it has resulted in poaching of rare wild tigers and other endangered species. Males who believe that this works think like this:

Tigers (presumably) have a great sex life; thus, eating a tiger's sexual organ will improve my sex life. You should be able to see what is wrong with this kind of thinking, especially in the absence of any evidence to support it.

Why should you be skeptical when you hear that eating the ground up penis of a tiger will increase the human male's sexual potency?

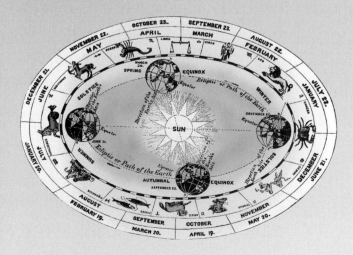

Why does the science of psychology urge you to be skeptical of astrology?

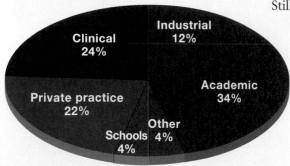

𝓕igure 1.3
Settings in Which Psychologists Work

More psychologists work in academic settings (34%), such as colleges and universities, than any other setting. However, clinical (24%) and private practice (22%) settings, both of which are contexts in which many psychologists in the mental health professions work, combined, make up almost half of the total settings.

Careers in Psychology

Still others work in business and industry, designing more efficient criteria for hiring. In short, psychology is a field with many areas of specialization (figure 1.3).

Careers in Psychology

You might already be wondering whether to major in psychology. Students who major in psychology often find that the subject matter is highly interesting. You have already encountered some of these interesting topics in this first chapter—including exploring the brain's role in behavior, figuring out ways to help children think critically, and analyzing why youths kill people. In the remaining chapters, you will encounter hundreds more of these truly fascinating inquiries in psychology.

Not only will you gain considerable knowledge and understanding of mind and behavior by majoring in psychology, but majoring in psychology will equip you with a rich and diverse portfolio of skills that will serve you well in undertaking many different types of work, both practical and professional. A major in psychology can help you improve your research skills, measurement and computing skills, problem-solving and critical thinking skills, and writing skills (Hayes, 1997). Integrating these skills, which span the arts and sciences, will provide you with unique qualifications. Even if you are not a psychology major or do not plan to major in psychology, this course and others in psychology can provide you with a richer, deeper understanding of many areas of life.

Psychology can not only give you a rich knowledge base and a great repertoire of skills, it also pays reasonably well (Sternberg, 1997a). Psychologists earn well above the median salary in North America. It is unlikely that you will live in a palatial mansion by majoring in psychology, but it is also unlikely that you will go broke. Although psychology is unlikely to make you fantastically wealthy, it will help you to improve peoples' lives, understand yourself and others, possibly advance the state of knowledge in the field, and have an enjoyable time while you are doing these things.

An undergraduate degree in psychology can provide you with access to a variety of jobs. For a list of some of the job possibilities in business, social/human services, and research, see figure 1.4. If you choose a career in psychology, you can greatly expand your opportunities (and your income) by getting a graduate degree, either a master's or a doctorate.

Where do psychologists work? Slightly more than one-third are teachers, researchers, or counselors at colleges or universities. Most other psychologists work in clinical and private practice settings (see figure 1.3).

Areas of Specialization in Psychology

If you go to graduate school, you will be required to specialize in a particular area of psychology. Following is a list of some of the specializations: clinical and counseling; community; experimental; physiological psychology and neuroscience; developmental; social; personality; school and educational; industrial and organizational; cross-cultural; psychology of women; health; forensic; and sports. Sometimes the categories are not mutually exclusive. For example, some social psychologists are also experimental psychologists.

Clinical and counseling psychology *is the most widely practiced specialization in psychology: clinical and counseling psychologists diagnose and treat people with psychological problems* (see table 1.1). The work of clinical psychologists often does not differ from that of counseling psychologists, although a counseling psychologist sometimes deals with people who have less serious problems. In many instances, counseling psychologists work with students, advising them about personal problems and career planning.

"Well, you don't look like an experimental psychologist to me."

Some Job Possibilities for Students with an Undergraduate Degree in Psychology

Following is a brief list of some job possibilities that students with an undergraduate degree in psychology may find available (Jalbert, 1996):

Business
- personnel administrator
- public relations
- sales representative
- admissions recruiter
- textbook representative
- advertising
- insurance agent
- management trainee
- retail sales management
- loan officer

Social/Human Services
- case worker
- youth counselor
- employment counselor
- fund-raising specialist
- alumni affairs coordinator
- mental health aide
- parent educator
- drug abuse counselor

Research
- research assistant
- trainee for product research companies
- marketing researcher
- grant and report writer
- information specialist/researcher
- research analyst
- statistical assistant

Figure 1.4
Some Job Possibilities for Students with an Undergraduate Degree in Psychology

Clinical psychologists are different from psychiatrists. Typically a clinical psychologist has a doctoral degree in psychology, which requires 3 to 4 years of graduate work, plus 1 year of internship in a mental health facility. **Psychiatry** *is a branch of medicine practiced by physicians with a doctor of medicine (M.D.) degree who subsequently specialize in abnormal behavior and psychotherapy.* Clinical psychologists and psychiatrists are both interested in improving the lives of people with mental health problems. One important distinction is that psychiatrists can prescribe drugs, whereas clinical psychologists cannot.

Community psychology *focuses on providing accessible care for people with psychological problems.* Community-based mental health centers are one means of providing such services as outreach programs to people in need, especially those who have traditionally been underserved by mental health professionals. Community psychologists view human behavior in terms of adaptation to resources and to one's situation. They work to create communities that are more supportive of residents by pinpointing needs, by providing needed services, and by teaching people how to gain access to resources already available. Finally, community psychologists are also concerned about *prevention.* They try to prevent mental health problems by identifying high-risk groups and then intervening to provide appropriate services and by stimulating new opportunities in the community.

Experimental psychology *involves areas in which psychologists often conduct basic research and use an experimental strategy.* Among the main areas that experimental psychologists study are sensation and perception, cognitive processes (such as memory), learning, motivation, and emotion.

Behavioral neuroscience and comparative psychology *focus on biological processes, especially the brain's role in behavior.* Many of these scientists use animals in their research and investigate a range of topics from how the brain processes information to the effects of hormones on behavior.

Nonacademic Careers in Psychology

CPA's Divisions
APA's Divisions
Community Psychology
Behavioral Neuroscience and Comparative Psychology

Clinical Psychology
Counseling Psychology

Industrial/Organizational Psychology

Specialties in the Fields of Clinical and Counseling Psychology, and in Industrial and Organizational Psychology

Clinical and Counseling Psychology*

Psychotherapy
With many subspecialties such as family therapy, group therapy, drug therapy, individual therapy, biofeedback, and sex therapy

Clinical Child Psychology
Assessment (giving tests), severely disordered children, learning disabilities, reading problems, mental retardation, and parent education

Behavior and Mental Disorders
Alcoholism, delinquency, crime, suicide, eating disorders, and depression

Medical Psychology
Often working in hospitals in concert with physicians and other medical personnel, hospital care

Gerontology
Specializing in the growing area of older adults' mental disturbances

Community Mental Health
Working in community mental health clinics

Physically Handicapped
Working with the disabled, blind, and hearing impaired

Industrial and Organizational Psychology*

Management and Organization
Behavior in organizations, labor-management relations, human relations, and compensation

Personnel
Career development and training, job satisfaction and attitudes toward work, selection and placement of employees, retirement

Vocational Counseling
Personal or adjustment counseling, test construction, diagnosis and assessment, rehabilitation counseling, employee counseling, employment counseling, and counseling disabled and handicapped employees

Advertising
Evaluation of how people perceive and think about advertisements, examination of motivational and emotional factors involved in advertising effectiveness

Marketing
Consumer surveys, market analysis

*These lists are meant to be exemplary, not exhaustive.

Developmental psychology *is concerned with how we become who we are, from conception to death.* In particular, developmental psychologists focus on the biological and environmental factors that contribute to human development. For many years the major emphasis was on child development. However, an increasing number of today's developmental psychologists show a strong interest in adult development and aging. Their inquiries range across the biological, cognitive, and social domains of life.

Social psychology *deals with people's social interactions, relationships, social perceptions, and attitudes.* Social psychologists believe we can better understand mind and behavior if we know something about how people function in groups.

Personality psychology *focuses on the relatively enduring traits and characteristics of individuals.* Personality psychologists study such topics as self-concept, aggression, moral development, gender roles, and inner or outer directedness.

School and educational psychology *is concerned with children's learning and adjustment in school.* School psychologists work in elementary and secondary school systems, testing children, making recommendations about educational placement, and working on educational planning teams. Educational psychologists work at colleges and universities, teach classes, and do research on teaching and learning.

Industrial/organizational psychology *deals with the workplace, focusing on both the workers and the organizations that employ them.* Industrial/organizational psychologists are concerned with training employees, improving working conditions, and developing criteria for selecting employees. For example, an organizational psychologist might recommend that a company adopt a new management structure that would increase communication between managers and staff. The background of industrial and organizational psychologists often includes training in social psychology.

Cross-cultural psychology *examines the role of culture in understanding behavior, thought, and emotion.* Cross-cultural psychologists compare the nature of psychological processes in different cultures, with a special interest in whether or not psychological phenomena are universal or culture specific. The International Association for Cross-Cultural Psychology promotes research on cross-cultural comparisons and awareness of culture's role in psychology.

The **psychology of women** *emphasizes the importance of promoting the research and study of women,* integrating this information about women with current psychological knowledge and beliefs, and applying the information to society and its institutions. The Section on Women and Psychology (SWAP), now the second-largest division of the Canadian Psychological Association, was formed in 1976.

Health psychology *is a multidimensional approach to health that emphasizes psychological factors, lifestyle, and the nature of the health care delivery system.* Health psychologists may work in physical or mental health areas. Some are members of multidisciplinary teams that conduct research or provide clinical services.

Forensic psychology *is the field of psychology that applies psychological concepts to the legal system.* Social and cognitive psychologists increasingly conduct research on topics related to psychology and law. Forensic psychologists are also hired by legal teams to provide input about many aspects of a trial.

THINKING ABOUT PSYCHOLOGY AND LIFE

Which Areas of Psychology Interest You the Most?

PSYCHOLOGY has many diverse areas, ranging from exploring the brain's role in behavior to understanding how we develop as human beings to helping people with their psychological problems. Think about the areas of psychology described in the text. Which areas interest you the most? Go through the list of areas below and rank them from 1 (most interesting) to 11 (least interesting).

_____ Clinical and Counseling Psychology
_____ Community Psychology
_____ Experimental Psychology
_____ Physiological Psychology and Neuroscience
_____ Developmental Psychology
_____ Social Psychology
_____ Personality Psychology
_____ School and Educational Psychology
_____ Industrial/Organizational Psychology
_____ Cross-Cultural Psychology
_____ The Psychology of Women
_____ Health Psychology
_____ Forensic Psychology
_____ Sports Psychology

When you have finished studying this book and completed the course, you might want to return to this exercise to see if and how your rankings are different.

Educational Psychology
Health Psychology
Forensic Psychology

SUMMARY TABLE 1.2
Psychology and Life: What Matters;
Psychology's Careers and Areas of Specializations

Concept	Processes/ Related Ideas	Characteristics/Description
Psychology and Life: What Matters	Ten Themes	Biological processes, environmental processes, mental processes, the social world, culture, individual variations, science, conceptual diversity, controversies, and critical thinking all matter.
Psychology's Careers and Specializations	Careers in Psychology	Majoring in psychology can open up many career opportunities, and the field of psychology is highly interesting to many people. Majoring in psychology will not only provide you with considerable knowledge about mind and behavior, it will also help you improve in many skill areas. And careers in psychology pay reasonably well. A graduate degree will greatly expand your opportunities (and your income). Careers range from improving the lives of people with mental problems to teaching at a university and conducting research.
	Areas of Specialization	These include clinical and counseling; community; experimental; behavioral neuroscience and comparative psychology; developmental; social; personality; school and educational; industrial/organizational; cross-cultural; women's psychology; health psychology; forensic psychology; and sport psychology.

Sport Psychology

Psych Web

Sport psychology *is the field of psychology that applies psychology's principles to improving sport performance and enjoying sport participation.* Sports psychology is a relatively new field but is rapidly gaining acceptance. At the 1996 Olympics, many psychologists worked with U.S. and Canadian athletes and coaches.

In sum, the avenues an individual can follow as a psychologist are richly varied. We have only touched on this enormous variety in our description of psychology's main areas. For example, within each area numerous specializations are possible. Table 1.1 lists some specializations available in clinical and counseling psychology and in industrial/organizational psychology. Salaries are especially good in the area of industrial and organizational psychology.

At this point we have studied a number of ideas about what matters in psychology, as well as psychology's careers and areas of specialization. An overview of these ideas is presented in summary table 1.2. In this chapter, we have touched on psychology's role as a science on several occasions. In the next chapter, we will extensively explore psychology's scientific makeup.

Overview

Overview

WE BEGAN THIS CHAPTER by exploring these aspects of psychology: How it is defined, the beginnings of psychology as a science, and early and contemporary approaches to psychology. We examined ten themes that matter in psychology and life: biological processes, environmental processes, mental processes, the social world, culture, individual variations, science, conceptual diversity, controversies, and critical thinking. We also read about psychology's careers and areas of specialization.

Don't forget that you can obtain a more detailed overview of the chapter by studying again the two summary tables of pages 16 and 28.

WHAT IS PSYCHOLOGY?

Exploring Psychology

- Defining Psychology
- The Beginnings of Psychology as a Science
- Early and Contemporary Approaches to Psychology

Psychology and Life: What Matters

- Biological Processes Matter
- Environmental Processes Matter
- Mental Processes Matter
- The Social World Matters
- Culture Matters
- Individual Variations Matter
- Science Matters
- Conceptual Diversity Matters
- Controversies Matter
- Critical Thinking Matters

Psychology's Careers and Areas of Specialization

- Careers in Psychology
- Areas of Specialization in Psychology

Key Terms

psychology 5
science of psychology 5
behavior 5
mental processes 5
natural selection 6
structuralism 7
functionalism 7
behavioral approach 8
social cognitive theory 8
psychoanalytic approach 10
humanistic approach 10

cognitive approach 11
information processing 11
behavioral neuroscience
    approach 11
evolutionary psychology
    approach 12
sociocultural approach 12
culture 12
ethnicity 13
gender 13
sex 13

eclectic approach 14
critical thinking 22
clinical and counseling
    psychology 24
psychiatry 25
community psychology 25
experimental psychology 25
behavioral neuroscience and
    comparative psychology 25
developmental psychology 27
social psychology 27

personality psychology 27
school and educational
    psychology 27
industrial/organizational
    psychology 27
cross-cultural psychology 27
psychology of women 27
health psychology 27
forensic psychology 27
sport psychology 28

Key People

Charles Darwin 6
Johannes Müller 6
Wilhelm Wundt 6
E. B. Titchener 7
William James 7
Ivan Pavlov 8

B. F. Skinner 8
Albert Bandura 8
Sigmund Freud 9
Erik Erikson 10
Carl Rogers 10

Abraham Maslow 10
Herbert Simon 11
D.O. Hebb 11
Roger Sperry 12
David Buss 12

Steven Pinker 12
John Berry 13
Diane Halpern 22
Sandra Pyke 22

Psychology Checklist

How much have you learned since the beginning of the chapter? Use the following statements to help you review your knowledge and understanding of the chapter material. First, read the statement and mentally or briefly demonstrate on paper that you can outline and discuss the relevant information.

_____ I know how to define psychology.
_____ I can describe the beginnings of psychology as a science.
_____ I can discuss psychology's seven main early and contemporary approaches.
_____ I know what it means to take an eclectic approach in psychology.

_____ I can describe the ten main themes that were examined in regard to what matters in psychology.
_____ I can discuss careers in psychology.
_____ I can profile the main areas of specialization in psychology.

For any items that you did not check off, go back and locate the relevant material in the chapter. Review the material until you feel you can check off the item. You may want to use this checklist later in preparing for an exam.

Taking It to the Net

1. The American Psychological Association requires that clinical psychologists have either a PhD or PsyD. Although both study clinical issues and techniques, PhD programs are generally more research oriented, while PsyD programs are more applied. The Canadian Psychological Association does not yet endorse the PsyD designation, preferring the PhD research-practitioner model. Regardless, are you interested in research? Do you think it is important for a clinician to be involved in research in psychology? What kinds of things do researchers in clinical psychology study?

2. Evolutionary psychology emphasizes the role of adaptation and survival of the fittest in explaining behavior. For example, eating healthy food is a behavior that results in looking and feeling better, which results in more opportunities to procreate and pass on our genes. In your opinion, what adaptive problem is solved by be-

haviors such as anxiety and depression? Furthermore, can you think of how these behaviors will continue to evolve in the future?

3. The behavioral approach to psychology emphasizes observable behavior and its environmental determinants (i.e., the cause and effect of behavior we can see). In contrast, the cognitive approach emphasizes mental processes (i.e., our thoughts and ideas about ourselves and the world around us). Some psychologists have in turn combined these two approaches to employ a cognitive-behavioral approach to therapy. Explain how the two branches of psychology can be combined to explain and treat abnormal behavior such as anxiety. Do you think that cognitive-behavioral therapy is a viable approach?

Connect to http://www.mcgrawhill.ca/college/santrock to find the answers!

Resources for Psychology and Life

Canadian Psychological Association
151 Rue Slater Street, Suite 205
Ottawa, Ontario
K1P 5H3
613-237-2144
http://www.cpa.ca/

The Canadian Psychological Association is the predominant organization representing psychologists in Canada. CPA offers information about psychology to students and offers many benefits to student affiliate members.

American Psychological Association
750 First Street, NE
Washington, DC 20002-4242
202-336-5500
http://www.apa.org/

The American Psychological Association is the largest organization of psychologists in the United States. It publishes a number of journals on different psychological topics and the free booklet *Careers in Psychology,* which describes a wide range of career opportunities in psychology. Undergraduate students, including Canadians, are welcome to join the APA.

American Psychological Society
1010 Vermont Avenue, NW, Suite 1100
Washington, DC 20005
202-783-2077
http://www.psychologicalscience.org/

The American Psychological Society promotes and advances research and applications in psychology. Student affiliate memberships are available.

How to Think Like a Psychologist (1996)
by Donal McBurney
Upper Saddle River, NJ: Prentice-Hall

This book focuses on misconceptions and impediments to understanding psychology. Using a question-answer format, it evaluates such questions as why do psychologists have so many theories, why do I have to learn about so many methods, why do I have to learn about the brain, can you prove there is no ESP, how can psychology be a science when everybody is unique, and why can't psychologists predict who will commit a violent act?

Is Psychology the Major for You? (1987)
by P. J. Woods and C. S. Wilkinson
Washington, DC: American Psychological Association

This book is must reading for any student interested in a career in psychology. It explains how a psychology degree can be valuable preparation for many diverse careers, including careers in human services, management, and marketing.

Library Use: A Handbook for Psychology (1992, 2nd ed.)
by Jeffrey Reed and Pam Baxter
Washington, DC: American Psychological Association

This book will show you how to select, define, and locate topics for a library search in psychology. The topics chosen appeal to the interests of many psychology students, and you don't need to have highly technical knowledge to use this book.

Encounters with Great Psychologists: Twelve Dramatic Portraits (1989)
by John Kunkel
Toronto: Wall & Thompson

These twelve partly fictionalized accounts of conversations with famous psychologists captures their dedication to psychology.

The Story of Psychology (1993)
by Morton Hunt
New York: Doubleday

This engaging, well-written book journeys through psychology's history and portrays its founders, pioneers, and contemporary figures.

Chapter 2

CHAPTER OUTLINE

SCIENTIFIC RESEARCH AND THE SCIENTIFIC METHOD

Exploring the Science Side of Psychology

The Scientific Method and Its Steps

WHO WILL THE PARTICIPANTS BE?

RESEARCH METHODS

Observation

Interviews and Questionnaires

Case Studies

Standardized Tests

Physiological Research

Correlational Research

Experimental Research

Multiple Research Methods

RESEARCH CHALLENGES

Ethics and Values

Gender, Culture, and Ethnicity

Reading and Understanding Research Journals

Being a Wise Consumer of Information About Psychology

Psychology's Scientific Methods

"*Truth* is arrived at by the painstaking process of eliminating the untrue."

Sir Arthur Conan Doyle
British Physician and Detective-Story Writer, 20th Century

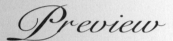

Preview

IN THIS CHAPTER, we will study the essence of what makes psychology a science: its research methods. It is these methods that differentiate a discipline like psychology from a discipline like philosophy. Philosophers seek truth by thinking about thinking and discussing thinking. Psychologists use scientific methods to seek truth. These are among the questions we will explore in this chapter:

• How might the scientific method provide more valid evidence than personal experience?

• How do psychologists select participants for their studies?

• What kinds of methods do psychologists use to obtain information?

• What ethical issues are involved in psychological research?

• What does it take to become a wise consumer of information about psychology?

WHEN YOU TURN ON the evening news or open a newspaper or magazine, you are bombarded with reports about recent research results in medicine, nutrition, and psychology. You are told that a particular vitamin minimizes the risk of cancer; that a particular educational program is effective in helping persons with mental disabilities cope in social situations; that certain nutritional factors, such as eating a healthy, balanced breakfast, help young children concentrate in school; and that certain styles of parenting produce mentally healthy or mentally unhealthy children. How do you respond to this barrage of information? Many of us immediately double our intake of the vitamin in question, vote for candidates who support the educational programs that agree with the latest research on the issue, and make a mental note of (or if you are already a parent, apply) the parenting strategies that you hear produce "healthy" children.

What we know, *or think we know,* about scientific research affects nearly every aspect of daily life, from deciding what foods to eat, to deciding how to vote, and even to deciding what to say to a frightened child in our care. We live in the information age. Research results are no longer the domain of the experts who carry out the studies or the paid professionals who carefully examine and apply the results on a case-by-case basis. For better or for worse, the mass media in our society make research results in psychology the property and concern of every aware Canadian citizen. As a member of society, by voting and paying taxes, you affect the course of scientific research in helping to determine not only which studies scientists carry out, but how they will affect your life in terms of the funding that you will make available for implementing the results of the studies. You will see in this chapter that properly conducted scientific research is a powerful tool for uncovering the laws of physical and mental nature. You will see also that this tool has limits. While scientific inquiry in psychology is the most sophisticated and accurate way of acquiring information about the laws of human behavior, it is also a slow and painstaking process. The results we come to believe from scientific inquiry are rarely the results of a single study;

rather, they derive from mountains of data, collected over many years, that converge on a single conclusion, such as "Smoking tobacco causes cancer." The purpose of this chapter is to make you skeptical and to make you aware, not of the truth or falsehoods of the "scientific" claims that you encounter daily, but of the factors you need to understand in order to evaluate the basis of such claims.

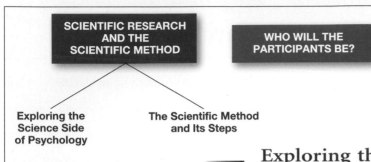

SCIENTIFIC RESEARCH AND THE SCIENTIFIC METHOD

WHO WILL THE PARTICIPANTS BE?

Exploring the Science Side of Psychology

The Scientific Method and Its Steps

Scientific Research and the Scientific Method

In defining psychology in chapter 1, we said that it is the scientific study of behavior and mental processes. Let's further examine what we mean when we call psychology a science.

Exploring the Science Side of Psychology

It is sometimes said that experience is the most important teacher. We do get a great deal of knowledge from personal experience. We generalize from what we observe and frequently turn memorable encounters into lifetime "truths." But how valid are these personal conclusions? As we mentioned in chapter 1, sometimes we err in making personal observations or misinterpret what we see and hear. Chances are, you can think of many situations in which you thought other people read you the wrong way, just as they feel that you misread them. And when our judgments are based on personal experiences, we also aren't always totally objective because we sometimes base our judgments on a need to protect our ego and self-esteem (McMillan, 2000).

Scientific research *is objective, systematic, and testable.* It reduces the likelihood that information will be based on personal beliefs, opinions, and emotions. Can a scientific approach give us more accurate information about psychology? Some people have difficulty thinking of psychology as being a science in the same way that physics, chemistry, and biology are sciences. Can a discipline that studies why people are attracted to each other, how they reason about moral values, and the way ethnicity affects identity be equated with disciplines that examine gravity, the molecular structure of a compound, and the flow of blood in the circulatory system? Science is not defined by *what* it investigates but by *how* it investigates. Whether you study photosynthesis, butterflies, Saturn's moons, or why some people bite their fingernails more than others do, it is the way you study them that makes your approach scientific or not.

Science and Research Methods

Science is not defined by what *it studies but by* how *it investigates it. Photosynthesis, butterflies, Saturn's moons, or relationships among people can all be studied in a scientific manner.* What are some areas of psychology, other than relationships among people, that science can appropriately be used to investigate?

To be a scientist is to be curious and skeptical. Consider these statements:

- Love is blind.
- Happiness is the key to success.
- People have mental disorders because society makes them that way.
- Communication with spirits is possible.

When scientists hear claims like these, they want to know if they are based on *good scientific research.* Such claims spark a psychologist's curiosity and skepticism. Psychology seeks to sort fact from fancy by thinking critically about, and scientifically studying, mind and behavior.

The Scientific Method and Its Steps

The scientific method is widely used by psychologists when they study behavior and mental processes. Scientific research is based on the **scientific method,** *an approach that can be used to discover accurate information. It includes these steps: Conceptualize a problem, collect data, draw conclusions, and revise research conclusions and theory.* We will apply the scientific method to aggressive behavior and violence to provide a common thread for their discussion and to help you understand them.

Conceptualize a Problem   The problem we have chosen is whether people become aggressive by observing other people's aggressive actions. Conceptualizing a problem might not seem like a difficult task. However, a common difficulty that many students (undergraduate and graduate) have is that they state the problem they want to study in vague, general terms. For example, a student might say, "I want to study aggression" or "I want to study why people become violent." That is a start, but it is important to go beyond a general description of a problem by narrowing and zeroing in on what you want to study. Do you want to study aggression's biological dimensions? environmental determinants? Do you want to study strategies for reducing aggression? For example, here is a specific problem that can be studied with regard to aggression's biological dimensions: What role does the hormone testosterone play in males' aggressive behavior? And here is a specific problem that can be studied in regard to strategies for reducing aggression: Does keeping children from watching aggression on TV decrease their aggressive behavior?

Operational Definition   In conceptualizing a problem, psychologists use an **operational definition,** *which consists of describing as precisely as possible the aspects of a problem and how it is to be studied in terms of observable events that can be measured.* By using operational definitions, psychologists eliminate some of the fuzziness and loose ends that easily creep into thinking about a problem and studying it. Operational definitions also make concepts public by being very specific about what observational measurements define them. An operational definition frees a concept from any particular individual's feelings and intuitions, allowing it to be studied by anyone who can conduct the measurable operations.

To see the importance of an operational definition, consider a concept like "depression." "Feeling sad" is not an operational definition of depression. Depression might be operationally defined as experiencing, for 2 weeks or longer, a major depressive episode, depressed characteristics such as lethargy and hopelessness, and impaired daily

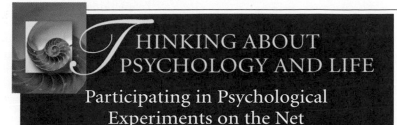

Exploring Pseudoscience

On Being a Scientist

functioning. Further, for the definition to be operational, there would have to be clear ways to measure depression, such as through an interview, survey, or observations.

Albert Bandura examined aggression's many dimensions and possible determinants. He chose to focus on whether children learn to be aggressive from watching other people be aggressive (Bandura, 1965). In this first step in the scientific method, Bandura identified a problem to study and used operational definitions to precisely describe aggression and how it was to be studied. Imitative aggression was operationally defined as observable physical and verbal behaviors shown by children as agreed upon by two independent judges. Bandura also operationally defined the procedure by which children observed a model in considerable detail. Following is an excerpt from one portion of the procedure, which clearly reveals how precise psychologists are when they conduct studies:

> The children were brought individually to a semi-darkened room. The experimenter informed the children that she had some business to attend to before they could proceed to the "surprise playroom," but that during the waiting period the child might watch a television program. After the child was seated, the experimenter walked over to the television console, ostensibly tuned in a program and then departed. A film of approximately 5 minutes duration depicting the model's responses was shown on a glass lenscreen in the television console by means of a rear projection arrangement, screened from the child's view by large panels. The televised form of presentation was utilized primarily because attending responses to televised stimuli are strongly conditioned in children and this procedure would therefore serve to enhance observation which is a necessary condition for imitative learning. (Bandura, 1965, p. 590)

Consider how much more precise this operational definition of the research procedure is than to just say, "The children will observe a model behave aggressively in a room" (which does not adequately operationally define the procedure).

Theory and Hypotheses   Theories might be used in conceptualizing a problem. A **theory** *is a coherent set of interrelated ideas that helps to make predictions and explain data.* A theory generates **hypotheses,** *which are specific assumptions or predictions that can be tested to determine their accuracy.* Theories that have withstood the test of time have confirmed a lot of hypotheses (Stanovich, 1998).

You might recall from chapter 1 our description of Bandura's social cognitive theory, a theory that emphasizes that both experiences and thoughts influence behavior. As part of his social cognitive theory, Bandura believes that observational learning is a key process. Bandura and others have conducted many research studies within this general theoretical framework. In his study of aggression, one of the hypotheses that Bandura (1965) tested was this: *Children who watch a model be either reinforced or given no consequence for being aggressive will be more likely to imitate the model than when the model is punished for being aggressive.* The reinforcement consisted of the model being given candy and soft drinks along with words of praise for a superb performance. The punishment consisted of another adult shaking a menacing finger at the aggressive model and saying, "Hey, you big bully. You quit picking on that clown. I won't tolerate it."

Generating Research Ideas

Collect Information (Data)   The second step in the scientific method is to collect data. Psychologists use research methods to collect data about the problem they are studying. Later in the chapter we will discuss many aspects of research methods, including how psychologists select the participants they want to study and how they design a study. In Bandura's study, the participants were young boys and girls who observed an adult model act aggressively and be reinforced, punished, or receive no consequences for the aggressive behavior. Bandura collected data about how aggressively the children acted after they watched the adult behave aggressively.

Draw Conclusions   The scientific method's third step is to draw conclusions. Once psychologists collect data, they use mathematical (statistical) procedures to understand what the data mean. Then they draw conclusions. In Bandura's study, the data

Statistics Resources

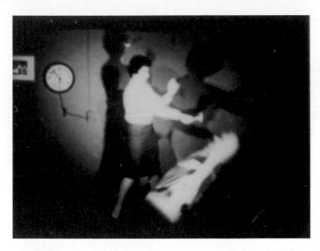 

$\mathcal{F}$igure 2.1
Bandura's Study of Observational Learning

(Left) In Bandura's study, young children watched an adult act aggressively by punching a Bobo doll (a large plastic inflated toy with a clown-like appearance) and subsequently the adult was reinforced, punished, or given no consequences for the aggressive action. *(Right)* Subsequently, the children were more likely to imitate the adult's aggressive actions when the adult model was reinforced or given no consequences than when punished.

that had been collected were statistically analyzed. Based on this analysis, Bandura concluded that children who saw adults be either reinforced or given no consequences for behaving aggressively are more likely to engage in aggressive actions themselves than are children who saw adults be punished for their aggressive actions (see figure 2.1).

Revise Research Conclusions or Theory

The final step in the scientific method involves revising research conclusions in an area or theory. For example, psychologists have developed a number of theories about why people become aggressive. Data, such as those collected by Bandura, force psychologists to examine existing theories to see if they still hold up. For example, when Bandura conducted his research, the main theories of aggression were that aggression is a biological drive or occurs because it gets rewarded. Bandura's research, along with other similar studies, caused psychologists to recognize that aggression also occurs because of observational learning, not just because of a biological drive and reinforcement. Figure 2.2 provides a visual representation of the scientific method's steps applied to Bandura's observational learning study.

It is important to mention that a revision of theory usually occurs only after a number of studies produce similar results. In the case of observational learning's role in aggression, many researchers have found that when children watch people act aggressively, the children become more aggressive themselves (Coie & Dodge, 1998).

Who Will the Participants Be?

Who the participants will be is an important question that every researcher who conducts a study must answer. Will they be people or animals? Will they be children or adults, or both? Will they be males or females, or both? Will they all be of a single ethnicity, such as Anglo-Canadian, or will they come from a diversity of ethnic groups?

When psychologists conduct a study, they usually want to be able to draw conclusions that will apply to a larger group of people (or animals) than the participants they actually study. Thus, an investigator might conduct a study of 300 married couples in Toronto, who have a history of the husband abusing the wife, but the investi-

Step 1
CONCEPTUALIZE A PROBLEM

Bandura identified this problem: Determining whether children learn to become aggressive by observing adults behave aggressively. He operationally defined the study by precisely defining how aggression would be measured and how the research would be conducted. Bandura's social cognitive theory served as the theoretical orientation of the study. The specific hypothesis tested in this study was: Children who watch a model being reinforced for being aggressive or being given no consequences will be more likely to imitate the model than when the model is punished for being aggressive.

Step 2
COLLECT INFORMATION (DATA)

Bandura presented young children with an adult model who engaged in aggressive behavior and was either reinforced, punished, or given no consequences. The children were subsequently observed to determine if watching the model act aggressively under these conditions increased their aggression.

Step 3
DRAW CONCLUSIONS

Bandura statistically analyzed the data he collected and found that children who watched an adult act aggressively and be reinforced or receive no consequences subsequently increased their own aggression more than when the model was punished for aggressive actions.

Step 4
REVISE RESEARCH CONCLUSIONS AND THEORY

Bandura's research, along with other research that obtained similar results, stimulated psychologists to add observational learning to the list of factors (such as biological drives and reinforcement) that cause children to behave aggressively.

Figure 2.2
The Scientific Method Applied to Bandura's Study of Observational Learning and Aggression

gator might want the results to apply to all married couples with a history of wife abuse in Canada. A **population** *is the entire group about which the investigator wants to draw conclusions.* In this particular study of spousal abuse, the population is all couples in Canada in which men abuse their wives. A **sample** *is a subset of the population chosen by the investigator for study.* In this spousal abuse study, the sample is the 300 couples in Toronto. Why does a sample need to be used rather than the population? Because it is impractical to survey the entire population.

The target population to which the investigator wants to generalize varies with the study. For example, in a study of the effects of televised violence on boys' aggression, the population might be all 3- to 5-year-old boys in Canada. In a study of how people think critically, the population might be all humans. In a study of whether chimpanzees have language, the population might be all chimpanzees.

Generalization from the sample to the population can be made only if the sample is representative (which means "typical") of the population. For example, in the study of 300 couples in which the husbands abuse their wives, a disproportionate number of them may have had income in the poverty range and were Anglo-Canadians. Thus, caution would be warranted in generalizing the results to the entire Canadian population of couples in which the husbands abuse their wives, especially those in higher income brackets and from other ethnic groups.

In a **random sample,** *every member of the population has an equal chance of being selected.* In the study of spousal abuse, a representative sample would mirror the population in terms of such factors as age, socioeconomic status, age at marriage, geographic location, religion, and so forth.

Appropriate sampling methods aren't always followed (Heiman, 1995; Benjafield, 1994). Newspapers and magazines often conduct surveys of their readership. Those who participate by mailing or calling in their opinions probably feel more strongly about the issue than those who do not respond. Issues such as whether or not drunk driving laws should be tougher or whether premarital sex is morally wrong are likely to spur those with strong feelings into action. For example, when a magazine like *Playboy* surveys its readers on sexual attitudes, the results show far more permissiveness than if a random sample of adults in North America were asked about their sexual attitudes.

It is easy to get the impression that psychological research is worthless if it is not based on a random sample. However, random sampling is important in some types of research, much less important in others. If a researcher wants to know how often spousal abuse occurs in Canada, obtaining a random sample is important. However, in many research studies, psychologists are interested in studying specific aspects of behavior under specific conditions, in which case they deliberately do not obtain a random sample. In these studies, they might want people with certain characteristics well represented. Thus, in a study of spousal abuse, a researcher might study 50 couples in which the wife had been married before and 50 couples in which she had not; this researcher is interested in discovering whether the previous marriage of the wife affects the incidence and nature of spousal abuse.

SUMMARY TABLE 2.1
Scientific Research and the Scientific Method; Who Will the Participants Be?

Concept	Processes/ Related Ideas	Characteristics/Description
Exploring the Science Side of Psychology	Its nature	Personal experiences don't always give us valid information. Science seeks to provide accurate information. A discipline is a science not because of *what* it investigates but because of *how* it investigates. Scientific research is objective, systematic, and testable.
The Scientific Method and Its Steps	What is the scientific method?	The scientific method is an approach that is used to discover accurate information about phenomena, including mind and behavior. It includes these steps: Identify a problem, collect information (data), draw conclusions, and revise research conclusions and theory.
	Conceptualize a problem	In defining and studying a problem, it is important to avoid stating the problem in vague, general terms. Psychologists create an operational definition of a problem, which consists of describing as precisely as possible the aspects of a problem and how it should be studied in terms of observable events that can be measured. A theory is a coherent set of interrelated ideas that helps to make predictions and explain data. A theory has hypotheses, which are specific assumptions or predictions that can be tested to determine their accuracy.
	Collect data	In collecting data, investigators choose from a variety of research methods.
	Draw conclusions	Once psychologists collect data, they analyze them using mathematical (statistical) procedures in order to understand their meaning.
	Revise research conclusions and theory	A revision of research conclusions and theory usually occurs only when a number of studies produce similar results.
Who Will the Participants Be?	Their nature	When psychologists conduct a study, they usually want to be able to draw conclusions that will apply to a larger group of people (or animals) than the participants they actually study. A population is the entire group of participants about which the investigator wants to draw conclusions. The sample is a subset of the population chosen by the investigator for study. Generalization from the sample to the population can be made if the sample is representative of the population. In a random sample, every member of the population has an equal chance of being selected. In a number of instances, researchers deliberately do not select a random sample but rather one that has people with certain characteristics represented. Appropriate sampling is not always followed, which can lead to biased results.

It also should be pointed out that in many areas of psychology, generalization comes from similar findings across a number of studies rather than from random sampling within a single study. If five or six studies conducted with varied samples (maybe one in Winnipeg with low-income and middle-income ethnic minority participants; another in Vernon, B.C., with middle-income White participants; and others with somewhat similar or different participant characteristics) all find that frequent conflict and one or more incidents of physical abuse in a previous marriage are related to future spousal abuse, then we gain better confidence that these findings can be generalized to the population.

At this point we have studied many ideas about scientific research, the scientific method, and who the participants will be in a research study. An overview of these ideas is presented in summary table 2.1.

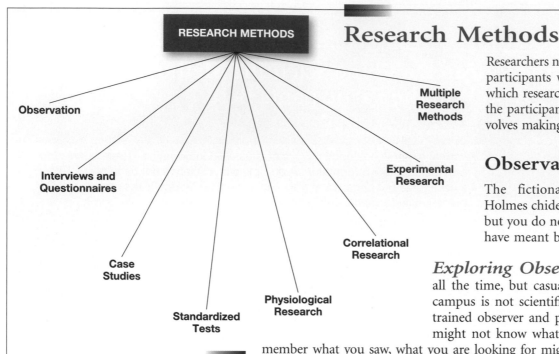

RESEARCH METHODS

- Observation
- Interviews and Questionnaires
- Case Studies
- Standardized Tests
- Physiological Research
- Correlational Research
- Experimental Research
- Multiple Research Methods

Research Methods

Researchers not only must determine who their participants will be, they also have to decide which research methods they will use to study the participants. You will discover that this involves making quite a few decisions.

Observation

The fictional English detective Sherlock Holmes chided his assistant, Watson, "You see but you do not observe." What might Holmes have meant by this comment?

Exploring Observation   We look at things all the time, but casually watching a friend cross the campus is not scientific observation. Unless you are a trained observer and practice your skills regularly, you might not know what to look for, you might not remember what you saw, what you are looking for might change from one moment to the next, and you might not communicate your observations effectively.

For observations to be effective, we have to know what we are looking for, whom we are observing, when and where we will observe, how the observations will be made, and in what form they will be recorded. That is, we need to observe in some *systematic* way (Zeren & Makosky, 1995). Consider aggression. Do we want to study verbal or physical aggression, or both? How will we know it when we see it? If one man punches another in the arm, will we mark that down as aggression? If both men are laughing and one punches the other in the arm, will we still count the punch as aggression? Do we want to study men, or women, or children, or all of these? Do we want to evaluate them in a university laboratory, at work, at play, in their homes, or at all of these locations? Do we want to audiotape or videotape their behavior, or

This researcher is using observation as part of a research study on infant development. Videotaped observation has allowed researchers to become increasingly precise in coding various behaviors because they can play the tape over and over to discover micro aspects of behavior.

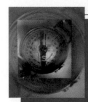

EXPLORATIONS IN PSYCHOLOGY
Hans, the Clever Horse

TO UNDERSTAND the importance of controlled observation in psychology, we will consider a horse by the name of Hans who lived in Germany in the early 1900's. According to experts, Hans could reason and "talk." Hans had been trained by a retired math teacher, Mr. von Osten, to communicate by tapping his forefoot and moving his head. A head nod meant yes, while a shake suggested no. Mr. von Osten developed a code for verbal information in which each letter was represented by a pair of numbers. The letter A was coded as one tap, pause, one tap, and the letter I was three taps, pause, two taps. Once Hans learned to tap his foot or move his head when questioned, he was given simple problems and then fed a piece of bread or carrot for correct responses. By the end of his training, Hans could spell words spoken to him, and he excelled in math. He became a hero in Germany— his picture was on liquor bottles and toys. Experts were so impressed that an official commission of thirteen scientists, educators, and public officials examined the horse, testing him to see if he really could do all of the things claimed. They came away even more impressed and issued a statement saying that there was no evidence of any intentional influence or aid on the part of Hans' questioners.

But one scientist was not so sure that Hans was as intelligent as he had been portrayed. Oskar von Pfungst, a very sharp observer, had detected that Hans always faced his questioner. Von Pfungst hypothesized (developed the hunch or belief) that this might have something to do with his math ability. He set up a very simple experiment. He wrote numbers on a card and held them up one at a time, asking Hans to tap out the numbers written on each card. Half of the cards von Pfungst held so that only Hans, not von Pfungst, could see what was on them. With the cards von Pfungst could see, Hans was his usual brilliant self, getting 92 percent of them correct. But for the numbers von Pfungst could not see, Hans was no longer a brilliant horse, getting only 8 percent correct.

Von Pfungst repeated the experiment over and over again with nearly the same results. He then carefully observed Hans with his other questioners, including von Osten. As soon as they stated the problem to Hans, most questioners would turn their head and upper body slightly. When the correct number of foot taps had been made by Hans, the questioner would move his head upward. Despite his years of work with the horse, Mr. von Osten had never dreamed that Hans had learned to "read" him. Von Osten commented that he actually was angry at the horse and felt betrayed by him.

Thus we can see that experts sometimes can be wrong and that what sometimes seems to be the truth may be a false impression. Even experts can be fooled if they don't make appropriate use of research procedures to check their observations.

---

both? A common way to record observations is to write them down, using shorthand or symbols; however, psychologists increasingly use tape recorders, video cameras, special coding sheets, and one-way mirrors to make observations more efficient. To read further about the importance of systematic observation in accurately obtaining information about behavior, see Explorations in Psychology.

Laboratory Observation   When we observe, we often need to *control* certain factors that determine behavior but are not the focus of our inquiry. For this reason much of psychology's research is conducted in a **laboratory,** *a controlled setting with many of the complex factors of the "real world" removed.* For example, Bandura's (1965) study of observational learning and aggression that we described earlier was conducted in a laboratory. By conducting his research in a laboratory with adults the child did not know, Bandura controlled when the child witnessed aggression, how much aggression the child saw, and what form the aggression took. Bandura could not have conducted his experiment as effectively if other factors, such as parents, siblings, friends, television, and a familiar room, had been present.

Laboratory research, however, does have some drawbacks. First, it is almost impossible to conduct research without the participants' knowing they are being studied. Second, the laboratory setting is unnatural and therefore can cause the participants to behave unnaturally. Research participants usually show less aggressive

"For crying out loud; gentlemen! That's us! Someone's installed the one-way mirror in backward!"

behavior in a laboratory than in a more familiar or natural setting, such as a park or at home. They also show less aggression when they are aware they are being observed than when they are unaware they are being observed. Third, people who are willing to come to a university laboratory are unlikely to represent groups from diverse cultural backgrounds. Those who are unfamiliar with university settings, and with the idea of "helping science," may be intimidated by the setting. Fourth, some aspects of mind and behavior are difficult if not impossible to examine in the laboratory. Certain types of stress are difficult (and unethical) to study in the laboratory. Alcohol, for instance, consistently increases aggression in an individual who is provoked. In 1985 a riot broke out at a soccer game in Brussels, Belgium. The English fans, intoxicated by alcohol, aroused by the competition, and taunted by the Italian fans, attacked the Italians. As the Italians retreated, they were crushed against a wall—the death toll was 38. Recreating circumstances in a laboratory that even remotely resemble the Brussels soccer game is impossible and unethical.

Naturalistic Observation   Although laboratory research is a valuable tool for psychologists, naturalistic observation provides insight that we sometimes cannot achieve in the laboratory (Pellegrini, 1996). In **naturalistic observation,** *psychologists observe behavior in real-world settings and make no effort to manipulate or control the situation.* Psychologists conduct naturalistic observations at soccer games, day-care centers, university dormitories, rest rooms, corporations, shopping malls, restaurants, dances, and other places people live in and frequent. In contrast to Bandura's observations of aggression in a laboratory, some psychologists use naturalistic methods to observe the aggression of children in nursery schools, the aggression of marital partners at home, and the arguments and violence of people at sporting events and political protests (Mahoney, 1995; Pence, 1988).

Jane Goodall was a young woman when she made her first trip to the Gombe Research Center in Tanzania, Africa. Fascinated by chimpanzees, she dreamed about a career that would allow her to explore her hunches about the nature of chimpanzees. She embarked on a career in the bush that involved long and solitary hours of careful, patient observation. A specialist in animal behavior, her observations spanned 30 years, years that included her marriage, the birth of her son, untold hardship, and inestimable pleasure. Due to her efforts, our understanding of chimpanzees in natural settings dramatically improved. What are some other aspects of behavior that could be studied by using naturalistic observation?

Even though naturalistic observation can provide valuable information about how people behave in real-world settings, it has some drawbacks. As with laboratory observation, observers often have difficulty making their presence unobtrusive so they don't affect the participants. To combat the problem of participants' reacting to being observed, researchers usually observe long enough for people to become accustomed to being observed and to begin to behave more naturally. Also, naturalistic observation provides less control over the study's conditions than laboratory observation does.

Interviews and Questionnaires

Sometimes the best and quickest way to get information from people is to ask them for it. An **interview** involves asking questions to find out about a person's experiences and attitudes. Most interviews occur face-to-face, although they can take place over the telephone. Some interview questions are unstructured and open-ended, such as "Tell me about your aggressive tendencies" or "How violent would you say your marriage is?" Other interview questions are more structured and ask about more specific things. For example, a structured interview question might ask, "How many times have you and your marital partner argued in the last month: 0, 1–2, 3–5, 6–10, 10–30, every day?" One shortcoming of an interview is **social desirability,** *the tendency of participants to tell the interviewer what they think is socially acceptable or desirable rather than what they truly feel or think.* For example, a woman might not want to reveal the actual torment she has gone through because of her husband's abuse.

"*Would you say Attila is doing an excellent job, a good job, a fair job, or a poor job?*"

Questionnaires (or surveys) *are similar to structured interviews except that the respondents read the questions and mark their answers on paper instead of verbally responding to an interviewer.* A major advantage of questionnaires is that they can be given to large numbers of people easily (some now appear on the Internet). Good surveys have concrete, specific, and unambiguous questions. Social desirability is a problem for questionnaires just as it is for interviews (Krosnick, 1999).

Case Studies

A **case study** *is an in-depth look at a single individual; this method is used mainly by clinical psychologists when, for either practical or ethical reasons, the unique aspects of an individual's life cannot be duplicated.* A case study provides information about one person's fears, hopes, fantasies, traumatic experiences, upbringing, family relationships, health, or anything that helps the psychologist understand the person's mind and behavior.

Traumatic experiences have produced some truly fascinating case studies in psychology. Consider the following. A 26-year-old schoolteacher met a woman with whom he fell intensely in love. But several months after their love affair began, the schoolteacher became depressed, drank heavily, and talked about suicide. The suicidal ideas progressed to images of murder and suicide. His actions became bizarre. On one occasion he punctured the tires of his beloved's car. On another he stood on the side of the road where she passed frequently in her car, extending his hand in his pocket so she would think he was holding a gun. Only eight months after meeting her, the teacher shot her while he was a passenger in the car she was driving. Soon after the act, he ran to a telephone booth to call his priest. The girlfriend had died (Revitch & Schlesinger, 1978).

This case reveals how depressive moods and bizarre thinking can precede violent acts, such as murder. Other vivid case studies appear throughout this text, among

Standardized tests require individuals to answer a series of written or oral questions. The individual on the right is being given a standardized test of intelligence. Other than standardized tests, what other methods might be used to assess intelligence?

Standardized Tests

Physiological Research

them a woman with three personalities, each of which is unaware of the others, and a modern-day wild child named Genie, who lived in near total isolation during her childhood.

Case histories provide dramatic, in-depth portrayals of people's lives, but we must be cautious when generalizing from this information. The subject of a case study is unique, with a genetic makeup and experiences no one else shares. In addition, case studies involve judgments of unknown reliability. Psychologists who conduct case studies rarely check to see if other psychologists agree with their observations.

Standardized Tests

Standardized tests *require people to answer a series of written and/or oral questions, and they have two distinct features: (1) An individual's score is totaled to yield a single score, or set of scores, that reflects something about that individual; and (2) the individual's score is compared with the scores of a large group of similar people to determine how the individual responded relative to others.* Scores are often stated in terms of percentiles. For example, suppose you scored in the 92nd percentile on the WAIS-R, the Wechsler Adult Intelligence Scale-Revised. This means that 92 percent of a large group of individuals who previously took the test received scores lower than yours. Among the most widely used standardized tests in psychology are the WAIS-R, the Stanford-Binet intelligence test and the Minnesota Multiphasic Personality Inventory (MMPI).

To continue our look at how psychologists use different methods to evaluate aggression, consider the MMPI, which includes a scale to assess an individual's delinquency and antisocial tendencies. The items on this scale ask you to respond whether or not you are rebellious, impulsive, and have trouble with authority figures. The 26-year-old teacher who murdered his girlfriend would have scored high on a number of the MMPI scales, including one designed to measure how strange and bizarre our thoughts and ideas are.

The main advantage of standardized tests is that they provide information about *individual differences* among people. But information obtained from standardized tests does not always predict behavior in nontest situations. Standardized tests are based on the belief that a person's behavior is consistent and stable. Although personality and intelligence, two of the primary targets of standardized tests, have some stability, they can vary, depending on the situation. For example, a person may perform poorly on a standardized intelligence test in an office setting but display a much higher level of intelligence at home where he or she is less anxious. This criticism is especially relevant for members of minority groups, some of whom have been inappropriately classified as mentally retarded on the basis of their scores on intelligence tests. And cross-cultural psychologists caution that while many psychological tests developed in Western cultures might work reasonably well in Western cultures, they might not always be appropriate in other cultures (Cushner & Brislin, 1995). For example, people in other cultures simply might not have had as much exposure to the information on the test.

Physiological Research

An additional method that psychologists use is physiological research. Research on the biological basis of behavior and technological advances continue to produce remarkable insights about mind and behavior. For example, researchers have found that electrical stimulation of certain areas of the brain turns docile, mild-mannered people into hostile, vicious attackers; and higher concentrations of some hormones have been associated with anger in adolescents (Tremblay & Schaal, 1995).

In a recent study of men who had a history of battering their wives, couples' bodies were monitored with electronic sensors during discussions about marital problems

(Jacobsen & Gottman, 1998). One type of these violent men (called "cobras" by the researchers) sounded and looked aggressive but were very calm physiologically. The other type of violent men (called "pit bulls" by the researchers) became internally aroused during discussions about marital problems, never letting up on their wives.

Because much physiological research cannot be carried out with humans, psychologists sometimes use animals. Animal studies permit researchers to control genetic background, diet, experiences during infancy, and countless other factors. In studying humans, psychologists treat these factors as random variation, or "noise," that can interfere with accurate results. In addition, animal researchers can investigate the effects of some treatments (brain implants, for example) that would be unethical with humans. Moreover, it is possible to track the entire life span of some animals over a relatively short period of time. Laboratory mice, for instance, have a life span of approximately 1 year.

With regard to aggression, we know that castration turns ferocious bulls into docile oxen by acting on the male hormone system. After a number of breedings of aggressive mice, researchers have created mice who are absolutely ferocious (Manning, 1989). Do these findings with animals apply to humans? Hormones and genes do influence human aggression, but the influence is less powerful than in animals. Because humans differ from animals in many ways, one disadvantage of research with animals is that the results might not apply to humans.

Correlational Research

In **correlational research**, *the goal is to describe the strength of the relation between two or more events or characteristics.* Correlational research is useful because the more strongly two events are correlated (related, or associated), the more effectively we can predict one from the other.

Continuing with our theme of applying research methods to aggression, let's examine the correlation between children's viewing of violence on TV and their aggressive behavior. In one study, long-term exposure to television violence was correlated with the likelihood of aggression in adolescent boys (Belson, 1978). Those who watched the most aggression on television were the most likely to commit a violent action, swear, be aggressive in sports, threaten violence toward another boy, write slogans on walls, or break windows.

Can we conclude from this study that television violence causes aggression? The answer is no. We can only say that watching violence on television is *associated* (or *related* or *correlated*) with acting aggressively. Remember this important research principle: *Correlation does not equal causation.* We cannot say that watching TV violence causes aggression in this study because it is possible that a third factor, such as genetic tendency, temperament, or inadequate parenting, underlies their association.

To ensure that you understand correlation, let's consider another example. People who make a lot of money have higher self-esteem than their counterparts who make less money (see figure 2.3). We could mistakenly interpret this to mean that making a lot of money causes high self-esteem.

Because some physiological research cannot be carried out with humans, psychologists might use animals in their research. Shown here are two previously peaceful monkeys in which the researcher has electrically stimulated a specific region of their brains (the limbic system). When their limbic system is electrically stimulated, they show rage. Can you think of other research topics that might be effectively studied with animals?

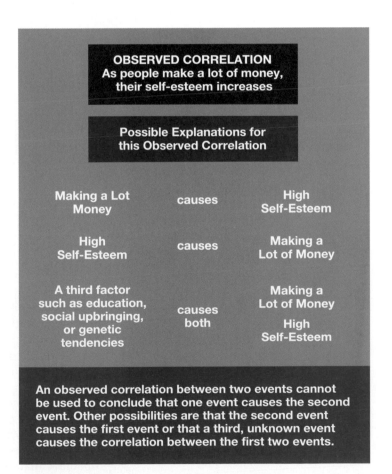

OBSERVED CORRELATION
As people make a lot of money, their self-esteem increases

Possible Explanations for this Observed Correlation

Making a Lot Money	causes	High Self-Esteem
High Self-Esteem	causes	Making a Lot of Money
A third factor such as education, social upbringing, or genetic tendencies	causes both	Making a Lot of Money / High Self-Esteem

An observed correlation between two events cannot be used to conclude that one event causes the second event. Other possibilities are that the second event causes the first event or that a third, unknown event causes the correlation between the first two events.

Figure 2.3
Possible Explanations of Correlational Data

Correlational Research Designs

Experimental Research

There are two other interpretations that we need to consider. First, it could be that developing high self-esteem causes people to make a lot of money. Second, a third factor, such as education, social upbringing, or genetic tendencies, could cause the correlation between making a lot of money and high self-esteem. Throughout this text you will read about numerous correlational research studies. Keep in mind how easy it is to assume causality when two events or characteristics are merely correlated. Only experimental research allows the inference of causality.

Experimental Research

First we will describe how experimental research is conducted, and then we will discuss why researchers must be cautious when conducting such research.

How Experimental Research Is Conducted   **Experimental research** *allows psychologists to determine behavior's causes.* Psychologists accomplish this task by performing an **experiment,** *a carefully regulated procedure in which one or more factors believed to influence the behavior being studied are manipulated and all other factors are held constant.* If the behavior under study changes when a factor is manipulated, we say that the manipulated factor causes the behavior to change. Psychologists conduct experimental research to determine cause-and-effect relationships between events, something correlational research cannot do. *Cause* is the event being manipulated. *Effect* is the behavior that changes because of the manipulation. Nothing is manipulated in correlational research, but in experimental research the researchers actively change an event to see its effect on behavior.

Experiments involve at least one independent variable and one dependent variable. The **independent variable** *is the manipulated, influential, experimental factor.* The label *independent* is used because this variable can be changed independent of other factors to determine its effect on the dependent variable. Researchers have a vast array of options open to them in selecting an independent variable. In one experimental study, the researchers chose as the independent variable the amount and type of television violence that young children saw (Steuer, Applefield, & Smith, 1971). The **dependent variable** *is the factor that is measured in an experiment.* It can change as the independent variable is manipulated. The label dependent is used because this variable depends on what happens to the participants in the experiment. In the study of the relationship between television violence and aggression, the dependent variable was the children's aggressive behavior.

Experiments also involve one or more experimental groups and one or more control groups. An **experimental group** *is a group whose experience is manipulated.* In the study relating television violence and aggression, the experimental group was the children who saw television violence. A **control group** *is a comparison group that is treated in every way like the experimental group except for the manipulated factor.* The control group serves as a baseline against which the effects of the manipulated condition can be compared. In the study relating television violence and aggression, the control group was the group of children who also watched TV but did not see television violence.

Another important aspect of experimental research is **random assignment,** *which occurs when researchers assign participants to experimental and control groups by chance.* This practice reduces the likelihood that the experiment's results will be due to any preexisting differences between groups. For example, in the study relating television violence and aggression, random assignment decreased the probability that the two groups of children differed on such factors as aggressive tendencies, prior exposure to TV violence, intelligence, health, socioeconomic status, and so on.

To summarize the experimental research on television violence and aggression, young children were randomly assigned to one of two groups: one (the experimental group) watched television shows taken directly from violent Saturday-morning cartoon offerings on 11 different days; the second group (control group) watched television cartoon shows with all of the violence removed. The young children subsequently were observed during their play at preschool. The young children who saw the violent TV cartoon shows kicked, choked, and pushed their playmates more than their counterparts who saw the TV cartoon shows with the violence removed. Because this is experimental research, we can conclude that in this study TV violence *caused* an increase in the children's aggressive behavior (see figure 2.4).

Throughout our coverage of psychology's research methods, we have discussed the study of aggression and violence as an illustration. To obtain a further glimpse of how these methods can be used in psychological research, see figure 2.5, which illustrates the application of these methods to the study of dreaming.

Experimental Research Cautions   Although experimental research has considerable power to discover behavior's causes, such research must be done

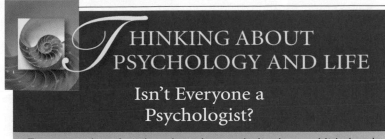

THINKING ABOUT PSYCHOLOGY AND LIFE

Isn't Everyone a Psychologist?

EACH OF US has theories about human behavior, and it is hard to imagine how we could get through life without them. In this sense, we are all psychologists. However, the theories of psychology that we carry around and the way we obtain support for our theories are often quite different from the way psychologists go about theorizing and collecting data about an issue or topic (Stanovich, 1998).

Think for a few moments about your views of human behavior. How did you arrive at them? Might at least some of them be biased? Now think about what you have read in this chapter and chapter 1 about the science of psychology. How is our personal psychology different from scientific psychology? Which one is more likely to be accurate? Why? Although our personal psychology and scientific psychology are often different, in what ways might they be similar?

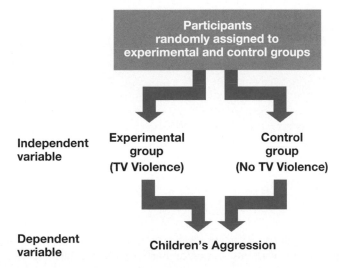

Figure 2.4

An Experimental Research Study: The Effects of TV Violence on Young Children's Aggression

In this example of experimental research, young children were randomly assigned to one of two groups: the experimental group who saw TV violence and the control group who did not. The independent variable (which is always the manipulated variable) was the amount of violence the children saw. The dependent variable was the children's aggression shown at play. The researchers found that TV violence caused children's aggressive behavior to increase. We can use the word *cause* because this is an experimental study.

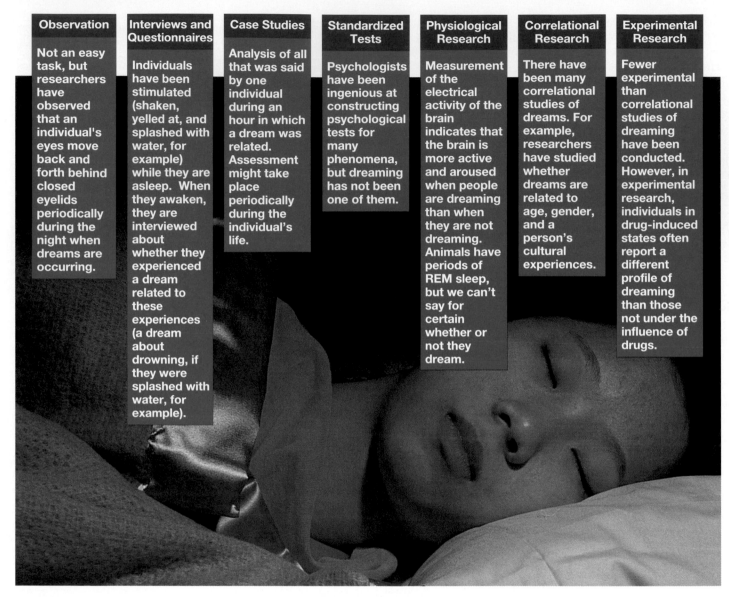

Observation	Interviews and Questionnaires	Case Studies	Standardized Tests	Physiological Research	Correlational Research	Experimental Research
Not an easy task, but researchers have observed that an individual's eyes move back and forth behind closed eyelids periodically during the night when dreams are occurring.	Individuals have been stimulated (shaken, yelled at, and splashed with water, for example) while they are asleep. When they awaken, they are interviewed about whether they experienced a dream related to these experiences (a dream about drowning, if they were splashed with water, for example).	Analysis of all that was said by one individual during an hour in which a dream was related. Assessment might take place periodically during the individual's life.	Psychologists have been ingenious at constructing psychological tests for many phenomena, but dreaming has not been one of them.	Measurement of the electrical activity of the brain indicates that the brain is more active and aroused when people are dreaming than when they are not dreaming. Animals have periods of REM sleep, but we can't say for certain whether or not they dream.	There have been many correlational studies of dreams. For example, researchers have studied whether dreams are related to age, gender, and a person's cultural experiences.	Fewer experimental than correlational studies of dreaming have been conducted. However, in experimental research, individuals in drug-induced states often report a different profile of dreaming than those not under the influence of drugs.

$\mathcal{F}$igure 2.5
Psychology's Research Methods Applied to Dreaming

cautiously, with safeguards (Vadum & Rankin, 1998). Certain expectancies and biases on the part of experimenters and/or participants can tarnish results.

Experimenters can subtly influence their research participants, in many cases unknowingly. **Experimenter bias** *occurs when the experimenter's own expectations influence the outcome of the research.* In a classic study, Robert Rosenthal (1996) turned college students into experimenters. They were randomly assigned rats from the same litter. However, half of the students were told that their rats were "maze bright," while the other half were told that their rats were "maze dull." The students then conducted experiments to test their rats' ability to navigate mazes. The results were stunning. The so-called "maze-bright" rats were more successful than the "maze-dull" rats at running the mazes. The only explanation for the results is that the college students' expectations affected the performance of the rats. In subsequent studies, researchers have demonstrated that experimenter's expectations influence not only rodent behavior but human behavior as well (Rosenthal, 1994).

Research participant bias *reflects research participants' beliefs about how they are expected to behave.* Research participants routinely have expectations about what they are supposed to do and how they should behave. Imagine that researchers hypothesize that a particular new drug will decrease violent behavior. They randomly assign the participants to an experimental group (those who receive the drug) and a control group (those who do not). After 3 months, the experimental group shows less violent behavior than the control group. It seems as though we could conclude that the drug caused violent behavior to decrease. However, the effects might be due to the expectations of the participants in the experimental group, not to the drug itself. Possibly because they expected to be less violent, they were violent less often. The **placebo effect** *occurs when participants' expectations, rather than the experimental treatment, produce the desired outcome.*

How might this placebo effect be reduced? In studies like the one we just described, the researchers can give the control group a *placebo.* In this case, the placebo might be a sugar pill. The control group participants are not told that it is a placebo. Thus, both the experimental and the control groups think they are getting the drug. In any study, researchers try to minimize the participants' expectations or cancel them out across the groups by making them as identical as possible.

Might we be able to design an experiment in which neither the experimenter's nor the participants' expectancies affect the outcomes? Yes, and it is called a **double-blind experiment,** *in which neither the experimenter nor the participants are aware of which participants are in the experimental group and which are in the placebo control group until the results are calculated.* If the study of drug treatment for violence is conducted in a double-blind manner, the experimenter and the participants would be kept in the dark about which group is receiving the drug and which is getting the placebo. A double-blind study allows researchers to tease apart the actual effects of the independent variable from the experimenter's and the participants' enthusiasm for it.

THINKING ABOUT PSYCHOLOGY AND LIFE
No Magic Bullet

IN OUR DESCRIPTION of experimental research, we concluded that TV violence caused young children's aggressive behavior to increase. It is easy to fall into the trap of thinking that TV violence is the *only* cause of children's aggression. That is not what the study's findings meant.

Always keep in mind one of psychology's most important lessons, which was highlighted in chapter 1: Behavior has multiple determinants. Just because researchers find a causal connection between variable *A* and variable *B* does not mean that variable *A* is the only cause of variable *B*. That is, variable *A* is not a magic bullet that by itself brings about a change in variable B (Stanovich, 1998). Like other behaviors, children's aggressive behavior has multiple determinants, and TV violence is but one of them. Can you think of what some other determinants of children's aggression might be? Think about such factors as heredity, hormones, parenting, poverty, and the violence in society other than what is shown on TV. See if you can add to this list.

Let's consider another experimental study. In this study, the researchers find that when people are given a particular drug they become less depressed. Does that mean that too much or too little of a drug in people's brains causes depression? What might be some other causes of depression?

Multiple Research Methods

We have described seven types of research methods to give you a broad sense of the strategies and measures that psychologists use in conducting research. Although we presented the methods separately, researchers often use more than one of them in conducting a research study. For example, researchers might select a correlational or experimental research method in setting up the study. In the same study, they might choose from among observation, surveys/interviews, standardized tests, or physiological methods to measure the problem they are investigating. In Bandura's (1965) study of observational learning and aggression that was presented earlier, an experimental research method was followed and the children's aggression was assessed with the research method of observation. In the study of married couples in which the husbands had a history of battering their wives that was discussed earlier (Jacobsen & Gottman, 1998), a correlational research method was used, and observations and physiological methods were used to assess the participants' behavior.

At this point we have studied many ideas about research methods. An overview of these methods is presented in summary table 2.2.

SUMMARY TABLE 2.2
Research Methods

Concept	Processes/ Related Ideas	Characteristics/Description
Observation	Exploring observation	Observation is an important research method in psychology. For observation to be effective, it must be done in a systematic manner. Observation can be done in a laboratory or in naturalistic settings.
	Laboratory observation	A laboratory is a controlled setting with many of the complex factors of the "real world" removed. Laboratory research provides considerable control over research, but criticisms of it have been made.
	Naturalistic observation	Naturalistic observation is done in real-world settings and no effort is made to manipulate or control the situation. However, reactivity to being observed can be a problem, and naturalistic observation provides less control over the study's conditions than laboratory research.
Interviews and Questionnaires	Their nature	An interview involves asking questions to find out about a person's experiences and attitudes. One shortcoming of interviews is social desirability. Questionnaires (or surveys) are similar to structured interviews except that respondents mark their answers on paper rather than verbally responding to an interviewer.
Case Studies	Their nature	These are in-depth looks at a single individual used mainly by clinical psychologists when, for either practical or ethical reasons, the unique aspects of the person's life cannot be duplicated. Caution needs to be exercised in generalizing to other people because of the uniqueness of the information.
Standardized Tests	Their nature	These require people to answer a series of written and/or oral questions. Standardized tests have two distinct features: (1) An individual's score is totaled to yield a single score, or set of scores, (2) the individual's score is compared with scores of a large group of similar people to determine how the individual responded relative to others.
Physiological Research	Its nature	This research provides insight about the biological dimensions of mind and behavior. Because much physiological research cannot be carried out with humans, psychologists often study animals when they conduct this type of research.
Correlational Research	Its nature	In correlational research, the goal is to describe the strength of the relation between two or more events or characteristics. An important research principle is that correlation does not equal causation. When there is a correlation between two events, the first could cause the second, the second could cause the first, or a third, unknown factor could cause the correlation between the first two factors.
Experimental Research	How experimental research is conducted	Experimental research allows psychologists to determine behavior's causes. This is accomplished by conducting an experiment, which involves examining the influence of at least one independent variable (the manipulated, influential, experimental factor) on one or more dependent variables (the measured factor). Experiments involve the random assignment of participants to one or more experimental groups (the group whose experience is being manipulated) and one or more control groups (a comparison group that is treated in every way like the experimental group except for the manipulated factor).
	Experimental research cautions	Some cautions need to be exercised in conducting experiments because expectancies and biases on the part of both experimenters and participants can tarnish results. These cautions involve experimenter bias (when the experimenter's expectations influence the experiment's outcome) and research participant bias (which reflects the beliefs that participants have about how they are expected to behave). The placebo effect occurs when participants' expectations, rather than the experimental treatment, produce the desired outcome. The placebo effect can be reduced by including a placebo control group. In a double-blind experiment, neither the experimenter nor the participants are aware of which participants are in the experimental group and which are in the placebo control group until the results are calculated.
Multiple Research Methods	Their nature	Researchers often use more than one research method in a research study—for instance, an experimental or correlational method and observation or physiological methods.

Research Challenges

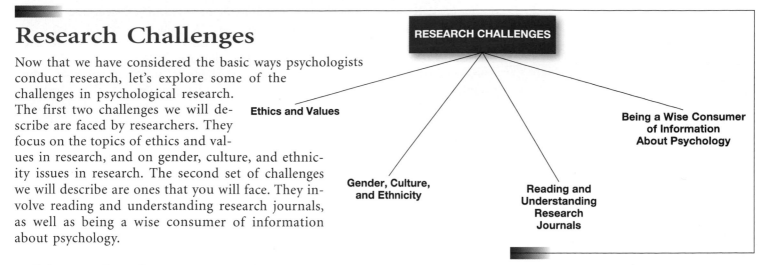

Now that we have considered the basic ways psychologists conduct research, let's explore some of the challenges in psychological research. The first two challenges we will describe are faced by researchers. They focus on the topics of ethics and values in research, and on gender, culture, and ethnicity issues in research. The second set of challenges we will describe are ones that you will face. They involve reading and understanding research journals, as well as being a wise consumer of information about psychology.

Ethics and Values

To begin our inquiry into ethics and values, let's explore why they are important in psychological research.

Why Are Ethics and Values Important in Psychological Research?

There are three reasons why you need to know about ethics and values in psychology (and in other related disciplines). The first, and most important, is that we are active members of society in the age of information and technology. At the beginning of this chapter, we read about some of the ways that the results of scientific research in psychology and other domains affect our daily lives. As technology advances, the tools and methods available to scientists are becoming more and more sophisticated. Research in Canada and in many other countries is often supported by government grants. Since the allocation of grant money is highly competitive—not only within the scientific community, but also between science and other government-sponsored projects—we must continually set an agenda prioritizing the lines of research we believe are the most beneficial to society. In recent years, for example, the crisis of AIDS has necessitated a shifting of priorities in ways that could not have been anticipated only a decade ago. In addition to questions about what lines of research are important and beneficial, with the explosion in technology society must grapple with looming ethics questions concerning research applications that were unimaginable only a few decades ago (Kimmel, 1996). Should parents be able to determine the sex of their children? Should embryos left over from procedures for increasing fertility in sterile couples be frozen and potentially be used in other research; or should they be discarded?

Science must walk a fine line between the pursuit of knowledge and the application of such knowledge (Hoagwood, Jensen, & Fischer, 1996). What science learns through research, society must continually evaluate and apply in ways that it deems ethical. The same line of research that might some day enable previously sterile couples to have children might also enable prospective parents "to call up and order" the characteristics they prefer in their children. Similarly, the knowledge that might someday noticeably tip the balance of males and females in the world might also prevent suffering and unnecessary death. The line of research that enables previously sterile couples to have children is the line of research capable of creating excess frozen embryos to be passed about in the courts as a part of divorce settlement: the house, the car, and the frozen embryos.

The second reason that you need to understand ethics and values in psychology is that some, if not all, of you will undoubtedly serve as participants in psychological research at some point in your life. As such, you need to know about your rights as a participant and about the responsibilities researchers have in assuring that these rights are carefully safeguarded. For the time being, questions concerning ethics in research in psychology are somewhat less dramatic than the analogous questions discussed in the biological sciences. Nonetheless, the issues concerning ethics in research are just as real in psychology as in these other domains. When Anne and Pete, two 19-year-old university students, agreed to participate in an investigation of dating couples, they did not consider the possibility that the questionnaire they completed would stimulate them to think about issues that might lead to conflict in their relationship, and possibly even end it. One year after the study was conducted, 9 of 10 participants said they had discussed their answers with their dating partner (Rubin & Mitchell, 1976). In most instances the discussions helped to strengthen the relationships. But in some cases the participants used the questionnaire as a springboard to discuss problems or concerns previously hidden. One participant said, "The study definitely played a role in ending my relationship with Larry." In this case, the couple had different views about how long they expected to be together. She was thinking of a short-term dating relationship only, while he was thinking in terms of a lifetime. Their answers to the questions brought the disparity in their views to the surface and led to the end of their relationship.

The last, but by no means the least, of the reasons you need to know about ethics and values in conducting psychological research is that many of you may some day be experimenters. This may take the form of carrying out an experimental project in a psychology course, in graduate school, or ultimately in a career in experimental psychology. Students, even very smart and concerned students, frequently do not consider the rights of the participants who serve in their experiments. One student might think, "I volunteer in a home for the mentally retarded several hours per week. I can use the residents of the home in my study to see if a particular treatment helps improve the residents' memory for everyday tasks." We will see below that well-meaning, kindly, and considerately conceived studies like this one, without proper permissions and consents from the people responsible for the welfare of these individuals, constitute flagrant violations of the rights of the participants. We next turn to the exact nature of these rights and the concomitant responsibilities of experimenters.

Psychologists' Ethical Principles

Ethics Guidelines of the Canadian Psychological Association

At first glance, you would not imagine that a questionnaire on dating relationships would have any impact on those who participate in the research. But psychologists increasingly recognize that considerable caution must be taken to ensure the well-being of the participants in a psychological study. Today universities have review boards that evaluate the ethical nature of research conducted at their institutions. Proposed research plans must pass the scrutiny of a research ethics committee before the research can be initiated. In addition, the Canadian Psychological Association (CPA) has developed unique ethics guidelines for its members (Sinclair, 1998).

The code of ethics adopted by the CPA, like those of the American Psychological Association (APA), instructs psychologists to protect their participants from mental and physical harm. The participants' best interests need to be kept foremost in the researcher's mind (Rosnow, 1995; Dobson & Breault, 1998). The CPA's guidelines include the requirement of **informed consent,** *which means that all participants must know what their participation will involve and any risks that might develop.* For example, research participants on dating should be told beforehand that a questionnaire might stimulate thoughts about issues in their relationship that they have not considered. Participants should also be informed that in some instances a discussion of the issues raised might improve their relationship, while in others it might worsen the relationship and even end it. Even after informed consent is given, participants must retain the right to withdraw from the study at any time and for any reason.

Another important aspect of ethics in research is **confidentiality:** *researchers are responsible for keeping all of the data they gather on individuals completely confidential and, when possible, completely anonymous.*

Yet another responsibility of researchers is **debriefing,** *which consists of informing participants of the purpose and methods used in a study after the study has been completed.* In most cases it is possible to inform participants in a general manner about the purpose of the research beforehand without "giving away" the predicted results, which could create participants' expectations that the experimenter wants them to behave in a certain way. When this is not possible, participants must be debriefed after the research has been completed.

Deception is an ethical issue that psychologists debate extensively (Whitley, 1996). In some circumstances, telling the participant beforehand what the research study is about substantially alters the participant's behavior and invalidates the researcher's data by creating research participant bias. For example, suppose a psychologist wants to know whether bystanders will report a theft. A mock theft is staged, and the psychologist observes which bystanders report it. Had the psychologist informed the bystanders beforehand that the study intended to discover the percentage of bystanders who will report a theft, the whole study would have been undermined. In all cases, the psychologist must ensure that the deception will not harm the subject and that the subject will be told the complete nature of the study (debriefed) as soon as possible after the study is completed (Chastain & Landrum, 1999).

Values   Questions are asked not only about the ethics of psychology, but also about the values of psychology. Values involve standards about what is worthwhile and desirable (Pettifor, 1998). Some psychologists argue that psychology should be value-free and morally neutral. From their perspective, the psychologist's role as a scientist is to present facts in as value-free a fashion as possible (Kimble, 1989). Others believe that, since psychologists are human, they are not value-free, even if they try to be. On the other hand, some people argue that psychologists should take stands on value-laden issues (Neufeldt, 1989). For example, if research shows that day care in the first year of life is harmful to children's development, shouldn't psychologists support reforms to improve day care or mandates to have businesses give one parent up to a year of paid leave after the child is born? More information about psychology and values appears in Explorations in Psychology.

How Ethical Is Research with Animals?   Psychologists who make use of animals in their research have frequently been the target of animal welfare and animal rights activists, who often chant slogans like "Psychologists are killing our animals!" and "Stop the pain and abuse!"

For generations, some psychologists have used animals in their research, which has provided a better understanding of, and solutions for, many human problems. Neal Miller, a leading figure in contemporary psychology who has made important discoveries about the effects of biofeedback on health, listed the following areas where animal research has benefited humans (Miller, 1985):

- Psychotherapy and behavioral medicine
- Rehabilitation of neuromuscular disorders
- Understanding and alleviating effects of stress and pain
- Discovery and testing of drugs to treat anxiety and severe mental illness
- Knowledge about drug addiction and relapse
- Treatments to help premature infants gain weight so they can leave the hospital sooner
- Knowledge about memory used to alleviate deficits of memory in old age

How widespread is animal research in psychology? Relatively few CPA members use animals in their research. Rats and mice are by far the most widely used, accounting for 90 percent of all psychological research with animals. How widespread is abuse to animals in psychological research? According to animal welfare and rights activists, it is extensive. It is true that researchers sometimes use procedures that would be unethical with humans, but they are guided by a stringent set of

Ethical Guidelines in Animal Research

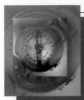

EXPLORATIONS IN PSYCHOLOGY
Psychology and Values

CONTROVERSY SWIRLS about the issue of whether psychology is value free. As a science, psychology is dedicated to discovering facts about behavior and creating theories to explain those facts. In this abstract description, values do not crop up. The scientific system requires only that psychology discover the most dependable facts and generate the best theories possible (Kimble, 1989). Is this reality, though? No, reality is more complex (Reed, Turiel, & Brown, 1995; Seligman, Olson, & Zanna, 1996). Psychology deals with living organisms. Consider how the following experiences, characteristics, and attitudes of researchers might influence their choice of research questions:

- Being a divorced single parent. Might this person be drawn to studying a topic such as a lack of parental involvement in children's development on the part of noncustodial fathers?
- Being a political conservative who values the right to own a gun. Might this person be interested in studying a topic like aggression and violence, or possibly the development of political attitudes?
- Being a person from an ethnic minority background who has experienced prejudice. Might this individual be intrigued by the factors that influence people to develop racist attitudes and ways to reduce racism?

Consider how people's values are reflected in their answers to the following questions:

- Should there be a ban on sexually explicit books or freedom of literary expression?
- Does the public have a right to know or should an individual have a right to privacy?

- Should retribution or rehabilitation be the goal of criminal codes?
- Which is the best decision, "freedom of choice" or "right to life"?

Might people with very different values perceive and label the same behavior differently? One individual might call a particular kind of sexual act a "sexual variation," another might label the same act "sick." One person might label a female's behavior "too aggressive," another might call the same behavior "competent." One individual might observe a male's long hours of work and label the behavior "overachieving" or "workaholic," another might call the same behavior "maximizing potential."

When psychologists are called on as experts, they often make statements and recommendations that are also laden with values. The therapist you consult about your problems may have certain personal values about sexual conduct that influence the advice he gives; the professor in your class may have certain personal values about moral behavior, child rearing, and how to get ahead in life that she communicates to you; and a psychologist interviewed on CBC's *Newsworld* may have certain values about government's responsibility in caring for the homeless, an adolescent's level of responsibility in dealing cocaine, and a mentally disordered individual's responsibility in committing mass murder. In sum, although psychology often strives to reduce the role of values as it seeks the truths of human behavior, in the court of life, which is psychology's setting, values and psychology are difficult to disentangle (Evans, 1997).

standards that address such matters as housing, feeding, and the psychological well-being of animals. Researchers are required to weigh the potential benefit of the research against the possible harm to the animal and to avoid inflicting unnecessary pain. Animal abuse is simply not as common as animal activist groups charge. However, stringent ethical guidelines must be followed when animals or humans are the subjects in psychological research (Herzog, 1995).

Gender, Culture, and Ethnicity

Is some psychological research gender biased? Might other research sometimes involve culture and ethnic bias?

Gender Bias   Too often psychological research has had a gender bias (Stark-Adamec & Kimball, 1983, 1984; Anselmi, 1998; Rickabaugh, 1998). For too long, the female experience was subsumed under the male experience. A good example can be drawn from Carol Gilligan's critique of work on moral development (Gilligan, 1982, 1996). The most widely known theory of moral development was proposed by a male (Lawrence Kohlberg) in a male-dominant society (the United States), and males were the main participants in research used to support the theory for many years. Further, the highest level of moral development has often been portrayed as based on a principle of "justice for the individual" (Kohlberg, 1976). However, more recent theorizing notes that male bias emphasizes the individual and autonomy, and suggests incorporating a care perspective that focuses on relationships and connections with others (Gilligan, 1982, 1996).

In a similar vein, some researchers believe that gender differences in mathematics have often been exaggerated and have been fueled by societal bias (Hyde & Plant, 1995). Denmark, Russo, Frieze & Eschuzur (1988) argue that too often when gender differences are found, they are magnified. For example, a researcher might report in a study that 74 percent of men had good spatial reasoning skills while only 67 percent of the women did, and go on to talk about the differences in their mathematical achievement. In reality, this might be a small difference that would disappear if the study were repeated, and the study might have methodological problems that don't allow such strong interpretations.

In response to such problems, Stark-Adamec & Kimball (1983, 1984) proposed a set of guidelines for the conduct of nonsexist research which were adopted in 1983 as policy by the Canadian Psychological Association. They argued that only nonsexist research can improve the status and quality of life of women. In contrast, sex-bias in psychological research is largely unintentional and due to a persistent lack of awareness of the issues and factors involved. Given the implications of such research for women—in terms of quality of life, physical and psychological health and equal opportunity—the support, conduct, and publication of sex-biased research is unscientific and unethical.

Cannie Stark-Adamec, now of the University of Regina, along with Meredith Kimball, of Simon Fraser University, has developed a number of guidelines for nonsexist research. Stark and others believe that psychology needs to be challenged to examine the world in a new way, one which incorporates girls' and women's perspectives. What are some areas of psychology that could benefit from reduced gender bias?

If we are concerned about equal rights in research, then, we should consider questions such as the following (Tetreault, 1997; Stark-Adamec, 1992):

- How might gender be a bias that influences the choice of theory, questions, hypotheses, participants, and research design?
- How might research on topics of primary interest to females, such as relationships, feelings, and empathy, challenge existing theory and research?
- How has research that has exaggerated gender differences between females and males influenced the way people think about females?

Cultural and Ethnic Bias   We need to include more people from diverse ethnic groups in psychological research (Graham, 1992). Historically, people from ethnic minority groups (Aboriginal peoples, West Indian blacks, S.E. Asians, Chinese, etc.) have been discounted from most research in Canada and simply thought of as variations from the norm or average. These nonmainstream individuals have been viewed as confounds or "noise" in data. Consequently, researchers have deliberately excluded them from the samples they have selected (Ryan-Finn, Cause,

Through the Eyes of Psychologists

Sandra Graham, *UCLA*

"Academic psychology cannot maintain its integrity by continuing to allow ethnic minorities to remain marginalized in mainstream research."

& Grove, 1995). Because individuals from diverse ethnic groups have been excluded for so long, there is likely more variation in people's real lives than research data have indicated in the past (Stevenson, 1995).

Researchers also have tended to use "ethnic gloss" when they select and describe diverse ethnic groups (Trimble, 1989). **Ethnic gloss** *is using an ethnic label such as Aboriginal Peoples or Chinese in a superficial way that portrays an ethnic group as being more homogeneous than it really is.* For example, a researcher might describe a research sample like this: "The participants were 20 Aboriginal peoples, 20 Chinese, and 20 Anglo-Canadians." A more complete description of the Aboriginal group might be something like this: The 20 Aboriginal participants were of Micmac origin and were equally divided into four groups of five: one group was from Fort Folly, New Brunswick; another group was from Pictou Landing First Nation, in Trenton, Nova Scotia; a third was from the Abegweit Band, in Cornwall, Prince Edward Island. The fourth group was off-reserve, living and working in the greater Halifax area. All participants were functionally trilingual (Micmac, English, French) and were born on one of the three reserves mentioned here. Ethnic gloss can cause researchers to obtain samples of ethnic groups that are not representative of the group's diversity, which can lead to overgeneralization and stereotyping.

Reading and Understanding Research Journals

A research challenge that you might face involves reading and understanding research journals. Regardless of the career you pursue, you can benefit from learning about the journal process. Possibly as a student you will be required to look up original research in journals as part of writing a paper. During or after university, you might want to consult journals to obtain information about some aspect of a career or your personal life. And as an inquiring person, you might want to look up information in journals after you hear or read about something that piques your curiosity.

A *journal* publishes scholarly and academic information, usually in a specific domain—like physics, math, sociology, or, in the case of our interest, psychology. Scholars in these fields publish most of their research in journals, which are the core information in virtually every academic discipline.

Journal articles are usually written for other professionals in the field of the journal's focus—such as geology, anthropology, or, again in our case, psychology. Because the articles are written for other professionals, they might contain technical language and specialized terms that are difficult for nonprofessionals to understand. As you move through this course, you will be learning a great deal more about the specialized field of psychology, which should improve your ability to understand journal articles in this field.

An increasing number of journals publish information about psychology. Some of these journals focus on psychology in general. These

Research journals are the core of information in virtually every academic discipline. Those shown here are among the increasing number of research journals that publish information about psychology. What are the main parts of a research article that present findings from original research?

include *Canadian Psychology, American Psychologist, Psychological Science, Psychological Bulletin,* and *Psychological Review.* Others are more aligned with areas of specialization in psychology. These more specialized journals include *Canadian Journal of Experimental Psychology, Journal of Experimental Psychology, Behavioral Neuroscience, Developmental Psychology, Journal of Abnormal Psychology, Journal of Personality and Social Psychology, Gender Roles, Journal of Applied Psychology,* and *Canadian Journal of Community Mental Health.*

In psychology, many journal articles are reports of original research. A number of journals also include, or focus exclusively, on reviews of research or theoretical ideas. Many journals are highly selective about what they publish. Every journal has a board of experts that evaluates articles submitted for publication. One or more of the experts carefully examines the submitted paper and accepts or rejects it based on such factors as its contribution to the field, theoretical relevance, methodological excellence, and clarity of writing. Some prestigious journals reject as many as 80 to 90 percent of submitted articles because they fail to meet the journal's standards.

Where do you find research journals such as those listed above? Your university library likely has one or more of the journals we listed as well as many others. Some public libraries also carry research journals.

Research journal articles that are reports of original research follow this format: abstract, introduction, method, results, discussion, and references. The *abstract* is a brief summary that appears at the beginning of an article. The abstract lets readers quickly determine whether the article is relevant to their interests and whether they want to read the article. The *introduction,* as its title suggests, introduces the problem or issue that is being studied. It includes a concise review of research relevant to the topic, theoretical underpinnings, and one or more hypotheses to be tested. The *method* section consists of a clear description of the participants evaluated in the study, the research methods used, and the procedures that were followed. The method section should be sufficiently clear and detailed so that by reading it another researcher could repeat some portion of the study or replicate the entire study. The *results* section includes statistical analyses that are often difficult for nonprofessionals to understand. The *discussion* section describes the author's conclusions, inferences about, and interpretation of what was found. Statements are usually made about whether the hypotheses presented in the introduction were supported, limitations of the study, and suggestions for future research. The last part of the journal article is called *references,* which gives bibliographic information for every source cited in the article. The reference section is often a good source for finding other articles relevant to the topic of the paper, if you are interested.

Psychology Research Journals

Being a Wise Consumer of Information About Psychology

Psychological research is increasingly talked about in the media. Television, radio, newspapers, and magazines all frequently report on research that is likely to be of interest to the general public. Many educational and psychological organizations regularly supply the media with information about research. In many cases, this information has been published in professional journals or presented at national meetings, and most universities have a media relations department that contacts the press about current research by their faculty.

Not all psychological information that is presented for public consumption comes from professionals with excellent credentials and reputations at universities or in applied mental health settings. Because journalists, television reporters, and other media personnel are not trained in psychology, it is not an easy task for them to sort through the widely varying material they see and make a sound decision about the best psychological information to present to the public.

Through the Eyes of Psychologists

Keith Stanovich, *University of Toronto*

"Media presentations of psychology are just as misleading as they ever were."

Unfortunately, the media often focus on sensationalistic and dramatic psychological findings. They want you to read what they have written or stay tuned to their channel. They hope to capture your attention and keep it by presenting dramatic, sensationalistic, and surprising information. As a consequence, media presentations of psychological information tend to go beyond what actual research articles and clinical findings really say.

Even when excellent research is presented to the public, it is difficult for media personnel to adequately inform people about what has been found and the implications for their lives. For example, throughout this text you will be introduced to an entirely new vocabulary. Each time we present a new concept we precisely define it and give examples of it as well. We have an entire book to carry out our task of carefully introducing, defining, and elaborating on key concepts and issues, research, and clinical findings. The media, however, do not have the luxury of time and space to detail and specify the limitations and qualifications of research. They often have only a few minutes or a few lines to summarize as best they can the complex findings of a study or a psychological concept.

Research on Groups and the Individual Needs of the Consumer

Being a wise consumer of information about psychology involves understanding that most research focuses on groups, yet the consumer has individual needs. Individual variations about how participants respond is often not the focus of research. For example, if researchers are interested in the effects of divorce on an adult's ability to cope with stress, they might conduct a study of 50 divorced women and 50 married women. They might find that divorced women, as a group, cope more poorly with stress than married women do. This applies to divorced women as a group, and it is group results that are commonly reported in the media. In this particular study, some of the divorced women were coping better than some of the married women—not as many, but some. Indeed, it is entirely possible that of the 100 women in the study, the 2 or 3 women who were coping the best with stress were divorced women. It would still be accurate, though, to report the findings as showing that married women (as a group) coped more effectively with stress than divorced women (as a group) did.

As a consumer of psychological information, you want to know what the information means for you *individually,* not necessarily what it means for the group. The failure of the media to distinguish adequately between research on groups and the individual needs of consumers is not entirely their fault. Researchers have not adequately done this either. Researchers often fail to examine the overlap between groups and present only the differences that are found. When those differences are reported, too often they are stated as if there were no overlap in the findings for the groups being compared (in our example, divorced women and married women), when in reality there was substantial overlap. If you read a report in a research journal or the media that states that divorced women coped more poorly with stress than married women did, it does not mean that all divorced women coped more poorly. It simply means that as a group, married women coped better—it does not mean that if you are a divorced woman, you cope more poorly than married women do.

Overgeneralization Based on a Small Sample

There often isn't space or time in media presentations of psychological information to go into details about the nature of the sample. Sometimes you will get basic information about sample size—whether it is based on 10 subjects, 50 subjects, or 200 subjects, for example. In many cases, small or very small samples require that care be exercised in generalizing to a larger population of individuals. For example, if a study of divorced women is based on only 10 or 20 divorced women, study findings may not generalize to all divorced women because the sample investigated may have some unique characteristics. The sample might have a high income, be of English descent, be childless, live in a small town in Manitoba, and be undergoing psychotherapy. In this study, then, we would clearly be making unwarranted generalizations if we thought the findings might automatically characterize divorced women who have moderate to low incomes, are from other ethnic backgrounds, have children, are living in different contexts, and are not undergoing psychotherapy.

A Single Study Is Usually Not the Defining Word About an Issue or Problem
The media might identify an interesting piece of research or a clinical finding and claim that it is something phenomenal with far-reaching implications. While such studies and findings do occur, it is rare for a single study to provide earth-shattering and conclusive answers, especially answers that apply to all people. In fact, in most psychological domains where there are many investigations, finding conflicting results about a particular topic or issue is not unusual. Answers to questions in research usually emerge after many scientists have conducted similar investigations that yield similar conclusions. Thus, a report of one research study should not be taken as the absolute, final answer on a problem.

In our example of divorce, if one study reports that a particular therapy conducted by a therapist has been especially effective with divorced adults, we should not conclude that the therapy will work as effectively with all divorced adults and with other therapists until more studies are conducted.

Causal Conclusions Cannot Be Drawn from Correlational Studies
Drawing causal conclusions from correlational studies is one of the most common mistakes made by the media. In studies in which a true experiment has not been conducted (in an experiment, subjects are randomly assigned to treatments or experiences), two variables or factors might have only a *noncausal* relation to each other. Remember from our discussion of correlation earlier in the chapter that causal interpretations cannot be made when two or more factors are simply correlated. We cannot say that one causes the other. In the case of divorce, a headline might read "Low income causes divorced women to have a high degree of stress." We read the article and find out the headline was derived from the results of a research study. Since we obviously cannot, for ethical or practical purposes, randomly assign women to become divorced or stay married, and for the same reasons we cannot randomly assign divorced women to be poor or rich, this headline is based on a correlational study, on which such causal statements cannot be accurately based. The low income might have caused the divorced women to have low self-esteem, but for some of the women low self-esteem might have hurt their chances for having a higher income. Their low self-esteem may be related to other factors as well—factors such as inadequate societal supports, a history of criticism from an ex-husband, and so on.

Always Consider the Source of the Psychological Information and Evaluate Its Credibility
Studies conducted by psychologists are not automatically accepted by the research community. The researchers must usually submit their findings to a research or clinical journal where it is reviewed by their colleagues, who make a decision about whether to publish the paper or not. While quality of research and clinical findings in journals is not uniform, in most cases papers have undergone far greater scrutiny and careful consideration of the quality of the work than for what is reported in the media. Within the media, though, a distinction can usually be drawn between what is presented in respected newspapers, such as *The Globe and Mail* and *National Post,* as well as credible magazines, such as *Time* and *Maclean's,* and much less respected and less credible tabloids, such as the *National Inquirer.*

At this point we have discussed many ideas about research challenges. An overview of these ideas is presented in summary table 2.3. In the next chapter, we continue our journey through psychology's many areas, turning our attention to mind and behavior's biological foundations and neuroscience's fascinating exploration of the brain.

Summary Table 2.3
Research Challenges

Concept	Processes/ Related Ideas	Characteristics/Description
Ethics and Values	Why are ethics and values important in psychological research?	There are three reasons: (1) We are active members of society in the age of information and technology; (2) some, if not, all of you will participate in psychological research at some point in your life, so you need to know about researchers' responsibilities; and (3) many of you may some day be experimenters.
	Ethics guidelines of the Canadian Psychological Association	Researchers must ensure the well-being of participants. The risk of physical and mental harm must be minimal. The Canadian Psychological Association has precise ethics guidelines that include informed consent, confidentiality, and debriefing. Deception is an ethical issue that is debated by psychologists.
	Values	Whether psychology should be value-free is a topic of continuing controversy.
	How ethical is research with animals?	Controversy also swirls around the use of animals in psychological research, although abuse is not as widespread as some activists charge.
Gender, Culture and Ethnicity	Gender bias	Too often psychological research has had gender bias. Among the questions being generated are how such bias might influence the choice of theory, questions, hypotheses, research topics, participants, and research design.
	Cultural and ethnic bias	We need more people from diverse ethnic groups in psychological research. When individuals from ethnic minority groups are research participants, ethnic gloss needs to be considered.
Reading and Understanding Research Journals	Their nature	Regardless of the career you pursue, you can benefit from learning about the journal process and reading journals. Research journal articles that report original research follow this format: abstract, introduction, method, results, discussion, and references.
Being a Wise Consumer of Psychological Information	Research on groups and the individual needs of the consumer	Most research focuses on groups yet the consumer has individual needs. The media often fail to make this distinction and researchers have not done this adequately either. Too often results are reported as if the groups being compared did not overlap, when in reality there was substantial overlap.
	Overgeneralization based on a small sample	The media often do not go into details about the sample size of research they report and often overgeneralize about findings based on a small sample.
	A single study is usually not the defining word about an issue or problem	Answers to research questions usually emerge after many scientists have conducted similar investigations that produce similar conclusions rather than on a single study.
	Causal correlations cannot be drawn from correlational studies	Drawing causal conclusions from correlational studies is a common mistake made by the media. Remember that correlation does not equal causation.
	Always consider the source of the psychological information and evaluate its credibility	Research journals have more credibility than newspapers and magazines, although some popular media provide sounder psychological information than others.

Overview

WE BEGAN THIS CHAPTER by discussing these aspects of scientific research and the scientific method: the science side of psychology and the scientific method and its steps. Then we turned our attention to who the participants will be in a research study. Our coverage of research methods focused on observation, interviews and questionnaires, case studies, standardized tests, physiological research, correlational research, experimental research, and multiple research methods. We also studied these research challenges: ethics and values; gender, culture, and ethnicity; reading and understanding research journals; and being a wise consumer of information about psychology.

Don't forget that you can obtain a more detailed overview of the chapter by studying again the three summary tables on pages 39, 50, and 60.

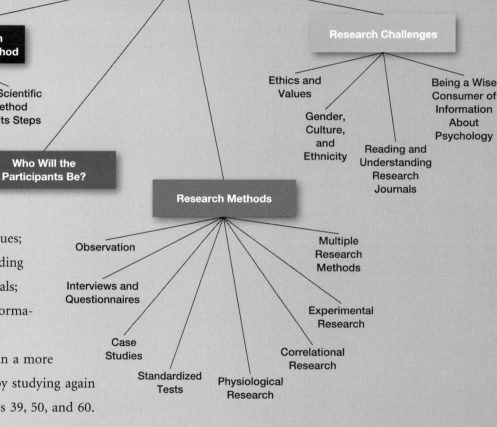

Key Terms

scientific research 34
scientific method 35
operational definition 35
theory 36
hypotheses 36
population 38
sample 38
random sample 38

laboratory 41
naturalistic observation 42
interview 43
social desirability 43
questionnaires (surveys) 43
case study 43
standardized tests 44
correlational research 45

experimental research 46
experiment 46
independent variable 46
dependent variable 46
experimental group 46
control group 46
random assignment 46
experimenter bias 48

research participant bias 49
placebo effect 49
double-blind experiment 49
informed consent 52
confidentiality 52
debriefing 53
ethnic gloss 56

Key People

Key People

Albert Bandura 36
Florence Denmark 55

Psychology Checklist

Checklist

How much have you learned since the beginning of the chapter? Use the following statements to help you review your knowledge and understanding of the chapter material. First, read the statement and mentally or briefly demonstrate on paper that you can outline and discuss the relevant information.

_____ I know what the scientific method is and can discuss its steps.
_____ I have a good command of what is meant by an operational definition, theory, and hypothesis.
_____ I can describe how psychologists select participants for their studies.
_____ I can discuss the numerous research methods psychologists use.

_____ I know what correlational and experimental research are, and some cautions about each of these methods.
_____ I am aware of ethics and values in psychological research.
_____ I can describe issues in research that involve gender, culture, and ethnicity.
_____ I understand how to be a wise consumer of information about psychology.

For any items that you did not check off, go back and locate the relevant material in the chapter. Review the material until you feel you can check off the item. You may want to use this checklist later in preparing for an exam.

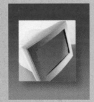

Taking It to the Net

The Net

1. The Canadian Psychological Association (CPA) has strict ethical guidelines for research on human subjects. How do you think these issues apply to research on animals? Can you justify the use of animals in medical and psychological research? What about in cosmetic research? Think about your answers on both a subjective level and a more personal level (e.g., would you turn down medical procedures for yourself or a loved one because they were developed at the expense of animals?).

2. Internal validity is a major research challenge. It determines whether there is a cause-effect relationship between the independent and dependent variables. Consider an experiment in which we are studying the effects of caffeine on memory. We give the entire group of participants a reading passage and tell them to remember as much as they can. We then split the participants into two groups: one will be given three cups of coffee and the other will receive no coffee. We then give both groups a test of recall on the reading passage, and find that the group who had no coffee remembered more. What are the dependent and independent variables of this experiment? What are some sources of threat to internal validity, and how can they be controlled?

3. In today's media, we are inundated with scientific claims. We read about new products, medications, and services that claim to be more effective than they really are. One typical tool is statistics, which is often used to exaggerate research findings to suit the needs of the experimenter. Claims based on exaggerated data are also known as junk science. What are some other tools of junk science? Use your Internet researching skills to find a scientific claim that is based on junk science and describe what methods are used to skew the results of the research.

Connect to http://www.mcgrawhill.ca/college/santrock to find the answers!

Resources for Psychology and Life

Canadian Code of Ethics for Psychologists (1991)

    Canadian Psychological Association
    151 Slater Street, Suite 205
    Ottawa, Ontario
    K1P 5H3

The code of ethics governing psychological research in Canada is available from the CPA at the above address. It can also currently be found online at the CPA Web site (http://www.cpa.ca/) at this URL: http://www.cpa.ca/ethics.html.

Ethics for Psychology (1994)

    by Mathilda Center, Bruce Bennett, Stanley Jones, and
    Thomas Nagey
    Washington, DC: American Psychological Association

This book provides an overview of the process of ethical decision making and describes the nature of the American Psychological Association. The ethical standards that guide psychological research are clearly spelled out.

Guidelines for Ethical Conduct in the Care and Use of Animals (1993)

    Science Directorate
    American Psychological Association
    750 First Street, NE
    Washington, DC 20002–4242

This pamphlet was developed by the American Psychological Association's Committee on Animal Research and Ethics (CARE). It profiles guidelines for the appropriate care and use of animals in research.

The Law, Standards of Practice, and Ethics in the Practice of Psychology (1997)

    by David Evans
    Toronto: Emond Montgomery Publications

This book goes beyond a treatment of codes of ethics in psychological research to an in-depth consideration of the relationship of the practice of psychology to society at large.

How to Think Straight About Psychology (1998, 5th ed.)

    by Keith Stanovich
    New York: Longman

This charming text explores how psychologists think about behavior, with a special emphasis on creating and defending arguments about the validity of cause-and-effect relations. The author offers many examples of classic research in psychology and also explores why psychologists struggle to gain respect from other sciences. The author refers to psychology as the "Rodney Dangerfield of the sciences" because of its image problem. Among the important psychological concepts examined by Stanovich are operationism, converging evidence, experimental control, the role of statistics, correlation, and causation.

Science Free of Sexism: A Psychologist's Guide to the Conduct of Nonsexist Research (1984)

    by Cannie Stark-Adamec & Meredith Kimball
    Stark-Adamec, C., & Kimball, M. (1984). Science free of sexism:
    A psychologist's guide to the conduct of nonsexist research.
    Canadian Psychology, 25(1), 23-34.

This article presents CPA-sanctioned guidelines for avoiding sexism in research. A copy of these guidelines can currently also be found online at the CPA Web site (http://www.cpa.ca/) at this URL: http://www.cpa.ca/guide6L.html.

Thinking Critically about Research Methods (1994)

    by John Benjafield
    Boston: Allyn and Bacon

This book offers a solid high-level treatment of the issues involved in conducting psychological research.

Publication Manual of the American Psychological Association (4th ed., 1994)

    Washington, DC: American Psychological Association

This is the style manual used by researchers and students in psychology and other behavioral and social sciences. The manual provides publication information that includes the topics of organization, writing, submitting manuscripts, reducing bias in the language, referencing, and general policies and ethics in scientific publication.

The Science Game: An Introduction to Research in the Social Sciences

    by Sandra Pyke and Neil Agnew
    Englewood Cliffs, NJ: Prentice Hall

This popular book covers, in an entertaining and informative way, a number of important ideas about conducting research in psychology.

Chapter 3

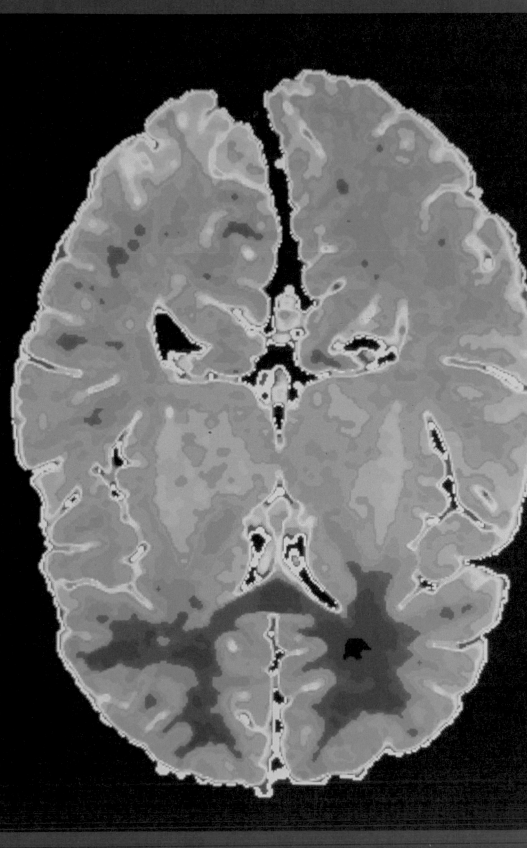

CHAPTER OUTLINE

BIOLOGICAL FOUNDATIONS

Heredity

The Evolutionary Perspective

Nature and Nurture

THE FIELD OF NEUROSCIENCE, THE NERVOUS SYSTEM, AND NEURONS

The Field of Neuroscience

The Organization of the Nervous System

Neurons

Glial Cells

BRAIN STRUCTURE AND FUNCTION

Embryological Development and Levels in the Brain

Neocortex

The Cerebral Hemispheres and Split-Brain Research

Integration of Function in the Brain

EXPLORING THE BRAIN

Brain Damage, Plasticity, and Repair

Techniques for Studying the Brain

The Brain and the Endocrine System

Biological Foundations and Neuroscience

Preview

ORGANISMS ARE NOT like billiard balls, moved by simple external forces to predictable positions. Biological foundations and environmental experiences work together to make us who we are. Of the biological structures that have evolved, none is more important than the three-pound universe inside of your skull—the brain. Much of this chapter focuses on the brain's role in behavior and mental processes. These are some of the questions we will explore in this chapter:

- How do nature and nurture interact to influence people's behavior?
- What is the field of neuroscience all about?
- What happens to people's behavior when the connections between the brain's two hemispheres are severed?
- What techniques do scientists use to "see inside" the brain?

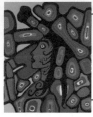

Images of Psychology and Life
The Jim and Jim Twins

Jim Springer and Jim Lewis are identical twins. They were separated at the age of 4 weeks and didn't see one another again until they were 39 years old. Even so, they share uncanny similarities that read more like fiction than fact. For example, they have both worked as part-time deputy sheriffs, have vacationed in Florida, have driven Chevrolets, have had dogs named Toy, and have married and divorced women named Betty. In addition, one twin named his son James Allan, and the other named his son James Alan. Both like math but not spelling, and both enjoy carpentry and mechanical drawing. They have both chewed their fingernails down to the nubs and have almost identical drinking and smoking habits. Both have had hemorrhoids, put on ten pounds at about the same time, and first suffered headaches at the age of 18. They also have similar sleep patterns.

Jim and Jim have some differences as well. One wears his hair over his forehead, whereas the other wears it slicked back with sideburns. One expresses himself better verbally; the other is more proficient in writing. For the most part, however, they are more alike than different.

The Jim and Jim twins were part of the Minnesota Study of Twins Reared Apart, directed by Thomas Bouchard and his colleagues (1996). The researchers brought

The Jim twins: how coincidental? Springer, right, and Lewis were unaware of each other for 40 years.

identical (genetically identical because they come from the same fertilized egg) and fraternal (genetically dissimilar because they come from different fertilized eggs) twins from all over the world to Minneapolis to investigate the psychological aspects of the twins' lives. For example, the twins were interviewed and asked more than 15,000 questions about their family and childhood environment, personal interests, vocational orientation, values, and aesthetic judgments. Detailed medical histories were obtained, including information about their smoking, diet, and exercise habits. The researchers also took chest X rays, and gave heart stress tests, as well as EEGs (brain-wave tests). The twins were also given a number of personality, ability, and intelligence tests (Bouchard & others, 1981).

Critics of conclusions drawn about the genetic basis of behavior in the Minnesota twins study point out that some of the separated twins had been together several months prior to their adoption, that some twins had been reunited prior to their testing (in some cases a number of years earlier), that adoption agencies often place twins in similar homes, and that even strangers who spend several hours together and start comparing their lives are likely to come up with coincidental similarities (Adler, 1991). Still, even in the face of such criticism, the Minnesota study demonstrates the interest scientists have shown in the genetic basis of behavior.

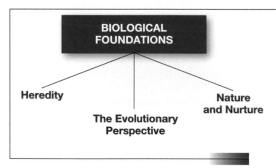

BIOLOGICAL FOUNDATIONS

Heredity

The Evolutionary Perspective

Nature and Nurture

Biological Foundations

In the words of twentieth-century French essayist Antoine de Saint-Éxupéry, "The seed of the cedar will become cedar, the seed of the bramble can only become bramble." An English proverb says, "That which comes of a cat will catch mice." Why does the bramble become only bramble? Why does the cat catch mice? No matter what the species, there must be a mechanism used to pass the message of inheritance from one generation to the next. That mechanism is heredity.

Heredity

You began life as a single cell, a fertilized human egg, weighing about one-twenty-millionths of an ounce. From this single cell, you developed into a human being made of trillions of cells. The nucleus of each human cell contains 46 **chromosomes**, *which are threadlike structures that come in 23 pairs, one member of each pair coming from each parent.* Chromosomes contain the remarkable genetic substance **deoxyribonucleic acid,** or **DNA,** *a complex molecule that contains genetic information* (see figure 3.1). **Genes,** *the units of hereditary information, are short segments of chromosomes, composed of DNA.* Genes act like blueprints for cells to reproduce themselves and manufacture the proteins that maintain life.

Although we have a long way to go before we unravel all the mysteries about the way genes work, some aspects of heritability are well understood. Every person has two genes for each characteristic governed by heredity. When genes combine to determine our characteristics, some genes are dominant. According to the **dominant-recessive genes principle,** *if one gene of a pair is dominant and one is recessive, the dominant gene exerts its effect, overriding the potential influence of the recessive gene.* A recessive gene exerts its influence only if both genes of a pair are recessive. If you inherit a recessive gene from only one parent, you may never know you carry the gene. In the world of dominant-recessive genes, brown eyes, farsightedness, and dimples rule over blue eyes, nearsightedness, and freckles. If you inherit a recessive gene for a trait from both of your parents, you will show the trait. That's why two brown-eyed parents can have a blue-eyed child: Each parent would have a dominant gene for brown eyes and a recessive gene for blue eyes. Since dominant genes override recessive genes, the parents have brown eyes. However, the child can inherit a recessive gene for blue eyes from each parent. With no dominant gene to override them, the recessive genes make the child's eyes blue.

Another aspect of understanding heredity involves the distinction between genotype and phenotype. **Genotype** *is the person's genetic heritage, the actual genetic material.* However, not all of this genetic material is apparent in a person's observed and measurable characteristics. **Phenotype** *is the way an individual's genotype is expressed in observable, measurable characteristics.* Phenotypes include physical characteristics (such as height, weight, and eye color) and psychological characteristics (such as intelligence and personality).

For each genotype, a range of phenotypes can be expressed. Imagine that we could identify all of the genes that would make a person introverted (shy) or extraverted (outgoing). Would measured introversion–extraversion be predictable from knowledge of specific genes? The answer is no, because even if the genetic model were adequate, introversion–extraversion is a characteristic that is influenced not only by heredity but also by experiences. For example, parents can guide a shy child to become more social.

The Human Genome Project (a genome is a complete set of genes), begun in the late 1970s, has as its goal the construction of the first detailed map of every human gene. Genetic engineers hope to use the knowledge derived from the project to reverse the course of many natural diseases. Recently, they have isolated the genes for Huntington's disease, Lou Gehrig's disease, the so-called bubble-boy disease, and a common form of colon cancer, among others.

The simple model of genes developed by Gregor Mendel at the beginning of the twentieth century with garden peas—in which the color of a flower is determined by a single gene—is almost never seen in human DNA. For example, a complex gene like the one that causes cystic fibrosis can go wrong in a vast number of locations. So far scientists already have identified 350 sites where the cystic fibrosis gene is disconfigured.

When 80,000 genes from one parent combine at conception with the 80,000 genes of the other parent, the number of possible combinations—in the trillions—is staggering. No wonder scientists are struck by the complexity of genetic transmission (Hartwell & others, 2000).

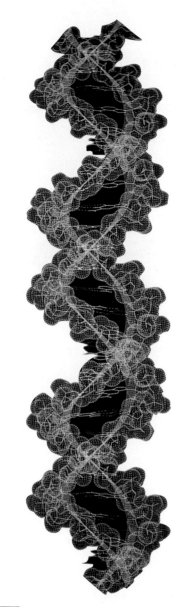

𝒻igure 3.1
The Remarkable Substance
Known as DNA

Landmarks in the History of Genetics
Human Genome Project
Heredity Resources

Cynthia Cushall is evidence of the positive results of gene mapping. Three years after receiving gene therapy treatments, Cynthia no longer has to live in a plastic bubble to be protected from infection. What might the future hold for gene mapping?

Evolution
Evolutionary Psychology
Handbook of Evolutionary Psychology

The Evolutionary Perspective

Humans are relative newcomers to Earth. If we consider evolution in terms of a calendar year, humans arrived on the planet late in December (Sagan, 1980). Despite our brief existence, we have established ourselves as the most dominant species. As our earliest ancestors left the forests to form hunting societies on the grassy savannas, their thinking and behavior changed. How did these changes in thinking and behavior come about?

Natural Selection   Over time entire species can change through **natural selection,** *the evolutionary process that favors genes that code for design features most likely to lead to reproduction and survival.* Also known as "the survival of the fittest," natural selection lies at the heart of Charles Darwin's (1859) theory of evolution (Volpe & Rosenbaum, 2000). Darwin, a nineteenth-century naturalist, sailed to South America to study a multitude of plant and animal species in their natural surroundings. He observed that most organisms reproduce at rates that should result in overpopulation, yet somehow populations remain nearly constant.

Darwin reasoned that each new generation must engage in an intense, constant struggle for food, water, and other resources. In the course of this struggle, many of the young would die. Those who survive would be those who were better adapted to their environment. The survivors would reproduce and, in turn, pass on some of their characteristics to the next generation. Over the course of many generations, the organisms with the characteristics needed for survival (speed and sharp claws in predators or thick fur in Arctic animals, for instance) would make up an increasingly larger percentage of the population. Over many, many generations, this process could modify the entire population (Mader, 2000). If environmental conditions were to change, however, other characteristics might be needed and would move the process in a different direction.

Over a million species have been classified, from bacteria to blue whales, with many varieties of beetles in between. The work of evolution produced the animal mind (Shettleworth, 1998) and the extended period of parental care human beings give their offspring. Generally, evolution proceeds at a very slow pace. The lines that led to the emergence of human beings and the great apes diverged about 14 million years ago. Modern humans, *Homo sapiens,* came into existence only about 50,000 years ago, and civilization as we know it began about 10,000 years ago. No sweeping evolutionary changes in humans have occurred since then—for example, our brains haven't become 10 times bigger, we haven't developed a third eye, and we haven't evolved flight.

Evolutionary Psychology   In chapter 1, we introduced evolutionary psychology as psychology's newest approach. The **evolutionary psychology approach** *emphasizes the importance of adaptation, reproduction, and "survival of the fittest" in explaining behavior* ◄ ▥ P. 12.

David Buss (1995) recently described the basic principles of evolutionary psychology. Mechanisms (both psychological and physiological) are the product of evolution by selection. These mechanisms owe their existence to the successful solution to an adaptive problem that humans faced in ancestral environments. The adaptive problems are numerous, and they are all related to successful survival and reproduction, with reproduction being the engine that drives evolution, and survival being important because it aids reproduction. According to Martin Daly and Margo Wilson, these problems include parenthood (Daly & Wilson, 1998), homicide (Daly & Wilson, 1988), and motivation and emotion (deCatanzaro, 1999).

Evolutionary psychologists believe that their approach provides an umbrella for unifying the diverse fields of psychology. Not all psychologists agree. Some argue that it is unlikely that one approach can unify the diverse, complex field of psychology

Through the Eyes of Psychologists

Martin Daly & Margo Wilson, *McMaster University*

"Sex is so pervasive a factor in our lives and in the world about us that we can easily overlook the fundamental ways in which it challenges our understanding."

(Graziano, 1995). Others stress that evolutionary approaches do not account for cultural diversity (Paludi, 1998).

Nature and Nurture

Although genes play a role in human behavior, they alone do not determine who we are. Genes exist within the context of a complex environment; biologists who study even the simplest animals agree it is virtually impossible to separate the effects of an animal's genes from the effects of its environment (Lewis, 1999). **Environment** *refers to all of the surrounding conditions and influences that affect the development of living things.* Environment includes the food we eat, the air we breathe, and the many different physical and social contexts we experience—the cities and towns we live in; our relationships with our parents, peers, and teachers; and our continuing interactions at work, at home, and at play. The term **nurture** *is often used to describe an organism's environmental experiences.* The term **nature** *is often used to describe an organism's biological inheritance.* The interaction of nature and nurture, genes and environment, influences every aspect of mind and behavior (Brown, 1995; Mader, 2000).

McGill psychologist Donald Hebb used to offer a useful analogy: what is the relevant contribution of height and width to the area of a rectangle? Of course both dimensions are absolutely essential; if either is reduced to zero, there is no rectangle any more. Similarly, if an attractive, popular, intelligent girl is elected president of her senior high school class, her success is due to both heredity and the environment. In sum, both genes and environment are necessary for a person to even exist (Scarr & Weinberg, 1980). Similarly, both contribute to the development of a person's intelligence, temperament, height, ability to skate or read, and so on (Gottleib, Wahlsten, & Lickliter, 1998).

Further, the relative contributions of heredity and environment are not additive, as in such-and-such a percentage of nature, such-and-such a percentage of experience (Johnson, 2000; Tamarin, 1999). Nor is it accurate to say that full genetic ex-

THINKING ABOUT PSYCHOLOGY AND LIFE
Nature, Nurture, and Politics

MIGHT A PERSON'S VIEWS on how strongly heredity or environment influences behavior be a lens for knowing their political leanings? Spend a few minutes thinking about this question. What is your view on how strongly heredity influences behavior? on how strongly environment influences behavior? What are your political leanings?

The more powerful heredity is, the less potent are such human qualities as free will, capacity to choose, and a sense of responsibility for these choices. That is, people tend to think that if it's in your genes, you are not accountable. This kind of thinking allows alcoholics to think that they are helpless victims of their biology rather than willful agents with control over their bodies. Genetic determinism can free families of responsibility, yet lock them in their suffering.

At the political level, biological determinism now colors all sorts of debates on issues such as health care, juvenile justice, and welfare reform. The effort to dismantle social programs is fueled by the belief that government interventions (the nurturing side of the nature-nurture debate) don't work very well and by the attitude that society can't make up for every citizen's bad luck. Conservative politicians take this stance, while liberal politicians are more likely to believe that environment makes a big difference in people's behavior. Political liberals are more likely to favor programs like early childhood education and day care, which reflect environmental changes to improve the lives of children. As onetime McMaster University psychologist Leon Kamin notes, one of the simplest ways to find out someone's political leanings is to ask them where they stand on the nature-nurture issue (Herbert, 1997). Try this out with several of your friends.

Behavior Genetics

SUMMARY TABLE 3.1
Biological Foundations

Concept	Processes/ Related Ideas	Characteristics/Description
Heredity	Chromosomes, DNA, and Genes	The nucleus of each human cell contains 46 chromosomes that are composed of DNA. Genes are short segments of DNA and act as blueprints for cells to reproduce and manufacture proteins that maintain life. The dominant-recessive genes principle states that if one gene pair is dominant and one is recessive, the dominant gene overrides the recessive gene; a recessive gene exerts its influence only if both genes of a pair are recessive. Genotype is the person's genetic heritage, the actual genetic material. Phenotype is the way an individual's genotype is expressed in observable, measurable characteristics.
The Evolutionary Perspective	Natural Selection	Over time, entire species can change through natural selection, the evolutionary process that favors genes that result in design features most likely to lead to reproduction and survival.
	Evolutionary Psychology	This contemporary approach emphasizes the importance of adaptation, reproduction, and "survival of the fittest" in explaining behavior. In evolutionary psychology, psychological mechanisms are the result of evolution. Critics argue that evolutionary psychology does not adequately take cultural diversity into account.
Nature and Nurture	Gene-Environment Interaction	The term *nature* is often used to refer to an organism's biological inheritance. The term *nurture* is often used to refer to an organism's environmental experiences. Every behavior is, to some degree, the product of both genetic heritage and environment, or what is called gene-environment interaction.

pression happens once, around conception or birth, after which we take our genetic legacy into the world to see how far it gets us. Genes produce proteins throughout the life span, in many different environments. Or they don't produce these proteins, depending on how harsh or nourishing those environments are.

At this point, we have discussed some important ideas about heredity, evolution, and nature and nurture. A summary of these ideas is presented in summary table 3.1. Of all the aspects of human behavior that have evolved, none helps us adapt to our world more than the brain does. To its knowns and unknowns we now turn.

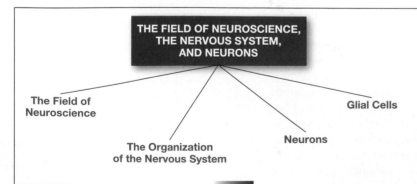

The Field of Neuroscience, the Nervous System, and Neurons

With "wiring" more complex than any computer, the human brain is the most complicated organization of matter we know of. Let's explore the field that studies this complex three-pound universe within our skulls.

The Field of Neuroscience

The **nervous system** *is the body's electrochemical communication circuitry, made up of billions of neurons.* The nervous system's central command system, the brain, controls all of your thoughts and movements. It weighs about three pounds and is slightly

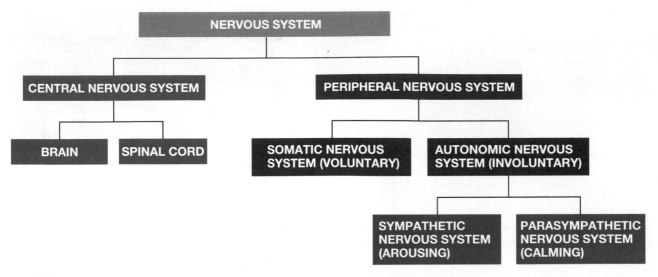

Major Divisions of the Human Nervous System

larger than a grapefruit. With its "crinkled" outer layer, it looks like a large, shelled walnut. Inside, the brain has the consistency of undercooked custard or a ripe avocado. **Neurons,** *or nerve cells, are the nervous system's basic units.* Highly organized, your nervous system is continuously at work processing information about everything you do, whether you are taking out the garbage, spotting a loved one across a crowded room, or preparing a speech (Conlan & others, 1999).

Not long ago the disciplines that studied the nervous system were virtually isolated from each other. Neuroanatomy studied the neuron's physical structure, neurophysiology investigated how neurons function, neurochemistry analyzed the neuron's chemical activity, and physiological psychology (which is now called behavioral neuroscience or biological psychology) focused on the nervous system's connections with behavior (Beatty, 1995). Such designations continue today, but these once-disparate disciplines increasingly overlap (Thalman, 1999). Today **neuroscience** *is the umbrella term for the multidisciplinary study of the nervous system.* ◀▥ P. 11. The Society for Neuroscience, the professional society for all types of neuroscientists, was founded in 1970 with 600 charter members and has grown to more than 25,000 members today.

Neuroscience
Internet Neuroscience Resources
Exploring Neuroscience

The Organization of the Nervous System

When Emerson said, "The world was built in order and the atoms march in tune," he must have had the human nervous system in mind. This truly elegant system is highly ordered and organized. It is at work processing information in everything we do, whether stumbling across a tiger in the jungle or stretching out for a lazy nap on a hammock. The human nervous system is made up of bundles of nerve cells.

The nervous system is divided into two parts: the central nervous system and the peripheral nervous system. The **central nervous system (CNS)** *is made up of the brain and spinal cord.* More than 99 percent of all neurons (nerve cells) in our body are located in the CNS. The **peripheral nervous system** *is the network of nerves that connects the brain and spinal cord to other parts of the body.* The peripheral nervous system brings information to and from the brain and spinal cord and carries out the commands of the CNS to execute various muscular and glandular activities. Figure 3.2 displays the hierarchical organization of the nervous system's major divisions.

The two major divisions of the peripheral nervous system are the somatic nervous system and the autonomic nervous system. The **somatic nervous system** *consists of sensory nerves, which convey information from the skin and muscles to the CNS*

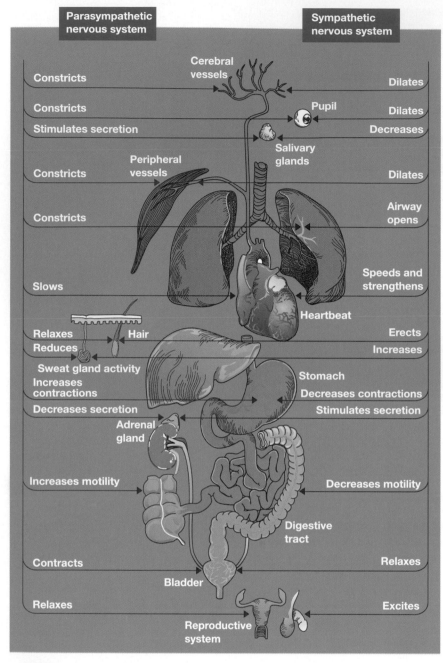

Parasympathetic nervous system

Constricts — Cerebral vessels — Dilates

Constricts — Pupil — Dilates

Stimulates secretion — Salivary glands — Decreases

Constricts — Peripheral vessels — Dilates

Constricts — Airway opens

Slows — Heartbeat — Speeds and strengthens

Relaxes — Hair — Erects

Reduces — Increases

Sweat gland activity

Increases contractions — Stomach — Decreases contractions

Decreases secretion — Stimulates secretion

Adrenal gland

Increases motility — Decreases motility

Digestive tract

Contracts — Bladder — Relaxes

Relaxes — Reproductive system — Excites

Sympathetic nervous system

*F*igure 3.3
Autonomic Nervous System

Parasympathetic and sympathetic divisions. The sympathetic system is at work when we are aroused; the parasympathetic system is at work when we are calm. Both systems influence most organs. For example, the sympathetic system speeds and strengthens heartbeat; the parasympathetic system slows heartbeat.

Neural Processes

Neurons: Our Internal Galaxy

about such matters as pain and temperature, and motor nerves, which inform muscles when to act. The **autonomic nervous system** *takes messages to and from the body's internal organs, monitoring such processes as breathing, heart rate, and digestion.* It too is divided into two parts, the **sympathetic nervous system,** *the division of the autonomic nervous system that arouses the body,* and the **parasympathetic nervous system,** *the division of the autonomic nervous system that calms the body* (see figure 3.3).

To get a better feel for how the human nervous system works, imagine that you are preparing to give a speech in a class. As you go over your notes one last time, your peripheral nervous system carries information about the notes to your central nervous system. Your central nervous system processes the marks on the paper, interpreting the words as you memorize key points and plan ways to keep the audience interested. After studying the notes several minutes longer, you scribble a joke midway through them. Your peripheral nervous system is at work again, conveying to the muscles in your arm and hand the information from your brain that enables you to make the marks on the paper. The information transmitted from your eyes to your brain and from your brain to your hand is being handled by the somatic nervous system. This is your first speech in a while, so you are a little uptight. As you think about getting up in front of the class, your stomach feels queasy and your heart begins to thump. This is the sympathetic division of the autonomic nervous system functioning as you become aroused. You regain your confidence after reminding yourself that you know the speech cold. As you relax, the parasympathetic division of the autonomic nervous system is working.

Neurons

So far we have described the nervous system's major divisions. But there is much more to the intriguing story of how the nervous system processes information. Let's focus on the details of the nervous system and find out more about the cells, chemicals, and electrical impulses that are the nuts and bolts of this operation.

Neuron Pathways Remember from earlier in the chapter that the neuron is the nervous system's basic unit. Information flows into the brain, within the brain, and out of the brain along specialized neurons known as afferent nerves, interneurons, and efferent nerves. **Afferent nerves,** *or sensory nerves, carry information to the brain.* The word *afferent* comes from the Latin word meaning "bring to." **Efferent nerves,** *or motor nerves, carry the brain's output.* The word *efferent* is derived from the Latin word meaning "bring forth."

To see how afferent and efferent nerves work, let's consider a well-known reflex, the knee jerk. When your knee jerks in response to a tap just below your kneecap, afferent cells transmit information directly to efferent cells in the spinal cord, so the information processing is quick and simple. Because the information involving the knee jerk is processed at the spinal cord, it does not require the brain's participation.

More complex information processing is accomplished by passing the information through systems of **interneurons,** *central nervous system neurons that mediate sensory input and motor output.* Interneurons make up most of the brain. For example, as you read the notes for your speech, the afferent input from your eye is transmitted to your brain, then passed through many interneuron systems, which translate (process) the patterns of black and white into neural codes for letters, words, associations, and meanings. Some of the information is stored in the interneuron systems for future associations and, if you read aloud, some is output as efferent messages to your lips and tongue.

Your gift of speech is possible because human interneuron systems are organized in ways that permit language processing. Although the neurons in a canary's brain are exactly the same as those in a frog's brain, frogs croak and canaries sing because the neurons are organized differently in the two brains. The interneurons in the frog's vocalization system are connected in such a way that they produce croaking, whereas the canary's produce singing. This is why the study of brain organization—the anatomy and fine structure of the brain—is so important. Brain organization is the key to understanding all of the complex and wondrous things that brains do. We'll tackle the brain's anatomy later; first, let's examine neurons in greater detail.

The Structure of the Neuron   Neurons handle information processing in the nervous system at the cellular level. There are about 100 billion neurons in the human brain. The average neuron is as complex as a small computer, and has as many as 15,000 physical connections with other cells. At times the brain may be "lit up" with as many as a quadrillion connections.

The three basic parts of the neuron are the cell body, the dendrites, and the axon (see figure 3.4). The neuron's **cell body** *contains the nucleus, which directs the manufacture of the substances the neuron uses for its growth and maintenance.* Most neurons are created very early in life and will not be replaced if they are destroyed, although their shape, size, and connections can change throughout their life span.

The **dendrite** *is the receiving part of the neuron, serving the important function of collecting information and orienting it toward the cell body.* Most nerve cells have a number of dendrites. Although there are many dendrites radiating from the cell body of the neuron, there is usually only one axon. The **axon** *is the part of the neuron that carries information away from the cell body to other cells.* The axon is much thinner and longer than a dendrite and looks like an ultrathin cylindrical tube. The axon of a single neuron may extend all the way from the top of the brain to the base of the spinal cord, a distance of over three feet. In turn, the axon branches into many *axon terminals,* each of which ends in a *terminal button.* A **myelin sheath,** *a layer of fat cells that insulates the axon, encases most axons.* Not only does the myelin sheath serve as insulation for the nerve cell, it also helps the nerve impulse to travel faster. The myelin sheath developed as brains evolved and became larger, which made it necessary for information to travel over long distances in the nervous system. This is similar to the appearance of freeways and turnpikes as cities grew. The newly developed roadways keep the fast-moving long-distance traffic from getting tangled up with slow-moving traffic.

The Nerve Impulse   Neurons send information down the axon as brief impulses, or waves, of electricity. Perhaps in a movie you have seen a telegraph operator sending a series of single clicks down a telegraph wire to the next station. That is what neurons do. To send information to other neurons, they send a series of single, electrical clicks down their axons. By changing the rate and timing of the clicks,

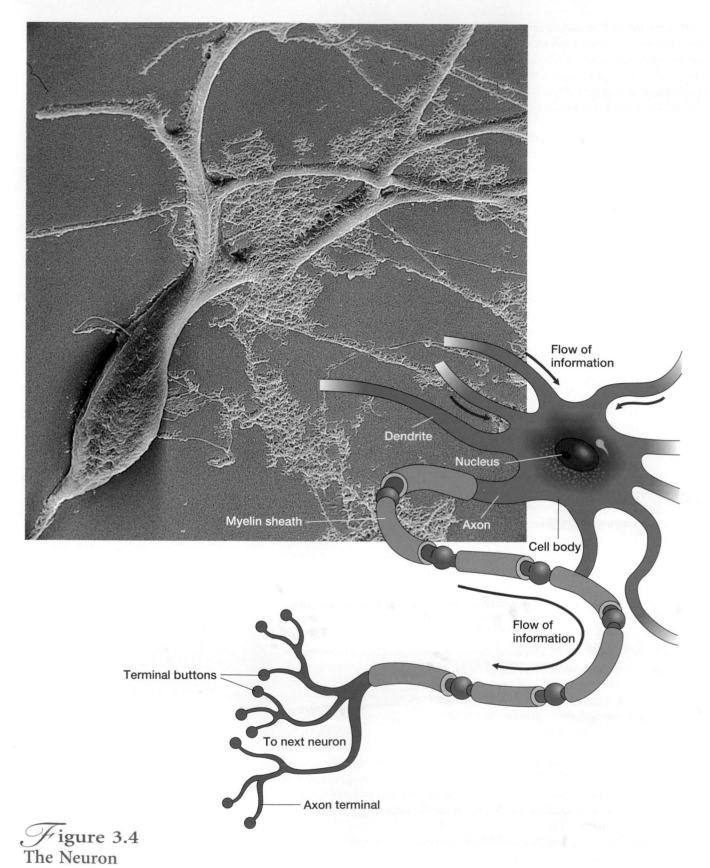

Figure 3.4
The Neuron

The cell body receives information from the dendrites of other neurons *(top)*. Information leaves the cell body and travels to other neurons, muscles, or glands through the axon *(bottom)*. A myelin sheath covers most axons and speeds information transmission. As it ends, the axon branches out into axon terminals which end in terminal buttons. An actual neuron is shown in the large photograph. Notice the branching dendrites at the top and the cell body at the bottom left.

the neuron can vary the nature of the message it sends. As you reach to turn this page, hundreds of such clicks will stream down the axons in your arm to tell your muscles just when to flex and how vigorously.

The wave of electrical charge that sweeps down the axon abides by the **all-or-none principle,** *which means that once the electrical impulse reaches a certain level of intensity, it fires and moves all the way down the axon, remaining at the same strength throughout its travel.* The electrical impulse traveling down an axon is much like a fuse to a firecracker. It doesn't matter whether a match or blowtorch is used to light the fuse; as long as a certain minimal intensity has been reached, the spark travels quickly and at the same level of strength down the fuse until it reaches the firecracker.

To understand how a neuron, which is a living cell, creates and sends electrical signals, we need to examine this cell and the fluids in which it floats. A neuron is a balloonlike bag filled with one kind of fluid and surrounded by a slightly different kind of fluid. A piece of this balloon-like bag is stretched and pulled to form a long, hollow tube, which is the axon. The axon tube is very thin; a few dozen in a bundle would be about the thickness of human hair.

To see how the neuron creates electrical signals, we must look at two things: the particles that float in the fluids and the actual wall of the cell, the membrane. The important particles in the fluids are ions of the elements sodium and chloride (which we get from common table salt—sodium chloride) and potassium. **Ions** *are electrically charged particles.* The neuron creates electrical signals by moving these charged ions back and forth through its membrane; the waves of electricity that are created sweep along the membrane (Armstrong, 1999).

How does the neuron move these ions? It's really fairly simple; the membrane, the wall of our balloon, is covered with hundreds of thousands of small gates or *ion channels,* that open and close to let the ions pass in or out to the cell. Normally, when resting or not sending information, the ion channels for sodium are closed, and those for potassium and chloride are partly open. Therefore, the membrane is in what is called a semipermeable state, and the ions separate; sodium is kept outside, lots of potassium ends up inside, and much of the chloride is inside. Because the ions are separated, a charge is present along the membrane of the cell (see figure 3.5). **Resting potential** *is the stable, negative charge of an inactive neuron.* That potential, by the way, is about one-fourteenth of a volt, so fourteen neurons could make a one-volt battery. The electric eel's 8,400 cells could generate 600 volts.

When the neuron gets enough excitatory input to cause it to send a message, the sodium channels at the base of the axon open briefly, then shut again. While those channels are open, sodium rushes into the axon, carrying an electrical charge, and that charge causes the next group of channels on the axon to flip open briefly. And so it goes all the way down the axon, just like a long row of cabinet doors opening and closing in sequence. After the sodium channels close, potassium ions flow out of the cell and bring the membrane charge back to the resting condition. **Action potential** *is the brief wave of electrical charge that sweeps down the axon* (see figure 3.6).

Synapses and Neurotransmitters

What happens once the neural impulse reaches the end of the axon? Neurons do not touch each other directly, but communicate across the synapse. The story of the connection between one neuron and another is one of the most intriguing and highly researched areas of contemporary neuroscience. **Synapses** *are tiny gaps between neurons.* Most synapses are between the axon of one neuron and the dendrites or cell body of another neuron.

How does information get across this gap to the next neuron? The end of an axon branches out into a number of fibers that end in structures called terminal buttons. Neurotransmitters are found in the tiny *synaptic vesicles* (chambers)

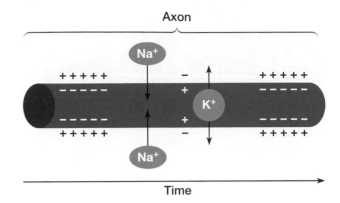

Figure 3.5
Movement of Sodium and Potassium Ions Down the Axon and the Action Potential

Electrical/chemical changes in the neuron produce an action potential. The sodium and potassium ions are shown moving into and out of the axon. As the nerve impulse moves down the axon, electrical stimulation of the membrane makes it more permeable to sodium ions (Na^+). Sodium rushes into the axon, carrying a positive electrical charge, and that charge causes the next group of gates on the axon to flip open briefly. So it goes, all the way down the axon. After the sodium gates close, potassium ions (K^+) flow out of the cell, and the neuron returns to its resting state with a slight negative charge.

Action Potential

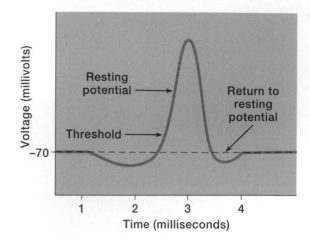

Neurotransmitters

$\mathscr{F}$igure 3.6
Action Potential

The action potential is shown on this graph in terms of its electrical voltage. The action potential is the positive charge in the cell generated by the influx of sodium (Na^+) ions. In the example shown here, the wave of electrical charge reaches about 40 millivolts. After the sodium gates close, potassium ions (K^+) flow out of the cell and bring the voltage back to its resting potential.

located in the terminal buttons. **Neurotransmitters** *are chemical substances that carry information across the synaptic gap to the next neuron.* The molecules of these chemical substances wait for a nerve impulse to come down through the axon. Once the nerve impulse reaches the terminal buttons, the electrical signal causes the synaptic vesicles to migrate to the edge of the terminal buttons. At the edge, the vesicles burst open, and the neurotransmitter molecules spew forth into the gap between the two neurons. In the synaptic gap, the neurotransmitter molecules diffuse across the synapse in random motion, and some land on receptor sites in the next neuron, where they fit like small keys in equally small locks. The key in the lock, in turn, opens a "door" and electrical signals begin to sweep through the next neuron. Think of the synapse as a river that cuts two sections of a road in two. When a truck gets to the river via the road on one side of the river, it crosses the water by ferry and rolls right onto the second section of road to continue its journey. Similarly, a message in the brain is "ferried" across the synapse by a neurotransmitter, which pours out of the end of the cell just as the message approaches the synapse. The operation of the synapse and neurotransmitters is illustrated in figure 3.7.

More than fifty neurotransmitters, each with a unique chemical makeup, have been discovered, and the list will probably grow to a hundred or more in the near future (Johnson, 2000). Most creatures that have been studied, from snails to whales, use the same neurotransmitter molecules that our own brains use. And many animal venoms, such as that of the black widow, actually are neurotransmitter-like substances that disturb neurotransmission.

What are some of these neurotransmitters and how are they related to our behavior? **GABA,** *gamma aminobutyric acid, is a neurotransmitter that inhibits the firing of neurons and is found throughout the central nervous system.* It is believed to be the neurotransmitter in as many as one-third of the brain's synaptic connections. GABA is important in the brain because it keeps many neurons from firing. This inhibition helps to control the preciseness of the signal being carried from one neuron to the next. Low levels of GABA are linked with anxiety. Valium and other antianxiety drugs increase GABA's inhibitory effects.

Acetylcholine (ACh) *is a neurotransmitter that usually stimulates the firing of neurons and is involved in the action of muscles, learning, and memory.* The venom of the black widow spider causes ACh to gush through the synapses between the spinal cord and skeletal muscles, producing violent spasms. The drug curare, found on the tips of some South American Indians' poison darts, blocks some receptors for ACh, paralyzing muscles.

Norepinephrine *is a neurotransmitter that usually inhibits the firing of neurons in the central nervous system, but excites the heart muscles, intestines, and urogenital tract. It is involved in the control of alertness and wakefulness.* Too little norepinephrine is also associated with depression; too much, with agitated, manic states.

Dopamine *is a neurotransmitter that is mainly inhibitory. It is involved in the control of voluntary movement.* Low levels of dopamine are associated with Parkinson's disease; high levels are associated with schizophrenia, a severe mental disorder.

Serotonin *is a neurotransmitter that is primarily inhibitory. It is involved in the regulation of sleep and depression.* The antidepressant drug Prozac works by restricting the movement of serotonin across synapses.

Endorphins *are natural opiates that mainly stimulate the firing of neurons. They increase pleasure and reduce pain.* As early as the fourth century B.C. the Greeks used the wild poppy to induce euphoria. However, it was not until more than 2,000 years later that the magical formula behind opium's addictive action was discovered. In the early 1970s, scientists found that opium plugs into a sophisticated system of natural opiates that lie deep within the brain's pathways (Pert, 1999; Pert & Snyder, 1973). The system involves neurotransmitters called endorphins, which shield the body from

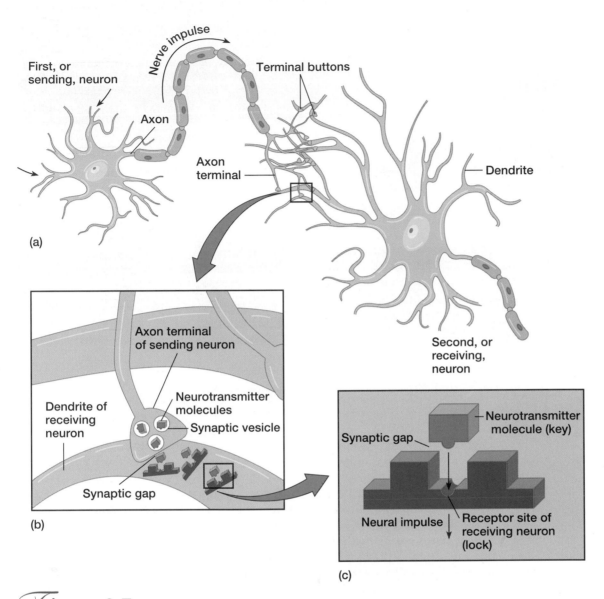

Figure 3.7
How Synapses and Neurotransmitters Work

(a) When an axon reaches its destination, it branches out into a number of fibers that end in terminal buttons. There is a tiny gap between these terminal buttons at the tip of the axon terminal and the next neuron. (b) When it reaches the terminal buttons, the neural impulse releases tiny chemical molecules that are stored in synaptic vesicles in the knobs. These chemical substances are called neurotransmitters. They diffuse across the synaptic gap between the sending and receiving neurons. Some of them land on receptor sites in the next neuron, where the neural impulse continues its travel. (c) Neurotransmitter molecules fit like small keys in equally small locks, once they reach the receptor site in the receiving neuron. The key in the lock opens the "door," and a neural impulse begins to travel through the second neuron.

pain and elevate feelings of pleasure. A long-distance runner, a woman giving birth, and a person in shock after a car wreck all have elevated levels of endorphins. Figure 3.8 summarizes information about the six neurotransmitters we have discussed.

In the description of neurotransmitters, we indicated that the actions of some neurotransmitters stimulate, or excite, neurons to fire whereas those of other neurotransmitters inhibit neurons from firing. Some neurotransmitters are both excitatory and inhibitory, depending on what the information-processing job is. As the neurotransmitter moves across the synaptic gap to the receiving neuron, its molecules

Neurotransmitter	Description/Functions
GABA	Inhibits firing of neurons; low levels linked with anxiety; Valium and other antianxiety drugs increase GABA's inhibitory effects
Acetylcholine (Ach)	Usually stimulates firing of neurons; involved in action of muscles, learning, and memory
Norepinephrine	Usually inhibits firing of neurons; involved in control of alertness and wakefulness; too little is associated with depression, too much with agitated, manic states
Dopamine	Mainly inhibitory; involved in control of voluntary movement; low levels associated with Parkinson's disease; high levels associated with schizophrenia
Serotonin	Mainly inhibitory; involved in the regulation of sleep and depression; the antidepressant Prozac works by blocking the reabsorption and removal of serotonin from synapses
Endorphins	Natural opiates that mainly stimulate firing of neurons; involved in pleasure and pain

Figure 3.8
Description and Functions of Neurotransmitters

Drugs, the Brain, and Behavior

might spread out or be confined to a small space. The molecules might come in rapid sequence or be spaced out. The receiving neuron must integrate all of this information and decide whether or not to fire.

Another important point is that most drugs that influence behavior do so mainly by influencing neurotransmitters (Shier, Butler, & Lewis, 2000). Drugs can mimic or increase the effects of a neurotransmitter, or they can block those effects. An **agonist** *is a drug that mimics or increases a neurotransmitter's effects.* For example, the drug morphine mimics the action of endorphins by stimulating receptors in the brain involved with pleasure and pain. An **antagonist** *is a drug that can block a neurotransmitter's effects.* As we mentioned earlier, the antidepressant Prozac can block the effects of serotonin.

So far in our discussion of the brain's cells, we have focused on neurons. As we see next, another type of cell also is present in the brain.

Glial Cells

The Spanish neuroanatomist Santiago Ramón y Cajal discovered that the brain is made up of two types of cells—neurons, or nerve cells, and **glial cells,** *non-neuron cells that provide supportive and nutritive functions.* Somewhat amazingly, there are many more glial cells in the nervous system than there are neurons. Ramón y Cajal used advances in microscope techniques to discover the glial cells early in the twentieth century. He described the cells as looking like glue between the nerve cells.

Unfortunately, we do not know as much about glial cells as we do about neurons. We do know that glial cells do not have axons or dendrites, and they are not specialized to send or receive information. They probably function as physical supports for neurons. They seem to regulate the internal environment of the brain, especially the fluid surrounding neurons, and provide nutrition for neurons. For example, neurons placed in a solution containing glial cells grow more rapidly and prolifically than neurons floating in the same solution without glial cells (Kennedy & Folk-Seang, 1986). The myelin sheath that covers most axons is made up of one kind of glial cell.

Summary Table 3.2
The Field of Neuroscience, the Nervous System, and Neurons

Concept	Processes/ Related Ideas	Characteristics/Description
The Field of Neuroscience	Its Nature	The nervous system is the body's electrochemical circuitry, made up of billions of neurons. Neurons, or nerve cells, are the nervous system's basic units *Neuroscience* is the umbrella term for the multidisciplinary study of the nervous system.
The Organization of the Nervous System	Central Nervous System	The central nervous system consists of the brain and spinal cord; it contains more than 99 percent of all neurons.
	Peripheral Nervous System	The peripheral nervous system is a network of nerves that connect the brain and spinal cord to other parts of the body. Two major divisions are the somatic nervous system and the autonomic nervous system. The autonomic nervous system is divided into the sympathetic and parasympathetic systems.
Neurons	Neuron Pathways	Afferent nerves (sensory nerves) carry input to the brain; efferent nerves (motor nerves) carry output away from the brain; interneurons do most of the information processing within the brain.
	Structure of the Neuron	The three basic parts of the neuron are the cell body, dendrite, and axon. The myelin sheath speeds information transmission.
	The Nerve Impulse	Neurons send information in the form of brief impulses, or "waves," of electricity. These waves are called the action potential and operate according to the all-or-none principle.
	Synapses and Neurotransmitters	Synapses are gaps between neurons. The neural impulse reaches the axon terminal and stimulates the release of neurotransmitters from tiny vesicles. These carry information to the next neuron, fitting like keys in locks. Important neurotransmitters include GABA, acetylcholine, norepinephrine, serotonin, and endorphins. Some neurotransmitters are excitatory, others are inhibitory. Agonists are drugs that mimic or increase a neurotransmitter's effects. Antagonists are drugs that block a neurotransmitter's effects.
Glial Cells	Their Nature	They provide support for neurons and are thought to be involved in the regulation and nutrition of neurons.

At this point we have discussed a number of ideas about the field of neuroscience, the nervous system, and neurons. An overview of these ideas is presented in summary table 3.2.

Brain Structure and Function

Most of the information we have covered about the brain has been about one or two cells. Earlier we indicated that about 99 percent of all neurons in the nervous system are located in the brain and the spinal cord. Neurons do not simply float in the brain. Connected in precise ways, they compose the various structures of the brain (Smock, 1999).

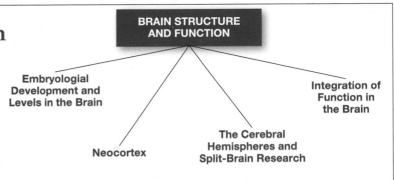

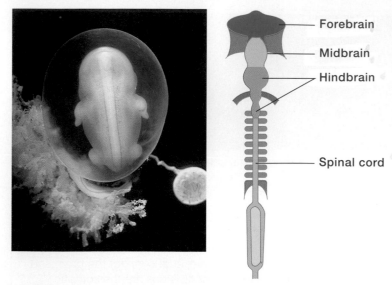

*F*igure 3.9
Embryological Development of the Nervous System

In this photograph you can see the primitive, tubular appearance of the nervous system at 6 weeks in the human embryo. The drawing shows the major brain regions and spinal cord as they appear early in the development of a human embryo.

Brain and Mind

Embryological Development and Levels in the Brain

As a human embryo develops inside the womb, the nervous system begins as a long, hollow tube on the embryo's back. At three weeks or so after conception, the brain forms into a large mass of neurons and loses its tubular appearance.

The elongated tube changes shape and develops into three major divisions: the hindbrain, which is the portion of the brain adjacent to the spinal cord; the midbrain, which is above the hindbrain; and the forebrain, which is the highest region of the brain (O'Rahilly & Muller, 1999) (see figure 3.9).

Hindbrain   The **hindbrain,** *located at the skull's rear, is the lowest and evolutionarily oldest portion of the brain. The three main parts of the hindbrain are the medulla, cerebellum, and pons.* Figure 3.10 shows the location of these brain structures as well as some of the forebrain's main structures. The **medulla** *begins where the spinal cord enters the skull. It helps to control our breathing and regulates a portion of reflexes that allow us to maintain an upright posture.* The **cerebellum** *extends from the rear of the hindbrain and is located just above the medulla. It consists of two rounded structures thought to play important roles in motor behavior.* Leg and arm movements are coordinated at the cerebellum, for example. When we play golf, practice the piano, or perfect our moves on the dance floor, the cerebellum is hard at work. If a higher portion of the brain commands us to write the number 7, it is the cerebellum that integrates the muscular activities required to do so. If the cerebellum becomes damaged, our movement becomes uncoordinated and jerky. The **pons** *is a bridge in the hindbrain that contains several clusters of fibers involved in sleep and arousal.*

Midbrain   The **midbrain,** *located between the hindbrain and forebrain, is an area where many nerve-fiber systems ascend and descend to connect the higher and lower portions of the brain.* In particular, the midbrain relays information between the brain and the eyes and ears. Visual attention, for example, is linked to one midbrain **nucleus** (*group of specialized nerve cells in the brain or spinal cord*), the *superior colliculus.* Parkinson's disease, a deterioration of movement that produces rigidity and tremors in the elderly, damages a section near the bottom of the midbrain.

Two systems in the midbrain are of special interest. One is the **reticular formation** (see figure 3.11), *a diffuse collection of neurons involved in stereotyped patterns of behavior such as walking, sleeping, or turning to attend to a sudden noise.* The other system consists of small groups of neurons that use the special neurotransmitters serotonin, dopamine, and norepinephrine. These three groups contain relatively few cells, but they send their axons to a remarkable variety of brain regions, perhaps explaining their involvement in high-level, integrative functions (Shier, Butler, & Lewis, 1999).

It is not the hindbrain or midbrain that separates humans from animals, however. In humans, it is the forebrain that becomes enlarged and specialized.

Forebrain   You try to understand what all of these terms and parts of the brain mean. You talk with friends and plan a party for this weekend. You remember it has been 6 months since you went to the dentist. All of these experiences and millions more would not be possible without the **forebrain,** *the highest and evolutionarily newest region of the human brain. Among its most important structures are the limbic system, amygdala, hippocampus, thalamus, basal ganglia, hypothalamus, and neocortex,* each of which we will discuss in turn.

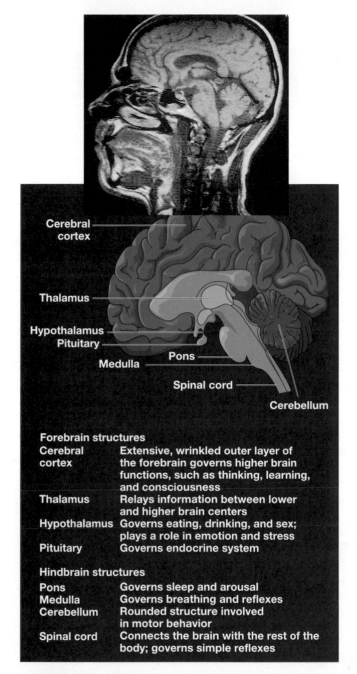

Forebrain structures

Cerebral cortex	Extensive, wrinkled outer layer of the forebrain governs higher brain functions, such as thinking, learning, and consciousness
Thalamus	Relays information between lower and higher brain centers
Hypothalamus	Governs eating, drinking, and sex; plays a role in emotion and stress
Pituitary	Governs endocrine system

Hindbrain structures

Pons	Governs sleep and arousal
Medulla	Governs breathing and reflexes
Cerebellum	Rounded structure involved in motor behavior
Spinal cord	Connects the brain with the rest of the body; governs simple reflexes

Figure 3.10
Structure and Regions in an Actual Image of the Human Brain

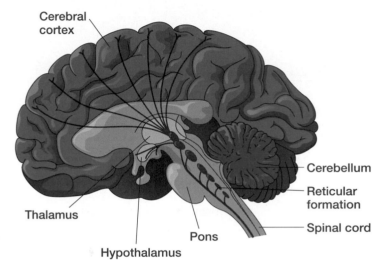

Figure 3.11
The Reticular Formation

The reticular formation is a network of nerve fibers that runs through the brain stem. The arrows shown radiating from the brain stem are drawn to show the connections of the reticular formation to the higher portions of the brain in the neocortex. The reticular formation is involved in arousal and attention.

Limbic System   The **limbic system,** *a loosely connected network of structures under the cerebral cortex, plays important roles in both memory and emotion.* Its two principal structures are the amygdala and hippocampus (see figure 3.12).

The **amygdala** *(from the Latin for "almond" shape) is a limbic system structure located within the base of the temporal lobe. It is involved in the discrimination of objects that are important in the organism's survival, (such as appropriate food, mates, and social rivals) and in emotion (through its many connections with higher and lower portions of the brain)* (LeDoux, 1999). Neurons in the amygdala often fire selectively at the sight of such stimuli, and lesions in the amygdala can cause animals to attempt to eat, fight, or mate with inappropriate objects such as chairs.

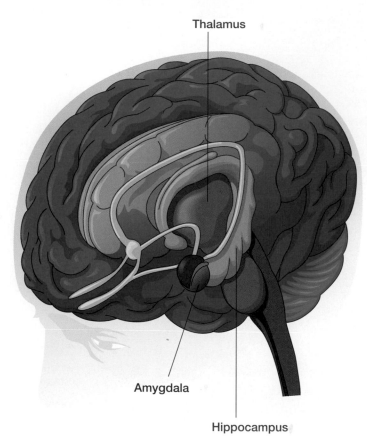

Thalamus

Amygdala

Hippocampus

ℱigure 3.12
The Limbic System

The two main structures of the limbic system are the amygdala, which is involved in the discrimination of objects that are important for the organism's survival and in emotion; and the hippocampus, which is involved in memory.

The **hippocampus** *is a limbic system structure that has a special role in the storage of memories.* Individuals suffering extensive hippocampal damage simply cannot retain any new conscious memories after the damage. It is fairly certain, though, that memories are not stored "in" the limbic system. Instead, the limbic system seems to control what parts of all the information passing through the cortex should be "printed" into durable, lasting neural traces in the cortex (Gluck, 1996).

Thalamus   The **thalamus** *is a forebrain structure that sits at the top of the brain stem in the central core of the brain. It serves as a very important relay station, functioning much like a telephone switchboard.* While one area of the thalamus works to orient information from the sense receptors (hearing, seeing, and so on), another region seems to be involved in sleep and wakefulness, having ties with the reticular formation (see figure 3.11 for the location of the thalamus).

Basal Ganglia   The **basal ganglia** *are forebrain structures essential to starting and stopping voluntary movements.* Individuals with damage to basal ganglia suffer from either unwanted movement (such as constant writhing or jerking of limbs) or too little movement (as in the slow and deliberate movements of those with Parkinson's disease).

Hypothalamus   The **hypothalamus,** *much smaller than the thalamus and about the size of a kidney bean, is a forebrain structure located just below the thalamus. The hypothalamus monitors three enjoyable activities—eating, drinking, and sex; it helps direct the endocrine system through the pituitary gland; and it is involved in emotion, stress, and reward.* Perhaps the best way to describe the function of the hypothalamus is in terms of a regulator. It is sensitive to changes in the blood and neural input, and it responds by influencing the secretion of hormones and neural outputs. For example, if the temperature of circulating blood near the hypothalamus is increased by just 1 or 2 degrees, certain cells in the hypothalamus start increasing their rate of firing. As a result, a chain of events is set in motion. Increased circulation through the skin and sweat glands occurs immediately to release this heat from the body. The cooled blood circulating to the hypothalamus slows down the activity of some of the neurons there, stopping the process when the temperature is just right—37.1 degrees Centigrade. These temperature-sensitive neurons function like a finely tuned thermostat in returning the body to a balanced state.

The hypothalamus is also involved in emotional states, playing an important role as an integrative location for handling stress. Much of this integration is accomplished through the hypothalamus' action on the pituitary gland, located just below it. If some areas of the hypothalamus are electrically stimulated, a feeling of pleasure results. In a classic experiment, McGill researchers James Olds and Peter Milner (1954) implanted an electrode in the hypothalamus of a rat's brain. When the rat ran to a corner of an enclosed area, a mild electric current was delivered to its hypothalamus. The researchers thought the electric current was punishment for the rat and would cause it to avoid the corner. Much to their surprise, the rat kept returning to the corner. Olds and Milner believed they had discovered a pleasure center in the hypothalamus.

Olds (1958) conducted further experiments and found that rats would press bars until they dropped over from exhaustion just to continue to receive a mild electric shock to their hypothalamus. One rat pressed a bar more than 2,000 times an hour for a period of 24 hours to receive the stimulus to its hypothalamus (see figure 3.13). Today researchers agree that the hypothalamus is involved in pleasurable feelings, but that other areas of the brain, such as the limbic system and a bundle of fibers in the forebrain, are also important in the link between brain and pleasure as well (Milner, 1991).

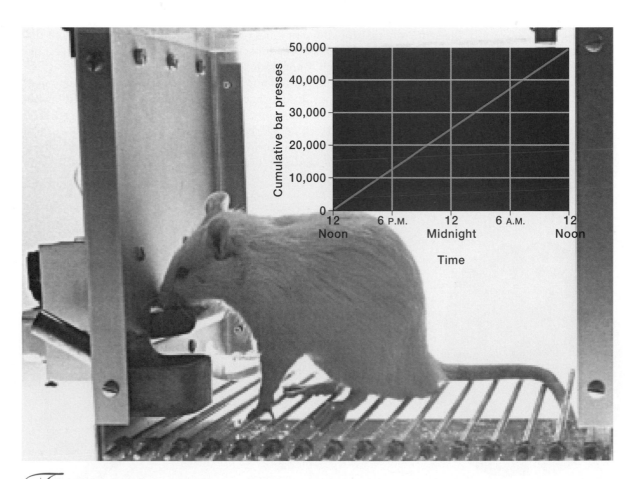

Figure 3.13
Results of the Experiment by Olds (1958) on the Role of the Hypothalamus in Pleasure

The graphed results for one rat show that it pressed the bar more than 2,000 times an hour for a period of 24 hours to receive the stimulus to its hypothalamus. One of the rats in Olds and Milner's experiments is shown pressing the bar to receive stimulation to its hypothalamus.

The Olds studies have implications for drug addiction. In the Olds studies, the rat pressed the bar mainly because of a positive reinforcing effect (pleasure), not because it wanted to avoid or escape a negative withdrawal effect (pain). Cocaine users talk about the drug's ability to heighten pleasure in food, in sex, and in a variety of activities, highlighting the reward aspects of the drug (Restak, 1988).

Neocortex

The Neocortex

The **neocortex** *is a region of the forebrain that is the most recently developed part of the brain in the evolutionary scheme.* The neural tissue that comprises the neocortex is the largest part of the brain by volume (about 80 percent) and covers the lower portions of the brain almost like a large cap. Let's look at the neocortex in more detail.

The wrinkled surface of the neocortex is divided into two halves (see figure 3.14). These two halves are called hemispheres, and each is divided into four lobes—frontal, parietal, temporal, and occipital (see figure 3.15). The **occipital lobe,** *the portion of the neocortex at the back of the head, is involved in visual functioning* (Milner & Goodale, 1995). The **temporal lobe,** *the portion of the neocortex just above the ears, is involved in hearing.* The **frontal lobe,** *the portion of the neocortex behind the forehead, is involved in the control of voluntary muscles, intelligence, and personality.* Figure 3.16 describes a fascinating case that illustrates how damage to the frontal lobe can significantly alter personality. The **parietal lobe,** *the portion of the neocortex at the top of the head and toward the rear, is involved in bodily sensation.*

In the same way that the different lobes of the neocortex are associated with different processes, different regions of the lobes have different jobs. Scientists have determined this primarily through topographic mapping.

Projection maps are widely used topographical maps made by stimulating areas of the brain and detecting the resulting behavior or by recording the electrical activity of the neocortex during certain behaviors. Wilder Penfield (1947), a neurosurgeon at the Montreal Neurological Institute, worked with a number of patients who had a severe form of epilepsy. Penfield often performed surgery to remove portions of the epileptic patients' brains, but he was concerned that removing a portion of the brain

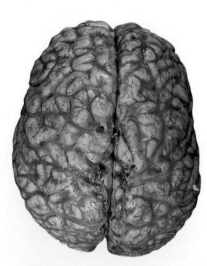

Figure 3.14
The Human Brain's Two Hemispheres
The two halves (hemispheres) of the human brain can be seen clearly in this photograph.

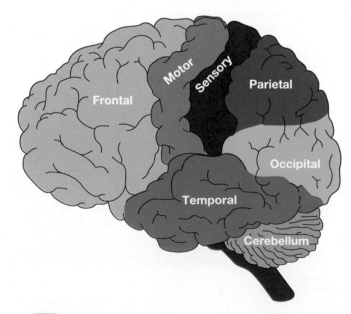

Figure 3.15
The Brain's Four Lobes
Shown here are the locations of the brain's four lobes: occipital, temporal, frontal, and parietal.

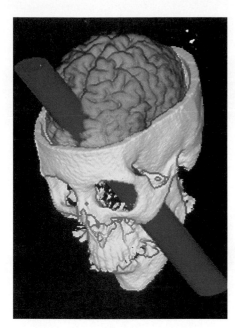

Phineas T. Gage, a 25-year-old foreman who worked for the Rutland and Burlington Railroad in Vermont, met with an interesting experience on September 13, 1848. Phineas and several co-workers were using blasting powder to construct a roadbed. The crew drilled holes in the rock and gravel, poured in the blasting powder, and then tamped down the powder with an iron rod. While Phineas was still tamping it down, the powder blew up, driving the iron rod up through the left side of his face and out through the top of his head. Though the wound in his skull healed in a matter of weeks, Phineas became a different person. He had been a mild-mannered, hardworking, emotionally calm individual prior to the accident, well liked by all who knew him. Afterward, he became obstinate, moody, irresponsible, selfish, and incapable of participating in any planned activities. The location of damage was the frontal lobe and it significantly altered Phineas's personality.

Figure 3.16
The Injury to Phineas T. Gage

might impair some of the individuals' functions. Penfield's solution was to map the cortex during surgery by stimulating different cortical areas and observing the responses of the patients, who were given a local anesthetic so they would remain awake during the operation. He found that, when he stimulated certain sensory and motor areas of the brain, different parts of a patient's body moved (see figure 3.17). For both sensory and motor areas, there is a point-to-point relation between a part of the body and a location on the neocortex (see figure 3.18). The face and hands are given proportionally more space than other body parts. Because the face and hands are capable of finer perceptions and movements than are other body areas, they need more neocortex representation (Penfield & Rasmussen, 1950).

The point-to-point mapping of sensory fields onto the cortex's surface is the basis of our orderly and accurate perception of the world (Fox, 1996). When something touches your lip, for example, your brain knows what body part has been touched (your lip) because the nerve pathways from your lip are the only pathways that project to the lip region of the sensory cortex. This arrangement is analogous to the private hot line that connects Washington and Moscow. If the red phone rings in the president's office in Washington, the call must be from Moscow, because Moscow is the only city that is connected to the other end of the hot line. In the sensory cortex, every small region has its own neural hot line bringing in information directly from the corresponding part of the sensory field. In our telephone analogy, it would be as if the president (the cortex) had hundreds of telephones, each one connected to the capital city of a different country. Which phone was ringing would indicate which country (which part of the sensory field) had a message to convey.

One familiar example of what happens when these neural hot lines get connected the wrong way is seen in Siamese cats. Many Siamese cats have a genetic defect that causes the pathways from the eyes to connect to the wrong parts of the visual cortex during development. The result is that these cats spend their lives looking at things cross-eyed in an effort to "straighten out" the visual image of their visual cortex.

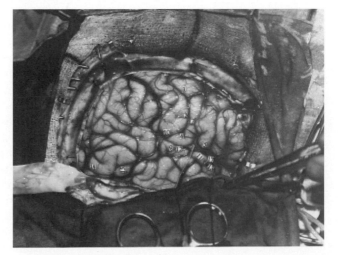

Figure 3.17
Penfield's Research
Penfield stimulated specific locations with a very thin electric probe. When he stimulated a specific area, the patient opened his mouth, sneezed, and began chewing.

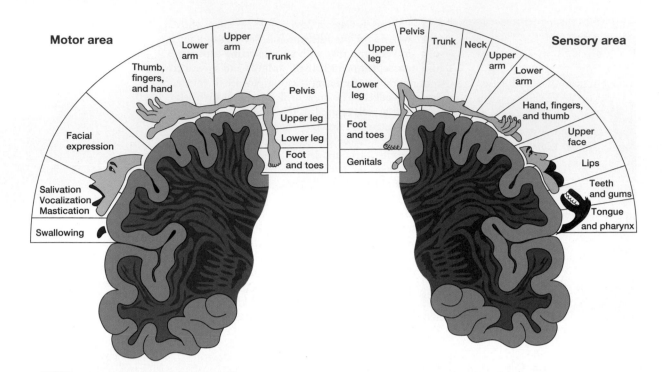

Motor area

Thumb, fingers, and hand

Lower arm

Upper arm

Trunk

Pelvis

Upper leg

Lower leg

Foot and toes

Facial expression

Salivation
Vocalization
Mastication

Swallowing

Pelvis

Trunk

Neck

Upper leg

Lower leg

Foot and toes

Genitals

Upper arm

Lower arm

Sensory area

Hand, fingers, and thumb

Upper face

Lips

Teeth and gums

Tongue and pharynx

𝓕igure 3.18

Disproportionate Representation of Body Parts in the Motor and Sensory Areas of the Cortex

As can be seen in this drawing, the amount of cortex allotted to a body part is not proportionate to the body part's size. Instead, the brain has more space for body parts that require precision and control. Thus, the thumb, fingers, and hand require more brain tissue than do the upper leg and upper arm.

So far our description of the neocortex has focused on sensory and motor areas, but more than 75 percent of the neocortex is made up of areas called the association cortex. The **association cortex** *(or association areas) is the region of the neocortex involved in our highest intellectual functions, such as thinking and problem solving.* The neurons in the association cortex communicate with each other and with neurons in the motor area of the cortex.

Of special interest is the finding that damage to a specific part of the association cortex often does not result in a specific loss of function. With the exception of language areas (which are localized), loss of function seems to depend more on the extent of damage to the association areas than to the specific location of the damage. By observing brain-damaged individuals and using the mapping technique, scientists have found that the association cortex is involved in linguistic and perceptual functioning. The largest portion of association areas is located in the frontal lobe, directly under the forehead. Damage to this area does not lead to sensory or motor loss. Indeed, it is this area that may be most directly related to thinking and problem solving. Early experimentation even referred to the frontal lobe as the center of intelligence, but research suggests that frontal lobe damage may not result in a lowering of intelligence. Planning and judgment are characteristics often associated with the frontal lobe. Personality may also be linked with the frontal lobe. Recall the misfortune of Phineas Gage, whose personality radically changed after he experienced frontal lobe damage.

One of the truly fascinating areas of inquiry in contemporary neuroscience concerns the nature of difference between the brains of men and women (Kimura, 1987). University of Western Ontario neuroscientist Doreen Kimura (1999) has explored how hormones actually "reorganize" the brain early in life. Drawing upon behavioral, neurological and endocrinological studies, she theorizes how the sexes end up with distinct problem-solving abilities. Levy (1974) presented evidence that differences between the brains of men and women may involve differences between the two hemispheres of the brain and the nature of the connection between them.

You have learned that the neocortex is divided into two hemispheres. The fascinating story of information processing in the neocortex involves lobes, maps, and differences between brains, but it could not be completely told without knowing more about how the two sides, or hemispheres, of the brain work.

The Cerebral Hemispheres and Split-Brain Research

At the beginning of our discussion of the cerebral cortex, we indicated that it is divided into two halves—left and right (see figure 3.17). Might these hemispheres have different functions? In 1861, French surgeon Paul Broca saw a patient who had suffered an injury to a precise part of his left hemisphere about 30 years earlier. The patient became known as Tan after the only word he could speak. He suffered from *aphasia,* a language disorder associated with brain damage. Today we refer to this region of the brain as Broca's area, which plays an important role in the production of speech. Another left-hemisphere area involved in language is *Wernicke's area,* which, if damaged, causes problems in comprehending language. More recently, the Wernicke-Geschwind model (see figure 3.19) has been proposed to explain how these two areas collaborate with others to explain what happens when a spoken word is presented and the individual repeats the word out loud (Geschwind & Galaburda, 1987).

Today, there continues to be considerable interest in the degree to which the brain's left hemisphere or right hemisphere is involved in various aspects of thinking, feeling, and behavior (Carlson, 1999). For many years scientists speculated that the **corpus callosum,** *a large bundle of axons that connects the brain's two hemispheres,* had something to do with relaying information between the two sides. Roger Sperry (1974) confirmed this in an experiment in which he cut the corpus callosum in cats. He also severed certain nerves leading from the eyes to the brain. After the operation, Sperry trained the cats to solve a series of visual problems with one eye blindfolded. After the cat learned the task, say with only its left eye uncovered, its other eye was blindfolded and the animal was tested again. The "split-brain" cat behaved as if it had never learned the task. It seems that the memory was stored only in the left hemisphere, which could no longer directly communicate with the right hemisphere.

Further evidence of the corpus callosum's function has come from experiments with patients who have severe, even life-threatening, forms of epilepsy. Epilepsy is caused by electrical "brainstorms" that flash uncontrollably across the corpus callosum. W. J. is one of the most famous cases. Neurosurgeons severed the corpus callosum of an epileptic patient now known as W. J. in a final attempt to reduce his unbearable seizures. Sperry (1968) examined W. J. and found that the corpus callosum functions the same in humans as in animals—cutting the corpus callosum seemed to leave the patient with "two separate minds" that learned and operated independently.

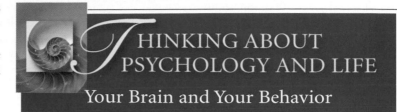

THINKING ABOUT PSYCHOLOGY AND LIFE
Your Brain and Your Behavior

WHICH AREAS of your brain are most likely to be involved when you do the following?

- Fall asleep
- Think critically
- Yell at someone
- Shoot a basketball
- Look at a painting
- Get hungry
- Say a word correctly

Aphasia

Corpus Callosum

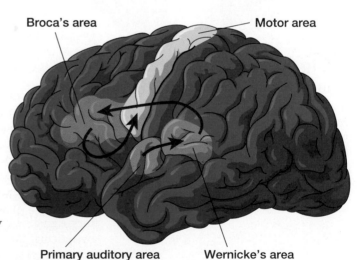

Figure 3.19
The Wernicke-Geschwind Model

When a word is heard and repeated aloud, the ear sends action potentials to the primary auditory area where the sound is first analyzed. It then goes to Wernicke's area where a sound-based code is retrieved and the word is understood. It then goes to Broca's area where the instructions to speak the word are assembled. Finally, these instructions are sent to the motor cortex which activates the appropriate parts of the speech system.

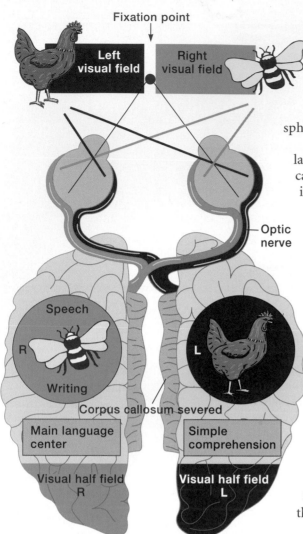

Fixation point

Left visual field

Right visual field

Optic nerve

Speech

R

Writing

L

Corpus callosum severed

Main language center

Simple comprehension

Visual half field R

Visual half field L

Figure 3.20
Visual Information in the Split Brain

In a split-brain patient, information from the visual field's left side projects only to the right hemisphere. Information from the visual field's right side projects only to the left hemisphere. Because of these projections, stimuli can be presented to only one of a split-brain patient's hemispheres.

The right hemisphere, it turns out, receives information only from the left side of the body, and the left hemisphere receives information only from the right side of the body. When you hold an object in your left hand, for example, only the right hemisphere of your brain detects the object. When you hold an object in your right hand, only the left hemisphere of the brain detects the object (see figure 3.20). Because you have a normal corpus callosum, both hemispheres receive this information.

The most extensive research on the brain's two hemispheres involves language. A common misconception is that virtually all language processing is carried out in the brain's left hemisphere. Speech and grammar can be localized to the left hemisphere in most people. However, understanding such aspects of language as appropriate use of language in different contexts, metaphor, and much of humor involves the right hemisphere.

Speculation continues about the brain's hemispheric specialization—the notion that the two hemispheres function in different ways and that some psychological processes are restricted almost exclusively to one hemisphere or the other (Saravi, 1993). In fact, people commonly use the phrases *left-brained* and *right-brained* to say which hemisphere is dominant. Explorations in Psychology addresses the nature of hemispheric specialization and separates fact from fantasy regarding a number of related myths.

Integration of Function in the Brain

How do all of the various brain regions cooperate to produce the wondrous complexity of thought and behavior that characterize humans? Part of the answer to this question, such as how the brain solves a murder mystery or writes a poetic essay, is beyond the grasp of neuroscience. Still, we can get a sense of integrative brain function by considering something like the act of escaping from a burning building. A simplistic view might be that such behavior was controlled by an "escaping from danger" center in the brain. Let's compare that view with a more contemporary one.

Imagine you are sitting at your desk writing letters when fire breaks out behind you. The sound of crackling flames is relayed from your ear, through the thalamus, to your auditory cortex, and on to the auditory association cortex. At each stage, the stimulus energy has been processed to extract information, and at some stage, probably at the association cortex level, the sounds are finally matched with something like a neural memory representing previous sounds of fires you have heard. The association "fire" sets new machinery in motion. Your attention (guided in part by the reticular formation) swings to the auditory signal being held in your association cortex, and simultaneously (again guided by reticular systems) your head turns toward the noise. Now your visual association cortex reports in: "Objects matching flames are present." In other association regions, the visual and auditory reports are synthesized ("We have things that look and sound like fire"), and neural associations representing potential actions ("flee") are activated. However, firing the neurons that code the plan to flee will not get you out of the chair. The basal ganglia must become engaged, and from there the commands will arise to set the brain stem, motor cortex, and cerebellum to the task of actually transporting you out of the room.

Which part of your brain did you use to escape? Virtually all systems had a role; each was quite specific, and together they generated the behavior. By the way, you would probably remember an event such as a fire in your room. That is because your

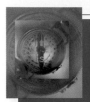

TO MOST SCIENTISTS, the concept of the brain as split into two tidy halves—one being the source of creativity, the other the source of logical thinking—is simplistic. Sandra Witelson, a neuroscientist at McMaster University, points out that no complex function—music, art, reading, or whatever—can be assigned to one single hemisphere or the other. Complex thinking in normal people involves communication between both sides of the brain.

The real issue is the degree to which bihemispheric representation of functions may vary in left-hander vs right-handers (Witelson, 1985), women vs. men (Witelson & Kigar, 1992), geniuses vs. normal people (Witelson, Kigar, & Harvey, 1999), and even homosexual vs. heterosexual people (McCormick, & Witelson, 1994).

The left-brain, right-brain myth originated in Roger Sperry's split-brain studies. Recall that Sperry examined people whose corpus callosum had been severed and found that after surgery the two sides of the brain learned and operated independently. Unfortunately, the media oversimplified the complexity of Sperry's findings. Media reports indicated that when you work on a novel, only your left hemisphere is busy. Switch to creating an oil painting and only your right brain is working. People became either right-brained (artistic) or left-brained (logical). Figure 3.A gives an example of the either/or oversimplification of the brain's two hemispheres.

Roger Sperry did discover that the left hemisphere is superior in the logic used to prove geometric theorems. But in everyday life, our problems involve integrating information and drawing conclusions. In these instances, the right brain's functions are crucial. In virtually all activities, there is an interplay between the brain's two hemispheres (Hoptman & Davidson, 1994). Phil Bryden described this interplay as *complementary specialization* (Bryden, 1986). For example, in reading, the left hemisphere comprehends syntax and grammar, which the right does not. However, the right brain

Neuroscientist Sandra Witelson has conducted extensive research on communication between the two hemispheres of the brain. What conclusions does she reach about left-brain–right-brain functioning?

is better at understanding a story's intonation and emotion. The same is true for music and art. In some musical skills, such as recognizing chords, the right hemisphere is better. In others, such as distinguishing which of two sounds came first, the left hemisphere takes over.

Another offshoot of the left-brain, right-brain hoopla is speculation that more right-brain activities and exercises should be incorporated into schooling (Edwards, 1979). In schools that rely heavily on rote learning to instruct students, children would probably benefit from exercises in intuitive thought and holistic thinking. But this deficiency in school curricula has nothing to do with left-brain, right-brain specialization (Segalowitz, 1983).

Further evidence of the brain's hemispheric flexibility and resilience involves 13-year-old Brandi Binder (Nash, 1997). She developed such a severe case of epilepsy that UCLA surgeons removed her right cortex at age 6. She lost virtually all control over muscles on the left side of her body, the side controlled by the right side of the brain. Yet today, after years of therapy ranging from leg lifts to math and music training, Binder is an A student. She loves music, math, and art, which are usually associated with the right side of the brain. Her recuperation is not 100 percent. For example, she has never regained the use of her left arm. However, her recovery is remarkable and shows that if there is a way to compensate, the brain will find it.

There is so much more to understanding brain function and organization than characterizing people as right- or left-brained. After all, we are trying to understand the most complex pieces of matter in the known universe.

Brandi Binder is evidence of the brain's hemispheric flexibility and resilience. Despite having the right side of her cortex removed because of a severe case of epilepsy, Brandi engages in many activities often portrayed as only "right-brain" activities. She loves music, math, and art, and is shown here working on one of her paintings.

HOW THE BRAIN DIVIDES ITS WORK

𝓕igure 3.A
Stereotyped Myths About Left Brain, Right Brain
Is left-brain, right-brain specialization all-or-none, as this drawing implies? No. © *Roy Doty/Newsweek*

SUMMARY TABLE 3.3
Brain Structure and Function

Concept	Processes/ Related Ideas	Characteristics/Description
Embryological Development	Embryological Development	A neural tube develops into the hindbrain (lowest level), midbrain (middle level), and forebrain (highest level).
Levels in the Brain	Hindbrain	The hindbrain is located at the skull's rear and has three main structures: medulla (helps to control breathing and regulates reflexes that allow an upright position), cerebellum (involved in motor behavior), and pons (bridge involved in sleep and arousal).
	Midbrain	The midbrain is located between the hindbrain and the forebrain. It is an area where many fibers ascend and descend to connect higher and lower areas of the brain. There are two main systems in the midbrain: The reticular formation is involved in stereotyped patterns of behavior such as walking, sleeping, or turning toward a sudden noise. The other system consists of a number of nuclei that use special neurotransmitters.
	Forebrain	The forebrain is the highest region of the human brain. Its structures include the limbic system (involved in memory and emotion), amygdala (involved in discrimination of objects and emotion), hippocampus (involved in storage of memories), thalamus (important relay station), basal ganglia (involved in starting and stopping voluntary movements), hypothalamus (monitors eating, drinking and sex; helps direct the endocrine system through links with the pituitary gland; and is involved in emotions, stress, and reward), and the neocortex.
Neocortex	Its Nature	The neocortex is the region of forebrain that is divided into two hemispheres, each of which is divided into four lobes—occipital lobe, which is involved in visual functioning; temporal lobe, which is involved in hearing; frontal lobe, which is involved in the control of voluntary muscles; and parietal lobe, which is involved in bodily sensation. Projection maps have helped scientists determine the neocortex's role in different behaviors. The neocortex can be divided into sensory, motor, and association areas.
The Cerebral Hemispheres and Split-Brain Research	Their Nature	Broca's area (production of speech) and Wernicke's area (comprehension of language) are located in the brain's left hemisphere and, according to the Wernicke-Geschwind model, are involved in speaking a read word. The corpus callosum is a bundle of axons that connects the brain's two hemispheres. Pioneered by Sperry, split-brain research involves severing the corpus callosum. In normal individuals, the two hemispheres work together to process information. A number of myths have developed that exaggerate left-brain and right-brain functions.
Integration of Function in the Brain	Its Nature	Most psychological functions do not involve a single structure in the brain, but rather, the integration of information by a number of structures.

limbic circuitry would likely have issued the "start print" command when the significant association "fire" was first triggered. The next time the sounds of crackling flames reach your auditory association cortex, the associations triggered will include those of this most recent escape. In sum, there is considerable integration of function in the brain (Gevins, 1999).

At this point we have studied a number of ideas about structure and function in the brain. An overview of these ideas is presented in summary table 3.3.

Exploring the Brain

Other topics important for understanding the brain include these: What is the nature of brain damage, plasticity, and repair? What techniques can be used to study the brain? How do the brain and endocrine system work together?

EXPLORING THE BRAIN

Brain Damage, Plasticity, and Repair

Techniques for Studying the Brain

The Brain and the Endocrine System

Brain Damage, Plasticity, and Repair

If the brain is damaged through injury or illness, does it have the capacity to repair itself? Are there external ways we can restore some or all of the brain's functioning after it has been damaged?

The Brain's Plasticity and Capacity for Repair
Brain damage can produce horrific effects, including paralysis, sensory loss, memory loss, and personality deterioration. When such damage occurs, can the brain recover some or all of its functions? Recovery from brain damage varies considerably (Garraghty, 1996).

Plasticity *is the brain's capacity to modify and reorganize itself following damage.* In one study, researchers surgically removed part of the monkeys' somatosensory cortex. Later the somatosensory cortical map shifted to intact adjacent parts of the parietal lobes, restoring the body's ability to experience sensations (Fox, 1984).

The human brain shows the most plasticity in young children before the functions of the cortical regions become entirely fixed (Kolb, 1989). For example, if the speech areas in an infant's left hemisphere are damaged, the right hemisphere assumes much of this language function. However, after age 5, permanent damage to the left hemisphere can permanently disrupt language ability (Kolb and others, 1998).

A key factor in recovery is whether some, or all, of the neurons in an affected area are just damaged or completely destroyed (Black, 1999; Carlson, 1999). If the neurons are not completely destroyed, brain function often becomes restored over time. Unlike some fish and amphibians who can regenerate neurons, our central nervous system cannot. Once a human neuron is lost, it is gone forever.

Even though new neurons can't be regenerated in humans, other repair mechanisms exist (Azar, 1996). They include:

- *Collateral sprouting,* in which the axons of some healthy neurons adjacent to damaged cells grow new branches.
- *Substitution of function,* in which the damaged region's function is taken over by another area, or areas, of the brain. This is what happened in the example of the right hemisphere taking over the speech function of the damaged left hemisphere in infants.

To read further about the brain's plasticity, see the fascinating story of the Mankato nuns in Explorations in Psychology.

Brain Tissue Implants
The brain's capacity to repair itself may restore some lost functions following damage, but not in all cases. In recent years, considerable excitement has been generated about **brain grafts,** *which involve implanting healthy tissue into damaged brains.* The potential success of brain grafts is much better when brain tissue from the fetal stage (an early stage in prenatal development) is used. The neurons of the fetus are still growing and have a much higher probability of making connections with other neurons than do the neurons of

Brain Disorders
Repairing the Damaged Brain

University of Lethbridge neuroscientist Bryan Kolb suffered some loss of vision from a right occipital stroke, which he correctly self-diagnosed. He then wrote about his recovery in the Canadian Journal of Psychology *(Kolb, 1990). Another Canadian, documentary filmmaker Bonnie Klein, suffered a catastrophic brain stem stroke. She described her remarkable recovery in* Slow Dance: A Story Of Love, Stroke, And Disability *(Klein, 1997).*

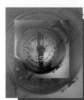

EXPLORATIONS IN PSYCHOLOGY
The Brains of the Mankato Nuns

NEARLY 700 NUNS in a convent in Mankato, Minnesota, are the largest group of brain donors in the world. By examining the nuns' donated brains, as well as others, neuroscientists are beginning to understand that the brain has a remarkable capacity to change and grow, even in old age. The Sisters of Mankato lead an intellectually challenging life, and brain researchers have recently found that stimulating the brain with mental exercises can cause neurons to increase their dendritic branching (Snowden, 1995) (see figure 3.B).

The capacity of the brain to change offers new possibilities for preventing and treating brain diseases, helping to explain why some individuals can

- Delay the onset of Alzheimer's disease symptoms for years; the more educated people are, the less likely they are to develop Alzheimer's, probably because intellectual activity develops surplus brain tissue that compensates for tissue damaged by the disease.
- Recover better from strokes. Researchers have found that even when areas of the brain are permanently damaged by stroke, new message routes can be created to get around the blockage or to resume the function of that area.
- Feel sensation in missing limbs. Scientists no longer believe that the complaints of pain in amputated body parts are psychosomatic. The sensations, which eventually fade, likely are the brain's way of keeping once-busy neurons active, providing evidence that areas of the brain no longer useful can be taken over by nearby regions of the cortex.

Figure 3.B
The Brains of the Mankato Nuns

Sister Marcella Zachman *(inset, left)* finally stopped teaching at age 97. Now, at 99, she helps ailing nuns exercise their brains by quizzing them on vocabulary or playing a card game called Skip-Bo, at which she deliberately loses. Sister Mary Esther Boor *(inset, right),* also 99 years of age, is a former teacher who keeps alert by doing puzzles and volunteering to work the front desk. *Large photo:* A technician holds the brain of a deceased Mankato nun. The nuns donate their brains for research that explores the effects of stimulation on brain growth. This research is supported by the U.S. National Institute on Aging.

adults. In a number of studies, researchers have damaged part of a rat's (or some other animal's) brain, waited until the animal recovered as much as possible by itself, and assessed its behavioral deficits. Then they took the corresponding area of a fetal rat's brain and transplanted it into the damaged brain of the adult rat. In these studies, the rats that received the brain transplants demonstrated considerable behavioral recovery (Dunnett, 1989).

Might such brain grafts be successful with humans suffering from brain damage? One problem is finding donors. Aborted fetuses are a possibility, but they raise ethical issues. Another possibility has been attempted with individuals who have Parkinson's disease, a neurological disorder that affects about 200,000 people in Canada. Parkinson's disease impairs coordinated movement to the point that just walking across a room can be a major ordeal. Brain grafters have tried to substitute adrenal gland tissue for brain tissue. Why adrenal gland tissue? Parkinson's disease damages neurons in an area of the brain that secretes the neurotransmitter dopamine. Adrenal gland cells produce dopamine. Early reports of adrenal gland transplants in Parkinson's patients were promising, but the long-term effects have been less so (Lewin, 1988).

The potential for brain grafts also exists for individuals with Alzheimer's disease, which is characterized by a progressive decline in intellectual functioning. Brain destruction in Alzheimer's disease involves the degeneration of neurons that function in memory. Such degenerative changes can be reversed in rats (Gage & Bjorklund, 1986). However, as yet no success with brain grafts with Alzheimer's patients has been reported. Nonetheless, the future holds promise that such grafts may someday be possible in humans.

Techniques for Studying the Brain

Earlier we discussed research by Wilder Penfield and James Olds in which electrodes were inserted into living brains in order to study brain functions. Neuroscientists no longer have to perform surgery on living patients or cadavers to study the brain. Sophisticated techniques allow researchers to "look inside" the brain while it is at work. Let's examine some of these fascinating techniques.

High-powered microscopes are widely used in neuroscience research. Neurons are stained with the salts of various heavy metals such as silver and lead. These stains coat only a small portion of any group of neurons. The stains allow neuroscientists to view and study every part of a neuron in microscopic detail.

Also widely used, the **electroencephalograph** (EEG) *records the electrical activity of the brain.* Electrodes placed on the scalp detect brain-wave activity, which is recorded on a chart known as an electroencephalogram (see figure 3.21). This device has been used to assess brain damage, epilepsy, and other problems.

An EEG measures the pooled activity of millions of neurons beneath each electrode. In contrast, in single-unit recording, a measure of a single neuron's electrical activity, a thin wire or *microelectrode,* is inserted in or near an individual neuron (Seidemann and others, 1996). The neuron's activity is transmitted to an amplifier, which allows researchers to display information about the activity.

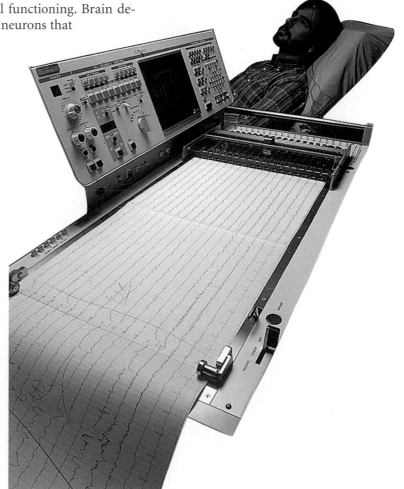

Figure 3.21
An EEG Recording

The electroencephalograph (EEG) is widely used in sleep research. It has led to some major breakthroughs in understanding sleep by showing how the brain's electrical activity changes during sleep.

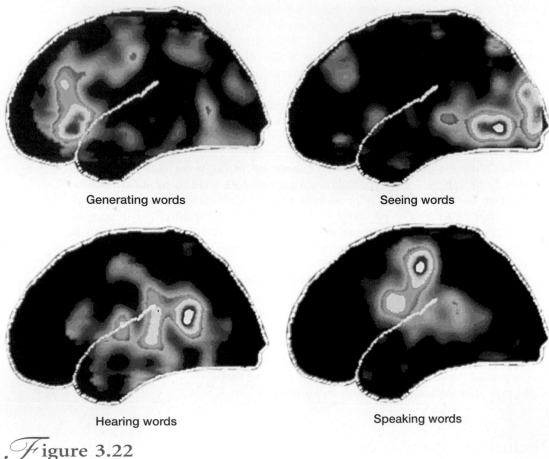

Generating words   Seeing words

Hearing words   Speaking words

*F*igure 3.22
PET Scan

This PET scan of the left brain's hemisphere contrasts the different areas used in aspects of language activity: Generating words, hearing words, seeing words, and speaking words.

For years X rays have been used to determine damage inside or outside our bodies, both in the brain and in other locations. But a single X ray of the brain is hard to interpret because it shows the three-dimensional nature of the brain's interior in a two-dimensional image (Goel, 1995). **Computer-assisted axial tomography (CAT scan)** *is three-dimensional imaging obtained from X rays of the head that are assembled into a composite image by computer.* The CAT scan provides valuable information about the location of damage due to a stroke, language disorder, or loss of memory.

Positron-emission tomography (PET scan) *measures the amount of glucose in various areas of the brain, then sends this information to a computer.* Because glucose levels vary with the levels of activity throughout the brain, tracing the amounts of glucose generates a picture of activity level throughout the brain (Fiez & others, 1996; Goel and others, 1997). Figure 3.22 shows PET scans of people's brain activity while they are hearing, seeing, speaking, and thinking.

Another technique is **magnetic resonance imaging (MRI),** *which involves creating a magnetic field around a person's body and using radio waves to construct images of the person's brain tissues and biochemical activities.* MRI provides very clear pictures of the brain's interior, does not require injecting the brain with a substance, and does not pose a problem of radiation overexposure (Toga, 1998; Toga & Mazziota, 1999).

At this point we have discussed many different aspects of the brain and techniques for studying it. One more important aspect of the body's biological makeup deserves further attention—the endocrine system.

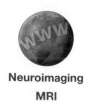

Neuroimaging
MRI

The Brain and the Endocrine System

Recall that the autonomic nervous system involves connections with internal organs, regulating processes like respiration, heart rate, and digestion. The autonomic nervous system acts on the endocrine glands to produce a number of important physiological reactions to strong emotions such as rage and fear.

The **endocrine glands** *are a set of glands that release their chemical products directly into the bloodstream. Hormones are chemical messengers manufactured by the endocrine glands.* Hormones travel more slowly than nerve impulses. The bloodstream conveys hormones to all parts of the body, and the membrane of every cell has receptors for one or more hormones.

The endocrine glands consist of the hypothalamus and the pituitary gland at the base of the brain, the thyroid and parathyroid glands at the front of the neck, the adrenal glands just above the kidneys, the pancreas in the abdomen, and the ovaries in the female's pelvis and the testes in the male's scrotum (see figure 3.23). Other hormones are produced as well, including several in the gastrointestinal tract that control digestion. In much the same way that the brain's control of muscular activity is constantly monitored and altered to suit the information received by the brain, the action of the endocrine glands is continuously monitored and changed by the nervous, hormonal, and chemical information sent to them (Mader, 1999).

The **pituitary gland** *is an important endocrine gland that sits at the base of the skull and is about the size of a pea; the pituitary gland controls growth and regulates other glands* (see figure 3.24). The anterior (front) part of the pituitary is

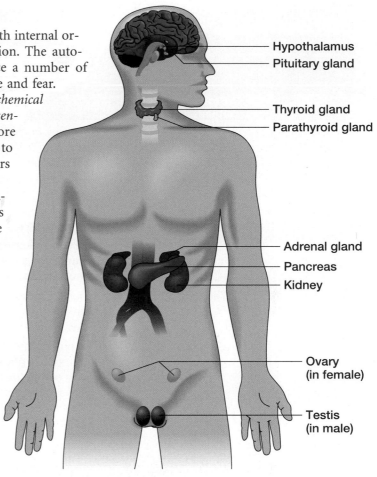

Hypothalamus
Pituitary gland

Thyroid gland
Parathyroid gland

Adrenal gland
Pancreas
Kidney

Ovary
(in female)

Testis
(in male)

*F*igure 3.23
The Major Endocrine Glands

The pituitary gland releases hormones that regulate the hormone secretions of the other glands. The pituitary gland is itself regulated by the hypothalamus.

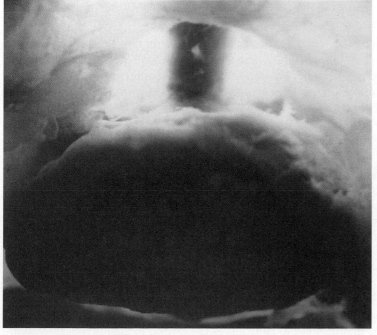

*F*igure 3.24
The Pituitary Gland

The pituitary gland, which hangs by a short stalk from the hypothalamus, regulates the hormone production of many of the body's endocrine glands. Here it is enlarged 30 times.

Summary Table 3.4
Exploring the Brain

Concept	Processes/ Related Ideas	Characteristics/Description
Brain Damage, Plasticity, and Repair	The Brain's Plasticity and Capacity for Repair	Recovery from brain damage varies considerably. Plasticity is the brain's capacity for modification and reorganization following damage. If neurons in the central nervous system are destroyed, they cannot be regenerated. Plasticity is greater in young children than in adults. Collateral sprouting and substitution of function are two mechanisms of repair in the brain.
	Brain Tissue Implants	Brain grafts involve implanting healthy tissue into damaged brains. The most successful brain grafts involve the use of fetal brain tissue, but this procedure raises ethical issues. The potential for brain grafts exists for individuals with Parkinson's disease and with Alzheimer's disease. Brain grafts have been much more successful with animals than with humans.
Techniques for Studying the Brain	Their Nature	Among the most widely used techniques are high-powered microscopes, the electroencephalograph, single-unit recordings, the CAT scan, the PET scan, and magnetic resonance imaging (MRI).
The Brain and Endocrine System	Linkages	The autonomic nervous system acts on the endocrine glands to produce a number of physiological reactions to strong emotions such as rage and fear. The endocrine glands discharge their chemical products into the bloodstream. These chemical products, called hormones, can travel to all parts of the body. The pituitary gland and the adrenal glands are important parts of the endocrine system.

known as the master gland, because almost all of its hormones direct the activity of target glands elsewhere in the body. For example, follicle-stimulating hormone (FSH) produced by the pituitary monitors the level of sex hormones in the ovaries of females and testes of males. Though most pituitary hormones influence a specific organ, growth hormone (GH) acts on all tissues to produce growth during childhood and adolescence. Dwarfs have too little of this hormone, giants too much.

The **adrenal glands** *play an important role in our moods, our energy level, and our ability to cope with stress.* Each adrenal gland secretes epinephrine (also called adrenaline) and norepinephrine (also called noradrenaline). While most hormones travel rather slowly, epinephrine and norepinephrine do their work quickly. Epinephrine helps a person get ready for an emergency by acting on smooth muscles, the heart, stomach, intestines, and sweat glands. Epinephrine also stimulates the reticular formation, which in turn arouses the sympathetic nervous system, and this system subsequently excites the adrenal glands to produce more epinephrine. Norepinephrine also alerts the individual for emergency situations by interacting with the pituitary and the liver. You may remember that norepinephrine also functions as a neurotransmitter when released by neurons. In the case of the adrenal glands, norepinephrine is released as a hormone. In both instances, norepinephrine conveys information—in the first instance to neurons, in the second to glands (Raven & Johnson, 1999).

At this point we have studied a number of ideas about exploring the brain. An overview of these ideas is presented in summary table 3.4. In the next chapter, we will examine sensation and perception, including the brain's role in the visual and auditory senses.

Overview

Overview

We began this chapter by exploring these aspects of biological foundations: heredity, evolution, and nature/nurture. Next, we studied neuroscience, the nervous system, and neurons. This included examining what the field of neuroscience is about, the organization of the nervous system, neurons, and glial cells. Our coverage of brain structure and function focused on embryological development and levels in the brain, the neocortex, cerebral hemispheres and split-brain research, and integration of function in the brain. In the final section of the chapter we explored these aspects of the brain: brain damage, plasticity, and repair, techniques for studying the brain, and the brain and endocrine system.

Don't forget that you can obtain a more detailed overview of the chapter by again studying the four summary tables on pages 70, 79, 90, and 96.

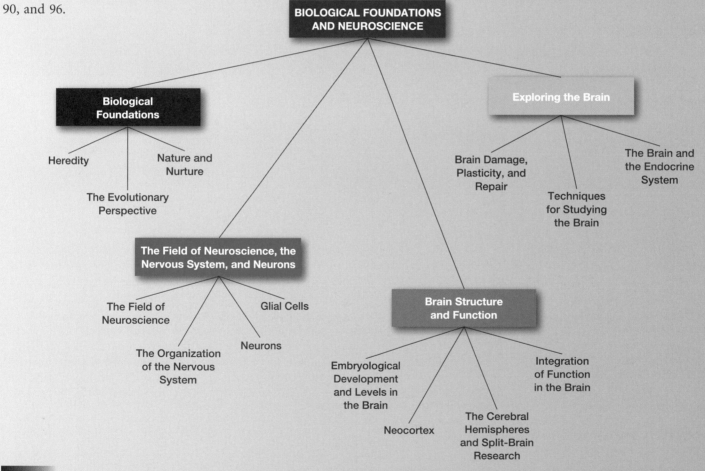

Key Terms

chromosomes 66
deoxyribonucleic acid (DNA)
   66
genes 66
dominant-recessive genes
   principle 66
genotype 67
phenotype 67
natural selection 68
evolutionary psychology
   approach 68
environment 69
nurture 69
nature 69
nervous system 70
neurons 71
neuroscience 71
central nervous system (CNS)
   71
peripheral nervous system 71
somatic nervous system 71

autonomic nervous system 72
sympathetic nervous system
   72
parasympathetic nervous
   system 72
afferent nerves 72
efferent nerves 72
interneurons 73
cell body 73
dendrite 73
axon 73
myelin sheath 73
all-or-none principle 75
ions 75
resting potential 75
action potential 75
synapses 75
neurotransmitters 76
GABA 76
acetylcholine (ACh) 76
norepinephrine 76

dopamine 76
serotonin 76
endorphins 76
agonist 78
antagonist 78
glial cells 78
hindbrain 80
medulla 80
cerebellum 80
pons 80
midbrain 80
reticular formation 80
forebrain 80
limbic system 81
amygdala 81
hippocampus 82
thalamus 82
basal ganglia 82
hypothalamus 82
neocortex 84
occipital lobe 84

temporal lobe 84
frontal lobe 84
parietal lobe 84
association cortex (association
   areas) 86
corpus callosum 87
plasticity 91
brain graft 91
electroencephalograph (EEG)
   93
computer-assisted axial
   tomography (CAT scan) 94
positron-emission tomography
   (PET scan) 94
magnetic resonance imaging
   (MRI) 94
endocrine glands 95
pituitary gland 95
adrenal glands 96

Key People

Thomas Bouchard 65
Charles Darwin 68
David Buss 68

Martin Daly and Margo
   Wilson 69
Santiago Ramón y Cajal 78

James Olds and Peter Milner 83
Wilder Penfield 84
Paul Broca 87

Roger Sperry 87
Sandra Witelson 89
Bryan Kolb 91

Psychology Checklist

BIOLOGICAL FOUNDATIONS AND NEUROSCIENCE

How much have you learned since the beginning of this chapter? Use the following statements to help you review your knowledge and understanding of the chapter material. First, read the statement and mentally or briefly demonstrate on paper that you can outline and discuss the relevant information.

_____ I can state some basic ideas about heredity, the evolutionary perspective, and how nature and nurture interact to influence behavior.

_____ I know what the nervous system is and what neurons are, and I can discuss what the field of neuroscience is about.

_____ I am aware of how the nervous system is organized.

_____ I can describe how neurons process information.

_____ I know the roles of glial cells in the nervous system.

_____ I can discuss the brain's embryological development.

_____ I can outline the structures and functions of the hindbrain, midbrain, and forebrain.

_____ I know how the neocortex is organized and can discuss its functions.

_____ I can describe how function is integrated in the brain.

_____ I am aware of the brain's plasticity and capacity for repair.

_____ I can discuss the techniques scientists use to study the brain.

_____ I know how the endocrine system processes information.

For any items that you did not check off, go back and locate the relevant material in the chapter. Review the material until you feel that you can check off the item. You may want to use this checklist later in preparing for an exam.

Taking It to the Net

1. Have you ever seen a picture of the brain? Brain-imaging techniques have developed rapidly over the past half century. New technology has allowed us to see the brain in an entirely new way. Keeping in mind that each tool allows us to derive different information, describe the major imaging techniques, giving examples of when each would be employed. Which technique gives a color representation of the brain? Why is color used?

2. Prozac, a popular antidepressant drug, is a selective serotonin reuptake inhibitor (SSRI). Other popular SSRIs include Zoloft and Paxil. They alleviate symptoms of depression by affecting the reuptake of serotonin in the brain. Using the information provided at the web site listed below, explain the process of reuptake and how SSRIs inhibit the process of normal reuptake. What can you infer about the causal nature of depression? Do you think that is the only cause of depressive symptoms?

3. You have probably heard at one time or another that you are a "left-brained" or "right-brained" person. These expressions are usually used to describe your personality in terms of what we know about brain laterality. Can we, in fact, be left- or right-brained? What does that mean? Furthermore, what percentage of your brain do you actually use? Do you think you can learn to use more of your brain?

Connect to http://www.mcgrawhill.ca/college/santrock to find the answers!

Resources for Psychology and Life

Brain, Mind, and Behavior (1988, 2nd ed.)
by F. E. Bloom, A. Lazerson, and L. Hofstader
New York: W. H. Freeman

This book is part of a multimedia teaching package involving the Public Broadcasting System's eight-part series "The Brain." The beauty of the brain is captured in both photographs and well-written essays on its many facets.

Classic Cases in Neuropsychology (1996)
by Chris Code, Claus Wallesch, Yves Joanette, and Andres Lecours
Hillsdale, NJ: Erlbaum

This book explores classic case studies that have shaped our knowledge about the way the brain works.

Cognition, Evolution, and Behavior (1998)
By Sara Shettleworth
New York: Oxford University Press

This book raises issues that are intrinsically interdisciplinary as it probes the evolution of the animal mind and questions the relationship between the human mind and the minds of other species.

The Double Helix (1968)
by J. D. Watson
New York: New American Library

This is a personalized account of the research leading up to one of the most provocative discoveries of the twentieth century—the DNA molecule. Reading like a mystery novel, it illustrates the exciting discovery process in science.

The Evolution of Desire (1994)
by David Buss
New York: Basic Books

David Buss, one of evolutionary psychology's architects, weaves a fascinating account of how our evolutionary past shapes human sexuality and love.

Human Growth Foundation
7777 Leesburg Pike
Falls Church, VA 22043
703-883-1773

This organization seeks to promote better understanding of human growth problems caused by pituitary gland irregularities. Information about hormone-related problems is available as well as recommendations for educational programs.

Left Brain, Right Brain (1994)
by S. P. Springer and G. Deutsch
New York: W. H. Freeman

This book includes an up-to-date description of research on the roles of the brain's two hemispheres in a number of areas.

Heart and Stroke Foundation of Canada
222 Queen Street
Suite 1402
Ottawa, Ontario, K1P 5V9

This foundation provides information on the effects of stroke on the brain, and on recovery programs. The HSF can also be reached on the Web at this URL: http://www.hsf.ca/

Parkinson Foundation of Canada
710-390 Bay Street
Toronto, ON M5H 2V2
416-366-0099
1-800-565-3000

This foundation is dedicated to heightening public awareness, raising funds for research, developing literature and materials and distributing them to individuals and organizations across Canada, and providing services to support persons with Parkinson's and their families and caregivers. Their newsletter *Network* is published five times a year.

Chapter 4

CHAPTER OUTLINE

DETECTING AND PERCEIVING THE WORLD

Defining Sensation and Perception

Thresholds

Signal Detection Theory

THE VISUAL SYSTEM

The Visual Stimulus and the Eye

From Eye to Brain and Neural-Visual Processing

Sensory Adaptation

Color Vision

THE AUDITORY SYSTEM

The Nature of Sound and How We Experience It

Structures and Functions of the Ear

Theories of Hearing

Neural-Auditory Processing

OTHER SENSES

The Skin Senses

The Chemical Senses

The Kinesthetic and Vestibular Senses

PERCEPTION

Attention

Principles of Perception

Illusions

Issues in Perception

Sensation and Perception

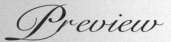

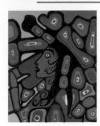

Images of Psychology and Life
To Feel or Not to Feel?

MISS C. came from the West to study at McGill. Her father worried about her. As a child she had suffered severe burns kneeling on a radiator and had bitten off the tip of her tongue chewing food. McGill psychologist Gordon McMurray (1950) confirmed that she was congenitally unable to feel pain. She did not feel much of anything: strong electric shocks, very hot water, or being sharply pinched. You might think the absence of pain a blessing but for Miss C. it was a death sentence. Her joints fell apart because she never shifted her weight when standing, rolled over in her sleep, or avoided awkward postures. Her joints became chronically inflamed and she died of massive infections at age 29. Other children like her have accidentally pulled out their own teeth and almost died from ruptured appendixes (Melzack, 1973).

Mrs. G.E.A. fell and hurt her foot, which turned black and blue. She began to experience episodes of pain in her foot, which began with her toes feeling dead. Then she would experience intense pain during which her toes felt like they were bursting and on fire. Her toes could not stand even the lightest touch. Mrs. G.E.A. had no obvious physical problem in her foot. Fortunately for her, some injections of an anesthetic relieved her symptoms; others have not been so lucky. Stimuli as mild as a puff of air have given rise to pain so chronic and severe that repeated multiple surgery has not helped (Melzack, 1973).

And so it goes with our other senses as well. The world of our experience is created for us by the functioning, or malfunctioning, of our sensory and perceptual systems (see Sacks, 1985, for more examples). We can experience the tortures of hell on earth or the joys of a multi-hued sunrise in Halifax, a crisp winter's morning skiing in Banff, or a gourmet meal in Quebec City, depending on the functioning of our sensory and perceptual systems. How our brain takes information from our senses and transforms it into our lived experience is one of the most intriguing questions in all of psychology.

Preview

EACH OF US has a number of sensory and perceptual systems to detect, process, and interpret what we experience in our environment. Sensing and perceiving involve a complex and sophisticated visual system, an auditory system that is an elaborate engineering marvel compacted into a space the size of an Oreo cookie, and other processes that inform us about soft caresses and excruciating pain, sweet and sour tastes, floral and peppermint odors, and whether our world is upside down or right side up.

These are some of the questions we will explore in this chapter:

• How close does an approaching bumblebee have to be before you can hear it buzzing?
• What factors are involved in an air traffic controller's detection of a plane where it is not supposed to be?
• How do we see, hear, touch, feel pain, taste, and smell?
• How do artists use perceptual cues to portray depth in their paintings?
• Why do you see illusions?
• Can some people actually perceive the world through something other than normal sensory pathways; that is, do they have extrasensory perception?

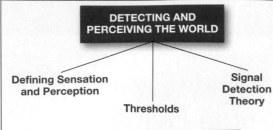

Defining Sensation and Perception

Thresholds

Signal Detection Theory

Detecting and Perceiving the World

How can sensation and perception be defined? How do we detect the sensory world?

Defining Sensation and Perception

How do you know the color of grass, that a smell is sweet, that a sound is a sigh, and that the lights around the shore are dim? You know these things because of your *senses.* All outside information comes into us through our senses. Without vision, hearing, touch, taste, smell, and other senses, your brain would be isolated from the world: you would live in a dark silence—a tasteless, colorless, feelingless void.

Sensation *is the process of detecting and encoding stimulus energy in the world.* Stimuli emit physical energy—light, sound, and heat, for example. The sense organs detect this energy and then transform it into a code that can be transmitted to the brain. The first step in "sensing" the world is the work of receptor cells, which respond to certain forms of energy. The retina of the eye is sensitive to light, and special cells in the ear are sensitive to sound, for example. This physical energy is transformed into electrical impulses; the information carried by these electrical impulses travels through nerve fibers that connect the sense organs with the central nervous system. Once in the brain, information about the external world travels to the appropriate area of the cerebral cortex (Halliday, 1998).

Perception *is the brain's process of organizing and interpreting sensory information to give it meaning.* The retinas of our eyes record a fast-moving silver object in the sky, but they do not "see" a passenger jet: our eardrum vibrates in a particular way, but it does not "hear" a Beethoven symphony. Organizing and interpreting what is sensed—"seeing" and "hearing" meaningful patterns in sensory information—is perception.

In our everyday lives, the two processes of sensation and perception are virtually inseparable. When the brain receives information, for example, it automatically interprets and responds to the information. Because of this, most contemporary psychologists refer to sensation and perception as a unified information-processing system (Goldstein, 1999).

Psychophysics
Perception & Psychophysics

Thresholds

How close does an approaching bumblebee have to be before you can hear its buzzing? How far away does a brewing coffeepot have to be for you to detect the smell of coffee? How different does the percentage of fat have to be for you to taste a difference between the "low-fat" and "regular" versions of your favorite ice cream?

Questions like those just posed are answered by **psychophysics,** *the field that studies links between the physical properties of stimuli and a person's experience of them.* For example, an experiment in psychophysics might examine the relation between the rate at which a light flashes and a participant's ability to see individual flashes.

Absolute Threshold   A basic problem for any sensory system is its ability to detect varying degrees of energy in the environment. This energy can take the form of light, sound, chemical, or mechanical stimulation. How much of a stimulus is necessary for you to see, hear, taste, smell, or feel something? One way to address these questions is to assume that each of us has an **absolute threshold,** *or minimum amount of energy that we can detect.* When a stimulus has less energy than

this absolute threshold, we cannot detect its presence; when the stimulus has more energy than the absolute threshold, we can detect the stimulus. An experiment with a wristwatch or a clock will help you understand the principle of absolute threshold. Find a wristwatch or clock that ticks; put it on a table and walk far enough across the room so that you no longer hear the ticking. Then gradually move toward the wristwatch or clock. At some point you will begin to hear the ticking. Hold your position and notice that occasionally the ticking fades and you may have to move forward to reach the threshold; at other times it may become loud and you can move backward.

In this experiment, if you measure your absolute threshold several times, you will likely record several different distances for detecting the stimulus. For example, the first time you try it, you might hear the ticking at 25 feet from the clock. But you probably won't hear it every time at 25 feet. Maybe you hear it only 38 percent of the time at this distance but hear it 50 percent of the time at 20 feet away and 65 percent of the time at 15 feet. Also, people have different thresholds because some people have better hearing than others and some people have better vision than others. Figure 4.1 shows one person's idealized absolute threshold for detecting a clock's ticking sound. Measured absolute threshold has been arbitrarily decided by psychologists to be the point at which the individual detects the stimulus 50 percent of the time—in this case 20 feet away. Using the same clock, another person might have a measured absolute threshold of 26 feet, and yet another at 18 feet. The approximate absolute thresholds of five different senses are listed in table 4.1.

Under ideal circumstances, our senses have very low absolute thresholds, and so we can be remarkably good at detecting small amounts of stimulus energy. You can demonstrate this to yourself by using a sharp pencil point to carefully lift a single hair on your forearm. You will probably be surprised to realize that for most of us this tiny bit of pressure on the skin is easily detectable. You might also be surprised to learn in table 4.1 that the human eye can see a candle flame at 30 miles on a dark, clear night. But our environment seldom gives us ideal conditions to detect stimuli. If the night is cloudy and the air is polluted, for example, you would have to be much closer to see the flicker of a candle flame. And other lights on the horizon—car or house lights—might hinder your ability to detect the candle's flame. **Noise** *is the term given to irrelevant and competing stimuli.* For example, suppose someone speaks to you from the doorway of the room where you are sitting. You might fail to respond because your roommate is talking on the phone and a CD player is blaring out your favorite song. We usually think of noise as being auditory, but the psychological meaning of the term noise also involves other senses. The pollution, cloudiness, car lights, and house lights are forms of visual noise that hamper your ability to see a candle flame from a great distance.

We have discussed sensations that are above an individual's threshold of awareness, but what about the possibility that we experience the sensory world at levels below our conscious detection? To learn more about this controversial possibility, turn to Explorations in Psychology.

Difference Threshold   In addition to studying the amount of stimulation required for a stimulus to be detected, psychologists investigate the degree of difference that

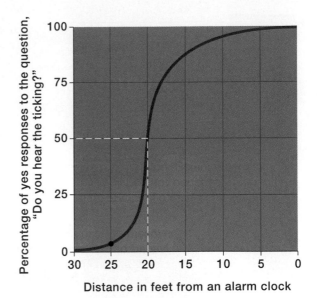

Figure 4.1
Measuring Absolute Threshold

Absolute threshold is the minimum amount of energy we can detect. To measure a person's absolute threshold, psychologists have arbitrarily decided to use the criterion of detecting the stimulus 50 percent of the time. In the graph shown here, the person's measured absolute threshold for detecting the ticking clock is at a distance of 20 feet.

Research on Subliminal Perception

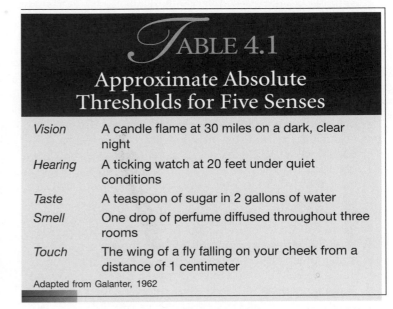

TABLE 4.1 Approximate Absolute Thresholds for Five Senses	
Vision	A candle flame at 30 miles on a dark, clear night
Hearing	A ticking watch at 20 feet under quiet conditions
Taste	A teaspoon of sugar in 2 gallons of water
Smell	One drop of perfume diffused throughout three rooms
Touch	The wing of a fly falling on your cheek from a distance of 1 centimeter

Adapted from Galanter, 1962

EXPLORATIONS IN PSYCHOLOGY
Analyzing Subliminal Perception

ARE YOU CURIOUS ABOUT whether you can be influenced by messages you are not even aware of? According to Canadian psychologists Philip Merikle and Meredith Daneman, subliminal perception has long fascinated psychologists (Merikle & Daneman, 1998). An experiment by Fowler and colleagues (1981) provides some supportive evidence. In this experiment, words were flashed so rapidly that the subjects could not tell what they were seeing. Subsequently, the subjects were shown two words (such as *hotel* and *book*) and asked which was most like the subliminally presented word (*lodge*). Somewhat amazingly, the subjects answered most questions correctly. A possible explanation for these results is that sensory information too faint to be recognized consciously may be picked up by sensory receptors and transmitted to the brain at a level beneath conscious awareness.

More recently, researchers have verified these findings that people's performance can sometimes be affected by stimuli that are too faint to be recognized at a conscious level (Greenwald, Draine & Abrams, 1996). One interesting approach has been to study the memories of people under general anaesthesia for surgery (Merikle & Daneman, 1996). Early reports suggested that positive comments during anesthesia could speed up postoperative recovery. Subsequent research, however, has failed to support this idea. On the other hand, specific information IS remembered following surgery, as long as testing occurs within 36 hours (Merikle & Daneman, 1996). You might be interested in just how this sort of research is carried out. For example, Bonebakker and colleagues (1996) presented words via headphones to patients under anesthesia during surgery for elective procedures.

An area involving subliminal perception that has generated great controversy is whether subliminal messages are embedded in rock music. Some rock groups have allegedly inserted satanic messages played backward in their music. According to this theory, when the music is played normally (forward), the messages are not consciously perceived, but they influence our behavior in a subliminal way. Researchers have not found any evidence whatsoever that backward satanic messages exist or, if they do, that they influence our behavior (McIver, 1988). Begg, Needham & Bookbinder (1993) presented subjects with digitized statements played backwards or forwards and then tested subject's recognition. While subjects did have some ability to recognize backward statements, they showed no evidence that they understood them. Thus, the forward meaning of the backward statements does not "leak" through even when the back-

Mötley Crüe's Shout at the Devil *album has been one of the targets of groups who believe that backward messages are embedded in songs. The protesters say that this album has the phrase* Backward mask where are you, oh. Lost in error, Satan. *However, researchers have been unable to find any evidence whatsoever that these and other satanic messages are encoded in the music or that, if they are, they can influence behavior.*

ward statements are, in themselves, memorable. Investigators have found that people's perceptions of whether or not these messages exist is largely a function of what they expect to hear. In one experiment, when told beforehand that a message of satanic quality would influence them, participants were more likely to hear the message. With no such expectation, participants did not hear the message (Vokey & Read, 1985). And in a recent study, individuals failed to detect any information in subliminal self-help auditory tapes (Moore, 1995).

What can we conclude? First, weak sensory stimuli can be registered by sensory receptors and possibly encoded in the brain beneath conscious awareness. Second, no evidence supports the claims of advertisers and rock music critics that such sensory registration has any substantial impact on our thoughts and behavior. Rather, evidence suggests that we are influenced extensively by those sounds and views we are consciously aware of and can attend to efficiently (Smith & Rogers, 1994).

must exist between two stimuli before this difference is detected. This **difference threshold,** *or just noticeable difference (jnd), is the smallest difference in stimulation required to discriminate one stimulus from another 50 percent of the time.* An artist might detect the difference between two similar shades of color. A tailor might determine a difference in the texture of two fabrics by feeling them. How different must the colors and textures be for these people to determine the difference? Just as the absolute threshold is determined by a 50 percent detection rate, the difference threshold is the point at which a person reports that two stimuli are different 50 percent of the time.

An important aspect of difference thresholds is that the threshold increases with the magnitude of the stimulus. You may notice when your roommate turns up the volume on the stereo by even a small amount when the music is playing softly. But if he or she turns the volume up an equal amount when the music is playing very loudly, you may not notice. More than 150 years ago, E. H. Weber, a German psychologist, noted that, regardless of their magnitude, two stimuli must differ by a constant proportion to be detected. **Weber's law** *is the principle that two stimuli must differ by a constant minimum percentage (rather than a constant amount) to be perceived as different.* Weber's law generally holds true. For example, we add 1 candle to 60 candles and notice a difference in the brightness of the candles; we add 1 candle to 120 candles and do not notice a difference. We discover, though, that adding 2 candles to 120 candles does produce a difference in brightness. Adding 2 candles to 120 candles is the same proportionately as adding 1 candle to 60 candles. The exact proportion varies with the stimulus involved. For example, a change in a tone's pitch of 3 percent can be detected, but in taste a 20 percent change is required for a person to detect a difference, and in smell a 25 percent change is required.

Through the Eyes of Psychologists

Ronald Melzack, *McGill University*

"At any instant in time, millions of nerve impulses arrive at the brain from all the body's sensory systems. How can all this be integrated in a constantly changing unity of experience?"

Signal Detection Theory

Signal detection theory *is the theory that sensitivity to sensory stimuli depends on a variety of factors besides the physical intensity of the stimulus and the sensory abilities of the observer.* These factors include individual and contextual variations such as fatigue, expectancy, and the urgency of the moment. Let's consider the case of two air traffic controllers with exactly the same sensory ability to detect blips on a radar screen. One is monitoring the radar screen while working overtime late into the night and is feeling fatigued. The other is watching the screen in the morning after having a good night's sleep. The fatigued radar operator fails to see a blip indicating that a small private plane is flying too close to a large passenger jet, and the two collide. However, in a similar situation, the well-rested controller detects a private plane intruding in the air space of a large passenger jet and contacts the small private plane's pilot, who then changes course. Consider also the circumstance of two individuals at a dentist's office. One begins to "feel" pain the instant the drill touches the tooth's surface, the other doesn't "feel" pain until the dentist drills deep into a cavity.

Not only does our *sensitivity* to a stimulus vary over time, but our response *criterion,* our willingness to report that we have detected a stimulus, also complicates matters. For example, we may hear a noise but be unwilling to say that we have, out of fear, concern, politeness, or because that is what we think we are expected to say. Alternately, we may fail to hear a noise but say that we did, for the same reasons. Fortunately, signal detection theory provides a mathematical way to separate out a person's sensitivity to a stimulus from his or her response criterion (how willing he or she is to say "yes").

At this point you should have a basic understanding of sensation and perception, the thresholds of sensory awareness, and signal detection theory. An overview of these ideas is presented in summary table 4.1. Now let's turn to each of the senses, beginning with the sense we know the most about: vision.

SUMMARY TABLE 4.1
Detecting and Perceiving the World

Concept	Processes/ Related Ideas	Characteristics/Description
Defining Sensation and Perception	Their Nature	Sensation is the process of detecting and encoding stimulus energy in the world. Perception is the process of organizing and interpreting sensory information. Most contemporary psychologists refer to sensation and perception as a unified information-processing system.
Thresholds	Absolute Threshold	Psychophysics is the field that studies links between the physical properties of stimuli and a person's experience of them. A basic problem for any sensory system is to detect varying degrees of energy in the environment. One way to cope with this problem is to assume that each of us has an absolute threshold, or minimum amount of energy we can detect.
	Difference Threshold	The difference threshold, or just noticeable difference (jnd), is the smallest difference in stimulation required to discriminate one stimulus from another 50 percent of the time. Weber's law is the principle that two stimuli must differ by a constant minimum percentage (rather than a constant amount) to be perceived as different. Weber's law generally holds true.
Signal Detection Theory	Its Nature	This is the theory that sensitivity to sensory stimuli depends on a variety of factors besides the physical intensity of the stimulus and the sensory abilities of the observer. These factors include individual and contextual variations as well as response criterion.

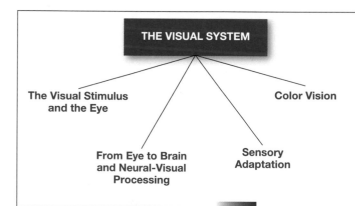

The First Steps of Visual Perception

The Visual System

We see a world of shapes and sizes—some stationary, others moving, some in black and white, others in color. But how? What is the machinery that enables us to experience this marvelous landscape?

The Visual Stimulus and the Eye

To understand our sense of vision, we need to know some basic facts about light, the energy that makes vision possible. **Light** *is a form of electromagnetic energy that can be described in terms of wavelengths.* Waves of light are much like the waves formed when a pebble is tossed into a lake. The **wavelength** *is the distance from the peak of one wave to the peak of the next.* Visible light's wavelengths range from about 400 to 700 nanometers (a nanometer is one-billionth of a meter and is abbreviated nm). The difference between visible light and other forms of electromagnetic energy is its wavelength. Outside the range of visible light are longer radio and infrared radiation waves, and shorter ultraviolet and X rays (see figure 4.2). These other wavelengths continually bombard us, but we do not see them. Why do we see only the narrow band of the electromagnetic spectrum between 400 and 700 nanometers? The most likely answer is that our visual system evolved in the sun's light. Thus, our visual system is able to perceive the spectrum of energy emitted by the sun. By the time sunlight reaches the earth's surface, it is strongest in the 400 to 700 nanometer range.

The purpose of the eye is not unlike that of a camera: to get the best possible "picture" of the world. A good picture is one that is in focus, is not too dark or too light, and has good contrast between the dark and light parts. Each of several

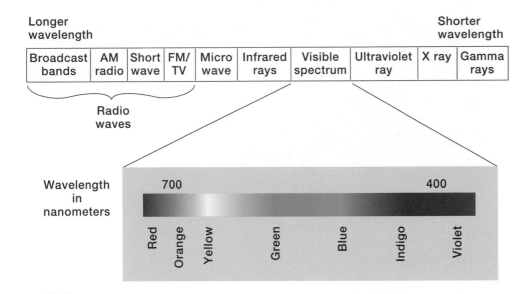

Figure 4.2
The Electromagnetic Spectrum and Visible Light

Visible light is only a narrow band in the electromagnetic spectrum. Visible light wavelengths range from about 400 to 700 nanometers. X rays are much shorter, and radio waves are much longer.

structures in the eye plays an important role in this process. By looking closely at your eyes in the mirror, you notice three parts—the sclera, iris, and pupil (figure 4.3). The **sclera** is the white outer part of the eye that helps to maintain the shape of the eye and to protect it from injury. The **iris** *is the colored part of the eye*, which can range from light blue to dark brown. The **pupil,** *which appears black, is the opening in the center of the iris.* The iris contains muscles that function to control the size of the pupil and, hence, the amount of light that gets into the eye. This allows the eye to function optimally under different conditions of illumination, which can range in the course of a normal day from the darkest of basements to the brightest of summer sunshine. To get a good "picture" of the world, the amount of light that enters the eye needs to be adjustable. In this sense, the pupil acts like the aperture of a camera, opening to let in more light when it is needed and closing to let in less light when there is too much.

You can demonstrate changes in the size of your own pupil by looking at your eyes in the mirror and turning the room lights up and down. (You obviously need to try this in a room with sufficient light to see your eyes even when the lights are turned all the way down.) As you turn down the room light, the pupil will begin to enlarge to let in more light; as you turn the room lights back up, the pupil opening will shrink to let in less light.

If the eye is to act like a camera, in addition to having the right amount of light, the image has to be in focus at the back of the eye. Two structures serve this purpose: the **cornea,** *which is a clear membrane just in front of the eye*, and the **lens of the eye,** *which is a transparent and somewhat flexible ball-like entity filled with a gelatinous material.* The function of both of these structures is to bend the light falling on the surface of the eye just enough to focus it at the back of the eye. The curved surface of the cornea does most of this bending, while the lens "fine-tunes" the focus as needed. When you are looking at far-away objects, the lens has a relatively flat shape. This is because the light reaching the eye from far-away objects is parallel and the bending power of the cornea is sufficient to keep things in focus. The light reaching the eye from objects that are close, however, is more scattered and so more bending of the light is required to achieve focus. This focusing is done by a process called

Seeing, Hearing, and Smelling the World

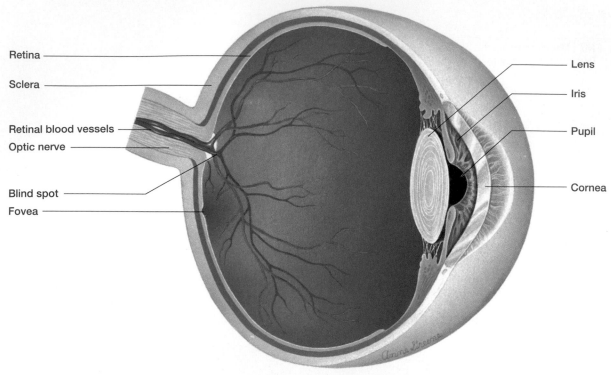

Retina
Sclera
Retinal blood vessels
Optic nerve
Blind spot
Fovea
Lens
Iris
Pupil
Cornea

Figure 4.3
Main Structures of the Eye

Copyright © 1997 The McGraw-Hill Companies, Inc.

accommodation, *in which the lens changes its curvature.* Without this fine-tuning ability, it would be difficult to focus on objects that are close to us, like needlework or reading. As we age, we may develop *presbyopia.* The lens of our eye loses its flexibility and, hence, its ability to change from its normal flattened shape to the rounder shape needed to bring objects into close focus. This is why many people with normal vision throughout their young adult life require reading glasses when they get older.

The parts of the eye that we have discussed so far work together to get the best possible picture of the world. All of this effort, however, would be for naught without a method for keeping or "recording" the images we take of the world. In a camera, film serves just such a purpose. Film is made of a material that responds to light. Likewise, the **retina** *is the light-sensitive surface in the back of the eye that houses light receptors called rods and cones.* Making an analogy between the film of a camera and the retina, however, vastly underestimates the complexity and elegance of the retina's design. Even after decades of intense study, the full marvel of this structure is far from understood.

Because the retina is so important to vision, we need to study its makeup more closely. **Transduction** *involves the conversion of one form of energy into another.* In sensation, this consists of converting stimulus energy into neural impulses. There are two kinds of receptors in the retina—rods and cones—and they turn the electromagnetic energy of light into action potentials that can be processed by the nervous system. **Rods** *are receptors in the retina that are sensitive to light but are not very useful for color vision.* Thus, they function well under low illumination; as you might expect, they are hard at work at night. **Cones** *are the receptors that we use for color perception.* Like the rods, cones are light sensitive. However, they require more light than the rods do to respond, and so they operate best in daylight or under high illumination.

The rods and cones in the retina are receptors that transduce light into neural impulses by means of a photochemical reaction. The breakdown of the chemicals (*rhodopsin* in rods and *iodopsin* in cones) produces a neural impulse that is first trans-

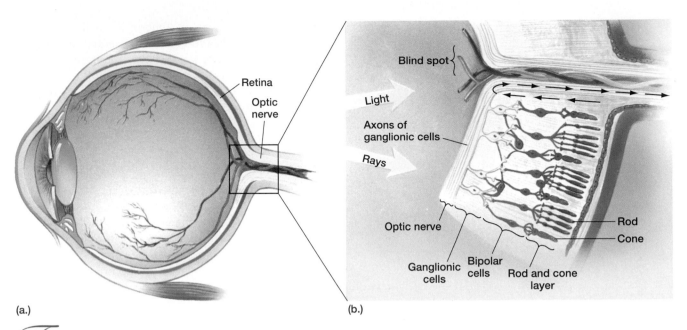

(a.)   (b.)

𝓕igure 4.4
Direction of Light in the Retina

(a) Light passes through the cornea, pupil, and lens. Then it falls on the retina, a light-sensitive surface. *(b)* In the retina, light first triggers a photochemical reaction in the rods and cones. Next, the bipolar cells are activated, which in turn activate the ganglion cells. Then light information is transmitted into the optic nerve, which carries information to the brain. The arrows indicate the sequence in which light information moves in the retina.   Copyright 1997 © The McGraw-Hill Companies, Inc.

mitted to the bipolar cells and then moves down to the ganglion cells (see figure 4.4). The nerve impulse then passes along the axons of the ganglion cells, which make up the optic nerve.

Rods and cones are involved in different aspects of vision and differ both in how they respond to light and in their distribution on the surface of the retina. The most important part of the retina is the **fovea,** *which is a minute area in the center of the retina where vision is at its best.* The fovea is able to resolve much finer detail than any other part of the retina and contains only cones. The fovea is vitally important to many visual tasks (try reading out of the corner of your eye!). By contrast, rods are found on the *periphery* (outer boundary) of the retina around the central fovea. As their name suggests, rods are long and cylindrical. Since they require little light to respond, they work best under conditions of low illumination. Because of this light sensitivity and the rods' location on the retina, we are able to detect fainter spots of light on the peripheral retina than at the fovea. It has been known for centuries that if you want to see a very faint star, you should gaze slightly to the right or left of the star.

Finally, there is one place on the retina that contains neither rods nor cones. Not surprisingly, this area is called the **blind spot;** *it is the place on the retina where the optic nerve leaves the eye on its way to the brain* (see figure 4.4(b)). We cannot see anything that reaches only this part of the retina. To experience your blind spot, see figure 4.5.

𝓕igure 4.5
The Eye's Blind Spot

There is a normal blind spot in your eye, a small area where the optic nerve leads to the brain. To find your blind spot, hold this book at arm's length, cover your left eye, and stare at the red pepper on the left with your right eye. Move the book slowly toward you until the yellow pepper disappears. To find the blind spot in your left eye, cover your right eye, concentrate on the yellow pepper, and adjust the book until the red pepper disappears.

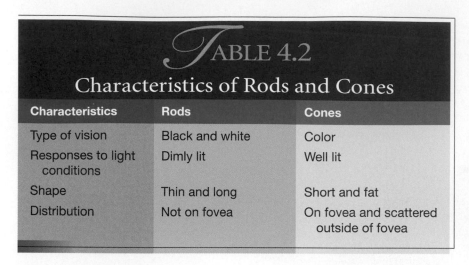

TABLE 4.2

Characteristics of Rods and Cones

Characteristics	Rods	Cones
Type of vision	Black and white	Color
Responses to light conditions	Dimly lit	Well lit
Shape	Thin and long	Short and fat
Distribution	Not on fovea	On fovea and scattered outside of fovea

A summary of some of the main characteristics of rods and cones is presented in table 4.2. So far we have studied the importance of light and structures of the eyes. The journey of vision now leads us to the brain and how it processes visual information.

From Eye to Brain and Neural-Visual Processing

The optic nerve leads out of the eye toward the brain carrying information about light. Stimuli in the left visual field are registered in the right half of the retina in both eyes, and stimuli in the right visual field were registered in the left half of the retina in both eyes. At the point called the *optic chiasm* the optic nerve fibers divide, and approximately half of the nerve fibers cross over the midline of the brain. The visual information originating in the right halves of the two retinae is then transmitted to the left side of the occipital lobe in the back of the brain; the visual information originating in the left halves of the retinae is transmitted to the right side of the occipital lobe ◀⃤ P. 84. What all of these crossings mean is that what we see in the left side of our visual field ends up in the right side of our brain, and what we see in the right visual field ends up in the left side of our brain (see figure 4.6).

The visual cortex in the occipital lobe combines information from both eyes and is responsible for higher levels of visual processing (Farah, 1999). **Feature detectors** *are neurons in the brain's visual system that respond to particular lines or other features of a stimulus* ◀⃤ P. 72. Canadian David Hubel and Swede Torsten Wiesel (1965) won a Nobel Prize for their research on feature detectors. By recording the activity of a *single* neuron in a cat while it looked at patterns that varied in size, shape, color, and movement, they found that the visual cortex has neurons that are individually sensitive to different types of lines and angles. For example, one neuron might show a sudden burst of activity when stimulated by lines of a particular angle; another neuron might fire only when moving stimuli appear; yet another neuron might be stimulated when the object in the visual field has a combination of certain angles, sizes, and shapes. Figure 4.7 illustrates Hubel and Wiesel's research on feature detectors in monkeys.

Hubel and Wiesel's discovery led to a revolutionary idea. While we are perceiving a unified scene, the brain is dissecting the view into many parts, each of which triggers a different set of neurons. One set of neurons responds to color and form, another only to motion. The challenge today is figuring out how the brain, once it has broken the sensory landscape into pieces, stitches them back together again (Milner & Goodale, 1995; Brownlee, 1997; Mountcastle, 1998).

Sensory Adaptation

Turning out the lights in your bedroom at night, you stumble across the room to your bed, completely blind to the objects around you. Gradually you *dark adapt,* as the objects in your room reappear and become more and more clear. The ability of the visual system to dark adapt is an example of the principle of **sensory adaptation**—*a change in the responsiveness of the sensory system based on the average level of surrounding stimulation.* You have experienced sensory adaptation countless times in your life—adapting to the temperature of a shower, to the water in an initially "freezing" swimming pool, or to the smell of the Thanksgiving dinner that is wonderful to the arriving guests but almost undetectable to the cook who slaved over it all day. These are examples of sensory adaptation. While all senses adapt to prolonged stimulation, we will take up this topic using vision as an example since you have just learned about the mechanisms involved in adapting to light.

Let's return to our example of adapting to the dark. When you turn out the lights, everything is black. Conversely, when you step out into the bright sunshine after spending some time in a dark basement, your eyes are flooded with light, everything appears too light, and you must *light adapt*. When we talked about the purpose of the eye, we said that the eye needs to get a good picture of the world. Good pictures have sharp contrasts between dark and light parts. We have already seen that the pupil serves an important function in adjusting the amount of light that gets into the eye and therefore helping to preserve the contrast between dark and light in our picture. Additionally, structures throughout the visual system also adapt. You might have noticed that the change in the size of the pupil as you dim or brighten the lights happens very quickly. You also might have noticed that when you turn out the lights in your bedroom, the contrast between dark and light continues to improve for nearly 20 minutes. This is because both the rods and the cones in the visual system adapt or adjust their response rates on the basis of the average light level of the surrounding room. This adaptation takes longer than the pupil adjustment. All of these mechanisms allow the visual system to preserve the contrast in the images it takes of the world over an extremely large range of background illumination conditions. We do, however, pay for our ability to adapt to the average level of light in our environment. It takes precious *time* to adapt, say when driving out of a dark tunnel under a mountain into the glistening and blinding reflection of the sun off the snow.

Color Vision

We spend a lot of time thinking about color—the color of the car we want to buy, the color we are going to paint the walls of our room, the color of the clothes we wear. We can change our hair color or even the color of our eyes to make us look more attractive.

What Is Color?   The human eye registers light wavelengths between 400 and 700 nm, which we see as different colors of light. This is what was shown in figure 4.2. However, lightwaves themselves have no color. The sensations of color reside in the visual system of the observer. So, if we talk about red light, we refer to the wavelengths of light that evoke the sensation of red. Objects appear a certain color to us because they reflect specific wavelengths of light to our eyes. These wavelengths are split apart into a spectrum of colors when the light passes through a prism, as in the formation of a rainbow. We can remember the colors of the light spectrum by thinking of an imaginary man named ROY G. BIV, for the colors red, orange, yellow, green, blue, indigo, and violet.

If you go into a paint store and ask for some red paint, the salesperson will probably ask you what kind of paint you want—such as dark or light, pinkish or more crimson, pastel or deep, and so on. These variations in the shade of red are due to differences in their hue, saturation, and brightness.

A color's **hue** *is based on its wavelength*. As shown in figure 4.2, the longest wavelengths seen by the human eye (about 700 nm) appear as red, the shortest (about 400 nm) appear as violet. A color's **saturation** *is based on its purity*. The purity of a color is determined by the amount of white light added to a single wavelength of color. The color tree shown in figure 4.8 can help us understand saturation. Colors that are very pure have no white light. They are located outside of the color tree. As we move toward the color tree's interior, notice how the saturation of color changes. The closer we get to the

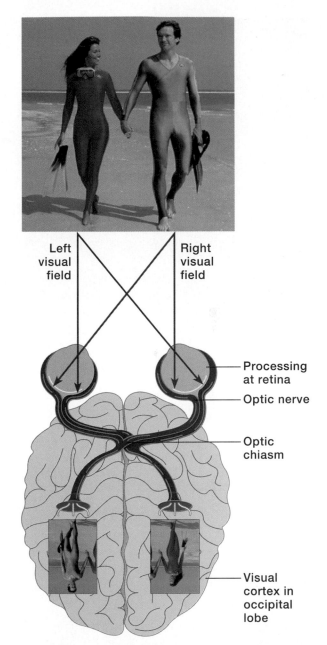

Left visual field   Right visual field

Processing at retina

Optic nerve

Optic chiasm

Visual cortex in occipital lobe

𝓕igure 4.6
Visual Pathways to and Through the Brain

Light from each side of the visual field falls on the opposite side of each eye's retina. Visual information then travels along the optic nerve to the optic chiasm, where most of the visual information crosses over to the other side of the brain. From there visual information goes to the occipital lobe at the rear of the brain. What all of the crossings mean is that what we see in the left side of our visual field (in this figure, the woman) ends up in the right side of our brain, and what we see in the right visual field (the man) ends up in the left side of our brain.

𝓕igure 4.7
Hubel and Wiesel's Research on Visual Information Processing

This photograph shows an electrode inserted into a monkey's neuron at a location in the visual system. Various light stimuli are projected onto a screen in front of the animal's eyes.

tree's center, the more white light has been added to the single wavelength of a particular color. That is, the deep colors at the edge fade into the more pastel colors toward the center. When saturation is added to hue, we see a much larger range of colors—pink and crimson as well as basic red, for example. However, another dimension is also involved in color—brightness. A color's **brightness** *is based on its intensity*. White has the most brightness, black the least.

Theories of Color Vision   The study of human color vision using psychological methods is well-developed (Kaiser & Boynton, 1996). A century before it was possible to study the anatomical and neurophysiological basis of color perception, psychological studies had discovered many of the basic principles of our color vision. These studies resulted in two main theories, each of which turned out to be correct.

The first color vision theory we discuss is based upon the fact that there are actually three different types of cone (red, green, and blue), each relying upon an iodopsin that best absorbs a different wavelength of visible light. The **trichromatic theory** *states that color perception is based on the existence of three types of receptors that are maximally sensitive to different, but overlapping, ranges of wavelengths*. The trichromatic theory of color vision was proposed by Thomas Young in 1802 and extended by Hermann von Helmholtz in 1852. The theory is based on the results of experiments on human color-matching abilities. These experiments show that a person with normal vision can match any color in the spectrum by combining three other wavelengths. In this type of experiment, individuals are given a light of a single wavelength and are asked to combine three other single-wavelength lights to match the first light. They can do this by changing the relative intensities of the three lights until the color of the combination light is indistinguishable from the color of the first light. Young and Helmholtz reasoned that if the combination of any three wavelengths in different intensities is indistinguishable from any single pure wavelength, the visual system must be basing its perception of color on the relative responses of three receptor systems.

Further support for the trichromatic theory is found in the study of color blindness (see figure 4.9). The term *color blind* is somewhat misleading. Complete color blindness is rare, involving 1 in 300,000 people (Coren, Ward & Enns, 1999), and means that all three kinds of cone are not functioning in that person. In contrast, *color deficient* people, who can see some colors but not others, are either monochromats or dichromats. **Monochromats** *are people with only one kind of cone*. **Dichromats** *are people with only two kinds of cones*. The nature of color deficiency depends

𝓕igure 4.8
A Color Tree Showing Color's Three Dimensions: Hue, Saturation, and Brightness

Hue is represented around the color tree, saturation horizontally, and brightness vertically.

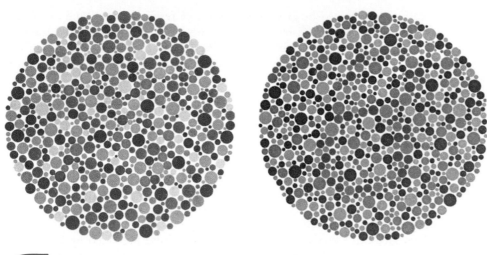

**igure 4.9**

Examples of Stimuli Used to Test for Color Blindness

In the left circle, people with normal vision see the number 16, but people with red-green color blindness do not. In the right circle, people with normal vision detect the number 8, but those with red-green color blindness see one number or none. A complete color blindness assessment involves the use of fifteen stimuli.

The above has been reproduced from Ishihara's Tests for Colour Blindness published by Kanehara & Co., Ltd., Tokyo, Japan, but tests for color blindness cannot be conducted with this material. For accurate testing, the original plates should be used.

on which of the three kinds of cones is inoperative. Recall that the three different cone systems are red, green, and blue. For example, in the most common form of color blindness, the green cone system malfunctions in some way. Green is indistinguishable from certain combinations of blue and red. Interestingly, the vast majority of people suffering from color blindness or color deficiency are men. And, of course, **trichromats** *are people with normal color vision, having all three kinds of cone receptors.*

The German physiologist Ewald Hering was not completely satisfied with the trichromatic theory of color vision. Hering observed that some colors cannot exist together whereas others can. For example, it is easy to imagine a greenish-blue or a reddish-yellow, but nearly impossible to imagine a reddish-green or a bluish-yellow. Hering also observed that trichromatic theory could not adequately explain **afterimages,** *sensations that remain after a stimulus is removed.* See figure 4.10 to experience an afterimage. Color afterimages are common and they involve complementary colors. Such information led Hering to propose that the visual system treats colors as *opponent pairs:* red-green and blue-yellow. Further, Hering proposed that the visual system must include two types of color-sensitive

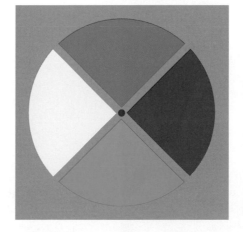

igure 4.10

Negative Afterimage—Complementary Colors

If you gaze steadily at the dot in the colored panel on the left for a few moments, then shift your gaze to the gray box on the right, you will see the original hues change into their complementary colors. The blue appears as yellow, the red as green, the green as red, and the yellow as blue. This pairing of colors has to do with the fact that color receptors in the eye are apparently sensitive as pairs; when one color is turned off (when you stop staring at the panel), the other color in the receptor is briefly "turned on." The afterimage effect is especially noticeable when you spend time painting walls or objects in bright colors.

cells; one responding to red or green and the other responding to blue or yellow. Each cell responds in opposite fashion to its two opponent colors. Consider the red-green cell, for example. It will increase its response rate when red is shown but decrease it when green is shown. When both colors are presented, the cell cannot respond in both ways at once and so a whitish color is seen.

Hering's view is called **opponent-process theory,** *which states that cells in the visual system respond to red-green and blue-yellow colors; a given cell might be excited by red and inhibited by green, while another cell might be excited by yellow and inhibited by blue.* Researchers have found that opponent-process theory does explain afterimages (Hurvich & Jameson, 1969; Jameson & Hurvich, 1989). If you stare at red, for instance, your red-green system seems to "tire," and when you look away, it rebounds and gives you a green afterimage. Also, if you mix equal amounts of opponent colors, such as blue and yellow, you see gray; figure 4.11 illustrates this principle.

We have seen that the trichromatic theory of color perception is correct in that we do in fact have three kinds of cone receptors like those predicted by Young and Helmholtz. Then how can the opponent-process theory also be correct? The answer is that the red, blue, and green cones in the retina are connected to retinal ganglion cells in such a way that the three-color code is immediately translated into the opponent-process code (see figure 4.12). For example, a green cone might inhibit and a red cone might excite a particular ganglion cell. Thus, *both* the trichromatic and opponent-process theory are correct—the eye and the brain use both methods to code colors.

Our discussion of theories of color vision illustrates an important feature of psychology that we described in chapter 1. Science often progresses when conflicting

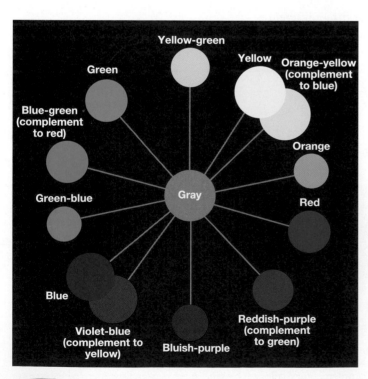

*F*igure 4.11
Color Wheel

Colors opposite each other produce the neutral gray in the center when they are mixed. For instance, blue-green is the complement of red.

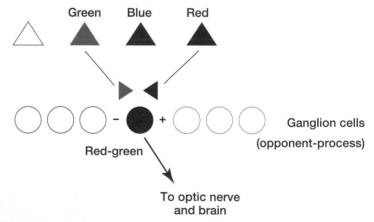

*F*igure 4.12
Trichromatic and Opponent-Process Theories: Transmission of Color Information in the Retina

Cones responsive to green, blue, or red light form a trichromatic receptor system in the retina. As information is transmitted to the retina's ganglion cells, opponent-process cells are activated. As shown here, a retinal ganglion cell is inhibited by a green cone (−) and excited by a red cone (+), producing red-green color information.

Summary Table 4.2
The Visual System

Concept	Processes/ Related Ideas	Characteristics/Description
The Visual Stimulus and the Eye	Their Nature	Light is a form of electromagnetic energy that can be described in terms of wavelengths. The wavelength is the distance from the peak of one wave of light to the next. The receptors in the human eye are sensitive to wavelengths from 400 to 700 nm. Key parts of the eye are the sclera, iris, pupil, and cornea. The lens and the cornea bend the light falling on the surface of the eye just enough to focus it on the back of the eye. The retina is the light-sensitive surface in the back of the eye, consisting of light receptors called rods (which function well under low illumination), cones (which function in color vision), and different neurons.
From Eye to Brain and Neural-Visual Processing	The Nature of Transmission	The optic nerve transmits neural impulses to the brain. Because of crossovers of nerve fibers, what we see in the left visual field is registered in the right side of the brain and vice versa. Visual information reaches the occipital lobe of the brain, where it is further integrated. Hubel and Wiesel discovered that neurons in the visual cortex can detect features of our visual world such as line, angle, and size.
Sensory Adaptation	Its Nature	Sensory adaptation involves weakened sensory response after prolonged stimulation.
Color Vision	What Is Color?	Objects appear in color because they reflect certain wavelengths of light between 400 and 700 nm. Important properties of color are hue (based on wavelength content), saturation (based on purity), and brightness (based on intensity).
	Theories of Color Vision	Scientists have found support for two theories. The trichromatic theory states that color perception is based on the existence of three types of receptors, which are maximally sensitive to different, but overlapping, ranges of wavelengths. This theory is also called the Young-Helmholtz theory and emphasizes the colors of red, green, and blue. The trichromatic theory explains color blindness but not afterimages. The opponent-process theory does explain afterimages. The opponent-process theory, developed by Hering, states that cells in the visual system respond to red-green and blue-yellow colors. Researchers have found that the red, blue, and green cones are connected to the retinal ganglion cells in such a way that the three-color code is translated into the opponent-process code. Thus, both theories are right—the eye and the brain use both methods to code colors.

ideas are posed and investigated. In many instances, as with color vision, a compromise solution may work best.

Our tour of the visual system has been extensive—you have read about the light spectrum, the structures of the eye, neural-visual processing, and the marvels of color vision. To help you remember the main themes of the visual system, see summary table 4.2. Next you will study the second most researched sensory system—hearing.

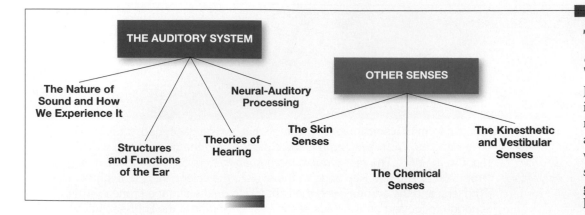

The Auditory System

Just as light provides us with information about the environment, so does sound. Think about what life would be like without music, the rushing sound of ocean waves, or the gentle voice of someone you love. Sounds in the world tell us about the approach of a person behind us, an approaching car, the force of the wind outside, the mischief of a 2-year-old, and, perhaps most importantly, the kinds of information that we transmit through language and song (Bregman, 1990).

Auditory Perception

Sound Waves

The Nature of Sound and How We Experience It

At a rock concert you may have felt the throbbing pulse of loud sounds or sensed the air vibrations around you. Bass instruments are especially effective at creating mechanical pulsations. When a bass is played loudly we can sense air molecules being pushed forward in waves from the speaker. **Sounds,** *or sound waves, are vibrations in the air that are processed by our auditory (or hearing) system.*

Remember that we described light waves as being much like the waves fanned when a pebble is tossed into a lake, with concentric circles moving outward from where the pebble entered the water. Sound waves are similar. They vary in wavelength, which determines the **frequency** *of the sound wave or the number of cycles (or full wavelengths) that pass through a point in a given time* (see figure 4.13). Frequency is measured in *Hertz (Hz), sometimes also called cps (cycles per second).* **Pitch** *is the perceptual interpretation of the frequency of sound.* High-frequency sounds are perceived as having a high pitch, low-frequency sounds are perceived as having a low pitch. A soprano voice sounds high-pitched, a bass voice sounds low-pitched. As in the case of vision, human sensitivity is limited to a range of sound frequencies: about 20–20,000 Hz (Coren, Ward & Enns, 1999). In contrast, dogs can hear higher frequencies than humans.

Sound waves vary not only in frequency but also in amplitude. The sound wave's **amplitude** *is measured in decibels (dB), the amount of pressure produced by a sound wave relative to a standard;* the typical standard is the weakest sound the human ear can detect. Thus, zero decibels would be the softest noise detectable by humans.

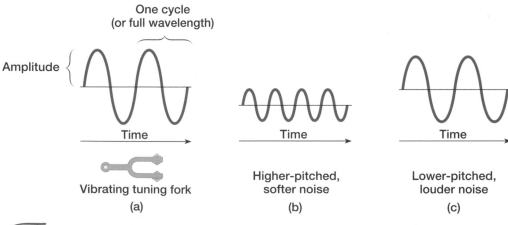

ℱigure 4.13
Frequency and Amplitude of Sound Waves

(a) A tuning fork is an instrument with two prongs that produces a tone when struck. You may have seen one in a music classroom or science laboratory. The vibrations of the tuning fork cause air molecules to vibrate like a musical instrument, producing a sound-wave pattern like the one shown. *(b)* Wavelength determines the frequency of the sound wave, which is the number of cycles, or full wavelengths, that can pass through a point in a given time. In the tuning fork example, two cycles (full wavelengths) have occurred in the time frame shown. In the sound waves shown here, four cycles have occurred in this time frame, so this sound wave has a higher frequency than the sound wave with the tuning fork; hence, it has a higher pitch. *(c)* The amplitude of the sound wave is the change in pressure created by the sound wave and is reflected in the sound wave's height. This sound wave has a smaller amplitude than the sound wave shown with the tuning fork; thus, it does not sound as loud.

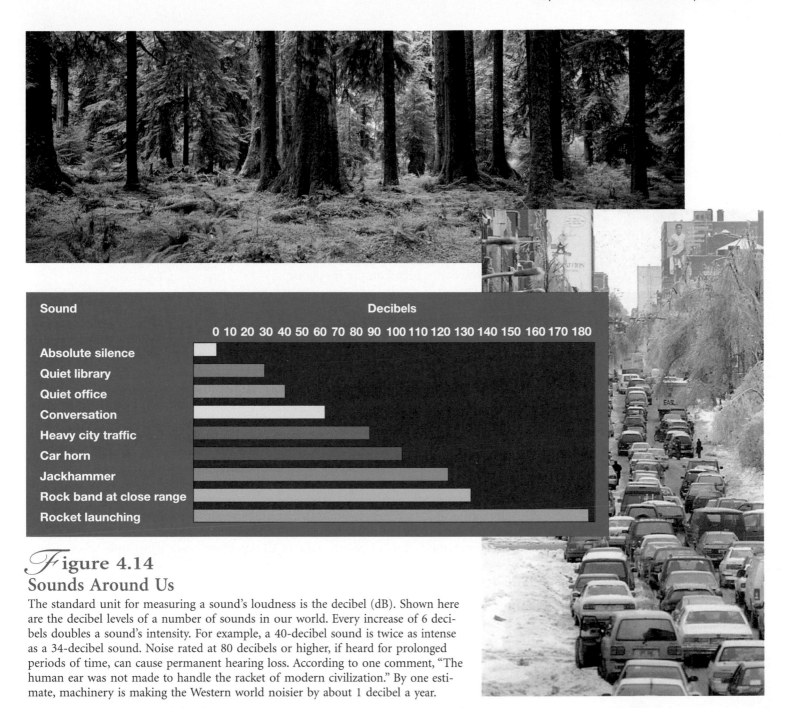

Sound	Decibels
	0 10 20 30 40 50 60 70 80 90 100 110 120 130 140 150 160 170 180
Absolute silence	
Quiet library	
Quiet office	
Conversation	
Heavy city traffic	
Car horn	
Jackhammer	
Rock band at close range	
Rocket launching	

ℱigure 4.14
Sounds Around Us

The standard unit for measuring a sound's loudness is the decibel (dB). Shown here are the decibel levels of a number of sounds in our world. Every increase of 6 decibels doubles a sound's intensity. For example, a 40-decibel sound is twice as intense as a 34-decibel sound. Noise rated at 80 decibels or higher, if heard for prolonged periods of time, can cause permanent hearing loss. According to one comment, "The human ear was not made to handle the racket of modern civilization." By one estimate, machinery is making the Western world noisier by about 1 decibel a year.

Noise rated at 80 decibels or higher, if heard for prolonged periods of time, can cause permanent hearing loss. A quiet library is about 30 decibels, a car horn about 90 decibels, a rock band at close range 130 decibels, and a rocket launching 180 decibels. Noise levels have risen in recent years (Staples, 1996).The decibel levels of various sounds are shown in figure 4.14. **Loudness** *is the perception of a sound wave's amplitude.* In general, the higher the amplitude of the sound wave, the louder the sound is perceived to be. In the world of amplitude, this means that air is moving more vigorously for loud sounds and less vigorously for soft sounds.

So far we have been describing a single sound wave with just one frequency. This is similar to the single wavelength or pure colored light we just discussed in the context of color matching. Most sounds, however, including those of speech and music, are complex sounds. **Complex sounds** *are those in which numerous frequencies of sound blend together.* **Timbre** *is the tone color or perceptual quality of a sound.* Timbre

Auditory Perception Demonstrations

differences are what make the difference between a trumpet and a trombone playing the same note. Further, complex sounds themselves combine to produce more complex sequences, such as musical melodies (Cuddy, 1993).

Structures and Functions of the Ear

What happens to sound waves once they reach your ear? How do various structures of the ear transform sound waves of expanded and compressed air so they can be understood by the brain as sound? The function of the ear is analogous to the function of the eye. The ear serves the purpose of transducing and transmitting a high-fidelity version of sounds to the brain for analysis and interpretation. Just as an image needs to be in focus and sufficiently bright for the brain to interpret it, a sound needs to be transmitted in a way that preserves information about its location: its frequency, which helps us distinguish the voice of a child from that of an adult; its amplitude, which helps us tell how loud a sound is; and its timbre, which allows us to identify the voice of a friend on the telephone.

The ear is divided into the *outer ear, middle ear,* and *inner ear* (the major structures of the ear are shown in figure 4.15). The **outer ear** *consists of the pinna and the external auditory canal.* The pinna is the outer visible part of the ear (elephants have very large ones). Its shape helps us to localize sounds by making the sound different in front of us than behind us. The pinnae of many animals such as dogs are movable and serve a more important role in sound localization than do the pinnae of humans. Dogs will prick up their ears toward the direction of a faint and interesting sound.

After passing the pinna, sound waves are then funneled through the external auditory canal to the middle ear. The **middle ear** *has four main parts: eardrum (tympanic membrane), hammer (malleus), anvil (incus), and stirrup (stapes).* The eardrum is the first structure that sound touches in the middle ear. The eardrum is a membrane that vibrates in response to a sound. The vibrations are then transmitted to the three smallest bones in the human body—the hammer, anvil, and stirrup. The middle ear bones translate the sound waves in air into sound waves in fluid (lymph) so they can be processed further in the inner ear. Most of us know that sound travels far more easily in air than in fluid. When we are swimming underwater, loud shouts from the side of the pool are barely detectable to us. Sound waves entering the ear travel in air until they reach the inner ear, at which point they will begin to be transmitted through body fluids. At this border between air and fluid, sounds meet the same kind of resistance that shouts directed at an underwater swimmer meet when they hit the surface of the water. The hammer, anvil, and stirrup act like a lever to amplify the sound waves before they reach the liquid-filled inner ear.

The main parts of the **inner ear** *are the oval window, cochlea, and the organ of Corti.* The stirrup is connected to the oval window, which is a membrane like the eardrum and transmits the waves to the cochlea. The **cochlea** *is a long tubular fluid-filled structure that is coiled up like a snail.* The **basilar membrane** *is housed inside the cochlea and runs its entire length.* The **organ of Corti,** *also running the length of the cochlea, sits on the basilar membrane and contains the ear's sensory receptors, which change the energy of the sound waves into nerve impulses that can be processed by the brain.* Hairlike sensory receptors in the organ of Corti are stimulated by vibrations of the basilar membrane. Sound waves traveling in the fluid of the inner ear cause these hairlike receptors to move. This movement generates nerve impulses, which vary with the frequency and extent of the membrane's vibrations. These nerve impulses, sent via the auditory nerve, are interpreted as sound by the brain.

Theories of Hearing

One of the auditory system's mysteries is how the inner ear registers the frequency of sound (Warren, 1999). Two theories have been proposed to explain this mystery: place theory and frequency theory. **Place theory** *is a theory of hearing which states*

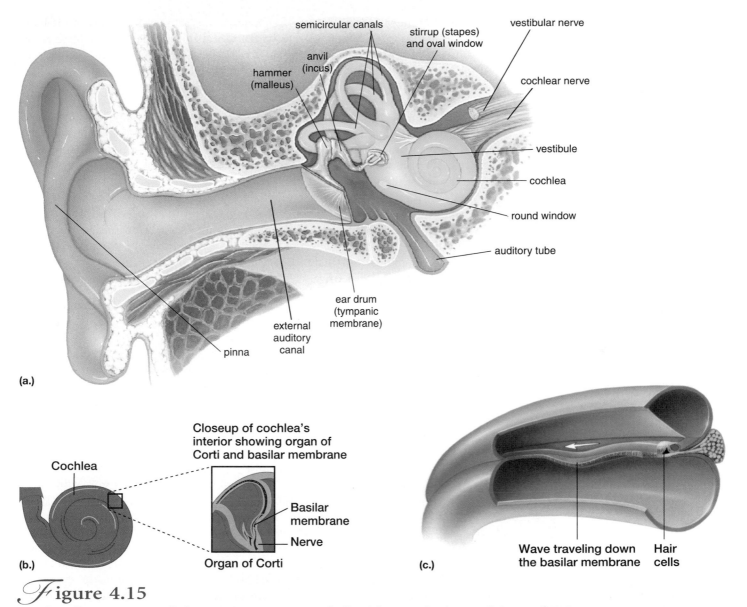

(a.)

(b.)   Cochlea   Closeup of cochlea's interior showing organ of Corti and basilar membrane   Basilar membrane — Nerve   Organ of Corti

(c.)   Wave traveling down the basilar membrane   Hair cells

ℱigure 4.15
Major Structures of the Human Ear and the Transmission of Sound Waves

(a) The main structures of the external, middle, and inner ear. *(b)* This closeup of the cochlea's interior shows the organ of Corti and the basilar membrane. *(c)* This enlarged drawing was made by unwinding the snail-like structure of the cochlea and cutting it open. The sound wave is shown traveling down the membrane and stimulating hair cells.

that each frequency produces vibrations at a particular location on the basilar membrane. Georg von Békésy won a Nobel Prize in 1961 for his research on the basilar membrane. Von Békésy (1960) studied the effects of vibration applied at the oval window on the basilar membrane of human cadavers. Through a microscope, he saw that this stimulation produced a traveling wave on the basilar membrane. A traveling wave is like the ripples that appear in a pond when you throw in a stone. However, since the cochlea is a long tube, the ripples can travel in only one direction, from the end of the cochlea where the oval window is placed to the far tip of the cochlea. High-frequency vibrations create traveling waves that maximally displace (or move) the area of the basilar membrane next to the oval window; low-frequency vibrations maximally displace areas of the membrane closer to the tip of the cochlea.

Place theory adequately explains high-frequency sounds but fares poorly with low-frequency sounds. A high-frequency sound stimulates a very precise area on the basilar membrane. By contrast, a low-frequency sound causes a large part of the basilar membrane to be displaced, so it is hard to localize the "maximal displacement" of the basilar membrane. Because humans can hear low-frequency sounds better than can be predicted by looking at the precision of the basilar membrane's response to these sounds, some other factors must be involved. **Frequency theory** *states that the perception of a sound's frequency is due to how often the auditory nerve fires.* Higher-frequency sounds cause the auditory nerve to fire more often than do lower-frequency sounds. One problem with frequency theory is that a single neuron has a maximum firing rate of about 1,000 times per second. Because of this limitation, frequency theory cannot be applied to tones with frequencies that would require a neuron to fire more than 1,000 times per second.

To deal with this limitation, a modification of place theory called the **volley principle** *states that neural cells can fire neural impulses in rapid succession, producing a volley of impulses.* This alternate rapid neural firing attains a combined frequency above 1,000 times a second. Thus, frequency theory better explains the perception of low-frequency sounds and place theory provides a better explanation of high-frequency sounds. Both theories may be correct with sounds of low and high frequencies signaled with different neural coding schemes.

Neural-Auditory Processing

As we saw in the visual system, once energy from the environment is picked up by our receptors, it must be transmitted to the brain for processing and interpretation. An image on the retina does not a Picasso make—likewise, a pattern of receptor responses in the cochlea does not a symphony make! In the retina, we saw that the responses of the rod and cone receptors feed into ganglion cells in the retina and leave the eye via the optic nerve. In the auditory system, the **auditory nerve** *carries neural impulses to the brain's auditory areas* ◀⫘ P. 84. Auditory information moves up the auditory pathway in a more complex manner than does visual information in the visual pathway. Many synapses occur in the ascending auditory pathway, with some fibers crossing over the midline and others proceeding directly to the hemisphere on the same side as the ear of reception. The auditory nerve extends from the cochlea to the brain stem, with some fibers crossing over the midline. The cortical destination of most of these fibers is the temporal lobes of the brain (beneath the temples of the head).

Now that we have described the visual and auditory systems in some detail, we turn to a number of other sensory systems—the skin senses, the chemical senses (smell and taste), and the kinesthetic and vestibular senses. As you can tell, we have more than the traditional five senses of sight, hearing, taste, touch, and smell.

Other Senses

In addition to our visual and auditory senses, we also have other senses that detect information in the environment. They include the skin senses, the chemical senses, and the kinesthetic and vestibular senses.

The Skin Senses

We know when a friend has a fever by putting our hand to her head; we know how to find our way to the light switch in a darkened room by groping along the wall; and we know whether or not a pair of shoes is too tight by the way the shoes touch different parts of our feet when we walk. Many of us think of our skin as a canvas rather than a sense. We color it with cosmetics, dyes, and tatoos. But the skin is our largest sensory system, draped over the body with receptors for touch, temperature, and pain. These three kinds of receptors form the cutaneous senses. A large variety of important information comes to us through our ability to detect touch.

Touch   Touch is a sense we often take for granted. As we saw in the earlier discussion on detection, our ability to respond to touch is astounding. Raising a single hair on your forearm with the sharp point of a pencil should convince you of this. What do we detect when we feel "touch"? What kind of energy does our sense of touch pick up from our external environment? In vision, we detect electromagnetic energy or light. In audition, we detect the vibrations of air or soundwaves pressing against our eardrum. In touch, we detect mechanical energy, or pressure against the skin. The lifting of a single hair causes pressure on the skin around the shaft of hair. This tiny bit of mechanical pressure at the base of the hair is sufficient for us to detect the "touch" of the pencil point! More commonly, we detect the mechanical energy of the pressure of a car seat against our buttocks, or the pressure of a pencil in our hands. Is this kind of energy so different than the kind of energy we detect in vision or audition? Sometimes the only difference is one of intensity—the sound of a rock band playing softly is auditory stimulus, but at the high volumes that make a concert hall reverberate, such an auditory stimulus is *felt* as mechanical energy pressing against your skin.

Just as our visual system is more sensitive to images on the fovea than to images in the peripheral retina, our sensitivity to touch is not equally good across all areas of the skin. As you might expect, human toolmakers need to have excellent touch discrimination in their hands, but much less touch discrimination in other parts of the body such as the torso or legs. This amounts to having more space in the brain to analyze touch signals coming from the hands than from the legs (Penfield & Rasmussen, 1950; see figure 3.18).

Temperature   Beyond the need to sense physical pressure on the skin, we need to detect temperature, even in the absence of direct contact with the skin. **Thermoreceptors,** which are located under the skin, respond to increases and decreases in temperature. Thermoreceptors not only serve a general function of sensing temperature changes at or near our skin, but also provide input to keep our body's temperature regulation at 98.6 degrees Fahrenheit. Thermoreceptors come in two types: warm and cold (warm thermoreceptors respond to the warming of the skin, and cold thermoreceptors respond to the cooling of the skin).

Pain

Pain   When skin contact takes the form of a sharp pinch, our sensation of mechanical pressure changes from touch to pain. When a pot handle is so hot that it burns your hand, your sensation of temperature becomes one of pain. Many kinds of stimuli can cause pain. Intense stimulation of any sense can produce pain—too much light, very loud sounds, very spicy food, for example. Our ability to sense pain is vital for our survival as a species. **Pain** *is the sensation that warns us that damage to our bodies is occurring*. It functions as a quick-acting system that tells the motor systems of the brain that they must minimize or eliminate this damage. A hand touching a hot stove must be pulled away; ears should be covered up when one walks by a loud pavement drill; chili should be buffered with some crackers.

Pain receptors are dispersed widely throughout the body (Beatty, 1995). Although all pain receptors are anatomically similar, they differ in the type of physical stimuli to which they best respond. Mechanical pain receptors respond mainly to pressure, such as when a sharp object is encountered. Heat pain receptors respond primarily to strong heat that is capable of burning tissue. Other pain receptors have a mixed function, responding to both types of painful stimuli. Many pain receptors are chemically sensitive, responding to a range of pain-producing substances.

While we have seen that sensations are affected by factors such as motivation and expectation, the sensation of pain is especially susceptible to these factors (Philips & Rachman, 1996). Cultural and ethnic contexts, also, can greatly determine the degree to which an individual experiences pain (Rollman, 1998). For example, one pain researcher described a ritual performed in India in which a chosen person travels from town to town delivering blessings to the children and the crops while suspended from metal hooks embedded in his back (Melzak, 1973). The chosen person apparently re-

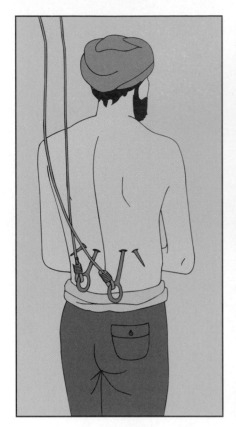

$\mathscr{F}$igure 4.16
Hook-Swinging Ceremony

(Left) Two steel hooks are shown hanging from the back of an Asian Indian participating in a hook-swinging ceremony. *(Right)* The man hangs onto ropes as a cart takes him from village to village. After he blesses each child and farm field in the village, he swings freely, suspended by the hooks in his back (after Kosambi, 1967).

Taste and Smell

ports no sensation of pain and appears to be in ecstasy (see figure 4.16).

An influential theory of pain perception that offers insight into how cognitive and emotional factors might exert such dramatic influences on the experience of pain was developed by McGill psychologists Ronald Melzack and Patricia Wall (1965, 1988). They proposed the **gate-control theory,** *which states that the spinal column contains a neural gate that can be opened (allowing perception of pain) or closed (blocking perception of pain).* In this account, the brain can send signals downward to the dorsal horns of the spinal cord to close the gate, and hence suppress the sensation of pain (see figure 4.17). Gate-control theory has been proposed as an explanation for the effects of **acupuncture,** *a technique in which thin needles are inserted at specific points in the body to produce various effects such as local anesthesia* (figure 4.18). Gate-control theory of pain assumes that the presence of acupuncture needles somehow manages to shut the pain gate, inhibiting the experience of pain. Gate-control theory may also explain the fact that gentle pressure on the skin, such as lightly rubbing the skin, seems to inhibit the pain signal. The theory does not, however, explain *phantom limb pain,* felt by an amputee in the area of the missing limb, and has recently been revised to do so (Melzack, 1993).

The Chemical Senses

We've seen that the information impinging on our senses comes in many diverse forms: electromagnetic energy in vision, soundwaves in audition, and mechanical pressure and temperature in the cutaneous senses. The last two senses we will study are responsible for processing chemicals in our environment. With taste we detect chemicals that have been dissolved in saliva and with the sense of smell we detect airborne chemicals. Taste and smell are frequently stimulated simultaneously. We sometimes only realize the strong links between the two senses when a nasty cold and nasal congestion seem to take the pleasure out of eating. Our favorite foods become "tasteless" without the smells that characterize them. Despite this link, we will see that our senses of taste and smell have lives and functions all their own.

Taste   What would life be with no sense of taste? For anyone who has tried to diet, "not worth living" is an all-too-often way of responding. The thought of giving up a favorite taste, such as chocolate or butter, can be a very depressing thought. We use our sense of taste to select food and to regulate food intake. While it is not so easy to see or smell mold on a blueberry, a small taste is enough to prompt you to sense that the fruit is no longer fit for consumption. Beyond that, the pleasure associated with the taste of food depends on many aspects of our body's need for a particular food (Bartoshuk & Beauchamp, 1994). The taste of devil's food cake can be very pleasurable when we are hungry yet almost revolting after eating a banana split.

It is not the prettiest sight you've ever seen, but try this anyway. Take a drink of milk and allow it to coat your tongue. Then go to a mirror, stick out your tongue, and look carefully at its surface. You should be able to see rounded bumps above the surface of your tongue. Those bumps, called **papillae,** *contain your taste buds, which*

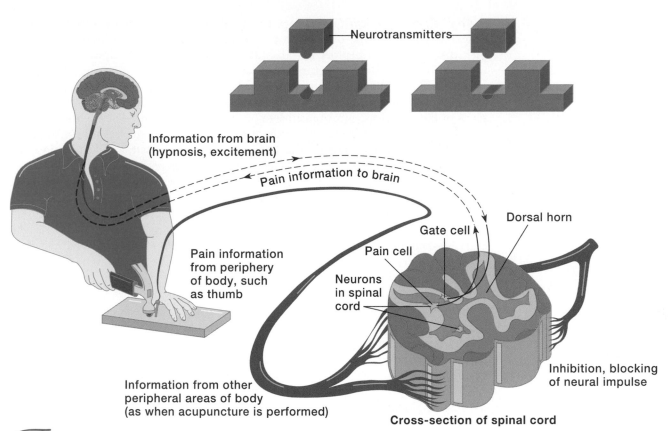

Neurotransmitters

Information from brain
(hypnosis, excitement)

Pain information to brain

Dorsal horn

Gate cell

Pain cell

Neurons in spinal cord

Pain information
from periphery
of body, such
as thumb

Inhibition, blocking
of neural impulse

Information from other
peripheral areas of body
(as when acupuncture is performed)

Cross-section of spinal cord

Figure 4.17
Gate-Control Theory of Pain

In the case of hitting your thumb with a hammer, pain signals initially go through the spinal cord and then to the brain. Gate-control theory states that pain information can be blocked in the spinal cord. Pain pathways from the periphery of the body (thumb, foot, etc.) make a synaptic connection in the spinal cord and then ascend to the brain. Interneurons can inhibit transmission through these pathways, as shown in the drawing above. When a strong peripheral stimulus (as applied during acupuncture) comes into the spinal cord, this can turn on the interneuron and close the gate in the pain pathway. Also, when a signal comes down from the brain (during hypnosis or the excitement of athletic competition), it, too, can turn on the interneuron and close the gate. The gate is not a physical structure that actually opens and shuts; rather, the gate is the inhibition of neural impulses. Neurotransmitters are involved in gate control, but much remains to be known about their identity.

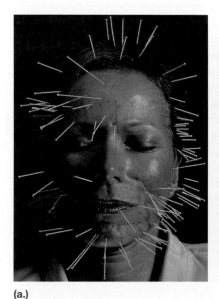

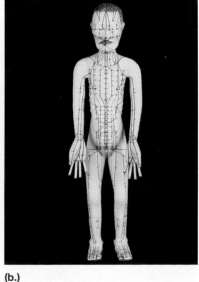

Figure 4.18
Acupuncture

(a) This woman is being treated for pain by an acupuncturist. (b) Acupuncture points are carefully noted on this nineteenth-century Japanese papier-mâché figure. In their adaptation of the Chinese methodology, the Japanese identified 660 points.

(a.)   (b.)

are the receptors for your taste. About 10,000 of these taste buds are located on your tongue. As in all of the other sensory systems we have discussed, the information picked up by these receptors is transmitted to the brain for analysis and response (spitting something out, for example) when it is necessary.

The taste qualities we respond to can be categorized as sweet, sour, bitter, and salty. Though all areas of the tongue can detect each of the four tastes, different regions of the tongue are more sensitive to one taste than another. The tip of the tongue is the most sensitive to sweet; the rear of the tongue is the most sensitive to bitter; just behind the area for sweet is the area most sensitive for salt; and just behind that is the most sensitive area for sour. While the tastes we experience can be categorized along these dimensions, our tasting ability goes far beyond them. Most of us pride ourselves on being able to discriminate different brands of ice cream; caffeinated and decaffeinated soda, coffee, and tea; and the many variations of product substitutes that are supposed to be better for us than the standard high-cholesterol, high-sugar, and high-fat culinary pleasures. Think of the remarkable range of tastes that you have which are generated by variations and combinations of the four basic taste qualities (sweet, sour, bitter, and salty).

Olfaction

Smell   A good way to begin our discussion of smell is to consider the many functions it serves. It is often easier to understand the importance of smell when we think about animals with more sophisticated senses of smell than our own. A dog, for example, can use its sense of smell to find its way back from a lone stroll, distinguish friend from foe, or even (with some practice!) detect illegal drugs concealed in a suitcase. In fact, dogs can detect odors in concentrations 100 times lower than those detectable by humans. In comparison to the nasal feats of the average dog, we might be tempted to believe that the sense of smell has outlived its usefulness in humans. What do we use smell for? For one, humans need the sense of smell to decide what to eat. We can distinguish rotten food from fresh food, and remember (all too well) which foods have made us ill in the past. The smell of a food that has previously made us ill is often, by itself, enough to make us feel nauseous. Second, while tracking is a function of smell that we often associate only with animals, humans are competent odor trackers. We can follow the smell of gas to a leak, the smell of smoke to a fire, or the smell of a hot apple pie to a windowsill.

What physical equipment do we use to process odor information? Just as the eyes scan the visual field for objects of interest, and the pinnae prick up to direct attention to sounds of interest, the nose is not a passive instrument. We actively sniff when we are trying to track down the source of a fire, or of a burned-out fluorescent light. The receptor cells for smell are located in the roof of the nasal cavity (see figure 4.19), so sniffing has the effect of maximizing the chances of detecting an odor (Doty & Muller-Schwarze, 1992). The **olfactory epithelium,** *located at the top of the nasal cavity, contains a sheet of receptor cells for smell.* These receptor sites are covered with millions of minute hairlike antennae, or *cilia,* that project through the mucus in the top of the nasal cavity and make contact with air on its way to the throat and lungs.

How good are you at identifying smells? Without practice, most people do a rather

Many animals have a stronger sense of smell than humans do. Dogs especially have a powerful olfactory sense. Watson, a Labrador retriever, has reliably pawed his owner 45 minutes before her epileptic seizures begin, giving her time to move to a safe place. How does the Labrador do this? The best hypothesis is that the dog smells the chemical changes known to precede epileptic seizures.

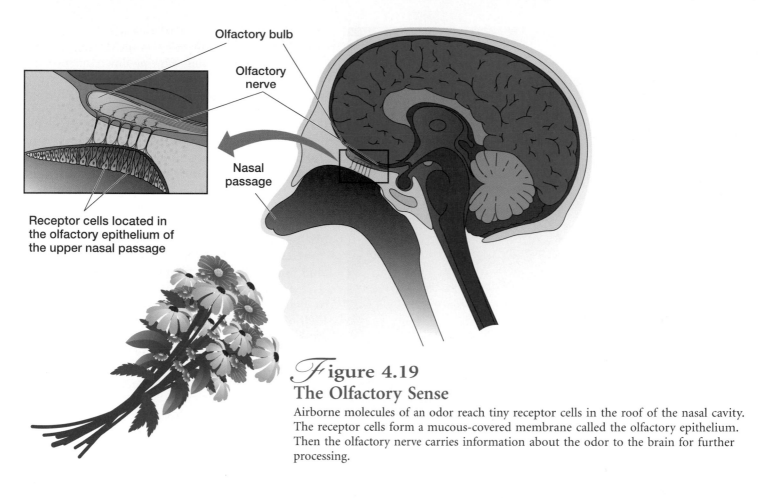

Olfactory bulb

Olfactory nerve

Nasal passage

Receptor cells located in the olfactory epithelium of the upper nasal passage

Figure 4.19
The Olfactory Sense

Airborne molecules of an odor reach tiny receptor cells in the roof of the nasal cavity. The receptor cells form a mucous-covered membrane called the olfactory epithelium. Then the olfactory nerve carries information about the odor to the brain for further processing.

poor job of identifying odors. But the human olfactory sense can be improved. Perfumers, as perfume testers are called, can identify between 100 and 200 different fragrances.

The Kinesthetic and Vestibular Senses

You know the difference between walking and running and between lying down and sitting up. To perform even the simplest acts of motor coordination, like reaching out to take a book off a library shelf or getting up out of a chair, the brain must be constantly receiving and coordinating information from every part of the body. Your body has two kinds of senses that provide information about your movement and orientation in space: the **kinesthetic senses** *provide information about movement, posture, and orientation,* and the **vestibular sense** *provides information about balance and movement.*

No specific organ contains the kinesthetic senses. Instead, they are embedded in muscle fibers and joints. As we stretch and move, these receptors signal the state of the muscle. Kinesthesia is a sense that you often don't even notice until it is gone. Try walking when your leg "is asleep," or smiling (never mind talking) when you've just come from a dentist's office and you are still under the effects of novocaine. Perhaps the sophistication of kinesthesis can be best appreciated when we think in terms of memory. Even a mediocre typist can bang out twenty words per minute—but how many of us could write down the order of the letters on a keyboard without looking? We say that our fingers remember the positions of the keys. Typing is a skill that relies on very coordinated sensitivity to the orientation, position, and movements of our fingers. Likewise, the complicated movements a ballet dancer uses to perform cannot be written down or communicated easily using language. They involve nearly every muscle and joint in the body.

The vestibular sense tells us whether our head (and hence usually our body) is tilted (e.g., Zikovitz & Harris, 1999), moving, slowing down, or speeding up. It works in concert with the kinesthetic senses to coordinate our proprioceptive feedback, which is information about the position of our limbs and body parts in relation to other body parts. Consider the combination of sensory abilities involved in the motion of hockey players skating down the ice with the puck cradled and pushed forward with the hockey stick. The hockey players are responding simultaneously to a multitude of sensations including those produced by the slickness of the ice, the position of the puck, the speed and momentum of the forward progression, and the requirements of the play to turn and to track the other players on the ice.

The **semicircular canals,** *located in the inner ear, contain the sensory receptors that detect head motion that is caused when we tilt or move our heads and/or bodies* (see figure 4.20). These canals consist of three fluid-filled circular tubes that lie in the three planes of the body—right-left, front-back, and up-down. We can picture these as three intersecting hula hoops.

As you move your head, the fluid of the semicircular canals flows in different directions and at different speeds (depending upon the force of the head movement). Our perception of head movement and position is determined by the movements of these receptor cells. This ingenious system of using the motion of fluid in tubes to sense head position is not unlike the system we learned about in audition. In audition, though, the fluid movement in the cochlea is caused by the pressure sound exerts on the oval window, whereas in the vestibular sense the movements we sense are real movements of the head and body.

The combination of kinesthetic and vestibular senses is supplemented by information from vision (Harris & Jenkin, 1998). This simple principle has made many an amusement park and large-screen movie theater profitable. When films are shown on screens that are large enough to fill our visual field, such as those found in many theme parks, the motion you perceive on the screen can make you feel like you are moving. An exciting new area of research involves the role of kinesthetic cues in the exploration and creation of *virtual environments,* computer-generated worlds, which may be best experienced while wearing 3-D stereo goggles (Harris, Jenkin, & Zikovitz, 1999).

At this point we have discussed a number of ideas about the auditory, skin, chemical, kinesthetic, and vestibular senses. A summary of these ideas is presented in summary table 4.3.

Our eyes take in the light reflecting off of objects around us. However, our brain pays attention to only part of the scene. For example, when you are looking for a pen on a messy desk, you scan the surface without noticing the papers scattered across it. Next, we examine such aspects of perception, beginning with attention.

(a.)

(b.)

*F*igure 4.20
The Semicircular Canals and Vestibular Sense

(a) This is a photograph of the semicircular canals located in the ear. The semicircular canals play an important role in the vestibular sense. The three canals are roughly perpendicular to each other in the three planes of space. Any angle of head rotation is registered by hair cells in one or more semicircular canals in both ears. *(b)* The semicircular canals provide feedback to the gymnast's brain as her body and head tilt in different directions.

Summary Table 4.3
The Auditory System and Other Senses

Concept	Processes/ Related Ideas	Characteristics/Description
The Auditory System	The Nature of Sound and How We Experience It	Sounds or sound waves are vibrations in the air that are processed by the auditory (or hearing) system. Sound waves vary in wavelength, which determines the frequency of the sound wave or the number of Hertz (or full wavelengths) that pass through a point in a given time. Pitch is the perceptual interpretation of the frequency of sound. Amplitude is measured in decibels (dB), the amount of pressure produced by a sound wave relative to a standard. Loudness is the perception of a sound wave's amplitude. Complex sounds are those in which numerous frequencies of sound blend together. We experience the particular combination of frequencies in a sound as the quality or timbre of a sound.
	Structures and Functions of the Ear	The ear serves the function of transmitting a high-fidelity version of sounds in the world to the brain for analysis and interpretation. The ear is divided into the outer ear, middle ear, and inner ear. The outer ear consists of the pinna and the external auditory canal. The middle ear consists of the eardrum, hammer, anvil, and stirrup. The main parts of the inner ear are the oval window, cochlea, and the organ of Corti. The basilar membrane, located inside the cochlea, is where vibrations are changed into nerve impulses.
	Theories of Hearing	Place theory states that each frequency produces vibrations at a particular spot on the basilar membrane. Frequency theory states that the perception of a sound's frequency is due to how often the auditory nerve fires. Volley theory is a modification of place theory, stating that high frequencies can be signaled by teams of neurons that fire at different offset times to create an overall firing rate that could signal a very high frequency. Frequency theory is better at explaining lower-frequency sounds, volley and place theories higher-frequency sounds.
	Neural-Auditory Processing	Information about sound is carried from the cochlea to the brain by the auditory nerve. Information is integrated in the temporal lobe.
Other Senses	The Skin Senses	The skin senses consist of the senses of touch, temperature, and pain. In touch, we detect mechanical energy, or pressure against the skin. Thermoreceptors, which are located under the skin, respond to increases and decreases in temperature. Pain is the sensation that warns us that damage to our bodies is occurring. Gate-control theory states that the spinal column contains a neural gate that can be opened (allowing the perception of pain) or closed (blocking the perception of pain). Gate-control theory has been proposed as one explanation of acupuncture, a technique in which thin needles are inserted at specific points in the body to produce various effects, including local anesthesia. Gate-control theory does not completely explain how we experience pain.
	The Chemical Senses	The chemical senses consist of taste and smell. We use our sense of taste to select food and to regulate food intake. Papillae are rounded bumps above the surface of the tongue that contain taste buds, the receptors for taste. The taste qualities we can respond to are classified as sweet, sour, bitter, and salty. The functions of smell include guiding our decisions about what to eat, tracking, and communication. The olfactory epithelium, located at the top of the nasal cavity, contains a sheet of receptor cells for smell.
	The Kinesthetic and Vestibular Senses	The kinesthetic senses provide information about movement, posture, and orientation, while the vestibular sense provides information about balance and movement. The semicircular canals, located in the inner ear, contain the sensory receptors that detect head motion that is caused when we tilt or move our heads and/or bodies.

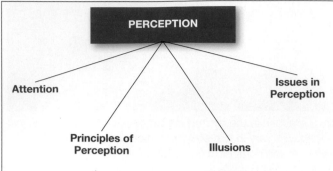

Perception

Earlier in this chapter we said that perception is the brain's process of organizing and interpreting sensory information to give it meaning ◀▥ P. 102. When perception goes to work, sensory receptors have received energy from stimuli in the external world and sensory organs have processed and transformed the information so it can be transmitted to the brain. Perception is a creation of the brain; it is based on input extracted from sensory organs, such as the eye, ear, and nose. But perception goes beyond this input. The brain uses past experience (information previously extracted) as a basis for making educated guesses, or interpretations, about the state of the outside world.

Attention

The world holds a lot of information to perceive. Right now you are perceiving the letters and words that make up this sentence. Now look around the setting where you are and pick out something to look at other than this book. After that curl up the toes on your right foot. In each of these circumstances, you engaged in **selective attention,** *which involves focusing on a specific aspect of experience while ignoring others.* The *cocktail party effect,* the ability to attend selectively to one voice among many, is an example of selective attention.

Not only is attention selective, it also is *shiftable.* If the telephone rings while you are studying, you shift your attention from studying to the telephone. If you go to an art museum, you look at one painting, then another, then others, moving your attention from one painting to the next. And as you look at each painting, you shift your vision from one part of the painting to another, seeking to understand it better.

Why do we pay attention to some aspects of our experience and block out others? What you attend to is influenced by your motivation and interests. Art is one of my interests, so I will be more likely to attend to an advertisement for an art show than someone who has no interest in art. A person who is interested in sports is more likely to attend to an announcement that a basketball game will be

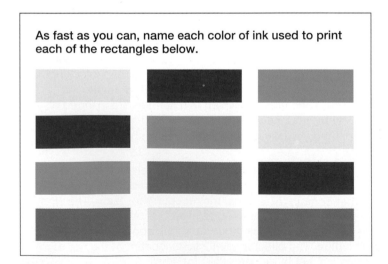

*F*igure 4.21
The Stroop Effect

Before reading further, make sure you have read the instructions above and completed the tasks. You probably had little or no difficulty in naming the colors of the rectangles in the left-hand set. However, you likely stumbled more when you were asked to name the color of ink used to print each word in the right-hand set. This demonstration of automaticity in perception is called the Stroop effect.

on TV tonight than someone who is not interested in sports. There are also several features of stimuli that cause people to attend to them. Novel stimuli (those that are different or unusual) often attract our attention. If a Ferrari convertible whizzes by, you are more likely to notice it than if it were a Ford. Size, color, and movement also influence our attention. Objects that are large, vividly colored, or moving are more likely to grab our attention than objects that are small, dull-colored, or stationary.

Highly practiced and familiar stimuli, such as your own name, are often perceived so automatically it is almost impossible to ignore them. The **Stroop effect** *is an example of automatic perception in which it is difficult to name the colors in which words are printed when the actual words refer to different colors.* To experience the Stroop effect, see Figure 4.21. In most instances, the highly practiced and almost automatic perception of word meaning makes reading easier (Lowe & Mitterer, 1982). However, this same automaticity makes it hard to ignore the meaning of color words when they are printed in a different color (MacLeod, 1992; Besner and Stolz, 1999). Thus the Stroop effect represents a failure of selective attention.

Although attention plays an important role in perception, what we ultimately see, or interpret, also depends on a number of important principles of perception that involve specific characteristics of sensory stimuli.

Principles of Perception

Principles of perception include those involving shape perception, depth perception, motion perception, and perceptual constancy.

Shape Perception   Think about the world of shapes—buildings against the sky, boats on the horizon, letters on this page. We see these shapes because they are marked off from the rest of what we see by **contour**, *a location at which a sudden change of brightness occurs* (Elder & Zucker, 1993). As you look at this page, you see letters, which are shapes, in a field or background, the white page (e.g., Elder & Zucker, 1998). The **figure-ground relationship** *is the principle by which we organize the perceptual field into stimuli that stand out (figure) and those that are leftover (ground).* Some figure-ground relationships, though, are highly ambiguous, and it is difficult to tell what is figure and what is ground. A well-known ambiguous figure-ground relationship is shown in figure 4.22.

As you look at the figure, your perception is likely to shift between seeing two faces or seeing a single goblet. Another example of figure-ground ambiguity is found in the work of artist M. C. Escher, which keeps us from favoring one figure over another seemingly because spatial location and depth cues are not provided (see figure 4.23).

One group of psychologists—the Gestalt psychologists—has been especially intrigued by how we perceive shapes. According to **Gestalt psychology,** *people naturally*

THINKING ABOUT PSYCHOLOGY AND LIFE
Counting Aces of Spades

PLACE YOUR HAND over the bottom set of cards. Now as quickly as you can count how many aces of spades you see in the top set.

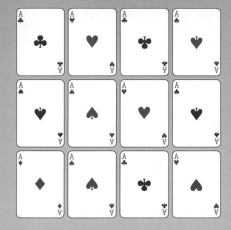

Now place your hand over the top set of cards. Quickly count the number of aces of spades in the set of 12 cards below.

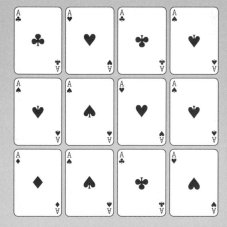

Most people report that they see 2–3 aces of spades in the top set of 12 cards. However, if you look closely, there are 5. Two of the aces of spades are black and three are red. When people look at the bottom set of 12 cards they are more likely to count 5 aces of spades. Why the difference in what we perceive? The answer lies in our perceptual expectations: We expect the aces of spades to be black because that is how they are presented in a regular deck of cards. We don't expect them to be colored red, so it is easy to skip right over the red-colored ones. Interestingly, young children are more accurate at this task than adults. Why? Because they have not built up the perceptual expectation that aces of spades are black.

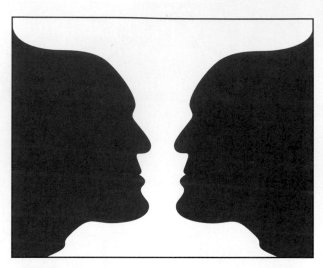

Figure 4.22
Reversible Figure-Ground Pattern
Either a goblet or a pair of silhouetted faces in profile can be seen.

Figure 4.23
Sophisticated Use of the Figure-Ground Relationship in Escher's Woodcut *Relativity* (1938)

The Joy of Visual Perception

organize their perceptions according to certain patterns; Gestalt is a German word that means "configuration" or "form." One of Gestalt psychology's main principles is that the whole is not equal to the sum of its parts. For example, when you watch a movie, the "motion" you see in the film cannot be found in the film itself; if you examine it, you see only separate frames at a rate of many per second. When you watch the film you perceive a whole that is very different from the separate individual pictures that are the whole's parts.

The figure-ground relationship just described is another Gestalt principle. Three other Gestalt principles are closure, proximity, and similarity. The principle of *closure* states that when individuals see a disconnected or incomplete figure, they fill in the spaces and see it as a complete figure (see figure 4.24a). The principle of *proximity* states that when individuals see objects closer to each other, they tend to group them together (see figure 4.24b). The principle of *similarity* states that the more similar objects are, the more likely we are to group them together (see figure 4.24c).

Depth Perception   The images of the world we see appear on our retinas in two-dimensional form, yet we see a three-dimensional world. **Depth perception** *is the ability to perceive objects three-dimensionally*. Look at the setting where you are. You don't see it as flat. You see some objects farther away, some closer. Some objects overlap each other. The scene and objects that you are looking at have depth. How do you see depth? To see a world of depth, we use two kinds of information, or cues—binocular and monocular. We have two eyes, which view the world from slightly different places. **Binocular cues** *are depth cues that are based on the combination of the images on the left and right eyes and on the way the two eyes work together*. **Monocular cues** *are depth cues that can be extracted from the image in one eye, either the left or the right eye*.

Because we have two eyes, we get two views of the world, one from each eye (Regan, 1991). The pictures are slightly different because the eyes are in slightly different positions. Hold your hand about 10 inches from your face, and alternately close and open your left and right eyes, so only one eye is open at a time. The image of your left hand will appear to jump back and forth. This is because the image of your

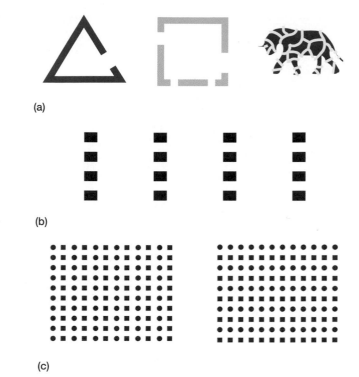

(a)

(b)

(c)

Examining Art for Perceptual Cues and Organization

ARTISTS MAKE extensive use of perceptual cues and organization in their work. Some artists have even specifically manipulated these cues to create their art. You just saw an example on the previous page (Figure 4.23). Here, M.C. Escher has playfully created an impossible scene, which could not exist in real life. Many of M.C. Escher's pieces present us with similar perceptual challenges. Some other artists who challenge us by manipulating perceptual cues include the Surrealist Rene Magritte, the Cubist Pablo Picasso, and the founder of optical art, Vassely Vasserely.

To further your knowledge and understanding of how painters use perceptual cues and organization, go to a museum and look closely at paintings from different schools such as neoclassical, impressionist, and expressionist. If you don't have access to a museum, go to the library and look closely at some art books that represent different schools of painting and engage in a similar exercise.

$\mathscr{F}$igure 4.24
Gestalt Principles of Closure, Proximity, and Similarity

(a) Closure: When we see disconnected or incomplete figures, we fill in the spaces and see them as complete figures. *(b)* Proximity: When we see objects that are near each other, they tend to be seen as a unit. You are likely to perceive the grouping as 4 columns of 4 squares, not 1 set of 16 squares. *(c)* Similarity: When we see objects that are similar to each other, they tend to be seen as a unit. In this display, you are likely to see vertical columns of circles and squares in the left box but horizontal rows of circles and squares in the right box.

hand is in a slightly different place on the left and right retinas. The **disparity**, or *difference of the image in the two eyes,* is the cue the brain uses for binocular vision, also known as *stereopsis* (Howard & Rogers, 1995). Both images are combined in the brain, and the disparities between the images of objects in the two eyes gives us information about the three-dimensionality of the world (Schneider, Moraglia, & Speranza, in press).

The perception of depth from disparity can be demonstrated as in figure 4.25, based on a principle for presenting stereoscopic information from a single two-dimensional image (Tyler, 1983). These kinds of displays have become extremely popular in recent years and can now be found in art books, on greeting cards, and on posters in specialty shops; around the turn of the century, stereograms were similarly popular when stereoviewers became easily available.

In addition to having an indication of the depth of objects from the difference between the two-eye images, our perception of depth also makes use of a number of monocular cues, or cues available from a single-eye image. These are powerful cues and under normal circumstances can provide a very compelling impression of depth. Try closing one eye—your perception of the world still retains many of its three-dimensional qualities. Some examples of monocular cues are as follows:

1. *Aerial perspective.* Pollution and water vapor in the air scatter light waves, giving distant objects a hazy appearance.
2. *Familiar size.* This cue to the depth and distance of objects is based on what we have learned from experience about the standard sizes of objects. We know how large oranges tend to be, so we can tell something about how far away an orange is likely to be by the size of its image on the retina.
3. *Height in the field of view.* All other things being equal, objects that are higher in a picture are seen as farther away.

Stereoscopic Imagery
Vision and Art

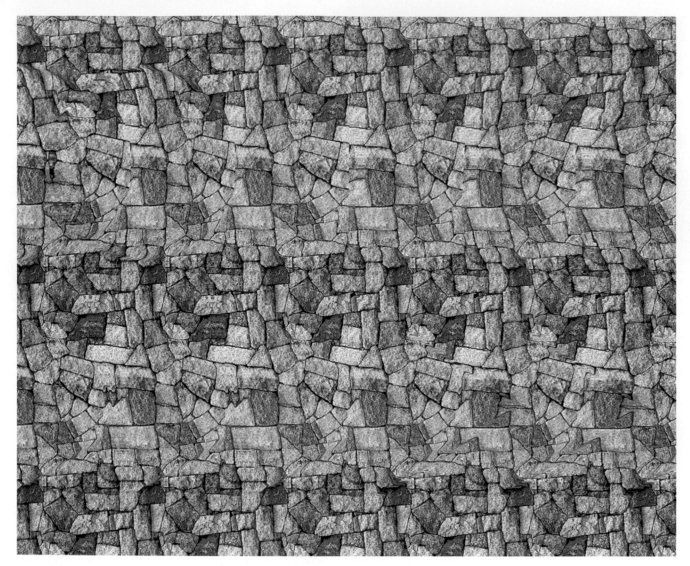

$\mathcal{F}$igure 4.25
A Stereogram

Seen in the right way, this figure contains 3 three-dimensional objects: a sphere in the top left, a pyramid in the top right, and a curved pointed conical figure in the center at the bottom. They may take a moment or two to see, but when you see them, they will be astoundingly clear and three-dimensional. There are two ways to see the three-dimensional objects in this figure. Technique 1: Cross your eyes by holding your finger up between your face and the figure. Look at the tip of your finger, and then slowly move your finger back and forth, toward and away from the figure, being careful to maintain focus on your finger. When the correct distance is reached, the three-dimensional objects will pop out at you. Technique 2: Put your face very close to the figure, so that it is difficult to focus or converge your eyes. Wait a moment, and begin to pull your face very slowly back from the figure. The picture should appear blurred for a bit, but when a good distance is reached should snap into three-dimensionality. Regardless of the technique you try, be patient! You may have to try one or both of these techniques a few times. The difficulty is that your eyes will try to converge at the distance of the page (very sensible of them!)—but you will be able to perceive this illusion only if you can trick them into converging elsewhere, either in front of the page, as will happen in technique 1, or perfectly parallel and unconverged, as will happen in technique 2. Note: Some people will not be able to see the three-dimensionality in these figures at all, for one of several reasons. First, some of us have eyes much too well adapted to the real world to be convinced to converge in the "wrong place," given the image data appearing on the retinas! Second, some very common visual deficits that can yield appreciable differences between the quality of the image on the left and right retinas can affect the development of normal stereopsis, or binocular vision. The brain requires comparable image quality from the two eyes in the first few years of life to develop a high degree of stereoacuity. When this is not the case, the development of binocular neural mechanisms, which need to compare information in the two eyes, can be affected and can pose problems in processing the *pure* stereoscopic information in this figure. The information in this figure is purely stereoscopic because other kinds of cues to depth, like shading and perspective, are not available.

𝓕igure 4.26
An Artist's Use of the Monocular Cue of Linear Perspective

Lawren Harris, of Canada's Group of Seven, used linear perspective to give the perception of depth to his painting *Miners' Houses, Glace Bay.* AGO No. 69/122.

4. *Linear perspective.* This cue is based on the fact that objects farther away take up less space on the retina. As shown in figure 4.26, as an object recedes into the distance, parallel lines in the scene appear to converge.

5. *Overlap.* An object that partially conceals or overlaps another object is perceived as closer.

6. *Shading.* This cue involves changes in perception due to the position of the light and the position of the viewer. Consider an egg under a desk lamp. If you walk around the desk, you will get different shading patterns on the egg.

7. *Size in the field of view.* All other things being equal, objects that are smaller are seen to be farther away.

8. *Texture gradient.* Texture becomes more dense and finer, the farther away it is from the viewer (see figure 4.27).

Depth perception is especially intriguing to artists. They face a problem because the real world is three-dimensional and they have to paint on a two-dimensional canvas. Artists often use monocular cues to give the feeling of depth to their paintings. Indeed, monocular cues have become so widely used by artists that they have also been called *pictorial cues.* To learn more about art and perception, turn to Explorations in Psychology.

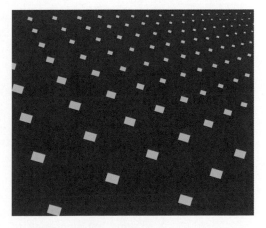

𝓕igure 4.27
Texture Gradient

The gradients of texture create an impression of depth on a flat surface.

EXPLORATIONS IN PSYCHOLOGY
The Perceptual Worlds in Art

LOOK AT FIGURE 4.A. If you stood very close to this painting and looked at one area, you would see only daubs of colored pigments on a canvas. If you stood back and considered the whole painting, however, you would see the brilliantly colored landscape with a tree, a village, a church, and a turbulent sky. The painting is nineteenth-century Dutch artist Vincent van Gogh's masterpiece *Starry Night*. This is not likely the scene most of us would paint if we were trying to recreate the real world. Stars do not race about in frenzied whirlpools. What caused van Gogh to paint *Starry Night* the way he did? For one thing, he was a tormented, intense, mystical man. Some of the torment, and a kind of ecstasy, are built into the painting. Another artist, not experiencing van Gogh's mental anguish, would likely have painted the same starry night very differently.

Was van Gogh painting what he actually saw? We don't know the answer to

Figure 4.A
Vincent van Gogh's *Starry Night*

Van GOGH, Vincent. *The Starry Night* (1889). Oil on canvas, 29 × 36¼″ (73.7 × 92.1 cm). The Museum of Modern Art, New York. Acquired through the Lillie P. Bliss Bequest. Photograph © 1996 The Museum of Modern Art, New York.

Figure 4.B
Raphael's *Fire in the Borgo*

The Renaissance masters used depth cues to give their paintings three-dimensional appearance. Notice the detailed attention to perspective, such as how the roofs above the columns extend backward. Notice also the smaller size of the people in the distance and the overlapping of people and buildings.

that question, but we do know that, at some points in history, artists have strived to mirror the world just as it appears to their eyes; at others they have deliberately distorted reality. The Renaissance masters tried to paint the world as accurately as possible, as if their canvas were a photograph (see figure 4.B). They relied on many of the cues for depth perception to portray three-dimensional reality on a flat surface.

For example, Impressionist painters, like British Columbia artist Emily Carr, focused on the impression a scene makes on the observer instead of trying to paint the scene as accurately as possible. She strove to capture the viewer's perception of nature's fleeting sensations of light. Her technique involved the creation of a patchwork of varying daubs of brightly colored paint (see figure 4.C). When you look at an Emily Carr painting up close, you see individual patches of color; however, when

Emily Carr, *Old Time Coast Village*. VAG 42.3.4, Vancouver Art Gallery/Trevor Mills.

Figure 4.C
Emily Carr's *Old Time Coastal Village*

you stand away from the painting, the individual patches of color blur and mix together.

Many modern painters moved even further away from recreating the world we actually see. In the twentieth century, Pablo Picasso liked to place varying geometrical forms (circles, triangles, rectangles, for example) together and challenge observers to interpret what he had painted. Look at Picasso's painting in figure 4.D. Can you tell what it is without looking at the figure legend?

As can be seen, understanding perception's role in art is complex, involving not only the artist's perceptions but also the perceptions of the art's observers. Artists paint not only what they see but also what they know, and what observers perceive a painting to be is influenced by their experiences. Van Gogh's *Starry Night* might be perceived as a bombing raid by a Londoner who experienced the German blitz in World War II; as a hallucinatory vision by someone under the influence of drugs or a fever; as the way the sky always looks by someone with a particular visual disorder; and as weird or bizarre by someone who views nature in meticulous, ordered ways. Above all else, art is artist, observer, and communication, not unlike a "perceptual conversation" between one person's view of the world and another person's view of the world.

Figure 4.D
Picasso's *Nude Woman*

Look at the painting and think about the way some of the Gestalt principles of perception are incorporated. The nude is an incomplete figure. You have to fill in the spaces to make it complete. Remember that this is the principle of closure. The principles of proximity and similarity cause you to see the two objects toward the bottom of the painting as feet.

Movement Aftereffects

Figure 4.28
Movement Aftereffects

This is an example of a geometric pattern that produces afterimages in which motion can be perceived. If the center of the pattern is fixated for approximately 10 seconds and then the afterimage is projected on a plain white surface, rotary motion is usually perceived.

Motion Perception   During the course of each day, we perceive objects that move—other people, cars, planes, animals. Why are we able to perceive motion? First, we have neurons that are specialized to detect motion. Second, feedback from our body tells us whether we are moving or someone or an object is moving. For example, you move your eye muscles as you watch a ball coming toward you. Third, the environment we see is rich in cues that give us information about movement. For example, when we run, we can tell that the background is moving.

Psychologists are interested in both real movement and **apparent movement,** *which occurs when an object is stationary but we perceive it to be moving.* An example of apparent movement can be experienced at an IMAX theater. Specially-produced films are shown on six-story tall screens that fill your entire visual field. Airplanes, whales, jaguars, or spacecraft appear to move right out of the screen towards the audience. Scenes filmed from roller coasters or cars can induce strong sensations of "movement" in the audience as well. A powerful sound system broadcast in surround sound enhances the experience. More recently, 3-D films have been produced for the IMAX screen, compounding the intensity of the experience.

Two forms of apparent motion are stroboscopic motion and movement aftereffects. **Stroboscopic motion** *is the illusion of movement created when a rapid stimulation of different parts of the retina occurs—motion pictures are a form of stroboscopic motion.* **Movement aftereffects** *happen when we watch continuous movement and then look at another surface, which then appears to move in the opposite direction.* Figure 4.28 provides an opportunity to experience movement aftereffects.

Perceptual Constancy   Retinal images are constantly changing as we experience our world. Even though the stimuli that fall on the retinas of our eyes change as we move closer or farther away from objects, or look at objects from different orientations and in light or dark settings, we perceive objects as constant and unchanging. We experience three types of perceptual constancies: size constancy, shape constancy, and brightness constancy. **Size constancy** *is the recognition that an object remains the same size even though the retinal image of the object changes* (see figure 4.29). **Shape constancy** *is the recognition that an object remains the same shape even though its orientation to us changes.* Look around the room in which you are reading this book. You probably see objects of various shapes—chairs and tables, for example. If you walk around the room, you will see these objects from different sides and angles. Even though the pattern of light falling on the retina, the *retinal image* of the object, changes as you walk, you still perceive the objects as being the same shape (see figure 4.30). **Brightness constancy** *is the recognition that an object retains the same degree of brightness even though different amounts of light fall on it.* For example, regardless of whether you are reading this book indoors or outdoors, the white pages and the black print do not look any different to you in terms of their whiteness or blackness.

How are we able to resolve the discrepancy between a retinal image of an object and its actual size, shape, and brightness? Experience is important. For example, no matter how far away you are from your car, you know how large it is. Not only is familiarity important in size constancy, but so are binocular and monocular depth cues ◀︎▥ P. 130. Even if we have never previously seen an object, these cues provide us with information about an object's size. Many visual illusions are influenced by our perception of size constancy.

Illusions

Our perceptual interpretations are usually correct. For example, on the basis of a change in color or texture, we can conclude that a dog is on the rug. On the basis of a continuous increase in size, we conclude that a train is coming toward us. Sometimes, though, the interpretations or inferences are wrong, with the result being an illusion that is a misperception.

A **visual illusion** *occurs when two objects produce exactly the same retinal image but are perceived as different images.* Illusions are incorrect, but they are not abnormal. They can provide insight into how our perceptual processes work (Nakamizo, Ono, & Medin, 1999; Rinkenauer, Mattes, & Ulrich, 1999). More than two hundred different types of illusions have been discovered; we will study six.

One of the most famous is the Müller-Lyer illusion, illustrated in figure 4.31. The two horizontal lines are exactly the same length, although *b* looks longer than *a*. Another illusion is the horizontal-vertical illusion in which a vertical line looks longer than a horizontal line even though the two are equal (see figure 4.32). In the Ponzo illusion (see figure 4.33), the top line looks much longer than the bottom line.

𝓕igure 4.29
Size Constancy
Even though our retinal image of the hot air balloons changes, we still perceive the different balloons as being approximately the same size. This illustrates the principle of size constancy.

𝓕igure 4.30
Shape Constancy
The various projected images from an opening door are quite different, yet you perceive a rectangular door.

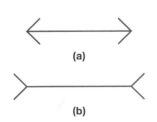

(a)

(b)

𝓕igure 4.31
Müller-Lyer Illusion
The two lines are exactly the same length, although (b) looks longer than (a).

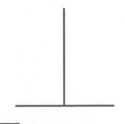

𝓕igure 4.32
The Horizontal-Vertical Illusion
The vertical line looks longer than the horizontal line, but they are the same length.

© Sidney Harris

*F*igure 4.33
Ponzo Illusion

The top line looks much longer than the bottom line, but they are equal in length.

Visual Illusions
Exploring Visual Illusions

Why do these illusions trick us? One reason is that we mistakenly use certain cues for maintaining size constancy. For example, in the Ponzo illusion we see the upper line as being farther away (remember that objects higher in a picture are perceived as being farther away). The Müller-Lyer illusion, though, is not so easily explained. We might make our judgments about the lines by comparing incorrect parts of the figures. For example, when people were shown the Müller-Lyer illusion with the wings painted a different color than the horizontal lines, the illusion was greatly reduced (Coren & Girgus, 1972). Shortly we also will discuss how cultural experiences influence an individual's perception of the Müller-Lyer illusion.

Another well-known illusion is the moon illusion (see figure 4.34). The moon is 2,000 miles in diameter and 289,000 miles away. Because both the moon's size and its distance from us are beyond our own experience, we have difficulty judging just how far away it really is. When the moon is high in the sky, directly above us, little information is present to help us judge its distance—no texture gradients or stereoscopic cues exist, for example. But when the moon is on the horizon, we can judge its distance in relation to familiar objects—trees and buildings, for example—which makes it appear farther away. The result is that we estimate the size of the moon as much larger when it is on the horizon than when it is overhead.

The devil's tuning fork is another fascinating illusion. Look at figure 4.35 for about 30 seconds, then close the book. Now try to draw the tuning fork. You undoubtedly found this a difficult, if not impossible, task. Why? Because the figure's depth cues are ambiguous, you had problems correctly interpreting it.

In our final example of an illusion, a "doctored" horrific face seen upside down goes unnoticed. Look at figure 4.36—you probably recognize this famous face as Margaret Thatcher. What seems to be an ordinary portrait is actually doctored. The mouth and eyes have been cut out from the original and pasted back on upside

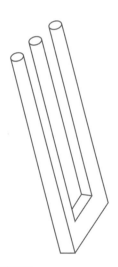

*F*igure 4.35
Devil's Tuning Fork

*F*igure 4.34
Moon Illusion

When the moon is on the horizon, it looks much larger than when it is high in the sky, directly above us. Why does the moon look so much larger on the horizon?

down. If you turn this book upside down, the horrific look is easily seen. The "Thatcher" illusion may take place because the mouth is so far out of alignment that we simply cannot respond to its expression; it is still a fearsome face, but we do not see that, and we may have a difficult time telling what really is the top of the mouth in the picture.

Issues in Perception

In chapter 1 we indicated that psychology is filled with controversies. So it is in the field of perception. To begin our tour of perception issues, let's explore two competing approaches to perception.

THINKING ABOUT PSYCHOLOGY AND LIFE
Inventing a Video Game

IMAGINE THAT YOU ARE unleashing your creative skills to invent a new video game (Zakrajsek, 1999). What applications of sensation and perception that you have learned about in this chapter will you need to call on to create the video game? In answering this question, consider vision, monocular cues to depth perception, the visual field sound, and the game's controls.

Approaches to Perception.   Two main approaches to understanding perception are the information-processing approach and the ecological approach.

The **information-processing approach** *states that perception is the process of representing information from the world internally.* As information from the world is processed, it undergoes a series of manipulations. For example, the individual cognitively constructs an image of the world based on sensory input plus information retrieved from memory. When asked what the purpose of vision is, one of information processing's main architects, David Marr (1982), answered: *To create a three-dimensional representation or map of the world in the brain.* That is, vision's purpose includes navigating through the environment without bumping into things; being able to grasp things; and creating a representation of visual objects that can be compared with representations in memory. For information-processing psychologists, an important function of perception is to help people construct an understanding of the world.

The **ecological approach** *states that perception's function is to bring the organism into contact with the environment and increase its adaptation.* A key aspect of perceptual adaptation is to be able to detect perceptual invariants (aspects of perception that remain intact) in a constantly changing world. An important claim of the ecological approach is that even complex things (such as a spatial layout) can be perceived directly without any cognitive construction. Information is out there in the environment, say the ecological enthusiasts, and perception's function is to detect it.

This main architect of the ecological approach, James J. Gibson (1966) answered the question of what perception is for this way: *Perception is for action.* In Gibson's view, an object is what you can do with it. In an environment with an object in motion, such as a baseball, the brain detects "how much time I have to get my glove up to catch the ball." Thus, the ecological approach's external emphasis on perception's role in action contrasts with the information-processing approach's emphasis on perception's role in internally constructing understanding (See figure 4.37).

Is Perception Learned or Innate?   One long-standing question
in psychology is whether perception is learned or innate (inborn). Researchers have tried to unravel this nature/nurture question on depth perception in a number of ways: experiments with infants, studies of individuals who recover from blindness, and cross-cultural studies about how people perceive their world.

The Visual Cliff   An experiment by Eleanor Gibson and Richard Walk (1960) indicates that by at least 6 months of age infants have an understanding of depth. Gibson and Walk constructed a miniature cliff with a shallow side and

Figure 4.36
Why Does This Famous Face Look So Different When You Turn the Book Upside Down?

Information-Processing Approach   **Ecological Approach**

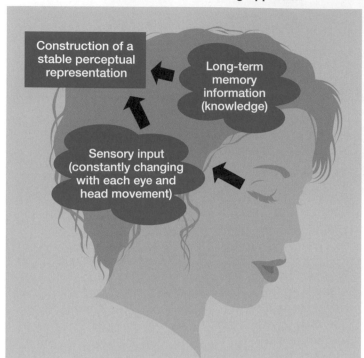
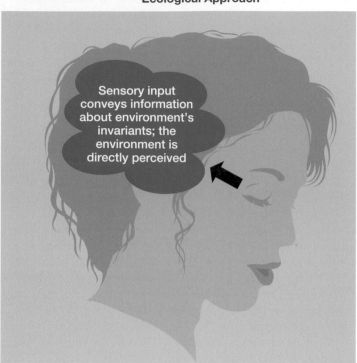

*F*igure 4.37
Information-Processing and Ecological Approaches to Perception

*F*igure 4.38
The Visual Cliff

The visual cliff was developed by Eleanor Gibson and Richard Walk (1960). The infant shown here hesitates as he moves onto the glass-covered dropoff, the deep side of the visual cliff. Even when coaxed by their mothers, infants are still reluctant to venture out onto the deep dropoff, indicating they can perceive depth.

a dropoff that was covered by firm glass (see figure 4.38). This structure is known as a *visual cliff*. Infants old enough to crawl (6 months and older) were placed on the shallow side. The infants stayed in place rather than venture out onto the glass-covered dropoff, indicating that they perceived depth. However, infants at 6 months are old enough to have encountered many situations where they could have *learned* to perceive depth, so the visual cliff experiment failed to provide convincing evidence that depth perception is innate. Whether or not infants younger than 6 months perceive depth is controversial.

Other studies have shown that during the first month of life, human infants turn away to avoid objects that move directly toward them, but do not turn away when objects move toward them at angles that would not collide with them (Ball & Tronick, 1971). And animals with little visual experience—including day-old goats and just-hatched chicks—respond just as 6-month-old human infants do; they remain on the visual cliff's shallow side and do not venture out onto the glass-covered dropoff. These studies suggest that some of the ability to perceive depth is innate.

Recovery from Blindness   In further attempts to determine whether or not depth perception is innate, psychologists have also studied people who were born blind, or became blind shortly after birth, and whose sight later was restored by medical procedures. If the ability to interpret sensory information is innate, such people should be able to see their world clearly after they recover from the operation. Consider S. B., blind since birth, who had a successful corneal transplant at the age of 52 (Gregory, 1978). Soon after S. B.'s bandages were removed, he was able to recognize common objects, identify the letters of the alphabet, and tell time from a clock. However, S. B. had some perceptual deficiencies. While his eyes functioned effectively, S. B. had difficulty perceiving objects he had not previously touched (see figure 4.39).

The findings for formerly blind persons also do not answer the question of whether or not perception is innate or learned. Some people recognize objects soon after their bandages are removed; others require weeks of training before they recognize such simple shapes as a triangle. Neural connections, such as those between the eyes and the brain, can deteriorate from disuse. So a person whose sight has been restored after a lifetime of blindness may have an impaired ability to perceive visual information. Further, previously blind adults, unlike infants, have already experienced the world through their nonvisual senses, such as touch and hearing, and those perceptual systems may continue to contribute to their perception after they regain their vision.

Culture and Perception   While our biological inheritance equips us with some elegant perceptual capabilities, our experiences also contribute to how we perceive the world (Berry and others, 1992). Some cross-cultural psychologists have proposed that the demands of different cultures lead to greater emphasis on certain senses (Wober, 1966). For example, hunters who have to stalk small game animals may develop their kinesthetic senses more than office workers in highly industrialized nations.

Cross-cultural psychologists have been especially interested in how people from different cultures perceive visual illusions (Segall & others, 1990). The **carpentered-world hypothesis** *states that people who live in cultures in which straight lines, right angles, and rectangles predominate (for instance, in which most rooms and buildings are rectangular and many objects, such as city streets, have right angles) should be more susceptible to illusions involving straight lines, right angles, and rectangles than are people who live in noncarpentered cultures* (figure 4.40). This tendency enhances the Müller-Lyer illusion and makes people from carpentered environments more susceptible to it than people from noncarpentered environments are. For example, the Zulu in isolated regions of southeastern Africa live in a world of open spaces and curves. Their huts are round with round doors, and they even plow their fields in curved, rather than straight, furrows. According to the carpentered-world hypothesis, the Zulu would not be very susceptible to the Müller-Lyer illusion. Cross-cultural psychologists have found this to be the case (Segall, Campbell, & Herskovits, 1963).

Nature/Nurture Conclusions   It seems that both nature and nurture are responsible for the way we perceive the world ◀▦ P. 69. One view of how the two influences interact to shape perception is that all people, regardless of culture, have the same perceptual processes and the same potential for perceptual development, but cultural factors determine what is learned and at what age (Kagitcibasi, 1995). So far we have discussed perception in terms of shape, depth, constancy, illusion, and whether or not perception is innate or learned. Now we turn our attention to a topic related to perception that stimulates a lot of curiosity.

Extrasensory Perception   Our eyes, ears, mouth, nose, and skin provide us with sensory information about the external world. Our perceptions are based on our interpretation of this sensory information. Some people, though, claim they can perceive the world through something other than normal sensory pathways. **Extrasensory perception (ESP)** *is perception that occurs without the use of any known sensory process.* Most psychologists do not believe in ESP (Alcock, 1981, 1987, 1998); however, a few of them investigate it.

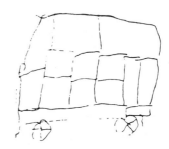

𝒻igure 4.39
S. B.'s Drawing of a Bus After Recovering from Blindness

S. B. drew the bus at the top 48 days after a corneal transplant restored his vision, and he drew the bus at the bottom a year after the operation. Both drawings reflect more detail for the parts of the bus S. B. used or touched while he was blind than the parts he did not use or touch. In the bottom drawing, notice the absence of the front of the bus, which S. B. never touched.

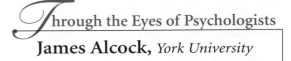

𝒯hrough the Eyes of Psychologists

James Alcock, *York University*

"Parapsychology is best described as being belief in search of data rather than data in search of an explanation."

𝓕igure 4.40
The Carpentered-World Hypothesis

The Zulu live in isolated regions of southeastern Africa in a world of open spaces and curves. Their huts are round with round doors, and they even plow their fields in curved, rather than straight, furrows. As the carpentered-world hypothesis would predict, the Zulu are not very susceptible to the Müller-Lyer illusion.

𝓕igure 4.41
An Experimental Situation Involving an Attempt to Demonstrate Telepathy

At the top *(blue insert)*, a person in one room tries to "send" a message through thought to a person (the subject) in another room. The sender selects a card and then attempts to relay the information mentally to the subject. The subject then selects a card, and it is compared to the one previously chosen by the sender to see if the cards match. If the mind-to-mind communication occurs beyond levels of chance, then it would be argued that telepathy has taken place.

Extrasensory experiences fall into three main categories. The first is **telepathy,** *which involves the transfer of thought from one person to another.* For example, this skill is supposedly possessed by people who can "read" another person's mind. If two people are playing cards and one person can tell what cards the other person picked up, telepathy is taking place (see figure 4.41). **Precognition** *involves "knowing" events before they happen.* For example, a fortune-teller might claim to see into the future and tell you what will happen to you in the coming year. Or an astrologer might predict that a major hurricane will strike in Halifax in September of next year. **Clairvoyance** *involves the ability to perceive remote events that are not in sight.* For example, a person at a movie theatre senses a burglar breaking into his house at that moment. **Psychokinesis,** closely associated with ESP, *is the mind-over-matter phenomenon of being able to move objects without touching them, such as mentally getting a chair to rise off the floor or shattering a glass merely by staring at it.*

One of the most famous claims of ESP involved Uri Geller, a psychic who supposedly performed mind-boggling feats. Observers saw Geller correctly predict the number on a die rolled in a closed box eight out of eight times, reproduce drawings hidden in sealed envelopes, bend forks without touching them, and start broken watches. While he had worked as a magician, Geller claimed his supernatural powers were created by energy sent from another universe. Careful investigation of Geller's feats revealed they were nothing more than a magician's tricks. For example, in the case of the die, Geller was allowed to shake the box and open it himself, giving him an opportunity to manipulate the die (Randi, 1980).

Through their astonishing stage performances, many psychics are very convincing. They seem able to levitate tables, communicate with spirits, and read an audience member's mind. Many psychics, like Uri Geller, are also magicians who have the ability to perform sleight-of-hand maneuvers and dramatic manipulations that go unnoticed by most human eyes. One magician's personal goal, though, is to expose the hoaxes of the psychics. James Randi (1980) has investigated a number of psychics' claims and publicized their failures. More about Randi's debunking of supposed psychic powers is presented in Explorations in Psychology.

Scientists have also examined ESP in experimental contexts. Some ESP enthusiasts believe the phenomena are more likely to occur when a subject is totally relaxed and deprived of sensory input. In this kind of ESP experiment, the subject lies down and half a Ping-Pong ball is placed over each eye. An experimenter watches through a one-way mirror from an adjacent room, listening to and recording the subject's statements. At an agreed-upon time someone from another location concentrates on the message to be sent mind to mind.

Carl Sargent (1987) has used this procedure in a number of telepathy experiments and reported a great deal of success. In one experiment, Sargent had a "sender" mentally transmit an image of one of four pictures selected from one of 27 randomly selected sets of four pictures. Immediately afterward, the experimenter and the subject examined a duplicate set of four pictures and together judged and ranked their degree of correspondence with the subject's recorded impression. Experimental psychologist Susan Blackmore (1987) was skeptical about Sargent's ESP success, so she visited his laboratory at Cambridge University in England as an observer. When the subject was shown four pictures, the success rate expected by chance was 25 percent (one of four pictures). In the experimental sessions observed by Blackmore, the subjects' hit rate was 50 percent, far exceeding chance.

Sargent supposedly invokes a number of elaborate procedures to protect randomization, experimenter bias, unbiased selection by the subject, and so on. Blackmore was still skeptical, finding some disturbing flaws in the way Sargent's

EXPLORATIONS IN PSYCHOLOGY
Debunking Psychics' Claims

A WOMAN REPORTS that she has power over the goldfish in a huge 50-gallon tank. She claims that she can will them to swim to either end of the tank. As soon as she wills it, the fish take off.

Under the careful scrutiny of James Randi, this woman's account turned out to be just another fish story. The woman had written Randi, a professional magician, who has a standing offer of $10,000 to anyone whose psychic claims withstand his analysis. In the case of the woman and her goldfish, Randi received a letter from her priest validating her extraordinary power. Randi talked with the priest, who told him that the woman would put her hands in front of her body and then run to one end of the tank. The fish soon followed. Since the fish could see out of the tank just as we can see into it, Randi suggested that she put opaque brown wrapping paper over one end of the tank and then try her powers. The woman did and called Randi about the result, informing him that she had discovered something new about her powers: that her mind could not penetrate the brown paper. The woman believed that she had magical powers and completely misunderstood why Randi had asked her to place the brown paper over the fish tank.

Magician James Randi (right) has investigated a large number of psychics' claims. No one has yet won Randi's standing offer of $10,000 to anyone whose psychic claims withstand his analysis.

No one has claimed Randi's $10,000 prize, but he has been called to investigate several hundred reports of supernatural and occult powers. Faith healers have been among those he has evaluated. Randi has witnessed individuals yelling and dancing up and down, saying they are healed of such maladies as cancer and diabetes. When asked how they know they are healed, they usually say it is because they no longer have the disease or because the faith healer told them so. On checking back with the "healed" a week later, Randi has found diabetics taking insulin and a cancer patient resuming radiation therapy. In some cases, their health has dramatically worsened, as in the case of a diabetic who had to be taken to the hospital because he had stopped his insulin treatment. When asked if they still believed in the faith healer's treatment, it is not unusual to hear these individuals say that they just did not believe strongly enough.

Randi (1997) makes the distinction between the tricks of magicians like him, and the work of psychics and faith healers. He says that magic is done for entertainment, the other for swindling.

experiments were conducted. In some sessions, he did the randomization of the picture himself, putting himself where he could manipulate the ordering of the pictures. In other sessions, he came in while the subject was judging the pictures and "pushed" the subject toward the picture that had been "transmitted" by the "sender." Further, as Jim Alcock (1981) stresses, parapsychologists are often statistically unsophisticated, uncritically accepting any unexplained departure from chance results as evidence in favor of ESP.

No one has been able to replicate the high hit rates in Sargent's experiments. Proponents of ESP such as Sargent claim they have demonstrated the existence of ESP, but critics such as Alcock and Blackmore demand to see or experience the same phenomena themselves. Replication is one of the hallmarks of scientific investigation, yet replication has been a major thorn in the side of ESP researchers. ESP phenomena have not been reproducible when rigorous experimental standards are applied (Bates, 1995; Hines, 1988) ◄ IIII P. 34.

At this point, we have discussed a number of ideas about perception. To help you sort out the main concepts in this discussion, turn to summary table 4.4.

Extrasensory Perception
James Randi

SUMMARY TABLE 4.4
Perception

Concept	Processes/Related Ideas	Characteristics/Description
Attention	Its Nature	Selective attention involves focusing on a specific aspect of experience while ignoring others. Not only is attention selective, it also is shiftable. Attention is influenced by a person's motivation and interests, as well as characteristics of stimuli, such as novelty. The Stroop effect is an example of automatic perception in which it is difficult to say words for colors that are printed in a different color.
Principles of Perception	Shape Perception	Shape is perceived because it is marked off by contour. Gestalt psychologists developed a number of principles of perceptual organization, a fundamental one being that the whole is not equal to the sum of its parts.
	Depth Perception	Depth perception is our ability to perceive objects as three-dimensional. To see a world of depth, we use binocular cues, such as retinal disparity and convergence, and monocular cues (also called pictorial cues), such as linear perspective, texture gradient, relative size, interposition, shadowing, and aerial perspective.
	Motion Perception	Motion perception focuses both on real movement and apparent movement. Stroboscopic motion and movement aftereffects are two prominent forms of apparent movement.
	Perceptual Constancy	This concept includes size, shape, and brightness constancy. Experience with objects and distance cues help us to see objects as unchanging.
Illusions	Their Nature	Illusions occur when two objects produce exactly the same retinal image but are perceived as different images. Among the more than 200 different illusions are the Müller-Lyer illusion and the moon illusion. Perceptual constancies and cultural experiences are among the factors thought to be responsible for illusions.
Issues in Perception	Approaches to Perception	Two main approaches are the information-processing approach and the ecological approach. The information-processing approach states that perception is the process of internally representing information from the world. The individual cognitively constructs an image of the world based on sensory input plus information retrieved from memory. The ecological approach states that perception's function is to bring the organism into contact with the world and increase its adaptation. A key aspect of perceptual adaptation in the ecological view is to be able to detect perceptual invariants. In the ecological view, the world is perceived directly and perception is for action.
	Is Perception Innate or Learned?	Experiments using the visual cliff with young infants and animals indicate that some of the ability to perceive depth is likely innate. Studies of formerly blind adults are inconclusive as to whether perception is innate or learned. Cross-cultural studies suggest that experiences contribute to how people perceive the world. A wise conclusion is this: Perception is influenced by nature and nurture.
	Extrasensory Perception	Extrasensory perception is perception that does not occur through normal sensory channels. Three main forms are telepathy, precognition, and clairvoyance. Psychokinesis is a closely related phenomenon. The claims of ESP enthusiasts have not held up to scientific scrutiny.

Overview

Overview

WE BEGAN THIS CHAPTER by evaluating how people detect and perceive the world; we defined sensation and perception and also discussed thresholds and signal detection theory. Next we read about the visual sense—the visual stimulus and the eye, from eye to brain and neural-visual processing; and the auditory system—the nature of sound and how we experience it, structures and functions of the ear, theories of hearing, and neural-auditory processing. We also learned about the skin, chemical, kinesthetic, and vestibular senses. Our coverage of perception focused on attention, principles of perception, illusions, and issues in perception. Don't forget that you can obtain a more detailed overview of the chapter by again studying the four summary tables on pages 106, 115, 127, and 144.

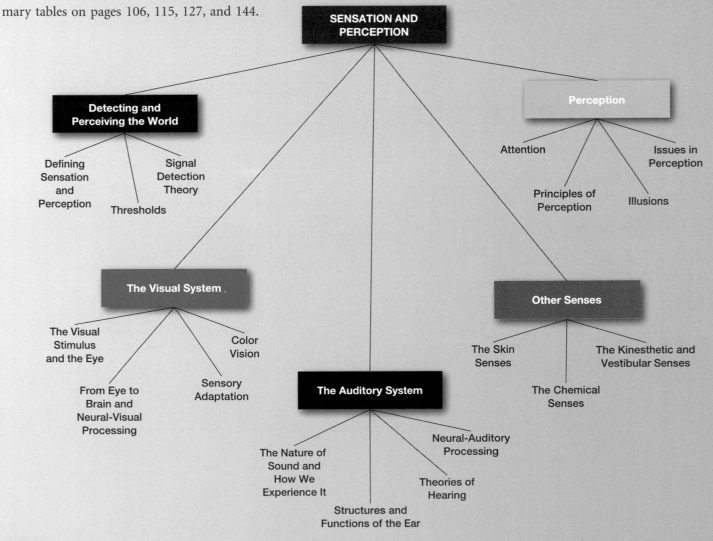

Key Terms

sensation 102
perception 102
psychophysics 102
absolute threshold 102
noise 103
difference threshold 105
Weber's law 105
signal detection theory 105
light 106
wavelength 106
sclera 107
iris 107
pupil 107
cornea 107
lens of the eye 107
accommodation 108
retina 108
transduction 108
rods 108
cones 108
fovea 109
blind spot 109

feature detectors 110
sensory adaptation 110
hue 111
saturation 111
brightness 112
trichromatic theory 112
monochromats 112
dichromats 112
trichromats 113
afterimages 113
opponent-process theory 114
sounds 116
frequency 116
pitch 116
amplitude 116
loudness 117
complex sounds 117
timbre 117
outer ear 118
middle ear 118
inner ear 118
cochlea 118

basilar membrane 118
organ of Corti 118
place theory 118
frequency theory 120
volley principle 120
auditory nerve 120
thermoreceptors 121
pain 121
gate-control theory 122
acupuncture 122
papillae 122
olfactory epithelium 124
kinesthetic sense 125
vestibular sense 125
semicircular canals 126
selective attention 128
Stroop effect 129
contour 129
figure-ground relationship 129
Gestalt psychology 129
depth perception 130

binocular cues 130
monocular cues 130
disparity 131
apparent movement 136
stroboscopic motion 136
movement aftereffects 136
size constancy 136
shape constancy 136
brightness constancy 136
visual illusion 137
information-processing approach 139
ecological approach 139
carpentered-world hypothesis 141
extrasensory perception (ESP) 141
telepathy 142
precognition 142
clairvoyance 142
psychokinesis 142

Key People

E. H. Weber 105
David Hubel and Torsten Wiesel 110

Thomas Young and Hermann von Helmholtz 112
Ewald Hering 113
Georg von Békésy 119

Ronald Melzak and Patrick Wall 122
David Marr 139
James J. Gibson 139

Eleanor Gibson and Richard Walk 139
James Randi 139
James Alcock 141

Psychology Checklist
SENSATION AND PERCEPTION

How much have you learned since the beginning of the chapter? Use the following statements to help you review your knowledge and understanding of the chapter material. First, read the statement and mentally or briefly demonstrate on paper that you can outline and discuss the relevant information.

_____ I know how to define sensation and perception.
_____ I can discuss different types of thresholds.
_____ I can describe what signal detection theory is.
_____ I can discuss the visual stimulus and the eye.
_____ I am aware of how information is transmitted from the eye to the brain and of what neural-visual processing is.
_____ I can describe what sensory adaptation is.
_____ I know about color vision, including different theories about it.
_____ I can discuss the nature of sound and how people experience it.

_____ I know about the ear's structures and functions.
_____ I am aware of what neural-auditory processing is.
_____ I can describe the skin senses and chemical senses, as well as the kinesthetic and vestibular senses.
_____ I can discuss the nature of attention.
_____ I know about the principles of perception involved in shape perception, depth perception, motion perception, and perceptual constancy.
_____ I can describe the nature of illusions.
_____ I can evaluate issues in perception that involve approaches to perception, whether perception is innate or learned, and extrasensory perception.

For any item that you did not check off, go back and locate the relevant material in the chapter. Review the material until you feel that you can check off the item. You may want to use this checklist later in preparing for an exam.

Taking It to the Net

1. Noise-induced hearing loss (NIHL) is an extremely widespread, yet underreported, problem. Sounds that are loud enough to damage sensitive inner-ear structures can produce hearing loss that is not reversible by any available medical or surgical treatment. We are inundated with sounds throughout the day that reduce our normal hearing capabilities. What ear structures are affected by loud noise, and at what level does noise become dangerous? Give examples of dangerous noise that you are exposed to on a daily basis and what you can do to reduce the risk of NIHL.

2. Have you ever seen a visual illusion? A visual illusion occurs when two discrete objects produce identical retinal images, but are perceived as being different. They occur because we rely on certain visual cues to explain visual stimuli, and when the cues are deliberately used to deceive us, we perceive images as being different. One such illusion is the Hering illusion. Explain the phenomenon of the Hering illusion. What do you see? Why do you see that? What occurs in your visual system that could account for this illusion?

3. One important aspect of driving automobiles is being aware of your driving "blind spot." It can obstruct your view and/or cause you to miss seeing another car or person. A similar effect occurs in our actual eyes. A certain spot on our eyes is completely without the ability to see. Where is the blind spot in the human eye, and why does it exist? Give your answer in terms of both the biological structures of the eye and subjective perceptual experience. How does your eye react when stimuli in and surrounding the blind spot are altered? Does it adjust for these changes?

Connect to http://www.mcgrawhill.ca/college/santrock to find the answers!

Resources for Psychology and Life

Human Behavior in Global Perspective (1990)
by Marshall Segall, Pierre Dasen, John Berry, and Ype Poortinga
New York: Pergamon

Segall's research has made important contributions to an understanding of cultural influences on perception.

The Canadian National Institute for the Blind
CNIB National Communications
1929 Bayview Avenue
Toronto, Ontario M4G 3E8
http://www.cnib.ca/

In the words of the CNIB mission statement: "Whether it's helping children become literate in Braille, aiding adults in acquiring workplace skills, or teaching seniors the daily living skills that can help them continue to lead independent lives, the CNIB has always been guided by a key principle: people who are blind or visually impaired can be as productive, fulfilled, and happy as sighted people."

Canadian Association of the Deaf
Suite 203, 251 Bank Street
Ottawa, Ontario K2P 1X3
http://www.cad.ca/

This organization describes itself as "the national consumer organization of the deaf people of Canada. It combines the purposes of a research and information centre, an advisory council, a representative body, a self-help society, and a community action organization."

Pseudoscience and the Paranormal (1988)
by Terence Hines
Buffalo, NY: Prometheus Books

This comprehensive book examines the empirical evidence behind virtually all forms of alleged paranormal and pseudoscientific phenomena, including biorhythms, graphology, plant perception, subliminal perception, astrology, and UFO abductions. The author analyzes the puzzling question of why people continue to believe in the reality of the supernatural in spite of overwhelming evidence against it.

Seeing: Illusion, Brain, and Mind (1980)
by J. P. Frisby
New York: Oxford University Press

This fascinating book presents many illusions and describes attempts to explain them.

Sensation and Perception (1999, 5th ed.)
by Stanley Coren, Lawrence Ward & James Enns
Fort Worth, TX: Harcourt Brace

This current textbook provides in-depth coverage of many topics in sensation and perception.

The Story of My Life (1970)
by Helen Keller
New York: Airmont

This fascinating portrayal of Helen Keller's life as a blind person provides insights into blind people's perception of the world and how they use other senses.

Chapter 5

CHAPTER OUTLINE

WHAT IS CONSCIOUSNESS?

SLEEP

Why Do We Sleep?

Sleep and Circadian Rhythms

Sleep Deprivation and Sleep Needs

Stages of Sleep

The Neural Basis of Sleep

Sleep Disorders

DREAMS

The Interpretation of Dreams

More About Dreams

HYPNOSIS

Definition and History

The Hypnotic State: Features and Individual Differences

Theories of Hypnosis

Applications of Hypnosis

PSYCHOACTIVE DRUGS

The Uses of Psychoactive Drugs

Types of Psychoactive Drugs

Exploring Addiction and Drug Abuse

States of Consciousness

Images of Psychology and Life
Colin Kemp's Tragic Night Terror

> *"The ultimate gift of conscious life is a sense of mystery that encompasses it."*
>
> Lewis Mumford
> *American Cultural Historian, 20th Century*

Preview

MOST OF US take for granted our nightly sojourn in the realm of sleep. But as you will see shortly, the experiences of one man, Colin Kemp, stimulate us to wonder about the nature of sleep and states of consciousness. These are some of the questions we will explore in this chapter:

- What are some different states of consciousness we experience?
- Why do we sleep? How much sleep do we need? What happens when we are deprived of sleep?
- Can you influence what you dream about?
- Can everyone be hypnotized?
- Why do people take psychoactive drugs?
- What are some strategies for preventing and treating drug abuse?

IT WAS AUGUST 1985, and Colin Kemp, a 33-year-old salesman in Caterham, England, went to sleep as usual. About two hours later, he was confronted by two soldiers in his bedroom. They started to chase him. One soldier had a knife, the other a gun. Kemp ran away from them as fast as he could, but he wasn't fast enough. Kemp wrestled with the knife-wielding soldier. The other soldier aimed his gun at Kemp's head. Kemp tripped him, gripped his neck, and began choking him, but he slipped away. He turned, aimed the gun at Kemp, and fired. Kemp awoke in a state of panic, sweat pouring down his head. In a frenzy of terror, he turned to his wife, who was lying next to him in bed. She was dead. Kemp had strangled her, not the soldier.

A trial was held nine months later. Kemp said he was asleep when he killed his wife, pleading not guilty to the murder charge because he had intended to kill the solider, not his wife. Psychiatrists testified on Kemp's behalf, instructing the jury that Kemp was having a night terror at the time he killed his wife. *Night terrors* are characterized by sudden arousal from sleep and intense fear, usually accompanied by a number of physiological reactions such as rapid heart rate and breathing, loud screams, heavy perspiration, and physical movement. In most instances, the individual has little or no memory of what happened during the night terror.

Kemp experienced night terrors on two occasions prior to the fatal event. Both times he was being chased during his sleep. In one of the night terrors, he punched at his wife. She awakened and asked what was happening. The second time he kicked her in the back. Strangling someone to death is a much more elaborate and sustained activity than kicking an individual in the back. Is it possible that an action like Kemp's—strangling someone to death—could actually take place during sleep? The jury apparently thought so. They acquitted Kemp.

They viewed his act as an unconscious one. That is, the jury concluded that Kemp was not aware of what he was doing (Restak, 1988). One final note: Be aware that night terrors rarely lead to such extreme behavior as Colin Kemp's.

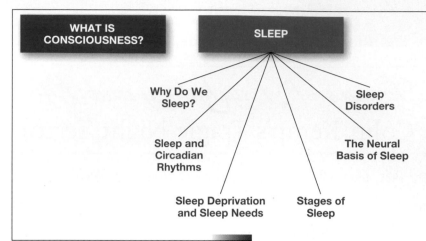

The Nature of Consciousness
Internet Resources on Consciousness

What Is Consciousness?

For much of the twentieth century, psychologists shunned the slippery, subjective trappings of consciousness that intrigued their predecessors in the late nineteenth century. Instead, they focused on overt behaviors and the rewards and punishments that determined those behaviors (Skinner, 1938; Watson, 1913). Recently, though, the study of consciousness has gained widespread respectability in cognitive science (Baars, 1999; Nelson, 1996). For the first time in many decades, psychologists from many different fields are interested in consciousness, including its relation to unconsciousness (Cohen & Schooler, 1996; Grossenbacher, 1999; Schacter, 1999). As we go through our lives, we process information at different levels of awareness. We are aware of some of the processing, unaware of other processing (Hunt, 1995).

Although there is still disagreement about the nature of consciousness, we can define **consciousness** *as awareness of both external and internal stimuli or events.* The external events include what you attend to as you go through your day—the comment your best friend just made about your new hairstyle, the car in front of you that just swerved to miss a dog, the music you are listening to on your Walkman, for example. Internal events include your awareness of your sensations—my headache just returned, I'm breathing too fast, my stomach's rumbling—as well as your thoughts and feelings—I'm really having trouble in biology this semester, I'm anxious about the exam next week, I'm happy Marsha is coming with me to the game tonight.

The contents of our awareness may change from one moment to the next, since information can move rapidly in and out of consciousness. Many years ago, William James (1890/1950) described the mind as a **stream of consciousness**—*a continuous flow of changing sensations, images, thoughts, and feelings.* Our minds race from one topic to the next—from thinking about the person who is approaching us, to how well we feel, to what we are going to do tomorrow, to where we are going for lunch.

While William James was interested in charting the shifting nature of our stream of consciousness, remember that Sigmund Freud (1900/1953) believed that most of our thoughts are unconscious. **Unconscious thought,** *according to Freud, is a reservoir of unacceptable wishes, feelings, and thoughts that are beyond conscious awareness.* Unconscious thought has nothing to do with being unconscious after being knocked out by a blow on the head in a boxing match, being anesthetized, or falling into a coma.

According to Freud, unconscious thoughts are too laden with anxiety and other negative emotions for consciousness to admit them. For example, a young man who is nervous around women breaks into a cold sweat as a woman approaches him. He is unconscious of the fact that his fear of women springs from the cold, punitive way his mother treated him when he was a child. Freud believed that one of psychotherapy's main goals was to bring unconscious thoughts into conscious awareness so they can be addressed and dealt with.

Freud accurately recognized that consciousness is not simply a matter of being aware or unaware. Sometimes consciousness is highly focused and alert; at other times it is more passive. Even sleep, once thought to be completely passive and unconscious, is now known to have active and at least minimally conscious properties. According to McMaster University psychologist Larry Jacoby, one important distinction is that between controlled and automatic processes.

Controlled processes *represent the most alert states of consciousness, in which individuals actively focus their efforts toward a goal.* Controlled processes require focused attention and interfere with other ongoing activities. In memory, this means being aware that you are trying to remember (Kelley & Jacoby, 1996). Consider Renée, who is learning how to use her new personal computer. She is completely absorbed in reading and memorizing parts of the tutorial manual that accompanies the computer—she doesn't hear her roommate humming to herself or the song on the radio. This state of focused awareness is what is meant by controlled processes.

Once Renée learns how to use the software, using the keyboard becomes almost automatic; that is, she doesn't have to concentrate so hard on how to perform each of the steps required to get the computer to do something. Two weeks ago she had to stop and concentrate but now her fingers fly across the computer keyboard. This kind of consciousness involves automatic processes. **Automatic processes** *are forms of consciousness that require minimal attention and do not interfere with other ongoing activities.* Automatic processes require less conscious effort than controlled processes. In memory this means remembering without deliberately trying (Jacoby, 1998). When we are awake, our automatic behaviors should be thought of as lower in awareness than controlled processes, rather than not conscious at all.

"If you ask me, all three of us are in different states of awareness."

Daydreaming *is another form of consciousness that involves a low level of conscious effort.* Daydreaming lies somewhere between active consciousness and dreaming while we are asleep. It is a little like dreaming when we are awake. Daydreams usually start spontaneously when what we are doing requires less than our full attention. Mind-wandering is probably the most obvious type of daydreaming. We regularly take brief side trips into our own private kingdoms of imagery and memory even as we read, listen, or work. When we daydream we often drift off into a world of fantasy. We imagine ourselves on dates, at parties, on television, at faraway places, at another time in our lives. Sometimes our daydreams are about ordinary, everyday events, such as paying the rent, getting our hair done, or dealing with someone at work. This semiautomatic thought flow can be useful. As you daydream while you shave, iron a pair of pants, or walk to the store, you may be making plans or solving a problem. Daydreams can remind us of important things ahead. Daydreaming keeps our minds active while helping us to cope, to create, and to fantasize.

When we sleep and dream, our level of awareness is lower than when we daydream, but we no longer think of being asleep as the complete absence of consciousness. Sleep and dreams, though, are at very low levels of consciousness.

So far the states of consciousness we have described are normal everyday occurrences in each of our lives. An **altered state of consciousness** *occurs when a person is in a mental state that noticeably differs from normal awareness.* Drugs, meditation, traumas, fatigue, hypnosis, and sensory deprivation produce altered states of consciousness. Interestingly, it is also possible that new media, such as television, video games, the Internet, and virtual reality can also alter consciousness (Preston, 1998). Whether a state of consciousness is described as normal or altered depends on how the word *normal* is defined. Someone who drinks a caffeinated soda to increase alertness, for instance, is considered to be in a normal state of consciousness. But someone who takes a drug that induces hallucinations, such as LSD, is considered to be in an altered state of consciousness. In Explorations in Psychology, we discuss the role that altered states of consciousness played in the origin of some of the world's great religions.

As you can see, our states of consciousness are many, varied, and complex (Rose, 1999). A summary of some of the main forms of consciousness and their level of awareness or unawareness is presented in figure 5.1. Now we turn our attention to the fascinating world of sleep and dreams.

HIGH-LEVEL AWARENESS	Controlled processes	High level of awareness, focused attention required		This student is using controlled processes that require focused concentration.
LOWER-LEVEL AWARENESS	Automatic processes	Awareness, but minimal attention required		This woman is an experienced computer operator. Her maneuvers with the keyboard are automatic, requiring minimal awareness.
	Daydreaming	Low level of awareness and conscious effort, somewhere between active consciousness and dreaming while asleep		Our daydreams often start spontaneously when what we are doing requires less than our full attention.
	Altered states of consciousness	A mental state noticeably different from normal awareness; produced by drugs, trauma, fatigue, hypnosis, meditation, and sensory deprivation		Shown here is a woman being hypnotized.
	Sleep and dreams	No longer thought of as the absence of consciousness, but they are at very low levels of consciousness		All of us dream while we sleep, but some of us dream more than others.
NO AWARENESS	Unconscious mind (Freudian)	Reservoir of unacceptable wishes, feelings, and memories, often with sexual and aggressive overtones, that are too anxiety provoking to be admitted to consciousness		The woman shown lying on the couch is undergoing psychoanalytic therapy to reveal her unconscious thoughts.
	Unconscious (non-Freudian)	Being knocked unconscious by a blow or when we are anesthetized; deep prolonged unconsciousness characterizes individuals who go into a coma as the result of injury, disease, or poison		Unconsciousness can result from an injury, such as a blow to the head.

Figure 5.1
Forms of Consciousness and Levels of Awareness

EXPLORATIONS IN PSYCHOLOGY
Altered States of Consciousness and the World's Great Religions

- YEMENITE JEWS in a Jerusalem synagogue, wrapped in their prayer shawls, barefoot, sitting cross-legged, and swaying back and forth recite the Torah.
- Dar Jo and Lai Sarr, Zen monks, explore the Buddha-nature at the center of their beings through zazen meditation, meditative walking, and chanting sutras.
- Coptic Christians in Cairo, Egypt, emit an eerie and spine-tingling cry of spiritual fervor.
- Muslims in Pakistan fast from dawn to dusk during the month of Ramadan, consistent with the fourth pillar of Islam.

Today billions of people around the world guide their lives by the tenets of Judaism, Christianity, Islam, and Buddhism (Hood, 1995). Most religions involve the practice of altered states of consciousness as expected parts of religious ritual, whether the altered state is derived through meditation, prayer, fasting, or substance use.

Many of the world's great religions began with a moment of revelation, an ecstatic moment infused with such mystery, power, and beauty that it forever altered the founding prophet's consciousness (Paloutzian, 1996). God called Abraham, bidding him to leave his homeland in Mesopotamia to seek a promised land known as Canaan. There he founded a religious faith, Judaism, whose followers were to enjoy a special relationship with the creator of heaven and earth. In the Christian religion, death could not vanquish Jesus in A.D. 29; following his death, Jesus appeared in a revelation to Paul, who then became a believer in Christ's resurrection and traveled widely to preach Christianity. In the Islamic religion, Mohammed saw a vision and heard a voice in the year A.D. 610 that would alter his life; the angel Gabriel came to Mohammed and said, "Mohammed, thou art a messenger of God."

Mystical revelation did not play a role in the creation of Buddhism. In the late sixth century B.C., Siddhartha Gautama (Buddha) developed enlightenment without assistance from any teachers or divine revelation. The Buddhist path to enlightenment involves meditating—turning inward to discover that within oneself is the origin of the world, the end of the world, and the way to all goals (Hunt, 1995).

Regardless of whether you believe in the teachings of any of the world's religions, you can see the importance of altered states of consciousness as a critical component in the foundation or practice of the religions of the world. Can you identify how altered states of consciousness might play a role in your own religious tradition?

Among those who practice altered states of consciousness in the world's religions are (a) Zen monks who explore the Buddha-nature at the center of their beings and (b) Muslims in Pakistan who fast from dawn to dusk during the month of Ramadan as the fourth pillar of Islam. What are some other ways that altered states of consciousness might be involved in religion?

The Nature of Sleep

Jet Lag and Circadian Rhythms

Sleep

Each night something lures us from work, from play, and from our loved ones into a solitary state. It is sleep, which claims about one-third of the time in our lives, more than any other pursuit. This alluring realm of mental escapades we enter each night has intrigued philosophers and scientists for centuries. Those who investigated sleep were primarily interested in its role as a springboard for dreams. We no longer regard sleep as the complete absence of consciousness. Now we know that sleep involves much more (Broughton & Ogilvie, 1992).

Why Do We Sleep?

There are two main theories about why we sleep—repair theory and ecological theory. **Repair theory** *holds that sleep restores, replenishes, and rebuilds our brains and bodies, which somehow are worn out or used up by the day's waking activities.* This idea fits with the feeling of being "worn out" before we sleep and "restored" when we wake. Aristotle proposed a repair theory of sleep centuries ago, and most experts today believe in some version of repair (Dement, 1999; Hirshkowitz, Moore, & Minhoto, 1997).

Ecological theory *is a relatively recent view of why we sleep. This evolutionary-based approach argues that the main purpose of sleep is to prevent animals from wasting their energy and harming themselves during those parts of the day or night to which they have not adapted.* For example, it was not adaptive for our ancestors to fumble around in the dark, risking accidents or attack by large predators such as lions and tigers. So, like the chimpanzees who slept safely in treetops, our ancestors presumably hid and slept through the night.

In today's world, ecological factors are still important for animals in the wild. With good hiding places, small prey animals (such as mice and rabbits) sleep regularly and safely all through the daylight hours. By contrast, large animals that cannot hide, such as horses and cows, show scanty and irregular sleep patterns. Thus, body weight and danger of attack are important factors in determining how much sleep animals get. The total sleep of different animals ranges from slightly less than 3 to almost 20 hours of every 24-hour period (Webb, 1993) (see figure 5.2).

Both repair theory and ecological theory have merit. Repair theory accounts for the results of sleep deprivation. That is, not getting enough sleep makes us sleepy and getting sleep helps us to recover. Ecological theory explains the wide range of sleep and timing of sleep in animals. Possibly sleep was originally important for keeping humans out of harm's way but since has evolved to allow for restoration.

Sleep and Circadian Rhythms

We are unaware of most of our body's rhythms—for example, the rise and fall of hormones in the bloodstream, accelerated and decelerated cycles of brain activity, highs and lows in body temperature. Some rhythms are *circadian* (from the Latin words *circa* meaning "about" and *dies* meaning "day"). A **circadian rhythm** *is a daily behavioral or physiological cycle; an example is the 24-hour sleep/wake cycle.*

One circumstance in which the circadian rhythm of the human sleep/wake cycle may become desynchronized is *jet lag,* which occurs when we take a long cross-country or transoceanic flight. If you fly from Vancouver to Halifax and then go to bed at 11 P.M. Atlantic time, you may have trouble falling asleep because your body is still on Pacific time. Even if you sleep for 8 hours that night, you may find it hard to wake up at 7 A.M. Atlantic time, because your body

*𝓕*igure 5.2

From Bats to Horses: The Wide Range of Sleep in Animals

Animal	Hours of Sleep Per 24-Hour Period
Bat	19.9
Armadillo	18.5
Cat	14.5
Fox	9.8
Rhesus monkey	9.6
Rabbit	8.4
Human	8.0
Cow	3.9
Sheep	3.8
Horse	2.9

thinks it is 4 A.M. If you stay in Halifax for several days, your body will adjust to the new schedule.

The phase shift that occurred when you flew from Vancouver to Halifax means your body time is out of phase, or synchronization, with clock time. When jet lag occurs, it is the result of two or more body rhythms being out of sync. You usually go to bed when your body temperature begins to drop, but, in your new location, you may be trying to go to bed when it is rising. When you wake up in the morning, your adrenal glands release large doses of cortisol. In your new geographical location, the glands may be releasing this chemical just as you are getting ready for bed at night.

Another circumstance in which circadian rhythms may become desynchronized is when shift workers change their work hours. Shift rotation might have been one of the causes of the nuclear accident at Three Mile Island (Moore-Ede, Sulzman, & Fuller, 1982). The team of workers monitoring the nuclear plant when the incident took place had been placed on night shift just after a six-week period of constant shift rotation.

Not all shift workers are affected equally (Monk, 1993). A small proportion actually prefer shift work. People over 50, those who require more than nine hours of sleep a night, and those with a tendency to be "morning types" (get up early, go to bed early) are the most adversely affected by shift work.

What can help shift workers adjust to their schedule? Use of daylight levels of artificial illumination at work on the night shift and precise specification of eight hours of total darkness at home from 9 A.M. to 5 P.M. can dramatically speed up the realignment of circadian rhythms (Czeilse and others, 1990). Although sleeping pills can improve daytime sleep, they don't affect circadian realignment and their long-term use is not recommended.

In Canada the impact of the disruption of circadian rhythms stems from the fact that days are short in the winter and long in the summer. The especially short days of winter result in higher incidences of *seasonal affective disorder* (SAD), a seasonal form of depression accompanied by increased appetite and *hypersomnia,* or excessive sleepiness. Perhaps not surprisingly, some patients can suffer from summer SAD when days get especially long. The symptoms are the opposite of those reported in winter SAD: decreased appetite and insomnia (Wehr & Rosenthal, 1989). As you might imagine, the effects of winter and summer SAD become exacerbated the further north you live. People who live north of the Arctic Circle can face months of endless night and months of endless day.

Winter SAD can be treated, either with some forms of medication or with daily exposure to white light (Tam, Lam, & Levitt 1995). Using light bulbs which emit the full spectrum of sunlight may be especially helpful. Also, York University psychologist Shimon Amir has found that the circadian clock can be reset, mainly with ultra-short light flashes (Arvanitogiannis & Amir, 1999).

As researchers became intrigued by the role of biological rhythms, naturally they were curious about what happens when an individual is completely isolated from all *zeitgebers:* clocks, calendars, night, the moon, the sun, and other indices of time (Kales, 1970; Siffre, 1975). French scientist Michel Siffre entered Midnight Cave near Del Rio, Texas, on February 14, 1972. A small nylon tent deep within the cave was Siffre's home for six months. Because Siffre could not see or sense the sun rising and setting in the cave, he began to live by biological cycles instead of by days.

Siffre referred to each one of his sleep/wake cycles as a day. Siffre's days closely resembled a 24-hour cycle throughout the six months in the cave, although they were slightly longer and more varied toward the end of the six months. Near the end of his stay in the cave, occasionally Siffre's days were very long, but most still averaged about 28 hours.

Sleep researchers are recording Randy Gardner's (he's the person doing the pushups) behavior during his 264-hour period of sleep deprivation. Most people who try to stay up even one night have difficulty remaining awake from 3 to 6 A.M. Why shouldn't you follow Gardner's sleep deprivation example?

The photograph shows the interior of the cave where Michel Siffre lived for six months. What were Siffre's sleep/wake cycles like?

Interestingly, the natural circadian rhythm, or *free-running cycle*, of most animals, including humans, is 25 to 26 hours, but our internal clocks easily adapt to the 24-hour rhythms (light, sounds, warmth) of the turning earth. When we are isolated from environmental cues, our sleep/wake cycles continue to be rather constant but typically longer than 24 hours, as the experience of Michel Siffre showed.

Sleep Deprivation and Sleep Needs

How long can people go without sleep and still function? One 17-year-old high school student, Randy Gardner, went without sleep for 264 hours (about 11 days), the longest observed period of total sleep deprivation. He did it as part of a science fair project (Dement, 1978). Carefully monitored by sleep researchers, Randy did suffer some hallucinations, speech, and movement problems. However, on the last night he played arcade games with sleep researcher William Dement and consistently beat him. Randy recovered fully after a 14 hour 40 minute restorative sleep. Randy's story is exceptional in that he was able to maintain a high level of physical activity and received national TV coverage, which helped him stay awake. Even then, he almost fell asleep several nights, but his observers would not let him close his eyes. In more normal circumstances, individuals have far more difficulty staying awake all night, especially between 3:00 and 6:00 A.M.

Although Randy Gardner was able to go about 11 days without sleep, the following discussion should convince you that even getting 60 to 90 minutes less sleep than you need each night can harm your ability to perform optimally the next day. As we will also see, it doesn't take very long for sleep deprivation to play havoc with our lives.

According to the University of Ottawa's Roger Broughton, excessive daytime sleepiness is a major clinical problem. Maas (1998) argues that 50 percent of the American population is sleep deprived and a similar proportion report trouble sleeping on any given night. With adequate sleep you give yourself the opportunity to perform at peak level the next day.

On-Line Circadian Rhythm Experiment
Biological Clocks and Rhythms

The average North American gets just under 7 hours of sleep a night (National Commission on Sleep Disorders Research, 1993). Many sleep researchers believe people need to deposit at least 8 hours of sleep in their nightly sleep debt account to stay fully alert and optimize their performance the next day (Maas, 1998). A sleep debt can build quickly, not unlike finance charges on an unpaid bank balance, when you are burning the candle at both ends. Consider a medical technician who tried to get by on about 4 hours of sleep a night—ironically, at a sleep disorders center—so she could take care of her infant daughter during the day. Before long, she developed heart palpitations, dizziness, a fear of driving, and wide mood swings from being up 20 hours a day. In time she might even have become violent (Broughton & Shimsu, 1995).

Some sleep researchers argue that we can benefit from sleeping more than eight hours a night. At one sleep center, the alertness of 8-hour sleepers who claimed to be well-rested increased when they slept two more hours (Roehrs & Roth, 1998). Why are we getting too little sleep? Work and school pressures and family and social obligations often lead to long days and irregular sleep/wake schedules. Not having enough hours in a day, we cheat on our sleep. Most people need to get about 60 to 90 minutes more sleep each day than they presently get.

Stages of Sleep

Stages of sleep correspond to massive electrophysical changes throughout the brain, as the fast, irregular, and low-amplitude activity of wakefulness is replaced by the regular, slow, high-amplitude waves of deep sleep (Ogilvie, 1993; Ogilvie & Harsh, 1994). The invention of the electroencephalograph (EEG) led to some major breakthroughs in understanding sleep by revealing how the brain's electrical activity changes during sleep ◀━━ P. 93. Figure 5.3 shows the EEG patterns for various sleep stages. Coupled with behavioral measures, we now have an even better understanding of how and when we fall asleep.

Alpha waves *make up the EEG pattern of individuals who are awake but relaxed.* As your breathing slows and your brain waves slow further, you enter the somewhat irregular wave pattern of stage 1 sleep. **Sleep spindles** *are brief bursts of higher-frequency waves that periodically occur during stage 2 sleep.* Stage 2 lasts up to 20 minutes. Beginning in stage 3 and increasingly in stage 4, **delta waves,** *which are large, slow brain waves associated with deep sleep, appear.* Together, stages 3 and 4 are often referred to as "deep sleep." The sleeper who awakens during deep sleep often appears confused, and it is during stage 4 sleep that sleepwalking, sleeptalking, and bed-wetting most often occur.

After about 90 minutes of sleep, much of which is spent in stages 3 and 4, the sleeper moves restlessly and drifts up through the sleep stages toward wakefulness. But instead of reentering stage 1, the person enters a different form of sleep called "rapid eye movement" (REM) sleep. **REM sleep** *is a periodic, active stage of sleep during which dreaming occurs.* During REM sleep, the EEG pattern shows fast waves similar to those of relaxed wakefulness and the sleeper's eyeballs move up and down and from left to right (see figure 5.4).

A person who is awakened during REM sleep is more likely to report having dreamed than when awakened at any other stage. Even people who claim they rarely dream frequently report dreaming when they are awakened during REM sleep. The longer the period of REM sleep, the more likely a person will report dreaming. Dreams do occur during slow-wave or non-REM sleep, but the frequency of dreams in the other stages is relatively low.

Through the Eyes of Psychologists

Roger Broughton, *University of Ottawa*

"Excessive daytime sleepiness is a major clinical symptom which has significant socioeconomic impact and is a leading cause of vehicular, occupational and home accidents."

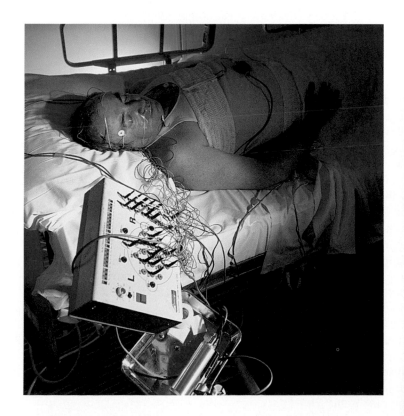

Figure 5.3
Stages of Sleep and EEG Recordings of Brain Waves

Note: Above: An individual being monitored in a sleep experiment.
Right: EEG recordings of brain waves in different stages of sleep.

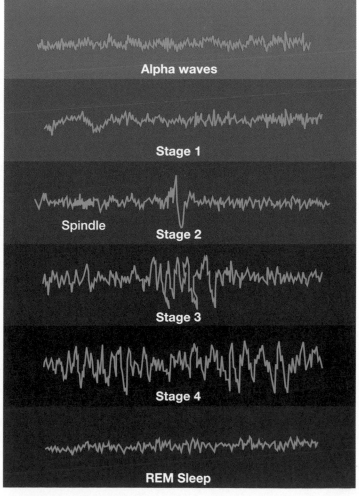

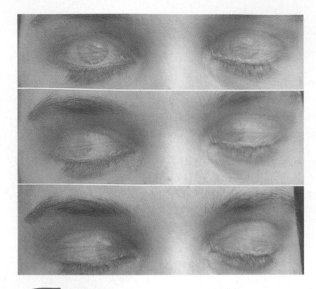

𝒻igure 5.4
REM Sleep
During REM sleep, our eyes move rapidly. Although rapid eye movements are not like the eye movements we make when scanning an image, they do suggest that we were observing the images we see moving in our dreams.

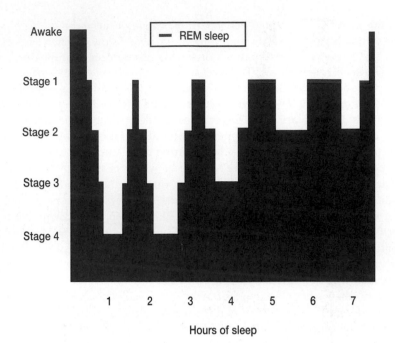

𝒻igure 5.5
The Changing Rhythms of Sleep
During a typical night's sleep, REM sleep (shown in red) increases during the latter part of the night. Stages 3 and 4 dominate sleep early in the night but decrease dramatically toward the end of a night's sleep.

So far we have described a normal cycle of sleep, which consists of four stages, plus REM sleep. There are several important points to remember about the nature of these stages (see figure 5.5). One of these cycles lasts about 90 minutes and recurs several times during the night. We get more deep sleep (stage 4) in the first half of a night's sleep than in the second half. The majority of REM sleep takes place during the latter part of a night's sleep, when the REM period becomes progressively longer. The night's first REM period might last for only about 10 minutes, the final REM period for as long as an hour.

The amount of REM sleep changes over the life span. As indicated in figure 5.6, the percentage of total sleep made up of REM sleep is especially large in early infancy (almost 8 hours). Elderly adults engage in less than one hour of REM sleep a night. Figure 5.6 also reveals how the amount of total sleep changes from approximately 16 hours at the beginning of infancy to less than 6 hours in old age.

These dramatic developmental changes in REM sleep raise questions about its function. For young infants, REM sleep might play a role in stimulating the brain and contributing to its growth. Remember from chapter 1 that an enriched environment contributes to brain growth. Because most of a young infant's time is spent in sleep, REM sleep could be nature's way of stimulating the brain.

REM sleep might also contribute to memory. Researchers have presented individuals with unique phrases before they go to bed (Empson & Clarke, 1970). When they are awakened just before they begin REM sleep, they remember less the next morning than when they are awakened during the other sleep stages.

𝒯hrough the Eyes of Psychologists
Robert Ogilvie, *Brock University*

"From the earliest moments of human thought, people have wondered about the relationship between waking and sleeping."

The Neural Basis of Sleep

For many years researchers thought sleep occurred in the absence of enough sensory stimulation to keep the brain awake. Without stimuli, the brain was believed to just "slow down," producing sleep. But researchers realized that sleep comes and goes without any obvious change in the amount of environmental stimulation. Theorists suggested we might have an internal "activating system" in the reticular formation that keeps the brain activated, or awake, all day (Hobson & McCarley, 1977). According to this theory, "fatigue" of the so-called activating system, or an accumulation of some "sleep toxin" that chemically depresses the activating system, induced sleep.

The contemporary view of sleep is radically different. As you have learned, the brain does not "stop" during sleep, but instead carries out complex processes that produce both REM and non-REM sleep behaviors. In fact, at the cellular level, many neurons fire faster during sleep than in a waking state.

The puzzle is not completely solved, but some of the major pieces of the brain's machinery involved in sleep have been identified. Non-REM sleep, for example, requires the participation of neurons in both the forebrain and the medulla. REM sleep is a period of especially intense brain activity, also requiring the cooperation of a number of brain systems. To read further about the brain's role in sleep and in learning, turn to Explorations in Psychology.

Sleep Disorders

According to Sleep/Wake Disorders Canada, more than two million Canadians, 7 percent, suffer from sleep disorders. A 1995 Gallup poll found that 49 percent of American adults were suffering from sleep disorders, a 15 percent increase from 1991. The increase in sleep disorders is likely due to the increasingly frantic pace of work, work pressures, and an aging population (Aldrich, 1999). Amazingly, 95% of individuals with sleep disorders go undiagnosed and untreated, many of them struggling through the day feeling unmotivated and exhausted (National Commission on Sleep Disorders Research, 1993).

Sleep Disorders

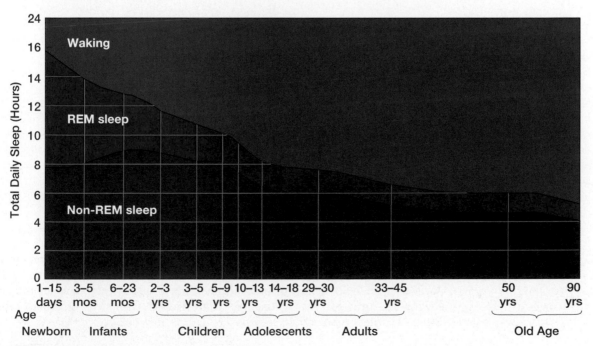

Figure 5.6
Sleep Across the Human Life Span

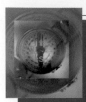

EXPLORATIONS IN PSYCHOLOGY
Can We Learn While We Are Asleep?

KING HENRY IV OF FRANCE once said, "Great eaters and great sleepers are incapable of anything else that's great." But King Henry had not seen the recent sleep research that raises the possibility that learning might take place while we are asleep.

Two recent studies, one on rats and one on university students, demonstrated the value of sleep in strengthening memories from the previous day. To remember where you have been or to learn a new skill, sleep seems to help.

In one of the studies, researchers fitted rats with recording devices that detected simultaneous firings of nerve cells in the hippocampus, a brain structure involved in remembering a new place (Wilson & McNaughton, 1994). When the rats were allowed to explore new locations, different hippocampus cells fired electrical impulses. The researchers found that the nerve cells most likely to fire together during sleep were the ones that fired together during daytime exploration. Apparently, the rat's brain uses sleep as an opportunity to strengthen memories from the previous day's activities.

This type of memory—of places, events, or facts—is called *declarative memory*. Neuroscientists have documented that the hippocampus plays an important role in declarative memory (Tulving & Moscovitsch, 1998). Another type of memory, *procedural memory*, which involves learning skills or habits, like driving a car, does not seem to be based in the hippocampus. Rather, such repetition of tasks trains the brain's outer layer of "thinking" nerve cells to perform the job more automatically.

Researchers had thought that sleep strengthens declarative memory, but they saw no reason why sleep should improve procedural memory. However, in one recent study the results suggested otherwise (Karni & others, 1994). University students were trained to recognize subtle differences in visual patterns: to identify the shape of a figure in a pattern. They improved their performance with practice, and performed the task better after a good night's sleep than at the end of the previous day's practice session, suggesting that their brains were doing something during sleep to enhance the newly learned skill. Actually, earlier research had shown that performance improves after an 8- to 10-hour lag, even if the lag is during the day and the performers are awake during it. The new study documented that the improvement also occurs during sleep.

In this chapter, we have learned that all sleep is not alike—for example, some is slow-wave sleep, other involves REM sleep. Might one phase of sleep enhance learning more than others? In the learning-task sleep study, the researchers monitored the students' brain waves to detect when REM sleep was occurring and rang a bell anytime they began to drift off into REM sleep (Karni & others, 1994). In another trial, the bell went off only during slow-wave sleep.

Apart from the obvious results—such as the students' being a little testy the next day from having their sleep interrupted—some interesting findings emerged in their ability to tell the shape of a pattern. If slow-wave sleep was disrupted, the students still scored better on the tasks than they had the previous day. But if REM sleep was disrupted, the sleep did the students no good and their skill was not improved. Thus, something about REM sleep might hold a key to strengthening this type of memory. Old skills, in which memories are presumably already strong enough, were not diminished by REM sleep deprivation in this study. So, presumably, REM sleep facilitates the learning of new skills (Siegfried, 1994).

But what about material that is presented to individuals during sleep? Could you possibly enhance your performance on tests or learn a foreign language by being presented with information while you are sleeping? The research evidence suggests that sleep learning is ineffective when measured in terms of an individual's ability to consciously remember material presented during sleep (Druckman & Bjork, 1994). So playing back a tape recording of your professor's lecture while you are sleeping will not improve your knowledge of the material.

Sometimes the symptoms of sleep disorders are bizarre and sufferers might not understand their own actions (Maas, 1998). They might be afraid of the stigma associated with their behavior and be unwilling to admit they have a problem. Following are some real-life experiences of individuals with sleep disorders (American Sleep Disorders Association, 1998):

—A sleeping woman who awakened to find herself in a grocery store aisle wheeling a cart filled with 56 boxes of cornflakes
—An air traffic controller whose only way to keep from falling asleep at work was to stand up all night and never sit down

—A man in the back of a moving trailer who sleep-walked out the back door and was killed on the highway

At first glance, these experiences may seem humorous but sleep disorders can cause a great deal of suffering and even death, as it did for the sleepwalker.

Insomnia   Insomnia *is a common sleep problem; put simply, it is the inability to sleep.* Insomnia can involve a problem in falling asleep, waking up during the night, or waking up too early (Davies, 1999). As many as one in ten Canadians has insomnia. It is more common among women, older adults, thin people, depressed or stressed people, and people who are poor (Devries, 1998).

We spend large sums of money, especially on drugs, trying to sleep better (Graber, Garber, & Govin, 1999). In 1997, about one million Canadians over the age of 11 used sleeping pills (Health Canada, 1999). Many sleep experts now believe that physicians have been too quick to prescribe sedatives for insomniacs. Sedatives reduce the amount of time a person spends in stage 4 and REM sleep, and can disrupt the restfulness of sleep. There is some danger of overdose, and over time *tolerance* can develop; sedatives lose their effectiveness, requiring ever greater dosages to achieve the same effect.

If possible, then, sedatives and nonprescription sleeping pills should be used with caution and only for short-term sleep problems. Also, when a person stops using them after several nights, bad dreams and even more insomnia are likely to appear. Sleep experts say they can be used on a temporary basis for short-term insomnia, such as jet lag, the loss of a loved one, or anticipation of a stressful event, such as giving a speech. However, sleeping pills should never be used for chronic insomnia, which lasts six months or more.

Recently, there has been considerable interest in the hormone *melatonin* for reducing insomnia. Melatonin is naturally secreted by the brain's pineal gland in response to darkness. Not only has melatonin been touted as an antidote for insomnia, it has also been promoted as an anti-aging remedy. Research on melatonin's role in inducing sleep and slowing aging is in its early phases with no definitive conclusions reached as yet. One of the potential risks of melatonin is its irregular quality in health-food stores.

Some good strategies for reducing insomnia are shown in figure 5.7.

Sleepwalking and Sleeptalking   Somnambulism *is the formal term for sleepwalking, which occurs during the deepest stages of sleep.* For many years experts believed somnambulists were acting out their dreams. But somnambulism occurs during stages 3 and 4, early in the night, the time when a person is least likely to dream. Sleepwalking is most common in children, although some adults also sleepwalk. Like the case of Colin Kemp and his night terror, there are rare cases of sleepwalkers murdering and being acquitted (e.g. Broughton and others, 1994).

It is safe to awaken sleepwalkers, and it's probably a good idea since they might harm themselves or others as they roam through the night (Swanson, 1999). The most effective treatment for sleepwalking is to institute safety measures, such as erecting gates and locking all doors and windows. Hypnosis, which we will discuss later in the chapter, might be helpful with adults (Mindell, 1996).

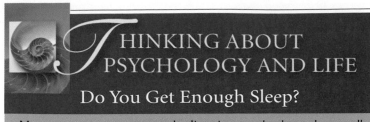

THINKING ABOUT PSYCHOLOGY AND LIFE

Do You Get Enough Sleep?

MANY UNIVERSITY STUDENTS don't get enough sleep. In a poll of U.S. college freshman, more than 80 percent said they stayed up all night at least once during the year (Sax & others, 1995). To evaluate whether you are sleep deprived, answer the following questions yes or no.

Yes	No	
____	____	I need an alarm clock to wake up at the appropriate time.
____	____	It's a struggle for me to get out of bed in the morning.
____	____	I feel tired, irritable, and stressed out during the week.
____	____	I have trouble concentrating.
____	____	I have trouble remembering.
____	____	I feel slow with critical thinking, problem solving, and being creative.
____	____	I often fall asleep watching TV.
____	____	I often fall asleep in boring meetings or lectures in warm rooms.
____	____	I often fall asleep after heavy meals or after low doses of alcohol.
____	____	I often fall asleep within five minutes of getting into bed.
____	____	I often feel drowsy while driving.
____	____	I often sleep extra hours on weekend mornings.
____	____	I often need a nap to get through the day.
____	____	I have dark circles around my eyes.

According to psychologist James Maas (1998), who developed this quiz, if you responded yes to three or more of these items you probably aren't getting enough sleep. Later in the chapter we will describe some good strategies for reducing insomnia that will help you get the sleep you need to optimize your performance the next day and be healthy.

1.	Reduce stress as much as possible
2.	Exercise regularly (but not just before you go to bed)
3.	Keep mentally stimulated during the day
4.	Become a good time manager
5.	Eat a proper diet
6.	Stop smoking
7.	Reduce caffeine intake
8.	Avoid alcohol, especially near bedtime
9.	Take a warm bath before bed
10.	Maintain a relaxing atmosphere in the bedroom
11.	Clear your mind at bedtime
12.	Before going to bed, engage in a relaxation technique such as listening to a tape designed for relaxation
13.	Learn to value sleep
14.	If necessary, contact the health service at your college or university for advice about your sleeping problem

Figure 5.7
Strategies for Reducing Insomnia

Sleep Apnea

Another quirky night behavior is sleeptalking. Most sleeptalkers are young adults, but sleeptalkers come in all ages. If you interrogated a sleeptalker, could you find out what he did last Thursday night? Probably not. Although he may speak to you and make fairly coherent statements, the sleeptalker is soundly asleep. Most likely the sleeptalker will mumble some response to your question, but don't count on its accuracy.

Nightmares and Night Terrors   A **nightmare** *is a frightening dream that awakens the sleeper from REM sleep.* A nightmare's content invariably involves danger—being chased, robbed, raped, murdered, or thrown off a cliff. Most of us have had nightmares, especially when we were young children. Nightmares peak at three to six years of age and then decline, although the average university student experiences four to eight nightmares a year and the average adult 25 years and older has one or two a year (Hartmann, 1993). When people report an increase in the number of nightmares they have, or worsening nightmares, they are often associated with an increase in life stress, such as loss of a relationship, conflict, or some type of negative event (Belicki, Chambers & Ogilvie, 1997).

At the beginning of this chapter, we described the tragic night terror of Colin Kemp. Remember that a **night terror** *is characterized by sudden arousal from sleep and intense fear, usually accompanied by a number of physiological reactions such as rapid heart rate and breathing, loud screams, heavy perspiration, and physical movement.* Night terrors (also called sleep terrors) are less common than nightmares. Unlike nightmares, night terrors occur in slow-wave, non-REM sleep. As many as 6 percent of children have night terrors, with the peak at 5 to 7 years of age and a decrease thereafter. For both nightmares and night terrors, try to awaken and provide soothing reassurance to the person. Children do not usually remember their night terrors in the morning.

Treatment for nightmares and night terrors in adults often involves the use of anxiety reduction techniques, such as relaxation and imagery. We will describe how these techniques are carried out in chapter 6 ("Learning") and chapter 14 ("Therapies").

Narcolepsy   **Narcolepsy** *is the overpowering urge to fall asleep.* The urge is so strong that the person may fall asleep while talking or standing up. Narcoleptics immediately enter REM sleep rather than moving through the sleep stages. Narcoleptics experience severe embarrassment, academic decline and feelings of loss of self-worth (Broughton & Broughton, 1994). Researchers suspect that narcolepsy is inherited, because it runs in families. It may also be related to a disorder of the body's circadian rhythms.

Sleep Apnea   **Sleep apnea** *is a sleep disorder in which individuals stop breathing because the windpipe fails to open or brain processes involved in respiration fail to work properly.* Individuals with sleep apnea experience numerous brief awakenings during the night so they can breathe better, although they are not usually aware of their awakened state. During the day these people may feel sleepy because they were deprived of sleep at night. This disorder is most common among infants and people over the age of 65.

One million Canadians and thirty million Americans suffer from sleep apnea, a temporary cessation of breathing during sleep that is potentially life-threatening, especially if it occurs when the individual has taken a sleeping pill or had too much alcohol. Being overweight is also a risk factor for sleep apnea (Culebras, 1996).

SUMMARY TABLE 5.1
States of Consciousness and Sleep

Concept	Processes/ Related Ideas	Characteristics/Description
States of Consciousness	Their Nature	Consciousness is awareness of both external and internal stimuli and events. Consciousness is a rich, complex landscape of the mind, consisting of processes at varying levels of awareness. Among the many forms of consciousness are controlled processes, automatic processes, daydreaming, altered states of consciousness, sleep and dreams, unconscious thought (Freudian), and unconsciousness (non-Freudian, such as an anesthetized state).
Sleep	Why Do We Sleep?	We sleep for restoration and repair (repair theory) and to keep us from wasting energy and risking harm during the time of day or night to which we are not adapted (ecological theory).
	Sleep and Circadian Rhythms	A circadian rhythm is a cycle of about 24 hours. The human sleep/wake cycle is an important circadian rhythm. This cycle can become desynchronized. Individuals isolated in caves for months continue to approximate a 24-hour cycle, although at times the cycle is slightly longer.
	Sleep Deprivation and Sleep Needs	Individuals have gone without sleep as long as 11 days and, after a restorative sleep, seem to show no serious ill effects. In more normal circumstances, individuals have more difficulty staying awake all night, especially from 3 to 6 A.M. The average North American gets just under 7 hours of sleep a night. An increasing number of sleep researchers believe that 8 hours or more are needed to function optimally the next day. Sleep debts can build quickly and jeopardize health and well-being.
	Stages of Sleep	Different stages of sleep are measured by the electroencephalograph (EEG), which measures the brain's electrical activity. Alpha waves occur when we are in a relaxed state. When we sleep we move from light sleep in stage 1 to deep sleep in stage 4 (delta waves). Then we go directly into REM sleep, where dreams occur. Each night we go through a number of these sleep cycles. REM sleep peaks in early infancy and then declines. REM sleep may be involved in the brain's growth and memory.
	The Neural Basis of Sleep	Early views emphasized environmental stimulation and subsequently an internal activating system in the reticular formation. The contemporary view states that the brain is actively engaged in producing sleep behaviors, and different neurotransmitters are involved.
	Sleep Disorders	Among the most prominent are insomnia, sleepwalking and sleeptalking, nightmares and night terrors, narcolepsy, and sleep apnea.

Treatment of sleep apnea includes surgery to remove the airway obstruction, weight loss for individuals in which obesity plays a role, position restriction for individuals in which the apnea occurs only in certain positions, avoidance of alcohol and other depressant drugs, nasal decongestants, anti-inflammatory agents, and other pharmacological agents.

At this point we have discussed many ideas about states of consciousness and sleep. An overview of these ideas is presented in summary table 5.1. We've toured the fascinating world of sleep and seen that dreams usually occur during REM sleep. Let's now explore the fascinating world of dreams in greater detail.

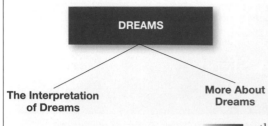

DREAMS

The Interpretation
of Dreams

More About
Dreams

Dream Analysis

Dreams

Ever since the dawn of language, dreams have been imbued with historical, personal, and religious significance. As early as 5000 B.C. Babylonians recorded and interpreted their dreams on clay tablets. Egyptians built temples in honor of Serapis, the god of dreams. People occasionally slept in these temples in the hope that Serapis would appear in their dreams and either heal them or tell them what to do to be healed. Dreams are described at length in more than seventy passages in the Bible, and in many primitive cultures dreams are an extension of reality. For example, there is an account of an African chief who dreamed that he had visited England. On awakening, he ordered a wardrobe of European clothes. As he walked through the village in his new wardrobe, he was congratulated for having made the trip. Similarly, Cherokee Indians who dreamed of being bitten by a snake were treated for the snakebite.

Today, we still try to figure out what dreams mean (see figure 5.8). Much of the interest stems from psychoanalysts who have probed the unconscious mind to understand the symbolic content of dreams. Although we do have concrete information regarding sleep stages, there is little scientific data to explain why we dream or what the dreams mean ◀▥ P. 48.

The Interpretation of Dreams

Many of us dismiss the nightly excursion into the world of dreams as a second-rate mental activity, unworthy of our rational selves. By focusing only on the less mysterious waking world, we deny ourselves the opportunity of chance encounters with distant friends, remote places, dead relatives, gods, and demons. But what, if anything, do our dreams really mean? Let's now explore three approaches that attempt to explain the nature of dreaming.

Freud's Theory   In Freud's (1900) theory, the reason we dream is **wish fulfillment**, *an unconscious attempt to fulfill needs (especially for sex and aggression) that cannot be expressed, or go ungratified during waking hours.* For example, people who are sexually inhibited while awake would likely have dreams with erotic content. Those who have strong aggressive tendencies but hold anger in while awake likely would have dreams filled with violence and hostility. Freud also stressed that dreams often contain memories of infancy and childhood experiences, especially events associated with parents. And he said our dreams frequently contain information from the day or two preceding the dream. In his view, many of our dreams reflect combinations of these distant early experiences with our parents and more recent daily events. Freud believed that the task of dream interpretation is a difficult one because we successfully disguise wish fulfillment when we dream. Note that the term *wish fulfillment* does not mean that all dreams reflect hopes; some reflect fears.

Freud distinguished between a dream's manifest and latent content. **Manifest content** *is the dream's surface content, which contains dream symbols that distort and disguise the dream's true meaning.* **Latent content** *is the dream's hidden content, its unconscious meaning.* For example, in Freud's view, a person might have a dream that included snakes and neckties. The snakes and neckties are the dream's manifest content. Another person might have a dream about a king or a president. However, Freud said that such dreams are symbols for underlying latent content (in these cases the snakes and neckties symbolize a male's genitals and the king or president symbolized a father or the therapist). Freud thought that once the therapist understood a client's symbolism, the nature of the dream could then be interpreted.

A final point to be made about Freud's dream theory involves its scientific merit. Researchers have found it extremely difficult to devise appropriate methods to even attempt to verify his dream theory.

Cognitive Theory The **cognitive theory of dreaming** *proposes that dreaming can best be understood by relying on the same cognitive concepts that are used in studying the waking mind.* That is, dreaming involves processing information, memory, and possibly problem solving. Unlike Freud's theory, in the cognitive theory of dreaming there is no search for the hidden, symbolic content of dreams (Foulkes, 1993, 1999).

Rather than being an arena in which to play out our unsatisfied needs, dreams might be a mental realm where we can solve problems and think creatively. For example, the Scottish author Robert Louis Stevenson (1850–1894) claimed he got the idea for *Dr. Jekyll and Mr. Hyde* in a dream. Elias Howe, attempting to invent a machine that sewed, reportedly dreamed he was captured by savages carrying spears with holes in their tips. Upon waking, Howe realized he should place the hole for the thread at the end of the needle, not the middle. Dreams may spark such gifts of inspiration because, in unique and creative ways, they weave together current experiences with the past.

***F*igure 5.8**
Artists' Portrayals of Dreams
Through the centuries, artists have been adept at capturing the enchanting or nightmarish characteristics of our dreams. *(Right)* Dutch painter Hieronymus Bosch (1450–1516) captured both the enchanting and frightening world of dreams in *The Garden of Delights. (Above left)* In *The Nightmare,* Henry Fuseli (1741–1825) portrayed the frightening world of nightmarish dreams by showing a demon sitting on a woman having a nightmare. *(Bottom left)* Marc Chagall painted a world of dreams in *I and the Village.*
Chagall, Marc. I AND THE VILLAGE. 1911. Oil on canvas 6' 3 5/8" x 59 5/8" (192.1 x 151.4 cm) The Museum of Modern Art, New York. Mrs. Simon Guggenheim Fund. Photograph © 1999 The Museum of Modern Art, New York.

Activation-Synthesis Theory   **Activation-synthesis theory** *states that dreams are powered by the spontaneous firing of neurons.* Dreams reflect the brain's efforts to make sense out of, or find meaning in, the neural activity that takes place during sleep. In this view, the brain's activity involves a great deal of random activity. Dreams are an attempt to make sense of this chaos (McCarley, 1989). The sudden, uncoordinated eye movements of REM sleep make the dreamworld move in odd ways; for instance, it might include magic carpets over an undulating landscape. Dreams tend to truncate, dissolve, or shift suddenly in midstream. Freud explained this as the dreamer's attempt to elude the unpleasant and the taboo. In activation-synthesis theory, this shifting is due to normal cycles of neural activation (Hobson, 1999). One group of cells simply runs its course, another set is activated and a new dream landscape emerges. In sum, in the activation-synthesis view, dreams are merely a glitzy side show, not the main act (Hooper & Teresi, 1993).

More About Dreams

The world of dreams raises some intriguing questions. Let's explore four of these.

Do People Dream in Color?   Some people say they dream only in black and white, but virtually everyone's dreams contain color. However, we often forget the color by the time we awaken and recall the dream. Some people claim that certain colors have fixed meanings in their dreams—white for purity, red for passion, green for vitality, black for evil or death, for example. However, no evidence has been found to support this belief. Red may stand for passion in one dream, danger in another, and anger in yet another dream.

Do Animals Dream?   It is impossible to say for certain whether or not animals dream; we know they have periods of REM sleep, so it is possible that they do. But dogs' twitching and howling during sleep, for instance, should not be taken as evidence that they are necessarily dreaming.

Do Males and Females Dream About Different Things?
According to extensive assessments of what males and females dream about, the dreams of males are more likely than those of females to include content about males, aggression, torso/anatomy, sexuality, and dreamer-involved success (Domhoff & Schneider, 1998). The dream content of females is more likely to include females, friends, and victimization. In these surveys, about 80 percent of the dreams of both males and females have negative emotions present.

Why Can't We Remember All of Our Dreams?   Everyone dreams, but some of us remember our dreams better than others. It's not surprising that no one remembers all their dreams, since dreaming occurs at such a low level of consciousness. It is also no surprise that the accuracy of our later waking memory for dreams should be open to question (Bernstein & Belicki, 1996). Psychoanalytic theory suggests we forget most of our dreams because they are threatening, but there is no evidence to support this belief. We remember our dreams best when we are awakened during or just after a dream. Similarly, the dreams we have just before we awaken are the ones we are most likely to remember. People whose sleep cycles have long periods between their last REM stage and awakening are more likely to report they don't dream at all or rarely remember their dreams.

At this point we have studied a number of ideas about dreaming. An overview of these ideas is presented in summary table 5.2. Next, we will turn our attention to hypnosis.

The Study of Dreams
Exploring Dreams

*S*UMMARY *T*ABLE 5.2
Dreams

Concept	Processes/Related Ideas	Characteristics/Description
The Interpretation of Dreams	Freud's Theory	Freud's psychoanalytic theory states that dreams are the unconscious wish fulfillment of needs unmet during waking states. Freud believed that dreams often involve a combination of early childhood experiences and daily residue. He stressed that dreams have rich, symbolic content and distinguished between a dream's manifest content and latent content. Researchers have found it extremely difficult to devise appropriate methods to even attempt to verify Freud's dream theory.
	Cognitive Theory	Cognitive theory proposes that dreaming can best be understood by relying on the same cognitive concepts that are used in studying the waking mind. That is, dreaming involves processing information, memory, and possibly problem solving.
	Activation-Synthesis Theory	This theory states that dreams are powered by the spontaneous firing of neurons. Dreams reflect the brain's efforts to make sense out of or find meaning in the neural activity that takes place during sleep.
More About Dreams	Do People Dream in Color?	Virtually everyone's dreams contain color. Colors don't have fixed meanings in dreams.
	Do Animals Dream?	It is impossible to say whether animals dream or not, although they do have periods of REM sleep.
	Do Females and Males Dream About Different Things?	Males' dreams have more content about males, aggression, torso/anatomy, sexuality, and dreamer-involved success. Females' dreams are more likely to be about females, friends, and victimization.
	Why Can't We Remember All of Our Dreams?	We can't remember them because dreaming occurs at such a low level of consciousness. We remember our dreams best when we are awakened during or just after a dream.

Hypnosis

A young cancer patient is about to undergo a painful bone marrow transplant procedure. A man directs the boy's attention, asking him to breathe with him and listen carefully. The boy becomes absorbed in a pleasant fantasy—he is riding a motorcycle over a huge pizza, dodging anchovies and maneuvering around chunks of mozzarella. Minutes later the procedure is over. The boy is relaxed and feels good about his self-control. The doctor successfully used hypnosis as a technique to help the young cancer patient control pain.

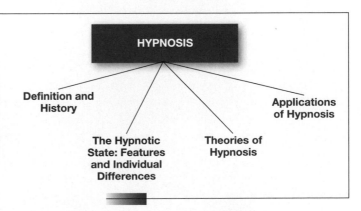

Definition and History

Hypnosis *is a psychological state of altered attention and awareness in which the individual is unusually receptive to suggestions.* Hypnosis has been used since the beginning of recorded history (Spanos & Chaves, 1991). It has been associated with religious ceremonies, magic, the supernatural, and many erroneous theories. Today hypnosis is recognized as a legitimate process in psychology and medicine, although much is yet to be learned about how it works (Kirsch & Linn, 1998).

Hypnosis

Through the Eyes of Psychologists

Ernest Hilgard,
Stanford University

"Of all states of consciousness, none raises more questions than the hypnotic state. Once associated with the bizzare and the occult, hypnosis has now become the subject of rigorous scientific investigation."

In the eighteenth century the Austrian physician Franz Anton Mesmer cured his patients by passing magnets over their bodies. Mesmer said the problems were cured by "animal magnetism," an intangible force that passes from therapist to patient. In reality, the cures were due to some form of hypnotic suggestion. Mesmer's claims were investigated by a committee appointed by the French Academy of Science. The committee agreed that Mesmer's treatment was effective; however, they disputed his theoretical claims about animal magnetism and prohibited him from practicing in Paris. Mesmer's theory of animal magnetism was called mesmerism, and even today we use the term *mesmerized* to mean hypnotized or enthralled.

The Hypnotic State: Features and Individual Differences

There are four requirements for hypnosis to succeed. First, distractions are minimized and the person to be hypnotized is made comfortable. Second, the person is told to concentrate on something specific, such as an imagined scene or the ticking of a watch. Third, the individual is told what to expect in the hypnotic state (such as relaxation or a pleasant floating sensation). Fourth, the hypnotist suggests certain events or feelings that he knows will occur or observes occurring (such as "Your eyes are getting tired"). When the suggested effects occur, the individual interprets them as being caused by the hypnotist's suggestions and accepts them as an indication that something is happening. This increases the person's expectations that the hypnotism will make things happen in the future and makes him even more suggestible.

Do you think you could be hypnotized? What about your friends—are they more or less likely to be influenced by hypnosis than you? For as long as hypnosis has been studied, about 200 years, we've known that some people are more easily hypnotized than others. In fact, about 10 to 20 percent of the population are very susceptible to hypnosis, 10 percent or less cannot be hypnotized at all, and the remainder fall somewhere in between (Hilgard, 1965). There is no simple way to tell whether you can be hypnotized. But if you have the capacity to immerse yourself in imaginative activities—listening to a favorite piece of music or reading a novel, for example—you are a likely candidate. People susceptible to hypnosis become completely absorbed in what they are doing, removing the boundaries between themselves and what they are experiencing in their environment.

Theories of Hypnosis

Ever since Anton Mesmer proposed his theory of "animal magnetism," psychologists have been trying to figure out why hypnosis works. Contemporary theorists are divided on their answers to the following question: Is hypnosis a special cognitive state, or is it simply a form of learned social behavior?

Special Process Theory Ernest Hilgard (1977) proposed the **special process theory,** *which states that hypnotic behavior involves a special cognitive state that is different than nonhypnotic behavior.* Hypnotic responses are involuntary and involve a hidden observer. The hidden observer allows the person to be fully aware of what is happening yet maintain passive

In special process theory, hypnotic responses, elicited by suggestions, are involuntary. In the situation shown here, the brain activity of a hypnotized individual is being monitored.

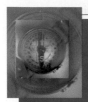

EXPLORATIONS IN PSYCHOLOGY
Is Hypnosis a Window to Forgotten Events?

HYPNOSIS HAS been used to enhance people's ability to accurately recall forgotten events (Yuille & McEwan, 1985). For example, police departments sometimes arrange to have eyewitnesses to crimes hypnotized, in the hope that this will significantly improve their recall.

Most research now indicates that hypnosis does not dramatically improve the accuracy of recall and does not increase the accuracy with which witnesses identify perpetrators whom they have observed commit mock crimes (Lynn, Rhue, & Spanos, 1994). Although subjects do sometimes recall new information under hypnosis, they may also recall new information when motivated by nonhypnotic instructions (Frischoltz, 1995). Also, when hypnotic (and sometimes nonhypnotic) procedures are used to obtain new information from witnesses, the new information is often inaccurate. And in most real-life circumstances, there is nothing that enables either the witnesses or the interviewer to discriminate between accurate and inaccurate aspects of recall.

Hypnotic subjects can be influenced by leading questions. For example, hypnotic subjects might be asked, "What color was the subject's mustache?" The subjects then often create an image of the suspect they saw and supply the suspect with a mustache, even though the actual suspect did not have a mustache. If these witnesses later see a police lineup that has a suspect with a mustache, they might misidentify that suspect as the perpetrator.

In a number of studies, witnesses who have been given hypnotic interviews are more confident about the inaccurate aspects of their recall or about misidentifications than are nonhypnotized witnesses. On the basis of such findings, as well as research revealing that hypnotic subjects are susceptible to lead-ing questions, Martin Orne (1959) proposed that the recall of hypnotic witnesses might reflect *pseudomemories*—false memories that are confidently believed in as real memories. Orne further stressed that because hypnotic witnesses have so much confidence in their pseudomemories, they are effectively immunized against cross-examination.

However, other researchers have found that pseudomemories occur as frequently in nonhypnotic subjects as in hypnotic subjects. And several studies have reported that hypnotic testimony is no more resistant to cross-examination than nonhypnotic testimony.

Because of the mixed research evidence, in Canada, hypnotic testimony can, at best, be used as corroborative evidence. It has even been banned in some American states. Clearly, if hypnotic testimony is to be admitted, extreme caution needs to be exercised in administering hypnotic procedures to victims and witnesses.

Why should extreme caution be exercised when evaluating memories generated by hypnotic testimony?

involvement. Hilgard discovered this dual involvement during a classroom demonstration in which he hypnotized a student. Hilgard induced deafness in the student and showed that the person was completely unresponsive to any sounds around him—conversation, noise, taunts. Then a student from the class asked if the hypnotized individual was really as unresponsive to sounds as he seemed. Hilgard, being a flexible teacher, asked the person to raise a finger if a part of him could still hear. To the surprise of Hilgard and the rest of the class, the student raised his finger, suggesting a divided consciousness in which a part of the student's mind was passively aware of what was happening.

What are some different theories about hypnosis? What are some applications of hypnosis?

Hypnosis Applications

Nonstate Theory   Carleton professor Nick Spanos was a major architect of a second theory of hypnosis, **nonstate theory**, *which proposes that individuals who become hypnotized are under the social influence of the hypnotist*. They are carrying out the social role of being a good hypnotic subject and letting the hypnotist direct their imaginative thinking. In this view, hypnotized individuals might appear to surrender their voluntary control to conform to situational demands (Spanos, 1989, 1991). However, according to nonstate theory, they are not partitioned into a divided consciousness of actor and observer as Hilgard suggested.

The special process and nonstate theories are not necessarily incompatible. Perhaps both divided consciousness (special process theory) and social influence (nonstate theory) are involved in many instances of hypnosis (Kihlstrom & McConkey, 1990).

Applications of Hypnosis

Hypnosis is widely used in psychotherapy, medicine and dentistry, criminal investigation, and sports. Hypnosis has been used in psychotherapy to treat alcoholism, somnambulism, suicidal tendencies, overeating, and smoking. One of the least effective, but most common, applications of hypnosis is to help people stop overeating and quit smoking. Hypnotists direct their patients to stop these behaviors, but dramatic results rarely are achieved unless the patient is already highly motivated to change. The most effective use of hypnosis is as an adjunct to different forms of psychotherapy.

A long history of research and practice clearly has demonstrated that hypnosis can reduce the experience of pain (Crasilneck, 1995). However, not everyone is hypnotizable enough to experience this effect. The effectiveness of hypnosis in increasing muscular strength and endurance, as well as sensory thresholds, has not been demonstrated (Druckman & Bjork, 1994).

There is also considerable interest today in the application of hypnosis to help people recall forgotten events. To read about this fascinating topic, turn to Explorations in Psychology.

At this point we have studied a number of ideas about hypnosis. An overview of these ideas is presented in summary table 5.3.

In our discussion of hypnosis, we have seen that, in the special process view, hypnosis alters the person's state of consciousness. Next we will see that ever since the dawn of human history people have used drugs to alter consciousness, to "get high."

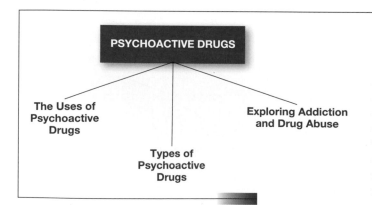

Psychoactive Drugs

During one phase of his medical career, Sigmund Freud experimented with therapeutic uses of cocaine. He was searching for possible medical applications, such as a painkiller for eye surgery. He soon found that the drug induced ecstasy. He even wrote to his fiancée and told her how just a small dose of cocaine produced lofty, wonderful sensations. As it became apparent that some people became psychologically addicted to cocaine, and after several died from overdoses, Freud quit using the drug. Cocaine is just one of many drugs taken to alter consciousness.

The Uses of Psychoactive Drugs

Psychoactive drugs *act on the nervous system to alter our state of consciousness, modify our perceptions, and change our moods*. Ever since the ancients first sat entranced in front of the communal fire, humans have searched for substances they hoped

SUMMARY TABLE 5.3
Hypnosis

Concept	Processes/ Related Ideas	Characteristics/Description
Definition and History	Their Nature	Hypnosis is a psychological state of altered consciousness in which the subject is unusually receptive to suggestion. The history of hypnosis began with Franz Anton Mesmer and his belief in animal magnetism.
The Hypnotic State: Features and Individual Differences	Their Nature	Hypnosis involves reducing distracting stimuli and making the subject comfortable, getting the individual to concentrate, and suggesting what is to be experienced in the hypnotic state. About 10 to 20 percent of the population is highly susceptible to hypnosis, about 10 percent cannot be hypnotized at all, and the remainder fall in between. People who have the ability to immerse themselves in imaginative activities are good candidates for hypnosis.
Theories of Hypnosis	Special Process Theory	Hilgard proposed the special process theory, which states that hypnotic behavior involves a special cognitive state that is different than nonhypnotic behavior. Hypnotic responses are involuntary and involve a hidden observer.
	Nonstate Theory	Spanos proposed nonstate theory, which states that individuals who become hypnotized are under the social influence of the hypnotist. They are carrying out the social role of being a good hypnotic subject and letting the hypnotist direct their imaginative thinking.
Applications	Their Nature	Hypnosis has been widely applied, with mixed results, to a variety of circumstances, including psychotherapy, medicine, dentistry, criminal trials, and sports.

would produce pleasurable sensations and alter their state of consciousness. Among the substances that alter consciousness are alcohol, hemp and cactus plants, mushrooms, poppies, and tobacco, an herb that has been smoked and sniffed for more than 400 centuries.

Human beings are attracted to psychoactive substances because they help them adapt to an ever-changing environment. Smoking, drinking, and taking drugs reduce tension and frustration, relieve boredom and fatigue, and in some cases help us escape from the harsh realities of the world (Hales, 1999). Psychoactive drugs provide us with pleasure by giving us inner peace, joy, relaxation, kaleidoscopic perceptions, surges of exhilaration, and prolonged heightened sensation. They may be useful in helping us to get along in our world. For example, amphetamines can keep us awake all night so we can study for an exam. We might also take drugs because we are curious about their effects, in some cases because of sensationalistic accounts in the media. We might wonder if the drugs described can provide us with unique, profound experiences. We also take drugs for social reasons, hoping they will make us feel more at ease and happier in our interactions and relationships with others.

The use of psychoactive drugs for such personal gratification and temporary adaptation, however, can carry a high price tag: drug dependence, personal and social disorganization, and a predisposition to serious and sometimes fatal diseases (Goldberg, 2000). What was initially intended as enjoyment and adaptation can eventually turn into sorrow and maladaptation. For example, drinking may initially help people relax and forget about their worries. But then they may begin to drink more and more, until the drinking becomes an addiction that destroys relationships and careers, and leads to physical and psychological damage, including permanent liver damage and major depression. As a person continues to take a psychoactive drug, the

The Pleasure System, Drugs, and Society

body develops a **tolerance,** *which means that a greater amount of the drug is needed to produce the same effect.* The first time someone takes 5 milligrams of Valium, for example, the drug will make them feel very relaxed. But after taking the pill every day for 6 months, the person may need to take 10 milligrams to achieve the same calming effect.

Physical dependence *is the physical need for a drug that is accompanied by unpleasant withdrawal symptoms when the drug is discontinued.* **Psychological dependence** *is the strong desire and craving to repeat the use of a drug because of various emotional reasons, such as a feeling of well-being and reduction of stress.* Both physical and psychological dependence mean that the psychoactive drug is playing a powerful role in the person's life (Avis, 1999).

Types of Psychoactive Drugs

Three main types of psychoactive drugs are depressants, stimulants, and hallucinogens.

Depressants   **Depressants** *are psychoactive drugs that slow down mental and physical activity.* Among the most widely used depressants are alcohol, barbiturates, tranquilizers, and opiates.

Alcohol   We do not always think of alcohol as a drug, but it is an extremely powerful one. Alcohol acts upon the body as a depressant and slows down the brain's activities. This might seem surprising, since people who normally tend to be inhibited may begin to talk, dance, or socialize after a few drinks, but people "loosen up" after one or two drinks because the brain areas involved in controlling inhibition and judgment *slow down.* As people drink more, their inhibitions become even further reduced and their judgments become increasingly impaired. Activities requiring intellectual functioning and skill, such as driving, become impaired as more alcohol is consumed. Eventually the drinker becomes drowsy and falls asleep. With extreme intoxication, a person may even lapse into a coma and die. These effects vary according to how the person's body metabolizes alcohol, body weight, the amount of alcohol consumed, and whether previous drinking has led to tolerance (Clayton, 1999).

Alcohol is the most widely used drug in our society. A 1992 Gallup Poll revealed that 13 million Americans call themselves alcoholics. Alcoholism is the third leading killer in the United States. In Canada in 1996–7, about 3.2 million people drank five or more drinks on one occasion 12 or more times in the previous 12 months, thus qualifying as heavy drinkers (Health Canada, 1999). Over one million people drank to this extent on a weekly basis (although such operational definitions are open to question, DeCourville & Sadava, 1997; Chaikelson and colleagues, 1994). Each year, over 1,400 Canadians are killed, and 92,000 injured, by drunk drivers (Health Canada. 1999). More than 60 percent of homicides involve the use of alcohol by either the offender or the victim, while 65 percent of aggressive sexual acts against women involve the use of alcohol by the offender.

A special concern is the high rate of alcohol use by adolescents and university students in Canada and the United States (Dimeff, 1999; Statistics Canada, 1999). In the 1990s, drug use by young adolescents increased considerably, and alcohol is the substance they abuse the most.

Many Canadian and American university students say they binge-drink (that is, have had five or more drinks in a row at least once in the last two weeks) (Johnston, O'Malley, & Bachmann, 1998. Health Canada, 1999). In an American survey on 140 campuses, binge-drinking students were 11 times more likely to fall behind in school and twice as likely to have unprotected sex than college students who did not drink (Weschsler and others, 1994).

Alcoholism *is a disorder that involves long-term, repeated, uncontrolled, compulsive, and excessive use of alcoholic beverages that impair the drinker's health and social relationships.* If you struggle to manage alcohol use, chances are good that you are not the only person in your family who had this problem. Family studies consistently

Clearinghouse for Drug Information
Drugs and Behavior Links

Alcohol and the Brain

Alcohol Self-Evaluation
Alcoholism

find a high frequency of alcoholism in the first-degree relatives of alcoholics (Hannigan & others, 1999).

In one review of research on family alcoholism, when the father was an alcoholic, both sons and daughters had increased rates of alcoholism; when the mother was an alcoholic, increased rates of alcoholism occurred only for daughters (Pollock & others, 1987). Twin studies of alcoholism have revealed a modest influence of heredity (Sher, 1991), while adoption studies document the contribution of biological relatives' alcoholism to alcoholism in male adoptees (Sher, 1993). Research along these lines has persuaded many psychologists that heredity plays an important role in alcoholism (Goodwin, 1998). However, the precise genetic mechanism has not yet been identified.

Although family, twin, and adoption studies reveal a genetic influence on alcoholism, environmental factors also play an important role. Thus, many alcoholics do not have close relatives who are alcoholics (Sher, 1993). According to tension reduction theory, alcoholics have learned to reduce anxiety through drinking. Alternately, interaction theory sees alcoholism as rooted in an interaction between person variables, like the tendency to experience anxiety, and situational variables, like the availability of alcohol (Sadava, 1987). Cultural variations in alcohol use also underscore the role of the environment. Like other behaviors and problems, alcoholism is multiply determined and has multiple pathways of development (Sobell & Sobell, 1993). Later in the chapter, we will explore the prevention and treatment of alcoholism in our discussion of addiction and drug abuse.

Barbiturates   Barbiturates, *such as Nembutal and Seconal, are depressant drugs that are used to induce sleep.* In heavy dosages, they can lead to impaired memory and decision making. When combined with alcohol (for instance, sleeping pills taken after a night of binge-drinking), the result can be lethal. Barbiturates by themselves can also produce death in heavy dosages, which makes them the drug most often chosen in suicide attempts. Abrupt withdrawal from barbiturates can produce seizures.

Tranquilizers   Tranquilizers, *such as Valium and Xanax, are depressant drugs that reduce anxiety and induce relaxation.* Unlike barbiturates, which are often given to induce sleep, tranquilizers are usually given to calm an anxious, nervous individual. Tranquilizers are among the most widely used drugs in North America and can produce withdrawal symptoms when individuals stop taking them.

Opiates   Opiates, *which consist of opium and its derivatives, depress the central nervous system's activity.* The most common opiate drugs—morphine and heroin—affect synapses in the brain that use endorphins as their neurotransmitter. When these drugs leave the brain, the affected synapses become understimulated. For several hours after taking an opiate, a person feels euphoric and relieved of pain and has an increased appetite for food and sex. Morphine is sometimes used medically as a painkiller. But the opiates are among the most physically addictive drugs, leading to craving and painful withdrawal when the drug becomes unavailable.

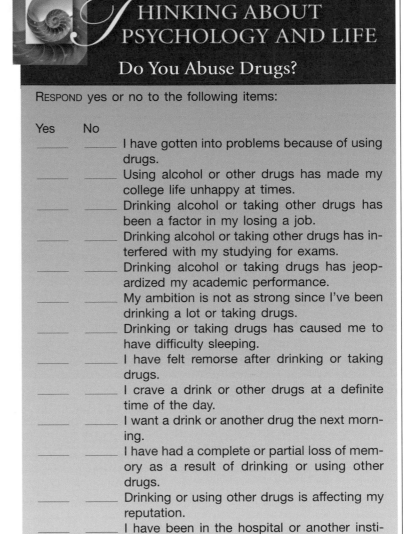

THINKING ABOUT PSYCHOLOGY AND LIFE
Do You Abuse Drugs?

RESPOND yes or no to the following items:

Yes   No
____ ____ I have gotten into problems because of using drugs.
____ ____ Using alcohol or other drugs has made my college life unhappy at times.
____ ____ Drinking alcohol or taking other drugs has been a factor in my losing a job.
____ ____ Drinking alcohol or taking other drugs has interfered with my studying for exams.
____ ____ Drinking alcohol or taking drugs has jeopardized my academic performance.
____ ____ My ambition is not as strong since I've been drinking a lot or taking drugs.
____ ____ Drinking or taking drugs has caused me to have difficulty sleeping.
____ ____ I have felt remorse after drinking or taking drugs.
____ ____ I crave a drink or other drugs at a definite time of the day.
____ ____ I want a drink or another drug the next morning.
____ ____ I have had a complete or partial loss of memory as a result of drinking or using other drugs.
____ ____ Drinking or using other drugs is affecting my reputation.
____ ____ I have been in the hospital or another institution because of my drinking or taking drugs.

University students who responded yes to items similar to these on the Rutgers Collegiate Abuse Screening Test were more likely to be substance abusers than those who answered no. If you responded yes to just 1 of the 13 items on this screening test, consider going to your university health or counseling center for further screening.

The Opiates

Cocaine
Effects of Cocaine on the Brain

Recently, another hazardous consequence of opiate addiction has surfaced: AIDS. Most heroin addicts inject the drug intravenously. When they share their needles, blood from the needles can be passed on. A full 20 percent of adult AIDS cases in Canada were attributed to intravenous drug use transmission in 1997, compared with only 2 percent prior to 1990 (Health Canada, 1999).

Stimulants   Stimulants *are psychoactive drugs that increase the central nervous system's activity.* The most widely used stimulants are caffeine, nicotine (in cigarettes), amphetamines, and cocaine. Coffee, tea, and caffeinated soft drinks are mild stimulants. We will discuss amphetamines, cocaine, and caffeine here but will save nicotine for chapter 15 (Health, Stress, and Coping).

Amphetamines   Amphetamines are widely prescribed, often in the form of diet pills. They are also called "pep pills" and "uppers." Amphetamines increase the release of the neurotransmitter dopamine, which increases the user's activity level and pleasurable feelings.

Cocaine   Cocaine comes from the coca plant, native to Bolivia and Peru. For centuries Bolivians and Peruvians have chewed on the plant to increase their stamina. Today cocaine is either snorted or injected in the form of crystals or powder. The effect is a rush of euphoria, which eventually wears off, followed by depression, lethargy, insomnia, and irritability. Cocaine can trigger a heart attack, stroke, or brain seizure.

When animals and humans chew coca leaves, small amounts of cocaine gradually enter the bloodstream, without any apparent adverse effects. However, when extracted cocaine is sniffed, smoked, or injected, it enters the bloodstream very rapidly, producing a rush of euphoric feelings that lasts for about 15 to 30 minutes. Because the rush depletes the supply of the neurotransmitters dopamine and norepinephrine in the brain, an agitated, depressed mood usually follows as the drug's effects decline.

Crack *is an intensified form of cocaine, consisting of chips of pure cocaine that are usually smoked.* Crack is believed to be one of the most addictive substances known, being much more addictive than heroin, barbiturates, and alcohol. In the U.S., emergency-room admissions related to crack have soared from less than 600 cases in 1985 to more than 15,000 a year in the early 1990s.

Treatments for cocaine addiction have not been very successful. Cocaine's addictive properties are so strong that 6 months after treatment, more than 50 percent of cocaine abusers return to the drug. Experts on drug abuse believe the best approach to reduce cocaine addiction is through prevention programs.

Caffeine   Often overlooked as a drug, caffeine is the most widely used psychoactive drug in the world. Caffeine is a stimulant and a natural component of various plants that are the sources of coffee, tea, and cola-flavored soft drinks. Caffeine is also present in chocolate and many nonprescribed medications. The stimulating effects of caffeine are often perceived as beneficial, but some people experience unpleasant effects. *Caffeinism* is the term given to overindulgence of caffeine. It is characterized by mood changes, anxiety, disruption of sleep, and possibly other problems. Caffeinism often develops in individuals who consume 5 to 7 cups of coffee (500–700 mgs of caffeine) each day. Frequent symptoms of caffeinism are insomnia, irritability, headaches, ringing in the ears, dry mouth, increased blood pressure, and digestive problems.

Caffeine activates the pleasure centers of the brain, so it is not surprising that it is difficult to "kick the caffeine habit." When individuals remove caffeine from their diet, they typically initially incur headaches, lethargy, apathy, and concentration difficulties. These symptoms of withdrawal are usually mild and tolerable and subside after a brief period of time.

Hallucinogens   **Hallucinogens** *are psychoactive drugs that modify a person's perceptual experience and produce visual images that are not real.* Hallucinogens are also called "psychedelic" (meaning "mind-altering") drugs. Marijuana has a milder hallucinogenic effect, LSD a stronger one.

Marijuana   Marijuana is the dried leaves and flowers of the hemp plant *Cannabis sativa,* which originated in central Asia but is now grown in most parts of the world. The plant's dried resin is known as hashish. The active ingredient in marijuana is THC, which stands for the chemical delta-9-tetrahydrocannabinol. This ingredient does not resemble the chemicals of other psychoactive drugs and does not affect a specific neurotransmitter. Rather, marijuana disrupts the membranes of neurons and affects the functioning of a variety of neurotransmitters and hormones.

The physical effects of marijuana include increases in pulse rate and blood pressure, reddening of the eyes, coughing, and dryness of the mouth. Psychological effects include a mixture of excitatory, depressive, and mildly hallucinatory characteristics, making it difficult to classify the drug. Marijuana can trigger spontaneous unrelated ideas, distorted perceptions of time and place, increased sensitivity to sounds and colors, and erratic verbal behavior. Marijuana can also impair attention and memory. When used daily in large amounts, marijuana can also alter sperm count and change hormonal cycles; it might be involved in some birth defects. Marijuana use declined during the 1980s, but an upsurge in its use has occurred in the 1990s (Johnston, O'Malley, & Bachman, 1998; Statistics Canada, 1999). Possible medical uses of marijuana include treating glaucoma, chemotherapy-caused nausea and vomiting, and AIDS-related weight loss (Avis, 1999).

Hallucinogenic Drugs
Marijuana

LSD   LSD (lysergic acid diethylamide) is a hallucinogen that even in low doses produces striking perceptual changes. Objects change their shape and glow. Colors become kaleidoscopic, fabulous images unfold as users close their eyes. Designs swirl, colors shimmer, bizarre scenes appear. Sometimes the images are pleasurable; sometimes they are grotesque. Figure 5.9 shows one kind of perceptual experience that a number of LSD users have reported. LSD can influence the user's perception of time as well. Time often seems to slow down dramatically, so that brief glances at objects are experienced as deep, penetrating, and lengthy examinations, and minutes often seem to be hours or days.

LSD's effects on the body can include dizziness, nausea, and tremors. LSD acts primarily on the neurotransmitter serotonin in the brain, though it can affect dopamine as well. Emotional and cognitive effects may include rapid mood swings or impaired attention and memory. LSD was popular in the late 1960s and early 1970s, but its popularity dropped after its unpredictable effects became well publicized. However, a recent increase in LSD use by high school and university students has been reported (Johnston, O'Malley, & Bachman, 1998; Statistics Canada, 1999).

We have discussed many aspects of three main classes of psychoactive drugs—depressants, stimulants, and hallucinogens. Figure 5.10 provides an overview of these drugs' medical uses, short-term effects, overdose effects, health risks, and physical/psychological dependence.

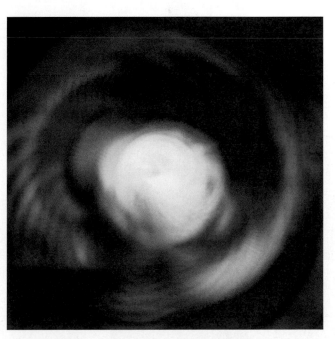

Exploring Addiction and Drug Abuse

Let's further examine drugs and their effects on behavior by studying addiction and then turn to the prevention and treatment of drug abuse.

Figure 5.9
LSD-Induced Hallucination

Under the influence of hallucinogenic drugs, such as LSD, several users have reported seeing images that have a tunnel effect like the one shown here.

One glass of wine equals one can of beer in alcoholic content.

Cocaine is extracted from coca plants.

Cannabis paraphernalia, drug equipment or gadgets, is usually sold in "head shops" for use in smoking marijuana.

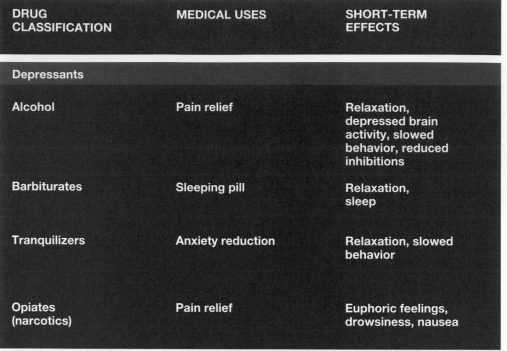
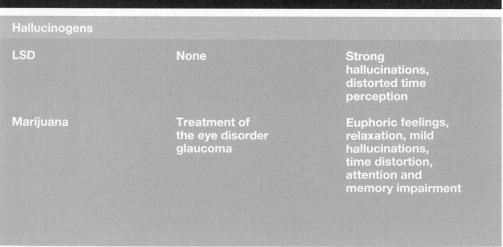

DRUG CLASSIFICATION	MEDICAL USES	SHORT-TERM EFFECTS
Depressants		
Alcohol	Pain relief	Relaxation, depressed brain activity, slowed behavior, reduced inhibitions
Barbiturates	Sleeping pill	Relaxation, sleep
Tranquilizers	Anxiety reduction	Relaxation, slowed behavior
Opiates (narcotics)	Pain relief	Euphoric feelings, drowsiness, nausea
Stimulants		
Amphetamines	Weight control	Increased alertness, excitability; decreased fatigue, irritability
Cocaine	Local anesthetic	Increased alertness, excitability, euphoric feelings; decreased fatigue, irritability
Hallucinogens		
LSD	None	Strong hallucinations, distorted time perception
Marijuana	Treatment of the eye disorder glaucoma	Euphoric feelings, relaxation, mild hallucinations, time distortion, attention and memory impairment

$\mathcal{F}$igure 5.10

Psychoactive Drugs: Depressants, Stimulants, and Hallucinogens

OVERDOSE	HEALTH RISKS	RISK OF PHYSICAL/ PSYCHOLOGICAL DEPENDENCE
Disorientation, loss of consciousness, even death at high blood-alcohol levels	Accidents, brain damage, liver disease, heart disease, ulcers, birth defects	Physical: moderate; psychological: moderate
Breathing difficulty, coma, possible death	Accidents, coma, possible death	Physical and psychological moderate to high
Breathing difficulty, coma, possible death	Accidents, coma, possible death	Physical: low to moderate; psychological: moderate to high
Convulsions, coma, possible death	Accidents, infectious diseases such as AIDS	Physical: high; psychological: moderate to high

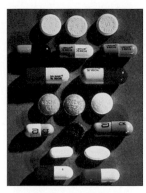

Tranquilizers are used for reducing anxiety and inducing relaxation.

| Extreme irritability, feelings of persecution, convulsions | Insomnia, hypertension, malnutrition, possible death | Physical: possible; psychological: moderate to high |
| Extreme irritability, feelings of persecution, convulsions, cardiac arrest, possible death | Insomnia, hypertension, malnutrition, possible death | Physical: possible; psychological: moderate (oral) to very high (injected or smoked) |

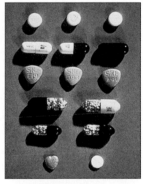

Amphetamines are stimulants used to increase alertness and energy.

| Severe mental disturbance, loss of contact with reality | Accidents | Physical: none; psychological: low |
| Fatigue, disoriented behavior | Accidents, respiratory disease | Physical: very low; psychological: moderate |

Shown here is a private, illegal laboratory for manufacturing LSD.

Addictions
Drug Abuse Links

Addiction   Addiction *is a pattern of behavior characterized by an overwhelming involvement in using a drug and securing its supply.* This can occur despite adverse consequences associated with the use of the drug. There is a strong tendency to relapse after quitting or withdrawal. Withdrawal symptoms consist of significant changes in physical functioning and behavior. Depending on the drug, these symptoms might include insomnia, tremors, nausea, vomiting, cramps, elevation of heart rate and blood pressure, convulsions, anxiety, and depression when a physically dependent person stops taking the drug. Experts on drug abuse use the term *addiction* to describe either a physical or psychological dependence on the drug or both (Carroll, 1999; Pinger & others, 1998).

Controversy continues about whether addictions are diseases (Ray & Ksir, 1999). The **disease model of addiction** *describes addictions as biologically based, lifelong diseases that involve a loss of control over behavior and require medical and/or spiritual treatment for recovery.* In the disease model, addiction is either inherited or bred into a person early in life. Current or recent problems or relationships are not believed to be causes of the disease. Once involved in the disease, you can never completely rid yourself of it, according to this model. The disease model has been strongly promoted and supported by the medical profession and Alcoholics Anonymous (AA).

Critics argue that the disease approach is not the best one because the biological mechanisms that might account for addictive behavior have not been identified. It keeps people from developing self-control, it stigmatizes people with labels such as *addict* and *alcoholic,* in some cases for life, and it dispenses a rigid program of therapy rather than advocating more flexible approaches. Also, addiction is not necessarily life-long (Grabowski, 1999). Two critics of the disease model, Stanton Peele and Archie Brodsky (1991), believe that addiction is a habitual response and a source of gratification or security. They say that an addiction can involve *any* attachment or sensations that grow to such proportions that they impair the person's life—including drugs, food, gambling, shopping, love, and sex. In this view, the "hook" of the addiction—what keeps people coming back to it—is that it provides people with feelings and gratifying sensations they are not able to get in other ways. Peele and Brodsky believe that understanding addiction requires that it be placed in the proper context, as part of people's lives, their personalities, their relationships, their environments, and their perspectives. They call their model the "life-process" model. In sum, the **life-process model of addiction** *argues that addiction is not a disease but rather a habitual response and a source of gratification or security that can be understood only in the context of social relationships and experiences.*

Each of these views of addiction—the disease model and the nondisease, life-process model—has its supporters.

Prevention and Treatment of Drug Abuse   Prevention of drug abuse is an admirable goal. Let's explore some strategies for accomplishing this and examine treatment programs for drug abuse.

Prevention programs have focused on three goals: primary, secondary, and tertiary prevention, with the greatest emphasis being targeted at primary and tertiary prevention. **Primary prevention** *is prevention that attempts to stop people from taking drugs by helping them to not start.* Primary prevention programs are increasingly being initiated with elementary school children. The most recent primary prevention models are based on the belief that early prevention works best, especially through the influence of respected role models who advocate abstinence from drugs and through peer pressure (Pentz, 1993).

Secondary prevention *is an attempt to minimize the harm caused by drug use with a high-risk population or with a group that is involved in experimental or occasional use.* In high schools, secondary prevention often involves attempts to reduce alcohol or tobacco use. Recognizing that a majority of high school students drink at least occasionally, secondary prevention programs focus on the hazardous consequences of drinking and driving. Other secondary prevention programs include crisis counseling and drug-abuse counseling for individuals whose drug use has gone beyond experimental or occasional use.

Tertiary prevention *consists of treatment for people who abuse drugs. Tertiary prevention programs include medical treatment, residential facilities, and rehabilitation.*

Two factors stand out when the successful components of drug-abuse prevention are analyzed: intensive individualized attention and community-wide, multiagency collaboration (Dryfoos, 1990). The Canadian government has recently revised a national drug strategy (Health Canada, 1998) to oversee provincial and community initiatives. Seven components provide a framework for this strategy: research and knowledge dissemination, prevention programming, treatment and rehabilitation, legislation, enforcement and control, and international co-operation. The basic philosophy of community-wide programs (see e.g. Pentz, 1993) is that a number of different programs concerned with primary, secondary and tertiary prevention must be in place for men and women (Blackwell, Thurston, & Graham, 1996).

Children who grow up in families in which they are given considerable nurturance and support are less likely to become drug abusers than children who are neglected and not given adequate support and attention from their parents (Brook & others, 1990). When high-risk children or adolescents become attached to a responsible adult who gives them attention and responds to their needs, their risk status declines. In one successful substance-abuse program, a student assistance counselor was available full-time for individual counseling and referral for treatment.

The importance of prevention and early intervention is underscored when the percentage of individuals who recover from alcoholism is examined (Sales, 1999). Despite occasional positive claims that you see in the media, the stunning reality is that no single inpatient, outpatient, counseling, self-help, or drug treatment has been shown to reduce relapse rates for alcoholism over the long term (Seligman, 1993; Seligman & Rosenhan, 1998). When researchers evaluate the effects of drug treatment programs over the short term, such as 6 months, they often find positive results, with about two-thirds of individuals still abstinent this long after treatment. However, an analysis of more than 100 long-term studies on thousands of alcoholics revealed that no one treatment was better than the others and that no one type of treatment was superior to no treatment at all (Emrick, 1982; Goodwin, 1988; Seligman, 1993).

About one-third of alcoholics recover whether they are in a treatment program or not. This figure was found by George Vaillant (1983, 1992) in a long-term study of 700 individuals over 50 years and has consistently been found by other researchers as well. Vaillant describes the "one-third rule" for alcoholism: by age 65, one-third are dead or in terrible shape, one-third are abstinent or drinking socially, and one-third are still trying to beat their addiction. In his extensive research, Vaillant did reveal that a positive outcome and recovery from alcoholism are predicted by certain factors: (1) a strong negative experience related to drinking, such as a serious medical emergency or condition; (2) finding a substitute dependency to compete with alcohol abuse, such as meditation, exercise, or overeating (which of course has its own negative health consequences); (3) having new social supports (such as a concerned, helpful employer or a new marriage); and (4) joining an inspirational group, such as a religious organization or AA.

At this point we have discussed many ideas about psychoactive drugs. An overview of these ideas is presented in summary table 5.4. One topic we evaluated in this chapter was whether people can learn while they are sleeping. In the next chapter, we focus our attention exclusively on the topic of learning.

Summary Table 5.4
Psychoactive Drugs

Concept	Processes/ Related Ideas	Characteristics/Description
The Uses of Psychoactive Drugs	Their Nature	Psychoactive drugs act on the central nervous system to alter states of consciousness, modify perceptions, and alter mood. They have been used since the beginning of recorded history for pleasure, utility, curiosity, and social reasons. Tolerance means that a greater amount of a drug is needed to produce the same effect. Physical dependence is the physical need for the drug that is accompanied by unpleasant withdrawal symptoms when the drug is discontinued. Psychological dependence is the strong desire and craving to repeat the use of a drug for various emotional reasons, such as a feeling of well-being and the reduction of stress the drug produces.
Types of Psychoactive Drugs	Depressants	Depressants are psychoactive drugs that slow down mental and physical activity. Depressants include alcohol, barbiturates, tranquilizers, and opiates. Alcohol is the most widely used drug in North America and the third leading killer. Special concerns are the high use of alcohol by adolescents and university students. Alcoholism is a disorder that involves long-term repeated, uncontrolled, compulsive, and excessive use of alcoholic beverages that impairs the drinker's health and social relationships. Both nature and nurture are involved in alcoholism. Barbiturates are depressant drugs that are used medically to induce sleep. Tranquilizers are depressant drugs that reduce anxiety and induce relaxation. Opiates, which consist of opium and its derivatives, depress the central nervous system's activity. The most common opiate drugs are morphine and heroin.
	Stimulants	Stimulants are psychoactive drugs that increase central nervous system activity. The most widely used stimulants are caffeine, nicotine, amphetamines, and cocaine. Cocaine provides a euphoric rush that is followed by depression, lethargy, insomnia, and irritability. Cocaine can even trigger a heart attack, stroke, or brain seizure. Crack is an intensified form of cocaine and is believed to be one of the most addictive drugs. Treatments for cocaine addiction have not been very successful. Caffeine also is a stimulant and might be the most widely used psychoactive drug in the world. A special concern is caffeinism, an overindulgence that is associated with a variety of psychological and physical problems.
	Hallucinogens	Hallucinogens are psychoactive drugs that modify perceptual experiences and produce visual images that are not real. Marijuana and LSD are hallucinogens. Marijuana produces a mixture of excitatory, depressive, and mildly hallucinatory psychological effects. LSD is a stronger hallucinogen than marijuana. Both marijuana use and LSD use increased in the 1990s.
Exploring Addiction and Drug Abuse	Addiction	Addiction is a pattern of behavior characterized by an overwhelming involvement with using a drug and securing its supply. Two views of addiction are the disease model and the life-process model.
	Prevention and Treatment of Drug Abuse	Three forms of prevention/treatment are primary, secondary, and tertiary. Successful drug-abuse programs for children and youth have two significant components: (1) intensive individualized attention, and (2) community-wide, multiagency collaboration. Analyses of treatment programs for alcoholics over the short term show some positive results but over the long term reveal that no one treatment program is better than others and that no one treatment is superior to no treatment at all. About one-third of alcoholics recover with no treatment. However, Vaillant's research did reveal some factors that predict a positive outcome and recovery from alcoholism.

Overview *Overview*

WE BEGAN THIS CHAPTER by discussing the nature of consciousness. Then we examined these aspects of sleep: why we sleep, sleep and circadian rhythms, sleep deprivation and sleep needs, the neural basis of sleep, and sleep disorders. We also studied the interpretation of dreams and many other aspects of dreams. Our coverage of hypnosis focused on its definition and history, the hypnotic state (features and individual differences), theories of hypnosis, and applications. We evaluated these aspects of psychoactive drugs: their uses, their types, and addiction and drug abuse.

Don't forget that you can obtain a more detailed overview of the chapter by again studying the four summary tables on pages 163, 167, 171, and 180.

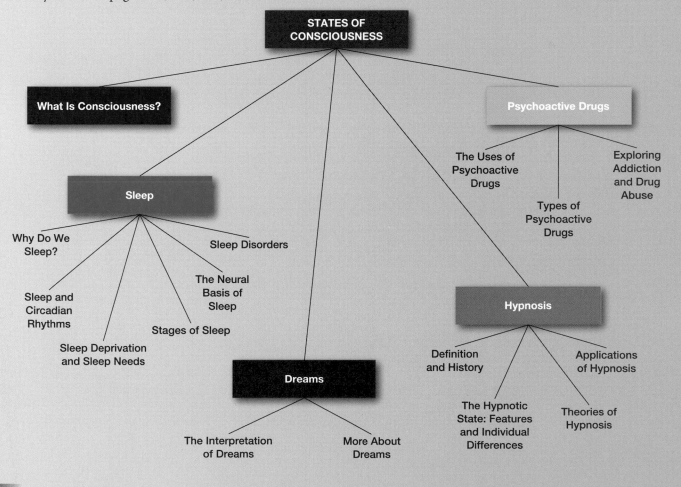

Key Terms

consciousness 150
stream of consciousness 150
unconscious thought 150
controlled processes 150
automatic processes 151
daydreaming 151
altered states of consciousness 151
repair theory 154
ecological theory 154
circadian rhythm 154
alpha waves 157
sleep spindles 157

delta waves 157
REM sleep 157
insomnia 161
somnambulism 161
nightmare 162
night terror 162
narcolepsy 162
sleep apnea 162
wish fulfillment 164
manifest content 164
latent content 164
cognitive theory of dreaming 165

activation-synthesis theory 166
hypnosis 167
special process theory 168
nonstate theory 170
psychoactive drugs 170
tolerance 172
physical dependence 172
psychological dependence 172
depressants 172
alcoholism 172
barbiturates 173
tranquilizers 173

opiates 173
stimulants 174
crack 174
hallucinogens 175
addiction 178
disease model of addiction 178
life-process model of addiction 178
primary prevention 178
secondary prevention 178
tertiary prevention 179

Key People

William James 150
Sigmund Freud 150

Roger Broughton 157
Bob Ogilvie 158

Ernest Hilgard 168
Nick Spanos 170

Psychology Checklist
STATES OF CONSCIOUSNESS

How much have you learned since the beginning of the chapter? Use the following statements to help you review your knowledge and understanding of the chapter material. First, read the statement and mentally or briefly demonstrate on paper that you understand and can discuss the relevant information.

_____ I know what consciousness is and can profile different states of consciousness.
_____ I am aware of why we sleep.
_____ I can describe the nature of sleep and circadian rhythms.
_____ I can discuss the effects of sleep deprivation and how much sleep people need to function optimally.
_____ I can describe the stages of sleep people go through.
_____ I know about the brain's role in sleep.
_____ I can discuss different sleep disorders.

_____ I can describe the nature of dreams, including different theories of dreams.
_____ I know what hypnosis is and the features and individual variations involved in the hypnotic state.
_____ I can discuss theories of hypnosis.
_____ I can describe applications of hypnosis.
_____ I can discuss the uses of psychoactive drugs.
_____ I can profile the different types of psychoactive drugs.
_____ I know about the nature of addiction and prevention/treatment of drug abuse.

For any items that you did not check off, go back and locate the relevant material in the chapter. Review the material until you feel you can check off the item. You may want to use this checklist later when you are preparing for an exam.

Taking It to the Net

1. Do you require a lot of sleep, or can you function well with only a few hours sleep? Many of your friends probably differ greatly in the amount of sleep they need. Generally, however, we all need around the same amount of sleep to remain healthy. How much do you think we need? What happens to you if you don't get enough sleep? You may try to "catch up on your sleep," but does this really work? Explain the notion of sleep debt and how it relates to you.

2. Many university students travel home during Thanksgiving and Christmas break. If you have traveled long distances, you might have experienced jet lag. Jet lag can play interesting tricks on your mind, confusing you and making you tired. Explain why traveling long distances results in jet lag. How do you achieve it and what can you do to prevent it?

3. You have probably seen or heard things in the media about hypnotism. Maybe you have seen a hypnotist at your college, making students do strange and humorous things while under a trance. Do you think everyone can be hypnotized? You might also know that hypnosis has been used in psychotherapy for a variety of clinical applications. How does hypnosis work? Can memory be improved with hypnosis?

Connect to http://www.mcgrawhill.ca/college/santrock to find the answers!

Resources for Psychology and Life

Sleep/Wake Disorders Canada
3080 Yonge St, Suite 5055,
Toronto, ON M6A 2A4
Website currently at: http://www.geocities.com/
HotSprings/1837/

An excellent resource, particularly for persons recently diagnosed with any sleep disorder.

Power Sleep: The Revolutionary Program that Prepares Your Mind for Peak Performance
by James Maas (1998)
New York: Villard

Maas argues that many Americans do not function at their peak performance because they get too little sleep. He provides strategies for helping people get the sleep they need.

Sleep Thieves: An Eye-Opening Exploration Into the Science and Mysteries of Sleep
by Stanley Coren (1996)
New York: The Free Press

This volume is a light-hearted coverage of the degree to which our society has fallen into sleep debt.

Association for the Study of Dreams
P.O. Box 1600
Vienna, VA 22183
703-242-8889

This association provides an international, interdisciplinary forum for furthering knowledge about dreams. Medical professionals, psychologists, educators, and students are welcomed as members. The group publishes a quarterly newsletter.

The Chemistry of Consciousness (1994)
by J. A. Hobson
Boston: Little, Brown

This book on the neurobiological basis of dreaming is written by one of the field's leading researchers.

Theories of Hypnosis: Current Models and Perspectives (1993)
edited by Steven Lynn and Judith Rhue
New York, NY: Guilford Press

This volume focuses on theories of hypnosis, including excellent chapters by Canadian researchers. Special process theory is defended (Hilgard, Bowers & Davidson) as is nonstate theory (Spanos). A synthesis of the two (Nadon, Laurence & Perry) can also be found here.

Alcoholics Anonymous World Services
475 Riverside Drive
New York, NY
212-878-3400

Alcoholics Anonymous (AA) provides support groups for individuals with drinking problems or other addictive behaviors. Most communities have local chapters of AA.

Canadian Centre on Substance Abuse
75 Albert Street, Suite 300
Ottawa, ON K1P 5E7
Website: http://www.ccsa.ca/

The Centre promotes informed debate on substance abuse issues, disseminates information on the nature, extent and consequences of substance abuse, and supports and assists organizations involved in substance abuse treatment, prevention, and educational programming.

Centre for Addiction and Mental Health
33 Russell Street
Toronto, ON M5S 2S1
Website: http://www.camh.net/

Created in 1998 through the successful merger of the Addiction Research Foundation, the Clarke Institute of Psychiatry, the Donwood Institute and the Queen Street Mental Health Centre, the Centre for Addiction and Mental Health is a teaching hospital fully affiliated with the University of Toronto. Excellent research resources are available here.

Chapter 6

CHAPTER OUTLINE

WHAT IS LEARNING?

CLASSICAL CONDITIONING

Pavlovian Conditioning

Temporal Contiguity and Contingency

Extinction, Generalization, and Discrimination

How Classical Conditioning Works: Pavlov and the Contemporary Perspective

Classical Conditioning in Humans

Evaluating Classical Conditioning

OPERANT CONDITIONING

What Operant Conditioning Is

Thorndike's Law of Effect

Skinner's Operant Conditioning

Applications of Operant Conditioning

OBSERVATIONAL LEARNING

COGNITIVE FACTORS IN LEARNING

Expectations and Cognitive Maps

Insight Learning

BIOLOGICAL AND CULTURAL FACTORS IN LEARNING

Biological Factors

Cultural Factors

Learning

Images of Psychology and Life
Learning to Die

> "To learn is a natural pleasure."
>
> Aristotle
> *Greek Philosopher, 4th Century B.C.*

Preview

THE ABILITY TO LEARN is a remarkable and enchanting gift. When we think about learning, we might come up with an image of someone sitting at a desk and studying a book. Studying does involve learning, but learning is much more than just studying. You will see in this chapter that learning applies to many areas of acquiring new behaviors, skills, and knowledge. These are some of the questions we will explore:

- What is learning?
- How do people learn to fear things?
- How would you go about teaching a pigeon to play table tennis or guide a missile?
- Why is punishment often not a good choice when you want to change behavior?
- What are some good strategies for improving self-control?
- How much do we learn by observing others do something?
- What roles do biology and culture play in learning?

WE HUMANS MUST LEARN almost everything. We do so with classical conditioning, operant conditioning and/or observational learning, all discussed in this chapter. Most of the time learning is, as Aristotle suggests, a positive experience. But that is not always the case. As we shall see in this chapter, we may also learn our fears, our phobias, and our addictions through the same mechanisms. In extreme cases, we can learn enough to literally kill us.

For years, many deaths due to drug overdoses were a mystery. Addicts recovering from nearly-fatal drug overdoses commonly reported that they had not taken higher-than-normal dosages and that drug impurity was not a factor. It was not until Shepard Siegel (1999) from McMaster University applied classical conditioning principles to these cases that the puzzle was solved.

It turned out that the common thread in these mysterious deaths was that that the addicts had "shot up" in a new environment. Siegel (1979) confirmed that new environments could be responsible by showing that rats are able to tolerate higher doses of heroin in a familiar as opposed to an unfamiliar environment. The injection of the drug (an unconditioned stimulus) leads to a dramatic bodily response (an unconditioned response). Over time the addict builds up drug *tolerance,* requiring ever-higher dosages to get the same "high." Siegel (1983) explained the build-up of tolerance in classical conditioning terms.

In August of 1996, 35-year-old Steven Chuvalo was found dead of a drug overdose at a Toronto home. His father, ex-Canadian boxing champion George Chuvalo, has been fighting back the only way he knows how. He's been travelling across Canada, visiting every high school that he can and warning kids about the danger of drugs. Did Steven Chuvalo mean to kill himself or was it an accident? Could classical conditioning have contributed? How is classical conditioning involved in some cases of drug overdose?

The setting of the drug use (the sight of the needle, the room, etc.) comes to predict the drug injection (it becomes a conditioned stimulus). The setting also comes to trigger a conditioned compensatory response, one in which the nervous system attempts to counteract the massive effects of the drug with an *opponent process*. This opponent bodily response accounts for the tolerance. As more tolerance builds up, the addict must increase the dosage, leading to a larger compensatory response, and so on.

Suppose an addict has a long history of shooting up in the same place, say his room. He has built up considerable drug tolerance, due to the opponent process triggered by familiar cues in his room. Now suppose the addict shoots up with his usual high dosage in an unfamiliar room. His familiar surroundings cannot act as a conditioned stimulus to trigger the usual compensatory response and so the drug acts more strongly than usual. The result can easily be an overdose, sometimes ending in the death of the addict (Siegel & others, 1982).

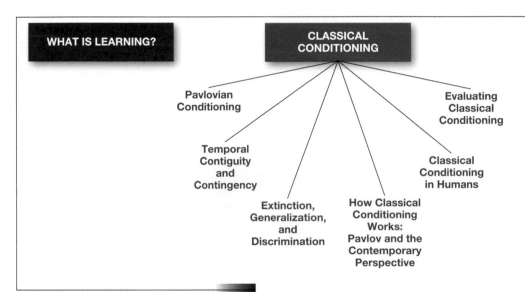

What Is Learning?

In learning how to use a computer, you might make some mistakes along the way, but at some point you will get the knack of how to use it. You will change from being someone who could not operate a computer to being one who can. Learning anything new involves change. Once you have learned to use a computer, the skill does not usually leave you. Once you learn how to drive a car, you do not have to go through the process again. Learning involves a relatively permanent influence on behavior. You learned how to use a computer through experience with the machine. Through experience you also learned that you have to study to do well on a test, that when you go to a rock concert there is usually a warm-up act, and that a hat trick in hockey is scoring three goals in a game. Putting these pieces together, we arrive at a definition of **learning:** *a relatively permanent change in behavior that occurs through experience.*

Psychologists explain our many experiences with a few basic learning processes. We respond to things that happen to us, we act and experience consequences for our behavior, and we observe what others say and do. These three aspects of experiences form the three main types of learning we will study in this chapter—classical conditioning (responding), operant conditioning (acting), and observational learning (observing). As we study the nature of learning, you will discover that early approaches investigated the way experience and behavior are connected without referring to cognitive or mental processes. In recent years, cognitive processes have assumed a more important role in learning. We will discuss more recent cognitive approaches to learning later in the chapter, but first we will examine classical conditioning.

Learning Theories and Applications

Classical Conditioning

It is a nice spring day. A father takes his baby out for a walk. The baby reaches over to touch a pink flower and is badly stung by the bumblebee sitting on the petals. The next day, the baby's mother brings home some pink flowers. She removes a flower from the arrangement and takes it over for her baby to smell. The baby cries loudly as soon as she sees the pink flower. The baby's panic at the sight of the pink flower illustuates the learning process of **classical conditioning,** *in which a neutral stimulus becomes associated with a meaningful stimulus and acquires the capacity to elicit a similar response.*

Pavlovian Conditioning

In the early 1900s, the Russian physiologist Ivan Pavlov investigated the way the body digests food ◀▥ P. 8. As part of his experiments, he routinely placed meat powder in a dog's mouth, causing the dog to salivate. Pavlov began to notice that the meat powder was not the only stimulus that caused the dog to salivate. The dog salivated in response to a number of stimuli associated with the food, such as the sight of the food dish, the sight of the individual who brought the food into the room, and the sound of the door closing when the food arrived. Pavlov recognized that the dog's association of these sights and sounds with the food was an important type of learning, which came to be called classical conditioning.

Pavlov wanted to know *why* the dog salivated to various sights and sounds before eating the meat powder. He observed that the dog's behavior included both learned and unlearned components. The "unlearned" part of classical conditioning is based on the fact that some stimuli automatically produce certain responses apart from any prior learning; in other words they are inborn or innate. **Reflexes** *are automatic stimulus-response connections.* They include salivation in response to food, nausea in response to bad food, shivering in response to low temperature, coughing in response to the throat being clogged, pupil constriction in response to light, and withdrawal in response to blows or burns. An **unconditioned stimulus (US)** *is a stimulus that produces a response without prior learning; food was the US in Pavlov's experiments.* An **unconditioned response (UR)** *is an unlearned response that is automatically elicited by the US. In Pavlov's*

If a bee stings this young girl while she is holding a pink flower, how would classical conditioning explain her panic at the sight of pink flowers in the future?

Pavlov (the white-bearded gentleman in the center) is shown demonstrating the nature of classical conditioning to students at the Military Medical Academy in Russia. © The Granger Collection, New York

experiments, the saliva that flowed from the dog's mouth in response to food was the UR. In the case of the baby and the flower, the baby's learning and experience did not cause her to cry when the bee stung her. Her crying was unlearned and occurred automatically. The bee's sting was the US and the crying was the UR.

In classical conditioning, the **conditioned stimulus (CS)** *is a previously neutral stimulus that eventually elicits the conditioned response after being associated with the unconditioned stimulus.* The **conditioned response (CR)** *is the learned response to the conditioned stimulus that occurs after CS-US pairing* (Pavlov, 1927). In studying the salivary response, Pavlov rang a bell before giving meat powder to a dog. Until then, ringing the bell did not much affect the dog, except perhaps to wake it from a nap. The bell was a neutral stimulus with respect to salivation. But the dog began to associate the bell's sound with the food and salivated when it heard the bell. The bell had become a conditioned (learned) stimulus (CS) and the salivation a conditioned response (CR). During *acquisition,* then, repeated CS–US pairings have the effect of strengthening the conditioned association. Before conditioning, the bell and the food were unrelated. After their association, the bell (now a CS) produced a CR (salivation). For the unhappy baby, the flower was the baby's bell, or CS, and crying was the CR after the sting (US) and the flower (CS) were paired.

Classical conditioning is a form of **associative learning,** *which involves learning that two events are related or linked.* In classical conditioning, the learned association involves the link between two stimuli (CS and US). A summary of how classical conditioning works is shown in figure 6.1.

Classical Conditioning

Temporal Contiguity and Contingency

The interval between the CS and the US is one of the most important aspects of classical conditioning (DeCola & Fanselow, 1995; Weidemann, Georgilas, & Kehoe, 1999). It is important because it defines the **contiguity,** *or degree of association,* of the stimuli. Conditioned responses develop when the interval between the CS and US is very short, as in a matter of seconds. In many instances optimal spacing is a fraction of a second (Kimble, 1961). In Pavlov's work, if the bell rang 20 minutes after the presentation of the food, the dog probably would not associate the bell with the food.

Robert Rescorla (1966, 1988) believes that for classical conditioning to take place, it is important to have not only temporal contiguity in the CS-US connection, but also contingency. **Contingency (in classical conditioning)** *involves the predictability of the occurrence of one stimulus from the presence of another.* For example, a flash of lightning is usually followed by the sound of thunder. Thus, if you see lightning, you might put your hands over your ears or lean away in anticipation of the thunder.

Extinction, Generalization, and Discrimination

Pavlov rang the bell repeatedly in a single session and did not give the dog any food. Eventually the dog stopped salivating. This result is **extinction,** *which in classical conditioning is the weakening of the conditioned response in the absence of the unconditioned stimulus.* Without continued association with the unconditioned stimulus (US), the conditioned stimulus (CS) loses its power to elicit the conditioned response (CR). Over time, after her bee sting, the baby encountered many pink flowers and was not stung by a bee. Consequently, her fear of pink flowers subsided and eventually disappeared. The pink flower (CS) lost its capacity to elicit fear (CR) when the flower was no longer associated with bee stings (US) and the pain and fear they cause (UR).

Extinction is not always the end of the conditioned response. The day after Pavlov extinguished the conditioned salivation at the sound of a bell, he took the dog to the laboratory and rang the bell, still not giving the dog any meat powder. The dog salivated, indicating that an extinguished response can spontaneously recur. **Spontaneous recovery** *is the process in classical conditioning by which a conditioned response can recur after a time delay without further conditioning.* In the case of the baby, even

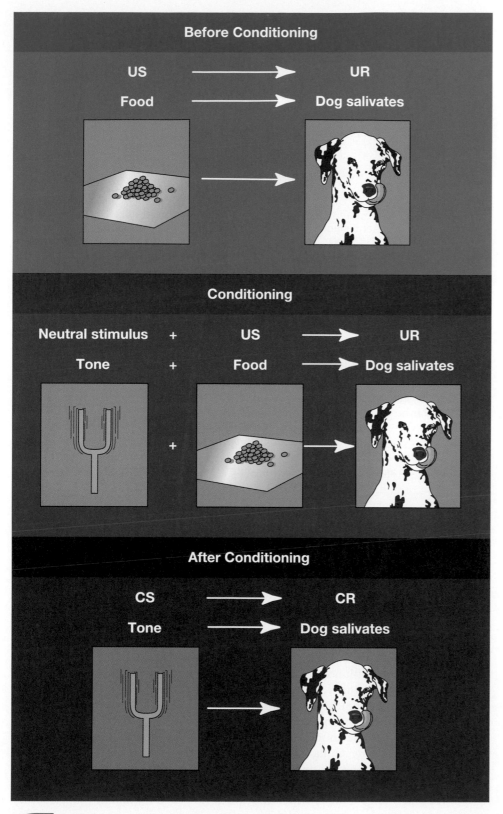

$\mathcal{F}$igure 6.1
Pavlov's Classical Conditioning

In one experiment, Pavlov presented a neutral stimulus (tone) just before an unconditioned stimulus (food). The neutral stimulus became a conditioned stimulus by being paired with the unconditioned stimulus. Subsequently, the conditioned stimulus (tone) by itself was able to elicit the dog's salivation.

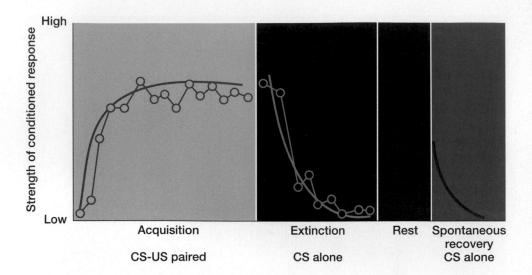

$\mathscr{F}$igure 6.2
The Strength of a Classically Conditioned Response During Acquisition, Extinction, and Spontaneous Recovery (after Pavlov, 1927)

During acquisition the conditioned stimulus (CS) and unconditioned stimulus (US) are associated. The dots are actual data points and the curve represents the ideal. As can be seen, when this occurs, the strength of the conditioned response (CR) increases. During extinction the CS is presented alone, and, as can be seen, this results in a decrease of the CR. After a rest period, spontaneous recovery appears, although the strength of the CR is not nearly as great at this point as it was after a number of CS–US pairings. When the CS is presented alone again after spontaneous recovery, the response is extinguished rapidly.

though she saw many pink flowers after her first painful encounter and was not "stung" by them, she showed some signs of fear from time to time. Over time her conditioned fear (CR) to pink flowers (CS) diminished; she showed less tendency to recover her fear of pink flowers spontaneously, especially since she did not experience further painful stings (US). Figure 6.2 shows the sequence of acquisition, extinction, and spontaneous recovery. Spontaneous recovery can occur several times, but as long as the conditioned stimulus is presented alone, spontaneous recovery becomes weaker and eventually ceases to occur (Goddard, 1997).

After many conditioning trials, Pavlov found that the dog salivated in response not only to the tone from the tuning fork, but to other sounds, such as a whistle. Pavlov did not pair these sounds with the unconditioned stimulus of the food. He discovered that the more similar the noise was to the original sound of the tone, the stronger was the dog's salivary flow. In the example of conditioned fear of pink flowers, the baby not only cried at the sight of pink flowers, but she also now cries at the sight of red and orange flowers. **Generalization** *in classical conditioning is the tendency of a new stimulus that is similar to the original conditioned stimulus to elicit a response that is similar to the conditioned response.*

Stimulus generalization is not always beneficial. For example, the cat who generalizes from a minnow to a piranha has a major problem; therefore it is important to discriminate between stimuli. **Discrimination** *in classical conditioning is the process of learning to respond to certain stimuli and not to respond to others.* To produce discrimination, Pavlov gave food to the dog only after ringing the bell and not after any other sounds. In this way, the dog learned to distinguish between the bell and other sounds. Similarly, the baby was not stung and did not cry when seeing blue flowers, thus discriminating between blue and pink flowers.

How Classical Conditioning Works: Pavlov and the Contemporary Perspective

Stimulus substitution *was Pavlov's theory of how classical conditioning works; it states that the nervous system is structured in such a way that the CS and US bond together and eventually the CS substitutes for the US.* However, if the CS substitutes for the US, the two stimuli should produce similar responses. This does not always happen. Using a shock as a US often elicits flinching and jumping, whereas a light (CS) paired with a shock may cause the organism to be immobile, for example.

Information theory *is one contemporary explanation of why classical conditioning works; it stresses that the key to understanding classical conditioning focuses on the information an organism gets from the situation.* Some years ago, E. C. Tolman (1932) said the information value of the CS is important in telling the organism what will follow. In Tolman's words, the organism uses the CS as a sign or expectation that a US will follow. Tolman's belief that the information the CS provides is the key to understanding classical conditioning was a forerunner of contemporary thinking.

In one contemporary view of classical conditioning, an organism is seen as an information seeker using logical and perceptual relations among events, along with preconceptions, to form a representation of the world (Rescorla, 1988, 1996). The contemporary view still recognizes contiguity between the CS and US as important in classical conditioning, but it emphasizes that what is important about the CS-US connection is the information the stimuli give the organism (Kohn & Kalat, 1995).

A classic experiment conducted by Leon Kamin (1968) illustrates the importance of an organism's history and the information provided by a conditioned stimulus in classical conditioning. A rat was conditioned by repeatedly pairing a tone (CS) and a shock (US), until the tone alone produced a strong conditioned response (fear). The tone continued to be paired with the shock, but a light (a second CS) was turned on each time the tone was sounded. Even though the light (a CS) and the shock (US) were repeatedly paired, the rat showed no conditioning to the light. The light by itself produced no CR. Conditioning to the light was blocked, almost as if the rat had not attended to it. The rat apparently used the tone as a signal to predict that a shock would be forthcoming; it did not need to learn information about the light's pairing with the shock, because that information was redundant, the information having already been learned in the pairing of the tone and the shock. In this experiment, conditioning was governed not by the contiguity of the CS and US but, rather, by the rat's history and the information it received. Contemporary classical conditioning researchers are exploring further the role of information in an organism's learning (Domjan, 1996; Fanselow, DeCola, & Young, 1993).

Classical Conditioning in Humans

Since Pavlov's experiments, individuals have been conditioned to respond to the sound of a buzzer, a glimpse of light, a puff of air, or the touch of a hand (Woodruff-Pak, 1999). Classical conditioning has a great deal of survival value for the individual (Vernoy, 1995). Because of classical conditioning, we jerk our hands away before they are burned by fire. Classical conditioning is also at work when a tranquil scene—such as an empty beach with waves lapping onto the sand—is described and the harried executive relaxes as if she were actually lying on that beach.

You will note that their ability to comprehend, assess and process information increases dramatically when Professor Podhertz throws in the cat.

© Leo Cullum

*T*hrough the Eyes of Psychologists

Robert Rescorla, *University of Pennsylvania*

"Classical conditioning is now described as the learning of relations among events so as to allow the organism to represent its environment."

A **phobia** *is an irrational fear.* Classical conditioning provides an explanation of these and other fears. The famous behaviorist John Watson conducted an investigation to demonstrate classical conditioning's role in phobias. A little boy named Albert was shown a white laboratory rat to see if he was afraid of it. He was not. As Albert played with the rat a loud noise was sounded behind his head. As you might imagine, the noise caused little Albert to cry. After only seven pairings of the loud noise with the white rat, Albert began to fear the rat even when the noise was not sounded. Albert's fear was generalized to a rabbit, a dog, and a sealskin coat.

Today we could not ethically conduct such an experiment. Especially noteworthy is the fact that Watson and his associate did not remove Albert's fear of rats, so presumably this phobia remained with him after the experiment (Watson & Raynor, 1920). The experiment with little Albert was conducted in the early part of the twentieth century when there was less concern about the ethical aspects of research. As we saw in Chapter 2 ("Psychology's Scientific Methods"), today psychologists must adhere to strict ethical guidelines when they conduct research. Today, the little Albert study would not be approved under the ethical guidelines of the Canadian and American Psychological Associations.

Watson was right about how many of our fears can be learned through classical conditioning. We might develop a fear of the dentist because of a painful experience, fear driving after having been in an automobile accident, and fear dogs after having been bitten by one.

If we can produce fears by classical conditioning, we should be able to eliminate them using conditioning procedures. **Counterconditioning** *is a classical conditioning procedure for weakening a CR by associating the fear-provoking stimulus with a new response incompatible with the fear.* Though Watson did not eliminate little Albert's fear of white rats, an associate of Watson's, Mary Cover Jones (1924), did eliminate the fears of a 3-year-old boy named Peter. Peter had many of the same fears as Albert; however, Peter's fears were not produced by Jones. Among Peter's fears were white rats, fur coats, frogs, fish, and mechanical toys. To eliminate these fears, a rabbit was brought into Peter's view but kept far enough away that it would not upset him. At the same time the rabbit was brought into view, Peter was fed crackers and milk. On each successive day the rabbit was moved closer to Peter as he ate crackers and milk. Eventually Peter reached the point where he would eat the food with one hand and pet the rabbit with the other. The feeling of pleasure produced by the crackers and milk was incompatible with Peter's feeling of fear of the rabbit, and fear was extinguished through counterconditioning.

Some of the behaviors we associate with health problems or mental disorders can involve classical conditioning. Certain physical complaints—asthma, headaches, ulcers, and high blood pressure, for example—can partly be the products of classical conditioning. We usually say that such health problems are caused by stress, but often what happened is that certain stimuli, such as a boss's critical attitude or a wife's threat of divorce, are conditioned stimuli for physiological responses. Over time, the frequent presence of the physiological responses may produce a health problem or disorder. A boss's persistent criticism may cause an employee to develop muscle tension, headaches, or high blood pressure. Anything associated with the boss, such as work itself, can then trigger stress in the employee (see figure 6.3).

Classical conditioning is not restricted to unpleasant emotions. Among the things in our life that produce pleasure because they have become conditioned might

In 1920, nine-month-old Albert was conditioned to fear a white rat by pairing the rat with a loud noise. When little Albert was subsequently presented with other stimuli similar to the white rat, such as the rabbit shown here with little Albert, he was afraid of them, too. This illustrates the principle of stimulus generalization in classical conditioning. What are some other examples of generalization in classical conditioning?

Courtesy of Professor Benjamin Harris

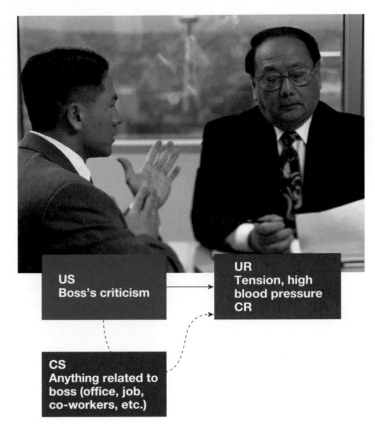

*F*igure 6.3
Classical Conditioning: Boss's Criticism and High Blood Pressure

be the sight of a rainbow, a sunny day, or a favorite song. If you have a positive romantic experience, the location where that experience took place can become a conditioned stimulus. This is the result of the pairing of a place (CS) with the event (US). Sometimes, though, classical conditioning involves an experience that is both pleasant and deviant from the norm. Consider a fetishist who becomes sexually aroused by the sight and touch of certain clothing, such as undergarments or shoes. The fetish may have developed when the fetish object (undergarment, shoe) was associated with sexual arousal, especially when the individual was young. The fetish object becomes a conditioned stimulus that can produce sexual arousal by itself (Chance, 1979).

Evaluating Classical Conditioning

Pavlov described learning in terms of classical conditioning. While classical conditioning helps us to learn about our environment, we learn about our world in other ways, too. Classical conditioning describes the organism as *responding* to the environment, a view that fails to capture the active nature of the organism and its influence on the environment. Next, we study a major form of learning that places more emphasis on the organism's *activity* in the environment—operant conditioning.

Before turning to that discussion, however, let's review the main themes of classical conditioning. Summary table 6.1 will help you with this review and will provide information about the basic nature of learning.

SUMMARY TABLE 6.1
The Nature of Learning and Classical Conditioning

Concept	Processes/ Related Ideas	Characteristics/Description
What Is Learning?	Its Nature	Learning is a relatively permanent change in behavior due to experience. How we respond to the environment (classical conditioning), how we act in the environment (operant conditioning), and how we observe the environment (observational learning) are the most important ways in which we experience. Early approaches emphasized connections between environment and behavior; many contemporary approaches stress that cognitive factors mediate environment-behavior connections.
Classical Conditioning	Pavlovian Conditioning	Pavlov discovered that an organism learns the association between an unconditioned stimulus (US) and a conditioned stimulus (CS). The US automatically produces the UR (unconditioned response). After conditioning (CS-US pairing), the CS elicits the CR (conditioned response) by itself. Generalization, discrimination, and extinction are also involved. Classical conditioning is a form of associative learning, which involves learning that two events are related or linked. In classical conditioning, the learned association involves the link between two stimuli (CS and US).
	Temporal Contiguity and Contingency	Pavlov argued that for classical conditioning to take place, the CS–US connection has to have temporal contiguity. Rescorla believes the CS–US connection also has to involve contingency in that one stimulus has to be able to predict the presence of the other stimulus.
	How Classical Conditioning Works: Pavlov and the Contemporary Perspective	Pavlov explained classical conditioning in terms of stimulus substitution but one modern explanation is based on information theory.
	Classical Conditioning in Humans	Classical conditioning has survival value for humans, as when we develop a fear of hazardous conditions. Irrational fears are explained by classical conditioning. Counterconditioning has been used to eliminate fears.
	Evaluating Classical Conditioning	Classical conditioning is important in explaining the way learning in animals occurs. It is not the only way humans learn and fails to capture the active nature of an organism in the environment.

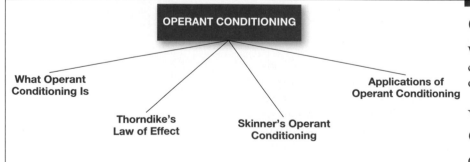

Operant Conditioning

We have discussed one major type of learning—classical conditioning. Now let's explore a second major type—operant conditioning.

What Operant Conditioning Is

Classical conditioning excels at explaining how neutral stimuli become associated with unlearned, involuntary responses, but it is not as effective in explaining voluntary behaviors, such as studying hard for a test, playing slot machines in Las Vegas, or teaching a pigeon to play ping-pong. Operant conditioning is usually better than

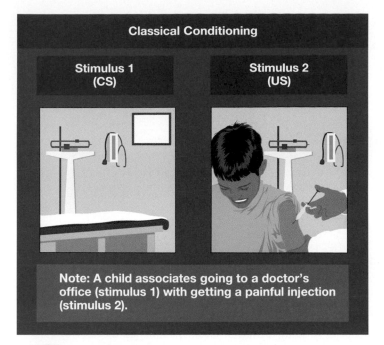

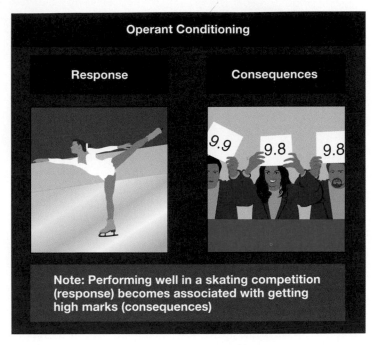

$\mathcal{F}$igure 6.4
Associative Learning: Comparing Classical and Operant Conditioning

classical conditioning at explaining voluntary behavior. The concept of operant conditioning was developed by the American psychologist B. F. Skinner (1938) ◀▥ P. 8. **Operant conditioning** *(or instrumental conditioning) is a form of learning in which the consequences of behavior produce changes in the probability of the behavior's occurrence.* Skinner chose the term *operant* to describe the behavior of the organism—the behavior operates on the environment, and the environment in turn operates on the behavior.

When we described classical conditioning earlier, we said that it is a form of associative learning. Operant conditioning is also a form of associative learning. However, in classical conditioning the association is between two stimuli, whereas in operant conditioning the association is between a response and its consequences (see figure 6.4). For example, in operant conditioning, performing a great skating routine in competition (response) is likely to result in a high score from the judges (consequences). Recall also that we said operant conditioning involves a contingency between the organism's response and its consequences. For example, a simple operant might be pressing a lever that leads to the delivery of food; the delivery of food is contingent on pressing the lever.

Operant Conditioning

Thorndike's Law of Effect

Although B. F. Skinner has emerged as the primary figure in operant conditioning, E. L. Thorndike's experiments established the power of consequences in determining voluntary behavior. At about the same time Ivan Pavlov was conducting classical conditioning experiments with salivating dogs, American psychologist E. L. Thorndike was studying cats in puzzle boxes. Thorndike put a hungry cat inside a box and a piece of fish outside. To escape from the box, the cat had to learn how to open the latch inside the box. At first the cat made a number of ineffective responses. It clawed or bit at the bars and thrust its paw through the openings. Eventually the cat accidentally stepped on the treadle that released the door bolt. When the cat returned to the box, it went through the same random activity until it

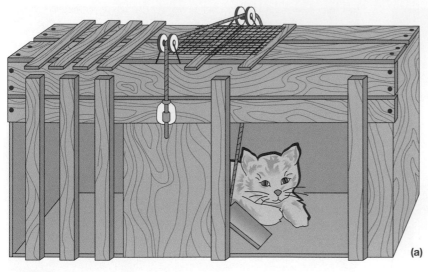

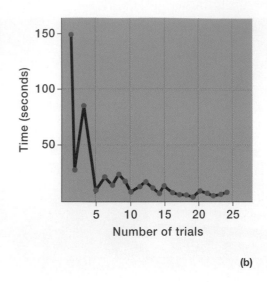

Figure 6.5
Thorndike's Puzzle Box and the Law of Effect

(a) A box typical of the puzzle boxes Thorndike used in his experiments with cats to study the law of effect. Stepping on the treadle released the door bolt. A weight attached to the door then pulled the door open and allowed the cat to escape. (b) One cat's learning curve over 24 separate trials. Notice how the cat learned to escape much more quickly after about five trials, after it had learned the consequences of its behavior.

B. F. Skinner
Positive Reinforcement
Skinner on Audio

stepped on the treadle once more. In subsequent trials, the cat made fewer and fewer random movements, until it immediately clawed the treadle to open the door (see figure 6.5). The **law of effect,** *developed by Thorndike, states that behaviors followed by positive outcomes are strengthened, whereas behaviors followed by negative outcomes are weakened.*

The key question for Thorndike was how the correct stimulus-response bond strengthens and eventually dominates incorrect stimulus-response bonds. According to Thorndike, the correct S-R association strengthens and the incorrect association weakens because of the *consequences* of the organism's actions. Thorndike's view is called *S-R theory* because the organism's behavior is due to a connection between a stimulus and a response. As we see next, Skinner's operant conditioning approach expanded Thorndike's basic ideas.

Skinner's Operant Conditioning

Earlier we indicated that Skinner described operant conditioning as a form of learning in which the consequences of behavior lead to changes in the probability of that behavior's occurrence. The consequences—reinforcement or punishment—are contingent on the organism's behavior. First we will tackle reinforcement, then we will discuss punishment.

Positive and Negative Reinforcement
Reinforcement means "to strengthen." In **positive reinforcement,** *the frequency of a response increases because it is followed by a rewarding stimulus.* For example, if someone you meet smiles at you and the two of you talk for some time, the smile has reinforced your talking. Similarly, complimenting someone you are attracted to might make that person more receptive to your advances and increase the probability that you will get to know the person better. The same principle of positive reinforcement is at work when an animal trainer teaches a dog to "shake hands" by giving it a piece of food when it lifts its paw.

Conversely, in **negative reinforcement** *the frequency of a response increases because it is followed by the removal of an aversive (unpleasant) stimulus.* For example, your father nags at you to clean out the garage. He keeps nagging. Finally you get tired of the nagging and clean out the garage. Your response (cleaning out the garage) removed the unpleasant stimulus (nagging). Taking an aspirin works the same way. Taking aspirin is reinforced when this behavior is followed by a reduction in pain.

To understand the distinction between positive and negative reinforcement, remember that "positive" and "negative" don't have anything to do with "good" and "bad." And just keep remembering that they are procedures in which something is given (positive reinforcement) and something is removed (negative reinforcement). Figure 6.6 provides another example to further help you understand the distinction between positive and negative reinforcement.

"Once it became clear to me that, by responding correctly to certain stimuli, I could get all the bananas I wanted, getting this job was a pushover."

Mechanisms of Learning Are the Same in All Species

One of Skinner's basic beliefs was that the mechanisms of learning are the same for all species. This belief led him to an extensive study of animals in the hope that the basic mechanisms of learning could be understood with organisms that were simpler than humans.

For example, during World War II, Skinner constructed a rather strange project—a pigeon-guided missile. A pigeon in the warhead of the missile operated the flaps on the missile and guided it home by pecking at an image of a target. How could this possibly work? When the missile was in flight, the pigeon pecked the moving image on a screen. This produced corrective signals to keep the missile on its course. The pigeons did their job well in trial runs, but top Navy officials just could not accept pigeons piloting their missiles in a war. Skinner, however, congratulated himself on the degree of control he was able to exercise over the pigeons (see figure 6.7).

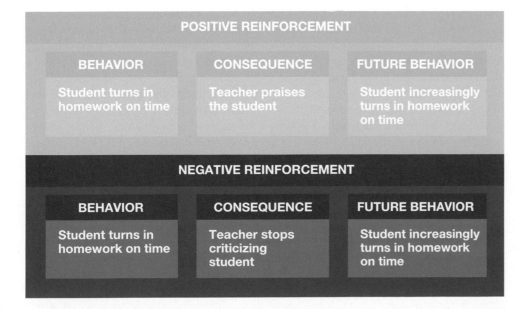

POSITIVE REINFORCEMENT

BEHAVIOR	CONSEQUENCE	FUTURE BEHAVIOR
Student turns in homework on time	Teacher praises the student	Student increasingly turns in homework on time

NEGATIVE REINFORCEMENT

BEHAVIOR	CONSEQUENCE	FUTURE BEHAVIOR
Student turns in homework on time	Teacher stops criticizing student	Student increasingly turns in homework on time

*F*igure 6.6
Positive and Negative Reinforcement

Following the pigeon experiment, Skinner (1948) wrote *Walden Two*, a novel in which he presented his ideas about building a scientifically managed society. Skinner envisioned a utopian society that could be engineered through behavioral control. Skinner viewed existing societies as poorly managed because people believe in myths such as free will. He pointed out that humans are no more free than pigeons are; denying that our behavior is controlled by environmental forces is to ignore science and reality, he argued. Skinner believed that in the long run we would be much happier when we recognized such truths, especially his concept that we could live a prosperous life under the control of positive reinforcement.

Skinner and other behaviorists have made every effort to study organisms under precisely controlled conditions so that the connection between the operant and the specific consequences could be examined in minute detail. One of the ways in which Skinner achieved such control was the development in the 1930s of the Skinner box (see figure 6.8). A device in the box would deliver food pellets into a tray at random. After a rat became accustomed to the box, Skinner installed a lever and observed the rat's behavior. As the hungry rat explored the box, it occasionally pressed the lever and a food pellet would be dispensed. Soon after, the rat learned that the consequences of pressing the lever were positive—it would be fed. Further control was achieved by soundproofing the box to ensure that the experimenter was the only influence on the organism. In many experiments the responses were mechanically recorded and the food (the stimulus) was dispensed automatically. Such precautions were designed to avoid human error.

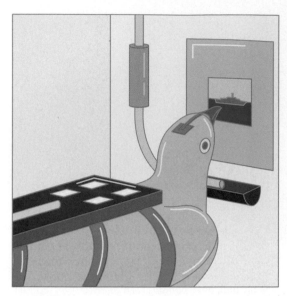

$\mathcal{F}$igure 6.7
Skinner's Pigeon-Guided Missile

Skinner wanted to assist the military by using pigeons' tracking behavior. A gold electrode covered the tip of the pigeons' beaks. Contact with the screen on which the image of the target was projected sent a signal informing the missile's control mechanism of the target's location. A few grains of food occasionally given to the pigeons maintained their tracking behavior.

Skinner Box

Time Interval   As with classical conditioning, learning is more efficient in operant conditioning when the interval between response and reinforcement is a few seconds rather than minutes or hours. An especially important distinction to remember is that learning is more efficient under *immediate* rather than delayed consequences (Holland, 1996). Information about the importance of this distinction in our everyday lives is presented in Explorations in Psychology.

Shaping   When a behavior takes time to occur, the learning process in operant conditioning can be shortened if an *approximation* of the desired behavior is rewarded. **Shaping** *is the process of rewarding approximations of desired behavior.* In one situation, parents used shaping to toilet train their two-year-old son. The parents knew all too well that the grunting sound the child made signaled he was about to fill his diaper. In the first week they gave him candy if they heard the sound within 20 feet of the bathroom. The second week he was given candy only if he grunted within 10 feet of the bathroom, the third week only if he was in the bathroom, and the fourth week, he had to use the toilet to get the candy (Fischer & Gochros, 1975). It worked!

Primary and Secondary Reinforcement   Positive reinforcement can be classified as primary reinforcement or secondary reinforcement, which focuses on a distinction between inborn, unlearned, and learned aspects of behavior. **Primary reinforcement** *involves the use of reinforcers that are innately satisfying; that is, they do not take any learning on the organism's part to make them pleasurable.* Food, water, and sexual satisfaction are primary reinforcers.

Secondary reinforcement *acquires its positive value through experience; secondary reinforcers are learned or conditioned reinforcers.* Hundreds of secondary reinforcers characterize our lives. For example, secondary reinforcers include such social situations as getting a pat on the back, praise, and eye contact. One popular story in psychology focuses on the use of eye contact as a secondary reinforcer to shape the behavior of a famous university professor, an expert on operant conditioning. Some students decided to train the professor to lecture from one corner of the classroom.

What are some other ways shaping can be used in learning?

They used eye contact as a reinforcer and began reinforcing successive approximations to the desired response. Each time the professor moved toward the appropriate corner, the students would look at him. If he moved in another direction, they looked away. By gradually rewarding successive approximations to the desired response, the students were able to get the professor to deliver his lecture from just one corner of the classroom. The well-known operant conditioning expert denies that this shaping ever took place. Whether it did or not, the story provides an excellent example of how secondary reinforcers can be used to shape behavior in real-life circumstances (Chance, 1979).

Another example also helps to understand the importance of secondary reinforcement in our everyday lives. When a student is given $25 for an A on her report card, the $25 is a secondary reinforcer. It is not innate, and it increases the likelihood the student will work to get another A in the future. Money is often referred to as a *token reinforcer*. When an object can be exchanged for some other reinforcer, the object may have reinforcing value itself, so it is called a token reinforcer. Gift certificates and poker chips are other token reinforcers.

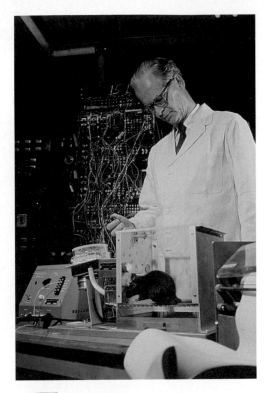

Schedules of Reinforcement

Most of the examples of reinforcement we have discussed so far have involved **continuous reinforcement,** *in which a response is reinforced every time it occurs*. When continuous reinforcement occurs, organisms learn rapidly. However, when reinforcement stops, extinction also takes place quickly. If a pay telephone we tend to use starts "eating" our coins and not giving us a dial tone, we quickly stop putting in more coins. However, several weeks later, we might try it again hoping it now works properly (which illustrates spontaneous recovery).

Figure 6.8
B. F. Skinner conducting an operant conditioning study in his behavior laboratory.

Partial reinforcement *involves a response being reinforced only a portion of the time*. Most of life's experiences involve partial reinforcement, not continuous reinforcement. A golfer does not win every tournament she enters; a chess whiz does not win every match he plays; a student is not patted on the back each time she solves a problem. **Schedules of reinforcement** *are "timetables" that determine when a response will be reinforced*. The four main schedules of reinforcement are fixed-ratio, variable-ratio, fixed-interval, and variable-interval.

A **fixed-ratio schedule** *reinforces a behavior after a set number of responses*. Fixed-ratio schedules are often used to increase production. For example, a salesperson might have to sell a specific number of items to get a commission. Also referred to as "piece work," such schedules are commonly used in Canada's fruit growing regions, where a picker might be paid for every 50 or 100 pieces of fruit picked. One characteristic of fixed-ratio schedules is that performance often drops off just after reinforcement.

In contrast, slot machines are on a **variable-ratio schedule,** *a timetable in which responses are rewarded an average number of times, but on an unpredictable basis*. For example, a slot machine might pay off at an average of every 20 times, but unlike a fixed-ratio schedule, the gambler cannot tell when this payoff will be. The slot machine might pay off twice in a row and then not again until after 58 coins have been inserted. This averages out to a reward every 20 responses, but when the reward will be given is unpredictable. Variable-ratio schedules produce high, steady rates of responding and greater resistance to extinction than the other three schedules. These properties are partly responsible for the appeal of gambling and the rise of pathological gambling in Canada (Ladouceur, 1996) and the associated social costs (Ladouceur & others, 1994). Fortunately, an understanding of the contingencies which produce gambling addiction can also help in treatment (Sylvain, Ladouceur, & Boisvert, 1997).

The remaining two reinforcement schedules are determined by *time elapsed* since the last behavior was rewarded. A **fixed-interval schedule** *reinforces the first appropriate response after a fixed amount of time has elapsed*. For example, you might get a reward the first time you put money in a slot machine after every 10-minute period has elapsed. The behavior of politicians campaigning for reelection often reflects a fixed-interval schedule of reinforcement. After they have been elected, they

Slot machines are on a variable-ratio schedule of reinforcement. What does this mean?

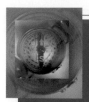

EXPLORATIONS IN PSYCHOLOGY
The Role of Immediate and Delayed Consequences in Developing Self-Control

- "THAT DOUBLE-DUTCH chocolate dessert is just too good to pass up."
- "I know I should start exercising more but I guess I'm just too lazy to get started."
- "I've got an important paper due tomorrow morning. Why am I here at this party? Why aren't I home writing the paper?"

If you are like most people, self-control problems like these crop up in your life, unfortunately all too frequently. We often describe ourselves as not having enough willpower to handle these situations. Actually, many of these situations reflect a conflict between immediate and delayed consequences of behavior involving various combinations of reinforcers and punishers (Martin & Pear, 1999).

Immediate Small Reinforcers Versus Delayed Strong Punishers

One reason obesity is a major health problem is that eating is a behavior with immediate positive consequences—food tastes very good and quickly provides a pleasurable feeling. Although the potential delayed consequences of overeating are negative (obesity and other possible health risks), immediate consequences are difficult to override. When the delayed consequences of behavior are punishing and the immediate consequences are reinforcing, the immediate consequences usually win, even when the immediate consequences are small reinforcers and the delayed consequences are major punishers. Smoking and drinking follow a similar pattern. The immediate consequences of smoking are reinforcing for most smokers—the powerful combination of positive reinforcement (tension relief, energy boost) and negative reinforcement (removal of craving, "nicotine fit"). The punishing aspects of smoking are primarily long-term, including shortness of breath, a sore throat, coughing, emphysema, heart disease, lung cancer, and other cancers. The immediate pleasurable consequences of drinking override the delayed consequences of a hangover or even alcoholism.

Immediate Small Reinforcers Versus Delayed Stronger Reinforcers

Self-control problems are also brought about by the choice we face between obtaining a small immediate reinforcer and waiting for a delayed but much-higher-valued reinforcer. For example, you can spend your money now on clothes, trinkets, parties, and the like or save your money and buy a house or car later. In another circumstance, you can play around now and enjoy yourself, which produces immediate small reinforcers, or you can study hard over a long period of time, which can produce delayed stronger reinforcers such as good grades, scholarships to graduate school, and better jobs.

Immediate Punishers Versus Delayed Reinforcers

Why are some of us so reluctant to take up a new sport? To try a new dance step? To go to a social gathering? To do something different? One reason is that learning new skills often involves minor punishing consequences, such as initially looking stupid, not knowing what to do, having to put up with sarcastic comments from onlookers, and so on. In these circumstances, reinforcing consequences are often delayed. For example, it takes us a long time to become a good golfer or a good dancer and enjoy ourselves in these activities.

Immediate Weak Punishers Versus Strong Delayed Punishers

Why do so many of us postpone such activities as going to the dentist, scheduling minor surgery, or paying campus parking fines? In this kind of self-control problem, if we act immediately we experience a weak punisher—it hurts to get our teeth drilled, it is painful to have minor surgery, and it is not very pleasurable to pay a campus parking fine. However, the delayed consequences can be more punishing—our teeth can fall out, we might need major surgery, and our car might get towed away or we might get thrown in jail. All too often, though, immediate consequences win out in these self-control situations.

In these examples of different combinations of immediate and delayed consequences of our behavior, we have seen that immediate consequences often interfere with our ability to control our behavior. Later in the chapter you will find some suggestions for ways to improve self-control through behavioral strategies.

reduce their campaigning and then don't pick it up again heavily until just before the next election (which can be two to four years later). On a fixed-interval schedule, few responses are made until the time approaches that the behavior will likely be reinforced (in the example just mentioned, getting reelected), then the rate of responding picks up rapidly.

A **variable-interval schedule** *is a timetable in which a response is reinforced after a variable amount of time has elapsed.* On this schedule, the slot machines might reward you after 10 minutes, then after two minutes, then after 18 minutes, and so on. Pop quizzes are on a variable interval schedule. So is fishing—you don't know if the fish will bite in the next minute, in a half hour, in an hour, or at all. Because it is difficult to predict when a reward will come, behavior is slow and consistent on a variable-interval schedule.

Figure 6.9 shows how the different schedules of reinforcement result in different rates of responding.

Schedules of Reinforcement

Extinction, Generalization, and Discrimination   Remember from our discussion of classical conditioning that extinction, generalization, and discrimination are important principles. They are also important principles in operant conditioning.

Extinction   Extinction *in operant conditioning occurs when a previously reinforced response is no longer reinforced and there is a decreased tendency to perform the response.* Spontaneous recovery also characterizes the operant form of extinction. For example, a factory worker gets a monthly bonus for producing more than her quota. Then, as a part of economic tightening, the company decides that it can no longer afford the bonuses. When bonuses were given, the worker's productivity was above quota every month; once the bonus was removed, performance decreased.

Generalization   Generalization *in operant conditioning means giving the same response to similar stimuli.* For example, in one study pigeons were reinforced for pecking at a disc of a particular color (Guttman & Kalish, 1956). Stimulus generalization was tested by presenting the pigeons with discs of varying colors. As shown in figure 6.10, the pigeons were most likely to peck at the disc closest in color to the original. An example from everyday life involves a student who has great success in dating people who dress very neatly and not so good results with people who dress sloppily. The student subsequently seeks dates with people who dress neatly, the neater the better, and avoids dating sloppy dressers, especially the sloppiest.

Discrimination   Discrimination *in operant conditioning means responding to stimuli that signal that a behavior will or will not be reinforced* (Jenkins & Sainsbury, 1969). For example, you might look at two street signs, both made of metal, both the same color, and both with words on them. However, one sign says "Enter at your own risk" and the other reads "Please walk this way." The words serve as discriminative stimuli because the sign that says "Please walk this way" indicates that you will be rewarded for doing so. However, the sign that says "Enter at your own risk" suggests that the consequences may not be positive if you walk past it. As another example, consider that football players are far more likely to tackle people in a football stadium than in a church. Further, they tackle people with certain colors on a uniform (the opposing team's rather than their own). They also don't tackle certain other people in uniforms, such as cheerleaders, referees, and police officers.

Punishment   Let's explore what punishment is and why one type of punishment is usually not recommended by psychologists.

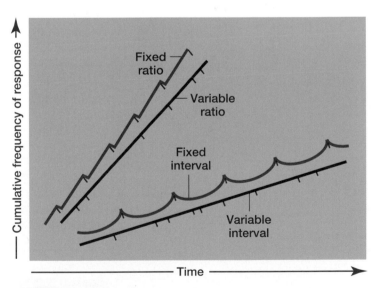

𝓕**igure 6.9**
Schedules of Reinforcement and Different Patterns of Responding

In this figure, each hash mark indicates the delivery of reinforcement. Notice on the fixed-interval schedule the dropoff in rate of responding after each response; on the variable-interval schedule the high, steady rate of responding; on the fixed-interval schedule the immediate dropoff in rate responding after reinforcement and the increase in rate of responding just before reinforcement (which results in a scallop-shaped curve); and on the variable-interval schedule the slow, steady rate of responding.

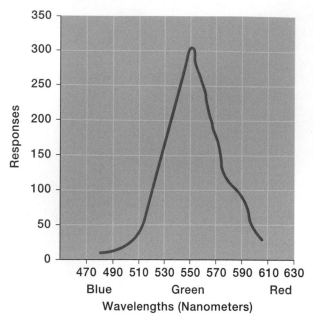

Figure 6.10
Stimulus Generalization

In the experiment by Guttman and Kalish (1956), pigeons initially pecked a disc of a particular color (in this graph, a green one with a wavelength of 550 nanometers) after they had been reinforced for this wavelength. Subsequently, when the pigeons were presented discs of colors with varying wavelengths, they were more likely to peck discs that were similar to the original disc.

Exploring What Punishment Is   Punishment *refers to a consequence that decreases the likelihood a behavior will occur.* For example, a child plays with an attractive matchbox and gets burned when one of the matches is lit. In the future, the child is less likely to play with matches. Figure 6.11 provides another illustration of punishment in which a student interrupts the teacher, the teacher verbally reprimands the student, and the student subsequently stops interrupting the teacher.

Punishment differs from reinforcement in the following way. In punishment, a behavior is weakened. In reinforcement, a behavior is strengthened. Also recall that we distinguished between positive reinforcement (a response increases because it is followed by a rewarding stimulus) and negative reinforcement (a response increases because it is followed by the removal of an aversive stimulus). So punishment is not the same as negative reinforcement. In punishment, a response decreases because of its consequences; in negative reinforcement, a response increases because of its consequences.

The following example should further help you distinguish between negative reinforcement and punishment. When an alcoholic consumes liquor to alleviate uncomfortable withdrawal symptoms, the probability that that person will use alcohol in the future is increased. The reduction of the withdrawal symptoms was a negative reinforcer for drinking. But if an inebriated alcoholic is seriously injured in a car wreck and subsequently quits drinking as much, punishment was involved because a behavior (drinking) was decreased.

The positive–negative distinction can also be applied to punishment, although it is not used as widely as in reinforcement. In **positive punishment**, *a behavior decreases when it is followed by an unpleasant stimulus.* In **negative punishment**, *a behavior decreases when a positive stimulus is removed from it.* Figure 6.12 compares positive reinforcement, negative reinforcement, positive punishment, and negative punishment.

Time-out *is a form of negative punishment in which a child is removed from a positive reinforcement.* It is generally recommended over presenting an aversive stimulus (positive reinforcement) as typically is done when punishment is administered. If a child is behaving in disruptive ways in the classroom, the teacher might put the child in a chair in the corner of the room facing away from the class or take the child to a time-out room.

Positive Punishment Is Often Not a Good Choice   Many people associate punishment with yelling at children or spanking them. An estimated 70 to 90 percent of North American parents have spanked their preschool children (Durrant, Broberg, & Rose-Krasnor, in press). Of those Canadian mothers who have spanked their children, one-third report doing so at least once or twice per week (Durrant, Broberg, & Rose-Krasnor, in press).

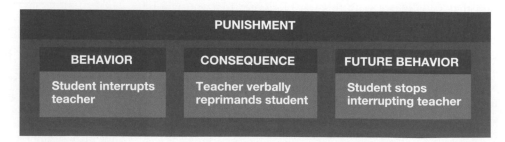

Figure 6.11
Punishment

Some people turn too quickly to aversive stimuli when trying to change a child's behavior. They might do this because they were harshly disciplined when they were growing up and they are just repeating how their parents dealt with them. Or it may be because they have developed a style of handling stress by yelling or screaming, feel they can effectively exercise power over their smaller charges, or are unaware of how positive reinforcement or other techniques, such as a time-out, can be used to improve children's behavior. However, remember that to satisfy a formal definition of punishment, the consequences have to decrease the behavior. All too often, though, aversive stimuli don't do what they are intended to do—namely, decrease an unwanted behavior (Edwards, 1999). In one study, the more mothers spanked their children, the more likely the children were to engage in antisocial behavior two years later, such as cheating, telling lies, being mean to others, bullying, getting into fights, and being disobedient (Strauss, Sugarman, & Giles-Sims, 1997).

Why do most psychologists usually recommend positive reinforcement or a time-out over using aversive stimuli that are involved in punishment? The reasons include the following (Santrock, in press):

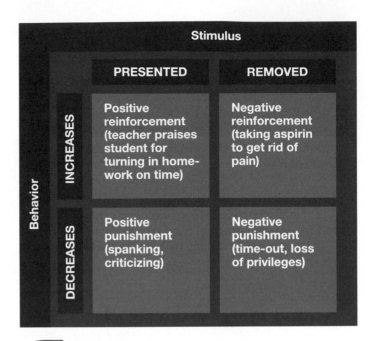

Figure 6.12
Positive Reinforcement, Negative Reinforcement, Positive Punishment, and Negative Punishment

- When intense punishment like yelling, screaming, or spanking is used, the adult is presenting children with an out-of-control model for handling stressful situations. The children might imitate this aggressive, out-of-control model.
- Punishment can instill fear, rage, or avoidance in children. Skinner's biggest concern was that punishment teaches organisms to avoid something. For example, a student who has a punitive teacher might dislike the teacher and not want to come to school.
- When children are punished, they can be so aroused and anxious that they can't concentrate clearly on their work for a long time after the punishment is given.
- Punishment tells people what not to do rather than what to do. When an adult makes a punishing statement such as "No, that's not right," he or she should always accompany it with positive feedback, such as "but why don't you try this."
- Punishment can be abusive. When parents discipline their children, they might not intend to be abusive but become so aroused when they are punishing the child that they become abusive (Adams, 1998).
- And, as mentioned earlier, what is intended as punishing can turn out to be reinforcing. In school, a child might learn that misbehaving will not only bring the teacher's attention but put the child in the limelight with classmates as well.

Applications of Operant Conditioning

A preschool child repeatedly throws his glasses and breaks them. A high school student and her parents have intense arguments. A university student is depressed. An elderly woman is incontinent. Operant conditioning procedures have helped such people to adapt more successfully and cope more effectively with their problems (Hersen & Miller, 1996; Luiselli & Cameron, 1998; Pierce & Epling, 1999).

Applied behavior analysis (behavior modification) *is the application of operant conditioning principles to change human behavior.* Consequences for behavior are established to ensure that more-adaptive actions are reinforced and less-adaptive ones are not (Baldwin & Baldwin, 1999; Kohlenberg, Tsai, & Kohlenberg, 1996). Advocates of behavior modification believe that many emotional and behavior problems are caused by inadequate (or inappropriate) response consequences (Alberto & Trautman, 1999). The child who throws down his glasses and breaks them may be receiving too

B. F. Skinner, *Behaviorist*

"The effective management of human behavior is jeopardized when we appeal to feelings and ideas in the explanation of behavior. In doing so, we neglect useful environmental contingencies."

Applied Behavior Analysis
Walden "U"

much attention from his teacher and peers for his behavior; they unwittingly reinforce an unacceptable behavior. In this instance, the parents and teachers would be instructed to divert attention from the destructive behavior and transfer it to a more constructive behavior, such as working quietly or playing cooperatively with peers (Harris, Wolf, & Baer, 1964).

Consider another circumstance. Barbara and her parents were on a collision course. Things got so bad that her parents decided to see a clinical psychologist. The psychologist, who had a behavioral orientation, talked with each family member, trying to get them to pinpoint the problem. The psychologist got the family to sign a behavioral contract that spelled out what everyone needed to do to reduce the conflict. Barbara agreed to (1) be home before 11 p.m. on weeknights; (2) look for a part-time job so she could begin to pay for some of her activities; and (3) refrain from calling her parents insulting names. Her parents agreed to (1) talk to Barbara in a low tone of voice rather than yell if they were angry; (2) refrain from criticizing teenagers, especially Barbara's friends; and (3) give Barbara a small sum of money each week for gas, makeup, and socializing, but only until she found a job.

Also consider Sam, a 19-year-old university student, who has been deeply depressed lately. His girlfriend broke off their relationship of two years, and his grades have been dropping. He decides to go to a psychologist who has a behavioral orientation. The psychologist enrolls him in the Coping with Depression course developed by Peter Lewinsohn (1987). Sam learns to monitor his daily moods and increase his ratio of positive to negative life events. The psychologist trains Sam to develop more efficient coping skills and gets Sam to agree to a behavioral contract, just as the psychologist did with Barbara and her parents.

Mary is an elderly woman who lives in a nursing home. In recent months she has become incontinent and is increasingly dependent on the staff for help with her daily activities. The behavioral treatment designed for Mary's problem involves teaching her to monitor her behavior and schedule going to the toilet. She is also required to do pelvic exercises. The program for decreasing Mary's dependence requires that the staff attend more to her independent behavior when it occurs and remove attention from dependent behavior whenever possible. Such strategies with the elderly have been effective in reducing problems with incontinence and dependence.

Behavior modification is used to teach couples to communicate more effectively, to encourage fathers to engage in more competent caregiving with their infants, to train autistic children's interpersonal skills, to help individuals lose weight, and to reduce an individual's fear of social situations. Another effective use of behavior modification is to improve an individual's self-control (Logue, 1995). Information about how this is accomplished is described in Explorations in Psychology.

Behavior modification is not only effective in therapy, but it has also been applied to the world of computers to promote better instruction. Some years ago, Skinner developed a machine to help teachers instruct students. The teaching machine engaged the student in a learning activity, paced the material at the student's rate, tested the student's knowledge of the material, and provided immediate feedback about correct and incorrect answers. Skinner hoped that the machine would revolutionize learning in schools, but the revolution never took place.

Today the idea behind Skinner's teaching machine is applied to computers, which help teachers instruct students. Research comparisons of computer-assisted instruction with traditional teacher-based instruction suggest that, in some areas, such as drill and practice on math problems, computer-assisted instruction can produce superior results (Kulik, Kulik, & Bangert-Drowns, 1985).

By now you should have a good feel for how operant conditioning works. A summary of the main themes of operant conditioning is presented in summary table 6.2.

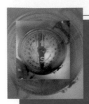

EXPLORATIONS IN PSYCHOLOGY
Using Behavior Modification to Improve Self-Control

CHANCES ARE EACH OF US could stand to change something about our lives. What would you like to change? What would you like to be able to control more effectively in your life? To answer these questions, you first have to specify your problem in a concrete way. For Al, this is easy—he is overweight and wants to lose 30 pounds. Stated even more precisely, he wants to consume about 1,000 fewer calories per day than he uses to give him a weight loss of about two pounds per week. Some problems are more difficult to specify, such as "wasting time," "having a bad attitude toward school," "having a poor relationship with —— ," or "being too nervous and worrying a lot." These types of problems have been called "fuzzies" because of their abstract nature (Mager, 1972). It is important to "unfuzzify" these abstract problems and make them more specific and concrete. Problems can be made more precise by writing out your goal and listing the things that would give you clear evidence that you have reached your goal.

A second important step in a self-control program is to make a *commitment* to change (Martin & Pear, 1999). Both a commitment to change and a knowledge of change techniques have been shown to help college students become more effective self-managers of their smoking, eating, studying, and relationship problems. Building a commitment to change requires you to do things that increase the likelihood you will stick to your project. First, tell others about your commitment to change—they will remind you to stick to your program. Second, rearrange your environment to provide frequent reminders of your goal, making sure the reminders are associated with the positive benefits of reaching your goal. Third, put in a lot of time and energy in planning your project. Make a list of statements about your project, such as "I've put a lot of time into this project; I am certainly not going to waste all of this effort now." Fourth, because you will invariably face temptations to backslide or quit your project, plan ahead for ways you can deal with temptation, tailoring these plans to your problem.

A third major step in developing a self-control program is to collect data about your behavior. This is especially important in decreasing excessive behaviors such as overeating and frequent smoking. One of the reasons for tracking your behavior is that it provides a reference point for evaluating your progress. When recording the frequency of a problem during initial observations, you should examine the immediate consequences that could be maintaining the problem (Martin & Pear, 1999).

A fourth major step in developing self-control is to design a self-control program. Many good self-control programs involve setting long-term and short-term goals, and developing a plan for how to reach the goals. Good self-control problems also usually include some type of self-talk, self-instruction, or self-reinforcement. For example, a person whose goal is to jog 30 minutes a day 5 days a week might say, "I'll never make it. It just won't work." This person can benefit by saying something like, "I know it's going to be tough, but I can make it." Also, individuals can engage in self-reinforcing statements or treat themselves. This might involve saying something like, "Way to go. You are up to 30 minutes three times a week. You are on your way." Or they might treat themselves to something like a movie, a new piece of clothing, or a new CD.

A fifth important aspect of improving your self-control is to make it last. One strategy is to establish specific dates for postchecks and to plan a course of action if your postchecks are not favorable. For instance, if your self-control program involves weight reduction, you might want to weigh yourself once a week. If your weight increases to a certain level, then you immediately go back on your self-control program.

Another strategy is to establish a buddy system by finding a friend or someone with a similar problem. The two of you set mutual maintenance goals. Once a month, get together and check each other's behavior. If your goals have been maintained, get together and celebrate in an agreed-upon way. Table 6.A summarizes the main steps in the self-control program we have described.

For other ideas on how to establish an effective self-control program tailored to your needs, you might want to contact the counseling center at your college or university. A good book on behavior modification or self-control also can be helpful—one is described in the suggested readings at the end of the chapter (Martin & Pear, 1999).

TABLE 6.A
Five Steps in Developing a Self-Control Program

1. Define the problem
2. Commit to change
3. Collect data about yourself
4. Design a self-control program
5. Make the program last—maintenance

Concept	Processes/Related Ideas	Characteristics/Description
What Operant Conditioning Is	Its Nature	Operant conditioning (or instrumental conditioning) is a form of associative learning in which the consequences of behavior produce changes in the probability of the behavior's occurrence.
	How It Differs from Classical Conditioning	In classical conditioning, the association is between two stimuli, but in operant conditioning the association is between a response and its consequence. Operant conditioning mainly involves voluntary behavior, while classical conditioning primarily involves involuntary behavior.
Thorndike's Law of Effect	Its Nature	It states that behaviors followed by a positive outcome are strengthened, whereas those followed by a negative outcome are weakened. Thorndike's view is referred to as S-R learning.
Skinner's Operant Conditioning	Positive and Negative Reinforcement	In positive reinforcement, the frequency of response is strengthened because it is followed by a rewarding stimulus. In negative reinforcement the frequency of a response increases because the response is followed by the removal of an aversive (unpleasant) stimulus.
	Mechanisms of Learning Are the Same in All Species	This belief led Skinner to extensively study animals in the hope that basic mechanisms of learning could be understood with organisms more simple than humans. Skinner and other behaviorists make every effort to study organisms under precisely controlled conditions, which led to the creation of the Skinner box. Skinner presented his ideas for a scientifically managed society in *Walden Two*.
	Time Interval	Immediate consequences are more effective than delayed consequences.
	Shaping	Shaping is the process of rewarding approximations of the desired behavior.
	Primary and Secondary Reinforcement	Primary reinforcement refers to innate reinforcers (food, water, sex): secondary reinforcement refers to reinforcers that acquire positive value through experience (money, smiles).
	Schedules of Reinforcement	Continuous reinforcement involves a response being reinforced every time it occurs. Partial reinforcement involves a response being reinforced only a portion of the time, which leads to greater resistance to extinction than continuous reinforcement. Four schedules of partial reinforcement are fixed-ratio, variable-ratio, fixed-interval, and variable-interval.
	Extinction, Generalization, and Discrimination	Extinction is a decrease in the tendency to perform the response brought about by unreinforced consequences of that response. Generalization means giving the same response to similar stimuli. Discrimination is the process of responding in the presence of one stimulus that is reinforced but not in the presence of another stimulus that is not reinforced.
	Punishment	Punishment refers to a consequence that decreases the likelihood that a behavior will occur. Punishment differs from reinforcement: in punishment a behavior is weakened, in reinforcement a behavior is strengthened. Just like reinforcement, punishment can be classified as positive or negative. In positive punishment, a behavior decreases when it is followed by a negative stimulus. In negative punishment, a behavior decreases when a positive stimulus is removed from it. Many psychologists think that positive reinforcement and negative punishment (time-out) are better choices than positive punishment.
Applications of Operant Conditioning	Their Nature	This refers to the use of learning principles to change maladaptive or abnormal behavior; applications focus on changing behavior by following it with reinforcement. Behavior modification is used widely to reduce maladaptive behavior. Among its applications are controlling aggressive behavior, reducing conflicts between parents and adolescents, coping with depression, helping elderly individuals function more independently, teaching by computer-assisted instruction, and improving self-control.

Observational Learning

Bandura (1986, 1994) believes that if we learned using only classical and operant conditioning, through trial-and-error, it would be very tedious and at times hazardous ◀▥ P. 8. Imagine, for example, teaching a 15-year-old to drive only by rewarding positive behavior (and not by explaining or demonstrating). Instead, many of our complex behaviors are the result of observing and imitating competent models who display appropriate behavior in solving problems and coping with their world (Striefel, 1998). Even animals use observational (or social) learning (Galef, Jr., 1990; Heyes & Galef, Jr., 1996), probably because it is an adaptive specialization (Lefebvre & Giraldeau, 1996). The capacity to imitate has been attributed to many birds and mammals (Moore, 1996).

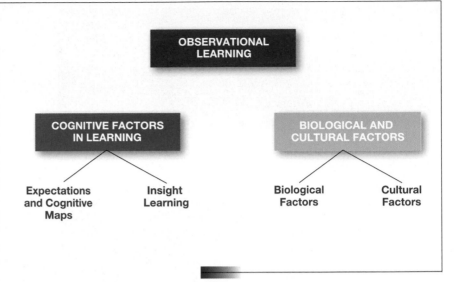

We initially encountered Bandura's ideas in Chapter 1, where we briefly introduced his social cognitive theory, and in Chapter 2, where we used his classic Bobo doll study of observational learning to demonstrate the steps in the scientific method. Let's now further explore his view of observational learning.

Observational learning, *also called imitation or modeling, is learning that occurs when a person observes and imitates someone's behavior.* The capacity to learn behavior patterns by observation eliminates tedious trial-and-error learning. In many instances observational learning takes less time than operant conditioning.

Bandura (1986) described four main processes that are involved in observational learning: attention, retention, motor reproduction, and reinforcement. For observational learning to take place, the first process that has to occur is *attention* (which we initially discussed in Chapter 4 because of its important role in perception). That is, before people can reproduce a model's actions, they must attend to what the model is saying or doing. You might not hear what a friend says if the stereo is blaring, or you might miss the teacher's analysis of a problem if you are admiring someone sitting in the next row. Imagine that you decide to take a class to improve your artistic skills. You need to attend to the instructor's words and hand movements. Attention to the model is influenced by a host of characteristics. For example, warm, powerful, atypical people command more attention than do cold, weak, typical people.

The next important process is *retention*. To reproduce a model's actions, you must code the information and keep it in memory so that it can be retrieved. A simple verbal description or a vivid image of what the model did assists retention. Memory is such an important cognitive process that the next chapter is devoted exclusively to it. In the example of taking a class to improve your art skills, you will need to remember what the instructor said and did in modeling good drawing skills.

Another process involved in observational learning is *motor reproduction*. People might attend to a model and code in memory what they have seen, but because of limitations in motor development they might not be able to reproduce the model's action. Thirteen-year-olds might hear Céline Dion sing with a heart-wrenchingly emotional yet soaring tone but be unable to reproduce her style. In the example of taking an art class to improve your art skills, you will need good motor reproduction skills to carry out what the instructor said to do.

A final process in Bandura's conception of observational learning involves *reinforcement,* or incentive conditions. On many occasions we may attend to what a model says or does, retain the information in memory, and possess the motor capabilities to perform the action, but we might fail to repeat the behavior because of inadequate reinforcement. This was demonstrated in one of Bandura's (1965) studies

Bandura's Theory

THINKING ABOUT PSYCHOLOGY AND LIFE

Models and Mentors in My Life

HAVING POSITIVE ROLE MODELS and mentors to observe and learn from can make important contributions to whether individuals develop optimally and reach their full potential. A mentor is someone you look up to and respect, who serves as competent model, and who is willing to work with you to help you achieve your goals. The role models and mentors could be your parents, teachers, an older peer, someone in the community. Spend a few minutes and think about the role models and mentors you have had in your life, including now. Do you remember any specific instances in which you watched them do or say something that had a lasting impact on you and you later modeled this behavior? List the most important role models and mentors in your life, then describe what you learned from them and how they helped your learning.

Role Models and Mentors	What I Learned from Them and How They Helped My Learning
1. _____	_____
2. _____	_____
3. _____	_____
4. _____	_____

A mentor can be very beneficial to students. If you currently don't have a mentor, think about the people at your university, or people in the community, that you respect and look up to. Consider asking one of these people to be a mentor for you.

---

in which children who had seen a model punished for aggression reproduced the model's aggression only when they were offered an incentive to do so ◀▥ P. 36. In the example of taking an art class, the instructor chooses one of your art pieces that you made during the class for display. This reinforcement encourages you to keep drawing and take another art skills class.

A summary of Bandura's model of observational learning is shown in figure 6.13.

Bandura views observational learning as an information-processing activity. As a person observes, information about the world is transformed into cognitive representations that serve as guides for action. As we see next, interest in the cognitive factors of learning has increased dramatically in recent years.

Cognitive Factors in Learning

In our study of learning we have had little to say about cognitive processes, except in our description of observational learning. In Skinner's operant conditioning view and Pavlov's classical conditioning view, no room is given to the possibility that cognitive factors such as memory, thinking, planning, or expectations might be important in learning. Many contemporary psychologists, including behavioral revisionists who recognize that cognition should not have been ignored in classical and operant conditioning, believe that learning involves much more than environment-behavior connections (Roberts, 1998).

In fact, the study of animal cognition has included research on animal counting (Olthof, Iden, & Roberts, 1997), memory (Brodbeck & Shettleworth, 1995) and spatial cognition (Shettleworth & Hampton, 1998). Let's explore some of these cognitive factors in learning: expectations, cognitive maps, and insight.

Expectations and Cognitive Maps

E. C. Tolman says that when classical and operant conditioning occur the organism acquires certain expectations. In classical conditioning the young boy fears the rabbit because he expects it will hurt him. In operant conditioning a woman works hard all week because she expects to be paid on Friday.

In his paper "Cognitive Maps in Rats and Men," Tolman (1948) articulated his belief that organisms select information from the environment and construct a cognitive map of their experiences. A **cognitive map** *is an organism's mental representation of the structure of physical space.* In Tolman's maze experiments, rats developed mental awareness of physical space and the elements in it. They used these cognitive maps to find where the food was located.

Tolman's idea of cognitive maps is alive and well today. Research has shown that many species develop cognitive maps of their surroundings, also referred to as spatial cognition. Consider, for example, a common Canadian bird, the black-capped chickadee. Black-capped chickadees store food in scattered locations and find it later using memory (Brodbeck & Shettleworth, 1995). According to Hampton & Shettleworth (1996), like other birds and animals that rely on excellent spatial memory in the wild, black-capped chickadees have a relatively enlarged hippocampus. As humans, when we move around in our environment, we also develop a cognitive map of where things are located, on both small and large scales. We have a cognitive map of where rooms are located in our house or apartment, and we have a cognitive map of where we are located in Canada, for example.

Tolman was not the only psychologist in the first half of the twentieth century who believed that cognitive factors play an important role in learning. So did Gestalt psychologist Wolfgang Kohler.

Insight Learning

Wolfgang Kohler, a German psychologist, spent four months in the Canary Islands during World War I observing the behavior of apes. While there he conducted two fascinating experiments. One is called the "stick problem," the other the "box problem." Though these two experiments are basically the same, the solutions to the problems are different. In both situations, the ape discovers that it cannot reach an alluring piece of fruit, either because the fruit is too high or it is outside of the ape's cage and beyond its reach. To solve the stick problem, the ape has to insert a small stick inside a larger stick to reach the fruit. To master the box problem, the ape must stack several boxes to reach the fruit (see figure 6.14).

According to Kohler (1925), solving these problems does not involve trial and error or mere connections between stimuli and responses. Rather, when the ape realizes that his customary actions are not going to get the fruit, he often sits for a period of time and appears to ponder how to solve the problem. Then he quickly gets up, as if he had a sudden flash of insight, piles the boxes on top of one another, and gets the fruit. **Insight learning** *is a form of problem solving in which the organism develops a sudden insight or understanding of a problem's solution.*

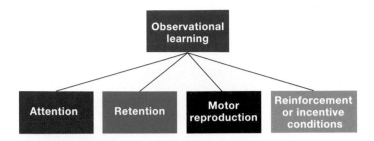

𝓕igure 6.13
Bandura's Model of Observational Learning
Bandura argues that observational learning consists of four main processes: attention, retention, motor reproduction, and reinforcement or incentive conditions. Consider a circumstance involving learning to ski. You need to attend to the instructor's words and demonstrations. You need to remember what the instructor did and her tips for avoiding disasters. You also need the motor abilities to reproduce what the instructor has shown you, and praise from the instructor after you have completed a few moves on the slopes should improve your motivation to continue skiing.

Biological and Cultural Factors in Learning

Albert Einstein had many special talents. He combined enormous creativity with great analytic ability to develop some of this century's most important insights about the nature of matter and the universe. Genes obviously provided Einstein extraordinary intellectual skills to think and reason on a very high plane, but cultural factors also undoubtedly contributed to Einstein's genius. Einstein received an excellent, rigorous European education, and later in the United States he experienced the freedom and support believed to be important in creative exploration. Would Einstein have been able to fully develop his intellectual skills and make such brilliant insights if he had grown up in a Third World country? Unlikely. Quite clearly both biological *and* cultural factors contribute to learning.

Biological Factors

We can't breathe under water, fish can't play table tennis, and cows can't solve math problems. The structure of an organism's body permits certain kinds of learning and inhibits others (Chance, 1999). For example, chimpanzees cannot learn to speak English because they lack the necessary vocal equipment. Some of us cannot solve difficult

Figure 6.14
Kohler's Box Problem Involving Insight Learning

Sultan, one of Kohler's brightest chimps, is faced with the problem of reaching a cluster of bananas overhead. Suddenly he solves the problem by stacking boxes on top of one another to reach the bananas. Kohler called this type of problem solving "insight learning."

calculus problems, others can, and the differences do not all seem to be the result of experiences.

Instinctive Drift   An example of biological influences on learning is **instinctive drift**, *the tendency of animals to revert to instinctive behavior that interferes with learning.* Consider the situation of Keller and Marion Breland (1961), students of B. F. Skinner, who used operant conditioning to train animals to perform at fairs, conventions, and in television advertisements. They used Skinner's techniques of shaping, chaining, and discrimination to teach pigs to cart large wooden nickels to a piggy bank and deposit them. They also trained raccoons to pick up a coin and place it in a metal tray. Although the pigs and raccoons, as well as other animals such as chickens, performed well at most of the tasks (raccoons became adept basketball players, for example—see figure 6.15), some of the animals began acting strangely. Instead of picking up the large wooden nickel and carrying it to the piggy bank, the pigs would drop the nickel on the ground, shove it with their snouts, toss it in the air, and then repeat these actions. The raccoons began to hold onto their coin rather than dropping it into the metal container. When two coins were introduced, the raccoons rubbed them together in a miserly fashion. Somehow these behaviors overwhelmed the strength of the reinforcement that was given at the end of the day. Why were the pigs and the raccoons misbehaving? The pigs were rooting, an instinct which is used to uncover edible roots. The raccoons engaged in an instinctive food-washing response. Their instinctive drift interfered with learning.

Preparedness and Taste Aversion   Some animals learn readily in one situation but have difficulty learning in slightly different circumstances. The difficulty might result not from some aspect of the learning situation but from the organism's predisposition (Seligman, 1970). **Preparedness** *is the species-specific biological predisposition to learn in certain ways but not others.*

Much of the evidence for preparedness comes from research on taste aversion (Garcia, 1989). Consider this situation: A psychologist went to dinner with his wife and ordered filet mignon with Béarnaise sauce, his favorite dish. Afterward they went to the opera. Several hours later, he became very ill with stomach pains and nausea. Several weeks later, he tried to eat Béarnaise sauce but couldn't bear it. The psychologist's experience involves *taste aversion,* another biological constraint on learning.

If an organism ingests a substance that poisons but does not kill it, the organism often develops considerable distaste for that substance. Rats that experience low levels of radiation after eating show a strong aversion to the food they were eating when the radiation made them ill. This aversion has been shown to last for as long as 32 days. Such long-term effects cannot be accounted for by classical conditioning, which would argue that a single pairing of the conditioned and unconditioned stimuli would not last that long (Garcia, Ervin, & Koelling, 1966). Radiation and chemical treatment of cancer often produces nausea in patients, and the resulting pattern of aversions often resembles those shown by laboratory animals.

Knowledge about taste aversion has been applied to balancing the ecological worlds of animals. For example, the livestock of farmers and ranchers may be threatened by wolves or coyotes. Instead of killing the pests or predators, the farmers feed them poisoned meat of their prey (cattle, sheep). The wolves and coyotes, poisoned but not killed, develop a taste aversion for cattle or sheep and, hence, are less of a threat to the farmers and ranchers. In this way, ranchers, farmers, cattle, sheep, wolves, and coyotes can live in a semblance of ecological balance.

Cultural Factors

In traditional views of learning, concepts such as culture have been given little or no attention. The behavioral orientation that dominated North American psychology for much of the twentieth century does focus on the cultural contexts of learning, but the organisms in those contexts have often been animals. When humans have been the subjects, there has been little or no interest in the cultural context.

How does culture influence learning? Most psychologists agree that the principles of classical conditioning, operant conditioning, and observational learning are universal and are powerful learning processes in every culture. However, culture can influence the *degree* to which these learning processes are used, and it often determines the *content* of learning  P. 12. For example, punishment is a universal learning process, but as we see next, its use and type show considerable sociocultural variation.

When behaviorism began its influential reign in North America between 1910 and 1930, child-rearing experts regarded the infant as capable of being shaped into almost any child. Desirable social behavior could be achieved if the child's antisocial behaviors were always punished and never indulged, and if positive behaviors were carefully conditioned and rewarded in a highly controlled and structured child-rearing regimen. The famous behaviorist John Watson (1928) authored a publication, *Infant Care*, that was the official U.S. government booklet for parents. This booklet advocated never letting children suck their thumb, and, if necessary, restraining the child by tying her hands to the crib at night and painting her fingers with foul-tasting liquids. Parents were advised to let infants "cry themselves out" rather than reinforce this unacceptable behavior by picking them up to rock and soothe them.

ℱigure 6.15
Instinctive Drift

This raccoon's skill in using its hands made it an excellent basketball player, but because of instinctive drift, the raccoon had a much more difficult time taking money to the bank.

However, from the 1930s to 1960s, a more permissive attitude prevailed and parents were advised to be concerned with the feelings and capacities of the child. Since the 1960s there has been a continued emphasis on the role of parental love in children's socialization, but experts now advise parents to play a less permissive and more active role in shaping children's behavior. Experts stress that parents should set limits and make authoritative decisions in areas where the child is not capable of reasonable judgment. However, they should listen and adapt to the child's point of view, should explain their restrictions and discipline, but not discipline the child in a hostile, punitive manner.

Despite the experts, most North American parents still spank. Why? One answer is culture; in this case the norms and sanctions of a nation or social group that support or deter the use of physical punishment. Studies of different cultures have shown considerable variability in the acceptance of this practice. In Barbados, for example, 77 percent of adults approve of lashing children with a belt or strap (Payne, 1989). In a 1992 sample of Canadians, 75 percent believed that spanking is acceptable under some circumstances (Durrant, 1996). In contrast, in 1994 only 11 percent of Swedes supported its use, even in its mildest forms (Statistics Sweden, 1996). Neither Canada nor the United States has a law that prohibits parents from spanking their children. However, Sweden passed just such a law in 1979 (Ziegert, 1983), becoming the first country in the world to do so (Finland, Denmark, Norway, Austria, and Cyprus have since passed similar laws).

Canadian researchers Joan Durrant and Linda Rose-Krasnor, along with Swede Anders Broberg, studied the use of physical punishment during mother-child conflicts in Canada and Sweden. They found that Canadian mothers had suffered more physical punishment in their childhoods and, in turn, used it more frequently with their children than did Swedish mothers, a good example of observational learning in action. The mothers most likely to prescribe physical punishment were those with more positive attitudes toward spanking and a stronger belief that the target behaviors were unstable and, therefore, changeable. This was true regardless of maternal age, education, and marital status, suggesting that the use of physical punishment is less a matter of personal characteristics than of cultural context (Durrant, Broberg, & Rose-Krasnor, in press).

The content of learning is also influenced by culture (Cole & Cole, 1996). We cannot learn about something we do not experience. The four-year-old who grows up among the Bushmen of the Kalahari Desert is unlikely to learn about taking baths or pouring water from one glass into another. Similarly, a child growing up in Chicago is unlikely to be skilled at tracking animals or finding water-bearing roots in the desert. Learning often requires practice, and certain behaviors are practiced much more often in some cultures than others. In Bali many children are skilled dancers by the age of 6, while Norwegian children are much more likely to be good skiers and skaters by that age. Children growing up in a Mexican village famous for its pottery may work with clay day after day, while children in a nearby village famous for its woven rugs and sweaters rarely become experts at making clay pots.

Since our last review, we have studied a number of ideas about observational learning, cognitive factors in learning, and biological/cultural factors in learning. A summary of these ideas is presented in summary table 6.3.

In this chapter, we studied some important cognitive factors in learning, such as expectations. We devote the entire next chapter to a very important cognitive process: memory.

SUMMARY TABLE 6.3
Observational Learning, Cognitive Factors, and Biological and Cultural Factors in Learning

Concept	Processes/ Related Ideas	Characteristics/Description
Observational Learning	Its Nature	Occurs when an individual observes someone else's behavior. Also called imitation or modeling. It is important to distinguish between what is learned and whether it is performed.
	Processes	Bandura believes that observational learning involves attention, retention, motor reproduction, and reinforcement or incentive conditions.
Cognitive Factors in Learning	Expectations and Cognitive Maps	Tolman reinterpreted classical and operant conditioning in terms of expectations. We construct cognitive maps of our experiences that guide our behavior; psychologists still study the nature of cognitive maps.
	Insight Learning	Kohler, like Tolman, was dissatisfied with the S-R view of learning. He believed that organisms reflect and suddenly gain insight into how a problem should be solved.
Biological and Cultural Factors in Learning	Biological Factors	Biological factors restrict what an organism can learn from experience. These constraints include instinctive drift, preparedness, and taste aversion.
	Cultural Factors	While most psychologists agree that the principles of classical conditioning, operant conditioning, and observational learning are universal, cultural customs can influence the degree to which these learning processes are used and culture often determines the content of learning.

Overview

WE BEGAN THIS CHAPTER by defining learning and then turned our attention to three main forms of learning: classical conditioning, operant conditioning, and observational learning. Our coverage of classical conditioning focused on Pavlovian conditioning, temporal contiguity and contingency, extinction, generalization, and discrimination, how classical conditioning works (Pavlov and the contemporary perspective), classical conditioning in humans, and an evaluation of classical conditioning. Our discussion of operant conditioning involved describing what it is, Thorndike's law of effect, many aspects of Skinner's operant conditioning, and applications of operant conditioning. We also studied observational learning. Next, we examined these cognitive factors in learning: expectations, cognitive maps, and insight learning. At the end of the chapter, we explored biological and cultural factors in learning.

Don't forget that you can obtain a more detailed overview of the chapter by again studying the three summary tables on pages 194, 206, and 212.

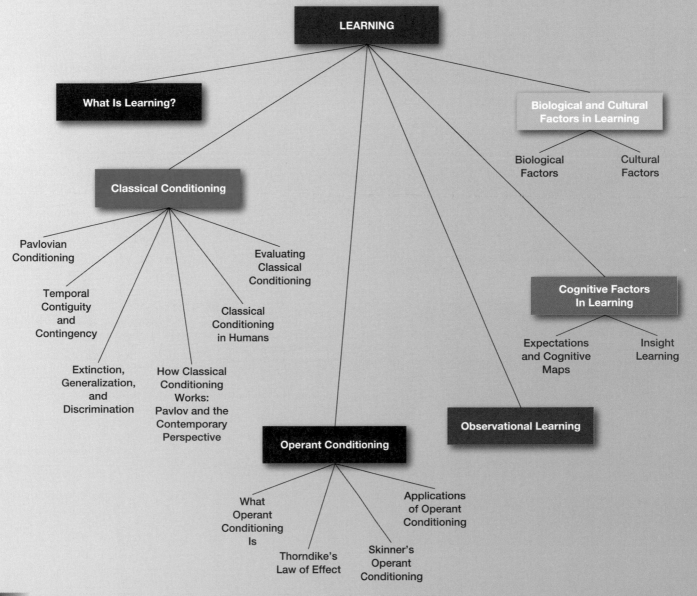

Key Terms

learning 186
classical conditioning 187
reflexes 187
unconditioned stimulus (US) 187
unconditioned response (UR) 187
conditioned stimulus (CS) 188
conditioned response (CR) 188
associative learning 188
contiguity 188
contingency (in classical conditioning) 188

extinction (in classical conditioning) 188
spontaneous recovery 188
generalization (in classical conditioning) 190
discrimination (in classical conditioning) 190
stimulus substitution 191
information theory 191
phobia 192
counterconditioning 192
operant conditioning 195
law of effect 196
positive reinforcement 196
negative reinforcement 197

shaping 198
primary reinforcement 198
secondary reinforcement 198
continuous reinforcement 199
partial reinforcement 199
schedules of reinforcement 199
fixed-ratio schedule 199
variable-ratio schedule 199
fixed-interval schedule 199
variable-interval schedule 201
extinction (in operant conditioning) 201
generalization (in operant conditioning) 201

discrimination (in operant conditioning) 201
punishment 202
positive punishment 202
negative punishment 202
time-out 202
applied behavior analysis (behavior modification) 203
observational learning 207
cognitive map 208
insight learning 209
instinctive drift 210
preparedness 210

Key People

Shepard Siegal 185
Ivan Pavlov 187
Robert Rescorla 188

E. C. Tolman 191
Leon Kamin 191
John Watson 192

Mary Cover Jones 192
B. F. Skinner 195
E. L. Thorndike 195

Albert Bandura 207
Wolfgang Kohler 209

Psychology Checklist

How much have you learned since the beginning of the chapter? Use the following statements to help you review your knowledge and understanding of the chapter material. First, read the statement and mentally or briefly on paper demonstrate that you understand and can discuss the relevant information.

_____ I know what learning is.
_____ I can discuss Pavlovian classical conditioning.
_____ I am aware of what extinction, generalization, and discrimination are in classical conditioning.
_____ I can describe classical conditioning in humans.
_____ I know how the contemporary view of classical conditioning differs from Pavlov's view.
_____ I can evaluate classical conditioning.
_____ I am aware of what operant conditioning is and how it differs from classical conditioning.

_____ I know what Thorndike's law of effect is.
_____ I can discuss Skinner's operant conditioning and principles, including ideas about positive reinforcement, negative reinforcement, positive punishment, and negative punishment.
_____ I can describe some applications of operant conditioning.
_____ I can discuss the nature of observational learning.
_____ I know about expectations and cognitive maps.
_____ I can discuss insight learning.
_____ I am aware of how biological factors influence learning.
_____ I can describe cultural factors in learning.

For any items that you did not check off, go back and locate the relevant material in the chapter. Review the material until you feel that you can check off the item. You may want to use this checklist later in preparing for an exam.

Taking It to the Net

1. Many colleges now offer online courses, available over the Internet. They use a method of learning called programmed instruction. Information is presented in steps, requiring the student to first complete one task before moving on to more difficult material. After each step, the student is given feedback on her work and a letter grade. This programmed instruction model adheres to a specific type of learning. Can you name it and identify its components? Do you think this is an effective way of learning? What are some criticisms of this type of learning?

2. Consider a summer job in which you are required to canvass for a window-cleaning company. You are given a territory to cover and asked to knock on people's doors to sign them up for window cleaning. You receive no base pay, but earn a significant amount in commission. Therefore, the more people you sign up for the service, the more you get paid. Moreover, your boss gives extra bonuses after every 10 people you sign up. Your boss is using the concept of reinforcement, and a specific schedule of reinforcement in particular. Which schedule of reinforcement is being used? Do you think that you will work harder this way than if you are paid a smaller amount every two weeks? Explain.

3. *Clockwork Orange*, a film by Stanley Kubrick based on the novel by Anthony Burgess, popularized the idea of behavior modification. The main character is a teenage thug whose violent acts lead to his eventual imprisonment. In prison, he opts for a sentence reduction by undergoing intensive behavior modification. This behavior modification resulted in rapid rehabilitation and eventual release from prison. Describe the behavior modification process and what it cost him. Do you think this is an effective method of rehabilitation? Explain your answer.

Connect to http://www.mcgrawhill.ca/college/santrock to find the answers!

Resources for Psychology and Life

Control: A History of Behavioral Psychology (1998)
by J.A. Mills
New York: New York University Press

This book explores the central and interrelated features that characterize North American behavioral psychology.

Behavior Modification: What It Is and How to Do It (1999, 6th ed.)
by G. Martin and R. Pear
Engelwood Cliffs, NJ: Prentice Hall

This excellent, easy-to-read book provides guidelines for using behavior modification to change behavior.

Social Foundations of Thought (1986)
by Albert Bandura
Englewood Cliffs, NJ: Prentice Hall

This book presents Bandura's cognitive social learning theory, which emphasizes reciprocal connections between behavior, environment, and person (cognition). Extensive coverage of observational learning is included.

Self-Control (1995)
by Alexandra Logue
Upper Saddle River, NJ: Prentice-Hall

This leading researcher evaluates specific areas of concern regarding self control—eating, drug abuse, education, money, lying, depression, suicide, and aggression. Logue also lists places to contact for further information about some of the clinical problems covered in the text.

Don't Shoot the Dog (1991)
by K. Pryor
New York: Simon & Schuster

This is a practical guide for applying the principles of reinforcement to everyday life. Topics include training animals, managing employees, coping with intrusive roommates, and improving self-control.

National Clearinghouse on Family Violence
Health Promotion and Programs Branch, Health Canada
Address Locator: 1907D1, Jeanne Mance Building
Tunney's Pasture, Ottawa, ON, K1A 1B4
1-800-267-1291 or (613) 957-2938
http://www.hc-sc.gc.ca/hppb/familyviolence/

The Clearinghouse is a national resource center for all Canadians seeking information about violence within the family and looking for new resources being used to address it.

Mentors (1992)
by T. Evans
Princeton, NJ: Peterson's Guides

This book describes how mentors can make a difference in children's lives, especially as a tutor in a one-to-one relationship.

Walden Two (1948)
by B. F. Skinner
New York: Macmillan

Skinner once entertained the possibility of a career as a writer. In this provocative book, he outlines his ideas on how a more complete understanding of the principles of operant conditioning can produce a happier life. Critics argue that his approach is too manipulative.

Chapter 7

CHAPTER OUTLINE

THE NATURE OF MEMORY

What Is Memory?

Exploring Memory

MEMORY ENCODING

Rehearsal

Deep Processing

Elaboration

Imagery

Organization

MEMORY STORAGE

Memory's Time Frames

Memory's Contents

Representing Memory

The Neurobiological Basis of Memory

MEMORY RETRIEVAL AND FORGETTING

Retrieval from Long-Term Memory

Autobiographical Memory

Emotional Memories

Forgetting

MEMORY AND STUDY STRATEGIES

Effective Strategies

Taking Good Notes

The PQ4R Method

Memory

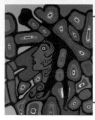

Images of Psychology and Life
M. K. and the Russian, S.

> "I come into the fields and spacious palaces of my memory, where are treasures of countless images of things of every manner."
>
> St. Augustine
> *Christian Church Father, 5th Century*

Preview

THERE ARE FEW moments when we are not steeped in memory. Memory can quietly stir, or spin off, with each step we take, each thought we think, each word we utter. Memory is the web of private images in which past and present are interwoven. It anchors the self in continuity. These are some of the questions we will explore in this chapter.

- How do memories get encoded, stored, and retrieved?
- What is the brain's role in memory?
- What are people most likely to remember about their lives?
- What role do emotional experiences play in memory?
- Why do we forget?
- What are some good memory and study strategies?

HOW IMPORTANT is memory to us? Consider the unfortunate case of M. K., a high school teacher who at the age of 43 was stricken with an acute episode of encephalitis (an inflammation of the brain caused by a virus, which, unless quickly treated, can cause serious brain damage). Within hours he lost access to almost all the memories he had formed during the previous 5 years. Worse still, he had virtually no memory of anything that happened to him after the onset of the encephalitis. Since the illness began, M. K. has learned a few names and a few major events over the years, and he can get around the hospital. M. K.'s tragic circumstance, in which a microscopic viral agent rendered him memoryless, conveys the emptiness of a life without memory.

The power of memory is also revealed in another, very different case. A Russian known only by the initial S. could remember a list of seventy items without making an error, and he had no difficulty recalling the list backward. S. once was asked to remember the following formula:

$$N \cdot \sqrt{d^2 \cdot \frac{85}{VX}} \cdot 3\sqrt{\frac{276^2 \cdot 86x}{n^2 V \cdot \pi 264}} \ n^2 b$$
$$= sv \frac{1624}{32^2} \cdot r^2 s$$

S. studied the formula for 7 minutes and then reported how he memorized it. The following portion of his response reveals how he made up stories to aid his memory:

Neiman (N) came out and jabbed at the ground with his cane ($\cdot$). He looked up at a tall tree, which resembled the square-root sign ($\div$), and thought to himself: "No wonder this tree has withered and begun to expose its roots. After all, it was here when I built these two houses" (d^2). Once again he poked his cane ($\cdot$). Then he said: "The houses are old, I'll have to get rid of them; the sale will bring in far more money." He had originally invested 85,000 in them (85).

S.'s complete story was four times this length. It must have been a powerful one, because 15 years later with no advance notice he recalled the formula perfectly.

Envious as we might be of S.'s remarkable memory, especially when taking university exams, S. suffered from it. He had to devise techniques for forgetting because he remembered virtually everything, no matter how trivial. He once commented that each word called up images, which collided with one another—the result sometimes was chaos. Forgetting was M. K.'s curse, but it was S.'s salvation.

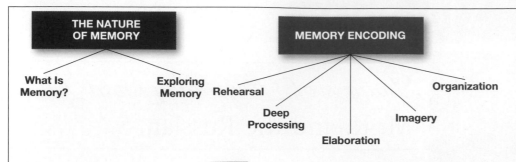

The Nature of Memory

Just what is memory? How necessary is it for our everyday functioning?

What Is Memory?

Memory *is the retention of information over time.* Psychologists study how information is initially placed or encoded into memory, how it is retained or stored after being encoded, and how it is found or retrieved for a certain purpose later ◀▥ P. 11.

Exploring Memory

Except for the annoying moments when memory fails or someone we know is afflicted with memory loss, most of us don't think much about how virtually everything we do or say depends on how smoothly our memory systems operate (Schacter, 1996, 1999). Take a moment and think about how important memory is in carrying out the simple task of meeting a friend at a restaurant. To begin with, you have to remember your friend's name and phone number. You have to bring to mind all of the information needed to execute the phone call. You have to use your memory of voices to determine whether the person answering the phone is your friend. To carry on the phone conversation with your friend, you have to access a vast dictionary of words, sounds, meanings, and syntax stored in your memory. At some point, you will have to sort through your memory of visits to restaurants, or recommendations of new ones, to decide on which restaurant is a good choice. You have to recall details of how to get to the restaurant. You also have to remember what else is going on in your life so that you don't plan to meet your friend when you have something else scheduled.

We rely on our memory systems to carry out similar feats every day of our lives. Human memory systems truly are remarkable when you think of how much information we put into our memory and how much we must retrieve to perform all of life's activities.

Human memory also has its imperfections, as we have all experienced. It is not unusual to find two people arguing about something that happened or didn't happen, each intensely confident that his or her memory is accurate and the other person remembers the circumstance inaccurately. Each of us has also had the frustrating experience of trying to remember someone's name or a place but not quite being able to retrieve it.

Other imperfections of memory surface in ongoing debates about the accuracy of memory in eyewitness testimony and the recovery of repressed experiences, both discussed later in this chapter. One dramatic example comes from a court case involving a father accused of the sexual abuse of his two daughters (Loftus, 1973). Under repeated questioning, the father began to "remember" episodes of abuse. In fact, a psychologist constructed a completely false story, which was repeatedly presented to the father, who responded by "remembering" that those events had happened as well. This underscores an important point about memory: we don't just coldly store and retrieve bits of data in computer-like fashion (Schacter, 1996, 1999). In the early study of memory, subjective experience was considered inappropriate subject matter. Today, however, scientists who study memory recognize its subjective nature and investigate how people reconstruct their own versions of the past. They recognize that the mind can distort, invent, and forget. And they know that emotions color memories. Clearly, we don't store judgment-free memories of reality.

Thus, the contemporary story of memory is about its phenomenal abilities, on the one hand, and its numerous limitations, on the other. In this chapter, we will

Memory and Cognition
Exploring Memory

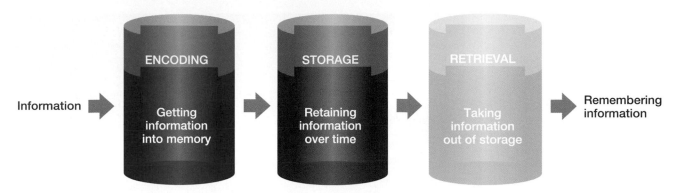

*F*igure 7.1
Processing Information in Memory
As you read about the many aspects of memory, remember that we cannot successfully remember information without successfully encoding, storing and retrieving that information.

profile these memory skills, as well as the ways memories can fail us. The next three sections of the chapter focus on encoding, storage, and retrieval. Although there are many complex dimensions to memory, thinking about memory in terms of these three domains should help you to understand it better (see figure 7.1). That is, for memory to work, we have to take information in, store it or represent it in some manner, and then retrieve it for some purpose later.

Encoding *involves how information gets into memory.* **Storage** *consists of the retention of information over time.* And **retrieval** *takes place when information is taken out of storage.* Let's now explore each of these important memory activities in greater detail.

Memory Encoding

In everyday experience, encoding has a lot in common with learning. When you are listening to a lecture, watching a movie, listening to music, or talking with a friend, you are encoding information into memory. Some information gets into memory virtually automatically, while getting other information in takes effort (Jacoby, 1998). Let's examine some encoding processes that require effort. These include our rehearsal of information, how deeply we process it, how extensively we elaborate it, our use of mental imagery, and how effectively we organize what we need to remember.

Rehearsal

Rehearsal *is the conscious repetition of information that increases the length of time that information stays in memory.* Imagine that you are looking up a phone number. If you can directly reach for the telephone, you probably won't have much trouble dialing the number, because the combined action of looking up the number and dialing it can take place quickly. But what if the telephone is not right by the phone book? Perhaps the phone book is in the kitchen and you want to talk privately on the phone in the bedroom. You will probably *rehearse* the number as you walk from the kitchen to the bedroom. Most of us experience a kind of "inner voice" that repeats the number again and again until we finally dial it. If our rehearsal is interrupted, we might lose the information.

Reheasal as defined here is referred to as *rote rehearsal* or *maintenance rehearsal,* rehearsal intended to maintain information in memory for short periods of time (Craik & Lockhart, 1972). When we have to remember information for long periods

SHALLOW PROCESSING	Physical and perceptual features are analyzed.	The lines, angles, and contour that make up the physical appearance of an object, such as a car, are detected.
INTERMEDIATE PROCESSING	Stimulus is recognized and labeled.	The object is recognized as a car.
DEEP PROCESSING	Semantic, meaningful, symbolic characteristics are used.	Associations connected with car are brought to mind—you think about the Porsche or Ferrari you hope to buy or the fun you and friends had on spring break when you drove a car to the beach.

Depth of processing

Figure 7.2
Depth of Processing
According to the levels of processing theory of memory, deep processing of stimuli produces better memory of them.

of time, as when we are studying for a test coming up next week, tomorrow, or even an hour from now, other strategies usually work better than maintenance rehearsal. A main reason rehearsal does not work well for retaining information over the long term is that rehearsal involves just repeating information by rote without imparting any meaning to it. Remembering information over the long term works better when we add meaning to it. As we see next, memory also usually works better when we process it at a deep level and elaborate it.

Deep Processing

After the discovery that rehearsal is not an efficient way to remember information over the long term, University of Toronto psychologists Fergus Craik and Robert Lockhart (1972) proposed that people process information at different levels. Their theory, **levels of processing theory**, *states that memory is on a continuum from shallow to deep, with deeper processing producing better memory.* The sensory or physical features of stimuli are analyzed first at a *shallow* level. This might involve detecting the lines, angles and contours of a printed word's letters, or a spoken word's frequency, duration, and loudness. At an *intermediate* level, the stimulus is recognized and given a label. For example, a four-legged, barking object is identified as a dog. Then, at the *deepest* level, information is processed semantically, in terms of its meaning. For example, if you saw the word *boat,* at the shallow level you might notice the shapes of the letters, at the intermediate level you might think of characteristics of the word (such as it rhymes with *coat*), and at the deepest level you might think about the kind of boat you would like to own and the last time you went fishing. Figure 7.2 depicts the levels of processing theory of memory. In other words, you're more likely to remember something if you process information at a deep, rather than shallow, level. In fact, even conventionally meaningless stimuli can be well-remembered if they are meaningfully processed (Mitterer & Begg, 1979).

Elaboration

Psychologists soon recognized that there is more to good memory than depth of processing. Within deep processing, the more extensive the processing, the better the memory (Craik & Tulving, 1975). **Elaboration** *is the extensiveness of processing at any given depth in memory.* For example, rather than memorizing the definition of *memory,* you would do better to come up with some examples of how information enters your mind, how it is stored, and how you can retrieve it. Thinking of examples of a concept is a good way to understand it. Self-reference is another effective way to elaborate information. For example, if the word *win* is on a list of words to remember, you might think of the last time you won a draw, or if the word *cook* appears, you might imagine the last time you cooked dinner. In general, elaborate processing of meaningful information, also referred to as *elaborative rehearsal* (Craik & Lockhart, 1972) is a good way to remember.

One reason elaborative rehearsal produces good memory is that it adds to the *distinctiveness* of the "memory codes" (Ellis, 1987). Distinctiveness describes the extent to which one memory differs from another in our memory. To remember some information, such as a name or a fact about geography, you need to search for the code that contains this information among the mass of codes contained in long-term memory. The search process is easier if the memory code is somehow highly distinctive (Hunt & Kelly, 1996). This is not unlike searching for a friend at a busy airport. If your friend is six feet tall and has flaming red hair, it will be easier to find him or her in the crowd. Also, as encoding becomes more elaborate, more information is stored. And as more information is stored, the more likely it is that this highly distinctive code will be easy to differentiate from other memory codes. For example, if you witness a bank robbery and observe that the getaway car was a red 1988 Pontiac with tinted windows and spinners on the wheels, your memory of the car is more distinctive than if you had noticed only that the getaway car was red.

Imagery

Imagery

How many windows are in your apartment or house? If you live in a dorm room with only one or two windows, this question might be too easy. If so, how many windows are in your parents' apartment or house? Few of us have ever memorized this information, but many of us believe we can come up with a good answer, especially if we use imagery to "reconstruct" each room. We take a mental walk through the house, counting windows as we go.

For years psychologists ignored the role of imagery in memory but the studies of University of Western Ontario psychologist Allan Paivio (1971, 1986) documented how imagery can improve memory. Paivio argued that memory is stored in one of two ways: as a verbal code or as an image code. For example, a picture can be remembered by a label (verbal code) or by a mental image. Paivio thinks that the image code, which is highly detailed and distinctive, produces better memory. The *dual-code hypothesis* claims that memory for images is better because the memory for the concept (image) is stored both as an imaginal code *and* as a verbal code, thus providing two potential avenues by which information can be retrieved.

Although imagery is now accepted as an important aspect of memory, there is controversy over whether we have separate codes for words and images (Pylyshyn, 1981). More about imagery appears later in the chapter when we discuss strategies for improving memory. For now, keep in mind that if you need to remember a list of things, forming mental images will help (Shepard, 1996). It will be especially helpful if you imagine two or more items interacting with each other (Begg, 1983).

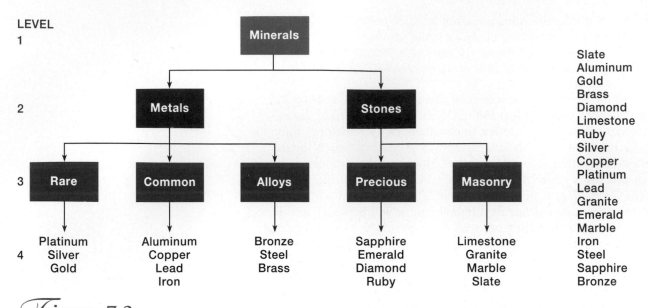

Figure 7.3
The Power of Organization in Memory

Memory works best when it is organized. In a 1969 study by Gordon Bower and his colleagues, participants remembered the words better when they were presented in a hierarchical format from general to specific (like the format shown above left) than when the words were presented in a random arrangement (above right).

Organization

Quickly recall the months of the year. How long did it take? What was your recall order? Your answers are probably "four to six seconds," and "natural order" (January, February, March, etc.). Now remember the months in alphabetical order. Did you make errors? How long did it take? It is much easier to recall the months naturally vs. alphabetically. This demonstration shows that your memory for the months of the year is organized. Indeed, one of memory's most distinctive features is its organization. If people are simply encouraged to organize material, their memory of the material improves, even if no warning is given that their memory will be tested (Mandler, 1980). In fact, when presented with unrelated lists of words, some people spontaneously reorganize the lists, as reflected in their recall order.

In many instances we remember information better when we organize it hierarchically (Bruning, Schraw, & Ronning, 1999). A *hierarchy* is a system in which items are organized from general to specific classes. Gordon Bower and his colleagues (1969) showed the importance of hierarchical organization in memory. Participants who were presented words in hierarchies remembered them better than those who were given the words in random groupings (see figure 7.3).

Chunking *is another beneficial organizational memory strategy that involves grouping or "packing" information into higher-order units that can be remembered as single units.* Chunking is a form of elaborative processing and works by making large amounts of information more manageable. For example, consider this simple list of words: *hot, city, book, forget, tomorrow,* and *smile.* Try to hold these words in memory for a moment, then write them down. If you recalled all seven words, you succeeded in holding 34 letters in your memory. Now try to hold the following in memory for a moment and then write it down:

O LDH ARO LDAN DYO UNGB EN

How did you do? As presented above, this string of letters is very difficult to remember. However, if you chunk the above letters to form the words "Old Harold and Young Ben," they become much easier to remember.

In summary, to encode something in memory more effectively you can rehearse

SUMMARY TABLE 7.1
The Nature of Memory and Encoding

Concept	Processes/ Related Ideas	Characteristics/Description
The Nature of Memory	What Is Memory?	Memory is the retention of information over time. Psychologists study how information is initially placed or encoded into memory, how it is retained or stored after being encoded, and how it is found or retrieved for a certain purpose later.
	Exploring Memory	We often take for granted how smoothly our memory systems work. Human memory is remarkable and allows us to carry out many feats every day of our lives. However, human memory also has its imperfections. Although there are many complex dimensions to memory, thinking about memory in terms of encoding (getting information into memory), storage (retaining information over time), and retrieval (taking memory out of storage) should help you understand it better.
Encoding	Rehearsal	Rehearsal is the conscious repetition of information that increases the length of time that information stays in memory. Rehearsal works best when we need to remember a list of numbers or items for a brief time. Many psychologists believe that when people want to remember information for longer time frames, other encoding strategies work better, especially when they impart meaning to what is to be remembered.
	Deep Processing	Craik & Lockhart's levels of processing theory states that memory processing occurs on a continuum from shallow to deep, with deeper processing producing better memory.
	Elaboration	The more elaboration involved, the better memory is. Elaboration is the extensiveness of processing at any given depth of memory.
	Imagery	Memory is stored either as a verbal code or as an image code. Paivio believes that the image code produces better memory because it is often detailed and distinctive.
	Organization	Memory works best when it is organized. Two ways to do this are hierarchical organization and chunking.

it, process it at a deep level, elaborate it, form imagery, organize it, and/or chunk it. At this point we have discussed a number of ideas about the nature of memory and encoding. An overview of these ideas is presented in summary table 7.1. Next, we turn our attention to how memory is stored.

Memory Storage

After we encode information, we need to retain or store the information. The three main stores of memory—sensory memory, working (or short-term) memory, and long-term memory—vary according to time. Let's explore these stores as well as other issues involved in retaining information.

Memory's Time Frames

We remember some information for less than a second, some for half a minute, and other information for minutes, hours, years, even a lifetime. Because memory often functions differently across these varied time intervals, we

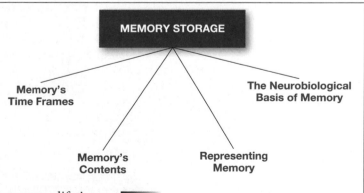

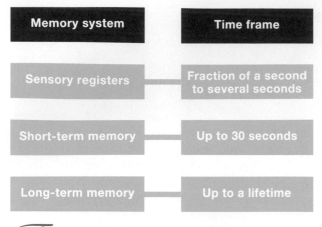

Memory system	Time frame
Sensory registers	Fraction of a second to several seconds
Short-term memory	Up to 30 seconds
Long-term memory	Up to a lifetime

Figure 7.4
Three Memory Stores that Vary According to How Long Memory Is Retained

can distinguish among different types of memory partly on the basis of their differing time frames. The three types of memory that vary according to their time frames are *sensory memory,* with time frames of a fraction of a second to several seconds; *working memory* (also often called short-term memory), with time frames of up to 30 seconds; and *long-term memory,* with time frames of up to a lifetime (see figure 7.4).

A Theory of Memory's Three Time Frames
An early popular theory of memory was formulated by Richard Atkinson and Richard Shiffrin (1968). The **Atkinson-Shiffrin theory** *states that memory involves a sequence of three stages: sensory memory, short-term (working) memory, and long-term memory* (see figure 7.5). As we have seen, much information makes it no further than the sensory memories of sounds and sights. This information is retained for only a brief instant. However, some information, especially that to which we pay attention, is transferred to short-term memory, where it can be retained for about 30 seconds (or longer with the aid of rehearsal). Atkinson and Shiffrin claimed that the longer information is retained in short-term memory through the use of rehearsal, the greater chance it has of getting into long-term memory. Notice in figure 7.5 that retrieval is used to search long-term memory and bring information back into short-term memory.

Some contemporary experts on memory, such as Alan Baddeley, believe that Atkinson and Shiffrin's theory is too simplified (Baddeley, 1993, 1998; Bartlett, 1998). They believe that memory doesn't always work in a neatly packaged three-stage sequence like Atkinson and Shiffrin proposed. They think that memory is far more complex and dynamic than this. For example, these contemporary experts believe that working memory uses long-term memory's contents in more flexible ways than simply retrieving information from it (Murdock, 1999). We will further discuss Baddeley's view of working memory shortly, but first we need to study sensory memory.

Sensory Memory
Sensory memory *holds information from the world in its original sensory form for only an instant, not much longer than the brief time it is exposed to the visual, auditory, and other senses.* Sensory memory is very rich and de-

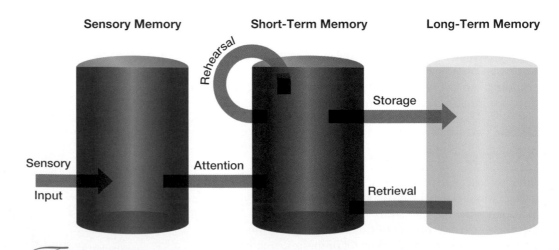

Figure 7.5
Atkinson and Shiffrin's Theory of Memory
In this model, sensory input goes into sensory memory. Through the process of attention, information moves into short-term memory, where it remains for 30 seconds or less, unless it is rehearsed. Then, the information goes into long-term memory storage; from here it can be retrieved for some purpose later.

tailed, but the information in it is very quickly lost unless certain processes are engaged in that transfer it into working or long-term memory.

Think about all the sights and sounds you encounter as you walk to class on a typical morning. Literally thousands of stimuli come into your fields of vision and hearing—cracks in the sidewalk, chirping birds, a noisy motorcycle, the blue sky, faces of hundreds of people. We do not process all of these stimuli, but we do process a number of them. In general, you process many more stimuli at the sensory level than you consciously notice. Sensory memory retains this information from your senses, including a large portion of what you think you ignore. But sensory memory does not retain the information very long. **Echoic memory** *(from the word* echo*) is the name given to auditory sensory memory in which information is retained for up to several seconds.* **Iconic memory** *(from the word* icon, *which means "image") is the name given to visual sensory memory in which information is retained only for about 1/4 second* (see figure 7.6). The sensory memory for other senses, such as smell and touch, has received little attention.

Figure 7.7
Sperling's Sensory Memory Experiment
This array of stimuli is similar to those flashed for about 1/20 of a second to the participants in Sperling's study.

Type of sensory memory	
Echoic	Iconic
Up to several seconds	About 1/4 second

Figure 7.6
Auditory and Visual Sensory Memory
If you hear this bird's call while walking through the woods, your echoic memory holds the information for several seconds. If you see the bird, your iconic memory holds the information for only about one-quarter of a second.

The first scientific research on sensory memory focused on iconic memory. In George Sperling's (1960) classic study, participants were presented with patterns of stimuli such as those in figure 7.7. As you look at the letters, you have no trouble recognizing them. But Sperling flashed the letters on a screen for only very brief intervals, about 1/20 second. After a pattern was flashed on the screen, the subjects could report only four or five letters. With such short exposure, reporting all 9 letters was impossible.

Some of the participants in Sperling's study reported feeling that, for an instant, they could *see* all nine letters within a briefly flashed pattern. But they ran into trouble when they tried to *name* all the letters they had initially *seen.* One hypothesis to explain this experience is that all nine letters were initially processed as far as iconic sensory memory. This is why all nine letters were *seen.* However, forgetting was so rapid that the participants could name only a handful of letters before they were lost from sensory memory.

Sperling decided to test this hypothesis. He reasoned that if all nine letters were actually processed in sensory memory, they should all be available for a brief time. To test this possibility, Sperling sounded a low, medium, or high tone just after a pattern of letters was shown. The participants were told that the tone was a signal to report only the letters from the bottom, middle, or top row, respectively. Under these conditions, the participants performed much better, suggesting a brief memory for most or all of the letters in the display.

Sensory Memory

Working or Short-Term Memory

Working memory, *also sometimes called short-term memory, is a limited-capacity memory system in which information is*

Short-Term Memory

Figure 7.8
A Theory of Working Memory

In Baddeley's theory of working memory the two subsystems—the visuospatial scratchpad and the articulatory loop—help the executive do its job. The visuospatial scratchpad involves our spatial imagery skills, the articulatory loop our language skills.

Through the Eyes of Psychologists

Alan Baddeley, MRC Applied Psychology Unit, Cambridge, England

"The concept of working memory provides a coherent framework for exploring the role of human memory in many aspects of cognition both within the laboratory and in the world outside."

retained for as long as 30 seconds, unless the information is rehearsed, in which case it can be retained longer. Compared with sensory memory, working memory is limited in capacity but can store information for a relatively longer duration. Its limited capacity was examined by George Miller (1956) in a classic paper with the catchy title, "The Magical Number Seven, Plus or Minus Two." Miller pointed out that on many tasks individuals are limited in how much information they can keep track of without external aids. Usually the limit is in the range of 7 ± 2 items. The most widely cited example of the 7 ± 2 capacity phenomenon involves **memory span,** *which is the number of digits an individual can report back in order after a single presentation of them.* Most university students can remember lists of 8 or 9 digits without making any errors. Longer lists, however, pose problems because they exceed your working memory capacity. If you rely on simple working memory to retain longer lists of items you probably will make errors.

As we saw earlier, by chunking information we can remember more than 7 ± 2 units of information. For example, we saw that when 34 letters were chunked into seven words they could be handled in our short-term memory. Thus, although short-term memory has limited capacity, chunking helps us to make the most of it.

Information stored in working memory lasts half a minute or less without rehearsal. However, if rehearsal is not interrupted, information can be retained indefinitely. Our rehearsal is often verbal, giving the impression of an inner voice, but it can also be visual or spatial, giving the impression of a private inner eye. One way to use your visualization skills is to maintain the appearance of an object or scene for a period of time after you have viewed it. People who are unusually good at this task are said to have *eidetic imagery,* or a photographic memory. All of us can do this to some degree, but a small number of individuals may be so good at maintaining an image they literally "see" the page of a textbook as they try to remember information during a test. However, eidetic imagery is so rare it has been difficult to study; some psychologists even doubt its existence (Gray & Gummerman, 1975).

Rehearsal is an important aspect of working memory, but there is much more we need to know about this type of memory. Working memory is a kind of mental "workbench" that lets us manipulate and assemble information when we make decisions, solve problems, and comprehend written and spoken language (Klatsky, 1984).

One theory of how working memory functions was proposed by British psychologist Alan Baddeley, (1990, 1995) (see figure 7.8). In this theory, working memory consists of a general "executive" and two subsystems that help the executive do its job. One of the subsystems is the articulatory loop, which is specialized to process language information. This is where rehearsal occurs. The other subsystem is the visuospatial scratchpad, which includes some of our spatial imagery skills, such as visualizing an object or a scene.

The idea of working memory has proven useful. Individual differences in working memory are related to performance in other cognitive domains (e.g. reading, Daneman & Merikle, 1996; verbal fluency, Daneman, 1991). We can also better understand how brain damage influences cognitive skills. For example, some amnesiacs perform well on working memory tasks, but show deficits in learning new information in long-term memory tasks. Another group shows the reverse pattern. One patient had good long-term memory despite having a two digit memory span (Baddeley, 1992)! Working memory deficits may also be involved in *Alzheimer's disease*—a progressive, irreversible brain disorder in older adults. The central executive of the working memory model may be the culprit, because Alzheimer's patients have difficulty coordinating different mental activities, one of the central executive's functions.

Long-Term Memory
Long-term memory *is a relatively permanent type of memory that holds huge amounts of information for a long period of time.* In one study, people remembered the names and faces of their high school classmates with considerable accuracy for at least 25 years (Bahrick,

Bahrick, & Whitlinger, 1975). The storehouse of long-term memory is indeed staggering. John von Neumann, a distinguished computer scientist, put the size at 2.8×10^{20} (280 quintillion) bits, which in practical terms means that our storage capacity is virtually unlimited. Von Neumann assumed we never forget anything, but even considering that we do forget things, we can hold several billion times more information than a large computer. Even more impressive is the efficiency with which we retrieve information. It usually takes only a moment to search through this vast storehouse to find the information we want. Who discovered America? What was the name of your first date? When were you born? Who developed the first psychology laboratory? You can, of course, answer these questions instantly.

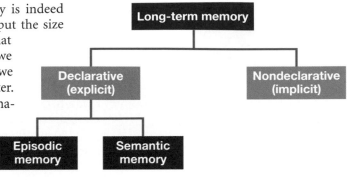

$\mathcal{F}$igure 7.9
Classification of Long-Term Memory's Contents

Memory's Contents

Just as different types of memory can be distinguished by how long they last—time frames of memory—memories within each time frame can be distinguished by their *content*. As we discussed earlier, the contents of sensory memory consist of memory for audition (echoic memory) and vision (iconic memory). Similarly, we learned that the contents of working memory vary according to at least two kinds of content—the articulatory loop, which holds information about speech, and the visuospatial scratchpad, which holds mental images. Therefore, it should be no surprise that the contents of long-term memory can also be differentiated.

Figure 7.9 shows a three-level organization of long-term memory's contents. In this hierarchical organization, memory is divided into the subtypes of declarative (explicit) memory and nondeclarative (implicit) memory. Declarative memory can be subdivided further into episodic and semantic memory. Let's now examine each of these categories.

Declarative and Nondeclarative Memory   Declarative memory *is the conscious recollection of information, such as specific facts or events, and, at least in humans, information that can be verbally communicated.* Because of its conscious and verbalizable nature, declarative memory has been called *explicit memory* (Graf & Schacter, 1985). Examples of declarative (or explicit) memory include recounting the events of a movie you have seen and describing a basic principle of psychology to someone. However, you do not need to be talking to be using declarative memory. Simply sitting and consciously reflecting about Einstein's theory of relativity, or the date you had last weekend, involves declarative memory.

Nondeclarative memory *is memory in which behavior is affected by prior experience without that experience being consciously recollected.* Because nondeclarative memory cannot be verbalized or consciously recollected, at least not in the form of specific events or facts, it is also called *implicit memory* (Graf & Schacter, 1985). One kind of example of nondeclarative memory involves skills such as playing tennis and typing. When you play tennis, you do so by remembering your past experience (i.e. you are not a beginner each time), but not in a verbalizable or normally conscious way. Endel Tulving (1985) refers to your memory for skills (the procedures you use to play tennis or type) as *procedural memory.*

The distinction between explicit and implicit memory has also illuminated forgetting in amnesiacs and the elderly. Amazingly, amnesiacs who perform poorly when given an explicit memory test such as cued recall perform just fine when an implicit memory task is used (Graf & Schacter, 1985). How can amnesiacs, who are supposed to be unable to remember, show what Cermak and his colleagues (1992) call a *dissociation* between explicit and implicit memory performance? Incidentally, Jacoby, Jennings & Hay (1996) have also shown that older people show the same dissociation. While we do know that the memory deficits of amnesiacs and the elderly are restricted to explicit memory, we do not yet know why.

Endel Tulving

Episodic and Semantic Memory   University of Toronto psychologist Endel Tulving (1972, 2000) has been a forceful advocate of distinguishing between two subtypes of declarative memory: episodic and semantic. **Episodic memory** *is the retention of information about the where and when of life's happenings.* For example, episodic memory includes what it was like when your younger brother or sister was born, what happened on your first date, what you were doing when Princess Diana died, and what you had for breakfast this morning (Tulving, in press). Episodic memory involves autobiographical episodes. We will return to this idea later in this chapter.

Semantic memory *is a person's knowledge about the world.* This includes a person's fields of expertise, general academic knowledge of the sort learned in school and everyday knowledge about meanings of words, famous individuals, important places, and common things. For example, semantic memory is involved in a person's knowledge of chess, knowledge of geometry, and knowledge of who Nelson Mandela and Mahatma Gandhi are. An important aspect of semantic memory is that it appears to be independent of an individual's personal identity with the past. You can access a fact—such as that Lima is the capital of Peru—and not have the foggiest notion of when and where you learned it.

Several examples help to clarify the distinction between episodic and semantic memory. Your memory of your first day on campus involves episodic memory. Your memory of the information you need to know to do well on your next psychology test involves semantic memory.

Consider also that in a certain type of amnesiac state, a person might forget entirely who she is—her name, family, career, and all other personal information about herself—yet she can talk and demonstrate general knowledge about the world. Her episodic memory is impaired, but her semantic memory is functioning. An especially dramatic case of this type, a young man named K. C., was reported by Endel Tulving (1989). After suffering a motorcycle accident, K. C. lost virtually all use of his episodic memory. The loss was so profound that he was unable to consciously recollect a single thing that had ever happened to him. At the same time, K. C.'s semantic memory was sufficiently preserved that he could learn about his past as a set of facts, just as he would learn about another person's life. He could report, for example, that the saddest day of his life was when his brother drowned about 10 years before. This sounds as if K. C. has episodic memory, but further questioning revealed that he had no conscious memory of the drowning event. He simply knew about the drowning because he was able to recall—apparently through use of his semantic memory—what he had been told about his brother by other members of his family.

Some aspects of the episodic/semantic distinction are summarized in figure 7.10. Although the distinctions listed have attracted considerable attention, they remain controversial. One criticism is that many cases of declarative memory are neither purely episodic nor purely semantic but fall in a gray area in between. Consider your memory for what you studied last night. You probably added knowledge to your semantic memory—that was, after all, the reason you were studying. You probably remember where you were studying, as well as when you started and about when you stopped. You can probably also remember some minor occurrences, such as a burst of loud laughter from the room next door or the coffee you spilled on the desk. Is episodic or semantic memory involved here? Tulving (1983) argues that semantic and episodic systems often work together in forming new memories. In such cases, the memory that is ultimately formed might consist of an autobiographical episode *and* semantic information.

Characteristic	Episodic Memory	Semantic Memory
Units	Events, episodes	Facts, ideas, concepts
Organization	Temporal	Conceptual
Affect	More important	Less important
Retrieval process	Deliberate (effortful)	Automatic
Retrieval report	"I remember"	"I know"
Education	Irrelevant	Relevant
Intelligence	Irrelevant	Relevant
Legal testimony	Admissible in court	Inadmissible in court

Source: From E. Tulving, *Elements of Episodic Memory,* p. 35.

𝓕igure 7.10
Some Characteristics That Differentiate Episodic and Semantic Memory

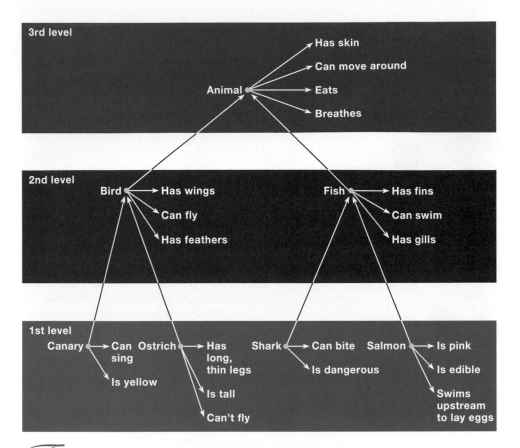

*F*igure 7.11
The Hierarchical Organization of Memory with Nodes (Branching Points) at Three Levels in the Hierarchy

Notice how the information becomes more detailed and specific as you move through the levels of the hierarchy in this model. Some psychologists have challenged this representation as too "clean" to portray the true complexity of our representation processes.

Representing Memory

We have seen that memory has three stores that vary by duration and that memory's contents can be differentiated into different categories. Another important aspect of memory storage is to understand how information is represented in memory. We will examine two main kinds of theories of this representation: network theories and schema theories.

Network Theories   One of the first network theories claimed that our memories can be envisioned as a complex network of nodes that stand for labels or concepts (see figure 7.11). The network was assumed to be hierarchically arranged with more-concrete concepts (canary, for example) nestled under more-abstract concepts (bird). More recently, cognitive psychologists realized that such hierarchical networks were too simple to describe the way human cognition actually works (Shanks, 1991). For example, people take longer to answer the true-or-false statement "An ostrich is a bird" than they do to answer the statement "A canary is a bird." Memory researchers now envision the network as more irregular and distorted: a *typical* bird, such as a canary, is closer to the node or center of the category *bird* than is the atypical ostrich. Figure 7.12 shows an example of the revised model, which allows for the typicality of information while retaining the original notion of node and network.

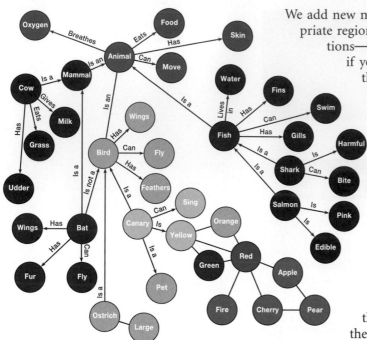

*F*igure 7.12

Revision of the Hierarchical Network View of How Information is Organized in Long-Term Memory

We add new material to this network by placing it in the middle of the appropriate region. The new material is gradually tied in—by meaningful connections—to the appropriate nodes in the surrounding network. That is why if you cram for a test, you will not remember the information over the long term. The new material is not woven into the long-term web. In contrast, discussing the material or incorporating it into a research paper interweaves it and connects it to other knowledge you have. These multiple connections increase the probability that you will be able to retrieve the information many months or even years later. The concept of multiple connections fits with our description of the importance of elaboration in memory that we discussed earlier in the chapter.

Schema Theories   Long-term memory has been compared to a library. Your memory stores information just as a library stores books. We retrieve information in a fashion similar to the process we use to locate and check out a book. But the process of retrieving information from long-term memory is not as precise as the library analogy suggests. When we search through our long-term memory storehouse we don't always find the *exact* "book" we want, or we might find the book we want but discover that only several pages are intact. We have to *reconstruct* the rest. When we reconstruct information, we often fit it into information that already exists in our mind. A **schema** *is a concept or framework that already exists in a person's mind and that organizes and interprets information.* Schemas from prior encounters with the environment influence the way we encode, make inferences about, and retrieve information (Jou, Shanteau, & Harris, 1996). Unlike network theories, which assume that retrieval involves specific facts, schema theory claims that long-term memory search is not very exact. We seldom find precisely what we want, or at least not all of what we want; hence, we have to reconstruct the rest. Our schemas support this reconstruction process, helping us fill in the gaps between our fragmented memories.

The schema theory of memory began with Sir Frederick Bartlett's (1932) studies of how people remember stories. Bartlett was concerned about how a person's background determines what they encode and remember about stories. Bartlett chose stories that sounded strange and were difficult to understand. He reasoned that a person's background, which is encoded in schemas, would reveal itself in the person's reconstruction (modification and distortion) of the story's content. For example, one of Bartlett's stories was called "War of the Ghosts," an English translation of an American Indian folktale. The story contained events that were completely foreign to the experiences of the middle- and upper-income British research participants. The War of the Ghosts story is presented in figure 7.13. The participants in Bartlett's study read the story twice then waited 15 minutes, at which time they were asked to write down the tale the best they could remember it.

What interested Bartlett was how differently the participants might reconstruct this and other stories from the original versions. The British participants used both their general schemas for daily experiences, and their schemas for adventurous ghost stories in particular, to reconstruct "War of the Ghosts." Familiar details from the story that "fit into" the participant's schemas were successfully recalled. But details that departed from the person's schemas were often extensively distorted. For example, the "something black" that came out of the Indian's mouth became blood in one reconstruction and condensed air in another. For one individual the two young men were hunting beavers rather than seals. Another person said the death at the end was due to a fever (this wasn't in the story).

*T*hrough the Eyes of Psychologists

Endel Tulving, *University of Toronto*

"Remembering events is a universally familiar experience. It is also a uniquely human one. As far as we know, members of no other species possess quite the same ability to experience again now, in a different situation and perhaps in a different form, happenings from the past, and know that the experience refers to an event that occurred in another time and place."

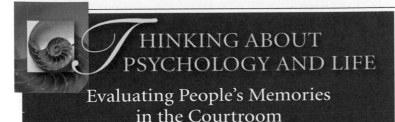

THINKING ABOUT PSYCHOLOGY AND LIFE

Evaluating People's Memories in the Courtroom

GET TOGETHER with several other students and go to the local courthouse. Observe part of a trial in a criminal court, domestic court, or even traffic court. Listen carefully to what the witnesses are saying. Are their memories likely to be completely accurate? What possible memory biases are at work in their descriptions of what they said took place? Do you think the trial might have had a different outcome if the jurors were aware that memory is often unreliable? If you can't make it to a courthouse, try watching part of a television trial to complete this exercise (Halpern, 1997). Some episodes from the television shows "Judge Judy" or "Judge Joe Brown" could serve the purpose of this exercise. Or you might try attending an on-campus judicial hearing.

There has been a flurry of interest in reconstructive memory, especially in the way people recall stories, give eyewitness testimony, remember their past, and recall conversations (Greene, 1999; Howe, 1995; Thompson & others, 1998). To learn more about the nature of reconstructive memory in eyewitness testimony turn to Explorations in Psychology.

We have schemas not only for stories but also for scenes or spatial layouts (a beach, a bathroom), as well as for common events (going to a restaurant, playing

Eyewitness Memory

One night two young men from Egulac went down to the river to hunt seals, and while they were there it became foggy and calm. Then they heard war cries, and they thought: "Maybe this is a war party." They escaped to the shore, and hid behind a log. Now canoes came up, and they heard the noise of paddles, and saw one canoe coming up to them. There were five men in the canoe, and they said:

"What do you think? We wish to take you along. We are going up the river to make war on the people."

One of the young men said: "I have no arrows."

"Arrows are in the canoe," they said.

"I will not go along, I might be killed. My relatives do not know where I have gone. But you," he said, turning to the other, "may go with them."

So one of the young men went, but the other returned home.

And the warriors went up the river to a town on the other side of Kalama. The people came down to the water, and they began to fight, and many were killed. But presently the young man heard one of the warriors say: "Quick, let us go home: that Indian has been hit." Now he thought: "Oh, they are ghosts." He did not feel sick, but they said he had been shot.

So the canoes went back to Egulac and the young man went ashore to his house, and made a fire. And he told everybody and said: "Behold I accompanied the ghosts, and we went to fight. Many of our fellows were killed, and many of those who attacked us were killed. They said I was hit, and I did not feel sick."

He told it all, and then he became quiet. When the sun rose he fell down. Something black came out of his mouth. His face became contorted. The people jumped up and cried.

He was dead.

Figure 7.13
The War of the Ghosts
When Sir Frederick Bartlett (1932) asked individuals to recall this story, they changed its details.

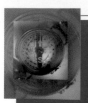

EYEWITNESS TESTIMONY may go wrong either because memories of events fade over time (Shepard, 1967) or because those memories contain errors (Schacter, 1995). When eyewitness testimony is inaccurate, the wrong person may go to jail (or even be put to death), or a person who committed a crime might not be prosecuted. Estimates are that between 2,000 and 10,000 people are wrongfully convicted each year in the United States alone because of faulty eyewitness testimony (Cutler & Penrod, 1995).

Much of the interest in eyewitness testimony focuses on distortion, bias, and inaccuracy in memory (Loftus, 1993a). In the O. J. Simpson murder trial, many people were puzzled when Simpson's housekeeper testified that his infamous white Bronco had not moved from its spot all evening, yet his limousine driver testified that he did not remember seeing the car when he arrived late that evening. This was only one of many variations that occurred across different witnesses in the high-profile Simpson trial and that regularly occur in other trials.

Unlike a videotape, memory can be altered by new information. In one study, students were shown a film of an automobile accident (Loftus, 1975). Some of the students were asked how fast the white sports car was going when it passed a barn. Other students were asked the same question without any mention of a barn. In fact, there was no barn in the film. However, 17 percent of the students who heard the question that included the barn mentioned it in their answer; only 3 percent of those whose question did not include the barn mentioned that they saw it. New information, then, can add or even replace existing information in memory.

A number of special issues compound difficulties in determining the truth based on eyewitness testimony. People of one ethnic group are less likely to recognize individual differences among people of another ethnic group (Brigham & others, 1982). Identification is further compromised when a witness has been drinking alcohol or taking a drug. Of these special issues, the difficulties surrounding the testimony of children can be daunting.

John Yuille of the University of British Columbia has written extensively on the psychology of eyewitness testimony, including the special problems involved with child witnesses (Yuille, & Wells, 1991). A main difficulty centers on the extreme suggestibility of children, making interviewing them a daunting task (Yuille, 1997). These problems are exacerbated when the case is one of sexual abuse (Raskin & Yuille, 1989). Pressures on children testifying in court may include the laying of criminal charges against a family member, a family member going to jail, the break of the family and/or the placing of the child under foster care. Coupled with children's natural suggestibility, such cases must be handled with special care (Raskin & Yuille, 1989).

O. J. Simpson's white Bronco grabbed our attention when it was televised live as he drove it along a Los Angeles freeway and he threatened suicide. Later, in the Simpson murder trial, different witnesses gave varying testimony about whether the Bronco had ever moved from its spot during the evening when Nicole Brown Simpson had been murdered. Possibly someone was lying, but it is also possible that witnesses reconstructed their memories honestly but differently.

The pressures on vulnerable children when they are called to testify, especially against family members, combined with their natural suggestibility, makes the validity of their testimony especially difficult to determine.

In sum, the problems with eyewitness testimony underscore how our memory is often not flawless. Like other memories, eyewitness memories are constructed and the constructions don't always match what actually happened.

"Why? You cross the road because it's in the script—that's why!"

©The New Yorker Collection 1986 Edward Koren from cartoonbank.com. All Rightes Reserved.

golf, writing a term paper). A **script** *is a schema for an event* (Schank & Abelson, 1977). Scripts often have information about physical features, people, and typical occurrences. This kind of information is helpful when people need to figure out what is happening around them. For example, if you are enjoying your after-dinner coffee in a restaurant and a man in a tuxedo comes over and puts a piece of paper on the table, your script tells you that the man is probably a waiter who has just given you the check.

So far in our coverage of memory storage we have studied the three time frames of storage, the differentiated content in storage, and how information is represented in storage. Next, we discuss where in the brain memories are stored.

The Neurobiological Basis of Memory

Yet another important aspect of memory storage is the brain's role in the retention of memory (Haberlandt, 1999). That is, where in the brain are memories stored?

Karl Lashley (1950) spent a lifetime looking for a location in the brain where memories are stored. He trained rats to discover the correct pathway in a maze and then cut out a portion of the animals' brains and retested their memory of the maze pathway. After experimenting with thousands of rats, Lashley found that the loss of various cortical areas did not affect rats' ability to remember the maze's path. Lashley concluded that memories are not stored in a specific location in the brain.

Many neuroscientists believe that memory is located in discrete sets or circuits of neurons ◄‖‖ P. 72. Brain researcher Larry Squire (1990), for example, says that most memories are probably clustered in groups of about 1,000 neurons. He points out that memory is distributed throughout the brain in the sense that no specific memory center exists. Many parts of the brain and nervous system participate in the memory of a particular event. Yet memory is localized in the sense that a limited number of brain systems and pathways are involved, and each probably contributes in different ways (Lynch, 1990).

Single neurons, of course, are at work in memory. Researchers who measure the electrical activity of single cells have found that some respond to faces, others to eye or hair color, for example. But for you to recognize your Uncle Albert, individual neurons that provide information about hair color, size, and other characteristics must act together.

Ironically, some of the answers to the complex questions about the neural mechanics of memory come from studies on very simple animals—the sea slug (Kandel & Schwartz, 1982) and the nematode (Wicks & Rankin, 1997). Eric Kandel and James Schwartz (1982) chose the sea slug, a large snail-without-a-shell, because of the simple architecture of its nervous system, which consists of only about 10,000 neurons.

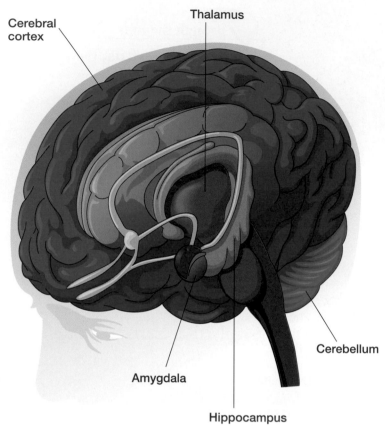

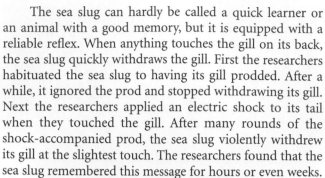

Cerebral cortex

Thalamus

Cerebellum

Amygdala

Hippocampus

Figure 7.14
Some Important Brain Structures That Are Involved in Memory

This drawing with some of the cerebral cortex stripped away lets you look into the brain's interior and see the location of four brain structures that play important roles in memory: hippocampus, thalamus, amygdala, and cerebellum.

The sea slug can hardly be called a quick learner or an animal with a good memory, but it is equipped with a reliable reflex. When anything touches the gill on its back, the sea slug quickly withdraws the gill. First the researchers habituated the sea slug to having its gill prodded. After a while, it ignored the prod and stopped withdrawing its gill. Next the researchers applied an electric shock to its tail when they touched the gill. After many rounds of the shock-accompanied prod, the sea slug violently withdrew its gill at the slightest touch. The researchers found that the sea slug remembered this message for hours or even weeks.

More important than the discovery that sea slugs had memories was the finding that memory seems to be written in chemicals. Shocking the sea slug's gill releases the neurotransmitter serotonin at the synapses, and this chemical release basically provides a reminder that the gill was shocked. This "memory" informs the nerve cell to send out chemical commands to retract the gill the next time it is touched. If nature builds complexity out of simplicity, then the mechanism used by the sea slug may work in the human brain as well. Chemicals, then, may be the ink with which memories are written.

While some neuroscientists are studying the cellular basis of memory, others are examining the broadscale architecture of memory in the brain. Neuroscientists have found that the hippocampus, part of the limbic system, and the thalamus, are involved in declarative memory (Mishkin & Appenzeller, 1987). The amygdala, also part of the limbic system, is critical for emotional memories. The cerebellum is involved in the implicit memory required to perform skills. Figure 7.14 shows the location of these structures in the brain.

Researchers are also using brain imaging techniques to reveal which areas of the brain are active when individuals are engaging in various memory activities ◀▥▥ P. 96. Using such memory imaging techniques as PET (positron emission tomograph, which depicts the activity of different brain regions by showing each area's consumption of sugar glucose), they have shown that:

- Deep encoding is specifically associated with activity in the brain's frontal lobe (Kapur & others, 1994)
- The parietal lobe is involved in the articulatory loop of working memory
- The temporal lobe is linked with priming of structurally visible objects, whereas the hippocampus is associated with the episodic recognition of these objects (Tulving & Markowitsch, 1998; Zola, 1996).
- Temporal lobe atrophy is related to dementia (Murtha and others, 1998).

To read further about the use of imaging techniques to explore the brain's role in memory, see Explorations in Psychology. As neuroscientists discover the identity of memory circuits in the brain, might we reach a point at which the psychological study of memory becomes unimportant? That's unlikely. First, we are far from working out all of the complexities of the neurochemical underpinnings in human memory. And second, even if we were successful in unraveling the neurochemistry of memory, each person's private kingdom of memories will remain intact.

At this point we have explored many aspects of memory storage. An overview of these ideas is presented in summary table 7.2. Now that we have studied how information gets into the brain (encoding) and how it is retained (storage), we need to learn about how we get information out of memory storage.

Brain Imaging

SUMMARY TABLE 7.2
Memory Storage

Concept	Processes/ Related Ideas	Characteristics/Description
Memory's Time Frame	A Theory of Memory's Three Time Frames	The Atkinson-Shiffrin theory states that memory occurs in a three-stage sequence: sensory memory to short-term (working) memory to long-term memory. Some contemporary experts believe this theory is too simplified, and that memory is more dynamic and complex than the theory implies.
	Sensory Memory	Sensory memory holds information from the world in its original form for only an instant, not much longer than the brief time it is exposed to the visual, auditory, and other senses. Visual sensory memory (iconic memory) retains information for about 1/4 second, auditory sensory memory (echoic memory) for several seconds. Sperling's classic study revealed that people have fleeting iconic memory.
	Working or Short-Term Memory	Working memory, sometimes also called short-term memory, is a limited-capacity memory system in which information is retained for as long as 30 seconds, unless the information is rehearsed, in which case it can be retained longer. According to George Miller, short-term memory's limitation is 7 ± 2 bits of information. In Baddeley's theory of working memory, an executive plus two subsystems—the phonological loop (language, rehearsal) and the visuospatial scratchpad (imagery)—are involved.
	Long-Term Memory	Long-term memory is a relatively permanent type of memory that holds huge amounts of information for a long period of time.
Memory's Contents	Declarative and Nondeclarative Memory	Memory can be divided into declarative (explicit) and nondeclarative (implicit) memory. Declarative memory can be further subdivided into episodic and semantic memory. Declarative (explicit) memory is the conscious recollection of information, such as facts and events, and, at least in humans, information that can be verbally communicated. Nondeclarative (implicit) memory refers to knowledge in the form of skills, habits, and cognitive operations that cannot be consciously remembered, at least in the form of events or facts. This makes implicit memory difficult, if not impossible, to communicate.
	Episodic and Semantic Memory	According to Endel Tulving, episodic memory is the retention of information about the where and when of life's happenings. Semantic memory is a person's knowledge about the world.
Representing Memory	Network Theories	Early network theories stressed that memories consist of a complex network of nodes that are hierarchically arranged. More-recent network theories stress the role of meaningful nodes in the surrounding network.
	Schema Theories	A schema is a concept or framework that already exists in a person's mind and that organizes and interprets information. Schema theory claims that long-term memory is not very exact and that we construct our past. There has been a flurry of interest in reconstructive memory in recent years, especially in the way people recall stories, give eyewitness testimony, remember their past, and recall conversations. Schemas for events are called scripts.
	The Neurobiological Basis of Memory	A main neurobiological issue regarding memory is the extent to which memory is localized or distributed. Single neurons are involved in memory, but some neuroscientists believe that most memories are stored in circuits of about 1,000 neurons. There is no specific memory center in the brain, but the hippocampus and thalamus are involved in declarative memory, the amygdala is critical for emotional memories, and the cerebellum is involved in the implicit memory required to perform skills.

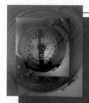

Explorations in Psychology
Cognitive Neuroscience: Watching Brain Activity During Memory Encoding

THE FIELD OF cognitive neuroscience is rapidly emerging as an important perspective (Kolb & Wishaw, 1999; Gazzaniga, Ivry, & Mangun, 1998). Cognitive neuroscience focuses on the brain's role in understanding cognitive activity.

One example of cognitive neuroscience research is scientists' exploration of the brain's role in remembering or forgetting experiences (Neergaard, 1998). Magnet resonance imaging (MRI) machines, which we described in Chapter 2, can measure split-second neural activity as a person's brain processes an experience.

In one research study, healthy volunteers were placed in MRI machines and one word was flashed every 2 seconds onto a screen inside (Wagner & others, 1998). Initially, the volunteers simply noted whether the words were in uppercase or lowercase letters. When they were given additional words, they were asked to determine, for each, whether what it designated was concrete, like *chair* or *book,* or abstract, like *love* or *democracy.* In this study, the participants showed more neural activity and better memory during the "concrete/abstract" word task than when they were asked to merely state whether the words were simply uppercase or lowercase. The researcher's conclusion: More-complex cognitive activity is linked with increased neural activity and improved memory.

In a second research study, healthy participants were shown color photographs of indoor and outdoor scenes while in an MRI machine (Brewer & others, 1998). They were not told that they would be given a memory test about the scenes. After the MRI scans, they were asked which pictures they remembered well, vaguely, or not at all. Their memories were compared to the brain scans. The longer the prefrontal lobes and a particular region of the hippocampus both lit up on the MRI scans, the better the participants remembered the scenes. Pictures paired with weak brain activity in these areas were forgotten.

MRI has also helped in the study of amnesia. For example, Levine & others, (1997) have used MRI scans to identify malfunctioning areas of the brain in selective retrograde amnesia. This new cognitive neuroscience research is helping scientists pinpoint the specific aspects of the brain involved in memory.

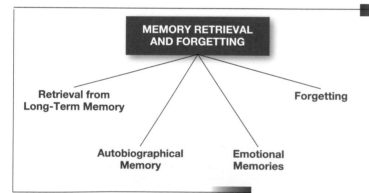

Memory Retrieval and Forgetting

Have you ever forgotten where you parked your car, your mother's birthday, or to meet a friend to study? Have you ever sat in a class taking an exam, unable to remember the answer to a question but remembering where on a page of your textbook a relevant, elusive concept was located?

Retrieval from Long-Term Memory

To retrieve something from your mental "data bank," you search your store of memory to find the relevant information. Let's explore several concepts related to retrieval.

Tip-of-the-Tongue Phenomenon

One glitch in retrieving information that we're all familiar with is the **tip-of-the-tongue phenomenon,** or **TOT state.** *It is a type of "effortful retrieval" that occurs when people are confident they know something but just can't quite seem to pull it out of memory* (Beattie & Coughlan, 1999; Brown & Nix, 1996). People in a TOT state usually can successfully retrieve characteristics of the word such as the first letter and the number of syllables but not retrieve the word itself.

In one study of the TOT state, participants were shown photographs of famous people and asked to say their names (Yarmey, 1973). The researcher found that people tended to use two strategies to try to retrieve the name of a person they thought they knew. One strategy was to pinpoint the person's profession. For example, one participant correctly identified the famous person as an artist but the artist's name, *Picasso*, remained elusive. Another retrieval strategy was to repeat initial letters or syllables—such as *Monetti, Mona, Magett, Spaghetti,* and *Bogette* in the attempt to identify Liza Minelli.

The TOT state arises because a person can retrieve some of the desired information but not all of it (Schacter, 1996). For example, when a person asks someone the identity of an individual who is standing next to Barbara at a social event, the person might not be able to recall Bill's name but might remember what he looks like and that his name begins with a *B*. A person's familiarity with a retrieval cue can induce a strong—sometimes spurious—feeling of knowing. For example, when the person cues the individual next to him about who is standing next to Barbara, the individual's familiarity with Bill might make him feel like he can easily retrieve Bill's name, but he might not be able to do so.

Serial Position Effect   Understanding how retrieval works also requires knowledge of the **serial position effect**—*that recall is superior for items at the beginning and at the end of a list.* If someone gave you the directions "Left on Spadina, right on Bloor, right on Yonge, left on King, and right on Jarvis," you would probably remember "Left on Spadina" and "right on Jarvis" more easily than the turns and streets in the middle. The **primacy effect** *refers to superior recall for items at the beginning of a list.* The **recency effect** *refers to superior recall for items at the end of the list.* Together with the relatively low recall of items from the middle of the list, this pattern makes up the serial position effect. See figure 7.15 for a typical serial position effect that shows a weaker primacy effect and a stronger recency effect. One application of primacy and recency effects is the advice to job candidates to try to be the first or last candidate interviewed.

How can primacy and recency effects be explained? The first few items in the list are easily remembered because they are rehearsed more often than later items (Atkinson & Shiffrin, 1968). Working memory is relatively empty when they enter, so there is little competition for rehearsal time. And since they get more rehearsal, they stay in working memory longer, and are more likely to be successfully encoded into long-term memory. In contrast, many items from the middle of the list drop out of working memory before being encoded into long-term memory. The last several items are remembered for different reasons. First, at the time these items are recalled, they might still be in working memory. Second, even if these items are not in working memory, their relative recency, compared to other list items, makes them easier to recall. For example, if you are a music fan, try remembering concerts you saw last year, or if you like the movies, try remembering the last ten movies you saw. You will probably find that the more recent concerts or movies are easier to remember than less recent ones.

Retrieval Cues and the Retrieval Task   Two other factors involved in retrieval are (a) the nature of the cues that can prompt your memory, and (b) the retrieval task that you set for yourself. If effective cues for what you are trying to remember do not seem to be available, you need to create them—a process that takes place in working memory. For example, if you have a "block" about remembering a new friend's name, you might go through the alphabet, generating names that begin with each letter. If you manage to stumble across the right name, you'll probably recognize it.

While cues help, your success in retrieving information also depends on the task you set for yourself. For instance, if you're simply trying to decide if something

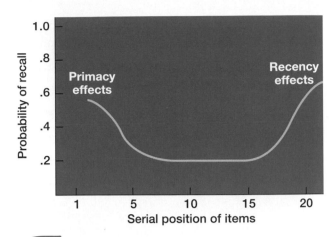

*F*igure 7.15
The Serial Position Effect
When a person is asked to memorize a list of words, the words memorized last are usually recalled best, those at the beginning next best, and those in the middle least efficiently.

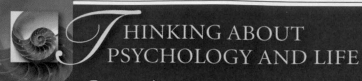

Generating Retrieval Cues

WE CAN LEARN to generate retrieval cues (Halpern, 1996). For example, memory researcher Elizabeth Loftus (1980) described the situation of going to a supermarket without a shopping list and forgetting what you were going to buy. She recommended going through different categories such as meats, dairy, cleaning supplies, desserts, and so on, then using these categories as retrieval cues for remembering your intended purchases.

To see how you can use categories to generate retrieval cues, write down the names of as many of your classmates from the middle or junior high school you attended as you can remember. When you run out of names, think about different locations and activities, such as math class, student council, eating lunch, basketball team, and so on. Did this help you to remember more of your classmates?

Memory Exercises

seems familiar, retrieval is probably a snap. Let's say you see a short, dark-haired woman walking toward you. You quickly decide she's someone who lives in the next dorm. But remembering her name or a precise detail, such as when you met her, can be harder. Such findings have implications for police investigations: A witness might be certain she has previously seen a face, yet she might have a hard time deciding if it was at the scene of the crime or in a mugshot.

The two factors just discussed—the presence or absence of good cues, and the retrieval task required—are involved in an important memory distinction: recall versus recognition memory. **Recall** *is a memory measure in which the individual must retrieve previously learned information, as on an essay test.* **Recognition** *is a memory measure in which the individual only has to identify ("recognize") learned items, as on multiple-choice tests.* Most university students prefer multiple-choice tests because they're easier than essay tests or fill-in-the blank tests. Recall tests, such as fill-in-the-blank tests, have poor retrieval cues. You are told to try to recall a certain class of information ("Discuss the factors that caused World War II"). In multiple-choice "recognition" tests, you merely judge whether a stimulus is familiar or not (Does it match something you experienced in the past?).

You have probably heard some people say that they are terrible at remembering names but they never forget a face. If you have made that claim yourself, try to actually recall a face. It's not so easy. Law enforcement officers know that witnesses often do a very poor job of describing a suspect, so in many cases they bring in an artist to reconstruct the suspect's face (see figure 7.16). Recalling faces is difficult. If you think you remember faces rather than names, it is probably because you are better at recognition than at recall.

Another consideration in understanding retrieval is the **encoding specificity principle,** *which states that associations formed at the time of encoding or learning tend to be effective retrieval cues.* For example, imagine that you have met someone whose occupation is tennis professional. If you encode that information along with such words as *racket, ball,* and *serve,* those words can be used as retrieval cues in trying to remember what the person's occupation is. Encoding specificity is compatible with our earlier discussion of elaboration. Recall that the more elaboration you use in encoding information, the better your memory of the information will be. Encoding specificity and elaboration reveal how interdependent encoding and retrieval are.

Retrieval also benefits from **priming,** *which involves activating particular connections or associations in memory.* In many cases, these associations are unconscious. Because the associations are primarily unconscious, priming has been categorized under nondeclarative or implicit memory (Kirsner & others, 1998).

In everyday life, priming is likely involved in unintentional acts of plagiarism (Schacter, 1996). For example, you propose an idea to a friend, who seems unimpressed by it or even rejects it outright. Weeks or months later, the friend excitedly describes your idea as if he had just come up with it himself. When you call your friend's attention to the fact that "his" idea is really "your" idea, you will likely face either heated denial or a sheepish apology born of a sudden dose of explicit memory.

Another practical example of priming involves those times when you are wandering the grocery store unable to remember one of the items you were supposed to buy. As you walk down the aisle you hear two people talking about fruit and that triggers your memory that you were supposed to buy raspberries. That is, hearing "fruit" primes your memory for raspberries.

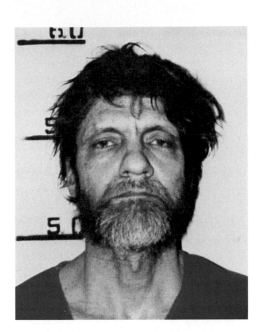

ℱigure 7.16
Remembering Faces

At left is the FBI artist's sketch of Ted Kaczynski. At right is a photograph of Kaczynski. The FBI widely circulated the artist's sketch, which was based on bits and pieces of observations people had made of the infamous Unabomber, in the hope that someone would recognize the Unabomber if they saw him. Would you have been able to recognize Kaczynski from the artist's sketch of him? Probably not. Although most people say they are very good at remembering faces, they are usually not as good as they think they are.

Autobiographical Memory

Our retrieval of information from long-term memory can involve personal memories. **Autobiographical memory** *is a person's recollections of his or her life experiences.* Autobiographical memory is a form of episodic memory, which we discussed earlier in the chapter. Whereas autobiographical memories are complex and can seem like they contain unending strings of stories and snapshots, researchers have found that these memories can be categorized (Schacter, 1996). For example, based on their research, Martin Conway and David Rubin (1993) sketch a structure of autobiographical memory that has three levels (see figure 7.17). The first level consists of *life time periods* (long segments of life that are measured in years and even decades); for example, you might remember something about your life in high school. The middle level in the hierarchy is made up of *general events* (these are extended composite episodes that are measured in days, weeks, or months); for example, you might remember a trip you took with your friends after you graduated from high school. The lowest level in the hierarchy is comprised of *event-specific knowledge* (individual episodes that are measured in seconds, minutes, or hours); for example, on your post-graduation trip, you might remember the exhilarating time you had when you took your first bungie-jump. When people tell their life stories, all three levels of information are usually present and intertwined.

We stitch together complex mixtures of personal knowledge about our past to form our life story (Thompson & others, 1998).

Level	Label	Description
Level 1	Life time periods	Long segments of time measured in years and even decades
Level 2	General events	Extended composite episodes that are measured in days, weeks, or months
Level 3	Event-specific knowledge	Individual episodes that are measured in seconds, minutes or hours

ℱigure 7.17
The Three-Level Hierarchical Structure of Autobiographical Memory

In most autobiographical memories there is some reality and some myth. Dan McAdams (1993) argues that these biographies of the self that connect the past and the present provide a set of memories that form the core of our personal identity. He says that our autobiographical memories are less about facts and more about meanings. They provide an embellished telling of the past. As people reconstruct their past in telling their autobiographical memories, their histories are made.

Emotional Memories

When we remember our life experiences, the memories are often wrapped in emotion. Let's begin our tour of emotional memories by examining flashbulb memories.

Flashbulb Memories

Flashbulb Memories   **Flashbulb memories** *are memories of emotionally significant events that people often recall with more accuracy and vivid imagery than everyday events.* An intriguing dimension of flashbulb memories is that several decades later people often remember where they were and what was going on in their lives at the time of such an event. Perhaps you can remember where you were when you first heard of the shootings at Columbine High School in 1999 or when Princess Diana died in 1997. We both still have vivid images of where we were when President Kennedy was shot in 1963—one of us (JS) was watching the University of Miami (Florida) football team play in the Orange Bowl while the other (JM) had just come home for lunch in Calgary while he was in grade 8. These memories seem to be part of an adaptive system that fixes in memory the details that accompany important events so they can be interpreted at a later time.

The vast majority of flashbulb memories are of a personal nature (Rubin & Kozin, 1984). University students were asked to report the three most vivid memories in their lives. Virtually all of these memories were of a personal nature rather than of nationally significant events or circumstances. The memories tended to center around an injury or accident, sports, members of the opposite sex, animals, deaths, the first week of university, and vacations. Students also answered questions about their memories of events that were most likely to produce flashbulb memories. Figure 7.18 shows which types of events more than 50 percent of the students said were of "flashbulb" quality.

Most people are confident about the accuracy of their flashbulb memories. Just how accurate are our flashbulb memories? Some flashbulb memories are accurate but most are probably not as photographically etched in our brain as we think. Some flashbulb memories deteriorate and change over time. However, flashbulb memories are far more durable and accurate than memories of day-to-day happenings. One reason that flashbulb memories are so durable is that they are often discussed and thought about in the days, weeks, and even years following an event. That was the case in President Kennedy's death, and it certainly has been and will be the case in Princess Diana's death. However, it's not just the discussion and rehearsal of information that make flashbulb memories so long-lasting. The emotions triggered by flashbulb events are also involved in their durability. Thus, if you have a flashbulb memory of Princess Diana's death, the emotional arousal you experienced when you heard about it also likely contributed to the flashbulb memory.

Earlier we indicated that the vast majority of flashbulb memories are of a personal nature. Some of these involve

Do you have a flashbulb memory for (left) the shootings at Columbine High School in 1999 or (right) Princess Diana's death in 1997? What is the nature of flashbulb memories?

emotionally uplifting experiences, as when a person remembers the positive emotional experience of high school graduation night. Other events might be at the opposite end of the emotional spectrum and involve personal trauma. What are the memories of those episodes in our lives like that involve personal trauma?

Personal Trauma In 1890, William James said that an experience can be so arousing emotionally as to almost leave a scar on the brain's tissue. Personal traumas that people experience are candidates for the type of emotionally arousing experience James was referring to. Some psychologists argue that memories for emotionally traumatic events are accurately retained, possibly forever, in considerable detail (Langer, 1991). There is good evidence that memory for traumatic events is usually more accurate than memory for ordinary events (Schacter, 1996). Consider the traumatic experience of children who were kidnapped at gunpoint on a school bus in Chowchilla, California, then buried underground for 16 hours before escaping. The children had the classic signs of traumatic memory—detailed and vivid recollections. However, when a child psychiatrist interviewed them four or five years after the chilling episode, she noted some striking errors and distortions in half of the children (Terr, 1988).

How can a traumatic memory be so vivid and detailed, yet at the same time have inaccuracies? A number of factors can be involved. Some children might have made perceptual errors at the time of encoding information because the episode was so shocking. Others might have distorted the information and recalled the episode as being less traumatic than it actually was, in order to reduce their anxiety about what happened. Others, in discussing the traumatic event with various people, might have incorporated bits and pieces of these persons' recollections of what happened into their own version of the event.

In sum, memories of real-life traumas are usually more accurate and long-lasting than memories of everyday events. However, memories of traumas are subject to some deterioration and distortion. In traumatic memories, the central part of the memory is almost always effectively remembered. Where distortion often arises is in the details of the traumatic episode.

Some cases of memory for personal trauma involve a mental disorder called *post-traumatic stress disorder,* which includes severe anxiety symptoms that can immediately follow the trauma or be delayed by months or even years until onset. This mental disorder can emerge as a consequence of exposure to any of several traumatic events, such as war, severe abuse (as in rape), and accidental disasters (such as a plane crash). The symptoms of this disorder can include "flashbacks" in which the individual relives the traumatic event in nightmares, or in an awake but dissociative-like state. They can also include difficulties with memory and concentration. We will have more to say about post-traumatic stress disorder in chapter 13 ("Abnormal Psychology").

Stress-related hormones likely play a role in memories that involve personal trauma. The release of stress-related hormones, which are signaled by the amgydala (see figure 7.14), likely account for some of the extraordinary longevity and vividness of emotional or traumatic experiences (Schacter, 1996).

Repressed Memories The emotional blows of personal trauma can produce distortions of memory or vivid reenactments of the event in memory. In the case of post-traumatic stress disorder, the event might be pushed beneath awareness only

Event	Percentage
A car accident you were in or witnessed	85
When you first met your roommate at Duke	82
The night of your high school graduation	81
The night of your senior prom (if you went or not)	78
An early romantic experience	77
A time you had to speak in front of an audience	72
When you got your admissions letter from Duke	65
Your first date—the moment you met him/her	57

The numbers refer to the percentages of university students who said these events triggered memories of "flashbulb" quality.

Figure 7.18
University Students' Flashbulb Memories
The numbers refer to the percentages of university students who said these events triggered memories of "flashbulb" quality.

Memory under Stress

Repressed Memories

False and Recovered Memories

EXPLORATIONS IN PSYCHOLOGY
Repressed Memories, Child Abuse, and Reality

THERE HAS BEEN a dramatic increase in reported memories of childhood sexual abuse that were allegedly repressed for many years. This increase corresponds with the growing understanding that the sexual abuse of children is, and has been, a massive problem in Canada (Gunn & Linden, 1994) as well as in the United States.

In 1991, popular actress Roseanne was on the cover of *People* magazine. She reported that her mother had been abusing her from the time Roseanne was an infant until she was 6 or 7 years of age, but that she had become aware of the abuse only recently during therapy. Other highly publicized cases of repressed memories of child abuse coming into awareness during therapy dot the pages of popular magazines and self-help books.

There is little doubt that actual childhood abuse is tragically common. Memory experts such as Elizabeth Loftus (1993b) and others (Kutchinsky, 1992) don't dispute that child abuse is a serious problem. What they take issue with is the way therapists get their clients to recall abuse. Therapists might help their clients to reconstruct a memory that is not real. Some clients who originally claimed they were abused have later recanted their accusations, blaming their abuse report on the therapist's leading inquiries (Belicki & others, 1993).

Few research studies offer convincing evidence about the extent to which repression of abuse actually occurs. At present, there are no satisfactory methods that can help us discover the answer. Although Loftus has demon-

Roseanne said that her mother abused her from the time she was an infant until she was 6 or 7 years old. Why have many psychologists questioned some of the reports of activation of repressed memories, such as Roseanne's?

strated the ease with which memories can be implanted in unsuspecting individuals, her critics say that her research might not accurately capture the actual trauma that occurs in abuse episodes.

Therapists and their clients are left with the chilling possibility that not all abuse memories recovered in therapy are real. In the absence of corroboration, some recollections might be authentic and others might not be.

According to Loftus (1993b), psychotherapists, counselors, social service agencies, and law enforcement personnel need to be careful about probing for horrors on the other side of some amnesiac barrier. They should be cautious in their interpretation of uncorroborated repressed memories that return later. Corroboration through other methods such as analyzing the sleep patterns and dreams of those who have possibly been sexually traumatized is another promising route (Belicki & Cuddy, 1996).

There is a final tragic risk involved in suggestive probing and uncritical acceptance of all allegations made by clients. These activities increase the probability that society in general will disbelieve the actual cases of child abuse that deserve extensive attention and evaluation. In general, any careless or uncritical acceptance of unreplicated findings in psychology, especially when they have a colorful element that attracts media attention, harms public attitudes toward the contributions of psychological research (Bruck & Ceci, 1999).

to reappear in vivid flashbacks months or even years later. Repression takes place when something shocking happens and the mind pushes all memory of the occurrence into some inaccessible part of the unconscious mind. At some later point, the memory might emerge in consciousness, as in the case of post-traumatic stress disorder.

In psychoanalytic theory, which we initially discussed in chapter 1, repression's main function is to protect the individual from threatening information. Repression doesn't erase a memory, it just makes it extremely difficult to remember it consciously. To read further about repressed memories, see Explorations in Psychology. We will have much more to say about repressed memories in our discussion of psychoanalytic theories in chapter 12 ("Personality") and chapter 14 ("Therapies").

Mood-Congruent Memory   Another aspect of emotional memories involves **mood-congruent memory,** *which means that people tend to remember information better when their mood is similar at encoding and retrieval.* Researchers have found that when people are in sad moods they are more likely to remember negative experiences, like failure and rejection, and that when they are in happy moods they are more likely to remember positive experiences, like success and acceptance (Mineka & Nugent, 1995). Unfortunately, for people who are depressed this means that they are likely to recall negative experiences, which only perpetuates their depression.

Now that we have studied many aspects of how we retrieve information, especially in the form of autobiographical and emotional memories, we turn our attention to why we forget.

Forgetting

Why do we forget? One of psychology's pioneers had some thoughts about this.

Ebbinghaus' Pioneering Research on Forgetting   Hermann Ebbinghaus (1850–1909), was the first individual to conduct scientific research on forgetting. In 1885, Ebbinghaus studied his own forgetting. He invented *nonsense syllables,* meaningless materials that are uncontaminated by prior learning. Examples of these consonant-vowel-consonant nonsense syllables include: *zeq, xid, lek, vut,* and *riy.* Ebbinghaus memorized a list of thirteen such nonsense syllables and then assessed how many of them he could remember. Even just one day later, he could only recall a few of the syllables. Ebbinghaus concluded that the most forgetting takes place soon after we learn something.

If we forget so quickly, why put effort into learning something? Fortunately, researchers have demonstrated that forgetting is not so extensive as Ebbinghaus envisioned (Baddeley, 1992). Ebbinghaus studied meaningless nonsense syllables. When we memorize more meaningful material, such as poetry, history, or the type of material in this text, forgetting is not so rapid and extensive. Let's now turn to some theories of why our long-term memory is vulnerable to forgetting.

Interference and Decay   Interference and decay have been proposed as two reasons people forget. **Interference theory** *states that we forget not because memories are actually lost from storage, but because other information gets in the way of what we want to remember.*

There are two kinds of interference: proactive and retroactive. **Proactive interference** *occurs when material that was learned earlier disrupts the recall of material learned later.* Remember that *pro-* means "forward in time." For example, suppose you had a good friend 10 years ago named *Mary,* and last night you met someone at a party named *Marie.* You might find yourself calling your new friend *Mary* because the old information *(Mary)* interferes with retrieval of new information *(Marie).* **Retroactive interference** *occurs when material learned later disrupts retrieval of information learned earlier.* Remember that *retro-* means "backward in time." Suppose you have become friends with *Marie* (and finally have gotten her name straight). If you find yourself sending a letter to your old friend *Mary,* you might address it to *Marie* because the new information *(Marie)* interferes with the old information *(Mary)* (see figure 7.19).

Proactive and retroactive interference *both* might be explained by cue-dependent forgetting. The reason *Mary* interferes with *Marie,* and the name *Marie* interferes with the name *Mary,* might be that the cue you are using to remember does not distinguish between the two memories. For example, if the cue you were using was "my good friend," it might evoke both names. This could result in retrieving the wrong name, or in a kind of blocking in which each name interferes with the other and neither comes to mind. Memory researchers have shown that retrieval cues (like *friend* in our example) can become overloaded, and when that happens we are likely to forget or to retrieve incorrectly.

Hermann Ebbinghaus (1850–1909) was the first psychologist to conduct scientific research on forgetting. What was the nature of this research?

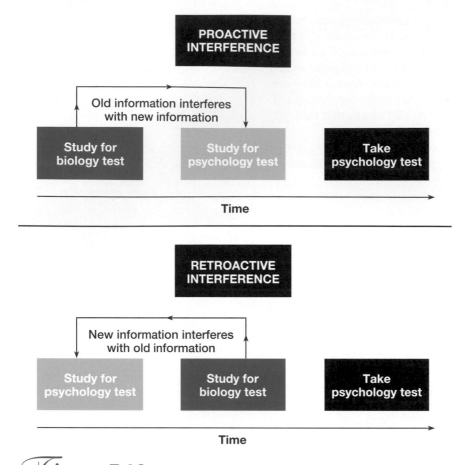

Although interference is involved in forgetting, it is not the whole story. **Decay theory** *states that when something new is learned, a neurochemical "memory trace" is formed, but over time this trace tends to disintegrate.* Decay theory suggests that the passage of time always increases forgetting. However, there is one circumstance in which older memories can be stronger than more recent ones. Older memories are sometimes more resistant to shocks or physical assaults on the brain than recent memories.

Amnesia   Consider the case of H. M. At the age of 27, H. M. underwent surgery to stop his epileptic seizures and emerged with his intelligence and most of his mental abilities intact, but the part of his brain that was responsible for laying down new memories (the hippocampus) was damaged beyond repair. This damage resulted in **amnesia,** *the loss of memory.* Although some types of amnesia clear up over time, H. M.'s amnesia endured. In the years following surgery, H. M.'s memory showed no improvement (Milner, Corkin & Teuber, 1968). The amnesia suffered by H. M. was anterograde in nature. **Anterograde amnesia** *is a memory disorder that affects the retention of new information or events.* What was learned before the onset of the condition is not affected. For example, H. M. could identify his friends, recall their names, and even tell stories about them—but only if he had known them before surgery. People who met H. M. after surgery remained virtual strangers, even if they spent thousands of hours with him. Most of H. M.'s postsurgical experiences were never encoded in his long-term memory. Oddly enough, H. M.'s short-term memory remained unchanged.

Amnesia also occurs in a second form, known as **retrograde amnesia,** *which involves memory loss for a segment of the past but not for new events.* It is much more common than anterograde amnesia, and frequently occurs when the brain is assaulted by an electrical shock or a physical blow—such as a head injury to a football player. The key difference from anterograde amnesia is that the forgotten information is *old* (prior to the event that caused the amnesia), and the person's ability to acquire new memories is not affected.

At this point we have studied many ideas about retrieval and forgetting. A summary of these ideas is presented in summary table 7.3. Next, we focus on another important dimension of memory—how we can improve it.

ℱigure 7.19
Proactive and Retroactive Interference

Pro- means "forward"; in proactive interference, old information has a forward influence by getting in the way of new material learned. *Retro-* means "backward"; in retroactive interference, new information has a backward influence by getting in the way of material learned earlier.

Amnesia

Exploring Amnesia

Ontario resident K.C. suffered a motorcycle accident which left him with an amazing form of retrograde amnesia. While K.C. could remember most of his general knowledge of the world, he lost pretty well everything he had ever known about his own past and never recovered it. That is, he had lost his episodic memory, but not his semantic memory, thus providing strong evidence in support of this distinction, which was advanced by Tulving (1972).

SUMMARY TABLE 7.3
Memory Retrieval and Forgetting

Concept	Processes/ Related Ideas	Characteristics/Description
Retrieval from Long-Term Memory	Tip-of-the-Tongue Phenomenon	This occurs when we can't quite pull something out of memory. The implication is that without good retrieval cues, information stored in memory is hard to find.
	Serial Position Effect	This influences retrieval, which is superior for items at the beginning of a list (primacy effect) and at the end of a list (recency effect).
	Retrieval Cues and the Retrieval Task	A key factor that makes retrieval effortful is the absence of effective cues. A second factor is the nature of the retrieval task, which, along with the presence or absence of retrieval cues, distinguishes recall and recognition memory. The encoding specificity principle states that associations formed at the time of encoding or learning tend to be effective retrieval cues. Retrieval also benefits from priming, which involves activating particular connections or associations in memory. In many cases, the associations are unconscious.
Autobiographical Memory	Its Nature	This refers to a person's recollections of his or her life experiences. Autobiographical memory has three levels: (1) life time periods, (2) general events, and (3) event-specific knowledge. Biographies of the self can connect the past and the present to form a portrait of our identity.
Emotional Memories	Flashbulb Memories	These are memories of emotionally significant events that people often recall with considerable accuracy and vivid imagery. Although flashbulb memories typically are more vivid and durable than memories for everyday events, they are subject to some deterioration and change.
	Personal Trauma	Memory for personal traumas is also usually more accurate than memory for ordinary events, but it too is subject to some distortion and inaccuracy. People tend to remember the core information about a personal trauma but might distort some of the details. Some cases of personal trauma result in post-traumatic stress disorder. The release of stress-related hormones, which are signaled by the amygdala, likely accounts for some of the extraordinary longevity and vividness of emotional or traumatic experiences.
	Repressed Memories	Personal trauma can cause individuals to repress emotionally laden information so that it is not accessible to the awareness of their conscious mind. Repression doesn't erase a memory, it just makes it extremely difficult to remember consciously.
	Mood-Congruent Memory	This principle states that people tend to remember information better when their mood is similar during encoding and retrieval.
Forgetting	Ebbinghaus' Pioneering Research on Forgetting	In 1885, Hermann Ebbinghaus tested his own memory of nonsense syllables. He discovered that his forgetting was rapid and extensive. However, researchers have found that we forget less than Ebbinghaus envisioned, especially when we learn meaningful material.
	Interference and Decay	Interference and decay have been proposed as two reasons people forget. Interference theory states that we forget, not because memories are actually lost from storage, but because other information gets in the way of what we want to remember. In proactive interference, material that was learned earlier disrupts the recall of material learned later. In retroactive interference, material learned later disrupts the retrieval of information that was learned earlier. Decay theory argues that when something new is learned, a memory trace is formed but, as time passes, this trace tends to deteriorate.
	Amnesia	Amnesia involves extreme memory deficits and comes in two forms. Anterograde amnesia is a memory disorder that prevents the retention of new information and events. Retrograde amnesia is a memory disorder that involves memory loss for a segment of the past but not for new events.

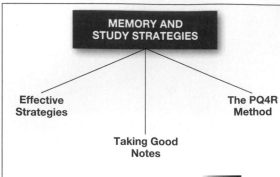

Memory Strategies
Memory Techniques

Memory and Study Strategies

Using the right memory and study strategies can help you improve your academic performance. Let's explore some of these strategies.

Effective Strategies

Effective memory and study strategies include paying attention, understanding the material, organizing, using mnemonics, asking yourself questions, spreading out and consolidating learning, cognitively monitoring your progress, and managing your time effectively.

Pay Attention and Minimize Distraction
Paying attention helps you remember something. If you want to remember something, give it your undivided attention. Monitor how well you pay attention. If you find yourself getting distracted, say a cue word or phrase like "Focus" or "Zero in" to yourself to increase your attention.

Understand the Material Rather Than Memorizing It By Rote
You will remember information over the long term if you understand it rather than just rehearsing and memorizing it by rote. Rehearsal works well for encoding information into short-term memory, but when you need to retrieve the information from long-term memory it is much less efficient. So, for most information, understand it, give it meaning, elaborate on it, and personalize it.

Organize What You Put Into Memory
You will remember information better if you organize it hierarchically. Arrange information, rework material, and give it a structure to help you remember it.

Use Mnemonic Strategies
Mnemonics *are specific memory aids for remembering information.* Mnemonic strategies can involve imagery and/or words. Following are three types of mnemonics:

- The **method of loci** *is a mnemonic strategy in which you develop an image of items to be remembered and store them in familiar locations (which is what "loci" means).* Rooms of houses or stores on a street are common locations used in this memory strategy. For example, if you need to remember a list of concepts, you can mentally place them in the rooms of a house you are familiar with, such as foyer, living room, dining room, kitchen, and so on. Then, when you need to retrieve the information, you imagine the house, mentally go through the rooms, and retrieve the concepts.
- *Acronyms* (creating a word from the first letters of items to be remembered) also can be used as a mnemonic strategy. For example, *Homes* can be used for remembering the Great Lakes: *H*uron, *O*ntario, *M*ichigan, *E*rie, and *S*uperior. Do you recall the acronym we used in chapter 4 to remember the colors in the light spectrum? It was an imaginary man named *ROY G. BIV* (*R*ed, *O*range, *Y*ellow, *G*reen, *B*lue, *I*ndigo, and *V*iolet).
- The **keyword method** *is a mnemonic strategy in which vivid imagery is attached to important words.* This method is often used for learning foreign vocabulary. Although the keyword method may sound complicated, by connecting vivid images of the words in questions, learning is made much easier.

Figure 7.20
The Keyword Method

The keyword method can be used to help you learn foreign vocabulary. To learn an association between the English *truck* and the French *camion,* you might notice that *camion* starts with the same sound as *camel,* and associate the keyword *camel* with a truck in an image, say, of a camel pulling a truck. Later, *camel* would provide a cue to retrieve *camion.*

Many experts on memory and study skills recommend that mnemonics be used mainly when you need to remember a list of items or specific facts. However, in most cases, memory for understanding is preferred over rote memorization.

Ask Yourself Questions

When you ask yourself questions about what you have read or an activity in class, you expand the number of associations you make with the information you need to retrieve. This self-questioning strategy can help you to remember. As you read, periodically stop and ask yourself questions, such as "What is the meaning of what I just read?" "Why is this important?" and "What is an example of the concept I just read?"

Spread Out and Consolidate Your Learning

Regularly review what you learn. You will benefit by distributing your learning over a longer period rather than cramming for a test at the last minute. Cramming tends to produce short-term memory that is processed in a shallow rather than a deep manner. A final, concentrated tune-up before the test instead of struggling to learn everything at the last minute is desirable (Halonen & Santrock, 1999).

Cognitively Monitor Your Progress

Cognitive monitoring *involves taking stock of your progress in an activity such as reading or studying.* For example, you might make sure that you summarize what you have read and restudy those parts of the material that were unclear. Also, if you are writing a paper for a course you will want to cognitively monitor your progress in terms of having the right resources to draw on, as well as having enough time to write a first draft and revise it one or more times.

Be a Good Time Manager and Planner

Managing your time effectively and planning out the necessary time to study will give you the hours you need to do well academically. How many hours a week do you spend studying for each hour you are in class? Study skills experts report that students who make high grades typically spend a minimum of two, and in many cases three, hours studying out of class for every hour they are in class. That means if you are in class 15 hours, you should be managing your time to study 30 to 45 hours outside of class each week if you want to make high grades.

THINKING ABOUT PSYCHOLOGY AND LIFE

Memory and Study Strategies

CANDIDLY RESPOND to the following items about your own memory and study strategies. Rate yourself 1 = never, 2 = some, 3 = moderate, 4 = almost always, and 5 = always. Then total your points.

	1	2	3	4	5
1. I'm good at focusing my attention and minimizing distractions.					
2. I study for understanding rather than memorizing material by rote.					
3. I organize information hierarchically as part of my memory strategies.					
4. I use mnemonic strategies when I have to memorize lists or specific facts.					
5. I ask myself questions about what I have read or about class activities.					
6. I spread out my studying and consolidate my learning.					
7. I cognitively monitor what I read and study.					
8. I am a good time manager and planner.					
9. I have a good note-taking system.					
10. I regularly review my notes.					
11. I use the PQ4R or a similar study system.					

TOTAL: _____

If you scored 50 to 55 points, you likely use good memory and study strategies. If you scored 45 to 49 points, you likely have some reasonably good memory and study strategies. If you scored below 45, spend some time working on improving your memory and study strategies. Most colleges and universities have a study skills center where specialists can help you.

Taking Good Notes

Taking good notes either from a lecture or a text benefits your memory. Don't write down everything the instructor says. It is impossible to do this anyway and it can prevent you from getting the big picture of what the instructor is communicating. Some good note-taking strategies include these:

- *Summarizing.* In this method, you listen for a few minutes and then write down the main idea that the instructor is trying to get across in that time frame. Then you listen for several more minutes and write down another idea, and so on.

SUMMARY TABLE 7.4
Memory and Study Strategies

Concept	Processes/ Related Ideas	Characteristics/Description
Effective Strategies	Memory and Study Strategies	These include paying attention and minimizing distraction, understanding the material rather than rotely memorizing it, organizing what you put into memory, using mnemonic strategies, asking yourself questions, spreading out and consolidating your learning, engaging in cognitive monitoring, as well as being a good time manager and planner.
Taking Good Notes	Its Nature	Don't take down everything the instructor says. Use a systematic strategy such as summarizing, outlining, concept maps, or the Cornell method. Get into the habit of reviewing your notes periodically.
The PQ4R Method	Its Nature	This system involves: Preview, Question, Read, Reflect, Recite, and Review.

- *Outlining.* You can outline what the instructor is saying, along the lines of how every chapter in this book is organized with "A"-level heads being the main topics, "B"-level heads as subtopics under the "A" heads, and "C"-level heads under the "B" heads.
- *Concept maps.* You can draw concept maps of what an instructor is saying, much like the concept maps you have studied at the end of each chapter in this book. The concept maps are similar to outlines but visually portray information in a spider-like format.
- *The Cornell Method.* Yet another note-taking strategy is the Cornell Method. It involves dividing an 8 1/2 × 11 sheet of paper into two columns by drawing a line down the page about 1/4 to 1/3 of the way from the left edge. You write your notes on the right 2/3 to 3/4 of the page. When you review your notes, you can then make notations and comments about the notes on the left side, which personalizes them for better understanding and retrieval.
- An excellent strategy is to get into the habit of reviewing your notes periodically rather than waiting to study them at the last minute before a test. Take a few minutes to review your notes just after a lecture if possible. This helps you to fill in information you might have missed but is still in your memory. And this strategy helps you to consolidate your learning.

The PQ4R Method

Various systems have been developed to help students remember information that they are studying. One of the earliest systems was called *SQ3R*, which stands for *Survey, Question, Read, Recite,* and *Review.* A more recently developed system is called **PQ4R,** *which stands for Preview, Question, Read, Reflect, Recite, and Review.* Thus, the PQ4R system adds an additional step to the SQ3R system: Reflect. This system can benefit you by getting you to meaningfully organize information, ask questions about it, reflect on it and think about it, and review it.

At this point we have discussed many ideas about memory and study strategies. An overview of these strategies is presented in summary table 7.4. In the next chapter, we continue our exploration of psychology's cognitive areas by studying thinking and language.

"You simply associate each number with a word, such as 'lipoprotein' and 3,467,009."

©Sidney Harris

Overview

WE BEGAN THIS CHAPTER by examining the nature of memory, evaluating what memory is and exploring memory's remarkable abilities and imperfections. Our coverage of memory encoding focused on rehearsal, deep processing, elaboration, imagery, and organization. We studied these aspects of memory storage: time frames, contents, representation, and neurological basis. We read about memory retrieval and forgetting, including ideas on retrieval from long-term memory, autobiographical memory, emotional memories, and forgetting. We discussed these dimensions of memory and study strategies: effective strategies, taking good notes, and the PQ4R method.

Don't forget that you can obtain a more detailed view of the chapter material by again studying the four summary tables on pages 223, 236, 245, and 248.

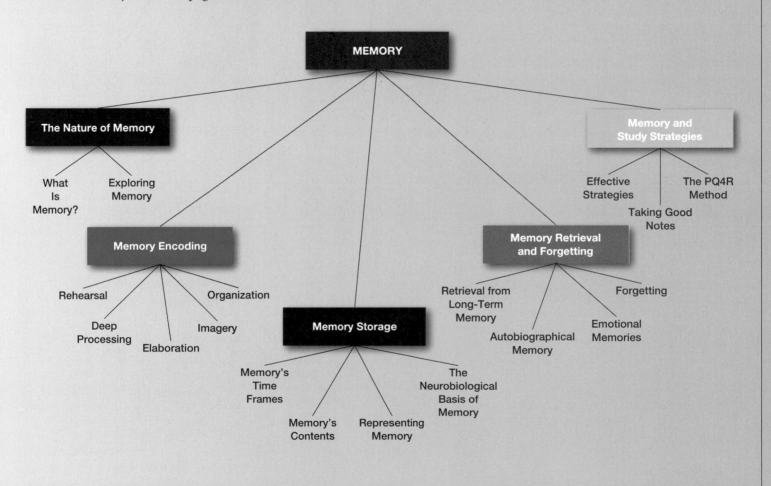

Key Terms

memory 218
encoding 219
storage 219
retrieval 219
rehearsal 219
levels of processing theory 220
elaboration 220
chunking 222
Atkinson-Shiffrin theory 224
sensory memory 224
echoic memory 225

iconic memory 225
working memory 225
memory span 226
long-term memory 226
declarative memory 227
nondeclarative memory 227
episodic memory 228
semantic memory 228
schema 230
script 233
tip-of-the-tongue (TOT) phenomenon 236

serial position effect 237
primacy effect 237
recency effect 237
recall 238
recognition 238
encoding specificity principle 238
priming 238
autobiographical memory 239
flashbulb memories 240
mood-congruent memory 243
interference theory 243

proactive interference 243
retroactive interference 243
decay theory 244
amnesia 244
anterograde amnesia 244
retrograde amnesia 244
mnemonics 246
method of loci 246
keyword method 246
cognitive monitoring 247
PQ4R 248

Key People

Fergus Craik and Robert Lockhart 220
Allan Paivio 221
Gordon Bower 222
Richard Atkinson and Richard Shiffrin 224

George Sperling 225
George Miller 226
Alan Baddeley 226
Endel Tulving 228

Sir Frederick Bartlett 230
John Yuille 232
Karl Lashley 233
Larry Squire 233

Eric Kandel and James Schwartz 233
Elizabeth Loftus 242
Hermann Ebbinghaus 243

Psychology Checklist

How much have you learned since the beginning of the chapter? Use the following statements to help you review your knowledge and understanding of the chapter material. First, read the statement and mentally or briefly demonstrate on paper that you understand and can discuss the relevant information.

_____ I can describe the basic nature of memory.
_____ I know how memories get encoded, including rehearsal, deep processing, elaboration, imagery, and organization.
_____ I can discuss memory's time frames, including the theory of three time frames.
_____ I can describe the nature of memory's contents.
_____ I know what declarative and nondeclarative memory are.
_____ I an evaluate how memory is represented.

_____ I can describe the neurobiological basis of memory.
_____ I know how memories are represented.
_____ I can discuss how people retrieve memories.
_____ I can describe autobiographical memory.
_____ I can evaluate emotional memories.
_____ I understand why people forget.
_____ I can describe the nature of amnesia.
_____ I know some good memory and study strategies.

For any items that you did not check off, go back and locate the relevant material in the chapter. Review the material until you feel that you can check off the item. You may want to use the checklist later in preparing for an exam.

Taking It to the Net

1. Have you ever used a rhyme or acronym to remember something for a test? These memory techniques are called mnemonics and they can be used to remember many different things. To illustrate the power of mnemonics, complete the rhyme, "Thirty days hath September, April, June, and November . . ." Do you think items learned with mnemonics are more enduring than items learned without such techniques? Describe the fundamental principles underlying the use of mnemonics.

2. Imagine you have just started a new job as a server in a restaurant. On your first day, you meet all of your friendly co-workers. Unfortunately, there are so many names you must remember, you begin to feel overwhelmed. Between the busboys, the cooks, the hostess, and the other servers, there are more than twenty names to remember. So, being a keen psychology student, you apply your knowledge of memory techniques to name/face recognition. Explain how you tackle this problem and what methods you use.

3. In the popular media, amnesia is most often associated with some kind of head injury. For instance, after a car accident, someone might forget the events leading up to the accident. They might even forget personal information, such as their name, the date, or their children's names. However, amnesia can occur as a result of events other than head injury. Stress, for instance, can lead to amnesia. Can you explain the process of how stress affects memory? What about trauma? Why do some trauma victims remember detailed events of the traumatic event while others recall nothing?

Connect to http://www.mcgrawhill.ca/college/santrock to find the answers!

Resources for Psychology and Life

The Oxford Handbook of Memory (in press)
  by Endel Tulving and Fergus Craik (Eds.)
  New York: Oxford University Press
By the time you read this, Tulving and Craik's book will have been published. Edited by two giants of memory research in Canada, this book epitomizes memory research as we move into the new millennium.

Searching for Memory (1996)
  by Daniel Schacter
  New York: Basic Books
This book, written by one of the memory field's leading researchers, provides numerous insights about memory. Chapters cover such high-interest topics as emotional memories, autobiographical memories, and amnesia.

Human Memory (1998, Rev. Ed.)
  by A. Baddeley
  Boston: Allyn & Bacon
Baddeley extensively reviews research on memory to support the development of his working memory model.

Remembering Our Past (1995)
  by David Rubin (ed.)
  New York: Cambridge
A number of contributors describe many dimensions of autobiographical memory.

Psychological Factors in Eyewitness Identification (1995)
  by Siegried Sporer, Roy Malpass, and Guenter Koehnken (eds.)
  Hillsdale, NJ: Erlbaum
Researchers from different fields address a variety of issues involving eyewitness identification.

Memory and Cognition
This research journal publishes articles on many aspects of memory and cognition.

Basic and Applied Memory Research, Vols. I and II (1996)
  by Douglas Hermann, Cathy McEvoy, Chris Hertzog, Paula Hertel, and Marcia Johnson (eds.)
  Hillsdale, NJ: Erlbaum
A wide array of topics in basic and applied memory research are evaluated.

The Myth of Repressed Memory (1994)
  by Elizabeth Loftus
  New York: St. Martin's Press
An accessible treatment of the dangers of using recovered memories in sexual abuse cases.

Fragment by Fragment: Feminist Perspectives on Memory and Child Sexual Abuse (in press)
  by M. Rivera (Ed.)
This book is worth reading in partial counterpoint to the Loftus book mentioned above.

Chapter 8

CHAPTER OUTLINE

THE COGNITIVE REVOLUTION IN PSYCHOLOGY

THINKING

What Is Thinking?

Forming Concepts

Solving Problems

Thinking Critically, Reasoning, and Making Decisions

LANGUAGE

What Is Language?

Biological and Environmental Influences

How Language Develops

Can Animals Use Language to Express Thought?

Language, Culture, and Cognition

Thinking and Language

Images of Psychology and Life
The Human Versus Big Blue, Cog, and CYC

Preview

THIS CHAPTER BUILDS on our earlier discussions of perception (Chapter 4), consciousness (Chapter 5), learning (Chapter 6), and memory (Chapter 7), each of which introduced important dimensions of cognitive psychology. We are now ready to explore how we think and use language, which are also central topics in cognitive psychology. These are some of the questions we will explore in this chapter:

• What is the cognitive revolution in psychology?
• How do people form concepts and solve problems?
• What are some obstacles to solving problems?
• What are some good strategies for thinking critically and making decisions?
• What is language and how does it develop?
• What are the best ways to talk to babies?
• Is there a best way to teach children to read?
• Do animals have language?

WHEN THE RUSSIAN chess champion Gary Kasparov faced off against an IBM computer named "Big Blue" in a celebrated chess match, he wasn't just after fame and money. By his own account, he was playing for me, you, and every member of the human species. He was trying, as he said, to "help defend our dignity."

Kasparov has competed against Big Blue on several occasions. In 1996, he barely escaped defeat. In 1997, he was not so fortunate. The computer won two games to one, with two matches ending in draws. Even Kasparov acknowledged that the computer had played a "humanlike" game.

Can machines like Big Blue actually "think" (Wright, 1996)? No one doubts Big Blue's chess skills, but at issue is whether it is a *thinking machine*. It uses "brute force" by computing zillions of calculations to arrive at decisions. On the topic of brute force, one organizer of an exclusively human chess tournament commented that you don't invite forklifts to weight-lifting competitions. Although relying on an almost

The Russian chess champion Gary Kasparov tied IBM's Big Blue in 1996, but in 1997, Big Blue (with its computing power doubled) sent Kasparov down to defeat.

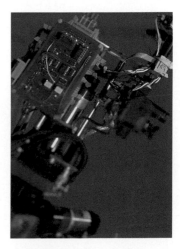

With eight Macintosh-type processors for a brain, Cog tries to learn the way human infants do. Can machines like this actually "think?"

253

endless number of mechanical rules, Big Blue also used some chess programs that sized up the state of play and reasoned strategically from there.

Rodney Brooks, a professor at MIT, built a computer and nicknamed it "Cog" (Dibbell, 1996). It is a vaguely person-shaped concoction of metal, plastic, and silicon, with cameras where eyes should be and eight 32-bit microprocessors for a brain. Brooks is trying to get Cog to learn about the world the way human babies do, programming and reprogramming itself through interactions with people and objects around it. One of Brooks' goals is to someday have a conversation with Cog about nothing in particular.

Douglas Lenant, who works at an artificial intelligence systems firm in Austin, Texas, has similar hopes for his brainchild, a sprawling data-rich computer program called CYC (as in enCYClopedic). While Brooks tries to get Cog to teach itself about the world, Lenant has already programmed more than a million rules into CYC. He types these into CYC's memory one assertion ("Bread is food," "You're wet when you sweat") at a time. He doesn't want to have to do this spoon-feeding forever. Ultimately, he hopes CYC will digest an encyclopedia whole and ask questions about whatever it doesn't understand.

The effort to build machines that think is more than four decades old now. Lenant's ideas represent one strategy in this effort, Brooks' another. Cog is a member of the bottom-up school. Inspired more by biological structures than by logical ones, the bottom-uppers don't bother trying to enter the rules of thought into their intelligent machines. Rather, they try to generate thought by building lots of small, simple programs and encouraging them to interact. There's no one place in Cog that you can point to as the seat of intelligence. Brooks says, "There's no there, there."

Lenant's approach follows the belief that symbolic knowledge makes the mind go round. That is, if you enter into the machine the logical structures through which we understand the world, you are on the road to recreating intelligence.

At present, neither Cog nor CYC has reached its creator's goal of mimicking human thinking. However, with the dramatic increase in machines' abilities, some researchers in this area believe that such efforts will lead to the creation of an intelligence that not only is different from our own, but more intelligent.

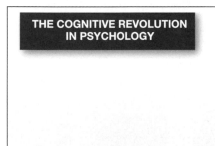

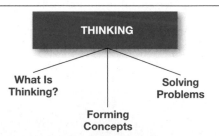

The Cognitive Revolution in Psychology

Behaviorism was a dominant force in psychology until the late 1950s and 1960s, when many psychologists began to realize that they could not understand or explain human behavior without making reference to mental processes (Gardner, 1985). The term *cognitive psychology* became a label for approaches that sought to explain observable behavior by investigating mental processes and structures that cannot be directly observed (Benjafield, 1997; Best, 1999).

Although behaviorists like John B. Watson had argued that psychology could not be a legitimate "scientific" discipline unless it restricted itself to the study and description of directly observable events, proponents of the cognitive revolution argued that scientific explanations usually explain the observable using terms or concepts that cannot be directly observed. For example, Isaac Newton explained the behavior of falling objects using the concept of gravitational force, a force that could not be directly observed.

A number of factors stimulated the growth of cognitive psychology ◀ P. 11. Probably none was more important than the development of computers. The first modern computer, developed by John von Neumann in the late 1940s, showed that inanimate machines could perform logical operations. This indicated that some mental operations might be modeled by computers, possibly telling us something about

The Information-Processing Approach

the way cognition works (Hochberg, in press). Cognitive psychologists often use the computer as an analogy to help explain the relation between cognition and the brain (Kirlik & Bisantz, 1999). The physical brain is described as the computer's hardware, cognition as its software (see figure 8.1).

Although the development of computers played an important role in psychology's cognitive revolution, inanimate computers and human brains function quite differently in some respects (Restak, 1988). For example, each brain cell, or neuron, is alive and can be altered in its functioning by many types of events in its biological environment. Current attempts to simulate the brain greatly simplify the behavior of neurons. The brain derives information about the world through a rich system of visual, auditory, olfactory, gustatory, tactile, and vestibular sensory receptors. Most computers receive information from a human who has already coded the information and represented it in a way that removes much of the ambiguity in the natural world. Attempts to use computers to process visual information or spoken language have achieved only limited success in highly constrained situations where much of the natural ambiguity is removed. The human brain also has an incredible ability to learn new rules, relationships, concepts, and patterns that it can generalize to novel situations. In comparison, current approaches to artificial intelligence are quite limited in their ability to learn and generalize (Benjafield, 1997).

Computers can do some things better than humans. Computers can perform complex numerical calculations much faster and more accurately than humans could ever hope to. Computers can also apply and follow rules more consistently and

Through the Eyes of Psychologists

Herbert Simon, *Carnegie Mellon University*

"You couldn't use a word like mind *in a psychology journal or you would get your mouth washed out with soap."*
(Referring to the first half of the twentieth century)

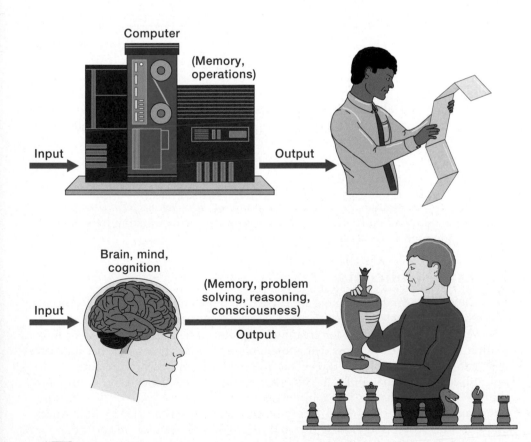

Figure 8.1
Computers and Human Cognition

An analogy is commonly drawn between the human cognition and the way computers work. The physical brain is analogous to a computer's hardware, and cognition (mental processes) is analogous to a computer's software.

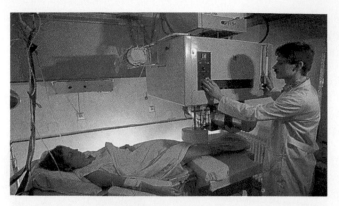

Artificial intelligence systems have been used to assist in medical diagnosis and treatment. What are some other ways they can be used?

with fewer errors than humans and represent complex mathematical patterns better than humans can. Although a computer can simulate certain types of learning that may improve its ability to recognize patterns or use rules of thumb to make decisions, it does not have the means to develop new learning goals. Furthermore, the human mind is aware of itself; the computer is not. Indeed, no computer is likely to approach the richness of human consciousness. In short, the brain's extraordinary capabilities will probably not be mimicked in a comprehensive manner by computers anytime in the near future.

The computer's role in cognitive psychology continues to increase, giving rise in recent years to a field called **artificial intelligence (AI)**, *the science of creating machines capable of performing activities that require intelligence when they are done by people.* AI is especially helpful in tasks requiring speed, persistence, and a vast memory (Hancock, 1999). For example, today we have chess-playing programs that can beat even the best players our species has to offer (as you saw in the Images section at the beginning of the chapter). Not only have these AI systems been applied to playing chess, but they have also been designed to assist in diagnosing medical illnesses and treatment, examining equipment failures, evaluating loan applicants, and advising students about which courses to take (Nickerson, 1999; Proctor, 1999).

Artificial intelligence systems attempt to mimic the way humans think (Dawson, 1998; Ellis & Humphreys, 1999). Next, we turn our attention to the way humans do their thinking.

Artificial Intelligence
Forming Concepts

Thinking

In earlier chapters, we studied how people perceive information (chapter 4, "Sensation and Perception") and how information is encoded, stored, and retrieved (chapter 7, "Memory"). Here we will study how we use this information when we think. To understand thinking, we will explore what it is, how concepts are formed, how problems can be solved, and different types of thinking, reasoning, and decision making.

What Is Thinking?

Thinking *involves mentally manipulating information, as when we form concepts, solve problems, reason, and make decisions.* We begin our tour of thinking by seeing why concepts are important and how they are formed.

Forming Concepts

Regardless of the kind of thinking we engage in, our thinking is fueled by **concepts,** *which are mental categories used to group objects, events, and characteristics.*

We have a special ability for creating categories to help us make sense of information in our world. We know that apples and oranges are fruits, but that they have different tastes and colors. We know that Porsches and Ford Escorts are automobiles, but also know that they differ in cost, speed, and prestige. How do we know these things? The answer lies in our ability to group them on the basis of their features. For example, Porsches and Ford Escorts have such things as an engine, four wheels, and a steering wheel, and provide transportation. By such features we know that they are both automobiles. In other words, we have a *concept* of what an automobile is.

Why are concepts important? If we did not have concepts, each object and event in our world would be unique to us. We would not be able to draw any kind of generalization. Concepts allow us to relate experiences and objects. Basketball, hockey, and track are sports. The concept of *sport* gives us a way to compare these activities. Neoclassicism, Impressionism, and Expressionism are all schools of art. The

Michelangelo's Libyan Sibyl, Sistine Chapel

Monet's "Palazzo Da Mula, Venice"

Figure 8.2
The Concept of Schools of Art

The concept of schools of art lets us compare paintings by different artists, such as these Neoclassicist, Impressionist, and Expressionist painters: Michelangelo (Neoclassicism), Monet (Impressionism), and Paul Klee (Expressionism).

Klee's "Dance You Monster to My Soft Song!"
Paul Klee, DANCE YOU MONSTER TO MY SOFT SONG!, 1972. Gift, Solomon R. Guggenheim, 1938. Photograph by Lee B. Ewing © The Solomon R. Guggenheim Foundation, New York. (FN 38.508)

concept *schools of art* lets us compare paintings by artists from these different schools (see figure 8.2).

Concepts grease the wheels of memory, making it more efficient so we don't have to "reinvent the wheel" each time we come across a piece of information. For example, we don't have to relearn what the Dow Jones Industrial Average is each time we pick up a newspaper. We already have the concept. Concepts also provide clues about how to react to an object or experience. For example, if we see a bowl of pretzels, our concept of food lets us know it is okay to eat them. Concepts allow us to associate classes of objects or events.

To further explore concept formation, suppose you are an avid tennis player but think your serve is weak. Paralleling the distinction between explicit and implicit memory discussed in the previous chapter, Lee Brooks (1978) of McMaster University has argued that concept learning may occur implicitly rather than explicitly. That is, your problem might be that you have only a vague concept of what a "killer" serve is really like. To get a feel for the concept you watch good players serve. Based on your observations, you develop an explicit hypothesis about the mechanics of an excellent serve. For example, you decide that the ball must be tossed high and that the server needs to swing the racket like a baseball pitcher throws an overhead pitch. You'll want to test the hypothesis in your own game to see if tossing the ball high and

Figure 8.3
When Is a Cup a "Cup"?

Which of these would you describe as the prototype for the concept "cup"? In one study, participants were most likely to choose number 5 (Labov, 1973). Some participants called number 4 a bowl and number 9 a vase because they were so different from the prototype.

swinging the racket like a baseball pitcher's overhead throw improves your serve.

Even though your tennis serve improves, chances are you'll still be somewhat dissatisfied. With a difficult concept (such as the mechanics of a good serve), you might need an expert—a professional tennis coach—to help you. The pro's concept is likely to include more features than the ones you discovered, as well as complex rules related to those features. For example, the pro might tell you that tossing the ball high helps, but that it works much better if you rotate the grip on your racket counterclockwise. In general, concepts with more features and more complicated rules are more difficult to learn. It is worth noting that someone may become an expert at, say, tennis, and yet be unable to explicitly describe how he or she does it. This explains why some experts are, nevertheless, poor coaches. The best coaches are those who can explicitly describe the complex rules underlying their expert knowledge of the field that they are in (Brooks, 1978).

Although psychologists have learned much about concept formation, some believe that the research has been too artificial. Eleanor Rosch (1973) argues that real-life concepts are less precise than those used in many psychology experiments. She says that real-life concepts often have "fuzzy boundaries." That is, it's not always clear exactly what features are critical to a concept. Consider the concept "cup." A little thought might suggest that cups (1) are concrete objects, (2) are concave, (3) can hold solids and liquids, (4) have handles, and (5) can be used to drink hot liquids. However, what about the cups in Chinese restaurants that don't have handles? And what about the poor-quality paper cups that conduct too much heat to be used for hot drinks? Although such objects lack certain "critical features" of cups, we still call them cups.

Rosch also believes that in considering how people think about concepts, prototypes (items that are typical of a category) are often involved. In **prototype matching**, *people decide whether an item is a member of a category by comparing it with the most typical item(s) of the category.* The more similar the item is to the prototype, the more likely a person will say it belongs in the category; the less similar, the more likely the person will judge that it doesn't belong in the category. For example, think of your concept of mountains: perhaps craggy and snow-covered like the Rocky Mountains. But some mountains, such the Laurentians, are not craggy at all. Thus, the Rockies are a more prototypical example of mountains than the Laurentians. When we consider the category of "mountain," we are more likely to use "Rockies" as the prototype than "Laurentians," despite the fact that many World Cup ski races have been held at Mont Sainte-Anne and Mont Tremblant. Nonetheless, members of a conceptual category can vary greatly and still have qualities that make them a member of that category. (See figure 8.3).

Solving Problems

It is impossible to solve problems without concepts. Think about driving, something many of us do every day. Signs and traffic signals every few blocks tell us to stop, yield, or proceed. Most of the symbols that keep traffic moving so smoothly are the brainchild of William Eno, the "father of traffic safety." Eno, born in New York City in 1858, became concerned about the horrendous traffic jams in the city. Horsedrawn vehicles were making street traffic dangerous. Eno published a paper about the urgency of street traffic reform. His proposed solutions to the problem created new concepts, such as the concepts "stop signs," "one-way streets," and "pedestrian islands," which continue to be important to traffic safety today (Bransford & Stein, 1993).

Like William Eno, we face many problems in the course of our everyday lives. These include trying to figure out the fastest way to get across town, planning how to get enough money to buy a CD player, working on a jigsaw puzzle, or estimating how much we owe in taxes. **Problem solving** *is an attempt to find an appropriate way of attaining a goal when the goal is not readily available.* Whatever the problem, we want to come up with the fastest and best solution possible. Next, we examine some steps in solving problems.

Steps in Solving Problems   Efforts have been made to specify the steps that individuals go through to solve problems effectively. Four such steps are (1) find and frame problems, (2) develop good problem-solving strategies, (3) evaluate solutions, (4) rethink and redefine problems and solutions over time.

(1) Find and Frame Problems   Before a problem can be solved, it has to be recognized. Identifying a key problem to solve is an important first step in problem solving (Mayer, 1999). Unfortunately, our society all too often discourages people from identifying problems. Many businesses, government agencies, and schools reprimand or fire employees who identify problems in the workplace. For example, increased incidences of cancer from asbestos might have been avoided if problems identified by employees had been acknowledged and acted on by people in authority. The pressure to ignore problems is so strong that the U.S. Congress finally passed a bill that provides protection for employees who are brave enough to persist in their fight to have the problems they identify recognized. It became known as the Whistle-Blower Protection Act.

Finding and framing problems often involves asking questions in creative ways (Goleman, Kaufman, & Ray, 1993). Bill Bowerman (inventor of Nike shoes) asked, "What happens if I pour rubber over a waffle iron?" Fred Smith (founder of Federal Express) asked, "Why can't there be reliable overnight mail service?" Godfrey Hounsfield (inventor of the CAT scan) asked, "Why can't we see what is inside the human body in three dimensions without cutting it open?" Masaru Ibuka (honorary chairman of Sony) asked, "Why don't we remove the recording function and speaker and put headphones on the player?"

Many of these questions were ridiculed at first. Other shoe companies thought Bowerman's waffle shoe was a "really stupid idea." Fred Smith proposed the idea of Federal Express during his days as a student at Yale and got a C on the paper. Godfrey Hounsfield was told that the CAT scan was impractical. And Masaru Ibuka was told, "A player without speakers—you must be crazy!"

In the past, most problem-solving exercises given to students have involved well-defined problems with well-defined definitions and operations for attaining the solutions. However, it is also important to learn to identify and deal with ill-defined problems. Many of life's real-world problems are ill-defined or vague, and don't have clearly defined ways of being solved. According to Sorrentino & Roney (1999), the ability to deal with vague situations, what they refer to as *uncertainty orientation,* is an important and unexplored personality characteristic. Consider the ill-defined problem of writing a paper for a psychology course. You have to proceed by narrowing down to a more specific problem such as deciding on the area of psychology (neuroscience, cognitive psychology, abnormal psychology, and so on) you will write about. You will then need to narrow your focus even further to find a specific problem within that area to write about, and so on. A good strategy is to weigh several specific alternatives before selecting one to write about. This type of exercise in finding and framing problems is an important aspect of problem solving.

(2) Develop Good Problem-Solving Strategies   Once you find a problem and clearly define it, you need to develop strategies for solving it. Among the effective strategies are setting subgoals, using algorithms, and utilizing heuristics.

Subgoaling *involves setting intermediate goals that put you in a better position of reaching the final goal or solution.* People might not solve a problem effectively because they don't generate subproblems or subgoals. Let's return to the problem of

Heuristics

THINKING ABOUT PSYCHOLOGY AND LIFE

The Candle, Nine-Dot, and Six-Matchstick Problems

The following three problems are often used to illustrate the concept of fixation in problem solving.

The Candle Problem

The problem here is how to mount a candle on a wall so that it won't drip wax on a table or floor while it is burning. How would you solve this problem?

The Nine-Dot Problem

Take out a piece of paper and copy the following arrangement of dots:

Without lifting your pencil, connect the dots using only four straight lines.

The Six-Matchstick Problem

The problem posed is: Given six matchsticks of equal length, arrange them to make four equilateral triangles, the sides of which are one stick long.

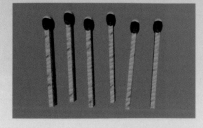

Solutions to the problems are presented at the end of the chapter.

writing a paper for a psychology course. What might be some subgoaling strategies? One might be locating the right books and research journals on the problem you have decided to study. At the same time you are searching for the right books and journals, you will likely benefit from establishing some subgoals in terms of what you need to accomplish along the way to your goal of a polished psychology paper. If the paper is due in two months, you might set a subgoal of a first draft of the paper two weeks before it is due, another subgoal of completing reading for the paper a month before it is due, and yet another subgoal of starting library research tomorrow.

Notice that in establishing the subgoals, we worked backward. Working backward in establishing subgoals is a good strategy. You first create a subgoal that is closest to the final goal and then work backward to the subgoal that is closest to the beginning of the problem-solving effort.

Algorithms *are strategies that guarantee a solution to a problem.* Algorithms come in different forms, such as using a formula, following a set of directions, or trying out all possible solutions. We often use algorithms in solving math problems by applying formulas, and when we follow the instructions to put something together, like a lawn chair or a table.

In some cases an algorithmic strategy might take a long time. Consider a person who is working on a crossword puzzle. She comes across c_nt_ _ker_ _ _ and looks to see what hint is given. It says, "Ill-tempered and quarrelsome." An algorithm for finding the correct word exists. She could try every possible alphabet combination in the six blank spaces and then check through a dictionary to see which one is correct. However, not many people would want to go through the more than one million steps in this algorithmic effort. Clearly, the algorithmic strategy of trying out all possible solutions should be applied to problems with a small number of possible solutions.

Instead of using an algorithm to solve this type of problem, most crossword-puzzle enthusiasts use **heuristics,** *which are strategies or rules of thumb that suggest a solution to a problem but do not guarantee an answer.* Thus, we know that certain combinations of letters are more likely to work than others. For example, in our attempt to find the correct word in the crossword puzzle, we know we need a vowel between *c* and *n*, so *b*, *q*, and a lot of other letters won't work. We also know that combinations of letters like *an* are acceptable between the *t* and *k*. We also know that it helps to sound out some words at this point. We come up with "contank" and "cantank." Then we get it: *cantankerous.*

In the real world, we are much more likely to face problems in which it is wise to use heuristics rather than algorithms. Heuristics help us narrow down the possible solutions to find the one that works.

(3) Evaluate Solutions Once we think we have solved a problem, we really won't know how effective our solution is until we find out if it actually works. It helps to have in mind a clear criterion for the effectiveness of the solution. For example, what will your criterion be for your psychology paper? Will it simply be getting it completed? receiving positive feedback on the paper? getting an A? having the instructor say that it is one of the best papers on the topic she has read?

(4) Rethink and Redefine Problems and Solutions over Time

An important final step in problem solving is to continually rethink and redefine problems (Bereiter & Scardamalia, 1993). People who are good at problem solving are more motivated to improve on their past performances and to make original contributions. Thus, you can examine the paper after it is returned by your instructor and use the feedback to think about ways to improve it. Sony continues to try to improve its Walkman, striving to make it lighter, smaller, and better sounding.

Obstacles to Solving Problems   Obstacles include becoming fixated and not being adequately motivated.

Becoming Fixated   It is easy to fall into the trap of becoming fixated on a particular strategy for solving a problem. **Fixation** *involves using a prior strategy and failing to look at a problem from a fresh, new perspective.* **Functional fixedness** *is one type of fixation in which individuals fail to solve a problem because they are fixated on a thing's usual functions.* If you have ever used a shoe to hammer a nail, you have overcome functional fixedness to solve a problem.

An example of a problem that requires overcoming functional fixedness is the Maier String Problem (Maier, 1931) (see figure 8.4). The problem is to figure out how to tie two strings together when they can't be reached at the same time and you must stand in one spot. If you hold one and then move it toward the other you cannot reach the second one. It seems as though you are stuck, but there is a pair of pliers on a table. Can you solve the problem?

The solution is to use the pliers as a weight, tying them to the end of one of the strings (see figure 8.5). Swing this string back and forth like a pendulum and grasp the stationary string. Your past experience with pliers makes this a difficult problem to solve. To solve the problem, you need to find a unique use for the pliers, in this case as a weight to create a pendulum.

Each of us occasionally gets into the mental rut of solving problems by using a particular strategy. A **mental set** *is a type of fixation in which an individual tries to solve a problem in a particular way that has worked in the past.* Both of us (the authors) had to overcome mental sets about using computers rather than typewriters for writing books. It took time to break out of the mental set of manual typing and subsequent manual spell-checking and editing. Once we did so, the problem goal of finishing a book became much easier. You might feel the same about some aspects of technology. A good strategy is to keep an open mind about such technological changes and monitor whether your mental set is keeping you from trying out new technology.

Lacking Motivation and Persistence   Individuals might have great problem-solving skills, but it hardly matters what talents they have if they are not motivated to use them (Sternberg & Spear-Swerling, 1996). It is especially important to be internally motivated to solve a problem and persist with effort at finding a solution. Some people give up too easily when they encounter a problem.

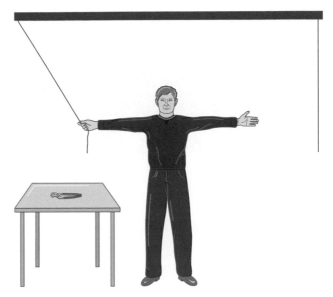

*F*igure 8.4
Maier String Problem
How can you tie the two strings together if you cannot reach them both at the same time?

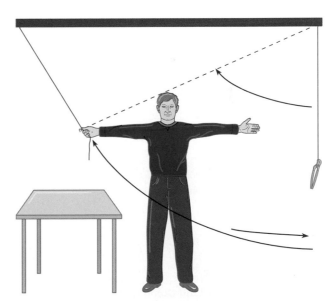

*F*igure 8.5
Solution to the Maier String Problem
Use the pliers as a weight to create a pendulum motion that brings the second string closer.

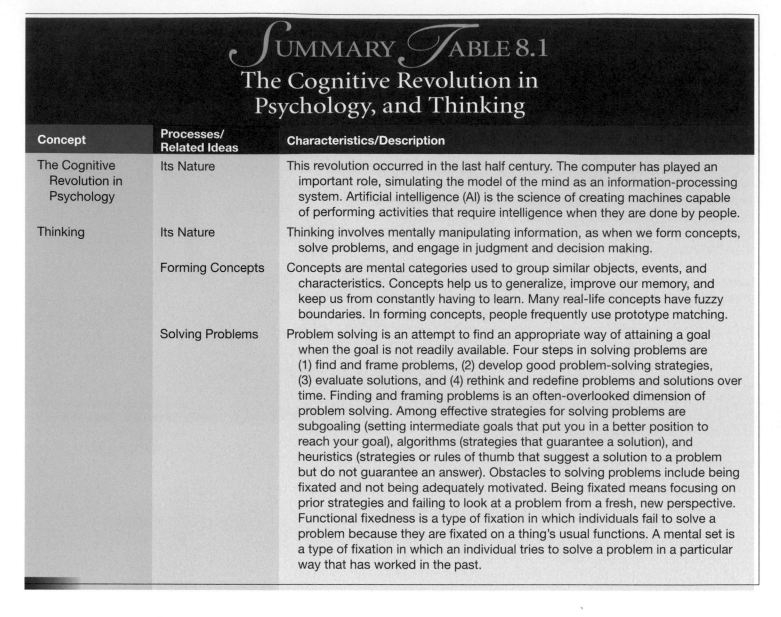

SUMMARY TABLE 8.1
The Cognitive Revolution in Psychology, and Thinking

Concept	Processes/Related Ideas	Characteristics/Description
The Cognitive Revolution in Psychology	Its Nature	This revolution occurred in the last half century. The computer has played an important role, simulating the model of the mind as an information-processing system. Artificial intelligence (AI) is the science of creating machines capable of performing activities that require intelligence when they are done by people.
Thinking	Its Nature	Thinking involves mentally manipulating information, as when we form concepts, solve problems, and engage in judgment and decision making.
	Forming Concepts	Concepts are mental categories used to group similar objects, events, and characteristics. Concepts help us to generalize, improve our memory, and keep us from constantly having to learn. Many real-life concepts have fuzzy boundaries. In forming concepts, people frequently use prototype matching.
	Solving Problems	Problem solving is an attempt to find an appropriate way of attaining a goal when the goal is not readily available. Four steps in solving problems are (1) find and frame problems, (2) develop good problem-solving strategies, (3) evaluate solutions, and (4) rethink and redefine problems and solutions over time. Finding and framing problems is an often-overlooked dimension of problem solving. Among effective strategies for solving problems are subgoaling (setting intermediate goals that put you in a better position to reach your goal), algorithms (strategies that guarantee a solution), and heuristics (strategies or rules of thumb that suggest a solution to a problem but do not guarantee an answer). Obstacles to solving problems include being fixated and not being adequately motivated. Being fixated means focusing on prior strategies and failing to look at a problem from a fresh, new perspective. Functional fixedness is a type of fixation in which individuals fail to solve a problem because they are fixated on a thing's usual functions. A mental set is a type of fixation in which an individual tries to solve a problem in a particular way that has worked in the past.

The Critical Thinking Community

At this point we have studied many ideas about the cognitive revolution and these aspects of thinking: its nature, forming concepts, and solving problems. An overview of these ideas is presented in summary table 8.1. Next, we continue our tour of thinking by examining different types of thinking, reasoning, and decision making.

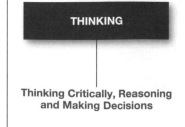

THINKING

Thinking Critically, Reasoning and Making Decisions

Thinking Critically, Reasoning, and Making Decisions

Aside from forming concepts and solving problems, other aspects of thinking include thinking critically, reasoning effectively, and making good decisions.

Thinking Critically   In chapter 1, we defined **critical thinking** *as thinking reflectively and productively and evaluating the evidence.* People who think critically grasp the deeper meaning of ideas, keep an open mind about different approaches and perspectives, and decide for themselves what to believe or do (Gardner, 1999; Runco, 1999). Critical thinking is currently of considerable interest to both psychologists and educators P. 22. However, critical thinking is not an entirely new idea. Educator John Dewey (1933) was working with a similar idea when he advocated teaching students to "think reflectively." Today, educators at all levels embrace the idea that an important outcome of education is to have students who think critically.

Jacqueline and Martin Brooks (1993) lament that so few schools teach students to think critically and develop a deep understanding of concepts. For example, many high school students read *Hamlet* but don't think deeply about it, never transforming their prior notions of power, greed, and relationships. Deep understanding occurs when people are stimulated to rethink their prior ideas.

In Brooks and Brooks' view, schools spend too much time on getting students to give a single correct answer in an imitative way rather than encouraging students to expand their thinking by coming up with new ideas and rethinking earlier conclusions. As we indicated in chapter 1, they believe that too often teachers ask students to recite, define, describe, state, and list rather than to analyze, infer, connect, synthesize, criticize, create, evaluate, think, and rethink. Too often we are inclined to stay on the surface of problems rather than stretching our minds and becoming deeply engaged in meaningful thinking (Bruning, Schraw, & Ronning, 1999).

Ellen Langer (1989, 1997; Moldoveanu & Langer, 1999) studies mindless behavior and encourages people to be more mindful. One of her favorite examples of mindless behavior involves the time she used a new credit card in a department store. The clerk noticed that she had not signed it and handed it to her to sign on the back. After passing the credit card through the machine, the clerk handed her a receipt to sign. Then the clerk held up the receipt Langer had signed and compared the signatures!

Langer's concept of mindfulness is similar to the way we described critical thinking earlier. She says that a mindful person (1) continues to create new ideas, (2) is open to new information, and (3) is aware of more than one perspective. By contrast, a mindless person is entrapped in old ideas, engages in automatic behavior, and operates from a single perspective. Langer believes that asking good questions is an important ingredient of mindful thinking.

THINKING ABOUT PSYCHOLOGY AND LIFE
Seeking Multiple Explanations

GOOD CRITICAL THINKERS often seek multiple or alternative explanations of something. They avoid believing something is due to a single cause. For example, consider 19-year-old Tom, a Native Canadian. He dropped out of university midway through his first year. Suppose you heard someone say, "Tom quit university because he wasn't smart enough to do university work."

• Is this statement a valid judgment or an unfortunate stereotype?
• Generate at least three other reasons Tom might have quit university.
• Speculate about how you can find out for certain which factors are responsible.

Critical Thinking Links
Schools for Thinking

Reasoning   What is reasoning? **Reasoning** *is the mental activity of transforming information to reach conclusions.* Reasoning is either inductive or deductive.

Inductive reasoning *involves reasoning from the specific to the general.* That is, it involves drawing conclusions about all members of a category based on observing some members (Bisanz, Bisanz, & Korpan, 1994). For example, suppose that in a literature class you read some of Shakespeare's plays and try to describe his idea of romantic love. Here, your inductive reasoning is being tapped. Applying concepts also challenges inductive reasoning, as when students use knowledge about research methods to evaluate science news (Zimmerman, Bisanz, &, Bisanz, 1998).

Analogies draw on inductive reasoning. An **analogy** *is a type of formal reasoning that involves four parts, with the relation between the first two parts being the same as the relation between the last two.* For example,

"For God's sake, think! Why is he being so nice to you?"

The New Yorker Collection. © 1998 Sam Gross from cartoonbank.com. All Rights Reserved

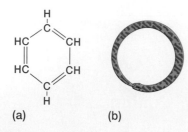

Figure 8.6
Use of Analogy in Problem Solving

The benzene ring *(a)* is one of the most important structures in organic chemistry. It was discovered by August Kekulé after he imagined how its structure might be analogous to a snake biting its tail *(b)*.

Mindfulness

Through the Eyes of Psychologists
Ellen Langer, *Harvard University*

"I didn't want to be thought of as mindless so I changed the name of what I was studying from mindlessness to mindfulness."

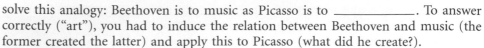

solve this analogy: Beethoven is to music as Picasso is to _____. To answer correctly ("art"), you had to induce the relation between Beethoven and music (the former created the latter) and apply this to Picasso (what did he create?).

Analogies can be helpful in solving problems, especially when they are visually represented (Mumford & Porter, 1999). Benjamin Franklin noticed that a pointed object drew a stronger spark than a blunt object when both were in the vicinity of an electrified body. Originally he believed this was an unimportant observation, but then, he realized that pointed rods of iron could be used to attract lightning, thus deflecting it from buildings and ships. August Kekulé discovered the ringlike structure of the benzene molecule in organic chemistry only after he visualized a snake biting its tail and saw the analogy to the structure of the benzene molecule (see figure 8.6). In many ways, analogies make the strange familiar and the familiar strange.

In contrast to inductive reasoning, **deductive reasoning** *is reasoning from the general to the specific.* When you learn about a general rule and then understand how it applies in some situations but not others you are engaging in deductive reasoning (Thompson, 1996). The fictional British detective Sherlock Holmes was a master at deductive reasoning. When solving a case, he sorted through a number of clues to zero in on the one correct solution to a murder. When psychologists, other scientists, and you use theories and intuitions to make predictions, then evaluate these predictions by making further observations, deductive reasoning is at work.

As with other forms of higher cognition, induction and deduction are carried out in the frontal lobes (Goel and others, 1997).

Making Decisions
Think of all the decisions you have to make in your life. Should I major in biology, psychology, or business? Should I go to graduate school right after college or get a job first? Should I establish myself in a career before settling down to have a family? Should I buy a house or rent? **Decision making** *involves evaluating alternatives and making choices among them.* In reasoning, people use established rules to draw conclusions. In contrast, when we make decisions, such rules aren't established and we don't know the consequences of the decisions (Tversky & Fox, 1995). Some of the information might be missing, and we might not trust all of the information we have (Matlin, 1998).

In one type of decision-making research, investigators study how people weigh the costs and benefits of various outcomes. They especially focus on whether people actually choose the outcome with the highest expected value (Smyth & others, 1994).

In choosing a college, you might have made up a list of pluses and minuses of going to different colleges (related to such factors as cost, quality of education, social life, and so on), then made a decision based on how the colleges fared on these criteria. In making your decision, you might have weighed some of these factors more heavily than others (such as cost, three points; quality of education, two points; and social life, one point).

In other instances when researchers study how people make decisions, they examine biases and flaws in decision making. In many cases, our decision-making strategies are well adapted to deal with a variety of problems (Nisbett & Ross, 1980). However, there are a number of biases and flaws that we are prone to make (Stanovich, 1999). Let's explore some of these.

Confirmation Bias **Confirmation bias** *is the tendency to search for and use information that supports our ideas rather than refutes them.* Thus, in solving a problem, I might have an initial hypothesis that something is going to work. I test out the hypothesis and find out that it is right some of the time. I conclude that my hypothesis was right rather than exploring the fact that it did not work some of the time. It is easy to detect the confirmation bias in the way that many people think. Consider politicians. They often accept news that supports their views and dismiss evidence that runs counter to their views. Consider also physicians who misdiagnose a patient because

𝓕igure 8.7
Belief Perseverance

Belief perseverance is a common bias that infiltrates our judgments. How is belief perseverance involved in thinking it improbable that Jim Carrey could be a dramatic actor (*The
Truman Show*) rather than a comic actor (*Ace Ventura, Pet Detective*)?

one or two symptoms fit with previous successful diagnoses they have made. In their
desire to confirm their diagnosis, they ignore symptoms that don't fit their diagnosis.
Our decisions can become further biased because we tend to seek out people whose
views confirm our own and tend to avoid acquaintances who have dissenting views.

In one study, Deanna Kuhn and her colleagues (1994) had participants listen to
an audiotaped reenactment of an actual murder trial. Subsequently, they were asked
what their verdict would be and why. Rather than considering and weighing possibilities against the evidence, many participants hurriedly composed a story that drew
only from evidence that supported their view of what happened. These participants
showed a confirmation bias by ignoring evidence that ran counter to their version
of events.

Belief Perseverance   Closely related to confirmation bias, **belief perseverance**
is the tendency to hold on to a belief in the face of contradictory evidence. People have
a difficult time letting go of an idea or strategy once they have embraced it.

Consider Jim Carrey (see figure 8.7). We have a hard time thinking of him in a
dramatic role because of the belief perseverance that he is a wild and crazy comic actor.

Overconfidence Bias   Overconfidence bias *is the tendency to have more confidence in our judgments and decisions than we should based on the relative frequency
of correct answers.* People are overconfident about how long people with a fatal disease will live, which businesses will go bankrupt, which psychiatric inpatients have

serious mental disorders, whether a defendant is guilty in a court trial, and which students will do well in graduate school (Kahneman & Tversky, 1995). People consistently have more faith in their judgments than predictions based on statistically objective measures indicate they should. For example, in one study, college students were asked to make predictions about themselves in the coming academic year (Vallone & others, 1990). They were asked to predict whether they would drop any courses, vote in an election, and break up with their girlfriend or boyfriend. Then they were asked to rate how confident they were in their predictions. At the end of the year, the accuracy of their predictions was examined. The results: The students were overconfident about what they thought would happen to them. For example, they were more likely to drop a class, not vote in an election, and break up with a girlfriend or a boyfriend than they had predicted.

Overconfidence can have consequences for people's lives (Matlin, 1998). For instance, in 1988, Captain Will Rogers was in charge of the USS *Vincennes* in the Persian Gulf. The ship's radar detected an unknown aircraft. Rogers had to make a decision about whether the aircraft was a civilian plane or an enemy ship attacking the USS *Vincennes.* His decision: Launch two missiles at the airplane. Both Rogers and the world soon learned that it was a civilian airplane. All 290 passengers on board were killed when it was shot down. A panel of decision-making experts concluded that Rogers had been overconfident about his original decision and had failed to verify critical factors in the situation (Bales, 1988).

Hindsight Bias   People are not only overconfident about what they predict will happen in the future (overconfidence bias), they also tend to be overconfident about circumstances that have already happened. **Hindsight bias** *is our tendency to falsely report, after the fact, that we accurately predicted an event.* In the case of Canadian Jim Carrey, many people thought he would never be successful as a dramatic actor. However, after the success of *The Truman Show,* some of these same people said that they knew all along he would be successful. As we write this, hockey season is getting ready to begin. Lots of people in different cities are predicting that their teams are going to make it to the Stanley Cup. Come spring, many of the same people will say, "I told you they weren't going to have a good season."

Availability Heuristic   Earlier in the chapter we described heuristics as rules of thumb that suggest a solution but do not ensure it will work. We will consider two heuristics that can produce flawed thinking: the availability heuristic and the representative heuristic. When we use the **availability heuristic** *we make a judgment about the probability of an event by recalling the frequency of the event's past occurrences.* When an event has recently occurred, we especially tend to overestimate its future occurrence. The media contribute to this prediction error by vividly exposing us to tornados, murders, diseases, and accidents. For example, if you saw a train wreck on television yesterday, you are more likely to estimate that train wrecks are more prevalent than if you had not seen the wreck.

Representativeness Heuristic   The **representativeness heuristic** *suggests that we make decisions based on how well something matches a prototype—that is, the most common or representative example.* Consider the following description of an individual's dinner companion: skilled at carpentry, proficient at wrestling, owns a pet snake, knows how to repair motorcycles, and has a police record. What is the probability that this person is a male? Most likely the description fits your prototype of a male more than a female, so you might estimate that there is a 9 in 10 chance the dinner companion is a male.

In this example, your prototype served you well because there are far more men than women in the population who fit the description. Sometimes, however, our prototypes do not take into account the frequency of events in the entire population.

SUMMARY TABLE 8.2
Thinking Critically, Reasoning, and Making Decisions

Concept	Processes/Related Ideas	Characteristics/Description
Critical Thinking	Its Nature	Critical thinking involves thinking reflectively and productively, and evaluating the evidence. Some critics argue that schools do not do a good job of guiding students to think critically. Langer says that too many people engage in mindless behavior, and she encourages us to be more mindful.
Reasoning	Its Nature	Reasoning is the mental activity of transforming information to reach conclusions. Inductive reasoning involves reasoning from the specific to the general. That is, it consists of drawing conclusions about all members of a category based on observing only some of them. Analogies draw on inductive reasoning. Deductive reasoning is reasoning from the general to the specific.
Decision Making	What Is It?	Decision making involves evaluating alternatives and making choices among them. One type of decision-making research studies how people weigh the costs and benefits of various outcomes. Another type studies people's biases and flaws in making decisions.
	Biases and Flaws	These biases and flaws involve confirmation bias (tendency to search for and use information that supports our ideas rather than refutes them), belief perseverance (tendency to hold on to a belief in the face of contradictory evidence), overconfidence bias (tendency to have more confidence in our judgments than we should, based on the relative frequency of correct answers), hindsight bias (tendency after the fact to falsely claim to have predicted an event), availability heuristic (making a judgment about the probability of an event by recalling the frequency of the event's past occurrences), and representativeness heuristic (making decisions based on how well something matches a prototype—that is, the most common representative or example).

For example, would you say the probability is greater that the dinner companion is a member of a motorcycle gang or a salesman? You would probably say there is a much greater chance that he is a member of a motorcycle gang, in which case you would be wrong. Why? Although only a very small percentage of the millions of the world's salesmen fit the description of the dinner companion, the total number represented by this percentage is greater than the total of motorcycle gang members who fit this description. Let's assume there are 10,000 members of motorcycle gangs in the world versus 100 million salesmen. Even if 1 of every 100 motorcycle gang members fits our description, there would be only 100 of them. If just 1 of every 100,000 salesmen fits our description, their number would total 1,000. So the probability is 10 times greater that the dinner companion is a salesman than a member of a motorcycle gang. Our lives involve many such instances in which we judge probabilities based on representativeness and fail to consider the population from which a sample is drawn.

At this point we have studied many ideas about these aspects of thinking: Critical thinking, reasoning, and decision making. An overview of these ideas is presented in summary table 8.2. Next, we will turn our attention to language, which provides us with a unique system for communicating our thoughts.

What Is Language?

Biological and Environmental Influences

Exploring Language

Language

In 1799, a nude boy was observed running through the woods in France. The boy was captured when he was 11 years old. He was called the Wild Boy of Aveyron and was believed to have lived in the woods alone for 6 years (Lane, 1976). When found, he made no effort to communicate. Even after a number of years, he never learned to communicate effectively. Sadly, a modern-day wild child named Genie was discovered in Los Angeles in 1970. Despite intensive intervention, Genie never acquired more than a primitive form of language. Both cases raise questions about the contribution of biology and environment to language, topics we will explore in depth later. First, though, we need to find out what language is.

What Is Language?

To explore what language is, we will first define it, then examine its rule systems.

Defining Language   **Language** *is a form of communication, whether spoken, written, or signed, that is based on a system of symbols.* Think how important language is in our everyday lives. We need language to speak with others, listen to others, read, and write. Our language enables us to describe past events in detail and to plan for the future. Language lets us pass down information from one generation to the next and create a rich cultural heritage.

All human languages have some common characteristics. These include infinite generativity and organizational rules. **Infinite generativity** *is the ability to produce an endless number of meaningful sentences using a finite set of words and rules.* This quality makes language a highly creative enterprise (Carroll, 1999). Language is characterized by a number of organizational rules that include phonology, morphology, syntax, and semantics, which we will discuss next.

Rule Systems   Language is made up of basic sounds, or phonemes (Lahari, 1999). **Phonology** *refers to a language's sound system.* Phonological rules ensure that certain sound sequences occur (for example, *sp, ba,* or *ar*) and others do not (for example, *zx,* or *qp*). A good example of a phoneme in the English language is /k/, the sound represented by the letter *k* in the word *ski* and the letter *c* in the word *cat.* Although the /k/ sound is slightly different in these two words, the variation is not distinguished, and the /k/ sound is described as a single phoneme. In some languages, such as Arabic, this kind of variation represents separate phonemes.

Morphology *refers to word formation.* Every word in the English language is made up of one or more morphemes. Some words consist of a single morpheme (for example, *help*), whereas others are made up of more than one morpheme (for example, *helper,* which has two morphemes, *help + er,* with the morpheme *-er* meaning "one who," in this case "one who helps"). However, not all morphemes are words (for example, *pre-, -tion,* and *-ing*). Just as the rules that govern phonemes ensure that certain sound sequences occur, the rules that govern morphemes ensure that certain strings of sounds occur in particular sequences.

Syntax *involves the ways words are combined to form acceptable phrases and sentences.* If someone says to you, "Bob slugged Tom" or "Bob was slugged by Tom," you know who did the slugging and who was slugged in each case because you share the same syntactic understanding of sentence structure. You also understand that the sentence "You didn't stay, did you?" is a grammatical sentence but that "You didn't stay, didn't you?" is unacceptable and ambiguous.

Semantics *refers to the meaning of words and sentences.* Every word has a set of semantic features (Garrod & Pickering, 1999). *Girl* and *woman,* for example, share many of the same semantic features as the word *female,* but differ semantically in

"If you don't mind my asking, how much does a sentence diagrammer pull down a year?"

© 1981 Thaves. Reprinted with permission.

regard to age. Words have semantic restrictions on how they can be used in sentences. The sentence *The bicycle talked the boy into buying a candy bar* is syntactically correct but semantically incorrect. The sentence violates our semantic knowledge that bicycles do not talk.

Biological and Environmental Influences

Is the ability to generate rules for language and then use them to create an infinite number of words the product of biological factors and evolution? Or is language learned and influenced by the environment?

Biological Influences   Estimates vary as to how long ago humans acquired language—about 100,000 years ago. In evolutionary time, then, language is a very recent acquisition. A number of experts believe that biological evolution undeniably shaped humans into linguistic creatures (Chomsky, 1957). The brain, nervous system, and vocal apparatus of our predecessors changed over hundreds of thousands of years. Physically equipped to do so, *Homo sapiens* went beyond grunting and shrieking to develop abstract speech. Language clearly gave humans an enormous edge over other animals and increased the chances of survival (Pinker, 1994) ◀▥ P. 12.

In the wild, chimps communicate through calls, gestures, and expressions, which evolutionary psychologists believe might be the roots of true language.

The famous linguist Noam Chomsky (1975) argues that language has strong biological underpinnings. In Chomsky's view, humans are biologically prewired to learn language at a certain time and in a certain way. Chomsky and many other language experts stress that the strongest evidence for language's biological basis resides in the fact that children all over the world acquire language milestones at about the same time developmentally and in about the same order, despite vast variations in the language input they receive from the environment. For example, in some cultures adults never talk to infants under one year of age, yet these infants still acquire language. Also, there is no convincing way to explain how quickly children learn language other than biological factors (Locke, 1999; Maratsos, 1999).

Environmental Influences   Behaviorists have advocated the view that language is primarily determined by environmental influences. For example, the famous behaviorist B. F. Skinner (1957) said that language is just another behavior, like sitting, walking, or running ◀▥ P. 203. He argued that all behaviors, including language, are learned through reinforcement. Albert Bandura (1977) later emphasized that language is learned through imitation ◀▥ P. 207.

However, virtually all language experts today agree that reinforcement and imitation cannot explain children's language development. Many children's sentences are novel in the sense that they have not previously heard them. Thus, a child might hear the sentence, "The plate fell on the floor" and then say "My mirror fell on the blanket" after the child drops the mirror on the blanket. Reinforcement (smiles, hugs, pats on the back, corrective feedback) and imitation (modeling of words and syntax) simply cannot explain this novel utterance.

Roger Brown (1973) spent long hours observing parents and their young children, searching for evidence that parents reinforce their children for speaking grammatically. He found that parents sometimes smiled and praised their children for sentences they liked, but that they also reinforced lots of ungrammatical sentences as well. Brown concluded that no evidence exists that reinforcement is responsible for the development of children's language rule systems.

Although reinforcement and imitation are not responsible for children's development of language rule systems, it is important that children interact with language-skilled people (Snow, 1999; Tracy, in press). The Wild Boy of Aveyron and Genie were not around such people when they were young children, and it clearly harmed their language development.

MIT linguist Noam Chomsky was one of the early architects of the view that children's language development cannot be explained by environmental input. In Chomsky's view, language has strong biological underpinnings, with children biologically prewired to learn language at a certain time and in a certain way.

EXPLORATIONS IN PSYCHOLOGY
How to Talk with Babies and Toddlers

In *Growing Up With Language,* linguist Naomi Baron (1992) provides a number of helpful ideas about ways that parents can facilitate their child's language development. A summary of her ideas follows:

Infants

- *Be an active conversational partner.* Initiate conversation with the infant. If the infant is in a daylong child-care program, ensure that the baby gets adequate language stimulation from adults.
- *Talk as if the infant understands what you are saying.* Adults can generate positive self-fulfilling prophecies by addressing their young children as if they understand what is being said. The process may take 4 to 5 years, but children gradually rise to match the language model presented to them.
- *Use a language style with which you feel comfortable.* Don't worry about how you sound to other adults when you talk with a child. Your effect, not your content, is more important when talking with an infant. Use whatever type of baby talk you feel comfortable with.

Toddlers

- *Continue to be an active conversational partner.* Engaging toddlers in conversation, even one-sided conversation, is the most important thing an adult can do to nourish a child linguistically.
- *Remember to listen.* Since toddlers' speech is often slow and laborious, parents are often tempted to supply words and thoughts for them. Be patient. Let toddlers express themselves, no matter how painstaking the process is or how great a hurry you are in.
- *Use a language style with which you are comfortable, but consider ways of expanding the child's language abilities and horizons;* use rhymes; ask questions that encourage answers other than "Yes"; actively repeat, expand, and recast the child's utterances; introduce new topics, and use humor in your conversation.

- *Adjust to a child's idiosyncrasies instead of working against them.* Many toddlers have difficulty pronouncing words and making themselves understood. Whenever possible, make toddlers feel that they are being understood.
- *Avoid gender stereotypes.* Don't let the toddler's sex unwittingly determine your amount or style of conversation. Many Canadian mothers are more linguistically supportive of girls than of boys, and many fathers talk less with their children than mothers do. Active and cognitively enriching initiatives from both mothers and fathers benefit both boys and girls.
- *Resist making normative comparisons.* Be aware of the ages at which a child reaches specific milestones (first word, first fifty words, first grammatical combination), but be careful not to measure this development rigidly against children of neighbors or friends. Such social comparisons can bring about unnecessary anxiety.

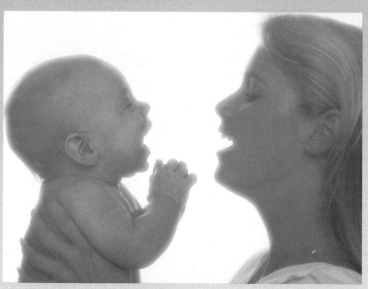

It is unquestionably a good idea for parents to begin talking to their babies right at the start. The best language teaching occurs when the talking is begun before the infant becomes capable of its first intelligible speech.

Talking to Babies

In one study, researchers observed the language environments of children from middle-income professional and welfare backgrounds, then examined the children's language development (Hart & Risley, 1995). All of the children developed normally in terms of learning to talk and acquiring all of the forms of English and basic vocabulary. However, there were enormous differences in the sheer amount of language the children were exposed to and the level of the children's language development.

SUMMARY TABLE 8.3
Language: Its Nature, and Biological and Environmental Influences

Concept	Processes/ Related Ideas	Characteristics/Description
What Is Language?	Defining Language	Language is a form of communication, whether spoken, written, or signed, that is based on a system of symbols. All human languages have some common characteristics. These include infinite generativity (the ability to produce an endless number of meaningful sentences using a finite set of words and rules) and organizational rules.
	Rule Systems	Language's organizational rules include phonology (the sound system of a language), morphology (the rules for combining morphemes, which are meaningful strings of sounds that contain no smaller meaningful parts), syntax (the ways words are combined to form acceptable phrases and sentences), and semantics (the meaning of words and sentences).
Biological and Environmental Influences	Biological Influences	A number of experts believe that biological evolution shaped humans into linguistic creatures. The famous linguist Noam Chomsky and others argue that the strongest evidence for language's biological basis resides in the fact that children all over the world acquire language milestones at about the same time developmentally and in about the same order, despite vast variations in the language input they receive from the environment.
	Environmental Influences	Behaviorists, such as Skinner and Bandura, have advocated that language is primarily determined by environmental influences, especially reinforcement and imitation, but the evidence suggests that reinforcement and imitation are not responsible for the development of children's language rule systems. However, it is important for children to interact with language-skilled people. Children are biologically prepared to learn language but benefit enormously from being bathed in a competent language environment from early in their development.

For example, in a typical hour, the middle-income professional parents spent almost twice as much time communicating with their children as the welfare parents did. The children from the middle-income professional families heard about 2,100 words an hour, their child counterparts in welfare families only 600 words an hour. The researchers estimated that by four years of age, the average welfare family child would have 13 million fewer words of cumulative language experience than the child in the average middle-income professional family. Amazingly, some of the three-year-old children from middle-class professional families had a recorded vocabulary that exceeded the recorded vocabulary of some of the welfare parents!

Thus, in the real world of learning language, children are neither exclusively biological linguists nor exclusively socially driven language experts (Ratner, 1993). As with all areas of psychology we have studied, it is important to take an interactionist view of how children learn language. That is, children are biologically prepared to learn language but benefit enormously from being bathed in a competent language environment from an early age (Pan & Snow, 1999; Snow, 1998). Some good strategies for how to provide this type of environment are discussed in Explorations in Psychology.

At this point we have studied a number of ideas about what language is and biological and environmental influences. An overview of these ideas is presented in summary table 8.3. Next, we explore how language develops.

Child Language

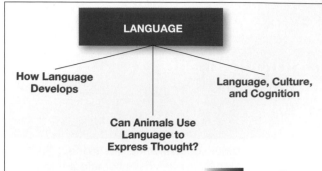

LANGUAGE

How Language Develops

Can Animals Use Language to Express Thought?

Language, Culture, and Cognition

How Language Develops

Most individuals in North America acquire a vocabulary of nearly 50,000 words in a language by the time they are adults. How does this development take place?

Early Development   Before babies ever say their first words, at the age of 10 to 13 months, they babble. Babbling—endlessly repeating sounds and syllables such as *bababa or dadada*—begins at about the age of three to six months and is determined by biological readiness, not reinforcement or the ability to hear (Locke, 1993). Even deaf babies babble for a time (Lenneberg, Rebelsky, & Nichols, 1965). Babbling probably allows the baby to exercise its vocal cords and helps develop articulation.

A child's first words name important people *(dada)*, familiar animals *(kitty)*, vehicles *(car)*, toys *(ball)*, food *(milk)*, body parts *(eye)*, clothes *(hat)*, household items *(clock)*, and greetings *(bye)*. These were babies' first words 50 years ago, and they are babies' first words today (Clark, 1983).

By the time children reach the age of 18 to 24 months, they usually utter two-word statements. They quickly grasp the importance of expressing concepts and the role that language plays in communicating with others (Plunkett & Schafer, 1999). To convey meaning in two-word statements, the child relies heavily on gesture, tone, and context. Children can communicate a wealth of meaning with two words; for instance:

Identification: See doggie.
Location: Book there.
Repetition: More milk.
Nonexistence: Allgone thing.
Negation: Not wolf.
Possession: My candy.
Attribution: Big car.
Agent-action: Mama walk.
Action-direct-object: Hit you.
Action-indirect-object: Give papa.
Action-instrument: Cut knife.
Question: Where ball? (Slobin, 1972)

These examples are from children whose first languages were English, German, Russian, Finnish, Turkish, and Samoan. Although these two-word sentences omit many parts of speech, they are remarkably succinct in conveying many messages. In fact, a child's first combination of words has this economical quality in every language. **Telegraphic speech** *is the use of short and precise words to communicate; it is characteristic of young children's two- or three-word combinations.* When we send a telegram, we are short and precise, excluding any unnecessary words. As a result, articles, auxiliary verbs, and other connectives usually are omitted. Of course, telegraphic speech is not limited to two-word phrases. "Mommy give ice cream" or "Mommy give Tommy ice cream" are also examples of telegraphic speech. As children leave the two-word stage, they move rather quickly into three-, four-, and five-word combinations (Blake, Quartaro & Onarati, 1993).

As we have just seen, language unfolds in a sequence. At every point in development, the child's linguistic interaction with parents and others obeys

Around the world, young children learn to speak in two-word utterances, in most cases at about 18 to 24 months of age. What implications does this have for the biological basis of language?

certain rules (de Villiers & de Villiers, 1999; MacWhinney, 1999). The concept of morphological rules was examined in a classic study by Jean Berko (1958). She presented preschool and first-grade children with cards such as the one shown in figure 8.8. The children were asked to look at the card while the experimenter read the words on it aloud. Then the children were asked to supply the missing word. This might sound easy, but Berko was interested not only in their ability to say the missing word but to say it correctly (with the ending that was dictated by the morphological rules). Thus, *wugs* is the correct response for the card in figure 8.8. Although the children's responses were not always completely accurate, they were much better than chance. What makes Berko's study so impressive is that the words were fictional, created solely for the purpose of the study. Thus, the children could not have based their answers on remembering past instances of hearing the words. Instead, they were forced to rely on *rules,* and their performance suggested that they did so successfully. Now that we have explored some aspects of early language development, let's examine an important question in this area.

This is a wug.

Now there is another one.
There are two of them.
There are two _____.

*F*igure 8.8
Stimuli in Berko's Classic Study of Children's Understanding of Morphological Rules
In Jean Berko's (1958) study, young children were presented cards such as this one with a "wug" on it. Then the children were asked to supply the missing word and say it correctly. "Wugs" is the correct response here.

Is There a Critical Period for Learning Language?   A critical period *is a period when there is learning readiness; beyond this period learning is difficult or impossible.* Almost all children learn one or more languages during their early years of development, so it is difficult to determine whether there is a critical period for language development. In the 1960s, Eric Lenneberg (1967) proposed a biological theory of language acquisition. He said that language is a maturational process and that there is a critical period between about 18 months of age and puberty during which a first language must be acquired. Central to Lenneberg's thesis is the idea that language develops rapidly and with ease during the preschool years as a result of maturation. Lenneberg provided support for the critical-period concept from studies of several atypical populations, including children and adults with damage in the left hemisphere of the brain, deaf children, and children with mental retardation (Tager-Flusberg, 1994, 1999). The children's brains had plasticity, and the children recovered their language skills but the adults did not. Lenneberg believed that adults had already passed the critical period during which plasticity of brain functioning allows reassignment and relearning of language skills.

The stunted language development of a modern "wild child" also supports the idea of a critical period for language acquisition. In 1970, a California social worker made a routine visit to the home of a partially blind woman who had applied for public assistance. The social worker discovered that the woman and her husband kept their 13-year-old daughter, Genie, locked away from the world. Kept in almost total isolation during her childhood, Genie could not speak or stand erect. She was forced to sit naked all day on a child's potty seat, restrained by a harness her father had made—she could move only her hands and feet. At night she was placed in a kind of straitjacket and caged in a crib with wire mesh sides and a cover. Whenever Genie made a noise, her father beat her. He never communicated with her in words but growled and barked at her.

Genie spent a number of years in extensive rehabilitation programs, such as speech and physical therapy (Curtiss, 1977; Rymer, 1993). She eventually learned to walk upright with a jerky motion and to use the toilet. Genie also learned to recognize many words and to speak in rudimentary sentences. At first she spoke in one-word utterances. Later she was able to string together two-word combinations such as "big teeth," "little marble," and "two hand." Consistent with the language development of most children, three-word combinations followed—for example, "small two cup." Unlike normal children, however, Genie did not learn how to ask questions and she doesn't understand grammar. Genie is not able

"No, Timmy, not 'I sawed the chair.' It's 'I saw the chair' or 'I have seen the chair.'"
© Glenn Bernhardt

Genie

What were Genie's experiences like? What implications do they have for language acquisition?

Bilingual Education

to distinguish between pronouns or passive and active verbs. Four years after she began stringing words together, her speech still sounded like a garbled telegram. And as an adult she speaks in short, mangled sentences, such as "Father hit leg," "Big wood," and "Genie hurt."

Bilingualism   Because Canada was founded by two peoples, the English and French, and because we have always opened our borders to peoples from other countries, many Canadians are bilingual. Partly as a consequence of the official Canadian government policy favoring bilingualism, by 1996, almost five million Canadians were able to carry on a conversation in both English and French (Statistics Canada, 1999). At the same time, even more Canadians were conversant in *either* English or French *and* another language. So no matter which way you look at it, Canada is a more or less bilingual country that has begun to recognize the advantages of bilingualism, official and otherwise.

In contrast, the United States is one of the few countries in the world in which most students graduate from high school knowing only their own language. Some U.S. states have recently passed laws declaring English to be their official language, so that schools are not obligated to teach minority children in languages other than English (Rothstein, 1998). In California in 1998, voters repealed bilingualism altogether (there is a large Spanish-speaking population there, as well as in other southern U.S. states). These developments make it increasingly difficult for American schools to teach academic subjects to immigrant children in their native languages (most often Spanish) while slowly and simultaneously adding English instruction, the preferred strategy of American schools for the last two decades (Romaine, 1999).

Research has consistently revealed that bilingualism does not interfere with performance in either language (Hakuta, 1999; Hakuta & Garcia, 1989). Children's use of their native language need not be restricted because it might interfere with learning a second language. In fact, a groundbreaking Canadian research program initiated by Wallace Lambert of McGill University has found that bilingual Canadian children actually perform better than unilingual children on both verbal and nonverbal measures of intelligence (Lambert & Anisfeld, 1969). Recently, Lambert and his colleagues (1993) have replicated and extended this work across a number of countries such as Israel, Singapore, and Switzerland.

Based on these findings, a Canadian program was developed to immerse English-speaking children in French for much of their early elementary school education in Quebec (Lambert & Tucker, 1972). Their English did not appear to have been harmed and their math scores, aptitude scores, and appreciation of French culture benefitted. Results such as these have influenced official Canadian government policy in favor of bilingual education (Noels & Clément, 1998).

Recently, Ellen Bialystok of York University (Bialystok, 1991) has clarified the contribution bilingualism can make to the development of intelligence and skills such as mathematics and reading. According to Bialystok, the link is via *metalinguistic awareness,* a knowledge of the properties and structures of language (Bialystok, in press). Bilingualism is beneficial because of the perspective gained from knowing and using a whole new set of linguistic signs and categories (Segalowitz, 1997). That is, the bilingual child learns early on, among other things, that the relationship between words and their referents is arbitrary. A child learning both English and French, for example, would learn that the family pet is referred to as a "dog" in one language but as a "chien" in the other. This makes it easier for the child to appreciate the distinction between his or her language and the world to which that language refers.

Children with more developed metalinguistic awareness can appreciate literacy earlier (Bialystok, 1997), likely because they more easily understand the symbolic relation between letters and sounds. Similarly, poor readers also have poor metalinguistic skills (Bialystok & Mitterer, 1987). Arguably, then, the advanced metalinguistic ability of bilingual children enables them to develop literacy more easily than unilingual children (Bialystok & Herman, 1999).

Linked to our earlier discussion of critical period is this question: Is it better to learn a second language as a child or as an adult? (Birdsong, 1999). Adults make faster initial progress but their eventual success in the second language is not as great as children's (Johnson & Newport, 1989). Children's ability to pronounce a second language with the correct accent also decreases with age, with an especially sharp decline occurring after the age of about 10 to 12 (Asher & Garcia, 1969). Adolescents and adults can become competent at a second language but this is a more difficult task than learning it as a child.

Following are some recommendations for working with linguistically and culturally diverse children (NAEYC, 1996):

• Recognize that all children are cognitively, linguistically, and emotionally connected to the language and culture of their home.
• Understand that second-language learning can be difficult. It takes time to become linguistically competent in any language.
• Recognize that children can and will acquire the use of a second language even when their home language is respected.

Reading   Another important school-related aspect of language involves how we read (Besner & Humphreys, 1990) and, therefore, the best way to teach children to read (Carr & Levy, 1990). The reading debate focuses on the whole-language approach versus the basic-skills-and-phonetics approach. The **whole language approach** *stresses that reading instruction should be parallel to children's natural language learning. Reading materials should be whole and meaningful.* In the whole language approach, reading is integrated with other skills, subjects, and real-world activities. This approach rests upon research showing that good readers can use their broader experience to treat texts as a meaningful whole (Masson & MacLeod, 1997), recognize familiar words as visual wholes (Buchanan & Besner, 1993), and fill in missing meanings when they cannot read a word.

Teaching Children to Read
Literacy and Reading

By contrast, the **basic-skills-and-phonetics approach** *emphasizes that reading instruction should stress phonetics and its basic rules for translating written symbols into sounds.* Early reading instruction should involve simplified materials. Only after they have learned phonological rules should children be given complex reading materials such as books and poems. This approach rests upon research showing that good readers can use phonetics to decipher unfamiliar words as required (Barron, 1994)

Which approach is best? Mitterer (1982) showed that different types of poor readers rely exclusively upon one or the other approach while good readers use both. A recently convened U.S. national panel concluded that a combination of the two approaches is the best strategy (Snow, 1998). The panel recommended that beginning readers be taught to sound out letters as the main way to identify unfamiliar words, the cornerstone of the basic-skills-and-phonetics approach. But the panel also endorsed several aspects of the whole language approach: encourage children, as they begin to recognize words, to predict what might happen in a story, draw inferences about stories, and write their own stories.

Psychologists have not only been curious about how human children learn language. As we see next, they are also intrigued by whether animals have language.

Can Animals Use Language to Express Thought?

Many animal species do have complex and ingenious ways to signal danger and to communicate about basic needs such as food and sex. For example, in one species

"Remember, don't talk sex, politics, or religion."

Reprinted courtesy of Omni Magazine © 1982.

of firefly the female has evolved to imitate the flashing signal of another species to lure the aliens into her territory. Then she eats them. But is this language in the human sense? And what about the animals who are our closest relatives, the great apes?

Chimpanzees and *Homo sapiens* have 98 percent of their genetic material in common. Chimpanzee behavior includes hunting, toolmaking, embracing, back patting, kissing, and holding hands. Do animals this closely related to us have language? Can we teach human language to them?

Some researchers believe apes can learn language. One celebrity in this field is a chimp named Washoe, who was adopted when she was about 10 months old (Gardner & Gardner, 1971). Since apes do not have the vocal apparatus to speak, the researchers tried to teach Washoe American Sign Language, which is one of the sign languages of the deaf. Washoe used sign language during everyday activities, such as meals, play, and car rides. In 2 years, Washoe learned 38 different signs, and by the age of 5 she had a vocabulary of 160 signs. Washoe learned how to put signs together in novel ways, such as *You drink* and *You me tickle*. A number of other efforts to teach language to chimps have had similar results (Premack, 1986).

The debate about chimpanzees' ability to use language focuses on two key issues: Can apes understand the meaning of symbols—that is, can they comprehend that one thing stands for another? And can apes learn syntax—that is, can they learn the kinds of mechanics and rules that give human language its creative productivity? The first of these issues may have been settled by Sue Savage-Rumbaugh and her colleagues (1993). These researchers found strong evidence that the chimps Sherman and Austin can understand symbols. For example, if Sherman or Austin is sitting in a room, and a symbol for an object is displayed on a screen, he will go into another room, find the object, and bring it back. If the object is not there, he will come back empty-handed (Cowley, 1988). Austin and Sherman can play a game in which one chimp points to a symbol for food (such as M&Ms), and the other chimp selects the food from a tray, then they both eat it. These observations are clear evidence that chimps can understand symbols (see figure 8.9).

Recent evidence concerning chimps' syntactic ability has come from a study of rare pygmy chimpanzees *(Pan paniscus),* also known as "bonobos." These chimps are friendlier and brighter than their cousins, and show some remarkable language abilities. For example, star pupil Kanzi is very good at understanding spoken English and has been shown to comprehend over 600 sentences, such as *Can you make the bunny eat the sweet potato?* (Savage-Rumbaugh, Shanker, & Taylor, 1998). Kanzi also produces fairly complex sentences using a response board hooked to a speech synthesizer. To read further about language in animals, turn to Explorations in Psychology.

The debate over whether or not animals can use language to express thoughts is far from resolved. Researchers agree that animals can communicate with each other and that some can manipulate language-like symbols with syntax that resembles that of young children. At the same time, it is clear that their language abilities do not show the same degree of generativity and complexity as adult human language.

Animal Communication

Language, Culture, and Cognition

Take a moment and reflect on several questions. Did the culture in which you grew up influence your language? Does language influence the way you think? Does thinking influence the nature of your language?

Language and Culture   Linguist Benjamin Whorf (1956) argued that language actually determines the way we think. Whorf and his student Edward Sapir were specialists in Native American languages, and they were fascinated by the possibility that speakers of different languages might view the world differently as the result of the languages they speak. Whorf's **linguistic relativity hypothesis** *states that language determines the structure of thinking and shapes our basic ideas.* The Inuit of the Far North, for instance, have a dozen or more words to describe the various textures, colors, and physical states of snow. Hopi Indians have no words for past and future. And Arabs have 6,000 words for aspects of the camel.

Our cultural experiences for concept shape a catalog of names that can be either rich or poor. An example of a name-rich concept in North America is the "automobile" (we use terms like *coupe, convertible, minivan, station wagon,* and many others, not to mention various makes and models). The *automobile* part of your mental library of names is the product of many years of experience with automobiles. You will probably see and think about them in finer gradations than people who live in the jungles of South America or on an isolated island in the Pacific Ocean. In this way, language acts as a window that filters the amount and nature of information that is passed on for further processing.

Critics of Whorf's theory say that words merely reflect, rather than cause, the way we think. The Inuits' adaptability and livelihood in the Far North depends on their capacity to recognize various conditions of snow and ice. A professional skier who is not Inuit might also know numerous words for snow, far more than the average person; and a person who doesn't know the words for the different types of snow might still be able to perceive these differences.

*F*igure 8.9
Chimps and Symbols

Sue Savage-Rumbaugh and her colleagues at the Yerkes Primate Center and Georgia State University have studied the basic question of whether chimps understand symbols. Their research suggests that the answer to this question is yes.

Eleanor Rosch (1973) found just that. She studied the effect of language on color perception among the Dani in New Guinea. The Dani have only two words for color—one that approximately means "white" and one that approximately means "black." If the linguistic relativity hypothesis were correct, the Dani would lack the ability to tell the difference between colors such as green, blue, red, yellow, and purple. But Rosch found that the Dani perceived colors just as we perceive them. As we know, color perception is biologically determined by receptors in the retinas in the eyes. Even though Whorf's linguistic relativity hypothesis missed the mark, researchers agree that although language does not determine thought, it can influence it.

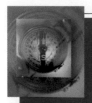

*E*XPLORATIONS IN *P*SYCHOLOGY
In Pursuit of Language in Animals:
Observations of Ake and Phoenix

IN QUICK SUCCESSION, a trainer forms four hand signals that mean "basket," "right," "Frisbee," and "fetch." A female dolphin named Ake has been taught the meaning of each sign but has never before been given this particular combination of signs. Nonetheless, Ake understands that this command tells her to go to the Frisbee to her right and take it to the basket. Ignoring a Frisbee floating at the left side of the pool, Ake moves to her right and scoops up the Frisbee floating there. She nudges it along the water's surface to a basket floating 30 feet away and flips it in. A shrill whistle tells her she has successfully completed her task, and she swims over to the trainer for a plump herring and a hug.

Ake is a seasoned veteran at the University of Hawaii Mammal Laboratory, directed by psychologist Louis Herman. Another veteran in Herman's lab is a dolphin named Phoenix, who, like Ake, has been trained and observed since 1979 (see figure 8.A). Herman wanted to discover whether the dolphins could master word order and syntax. Phoenix learned an acoustic language made up of computer-generated sounds, whereas Ake learned a visual system of hand signals. Phoenix's system involved a left-to-right grammar in which, for example, "Frisbee, in, basket" means "Place the Frisbee in the basket." In contrast, Ake learned an inverse grammar in which "basket, Frisbee, in" means the same thing—"Place the Frisbee in the basket." After receiving a message to place the Frisbee in the basket, as described at the beginning of this boxed feature, the dolphins will swim past other objects, retrieve the Frisbee, and place it as directed. The dolphins are even learning how to answer their trainers. When asked if a certain object is in their tank, the animals can answer by pressing one of two paddles for a yes or no response.

If animals like dolphins can be trained to communicate with a language-like system, do they use such a system in nature? Recently biologists and psychologists have carefully analyzed recordings of dolphins' whistles in the sea. Their findings reveal that each dolphin has a signature whistle that identifies it to others. The whistle also expresses emotional states—under stress, a dolphin's signature whistle changes pitch and duration. At present, though, there have been no data collected to support the contention that dolphins, chimpanzees, or any other nonhuman creatures use abstract symbols or syntax in the wild.

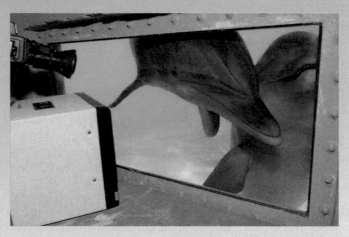

*F*igure 8.A
Phoenix and Ake, Two Dolphins in Herman's Studies
A TV monitor and camera near their tank's underwater-window allows Phoenix (*left*) and Ake to be observed by psychologists.

Language and Cognition

What about our memory and problem solving? What role does language play in these important cognitive activities? Memory is stored not only in terms of sounds and images, but also in words. When words are stored in memory, their processing is often deep and their retrieval more effortful.

Language helps us think, make inferences, tackle difficult decisions, and solve problems (Lycan, 1999). Language can be thought of as a tool for representing ideas. Some psychologists have argued that we cannot think without language, a proposition that has produced heated controversy. Is thought dependent on language, or is language dependent on thought? Language does provide a medium for representing abstract ideas. Our language rules are more sophisticated at an earlier point in our development than thought, suggesting that language is not always dependent on thought (Bruner, 1964).

Cognition might also be an important foundation for language (Gupta & Dell, 1999). Evidence that cognition is separate from language comes from studies of deaf children. On a variety of thinking and problem-solving tasks, deaf children perform at the same level as children of the same age who have no hearing problems. Some of the deaf children in these studies do not even have command of written or sign language (Furth, 1971).

So, thought can direct language, and language can direct thought (Jenkins, 1969). Language is virtually an unbounded symbol system, capable of expressing most thoughts, and language is the way we humans communicate most of our thoughts to each other. We do not always think in words, but undoubtedly our thinking would be greatly impoverished without them.

At this point we have studied many ideas about these aspects of language: how language develops, whether animals can be taught to express thought, and language, culture, and cognition. An overview of these ideas is presented in summary table 8.4. In this chapter, we explored the cognitive revolution in psychology, thinking, and connections between thinking and language. In the next chapter, we will continue our examination of cognitive psychology's domains by studying the concept of intelligence.

The linguistic relativity hypothesis states that our cultural experiences for a particular concept shape a catalog of names that can be either rich or poor. Consider how different your mental library of names for camel *might be if you had extensive experience with camels in a desert world and how different your mental library of names for* snow *might be if you lived in an arctic world of ice and cold. Despite its intriguing appeal, the linguistic relativity concept is controversial and many psychologists do not believe it plays a pivotal role in shaping thought.*

Through the Eyes of Psychologists

Ellen Bialystok, *York University*

"It is because metalinguistic awareness is consequential for other aspects of cognition, both linguistic and non-linguistic that its study is important."

SUMMARY TABLE 8.4
How Language Develops, Whether Animals Can Use Language to Express Thought, and Language, Culture, and Cognition

Concept	Processes/ Related Ideas	Characteristics/Description
How Language Develops	Early Development	Before babies say their first words, they babble. At 10 to 13 months, infants say their first words. Infants' early speech is telegraphic.
	Is There a Critical Period for Learning Language?	A critical period is a period when there is learning readiness; beyond this period learning is difficult or impossible. The stunted growth of children such as Genie supports the critical period notion. However, this concept is still controversial.
	Bilingualism	Researchers have found that bilingualism does not interfere with performance in either language and can improve cognitive development.
	Reading	The reading debate focuses on the whole language approach versus the basic-skills-and-phonetics approach. A recently convened panel of reading experts concluded that the best reading instruction combines these two approaches.
Can Animals Use Language to Express Thought?	The Nature of the Issue	Animals clearly can communicate, and chimps have been taught to use symbols. Whether animals have the same language abilities as humans continues to be debated.
Language, Culture, and Cognition	Language and Culture	Whorf's linguistic relativity hypothesis states that language determines the structure of thinking and shapes our basic ideas. Whorf's ideas are controversial.
	Language and Cognition	Thoughts and ideas are associated with words and ideas. Different languages also promote different ways of thinking. Language does not completely determine thought but does influence it. Language is important in many cognitive activities, such as memory and thinking. Cognitive activities also influence language.

Overview *Overview*

WE BEGAN THIS CHAPTER by exploring the cognitive revolution in psychology. Then we discussed these aspects of thinking: what it is, forming concepts, solving problems, thinking critically, reasoning, and making decisions. Our coverage of language focused on what it is, biological and environmental influences, how language develops, whether animals can use language to express thought, and language, culture, and cognition. Don't forget that you can obtain a more detailed overview of the chapter material by again studying the four summary tables on pages 262, 267, 271, and 280.

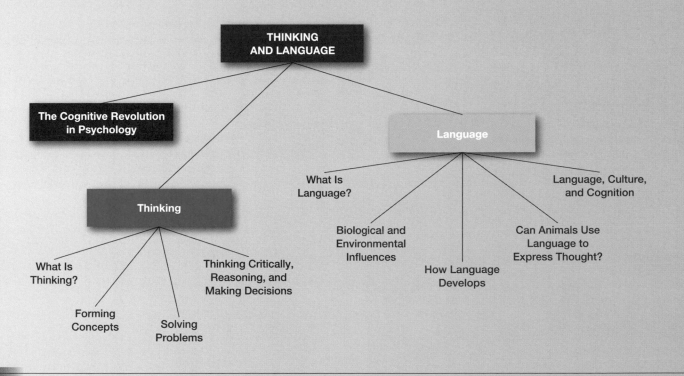

Key Terms *Key Terms*

artificial intelligence (AI) 256
thinking 256
concepts 256
prototype matching 258
problem solving 259
subgoaling 259
algorithms 260
heuristics 260
fixation 261
functional fixedness 261

mental set 261
critical thinking 262
reasoning 263
inductive reasoning 263
analogy 263
deductive reasoning 264
decision making 264
confirmation bias 264
belief perseverance 265
overconfidence bias 265

hindsight bias 266
availability heuristic 266
representativeness heuristic 266
language 268
infinite generativity 268
phonology 268
morphology 268
syntax 268
semantics 268

telegraphic speech 272
critical period 273
whole language approach 275
basic-skills-and-phonetics approach 275
linguistic relativity hypothesis 277

Key People

Eleanor Rosch 258

John Dewey 263

Ellen Langer 263

Noam Chomsky 269

B. F. Skinner 269

Albert Bandura 269

Roger Brown 269

Jean Berko 273

Wallace Lambert 274

Ellen Bialystok 274

Benjamin Whorf 277

Psychology Checklist
THINKING AND LANGUAGE

How much have you learned since the beginning of the chapter? Use the following statements to help you review your knowledge and understanding of the chapter material. First, read the statement and mentally or briefly demonstrate on paper that you can discuss the relevant information.

_____ I know about psychology's cognitive revolution.

_____ I can discuss how people form concepts.

_____ I am aware of what problem solving is and steps in problem solving.

_____ I can describe obstacles to solving problems.

_____ I can discuss the nature of critical thinking.

_____ I know how reasoning works.

_____ I can describe decision making, including biases and flaws that are involved.

_____ I know what language is and its rules systems.

_____ I can describe biological and environmental influences on language.

_____ I can discuss how language develops.

_____ I know about bilingualism and the educational issues involved.

_____ I am aware of the controversy about reading instruction.

_____ I can discuss whether animals can use language to express thought.

_____ I can describe linkages between language, culture, and thought.

For any items that you did not check off, go back and locate the relevant material in the chapter. Review the material until you feel you can check off the item. You may want to use this checklist later in preparing for an exam.

Taking It to the Net

1. Heuristics are rules of thumb that suggest a solution but do not ensure it will work. They help us narrow down possible solutions to problems. Often, however, heuristics are obstacles in solving problems because we are fixated on relying on these heuristics. Some problems require us to ignore heuristics in order to adequately solve them. Optical illusions often trick us into using heuristics that don't work. Explain how optical illusions are affected by these heuristic biases. How do you think this might relate to problems in your everyday life?

2. Have you ever had the experience of not being able to say what you mean? It is often a frustrating experience, in that you know what you want to say, but you can't find the words to say it. Imagine if you could never say what you wanted. Aphasia is a language disorder that affects the individual's ability to communicate their thoughts. Even though people with aphasia can think the words, they cannot say them. Do you think aphasics can communicate their thoughts by writing or typing them on a computer? Explain.

3. Have you ever heard of animals that are taught to communicate? One famous example is Washoe, a chimpanzee who was taught to use sign language. Washoe has used more than 1,000 taught signs in American Sign Language (Ameslan). Interestingly, she has since formed more than 200 signs that she was never taught. Why do you think psychologists want to teach chimps to communicate? What sorts of things can we learn from chimps who have language abilities?

Connect to http://www.mcgrawhill.ca/college/santrock to find the answers!

Resources for Psychology and Life

Genie (1993)
  by Russ Rymer
  New York: HarperCollins

In this book, Russ Rymer tells the poignant story of Genie, a child who grew up without language or any form of social training.

Growing Up With Language (1992)
  by Naomi Baron
  Reading, MA: Addison-Wesley

This book does an excellent job of conveying the appropriate role of parents in children's language development.

The IDEAL Problem Solver (1994, 2nd ed.)
  by John Bransford and Barry Stein
  New York: W. H. Freeman

This book discusses hundreds of fascinating problems and ways to effectively solve them.

Cognition (1997)
  by John Benjafield
  Upper Saddle River, N.J. : Prentice Hall

This book offers a solid and accessible introduction to cognitive psychology.

The Uncertain Mind: Individual Differences In Facing The Unknown (1999)
  by Richard Sorrentino & Christopher Roney
  New York: Psychology Press

The primary thesis of this book is that whether we orient more to uncertainty or to certainty is an extremely important dimension that people differ on.

In Other Words: The Psychology And Science Of Second Language Acquisition (1994)
  by Ellen Bialystok & Kenji Hakuta
  New York: Basic Books

Bilingualism is an important topic for Canadians and this book does an excellent job of covering the psychological and scientific issues.

Thinking Critically About Critical Thinking (1996)
  by Diane Halpern
  Mahway, NJ: Erlbaum

One of the leading experts on critical thinking, Diane Halpern, provides a number of exercises to stimulate your creative thinking.

Solutions to Problems in Thinking About Psychology and Life

The Candle Problem

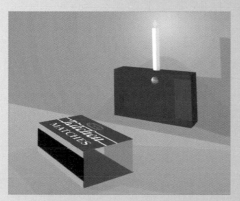

The solution requires a unique perception of the function of the box in which the matches came. It can become a candle-holder when tacked to the wall.

The Nine-Dot Problem

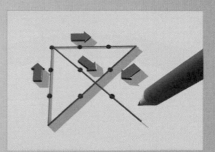

Most people have difficulty with this problem because they try to draw the lines within the boundaries of the dots. Notice that by extending the lines beyond the dots, the problem can be solved.

The Six-Matchsticks Problem

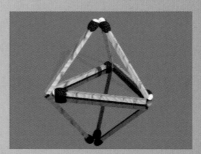

Nothing in the instructions said that the solution had to be two-dimensional.

Chapter

9

CHAPTER OUTLINE

THE NATURE OF INTELLIGENCE AND EARLY HISTORY OF ASSESSMENT

What Is Intelligence?

Early History of Assessment

INTELLIGENCE TESTS

How Tests Are Constructed and Evaluated

The Binet Tests and the Wechsler Scales

Group Tests

Aptitude and Achievement Tests

DO WE HAVE A SINGLE INTELLIGENCE OR MULTIPLE INTELLIGENCES?

Early Views

Contemporary Approaches

CONTROVERSIES AND ISSUES IN INTELLIGENCE

The Heredity-Environment Controversy

Culture and Ethnicity

The Use and Misuse of Intelligence Tests

THE EXTREMES OF INTELLIGENCE AND CREATIVITY

Mental Retardation

Giftedness

Creativity

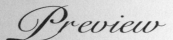

Preview

IN THIS CHAPTER, we continue discussing psychology's cognitive areas. Our focus will be on intelligence. You will see that the concept of intelligence is broad and that there is controversy over what intelligence is, as well as a number of other controversies such as whether intelligence tests are sometimes misused. These are some of the questions we will explore in this chapter:

• What is intelligence?
• How are intelligence tests constructed?
• Do we have a single intelligence or multiple intelligences?
• What roles do heredity and environment play in intelligence?
• How might intelligence tests be misused?
• What are some types of mental retardation?
• What does it mean to be gifted?
• How can people become more creative?

Images of Psychology and Life
Being Creative in "X"

FOR MANY YEARS psychologists have searched for what makes a person creative in general (Goleman, Kaufman, & Ray, 1993). However, Howard Gardner (1993) argues that you can't just say a person is creative in general, you have to say that she or he is creative in "X", that is, in a particular domain—such as writing, sculpture, biology, running an organization. Gardner believes that creativity is not like a fluid that can ooze in any direction in your life; instead, there are intelligences for domains, such as math, language, and music. A person can be highly innovative and imaginative in one of these domains and yet virtually draw blanks in the other domains. This leads Gardner to describe a creative person as someone who can regularly solve problems or come up with something novel that becomes a valuable product in a particular domain.

Van Gogh was creative in the domain of art, Shakespeare in the domain of writing plays and poetry, Einstein in the domain of physics, and Pierre Elliott Trudeau in the domain of politics. Van Gogh was not creative in writing, Shakespeare was not creative in math, Einstein was not creative in art, and Trudeau is not creative in biology. Gardner says that creative people are able to be creative in their domains on a regular basis—they aren't flashes in the pan. Creative people become immersed in the domain in which they work and constantly tinker with problems and ideas, asking, "What makes sense here, and what doesn't make sense?" And if it doesn't make sense, "What can I do about it?"

Gardner (1993) studied the lives of some of the twentieth century's most celebrated creative geniuses, such as Sigmund Freud in psychology, Martha Graham in dance, and Igor Stravinsky in music. He concluded that they did not just do something new. They literally changed, for years to come, the field or domain in which they worked. They all were extremely curious and passionate about their work and possessed these characteristics from an early age. They also showed a pattern of years of commitment to their domain and stretched their particular field, whether it was psychology, music, or dance, to achieve a creative breakthrough.

Gardner believes that each of us has a bent for a particular domain, an area in which we have a special talent or interest. Few of us will achieve the creative breakthroughs that Freud, Graham, and Stravinsky did, but it is important for us to examine our lives and skills to determine where our talents shine and where we struggle. In Gardner's view, thinking about intelligence and creativity in a general way obscures these domain-specific strengths and weaknesses.

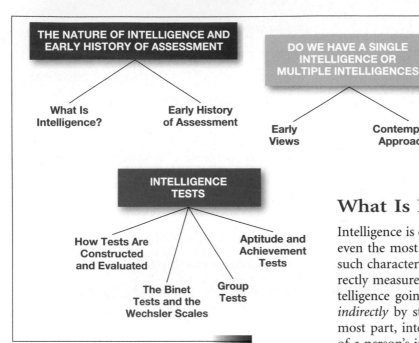

Mental Measurements Yearbook

The Nature of Intelligence and Early History of Assessment

Twentieth-century English novelist Aldous Huxley said that children are remarkable for their intelligence. What do people mean when they use the term *intelligence?*

What Is Intelligence?

Intelligence is one of our most prized possessions, yet it is a concept that even the most intelligent people have not been able to agree on. Unlike such characteristics as height, weight, and age, intelligence cannot be directly measured. We can't peel back a person's scalp and observe the intelligence going on inside. We can only evaluate a person's intelligence *indirectly* by studying the intelligent acts that people generate. For the most part, intelligence tests have been relied on to provide an estimate of a person's intelligence (Kail & Pellegrino, 1985).

Some experts describe intelligence as having verbal ability and problem-solving skills. Others describe it as the ability to adapt to and learn from life's everyday experiences. Combining these ideas, we arrive at a definition of **intelligence** *as verbal ability, problem-solving skills, and the ability to adapt to and learn from life's everyday experiences.*

The primary components of intelligence are very close to the mental processes (thinking and language) that we discussed in chapter 8. The differences in how we described thinking and language and how we will discuss intelligence lie in the concepts of individual differences and assessment. **Individual differences** *are the stable, consistent ways in which people are different from each other* ◀▥ P. 20. In terms of assessment, intelligence tests are designed to tell us whether a person can reason better than others who have taken the test. The two main areas of individual differences in psychology that have been emphasized the most are intelligence and personality. We will explore these individual differences in personality in chapter 12.

Early History of Assessment

The German psychologists who created psychology as a separate discipline, especially Wilhelm Wundt, were not interested in intelligence and its assessment. For them, psychology's appropriate subject matter was sensation and perception. They completely ignored the "higher mental processes," such as thinking and problem solving, that we equate with intelligence today. The early German psychologists were interested in the general laws of behavior; any differences between individuals were thought to be mistakes in measurements reflective of a young science. Before the close of the nineteenth century, however, proposals were made for a psychology of intelligence and individual differences.

In 1884 visitors to the International Health Exhibition at London's South Kensington Museum were invited to pay three pence each to enter Sir Francis Galton's "Anthropomorphic Laboratory" (Fancher, 1996). Galton tempted the visitors by offering

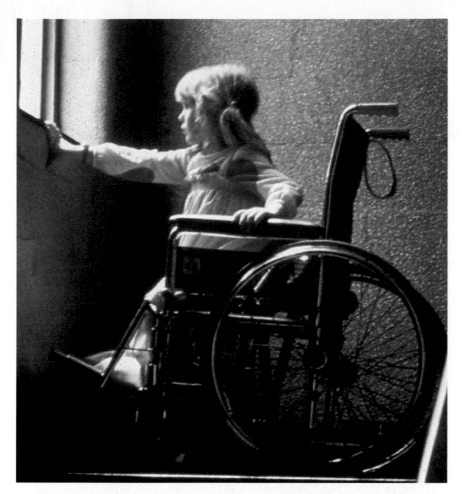

Intelligence includes not only verbal and problem-solving skills, but also the ability to adapt to and learn from life's everyday experiences, as exemplified in this young girl's adaptation to her inability to walk. What are some other examples of intelligence?

them a partial view of what was happening behind the trellised wall. Observers could see that each paying customer manipulated a number of interesting contrivances while an attendant wrote down information about their performance. By the exhibition's end, more than 9,000 men and women had been enticed into the laboratory. Without knowing it, they constituted the first large sample to take an intelligence test, though the term was not used at that time and a modern observer would find little similarity between the "tests" they took and the ones in use today. The battery of tests Galton administered measured such characteristics as head size, strength of hand grip, breathing capacity, reaction time, visual acuity, and memory for visual forms.

Sir Francis Galton is considered the father of mental tests (Boring, 1950). Like the early German psychologists, Galton believed that simple sensory, perceptual, and motor responses were the key dimensions of intelligence. In his laboratory, he attempted to discover systematic individual differences in these processes; however, his efforts produced no important findings about individual differences, possibly because of the sheer amount of data he collected. Although his research provided few conclusive results, Galton raised many important questions about intelligence—how it should be measured, what its components are, and the degree to which it is inherited—that we continue to study today.

The first North American psychologist to study individual differences was James McKeen Cattell. His most notable work was in the last decade of the nineteenth century. Like Galton, Cattell thought that sensory, perceptual, and motor processes represented the heart of intelligence. Cattell's battery of tests included asking university students to select the heavier of two weights and evaluating the speed with which they responded to a tone. He sought to discover a relation between these responses and achievement in university, but the results were disappointing. Cattell is credited with developing the label *mental test*. His research, like Galton's, provided few important conclusions about intelligence, but he, too, developed a tradition that paved the way for further studies of individual differences in intelligence.

Galton's focus on assessing sensory, perceptual, and motor processes was later overshadowed. Regardless, research continues on the relationship between intelligence and the speed of information processing (Miller & Vernon, 1996) and IQ and the speed of neural conduction (Rijsdijk, Boomsma, & Vernon, 1995).

Psychological Tests

Intelligence Tests

At some point in your life you have probably taken an intelligence test. Psychologist Robert Sternberg (1997) remembers his early experiences with intelligence tests. Sternberg eventually overcame his anxieties about IQ tests. He not only began performing better on them but when he was 13 he devised his own intelligence test and began using it to assess classmates—that is, until the school principal found out and scolded him. Sternberg became so fascinated by intelligence that he made its study one of his lifelong pursuits. Later in the chapter we will discuss his approach to intelligence. To begin, though, we need to explore how tests are constructed and evaluated, then examine the most widely used tests of intelligence.

How Tests Are Constructed and Evaluated

Measurement and testing have been involved in human decision making for centuries. The Chinese first developed formal oral tests of knowledge as early as 2200 B.C. The Chinese emperor Ta Yü conducted a 3-year cycle of "competency testing" of government officials. After three examinations, the officials were either promoted or fired (Sax, 1997). Tests have become commonplace in today's world as psychologists have sought more precise measurement of psychology's concepts (Wright, 1999). Any good test must meet three criteria—it must be reliable, it must be valid, and it must be standardized. We will consider each of these criteria.

Reliability   If a test that measures a characteristic is a stable and consistent test, scores should not significantly fluctuate because of chance factors, such as how much sleep you get the night before the test, who the examiner is, the temperature in the room where you take the test, and so on. **Reliability** *is the extent to which a test yields a consistent, reproducible measure of performance.* Reliability can be measured in several ways. **Test-retest reliability** *is the extent to which a test yields the same measure of performance when an individual is given the same test on two different occasions.* Thus, if we gave an intelligence test to a group of high school students today and then gave them the same test in 6 months, the test would be considered reliable if those who scored high on the test today generally score high on the test in 6 months. One limitation of test-retest reliability is that individuals sometimes do better the second time they take the test because they are familiar with it.

Alternative forms reliability *involves giving alternate forms of the same test on two different occasions.* The test items on the two forms of the test are similar but not identical. This strategy eliminates the chance of individuals performing better due to familiarity with the items, but it does not eliminate an individual's familiarity with the procedures and strategies involved in the testing. One difficulty with alternate forms reliability is creating two truly parallel alternative forms.

A third method of measuring reliability is **split-half reliability**, *which involves dividing the items into two halves, such as the first half of the test and second half of the*

Reliability and Validity

test. Individuals' scores on the two halves of the test are compared to determine how consistently they performed. When split-half reliability is high, we say that a test is *internally consistent.* For example, if we gave an intelligence test in which vocabulary items made up the first half of the test and logical reasoning items made up the second half, to be internally consistent individuals' scores would have to be similar on each half of the test. Sometimes psychologists compare individuals' scores on odd-numbered and even-numbered items as another means of establishing the internal consistency of a test.

Validity   A test may consistently measure an attribute, such as intelligence or personality, but this consistency does not ensure that we are measuring the attribute we want to measure (Embretson, 1999). A test of intelligence might actually measure something else, such as anxiety. The test might consistently measure how anxious you are and, thus, have high reliability but not measure your intelligence, which it purports to measure. **Validity** *is the extent to which a test measures what it is intended to measure.*

Like reliability, there are a number of methods to measure validity. One method is **content validity,** *which refers to the test's ability to test a broad range of the content that is to be measured.* For example, a final test in this class, if it is over the entire book, should sample items from each of the chapters rather than just two or three chapters. If an intelligence test purports to measure both verbal ability and problem-solving ability, the items should include a liberal sampling of items that reflects both of these domains. The test would not have high content validity if it asked you to define several vocabulary items but did not require you to reason logically in solving a number of problems.

One of the most important methods of measuring validity is **criterion validity,** *which is the test's ability to predict an individual's performance when assessed by other measures, or criteria, of the attribute.* For example, a psychologist might validate an intelligence test by asking the employers of the individuals who took the intelligence test how intelligent they are at work. The employers' perceptions would be another criterion for measuring intelligence. It is not unusual for the validation of an intelligence test to be another intelligence test. When the scores on the two measures overlap substantially, we say the test has high criterion validity. Of course, we may use more than one other measure to establish criterion validity. We might give the individuals a second intelligence test, get their employers' perceptions of their intelligence, and observe their behavior in real-life problem-solving situations ourselves.

Criterion validity can follow one of two courses, concurrent or predictive. **Concurrent validity** *is a form of criterion validity that assesses the relation of a test's scores to a criterion that is presently available (concurrent).* For example, a test might assess children's intelligence. Concurrent validity might be established by analyzing how the scores on the intelligence test correspond to the children's grades in school at this time.

Predictive validity *is a form of criterion validity that assesses the relation of a test's scores to an individual's performance at a point in the future.* For example, scores on an intelligence test might be used to predict whether the individual will be successful in university. Likewise, high school grades can be used for a similar purpose. Tests might also be developed to determine success as a police officer or pilot. Individuals take the test and then are evaluated *later* to see if they are indeed able to perform effectively in these jobs.

In considering reliability and validity, a test that is valid is reliable, but a test that is reliable is not necessarily valid. People can respond consistently on a test but the test might not be measuring what it purports to measure. To understand this, imagine that you have three darts to throw. If all three fall close together, you have reliability. However you have validity only if all three hit the bull's-eye (see figure 9.1).

Unreliable

Reliable but not valid

Valid and reliable

*F*igure 9.1
Links Between Reliability and Validity

The reliability and validity of a test can be illustrated by the dart-throwing analogy. If all the darts land in different places, then you have a lack of reliability, or consistency. If all the darts land in about the same place but far away from the bull's-eye, then you have reliability but a lack of validity. To be valid, though, all the darts have to hit the bull's-eye (which also means they have to be reliable).

Standardization of tests requires that uniform procedures be followed. What are some examples of these uniform procedures?

Standardization   Good tests are not only reliable and valid, they are standardized as well (Hopkins, 1998) ◀▥ P. 44. **Standardization** *involves developing uniform procedures for administering and scoring a test, as well as creating norms for the test.* Uniform testing procedures require that the testing environment be as similar as possible for all individuals. Without standardization, it is difficult to compare scores across individuals. If individuals take a test in a room where loud music is playing, they are disadvantaged compared to others who take the test in a quiet room. The test directions and the amount of time allowed to complete the test should be the same, for example. **Norms** *are established standards of performance for a test. Norms are created by giving the test to a large group of individuals representative of the population for whom the test is intended. This allows the test constructor to determine the distribution of test scores.* Norms inform us which scores are considered high, low, or average. For example, suppose you receive a score of 120 on an intelligence test; that number alone has little meaning. The score takes on meaning when we compare it with the other scores. If only 20 percent of the standardized group scored above 120, then we can interpret your score as high rather than low or average. Many tests of intelligence are designed for individuals from diverse groups. So that the tests are applicable to such different groups, many of them have norms—established standards of performance for individuals of different ages, socioeconomic statuses, and ethnic groups (Popham, 1999). Figure 9.2 summarizes the main themes of our discussion of how tests are constructed and evaluated.

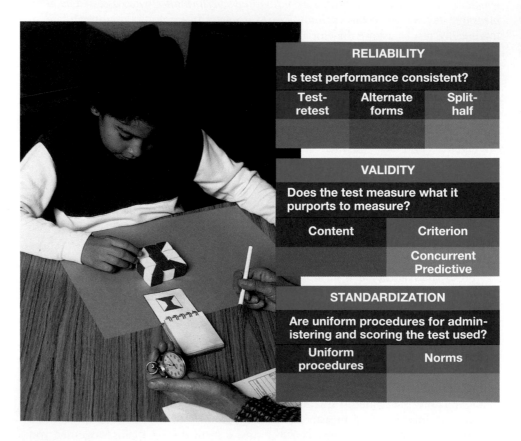

RELIABILITY
Is test performance consistent?

Test-retest	Alternate forms	Split-half

VALIDITY
Does the test measure what it purports to measure?

Content	Criterion
	Concurrent Predictive

STANDARDIZATION
Are uniform procedures for administering and scoring the test used?

Uniform procedures	Norms

𝓕**igure 9.2**
Test Construction and Evaluation

The Binet Tests and the Wechsler Scales

Intelligence tests can be administered to people on an individual basis or in a group. The two most widely used individual tests of intelligence are the Binet tests and Wechsler scales.

The Binet Tests   In 1904 the French Ministry of Education asked psychologist Alfred Binet to devise a method that would determine which students did not profit from typical school instruction. School officials wanted to reduce overcrowding by placing those who did not benefit from regular classroom teaching in special schools. Binet (Fancher, 1998) and his student Theophile Simon developed an intelligence test to meet this request. The test is referred to as the 1905 Scale and consisted of 30 items ranging from the ability to touch one's nose or ear when asked to the ability to draw designs from memory and define abstract concepts.

Binet developed the concept of **mental age** (**MA**), *which is an individual's level of mental development relative to others.* Binet reasoned that a mentally retarded child would perform like a normal child of a younger age. He developed norms for intelligence by testing 50 nonretarded children from the ages of 3 to 11. Children suspected of mental retardation were given the test and their performance was compared with children of the same chronological age in the normal sample. Average mental age (MA) scores correspond to chronological age (CA), which is age from birth. A bright child has an MA considerably above CA; a dull child has an MA considerably below CA.

The term **intelligence quotient** (**IQ**) *was devised in 1912 by William Stern. IQ consists of an individual's mental age divided by chronological age multiplied by 100:*

$$IQ = \frac{MA}{CA} \times 100$$

If mental age is the same as chronological age, then the individual's IQ is 100; if mental age is above chronological age, the IQ is more than 100; if mental age is below chronological age, the IQ is less than 100. Scores noticeably above 100 are considered above average; those considerably below are considered below average. For example, a 6-year-old child with a mental age of 8 would have an IQ of 133, whereas a 6-year-old child with a mental age of 5 would have an IQ of 83.

Over the years, extensive effort has been expended to standardize the Binet test, which has been given to thousands of children and adults of different ages selected at random from different parts of the world. By administering the test to large numbers of individuals and recording the results, it has been found that intelligence measured by the Binet approximates a normal distribution (see figure 9.3). A **normal distribution** *is symmetrical, with a majority of cases falling in the middle of the possible range of scores and few scores appearing toward the extremes of the range.*

Why were the Binet scales such a major advance over the earlier efforts of Galton and Cattell? Binet argued that intelligence could not be reduced to sensory, perceptual, and motor processes, as Galton and Cattell believed. Binet stressed that the core of intelligence consists of more complex mental processes such as memory, imagery, comprehension, and judgment. Galton and Cattell thought that children were untrustworthy subjects in psychological research, but Binet believed that a developmental approach was crucial for understanding the concept of intelligence. The developmental interest was underscored by the emphasis on the child's mental age in comparison to chronological age.

The Binet test has been revised many times to incorporate advances in the understanding of intelligence and intelligence testing. The many revisions are called the Stanford-Binet tests (Stanford University is where the revisions were done). Many of the revisions were carried out by Lewis Terman, who applied Stern's IQ concept to the test, developed extensive norms, and provided detailed, clear instructions for each problem on the test.

The current Stanford-Binet is given to individuals from the age of 2 through adulthood. It includes a wide variety of items, some requiring verbal responses,

Alfred Binet (1857–1911)

Alfred Binet constructed the first intelligence test after being asked to create a measure to determine which children could benefit from instruction in France's schools and which could not. Binet's 1905 scale measured more complex mental processes than Galton's and Cattell's tests.

Alfred Binet

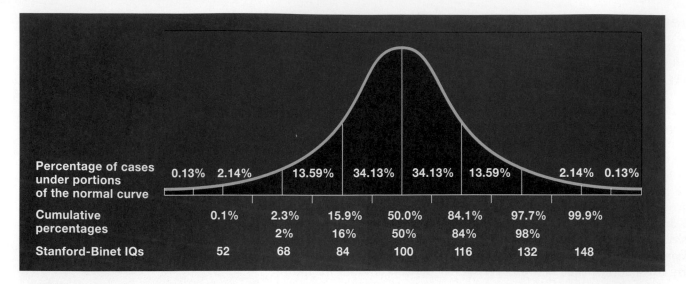

Percentage of cases under portions of the normal curve	0.13%	2.14%		13.59%	34.13%	34.13%	13.59%		2.14%	0.13%
Cumulative percentages		0.1%	2.3%	15.9%	50.0%	84.1%	97.7%	99.9%		
			2%	16%	50%	84%	98%			
Stanford-Binet IQs		52	68	84	100	116	132	148		

ℱigure 9.3
The Normal Curve and Stanford-Binet IQ Scores

The distribution of IQ scores approximates a normal curve. Most of the population falls in the middle range of scores. Notice that extremely high and extremely low scores are very rare. Slightly more than two-thirds of the scores fall between 84 and 116. Only about 1 in 50 individuals has an IQ of more than 132 and only about 1 in 50 individuals has an IQ of less than 68.

others nonverbal responses. For example, items that characterize a 6-year-old's performance on the test include the verbal ability to define at least six words, such as *orange* and *envelope*, and the nonverbal ability to trace a path through a maze. Items that reflect the average adult's intelligence include defining such words as *disproportionate* and *regard*, explaining a proverb, and comparing idleness and laziness.

The fourth edition of the Stanford-Binet was published in 1985. One important addition to this version is the analysis of the individual's responses in terms of four content areas: verbal reasoning, quantitative reasoning, abstract/visual reasoning, and short-term memory. A general composite score also is obtained to reflect overall intelligence. The Stanford-Binet continues to be one of the most widely used individual tests of intelligence.

The Wechsler Scales   Besides the Stanford-Binet, the other most widely used intelligence tests are the Wechsler scales, developed by David Wechsler. They include the Wechsler Adult Intelligence Scale–Revised (WAIS-R); the Wechsler Intelligence Scale for Children–III (WISC-III), to test children between the ages of 6 and 16; and the Wechsler Preschool and Primary Scale of Intelligence (WPPSI), to test children from the ages of 4 to 6½.

The Wechsler scales not only provide an overall IQ score but the items are grouped according to eleven subscales, six of which are verbal and five of which are nonverbal. This allows the examiner to obtain separate verbal and nonverbal IQ scores and to see quickly the areas of mental performance in which the individual is below average, average, or above average. The inclusion of a number of nonverbal subscales makes the Wechsler test more representative of verbal and nonverbal intelligence; the Binet test includes some nonverbal items but not as many as the Wechsler scales. Several of the Wechsler subscales are shown in figure 9.4.

Group Tests

The Stanford-Binet and Wechsler tests are individually administered intelligence tests. A psychologist approaches the testing situation as a structured interaction between the psychologist and the individual being tested. This provides an opportunity to sample the

VERBAL SUBSCALES

SIMILARITIES
An individual must think logically and abstractly to answer a number of questions about how things might be similar.

For example, "In what ways are boats and trains the same?"

COMPREHENSION
This subscale is designed to measure an individual's judgment and common sense.

For example, "Why do individuals buy automobile insurance?"

PERFORMANCE SUBSCALES

PICTURE ARRANGEMENT
A series of pictures out of sequence is shown to an individual, who is asked to place them in their proper order to tell an appropriate story. This subscale evaluates how individuals integrate information to make it logical and meaningful.

For example, "The pictures below need to be placed in an appropriate order to tell a story."

BLOCK DESIGN
An individual must assemble a set of multicolored blocks to match designs that the examiner shows. Visual-motor coordination, perceptual organization, and the ability to visualize spatially are assessed.

For example, "Use the four blocks on the left to make the pattern at the right."

Remember that the Wechsler includes 11 subscales, 6 verbal and 5 nonverbal. Four of the subscales are shown here.

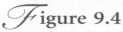igure 9.4

Sample Subscales of the Wechsler Adult Intelligence Scale–Revised

individual's behavior. During testing the psychologist observes the ease with which rapport is established, the level of energy and enthusiasm the individual expresses, and the degree of frustration tolerance and persistence the individual shows in performing difficult tasks. Each of these observations helps the psychologist understand the individual.

On some occasions, though, it is necessary to administer group intelligence tests, which are more convenient and economical than individual tests. For example, when

Should Parents Be Testing Their Own Child's IQ?

A CD-ROM, *Children's IQ and Achievement Test,* now lets parents test their child's IQ and how he or she is performing in relation to his or her grade in school. The company that makes the CD-ROM says that it helps to get parents involved in a constructive way with their children's education.

What might be some problems with parents giving their children an IQ test? In constructing your answer, consider whether intelligence is much more than just IQ, whether parents can objectively test their own child, and other cautions.

World War I began, Binet's test was already popular, and the idea of using tests to measure intelligence was generally accepted. The armed services thought it would be beneficial to know the intellectual abilities of its thousands of recruits. All of these people could not be tested individually. The result was the publication of the U.S. Army Alpha Test in 1917 to measure the intelligence of this large number of individuals on a group basis. In the same year, the U.S. Army Beta Test, mainly a performance test given orally, was designed for illiterate individuals who could not read the Army Alpha.

Though economical and convenient, group tests have some significant disadvantages. When a test is given to a large group, the examiner cannot establish rapport, determine the level of anxiety, and so on. Most testing experts recommend that, when important decisions are to be made about an individual, a group intelligence test should be supplemented by other information about the individual's abilities. For example, many children take ability tests at school in a large group. If a decision is to be made about placing a child in a special education class, it is a legal requirement that it not be based on a group intelligence test. The psychologist must administer an individual intelligence test, such as the Stanford-Binet or Wechsler, and obtain extensive additional information about the child's abilities outside the testing situation.

Have you taken the Canadian Achievement Tests (CAT) or the Canadian Test of Cognitive Skills (CTCS)? Yearly, many Canadian students take group tests like these. Or perhaps you have taken the Scholastic Aptitude Test (SAT)? More common in the U.S. than Canada, this test, like the CTCS, measures some of the same abilities as intelligence tests. However, the SAT and CTCS do not yield an overall IQ score; rather, these tests provide separate scores for skills such as verbal and mathematical ability.

Tests like the CTCS and SAT may be used to predict success in university, but they are only one of many pieces of information that determine whether a university admits a student. High school grades, the quality of the student's high school, letters of recommendation, individual interviews with the student, and special circumstances in the student's life are also taken into account.

In recent years, a controversy has developed over whether private coaching can raise a student's SAT scores. The student's verbal and mathematical abilities, which the SAT assesses, have been built over years of experience and instruction. Research shows that private coaching on a short-term basis cannot help raise SAT scores substantially. Researchers have found that, on the average, SAT preparation courses raise a student's scores only 15 points on the SAT's 200 to 800 scale (Kulik, Bangert-Drowns, & Kulik, 1984).

The latest controversy to hit the SAT is the discovery that certain items favor males. In one recent study, the answers of 100,000 students were analyzed. On 23 of 145 questions, one sex did better than the other. Males did better on all but two. Examples of questions that favored males included:

- "Dividends are to stockholders as. . . ." The answer is "royalties are to writers." Fifteen percent more males than females answered this item correctly.
- "The opposite of stamina is. . . ." The answer is "lack of endurance." Twelve percent more males answered this item correctly.

Educational Testing Service, responsible for the SAT's content, is revising the test by throwing out questions that are unusually difficult for females or males.

Aptitude and Achievement Tests

Psychologists distinguish between aptitude tests and achievement tests. **Aptitude tests** *predict an individual's ability to learn a skill or what the individual can accomplish with* *training.* **Achievement tests** *measure what a person has learned or the skills the person has mastered.* Aptitude tests measure future performance; achievement tests current performance. The CTCS (Canadian Test of Cognitive Skills) is an aptitude test. The tests you take in university that assess what you have learned are achievement tests. So is the CAT (Canadian Achievement Tests), which is used by Statistics Canada to track achievement of Canadian students.

The distinction between aptitude and achievement tests can be unclear. When someone gives a correct answer to a test item, it can be difficult to tell if the answer is correct because that person is naturally good at figuring out such answers (aptitude) or knew the answer through previous learning (achievement). Regardless, the CTCS and CAT can be used together to compare aptitude and achievement. Under-achievement, for example, would be indicated when a student received a higher CTCS than CAT score.

Do We Have a Single Intelligence or Multiple Intelligences?

Is it more accurate to describe intelligence as a general ability, or is intelligence made up of a number of specific abilities?

Early Views

Although the early Binet tests tapped some different cognitive skills (such as memory and comprehension), individuals' performance on these skills was lumped together to describe their general intellectual ability. Since Binet, other researchers have proposed that intelligence is best thought of as including a general ability along with some specific dimensions. Charles Spearman (1927) proposed that intelligence has two factors. **Two-factor theory** *is Spearman's theory that individuals have both general intelligence, which he called* g, *and a number of specific intelligences, which he called* s.

Spearman believed that these two factors accounted for a person's performance on an intelligence test. Many psychologists have followed up on Spearman's work. It is in this tradition that David Wechsler analyzed intelligence in terms of general and specific abilities (giving the individual an overall IQ but also providing information about specific subcomponents of intelligence).

However, some researchers abandoned the idea of a general intelligence and searched for specific factors only. **Multiple-factor theory** *is L.L. Thurstone's (1938) theory that intelligence consists of seven primary mental abilities: verbal comprehension, number ability, word fluency, spatial visualization, associative memory, reasoning, and perceptual speed.*

Contemporary Approaches

Two contemporary approaches that emphasize our multiple intellectual abilities have been proposed by Howard Gardner and Robert Sternberg.

Gardner's Seven Frames of Mind
One attempt to classify intelligence, developed by Howard Gardner (1983, 1993), includes seven components, although they are not the same as Thurstone's seven factors. The talents of Wayne Gretzky and Ludwig van Beethoven reflect the diversity of Gardner's concept of intelligence. Turn back the clock a few years. Gretzky, the Edmonton Oilers' superstar, springs into action. Scrambling to recover the puck behind his own net, he quickly weaves his way down the length of the ice, all the while processing the whereabouts of his six opponents and five teammates. As the crowd screams, Gretzky calmly looks one way, finesses his way past a defender, freezes the goaltender, and whirls a behind-the-back pass

Interview with Howard Gardner

*T*hrough the Eyes of Psychologists

Howard Gardner, *Harvard University*

"If by 2013 [the 30th anniversary of the publication of Gardner's Frames of Mind] there is a wider acceptance of the notion that intelligence deserves to be pluralized, I will be pleased."

Verbal Skills   *Math Skills*   *Spatial Skills*   *Movement Skills*

Musical Skills   *Insight about self*   *Insight about others*

$\mathcal{F}$igure 9.5
Gardner's Seven Frames of Mind

to a fast-breaking teammate, who scores an easy goal. Was there specific intelligence to Gretzky's movements and perception of the spatial layout of the hockey rink? Now

"You're wise, but you lack tree smarts."

we turn the clock back 200 years. A tiny boy just 4 years old is standing on the footstool in front of a piano keyboard practicing. At the age of 6, the young boy has been given the honor of playing concertos and trios at a concert. The young boy is Ludwig van Beethoven, whose musical genius was evident at a young age. Did Beethoven have a specific type of intelligence, one we might call musical intelligence?

Gretzky and Beethoven are two different types of individuals with different types of abilities. Gardner argues that Gretzky's talent reflects his movement intelligence and his ability to analyze the world spatially, and that Beethoven's talent reflects his musical intelligence. Beyond these three forms of intelligence, Gardner argues that we have four other main forms: verbal intelligence, mathematical intelligence, insightful skills for analyzing ourselves, and insightful skills for analyzing others (see figure 9.5).

Gardner believes that each of the seven intelligences can be destroyed by brain damage, that each involves unique cognitive skills, and that each shows up in exaggerated fashion in both the gifted and individuals who have mental retardation or autism (Solomon, Powell, & Gardner, 1999). Dustin Hoffman portrayed an individual with autism who had a remarkable computing

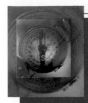

EXPLORATIONS IN PSYCHOLOGY
Project Spectrum

PROJECT SPECTRUM is an innovative attempt by Howard Gardner (1993) to apply his theory of multiple intelligences to educating children. Spectrum begins with the idea that every student has the potential to develop strengths in one or more areas.

What is a Spectrum classroom like? The classroom has rich and engaging materials that can stimulate a range of intelligences. Teachers do not try to evoke intelligences directly by using materials that are labeled "spatial" or "verbal." Rather, materials that relate to a combination of intelligence domains are used. For example, in a naturalist corner there are biological specimens that students can explore and compare. This area elicits students' sensory capacities and logical thinking skills. In a story-telling area, students create imaginative tales with stimulating props and design their own storyboards. This area encourages children to use their linguistic, dramatic, and imaginative skills. In a building corner, students can construct a model of their classroom and arrange small-scale photographs of the students and the teachers in their class. This area stimulates the use of spatial and personal skills. In all, the Spectrum classroom has 12 such areas that are designed to elicit students' multiple intelligences.

The Spectrum classroom can identify skills that are typically missed in a regular classroom. In one first-grade Spectrum classroom, a boy who was a product of a highly conflicted broken home was at risk for school failure. However, when Project Spectrum was introduced the boy was identified as especially skilled in one area. He was the best student in the class at taking apart and putting together common objects, such as a doorknob and a food grinder. His teacher became encouraged when she found that he possessed this skill and his overall school performance began to improve.

In addition to identifying unexpected strengths in students, Project Spectrum can also pinpoint undetected weaknesses. Gregory, who was especially skilled in math computation and conceptual knowledge, was doing very well in the first grade. However, he performed poorly in a number of Spectrum areas. Gregory did well only in the areas in which he needed to give a correct answer and

a person in authority gave it to him. As a result of the Spectrum Project, Gregory's teacher began to search for ways to encourage him to take risks on more open-ended tasks, to try things out in innovative ways, and to realize that it was okay to make mistakes.

Student in a Spectrum classroom engaged in a science project. What are Spectrum classrooms like?

ability in the movie *Rain Man.* This was illustrated when he helped his brother successfully gamble in Las Vegas by keeping track of all the cards that had been played.

There is currently considerable interest in applying Gardner's theory of multiple intelligences to children's education (Campbell, Campbell, & Dickinson, 1999; Fogarty & Bellanca, 1998). To read about these applications, see Explorations in Psychology.

Multiple Intelligences

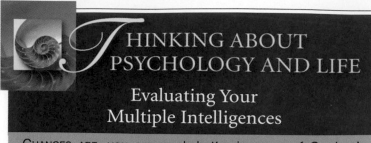

THINKING ABOUT PSYCHOLOGY AND LIFE

Evaluating Your Multiple Intelligences

CHANCES ARE, you are much better in some of Gardner's areas of intelligence than others. Answering the following questions candidly should give you a sense of what your intelligence profile looks like based on Gardner's scheme.

Verbal Thinking

Do you do well on verbal tests, like the verbal part of the SAT?

Are you a skilled reader and do you read prolifically?

Do you love the challenge of solving verbal problems?

Logical/Mathematical Thinking

Are you good at logically solving problems?

Do you think like a scientist?

Is math one of your favorite subjects?

Spatial Skills

Are you good at visualizing objects and layouts from different angles?

Do you have the ability to create maps of spaces and locations in your mind?

If you wanted to, could you be an architect?

Movement Skills

Do you have great hand-eye coordination?

Do you excel at sports?

Are you good at using your body to carry out an expression, as in dance?

Musical Skills

Do you play one or more musical instruments well?

Do you like to go to musical concerts?

Do you like to make up songs?

Insightful Skills for Self-Understanding

Do you know yourself well and have a positive view of yourself?

Are you in tune with your thoughts and feelings?

Do you have good coping skills?

Insightful Skills for Understanding Others

Are you good at "reading" people?

Do you like to work collaboratively with others?

Are you a good listener?

Which areas of intelligence do you excel in? Most everyone has one or more areas in which they do well and one or more areas in which they don't.

Sternberg's Triarchic Theory

While Gardner believes there are seven types of intelligence, Robert J. Sternberg (1986) thinks there are three. **Triarchic theory** *is Sternberg's theory that intelligence consists of componential intelligence, experiential intelligence, and contextual intelligence.* Consider Ann, who scores high on traditional intelligence tests such as the Stanford-Binet and is a star analytical thinker. Consider Jacques, who does not have the best test scores but has an insightful and creative mind. And consider Ng, a street-smart person who has learned to deal in practical ways with his world, although his scores on traditional IQ tests are low.

Sternberg calls Ann's analytical thinking and abstract reasoning "componential intelligence"; it is the closest to what we call intelligence in this chapter and what is commonly measured by intelligence tests. Jacques's insightful and creative thinking is called "experiential intelligence" by Sternberg. And Ng's street smarts and practical know-how is called "contextual intelligence" by Sternberg.

In Sternberg's view of componential intelligence, the basic unit in intelligence is a component, simply defined as a basic unit of information processing. Sternberg believes such components include the ability to acquire or store information; to retain or retrieve information; to transfer information; to plan, make decisions, and solve problems; and to translate our thoughts into performance.

The second part of Sternberg's model focuses on experience. According to Sternberg, intellectual people have the ability to solve new problems quickly, but they also learn how to solve familiar problems in an automatic, rote way so their minds are free to handle other problems that require insight and creativity.

The third part of the model involves practical intelligence—such as how to get out of trouble, how to replace a fuse, and how to get along with people. Sternberg describes this practical or contextual intelligence as all of the important information about getting along in the real world that you are not taught in school. He believes contextual intelligence is sometimes more important than the "book knowledge" that is often taught in school.

Sternberg (1997b) says that students with different triarchic patterns "look different" in school. Students with high analytic ability tend to be favored in conventional schooling. They often do well in direct instruction classes in which the teacher lectures and students are given objective tests. They are often considered "smart" students. They typically get good grades, do well on traditional IQ tests, and later get admitted to competitive universities. Students who are high in creative intelligence are often not in the top rung of their class. Sternberg says that many teachers have expectations about how assignments should be done and creatively intelligent students might not conform to those expectations. Instead of giving conformist answers, they give unique answers, for which they might get reprimanded or marked down. Like students high in creative intelligence, students who are practically intelligent often do not relate well to the demands of school. However, these students frequently do well outside of the classroom's walls. They may have excellent social skills and good common sense. As adults, they sometimes become successful managers, entrepreneurs, or politicians, yet have undistinguished school records.

Sternberg (1999) believes that few tasks are purely analytic, creative, or practical. Most tasks require some combination of these skills. For example, when students write a book report, they might (1) analyze the book's main themes, (2) generate new ideas about how the book could have been written better, and (3) think about how the book's themes can be applied to people's lives. Sternberg argues that what is important in teaching is to balance instruction related to all three types of intelligence. That is, students should be given opportunities to learn through analytical, creative, and practical thinking, in addition to the conventional strategy of having students memorize material.

Evaluating the Multiple Intelligences Approach   Gardner's and Sternberg's approaches have much to offer. They have stimulated us to think more broadly about what makes up people's intelligence. And they have motivated educators to develop programs that instruct students in different domains. However, some critics say that classifying such domains as musical skills (in Gardner's approach) is off base. They ask whether there are possibly other skills domains that Gardner has left out. For example, there are outstanding chess players, prizefighters, writers, politicians, lawyers, ministers, and poets. Yet we don't refer to chess intelligence, prizefighter intelligence, and so on. Other critics say that the research base to support the three intelligences of Sternberg and the seven intelligences of Gardner as the best way to characterize intelligence has not yet been developed.

At this point we have discussed many ideas about the nature of intelligence and its early history, intelligence tests, and whether we have a single intelligence or multiple intelligences. An overview of these ideas is presented in summary table 9.1.

Through the Eyes of Psychologists

Robert J. Sternberg,
Yale University

"My view of intelligence is quite different from the conventional one. Successful intelligence, as I view it, involves analytical, creative, and practical aspects."

Sternberg's Theory

Controversies and Issues in Intelligence

We have seen that intelligence is a complex and slippery concept with many competing definitions, theories, and tests. It is not surprising, therefore, that attempts to understand the nature of intelligence have been filled with controversy. Three controversies that currently share the spotlight are the following: (1) the degree to which intelligence is due to heredity or to environment, (2) the extent of ethnic differences and the role of culture in intelligence, and (3) the use and misuse of intelligence tests.

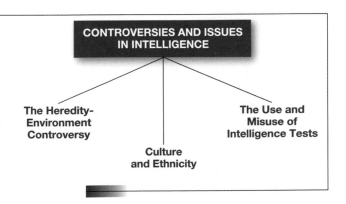

CONTROVERSIES AND ISSUES IN INTELLIGENCE

The Heredity-Environment Controversy

Culture and Ethnicity

The Use and Misuse of Intelligence Tests

The Heredity-Environment Controversy

Arthur Jensen (1969) sparked lively and, at times, hostile debate when he stated his theory that intelligence is primarily inherited and that environment and culture play only a minimal role in intelligence ◄||| P. 66. In one of his most provocative statements, Jensen claimed that genetics accounts for clear-cut differences in the average intelligence between races, nationalities, and social classes. A similar argument was recently made by Herrnstein and Murray (1994).

SUMMARY TABLE 9.1
The Nature of Intelligence and Early History of Assessment; Intelligence Tests; and Whether We Have a Single Intelligence or Multiple Intelligences

Concept	Processes/ Related Ideas	Characteristics/Description
The Nature of Intelligence and Early History of Assessment	What Is Intelligence?	Intelligence involves verbal ability, problem-solving skills, and the ability to adapt to and learn from life's everyday experiences. Interest in intelligence has focused on individual differences (the stable, consistent way people are different from each other) and assessment.
	Early History of Assessment	Sir Francis Galton is the father of mental tests. He believed that sensory, perceptual, and motor processes were at the core of intelligence. He tried to measure individual differences but found no formidable conclusions. James McKeen Cattell was the first North American to study individual differences in intelligence. He developed the label *mental test.*
Intelligence Tests	How Tests Are Constructed and Evaluated	A good test is reliable, valid, and standardized. Reliability is how consistently an individual performs on a test. Three forms of reliability are test-retest, alternate forms, and split-half. Validity is the extent to which a test measures what it is intended to measure. Validity can be assessed in terms of content validity and criterion validity. Criterion validity involves either concurrent or predictive validity. Standardization focuses on uniform procedures for administering and scoring a test; it also involves norms.
	The Binet Tests and the Wechsler Scales	Alfred Binet developed the first intelligence test, known as the 1905 Scale. He created the concept of mental age, whereas William Stern developed the concept of IQ. The Binet has been standardized and revised a number of times. The many revisions are called the Stanford-Binet. The test scores approximate a normal distribution and assess more complex cognitive abilities than Galton's and Cattell's did. The Stanford-Binet is given to individuals from the age of 2 through adulthood. Besides the Binet, the other most widely used individual tests of intelligence are the Wechsler scales, created by David Wechsler. These tests provide an overall IQ, verbal and performance IQs, and information about eleven subtests.
	Group Tests	These are convenient and economical, but they do not allow an examiner to monitor the testing closely. The Army Alpha and Beta tests were the first widely used group intelligence tests. The CTCS and SAT are group aptitude tests; the CAT is a group achievement test.
	Aptitude and Achievement Tests	Aptitude tests predict an individual's ability to learn a skill or the individual's future performance. Achievement tests assess what a person already knows. The distinction between these two types of tests is sometimes blurred.
Do We Have a Single Intelligence or Multiple Intelligences?	Early Views	The concept of mental age and IQ fits in the camp of viewing intelligence as a general ability. The Wechsler scales assess general intelligence and skills in specific areas. Spearman proposed the two-factor theory, which says people have a general ability (g) and specific abilities (s). Thurstone abandoned the idea of general intelligence. His multiple-factor theory proposed seven primary mental abilities.
	Contemporary Approaches	Gardner argues that intelligence consists of seven frames of mind (verbal, math, spatial, movement, music, insight about self, insight about others). There is currently considerable interest in applying his ideas to education. Sternberg proposed the triarchic theory, according to which intelligence comes in three forms: componential, experiential, and practical. There is much to offer in these views, although their research base has not been adequately developed.

Much of the research on intelligence and heredity relies upon comparisons of identical and fraternal twins. Identical twins have exactly the same genetic makeup. If intelligence is genetically determined, identical twins' IQs should be similar. Fraternal twins and ordinary siblings are less similar genetically, so their IQs should be less similar. Jensen (1969) found support for this argument.

Jensen (1998) places heredity's influence on intelligence at about 80 percent and thinks we can breed for intelligence. Just such an effort is being made today at the Repository for Germinal Choice. To read about the "Nobel Prize sperm bank" (so-called because it houses the sperm of several Nobel Prize winners as well as others), see Explorations in Psychology.

Significant criticisms have been leveled at Jensen's and Herrnstein and Murray's work. While experts generally agree that many minority groups score lower than Whites on IQ tests, many also raise serious questions about what this means. For instance, it has been argued that the tests are culturally biased against minority group members, an argument we shall return to shortly. Another criticism is that most investigations of heredity and environment do not include environments that differ radically. Thus, it is not surprising that many genetic studies show environment to be a fairly weak influence on intelligence (Fraser, 1995). Further, predictions about any individual based exclusively on that person's IQ are virtually useless.

Perhaps the most serious criticism has been championed by Douglas Wahlsten, of the University of Alberta (Wahlsten, 1994, 1996). Recall Jensen's claim that heredity's influence on intelligence is about 80 percent. Wahlsten claims that it makes no sense to treat heredity and environment as two separate, or *additive*, factors, contributing together like two friends giving $80 and $20 to buy a gift for another friend. Instead, Wahlsten argues, heredity and environment are *interactive*, or *multiplicative*, in their action. Recall Donald Hebb's (1958) argument ◀▥▥ P. 69 that the relationship of heredity and environment is like that of the height and width of a rectangle—it doesn't make sense to ask which is more important to the rectangle (Gottleib, Wahlsten, & Lickliter, 1998).

Thus, the interaction of heredity and environment is bi-directional. In one direction, each child's heredity helps determine its environment. For example, those nurturing a "naturally" less intelligent child may end up posing fewer intellectual challenges for that child and hence not stimulating that child's growth as much as they might a "naturally" brighter child. Conversely, each child's environment helps to determine how his or her heredity is expressed. For example, malnourishment stunts development, including that of intelligence. The two effects, then, are so intertwined that the study of the distribution of IQ scores in human populations or the study of the IQs of identical and fraternal twins cannot cleanly separate them. Thus any measure of the effect of heredity cannot be accurate and does not indicate any constraint on the modifiabilty of intelligence (Wahlsten, 1997).

This does not mean it is worthless to examine the role of heredity and environment in development. Wahlsten (Wahlsten & Gottlieb, 1997) makes it clear that carefully controlled animal studies, where it is possible to exert near-perfect control over the genetic make-up AND environmental experiences of the animals, can teach us much about the relationship between nature and nurture. It is just that human studies cannot use such control and hence cannot clearly separate the effects of heredity and environment.

In the end, the question is whether we are ever entitled to use the IQ scores of individuals or groups to justify failing to provide them with the best possible work or educational environments. Today, North American courts generally refuse to accept IQ scores as a basis for such a failure. Cognitive psychologist Robert J. Sternberg (1994) said that using one index—IQ—as a basis of policy judgment is not only irresponsible, it is dangerous. In the end, we are obliged to provide all individuals and all groups with the best environments possible so that they can develop to the fullest possible extent.

Today, most researchers agree that heredity does not determine intelligence to the extent Jensen and Herrnstein and Murray envisioned (Ceci, 1996). For most people, this means that modifying their environment can change their IQ scores considerably (Campbell & Ramey, 1993). It also means that programs designed to enrich

University of Alberta professor Douglas Wahlsten argues that it is not possible to sort out the relative effects of heredity and environment in determining the IQ of human individuals or groups. What are the details of his argument?

The Heredity-Environment Controversy

EXPLORATIONS IN PSYCHOLOGY
The Repository for Germinal Choice

DORAN (A NAME FROM the Greek word meaning "gift") learned all of the elements of speech by 2 years of age. An intelligence test showed that, at the age of 1, his mental age was 4. Doran was the second child born through the sperm bank. The sperm bank was founded by Robert Graham in Escondido, California, with the intent of producing geniuses. Graham collected the sperm of Nobel Prize–winning scientists and offered it free of charge to intelligent women of good stock, whose husbands were infertile.

One of the contributors to the sperm bank is physicist William Shockley, who shared the Nobel Prize in 1956 for inventing the transistor. During the 1960s and 1970s, Shockley received his share of criticism for preaching the genetic basis of intelligence. Two other Nobel Prize winners have donated their sperm to the bank, but Shockley is the only one who has been identified.

Are the progeny prodigies? It may be too early to tell. Except for Doran, little has been revealed about the children. Doran's genetic father was labeled "28 Red" in the sperm bank (the color apparently has no meaning). He is listed in the sperm bank's catalog as handsome, blond, and athletic, with high mathematical intelligence and several prizes for his classical music performances. One of his few drawbacks is that he passed along to Doran an almost one-in-three chance of developing hemorrhoids. Doran's mother says that her genetic contribution goes back to the royal court of Norway and to the poet William Blake.

The odds are not high that a sperm bank will yield that special combination of factors required to produce a creative genius. George Bernard Shaw, who believed that the influence of heredity on intelligence is strong, once told a story about a beautiful woman who wrote him saying that, with her body and his brain, they could produce marvelous offspring. Shaw responded by saying that unfortunately the offspring might get his body and her brain.

Not surprisingly, the Nobel Prize sperm bank is heavily criticized. Some say that brighter does not mean better. They also say that IQ is not a good indicator of social competence or human contribution to the world. Other critics say that intelligence is an elusive concept to measure and that it cannot reliably be reproduced, as the sperm bank is trying to do. Visions of the German gene program of the 1930s and 1940s are created. The German Nazis believed that certain traits were superior; they tried to breed children with such traits and killed people without them.

Although Graham's Repository of Germinal Choice (as the Nobel Prize sperm bank is formally called) is strongly criticized, consider its possible contributions. The repository does provide a social service for couples who cannot conceive a child, and individuals who go to the sperm bank probably provide an enriched environment for the offspring (Garelik, 1985).

Where do you stand on this controversial topic of breeding for intelligence? Do you think it is unethical? Can you see where it might bring hope for once childless parents?

Doran, conceived using sperm from the Repository for Germinal Choice

Dr. Robert Graham in the room that houses the sperm of Nobel Prize winners. What do you think about Graham's breeding for geniuses?

a person's environment can have a considerable impact, improving school achievement and the acquisition of skills needed for employability. While genetic endowment may always influence a person's intellectual ability, the environmental influences and opportunities we provide children and adults do make a difference.

In a study that was described initially in our coverage of environmental influences on language (chapter 8), researchers went into homes and observed how extensively parents from welfare and middle-income professional families talked and communicated with their young children (Hart & Risley, 1995) ◀▥ P. 270. They found that the middle-income professional parents were much more likely to talk and communicate with their young children than the welfare parents were. And how much the parents talked and communicated with their children in the first three years of their lives was correlated with the children's Stanford-Binet IQ scores at age 3 (the more they talked and communicated with their children, the higher the children's IQs were).

Keep in mind, though, that environmental influences are complex (Neisser & others, 1996). Growing up with all the "advantages," for example, does not necessarily guarantee success. Children from wealthy families may have easy access to excellent schools, books, travel, and tutoring, but they may take such opportunities for granted and fail to develop the motivation to learn and to achieve. In the same way, "poor" or "disadvantaged" does not automatically equal "doomed."

Researchers are increasingly interested in manipulating the early environment of children who are at risk for impoverished intelligence (Blair & Ramey, 1996) ◀▥ P. 17. The emphasis is on prevention rather than remediation. Many low-income parents have difficulty providing an intellectually stimulating environment for their children. Programs that educate parents to be more sensitive caregivers and train them to be better teachers, as well as support services, such as high quality Head Start programs, can make a difference in a child's intellectual development. The current trend is to conduct two-generation poverty interventions by working to improve the quality of life and skills of parents, as well as providing the child with an enriched environment (McLoyd, 1998).

Another argument for the importance of environment in intelligence involves the increasing scores of IQ tests around the world (Flynn, 1999). Scores on these tests have been increasing so fast that a high percentage of people regarded as having average intelligence at the turn of century would be considered below average in intelligence today (Hall, 1998) (see figure 9.6). If a representative sample of people today took the Stanford-Binet test used in 1932, about one-fourth would be defined as having very superior intelligence, a label usually accorded to fewer than 3 percent of the population. Because the increase has taken place in a relatively short period of time, it can't be due to heredity, but rather may be due to such environmental factors as the explosion in information people are exposed to as well as a much greater percentage of the population experiencing more education.

THINKING ABOUT PSYCHOLOGY AND LIFE
Can Intelligence Be Increased?

PSYCHOLOGISTS SUCH AS Howard Gardner, Robert Sternberg, and Douglas Wahlsten believe that intelligence can be increased considerably. Other psychologists such as Arthur Jensen contend that intelligence has such a strong hereditary basis that programs designed to increase intelligence are likely to have little success.

Which side do you come down on? Can intelligence be increased substantially through stimulating mental exercises and environmental experiences? Or is intelligence so strongly influenced by heredity that any efforts to increase intelligence are likely to fail? To read further about this issue, see a book to which a number of experts including Wahlsten, Gardner, Sternberg, and Jensen contributed articles—*Intelligence, Heredity, and Environment* (1997), edited by Sternberg and Elena Grigorenko.

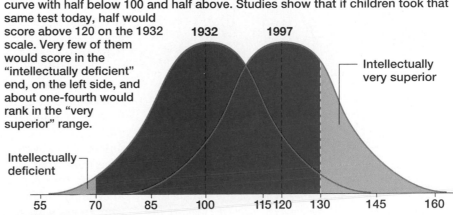

Figure 9.6
The Increase in IQ Scores from 1932 to 1997

Culture and Ethnicity

Are there cultural and ethnic differences in intelligence? Are standard intelligence tests biased? If so, can we develop tests that are culturally fair?

Cultural and Ethnic Comparisons   Native students tend to score 20 points lower on verbal scales and five points higher on performance scales of standardized intelligence tests when compared against White norms (McShane & Plas, 1984). In the U.S., African American and Latino children score below White children on standardized intelligence tests. On average, African American children score 10 to 15 points lower on IQ tests than White children do (Lynn, 1996). We are talking about average scores, though. Estimates also indicate that 15 to 25 percent of all African American schoolchildren score higher than half of all White schoolchildren, and many Whites score lower than most African Americans. This is because the distribution of scores for African Americans and Whites overlap.

There is, however, no evidence to support a genetic interpretation (Neisser & others, 1996). For example, Natives living further from "civilization" tend to have higher IQ scores than those living closer (Berry, 1976). Further, as African Americans have gained in socioeconomic status, their IQ gap has narrowed. Also, when disadvantaged African American children are adopted into middle-class families, their IQ scores more closely resemble national averages for middle-class children than for lower-class children (Scarr & Weinberg, 1983).

Cultural Bias and Culture-Fair Tests   Many early IQ tests were culturally biased, favoring people who were urban, middle-class and White rather than rural, lower class, and from a visible minority (Miller-Jones, 1989). For example, one question asked what should be done if you find a 3-year-old child in the street. The correct answer was "call the police." But visible minority inner-city children who perceive police as adversaries are unlikely to choose this answer. Similarly, children from rural areas might not choose this answer if there is no police force nearby. Such questions clearly do not measure the knowledge necessary to be "intelligent" in an inner-city neighborhood or in a rural area (Scarr, 1984). Another infamous example comes from Darou (1992) who gave what he thought was an unbiased IQ test question to a Canadian Native: "*Saw* is to *whine* as *snake* is to …?" The Native did not "correctly" answer "*hiss.*" He was from the far north and had never seen a snake. Besides, the saws he had used in the bush did not whine.

Even White Canadians do not perform identically to White Americans on IQ tests (Saklofske, 1996). Saklofske and others (1998) report that Canadian children score higher than American children on some WISC-III scales. The WAIS-R is also biased (Peckford, Templer & Ruff, 1975), especially the Information subtest (Pugh & Boer, 1989). Pugh & Boer (1991) studied problematic WAIS-R questions (e.g., about U.S. Senators) and suggested Canadian replacements (e.g., about Prime Ministers). Interestingly, even within a cultural group, an easy question in 1991 (when this research was published) might be harder to answer a decade later (e.g., Who is Gordon Lightfoot)?

Also, minority group members who do not speak English or speak nonstandard English may have difficulty understanding verbal questions framed in standard English, even if the test content is appropriate (Darou, 1992; Gibbs & Huang, 1989). Cultures also define intelligence differently (Rogoff, 1990) ◀▥ P. 19. Most European-heritage North Americans think of intelligence in terms of technical skills, but people in Kenya consider responsible participation in family and social life an integral part of intelligence. An intelligent person in Uganda is someone who knows what to do and then follows through with appropriate action. James Bay Cree value the visual pattern recognition skills necessary to find food (Darou, 1992). Intelligence to the Iatmul people of Papua,

"You can't build a hut, you don't know how to find edible roots and you know nothing about predicting the weather. In other words, you do terribly on our I.Q. test."

© *by Sidney Harris*

𝓕igure 9.7
Iatmul and Caroline Islander Intelligence
(*a*) The intelligence of the Iatmul people of Papua, New Guinea, involves the ability to remember the names of many clans.
(*b*) The Caroline Islands number 680 in the Pacific Ocean east of the Philippines. The intelligence of their inhabitants includes the ability to navigate by the stars.

New Guinea, involves remembering the names of up to 20,000 clans, and the islanders in the Caroline Islands value the talent of navigating by the stars (see figure 9.7).

As a result of such cases, researchers have tried to develop tests that accurately reflect a person's intelligence. **Culture-fair tests** *are intelligence tests that are intended to not be culturally biased.* Two types of culture-fair tests have been devised. The first includes questions that are familiar to people from all socioeconomic and ethnic backgrounds. For example, a child might be asked how a bird and a dog are different, on the assumption that virtually all children are familiar with birds and dogs. The second type of culture-fair test removes all verbal questions (e.g. Mawhinney, 1983). Figure 9.8 shows a sample question from the Raven Progressive Matrices Test. Even though tests such as the Raven Progressive Matrices are designed to be culture-fair, people with more education still score higher than those with less education do.

One test that takes into account the socioeconomic background of children is the SOMPA, which stands for System of Multicultural Pluralistic Assessment (Mercer & Lewis, 1978). This test can be given to children from 5 to 11 years of age, and

Cultural Bias and Testing

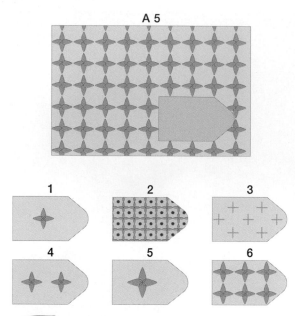

Figure 9.8
Sample Item from the Raven Progressive Matrices Test

Individuals are presented with a matrix arrangement of symbols, such as the one at the top of this figure and must then complete the matrix by selecting the appropriate missing symbol from a group of symbols.

"How are her scores?"

was especially designed for children from low-income families. Instead of relying on a single test, SOMPA is based on information from four different areas of the child's life: (1) verbal and nonverbal intelligence, assessed by the WISC-III; (2) social and economic background, obtained through a one-hour parent interview; (3) social adjustment to school, determined through a questionnaire that parents complete; and (4) physical health, assessed by a medical examination.

Why is it so hard to create culture-fair tests? Most tests tend to reflect what the dominant culture thinks is important (Sax, 1997). If tests have time limits, that will bias the test against groups not concerned with time. If languages differ, the same words might have different meanings for different language groups. Even pictures can produce bias because some cultures have less experience with drawings and photographs (Anastasi & Urbina, 1996). Even within the same culture, different groups could have different attitudes, values, and motivation, and this could affect their performance on intelligence tests. Items that ask why buildings should be made of brick are biased against children who have little or no experience with brick houses. Questions about railroads, furnaces, seasons of the year, distances between cities, and so on can be biased against groups who have less experience than others with these circumstances.

The Use and Misuse of Intelligence Tests

Psychological tests are tools. Like all tools, their effectiveness depends on the knowledge, skill, and integrity of the user. A hammer can be used to build a beautiful kitchen cabinet or it can be used as a weapon of assault. Like a hammer, psychological tests can be used for positive purposes or they can be badly abused. It is important for both the test constructor and the test examiner to be familiar with the current state of scientific knowledge about intelligence and intelligence tests.

Even though they have limitations, tests of intelligence are among psychology's most widely used tools. To be effective, though, intelligence tests must be viewed realistically. They should not be thought of as unchanging indicators of intelligence. They should be used in conjunction with other information about an individual, not relied on as the sole indicator of intelligence. For example, an intelligence test should not solely determine whether a child is placed in a special education or gifted class. The child's developmental history, medical background, performance in school, social competencies, and family experiences should be taken into account too.

The single number provided by many IQ tests can easily lead to stereotypes and expectations about an individual (Rosnow & Rosenthal, 1996). Many people do not know how to interpret the results of intelligence tests, and sweeping generalizations are too often made on the basis of an IQ score. For example, imagine that you are a teacher in the teacher's lounge the day after school has started in the fall. You mention a student—Johnny Jones—and a fellow teacher remarks that she had Johnny in class last year; she comments that he was a real dunce and points out that his IQ is 78. You cannot help but remember this information, and it might lead to thoughts that Johnny Jones is not very bright so it is useless to spend much time teaching him. In this way, IQ scores are misused and stereotypes are formed (Rosenthal & Jacobsen, 1968).

Ability tests can help a teacher group together children who function at roughly the same level in math or reading so they can

SUMMARY TABLE 9.2
Controversies and Issues in Intelligence

Concept	Processes/ Related Ideas	Characteristics/Description
The Heredity-Environment Controversy	Its Nature	Jensen's, as well as Herrnstein's and Murray's, argument that intelligence is primarily due to heredity has sparked a lively, and at times bitter, debate. According to Wahlsten, the partitioning of human intelligence into hereditary and environmental components is meaningless.
Culture and Ethnicity	Cultural and Ethnic Comparisons	There are cultural and ethnic differences in scores on intelligence tests, but the evidence suggests that they are not genetically based. In recent decades, the gap between African Americans and Whites on intelligence test scores has diminished as African Americans have experienced more socioeconomic opportunities.
	Cultural Bias and Culture-Fair Tests	Early intelligence tests favored White, middle-class urban individuals. Culture-fair tests are intelligence tests that are intended to not be culturally biased. Most intelligence psychologists believe they cannot replace traditional intelligence tests.
The Use and Misuse of Intelligence Tests	Their Nature	Despite limitations, when used by a judicious examiner, tests can be valuable tools for determining individual differences in intelligence. The tests should be used with other information about the individual. IQ scores can produce unfortunate stereotypes and expectations. Ability tests can help divide children into homogeneous groups; however, periodic testing should be done. Intelligence or a high IQ is not necessarily the ultimate human value.

be taught the same concepts together. However, when children are placed in tracks, such as "advanced," "intermediate," and "low," extreme caution needs to be taken. Periodic assessment of the groups is needed, especially with the "low" group. Ability tests measure *current* performance, and maturational changes or enriched environmental experiences may advance in a child's intelligence, requiring that she be moved to a higher group.

Despite their limitations, when used judiciously by a competent examiner, intelligence tests provide valuable information about individuals. There are not many alternatives to these tests. Subjective judgments about individuals simply reintroduce the bias the tests were designed to eliminate.

At this point we have discussed a number of ideas about issues and controversies in intelligence. An overview of these ideas is presented in summary table 9.2.

The Extremes of Intelligence and Creativity

Intelligence tests have been used to discover indications of mental retardation or intellectual giftedness, the extremes of intelligence. At times intelligence tests have been misused for this purpose. Keep in mind the theme that an intelligence test should not be used as the sole indicator of mental retardation or giftedness as we explore the nature of these intellectual extremes.

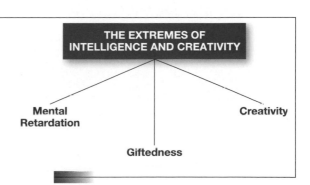

Mental Retardation

Mental Retardation

The main feature of mental retardation is inadequate intellectual functioning (Das & Naglieri, 1996). Before formal tests were developed to assess intelligence, individuals with mental retardation were identified by a lack of age-appropriate skills in learning and caring for themselves. Once intelligence tests were developed, numbers were assigned to indicate degrees of mental retardation. It is not unusual to find that, of two individuals with mental retardation with the same low IQ, one is married, employed, and involved in the community and the other requires constant supervision in an institution. These differences in social competence led psychologists to include deficits in adaptive behavior in their definition of mental retardation. **Mental retardation** *is a condition of limited mental ability in which the individual has low IQ, usually below 70 on a traditional intelligence test, has difficulty adapting to everyday life, and has an onset of these characteristics during the so-called developmental period—by age 18.* The reason for including developmental period in the definition of mental retardation is that we don't usually think of a university student who suffers massive brain damage in a car accident, resulting in an IQ of 60 as "mentally retarded." The low IQ and low adaptiveness should be evident in childhood, not following a long period of normal functioning that is interrupted by an insult of some form. Over 7.5 million North Americans fit this definition of mental retardation.

There are several classifications of mental retardation (Hallahan & Kaufmann, 2000). About 89 percent of individuals with mental retardation fall into the mild category, with IQs of 55 to 70. About 6 percent are moderately retarded, with IQs of 40 to 54; these people can attain a second-grade level of skills and may be able to support themselves as adults through some type of labor. About 3.5 percent of individuals with mental retardation are in the severe category, with IQs of 25 to 39; these individuals learn to talk and engage in very simple tasks but require extensive supervision. Less than 1 percent have IQs below 25; they fall into the profoundly mentally retarded classification and are in constant need of supervision (Minnes, in press).

Mental retardation may have an organic cause, or it may be social and cultural in origin. **Organic retardation** *is mental retardation caused by a genetic disorder or by brain damage; organic refers to the tissues or organs of the body, so there is some physical damage in organic retardation.* Down syndrome, one form of mental retardation, occurs when an extra chromosome is present in the individual's genetic makeup (see figure 9.9). It is not known why the extra chromosome is present, but it may involve the health or age of the female ovum or male sperm. Most people who suffer from organic retardation have IQs that range between 0 and 50.

Cultural-familial retardation *is a mental deficit in which no evidence of organic brain damage can be found; individuals' IQs range from 55 to 70.* Psychologists suspect that such mental deficits result from the normal variation that distributes people along the range of intelligence scores above 55, combined with growing up in a below-average intellectual environment. As children, those who are familially retarded can be detected in schools, where they often fail, need tangible rewards (candy rather than praise), and are highly sensitive to what others—both peers and adults—want from them. However, familially re-

Figure 9.9
A Child with Down Syndrome
What causes a child to develop Down syndrome? In which major classification of mental retardation does the condition fall?

tarded adults are usually invisible, perhaps because adult settings don't tax their cognitive skills as sorely and they can benefit from training (e.g. Feldman & Case, 1997). It may also be that the familially retarded increase their intelligence in adulthood.

Giftedness

There have always been people whose abilities and accomplishments outshine others'—the whiz kid in class, the star athlete, the natural musician.

What Is Giftedness?   People who are **gifted** *have above-average intelligence (an IQ of 120 or higher) and/or superior talent for something.* When it comes to programs for the gifted, most school systems select children who have intellectual superiority and academic aptitude. Children who are talented in the visual and performing arts (arts, drama, dance), athletics, or other special aptitudes tend to be overlooked.

Until recently giftedness and emotional distress were thought to go hand in hand. English novelist Virginia Woolf suffered from severe depression, for example, and eventually committed suicide. And Sir Isaac Newton, Vincent van Gogh, Anne Sexton, Socrates, and Sylvia Plath all had emotional problems. However, these are the exception rather than the rule; in general, no relation between giftedness and mental disorder has been found. Recent studies support the conclusion that gifted people tend to be more mature, have fewer emotional problems than others, and grow up in a positive family climate (Feldhusen, 1999; Feldman, 1997).

Characteristics of Gifted Children   Lewis Terman (1925) conducted an extensive study of 1,500 children whose Stanford-Binet IQs averaged 150. A popular myth is that gifted children are maladjusted, but Terman found in his study that they were not only academically gifted but also socially well adjusted. Many of these gifted children went on to become successful doctors, lawyers, and professors, and scientists.

Ellen Winner (1996) recently described three criteria that characterize gifted children, whether in art, music, or academic domains:

Gifted Children Links
Gifted Children and Education

1. *Precocity.* Gifted children are precocious. They begin to master an area earlier than their peers. Learning in their domain is more effortless for them than for ordinary children. In most instances, these gifted children are precocious because they have an inborn high ability in a particular domain or domains.
2. *Marching to their own drummer.* Gifted children learn in a qualitatively different way than ordinary children. One way that they march to a different drummer is that they need minimal help, or scaffolding, from adults to learn. In many instances, they resist any kind of explicit instruction. They also often make discoveries on their own and solve problems in unique ways.
3. *A passion to master.* Gifted children are driven to understand the domain in which they have high ability. They display an intense, obsessive interest and an ability to focus. They are not children who need to be pushed by their parents. They motivate themselves, says Winner.

Ten-year-old Alexandra Nechita recently burst onto the child prodigy scene. She paints quickly and impulsively on large canvases, some as large as 5 feet by 9 feet. It is not unusual for her to complete several of these large paintings in a week's time. Her paintings—in the modernist tradition—sell for up to $80,000 apiece. When she was only two years of age, Alexandra colored in coloring books for hours. She had no interest in dolls or friends. Once she started school, she would start painting as soon as she got home. And she continues to paint—relentlessly and passionately. It is, she says, what she loves to do.

Ten-year-old Alexandra Nechita is a gifted child in the domain of art. What are some characteristics of gifted children?

Teresa Amabile's Research

*T*hrough the Eyes of Psychologists

Teresa Amabile, *Brandeis University*

"Creative thinking skills include the ability to turn things over in your mind, like trying to make the strange familiar and the familiar strange."

Creativity

In the Images section at the beginning of this chapter we described Howard Gardner's view that, like intelligence, creativity is domain specific. Keep this important idea in mind as you read about creativity.

What Is Creativity? **Creativity** *is the ability to think about something in novel and unusual ways and come up with unique solutions to problems.* Thus, intelligence and creativity are not the same thing (Michael, 1999). This was recognized in Sternberg's account of intelligence and also by J. P. Guilford (1967). He distinguished between **convergent thinking,** *which produces one correct answer and is characterized by the kind of thinking required on conventional intelligence tests,* and **divergent thinking,** *which produces many answers to the same question and is more characteristic of creativity.* For example, a typical item on a conventional intelligence test is, "How many quarters will you get in return for 60 dimes?" By contrast, the following question has many possible answers. What image comes to mind when you hear the phrase "sitting alone in a dark room" or "Can you think of some unique uses for a paper clip?"

Are intelligence and creativity related? Although most creative people are quite intelligent, the reverse is not necessarily true. Many highly intelligent people (as measured by high scores on conventional tests of intelligence) are not very creative. And, if Sternberg had his way, creative thinking would become part of a broader definition of intelligence.

Paul MacCready is one of North America's most prolific inventors. His best-known invention is the Gossamer Condor, the first human-powered plane to travel a mile. MacCready's task was to design something stable and very light that would fly. This had to be done in a way different from any other airplane. MacCready's accomplishment won him a $100,000 prize and a place in the Smithsonian Institute next to the Wright Brothers' plane. MacCready says that asking the right questions and seeing things in a fresh way are critical for creativity.

Steps in the Creative Process

The creative process has often been described as a five-step sequence:

1. *Preparation.* You become immersed in a problem or an issue that interests you and arouses your curiosity.
2. *Incubation.* You churn ideas around in your head. This is the point at which you are likely to make some unusual connections in your thinking.
3. *Insight.* At this point, you experience the "Aha!" moment when all pieces of the puzzle seem to fit together (Gick & Lockhart, 1995).
4. *Evaluation.* Now you must decide whether the idea is valuable and worth pursuing. Is the idea really novel or is it obvious?
5. *Elaboration.* This final step often covers the longest span of time and the hardest work. This is what the famous twentieth-century American inventory Thomas Edison was talking about when he said that creativity is 1 percent inspiration and 99 percent perspiration.

Mihaly Csikszentmihalyi (pronounced ME-high CHICK-sent-me-high-ee) (1996) believes that the five-step sequence provides a helpful framework for thinking about how creative ideas are formed and developed. However, he argues that in reality creative people don't always go through the steps in a linear sequence. For example, elaboration is often interrupted by periods of incubation. Many fresh insights may also appear during incubation, evaluation, and elaboration. And in terms of a time frame, insight might last for years or it might only take a few hours. Sometimes the creative idea consists of one deep insight, at others a series of small ones.

Characteristics of Creative Thinkers

Creative thinkers tend to be characterized by the following (Perkins, 1984):

• *Flexibility and playful thinking.* Creative thinkers are flexible and play with problems, which gives rise to a paradox. Although creativity takes hard work, the work goes more smoothly if you take it lightly. In a way, humor greases the wheels of creativity (Goleman, Kaufmann, & Ray, 1993). When

Through the Eyes of Psychologists

Mihaly Csikszentmihalyi,
University of Chicago

"A genuinely creative accomplishment is almost never the result of a sudden insight, a lightbulb flashing in the dark, but comes after years of hard work."

Canadian short-story writer Alice Munro's stories reflect the intricate tapestry of her Ontario childhood. She says that she is "not an intellectual writer" but rather focuses on people, "The way they look, the way they sound, the way things smell, the way everything is that you go through every day." Relying on her intuition and rich language skills, she carefully crafts deeply creative stories that are richly associative and subtly connected, without being directly conscious of their underlying symbolic significance.

Leonard Cohen, Montreal-born singer-songwriter, poet, novelist and even filmmaker, writes songs that eloquently express the darker side of the human soul. He experiences his creativity as coming from a place beyond his personal control. Regardless, Cohen stresses that, for him, creating these songs is hard work: "I usually rewrite songs for a long time, sometimes for years. I keep trying to uncover what it is I am trying to say. I know that if I stop too soon I'll end up with slogans."

Jonas Salk, who invented the polio vaccine, says that his best ideas come to him at night when he suddenly wakes up. After about 5 minutes of visualizing problems he had thought about the day before, he begins to see an unfolding, as if a poem, painting, story, or concept is about to take form. Salk also believes that many creative ideas are generated through conversations with others who have open, curious minds and positive attitudes. Salk's penchant for seeing emergent possibilities often brought him in conflict with people who had orthodox opinions.

"What do you mean 'What is it?' It's the spontaneous, unfettered expression of a young mind not yet bound by the restraints of narrative or pictorial representation."

© Sidney Harris

you are joking around, you are more likely to consider any possibility. Having fun helps to disarm your inner censor that can condemn your ideas as off-base. **Brainstorming** *is a technique in which members of a group are encouraged to come up with as many ideas as possible, play off each other's ideas, and say practically whatever comes to mind.* Individuals are usually told to hold off from criticizing others' ideas until the end of the session.

• *Inner motivation.* Creative people are often motivated by the joy of creating. They tend to be less inspired by grades, money, or favorable feedback from others. Thus, creative people are more internally than externally motivated.
• *Willingness to risk.* Creative people make more mistakes than their less imaginative counterparts. It's not that they are less proficient, but that they come up with more ideas, more possibilities. They win some, they lose some. For example, the famous twentieth-century Spanish artist Pablo Picasso created more than 20,000 paintings. Not all of them were masterpieces. Creative thinkers learn to cope with unsuccessful projects and see failures as an important opportunity to learn.
• *Objective evaluation of work.* Despite the stereotype that creative people are eccentric and highly subjective, most creative thinkers strive to evaluate their work objectively. They may use an established set of criteria to make this judgment or rely on the judgments of respected, trusted others. In this manner, they can determine whether further creative thinking will improve their work.

Living a More Creative Life
Csikszentmihalyi (1996) interviewed ninety leading figures in art, business, government, education, and science to learn how creativity works. He discovered that creative people regularly engage in chal-

lenges that absorb them. Based on his interviews with some of the most creative people in the world, he concluded that the first step toward a more creative life is to cultivate your curiosity and interest. Here are his recommendations for doing this:

- *Try to be surprised by something every day.* Maybe it is something you see, hear, or read about. Become absorbed in a lecture or a book. Be open to what the world is telling you. Life is a stream of experiences. Swim widely and deeply in it, and your life will be richer.
- *Try to surprise at least one person every day.* In a lot of things you do, you have to be predictable and patterned. Do something different for a change. Ask a question you normally would not ask. Invite someone to go to a show or a museum you have never visited.
- *Write down each day what surprised you and how you surprised others.* Most creative people keep a diary, notes, or lab records to ensure that their experience is not fleeting or forgotten. Start with a specific task. Each evening record the most surprising event that occurred that day and your most surprising action. After a few days, reread your notes and reflect on your past experiences. After a few weeks, you might see a pattern of interest emerging in your notes, one that might suggest an area you can explore in greater depth.
- *When something sparks your interest, follow it.* Usually when something captures your attention, it is short-lived—an idea, a song, a flower. Too often we are too busy to explore the idea, song, or flower further. Or we think these areas are none of our business because we are not experts about them. Yet the world is our business. We can't know which part of it is best suited to our interests until we make a serious effort to learn as much about as many aspects of it as possible.
- *Wake up in the morning with a specific goal to look forward to.* Creative people wake up eager to start the day. Why? Not necessarily because they are cheerful, enthusiastic types but because they know that there is something meaningful to accomplish each day, and they can't wait to get started.
- *Take charge of your schedule.* Figure out which time of the day is your most creative time. Some of us are more creative late at night, others early in the morning. Carve out some time for yourself when your creative energy is at its best.
- *Spend time in settings that stimulate your creativity.* In Csikszentimihalyi's (1996) research, he gave people an electronic pager and beeped them randomly at different times of the day. When he asked them how they felt, they reported the highest levels of creativity when walking, driving, or swimming. These activities are semi-automatic in that they take a certain amount of attention while leaving some time free to make connections among ideas. Another setting in which highly creative people report coming up with novel ideas is the sort of half-asleep, half-awake state we are in when we are deeply relaxed or barely awake.

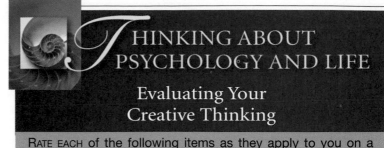

THINKING ABOUT PSYCHOLOGY AND LIFE

Evaluating Your Creative Thinking

RATE EACH of the following items as they apply to you on a scale from 1 = Not like me at all, 2 = Somewhat unlike me, 3 = Somewhat like me, and 4 = Very much like me.

	1	2	3	4
1. I am good at coming up with lots of new and unique ideas.				
2. I like to brainstorm with others to creatively find solutions to problems.				
3. I tend to be internally motivated.				
4. I'm a flexible person and like to play with my thinking.				
5. I like to be around creative people and learn from how they think.				
6. I like to be surprised by something every day and surprise others.				
7. I wake up in the morning with a mission.				
8. I search for alternative solutions to problems rather than giving a pat answer.				
9. I know which settings stimulate me to be creative and I try to spend time in those settings.				

Total your scores for all 9 items. My creativity score is _____. If you scored 32–36 points, you are likely a creative thinker. If you scored 27–31 points, you are inclined to be creative but could benefit from thinking about some ways to get more creativity in your life. If you scored 26 or below, seriously think about ways to become more creative. Again read the suggestions in the text for becoming a more creative person.

Csikszentmihalyi
Harvard Project Zero

SUMMARY TABLE 9.3
The Extremes of Intelligence and Creativity

Concept	Processes/Related Ideas	Characteristics/Description
Mental Retardation	Its Nature	Mental retardation is a condition of limited mental ability in which an individual has a low IQ (usually below 70 on a traditional intelligence test), has difficulty adapting to everyday life, and has these characteristics during the so-called developmental period—by age 18. Classifications of mental retardation range from mild (IQ of 55–70) to profound (IQ below 25). Mental retardation may have an organic cause (organic retardation) or it may be social and cultural in origin (cultural-familial retardation).
Giftedness	What Is Giftedness?	Individuals are described as gifted when they have above-average intelligence (an IQ of 120 or higher) and/or a special talent for something.
	Characteristics of Gifted Children	In Terman's study, gifted children were academically successful and socially well adjusted. Winner believes that gifted individuals are characterized by precocity, marching to the tune of a different drummer, and a passion to master.
Creativity	What Is Creativity?	Creativity is the ability to think about something in novel and unusual ways and come up with unique solutions to problems. Guilford distinguished between convergent thinking (which produces one correct answer and is characteristic of the kind of thinking required on conventional intelligence tests) and divergent thinking (which produces many answers to the same question and is more characteristic of creativity).
	Steps in the Creative Process	The creative process has often been described as a 5-step sequence: (1) preparation, (2) incubation, (3) insight, (4) evaluation, and (5) elaboration. However, in reality creative people don't always go through these steps in a linear sequence.
	Characteristics of Creative Thinkers	These include flexibility and playful thinking, inner motivation, willingness to risk, and objective evaluation of work.
	Living a More Creative Life	Csikszentmihalyi's recommendations: Be surprised by something every day; surprise at least one person every day; write down each day what surprised you and how you surprised others; when something sparks your interest, follow it; wake up in the morning with a specific goal to look forward to; take charge of your schedule; and spend time in settings that stimulate your creativity.

At this point we have discussed a number of ideas about the extremes of intelligence and creativity. An overview of these ideas is presented in summary table 9.3. In the next chapter, we will turn our attention to how we develop through the lifespan. Included in our exploration of human development will be ideas about how we develop intellectually.

Overview

Overview

WE BEGAN THIS CHAPTER by exploring what intelligence is and the early history of assessment. Our coverage of intelligence tests focused on how tests are constructed and evaluated, the Binet tests and Wechsler scales, group tests, as well as aptitude and achievement tests. We examined whether people have a single intelligence or multiple intelligences, studying early views and the contemporary approaches of Gardner and Sternberg. We evaluated these issues and controversies in intelligence: the heredity-environment controversy, culture and ethnicity, and the use and misuse of intelligence tests. We also read about the extremes of intelligence (mental retardation and giftedness) and creativity. Don't forget that you can obtain a more detailed overview of the chapter by again studying the three summary tables on pages 300, 307, and 314.

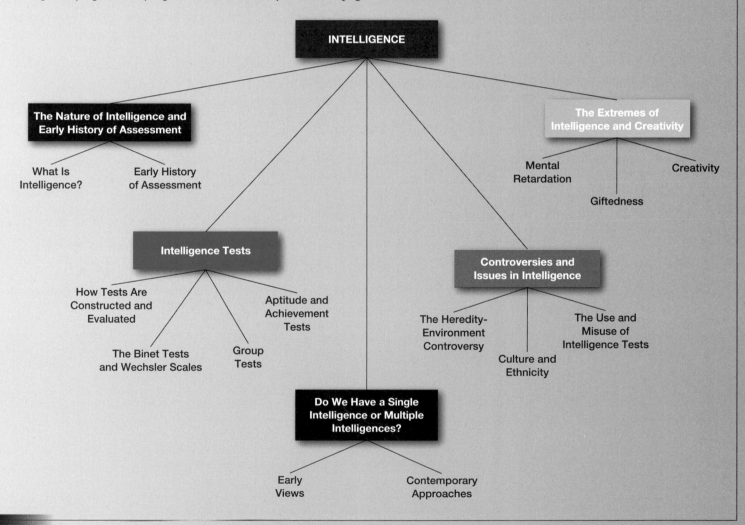

Key Terms

intelligence 286
individual differences 286
reliability 288
test-retest reliability 288
alternative forms reliability 288
split-half reliability 288
validity 289

content validity 289
criterion validity 289
concurrent validity 289
predictive validity 289
standardization 290
norms 290
mental age (MA) 291
intelligence quotient 291

normal distribution 291
aptitude tests 294
achievement tests 295
two-factor theory 295
multiple-factor theory 295
triarchic theory 298
culture-fair tests 305
mental retardation 308

organic retardation 308
cultural-familial retardation 308
gifted 309
creativity 310
convergent thinking 310
divergent thinking 310
brainstorming 312

Key People

Howard Gardner 285
Sir Frances Galton 286
James McKeen Cattell 287
Alfred Binet 291

David Wechsler 292
Charles Spearman 295
Robert Sternberg 298
Arthur Jensen 299

Richard Herrnstein and Charles Murray 301
Douglas Wahlsten 301

Lewis Terman 309
Ellen Winner 309
Mihaly Csikszentmihalyi 311

Psychology Checklist
INTELLIGENCE

How much have you learned since the beginning of the chapter? Use the following statements to help you review your knowledge and understanding of the chapter material. First, read the statement and mentally or briefly on paper demonstrate that you understand and can discuss the relevant information:

_____ I know what intelligence is and how to define it.
_____ I can describe the early history of studying intelligence.
_____ I can discuss how tests are constructed and evaluated, including reliability, validity, and standardization.
_____ I can describe the Binet tests and the Wechsler scales.
_____ I can discuss the multiple intelligence approaches of Gardner and Sternberg, including their educational applications.
_____ I am aware of the heredity-environment controversy in psychology.

_____ I know about issues of culture and ethnicity in psychology, including cultural comparisons and cultural bias.
_____ I can describe the uses and misuses of intelligence tests.
_____ I can discuss mental retardation.
_____ I am aware of what giftedness is, including characteristics of gifted children and Terman's gifted children.
_____ I can evaluate what creativity is, including steps in the creative process, characteristics of creative thinkers, and strategies for living a more creative life.

For any items that you did not check, go back and locate the relevant material in the chapter. Review the material until you feel that you can check off the item. You also may want to use this checklist later in preparing for an exam.

Taking It to the Net

1. The concept of intelligence is complex, encompassing many variables. In order to get into university, you may have had to take the Scholastic Aptitude Test (SAT). Guess what? You will have to take a similar test if you want to go on to graduate school (the GRE)! Are these tests of intelligence? If not, how do they differ from intelligence tests? Keep in mind the notion of predictability. Which test is used to predict success in university and/or occupational status? How well do these tests predict such successes?
2. Eric Clapton's albums have sold millions of copies over the last 20 years. His fans believe that he possesses incredible guitar skills and the ability to score beautiful music. Some psychologists have deemed his abilities a type of intelligence. Do you think musical intelligence is really a distinct type of intelligence? Explain your answer in terms of the definition of intelligence and the special abilities it takes to be musically gifted.
3. Mental retardation is a condition that affects cognitive and motor adaptive skills. It has been estimated over 7.5 million people in North America have mental retardation, affecting 25 times as many people as blindness. The criteria for mental retardation are based on IQ score, adaptive functioning, and age of onset. A diagnosis of mental retardation requires that the condition is present before the age of 18. What are the major causes of mental retardation? Can we prevent mental retardation? Explain.

Connect to http://www.mcgrawhill.ca/college/santrock to find the answers!

Resources for Psychology and Life

Creativity (1996)
by Mihaly Csikszentmihalyi
New York: HarperCollins

Csikszentmihalyi interviewed 90 creative stars in science, the arts, and other domains. He describes how they live, how they work, how they think.

Intelligence: Knowns and Unknowns
by Ulric Neisser (1996)
American Psychologist, 51, 77–102

This outstanding overview of what we know and don't know about intelligence is based on the input of a task force established by the Board of Scientific Affairs of the American Psychological Association. The task force concluded that much is known about intelligence but that many critical questions remain unanswered including the pathway by which genes produce their effects and the specific environmental factors that contribute to intelligence.

Encyclopedia of Creativity (1999)
by Marc Runco and Steven Pritzker (Eds.)
San Diego: Academic Press

Extensive, contemporary coverage of a wide range of topics on creative thinking by leading experts.

Gifted Children: Myths and Realities (1996)
by Ellen Winner
New York: Basic Books

Ellen Winner has studied gifted children for many years. In this recent book, she distinguishes the myths from the realities of gifted children. The distinctive abilities of gifted children are portrayed.

The Intelligence Men: Makers of the IQ Controversy (1985)
by Raymond Fancher
New York: Norton

This book covers the history of the concept of intelligence in a lively and engaging manner.

Creating Minds (1993)
by Howard Gardner
New York: Basic Books

Building on his framework of seven intelligences, ranging from musical intelligence to intelligence involved in understanding oneself, Gardner explores the lives of seven extraordinary individuals—Sigmund Freud, Albert Einstein, Pablo Picasso, Igor Stravinsky, T. S. Eliot, Martha Graham, and Mahatma Gandhi—each an outstanding exemplar of one kind of intelligence.

Assessment of Intellectual Functioning (1996, 2nd ed.)
by Lewis Aiken
New York: Plenum

This volume includes discussion of new tests and revisions of tests for assessing intelligence, testing in other countries and cultures, case materials and related psychological testing reports, and testing disabled individuals.

American Association on Mental Retardation
1719 Kalorama Road, NW
Washington, DC 20009
202-387-1968
800-424-3688

This North American organization works to promote the well-being of mentally retarded children and adults. Among the materials they have available is *Parents for Children, and Children for Parents: The Adoption Alternative.*

Chapter 10

CHAPTER OUTLINE

WHAT IS DEVELOPMENT?
Biological, Cognitive, and Socioemotional Processes
Periods of Development
Developmental Issues
CHILD DEVELOPMENT
Prenatal Development and Birth
Physical Development
Cognitive Development
Socioemotional Development
ADOLESCENCE
Historical Beginnings and the Nature of Adolescence
Physical Development
Cognitive Development
Socioemotional Development
ADULT DEVELOPMENT AND AGING
Physical Development
Cognitive Development
Socioemotional Development
Successful Aging
DEATH AND DYING

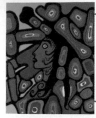

Images of Psychology and Life
Jessica Dubroff, Child Pilot

> " *I*n every child who is born, Under no matter what circumstances, And of no matter what parents, The potentiality of the human race Is born again. "
>
> James Agee
> *American Writer, 20th Century*

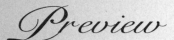

Preview

AS THE TWENTY-FIRST century approaches, children's well-being is one of our most important concerns. Development does not end with childhood, though, and intriguing questions are being raised about how much people can continue to change even when they are old. These are some of the questions we will explore in this chapter:

• What does it mean to "develop"?
• Is there a best age to be?
• How does the way children think change as they develop?
• How important is attachment to a caregiver in infancy?
• Is there a best way to parent children?
• What are some key aspects of adolescent development?
• Why do people age?
• Does everyone go through a midlife crisis?
• How can people age successfully?

THINK FOR A MOMENT about how your parents reared you. Were they permissive or controlling? Warm or cold? Later in the chapter we will examine styles of parenting based on such characteristics, but for now to encourage you to think about parenting, let's examine the tragic story of Jessica Dubroff.

In 1996, Jessica Dubroff took off in cold rain and died when her single-engine Cessna nosedived into a highway. Seven-year-old Jessica was only 4 feet, 2 inches tall and weighed just 55 pounds. What was she doing flying an airplane, especially in quest of being the youngest person ever to fly across the continent?

Jessica had been urged on by overzealous parents, by media drawn to a natural human-interest story, and by a U.S. Federal Aviation Administration that looked the other way. Jessica's feet did not even reach the rudder pedals. Overnight Jessica's death resulted in her becoming the poster child of parental and media exploitation. Some thought she had been granted too much freedom and had not been allowed to be a child.

Jessica's parents seemed determined to give their daughter independence from the beginning. She was delivered in a birthing tub without the benefit of a doctor or midwife. Her parents' philosophy was that real life is the best tutor, experience the best preparation for life. As a result, they kept Jessica and her brother (age 9) and sister (age 3) at home without filing a home-schooling plan with local authorities. Jessica had no dolls, only tools. Instead of studying grammar, she did chores and sought what her mother called "mastery." Jessica had few, if any, boundaries. Parenting consisted mainly of cheerleading.

Jessica became interested in flying after her parents gave her an airplane ride for her sixth birthday, only 23 months before her fatal crash. Her father admitted that the cross-country flight was his idea, but claimed that he had presented it to Jessica as a choice. The father became her press agent, courting TV, radio, and newspapers to publicize her flight.

After the crash, TV viewers were treated to a spectacle almost as disturbing as the accident itself. Jessica's mother said that if she had it to do over again, she would have done nothing differently. She also commented that she did everything she could to give Jessica freedom and choice. Developmental psychologists would counter that children should be given freedom and choice, but within the bounds of responsibility (Stengel, 1996).

Jessica's story is rare and tragic. However, the dangers of overachieving, of growing up too soon, of intensely focusing on a single activity, often show up in many different ways. The child actor grows up without an education. The adolescent tennis star mysteriously drops off the circuit to become a teenager. The young figure skater plots to club an opponent. Child athletes might ruin their bodies: ballerinas develop anorexia, teenage football players take steroids. Too many children have lives that are overscheduled, moving from one lesson to the next. They are being robbed of the time to develop coping skills that they need to deal with life's realities.

A vicious cycle has been set in motion. Parents who live vicariously through their children produce children who grow up feeling they have missed out on childhood, a time when play and its unstructured freedom should be prominent. Children should be allowed to have a well-rounded life, one that is not focused on achievement in a single domain.

We've been talking about Jessica Dubroff's development as a child. Let's now explore just what we mean by the term *development.*

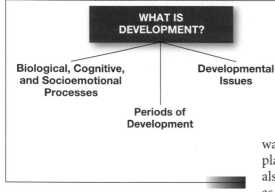

What Is Development?

As children, each of us traveled some common paths. Each of us—Leonardo da Vinci, Joan of Arc, Louis Riel, Martin Luther King, Jr., your authors, and you— walked at about the age of one, talked at about the age of two, engaged in fantasy play as a young child, and became more independent as an adolescent. Yet we are also unique. No one else in the world, for example, has the same set of fingerprints as you. Researchers who study child development are intrigued by children's universal characteristics as well as by their idiosyncrasies.

When we speak of **development,** *we mean a pattern of movement or change that begins at conception and continues throughout the life span.* Most development involves growth, although it also consists of decay (as in death). The pattern of change is complex because it is the product of several processes—biological, cognitive, and socioemotional.

Biological, Cognitive, and Socioemotional Processes

Biological processes *involve changes in an individual's physical nature.* Genes inherited from parents, the development of the brain, height and weight gains, motor skills, and the hormonal changes of puberty all reflect the role of biological processes in development.

Cognitive processes *involve changes in an individual's thought, intelligence, and language.* The tasks of watching a colorful mobile swinging above a crib, putting together a two-word sentence, memorizing a poem, solving a math problem, and imagining what it would be like to be a movie star all reflect the role of cognitive processes in children's development.

Socioemotional processes *involve changes in an individual's relationships with other people, changes in emotions, and changes in personality.* An infant's smile in response to her mother's touch, a young boy's aggressive attack on a playmate, a girl's development of assertiveness, and an adolescent's joy at the senior prom all reflect the role of socioemotional processes in children's development.

Remember as you read about biological, cognitive, and socioemotional processes that they are intricately interwoven. You will read about how socioemotional processes shape cognitive processes, how cognitive processes promote or restrict socioemotional processes, and how biological processes influence cognitive processes. Although it is helpful to study the various processes involved in children's development in separate sections of the chapter, keep in mind that you are studying the development of an integrated human child in whom mind and body are interdependent (see figure 10.1).

Periods of Development

For the purposes of organization and understanding, we commonly describe development in terms of periods. The most widely used classification of developmental periods involves the following sequence: prenatal period, infancy, early childhood, middle and late childhood, adolescence, early adulthood, middle adulthood, and late adulthood. Approximate age ranges are placed on the periods to provide a general idea of when a period first appears and when it ends.

The **prenatal period** *is the time from conception to birth.* It is a time of tremendous growth—from a single cell to an organism complete with a brain and behavioral capabilities, produced in approximately a nine-month period.

Infancy *is the developmental period that extends from birth to 18 or 24 months.* Infancy is a time of extreme dependence on adults. Many psychological activities are just beginning—language, symbolic thought, sensorimotor coordination, and social learning, for example.

Early childhood *is the developmental period that extends from the end of infancy to about 5 or 6 years; sometimes the period is called the preschool years.* During this time, young children learn to become more self-sufficient and to care for themselves, develop school readiness skills (following instructions, identifying letters), and spend many hours in play and with peers. First grade typically marks the end of this period.

Middle and late childhood *is the developmental period that extends from about 6 to 11 years of age, approximately corresponding to the elementary school years; sometimes the period is called the elementary school years.* Children master the fundamental skills of reading, writing, and arithmetic, and they are formally exposed to the larger world and its culture. Achievement becomes a more central theme of the child's world, and self-control increases.

Adolescence *is the developmental period of transition from childhood to early adulthood, entered approximately at 10 to 12 years of age and ending at 18 to 21 years of age.* Adolescence begins with rapid physical changes—dramatic gains in height and weight; changes in body contour; and the development of sexual characteristics such as enlargement of the breasts, development of pubic and facial hair, and deepening of the voice. At this point in development, the pursuit of independence and an identity are prominent. Thought is more logical, abstract, and idealistic. More and more time is spent outside of the family during this period.

Early adulthood *is the developmental period that begins in the late teens or early twenties and lasts through the thirties.* It is a time of establishing personal and economic independence; a time of career development; and for many a time of selecting a mate, learning to live with someone in an intimate way, starting a family, and rearing children.

Middle adulthood *is the developmental period that begins at approximately 35 to 45 years of age and extends into the sixties.* It is a time of expanding personal and social involvement and responsibility; of assisting the next generation in becoming competent, mature individuals; and of reaching and maintaining satisfaction in one's career.

Late adulthood *is the developmental period that begins in the sixties or seventies and lasts until death.* It is a time of adjustment to decreasing strength and health, life review, retirement, and adjustment to new social roles.

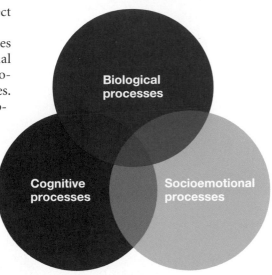

Figure 10.1
Changes in Development Are the Result of Biological, Cognitive, and Socioemotional Processes

These processes are interwoven as individuals develop.

Children's Issues

Health Canada: Children and Youth

National Institute of Child Health and Human Development

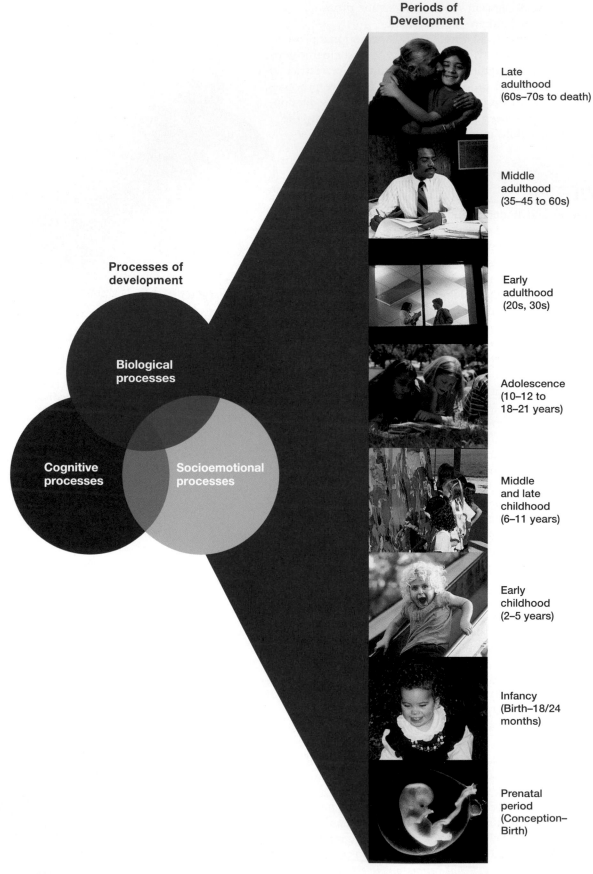

Periods of Development

Late adulthood (60s–70s to death)

Middle adulthood (35–45 to 60s)

Early adulthood (20s, 30s)

Adolescence (10–12 to 18–21 years)

Middle and late childhood (6–11 years)

Early childhood (2–5 years)

Infancy (Birth–18/24 months)

Prenatal period (Conception–Birth)

Processes of development

Biological processes

Cognitive processes

Socioemotional processes

𝓕igure 10.2 Processes and Periods of Development
The unfolding of life's periods of development is influenced by the interaction of biological, cognitive, and socioemotional processes.

The periods of the human life span are shown in figure 10.2, along with the processes of development—biological, cognitive, and socioemotional. As can be seen in figure 10.2, the interplay of biological, cognitive, and socioemotional processes produces the periods of the human life span.

In our description of the life span's periods, we placed approximate age bands on the periods; however, one expert on life-span development, Bernice Neugarten (1980), believes that we rapidly are becoming an age-irrelevant society. She says we are already familiar with the 28-year-old mayor, the 35-year-old grandmother, the 65-year-old father of a preschooler, the 55-year-old widow who starts a business, and the 70-year-old student. Neugarten says that she has had difficulty clustering adults into age brackets that are characterized by particular issues. She stresses that choices and dilemmas do not spring forth at 10-year intervals, and decisions are not made and then left behind as if they were merely beads on a chain. Neugarten argues that most adulthood themes appear and reappear throughout the human life span. The issues of intimacy and freedom can haunt couples throughout their relationship. Feeling the pressure of time, reformulating goals, and coping with success and failure are not the exclusive property of adults of any age.

Developmental Issues

Three important developmental issues focus on nature and nurture, continuity and discontinuity, and early and later experience.

Nature and Nurture   In chapter 3 ("Biological Foundations and Neuroscience"), we stressed that one of psychology's most important issues is the extent to which behavior is influenced by nature (heredity) or nurture (environment) ◀▥ P. 69. The nature-nurture issue is especially applicable to human development because it addresses the roles of heredity and environment in determining how we develop as human beings.

Some developmentalists emphasize the power of heredity in development. They argue that although the range of environments can be vast, the genetic blueprint produces some common developmental changes. We walk before we talk, speak one word before two words, grow rapidly in infancy and less so in early childhood, experience a rush of sexual hormones in adolescence, reach the peak of physical strength in late adolescence and early adulthood, then experience some decline. The nature proponents acknowledge that extreme environments—those that are psychologically barren or hostile—can depress development, but they believe that basic growth tendencies are genetically wired into humans.

By contrast, other developmentalists emphasize the importance of experiences in life-span development. Experiences run the gamut from the individual's biological environment (nutrition, medical care, drugs, and physical accidents) to the social environment (family, peers, schools, community, media, and culture).

Continuity and Discontinuity   Think for a moment about who you are. Did you become this person gradually, like the slow, cumulative growth of a seedling into a giant oak? Or did you experience sudden, distinct changes in your development, the way a caterpillar changes into a butterfly? For the most part, developmental psychologists who emphasize experience have described development as a gradual, continuous process; those who emphasize maturation have described development as a series of distinct stages.

THINKING ABOUT PSYCHOLOGY AND LIFE

Is There a Best Age to Be?

MIGHT PEOPLE BE HAPPIER in one developmental period than others? Consider adolescence, early adulthood, middle adulthood, and late adulthood. Do you think most people are happier in one of these periods than others? For example, when people are 15, 30, 50, and 70 might we find differences in whether people are happier at one of these ages than others? A woman in a psychology class John Santrock teaches spent about 10 minutes expounding on why 28 years of age is the best age to be. Essentially her argument was that at 28 a person is old enough to have experienced enough things in life to show maturity yet still be physically healthy and strong enough to fully enjoy life. Of course, many other students did not agree and asked her questions, such as, "If you are only 30 yourself, how do you know 28 is the best age to be?" and "Aren't there factors in many people's lives that might make a different age be best for them?"

Researchers have found no differences in how happy people are at different ages (Ingelhart & Rabier, 1996). Think some more about the different periods. Doesn't every period of the human life span have its highs and lows, hills and valleys? Get together with several other students and discuss what some of these uplifting and down-turning characteristics of different periods are.

Children and Poverty

"If you ask me, he's come too far too fast."

© The New Yorker Collection *1988 Lee Lorenz*
from cartoonbank.com. All Rights Reserved.

The view that stresses **continuity of development** *argues that development involves gradual, cumulative change from conception to death.* A child's first word, while seemingly an abrupt, discrete event, is actually the result of months of growth and practice. Similarly, while puberty might seem to happen overnight, it is actually a gradual process that occurs over several years.

The view that stresses **discontinuity of development** *argues that development involves distinct stages in the life span.* In this view, each of us passes through a sequence of stages that are qualitatively, rather than quantitatively, different. As a caterpillar changes into a butterfly, it does not become more caterpillar; it becomes a different kind of organism. Its development is discontinuous. Similarly, a child who earlier could think only in concrete terms becomes capable of thinking abstractly about the world. This is a qualitative, discontinuous change in development, not a continuous, quantitative change.

Early and Later Experience   The early-later experience issue has a long history and continues to be hotly debated among developmentalists (Cairns, 1998) ◀ IIIII P. 17. Some believe that unless infants experience warm, nurturant caregiving in the first year or so of life, their development will never be optimal (Bowlby, 1989). Plato was sure that infants who were rocked frequently became better athletes. Nineteenth-century New England ministers told parents in Sunday sermons that the way they handled their infants would determine their children's future character. The emphasis on the importance of early experience rests on the belief that each life is an unbroken trail on which a psychological quality can be traced back to its origin (Kagan, 1992).

The early-experience doctrine contrasts with the later-experience view that, rather than a statuelike permanence after change in infancy, development continues to be like the ebb and flow of a river. The later-experience advocates argue that children are malleable throughout development and that later sensitive caregiving is just as important as earlier sensitive caregiving (Lewis, 1997). A number of life-span developmentalists, who focus on the entire life span rather than only on child development, stress that too little attention has been given to later experiences in development (Baltes, Lindenberger, & Staudinger, 1998). They argue that early experiences are important contributors to development, but no more important than later experiences.

Conclusions About Developmental Issues   Most developmentalists do not take extreme positions on developmental issues. Development is not all nature or all nurture, not all continuity or all discontinuity, and not all early or later experience (Lerner, 1998; Santrock, 1999). Both nature and nurture, continuity and discontinuity, early experience and later experience characterize our development through the human life span. Regarding the nature-nurture issue, the key to development is the *interaction* of nature and nurture rather than either factor alone. For instance, an individual's cognitive development is the result of heredity-environment interaction, not heredity or environment alone.

Reproductive Health Resources

Child Development

Many special things have taken place in your life since you were born. But imagine . . . at one time you were a microscopic organism floating around in a sea of fluid in your mother's womb. As nineteenth-century American poet–essayist Samuel Taylor remarked, "The history of man for nine months preceding his birth is probably far more interesting and contains more stunning events than all the years that follow it."

Prenatal Development and Birth

Within a matter of hours after fertilization, a human egg divides, becomes a system of cells, and continues this mapping of cells at an astonishing rate. In a mere 9 months, there is a squalling bundle of energy that has its grandmother's nose, its father's eyes, and its mother's abundant hair.

(a)

(b)

(c)

ℱigure 10.3
Embryonic Period

(a) Embryo at 4 weeks. At about 4 weeks, an embryo is about 0.2 inches in length. The head, eyes, and ears begin to show. The head and neck are half the body length; the shoulders will be located where the whitish arm buds are attached. *(b)* Embryo at 8 weeks. At 8 weeks and 4 centimeters (1.6 inches), the developing individual is no longer an embryo, but a fetus. Everything that will be found in the fully developed human being has now begun to form. The fetal stage is a period of growth and perfection of detail. The heart has been beating for a month, and the muscles have just begun their first exercises. *(c)* Fetus at 4½ months. At 4½ months, the fetus is about 18 cm (just over 7 inches). When the thumb comes close to the mouth, the head may turn, and lips and tongue begin their sucking motions—a reflex for survival.

The Course of Prenatal Development   **Conception** *occurs when a single sperm cell from the male penetrates the female's ovum (egg). This process is also called fertilization.* A **zygote** *is a fertilized egg.* It receives one-half of its chromosomes from the mother, the other half from the father. The zygote begins as a single cell. After one week and many cell divisions, the zygote is made up of 100 to 150 cells. By the end of two weeks, the mass of cells attaches to the uterine wall. The **germinal period** *is these first two weeks after conception.*

During the **embryonic period,** *weeks three through eight after conception, some remarkable developments unfold* (see figure 10.3). *Before most women even know they are pregnant, the rate of cell differentiation intensifies, support systems for the cells form, and the beginnings of organs appear.* In the third week the neural tube that eventually becomes the spinal cord is forming. At about 21 days, eyes begin to appear, and by 24 days the cells of the heart begin to differentiate. During the fourth week, arm and leg buds emerge. At five to eight weeks, arms and legs become more differentiated, the face starts to form, and the intestinal tract appears. All of this is happening in an organism that by eight weeks weighs only ⅟₃₀ ounce and is just over one inch long.

The **fetal period** *begins two months after conception and lasts, on the average, for seven months. Growth and development continue their dramatic course, and organs ma-*

The Visible Embryo

ture to the point where life can be sustained outside the womb. At four months after conception, the fetus is about six inches long and weighs four to seven ounces. Prenatal reflexes become more apparent, and the mother feels the fetus move for the first time. At six months after conception, the eyes and eyelids are completely formed, a fine layer of hair covers the fetus, the grasping reflex appears, and irregular breathing begins. By seven to nine months, the fetus is much longer and weighs considerably more. In addition, the functioning of various organs steps up.

As these massive changes take place during prenatal development, some pregnant women tiptoe about in the belief that everything they do has a direct effect on the unborn child. Others behave more casually, assuming their experiences have little impact. The truth lies somewhere between these extremes. Although it floats in a comfortable, well-protected environment, the fetus is not totally immune to the larger environment surrounding the mother (Kopp, 1984).

A **teratogen** *(the word comes from the Greek word* tera, *meaning "monster") is any agent that causes a birth defect.* Rarely do specific teratogens, such as drugs, link up with specific birth defects, such as leg malformation, but the drug thalidomide is an exception. During the late 1950s, several hundred women took thalidomide early in pregnancy to prevent morning sickness and insomnia. Tragically, babies born to these mothers had arms and legs that had not developed beyond stumps.

The importance of women's health to the health of their offspring is nowhere better exemplified than when the mother is infected with human immunodeficiency virus (HIV), the virus that is believed to be the cause of acquired immune deficiency syndrome (AIDS). As the number of women infected with HIV increases, more newborns are born infected with HIV (Temoshok, 1998).

Between 15 and 30 percent of infants born to women infected with HIV become infected with the virus. AIDS is currently the sixth leading cause of death for children 1 to 4 years of age in the United States. By the end of 1997, one percent of Canadian AIDS cases (170) and deaths (105) were among children (Health Canada, 1998). Treatment can considerably reduce the rate of HIV transmission from an infected woman to her baby (Committee on Pediatric AIDS, 1998).

There are three ways a mother with HIV can infect her offspring: (1) during pregnancy, through the placenta (a life-support system of tissues); (2) during delivery, through contact with maternal blood and other fluids; and (3) after birth, through breast-feeding. HIV and AIDS will be discussed further in chapter 15, "Health Psychology."

Heavy drinking by pregnant women can also have devastating effects on offspring (Abel, 1984; Toth, Conner, & Streissguth, 1999). **Fetal alcohol syndrome (FAS)** *is a cluster of abnormalities that occur in children born to mothers who are heavy drinkers.* These abnormalities include a small head (microencephaly) and defective limbs, face, and heart. Most of these children are also below average in intelligence. Recently concern has increased about the well-being of the fetus when pregnant women drink even small amounts of alcohol. In summary, a woman who is pregnant or anticipates becoming pregnant should not drink any alcohol (Streissguth, 1997).

Pregnant women also should not smoke. Fetal and neonatal deaths, and preterm birth, are higher among mothers who smoke. Studies of whether smoking during pregnancy increases cancer risk in children are inconclusive and long-term studies into adulthood have not been conducted. However, in one recent study, urine samples from 22 of 31 newborns of mothers who smoke showed substantial amounts of one of the strongest carcinogens (NNK) in tobacco smoke; the urine samples of newborns whose mothers did not smoke did not contain the carcinogen (Hecht, 1998). In another study, prenatal exposure to cigarette smoking was related to poorer language and cognitive skills at four years of age (Fried & Watkinson, 1990).

Fetal Alcohol Syndrome
Touch Research Institute

Birth and the Newborn
The newborn is on a threshold between two worlds. In the womb the fetus exists in a dark, free-floating, low-gravity environment with a relatively warm, constant temperature. At birth, the newborn must quickly adapt to light, gravity, cold, and a buzzing array of changing stimuli.

THERE HAS BEEN great interest recently in the roles of touch and massage in improving the growth, health, and well-being of infants and children. This interest has been especially stimulated by a number of research investigations by Tiffany Field (1995), director of the Touch Research Institute at the University of Miami School of Medicine. In one study, 40 preterm infants who had just been released from an intensive care unit and placed in a transitional nursery were studied (Field, Scafidi, & Schanberg, 1987). Twenty of the preterm babies were given special stimulation with massage and exercise for three 15-minute periods at the beginning of 3 consecutive hours every morning for 10 weekdays. For example, each infant was placed on its stomach and gently stroked. The massage began with the head and neck and moved downward to the feet. It also moved from the shoulders down to the hands. The infant was then rolled over. Each arm and leg was flexed and extended; then both legs were flexed and extended. Next, the massage was repeated.

The massaged and exercised preterm babies gained 47 percent more weight than their preterm counterparts who were not massaged and exercised, even though both groups had the same number of feedings per day and averaged the same intake of formula. The increased activity of the massaged, exercised infants would seem to work against weight gain. However, similar findings have been discovered with animals. The increased activity may increase gastrointestinal and metabolic efficiency. The massaged infants were more active and alert, and they performed better on developmental tests. Also, their hospital stays were about 6 days shorter than those of the nonmassaged, nonexercised group, which saved about $3,000 per preterm infant. Field has recently replicated these findings with preterm infants.

In another study, Field (1992) gave the same kind of massage (firm stroking with the palms of the hands) to preterm infants who had been exposed to cocaine in utero. The infants also showed significant weight gain and improved scores on developmental tests. Currently, Field is using massage therapy with HIV-exposed preterm infants with the hope that their immune system functioning will be improved. Others she has targeted include infants of depressed mothers, infants with colic, infants and children with sleep problems, as well as children who have diabetes, asthma, and juvenile arthritis.

Field also reports that touch has been helpful with children and adolescents who have touch aversions, such as children who have been sexually abused, autistic children, and adolescents with eating disorders. Field is also studying the amount of touch a child normally receives during school activities. She hopes that positive forms of touch will return to school systems, where touching has been outlawed because of potential sexual-abuse lawsuits.

Shown here is Dr. Tiffany Field massaging a newborn infant. Dr. Field's research has clearly demonstrated the power of massage in improving the developmental outcome of at-risk infants. Under her direction the Touch Research Institute in Miami, Florida, was recently developed to investigate the role of touch in a number of domains of health and well-being.

A full-term infant has grown in the womb for the full 38 to 42 weeks between conception and delivery. A **preterm infant** *is an infant born prior to 38 weeks after conception.* While parents of preterm infants generally experience considerable parenting stress (Robson, 1997), whether a preterm infant will have developmental problems is less clear. Very small preterm infants and those who grow up in conditions of poverty are more likely to have problems than are those who are larger or live in higher socioeconomic conditions. Indeed, many larger preterm infants from middle- and high-income families do not have developmental problems. Nonetheless, more preterm infants than full-term babies have learning disorders (Kopp, 1984).

Researchers are continuing to unveil new ideas for improving the lives of preterm infants. One increasingly used technique is to regularly massage and gently exercise preterm infants. This technique is described in Explorations in Psychology.

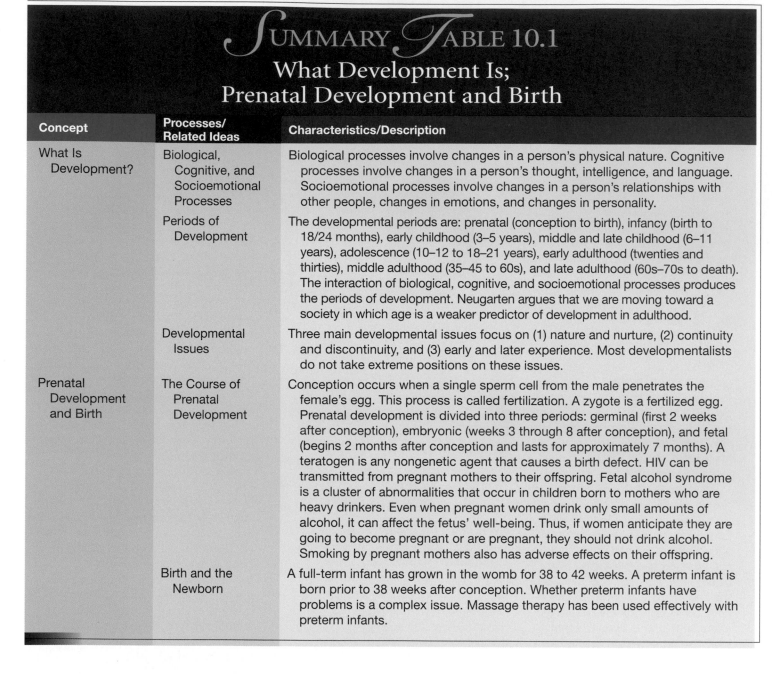

Summary Table 10.1
What Development Is;
Prenatal Development and Birth

Concept	Processes/Related Ideas	Characteristics/Description
What Is Development?	Biological, Cognitive, and Socioemotional Processes	Biological processes involve changes in a person's physical nature. Cognitive processes involve changes in a person's thought, intelligence, and language. Socioemotional processes involve changes in a person's relationships with other people, changes in emotions, and changes in personality.
	Periods of Development	The developmental periods are: prenatal (conception to birth), infancy (birth to 18/24 months), early childhood (3–5 years), middle and late childhood (6–11 years), adolescence (10–12 to 18–21 years), early adulthood (twenties and thirties), middle adulthood (35–45 to 60s), and late adulthood (60s–70s to death). The interaction of biological, cognitive, and socioemotional processes produces the periods of development. Neugarten argues that we are moving toward a society in which age is a weaker predictor of development in adulthood.
	Developmental Issues	Three main developmental issues focus on (1) nature and nurture, (2) continuity and discontinuity, and (3) early and later experience. Most developmentalists do not take extreme positions on these issues.
Prenatal Development and Birth	The Course of Prenatal Development	Conception occurs when a single sperm cell from the male penetrates the female's egg. This process is called fertilization. A zygote is a fertilized egg. Prenatal development is divided into three periods: germinal (first 2 weeks after conception), embryonic (weeks 3 through 8 after conception), and fetal (begins 2 months after conception and lasts for approximately 7 months). A teratogen is any nongenetic agent that causes a birth defect. HIV can be transmitted from pregnant mothers to their offspring. Fetal alcohol syndrome is a cluster of abnormalities that occur in children born to mothers who are heavy drinkers. Even when pregnant women drink only small amounts of alcohol, it can affect the fetus' well-being. Thus, if women anticipate they are going to become pregnant or are pregnant, they should not drink alcohol. Smoking by pregnant mothers also has adverse effects on their offspring.
	Birth and the Newborn	A full-term infant has grown in the womb for 38 to 42 weeks. A preterm infant is born prior to 38 weeks after conception. Whether preterm infants have problems is a complex issue. Massage therapy has been used effectively with preterm infants.

At this point we have studied a number of ideas about what development is, as well as prenatal development and birth. An overview of these ideas is presented in summary table 10.1. Next, we continue our exploration of development by examining children's physical development.

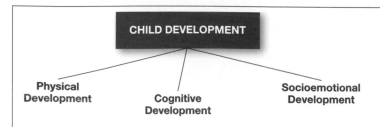

Physical Development

At no other time in a person's life will there be so many changes occurring so fast as during the first few years. During infancy, we change from virtually immobile, helpless beings to insatiably curious, talking creatures who toddle as fast as our legs can carry us.

Infancy   The newborn is not an empty-headed organism (Maurer & Maurer, 1988). It comes into the world already equipped with several genetically "wired" re-

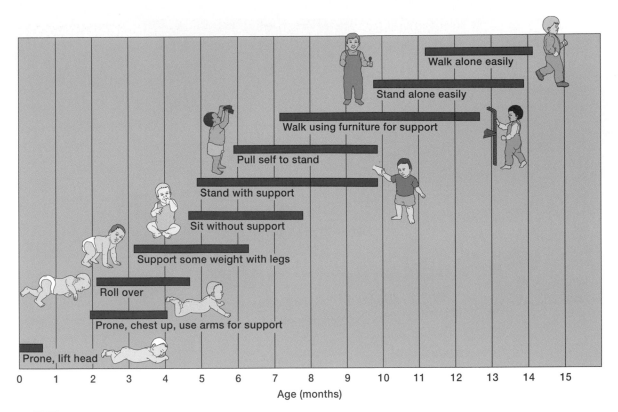

Walk alone easily

Stand alone easily

Walk using furniture for support

Pull self to stand

Stand with support

Sit without support

Support some weight with legs

Roll over

Prone, chest up, use arms for support

Prone, lift head

| 0 | 1 | 2 | 3 | 4 | 5 | 6 | 7 | 8 | 9 | 10 | 11 | 12 | 13 | 14 | 15 |

Age (months)

Figure 10.4
Developmental Accomplishments in Gross Motor Skills During the First 15 Months

flexes. For example, the newborn has no fear of water, naturally holding its breath and contracting its throat to keep water out. Some of the reflexes we possess as newborns persist throughout our lives—coughing, blinking, and yawning, for example. Others disappear in the months following birth as higher brain functions mature and we develop voluntary control over many behaviors (McDonnell, Corkum & Wilson, 1989). For example, by seven months we lose the sucking reflex (in which the infant automatically sucks an object touching the mouth).

The infant's physical development in the first two years of life is dramatic. At birth, the newborn has a large head relative to the rest of the body, and it needs constant support. Within 12 months, the infant becomes capable of sitting anywhere, standing, stooping, climbing, and often walking. During the second year, growth decelerates, but rapid increases in such activities as running and climbing take place. Figure 10.4 shows the average ages at which infants reach various motor milestones.

Canadian researchers, such as Darwin Muir of Queen's University, have made many significant contributions to our understanding of the development of the infant's senses. Infants respond to acoustic information before they are born (Kisilevsky, Muir & Low, 1992). Before the first year, infants can perceive rhythm and tempo (Trehub & Thorpe, 1989) and localize sounds (Muir, Clifton & Clarkson, 1989). By three months of age, infants can discriminate between a stranger's face and that of their mother (Barrera & Maurer, 1981). The ability to tell things apart by touch also shows some development during this period (Stack & Tsonis, in press).

As an infant walks, talks, runs, hears, looks, and touches, changes in its brain occur. Consider that it takes only nine months to go from a single cell to a brain and nervous system that contains approximately 100 billion nerve cells. However, at birth and in early infancy, neurons have only minimal connections. As the infant develops from birth to two years, the interconnection of neurons increases dramatically as the dendrites (the receiving parts) of the neurons branch out (see figure 10.5).

Zero to Three

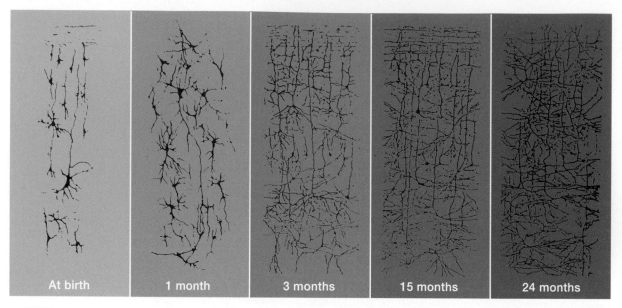

| At birth | 1 month | 3 months | 15 months | 24 months |

*F*igure 10.5
The Development of Dendritic Spreading
Note the increase in connections among neurons over the course of the first two years of life.

Child Development

Children's Education

Childhood   By their third birthday, children are full of new tricks such as climbing, skipping, and jumping. They are beginning to be able to make their body do what they want it to do, giving them a greater sense of self-control.

Catching, throwing, kicking, balancing, rolling, cutting, stacking, snapping, pushing, dancing, and swimming—preschool children perform these special feats and many, many more. As twentieth-century Welsh poet Dylan Thomas put it, "All the sun long they were running." The growth rate slows down in early childhood. Otherwise, we would be a species of giants. The growth and development of the brain underlie the young child's improvement in motor skills, reflected in activities such as the ability to hold a pencil and make increasingly efficient marks with it. A child's brain is closer to full growth than the rest of its body, attaining 75 percent of its adult weight by the age of 3 and 90 percent by age five.

The senses also mature during this period. For example, auditory sensitivity reaches adult levels by school age (Maurer & Maurer, 1988). Similarly, by age three children can visually focus on tiny images, such as letters of the alphabet and by about age six, which is normally when they are taught to read, they can scan a series of small letters.

In middle and late childhood, development is much smoother and more coordinated than in early childhood. While a preschool child can zip, cut, look, and dance, an elementary school child can zip, cut, look, and dance more efficiently and with more flair. Physical activities are essential for children to refine their developing skills. Child development experts believe children should be *active*, rather than *passive*, and should be able to plan and select many of their own activities. An ideal elementary school, for example, would include a gym and a safe, elaborate outdoor play area; a classroom with a fully equipped publishing center; and a science area with books to study, and animals and plants for observation. Children also need to "just" play. Education experts recognize that spontaneous play provides additional opportunities for children to learn.

At this point, we have discussed a number of ideas about what development is, the prenatal period and birth, and children's physical development. In the school atmosphere just described, in which children's education involves many opportunities for physical and self-initiated activities, not only is physical development enhanced, so is cognitive development, the topic to which we now turn.

Cognitive Development

Jean Piaget, the famous Swiss developmental psychologist, was a meticulous observer of his three children—Lucienne, Jacqueline, and Laurent. His books on cognitive development are filled with these observations. The following provide a glimpse of Piaget's observations of his children's cognitive development in infancy (Piaget, 1952).

- Toward the end of her fourth month, Lucienne is lying in her crib. Piaget hangs a doll over her feet. Lucienne thrusts her feet at the doll and makes it move. Afterward she looks at her motionless foot for a second, then kicks at the doll again. She has no visual control of her foot because her movements are the same whether she only looks at the doll or whether it is placed over her head. By contrast, she has tactile control of her foot because when she tries to kick the doll and misses, she slows her foot movements to improve her aim.
- At 11 months, while seated, Jacqueline shakes a little bell. She then pauses abruptly so she can delicately place the bell in front of her right foot; then she kicks the bell hard. Unable to recapture it, she grasps a ball and places it in the same location where the bell was. She gives the ball a firm kick.

For Piaget, such observations reflect the infant's cognitive development.

Piaget's Theory of Cognitive Development   Piaget (1896–1980) changed the way we think about children's minds. When Piaget's ideas were imported to North America in the 1960s, there was no theory available that explained how children's minds change as they age. Prior to Piaget, American psychologists had to choose from behaviorism, which emphasized that children receive information from the environment, or the IQ testing approach, which emphasized individual differences in children's intelligence. North American psychologists embraced Piaget's view that children *actively construct* their cognitive world and that they go through a series of stages in doing this.

In actively constructing their cognitive world, children use schemas. In chapter 7, "Memory," we defined a **schema** *as a concept or framework that already exists in a person's mind which organizes and interprets information.* In our discussion of memory we indicated that schemas help us to understand how people don't remember the past exactly but rather reconstruct it. Piaget's interest in schemas wasn't in terms of how people reconstruct the past but, rather, how they use schemas to organize and make sense out of their current experience.

Piaget (1952) said that two processes are responsible for how people use and adapt their schemas: assimilation and accommodation. **Assimilation** *occurs when individuals incorporate new information into existing knowledge.* That is, in assimilation people assimilate the environment to a schema. **Accommodation** *occurs when individuals adjust to new information.* That is, people accommodate their schemas to the environment. Consider this circumstance to see how assimilation and accommodation work: A young infant lunges at a rattle and tries to grasp it but is unable to pick it up. In this instance the infant has assimilated the rattle into the reaching schema of objects to be picked up. Over the course of several months and repeated attempts, the infant refines its movements and is able to pick up the rattle (accommodation). Consider how newborns reflexively suck everything that touches their lips. By sucking different objects, infants learn about the nature of these objects—their taste, texture, shape, and so on (assimilation). After several months of experience, though, they construct their understanding of the world differently. Some objects, such as fingers and the mother's breast, can be sucked, whereas others, such as fuzzy blankets, should not be (accommodation).

Jean Piaget, the famous Swiss developmental psychologist, changed the way we think about the development of children's minds.

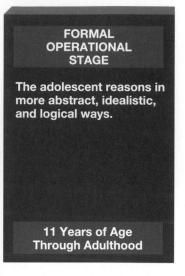

FORMAL OPERATIONAL STAGE

The adolescent reasons in more abstract, idealistic, and logical ways.

11 Years of Age Through Adulthood

CONCRETE OPERATIONAL STAGE

The child can now reason logically about concrete events and classify objects into different sets.

7 to 11 Years of Age

PREOPERATIONAL STAGE

The child begins to represent the world with words and images. These words and images reflect increased symbolic thinking and go beyond the connection of sensory information and physical action.

2 to 7 Years of Age

SENSORIMOTOR STAGE

The infant constructs an understanding of the world by coordinating sensory experiences with physical actions. An infant progresses from reflexive, instinctual action at birth to the beginning of symbolic thought toward the end of the stage.

Birth to 2 Years of Age

Figure 10.6
Piaget's Four Stages of Cognitive Development

Infant Cognition

Piaget also believed that we go through four stages in understanding the world (see figure 10.6). Each of the stages is age-related and consists of distinct ways of thinking. Remember, it is the *different* way of understanding the world that makes one stage more advanced than another. Knowing *more* information does not make the child's thinking more advanced, in Piaget's view. This is what Piaget meant when he said that the child's cognition is *qualitatively* different in one stage compared to another. Let's now examine Piaget's four stages.

The Sensorimotor Stage   The **sensorimotor stage,** *which lasts from birth to about 2 years of age, is the first Piagetian stage. In this stage, infants construct an understanding of the world by coordinating sensory experiences (such as seeing and hearing) with physical (motor) actions—hence the term sensorimotor.* It is nonsymbolic through much of its duration and object permanence is an important accomplishment. At the beginning of this stage, newborns have little more than reflexive patterns with which to work. By the end of the stage, two-year-olds show complex sensorimotor patterns and are beginning to use symbols in their thinking.

We live in a world of objects. Imagine yourself as a five-month-old infant and how you might experience the world. You are in a playpen filled with toys. One of the toys, a monkey, falls out of your grasp and rolls behind a larger toy, a hippopotamus. Would you know the monkey is behind the hippopotamus, or would you think it is completely gone? Piaget believed that "out of sight" literally was "out of mind" for young infants. At five months of age, you would not have reached for the monkey when it fell behind the hippopotamus. By eight months of age, though, infants begin to understand that out of sight is not out of mind. At this point, you would probably have reached behind the hippopotamus to search for the monkey, coordinating your senses with your movements.

Object permanence *is Piaget's term for one of the infant's most important accomplishments: understanding that objects and events continue to exist even when they cannot directly be seen, heard, or touched.* The most common way to study object permanence is to show an infant an interesting toy and then cover the toy with a sheet or a blanket. If infants understand that the toy still exists, they try to uncover it (see figure 10.7). Object permanence continues to develop throughout the sensorimotor period. For example, when infants initially understand that objects exist even when out of sight, they look for them only briefly. By the end of the sensorimotor stage, infants engage in a more prolonged and sophisticated search for an object.

In sum, we have seen that sensorimotor thought involves the ability to organize and coordinate sensations with physical movements, is nonsymbolic throughout its duration, and includes the development of object permanence. Next, we examine the second Piagetian cognitive stage.

The Preoperational Stage   The **preoperational stage** *is Piaget's second stage of cognitive development. Lasting from approximately two to seven years of age, it is more symbolic than sensorimotor thought, does not involve operational thought, is egocentric, and is intuitive rather than logical.*

Preschool children begin to represent their world with words, images, and drawings. Symbolic thoughts go beyond simple connections of sensorimotor information and physical action.

While preschool children can symbolically represent the world, they still cannot perform operations. **Operations,** *in Piaget's theory, are mental representations that are reversible.* Preschool children have difficulty understanding that reversing an action brings about the original conditions from which the action began. The following two examples will help you to understand Piaget's concept of reversibility. The preschool child may know that $4 + 2 = 6$ but not understand that the reverse, $6 - 2 = 4$, is true. Or let's say a preschooler walks to his friend's house each day but always gets a ride home. If you asked him to walk home one day he would probably reply that he didn't know the way since he had never walked home before.

A well-known test of whether a child can think "operationally" is to present a child with two identical beakers, A and B, filled with liquid to the same height (see figure 10.8). Next to them is a third beaker, C. Beaker C is tall and thin, while beakers A and B are wide and short. The liquid is poured from B into C, and the child is asked whether the amounts in A and C are the same. The four-year-old child invariably says that the amount of liquid in the tall, thin beaker (C) is greater than that in the short, fat beaker (A). The eight-year-old child consistently says the amounts are the same. The four-year-old child, a preoperational thinker, cannot mentally reverse the pouring action; that is, she cannot imagine the liquid going back from container C to container B. Piaget said that children such as this four-year-old girl have not grasped the concept of **conservation,** *a belief in the permanence of certain attributes of objects or situations in spite of superficial changes.*

The child's thought in the preoperational stage also is egocentric. By **egocentrism,** *Piaget meant the inability to distinguish between one's own perspective and someone else's perspective.* Piaget and Barbel Inhelder (1969) initially studied young children's egocentrism by devising the three mountains task (see figure 10.9). The child walks around the model of the mountains and becomes familiar with what the mountains look like from different perspectives. The child can see that different objects are on the mountains as well. The child is then seated on one side of the table on which the mountains are placed. The experimenter takes a doll and moves it to different locations around the table, at each location asking the child to select one photo from a series of photos that most accurately reflects the view the doll is seeing. Children in the preoperational stage often pick the photo that shows the view they have rather than the view the doll has.

Piaget also called preoperational thought *intuitive,* because when he asked children why they knew something, they often did not give logical answers, but offered personal insights or guesses instead. Yet, as Piaget observed, young children seem so sure that they know something, even though they do not use logical reasoning to arrive at the answer. Young children also have an insatiable desire to know their world, and they ask a lot of questions:

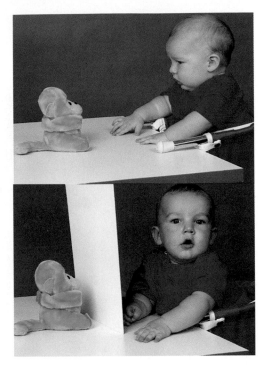

*F*igure 10.7
Object Permanence

Piaget thought that object permanence was one of infancy's landmark cognitive accomplishments. For this five-month-old boy, "out of sight" is literally out of mind. The infant looks at the toy monkey *(top),* but when his view of the toy is blocked *(bottom),* he does not search for it. Eventually, he will search for the hidden toy monkey, reflecting the presence of object permanence.

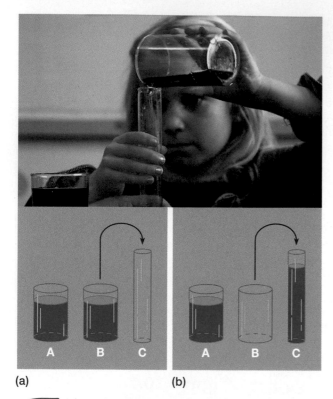

(a)   (b)

ℱigure 10.8
Piaget's Conservation Task

The beaker test is a well-known Piagetian test to determine whether a child can think operationally—that is, can mentally reverse actions and show conservation of the substance. *(a)* Two identical beakers are presented to the child. Then, the experimenter pours the liquid from B into C, which is taller and thinner than A or B. *(b)* The child is asked if these beakers (A and C) have the same amount of liquid. The preoperational child says no. When asked to point to the beaker that has more liquid, the preoperational child points to the tall, thin beaker.

"Why does a lady have to be married to have a baby?"
"Who was the mother when everybody was the baby?"
"Why do leaves fall?"
"Why does the sun shine?"

In sum, we have seen that preoperational thought is more symbolic than sensorimotor thought, is characterized by an inability to perform operations, is egocentric, and is intuitive rather than logical. Next, we explore the third Piagetian cognitive stage.

The Concrete Operational Stage   The **concrete operational stage** *is Piaget's third stage of cognitive development, which occurs from 7 to 11 years of age. Concrete operational thought involves using operations, and logical reasoning replaces intuitive reasoning, but only in concrete situations. It is characterized by a lack of abstract thinking, but classification skills are present.*

Earlier we described the beaker task that was too difficult for a preoperational child. Another well-known task to demonstrate operational thinking involves showing a child two identical balls of clay (see figure 10.10). The experimenter rolls one ball into a long, thin shape. The other is retained in its original ball shape. Then the child is asked if there is more clay in the ball or in the long, thin piece of clay. By the time children reach seven to eight years of age, most answer that the amount of clay is the same. To solve this problem correctly, children have to imagine that the clay ball is rolled out into a long, thin strip and then returned to its original round shape—imagination that involves a reversible mental action. Concrete operations allow the child to coordinate several characteristics rather than focusing on a single property of an object. In the clay example, the preoperational child is likely to focus on height *or* width. The child who has reached the stage of concrete operational thought coordinates information about both dimensions.

Many of the concrete operations identified by Piaget focus on the way children think about the properties of objects. One important skill at this stage of reasoning is the ability to classify or divide things into different sets or subsets and to consider their interrelations. Figure 10.11 shows an example of children's classification skills.

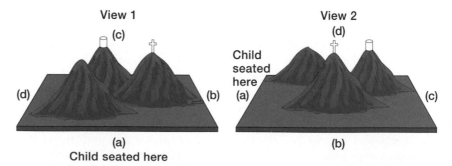

View 1   View 2

ℱigure 10.9
The Three Mountains Task

View 1 shows the child's perspective from where he or she is sitting. View 2 is an example of the photograph the child would be shown mixed in with others from different perspectives. To correctly identify this view, the child has to take the perspective of a person sitting at spot *(b)*. Invariably, a preschool child who thinks in a preoperational way cannot perform this task. When asked what a view of the mountains looks like from position *(b)*, the child selects a photograph taken from location *(a)*, the child's view at the time.

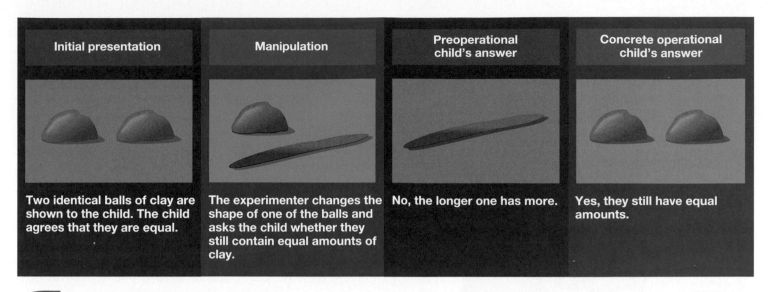

Initial presentation	Manipulation	Preoperational child's answer	Concrete operational child's answer
Two identical balls of clay are shown to the child. The child agrees that they are equal.	The experimenter changes the shape of one of the balls and asks the child whether they still contain equal amounts of clay.	No, the longer one has more.	Yes, they still have equal amounts.

𝒻igure 10.10
Preoperational and Concrete Operational Children: The Clay Example

In sum, we have seen that concrete operational thought involves operational thinking, logical reasoning in concrete but not abstract contexts, and classification skill. Next, we examine the fourth Piagetian cognitive stage.

The Formal Operational Stage   The **formal operational stage** *is Piaget's fourth and final stage of cognitive development entered at 11 to 15 years of age and continuing through the adult years. It is more abstract, idealistic, and logical than concrete operational thought.* Unlike elementary school children, adolescents are no longer limited to actual concrete experience as the anchor of thought. They can conceive make-believe situations, hypothetical possibilities, or purely abstract propositions. Thought also becomes more idealistic. Adolescents often compare themselves and others to ideal standards. And they think about what an ideal world would be like, wondering if they couldn't carve out a better world than the one the adult generation has handed to them.

At the same time adolescents think more abstractly and idealistically, they also think more logically. Adolescents begin to think more like a scientist thinks, devising plans to solve problems and systematically testing solutions. This type of problem solving has an imposing name. **Hypothetical-deductive reasoning** *is Piaget's name for adolescents' ability to develop hypotheses, or best hunches, about ways to solve problems, such as an algebraic equation.* They then systematically deduce, or conclude, which is the best path to follow to solve the problem. By contrast, children are more likely to solve problems in a trial-and-error fashion.

In sum, we have seen that formal operational thought is abstract, idealistic, and logical. Now that we have learned about Piaget's stages, let's evaluate the current status of his ideas in developmental psychology.

Evaluating Piaget   We have read about Freud in abnormal psychology, Skinner in learning, and Piaget in cognitive development. Freud altered the way we think about people's problems, and Skinner changed the way we look at how people learn. Likewise, Piaget completely opened up a new way of looking at how children's minds develop. All three are giants in their fields.

We owe to Piaget a long list of masterful concepts that have enduring power and fascination (Scholnick, 1999). These include the concepts of schemas, assimilation, accommodation, cognitive stages, object permanence,

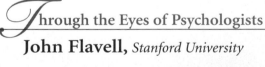
𝒯hrough the Eyes of Psychologists
John Flavell, *Stanford University*

"We owe to Piaget the present field of cognitive development with its image of the developing child, who through its own active and creative commerce with its environment, builds an orderly succession of cognitive structures en route to intellectual maturity."

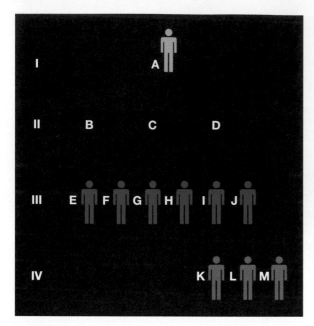

ℱigure 10.11
Classification Involving a Family Tree

One way to determine if children possess classification skills is to see if they can understand a family tree of four generations (Furth & Wachs, 1975). This family tree suggests that the grandfather (A) has three sons (B, C, & D), each of whom has two sons (E through J), and that one of these sons (J) has three sons (K, L, & M). A child who comprehends this classification system can move up and down a level (vertically), across a level (horizontally), and up and down and across a level (obliquely) within the system. A child who thinks in a concrete operational way understands that person J can, at the same time, be father, brother, and grandson, for example. A preoperational child cannot perform this classification and says that a father cannot fulfill these other roles.

egocentrism, and conservation. We also owe to Piaget the currently accepted vision of children as active constructive thinkers who manufacture their own development.

But just as Freud's and Skinner's views have been criticized, so have Piaget's (Lutz & Sternberg, 1999; Pascual-Leone & Johnson, 1999). Some cognitive abilities emerge earlier than Piaget thought. For example, Renée Baillargeon (1997) has documented that infants as young as four months of age know that objects continue to exist even when hidden (which Piaget did not think was possible until eight months of age). Memory and other forms of symbolic activity occur by at least the first half of the first year (much earlier than Piaget thought possible) (Mandler, 1998).

Formal operational thought does not emerge as consistently in early adolescence as Piaget envisioned. Many adolescents and even adults do not reason as logically as Piaget proposed. Thus, infants are more cognitively competent than Piaget thought, adolescents and adults less competent.

Piaget was interested in examining the species-general ways that all people go through cognitive stages, and he showed little interest in individual variations in people's thinking. Not surprisingly, he has been criticized for ignoring individual differences in thinking.

Robbie Case (1991) has championed the argument that Piaget's view places too much emphasis on grand stages and not enough on smaller, precise steps in solving problems. Information-processing psychologists believe that children's minds can be best understood by focusing more on strategies and skills, as well as how fast and efficiently people process information (Siegler, 1998; Keenan, Olson & Marini, 1998).

Piaget also did not think that culture and education play important roles in children's cognitive development. However, researchers have found that the age at which children acquire conservation skills is related to some extent with whether their culture provides relevant practice (Cole, 1999; Cole & Cole, 2000). The Russian psychologist Lev Vygotsky (1962) recognized that cognitive development does not occur in a sociocultural vacuum. In Vygotsky's view, the goal of cognitive development is to learn the skills that will allow you to be competent in your culture. To do this, he says that it is important to be guided and assisted by skilled members of the culture, much like being a cognitive apprentice (Rogoff, 1998). Vygotsky's view has become increasingly popular in education because of its emphasis on collaborative learning through interaction with skilled others.

In sum, today children's cognitive development is approached from plural points of view. Yet even though some of his ideas have been modified, Piaget still stands head and shoulders above all others in this field. It was his masterpiece that let us see how, as they develop, children's minds change in orderly, sequential ways (Scholnick & others, 1999).

Socioemotional Development

As children grow and develop, they are socialized by and socialize others—parents, siblings, peers, teachers, and others. Their small world widens as they grow older. We will begin this section by studying Erik Erikson's theory of how we develop socioemotionally.

Erikson's Theory of Socioemotional Development   Erik Erikson (1902–1994) spent his childhood and adolescence in Europe. After working as a psychoanalyst under Freud's direction, he came to the United States and taught at Harvard University. While he accepted some of Freud's beliefs, he disagreed with others. For example, while Freud argued that *psychosexual stages* are the key to understanding development, Erikson said that *psychosocial stages* are the key. In addition, while Freud stressed that personality is shaped in the first five years of life,

Erikson's Theory

Erikson emphasized lifelong development. In Erikson's (1968) view, people pass through eight stages in their journey through the human life span. The first four stages take place in childhood, the last four in adolescence and adulthood (see figure 10.12).

Each stage represents a developmental task or crisis that must be negotiated. For Erikson, the developmental task can be a turning point of increased vulnerability or enhanced potential. The more successfully people resolve the issues, the more competent they are likely to become.

Trust Versus Mistrust   Trust versus mistrust *is Erikson's first psychosocial stage, which occurs during the first year of life.* Trust is built when a baby's basic needs—such as comfort, food, and warmth—are met. If infants' needs are not met by responsive, sensitive caregivers, the result is mistrust. Trust in infancy sets the stage for a lifelong expectation that the world will be a good and pleasant place to live.

Autonomy Versus Shame and Doubt Autonomy versus shame and doubt *is Erikson's second stage, which occurs from one to three years of age.* The positive side of the stage involves developing a sense of independence and autonomy, the negative side a sense of shame and doubt. In seeking autonomy, toddlers assert their will. If they are restrained too much or punished too harshly, they are not likely to develop this sense of independence.

Erikson's stages	Developmental period
Integrity versus despair	Late adulthood (60s–)
Generativity versus stagnation	Middle adulthood (40s, 50s)
Intimacy versus isolation	Early adulthood (20s, 30s)
Identity versus identity confusion	Adolescence (10 to 20 years)
Industry versus inferiority	Middle and late childhood (elementary school years, 6 years– puberty)
Initiative versus guilt	Early childhood (preschool years, ages 3–5)
Autonomy versus shame and doubt	Infancy (second year)
Trust versus mistrust	Infancy (first year)

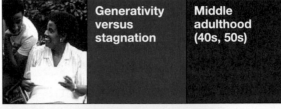

*F*igure 10.12
Erikson's Eight Life-Span Stages

Initiative Versus Guilt   Initiative versus guilt *is Erikson's third stage, which occurs from three to five years of age.* Asked to assume more responsibility for themselves, children develop initiative. If children are irresponsible or made to feel anxious, they might develop too much guilt. During the preschool years, children's social worlds widen and they are challenged to develop purposeful behavior and cope with these challenges. Erikson believed that young children are resilient. He said that most guilt is quickly compensated for by a sense of accomplishment.

Industry Versus Inferiority   Industry versus inferiority *is Erikson's fourth stage, which occurs from six years of age until puberty.* Industry is achieved by mastering knowledge and intellectual skills. When children don't attain this mastery, they can feel inferior. Erikson believed that at the end of early childhood's period of expansive imagination, children are ready to turn their energy to learning academic skills. If they don't, they might develop a sense of being incompetent and unproductive.

Identity Versus Identity Confusion   Identity versus identity confusion *is Erikson's fifth stage, which occurs during the adolescent years.* At this time individuals are faced with finding out who they are, what they are all about, and where they are going in life. If they don't adequately explore their identity, they emerge from this stage with a sense of identity confusion. Adolescents are confronted with many new roles and adult statuses, such as vocational and romantic. Parents need to allow adolescents to explore many different roles and paths within a particular role. If parents push an identity on adolescents without letting them adequately explore various roles and if a positive future path is not defined, identity confusion reigns.

Intimacy Versus Isolation   Intimacy versus isolation *is Erikson's sixth stage, which is experienced in the twenties and thirties (early adulthood).* At this time, individuals face the developmental task of forming intimate relationships with others. If they do not find intimacy in relationships with a partner and/or friends, they can develop a sense of social isolation. Erikson eloquently described intimacy as finding yourself yet losing yourself in another person.

Generativity Versus Stagnation   Generativity versus stagnation *is Erikson's seventh stage, which occurs in the forties and fifties (middle adulthood).* A chief concern is to assist the younger generation in developing and leading useful lives. This is what Erikson meant by generativity. The feeling of having done little or nothing for the next generation is what is meant by stagnation.

Integrity Versus Despair   Integrity versus despair *is Erikson's eighth and final stage, which individuals experience from the sixties on (late adulthood).* In late adulthood, people review their lives. If the retrospective glances reveal a life well spent, the person feels a sense of satisfaction—integrity is achieved. If the retrospective glances are negative, the person may feel a sense of despair.

Erikson did not believe that the proper solution to a stage is always completely positive. Some exposure or commitment to the negative side of a developmental task can be inevitable. For example, you can't trust all people under all circumstances and survive. Nonetheless, positive resolutions to a stage should dominate for optimal development to take place.

Evaluating Erikson's Theory   At a time when it was believed that most development takes place in childhood, Erikson charted how development is lifelong. His insights also helped to move us away from Freud's focus on sexuality and toward understanding the importance of successfully resolving different socioemotional tasks at different points in our lives. Erikson's ideas changed the way we think about some periods of development (Marcia, 1999). For example, Erikson encouraged us to look at adolescents not just as sexual beings, but as individuals seeking to find out who they are and searching to find their niche in the world. He informed us to not just think of middle-aged individuals as being in a state of decline but rather as having the important developmental task of contributing to the next generation.

Just as Piaget's theory has been criticized, so has Erikson's. Critics argue that the research base for Erikson's entire theory has not been developed. However, research on specific stages—such as identity versus identity confusion, as well as generativity versus stagnation—reveal that these are important developmental tasks at these points in our lives. Critics also say that Erikson's attempt to capture each stage with a single concept sometimes leaves out other important developmental tasks. For example, regarding early adulthood Erikson focused on intimacy versus isolation. However, another important developmental task in early adulthood involves careers and work, which were underplayed by Erikson.

However, such criticisms cannot tarnish Erikson's monumental contributions. He, along with Piaget, is a twentieth-century giant in developmental psychology.

Attachment   Erikson (1968) believes that the caregiver's responsive and sensitive behavior toward the infant during its first year provides an important foundation for later development. A number of contemporary developmental psychologists who study the process of "attachment" during infancy agree. Attachment usually refers to a strong relationship between two people in which each person does a number of things to continue the relationship. Many types of people are attached: relatives, lovers, a teacher and a student. In the language of developmental psychology, **attachment** *is the close emotional bond between the infant and its caregiver.*

Theories about infant attachment abound. Freud believed that the infant becomes attached to the person or object that provides oral satisfaction. For most infants, this is the mother, since she is most likely to feed the infant.

But researchers have questioned the importance of feeding in attachment. Harry Harlow and Robert Zimmerman (1959) evaluated whether feeding or contact comfort was more important to infant attachment. The researchers separated infant monkeys from their mothers at birth and placed them in cages where they had access to two artificial "mothers." One of the mothers was made of wire, the other of cloth. Half of the infant monkeys were fed by the wire mother, half by the cloth mother. The infant monkeys nestled close to the cloth mother and spent little time on the wire one, even when it was the wire mother that gave milk. This study clearly demonstrates that contact comfort, not feeding, is the crucial element in the attachment process (see figure 10.13).

In a famous study, Konrad Lorenz (1965) illustrated attachment behavior in geese. Lorenz separated the eggs laid by one goose into two groups. He returned one group to the goose to be hatched; the other group was hatched in an incubator. The goslings in the first group performed as predicted; they followed their mother as soon as they hatched. But those in the second group, who first saw Lorenz after hatching, followed him everywhere as if he were their mother. Lorenz marked the goslings and then placed both groups under a box. Mother goose and "mother" Lorenz stood aside as the box was lifted. Each group of goslings went directly to its "mother" (see figure 10.14). Lorenz called this process **imprinting,** *the tendency of an infant animal to form an attachment to the first moving object it sees and/or hears.*

For goslings, the critical period for imprinting is the first 36 hours after birth. There also appears to be a longer, more flexible "sensitive" period for attachment in human infants. A number of developmental psychologists believe that attachment to the caregiver in humans during the *first year* provides an important foundation for later development. This view has been especially emphasized by John Bowlby (1969, 1989) and Mary Ainsworth (1979). Bowlby believes the infant and the mother instinctively form an attachment. He believes the newborn is innately equipped to elicit the mother's attachment behavior; it cries, clings, smiles, and coos. Later the infant crawls, walks, and follows the mother. The infant's goal is to keep the mother nearby.

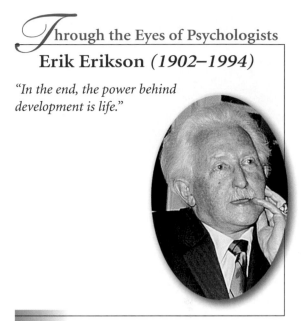

Through the Eyes of Psychologists

Erik Erikson (1902–1994)

"In the end, the power behind development is life."

Figure 10.13
Harlow's Classic "Contact Comfort" Study
Regardless of whether they were fed by a wire mother or by a cloth mother, the infant monkeys overwhelmingly preferred to be in contact with the cloth mother, demonstrating the importance of contact comfort in attachment.

Photo courtesy of Operation Migration

𝓕igure 10.14
Canadian William Lishman Leads a Flock of Imprinted Canada Geese on Their First Southward Migration

Inspired by Konrad Lorenz, William Lishman (along with Joseph Duff) experimented with helping orphaned Canada geese learn to migrate. Lishman's work was described in his autobiography, *Father Goose,* and was the subject of the film *Fly Away Home.*

Attachment

Research on attachment supports Bowlby's view that the infant's attachment to its caregiver intensifies at about 6 to 7 months (Schaeffer & Emerson, 1964).

Some babies have a more positive attachment experience than others (Levy, 1999). Ainsworth (1979) believes that the difference depends on how sensitive the caregiver is to the infant's signals (Pederson & others, 1998). Ainsworth says that in **secure attachment** *infants use the caregiver, usually the mother, as a secure base from which to explore the environment.* Infants who are securely attached are more likely to have mothers who are more sensitive, accepting, and expressive of affection toward them than those who are insecurely attached (Waters & others, 1995).

The securely attached infant moves freely away from the mother but also keeps tabs on her location by periodically glancing at her. The securely attached infant responds positively to being picked up by others, and when put back down, happily moves away to play. An insecurely attached infant, in contrast, avoids the mother or is ambivalent toward her. The insecurely attached infant fears strangers and is upset by minor, everyday sensations.

Not all developmentalists believe that a secure attachment in infancy is the only path to competence in life. Some developmentalists believe that too much emphasis is placed on the importance of the attachment bond in infancy. Jerome Kagan (1998), for example, believes that infants are highly resilient and adaptive. He argues that they are evolutionarily equipped to stay on a positive developmental course even in the face of wide variations in parenting. Kagan and others stress that genetic and temperament characteristics play more important roles in a child's social competence than the attachment theorists, such as Bowlby, Ainsworth, and Sroufe, are willing to acknowledge. For example, infants may have inherited a low tolerance for stress; this, rather than an insecure attachment bond, may be responsible for their inability to get along with peers.

Another criticism of attachment theory is that it ignores the diversity of socializing agents and contexts that exist in an infant's world (Thompson, 1991, 1998). In some cultures, infants show attachments to many people. In the African Hausa culture, both grandmothers and siblings provide a significant amount of care to infants (Harkness & Super, 1995). Infants in agricultural societies tend to form attachments to older siblings who are assigned a major responsibility for younger siblings' care. The attachments formed by infants in group care in Israeli kibbutzim provide another challenge to the singular attachment thesis.

Researchers recognize the importance of competent, nurturant caregivers in an infant's development. At issue, though, is whether or not secure attachment, especially to a single caregiver, is critical (Schneider-Rosen & Burke, 1999).

Temperament   As we mentioned, Jerome Kagan (1998) and others believe that temperament is an important dimension of development. **Temperament** *refers to an individual's behavioral style and characteristic way of responding.* A widely debated issue involves what the basic types of temperament are. Psychiatrists Alexander Chess and Stella Thomas (1977) believe that there are three basic types or clusters:

- *Easy child,* who is generally in a positive mood, quickly establishes regular routines in infancy, and adapts easily to new experiences
- *Difficult child,* who tends to react negatively and cry frequently, engages in irregular daily routines, and is slow to accept new experiences
- *Slow-to-warm-up child,* who has a low activity level, is somewhat negative, shows low adaptability, and displays a low intensity of mood

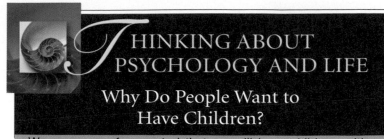

THINKING ABOUT PSYCHOLOGY AND LIFE

Why Do People Want to Have Children?

WE OFTEN TAKE for granted that we will have children, without considering why we will have them (Dickson & Harris, 1999). Why do you think couples should have children? If you are a female, what are your feelings about becoming a mother? If you are a male, what are your feelings about becoming a father? Is there a best age to become a mother or a father? What would that age be for you? Why? What are some reasons for not having children?

Other researchers argue that the basic factors in temperament are *emotionality* (tendency to be distressed), *sociability* (tendency to prefer the company of others to being alone), and *activity level* (tempo and vigor of movement) (Buss & Plomin, 1987).

Many parents don't become believers in temperament's importance until they have their second child (Rothbart & Bates, 1998). Parents typically view the firstborn child's behavior as due to the way they have socialized the child. However, management strategies that worked with the first child might not be as effective with the second child. Such differences in children's temperament, which appear very early in their lives, support the belief that "nature" as well as "nurture" influence development.

Good parenting involves paying attention to and respecting the child's individuality (Sanson & Rothbart, 1995). Temperament is an important dimension of this individuality (Thompson, 1999). Next, we explore further what is involved in good parenting.

Parenting   Even though many children spend a great deal of time in child-care situations away from the home, parents are still the main caregivers for the vast majority of the world's children. And parents have always wondered what the best way is to rear their children. "Spare the rod and spoil the child." "Children are to be seen and not heard." There was a time when parents took those adages seriously. But our attitudes toward children—and parenting techniques—have changed.

Parenting

Parenting Styles   At the beginning of the chapter we raised the issue of what the best way to parent is when we discussed Jessica Dubroff's tragic story. Diana Baumrind (1971, 1991) believes parents interact with their children in one of four basic ways. She classifies parenting styles as authoritarian, authoritative, neglectful, and indulgent.

Authoritarian parenting *is a restrictive, punitive style in which the parent exhorts the child to follow the parent's directions and to respect work and effort.* The authoritarian parent firmly limits and controls the child with little verbal exchange. Authoritarian parenting is associated with children's social incompetence. In a difference of opinion about how to do something, for example, the authoritarian parent might say, "You do it my way or else. . . .There will be no discussion!" Children of authoritarian parents are often anxious about social comparison, fail to initiate activity, and have poor communication skills.

Authoritative parenting *encourages children to be independent but still places limits and controls on their behavior. Extensive verbal give-and-take is allowed and parents are warm and nurturant toward the child.* Authoritative parenting is associated with children's social competence. An authoritative parent might put his arm around the child in a comforting way and say, "You know you should not have done that; let's talk about how you can handle the situation

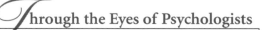

Through the Eyes of Psychologists

Mary Ainsworth,
University of Virginia

"It is an essential ground plan of the human species for an infant to become attached to a caregiver."

Children learn to love when they are loved

better next time." Children whose parents are authoritative tend to be socially competent, self-reliant, and socially responsible.

Neglectful parenting *is a style in which parents are uninvolved in their child's life.* This style is associated with the child's social incompetence, especially a lack of self-control. This type of parent cannot give an affirmative answer to the question, "It's 10 P.M. Do you know where your child is?" Children have a strong need for their parents to care about them. Children whose parents are neglectful might develop a sense that other aspects of the parents' lives are more important than they are. Children whose parents are neglectful tend to show poor self-control and do not handle independence well.

Indulgent parenting *is a style in which parents are involved with their children but place few demands on them.* Indulgent parenting is associated with children's social incompetence, especially a lack of self-control. Such parents let their children do what they want, and the result is the children never learn to control their own behavior and always expect to get their way. Some parents deliberately rear their children in this way because they believe the combination of warm involvement with few restraints will produce a creative, confident child. One boy whose parents deliberately reared him in an indulgent manner moved his parents out of their bedroom suite and took it over for himself. He was almost 18 years old and still had not learned to control his behavior; when he couldn't get something he wanted, he threw temper tantrums. As you might expect, he was not very popular with his peers. Children whose parents are indulgent never learn respect for others and have difficulty controlling their behavior.

There is more to understanding parent-child relationships than parenting style (Crouter & others, 1999; Lamb & others, 1999). For many years the socialization of children was viewed as a straightforward, one-way matter of indoctrination—telling small children about the use of spoons and potties, the importance of saying thank you, and not killing the baby brother. The basic philosophy was that children had to be trained to fit into the social world, so their behavior had to be shaped into that of a mature adult. The young child is not like the inanimate piece of stone the sculptor forms into a polished statue. **Reciprocal socialization** *is the process by which children socialize parents just as parents socialize children.* For example, children's smiles usually elicit positive overtures by parents. However, when children are difficult and aggressive, their parents are more likely to punish them. As another example of reciprocal socialization, consider adolescents. They lay guilt trips on parents, just as parents lay guilt trips on them.

A recent controversy about parenting focuses on the nature–nurture issue  P. 69. In a provocative book, *The Nurture Assumption,* Judith Harris (1998) argued that what parents do does not make a difference in their children's behavior. Spank them. Hug them. Read to them. Ignore them. Harris says it won't influence how they turn out. She argues that children's genes and peers are far more important than parents in children's development.

Harris is right that genes and peers matter, but wrong that parents don't. Numerous studies have revealed the importance of parents in child development. For example, when parents abuse their children, the children have problems in regulating emotions, becoming securely attached to others, developing competent peer relations, and adapting to school, and they develop anxiety and depression disorders (Cicchetti & Toth, 1998; Rogosch & others, 1995). Conversely, Rose-Krasnor and her colleagues (1996) trace the origins of social competence in children to early positive relationships with their mother. Child development expert, T. Berry Brazelton (1998) commented, "*The Nurture Assumption* is so disturbing it devalues what parents are trying to do. . . . Parents might say, 'If I don't matter, why should I bother?' That's terrifying and it's coming when children need a stronger home base."

The Mother's and Father's Roles   What do you think of when you hear the word *motherhood?* If you are like most people, you associate motherhood with a

Parenting and Genes

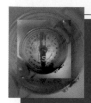

EXPLORATIONS IN PSYCHOLOGY
Child Care in North America

AS MORE women enter the workforce after pregnancy, and more of them are single parents, more families are relying on nonmaternal care for their infants and young children (Appelbaum & others, 1999; NICHD Early Child Care Research Network, 1997, in press; Peth-Pierce, 1998). Today, almost two-thirds of mothers with children under age 6 work outside the home. Most mothers return to work in their child's first 3 to 5 months of life, so their children spend much of their early lives in a variety of child-care arrangements.

Some child development experts argue that child care, especially as it is constituted in North America, poses risks for infants because healthy development requires caregiving by a single person. Yet others say that children can thrive in child care of high quality and that they are harmed only when the quality is poor.

The passing of the Canada Child Care Act (1998) focused attention on the quality of child care in Canada (Pence, 1989; Clifford & others, 1992). The emerging consensus is that high-quality child care does no harm and can sometimes even help children. For example, Schliecker, White and Jacobs (1991) found that child-care quality was related to vocabulary development, implicating lower-quality child-care settings. They also found that this effect was greater for single-parent mother-headed households. Turned around, high-quality child care can make a significant contribution to the development of a child's vocabulary, especially when that child comes from a single-parent family. The Canadian Transition to Child Care Study (McKim and others, 1999) examined the effect of child care on infant attachment. This study found that high-quality child care can actually counter the tendency of infants with a difficult temperament to experience insecure mother-infant attachment.

In the U.S., the National Institute of Child Health and Human Development (NICHD) undertook a *longitudinal* study (a study that follows the same individuals over time, usually several years or more) of the child-care experiences of children and their development. Researchers are assessing children over seven years of their lives, using multiple methods (trained observers, interviews, questionnaires, and testing) and measuring many facets of children's development (physical health, cognitive and socioemotional development).

Following are some of the results of this study to date:

• Infants from low-income families were more likely to receive low-quality child care than were their higher-income counterparts. Quality of care was based on such characteristics as group size, child-adult ratio, physical environment, caregiver characteristics (such as formal education, specialized training, and child-care experience), and caregiver behavior (such as sensitivity to children).
• Child-care in and of itself neither adversely affected nor promoted the security of infants' attachments to their mothers.
• Child-care quality, especially sensitive and responsive attention from caregivers, was linked with fewer child problems and better child language and cognitive abilities.

number of positive images, such as warmth, selflessness, dutifulness, and tolerance (Matlin, 1993). And while most women expect that motherhood will be happy and fulfilling, the reality is that motherhood has been accorded relatively low prestige in our society (Hoffnung, 1984). When stacked up against money, power, and achievement, motherhood unfortunately doesn't fare too well, and mothers rarely receive the appreciation they warrant. When children don't succeed or they develop problems, our society has had a tendency to attribute the lack of success or the development of problems to a single source—mothers. One of psychology's most important lessons is that behavior is multiply determined. So it is with children's development—when development goes awry, mothers are not the single cause of the problems, even though our society stereotypes them in this way.

A special concern of many contemporary mothers is whether working full-time in a career will harm their children's development. There is no evidence that this is the case (Parke & Buriel, 1998). Nonetheless, when working mothers place their children in child care (nonmaternal care), they worry about whether it will harm their children. This is a legitimate concern because much child care in North America is of poor quality. To read further about child care, see Explorations in Psychology.

SUMMARY TABLE 10.2
Children's Physical, Cognitive, and Socioemotional Development

Concept	Processes/Related Ideas	Characteristics/Description
Physical Development	Infancy	The newborn comes into the world with some genetically equipped reflexes. The infant's physical and sensory development in the first two years is extensive. Neuronal interconnections increase dramatically in the first two years.
	Childhood	Children gain more self-control over their body in early childhood. The child's brain development continues and is reflected in improved motor and sensory skills. In middle and late childhood, development is smoother and more coordinated.
Cognitive Development	Piaget's Theory	Piaget changed forever the way we think about children's minds. Piaget argued that children actively construct an understanding of the world. Children use schemas to understand their world. Two processes are responsible for how people use and adapt their schemas: assimilation and accommodation. Piaget also believed that we go through four stages in understanding the world: sensorimotor stage (0–2 years; involves coordinating sensory experiences with physical motoric actions, is nonsymbolic through most of its duration, and object permanence is an important accomplishment); preoperational stage (2–7 years; is more symbolic than sensorimotor thought, does not involve operational thought, is egocentric, and is intuitive rather than logical); concrete operational (7–11 years; involves using operations, logical thought replaces intuitive thought but only in concrete situations, abstract thinking is absent, and classification skills are present); formal operational thought (entered at 11–15 years, extends through adult years; thinking is more abstract, idealistic, and logical).
	Evaluating Piaget	Piaget is one of developmental psychology's giants. He gave us the model of the child as an active, constructivist thinker and a masterful list of concepts. Like all major theories, his has been criticized. Information-processing psychologists think he placed too much emphasis on grand stages; Vygotsky said he underplayed culture.
Socioemotional Development	Erikson's Theory	Erikson's theory is a psychosocial theory, while Freud's theory is a psychosexual theory. Erikson said development is lifelong, Freud thought the key changes took place in the first five years of life. Erikson theorized that people go through eight stages: trust vs. mistrust (1st year), autonomy vs. shame and doubt (1–3 years), initiative vs. guilt (3–5 years), industry vs. inferiority (6–puberty), identity vs. identity confusion (adolescence), intimacy vs. isolation (early adulthood), generativity vs. stagnation (middle adulthood), and integrity vs. despair (late adulthood). Erikson's stages represent developmental tasks that are turning points in people's lives.
	Evaluating Erikson's Theory	Like Piaget, Erikson is one of developmental psychology's giants. His emphasis on lifelong developmental changes was a major contribution. His theory has been criticized for not having a research base to support the grand scheme of eight stages.
	Attachment	Attachment is the close emotional bond between an infant and a caregiver. Harlow demonstrated the importance of contact comfort in attachment, Lorenz the importance of familiarity in attachment through his work on imprinting. Bowlby and Ainsworth believe that attachment in the first year is necessary for optimal development. Ainsworth described secure attachment as having the caregiver as a secure base from which to explore the environment. Critics of secure attachment say that biological factors such as temperament and the wider social world are not given enough attention.
	Temperament	Temperament is a person's behavioral style and characteristic ways of responding. Chess and Thomas proposed that there are three basic temperament styles: easy, difficult, and slow to warm up, although other classifications have been made. It is important for parents to be sensitive to the child's individuality, and temperament is an aspect of that individuality.
	Parenting	Baumrind described four parenting styles: authoritarian, authoritative, neglectful, and indulgent, with authoritative parenting (a combination of warmth, verbal give-and-take, and some limit setting) as optimal. Understanding parenting also involves understanding reciprocal socialization, the mother's role, and the father's role.

Children's socioemotional development can significantly benefit from interaction with a caring, accessible, and dependable father who fosters a sense of trust and confidence (Lamb, 1998; Snarey, 1998). The father's positive family involvement assumes special importance in developing children's social competence, because he is often the only male the child encounters on a regular day-to-day basis.

Father-mother cooperation and mutual respect help the child develop positive attitudes toward both males and females (Biller, 1993). It is much easier for working parents to cope with changing family circumstances and day-care issues when the father and mother equitably share child-rearing responsibilities. Mothers feel less stress and have more positive attitudes toward their husbands when they are supportive partners.

At this point we have discussed many ideas about children's cognitive and socioemotional development. An overview of these ideas is presented in summary table 10.2. Next, we continue our journey through the human life span by focusing on adolescence.

Fathers and Children

Adolescence

Twentieth-century poet-essayist Roger Allen once remarked, "In case you are worried about what's going to become of the younger generation, it's going to grow up and start worrying about the younger generation." Virtually every society has worried about its younger generation, but it was not until the beginning of the twentieth century that the scientific study of adolescence began.

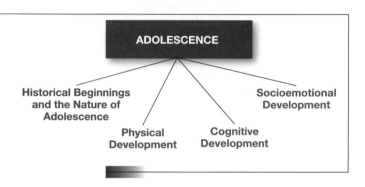

Historical Beginnings and the Nature of Adolescence

In 1904, psychologist G. Stanley Hall wrote the first scientific book on adolescence. Hall referred to the adolescent years as a time of "storm and stress." **The storm-and-stress view** *is Hall's concept that adolescence is a turbulent time charged with conflict and mood swings.* Thoughts, feelings, and actions oscillate between conceit and humility, good and temptation, happiness and sadness. The adolescent may be nasty to a peer one moment and kind the next moment. At one time the adolescent may want to be alone, yet seconds later seek companionship.

Too often adolescents have been stereotyped as abnormal and deviant. In addition to Hall, Freud described adolescents as sexually driven and conflicted. Young people of every generation have seemed radical, unnerving, and different to adults—different in how they look, how they behave, and the music they enjoy. But it is an enormous error to confuse the adolescent's enthusiasm for trying on new identities and enjoying moderate amounts of outrageous behavior with hostility toward parents and society. Acting out and boundary testing are time-honored ways in which adolescents move toward accepting, rather than rejecting, parental and societal values.

It does little good, and can do considerable disservice, to think of adolescence as a time of rebellion, crisis, pathology, and deviation. It's far more accurate to view adolescence as a time of evaluation, a time of decision making, a time of commitment as young people carve out their place in the world (Santrock, 1998). How competent they will become often depends on their access to a range of legitimate opportunities and long-term support from adults who care deeply about them.

Our discussion underscores an important point about adolescents: They do not make up a homogeneous group (Hauser, 1999). The majority of adolescents negotiate the lengthy path to adult maturity successfully, but too large a group does not. Ethnic, cultural, gender, socioeconomic, age, and lifestyle differences influence the

Healthy Adolescents

Adolescence is not best viewed as a time of crisis, rebellion, pathology, and deviation. Rather, a more accurate portrait is that adolescence is a time of evaluation, decision making, and commitment as youth seek to find out who they are and carve out a place for themselves in the world.

Biological Changes in Adolescence

actual life trajectory of every adolescent (Alsaker & Flammer, 1999). Different portrayals of adolescents emerge, depending on the particular group of adolescents being described (Brooks-Gunn, 1996). Later in our discussion of adolescence we will discuss at-risk youth, but first we need to explore some basic ideas about adolescents' physical, cognitive, and socioemotional development.

Physical Development

Imagine a toddler displaying all the features of puberty—a three-year-old girl with fully developed breasts or a boy just slightly older with a deep male voice. We would see this by the year 2250 if the age of puberty were to continue to decrease at its present pace. Menarche (the first menstruation) has declined from 14.2 years in 1900 to about 12.45 years today. Age of menarche has been declining an average of about four months a decade for the last century. We are unlikely, though, to see pubescent toddlers in the future because what happened in the last century is special. That something special is a higher level of nutrition and health. A lower age of menarche is associated with higher standards of living (Petersen, 1979).

Menarche is one event that characterizes puberty, but there are others as well. **Puberty** *is a period of rapid skeletal and sexual maturation that occurs mainly in early adolescence.* However, it is not a single, sudden event. We know when a young person is going through puberty, but pinpointing its beginning and its end is difficult. Except for menarche, which occurs rather late in puberty, no single marker heralds puberty. For boys, the first whisker or first wet dream could mark its appearance, but both may go unnoticed.

Hormonal changes characterize pubertal development. Hormones are powerful chemical substances secreted by the endocrine glands and carried through the body in the bloodstream. The concentrations of certain hormones increase dramatically during puberty (Dorn & Chrousos, 1996). **Testosterone** *is a hormone associated in boys with the development of genitals, an increase in height, and a change in voice.* **Estradiol** *is a hormone associated in girls with breast, uterine, and skeletal development.* In one study, testosterone levels doubled in girls but increased eighteenfold in boys during puberty; similarly, estradiol doubled in boys but increased eightfold in girls (Nottelmann & others, 1987). These hormonal and body changes occur on the average about two years earlier in females (10½ years) than in males (12½ years) (see figure 10.15).

Cognitive Development

As we noted earlier, cognitive development continues after the childhood years. Adolescents undergo some significant cognitive changes. We will briefly recap Piaget's view of adolescent cognitive development, then discuss adolescent egocentrism.

Piaget's Formal Operational Stage

Piaget said that adolescents enter a new stage of cognitive development from about 11 to 15 years of age, which he called the formal operational stage. Recall that Piaget believes that this stage is characterized by thought that is abstract, idealistic, and logical.

In actuality, not all adolescents are formal operational thinkers, at least not in terms of the logical thinking Piaget called *hypothetical-deductive reasoning.* For example, some adolescents still think at Piaget's concrete operational stage.

Adolescent Egocentrism   Adolescent thought, especially in early adolescence, is also egocentric. **Adolescent egocentrism** *involves the belief that others are as preoccupied with the adolescent as she herself is, the belief that one is unique, and the belief that one is indestructible* (Elkind, 1978). Attention-getting behavior, so common in adolescence, reflects egocentrism and the desire to be onstage, noticed, and visible. Imagine the eighth-grade boy who feels as if all eyes are riveted on his tiny facial blemish. Imagine also the sense of uniqueness felt by the following adolescent girl: "My mother has no idea about how much pain I'm going through. She has never been hurt like I have. Why did Bob break up with me?" And imagine the sense of indestructibility of two adolescent males drag racing down a city street. This sense of indestructibility may lead to drug use and suicide attempts.

Moral Development   Another aspect of cognitive development that changes during adolescence is reasoning about moral issues.

Kohlberg's Theory   Lawrence Kohlberg (1986) created eleven stories and asked children, adolescents, and adults some questions about the stories. One of the stories goes like this:

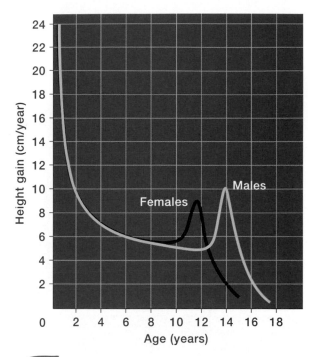

> In Europe a woman was near death from a special kind of cancer. There was one drug that the doctors thought might save her. It was a form of radium that a druggist in the same town had recently discovered. The drug was expensive to make, but the druggist was charging ten times what the drug cost him to make. He paid $200 for the radium and charged $2,000 for a small dose of the drug. The sick woman's husband, Heinz, went to everyone he knew to borrow the money, but he could get together only $1,000. He told the druggist that his wife was dying and asked him to sell it cheaper or let him pay later. But the druggist said, "No. I discovered the drug, and I am going to make money from it." Desperate, Heinz broke into the man's store to steal the drug for his wife. (Kohlberg, 1969)

$\mathcal{F}$igure 10.15
Pubertal Growth Spurt

On the average, the growth spurt that characterizes pubertal change occurs 2 years earlier for girls (age 10½) than for boys (age 12½).

After reading the story, the interviewee answers a series of questions about the moral dilemma. Should Heinz have done that? Was it right or wrong? Why? Is it a husband's duty to steal the drug for his wife if he can get it in no other way? Would a good husband do it? Did the druggist have the right to charge that much when there was no law actually setting a limit on the price? Why?

Based on the answers people gave to questions about this and other moral dilemmas, Kohlberg proposed that individuals go through three levels of moral development, each characterized by two stages (see figure 10.16). A key concept in understanding moral development, especially Kohlberg's theory, is **internalization,** *the developmental change from behavior that is externally controlled to behavior that is controlled by internal, self-generated standards and principles.*

The **preconventional level** *is Kohlberg's lowest level of moral thinking, in which the individual shows no internalization of moral values.* Moral thinking is based on punishments (stage 1) or rewards (stage 2) that come from the external world. In regard to the Heinz and the druggist story, at stage 1 an individual might say that Heinz should not steal the drug because he might get caught and sent to jail. At stage 2, the person might say he should not steal the drug because the druggist needs to make a profit on the drug.

The **conventional level** *is Kohlberg's second level of moral thinking, in which the individual has an intermediate level of internalization.* The individual abides by certain standards (internal), such as parents (stage 3) or society's laws (stage 4). At stage 3, an individual might say that Heinz should steal the drug for his wife because that is what society expects a good husband would do. At stage 4, the person might say that it is natural for Heinz to want to save his wife but that it still is always wrong to steal.

Lawrence Kohlberg, a pioneer in constructing a cognitive developmental theory of how people morally reason.

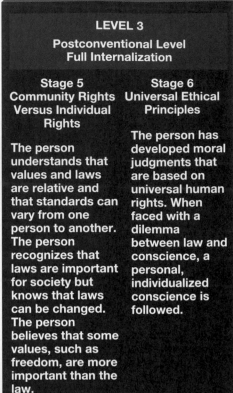

LEVEL 3
Postconventional Level
Full Internalization

Stage 5
Community Rights Versus Individual Rights

The person understands that values and laws are relative and that standards can vary from one person to another. The person recognizes that laws are important for society but knows that laws can be changed. The person believes that some values, such as freedom, are more important than the law.

Stage 6
Universal Ethical Principles

The person has developed moral judgments that are based on universal human rights. When faced with a dilemma between law and conscience, a personal, individualized conscience is followed.

LEVEL 2
Conventional Level
Intermediate Internalization

Stage 3
Interpersonal Norms

The person values trust, caring, and loyalty to others as the basis of moral judgments. Children often adopt their parents' moral standards at this stage, seeking to be thought of as a "good girl" or "good boy."

Stage 4
Social System Morality

Moral judgments are based on understanding and the social order, law, justice, and duty.

LEVEL 1
Preconventional Level
No Internalization

Stage 1
Punishment and Obedience Orientation

Children obey because adults tell them to obey. People base their moral decisions on fear of punishment.

Stage 2
Individualism and Purpose

Moral thinking is based on rewards and self-interest. Children obey when it is in their best interest to obey. What is right is what feels good and what is rewarding.

*F*igure 10.16
Kohlberg's Three Levels and Six Stages of Moral Development

Kohlberg's Theory

The **postconventional level** *is Kohlberg's highest level of moral thinking. Moral development is completely internalized and not based on others' standards.* The individual recognizes alternative moral courses, explores the options, and then develops a personal moral code. The code is among the principles generally accepted by the community (stage 5) or it is more individualized (stage 6). At stage 5, a person might say that the law was not set up for these circumstances, so Heinz can steal the drug. It is not really right, but he is justified in doing it. At stage 6, the individual evaluates alternatives, but recognizes that Heinz's wife's life is more important than a law.

Kohlberg believed these levels and stages occur in a sequence and are age-related. Some evidence for the sequence of Kohlberg's stages has been found, although few people reach stage 6 (Colby & others, 1983). Children are often in stages 1 and 2, although in the later elementary school years they may be in stage 3. Most adolescents are at stages 3 or 4.

Kohlberg believed that advances in moral development takes place because of the maturation of thought (especially Piaget's stages), opportunities for role-taking, and discussing moral issues with a person who reasons at a stage just above your own. In Kohlberg's view, parents contribute little to children's moral thinking because parent-child relationships are often too power-oriented.

Evaluating Kohlberg's Theory   Kohlberg's ideas stimulated considerable interest in the field of moral development. His provocative view continues to stimulate considerable research about how people think about moral issues (Narvaez & others, 1999; Thoma & Rest, 1999).

Kohlberg's theory also has its share of critics. One criticism is that moral reasons can always be a shelter for immoral behavior. When bank embezzlers and presidents are asked about their moral reasoning, what they say might be at Kohlberg's advanced stages, but their actual behavior might be filled with cheating, lying, and stealing. The cheaters, liars, and thieves might know what is right and what is wrong, but still *do* what is wrong.

A second major criticism of Kohlberg's view is that it does not adequately reflect relationships and concerns for others. The **justice perspective** *is a theory of moral development that focuses on the rights of the individual; individuals stand alone and independently make moral decisions. Kohlberg's theory is a justice perspective.* By contrast, the **care perspective** *is Carol Gilligan's (1982) theory of moral development that sees people in terms of their connectedness with others and focuses on interpersonal communication, relationships with others, and concern for others.* According to Gilligan, Kohlberg greatly underplayed the care perspective in moral development. She believes this may have happened because he was a male, most of his research was with males rather than females, and he used male responses as a model for his theory.

Gilligan (1996, 1998) also believes that girls reach a critical juncture in their development when they reach adolescence. Gilligan says that at the edge of adolescence, at about 11 or 12 years of age, girls become aware that their intense interest in intimacy is not prized by the male-dominated culture, even though society values females as caring and altruistic. The dilemma, says Gilligan, is that girls are presented with a choice that makes them appear either selfish (if they become independent and self-sufficient) or selfless (if they remain responsive to others). Gilligan states that as young adolescent girls experience this dilemma, they increasingly "silence" their distinctive voice. They become less confident and more tentative in offering their opinions, which often persists into adulthood. Some researchers believe this self-doubt and ambivalence too often translates into depression and eating disorders among adolescent girls.

Carol Gilligan with some of the students she has interviewed about the importance of relationships in a female's development. According to Gilligan (center), the sense of relationships and connectedness is at the heart of a female's development.

Socioemotional Development

Who are you and where are you headed in life? This is a central question in identity and the adolescent's socioemotional development. It is also a question that continues to be important in the college years and throughout adult development as well.

Identity Development   Recall from our earlier discussion that identity versus identity confusion is the fifth stage in Erikson's eight-stage life span

Gilligan's Care Perspective

"Do you have any idea who I am?"

© The New Yorker Collection 1988 *Edward Koren from cartoonbank.com. All Rights Reserved.*

Identity Development

What characterizes the most successful programs for intervening in adolescents' problems?

theory, occurring during the adolescent years. During adolescence, individuals enter what Erikson calls a "psychological moratorium"—a gap between the security of childhood and the autonomy of adulthood. In their search for identity, adolescents experiment with different roles. Those who successfully explore a number of alternatives emerge with a new sense of self that is both refreshing and acceptable; those who do not successfully resolve the identity crisis are confused, suffering what Erikson calls identity confusion. This confusion takes one of two courses: Individuals withdraw, isolating themselves from peers and family, or they lose themselves in the crowd. Adolescents want to decide freely for themselves such matters as what careers they will pursue, whether they will go to college, and whether they will marry. In other words, they want to free themselves from the shackles of their parents and other adults and make their own choices. At the same time, many adolescents have a deep fear of making the wrong decision and of failing. But as adolescents pursue their identity and their thoughts become more abstract and logical, they reason in more sophisticated ways. They are better able to judge what is morally right and wrong and become capable decision makers.

Identity is a self-portrait composed of many pieces, including these:

- The career and work path a person wants to follow (vocational/career identity)
- Whether a person is conservative, liberal, or a middle-of-the-roader (political identity)
- A person's spiritual beliefs (religious identity)
- Whether a person is single, married, divorced, and so on (relationship identity)
- The extent to which the person is motivated to achieve and is intellectual (achievement, intellectual identity)
- Whether a person is heterosexual, homosexual, or bisexual (sexual identity)
- Which part of the world or country a person is from and how intensely the person identifies with his/her cultural heritage (cultural/ethnic identity)
- The kinds of things a person likes to do, which can include sports, music, hobbies, and so on (interest)
- The individual's personality characteristics (such as being introverted or extraverted, anxious or calm, friendly or hostile, and so on) (personality)
- The individual's body image (physical identity)

Is an identity something that is cast in stone once you achieve it? No, people's lives can change and so can their identities. University plays an important role in many people's identity development because it is a setting where exploration and different views are encouraged (Santrock & Halonen, 1999).

At-Risk Youth   Adolescence is best viewed as a time of decision making and commitment rather than a time of crisis and pathology. However, a large subset of adolescents are at risk because their likelihood of becoming productive adults is limited. Four areas of special concern regarding a large portion of at-risk youth are delinquency, substance abuse, unprotected sex and adolescent pregnancy, and school-related problems (Dryfoos, 1990). Estimates are that as many as 25 percent of youth have three or more of these problems.

In an analysis of successful programs focused on at-risk youth, Joy Dryfoos (1990) found that two approaches had the widest application: providing individual attention to at-risk children and adolescents, and developing broad community-wide interventions. In successful programs, at-risk youth are attached to a responsible adult who pays attention to the adolescent's specific needs. For example, in substance abuse programs, a student assistance counselor might be available full-time for individual counseling. In delinquency prevention, a family worker might give "intensive" support to a predelinquent and the family so they will make the necessary changes to avoid repeated delinquent acts.

SUMMARY TABLE 10.3
Adolescence

Concept	Processes/ Related Ideas	Characteristics/Description
Historical Beginnings and the Nature of Adolescence	Historical Beginnings	G. Stanley Hall is the father of the scientific study of adolescence. In the early 1900s, he proposed the storm-and-stress view.
	Nature of Adolescence	Adolescence is a transition between childhood and adulthood that is best viewed as a time of evaluation, decision making, and commitment rather than as a time of rebellion, crisis, and pathology. Different portrayals of adolescence emerge, depending on the particular group of adolescents being described.
Physical Development	Its Nature	Puberty is a rapid change to maturation occurring mainly in early adolescence. Puberty has been occurring earlier in recent years. Puberty occurs roughly two years earlier for girls (10½) than for boys (12½).
Cognitive Development	Revisiting Piaget	Piaget argued that formal operational thought appears at 11 to 15 years of age. At this point, thought becomes more abstract, idealistic, and logical. However, not all adolescents are formal operational thinkers.
	Adolescent Egocentrism	This involves the belief that others are as preoccupied with you as you yourself are. It also involves the belief that you are unique and indestructible.
	Moral Development	Kohlberg proposed three levels (each with two stages) of moral development, which vary in the degree to which moral behavior is internalized: preconventional, conventional, and post conventional. Critics of Kohlberg's theory argue that moral thoughts do not always predict moral action. Gilligan also stresses that the theory is a justice perspective. She promotes a care perspective of morality and argues that early adolescence is a critical juncture in the development of females.
Socioemotional Development	Identity Development	Identity versus identity confusion is Erikson's fifth stage, which occurs during adolescence. Adolescents are in a psychological moratorium between childhood dependency and adult independence. The college years are an important time for identity changes.
	At-Risk Youth	Four problems characterize at-risk youth more than any others: substance abuse, delinquency, unprotected sex and adolescent pregnancy, and school-related problems. Many at-risk youth have more than one of these problems. Two approaches have had the best success in intervening in adolescent programs: (1) individual attention and (2) community-wide collaboration.

The basic concept of community-wide programs is that, to improve the lives of at-risk youth, a number of programs and services need to be in place (O'Donnell & others, 1999). For example, a substance abuse program might involve a community-wide health promotion that uses local media and community education in conjunction with a substance abuse prevention curriculum in the schools. A delinquency program might consist of a neighborhood development program that includes local residents in neighborhood councils who work with schools, police, courts, gang leaders, and the media.

At this point, we have discussed a number of ideas about adolescence. An overview of these ideas is presented in summary table 10.3. Next, we turn our attention to adult development and aging.

Helping Adolescents
Treating Adolescent Problems

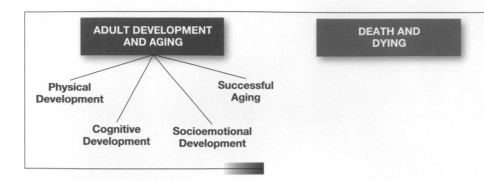

Adult Development and Aging

Menopause

Adult Development and Aging

Just as physical, cognitive, and socioemotional changes take place in the child and adolescent years, so too do they occur in the adult years. We will examine changes in the early, middle, and late adulthood years. Use this discussion as a springboard for thinking about your own development as an adult as well as for understanding your aging parents and grandparents.

Physical Development

Actress Bette Midler said that after 30 a body has a mind of its own. And comedian Bob Hope once remarked that middle age is when your age starts to show around your middle. How do we age physically as we go through the adult years?

Early and Middle Adulthood   Not only do we reach our peak performance during early adulthood, but we are also the healthiest then. Few young adults have chronic health problems. They have fewer colds and respiratory problems than they had as children. However, young adults rarely recognize that bad eating habits, heavy drinking, and smoking in early adulthood can impair their health as they age. Despite warnings on packages and in advertisements that cigarettes are hazardous to health, individuals actually increase their use of cigarettes as they enter early adulthood (Johnston, Bachman, & O'Malley, 1989). They also increase their use of alcohol, marijuana, amphetamines, barbiturates, and hallucinogens.

As we enter middle adulthood, we are more acutely concerned about our health status. We experience a general decline in physical fitness throughout middle adulthood and some deterioration in health. The three greatest health concerns at this age are heart disease, cancer, and weight. Cancer related to smoking often surfaces for the first time in middle adulthood.

Because North American culture stresses a youthful appearance, physical deterioration—graying hair, wrinkling skin, and a sagging body—in middle adulthood is difficult to handle. Many middle-aged adults dye their hair and join weight reduction programs; some even undergo cosmetic surgery to look young. In one study, middle-aged women focused more attention on their facial attractiveness than did the older or younger women. Middle-aged women also perceived that the signs of aging had a more detrimental effect on their appearance (Novak, 1977).

For women, middle age also means that menopause will occur. **Menopause** *is the time in middle age, usually in the late forties or early fifties, when a woman's menstrual periods cease completely.* The average age at which women have their last period is 52. A small percentage of women—10 percent—undergo menopause before 40. There is a dramatic decline in the production of estrogen by the ovaries. Estrogen decline produces some uncomfortable symptoms in some menopausal women—"hot flashes," nausea, fatigue, and rapid heartbeat, for example. Some menopausal women report depression and irritability, but in some instances these feelings are related to other circumstances in the women's life, such as becoming divorced, losing a job, caring for a sick parent, and so on (Dickson, 1990).

Research investigations reveal that menopause does not produce psychological problems or physical problems for the majority

What are some physical changes that women go through as they age?

of women (McKinlay & McKinlay, 1984). Although overall menopause is not the negative experience for most women it was once thought to be, the loss of fertility is an important marker for women—it means that they have to make final decisions about having children. Women in their thirties who have never had children sometimes speak about being "up against the biological clock" because they cannot postpone questions about having children much longer.

Estrogen replacement therapy is increasingly recommended for women who are making the transition to menopause (Stefanick, 1999). The American Geriatrics Association's recent recommendations include these (Bidikov & Meier, 1997):

- All middle-aged women should consider estrogen replacement therapy because it can reduce the risk of osteoporosis (loss of bone tissue), coronary disease, and menopausal symptoms such as hot flashes and sweating. However, the risk of estrogen replacement therapy can outweigh its benefits for women who are at risk for breast cancer.
- Women should actively participate in decision-making about using estrogen replacement therapy.

Do men go through anything like the menopause that women experience? Men do experience sex-related hormone declines in their fifties and sixties but they are usually not as precipitous as women's estrogen decline (Lemme, 1999).

Late Adulthood and Aging   The rhythm and meaning of human development eventually wend their way to late adulthood. To begin, we will explore the distinction between life span and life expectancy.

Life Span and Life Expectancy   We are no longer a youthful society. The concept of a period called "late adulthood" is a recent one—until the twentieth century, most individuals died before they were 65.

Developmentalists distinguish between life span and life expectancy. **Life span** *is the upper boundary of a species' life, the maximum number of years an individual can live.* The maximum number years human beings can live is about 120 years. As can be seen in figure 10.17, *Homo sapiens* is believed to have one of the longest, if not the longest, life spans.

Life expectancy *is the number of years that will probably be lived by the average person born in a particular year.* Improvements in medicine, nutrition, exercise, and lifestyle have increased our life expectancy an average of 30 additional years since 1900! (See figure 10.18.) The life expectancy of individuals born today in Canada is 78.6–81.4 years for women, 75.7 for men (Health Canada, 1998). One in three women born today is expected to live to be 100 or more years of age. The world's population of individuals 65 years of age and older doubled from 1950 to 1990, and the fastest growing segment of the population is the 85 years and over group. Thus, life expectancy has increased dramatically, but life span does not seem to have increased since the beginning of recorded history.

Biological Theories of Aging   Even if we are remarkably healthy through our adult lives, we begin to age at some point. What are some of the biological explanations of aging?

There are many of these theories, but two that especially merit attention are the cellular clock theory and the free-radical theory. Both of these theories look within the body's cells in an effort to unlock the mysteries of aging. The **cellular clock theory** *is Leonard Hayflick's (1977) view that cells can divide a maximum number of about 100 times, and that as we age, our cells become increasingly less capable of dividing.* Hayflick found that cells extracted from older adults, in their fifties to seventies, divided fewer than 100 times. Based on the way cells divide, Hayflick places the upper limit of the human life span at about 120

Species (common name)	Maximum life span (years)
Human	120
Galápagos turtle	100+
Indian elephant	70
Chinese alligator	52
Golden eagle	46
Gorilla	39
Common toad	36
Domestic cat	27
Domestic dog	20
Vampire bat	13
House mouse	3

*F*igure 10.17
Maximum Recorded Life Spans of Various Species

Aging Research

Time Period	Average Life Expectancy (in years)
Prehistoric times	18
Ancient Greece	20
Middle Ages, England	33
1620, Massachusetts Bay Colony	35
19th century, England	41
1900, USA	47
1915, USA	54
1954, USA	70
1999, Canada	79

*F*igure 10.18
Human Life Expectancy at Birth from Prehistoric to Contemporary Times

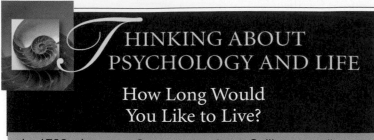

THINKING ABOUT PSYCHOLOGY AND LIFE

How Long Would You Like to Live?

In 1726, Jonathan Swift wrote about Gulliver traveling to many lands. In one land, Gulliver found the Stuldbrugs—people who were immortal. Even though they never died, they continued to age, becoming blind, crippled, immobile, in constant pain, and begging for their death. Gulliver's world was a world of science fiction, but it raises interesting issues about how long we would like to live and what we want our lives to be like when we become old. How long would you like to live? Why? Describe the oldest person you know. What is he or she like?

Frenchwoman Jeanne Louise Calumet pushed the upper boundary of the human life span, dying in 1997 at the age of 122. Greater ages have been claimed, but scientists say that the human life span is approximately 120 years of age. However, as genetic engineering continues to make progress, the possibility of altering cellular functioning to increase the human life span is raised. Some biologists have even brought up the possibility that in the future humans might live to be 400 years of age! What kinds of ethical issues are involved in genetically engineering cellular functioning to increase the human life span?

years. Thus, we rarely age to the end of our life span potential.

More recently in the 1990s, scientists have added an extension to the cellular clock theory. Hayflick didn't know why cells die. The answer may lie at the tip of chromosomes. Telomeres are DNA sequences that cap chromosomes, protecting them. Each time a cell divides, the telomeres of the daughter cells become shorter and shorter. After about 100 replications, the telomeres are dramatically reduced and the cell no longer can reproduce.

A second biological theory of aging is **free-radical theory,** *which states that people age because inside their cells unstable oxygen molecules known as free radicals are produced. These molecules ricochet around in the cells, damaging DNA and other cellular structures.* As the free radicals bounce around inside of cells, their damage can lead to a range of disorders, including cancer and arthritis.

A number of other biological theories of aging have been proposed. Theorized causes of aging range from a decline in the immune system's functioning to deficiencies in hormones.

Alzheimer's disease   Alzheimer's disease *is a progressive, irreversible brain disorder that is characterized by gradual deterioration of memory, reasoning, language, and eventually physical functioning.* Over 2.5 million Americans and 300,000 Canadians have this disease. One deficiency in the brains of individuals with Alzheimer's is in the important neurotransmitter acetylcholine (which we discussed in chapter 3, "Biological Foundations and Neuroscience") 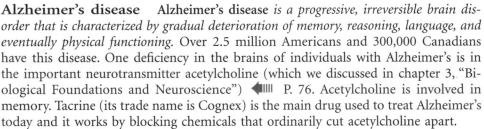 P. 76. Acetylcholine is involved in memory. Tacrine (its trade name is Cognex) is the main drug used to treat Alzheimer's today and it works by blocking chemicals that ordinarily cut acetylcholine apart.

Tacrine preserves a diminishing supply of acetylcholine for a while, but it does not attack the root cause of acetylcholine deficiency. Scientists now believe that Alzheimer's disease is the result of a complex unraveling of neural structure and function that involves many different cellular dimensions (Davis, 1999). Some clues are beginning to emerge that may help researchers eventually solve the Alzheimer puzzle. One clue is the possible role of free radicals, the unstable oxygen molecules we just discussed. But something that occurs earlier likely causes the oxidative damage to the free radicals. One candidate is a protein called "amyloid-beta," which might do its damage by activating immune system cells. Another possibility is that mutations in various genes cause abnormalities in the protein.

As we just mentioned, individuals with Alzheimer's have deficits in memory and thinking. Next, we explore the developmental course of such cognitive processes in adulthood.

Cognitive Development

Think back to when you were an adolescent, maybe taking an algebra class or writing a paper. How have you changed cognitively since then?

Early and Middle Adulthood   Piaget did not believe that you have changed cognitively at all since you were a young adolescent. He does not even think that a Ph.D. in physics thinks any differently than a formal operational thinking young adolescent. Piaget recognized that the physicist has more knowledge in a specific domain—physics. However, Piaget said that the way the physicist thinks is the same as a formal operational thinking adolescent. The physicist and the young adolescent both use logical thought to develop alternatives for solving a problem, then they deduce the correct solution from the options.

(Left) Former president Ronald Reagan was diagnosed with Alzheimer's at the age of 83. (Right) Canadian painter Joyce Wieland poses with a self-portrait, painted to "find out what I look like." She died in Toronto in 1998 of Alzheimer's.

Was Piaget right? He was right for some adolescents and some adults, but not for all. As we saw earlier, some adolescents are not formal operational thinkers and many adults never become formal operational thinkers.

Other psychologists believe that the absolute nature of adolescent logic and youth's buoyant optimism diminish in early adulthood (Labouvie-Vief, 1986). They argue that competent young adults are less caught up in idealism and tend to think logically and to adapt to life as circumstances demand. Less clear is whether our mental skills, especially memory, actually decline with age.

If there is a memory decline with age, it is more apparent in some types of memory tasks than others. Older adults do not forget how to drive a car (a well-established motor pattern) but they may have difficulty remembering the directions to the home of a new acquaintance (a task requiring new learning) (Rybash, Roodin, & Hoyer, 1999). Researchers are beginning to link age-related memory change to a decline in the **controlled processing** of information (Craik & Jacoby, 1996) ◀▦ P. 150. For example, Jane Dywan and Wendy Murphy of Brock University asked older and younger adults to read paragraphs which included italicized words that were to be ignored (Dywan & Murphy, 1996). When comprehension of the stories was tested, older adults were more likely to include the to-be-ignored information in their accounts of what they had read, altering the stories considerably. The distracting information was also familiar to the young adults but it did not intrude itself into their recollection of the stories. This ability to keep track of the source of information depends on controlled processing and becomes increasingly difficult as people age.

Late Adulthood and Aging   At age 70, John Rock introduced the birth control pill. And at age 76, Anna Mary Roberston, better known as Grandma Moses, took up painting and became internationally famous. And when Pablo Casals reached 95 years of age, a reporter called him the greatest cellist who ever lived but wondered why he still practiced six hours a day. Casals replied, "Because I feel like I am making progress."

The issue of intellectual decline through the adult years is a provocative one. David Wechsler (1972) whose intelligence scales you read about in chapter 9, concluded that intelligence peaks in early adulthood and then begins a continual decline until we die. But the issue of intellectual decline is more complex than Wechsler envisioned. Remember also from chapter 9 that many contemporary psychologists believe that intelligence comes in different forms ◀▦ P. 295. One of the most consistent findings is that when speed of processing information is involved, older adults do more poorly than their younger counterparts (Salthouse, 1994). They also tend to do more poorly on memory tasks than younger adults.

Alzheimer's Disease

Older adults might not be as quick with their thoughts as younger adults, but wisdom may be an entirely different matter. This elderly woman shares the wisdom of her experiences with a classroom of children.

Exploring Aging Issues

However, might there be some aspects of cognition that actually improve with age? One candidate is **wisdom** *which involves expert knowledge about the practical aspects of life.* Nonetheless, while wisdom may increase with age because of the buildup of life experiences we have, not every older person has wisdom (Baltes, Lindenberger, & Staudinger, 1998). Individual variations characterize all aspects of our cognitive life (Belsky, 1999).

Even for those aspects of cognitive aging that decline, such as memory, the possibility is raised that through education and training elderly adults can improve their cognitive skills (Luszcz & Bryan, 1999; Parke, Nisbett, & Hedden, 1999). Researchers have demonstrated that by using such memory strategies as organization and chunking, as well as mnemonics, older adults' memory can improve (Baltes, 1993; Willis & Schaie, 1994). However, while cognitive improvement is possible in older adults, many aging experts believe that older adults lose some of their plasticity they had earlier in development.

Socioemotional Development

As both Sigmund Freud and the nineteenth century Russian novelist Leo Tolstoy observed, adulthood's two most important themes are work and love. As we discuss socioemotional development in the adult years, you will see that indeed work and love are two of adulthood's most important domains.

Early and Middle Adulthood   Careers, work, and lifestyles are among the themes of early and middle adulthood for many people.

Careers and Work   Earning a living, choosing an occupation, and developing a career are important themes for people in their twenties and thirties. A few people seem to have known what they wanted to be ever since they were a child. But for many of us, choosing an occupation involves exploring a number of options during college and even beyond.

It is a good idea to keep up with the occupational outlook of various fields. An excellent resource is *The Occupational Outlook Handbook,* which is revised every two years. According to the most recent edition of the handbook (1998–1999), service-producing industries will account for the most new jobs, with business, health, and education services projected to account for 70 percent of the job growth through 2005. Jobs that require the most education and training will be the fastest growing and highest paying.

What are the most important skills that today's job applicants need? In a national survey of companies that employ college graduates, communication skills, interpersonal skills, and teamwork skills were at the top of the list (Collins, 1996) (see figure 10.19). All of these skills focus on communicating effectively.

Career interests continue to be an important dimension of life for many middle-aged adults. Midlife is a time when many people examine their career, evaluate what they have accomplished, and look to the future and see that they have a limited amount of time to accomplish what they want. However, many people reach the highest satisfaction in their careers during middle age and only about 10 percent of North Americans change careers at midlife. A recent concern of some middle-aged adults is the downsizing and early retirement programs of many companies.

Lifestyles   Should I get married? If I wait any longer, will it be too late? Will I get left out? Should I stay single or is it too lonely a life? If I get married, do I want to have children? How will it affect my marriage? These are questions that many young adults ask themselves as they try to figure out what they want their life to be about.

Oral Communication Skills 4.7
Interpersonal Skills 4.6
Teamwork Skills 4.5
Analytical Skills 4.4
Flexibility 4.3
Leadership Skills 4.2
Proficiency in Field of Study 4.2
Written Communication Skills 4.2
Computer Skills 4.1

Figure 10.19
The Skills That Employers Want a Job Candidate to Have

In a recent national survey of employers, the skills that employers want a job candidate to have were rated on a scale of 1 (extremely unimportant) to 5 (extremely important) (Collins, 1996). Notice how important communication skills—oral, interpersonal, teamwork—are to today's employers.

Until about 1930, the goal of a stable marriage was accepted as a legitimate endpoint of adult development. In the last 60 years, however, we have seen the emergence of the desire for personal fulfillment—both inside and outside a marriage—as a force that can compete with marriage's stability. The changing norm of male-female equality in marriage has produced relationships that are more fragile and intense than they were earlier in the twentieth century. More adults are remaining single longer in the 1990s, and the average duration of a marriage in the United States is currently just over nine years. The divorce rate, which increased astronomically in the 1970s, has begun to slow down, although it still remains very high. In Canada in 1996, 37 percent of marriages ended in divorce (Statistics Canada, 1999). Nevertheless, North Americans still show a strong preference for marriage—the proportion of women who never marry remained at about seven percent throughout the twentieth century, for example (Hernandez, 1988).

We often have idealistic expectations of marriage, which helps to explain our high divorce rate and dissatisfaction in marriage (Notarius, 1996). We expect our spouse to simultaneously be a lover, a friend, a confidant, a counselor, a career person, and a parent. Many myths about marriage contribute to these unrealistic expectations.

Many myths are also associated with being single, ranging from "the swinging single" to "the desperately lonely, suicidal single." Most singles are somewhere between these two extremes. The pluses of being single include time to make decisions about one's life, time to develop personal resources to meet goals, freedom to make autonomous decisions and pursue one's own schedule and interests, opportunities to explore new places and try out new things, and privacy. Common

"Your son has made a career choice, Mildred. He's going to win the lottery and travel a lot."

© 1985; Reprinted courtesy of Bunny Hoest.

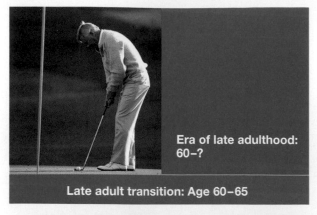

Era of late adulthood: 60–?

Late adult transition: Age 60–65

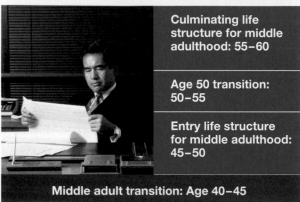

Culminating life structure for middle adulthood: 55–60

Age 50 transition: 50–55

Entry life structure for middle adulthood: 45–50

Middle adult transition: Age 40–45

Culminating life structure for early adulthood: 33–40

Age 30 transition: 28–33

Entry life structure for early adulthood: 22–28

Early adult transition: Age 17–22

Figure 10.20
Levinson's Periods of Adult Development

Middle Age Issues

problems of single adults include a lack of intimate relationships with others, loneliness, and finding a niche in a marriage-oriented society. Some single adults would rather remain single; others would rather be married.

Stage Theories of Adult Development   Psychologists have proposed different theories about adult development. Most theories address themes of work and love, career and intimacy. One set of theories proposes that adult development unfolds in stages ◀▦ P. 321.

Recall from our discussion of Erikson's theory earlier in the chapter that his eight stages of the human life span include one stage for early adulthood and one for middle adulthood. Erikson's early adulthood stage is intimacy versus isolation. Intimacy involves developing close, loving relationships and isolation involves the lonely feelings of not having a positive relationship with a partner and/or friends.

Erikson's middle adulthood stage is generativity versus stagnation. At this point in development, Erikson believes, it is important to contribute something meaningful to the next generation (generativity). If they do not, people in middle adulthood are left with a feeling of stagnation.

In *The Seasons of a Man's Life,* Daniel Levinson (1978) also described adult development as a series of stages. He extensively interviewed middle-aged male hourly workers, academic biologists, business executives, and novelists and concluded that developmental tasks must be mastered at a number of different points in adulthood (see figure 10.20).

In early adulthood, the two major tasks are exploring the possibilities for adult living and developing a stable life structure. The twenties represent the novice phase of adult development. By the end of a boy's teens, a transition from dependence to independence should occur. This transition is marked by a dream—an image of the kind of life the young man wants, especially in terms of marriage and a career. The novice phase is a time of experimenting and testing the dream in the real world.

Men actually determine their goals by the age of 28 to 33. During his thirties, a man usually works to develop his family life and career. In his late thirties, he enters a phase of becoming his own man (or BOOM, becoming one's own man, as Levinson calls it). By age 40, he reaches a stable point in his career; outgrows his earlier, more tenuous status as an adult; and now looks forward to the kind of life he will lead as a middle-aged adult.

In Levinson's view, the change to middle adulthood lasts about five years and requires that adults come to grips with four major conflicts that have existed since adolescence: (1) being young versus being old; (2) being destructive versus being constructive; (3) being masculine versus being feminine; and (4) being attached to others versus being separated from them. The success of the midlife transition depends on how effectively they can reduce these polarities and accept each of them as a part of their being. Levinson's original subjects were all males, but more recently he reported that these midlife issues hold for females as well (Levinson, 1978).

Erikson and Levinson emphasize that we go through a number of stages of adult development. In evaluating these theories, keep in mind they are based mainly on clinical observations rather than highly controlled research studies. Also, the perspectives tend to describe the stages as crises, especially in the case of Levinson's emphasis on a midlife crisis. Research on middle-aged adults reveals that few adults experience midlife in the tumultuous way described by Levinson. Individuals vary extensively in how they cope with and perceive midlife (Vaillant, 1977). In a recent large-scale study of 3,032 Americans, 25–74 years of age, a special focus was midlife development (Brim & others, 1999). The portrait of midlife was mainly positive, with only about 10 percent described as in a midlife crisis. Middle-aged individuals (40–65 years old) had lower anxiety levels and worried less than people under 40. The middle-aged individuals did report more negative life events than people under 40, but they showed considerable resiliency and good coping skills in the face of the stressors. The midlife individuals generally had few illnesses, but had poor physical fitness.

Rather than emphasizing that most people go through a midlife *crisis,* what actually happens is that most people experience a midlife *consciousness* (Santrock, 1999). That is, during middle age people do become aware of the young–old polarity and the shrinking time left in their lives. They do think about their role in contributing to the next generation. They do contemplate the meaning of life. But for most people, midlife consciousness does not become tumultuous and take on crisis proportions.

Life Events, Cohort Effects, and Social Clocks

Life events rather than stages may be responsible for changes in our adult lives. Events such as marriage, divorce, the death of a spouse, a job promotion, and being fired from a job involve varying degrees of stress and influence our development as adults (Holmes & Rahe, 1967). However, we also need to know about the many factors that mediate the influence of life events on adult development—physical health, intelligence, personality, family support, and income, for example (Hultsch & Plemons, 1979). In addition, we need to know how a person perceives the life events and how he or she copes with the stress involved. For instance, one person may perceive a divorce as highly stressful, whereas another person may perceive the same life event as a challenge. We also need to consider the person's life stage and circumstances. Divorce may be more stressful for an individual in his fifties who has been married for many years, for example, than for someone in her twenties who has been married only a few years. Individuals may cope with divorce more effectively at the beginning of the twenty-first century than people did at the beginning of the twentieth century because divorce has become more commonplace and accepted in today's society.

An increasing number of developmental psychologists stress that changing social expectations influence how different **cohorts**—*groups of individuals born in the same year or time period*—move through the life cycle. For example, people born during the Depression may have a different outlook on life than those born during the optimistic 1950s.

Bernice Neugarten (1980) believes that the social environment of a particular age group can alter its "social clock"—the timetable according to which individuals are expected to accomplish life's tasks, such as getting married, having children, and establishing themselves in a career. Social clocks act as guides for our lives. People who are somehow "out of sync" with these social clocks find their lives more stressful than those who are on schedule, says Neugarten. One study found that between the late 1950s and the late 1970s there was a dramatic decline in adults' beliefs that there is a "right age" for major life events and achievements (Passuth, Maines, & Neugarten, 1984).

Late Adulthood and Aging

Although we are in the evening of our lives in late adulthood, we were not meant to live out our remaining years passively (Hilleras & others, 1999). **Activity theory** *states that the more active and involved older people are, the more satisfied they are and the more likely it is that they will stay healthy.* Researchers have found that older people who go to church, attend meetings, take trips, and exercise are happier than those who simply sit at home (Stones & Kozma, 1989).

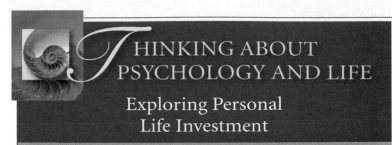

THINKING ABOUT PSYCHOLOGY AND LIFE
Exploring Personal Life Investment

TAKE A FEW MINUTES and evaluate yourself in terms of the domains of personal life investment described in figure 10.21. Rank-order the following from most important (1) to least important (7) in terms of your personal life investment—that is, how important they are in your life.

Domain	Ranking
work	_____
family	_____
friends	_____
independence	_____
cognitive fitness	_____
health	_____
thinking about life	_____

Now that you have thought about which of these domains is most important for you at your age, find at least one person from two age ranges other than your own in figure 10.21 and ask them to rank the domains in terms of their personal life investment. The age ranges are 25–34, 35–54, 55–65, 70–84, and 85–105. How do the other individuals' rankings of personal life investment compare with yours? Are your rankings and the rankings of the individuals of different ages the same as or different from those listed in figure 10.21? If you are a traditional-age university student (approximately 18–22), your age isn't represented in the adult life span study. Does your ranking of personal life investment match up with the 25- to 34-year-old age group? Regardless of your age, are there domains not listed above that are more important to you?

Social Aspects of Aging

Another aspect of understanding in late adulthood is life review. The nineteenth-century Danish philosopher Søren Kierkegaard said, "Life is lived forward, but understood backward." This is truer of late adulthood than of any other life span period. Kierkegaard's words reflect Erikson's final stage of integrity versus despair, which is a time of looking back to evaluate what we

Figure 10.21
Degree of Personal Life Investment at Different Points in Life

Shown here are the top four domains of personal life investment at different points in life. The highest degree of investment is listed at the top (for example, work was the highest personal investment from 25 to 34 years of age, family from 35 to 84, and health from 85 to 105).

have done with our lives. Recall from earlier in the chapter that the retrospective glances can be positive (integrity) or negative (despair).

Successful Aging

For too long, adult development and aging were looked at as processes of continual decline from early adulthood through the end of late adulthood (Smith & Baltes, 1999). Though some decline is inevitable as we age, many experts on aging believe that it is important to conceptualize aging more in terms of "success" than "decline" (Wong, 1989). The good news about aging is that with a proper diet, exercise, mental stimulation, good social relationships and support, and the absence of disease, many of our abilities decline very slowly. Leading an active rather than a passive life helps to slow aging. However, it is important to recognize that successful aging requires effort. Engaging in a regular exercise program requires effort for people of any age. So does practicing effective coping skills.

In thinking about successful aging through the adult years, an interesting question focuses on the personal life investments of people at different points in their lives. One recent study examined these personal life investments (Staudinger, 1996). As can be seen in figure 10.21, personal life investment varied somewhat, depending on the ages of the individuals. Work was most important for ages 25 to 34, then family became most important for ages 35 to 84. However, from age 85 to 105, health became the most important personal life investment. Clearly, successful aging for much of our adult life focuses on how effective we are at work, how loving our relationships are in our family, how good our friendships are, how healthy we are, and how cognitively fit we are.

Death and Dying

"I'd like to know what this show is all about before it's out," wrote the twentieth-century Danish poet and inventor Piet Hein. Death may come at any time, but it is during late adulthood that we realize our days are literally numbered. Societies throughout history have had philosophical or religious beliefs about death (Petrinovich, 1996). And most have some form of ritual to mark the passing from life to death. Some cultures hold a ceremonial meal accompanied by festivities. In others, mourners wear a black armband. Figure 10.22 shows two rituals that reveal cultural variations in dealing with death.

In most cultures, death is not viewed as the end of existence—although the biological body dies, the spirit lives on. This belief is held by many North Americans. Reincarnation, the belief that the soul is reborn in a new human body, is an important aspect of Hindu and Buddhist religions. Cultures often differ in their perception of death and their reaction to death. In the Gond culture of India, death is believed to be caused by magic and demons; Gonds react to death with anger. In the Tanala culture of Madagascar, death is thought to be caused by natural forces. The members of the Tanala culture react peacefully to death.

Elisabeth Kübler-Ross (1974) says that we go through five stages in facing death: denial and isolation, anger, bargaining, depression, and acceptance. Initially, the individual responds, "No, it can't be me. It's not possible." But denial is only a temporary defense. When the individual recognizes that denial can no longer be maintained, she often becomes angry and resentful. Now the individual's question becomes, "Why me?" Anger is often displaced onto physicians, nurses, family members, and even God. In the third stage, the dying person develops the hope that death can somehow be postponed or delayed. The individual now says, "Yes, me, but. . . ." The dying person often bargains and negotiates with God, offering a reformed life dedicated to God and the service of others for a few more months of life.

As the dying individual comes to accept the certainty of her death, she often enters a period of preparatory grief, becoming silent, refusing visitors, and spending much of the time crying or grieving. This behavior is a normal effort to disconnect the self from all love objects. Kübler-Ross describes the final stage, characterized by peace and acceptance of one's fate, as the end of the struggle, the final resting stage before death.

Not everyone goes through the stages in the sequence Kübler-Ross proposed. Indeed, Kübler-Ross herself says she has been misread, pointing out that she never believed every individual copes with death in a specific sequence. But she does maintain that the optimal way to cope with death is through the stages she has outlined.

But some individuals struggle until the very end, angrily hanging onto their lives. They follow the encouragement of Dylan Thomas: "Do not go gentle into that good night. Old age should burn and rave at close of day . . . rage, rage against the dying of the light." In these instances, acceptance of death never comes. People die in different ways and experience different feelings and emotions in the process: hope, fear, curiosity, envy, apathy, relief, even anticipation. They often move rapidly from one mood to another and in some instances two moods may be present simultaneously.

Those left behind after the death of an intimate partner suffer profound grief and often endure financial loss, loneliness, increased physical illness, and increased psychological disorders including depression (DeSpelder & Strickland, 1999). But how they cope with the crisis varies considerably. Widows outnumber widowers by

(a)

(b)

𝓕igure 10.22
Cultural Variations Regarding Death
(a) A New Orleans street funeral is in progress. (b) A deceased person's belongings are left on a mountainside in Tibet.

Death and Dying

SUMMARY TABLE 10.4
Adult Development and Aging; Death and Dying

Concept	Processes/ Related Ideas	Characteristics/Description
Adult Development and Aging	Physical Development	The peak of our physical skills usually comes in early adulthood, when it becomes easy to develop bad health habits. In middle adulthood, most individuals experience a decline in physical skills, some deterioration in health, and an increased interest in health matters. Menopause is a midlife biological marker for women, but it does not produce physical or psychological problems for most women. Human life expectancy has increased dramatically, but the human life span has remained virtually unchanged for centuries. Two biological theories of aging that focus on cellular functioning are cellular clock theory and free-radical theory. Based on the rate at which cells divide, the upper limit of the human life span is about 120 years. Alzheimer's disease is a progressive, irreversible brain disorder. Today, scientists believe Alzheimer's involves a complex unraveling of neural structure and function.
	Cognitive Development	An ongoing issue is how much intellectual decline takes place as people age, and when the decline takes place. In evaluating this issue it is important to consider which aspect of intelligence is being examined. For example, speed of processing and memory do decline as aging progresses, but wisdom likely increases. Even when decline takes place, cognitive strategies can be used to reduce the decline. There is less plasticity in cognitive functioning among older than younger adults, but there is some plasticity.
	Socioemotional Development	Careers and work are important dimensions of early adulthood. Adults must choose the type of lifestyle they want to follow—single, married, or divorced, for example. One set of adult personality theories proposes that adult development unfolds in stages (Erikson, Levinson).The midlife crisis is not as pervasive as Levinson proposed. However, most middle-aged adults experience a midlife consciousness that involves awareness of the young-old polarity and the shrinking amount of time left in life, generativity, and the meaning of life. Life events, cohort effects, and social clocks also are involved in understanding adult development. Everything we know about late adulthood suggests that an active lifestyle is preferable to disengagement. Erikson believes that the final issue in the life span to be negotiated is integrity versus despair, which involves a life review. For too long, adult development and aging were looked at as processes of continual decline. Today, more emphasis is given to successful aging.
Death and Dying	Their Nature	Death can come at any point in the life span, but in late adulthood we know it is near. Most societies have rituals that deal with death, although cultures vary in their orientation toward death. Kübler-Ross proposed five stages of coping with death, although they don't always occur in the sequence she proposed.

Bereavement and Grief

the ratio of 5 to 1 because women live longer than men, because women tend to marry men older than themselves, and because a widowed man is more likely to remarry. Widowed women are probably the poorest group in America, despite the myth of huge insurance settlements. Many are also lonely, and the poorer and less educated they are, the lonelier they tend to be. The bereaved are at increased risk for many health problems, including death. For both widows and widowers, social support helps them to adjust to the death of a spouse.

At this point we have discussed many ideas about adult development and aging, as well as death and dying. An overview of these ideas is presented in summary table 10.4. In this chapter we indicated that successful aging requires motivation and effort. In the next chapter, we will examine the topic of motivation, as well as emotion.

Overview

Overview

WE BEGAN THIS CHAPTER by examining what development is, including its biological, cognitive, and socioemotional processes, periods of development, and developmental issues. Our coverage of child development focused on prenatal development and birth, physical development, cognitive development, and socioemotional development. In studying adolescence, we evaluated its historical beginnings and nature, as well as physical, cognitive, and socioemotional changes. We also explored adult development and aging, including physical development, cognitive development, socioemotional development, and successful aging. And we read about death and dying.

Don't forget that you can obtain a more detailed overview of the chapter by again studying the four summary tables on pages 328, 344, 351, and 362.

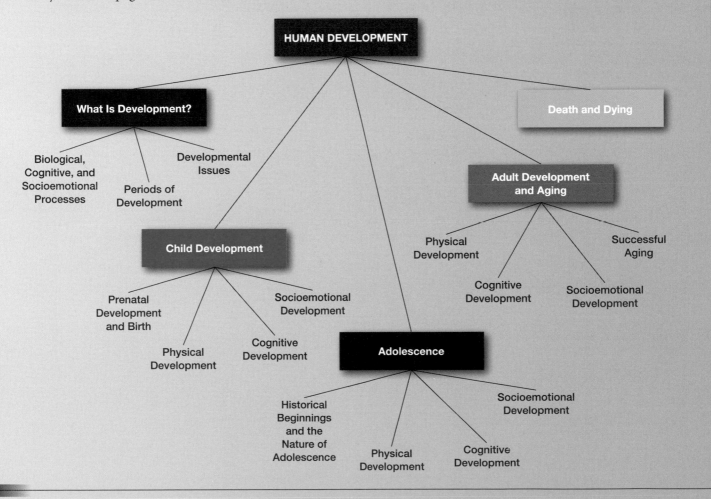

Key Terms

development 320
biological processes 320
cognitive processes 320
socioemotional processes 320
prenatal period 321
infancy 321
early childhood 321
middle and late childhood 321
adolescence 321
early adulthood 321
middle adulthood 321
late adulthood 321
continuity of development 324
discontinuity of development 324
conception 325
zygote 325
germinal period 325
embryonic period 325
fetal period 325

teratogen 326
fetal alcohol syndrome (FAS) 326
preterm infant 327
schema 331
assimilation 331
accommodation 331
sensorimotor stage 332
object permanence 332
preoperational stage 333
operations 333
conservation 333
egocentrism 333
concrete operational stage 334
formal operational stage 335
hypothetical-deductive reasoning 335
trust versus mistrust 337
autonomy versus shame and doubt 337

initiative versus guilt 338
industry versus inferiority 338
identity versus identity confusion 338
intimacy versus isolation 338
generativity versus stagnation 338
integrity versus despair 338
attachment 339
imprinting 339
secure attachment 340
temperament 341
authoritarian parenting 341
authoritative parenting 341
neglectful parenting 342
indulgent parenting 342
reciprocal socialization 342
storm-and-stress view 345
puberty 346
testosterone 346

estradiol 346
adolescent egocentrism 347
internalization 347
preconventional level 347
conventional level 347
postconventional level 348
justice perspective 349
care perspective 349
menopause 352
life span 353
life expectancy 353
cellular clock theory 353
free-radical theory 354
Alzheimer's disease 354
wisdom 356
cohorts 359
activity theory 359

Key People

Tiffany Field 327
Darwin Muir 329
Jean Piaget 331
Robbie Case 336
Lev Vygotsky 336
Erik Erikson 336

Harry Harlow and Robert Zimmerman 339
Konrad Lorenz 339
John Bowlby 339
Mary Ainsworth 339
Jerome Kagan 340

Alexander Chess and Stella Thomas 341
Diana Baumrind 341
G. Stanley Hall 345
Lawrence Kohlberg 347
Carol Gilligan 349

Leonard Hayflick 353
Daniel Levinson 358
Bernice Neugarten 359
Elisabeth Kübler-Ross 361

Psychology Checklist
HUMAN DEVELOPMENT

How much have you learned since the beginning of the chapter? Use the following statements to help you review your knowledge and understanding of the chapter material. First, read the statement and mentally or briefly on paper demonstrate that you understand and can discuss the relevant information.

_____ I know what development is, including its processes, periods, and issues.
_____ I can describe prenatal development and birth.
_____ I can discuss children's physical development.
_____ I am aware of what changes take place in children's cognitive development, including Piaget's theory.
_____ I know about children's socioemotional development, including Erikson's theory, attachment, and parenting.
_____ I can describe the historical beginnings of adolescence and the nature of adolescence.

_____ I can discuss the physical, cognitive, and socioemotional changes in adolescence, including identity development and Kohlberg's theory.
_____ I am aware of the physical changes that take place in adult development and the biological aspects of aging.
_____ I know about cognitive changes in adulthood and aging.
_____ I can describe socioemotional development in adulthood and aging, including theories of adult development.
_____ I can discuss successful aging.
_____ I can describe the nature of death and dying.

For any items that you did not check, go back and locate the relevant material in the chapter. Review the material until you feel that you can check off the item. You also may want to use this checklist later in preparing for an exam.

Taking It to the Net

1. Imagine you are playing with your 5-year-old cousin. You give her one quarter and she seems very pleased. Then, you playfully ask her if she wants to trade that quarter for three shiny new pennies. She looks at the quarter in her hand, looks at your hand, and gleefully says, "yes!" You ask her why, and she replies, "Because three is more than one." At what stage of cognitive development, according to Piaget, is your cousin right now? How do you know? What are some of the other common ways of thinking at this stage?

2. Early childhood care and development is essential to both individual children and society as a whole. This involves providing programs to communities, parents, and the children themselves. From a very early age (birth to age 8), children need to be supported in the development of their cognitive, social, and physical abilities. Children's development can be facilitated by instituting programs in communities throughout the world. Clearly the children benefit from such support, but how do you think society gains from early childhood intervention?

3. Although we usually associate development with the childhood years, key changes also occur in our aging years. As your grandparents will undoubtedly tell you, aging facilitates cognitive, physical, and social changes. One aspect of aging involves changes in our immune system. How is this system affected by aging? Why does this change occur? Explain the repercussions of such a change in our immune system.

Connect to http://www.mcgrawhill.ca/college/santrock to find the answers!

Resources for Psychology and Life

Handbook of Child Psychology (5th ed., Vols. 1–4) (1998)
 by William Damon (Ed.)
 New York: Wiley

This four-volume set includes detailed chapters about a wide range of topics in children's physical, cognitive, and socioemotional development.

The National Council on Aging
 1331 F Street, NW
 Washington, DC 20005
 202-347-8800
 http://www.ncoa.org

This organization is dedicated to increasing the well-being of older Americans. The council publishes a number of materials about aging and services available to older Americans. Although this is an American site, it is currently the best available.

Search Institute
 Thresher Square West
 700 South Third Street, Suite 210
 Minneapolis, NM 55415
 612-376-8955

The Search Institute has a large number of resources available for improving the lives of adolescents.

The Mind's Staircase: Exploring the Conceptual Underpinnings of Children's Thought and Knowledge (1991)
 by Robbie Case
 Hillsdale, NJ: Erlbaum

This is an excellent treatment of what is often referred to as the Neo-Piagetian position which seeks to further our understanding of Piagetian theory by making use of concepts from cognitive psychology.

Handbook of Parenting, Vols. I–IV (1995)
 by Mark Bornstein (ed.)
 Hillsdale, NJ: Erlbaum

These four volumes provide a wealth of information on a wide variety of parenting issues. Leading researchers discuss such topics as divorce, adoption, gifted children, ethnicity, day care, moral development, and poverty.

Child Development, Developmental Psychology, Journal of Research on Adolescence, and Journal of Gerontology

These are leading research journals in human development and they publish a wide array of articles on biological, cognitive, and socioemotional dimensions of development.

Infant Development: The Essential Readings (2000)
 by Darwin Muir
 Oxford, UK: Blackwell

An up-to-date treatment of infant development by one of Canada's most respected developmental psychologists.

Chapter 11

CHAPTER OUTLINE

SOME IDEAS ABOUT THE "WHYS" OF BEHAVIOR

Defining Motivation

Biological Influences

Cognitive Influences

Behavioral/Social/Cultural Influences

The Hierarchy of Motives

Issues in Motivation

HUNGER

Biological Factors

External and Cognitive Factors

Eating and Weight

SEXUALITY

Biological, Cognitive, Sensory/Perceptual, and Cultural Factors

The Human Sexual Response Cycle

Psychosexual Dysfunctions

Heterosexuality and Homosexuality

ACHIEVEMENT MOTIVATION

Need for Achievement

Person/Cognitive Factors

Cultural, Ethnic, and Socioeconomic Variations in Achievement

EMOTION

Defining Emotion

Biological Dimensions

Cognitive Dimensions

Behavioral Dimensions

Sociocultural Dimensions

Classifying Emotions

Motivation and Emotion

Images of Psychology and Life
Terry Fox's Marathon Run

Terry Fox attempted one of the greatest long-distance runs in history, but unfortunately he died of cancer before he could complete it. Averaging almost a marathon (26.2 miles) a day for five months, he ran 3,359 miles across Canada. What makes his feat truly remarkable is that Terry Fox had lost his leg to cancer and completed his grueling run with the aid of a prosthetic limb.

What motivated Terry Fox to complete his run? When he was hospitalized with cancer, he decided that if he survived he would do something to generate funds for cancer research. Many people feel overwhelmed by a cancer diagnosis and resign themselves to a lesser quality of life while they wait for the disease to run its course. Terry Fox, though, found a compelling reason to live. He concluded that his purpose in life was to go beyond himself and make a positive difference in the world. He felt renewed by his second chance.

Terry encountered unforeseen hurdles on his long run: severe headwinds, heavy rain, snow, and icy roads. These challenges took a toll. After his first month of running, he was only averaging eight miles a day, far less than he needed to accomplish if he was to finish his run before the worst of Canadian winter set in. Yet he managed to reach down inside himself to muster more motivation and energy to succeed. He kept going, picking up his pace in the second month to the point that he was back on track to reach his goal.

Terry Fox's accomplishments are all the more impressive when we consider that prior to his cancer diagnosis, he was only an average athlete and had a shy, introverted personality. Once his motivation had kicked in, he undertook one of the most meaningful runs in history. He learned to shed some of his shyness and began to give impassioned

Terry Fox undertook one of the greatest long-distance runs in history. What was his motivation?

Preview

WHEN YOU ARE MOTIVATED badly enough to get something, you will expend the energy and effort to get it. In this chapter, we will explore many aspects of motivation, evaluating why people do what they do, and emotion, examining our world of affect and feelings. Both motivation and emotion can regulate or modulate our behavior. For example, if you have a strong motivation to achieve, you might spend long hours studying and working. And your feelings of pride likewise can help to keep you on a path to achievement. These are some of the questions we will evaluate in this chapter:

- Are some needs more important to people than others?
- What explains why we get hungry? Is dieting harmful or beneficial?
- Why are people sexually motivated? What causes people to have a motivation for homosexual behavior?
- What are some good strategies for getting motivated to achieve?
- What happens to our bodies when we experience emotion?
- Can lie detectors accurately determine if people are lying?
- How do people express their emotions?
- Do women and men experience emotions differently?

speeches to thousands of people in an effort to persuade them to donate to cancer research. Terry's contributions go far beyond the funds he raised. His example stands as a testament to what motivation can accomplish even in the face of great adversity.

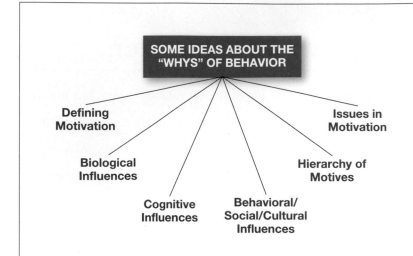

Motivation and Emotion

Some Ideas About the "Whys" of Behavior

Why do we do what we do? Let's explore this central question in motivation (Gardner & Tremblay, 1995).

Defining Motivation

We are all motivated, just motivated to do different things. Thus, some students are motivated to watch television, others to study for an exam. **Motivation** *involves the question of why people behave, think, and feel the way they do. Motivated behavior is energized, directed, and sustained.*

If you are hungry, you will probably put this book down and go to the refrigerator. If you are sexually motivated and have a partner, you might ask that person to engage in sexual behavior with you. If you are sexually motivated and don't have a partner, you might flirt with someone who attracts you. If you are motivated to achieve, you might stay in the library until midnight studying. When you are motivated, your behavior is energized and directed: you go to the refrigerator, to a party, to the library. Hunger, sex, and achievement are three important motivational areas of our lives—each of which we discuss in this chapter.

Motivations differ not only in kind, such as an individual's being motivated to eat rather than have sex, but also in intensity. We can speak of an individual as being more or less hungry, or more or less motivated to have sex. Let's now turn our attention to different ways psychologists conceptualize motivation, beginning with biological influences.

Biological Influences

Biological influences on motivation have been proposed in the form of instincts, needs and drives, and physiological factors such as brain processes and hormones. You will also see that ethology and evolutionary psychology propose biological views of motivation.

Instincts   An **instinct** *is an innate (unlearned), biological pattern of behavior that is assumed to be universal throughout a species.* Influenced by Darwin's evolutionary theory, American psychologist William McDougall (1908) argued that all behavior involves instincts. In particular, he said that we have instincts for acquisitiveness, curiosity, pugnacity, gregariousness, and self-assertion. At about the same time, Sigmund Freud (1917) argued that behavior is instinctually based. He believed that sex and aggression were especially powerful in motivating behavior ◀▥ P. 9.

It was not long before a number of psychologists had crafted laundry lists of instincts, some lists running into the thousands. However, it soon became apparent that what the early instinct theorists were doing was naming a behavior rather than explaining it. If we say that people have an instinct for sex, or for curiosity, or for acquisitiveness, these behaviors are not being explained, only named.

Although the early instinct approach of merely labeling behaviors as instincts landed in psychology's dust heap many years ago, the idea that some motivation is unlearned is still alive and well today. It is widely accepted that instinctive behavior is common in nonhuman species, and in chapter 10, "Human Development," we saw that human infants come into the world equipped with some unlearned instincts such as sucking. Most attachment theorists also believe that infants have an unlearned instinct for orienting toward a caregiver ◀▥ P. 339.

Needs and Drives   If you do not have an instinct for sex, maybe you have a need or a drive for it. A **drive** *is an aroused state that occurs because of a physiological need. A* **need** *is a deprivation that energizes the drive to eliminate or reduce the deprivation.* You might have a need for water, for food, or for sex. The need for food, for example, arouses your hunger drive. This motivates you to do something— to go out for a hamburger, for example—to reduce the drive and satisfy the need. As a drive becomes stronger, we are motivated to reduce it. This explanation is known as *drive reduction theory.*

Usually, but not always, needs and drives are closely associated in time. For example, when your body needs food, your hunger drive will probably be aroused. An hour after you have eaten a hamburger, you might still be hungry (thus, you need food), but your hunger drive might have subsided. From this example you can sense that drive pertains to a psychological state; need involves a physiological state.

The goal of drive reduction is **homeostasis,** *the body's tendency to maintain an equilibrium, or a steady state.* Literally hundreds of biological states in our bodies must be maintained within a certain range: temperature, blood-sugar level, potassium and sodium levels, oxygen, and so on. When you dive into an icy swimming pool, your body heats up. When you walk out of an air-conditioned room into the heat of a summer day, your body begins to cool down. These changes occur automatically in an attempt to restore your body to its optimal state of functioning.

Homeostasis is achieved in our bodies much like a thermostat in a house keeps the temperature constant. For example, assume that the thermostat in your house is set at 21 degrees. The furnace heats the house until a temperature of 21 degrees is reached, then the furnace shuts off. Without a source of heat, the temperature in the house eventually falls below 21 degrees. The thermostat detects this and turns the furnace back on again. The cycle is repeated so that the temperature is maintained within narrow limits. Today homeostasis is used to explain both physiological and psychological imbalances.

What is the status of drive reduction theory today? It has not been completely discarded, but most psychologists believe it does not provide a comprehensive framework for understanding motivation. Drive reduction theory states that people are motivated to reduce a drive. However, people often behave in ways that increase rather than reduce a drive. For example, they might skip meals in an effort to lose weight, which can increase their hunger drive rather than reduce it. Consider also people who seek stimulation and thrills, such as going bungee-jumping or riding a roller coaster. Instead of reducing a drive, they appear to be increasing their level of stimulation. In one study, monkeys

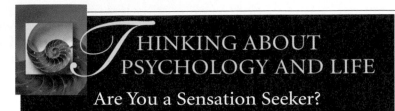

THINKING ABOUT PSYCHOLOGY AND LIFE
Are You a Sensation Seeker?

SENSATION SEEKING is defined as the motivation for varied, novel, and complex sensations and experiences (Zuckerman, 1979). High sensation seekers take physical and social risks just for the sake of the experiences. By responding to the items below you can get a sense of your motivation for sensation seeking.

For each of the following items, decide which of the two choices best describes your likes and feelings. If neither choice applies, choose the one that most describes you. Answer all of the items.

1. a. I like the tumult of sounds in a busy city.
   b. I prefer the peace and quiet of the country.
2. a. I dislike the sensations one gets when flying.
   b. I enjoy many of the rides in amusement parks.
3. a. I would like a job that would require a lot of traveling.
   b. I would prefer a job in one location.
4. a. I often wish I could be a mountain climber.
   b. I can't understand people who risk their necks climbing mountains.
5. a. I get bored seeing the same old faces.
   b. I like the comfortable familiarity of everyday friends.
6. a. I like to explore a strange city or section of town by myself, even if it means getting lost.
   b. I prefer a guide when I am in a place I don't know well.
7. a. I find people who disagree with my beliefs more stimulating than people who agree with me.
   b. I don't like to argue with people whose beliefs are sharply divergent from mine, since such arguments are never resolved.
8. a. I prefer more subdued colors in decoration.
   b. I like to decorate with bright colors.
9. a. When I have nothing to do or look at for any length of time, I get very restless.
   b. I often enjoy just relaxing and doing nothing.
10. a. Most people spend entirely too much money on life insurance.
    b. Life insurance is something that no one can afford to be without.
11. a. I don't like to drink coffee because it overstimulates me and keeps me awake.
    b. I like to drink coffee because of the lift it gives me.
12. a. The worst social sin is to be rude.
    b. The worst social sin is to be a bore.
13. a. The most important goal of life is to live it to the fullest and experience as much of it as you can.
    b. The most important goal of life is to find peace and happiness.
14. a. If I were a salesperson, I would prefer working on commission if I had a chance to make more money than I could on a salary.
    b. If I were a salesperson, I would prefer a straight salary rather than the risk of making little or nothing on a commission basis.
15. a. I like sharp or spicy foods.
    b. I prefer foods with a minimum of seasoning.

Count one point for sensation seeking for each of the following: 1a, 2b, 3a, 4a, 5a, 6a, 7a, 8b, 9a, 10a, 11b, 12b, 13a, 14a, 15a. If you answered 11 or more items this way, you probably have a strong motivation for sensation seeking. If you answered 5 items or less this way, you probably have a weak motive for sensation seeking. If you responded this way 6 to 10 times, you probably are in the average range of sensation seekers. The older one gets, the more sensation seeking scores go down.

solved simple problems just for the opportunity to watch a toy train (Butler, 1953). And a series of experiments suggested that college students could not tolerate sensory deprivation for more than two to three days, even though they were being paid for their participation (Bexton, Heron, & Scott, 1954). Also when people are curious and seek information, drive reduction does not seem to be involved.

Ethology and Evolutionary Psychology   Although psychologists rejected the biological concept of instinct many years ago, biology's role in motivation continues to be strong. Recall from chapter 10, "Human Development," that Konrad Lorenz (1965) conducted a classic study in which goslings became attached to Lorenz because he was the first moving object they saw after they were born ◀▥ P. 339. Lorenz interpreted the goslings' behavior as evidence of rapid innate learning within a critical time period. Lorenz's field is **ethology,** *the study of the biological basis of behavior in natural habitats.* Ethology emerged as an important theory because of the work of European zoologists such as Lorenz in the 1930s, who argued that behaviorism had gone too far in promoting environmental experiences in motivation.

In chapter 3, we also discussed the theory in psychology that is currently receiving the most attention for its emphasis on the biological and evolutionary basis of behavior: evolutionary psychology ◀▥ P. 68. According to evolutionary psychologists such as McMaster's Denys deCatanzaro (1999) and David Buss (1995), to understand motivation it is necessary to examine its evolutionary ties. They argue that the motivation for sex, aggression, achievement, and other behaviors is rooted in our evolutionary past. Thus, a species may be highly competitive because competitiveness provided an advantage and was passed down through the genes from generation to generation.

Physiological Processes   Our body's physiological makeup (such as brain processes and hormones) also represents another important aspect of biology's role in motivation. We will discuss these physiological mechanisms shortly when we explore hunger. In sum, although the concept of instinct did not survive, the views of ethologists and evolutionary psychologists, as well as physiological mechanisms, underscore biology's influence on the study of motivation.

Cognitive Influences

The contemporary view of motivation also emphasizes the importance of cognitive factors (Petri, 1996). Consider your motivation to do well in this class. Your confidence in your ability to do well and your expectation for success may help you to relax, concentrate better, and study more effectively. If you think too much about not doing well in the class and fear that you will fail, you can become too anxious and not perform as well. Your ability to consciously control your behavior and resist the temptation to party too much and avoid studying will improve your achievement, as will your ability to use your information-processing abilities of attention, memory, and problem solving as you study for and take tests ◀▥ P. 11.

Psychologists continue to debate the role of conscious versus unconscious thought in understanding motivation. Freud's legacy to contemporary psychoanalytic theory is the belief that we are largely unaware of why we behave the way we do. Psychoanalytic theorists argue that few of us know why we love someone, why we eat so much, why we are so aggressive, or why we are so shy. Although some cognitive psychologists have begun to study the role of the unconscious mind, for the most part they emphasize that human beings are rational and aware of their motivation. Humanistic theorists like Maslow (whose view we will explore shortly) also stress our ability to examine our lives and become aware of what motivates us.

Behavioral/Social/Cultural Influences

Environmental influences on motivation focus on the behavioral concept of incentives, as well as social/cultural influences.

Incentives   So far we have been discussing internal factors that motivate behavior (such as needs, drives, and thoughts). But aren't external factors also involved in motivation? Isn't external motivation at work when a person is not hungry but sees a familiar fast-food place and becomes motivated to go in and buy a hamburger?

External factors were added to motivation when psychologists developed the concept of **incentives,** *positive or negative stimuli or events that motivate behavior.* Incentives are motivation's external pull. The prospect of a lucrative income of $100,000+ is a positive incentive for going to medical school and becoming a doctor. The threat of an intruder is a negative incentive for purchasing a security system for a home.

Internal and external factors can work in tandem in motivating behavior. Think of internal factors as being like a "push" from inside to motivate behavior and external factors as being like a "pull" from outside to motivate behavior. You might be more likely to go into a fast-food restaurant and buy some food if you are hungry (the internal push) and you see the familiar sign for it (the external pull).

Social/Cultural Influences   As is true of much human behavior, environmental and sociocultural influences play an important role in motivation. Even "biological" motives have environmental and sociocultural underpinnings. Why does the same meal—say, steak, baked potato, and salad—satisfy our hunger so much more when we are seated near someone we love in a candle-lit room than in a noisy school cafeteria, for example? And consider the social motive of achievement. To fully understand achievement, we need to evaluate how parents and children interact, explore how peers compare one another, and examine the people we look up to as models of success, along with the standards for achievement in different cultures.

We have explored a number of different perspectives on motivation that consider biological, cognitive, and behavioral/social/cultural factors. Next, we turn our attention to a perspective that attempts to provide an integrative organization of various motives.

The Hierarchy of Motives

Is getting an A in this class more important than eating? If the person of your dreams told you that you were marvelous, would that motivate you to throw yourself in front of a car for the person's safety? According to Abraham Maslow (1954, 1971), our basic "needs" must be satisfied before our "higher" needs can be. Maslow's **hierarchy of motives** *states that individuals' main needs are satisfied in the following sequence: physiological, safety, love and belongingness, esteem, and self-actualization* (see figure 11.1). According to this hierarchy, people are motivated to satisfy their need for food before they are motivated to achieve, and their motivation for safety needs to be satisfied before their need for love.

Maslow's Hierarchy of Motives

Self-actualization

Esteem

Love and belongingness

Safety

Physiological

$\mathscr{F}$igure 11.1
Maslow's Hierarchy of Motives
Abraham Maslow developed the hierarchy of human motives to show how we have to satisfy certain basic needs before we can satisfy higher needs.

It is the need for self-actualization that Maslow has described in the greatest detail. **Self-actualization,** *the highest and most elusive of Maslow's needs, is the motivation to develop one's full potential as a human being.* According to Maslow, self-actualization is possible only after the other needs in the hierarchy are met. Maslow cautions that most people stop maturing after they have developed a high level of esteem and thus do not become self-actualized. Many of Maslow's writings focus on how people can reach the elusive motivational state of self-actualization. We will have more to say about self-actualization in the next chapter, "Personality."

The idea that human motives are hierarchically arranged is an appealing one. Maslow's theory stimulates us to think about the ordering of motives in our own lives. However, the ordering of the needs is somewhat subjective. Some people might seek greatness in a career to achieve self-esteem, while putting on hold their needs for love and belongingness.

Self-Actualization

Issues in Motivation

In our discussion of motivation's biological, cognitive, and behavioral/social/cultural underpinnings, we have encountered three important issues: (1) To what degree are we motivated by innate, unlearned, biological factors as opposed to learned, sociocultural, experientially based factors? (2) To what degree are we aware of what motivates us—that is, to what extent is our motivation conscious? (3) To what degree are we internally or externally motivated? These are issues that researchers continue to wrangle with and debate.

Keep in mind that, although we separated the biological, cognitive, and behavioral/social/cultural underpinnings of motivation for the purpose of organization and clarification, in reality they are often interrelated. For example, in the study of social cognition, psychologists call attention to how contextual/social factors interact with thinking to determine our motivation. Thus, a person's achievement motivation might be influenced by both the person's optimistic outlook (cognitive) and his or her relationship with an outstanding mentor (social).

At this point we have studied a number of basic ideas about the whys of behavior. An overview of these ideas is presented in summary table 11.1. Now we will turn our attention to some specific areas of motivation: hunger, sex, and achievement. These areas of motivation were chosen because they represent diverse aspects of motivation in our lives and reflect varying degrees of biological, cognitive, and behavioral/social/cultural influences. First, we will study hunger, which has strong biological underpinnings. Second, we will study sex, a bridge between biological and social motives. And third, we will evaluate the cognitive/social motive of achievement.

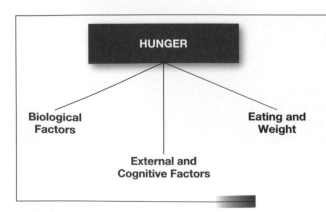

Hunger

Imagine that you live in the Bayambang area of the Philippines. You are very poor and have little food to eat. Hunger continuously gnaws at everyone in your village. Now imagine yourself as the typical Canadian, eating not only breakfast, lunch, and dinner, but snacking along the way—and maybe even raiding the refrigerator at midnight.

Food is an important aspect of life in any culture. Whether we have very little or large amounts of food available to us, hunger influences our behavior. What mechanisms explain why we get hungry?

SUMMARY TABLE 11.1
Some Ideas About the "Whys" of Behavior

Concept	Processes/Related Ideas	Characteristics/Description
Defining Motivation	Its Nature	Motivation involves the question of why people think, feel, and behave the way they do. Motivated behavior is energized, directed, and sustained.
Biological Influences	Instinct	An instinct is an innate (unlearned) biological pattern of behavior that is assumed to be universal throughout a species. The concept of instinct was popularized by McDougall at the beginning of the twentieth century. The idea that some of our motivation is unlearned and involves physiological factors is still present today.
	Needs and Drives	A drive is an arousal state that occurs because of a physiological need. A need is a deprivation that energizes the drive to eliminate or reduce the deprivation. Drive reduction theory was proposed as an explanation for motivation with the goal of drive reduction being homeostasis, the body's tendency to maintain an equilibrium. The concept of homeostasis is used to explain both physiological and psychological imbalances.
	Ethology and Evolutionary Psychology	Lorenz's ideas came from the field of ethology, the study of the biological basis of behavior in natural habitats. Ethologists argue that rapid innate learning often takes place in a critical period. Evolutionary psychologists also emphasize the biological and evolutionary basis of motivation.
	Physiological Processes	Motivation's biological basis also involves physiological processes such as brain processes and hormones.
Cognitive Influences	Their Nature	The contemporary view of motivation also emphasizes cognitive factors, including such information-processing abilities as attention, memory, and problem solving. Psychologists continue to debate the role of conscious versus unconscious thought in understanding motivation.
Behavioral/Social/Cultural Factors	Incentives	These are positive or negative external stimuli that motivate an individual's behavior.
	Social/Cultural Influences	These environmental factors also influence motivation. The role of behavioral, social, and cultural factors raises an important issue about motivation: Is behavior internally or externally motivated?
The Hierarchy of Motives	Maslow's view	According to Maslow's hierarchy of motives, our main needs are satisfied in this sequence: physiological, safety, love and belongingness, esteem, cognitive, aesthetic, and self-actualization. Maslow gave the most attention to self-actualization, the motivation to develop to one's full potential.
Issues in Motivation	Their Nature	Three important issues focus on (1) whether motivation is based on innate, unlearned, biological factors or learned, sociocultural, experiential factors; (2) to what degree we are aware of what motivates us; and (3) to what degree we are internally or externally motivated.

Biological Factors

You are sitting in class and it is 2 P.M. You were so busy today that you skipped lunch. As the professor lectures, your stomach starts to growl. For many of us, a growling stomach is one of the main signs that we are hungry. Psychologists have wondered for many years about the role of peripheral factors—such as the stomach, liver, and blood chemistry—in hunger.

Peripheral Factors   In 1912, Walter Cannon and A. L. Washburn conducted an experiment that revealed a close association between stomach contractions

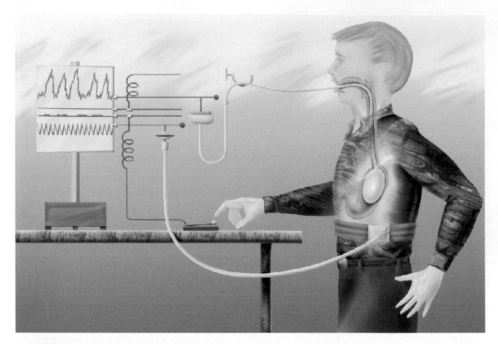

$\mathscr{F}$igure 11.2
Cannon and Washburn's Classic Experiment on Hunger

In this experiment, the researchers demonstrated that stomach contractions, which were detected by the stomach balloon, accompany a person's hunger feelings, which were indicated by pressing the key.

and hunger (see figure 11.2). As part of the procedure, a partially inflated balloon was passed through a tube inserted in Washburn's mouth and pushed down into his stomach. A machine that measures air pressure was connected to the balloon to monitor Washburn's stomach contractions. Every time Washburn reported hunger pangs, his stomach was also contracting. This finding, which was confirmed in subsequent experiments with other volunteers, led the two to believe that gastric activity was *the* basis for hunger.

Stomach signals are not the only factors that affect hunger. People whose stomachs have been surgically removed still get hunger pangs. Stomach contractions can be a signal for hunger, but the stomach can also send signals that stop hunger. We all know that a full stomach can decrease our appetite. In fact, the stomach actually tells the brain not only how full it is, but also how much nutrient is in the stomach load. That is why a stomach full of rich food stops your hunger faster than a stomach full of water. The same stomach hormone that helps start the digestion of food (called cholecystokinin, or CCK) reaches your brain through the bloodstream and signals you to stop eating.

Blood sugar (glucose) is another important factor in hunger, probably because the brain is critically dependent on sugar for energy. One set of sugar receptors is located in the brain itself, and these receptors trigger hunger when sugar levels get too low. Another set of sugar receptors is in the liver, which is the organ that stores excess sugar and releases it into the blood when needed. The sugar receptors in the liver signal the brain via the vagus nerve, and this signal can also make you hungry. Another important factor in blood-sugar control is the hormone insulin, which causes excess sugar in the blood to be stored in cells as fats and carbohydrates. Insulin injections cause profound hunger because they lower blood sugar drastically.

Psychologist Judith Rodin (1984) has further clarified the role of insulin and glucose in understanding hunger and eating behavior. She pointed out that when we eat complex carbohydrates such as cereals, bread, and pasta, insulin levels go up but then fall off gradually. When we consume simple sugars like candy bars and Cokes, insulin levels rise and then fall off sharply—the all-too-familiar "sugar low." Glucose levels in the blood are also affected by these complex carbohydrates and simple sugars in similar ways. The consequence is that we are more likely to eat within the next several hours after eating simple sugars than after eating complex carbohydrates. And the food we eat at one meal often influences how much we will eat at our next meal. So consuming doughnuts and candy bars, in addition to providing no nutritional value, sets up an ongoing sequence of what and how much we will probably crave the next time we eat.

Brain Processes   In chapter 3, "Biological Foundations and Neuroscience," we described the hypothalamus' important role in regulating important body functions, including hunger P. 82. More specifically, activity in two areas of the hypothalamus contributes to our understanding of hunger (see figure 11.3). The *lateral*

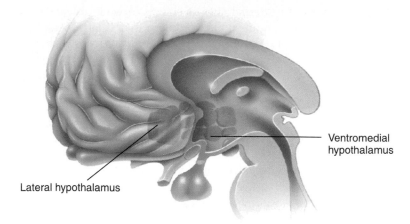

Ventromedial
hypothalamus

Lateral hypothalamus

𝓕igure 11.3
The Hypothalamus and Hunger

The hypothalamus plays an important role in regulating various body functions, one of which is hunger. More specifically, the lateral hypothalamus is involved in stimulating hunger and the ventromedial hypothalamus functions in restricting eating.

hypothalamus is involved in stimulating eating. When it is electrically stimulated in a well-fed animal, the animal begins to eat. And if this area of the hypothalamus is destroyed, even a starving animal will show no interest in food. The *ventromedial hypothalamus* is involved in reducing hunger and restricting eating. When this area of an animal's brain is stimulated, the animal stops eating. When the area is destroyed, the animal eats profusely and quickly becomes obese (see figure 11.4).

Today, neuroscientists believe that while the lateral and ventromedial hypothalamus play roles in hunger, there is much more to the brain's role in determining hunger than these on/off centers in the hypothalamus. They are exploring how neurotransmitters (recall from chapter 3 that these are chemical messengers that convey information from neuron to neuron) and neural circuits (clusters of neurons that often involve different parts of the brain) function in hunger ◀▥ P. 76.

Your internal physiological world is very much involved in whether or not you are hungry. But some external and cognitive factors are also involved.

External and Cognitive Factors

Might external cues stimulate hunger? Might the cognitive factor of self-control be involved in hunger?

External Cues   Psychologists are interested in how environmental cues might stimulate hunger. You may know someone who seems literally incapable of walking past an ice cream shop without stopping to eat a huge hot fudge sundae. Stanley Schachter (1971) believes that one of the main differences between obese and normal weight individuals is their attention to environmental cues for signals of when to eat. From this perspective, people of normal weight attend to internal cues for signals of when to eat—for example, when blood sugar level is low, hunger pangs are sensed in the stomach. In

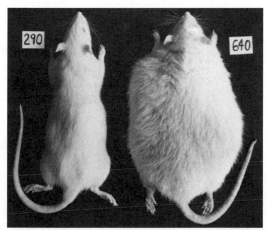

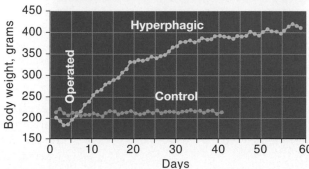

𝓕igure 11.4
The Ventromedial Hypothalamus (VMH) and Obesity in Rats

(top) A rat gained three times its normal body weight after a lesion was made in its VMH. *(bottom)* This graph displays the weight gain by a group of rats in which lesions were made in the VMH (hyperphagic) and by a group of rats in which no lesions were made (control). Notice how quickly the hyperphagic rats gained weight but that, after about one month, they virtually stopped gaining weight.

contrast, an obese person responds to external cues as signals of when to eat—how the food tastes, looks, and smells, for example. One problem that is left unresolved by Schachter's view is that not all people who have this special sensitivity to such cues are overweight (Rodin, 1984). Alternative perspectives have sought to integrate what we know about the importance of physiology and external cues in understanding obesity.

Self-Control   Rodin (1984) points out that not too long ago we believed that obesity was caused by such factors as unhappiness or responding to external food cues. According to Rodin, a number of biological, cognitive, and social factors are more important. We already discussed some important biological factors, including the roles of complex carbohydrates and simple sugars in insulin and glucose levels. In regard to external cues, Rodin says that while obese persons are more responsive to external food cues than normal-weight persons are, there are individuals at all weight levels who respond more to external than to internal stimuli. Many persons who respond to external cues also have the conscious ability to control their behavior and keep environmental food cues from externally controlling their eating patterns.

Eating and Weight

So far in our coverage of the hunger motive, we have explored some important factors that motivate a person to eat. In this section we examine other factors that influence the motivation to eat. In some cases, this motivation involves obesity and the ability of overweight individuals to become motivated to take off pounds and maintain the weight loss. In others, the motivation focuses on the motivation of individuals who are not overweight to be extremely thin.

Obesity
Heredity and Obesity

Obesity   Obesity is a serious and pervasive problem. Let's explore its pervasiveness and costs, as well as the roles that heredity, set point and metabolism, and environmental factors play in its development.

Pervasiveness and Costs   About one-third of the Canadian (Statistics Canada, 1999) and U.S. population are overweight enough to be at increased health risk. The prevalence of obesity has risen eight percent in the 1990s (Friedman & Brownell, 1998) and becomes more common with increased age, especially among women.

The health care costs linked to obesity are estimated to be $50 billion per year. Obesity is associated with increased risk of hypertension, diabetes, and cardiovascular disease.

Heredity   Until recently, the genetic component of obesity had been underestimated by scientists. Some individuals do inherit a tendency to be overweight. Only 10 percent of children who do not have obese parents become obese themselves, whereas 40 percent of children who become obese have one obese parent and 70 percent of children who become obese have two obese parents. Researchers have also documented that animals can be inbred to have a propensity for obesity (Blundell, 1984). Further, identical human twins have similar weights, even when they are reared apart. Estimates of the variance in body mass that can be explained by heredity range from 25 to 70 percent.

Set Point and Metabolism   The amount of stored fat in your body is an important factor in your **set point**, *the weight maintained when no effort is made to gain or lose weight.* Fat is stored in what are called adipose cells. When these cells are filled, you do not get hungry. When people gain weight—because of genetic predisposition, childhood eating patterns, or adult overeating—the number of their fat cells increases, and they might not be able to get rid of them. A normal-weight individual has 30 to 40 billion fat cells. An obese individual has 80 to 120 billion fat cells. Some scientists have proposed that these fat cells can shrink but might not go away.

Another factor in weight is **basal metabolism rate (BMR)**, *the minimal amount of energy an individual uses in a resting state.* BMR varies with age and sex. Rates decline precipitously during adolescence and then more gradually in adulthood; they are also slightly higher for males than females (see figure 11.5). Many people gradually increase their weight over many years. To some degree the weight gain can be due to a declining basal metabolism rate.

Environmental Factors   The human gustatory system and taste preferences developed at a time when reliable food sources were scarce. Our earliest ancestors probably developed a preference for sweets, because ripe fruit, which is a concentrated source of sugar (and calories), was so accessible. Today many people still have a "sweet tooth," but unlike our ancestors' ripe fruit that contained sugar *plus* vitamins and minerals, the soft drinks and candy bars we snack on today only fill us with empty calories.

Strong evidence of the environment's influence on weight is the doubling of the rate of obesity in the United States since 1900. This dramatic increase in obesity is likely due to greater availability of food (especially food high in fat), energy-saving devices, and declining physical activity. Obesity is six times more prevalent among women with low incomes than among women with high incomes. North Americans also are more obese than Europeans and people in many other areas of the world.

Dieting   Let's explore the diet scene in North America, restrained eating, whether diets work, the role of exercise in losing weight, and the potential harm and benefits of dieting.

The Diet Scene   Many interests are involved in the topic of dieting. These include the public, health professionals, policy makers, the media, and the powerful diet and food industries. On one side are the societal norms that promote a very lean, aesthetic body. This ideal is supported by billions a year in sales of diet books, programs, videos, foods, and pills. On the other side are health professionals and some members of the press. Although they recognize the high rate of obesity, they are frustrated by high relapse rates and the obsession with excessive thinness that can lead to chronic dieting and serious health risks (McFarlane, Polivy & McCabe, 1999; Brownell & Rodin, 1994).

Restrained Eating   One area related to dieting that psychologists have studied is restrained eating (Martins & Pliner, 1999). Too many people live their lives as one big long diet, interrupted by occasional hot fudge sundaes or chocolate chip cookies. **Restrained eaters** *are individuals who chronically restrict their food intake to control their weight.* Restrained eaters are often on diets, are very conscious of what they eat, and tend to feel guilty after splurging on sweets. An interesting characteristic of restrained eaters is that when they stop dieting, they tend to binge eat—that is, eat large quantities of food in a short time (McFarlane, Polivy, & Herman, 1998).

Do Diets Work?   Although many North Americans regularly embark on a diet, few are successful in keeping weight off long-term. Some critics argue

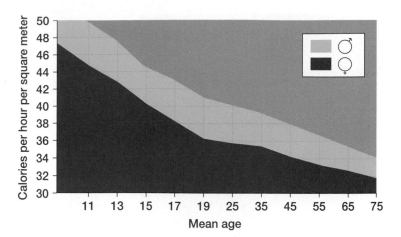

$\mathscr{F}$igure 11.5
Changes in Basal Metabolism Rate with Age
BMR varies with age and sex. Rates are usually higher for males and decline proportionately with age for both sexes.

Why People are Getting Fatter

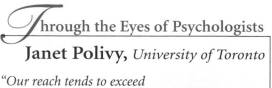
$\mathscr{T}$hrough the Eyes of Psychologists
Janet Polivy, *University of Toronto*

"Our reach tends to exceed our grasp where weight loss is concerned. Frustration and dissatisfaction are the understandable consequences."

Anorexia nervosa has become an increasing problem for adolescent girls and young adult women. What are some possible causes of anorexia nervosa?

Anorexia Nervosa

that all diets fail (Wooley & Garner, 1991). However, the weight of the evidence is that some individuals who go on diets do lose weight and maintain the loss (Brownell & Cohen, 1995). How often this occurs and whether some diet programs work better than others are still open questions.

Exercise   What we do know about losing weight is that the most effective programs include an exercise component. Exercise not only burns up calories, but continues to elevate the person's metabolic rate for several hours *after* the exercise. Also, exercise lowers a person's set point for weight, which makes it easier to maintain a lower weight (Bennett & Gurin, 1982).

Dieting: Harm or Benefit?   Dieting is a pervasive concern of many North Americans, but many people who are on diets should not be. A 10 percent reduction in body weight might produce striking benefits for an older, obese, hypertensive man but be unhealthy for a female university student who is not overweight. The pressure to be thin, and thus diet, is greatest among young women, yet they do not have the highest risk of obesity.

Even when diets do produce weight loss, they can place the dieter at risk for other health problems. One main concern focuses on weight cycling (commonly called "yo-yo dieting"), in which the person is in a recurring cycle of dieting and weight gain (Wadden & others, 1996). Researchers have found a link between frequent changes in weight and chronic disease (Brownell & Rodin, 1994). Also, liquid diets and other very-low calorie strategies are related to gall bladder damage.

With these problems in mind, when overweight people diet and maintain their weight loss, they become less depressed and reduce their risk for a number of health-impairing disorders (Christensen, 1996). Next, we will explore problems that occur at the other end of the weight spectrum—when people get so thin it impairs their health.

Anorexia Nervosa and Bulimia   **Anorexia nervosa** *is an eating disorder that involves the relentless pursuit of thinness through starvation.* Anorexia nervosa can eventually lead to death, as it did for popular singer Karen Carpenter in 1983.

Most anorexics are White adolescent or young adult females from well-educated, middle- and upper-income families. They distort their body image, perceiving themselves as overweight (Mussell & Mitchell, 1998). Many causes of anorexia have been proposed. One is the current fashion image of thinness. Another is that many anorexics grow up in families with high expectations. Unable to meet them, they turn to something they can control: their weight. In any case, the resulting anxiety (Buree, Papageorgis & Hare, 1990) can even lead to suicide (Coren & Hewitt, 1998). As we see next, while anorexics control their eating by restricting it, most bulimics often cannot.

Bulimia *is an eating disorder in which the individual consistently follows a binge-and-purge eating pattern.* The bulimic goes on an eating binge and then purges by self-induced vomiting or using a laxative. Like anorexia, bulimia is primarily a female disorder (Fairburn, 1995). Bulimia has become prevalent among traditional-age university women.

Bulimia can produce gastric and chemical imbalances in the body. Depression is common among bulimics. Polivy & Herman (1985) first proposed that chronic dieting may actually cause bingeing and Heatherton & Polivy (1993) have extended this line of reasoning to other eating disorders.

In chapter 15, "Health Psychology," we will further explore eating patterns and proper nutrition. At this point, we have evaluated many aspects of hunger. An overview of these ideas is presented in summary table 11.2. Next, we will continue our coverage of motivation by examining our motivation for sex.

SUMMARY TABLE 11.2
Hunger

Concept	Processes/Related Ideas	Characteristics/Discussions
Biological Factors	Peripheral Factors	Interest in the stomach's role in hunger was stimulated by Cannon's classic research, although stomach signals aren't the only factors that affect hunger. Blood sugar (glucose) is an important factor, probably because the brain is critically dependent on sugar for energy. Rodin helped clarify the role of insulin and glucose in understanding hunger and eating.
	Brain Processes	The hypothalamus plays an important role in regulating hunger. The lateral hypothalamus is involved in stimulating eating, the ventromedial hypothalamus in restricting eating. Today, neuroscientists are exploring the roles that neurotransmitters and neural circuits play in hunger.
External and Cognitive Factors	Their Nature	Schachter's research suggested that environmental cues are involved in the control of eating. However, not all people equally sensitive to external cues are overweight. Rodin argues that self-control is an important cognitive factor in understanding eating behavior.
Eating and Weight	Obesity	Obesity is a serious and pervasive problem, with about one-third of the Canadian and American population overweight enough to be at increased health risk. Heredity, set point, and basal metabolism are biological factors involved in obesity. Environmental factors also influence eating behavior. Our culture has changed from when our early ancestors ate natural fruits to the empty calories of many sweets today. The dramatic increase in obesity in the twentieth century underscores the importance of environmental factors in obesity as increasing numbers of people eat high-fat foods and lead more sedentary lives.
	Dieting	Many divergent interests are involved in the topic of dieting. One area related to dieting that is studied by psychologists is restrained eating. Most diets don't work, although some people do lose weight when they diet and maintain the loss. Exercise is an important component of a competent weight-loss program. Many people, especially females in their teens and early twenties, who go on a diet don't need to lose weight. The pressure to be thin can lead to harmful effects for people who are not overweight. However, when overweight people diet and maintain their weight loss, there are health benefits.
	Anorexia Nervosa and Bulimia	Anorexia nervosa is an eating disorder that involves the relentless pursuit of thinness through starvation. Bulimia is an eating disorder that involves a binge-and-purge eating pattern. Both disorders are common among young university women. They are serious health disorders and can even lead to death.

Sexuality

We do not need sex for everyday survival the way we need food and water, but we do need it for the survival of the species.

Biological, Cognitive, Sensory/Perceptual, and Cultural Factors

Our sexual motivation is fueled by many complex factors, including biological, cognitive, sensory/perceptual, and cultural.

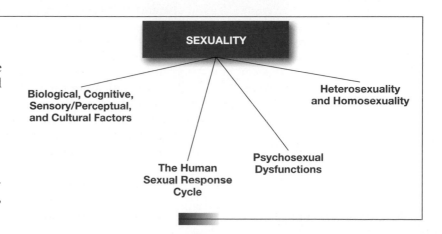

Biological Factors   Sex hormones are powerful chemicals that are controlled by the master gland in the brain, the pituitary ◀▥▥ P. 95. The two main classes of sex hormones are estrogens and androgens. **Estrogens,** *the most important of which is estradiol, influence the development of female physical sex characteristics and help to regulate the menstrual cycle.* Estrogens are produced by the ovaries. **Androgens,** *the most important of which is testosterone, promote the development of male genitals and secondary sex characteristics.* They influence sexual motivation in both sexes. Androgens are produced by the adrenal glands in males and females, and by the testes in males.

The secretion of sex hormones is regulated by a feedback system. The pituitary gland monitors hormone levels, but it is regulated by the hypothalamus. The pituitary gland sends out a signal to the testes or ovaries to manufacture the hormone. Then the pituitary gland, through interaction with the hypothalamus, detects when an optimal hormone level is reached and maintains this level.

The importance of the hypothalamus in sexual activity has been shown by electrically stimulating or surgically removing it. Electrical stimulation of certain hypothalamic areas increases sexual behavior; surgical removal of areas of the hypothalamus produces sexual inhibition. Electrical stimulation of the hypothalamus in a male can lead to as many as twenty ejaculations in one hour. The limbic system, which runs through the hypothalamus, also seems to be involved in sexual behavior. Its electrical stimulation can produce penile erection in males and orgasm in females.

In higher animals, the temporal lobes of the neocortex play an important role in moderating sexual arousal and directing it to an appropriate goal object ◀▥▥ P. 84. For example, temporal lobe damage in male cats impairs the animals' ability to select an appropriate partner. Male cats with temporal lobe damage try to copulate with everything in sight: teddy bears, chairs, even researchers. Temporal lobe damage in humans has also been associated with changes in sexual activity.

As we move from the lower to the higher animals, the role of hormones is less clear, especially in females (Crooks & Bauer, 1999). For human males, higher androgen levels are associated with sexual motivation and orgasm frequency (Booth, Johnson, & Granger, 1999; Knussman, Christiansen, & Couwenbergs, 1986; Udry & others, 1985). Nonetheless, sexual behavior is so individualized in humans that it is difficult to specify the effects of hormones.

Cognitive and Sensory/Perceptual Factors   From our experiences, we know that our cognitive world plays an important role in our sexuality (Crooks & Bauer, 1999). Thoughts and images are extensively involved in our sexual lives. We might be sexually attracted to someone but understand that it is important to inhibit our sexual urges until the relationship has time to develop and we get to know the person better. We have the cognitive capacity to think about the importance of not raping or inflicting sexual harm on others. We also have the cognitive capacity to generate sexual images. For example, some individuals become sexually aroused by generating erotic images and even reach orgasm while they are having fantasy images of sex (Whipple, Ogden, & Komisaruk, 1992).

Cognitive interpretation of sexual activity also involves our perception of the individual with whom we are having sex and his or her perception of us. We imbue our sexual acts with such perceptions as these: Is he loyal to me? What is our future relationship going to be like? How important is sex to her? What if she gets pregnant? Amid the wash of hormones in sexual activity is the cognitive ability to control, reason about, and try to make sense of the activity.

Not only are cognitive factors involved in sexual behavior, so are sensory/perceptual factors. The sensory system of touch usually predominates during sexual intimacy, but vision also plays an important role for some individuals ◀▥▥ P. 121. And we will see that smell has been proposed as a potential influence on sexual behavior, as have various foods and substances ◀▥▥ P. 124.

Men and women vary in how much touch and visual stimulation arouse their sexual motivation. In general, women are more aroused by touch, men by what they

Sexual behavior has its magnificent moments throughout the animal kingdom. Insects mate in midair, peacocks display their plumage, and male elephant seals have prolific sex lives. Experience plays a more important role in human sexual behavior. We can talk about sex with each other, read about it in magazines, and watch it on television and the movie screen.

see. This might explain why erotic magazines and X-rated movies are directed more toward males than toward females (Money, 1986). Women are more aroused by tender, loving touches that are coupled with verbal expressions of love than men are. Moreover, men are more likely to quickly become sexually aroused, whereas women's sexual arousal tends to build more gradually.

Might smell also be involved in sexual interest? **Pheromones** *are odorous substances released by animals that are powerful attractants.* Pheromones are involved when male guinea pigs are attracted by the urine of ovulating females. They are at work when all the male cats in a neighborhood know that a female cat is in heat. Several years ago Jovan developed a fragrance they claimed would attract men to women who wore it. The company advertised that the perfume contained a pheromone derived from human sweat. It was designed to lure human males just as pheromones attract male guinea pigs and cats. The fragrance was not the smashing success the perfumery anticipated, indicating there is far more to sexual attraction in humans than smell.

Various foods and substances also have been proposed as having a dramatic impact on sexual arousal. **Aphrodisiacs** *are substances that supposedly arouse a person's sexual desire and increase their capacity for sexual activity.* Recall from chapter 1 that we urged you to be skeptical about claims of how eating a ground up version of a tiger's penis would increase the male's sexual potency P. 23. Some foods, such as oysters, bananas, celery, tomatoes, and potatoes, are touted as aphrodisiacs. As with a tiger's genital parts, we urge you to be skeptical about these foods; they do not influence sexual behavior. A substance referred to as "Spanish fly" has also been promoted as a powerful aphrodisiac. This is not an effective sexual stimulant and can cause genital inflammation, tissue damage, and even death.

Pheromones

Cultural Factors   Sexual motivation is also influenced by cultural factors. The range of sexual values across cultures is substantial ◀‖‖‖ P. 19. Some cultures consider sexual pleasures to be "normal" or "desirable," other cultures view sexual pleasures as "weird" or "abnormal" (Caron, 1998). Consider the people who live on the small island of Ines Beag off the coast of Ireland. They are among the most sexually repressed people in the world. They know nothing about tongue kissing or hand stimulation of the penis, and nudity is detested. For both females and males, premarital sex is out of the question. Men avoid most sexual experiences because they believe that sexual intercourse reduces their energy level and is bad for their health.

Under these repressive conditions, sexual intercourse occurs only at night and takes place as quickly as possible as the husband opens his nightclothes under the covers and the wife raises her nightgown. As you might suspect, female orgasm is rare in this culture (Messinger, 1971).

By contrast, consider the Mangaian culture in the South Pacific. In Mangaia, young boys are taught about masturbation and are encouraged to engage in it as much as they like. At age 13, the boys undergo a ritual that initiates them into sexual manhood. First their elders instruct them about sexual strategies, including how to aid their female partner in having orgasms. Then, two weeks later, the boy has intercourse with an experienced woman who helps him hold back ejaculation until she can achieve orgasm with him. By the end of adolescence, Mangaians have sex virtually every day. Mangaian women report a high frequency of orgasm.

As reflected in the behavior of the people in these two different cultures, our sexual motivation is influenced by **sexual scripts.** *These are stereotyped patterns of expectancies for how people should behave sexually.* Two well-known sexual scripts are the traditional religious script and the romantic script. In the **traditional religious script,** *sex is accepted only within marriage.* Extramarital sex is taboo, especially for women. Sex means reproduction and sometimes affection. In the **romantic script,** *sex is synonymous with love.* If we develop a relationship with someone and fall in love, it is acceptable to have sex with the person whether we are married or not.

You are probably familiar with some sex differences in sexual scripts. Females tend to link sexual intercourse with love more than males do, and males are more likely to emphasize sexual conquest. Some sexual scripts involve a double standard, such as that it is okay for male adolescents to have sex but not females; and if the female gets pregnant, it's her fault for not using contraception.

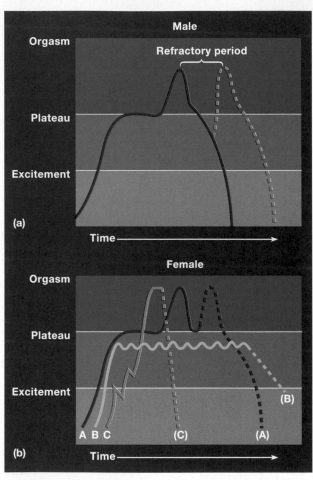

𝓕igure 11.6
Male and Female Sexual Response Patterns

(a) This diagram shows the excitement, plateau, orgasm, and resolution phases of the human male sexual response pattern. Notice that males enter a refractory period, which lasts from several minutes up to a day, in which they cannot have another orgasm. *(b)* This diagram shows the excitement, plateau, orgasm, and resolution phases of the human female sexual response pattern. Notice that female sexual responses follow one of three basic patterns. Pattern A somewhat resembles the male pattern, except that pattern A includes the possibility of multiple orgasm (the second peak in pattern A) without falling below the plateau level. Pattern B represents nonorgasmic arousal. Pattern C represents intense female orgasm, which resembles the male pattern in its intensity and rapid resolution.

The Human Sexual Response Cycle

How do humans respond physiologically during sexual activity? To answer this question, gynecologist William Masters and his colleague Virginia Johnson (1966) carefully observed and measured the physiological responses of 382 female and 312 male volunteers as they masturbated or had sexual intercourse. The **human sexual response pattern** *consists of four phases—excitement, plateau, orgasm, and resolution—as identified by Masters and Johnson* (see figure 11.6). The *excitement phase* begins erotic responsiveness; it lasts from several minutes to several hours, depending on the nature of the sex play involved. Engorgement of blood vessels and increased blood flow in genital areas and muscle tension characterize the excitement phase. The most obvious signs of response in this phase are lubrication of the vagina and partial erection of the penis.

The second phase of the human sexual response, called the *plateau phase,* is a continuation and heightening of the arousal begun in the excitement phase. The increases in breathing, pulse rate, and blood pressure that occurred during the excitement phase become more intense, penile erection and vaginal lubrication are more complete, and orgasm is closer.

The third phase of the human sexual response cycle is *orgasm*. How long does orgasm last? Some individuals sense that time is standing still when it takes place, but orgasm lasts for only about 3 to 15 seconds. Orgasm involves an explosive discharge of neuromuscular tension and an intense pleasurable feeling. However, orgasms are not all exactly alike. For example, females show three different patterns in the orgasm phase, as shown in figure 11.6: (a) multiple orgasms, (b) no orgasm, and (c) excitement rapidly leading to orgasm, bypassing the plateau phase; the third pattern most clearly corresponds to the male pattern in intensity and resolution.

Following orgasm, the individual enters the *resolution phase* in which blood vessels return to their normal state. One difference between males and females in this phase is that females may be stimulated to orgasm again without delay. Males enter a refractory period, lasting anywhere from several minutes to an entire day, in which they cannot have another orgasm. The length of the refractory period increases as men age.

Psychosexual Dysfunctions

Myths about females and males would have us believe that many women are uninterested in sexual pleasure and most men can hardly get enough. However, men and women have similar desires for sexual pleasure, and both sexes can experience psychological problems that interfere with the attainment of sexual pleasure. **Psychosexual dysfunctions** *are disorders that involve impairments in the sexual response pattern, either in the desire for gratification or in the inability to achieve it.* In disorders associated with the desire phase, both men and women show little or no sexual drive or interest. In disorders associated with the excitement phase, men may not be able to maintain an erection (McKinlay, 1999). In disorders associated with the orgasmic phase, both women and men reach orgasm too quickly or not at all. Premature ejaculation in men occurs when the time between the beginning of sexual stimulation and ejaculation is unsatisfactorily brief. Many women do not routinely experience orgasm in sexual intercourse, a pattern so common it can hardly be called dysfunctional. Inhibited male orgasm does occur, but it is much less common than inhibited female orgasm.

Psychosexual Dysfunction in Men
Psychosexual Dysfunction in Women
Viagra

The treatment of psychosexual dysfunctions has undergone nothing short of a revolution in recent years. Once thought of as extremely difficult therapeutic challenges, most cases of psychosexual dysfunction now yield to techniques tailored to improve sexual functioning (Bhugra & de Silva, 1998; Crooks & Bauer, 1999).

Attempts to treat psychosexual dysfunctions through traditional forms of psychotherapy, as if the dysfunctions were personality disorders, have not been very successful; however, new treatments that focus directly on each sexual dysfunction have reached success rates of 90 percent or more (McConaghy, 1993). For example, the success rate of a treatment that encourages women to enjoy their bodies and engage in self-stimulation to orgasm, with a vibrator if necessary, approaches 100 percent (Anderson, 1983). Some of these women subsequently transfer their newly developed sexual responsiveness to interactions with partners.

Recently, the most attention in helping individuals with a sexual dysfunction has focused on Viagra, a drug designed to conquer impotence. Its success rate is in the range of 60 to 80 percent, and its prescription rate has outpaced such popular drugs as Prozac (antidepressant) and Rogaine (baldness remedy) in first-year comparisons (Padma-Nathan, 1999). Viagra is also being taken by some women to improve their sexual satisfaction. However, Viagra is not an aphrodisiac; it won't work in the absence of desire. The possible downside of Viagra involves headaches in 1 of 10 men, seeing blue (because the eyes contain an enzyme similar to the one on which Viagra works in the penis, about 3 percent of users develop temporary

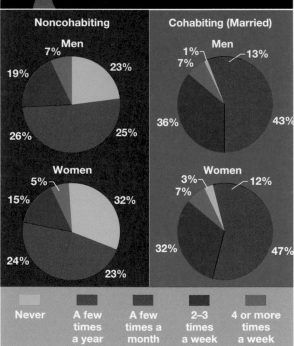

| Never | A few times a year | A few times a month | 2–3 times a week | 4 or more times a week |

Figure 11.7
Sex and Cohabitation
Percentages show noncohabiting and cohabiting (married) males' and females' responses to the question "How often have you had sex in the past year?"

Human Sexuality

vision problems ranging from blurred vision to a blue or green halo effect), and blackouts (Viagra can trigger a sudden drop in blood pressure). Also, scientists do not know the long-term effects of taking the drug, although in short-term trials it appears to be a relatively safe drug.

Heterosexuality and Homosexuality

Now we turn our attention to our sexual orientation and various aspects of heterosexuality and homosexuality.

Heterosexual Attitudes and Behavior   It is hard to accurately describe the sexual practices of diverse countries like Canada and the United States. The Kinsey report (1948) on Americans' sexual practices shocked North Americans by reporting that, among other observations, half of American men had engaged in extramarital affairs. However, Kinsey's results were not representative, because he recruited volunteers, including drifters and mental patients. Nevertheless, the Kinsey data were widely circulated and many people felt that they must be leading a more conservative sexual life than others.

Subsequent large-scale magazine surveys confirmed the trend toward permissive sexuality (Hunt, 1974). However, most magazine polls are also flawed. For example, surveys in *Playboy* and *Cosmopolitan* might appeal to subscribers who want to use the survey to brag about their sexual exploits.

Recently, more accurate data have been obtained using large random samples of men and women from all age groups in both Canada (Barrett & others, 1997) and the U.S. (Michael & others, 1994). Some of the key findings from these studies are:

• The frequency with which Canadians report they have sex is: daily (3%); several times a week (25%); once a week (25%); two or three times a month (14%); once a month (9%); hardly ever (13%); never (11%).
• Married couples have sex the most and are also the most likely to have orgasms when they do. Figure 11.7 portrays the frequency of sex for married and noncohabitating individuals in the past year.
• Adultery is the exception, not the rule. Seventy-five (U.S.) to 86 (Canada) percent of married men and 85 (U.S.) to 93 (Canada) percent of married women indicated that they have never been unfaithful.
• Men think about sex far more than women do—in the U.S. study, 54 percent of men said they think about it every day or several times a day, whereas 67 percent of women said they think about it only a few times a week or a few times a month.
• One Canadian poll asked if the respondent had two or more sexual partners in the previous year. The results ranged from a high of 32% for males 18-24 down to 0% for females 55-64. In the U.S. survey, only 17 percent of men and 3 percent of women said they have had sex with at least 21 partners.

In sum, North Americans' sexual lives are more conservative than previously believed. The overall impression is that sexual behavior is ruled by marriage and monogamy for most North Americans.

Within monogamous, married relationships, however, there is some evidence that sexual scripts are changing. In Quebec, for example, 80 percent of cohabiting heterosexual adults reported engaging in oral-genital sex (Samson and others, 1993). Further, the frequency of intercourse and oral-genital sex is correlated with both sexual satisfaction and general relationship satisfaction, suggesting that these behaviors are becoming a more accepted part of the sexual script for mature adults. To read

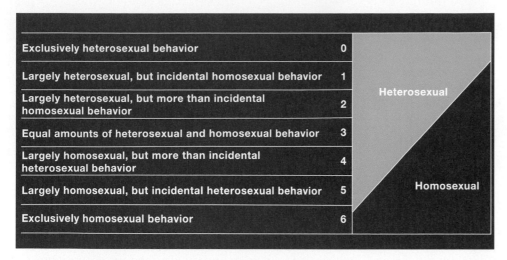

Exclusively heterosexual behavior	0
Largely heterosexual, but incidental homosexual behavior	1
Largely heterosexual, but more than incidental homosexual behavior	2
Equal amounts of heterosexual and homosexual behavior	3
Largely homosexual, but more than incidental heterosexual behavior	4
Largely homosexual, but incidental heterosexual behavior	5
Exclusively homosexual behavior	6

$\mathscr{F}$igure 11.8
The Continuum of Sexual Orientation

The continuum ranges from exclusive heterosexuality, which Kinsey and associates (1948) rated as 0, to exclusive homosexuality (6). People who are about equally attracted to both sexes (ratings 2 to 4) are bisexual.

further about the sexual landscape in North America and some of its myths, see Explorations in Psychology.

Homosexual Attitudes and Behavior   Until the end of the nineteenth century, it was generally believed that people were either heterosexual or homosexual. Today, it is more accepted to view sexual orientation along a continuum from exclusive heterosexuality to exclusive homosexuality rather than as an either/or proposition. Kinsey and his associates (Kinsey, Pomeroy, & Martin, 1948), described this continuum on a scale ranging from 0 (exclusive heterosexuality) to 6 (signifying exclusive homosexuality) (see figure 11.8). Some individuals are also **bisexual,** *being sexually attracted to people of both sexes.* In Kinsey's research, approximately 1 percent of individuals reported being bisexual (1.2 percent of males and 0.7 percent of females) and about 2 to 5 percent of individuals reported being homosexual (4.7 percent of males and 1.8 percent of females). In the recent U.S. survey, only 2.7 percent of the men and 1.3 percent of the women reported that they had had homosexual sex in the past year (Michael & others, 1994).

Why are some individuals homosexual and others heterosexual? Speculation about this question has been extensive, but no firm answers are available. Homosexuals and heterosexuals have similar physiological responses during sexual arousal and seem to be aroused by the same types of tactile stimulation. Investigators find no differences between homosexuals and heterosexuals in a wide range of attitudes, behaviors, and adjustments (Bell, Weinberg, & Mammersmith, 1981). Although homosexuality was once classified as a mental disorder, major psychiatric and psychological associations in Canada and the U.S. discontinued this classification in the 1970s.

Recently, researchers have explored the possible biological basis of homosexuality (Gladue, 1994). The results of hormone studies have been inconsistent. If male homosexuals are given male sex hormones (androgens), their sexual orientation doesn't change. Their sexual desire merely increases. However, in the second to fifth months after conception, exposure of the fetus to hormone levels characteristic of females might cause the individual (male or female) to become attracted to males (Ellis & Ames, 1987).

Sandra Witelson and her colleagues at McMaster University have also provided evidence that a biological factor is involved in the origins of sexual orientation. This includes finding different patterns of functional cerebral asymmetry (McCormick &

North American Sexual Behavior
Homosexuality

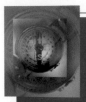

EXPLORATIONS IN PSYCHOLOGY
North America's Sexual Landscape and Its Myths

ACCORDING TO sexuality expert Bernie Zilbergeld (1992), dramatic changes in the sexual landscape have taken place in the last decade—from changing expectations of women to new definitions of masculinity, from the fear of disease to the renewed focus on long-term relationships. Sexuality's many myths have led to unrealistic expectations for our sexual lives. One man commented that he had learned so much misinformation about sex as a child that it was taking him the rest of his life to unlearn it. In middle age, he still can't believe how much stress he caused himself when he was younger and wishes he could apologize to the women who knew him in his earlier years. Among the sexual myths, according to Zilbergeld, are the myths that men need a large penis to satisfy a woman; that male and female orgasm are absolutely necessary for sexual satisfaction; that intercourse is the only real sexual act; that good sex has to be spontaneous (without planning or talking); and that it is virtually a crime when men have any questions, doubts, or problems in sex.

Too often people conceive of sex as a performance skill like race car driving or swimming. However, sex is best conceptualized as a form of communication within a relationship. Indeed, caring couples with good communication skills can usually survive most sexual problems, but uncaring couples with poor communication skills often do not have lasting relationships even if their sexual experiences are adequate or even good.

Although the majority of us manage to develop a mature sexuality, for most individuals there are some periods of vulnerability and confusion along the way. Many individuals have an almost insatiable curiosity about sexuality. Some wonder and worry about their sexual attractiveness, their ability to satisfy their sexual partner, and whether they will experience the ultimate sexual fantasy. Often our worries about our sexuality are fueled by media stereotypes about sexual potency and superhuman sexual exploits.

Witelson, 1994) and an increased incidence of left-hand preference (McCormick, Witelson & Kingstone, 1990) in gay men and lesbians compared with heterosexual people. With regard to anatomical structures, LeVay (1991) found that an area of the hypothalamus that governs sexual behavior is twice as large (about the size of a grain of sand) in heterosexual males as in homosexual males. This area was found to be about the same size in homosexual males and heterosexual females.

An individual's sexual orientation—homosexual, heterosexual, or bisexual—is most likely determined by a combination of genetic, hormonal, cognitive, and environmental factors (Baldwin & Baldwin, 1998). Most experts on homosexuality believe that no one factor alone causes homosexuality and that the relative weight of each factor can vary from one individual to the next. In effect, no one knows exactly why some individuals are homosexual. Scientists have a clearer picture of what does not cause homosexuality. For example, children raised by gay or lesbian parents or couples are no more likely to be homosexual than are children raised by heterosexual parents (Patterson, 1995). There is also no evidence that male homosexuality is caused by a dominant mother or a weak father, or that female homosexuality is caused by girls choosing male role models.

How can gays and lesbians adapt to a world in which they are a minority? According to psychologist Laura Brown (1989), gays and lesbians experience life as a minority in a dominant, majority culture. For lesbian women and gay men, developing a *bicultural identity* creates new ways of defining themselves. Brown believes that gays and lesbians adapt best when they don't define themselves in polarities, such as trying to live in an encapsulated gay or lesbian world completely divorced from the majority culture or completely accepting the dictates and bias of the majority culture. Balancing the demands of the two cultures—the minority gay/lesbian

An individual's sexual preference—heterosexual, homosexual, or bisexual—is most likely determined by a mix of genetic, hormonal, cognitive, and environmental factors.

SUMMARY TABLE 11.3
Sexuality

Concept	Processes/ Related Ideas	Characteristics/Discussions
Biological, Cognitive, Sensory/ Perceptual, and Cultural Factors	Biological Factors	Sex hormones are powerful chemicals that are controlled by the master gland in the brain, the pituitary. The two main classes of sex hormones are estrogens, the most important of which is estradiol, and androgens, the most important of which is testosterone. As we move from the lower to the higher animals, the role of hormones becomes less clear, especially in females.
	Cognitive and Sensory/ Perceptual Factors	Humans' thoughts and images are involved in their sexual lives. So are sensory/ perceptual factors. Females tend to be more sexually aroused by touch, males by visual stimulation. Pheromones are involved in sexual attraction in many nonhuman animals, but their role in humans has not been documented. Many "aphrodisiacs" have been proposed as sexual stimulants, but there is no clear evidence that anything we eat, drink, or inject has aphrodisiac qualities.
	Cultural Factors	Sexual motivation is also influenced by cultural factors, and sexual values vary extensively across cultures. Sexual scripts, such as traditional religious and romantic, influence sexual behavior.
The Human Sexual Response Cycle	Its Nature	Masters and Johnson mapped out the human sexual response cycle, which consists of four phases: excitement, plateau, orgasm, and resolution.
Psychosexual Dysfunctions	Their Nature	Psychosexual dysfunctions involve impairments in the sexual response cycle. Significant advancements in treating these dysfunctions have occurred in recent years.
Heterosexuality and Homosexuality	Heterosexual Attitudes and Behavior	Describing sexual practices in North America always has been challenging. The more recent Canadian and American work was a major improvement over the earlier survey by Kinsey. In that work, North Americans' sexual lives were portrayed as more conservative than in the earlier surveys.
	Homosexual Attitudes and Behavior	It is generally accepted to view sexual orientation along a continuum from exclusively heterosexual to exclusively homosexual. An individual's sexual orientation is likely the result of a combination of genetic, hormonal, cognitive, and environmental factors.

culture and the majority heterosexual culture—can often lead to more effective coping for homosexuals, says Brown.

At this point we have discussed a number of ideas about sexuality. An overview of these ideas is presented in summary table 11.3. Next, we continue our journey through different topics in motivation as we explore the motivation to be competent and to achieve.

Achievement Motivation

In our discussion of sexual motivation, we described biological, cognitive, and social aspects of the motivation. With achievement, we move away from biological factors and focus more on cognitive and social factors. Some people are highly motivated to succeed and spend considerable effort striving to excel. Others are not as motivated to succeed and don't work as hard to achieve. These two types of individuals vary in their achievement motivation.

Motivation and Learning

Need for Achievement

Need for achievement *is the desire to accomplish something, to reach a standard of excellence, and to expend effort to excel.* Borrowing from Henry Murray's (1938) theory and measurement of personality, psychologist David McClelland (1955) assessed achievement by showing individuals ambiguous pictures that were likely to stimulate achievement-related responses. The individuals were asked to tell a story about the picture, and their comments were scored according to how strongly they reflected achievement. Researchers have found that individuals whose stories reflect high achievement motivation have a stronger hope for success than fear of failure, are moderate rather than high or low risk takers, and persist with effort when tasks become difficult (Atkinson & Raynor, 1974).

McClelland (1978) also wondered if you could boost achievement behavior by increasing achievement motivation. To find out, he trained the businessmen in a village in India to become more achievement oriented, encouraging them to increase their hope for success, reduce their fear of failure, take moderate risks, and persist with a great deal of effort when tasks become difficult. Compared with village businessmen in a nearby town, the village businessmen who were trained by McClelland started more new businesses and employed more new people in the two years after the training.

Person/Cognitive Factors

In chapter 1, we explored Albert Bandura's social cognitive theory ◀|||| P. 8. Recall that Bandura believes that person/cognitive factors are an important aspect of understanding behavior. Let's examine what some of these person/cognitive factors are in understanding achievement, beginning with intrinsic/extrinsic motivation.

Intrinsic and Extrinsic Motivation   Earlier in this chapter we mentioned that whether motivation is internal (intrinsic) or external (extrinsic) is a key aspect of understanding motivation. This is especially true in the area of achievement.

Almost every boss, parent, or teacher has wondered whether or not to offer a reward to someone who does well (extrinsic motivation), or whether to let the individual's internal, self-determined motivation operate (intrinsic motivation). If someone is producing shoddy work, seems bored, or has a negative attitude, offering incentives may improve his or her motivation. But there are times when external rewards can diminish achievement motivation. One study showed that,

of students who already had a strong interest in art, those who did not expect a reward spent more time drawing than did their counterparts who knew they would be rewarded for drawing (Lepper, Greene, & Nisbett, 1973). According to University of Alberta psychologist Michael Enzle, a wide variety of events, such as deadlines, surveillance (Enzle & Anderson, 1993), and coercive rewards (Enzle, Roggeveen & Look, 1991) can reduce enjoyment of work, play and study.

Many psychologists believe intrinsic motivation has more positive outcomes than extrinsic motivation. They argue that intrinsic motivation is more likely to produce competent behavior and mastery motivation (Deci & Ryan, 1994; Harackiewicz, 1998). Especially important is the view that self-determination, which is intrinsic, produces a sense of personal control. Feehan & Enzle (1991) have shown that subjective control, even when it is illusory, acts to protect intrinsic motivation. The problem, then, with using a reward as an incentive is that individuals may perceive that the reward is what caused their achievement behavior rather than their own motivation to be competent.

Next, our attention shifts to attribution. As you read about attribution, you will see that intrinsic and extrinsic motivation are often one set of causes that individuals look to as they attempt to explain their behavior.

Intrinsic Motivation

Attribution   **Attribution theory** *states that individuals are motivated to discover the underlying causes of behavior as part of the effort to make sense out of the behavior.* In a way, attribution theorists say, people are like intuitive scientists, seeking the cause behind what happens.

The reasons individuals behave the way they do can be classified in a number of ways, but one basic distinction stands out above all others—the distinction between internal causes, such as the actor's personality traits or motives, and external causes, which are environmental, situational factors such as rewards or task difficulty (Heider, 1958). If university students do not do well on a test, do they attribute it to the teacher's plotting against them and making the test too difficult (external cause) or to their not studying hard enough (internal cause)? The answer to such a question influences how people feel about themselves. If students believe that their performance is the teacher's fault, they will not feel as badly as when they do poorly because they do not spend enough time studying.

An extremely important aspect of internal causes for achievement is *effort*. Unlike many causes of success, effort is under a person's control and amenable to change. The importance of effort in achievement is recognized even by children. In one study, third- to sixth-grade students felt that effort was the most effective strategy for good school performance (Skinner, Wellborn, & Connell, 1990).

Goal-Setting, Planning, and Monitoring   Goal-setting, planning, and self-monitoring are critical aspects of achievement. Goal-setting and planning often work in concert. Goals help individuals to reach their dreams, increase their self-discipline, and maintain interest.

Currently, there is considerable interest in studying people's self-generated goals (Schultheiss & Brunstein, 1999). Some examples of these goals are "personal projects," "life tasks," and "personal strivings." Personal projects can range from trivial pursuits (such as letting a bad haircut grow out) to life goals (such as becoming a good parent). Life tasks are problems individuals are currently working on. They usually focus on normal life transitions such as going to university, getting married, and entering an occupation. Many university students say that their life tasks revolve around academic achievement and social concerns (Cantor & Langston, 1989). Personal strivings represent what a person is typically trying to do. For example, someone might say that she typically tries to do well in school.

Researchers have found that individuals' achievement improves when they set goals that are specific, proximal, and challenging (Bandura, 1997; Schunk, 1996).

Motivating Students

THINKING ABOUT PSYCHOLOGY AND LIFE

How Goal-Directed Are You?

To EVALUATE HOW goal-directed you are, consider how much each of the following statements is like you or not like you:

- I set long-term and short-term goals.
- I set challenging goals that are neither too easy nor beyond my reach.
- I am good at managing my time and setting priorities to make sure I get the most important things done.
- I regularly make "to do" lists and successfully get most of these items done.
- I set deadlines and consistently meet them.
- I regularly monitor how well I'm progressing toward my goals and make changes in my behavior if necessary.
- When I am under pressure, I still plan my days and weeks in a clear, logical manner.
- I set task-involved, mastery goals rather than ego-involved or work-involved goals.

If most of your answers were that these descriptions characterize you then you are likely a goal-directed individual. If these statements do not characterize you, consider ways that you can become more goal-directed.

A fuzzy, nonspecific goal is "I want to be successful." A more concrete, specific goal is "I want to have a 3.5 average at the end of the semester." You can set long-term (distal) and short-term (proximal) goals. It is okay to set long-term goals, such as "I want to be a clinical psychologist," but if you do, make sure that you also create short-term goals, which are steps along the way. "Getting an A on the next psychology test" is an example of a short-term, proximal goal. So is "Doing all of my studying for this class by 4 P.M. Sunday." David McNally (1994), author of *Even Eagles Need a Push*, advises that when individuals set goals and plan, they should remind themselves to live their lives one day at a time. Make your commitments in bite-size chunks. A house is built one brick at a time, a cathedral one stone at a time. The artist paints one stroke at a time. You should also work in small increments.

Another good strategy is to set challenging goals. A challenging goal is a commitment to self-improvement. Strong interest and involvement in activities are sparked by challenges. Goals that are easy to reach generate little interest or effort. However, unrealistically high goals can bring failure and diminish self-confidence.

Achievement motivation researcher John Nicholls and his colleagues (Nicholls, 1979; Nicholls & others, 1990) distinguish among ego-involved goals, task-involved goals, and work-avoidant goals. Individuals with ego-involved goals strive to maximize favorable evaluations and minimize unfavorable ones. Thus, ego-involved individuals focus on how smart they will look and their ability to outperform others. By contrast, individuals who have task-involved goals focus more on mastering tasks. They concentrate on how well they can do the task and what they can learn. Individuals with work-avoidant goals try to exert as little effort as possible on a task. A good achievement strategy is to develop task-involved, mastery goals rather than ego-involved or work-avoidant goals.

Planning how to reach a goal and monitoring progress toward the goal are critical aspects of achievement (Eccles, Wigfield, & Schiefele, 1998). Researchers have found that high-achieving individuals monitor their own learning and systematically evaluate their progress toward their goal more than low-achieving individuals do (Zimmerman, Bonner, & Kovach, 1996).

Cultural, Ethnic, and Socioeconomic Variations in Achievement

People in North America are often more achievement-oriented than people in many other countries. One study of 104 societies revealed that parents in nonindustrialized countries placed a lower value on their children's achievement and independence and a higher value on obedience and cooperation than did the parents in industrialized countries (Barry, Child, & Bacon, 1959). In comparisons between Anglo-American children and Mexican and Latino children, the Anglo-American children were more competitive and less cooperative. For example, one study found that Anglo-American children were more likely to keep other children from gaining when they could not realize those gains themselves (Kagan & Madsen, 1972). Another study showed that Mexican children were more family-oriented whereas Anglo-American children tend to be more concerned about themselves

UCLA psychologist Sandra Graham is shown here talking with a group of young boys about motivation. Dr. Graham has conducted important research showing that middle-class African American children—like their White counterparts—have high achievement expectations and attribute their failures to lack of effort rather than to lack of luck.

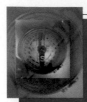

EXPLORATIONS IN PSYCHOLOGY
Comparing Math Achievement in Asian and North American Cultures

THE STIMULATION FOR Harold Stevenson's (1992, 1995, 1997) research is anchored in the poor performance of North American students on tests of mathematics and science in comparison to students in other countries, especially in Asia (Educational Testing Service, 1992; Atkin & Black, 1997). In one study, U.S. grade 8 and 12 students were below the overall national average of 20 countries in math problem solving, geometry, algebra, and calculus. Canadian students performed slightly better, although differences could be found from topic to topic (McKnight & others, 1987). In grade 8, Japanese students had the highest average scores of students, and in grade 12, Chinese students in Hong Kong had the highest scores, followed by Japanese students.

The Third International Mathematics and Science Study (TIMSS) is the largest and most ambitious international study of student achievement ever conducted. In 1994-95, it was conducted at five grade levels in more than 40 countries. Mathematics achievement data are available for the third (24 countries), fourth (25 countries), seventh (41 countries) and eighth (43 countries) grades, and the final year of secondary school (21 countries). The four top-ranked countries in grades 3, 4, 7 and 8 were Singapore, Korea, Japan, and Hong Kong. Canada's ranking was 13, 12, 18 and 19 respectively while that of the U.S. was 11, 10, 28 and 26. In the final year of secondary school, Canada was 9th while the U.S. was 19th but data for the Asian countries were not even available so these rankings would undoubtedly be considerably lower. Go to the Resources section at the end of the chapter to find a Web address for TIMSS so you can examine these statistics for yourself.

To learn more about the reasons for these large cross-cultural differences, Stevenson and his colleagues spent thousands of hours observing in classrooms, as well as interviewing and surveying teachers, students, and parents. Asian teachers spent more of their time teaching math than North American teachers did. For example, more than one-fourth of total classroom time in the first grade was spent on math instruction in Japan, compared with only one-tenth of the time in U.S. first-grade classrooms. Also, Asian students were in school an average of 240 days a year compared to 178 days in the U.S.

In addition to the substantially greater time spent on math instruction in Asian schools than in North American schools, differences in Asian and U.S. parents were found. U.S. parents had much lower expectations for their children's education and achievement than the Asian parents did. Also, U.S. parents were more likely to believe that their children's math achievement was due to innate ability, whereas Asian parents were more likely to say that their children's math achievement was the consequence of effort and training. Asian students were more likely than U.S. students to do math homework, and Asian parents were far more likely to help their children with their math homework than U.S. parents were (Chen & Stevenson, 1989).

In another cross-cultural comparison of math education, videotapes of eighth-grade teachers' instruction in the United States, Japan, and Germany were analyzed (Stigler & Hiebert, 1997). Differences among the countries included these: (1) Japanese students spent less time solving routine math problems and more time inventing, analyzing, and proving than U.S. or German students; (2) Japanese teachers engaged in more direct lecturing than American or German teachers; and (3) Japanese teachers were more likely to emphasize math thinking, whereas U.S. and German teachers were more likely to stress math skills (solving a specific problem or using a specific formula).

An important conclusion from these cross-cultural studies is that learning and achievement take time. The more time students spend on learning tasks, the more likely it is that they will learn the material and achieve high standards.

Asian students score considerably higher than North American students on math achievement tests. What are some possible explanations for these findings?

SUMMARY TABLE 11.4
Achievement

Concept	Processes/ Related Ideas	Characteristics/Discussions
Need for Achievement	Its Nature	Early interest focused on the need for achievement, defined as the desire to accomplish something, to reach a standard of excellence, and to expend an effort to excel.
Person/Cognitive Factors	Intrinsic/Extrinsic Motivation	Motivation can be described as intrinsic (internal) or extrinsic (external). Many psychologists believe it is important to emphasize intrinsic motivation, although some successful individuals are both intrinsically and extrinsically motivated.
	Attribution	Attribution theory states that people are motivated to discover the underlying causes of behavior as part of their effort to make sense out of the behavior. The main emphasis in attribution theory has focused on internal causes, especially effort, or external causes.
	Goal Setting, Planning, and Monitoring	These are critical aspects of achievement. Self-generated goals focus on such areas as personal projects, life tasks, and personal strivings. High achievers often set specific, proximal, and challenging goals. They are also likely to set task-involved, mastery goals rather than ego-involved or work-avoidant goals.
Cultural, Ethnic, and Socioeconomic Variations	Their Nature	Individuals in the United States are more achievement oriented than individuals in many other countries. A special concern is the achievement of individuals from various ethnic minority groups. Too often differences have become interpreted as "deficits" by middle-income, White standards. When researchers study both ethnicity and socioeconomic status in the same study, socioeconomic status is often a much better achievement predictor. Middle-income individuals fare better than their low-income counterparts in many achievement settings.

(Holtzmann, 1982). To read further about cross-cultural variations in achievement, see Explorations in Psychology.

Until recently, researchers studying achievement focused mainly on White males, and when achievement in ethnic minority groups has been studied, the cultural differences have too often been viewed against standards of achievements for White males. As a result, many researchers have reached the conclusion that ethnic minorities are somehow deficient when it comes to achievement (Gibbs & Huang, 1989). In the case of Canada's aboriginal peoples, for example, their negative attitudes toward mainstream notions of achievement and schooling can be traced directly to the horrendous disaster of early attempts to assimilate Canadian aboriginal populations through the residential school system (Barman, 1996).

In addition, most studies on ethnic minorities do not take into account *socioeconomic status* (SES), which is determined by a combination of occupation, education, and income. When ethnicity and socioeconomic status are taken into account in the same study, socioeconomic status tends to be a better predictor of achievement than ethnicity. Sandra Graham (1986) has found that middle-SES African American children, like their middle-SES White counterparts, have high expectations for their own achievement and understand that failure is often due to lack of effort rather than to luck.

At this point we have studied a number of ideas about achievement. An overview of these ideas is presented in summary table 11.4. Next, we continue our exploration of motivation and emotion, turning to the topic of emotion.

Emotion

Motivation and emotion are closely linked. Think about sex, which is often associated with joy; about aggression, which is usually associated with anger; and about achievement, which is associated with pride, joy, and anxiety. The terms *motivation* and *emotion* both come from the Latin word *movere*, which means "to move." Both motivation and emotion spur us into action.

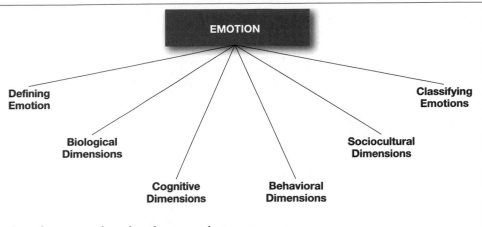

Just as with motivation, there are different kinds and intensities of emotions (Brehm, 1999). Not only can a person be motivated to eat rather than have sex, but be more or less hungry, or more or less interested in having sex. Similarly, a person can be happy or angry, and can be fairly happy or ecstatic, annoyed or fuming.

Defining Emotion

Defining emotion is difficult because it is not easy to tell when a person is in an emotional state. Are you in an emotional state when your heart beats fast, your palms sweat, and your stomach churns? Or are you in an emotional state when you think about how much you are in love with someone? Or when you smile or grimace? The body, the mind, and the face play important roles in understanding emotion. Psychologists debate how critical each is in determining whether we are in an emotional state. For our purposes, we will define **emotion** *as feeling, or affect, that can involve physiological arousal (a fast heartbeat, for example), conscious experience (thinking about being in love with someone, for example), and behavioral expression (a smile or grimace, for example).* Psychologists debate which of these components is the most important aspect of emotion and how they mix to produce emotional experiences (Cacioppo & Gardner, 1999).

Exploring Emotion

Emotion Research

The Autonomic Nervous System

Biological Dimensions

To further explore emotion, let's begin by examining the biological dimensions of emotion with a special focus on the first component of emotion we described: arousal.

Arousal   As you drive down a highway, the fog thickens. Suddenly you see a pile of cars in front of you. Your mind temporarily freezes, your muscles tighten, your stomach becomes queasy, and your heart feels like it is going to pound out of your chest. You immediately slam on the brakes and try to veer away from the pile of cars. Tires screech, windshield glass flies, and metal smashes. Then all is quiet. After a few short seconds you realize you are alive. You find that you can walk out of the car. Your fear turns to joy, as you sense your luck in not being hurt. In a couple of seconds, the joy turns to anger. You loudly ask who caused the accident.

The Autonomic Nervous System   As you moved through the emotions of fear, joy, and anger, your body changed. Recall from chapter 3, "Biological Foundations and Neuroscience," that the **autonomic nervous system (ANS)** *takes messages to and from the body's internal organs, monitoring such processes as breathing, heart rate, and digestion* ◀▥ P. 72. *The ANS is divided into the sympathetic (SNS) and parasympathetic (PNS) nervous systems* (see figure 11.9).

The **sympathetic nervous system** *is involved in the body's arousal being responsible for quick responses to a stressor, which is sometimes referred to as the fight-or-flight response.* The SNS immediately causes an increase in blood pressure, a faster heart

Sympathetic Nervous System		Parasympathetic Nervous System
Increases	Blood Flow to Brain	Decreases
Dilates	Pupils of Eyes	Constricts
Faster	Breathing Rate	Slower
Faster	Heartbeat	Slower
Increases	Skin Perspiration	Decreases
Decreases	Digestive Activity	Increases
Increases; stress hormones released	Adrenal Gland Activity	Decreases; stress hormones inhibited

Figure 11.9
Autonomic Nervous System

Polygraph Skepticism

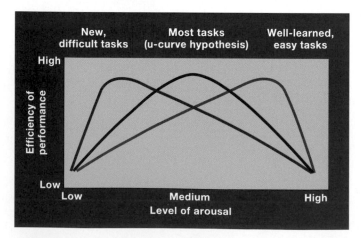

Figure 11.10
Arousal and Performance

The Yerkes-Dodson law states that optimal performance occurs under moderate arousal. However, for new or difficult tasks, low arousal may be best; for well-learned, easy tasks, high arousal can facilitate performance.

rate, more rapid breathing for greater oxygen intake, and more efficient blood flow to the brain and major muscle groups. All of these changes prepare us for action. At the same time the body stops digesting food, because this is not necessary for immediate action (which could explain why just before an exam, students are usually not hungry).

The **parasympathetic nervous system** *calms the body. Whereas the sympathetic nervous system prepares the individual for fighting or running away, the parasympathetic system promotes relaxation and healing.* When the PNS is activated, heart rate and blood pressure drop, stomach activity and food digestion increase, and breathing slows.

The sympathetic and parasympathetic nervous systems are important in understanding people's emotions. Some emotions are more activating than others. For example, when we are angry, our body becomes prepared for fighting and fleeing. Not surprisingly, anger is associated with elevated SNS activity such as heightened blood pressure and heart rate. Similarly, states of happiness and contentment are generally associated with lower SNS activation.

You have been asked to think about your emotional states in the face of an automobile crash and a university exam. Now put yourself in the situation of lying to someone. Because body changes predictably accompany emotional states, it was reasoned that a machine might be able to determine if a person is lying. The **polygraph** *is a machine used by examiners to try to determine if someone is lying; it monitors changes in the body— heart rate, breathing, and electrodermal response (an index detecting skin resistance to passage of a weak electric current)— thought to be influenced by emotional states.* To read further about the polygraph, see Explorations in Psychology.

Arousal and Performance   Early in this century, two psychologists described the role of arousal in performance. What is now known as the **Yerkes-Dodson law** *states that performance is best under conditions of moderate rather than low or high arousal.* At the low end of arousal you might be too lethargic to perform tasks well; at the high end you may not be able to concentrate. Think about how aroused you were the last time you took a test. If your arousal was too high, your performance probably suffered. If it was too low, you may not have worked fast enough to finish the test. Also think about performance in sports. Being too aroused usually harms athletes' performance. For example, a thumping heart and rapid breathing have been present on many golfers' missed putts and curlers' failed draw attempts. However, if these athletes' arousal is too low they may not concentrate well on the task at hand.

Moderate arousal often serves us best in tackling life's tasks, but there are times when low or high arousal produces optimal performance. For well-learned or simple tasks (signing your name, pushing a button on request), optimal arousal can be quite high. By contrast, when learning a task or doing something complex (such as solving an algebraic equation), much lower arousal is preferred. Figure 11.10 projects how arousal might influence easy, moderate, and difficult tasks. As tasks become more difficult, the ability to be alert and attentive, but relaxed, is critical to optimal performance.

EXPLORATIONS IN PSYCHOLOGY
Evaluating Lie Detectors

IN A TYPICAL POLYGRAPH TEST, a person is asked a number of neutral and key questions. If the person's heart rate, breathing, and electrodermal response increase substantially when the key questions are asked, the person is assumed to be lying. The polygraph has been widely used, especially in business, to screen new employees for honesty and to reveal employee theft.

However, the polygraph's effectiveness has been questioned (Saxe, Dougherty, & Cross, 1985). Heart rate and breathing can increase for reasons other than lying. Experts argue that the polygraph errs nearly 50 percent of the time, especially because it cannot distinguish between such feelings as anxiety and guilt (Iacono & Lykken, 1997). In other words, no unique physiological response to deception has been revealed (Lykken, 1987). Further, there are simple things people can do to avoid being detected while lying, such as tensing your muscles, biting your tongue and shifting your position in the chair. Although on occasion the mere presence of the polygraph and the subject's belief that the polygraph is accurate at detecting deception triggers confession, in too many cases the polygraph has been misused and misrepresented. These findings led to a 1987 Supreme Court of Canada decision rejecting polygraph testing as admissible evidence.

Some psychologists still defend the polygraph's use, saying that polygraph results are about as sound as other, admissible forms of evidence such as hair fiber analysis (Honts, 1998). The majority of psychologists, though, argue against the polygraph's use because of its inability to tell who's lying and who isn't (Iacono & Lykken, 1997; Saxe, 1998).

Recently, Michael Bradley of the University of New Brunswick Saint John has explored more sophisticated polygraphy methods such as the Guilty Knowledge Test (Bradley & Rettinger, 1992). Certain details of a crime may be known only by the investigating officers and the criminal. For example, if the criminal had stolen $500 in a yellow envelope from the bottom drawer of a desk the following sets of questions could be created. 1: You stole: $700, $400, $800, $500, $200? 2: The envelope with the money was: blue, red, yellow, brown, white? 3: The envelope with the money was in: a safe, a filing cabinet, a cupboard, a desk, a briefcase? The response to the first item in a new set is usually large so it is never the crime-relevant item. Excluding the first item, the responses to the other four items are compared. The criminal, because he or she knows the crime details, should have large physiological responses to each of the correct details. Innocent suspects, unaware of the relevant details, can only have large responses to them at random. In probability terms, they have a one in four (or 25 percent) chance of showing their largest response to the correct detail in any one set. Since, however, the joint probability of having the largest response on all three items is the multiple of the individual set probabilities there is only a .25 times 3 (or .75 percent) chance of being falsely considered guilty. If more items are used in the test or the sets are repeated, the probability of mistakenly identifying innocent suspects becomes vanishingly small.

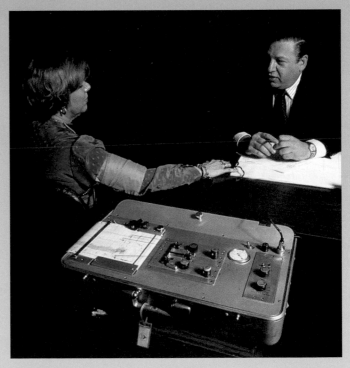

Examiners use a polygraph to tell if someone is lying; it monitors changes in the body believed to be influenced by emotional states. Controversy has swirled about the polygraph's use. Because of the polygraph's inaccuracy, in 1987 the Supreme Court of Canada rejected the use of polygraph testing as admissible evidence under Canadian law.

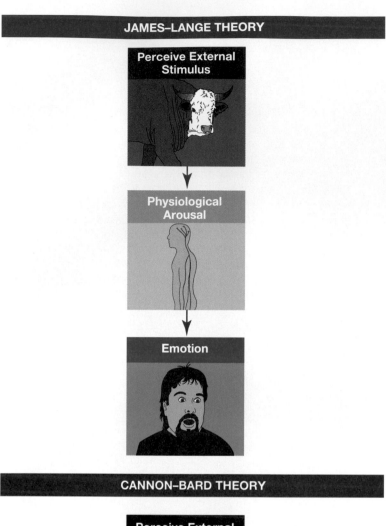

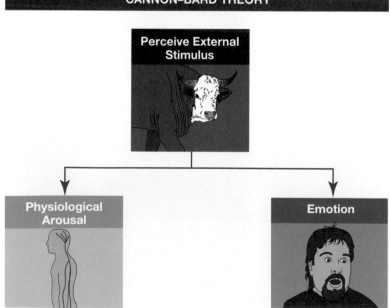

$\mathcal{F}$igure 11.11
James-Lange and Cannon-Bard Theories

James-Lange and Cannon-Bard Theories

Psychologists have developed a number of theories about the role of arousal in emotion. Imagine that you and your date are enjoying a picnic in the country. As you prepare to eat, a bull runs across the field toward you. Why are you afraid? Two well-known theories of emotion that involve physiological processes provide answers to this question.

Common sense tells you that you are trembling and running away from the bull because you are afraid. But William James (1890/1950) and Carl Lange (1922) said emotion works in the opposite way. The **James-Lange theory** *suggests that emotion results from physiological states triggered by stimuli in the environment. Emotion occurs after physiological reactions.* You see the bull scratching his hoof, and you begin to run away. The aroused body then sends sensory messages to the brain, at which point emotion is perceived. According to this theory, you do not run away because you are afraid, rather you are afraid because you are running away. In other words, you perceive a stimulus in the environment, your body responds, and you interpret the body's reaction as emotion. In one of James' own examples, you perceive you have lost your fortune, you cry, and then interpret the crying as feeling sad. This goes against the commonsense sequence of losing your fortune, feeling sorry, and then crying.

Walter Cannon (1927) objected to the James-Lange theory. To understand his objection, imagine the bull and the picnic once again. Seeing the bull scratching its hooves causes the hypothalamus of your brain to do two things simultaneously: first, it stimulates your autonomic nervous system to produce the physiological changes involved in emotion (increased heart rate, rapid breathing); second, it sends messages to your cerebral cortex where the experience of emotion is perceived. Philip Bard (1934) supported this theory, and so the theory became known as the **Cannon-Bard theory,** *the theory that emotion and physiological reactions occur simultaneously. In the Cannon-Bard theory, the body plays a less important role than in the James-Lange theory.* Figure 11.11 shows how the James-Lange and Cannon-Bard theories differ.

Neural Circuits and Neurotransmitters

Going beyond the early theories of emotion, contemporary emotion researchers are interested in more precisely charting the neural circuitry of emotions, especially specific emotions such as fear, and discovering the role of neurotransmitters in emotion.

In terms of neural circuits, in chapter 3, "Biological Foundations and Neuroscience," we described the amygdala as an almond-shaped part of the limbic system at the base of each of the brain's temporal lobes (see figure 11.12) ◄IIII P. 81. It houses circuits that color our experience with emotion. The amygdala not only receives simple signals (such as loud noises) from the brain's lower stations but also abstract, complex information from the brain's highest levels in the cerebral cortex. The amygdala in turn sends signals to many other parts of the brain, including the decision-making circuitry of the cerebral cortex's frontal lobes (Pinker, 1997).

The neural pathway of one emotion—fear—has been mapped well (Izard, Schultz, & Levinson, 1998). When an organism perceives an external stimulus (such as the raging bull), the neural message is transmitted to the thalamus (see figure 11.12). From there, the information moves along one of two pathways: (1) to the cerebral cortex where more extensive information processing takes place or (2) directly to the amygdala. The direct route from the thalamus to the amygdala does not require higher cortical processing. The direct route is rapid, automatic, and unconscious.

Thus, the amygdala appears to be an important structure in the neural circuitry of emotion through its many connections with other areas of the brain.

In addition to charting the main brain structures involved in neural pathways of emotions, researchers are also intrigued by the roles that neurotransmitters play in these pathways. Endorphins and dopamine might be involved in positive emotions such as happiness, and norepinephrine's function might be in regulating arousal (Panskepp, 1993; White & Milner, 1992) ◀▥ P. 76.

Much of what we have said about emotion has focused on its physiological basis. While physiological factors play important roles in emotion, cognitive processes are at work as well.

Cognitive Dimensions

Does emotion depend on the tides of the mind? Are we happy only when we think we are happy? Cognitive theories of emotion share an important point: emotion always has a cognitive component (Cornelius, 1996). Thinking is said to be responsible for feelings of love and hate, joy and sadness. While giving cognitive processes the main credit for emotion, the cognitive theories also recognize the role of the brain and body in emotion. That is, the hypothalamus and autonomic nervous system make connections with the peripheral areas of the body when emotion is experienced. According to cognitive theorists, body and thought are involved in emotion.

The Two-Factor Theory of Emotion
Stanley Schachter and Jerome Singer (1962) developed a theory of emotion that gave cognition a stronger role in emotion. The **two-factor theory of emotion** *is Schachter and Singer's theory that emotion is determined by two main factors: physiological arousal and cognitive labeling* (see figure 11.13). They argue that we look to the external world for an explanation of why we are aroused. We interpret the external cues present and label the emotion. For example, if you feel good after someone has made a pleasant comment to you, you might label the emotion "happy." If you feel bad after you have done something wrong, you may label the feeling "guilty."

To test their theory of emotion, Schachter and Singer (1962) injected subjects with epinephrine, a drug that produces high arousal. After volunteer subjects were given the drug, they observed someone else behave in either a euphoric way (shooting papers at a wastebasket) or an angry way (stomping out of the room). As predicted, the euphoric and angry behavior influenced the subjects' cognitive interpretation of their own arousal. When they were with a happy person, they rated themselves as happy; when they were with an angry person, they said they were angry. But this effect was found only when the subjects were not told about the true effects of the injection. When subjects were told that the drug would increase their heart

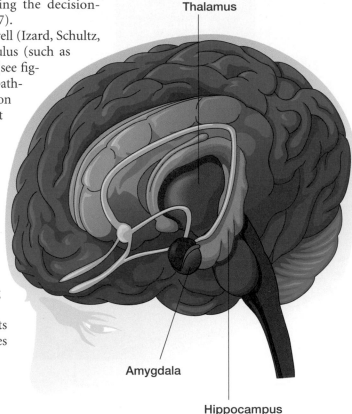

Thalamus

Amygdala

Hippocampus

𝒻igure 11.12
Important Structures in the Brain's Emotion Circuitry

The amygdala plays an important role in emotion through its many connections to other areas of the brain. For example, it has reciprocal connections with the cerebral cortex's frontal lobes, which are involved in abstract, complex information processing. In the specific emotion of fear, information is processed in the thalamus and then is either transmitted to the cerebral cortex and on to the amygdala or is directly transmitted to the amygdala.

The Emotional Brain

Psychophysiology and Emotion

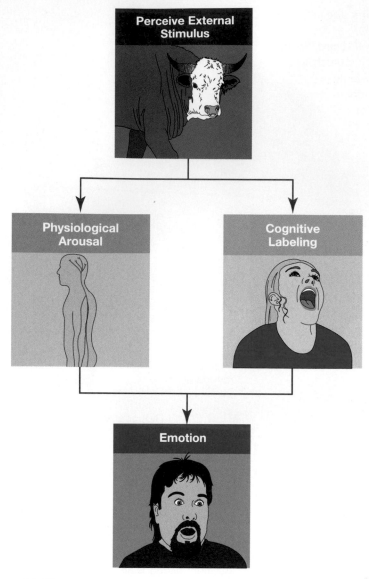

*F*igure 11.13
Schachter and Singer's Two-Factor Theory of
Emotion

**International Society for
Research on Emotions**

rate and make them jittery, they said the reason for their own arousal was the drug, not the other person's behavior.

Psychologists have had difficulty replicating the Schachter and Singer experiment but, in general, research supports the belief that misinterpreted arousal intensifies emotional experiences (Leventhal & Tomarken, 1986). An intriguing study substantiates this belief. It went like this: An attractive woman approached men while they were crossing the Capilano River Bridge in British Columbia. Only those without a female companion were approached. The woman asked the men to make up a brief story for a project she was doing on creativity (Dutton & Aron, 1974). By the way, the Capilano River Bridge sways precariously more than 200 feet above rapids and rocks (see figure 11.14). The female interviewer made the same request of other men crossing a much safer, lower bridge. The men on the Capilano River Bridge told more sexually oriented stories and rated the female interviewer more attractive than did men on the lower, less frightening bridge.

The Primacy Debate: Cognition or Emotion?

Richard Lazarus (1991) believes cognitive activity is a precondition for emotion. He says we cognitively appraise ourselves and our social circumstances. These appraisals, which include values, goals, commitments, beliefs, and expectations, determine our emotions. People may feel happy because they have a deep religious commitment, angry because they did not get the raise they anticipated, or fearful because they expect to fail an exam.

Robert Zajonc (1984) disagrees with Lazarus. Emotions are primary, he says, and our thoughts are a result of them. Who is right? Both are likely correct. Lazarus refers mainly to a cluster of related events that occur over a period of time, whereas Zajonc describes single events or a simple preference for one stimulus over another. Lazarus speaks about love over the course of months and years, a sense of value to the community, and plans for retirement; Zajonc talks about a car accident, an encounter with a snake, and liking ice cream better than spinach. Some of our emotional reactions are virtually instantaneous and probably don't involve cognitive appraisal, such as a shriek on detecting a snake. Other emotional circumstances, especially those that occur over a long period of time, such as a depressed mood or anger toward a friend, are more likely to involve cognitive appraisal.

Behavioral Dimensions

Remember that our definition of emotion includes not only physiological and cognitive components, but also a behavioral component. The behavioral component can be verbal or nonverbal. Verbally, a person might show their love for someone by professing it verbally or display their anger by saying some nasty things. Nonverbally, a person might smile, frown, show a fearful expression, droop their head, or slump their posture.

The most interest in the behavioral dimension of emotion has focused on the nonverbal behavior of facial expressions (Russell & Fernandez-Dols, in press).

Emotion researchers have been intrigued by people's ability to detect the emotion a person is experiencing on the basis of his or her facial expression. In a typical research study, individuals will be shown photographs like those in figure 11.15. In the research of Paul Ekman and his colleagues (Ekman & Friesen, 1984; Ekman &

*F*igure 11.14
Capilano River Bridge Experiment: Misinterpreted Arousal Intensifies Emotional Experiences

The precarious Capilano River Bridge in British Columbia is shown at left; the experiment is shown in progress at right. An attractive woman approached men while they were crossing the 200-foot-high bridge; she asked them to make up a story to help her out. She also made the same request on a lower, much safer bridge. The men on the Capilano River Bridge told sexier stories, probably because they were aroused by the fear or excitement of being up so high on a swaying bridge. Apparently they interpreted their arousal as sexual attraction for the female interviewer.

O'Sullivan, 1991), participants are usually able to identify these six basic emotions: happiness, anger, sadness, surprise, disgust, and fear.

Might our facial expressions not only reflect our emotions but also influence them? The **facial feedback hypothesis** *states that facial expressions can influence emotions as well as reflect them. In this view, facial muscles send signals to the brain, which help individuals recognize the emotion they are experiencing.* For example, we feel happier when we smile and sadder when we frown.

Support for the facial feedback hypothesis was found in an experiment by Ekman and his colleagues (1983). In this study, professional actors moved their facial muscles in very precise ways, such as raising their eyebrows and pulling them together, raising their upper eyelids, and stretching their lips horizontally back to their ears (you might want to try this out yourself). They were asked to hold their expression for 10 seconds, during which time the researchers measured their heart rate and body temperature. When they moved facial muscles in the way we described, they showed a rise in heart rate and a steady body temperature, physiological reactions that characterize fear. When the actors made an angry expression with their face (eyes have a penetrating stare, brows are drawn together and downward, and lips are pressed together or opened and pushed forward), their heart rate and body temperature both increased. The concept involved in the facial feedback hypothesis might sound familiar. It provides support for the James-Lange theory of emotion we discussed earlier—namely, that emotional experiences can be generated by changes in and awareness of our own bodily states.

Emotion Research Resources

*F*igure 11.15
Recognizing Emotions in Facial Expressions

Before reading further, look at the six photographs and determine the emotion reflected in each of the six faces. They are: *(top row across)* happiness, anger, sadness; *(bottom row across)* surprise, disgust, fear.

Paul Ekman's Research
Cultural Contexts and Emotion

Are the facial expressions that are associated with different emotions largely innate or do they vary considerably across cultures?

Sociocultural Dimensions

Culture and the Expression of Emotion   In *The Expression of the Emotions in Man and Animals,* Charles Darwin (1872/1965) argued that the facial expressions of human beings are innate, not learned; are the same in all cultures around the world; and evolved from the emotions of animals. Darwin compared the similarity of human snarls of anger with the growls of dogs and the hisses of cats. He compared the giggling of chimpanzees when they are tickled under their arms with human laughter.

Today psychologists still believe that emotions, especially facial expressions of emotion, have strong biological ties. For example, children who have been blind from birth and have never observed the smile or frown on another person's face, still smile or frown in the same way that children with normal vision do.

How does culture influence the expression of emotions? What role does gender play in emotion?

The universality of facial expressions and the ability of people from different cultures to accurately label the emotion that lies behind the facial expression has been extensively researched. Psychologist Paul Ekman's (1980, 1996) careful observations reveal that our many faces of emotion do not vary significantly from one culture to another. For example, Ekman and his colleague photographed people expressing emotions such as happiness, fear, surprise, disgust, and grief. They found that when they showed the photographs to other people from the United States, Chile, Japan, Brazil, and Borneo (an Indonesian island in the western Pacific Ocean), each person tended to label the same faces with the same emotions (Ekman & Friesen, 1968). In another study the focus was on the way the Fore tribe, an isolated Stone Age culture in New Guinea, matched descriptions of emotions with facial expressions (Ekman & Friesen, 1971). Before Ekman's visit, most of the Fore had never seen a Caucasian face. Ekman showed them photographs of American faces expressing emotions such as fear, happiness, anger, and surprise. Then he read stories about people in emotional situations. The Fore were able to match the descriptions of emotions with the facial expressions in the photographs. The similarity of facial expressions of emotions by persons in New Guinea and the United States is shown in figure 11.16.

While facial expressions of basic emotions appear to be universal across cultures, display rules for emotion are not culturally universal. **Display rules** *are sociocultural standards that determine when, where, and how emotions should be expressed.* For example, while happiness is a universally expressed emotion, when, where, and how it is displayed may vary from one culture to another. The same is true for other emotions such as fear, sadness, and anger. For example, members of the Utku culture in Alaska discourage anger by cultivating acceptance and by dissociating themselves from any display of anger. If a trip is hampered by an unexpected snowstorm, the Utku do not become frustrated, but accept the presence of the snowstorm and build an igloo. Most of us would not act as mildly in the face of subzero weather and barriers to our travel.

$\mathscr{F}$igure 11.16
Emotional Expressions in North America and New Guinea

At left are two North Americans; on the right are two members of the Fore tribe in New Guinea. Notice the similarity in their expressions of disgust and happiness. Psychologists believe that the facial expression of emotion is virtually the same in all cultures.

In addition to facial expressions, emotions are also expressed in many other nonverbal signals of body movement, posture, and gesture (Russell, 1999). Some basic nonverbal signals appear to be universal indicators of certain emotions, just as facial expressions are. For example, when people are depressed it shows not only in their sad facial expression, but also in their slow body movement, downturned head, and slumped posture.

Many nonverbal signals of emotion, though, vary from one culture to another (Cohen & Borsoi, 1996). For example, male-to-male kissing is commonplace in some cultures, such as Yemen (in the Middle East), but uncommon in other cultures, such as Canada, with the exception of Quebec. And the "thumbs up" sign, which in most cultures means either everything is OK or the desire to hitch a ride, is an insult in Greece, similar to a raised third finger in North America.

Nonverbal Communication of Emotions

Gender Influences   Unless you've been isolated on a mountaintop away from people, television, magazines, and newspapers, you probably know the master stereotype about gender and emotion: She is emotional, he is not. This stereotype is a powerful and pervasive image in our culture (Shields, 1991).

Is this stereotype supported when researchers study the nature of emotional experiences in females and males? Researchers have found that females and males are often more alike in the way they experience emotion than the master stereotype would lead us to believe. Females and males often use the same facial expressions, adopt the same language, and describe their emotional experiences similarly when they keep diaries about their life experiences. Thus, the master stereotype that females are emotional and males are not is simply that—a stereotype. Thus, for many emotional experiences, researchers do not find differences between females and males—both sexes are equally likely to experience love, jealousy, anxiety in new social situations, be angry when they are insulted, grieve when close relationships end, and be embarrassed when they make mistakes in public (Tavris & Wade, 1984).

When we go beyond the master stereotype and consider some specific emotional experiences, the context in which emotion is displayed, and certain beliefs about emotion, gender does matter in understanding emotion (Brannon, 1999; Shields, 1991). Consider anger. Men are more likely to show anger toward strangers, especially other men, when they

In the Middle Eastern country of Yemen, male-to-male kissing is commonplace, but in Canada, with the exception of Quebec, it is very uncommon.

feel they have been challenged, and men are more likely to turn their anger into aggressive action than women are.

Differences between females and males regarding emotion are more likely to occur in contexts that highlight social roles and relationships. For example, females are more likely than males to give accounts of emotion that include interpersonal relationships. And females are more likely to express fear and sadness than males, especially when communicating with their friends and family.

Classifying Emotions

Emotions are complex and varied. For example, there are more than 200 words for emotions in the English language. One way of classifying emotions is the wheel model.

The Wheel Model   A number of psychologists have classified the emotions we experience by placing them on a wheel. One such model was proposed by Robert Plutchik (1980) (see figure 11.17). He believes emotions have four dimensions: (1) They are positive or negative, (2) they are primary or mixed, (3) many are polar opposites, and (4) they vary in intensity. Ecstasy and enthusiasm are positive emotions; grief and anger are negative emotions. For example, think about your ecstasy when you get an unexpected A on a test, or your enthusiasm about the ski trip this weekend—these are positive emotions. In contrast, think about negative emotions, such as your grief when someone close to you dies or your anger when someone verbally attacks you. Positive emotions enhance our self-esteem; negative emotions lower our self-esteem. Positive emotions improve our relationships with others; negative emotions depress the quality of those relationships.

Plutchik also believes that emotions are like colors. Every color of the spectrum can be produced by mixing the primary colors. Possibly some emotions are primary, and if mixed together, they combine to form all other emotions. Happiness, disgust, surprise, sadness, anger, and fear are candidates for primary emotions. For example, combining sadness and surprise gives disappointment. Jealousy is composed of love and anger. Plutchik developed the emotion wheel to show how primary emotions work. Mixtures of primary emotions adjacent to each other combine to produce other emotions. Some emotions are opposites—love and remorse, optimism and disappointment.

To illustrate how positive emotions are involved in our lives, we will explore the nature of happiness. Then, to illustrate negative emotions in our lives, we will examine anger.

A Positive Emotion: Happiness   It was not until 1973 that *Psychological Abstracts,* the major source of psychological research summaries, included *happiness* as an index term. The recent interest in happiness focuses on positive ways we experience our lives, including cognitive judgments of our well-being (Parducci, 1996). That is, psychologists want to know what makes you happy and how you perceive your happiness. Many years ago, French philosopher Jean-Jacques Rousseau described the subjective nature of happiness this way: "Happiness is a good bank account, a good cook, and a good digestion."

In a recent review of research on happiness, having a good cook and a good digestion were not on the list of factors that contribute to our happiness, but the following were (Diener & Diener, 1998; Diener & others, 1999):

• Psychological and personality characteristics: high levels of self-esteem, optimism, extroversion, and personal control
• A supportive network of close relationships
• A culture that offers positive interpretations of most daily events
• Being engaged by work and leisure
• A faith that embodies social support, purpose, and hope

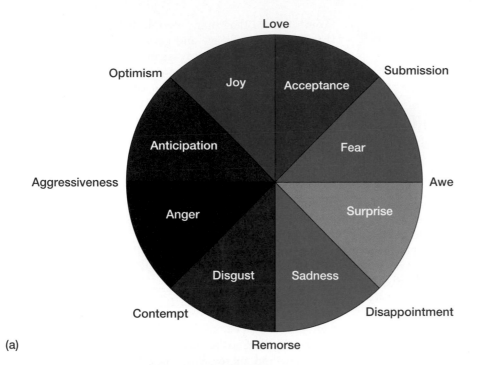

(a)

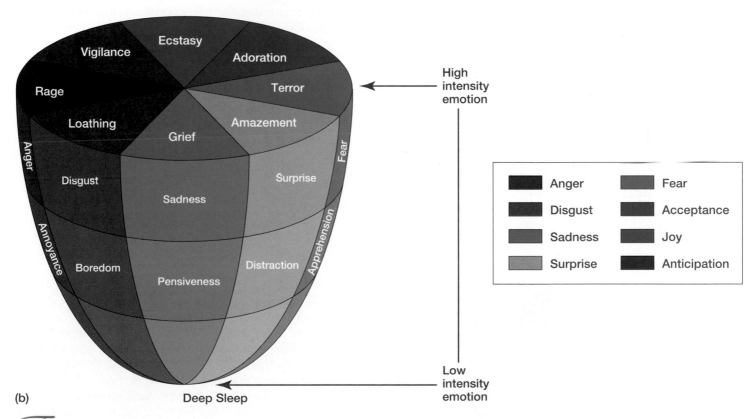

(b)

Figure 11.17
Plutchik's Classification of Emotions

(a) Plutchik theorized that people experience the eight basic emotions represented in the colored part of the emotion wheel (such as joy and sadness), as well as some combination of these (such as love being a combination of joy and acceptance). (b) The emotion solid illustrates how changes in intensity can modify each of the eight basic emotions. For example, notice how anger, when experienced intensely, becomes rage.

THINKING ABOUT PSYCHOLOGY AND LIFE

Pursuing the Good Life

CAROL RYFF AND BURTON SINGER (1998) recently proposed that living the good life primarily involves positive health. Furthermore, they argued that positive psychological health is most likely to be achieved by (1) leading a life of purpose, (2) having quality connections with others, (3) having positive self-regard, and (4) having mastery.

What do you think? What would your list of items be for living the good life? What about the subjective well-being of happiness? And what about intelligence and wisdom? Might they be important dimensions of living the good life? Some people might value intelligence and wisdom higher than happiness in living the good life (King & Pennebaker, 1998). The nineteenth-century English philosopher John Stuart Mill once said that it is better to be a dissatisfied human being than a satisfied pig. Better to be Socrates dissatisfied than a fool satisfied? Also, might there be a problem in measuring the good life?

Some factors that many people believe are involved in happiness (such as age and gender) are not.

But what about Rousseau's "good bank account?" Can we buy happiness? One study tried to find out if lottery winners are happier than other people (Brickman, Coates, & Janoff-Bulman, 1978). Major lottery winners were not happier than people who hadn't won when they were asked about the past, present, and the future. The people who hadn't won a lottery were actually happier doing life's mundane things such as watching television, buying clothes, and talking with a friend. Winning a lottery does not appear to be the key to happiness. Extremely wealthy people are not happier than people who can purchase the necessities. People in wealthy countries are not happier than people in poor countries. What is important, though, is having enough money to buy life's necessities.

Intense positive emotions—such as winning a lottery or getting a date with the person of your dreams—do not add much to a person's general sense of well-being because they are rare, and because they can decrease the positive emotion and increase the negative emotion we feel in other circumstances. For example, if you get a perfect grade on an essay, you may be overwhelmed with happiness at the time, but if your next essay gets a good, but not perfect grade, the previous emotional high can diminish your positive emotion the next time. It is the rare, if nonexistent, human being who experiences intense positive emotions and infrequent negative emotions week after week after week. According to Diener (1984), happiness boils down to the frequency of positive emotions and the infrequency of negative emotions.

You might wonder just how you objectively measure a subjective state such as happiness. Kozma & Stones (1980) developed the Memorial University of Newfoundland Scale of Happiness (MUNSH) for precisely this purpose. The MUNSH relies upon answers to 24 questions like "*Most of the things I do are boring or monotonous*" to produce a reliable and valid measure of happiness. While the original application of the MUNSH was with elderly people (Kozma, Stones & McNeil, 1991), it has since been applied to other groups.

Through the Eyes of Psychologists

Albert Kozma, *Memorial University of Newfoundland, and* **Michael Stones,** *Lakehead University*

"Because the subjective happiness of another person cannot be gauged directly, any form of objective measurement must be indirect."

A Negative Emotion: Anger

Anger is a powerful emotion. It has a strong impact not only on our social relationships, but also on the person experiencing the emotion (Norcross & Kobayashi, 1999). We can easily recount obvious examples of anger that often harm not only others but the angry individual as well—unrestrained and recurrent violence toward others, verbal and physical abuse of children, perpetual bitterness, the tendency to carry a "chip on the shoulder" in which a person overinterprets others' actions as demeaning, and the inability to inhibit the expression of anger.

What makes people angry? People often get angry when they feel they are not being treated fairly or when their expectations are violated. One researcher asked people to remember or keep records of their anger experiences (Averill, 1983). Most of the people said they became at least mildly angry several times a week; some said they became mildly angry several times a day. In many instances, the people said they got angry because they perceived that a friend or a loved one performed a misdeed. They especially got angry when they perceived the other person's behavior as unjustified, avoidable, and willful (Zillman, 1998).

Doesn't getting angry sometimes make us feel better and possibly help us cope better with our challenging lives? For example, Mark Twain once remarked, "When angry, count four; when very angry, swear." **Catharsis** *is the release of anger or aggressive energy by directly or vicariously engaging in anger or aggression; the catharsis hypothesis states that behaving angrily or watching others behave angrily reduces subsequent anger.*

Psychoanalytic theory promotes catharsis as an important way to reduce anger, arguing that people have a natural, biological tendency to display anger ◀▥ P. 9. From this perspective, taking out your anger on a friend or a loved one should reduce your subsequent tendency to display anger; so should heavy doses of anger on television and the anger we see in football, hockey, professional wrestling, and other aspects of our culture. Why? Because such experiences release pent-up anger.

Social cognitive theory argues strongly against this view ◀▥ P. 8. This theory states that by acting angrily, people are often rewarded for their anger, and that by watching others display anger, people learn how to be angry themselves. Which view is right? Research on catharsis suggests that acting angrily does not have any long-term power in reducing anger. If the catharsis hypothesis were correct, war should have a cathartic effect in reducing anger and aggression, but a study of wars in 110 countries since 1900 showed that warfare actually stimulated domestic violence (Archer & Gartner, 1976). Compared with nations that remained at peace, postwar nations had an increase in homicide rates. As psychologist Carol Tavris (1989) says in her book *Anger: The Misunderstood Emotion*, one of the main results of the ventilation approach to anger is to raise the noise level of our society, not to reduce anger or solve our problems. Individuals who are the most prone to anger get angrier, not less angry. Ventilating anger often follows this cycle: a precipitating event, an angry outburst, shouted recriminations, screaming or crying, a furious peak (sometimes accompanied by physical assault), exhaustion, and a sullen apology or just sullenness.

Every person gets angry at one time or another. How can we control our anger so it does not become destructive? Tavris (1989) makes the following recommendations:

1. When your anger starts to boil and your body is getting aroused, work on lowering the arousal by waiting. Emotional arousal will usually simmer down if you just wait long enough.
2. Cope with the anger in ways that involve being neither chronically angry over every little bothersome annoyance nor passively sulking, which simply rehearses your reasons for being angry.
3. Form a self-help group with others who have been through similar experiences with anger. The other people will likely know what you are feeling and together you might come up with some good solutions to anger problems.
4. Take action to help others, which can put your own miseries in perspective, as exemplified in the actions of the women who organized Mothers Against Drunk Drivers or any number of people who work to change conditions so that others will not suffer what they did.
5. Seek ways of breaking out of your usual perspective. Some people have been rehearsing their "story" for years, repeating over and over the reasons for their anger. Retelling the story from other participants' points of view often helps individuals to find routes to empathy.

At this point we have studied a number of ideas about emotion. An overview of these ideas is presented in summary table 11.5. Emotional self-awareness is an important aspect of being emotionally intelligent and earlier in the chapter we said that the degree to which we are aware of what motivates us is an important aspect of motivation. In the next chapter, you will also see that the unconscious-conscious dimension is a key aspect of understanding personality as well.

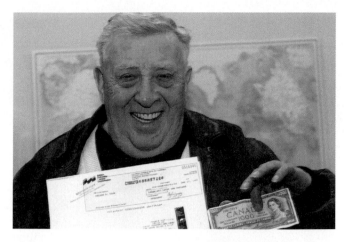

How might winning the lottery affect your happiness?

Anger
Emotional Intelligence

"My life is O.K., but it's no jeans ad."

SUMMARY TABLE 11.5
Emotion

Concept	Processes/ Related Ideas	Characteristics/Discussions
Defining Emotion	Its Nature	Emotion is feeling or affect that can involve (1) physiological arousal, (2) conscious experience, and (3) behavioral expression. Psychologists debate which of these ingredients is the most important and how they mix to produce emotion.
Biological Dimensions	Arousal	The autonomic nervous system and its two subsystems (sympathetic, which arouses the body, and parasympathetic, which calms the body) are involved in emotion. The polygraph is based on detecting changes in people's emotions, but it can be flawed.
	James-Lange and Cannon-Bard Theories	The James-Lange theory states that emotion results from physiological states triggered by environmental stimuli: Emotion follows physiological reactions. The Cannon-Bard theory states that emotion and physiological reactions occur simultaneously.
	Neural Circuits and Neurotransmitters	In contemporary biological views of emotion, neural circuitry and neurotransmitters are increasingly being highlighted. The amygdala especially plays an important role in this circuitry. The neural pathway of fear has been charted.
Cognitive Dimensions	The Two-Factor Theory	The two-factor theory of emotion is Schachter and Singer's theory that emotion is determined by two main factors: (1) physiological arousal and (2) cognitive labeling.
	Primacy Debate: Cognition or Emotion?	Lazarus believes cognition always directs emotion, whereas Zajonc argues that emotions are dominant. Both are probably right.
Behavioral Dimensions	Their Nature	Emotion has not only a physiological and cognitive component, but also a behavioral component. The most interest in the behavioral component has focused on facial expressions. Ekman and his colleagues have found that individuals can identify six basic emotions from facial expressions. The facial feedback hypothesis states that facial expressions can influence emotions as well as reflect them, and Ekman's research supports this hypothesis.
Sociocultural Dimensions	Culture	Most psychologists believe that facial expressions of basic emotions are the same across cultures. However, display rules, which involve nonverbal signals of body movement, posture, and gesture, vary across cultures.
	Gender	The master stereotype of gender and emotion is that she is emotional, he is not. When we go beyond the master stereotype and consider specific aspects of emotional experiences and the contexts in which emotion is displayed, gender matters in understanding emotion. Gender differences in emotion are most likely to occur in contexts that highlight social roles and relationships.
Classifying Emotions	The Wheel Model	Plutchik's wheel model portrays emotions in terms of four dimensions: (1) positive or negative, (2) primary or mixed, (3) polar opposites, and (4) intensity.
	A Positive Emotion: Happiness	Happiness involves such psychological and personality factors as high self-esteem, optimism, extraversion, and personal control; a supportive network of close relationships; a culture that offers positive interpretations of most daily events; being engaged by work and leisure; and a faith that embodies social support, purpose, and hope. Kozma & Stones developed the Memorial University of Newfoundland Scale of Happiness to measure happiness.
	A Negative Emotion: Anger	Anger has a strong impact on our social relationships. Catharsis is generally considered to be a poor strategy for dealing with anger.

Overview

To LEARN ABOUT MOTIVATION, we studied some ideas behind the whys of behavior: defining motivation, biological influences, cognitive influences, behavioral/social/cultural influences, the hierarchy of motives, and issues in motivation. Our coverage of hunger focused on biological factors, external and cognitive factors, as well as eating and weight. We studied these aspects of sexuality: biological, cognitive, sensory/perceptual, and cultural factors, the human sexual response cycle, psychosexual dysfunctions, as well as heterosexuality and homosexuality. We also examined many aspects of achievement motivation, including the need for achievement, person/cognitive factors, and cultural, ethnic, and socioeconomic variations in achievement. And we evaluated these aspects of emotion: defining emotion, biological dimensions, cognitive dimensions, behavioral dimensions, sociocultural dimensions, and classifying emotions.

Don't forget that you can obtain a more detailed overview of the chapter by again studying the five summary tables on pages 373, 379, 387, 392, and 406.

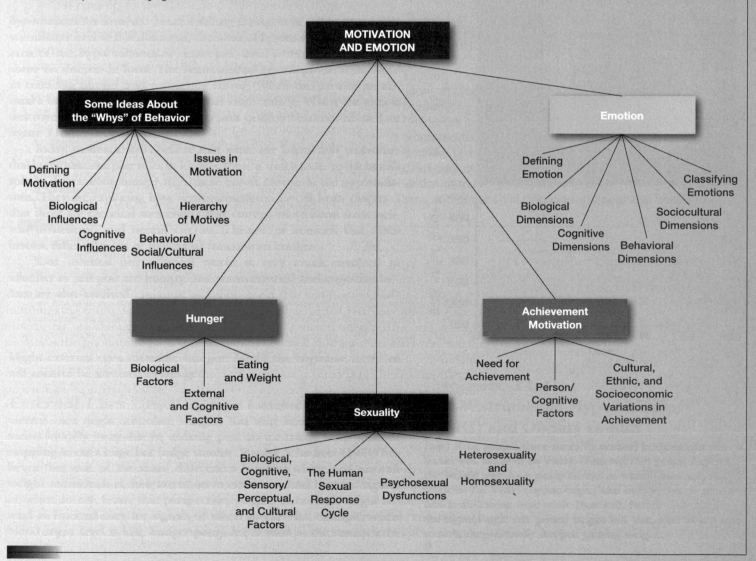

Key Terms

motivation 368
instinct 368
drive 369
need 369
homeostasis 369
ethology 370
incentives 371
hierarchy of motives 371
self-actualization 372
set point 376
basal metabolism rate (BMR) 377

restrained eaters 377
anorexia nervosa 378
bulimia 378
estrogens 380
androgens 380
pheromones 381
aphrodisiacs 381
sexual scripts 382
traditional religious script 382
romantic script 382
human sexual response pattern 382

psychosexual dysfunctions 383
bisexual 385
need for achievement 388
attribution theory 389
emotion 393
autonomic nervous system (ANS) 393
sympathetic nervous system 393
parasympathetic nervous system 394

polygraph 394
Yerkes-Dodson law 394
James-Lange theory 396
Cannon-Bard theory 396
two-factor theory of emotion 397
facial feedback hypothesis 399
display rules 400
catharsis 405

Key People

William McDougall 368
Konrad Lorenz 370
Abraham Maslow 371
Walter Cannon and A. L. Washburn 373
Judith Rodin 374
Stanley Schachter 375

Janet Polivy 377
William Masters and Virginia Johnson 382
Alfred Kinsey 384
David McClelland 388
Michael Enzle 389
Harold Stevenson 391

Sandra Graham 392
William James and Carl Lange 396
Stanley Schachter and Jerome Singer 397
Richard Lazarus 398

Robert Zajonc 398
Paul Ekman 398
Robert Plutchik 402
Ed Diener 404
Albert Kozma and Michael Stones 404

Psychology Checklist
MOTIVATION AND EMOTION

How much have you learned since the beginning of this chapter? Use the following statements to help you review your knowledge and understanding of the chapter material. First, read the statement and mentally or briefly on paper demonstrate that you understand the material and can discuss the relevant information.

_____ I know what motivation is and its biological, cognitive, and behavioral/social/cultural dimensions.

_____ I can describe Maslow's hierarchy of motives and self-actualization.

_____ I am aware of some important issues in motivation.

_____ I can discuss the biological, external, and cognitive factors in hunger.

_____ I can evaluate eating and weight, including ideas about obesity and dieting.

_____ I know about the biological, cognitive, sensory/perceptual, and cultural factors in sexuality.

_____ I can discuss the human sexual response cycle and sexual dysfunctions.

_____ I can evaluate heterosexual and homosexual attitudes and behavior.

_____ I can describe achievement motivation, especially the person/cognitive factors involved.

_____ I am aware of what emotion is and its biological, cognitive, behavioral, and sociocultural dimensions.

_____ I can discuss the ways emotions are classified and know about the nature of happiness and anger.

For any items that you did not check off, go back and locate the relevant material in the chapter. Review the material until you feel you can check off the item. You also may want to use this checklist later in preparing for an exam.

Taking It to the Net

1. Do you know someone who is always angry? Do you know someone who has a bad temper? Emotions are complex phenomena that affect the way we think and the way we behave. Consider, for example, a time when you have been really angry. Chances are, your anger altered the way you behaved, the thoughts you thought, and the things you said. Is emotion inherited? Why do you suppose some people are angrier than others? Explain.

2. Anorexia nervosa is an eating disorder that involves the relentless pursuit of thinness through starvation. Serious nutritional repercussions result from not eating. Hair falls out, teeth turn yellow and fall out, and bones become brittle and break easily. Ultimately, there comes a time when major organs are undernourished and the health of the person with anorexia is at serious risk. Anorexia nervosa is clearly a medical condition, but it is also a psychiatric disorder. Explain some of the psychological theories of anorexia nervosa. According to the *Diagnostic and Statistical Manual,* fourth edition *(DSM-IV),* what are the diagnostic criteria for anorexia nervosa?

3. Have you ever noticed that some people are really good at reading other people's emotions? They can look at you and know exactly how you are feeling. This is one component of emotional intelligence, a concept that has received considerable public interest recently. Some psychologists believe that emotional intelligence is a better predictor for success in business than IQ. What are the other components of emotional intelligence, and can it be improved? Why do you think it is called emotional *intelligence?*

Connect to http://www.mcgrawhill.ca/college/santrock to find the answers!

Resources for Psychology and Life

Alan Guttmacher Institute
111 Fifth Avenue
New York, NY 10003
212-254-5656
The Alan Guttmacher Institute is an especially good resource for information about sexuality.

Even Eagles Need a Push (1994)
by David McNally
This is an excellent book to get you motivated. A number of exercises and stories serve to get you energized and directed.

Why We Eat What We Eat (1996)
by Elizabeth Capaldi (ed.)
Washington, DC: American Psychological Association
Experts cut through popular myths about eating to present the latest research on how eating patterns develop. Topics include the development of food preferences and aversions, how eating patterns develop in childhood, how biology affects eating behavior, and how social contexts influence eating patterns.

Motivation and Emotion: Evolutionary, Physiological, Developmental, and Social Perspectives (1999)
by Denys deCatanzaro
Upper Saddle River, NJ: Prentice Hall
This up-to-date volume presents motivation and emotion within an integrated approach that assumes biological and psychological causes, including evolution, neuroscience, endocrinology, human development and culture.

Canada (1997)
by Michael Barrett, Alan King, Joseph Lévy, Eleanor Maticka-Tyndale & Alexander McKay

In R.T. Francoeur (Ed.). **The International Encyclopedia of Sexuality (Vol 1): Argentina to Greece.**
New York: Continuum
The only major summary of research on the sexual attitudes and practices of Canadians.

Third International Mathematics and Science Study (TIMSS)
http://timss.bc.edu/
Access the data yourself from the largest and most ambitious international study of student achievement ever conducted.

The Dance of Anger (1985)
by Harriet Lerner
New York: HarperPerennial
The Dance of Anger is written mainly for women about the anger in their lives, both their own anger and the anger of people they live with, especially men.

Telling Lies: Clues to Deceit in the Marketplace, Politics, and Marriage (1985)
by Paul Ekman
New York: W. W. Norton
Ekman describes how to read facial expressions and gestures to determine whether people are lying.

Sex in America (1994)
by Robert Michael, John Gagnon, Edward Laumann, and Gina Kolata
Boston: Little, Brown
This book reveals the extensive, surprising results of a large-scale, random-sample study of the sexual lives of Americans in the 1990s. The results suggested that Americans are more conservative in their sexual activities than was previously believed.

Chapter 12

CHAPTER OUTLINE

WHAT IS PERSONALITY?

PERSPECTIVES ON PERSONALITY

Psychoanalytic Perspectives

Behavioral and Social Cognitive Perspectives

Humanistic Perspectives

Trait Perspectives

PERSONALITY ASSESSMENT

Some Themes in Personality Assessment

Projective Tests

Self-Report Tests

Behavioral and Cognitive Assessment

COMPARING PERSPECTIVES ON PERSONALITY

Personality

Images of Psychology and Life
Everyday Descriptions of Personality

"*E*very person cries out to be read differently."

Simone Weil
French Philosopher, 20th Century

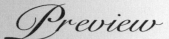

Preview

HOW DO THE images of personality we use in our everyday conversations about people correspond to the way psychologists describe personality? The images suggest that personality is a property of the individual that is related to how the individual functions in the world. These are some of the questions we will explore in this chapter:

• What is personality?
• How do the psychoanalytic perspectives portray personality? Is some of our personality unconscious? Is it tied to early experiences in our family?
• How do the humanistic perspectives describe personality? How important is the self in personality?
• What do the behavioral and social cognitive perspectives say are the key aspects of understanding personality?
• What is the trait perspective on personality? How much can our personality traits be modified by situations?
• What are some ways personality can be assessed?
• How do the main theoretical perspectives on personality stack up against each other on some key issues?

"She has a great personality."
"He has no personality."
"She is a personality."
"She has her mother's personality."

These statements reflect our everyday use of the term personality. You have probably used similar statements to describe someone you have known or known about. Let's look further at each of these statements (Peterson, 1988).

"She has a great personality." This statement is a positive evaluation. When you say this about a woman, it means you like something about her that does not involve looks, possessions, or status. There is something about her that makes you feel good when you are around her. Maybe it's the way she behaves, her attitude, her flair, her values, or even some of her quirks.

"He has no personality." This statement is also an evaluation, but it is a negative one. You do not really like this guy, but you might not dislike him either, unless you happen to be his university roommate or he is your boss. He makes your day boring. He has nothing unique that stamps him as very different from others: no passion, no weird hobby or unusual ability, and not much desire except just to go through life unnoticed. He can take or leave cross-country skiing or country music, he has no mismatched socks. He is almost like a piece of furniture.

Many celebrities, such as Canadian-born Michael J. Fox, are called "personalities." They are well known not just for what they do, but also for how they do it. Michael J. Fox's outgoing personality is a property of Michael J. Fox and is related to how he functions in the world. Of course, it is not just celebrities who have a personality. Each of us has a personality that is our property and is related to how we function in the world.

411

"She is a personality." Andy Warhol once said that in the future everyone will be famous for 15 minutes. Then it will be someone else's turn. Some of us make *Maclean's* magazine; most of us don't. People write about celebrities so noncelebrities can read about them. Many celebrities have unique personalities and we call them "personalities." Céline Dion, Jim Carrey, and Michael J. Fox are celebrities we think of as personalities. They are well known not just for what they do, but for how they do it. They play a role in our culture that becomes identified with the personality they bring to the role.

"She has her mother's personality." Many statements about personality focus on distinctive characteristics, what makes us different from others in some way. Personality is also used to make comparisons among individuals, describing common characteristics and similarities. Most of us have talked about the way certain people remind us of someone else we have known. They may have similar mannerisms. She holds grudges just like her mother does, for example. They may have similar temperaments. She is the life of the party and loves to be around people, just like her father. Many people look at their family members and see certain similar personality characteristics. For example, someone may say, "My brother is an introvert just like my cousin Robert." Or "My sister has my grandmother's personality—she has a stubborn streak a mile long."

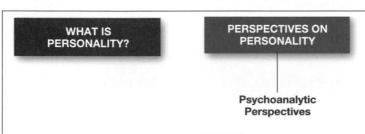

Psychoanalytic
Perspectives

Personality

**Journal of Personality
and Social Psychology**

What Is Personality?

Think about yourself for a moment. What are you *really* like? Are you outgoing or shy? Aggressive or calm? Intellectual or nonintellectual? Considerate or uncaring? Try to come up with seven or eight of these traits that reflect the way you respond to your world. In compiling this list, you chose personality characteristics that you probably feel are an enduring part of your makeup as a person. For example, if you said that you are an outgoing person, wouldn't you also say that you were outgoing a year ago and that you will probably be an outgoing person 1 year, 5 years, and 10 years from now? Most of us believe that we do have some enduring personality characteristics.

Now that you have thought about yourself in terms of your characteristics, think for a moment about how you would define personality. It's not that easy. Personality is one of those concepts that we think we understand but which can be quite difficult to verbally express. Our definition of personality includes enduring characteristics and adaptation: **Personality** *consists of enduring, distinctive thoughts, emotions, and behaviors that characterize the way an individual adapts to the world.*

We will be discussing a number of theoretical perspectives on personality (Endler & Parker, 1991). They ask why individuals react to the same situation in different ways. For example, *why* is Sam so talkative and gregarious, and Pierre so shy and quiet when they meet someone for the first time? *Why* is Gretchen so confident and Marie so insecure about upcoming job interviews? Some theorists believe that biological and genetic factors are responsible; others argue that life experiences are more important. Some theorists claim that the way we think about ourselves is the key to understanding personality, while others stress that the way we behave toward each other is more important (Endler, 1993; Friedman & Schustack, 1999).

The diversity of theories makes understanding personality a challenging undertaking (Maddi, 1996). Just when you think one theory has the correct explanation of personality, another theory will crop up and make you rethink your earlier conclusion. To keep from getting frustrated, remember that personality is a complex, multifaceted topic and no single theory has been able to account for all its aspects. Each theory has contributed an important piece to the personality puzzle. In fact, much of the information is *complementary* rather than contradictory. Together they let us see the total landscape of personality in all its richness (Feist & Feist, 1998).

Perspectives on Personality

The field of personality includes a number of theoretical perspectives. The main perspectives we will discuss are these: psychoanalytic, behavioral and social learning, humanistic, and trait theory and trait-situation interaction.

Psychoanalytic Perspectives

Initially we will describe some common characteristics of the psychoanalytic perspectives, then turn to Freud's theory of personality, then other important psychoanalytic theories, and finally evaluate the psychoanalytic perspectives.

Defining the Psychoanalytic Perspectives   **Psychoanalytic perspectives** *view personality as primarily unconscious (that is, beyond awareness) and as occurring in stages* ◀▥ P. 9. *Most psychoanalytic perspectives emphasize that early experiences with parents play an important role in sculpting personality.* Psychoanalytic theorists believe that behavior is merely a surface characteristic and that to truly understand someone's personality we have to explore the symbolic meanings of behavior and the deep inner workings of the mind. These characteristics are highlighted by the original architect of psychoanalytic theory: Sigmund Freud.

Freud's Theory   Loved and hated, respected and despised, Sigmund Freud, whether right or wrong in his views, has been one of the most influential thinkers of the twentieth century. Freud was a medical doctor who specialized in neurology. He developed his ideas about psychoanalytic theory from his work with psychiatric patients. He was born in Austria in 1856, and he died in London at the age of 83. Freud spent most of his life in Vienna, but he left the city near the end of his career to escape Nazi anti-Semitism.

As an eldest child, Freud was regarded as a genius by his brothers and sisters and doted on by his mother. Later we will see that one aspect of Freud's theory emphasizes a young boy's sexual attraction for his mother; it is possible that this aspect of his theory was derived from his own romantic attachment to his mother, who was beautiful and some 20 years younger than Freud's father.

In Freud's view, much more of our mind is unconscious than conscious. He envisioned our mind as a huge iceberg, with the massive part below the surface of the water being the unconscious part. Freud said that each of our lives is filled with tension and conflict; to reduce this tension and conflict we keep information locked in our unconscious mind. For Freud, the unconscious mind held the key to understanding behavior. Freud believed that even trivial behaviors have special significance when the unconscious forces behind them are revealed. A twitch, a doodle, a joke, a smile, each may have an unconscious reason for appearing. They often slip into our lives without our awareness. For example, Barbara is kissing and hugging Tom, whom she is to marry in several weeks. She says, "Oh, *Jeff,* I love you so much." Tom pushes her away and says, "Why did you call me Jeff? I thought you didn't think about him anymore. We need to have a talk!" You can probably think of times when these *Freudian slips* tumbled out of your own mouth.

Freud also believed that dreams hold important clues to our behavior ◀▥ P. 164, referring to them as "the royal road to the unconscious." He said dreams are unconscious representations of the conflict and tension in our everyday lives. Since the conflict and tension are too painful to handle consciously, they come out in our dreams. Much of the dream content is disguised in symbolism, requiring extensive analysis and probing to be understood. Freud's view of the mind as unconscious and symbolic has played an important role in understanding some movements in art, as discussed in Explorations in Psychology.

Sigmund Freud (1856–1939), the architect of psychoanalytic theory.

Psychoanalytic Theory
The Structure of the Unconscious

"Good morning beheaded—uh, I mean beloved."

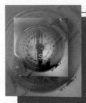

EXPLORATIONS IN PSYCHOLOGY
Freud, da Vinci, and Dali

BECAUSE OF its emphasis on symbolic and unconscious thought, psychoanalytic theory has been extensively applied to art and literature. The psychoanalytic formula is that creative works of art satisfy unconscious wishes; because these wishes are often unacceptable, they have to be disguised. Artistic techniques are used for this purpose. Freud (1908) examined Leonardo da Vinci's life and art, concluding that da Vinci was a man of extreme sexual inhibition brought about by castration anxiety. According to Freud, da Vinci channeled his sexual energy into creating well-known works of art such as the *Mona Lisa* (see figure 12.A). Freud believed that the Mona Lisa's mysterious smile was the smile of Leonardo's mother. How accurate was Freud's analysis of da Vinci and the Mona Lisa? As is the case with many ideas in psycho-

analytic theory, we don't have a scientific way to examine Freud's ideas on the role of symbolic and unconscious thought in the creative works of artists.

Although psychologists and art critics debate whether many works of art are unconsciously based, there is general agreement that the twentieth-century art movement known as Surrealism was heavily influenced by Freud's ideas. The Surrealists saw Freud's concept of the unconscious mind as the true source of untainted creativity. They thought that the conscious mind was too warped by the conventions and constraints of society to produce truly great works. Surrealist artists used a number of techniques to tap unconscious thoughts they could turn into paintings: dream analysis, automatic writing and drawing, and hypnosis. They threw paint onto canvas at random. They imitated primitive art. They used rags instead of brushes.

René Magritte and Salvador Dali are two of the best known Surrealist artists. Magritte painted memories of his dreams. He is famous for the distortion of perspective in his works. Dali used Freudian symbols to portray such sexual themes as guilt, masturbation, and intercourse (see figure 12.B). The Surrealists made a conscious effort to apply their unconscious thoughts to canvas. As with Freud's conclusions about da Vinci's sexually repressed thoughts about his mother, it is open to debate whether the Surrealists' works support the psychoanalytic view of creativity (Peterson, 1988).

Figure 12.A
The *Mona Lisa*. What was Freud's interpretation of her smile?

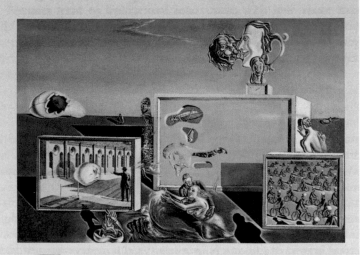

Figure 12.B
Salvador Dali, *Illumined Pleasures* (1929)

DALI, *Salvador*. Illumined Pleasures. (1929) Oil and collage on composition board, 93/8 × 133/4″ (23.8 × 34.7 cm). The Museum of Modern Art, New York. The Sidney and Harriet Janis Collection. Photograph © 1996 The Museum of Modern Art, New York.

The Structure of Personality   Freud (1917) believed that personality has three structures: the id, the ego, and the superego.

The **id** *is the Freudian structure of personality that consists of instincts, which are the individual's reservoir of psychic energy.* In Freud's view, the id is unconscious; it has no contact with reality. The id works according to the pleasure principle. The **pleasure principle** *is the Freudian concept that the id always seeks pleasure and avoids pain.*

It would be a dangerous and scary world if our personalities were all id. As young children mature, they learn they cannot slug other children in the face. They also learn they have to use the toilet instead of their diaper. As children experience the demands and constraints of reality, a new structure of personality is formed—the **ego,** *the Freudian structure of personality that deals with the demands of reality.* The ego is called the executive branch of personality because it makes decisions based on rationality. According to Freud, the ego abides by the **reality principle:** *It tries to bring the individual pleasure within the norms of society.* Few of us are cold-blooded killers or wild wheeler-dealers; we consider obstacles to our satisfaction that exist in our world. We recognize that our sexual and aggressive impulses cannot go unrestrained. The ego helps us to test reality, to see how far we can go without getting into trouble and hurting ourselves.

While the id is completely unconscious, the ego is partly conscious. It houses our higher mental functions—reasoning, problem solving, and decision making, for example. For this reason, the ego is referred to as the executive branch of the personality; like an executive in a company, it makes the rational decisions that help the company succeed.

The id and ego have no morality. They do not consider whether something is right or wrong. The **superego** *is the Freudian structure of personality that is the moral branch of personality.* The superego considers whether something is right or wrong. The superego is what we often refer to as our "conscience." Like the id, the superego does not consider reality; it doesn't deal with what is realistic, only with whether the id's sexual and aggressive impulses can be satisfied in moral terms. You are probably beginning to sense that both the id and the superego make life rough for the ego. Your ego might say, "I will have sex only occasionally and be sure to use an effective form of birth control." But your id is saying, "I want to be satisfied; sex feels so good." And your superego is at work too, "I feel guilty about having sex at all."

Remember that Freud considered personality to be like an iceberg; most of our personality exists below the level of awareness, just as the massive part of an iceberg is beneath the surface of the water. Figure 12.1 illustrates this analogy and how extensive the unconscious part of our mind is in Freud's view.

Defense Mechanisms   In addition to describing personality in terms of three structures (id, ego, and superego), Freud also said that defense mechanisms are important in understanding how personality works. The ego calls on a number of strategies to resolve the conflict between its demands for reality, the wishes of the id, and the constraints of the superego. **Defense mechanisms** *are the ego's protective methods*

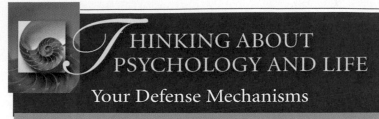

THINKING ABOUT PSYCHOLOGY AND LIFE
Your Defense Mechanisms

WE ALL USE defense mechanisms at one time or another in our lives. Some of us use them more than others. Examine figure 12.2 again to be sure you understand what the different defense mechanisms are like. For each of the following defense mechanisms, think about how you have used it in your life. If you don't think you have used it, in what future situations might you use it?

Repression
Rationalization
Displacement
Sublimation
Projection
Reaction Formation
Denial
Regression

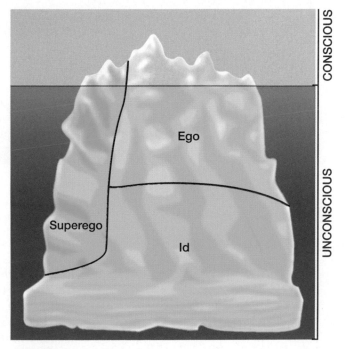

Figure 12.1
The Conscious and Unconscious Mind: The Iceberg Analogy

The analogy of the conscious and unconscious mind to an iceberg is often used to illustrate how much of the mind is unconscious in Freud's theory. The conscious mind is the part of the iceberg above water, the unconscious mind the part below water. Notice that the id is totally unconscious, while the ego and superego can operate at either the conscious or the unconscious level.

Defense Mechanism	How It Works	Example
Repression	The master defense mechanism; the ego pushes unacceptable impulses out of awareness, back into the unconscious mind.	A young girl was sexually abused by her uncle. As an adult, she can't remember anything about the traumatic experience.
Rationalization	The ego replaces a less acceptable motive with a more acceptable one.	A college student does not get into the fraternity of his choice. He says that if he had tried harder he could have gotten in.
Displacement	The ego shifts unacceptable feelings from one object to another, more acceptable object.	A woman can't take her anger out on her boss so she goes home and takes it out on her husband.
Sublimation	The ego replaces an unacceptable impulse with a socially acceptable one.	A man with strong sexual urges becomes an artist who paints nudes.
Projection	The ego attributes personal shortcomings, problems, and faults to others.	A man who has a strong desire to have an extramarital affair accuses his wife of flirting with other men.
Reaction Formation	The ego transforms an unacceptable motive into its opposite.	A woman who fears her sexual urges becomes a religious zealot.
Denial	The ego refuses to acknowledge anxiety-producing realities.	A man won't acknowledge that he has cancer even though a team of doctors has diagnosed his cancer.
Regression	The ego seeks the security of an earlier developmental period in the face of stress.	A woman returns home to mother every time she and her husband have a big argument.

*F*igure 12.2
Defense Mechanisms

Defense Mechanisms

for reducing anxiety by unconsciously distorting reality. In Freud's view, the conflicting demands of the personality structures produce anxiety. For example, when the ego blocks the pleasurable pursuits of the id, a person feels inner anxiety. This diffuse, distressed state develops when the ego senses that the id is going to cause some harm. The anxiety alerts the ego to resolve the conflict by means of defense mechanisms.

Repression *is the most powerful and pervasive defense mechanism, according to Freud; it works to push unacceptable id impulses out of awareness and back into the unconscious mind.* Repression is the foundation from which all other defense mechanisms work; the goal of every psychological defense is to *repress* or push threatening impulses out of awareness. Freud said that our early childhood experiences, many of which he believed were sexually laden, are too threatening and stressful for us to deal with consciously. We reduce the anxiety of this conflict through repression.

Among the other defense mechanisms we use to protect the ego and reduce anxiety are rationalization, displacement, sublimation, projection, reaction formation, denial, and regression. Figure 12.2 describes the defense mechanisms and gives an example of each.

Two final points about defense mechanisms need to be understood. First, they are unconscious; we are not aware we are calling on them to protect our ego and reduce anxiety. Second, when used in moderation or on a temporary basis, defense mechanisms are not necessarily unhealthy. For example, defense mechanisms such as denial can help a person cope with impending death. For the most part, though, we should not let defense mechanisms dominate our behavior and prevent us from facing life's demands.

The Development of Personality   As Freud listened to, probed, and analyzed his patients, he became convinced that their problems were the result of experiences early in life. Freud believed that we go through five stages of psychosexual development, and that at each stage of development we experience pleasure in one part of the body more than in others. **Erogenous zones,** *according to Freud, are parts of the body that have especially strong pleasure-giving qualities at particular stages of development.*

Freud thought that our adult personality is determined by the way we resolve conflicts between these early sources of pleasure—the mouth, the anus, and then the genitals—and the demands of reality. When these conflicts are not resolved, the individual may become fixated at a particular stage of development. **Fixation** *is the psychoanalytic defense mechanism that occurs when the individual remains locked in an earlier developmental stage because needs are under- or overgratified.* For example, a parent

GENITAL STAGE

Adolescence
and Adulthood

LATENCY STAGE

6 Years–Puberty

PHALLIC STAGE

3–6 Years

ANAL STAGE

$1\frac{1}{2}$–3 Years

ORAL STAGE

0–$1\frac{1}{2}$ Years

Figure 12.3
Freudian Stages

might wean a child too early, be too strict in toilet training the child, punish the child for masturbation, or "smother" the child with too much attention. We will return to the idea of fixation and how it may show up in an adult's personality, but first we need to learn more about the early stages of personality development. Figure 12.3 illustrates the five Freudian stages.

Oral stage *is the term Freud used to describe development during the first 18 months of life, in which the infant's pleasure centers on the mouth.* Chewing, sucking, and biting are chief sources of pleasure. These actions reduce tension in the infant.

The **anal stage** *is Freud's second stage of development, occurring between 1½ and 3 years of age, in which the child's greatest pleasure involves the anus or the eliminative functions associated with it.* In Freud's view, the exercise of anal muscles reduces tension.

THE FAR SIDE   By GARY LARSON

"So Mr. Fenton. . . . Let's begin with your mother."

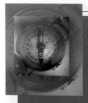

EXPLORATIONS IN PSYCHOLOGY
Freud's Oedipus Complex: Cultural and Gender Biases

THE OEDIPUS COMPLEX was one of Freud's most influential concepts relating early psychosexual relationships to later personality development. Freud developed this aspect of his theory during the Victorian era of the late 1800s when sexual interests, especially the female's, were repressed.

According to Freud, the phallic stage begins for a girl when she realizes she has no penis. He also believed that she recognizes the superiority of the penis to her anatomy, and thus develops *penis envy*. Blaming her mother for her lack of a penis, the girl renounces her love for her mother and becomes intensely attached to her father. Since her desire to have a penis can never be satisfied directly, Freud speculated that the young girl yearns for a penis substitute, a baby (especially a male baby). This female version of the Oedipus complex is sometimes referred to as the *Electra complex*. Freud believed that the Electra complex is never fully resolved but merely dissipates over time as the girl begins to identify with her mother and take on similar values and feminine behavior. As a result, Freud assumed that women do not develop as strong a conscience (superego) as do men.

Many psychologists believe Freud placed far too much emphasis on anatomy's role in personality development. Freud concluded, for example, that boys are likely to de-velop a dominant, powerful personality because they have a penis; without a penis, girls are predisposed to become submissive and weak. In basing his view of male/female differences in personality development on anatomical differences, Freud ignored the enormous impact of culture and experience.

More than half a century ago, the English anthropologist Brownislaw Malinowski (1927) observed the family dynamics of the Trobriand islanders of the Western Pacific and found that the Oedipus complex is not universal. In the Trobriand Islands, the biological father is not the head of the household; that disciplinarian role is reserved for the mother's brother. In Freud's view, this family constellation would not alter the Oedipus complex; the young boy should still vie for his mother's love and perceive his father as the hated rival, but Malinowski found no such conflict between fathers and sons in the Trobriand islanders. He did observe, however, that young boys feared the authoritarian, maternal uncle and directed negative feelings toward him. Malinowski's finding undermined Freud's Oedipus complex because it showed that the sexual relations within the family did not always create conflict and fear for a child.

The Oedipus Complex

The **phallic stage,** *Freud's third stage of development, occurs between the ages of 3 and 6. Its name comes from the Latin word* phallus, *which means "penis." During the phallic stage, pleasure focuses on the genitals as the child discovers that self-stimulation is enjoyable.*

In Freud's view the phallic stage has a special importance in personality development because this period triggers the Oedipus complex. This name comes from Greek mythology, in which Oedipus, the son of the King of Thebes, unwittingly killed his father and married his mother. The **Oedipus complex** *is the young child's development of an intense desire to replace the parent of the same sex and enjoy the affections of the opposite-sex parent.* As discussed in Explorations in Psychology, the Oedipus complex was not as universal as Freud believed; his concept was heavily influenced by the sociohistorical, cultural setting of turn-of-the-century Vienna.

At about five to six years of age, children recognize that their same-sex parent might punish them for their incestuous wishes. To reduce this conflict, the child identifies with the same-sex parent, striving to be like him or her. If the conflict is not resolved, though, the individual may become fixated at the phallic stage. Figure 12.4 illustrates some possible links between adult personality characteristics and fixation, sublimation, and reaction formation involving the phallic stage, as well as the oral and anal stage.

The **latency stage** *is the fourth Freudian stage of development, occurring approximately between six years of age and puberty; the child represses all interest in sexuality and develops social and intellectual skills.* This activity channels much of the child's

Stage	Adult Extensions (Fixations)	Sublimations	Reaction Formations
Oral	Smoking, eating, kissing, oral hygiene, drinking, chewing gum	Seeking knowledge, humor, wit, sarcasm, being a food or wine expert	Speech purist, food faddist, prohibitionist, dislike of milk
Anal	Notable interest in one's bowel movements, love of bathroom humor, extreme messiness	Interest in painting or sculpture, being overly giving, great interest in statistics	Extreme disgust with feces, fear of dirt, prudishness, irritability
Phallic	Heavy reliance on masturbation, flirtatiousness, expressions of virility	Interest in poetry, love of love, interest in acting, striving for success	Puritanical attitude toward sex, excessive modesty

Figure 12.4
Possible Links Between Adult Personality Characteristics and Fixation at Oral, Anal, and Phallic Stages

energy into emotionally safe areas and aids the child in forgetting the highly stressful conflicts of the phallic stage.

The **genital stage** *is the fifth and final Freudian stage of development, occurring from puberty on. The genital stage is the time of sexual reawakening; the source of sexual pleasure now becomes someone outside of the family.* Freud believed that unresolved conflicts with parents reemerged during adolescence. Once resolved, Freud believed, the individual would become capable of developing a mature love relationship and functioning independently as an adult.

Psychoanalytic Dissenters and Revisionists

Because Freud was among the first theorists to explore many new and uncharted regions of personality, some of his ideas have needed to be updated, others revised, and some have been tossed out altogether. In particular, Freud's critics have said his ideas about sexuality, early experience, social factors, and the unconscious mind were misguided (Adler, 1927; Erikson, 1968; Fromm, 1947; Horney, 1945; Jung, 1917; Kohut, 1977; Rapaport, 1967; Sullivan, 1953). The critics stressed the following:

- Sexuality is not the pervasive underlying force behind personality that Freud believed it to be.
- The first five years of life are not as powerful in shaping adult personality as Freud thought; later experiences deserve more attention.
- The ego and conscious thought processes play more dominant roles in our personality than Freud gave them credit for; we are not wed forever to the id and its instinctual, unconscious clutches. The ego has a separate line of development from the id; viewed in this way, achievement, thinking, and reasoning are not always tied to sexual impulses as Freud thought.
- Sociocultural factors are much more important than Freud believed. Freud placed more emphasis on the biological basis of personality by stressing the id's dominance.

Let's examine three theories by dissenters and revisionists of Freud's theory in greater detail—Horney's, Jung's, and Adler's theories.

Horney's Sociocultural Approach   Karen Horney (1885–1952) rejected the classical psychoanalytic concept that "anatomy is destiny" in favor of an approach that emphasized the importance of sociocultural factors in development. She cautioned that ideas such as "penis envy" were only hypotheses. She insisted that these hypotheses should be supported with observable data before they were accepted as fact.

Horney's Theory

Karen Horney (1885–1952) developed the first feminist criticism of Freud's theory. Horney's view emphasizes women's positive qualities and self-evaluation.

Through the Eyes of Psychologists

Nancy Chodorow, *University of California, Berkeley*

"The selves of women and men tend to be constructed differently— women's more in relationships, men's more in denials of self-other connections."

Jung's Theory
Jungian Links
Adler's Theory

Swiss psychoanalytic theorist Carl Jung developed the concepts of the collective unconscious and archetypes.

Horney pointed out that previous research about how women function was limited by the fact that those who described women, who influenced and represented the culture, and who determined the standards for suitable growth and development were men. She countered the notion of penis envy with the hypothesis that both sexes envy the attributes of the other, with men suffering "womb envy," coveting women's reproductive capacities. She also argued that women who feel "penis envy" are desirous only of the status that men have in most societies.

Horney also believed that the need for security, not sex or aggression, was the prime motive in human existence. Horney reasoned that when an individual's security needs are met they are able to develop their capacities to the fullest extent. She also suggested that people usually develop one of three strategies in their effort to cope with anxiety. First, individuals might *move toward* people, seeking love and support. Second, individuals might *move away* from people, becoming more independent. And third, individuals might *move against* people, becoming competitive and domineering. The secure individual uses these three ways of coping in moderation and balance, while the insecure individual often uses one or more of these strategies in an exaggerated fashion, becoming too dependent, too independent, or too aggressive.

Psychologists are still revamping psychoanalytic theory. Nancy Chodorow's (1978, 1989) feminist revision of psychoanalytic theory, for example, emphasizes that many more women than men define themselves in terms of their relationships, that many men use denial as a defense mechanism in regard to their relationships with others, and that emotions tend to be more salient to women's lives.

Jung's Analytical Psychology   Freud's contemporary Carl Jung (1875–1961) shared an interest in the unconscious, but he believed Freud underplayed the unconscious mind's role in our personality. Jung believed that the roots of personality go back to the dawn of human existence. The **collective unconscious** *is the impersonal, deepest layer of the unconscious mind, shared by all human beings because of their common ancestral past.* These common experiences have made a deep, permanent impression on the human mind (Harris, 1996). **Archetype** *is the name Jung gave to the emotionally laden ideas and images in the collective unconscious that have rich and symbolic meaning.* Jung believed that these archetypes emerge in art, religion, and dreams. He used archetypes to help people understand themselves.

Two common archetypes are *anima* (woman) and *animus* (man). Jung believed each of us has a passive "feminine" side and an assertive "masculine" side. We also have an archetype for self, which is often expressed in art. For example, the mandala, a figure within a circle, has been used so often Jung took it to represent the self (see figure 12.5). Another archetype is the *shadow,* our darker self. The shadow is evil and immoral. The shadow appears in many evil and immoral figures—Satan, Dracula, Mr. Hyde (of Jekyll and Hyde), and Darth Vader (of the *Star Wars* films) (Peterson, 1988) (see figure 12.6).

Adler's Individual Psychology   Alfred Adler (1870–1937) was another of Freud's contemporaries. In Adler's **individual psychology,** *people are motivated by purposes and goals, being creators of their own lives.* They are seen as responsible for their own lives. Unlike Freud, who believed in the power of the unconscious mind, Adler argued that people have the ability to consciously monitor their lives. He also believed that social factors are more important in shaping personality than sexual motivation (Silverman & Corsini, 1984).

Adler thought that everyone strives for superiority. Adler's concept of **striving for superiority** *emphasizes the human motivation to adapt, improve, and master the environment.* Striving for superiority is our response to feelings of inferiority that we all experience as infants and young children when we interact with people who are bigger and more powerful. We strive to overcome these feelings of inferiority because they are uncomfortable. **Compensation** *is Adler's term for the individual's attempt to overcome imagined or real inferiorities or weaknesses by developing one's abilities.* Adler believed that compensation was normal, and he said we often make up for a weakness in one ability by excelling in a different ability. For example, one person may be a mediocre student but compensate for this by excelling in athletics. **Overcompensation** *is Adler's term for the individual's attempt to deny rather than acknowledge a real situation, or the exaggerated effort to conceal a weakness.* Adler described two patterns of overcompensation. **Inferiority complex** *is the name Adler gave to exaggerated feelings of inadequacy.* **Superiority complex** *is his concept for exaggerated self-importance designed to mask feelings of inferiority.*

In summary, Adler's theory emphasized that people are striving toward a positive being and that they create their own goals. Their adaptation is enhanced by developing social interests and reducing feelings of inferiority. Like Jung, Adler has a number of disciples today.

Evaluating the Psychoanalytic Perspectives

Although psychoanalytic theories have diverged, they do share some core principles. Psychoanalytic theorists assert that our personality is determined both by current experiences and those from early in life. Two basic principles of psychoanalytic theory have withstood the test of time: early experiences do shape our personality, and personality can be better understood by examining it developmentally.

Another belief that continues to receive considerable attention is that we mentally transform environmental experiences. Psychologists also recognize that the mind is not all consciousness; unconscious motives lie behind some of our puzzling behavior. Psychoanalytic theorists' emphasis on conflict and anxiety leads us to consider the dark side of our existence, not just its bright side. Adjustment is not always an easy task, and the individual's inner world often conflicts with the outer demands of reality. And finally, psychoanalytic theories continue to force psychologists to study more than the experimental, laboratory topics of sensation, perception, and learning; personality and adjustment are rightful and important topics of psychological inquiry as well.

However, the main concepts of psychoanalytic theories have been difficult to test; they are largely matters of inference and interpretation. Researchers have not, for example, successfully investigated such key concepts as repression in the laboratory.

Much of the data used to support psychoanalytic theories have come from clinicians' subjective evaluations of clients; in such cases, it is easy for the clinician to see what she expects because of the theory she holds. Other data come from patients' recollections of the distant past (especially those from early childhood) and are of unknown accuracy. And psychoanalytic theories place too much weight on these early experiences within the family to shape personality. We retain the capacity for change and adaptation throughout our lives.

Some psychologists object that Freud overemphasized the importance of sexuality in understanding personality, and that Freud and Jung placed too much faith in the unconscious mind's ability to control behavior. Others object that the psychoanalytic perspectives provide a model of the person that is too negative and pessimistic. We are not born into the world with only a bundle of sexual and aggressive instincts. The demands of reality do not always conflict with our biological needs.

Figure 12.5
The Mandala as an Archetype of the Self

In his exploration of mythology, Carl Jung found that the self is often symbolized by a mandala, which is named for the Sanskrit word that means "circle." Jung believed that the mandala represents the self's unity.

Contemporary Psychoanalytic Views

Figure 12.6
Star Wars Characters as Archetypes of Good and Evil

In *Star Wars*, Ben Kenobi represented the archetype of good and Darth Vader the archetype of evil.

SUMMARY TABLE 12.1
The Nature of Personality,
and Psychoanalytic Perspectives

Concept	Processes/ Related Ideas	Characteristics/Description
What Is Personality?	Its Nature	Personality involves our enduring thoughts, emotions, and behaviors that characterize the way we adapt to the world. A key question is why different individuals respond to the same situation in different ways.
Psychoanalytic Perspectives	Defining the Psychoanalytic Perspectives	They view personality as primarily unconscious and as occurring in stages. Most psychoanalytic perspectives emphasize the importance of early experiences with parents in sculpting personality.
	Freud's Theory	Freud was one of the most influential thinkers of the twentieth century. He believed that most of the mind is unconscious, and that personality has three structures: id, ego, and superego. The id is the reservoir of psychic energy that tries to satisfy our basic needs. It is unconscious and operates according to the pleasure principle. The ego tries to provide us with pleasure by operating within the boundaries of reality. The superego is the moral branch of personality. The conflicting demands of these personality structures produce anxiety. Defense mechanisms protect the ego and reduce this anxiety. Repression is the master defense mechanism. Defense mechanisms are unconscious. Freud was convinced that problems develop because of childhood experiences. He said we go through five psychosexual stages: oral, anal, phallic, latency, and genital. If our needs are under- or overgratified at a particular stage, we can become fixated at that stage. During the phallic stage, the Oedipus complex is a major source of conflict.
	Psychoanalytic Dissenters and Revisionists	They criticized Freud for placing too much emphasis on sexuality and the first five years of life. They argued that Freud gave too little power to the ego, conscious thought, and sociocultural factors. Karen Horney believed that Freud did not emphasize sociocultural factors enough and that his theory has a masculine bias. Horney said the need for security, not sex or aggression, is our most important need. Carl Jung thought Freud underplayed the unconscious mind's role. He developed the concept of the collective unconscious and placed special emphasis on archetypes. Alfred Adler's theory is called individual psychology. It stresses that people are striving toward a positive being and that they create their own goals. Adler placed more emphasis on social motivation than Freud did.
	Evaluating the Psychoanalytic Perspectives	Strengths are an emphasis on the past, personality's developmental course, mental representation of the environment, unconscious mind, emphasis on conflict, and influence on psychology as a discipline. Weaknesses include the difficulty of testing the main concepts, the lack of an empirical data base and overreliance on reports from the past, too much emphasis on sexuality and the unconscious mind, a negative view of human nature, too much power given to early experience, and a male bias.

Many psychoanalytic theories of personality have a male bias, especially Freud's. Although Horney's theory helped to correct this bias, psychoanalytic theory continues to be revised today.

You should now have a sense of what personality is and the themes of psychoanalytic theories. A summary of these ideas is presented in summary table 12.1. Next we will discuss a view of personality *very* different from the psychoanalytic theories.

Behavioral and Social Cognitive Perspectives

John is engaged to marry Heather. Both have warm, friendly personalities, and they enjoy being with each other. Psychoanalytic theorists would say that their personalities are derived from long-standing relationships with their parents, especially their early childhood experiences. They would also argue that the reason for their attraction is unconscious; they are unaware of how their biological heritage and early life experiences have been carried forward to influence their adult personalities.

Behaviorists and social learning theorists would observe John and Heather and see something quite different. They would examine their experiences, especially their most recent ones, to understand the reason for John and Heather's attraction to one another. John would be described as rewarding Heather's behavior, and vice versa, for example. No reference would be made to unconscious thoughts, the Oedipus complex, defense mechanisms, and so on.

Defining the Behavioral and Social Cognitive Perspectives

The **behavioral and social cognitive perspectives** *emphasize the importance of studying environmental experiences and people's observable behavior to understand their personality. Social cognitive theory emphasizes person/cognitive factors in personality.*

At about the same time as Freud was interpreting his patients' unconscious minds through recollections of their childhood experiences, John B. Watson and Ivan Pavlov were conducting detailed observations of behavior under controlled laboratory conditions. Recall from chapter 6, "Learning," that Pavlov believed organisms learn through classical conditioning. Out of the behavioral tradition grew the belief that personality is observable behavior, learned through experiences with the environment. The two main versions of the behavioral and social cognitive perspectives are (1) behaviorism and (2) social cognitive theory.

Skinner's Behaviorism

In chapter 6, we described B. F. Skinner's approach to learning called *operant conditioning* ◀◻◻◻◻ P. 196. Skinner concluded that personality is the individual's *behavior,* which is determined by the *external environment.* Skinner believed we do not have to resort to biological or cognitive processes to explain personality (behavior). Some psychologists say that including Skinner among personality theorists is like inviting a wolf to a party of lambs because he took the "person" out of personality (Phares, 1984).

Behaviorists counter that you cannot pinpoint where personality is or how it is determined. In Skinner's view, personality simply consists of the collection of the person's observed, overt behaviors; it does not include internal traits or thoughts. For example, observations of Sam reveal that his behavior is shy, achievement-oriented, and caring. In short, these behaviors *are* his personality. According to Skinner, Sam is this way because the rewards and punishments in Sam's environment have shaped him into a shy, achievement-oriented, and caring person. Because of interactions with family members, friends, teachers, and others, Sam has *learned* to behave in this fashion.

Behaviorists who support Skinner's view would say that Sam's shy, achievement-oriented, and caring behavior may not be consistent and enduring. For example, Sam is uninhibited on Saturday night with friends at a bar, unmotivated to excel in English class, and occasionally nasty to his sister. In addition, Skinnerians believe that consistency in behavior comes from consistency in environmental experiences. If Sam's shy, achievement-oriented, and caring behavior is consistently rewarded, his pattern of behavior will likely be consistent. However, Skinner stressed that our behavior always has the capacity for change if new experiences are encountered. The issue of consistency in

PERSPECTIVES ON PERSONALITY

Behavioral and Social Cognitive Perspectives

Humanistic Perspectives

*T*hrough the Eyes of Psychologists

Walter Mischel, *Columbia University*

"Personality psychology is a field of great breadth, overlapping the neighboring areas of human development, abnormal behavior, emotion, cognition, learning, and social relations."

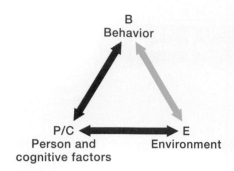

Bandura's Theory

$\mathscr{F}$igure 12.7
Bandura's Social Cognitive Theory

Bandura's social cognitive theory emphasizes reciprocal influences of behavior, environment, and person/cognitive factors.

Albert Bandura (above) and Walter Mischel are the architects of contemporary social cognitive theory.

personality is an important one. We will return to it on several occasions later in the chapter.

Since behaviorists believe that personality is learned and often changes according to environmental experiences and situations, it follows that by rearranging experiences and situations the individual's personality can be changed. For the behaviorist, shy behavior can be changed into outgoing behavior; aggressive behavior can be shaped into docile behavior; and lethargic, bored behavior can be shaped into enthusiastic, interested behavior.

Social Cognitive Theory Some psychologists believe the behaviorists are basically right when they say that personality is learned and influenced strongly by environmental experiences. But they think Skinner went too far in declaring that characteristics of the person or cognitive factors are unimportant in understanding personality. **Social cognitive theory** *states that behavior, environment, and person/cognitive factors are important in understanding personality* ◀▥ P. 8.

Albert Bandura (1986, 1997, 1998) and Walter Mischel (1973, 1995) are the architects of social cognitive theory's contemporary version, which was initially labeled *cognitive social learning theory* by Mischel (1973). Bandura says that behavior, environment, and person/cognitive factors interact in a reciprocal manner (see figure 12.7). Thus, in Bandura's view, the environment can determine a person's behavior (which matches up with Skinner's view), but there is much more to consider. The person can act to change the environment. Person/cognitive factors can influence a person's behavior and vice versa. Person/cognitive factors include self-efficacy (a belief that one can master a situation and produce positive outcomes), plans, and thinking skills. We will have much more to say about self-efficacy in chapter 15, "Health Psychology."

Remember from chapter 6, "Learning," that Bandura believes observational learning is a key aspect of how we learn. Through observational learning we form ideas about the behavior of others and then possibly adopt this behavior ourselves. For example, a young boy might observe his father's aggressive outbursts and hostile exchanges with people; when the boy is with his peers, he interacts in a highly aggressive way, showing the same characteristics as his father's behavior. Or a young executive adopts the dominant and sarcastic style of her boss. When this young woman interacts with one of her subordinates, she says, "I need this work immediately if not sooner; you are so far behind you think you are ahead!" Social cognitive theorists believe we acquire a wide range of such behaviors, thoughts, and feelings through observing others' behavior; these observations form an important part of our personality.

Social cognitive theorists also differ from the behavioral view of Skinner by emphasizing that we can regulate and control our own behavior, despite our changing environment (Metcalfe & Mischel, 1999). For example, another young executive who observed her boss behave in a dominant and sarcastic manner toward employees found the behavior distasteful and went out of her way to be encouraging and supportive of her subordinates. Someone tries to persuade you to join a particular social club on campus and makes you an enticing offer. You reflect on the offer, consider your interests and beliefs, and make the decision not to join. Your *cognition* (your thoughts) leads you to control your behavior and resist environmental influence in this instance.

Like the behavioral approach of Skinner, the social cognitive view emphasizes the importance of empirical research in studying personality. This research has focused on the processes that explain personality—the social and cognitive factors that influence what we are like as people. One process that Walter Mischel believes is important in understanding an individual's personality is delay of gratification, which is the ability to defer immediate satisfaction for a more desirable future outcome. For example, when you are in school you resist the temptation to slack off and have a good time now so you will be rewarded with good grades later. Again, the point is that we are capable of controlling our behavior rather than always being influenced by others.

Evaluating the Behavioral and Social Learning Perspectives

The behavioral and social cognitive theories emphasize that environmental experiences and situational influences determine personality. These approaches have fostered a scientific climate for understanding personality that highlights the observation of behavior. Social cognitive theory emphasizes both environmental influences and cognitive processes in explaining personality. This theory also suggests that people have the ability to control their environment.

Critics of both the behavioral and social learning perspectives take issue with several aspects of both perspectives. The behavioral view is criticized for ignoring the importance of cognition in personality and placing too much importance on the role of environmental experiences. Both approaches have been described as being too concerned with change and situational influences on personality and not paying adequate tribute to the enduring qualities of personality. Both views are said to ignore the role biology plays in personality. Both are labeled reductionistic, which means they try to explain the complex concept of personality in terms of one or two factors. The critics charge that the behavioral and social cognitive views are too mechanical, missing the most exciting, rich dimensions of personality. This latter criticism—that the creative, spontaneous, human dimensions of personality are missing from the behavioral and social cognitive perspectives—has been made on numerous occasions by humanists, whose perspective we consider next.

Humanistic Perspectives

Remember our example of the engaged couple, John and Heather, who were described as having warm, friendly personalities? Humanistic psychologists would say that John and Heather's warm, friendly personalities are a reflection of their inner selves. They would emphasize that a key to understanding their attraction is their positive perception of each other. John and Heather are not viewed as controlling each other or each other's behavior. Rather they have determined their own course of action and each has freely chosen to marry. No recourse to biological instincts or unconscious thoughts as reasons for their attraction occurs in the humanistic perspectives.

Association for Humanistic Psychology
Rogers' Theory

Defining the Humanistic Perspectives

The **humanistic perspectives** *stress the person's capacity for personal growth, freedom to choose one's own destiny, and positive qualities* ◀||||| P. 10. Humanistic psychologists believe each of us has the ability to cope with stress, control our lives, and achieve what we desire. Each of us has the ability to break through and understand ourselves and our world; we can burst the cocoon and become a butterfly, say the humanists.

You probably sense that the humanistic perspectives provide stark contrasts to the psychoanalytic perspectives, which is based on conflict, destructive drives, and little faith in human nature, and to the behavioral perspective, which, at its extreme, seems to reduce human beings to mere puppets on the strings of rewards and punishments. Carl Rogers and Abraham Maslow were the leading architects of the humanistic perspective.

Rogers' Approach

Like Freud, Rogers (1902–1987) began his inquiry about human nature with people who were troubled. In the knotted, anxious, defensive verbal stream of his clients, Rogers (1961) examined the conditioned, controlling world that kept them from having positive self-concepts and reaching their full potential as human beings.

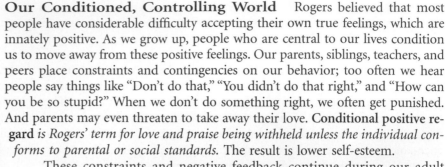

Carl Rogers, *(1902–1987)*

"In becoming a person, individuals drop one after another of their defensive masks with which they have faced life."

Our Conditioned, Controlling World   Rogers believed that most people have considerable difficulty accepting their own true feelings, which are innately positive. As we grow up, people who are central to our lives condition us to move away from these positive feelings. Our parents, siblings, teachers, and peers place constraints and contingencies on our behavior; too often we hear people say things like "Don't do that," "You didn't do that right," and "How can you be so stupid?" When we don't do something right, we often get punished. And parents may even threaten to take away their love. **Conditional positive regard** *is Rogers' term for love and praise being withheld unless the individual conforms to parental or social standards.* The result is lower self-esteem.

These constraints and negative feedback continue during our adult lives. The result tends to be that our relationships either carry the dark cloud of conflict or we conform to what others want. As we struggle to live up to society's standards, we distort and devalue our true self. And we might even completely lose our sense of self by mirroring what others want.

The Self   Through the individual's experiences with the world, a self emerges—this is the "I" or "me" of our existence. Rogers did not believe that all aspects of the self are conscious, but he did believe they are all accessible to consciousness. The self is a whole, consisting of one's self-perceptions (how attractive I am, how well I get along with others, how good an athlete I am) and the values we attach to these perceptions (good/bad, worthy/unworthy, for example). **Self-concept** *is a central theme in Rogers' and other humanists' views; self-concept refers to individuals' overall perceptions of their abilities, behavior, and personality.* In Rogers' view, a person who has an inaccurate self-concept is likely to be maladjusted.

In discussing self-concept, Rogers distinguished between the real self—that is, the self as it really is as a result of our experiences—and the ideal self, which is the self we would like to be. The greater the discrepancy between the real self and the ideal self, said Rogers, the more maladjusted we will be. To improve our adjustment, we can develop more positive perceptions of our real self, not worry so much about what others want, and increase our positive experiences in the world.

Unconditional Positive Regard, Empathy, and Genuineness   Rogers stressed that we can help a person develop a more positive self-concept through unconditional positive regard, empathy, and genuineness. Rogers said that we need to be accepted by others, regardless of what we do. **Unconditional positive regard** *is Rogers' term for accepting, valuing, and being positive toward another person regardless of the person's behavior.* Rogers recognized that when a person's behavior is below acceptable standards, inappropriate, or even obnoxious, the person still needs the respect, comfort, and love of others. Rogers strongly believed that unconditional positive regard elevates the person's self-worth. However, Rogers (1974) distinguished between unconditional positive regard directed at the individual as a person of worth and dignity and directed at the individual's behavior. For example, a therapist who adopts Rogers' view might say, "I don't like your behavior, but I accept you, value you, and care about you as a person."

Rogers also said we can help other people develop a more positive self-concept if we are *empathic* and *genuine*. Being empathic means being a sensitive listener and understanding another's true feelings. Being genuine means being open with our feelings and dropping our pretenses and facades. For Rogers, unconditional positive regard, empathy, and genuineness are three key ingredients of human relations. We can use these techniques to get other people to feel good about themselves and the techniques also help us to get along better with others.

The Fully Functioning Person   Rogers (1980) stressed the importance of becoming a fully functioning person—someone who is open to experience, is not very defensive, is aware of and sensitive to the self and the external world, and for the most part has a harmonious relationship with others. A discrepancy between our real self and our ideal self may occur; others may try to control us; and our world may have too little unconditional positive regard. But Rogers believed that we are highly resilient and capable of becoming a fully functioning person.

Humans' self-actualizing tendencies are reflected in Rogers' comparison of a person with a plant he once observed on the northern California coastline. As Rogers looked out at the waves furiously beating against the jagged rocks and shooting mountains of ocean spray into the air, he noticed the breakers pounding against a tiny sea palm tree 2 or 3 feet tall. The waves crashed against it, bending its slender trunk and whipping its leaves in a torrent of spray. Yet the moment the wave passed, the plant became erect, tough, and resilient once again. The plant took this incessant pounding hour after hour, week after week, possibly even year after year, all the time nourishing itself, maintaining its position, and growing. In this tiny tree, Rogers saw the tenacity of the human spirit and the ability of a living thing to push into a hostile environment and not only hold its own, but adapt, develop, and become itself. So it is with each of us, Rogers said.

Rogers believed that a person's basic tendencies are to actualize, maintain, and enhance life. He thought that the tendency for fulfillment—toward actualizing one's essential nature and attaining potential—is inborn in every person.

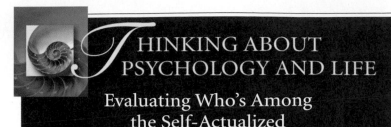

THINKING ABOUT PSYCHOLOGY AND LIFE
Evaluating Who's Among the Self-Actualized

THE FOLLOWING INDIVIDUALS were among the people identified as self-actualized by Maslow: Pablo Casals (cellist), Albert Einstein (physicist), Ralph Waldo Emerson (writer), William James (psychologist), Thomas Jefferson (politician), Abraham Lincoln (politician), Eleanor Roosevelt (humanitarian, diplomat), and Albert Schweitzer (humanitarian).

Maslow made up his list about three decades ago. Not all of his examples of self-actualized individuals were included here but there were considerably more men than women on the complete list. Most of the individuals were also from Western cultures. With Maslow's description of self-actualization in mind (including the characteristics of self-actualized individuals listed in figure 12.8), get together with some other students and brainstorm about who you would add to Maslow's list of self-actualized persons. For starters, consider Mahatma Gandhi (Indian political and spiritual leader) and Martin Luther King (clergyman, civil rights activist) (Endler, 1995), two individuals who were described as self-actualized by Maslow.

Maslow's Approach   Recall from chapter 11, "Motivation and Emotion," that another psychologist, Abraham Maslow (1908–1970), believed that self-actualization is the highest form of motivation ◀▥▥ P. 371. He also believed it is an important aspect of personality. Maslow was one of the most powerful figures in psychology's humanistic movement. He called the humanistic approach the "third force" in psychology—that is, an important alternative to the psychoanalytic and behavioral forces. Maslow pointed out that psychoanalytic theories place too much emphasis on disturbed individuals and their conflicts. Behaviorists ignore the person all together, he said.

Remember that Maslow (1954, 1971) believes our "basic" needs must be satisfied before our "higher" needs can be. According to Maslow's concept of **hierarchy of motives,** *individuals' needs must be satisfied in this sequence: physiological, safety, love and belongingness, esteem, and self-actualization.* Also recall that it is **self-actualization,** *the motivation to develop one's full potential as a human being, that Maslow focused on the most.* He believed self-actualization is the highest human need and that most people have difficulty reaching this level in their lives. Figure 12.8 describes the main characteristics that Maslow attributes to a self-actualized individual.

Self-Esteem   Interest in the self led to the belief that self-esteem is an important aspect of personality. **Self-esteem** *is the evaluative and affective dimension of self-concept. Self-esteem is also referred to as self-worth.*

Following are some of the issues and findings involving research on self-esteem (Baumeister, 1997):

• Does self-esteem fluctuate from day to day or remain stable? Most research studies have found it to be stable at least across a month or so of time (Baumeister, 1991). Self-esteem can change, especially in response to

Abraham Maslow

Through the Eyes of Psychologists

Abraham Maslow, *(1908–1970)*

"Self-actualizing stresses full humanness."

Maslow's Characteristics of Self-Actualized Individuals

Realistic orientation
Self-acceptance and acceptance of others and the natural world as they are
Spontaneity

Problem-centered rather than self-centered
Air of detachment and need for privacy
Autonomous and independent

Fresh rather than stereotyped appreciation of people and things
Generally have had profound mystical or spiritual, though not necessarily religious, experiences
Identification with humankind and a strong social interest

Tendency to have strong intimate relationships with a few special, loved people rather than superficial relationships with many people
Democratic values and attitudes
No confusion of means with ends
Philosophical rather than hostile sense of humor

High degree of creativity
Resistance to cultural conformity
Transcendence of environment rather than always coping with it

Figure 12.8
Maslow's Characteristics of Self-Actualized Individuals

transitions in life (such as graduating from high school or going to university) and to life events (such as getting a job or losing a job).

- Is self-esteem something very general or does it consist of a number of independent self-evaluations in different areas? That is, is it more appropriate to think of people having high or low self-esteem overall, or high or low self-esteem in specific areas of their lives, such as high in social, low in cognitive (academic)? Current thinking about this issue has evolved toward the conclusion that people do have a general level of self-esteem but can still have fluctuating levels of self-esteem in particular domains of their lives. (Fleming & Courtney, 1984).
- Low self-esteem is linked with depression (Harter, 1998). The failure to live up to one's standards is especially implicated in the connection between low self-esteem and depression.

An important point needs to be made about much of the research on self-esteem: It is correlational rather than experimental. Remember from our discussion in chapter 2, "Psychology's Scientific Methods," that correlation does not equal causation ◀ ‖‖‖ P. 45. Thus, if a correlational study finds an association between self-esteem and depression, depression could just as well cause poor self-esteem as much as poor self-esteem causes depression.

A topic of considerable interest is what can be done to increase the self-esteem of individuals with low self-esteem. Researchers have found that four main strategies help to improve self-esteem (Bednar, Wells, & Peterson, 1995; Harter, 1998): (1) identifying the causes of self-esteem, (2) experiencing emotional support and approval, (3) achieving, and (4) coping (see figure 12.9). The emphasis on experiencing emotional support and approval meshes with Carl Rogers' emphasis on unconditional positive regard that we discussed earlier in this chapter. Some psychologists argue that the most effective ways to improve self-esteem are to improve the person's achievement and coping skills. Rogers believes that when a person's achievement and coping skills improve, the individual's self-esteem is likely to follow suit. We will have much more to say about coping skills in chapter 15, "Health Psychology."

Evaluating the Humanistic Perspectives   The humanistic perspectives made psychologists aware that the way we perceive ourselves and the world around us are key elements of personality. Humanistic psychologists also reminded us that we need to consider the whole person and the positive bent of human nature. Their emphasis on conscious experience has given us the view that personality contains a well of "potential" that can be developed to its fullest.

A weakness of the humanistic perspective is that it is difficult to test. Self-actualization, for example, is not clearly defined. Psychologists are not certain how to study this concept empirically. Some humanists even scorn the experimental approach, preferring clinical interpretation as a data base. Verification of humanistic concepts has come mainly from clinical experiences rather than controlled, experimental studies. Some critics believe humanistic psychologists are too optimistic about human nature, overestimating the freedom and rationality of humans. And some critics say the humanists encourage self-love and narcissism.

We have seen that the behavioral and social cognitive perspectives, and the humanistic perspectives, take different paths to understanding personality. An overview of the main ideas in these perspectives is presented in summary table 12.2. Next we turn our attention to a fourth set of personality perspectives, the trait perspectives.

*F*igure 12.9
Four Main Strategies for Improving Self-Esteem

Trait Perspectives

Through the ages we have used an infinite variety of traits to describe ourselves and one another. More than 2,000 years ago Theophrastus described the stingy man, the liar, and the flatterer. A magazine article takes a modern swipe at the stingy man: Could a miser be lurking beneath the sensuous flesh and persuasive charm? Well, don't expect sapphires from him, if he itemizes who owes what when you're out Dutch-treat rather than splitting the bill, washes plastic party cups to reuse them, steams uncanceled stamps from letters, reshapes bent paper clips, has a dozen recipes for chicken wings, cuts his own hair, and wants rolls and butter included in his doggie bag (*Cosmopolitan*, September 1976, p. 148).

Think about yourself and your friends. How would you describe yourself? You might say that you're outgoing and sociable and that, in contrast, one of your friends is shy and quiet. You might refer to yourself as emotionally stable and describe one of your other friends as a bit skittish. Part of our everyday existence involves describing ourselves and others in terms of traits.

But traits have a deeper application as well. University of British Columbia psychologist Jerry Wiggins (e.g., Wiggins, 1997) has long been an advocate of the use of traits in both the construction of theories of personality and their measurement. Wiggins & Pincus (1992) also argued that trait approaches can be successfully applied to the study of people's lives.

Trait Theories   **Trait theories** *state that personality consists of broad dispositions, called traits, that tend to lead to characteristic responses.* In other words, people can be described in terms of the basic ways they behave, such as whether they are outgoing and friendly or whether they are dominant and assertive. People who have a strong tendency to behave in these ways are described as high on the traits; those

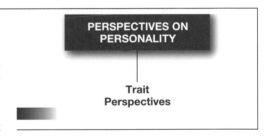

Trait Perspectives

Personality Traits

SUMMARY TABLE 12.2
The Behavioral and Social Cognitive Perspectives, and the Humanistic Perspectives

Concept	Processes/ Related Ideas	Characteristics/Description
Behavioral and Social Cognitive Perspectives	Defining the Behavioral and Social Cognitive Perspectives	They emphasize the importance of studying environmental experiences and a person's observable behavior to understand that person's personality. The contemporary version of social cognitive theory emphasizes person/cognitive factors in personality.
	Skinner's Behaviorism	This view emphasizes that cognition is unimportant in personality; personality is observed behavior, which is influenced by the rewards and punishments in the environment. Personality often varies according to the situation.
	Social Cognitive Theory	This theory, whose main architects are Bandura and Mischel, states that behavior, environment, and person/cognitive factors are important in understanding personality. In Bandura's view, these factors can reciprocally interact.
	Evaluating the Behavioral and Social Cognitive Perspectives	Strengths of both perspectives include emphases on environmental determinants and a scientific climate for investigating personality, as well as a focus on cognitive processes and self-control in the social cognitive approach. The behavioral view has been criticized for taking the "person" out of personality and for ignoring cognition. These approaches have not given adequate attention to enduring individual differences, to biological factors, and to personality as a whole.
Humanistic Perspectives	Defining the Humanistic Perspectives	They stress the person's capacity for personal growth and freedom, ability to choose one's own destiny, and positive qualities.
	Rogers' Approach	Each of us is a victim of conditional positive regard. The result is that the real self is not valued. The self is the core of personality; it includes both the real and ideal self. Rogers said we can help others develop a more positive self-concept in three ways: unconditional positive regard, empathy, and genuineness. Rogers also stressed that each of us has the innate, inner capacity to become a fully functioning person.
	Maslow's Approach	Maslow called the humanistic movement the "third force" in psychology. Maslow developed the hierarchy of needs concept with self-actualization being the highest human need.
	Self-Esteem	Self-esteem is the evaluative and affective dimension of the self. Self-esteem is also referred to as self-worth. Four main strategies for increasing self-esteem are (1) identifying the causes of low self-esteem, (2) emotional support and approval, (3) achievement, (4) coping.
	Evaluating the Humanistic Perspectives	They sensitized us to the importance of subjective experience, consciousness, self-conception, the whole person, and our innate, positive nature. Weaknesses focus on the absence of an empirical orientation, a tendency to be too optimistic, and an inclination to encourage self-love.

who have a weak tendency to behave in these ways are described as low on the traits. While trait theorists sometimes differ on which traits make up personality, they all agree that traits are the fundamental building blocks of personality (Cloninger, 1996; Matthews & Dreary, 1998).

Allport's View of Traits   Gordon Allport (1897–1967) believed that each individual has a unique set of personality traits. He argued that if a person's traits could be determined, it would be possible to predict the individual's behavior in various circumstances.

In going through an unabridged dictionary, Allport (1937) identified more than 4,500 personality traits. To impose some organization on the vast number of trait terms that might be used to describe an individual's personality, Allport grouped personality traits into three main categories: Central, secondary and cardinal.

Cardinal traits *are the most powerful and pervasive traits. When they are present, they dominate an individual's personality.* However, according to Allport, few people actually possess cardinal traits. We might think of some famous individuals as having these (Hitler's power, Mother Teresa's altruism). But most people aren't characterized by just one or two traits (unlike the way we think about Hitler or Mother Teresa). **Central traits** *are a limited number of traits (Allport believed most people have about 6 to 12 of these) that are usually adequate to describe most people's personalities.* For an example, an individual's personality might be described as friendly, calm, kind, and humorous. **Secondary traits** *are limited in frequency and least important in understanding an individual's personality.* They include particular attitudes and preferences, such as the type of food or music a person likes.

Eysenck's Dimensions of Personality   Hans Eysenck (1967) also tackled the task of determining the basic traits of personality. He gave personality tests to large numbers of people and analyzed each person's responses. Eysenck said that three main dimensions were needed to explain personality: (1) introversion–extraversion, (2) stable–unstable (known as the *neuroticism* dimension), and (3) psychoticism.

In terms of introversion–extraversion, an introverted person is quiet, unsociable, passive, and careful; an extraverted person is active, optimistic, sociable, and outgoing (Saklofske & Eysenck, 1994). In terms of stable–unstable, a stable person is calm, even-tempered, carefree, and has leadership possibilities; an unstable person is moody, anxious, restless, and touchy. Figure 12.10 shows these two basic dimensions in Eysenck's view. Eysenck believed that various combinations of these dimensions result in certain personality traits. For example, a person who is extraverted and unstable is likely to be impulsive. The third dimension, psychoticism, reflects the degree to which people are in contact with reality, control their impulses, and are cruel or caring toward others.

The Big Five Factors   Considerable interest continues to be generated in determining what the key factors of personality really are (Saucier & Ostendorf, 1999). In a number of areas, you have seen that psychologists are interested in pinning down the number and identity of factors involved in a concept. For example, in chapter 9, "Intelligence," we saw that Sternberg thinks intelligence is made up of three main factors and Gardner believes it is made up of seven.

The **big five factors of personality** *consists of emotional stability (neuroticism), extraversion, openness to experience, agreeableness, and conscientiousness* (see figure 12.11). A number of research studies point toward these factors as important dimensions of personality (Costa & McRae, 1995, 1998; David & Suls, 1999; Hogan, 1987).

Research on the big five includes the extent to which the factors appear in personality profiles in different cultures, how stable the factors are over time, and the role the factors might play in predicting physical and mental health (Wiggins, 1996).

Do the five factors show up in the assessment of personality in cultures around the world? There is increasing evidence that they do (Ozer & Reise, 1994). Researchers have found that some version of the five factors appears in people in countries as diverse as Canada, Finland, Poland, China, and Japan (Paunonen & others, 1992).

Using their five-factor personality test, Paul Costa and Robert McRae (1995) studied approximately a thousand university-educated men and women aged 20 to 96, assessing the same individuals over a period of many years. Data collection began in the 1950s to the mid 1960s and is ongoing. Costa and McRae concluded that

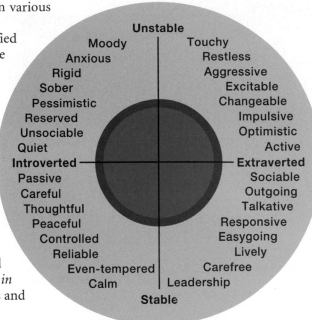

𝓕igure 12.10
Eysenck's Dimensions of Personality
Eysenck believed that for people without a psychological disorder, personality consists of two basic dimensions: (1) introversion–extraversion and (2) stability–instability. He thought that a third dimension—psychoticism—was needed to describe the personality of individuals with a psychological disorder.

Eysenck's View

The Big Five

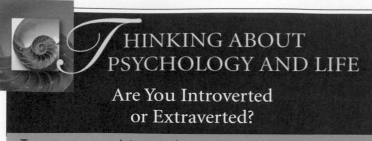

THINKING ABOUT PSYCHOLOGY AND LIFE

Are You Introverted or Extraverted?

To DETERMINE HOW introverted or extraverted you are, read each of the following 20 questions and answer either *yes* (if it is generally true for you) or *no* (if it is not generally true for you).

	Yes	No
1. Do you often long for excitement?		
2. Are you usually carefree?		
3. Do you stop and think things over before doing anything?		
4. Would you do almost anything for a dare?		
5. Do you often do things on the spur of the moment?		
6. Generally, do you prefer reading to meeting people?		
7. Do you prefer to have few but special friends?		
8. When people shout at you do you shout back?		
9. Do other people think of you as very lively?		
10. Are you mostly quiet when you are with people?		
11. If there is something you want to know about, would you rather look it up in a book than to talk to someone about it?		
12. Do you like the kind of work that you need to pay close attention to?		
13. Do you hate being with a crowd who plays jokes on one another?		
14. Do you like doing things in which you have to act quickly?		
15. Are you slow and unhurried in the way you move?		
16. Do you like talking to people so much that you never miss a chance of talking to a stranger?		
17. Would you be unhappy if you could not see lots of people most of the time?		
18. Do you find it hard to enjoy yourself at a lively party?		
19. Would you say that you were fairly self-confident?		
20. Do you like playing pranks on others?		

To arrive at your score for extraversion, give one point for each of the following items answered *yes*: #1, 2, 4, 5, 8. 9, 14, 16, 17, 19, and 20. Then give yourself one point for each of the following items answered *no*: #3, 6, 7, 10, 11, 12, 13, 15, 18. Add up all the points to arrive at a total score.

Your total score should be between 0 and 20. If your scores are very high (15–20), you are the "life of the party." You clearly prefer being with others to being alone. If your scores are very low (1–5), you are a loner. You find greater pleasure in solitary activities. If you are somewhere in between (6–14), you are flexible in how you prefer to spend your time. You can take pleasure in the company of others (especially if your score is in the higher range) but still manage to appreciate solitude.

considerable stability occurs in the five personality factors—emotional stability, extraversion, openness, agreeableness, and conscientiousness.

The notion that personality characteristics might influence vulnerability to illness and illness progression continues to attract widespread research attention. Much of this research, though, is conducted without reference to a unified framework of personality. The big five trait structure offers the potential for such a unified framework.

In one study, Costa and McRae's big five personality test, along with representative personality scales from health psychology (such as scales for personal control and self-esteem, optimism and hope, negative affectivity, and emotional control) were administered to two samples of male military recruits (Marshall & others, 1994). Variations in many of the health-related personality scales could be moderately explained by the big five factors. In health psychology research, neuroticism and extraversion have been given disproportionate attention (not surprisingly, given the prominence of these factors in theories of arousal and stress). The factors of conscientiousness and openness to experience have been especially neglected in research on personality's role in health and illness. Later in the chapter we will examine the tests that have been developed to assess the big five factors.

Research has generally supported the concept of the big five "general" traits, but some personality researchers believe they might not end up being the final list of supertraits. For example, some support has been found for two additional factors: excellent–ordinary and evil–decent, so the big five could become the big seven (Almagor, Tellegen, & Waller, 1995; Benet & Waller, 1995).

The Attack on Traits In his landmark book *Personality and Assessment* Walter Mischel (1968) criticized the trait view of personality as well as the psychoanalytic approach, both of which emphasize the internal organization of personality. Rather than viewing personality as consisting of broad, internal traits that are consistent across situations and time, Mischel said that personality often changes according to a given situation.

Mischel reviewed an array of studies and concluded that trait measures do a poor job of predicting actual behavior. For example, let's say Anne is described as an aggressive person. But when we observe her behavior we find that she is more or less aggressive depending on the situation—she might be aggressive with her boyfriend but almost submissive with her new boss. Mischel's view was called **situationism**, *which means that personality often varies considerably from one context to another.* Mischel's argument was an important one, but as we see next, many psychologists were not willing to abandon the trait concept altogether (Wiggins, 1997).

Trait-Situation Interaction Today, most psychologists in the field of personality are interactionists, including Mischel. They believe both trait (person) and situation variables are necessary to understand personality (Ackerman, Kyllonen, & Roberts, 1999; Edwards & Rothbard, 1999). They

Emotional Stability	Extraversion	Openness	Agreeableness	Conscientiousness
• Calm or anxious	• Sociable or retiring	• Imaginative or practical	• Softhearted or ruthless	• Organized or disorganized
• Secure or insecure	• Fun-loving or somber	• Interested in variety or routine	• Trusting or suspicious	• Careful or careless
• Self-satisfied or self-pitying	• Affectionate or reserved	• Independent or conforming	• Helpful or uncooperative	• Disciplined or impulsive

Figure 12.11
The Big Five Factors of Personality

also agree that the degree of consistency in personality depends on the kind of persons, situations, and behaviors sampled (Pervin, 1993; Mischel, 1995).

Suppose you want to assess the happiness of Bob, an introvert, and Petra, an extravert. According to trait-situation interaction theory, we cannot predict who will be happier unless we know something about the situations they are in. Imagine you get the opportunity to observe them in two situations, at a party and in a library.

Recent research has found that (1) the narrower and more limited a trait is, the more likely it will predict behavior; (2) some people are consistent on some traits and other people are consistent on other traits; and (3) personality traits exert a stronger influence on an individual's behavior when situational influences are less powerful (Walsh, 1995).

Cross-cultural psychologists believe that considering both the immediate setting *and* the broader cultural context leads to a better understanding of the situation's role in the way personality is expressed (Katigbak, Church, & Akamine, 1996). Also, University of Western Ontario psychologist Sampo Paunonen has investigated the measurement of personality across cultures (Paunonen & Ashton, 1998). It may be that trait approaches to personality depend upon the structure of language. One way to address this possibility is to look for the consistency of traits across cultures (Paunonen and others, 1992). Another approach is to use nonverbal assessment methods (Paunonen and others, in press).

At this point, we have studied a number of ideas about the trait perspectives. An overview of these ideas is presented in summary table 12.3. Now that we have explored the main theoretical perspectives in personality, we will turn our attention to another important aspect of studying personality: how it can be assessed.

Personality Assessment

PERSONALITY ASSESSMENT
Some Themes in Personality Assessment
Projective Tests
Self-Report Tests
Behavioral and Cognitive Assessment
COMPARING PERSPECTIVES ON PERSONALITY

"This line running this way indicates that you are a gregarious person, someone who really enjoys being around people. This division over here suggests that you are a risk taker; I bet you sometimes like to do things that are adventurous." These are the words you might hear from a palmist. Palmistry purports to "read" an individual's personality by interpreting the irregularities and folds in the skin of the hand. Each of these signs is interpreted in a precise manner. For example, a large mound of Saturn, the portion of the palm directly below the third joint of the middle finger, ostensibly relates to wisdom, good fortune, and prudence.

Summary Table 12.3
Trait Perspectives

Concept	Processes/ Related Ideas	Characteristics/Description
Trait Theories	Their Nature	Trait theories emphasize that personality involves the organization of traits within the individual. These traits are assumed to be essentially stable over time and across situations.
	Allport's View of Traits	Allport believed that each individual has a unique set of personality traits. He grouped personality traits into three main categories: cardinal, central, and secondary.
	Eysenck's Dimensions of Personality	Eysenck said that the basic dimensions of personality are (1) introversion–extraversion, (2) stability–instability (neuroticism), and (3) psychoticism.
	The Big Five Factors	There is much current interest in the big five factors in personality: emotional stability, extraversion, openness to experience, agreeableness, and conscientiousness.
	The Attack on Traits	Mischel's (1968) *Personality and Assessment* ushered in an attack on trait theory. Basically, the argument was that personality varies across situations more than trait theorists acknowledged.
Trait-Situation Interaction	Its Nature	Today most personality psychologists are interactionists. They believe that personality is determined by a combination of traits or person factors and the situation. Cross-cultural psychologists believe the situation involves both the immediate setting and the broader cultural context.

While palmists claim to provide a complete assessment of personality through reading lines in the hand, researchers debunk palmistry as quackery. Researchers argue that palmists give no reasonable explanation for their inferences about personality, and point out that the hand's characteristics can change through age and even exercise.

Even so, palmists manage to stay in business. They do so, in part, because they are keen observers—they respond to such cues as voice, general demeanor, and dress, which are more relevant signs of personality than the lines and folds on a person's palm. Palmists are also experts at offering general, trivial statements such as, "Although you are usually affectionate with others, sometimes you don't get along with people." This statement falls into the category of the **Barnum effect:** *If you make your predictions broad enough, any person can fit the description.* The effect was named after circus owner P. T. Barnum.

Some Themes in Personality Assessment

Assessment Journals

In contrast to palmists, psychologists use scientifically developed tests and methods to evaluate personality (Walsh & Betz, 1995). Most personality tests are designed to assess stable, enduring characteristics, free of situational influence (Hy & Loevinger, 1996). Further, many different tests have been constructed. For example, Douglas Jackson of the University of Western Ontario developed the widely cited *Personality Research Form (PRF)*. Based on Murray's (1938) theory of needs, the PRF was developed from a theoretical, rather than an empirical perspective. Jackson also developed the *Jackson Personality Inventory (JPI)*, which provides personality profiles of managers, executives, and professionals and has been instrumental in refining test development methodologies (Jackson, 1991).

Psychologists assess personality for different reasons. Clinical and school psychologists seek to understand, diagnose and treat an individual's psychological problems. Industrial psychologists and vocational counselors seek to help the individual select a career. And research psychologists seek to investigate the theories and dimensions of personality.

Projective Tests

A **projective test** *presents individuals with an ambiguous stimulus and then asks them to describe it or tell a story about it. Projective tests are based on the assumption that the ambiguity of the stimulus allows individuals to project into it their feelings, desires, needs, and attitudes.* The test is especially designed to elicit the individual's unconscious feelings and conflicts, providing an assessment that goes deeper than the surface of personality (Auerbach, 1999; Handler, 1999). Projective tests attempt to get inside of your mind to discover how you really feel and think, going beyond the way you overtly present yourself.

The Rorschach Inkblot Test

The **Rorschach inkblot test,** *developed in 1921 by the Swiss psychiatrist Hermann Rorschach, is a widely used projective test; it uses an individual's perception of inkblots to determine his or her personality.* The test consists of ten cards, half in black and white and half in color, which are shown to the individual one at a time (see figure 12.12). The person taking the Rorschach test is asked to describe what he or she sees in each of the inkblots. For example, an individual may say, "That looks like two people fighting." After the individual has responded to all ten inkblots, the examiner presents each of the inkblots again and inquires about the individual's earlier response. For example, the examiner might ask, "*Where* did you see the two people fighting?" and "*What* about the inkblot made the two people look like they were fighting?" Besides recording the responses, the examiner notes the individual's mannerisms, gestures, and attitudes.

How useful is the Rorschach in assessing personality? The answer to this question depends on one's perspective. From a scientific perspective, researchers are skeptical about the Rorschach (Feshbach & Weiner, 1996). Their disenchantment stems from the failure of the Rorschach to meet the criteria of reliability and validity. If the Rorschach were reliable, two different scorers should agree on the personality characteristics of the individual. If the Rorschach were valid, the individual's personality should predict behavior outside of the testing situation; that is, it should predict whether an individual will attempt suicide, become severely depressed, cope successfully with stress, or get along well with others. Conclusions based on research evidence suggest that the Rorschach does not meet these criteria of reliability and validity ◀⫶⫶ P. 288. This has led to serious reservations about the Rorschach's use in diagnosis and clinical practice.

Yet the Rorschach continues to enjoy widespread use in clinical circles; some clinicians swear by the Rorschach, saying it is better than any other measure at getting at the true, underlying core of the individual's personality (Sloan & others, 1996). They are not especially bothered by the Rorschach's low reliability and validity, pointing out that this is so because of the extensive freedom of response encouraged by the test. It is this freedom of response that makes the Rorschach such a rich clinical tool, say its advocates. In one survey, Rorschach-based testimony was legally challenged in only 6 of nearly 8,000 court cases (Weiner, Exner, & Sciara, 1996).

The Rorschach controversy continues (Baity & Hilsenroth, 1999; Murstein & Mathes, 1996). And it will probably not subside in the near future. Research psychologists will continue to criticize the low reliability and validity of the Rorschach; many clinicians will continue to say that the Rorschach is a valuable clinical tool, providing insights about the unconscious mind that no other personality test can.

Other Projective Tests

The **Thematic Apperception Test** (TAT), *which was developed by Henry Murray and Christina Morgan in the 1930s, is an ambiguous projective test designed to elicit stories that reveal something about an individual's personality.* The TAT consists of a series of pictures, each on an individual card (see figure 12.13). The person taking the TAT is asked to tell a story about each of the pictures, including events leading up to the situation described, the characters' thoughts and feelings, and how the situation turns out. It is assumed that the person projects her own unconscious feelings and thoughts into the story she tells. In

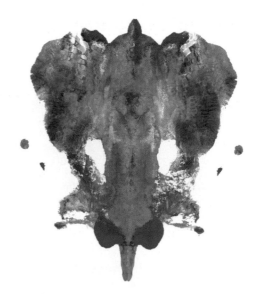

*$\mathscr{F}$*igure 12.12
Type of Stimulus Used in the Rorschach Inkblot Test

The Rorschach

"Rorschach! What's to become of you?"
© Sidney Harris

*𝓕*igure 12.13
Picture from the Thematic Apperception Test (TAT)

Reprinted by permission of the Publishers from Henry A. Murray, "Thematic Apperception Test," Cambridge, MA: Harvard University Press. Copyright © 1943 by the President and Fellows of Harvard College. © 1971 by Henry A. Murray.

addition to being used as a projective test in clinical practice, the TAT is used in research of achievement motivation (Cramer, 1999). Several of the TAT cards stimulate the telling of achievement-related stories, which enables the researcher to determine the person's need for achievement (McClelland & others, 1953).

Many other projective tests are used in clinical assessment. One test asks the individual to complete a sentence (for example "I often feel . . ." "I would like to . . ."); another test asks the individual to draw a person; and another test presents a word, such as *fear* or *happy,* and asks the individual to say the first thing that comes to mind. Like the Rorschach, these projective tests have their detractors and advocates; the detractors often criticize the tests' low reliability and validity, and the advocates describe the tests' abilities to reveal the underlying nature of the individual's personality better than more straightforward tests. Recently, another projective measure has generated considerable controversy—**graphology,** *the use of handwriting analysis to determine an individual's personality.* To read further about graphology and its lack of scientific status, turn to Explorations in Psychology.

Self-Report Tests

Unlike projective techniques derived from psychoanalytic perspectives, self-report tests, which are derived from the trait perspectives, do not attempt to assess an individual's hidden, unconscious personality. Rather, **self-report tests,** *also called objective tests or inventories, directly ask people whether items (usually true/false or agree/disagree) describe their personality traits or not.* For example, self-report personality tests include items such as:

- I am easily embarrassed.
- I love to go to parties.
- I like to watch cartoons on TV.

Self-report tests are questionnaires that include a large number of statements or questions like these. You respond with a limited number of choices (yes or no; true or false; agree or disagree). How do psychologists construct self-report tests of personality?

Constructing Self-Report Tests   Many of the early personality tests were based on **face validity,** *which is an assumption that the content of the test items is a good indicator of the individual's personality.* For example, if we developed a test item that asks you to respond whether or not you are introverted, and you answer, "I enjoy being with people," we accept your response as a straightforward indication that you are not introverted. Tests based on face validity assume that you are responding honestly and nondefensively, giving the examiner an accurate portrayal of your personality.

But not everyone is honest, especially when it concerns their own personality. Even if the individual is basically honest, he may be giving socially desirable answers. When motivated by **social desirability,** *individuals say what they think the interviewer wants to hear or what they think will make them look better.* For example, a basically lazy person might not want you to know this, and may try to present himself in a more positive way; therefore, he would respond negatively to the following item: "I fritter away too much time." Because of such responses psychologists realized they needed to go beyond face validity in constructing personality tests; they accomplished this by developing empirically keyed tests.

An **empirically keyed test** *relies on its items to predict some criterion.* Unlike tests based on face validity, in which the content of the items is supposed to be a good indicator of what the individual's personality is like, empirically keyed tests make no assumptions about the nature of the items. Imagine we want to develop a test that will determine whether or not applicants for a position as a police officer are likely to be competent at the job. We might ask a large number of questions of police officers, some of whom have excellent job records, others who have not performed as well. We would then use the questions that differentiate between competent and incompetent police officers on our test to screen job applicants. If the item, "I enjoyed reading poetry" predicts success as a police officer, then we would include it on the

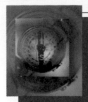

EXPLORATIONS IN PSYCHOLOGY
Being Skeptical About Graphology

CAN THE ANALYSIS of a person's handwriting provide insight into her personality? Examine the writing in figure 12.C to see the kinds of interpretations graphologists make. At least 3,000 firms in the United States use graphology when hiring individuals. In other countries, such as Israel and Japan, the use of graphological analysis in hiring is even more widespread. One survey found that 85 percent of all European firms use graphology as part of their employee-selection process (Levy, 1979). The managing editor of the journal *United States Banker* commented, "Graphoanalysis [graphology] reveals capabilities and aptitudes in an individual, many of which the applicant may not be aware of" (Van Deventer, 1983). Given the recent popularity of handwriting analysis in business hiring, it is important to examine whether it really does reveal anything about an individual's personality characteristics (Hines, 1988).

The research on graphology is almost totally negative (Furnham, 1988; Nevo, 1986). Dean and others (1992) have examined biases in the decision processes involved in graphology. One study typifies these negative results (Ben-Shakhar & others, 1986). Three professional graphologists were asked to assess the competence of 52 bank employees at their jobs and the nature of their relationships with co-workers. The samples consisted of brief autobiographical essays and responses to a short biographical questionnaire. The researchers also used information from the samples to make assessments about the employees' competence. The researchers' predictions and the graphologists' ratings were compared with the ratings by the employees' supervisors. The graphologists did no better than the researchers at matching the supervisors' ratings. In a second study, five graphologists did no better than chance when asked to predict the occupations of 40 successful professional men based on several pages of their handwriting. Carswell (1992) points out that, in Canada, because graphology lacks scientific validity, its practitioners may run the risk of civil or criminal liability from those who suffer damages as a result of its use.

If the research investigation of graphological claims is so negative, why is graphology so widely used and accepted? Graphological analysis has a mysterious, powerful ring to it. People are easily impressed by confident, so-called experts and assume they know what they are talking about. Positive, unscientific reports of graphologists' abilities appear frequently in magazines and business commentaries. People are fascinated by graphology and want to believe that their handwriting, because it is highly individual, reveals something about themselves. Also, graphologists' predictions, like those of palmists and astrologers, are usually very general and difficult to disprove.

---

1. Level of emotional responsiveness

Withdrawal   Objectiveness   Intensity

The backward slant at left indicates withdrawal, the vertical slant in the middle indicates objectiveness, and the forward slant on the right indicates intensity.

2. Social responsiveness

Repression   Lack of inhibition

Note the tight loops of the m and n on the left, which indicate repression, and the spread loops of the m and n on the right, which indicate a lack of inhibition.

3. Approach to achievement

Lack of self-confidence   Strong willpower

Note the low t-bar on the left, which indicates a lack of self-confidence, and the high t-bar on the right, which indicates strong willpower.

Figure 12.C
Some Graphological Interpretations

---

test even though it seems unrelated to police work. Next, we examine the most widely used empirically keyed personality test.

The Minnesota Multiphasic Personality Inventory (MMPI)

The **Minnesota Multiphasic Personality Inventory** (**MMPI**) *is the most widely used and researched self-report personality test.* The MMPI initially was constructed to assess "abnormal" personality tendencies and improve the diagnosis of individuals with

Journal of Personality Assessment MMPI-2

a mental disorder. A thousand statements were given to both mental patients and apparently normal people. How often individuals agreed with each item was calculated; only the items that clearly differentiated the psychiatric patients from the normal individuals were retained. For example, a statement might be included on the depression scale of the MMPI if patients diagnosed with a depressive disorder agreed with the statement significantly more than did normal individuals. For example, a statement with little face validity, such as "I sometimes tease animals," might be included on the depression scale, or any other scale, of the MMPI.

The MMPI was eventually streamlined to 550 items, each of which can be answered true, false, or cannot say. The items vary widely in content and include such statements as the following:

- I like to read magazines.
- I never have trouble falling asleep.
- People are out to get me.

A person's answers are grouped according to ten clinical categories, or scales, that measure problems such as depression, psychopathic deviation, schizophrenia, and social introversion.

The MMPI also includes four validity scales designed to indicate whether an individual is lying, careless, defensive, or evasive when answering test items. For example, if the individual responds "false" to a number of items, such as "I get angry sometimes," it would be interpreted that she is trying to make herself look better than she really is. We all get angry at least some of the time, so the individual who responds "false" to many such items is faking her responses. Another approach to verifying a test's validity is to time how long answers take (Holden & Kroner, 1992).

For the first time in its approximately 40-year history, the MMPI was revised in 1989. The revision is called the MMPI-2. It has a number of new items (for a total of 567 items), but the 10 clinical scales were retained as were several of the validity scales (such as the lie scale). New content scales were added to the MMPI-2. These include substance abuse, eating disorders, anger, self-esteem, family problems, and inability to function in a job.

The MMPI-2 continues to be widely used around the world to assess personality and predict outcomes (Butcher, 1999; Butcher, Lim, & Nezami, 1998). It has been so popular that it has been translated into more than 20 languages. Not only is it used by clinical psychologists to assess a person's mental health, it is also used to predict which individuals will make the best job candidates or which career an individual should pursue.

One trend is the increased use of computers to score the MMPI-2 (Finger & Ones, 1999; Iverson & Barton, 1999). Some critics argue that too often this has meant untrained individuals have been tempted to use the test in ways that it was not validated for.

Assessing the Big Five Factors   Earlier we indicated that there is great interest in the big five factors in personality: emotional stability, extraversion, openness, agreeableness, and conscientiousness. Paul Costa and Robert McRae (1992) constructed a test, the *Neuroticism Extraversion Openness Personality Inventory, Revised* (or *NEO-PI-R* for short), to assess the big five factors. Costa and McRae believe that the test can improve the diagnosis of personality disorders and help therapists understand how therapy might influence different types of clients. For instance, individuals identified as extraverts might prefer group whereas introverts might do better in individual psychotherapy.

Another measure used to assess the big five factors is Hogan's (1986) Hogan Personality Inventory (HPI). The Jackson Personality Inventory and the Personality Research Form have also been analyzed in terms of the big five factors (Paunonen & Jackson, 1996; Ashton & others, 1998). One way the HPI and the NEO-PI-R are used is to attempt to predict job success. Researchers have found that the HPI effectively predicts such job performance criteria as supervisor ratings and training course success (Wiggins & Trapnell, 1997).

*𝒯*hrough the Eyes of Psychologists

Douglas Jackson, *University of Western Ontario*

"Personality scale scores should be interpreted in the light of the assumptions and preconceptions guiding their development."

Evaluating Self-Report Tests   Adherents of the trait approach have strong faith in the utility of self-report tests. They point out that self-report tests have produced a better understanding of the nature of an individual's personality traits than can be derived from, for example, projective tests. However, some critics (especially psychoanalysts) believe the self-report measures do not get at the underlying core of personality and its unconscious determinants. Other critics (especially behaviorists) believe the self-report tests do not adequately capture the situational variation in personality and the ways personality changes as the individual interacts with the environment.

Exploring Personality Tests
Journal of Personality

Behavioral and Cognitive Assessment

Behavioral assessment attempts to obtain more objective information about an individual's personality by observing the individual's behavior directly ◀‖‖ P. 41. Instead of removing situational influences from personality as projective tests and self-report measures do, behavioral assessment assumes that personality cannot be evaluated apart from the environment. Behavior modification is an attempt to apply learning principles to change maladaptive behavior. Behavioral assessment of personality emerged from this tradition. For example, recall that the observer will often make baseline observations of the frequency of the individual's behaviors. This might be accomplished under controlled laboratory conditions or in more naturalistic circumstances. The therapist will then modify some aspect of the environment, such as getting parents and the child's teacher to stop giving the child attention when he engages in the aggressive behavior. After a specified period of time, the therapist will observe the child again to determine if the changes in the environment were effective in reducing the child's maladaptive behavior.

Sometimes, though, direct observations are impractical. What does a psychologist with a behavioral orientation then do to assess personality? She might ask individuals to make their own assessments of behavior, encouraging them to be sensitive to the circumstances that produced the behavior and the outcomes or consequences of the behavior. For example, a therapist might want to know the course of marital conflict in the everyday experiences of a couple. Figure 12.14 shows a spouse observation checklist that couples can use to record their partner's behavior.

The influence of social cognitive theory has increased the use of cognitive assessment in personality evaluation. The strategy is to discover what thoughts underlie the individual's behavior; that is, how do individuals think about their problems? What kinds of thoughts precede maladaptive behavior, occur during its manifestation, and follow it? Cognitive processes such as expectations, planning, and memory are assessed, possibly by interviewing the individual or asking him or her to complete a questionnaire. For example, an interview might include questions that address whether the individual overexaggerates his faults and condemns himself more than is warranted. A questionnaire might ask a person what her thoughts are after an upsetting event or it might assess the way she thinks during tension-filled moments.

It has been some time since we considered the different theoretical approaches to personality. Next, to conclude the chapter, we return to those theories and compare their orientation on a number of important issues involving personality.

Comparing Perspectives on Personality

Three important issues in personality are the degree to which it is innate or learned (biologically or experientially based); the degree to which it is conscious or unconscious; and the degree to which it is internally or externally determined.

1. *Innate versus learned.* Is personality due more to biological factors or more to environmental experiences? ◀‖‖ P. 68 (Ashton & others, 1998). Are individuals conceited and self-centered because they inherited the tendency to be conceited and self-centered from their parents, or did they learn to be that way through experiences with other conceited, self-centered individuals? Freud's theory has a strong biogenetic foundation, although many psychoanalytic revisionists have

Type of behavior	Item
Shared activities	We sat and read together. We took a walk.
Pleasing interactive events	My spouse asked how my day was. We talked about personal feelings. My spouse showed interest in what I said by agreeing or asking relevant questions.
Displeasing interactive events	My spouse commanded me to do something. My spouse complained about something I did. My spouse interrupted me.
Pleasing affectionate behavior	We held each other. My spouse hugged and kissed me.
Displeasing affectionate behavior	My spouse rushed into intercourse without taking time for foreplay. My spouse rejected my sexual advances.
Pleasing events	My spouse did the dishes. My spouse picked up around the house.
Displeasing events	My spouse talked too much about work. My spouse yelled at the children.

Figure 12.14
Items from the Spouse Observation Checklist

Couples are instructed to complete a more extensive checklist for fifteen consecutive evenings. Spouses record their partner's behavior, and they make daily ratings of their overall satisfaction with the spouse's behavior.

argued that he underestimated the power of environmental experiences and culture in determining personality. Behaviorism and humanism both endorse environment as a powerful determinant of personality, Skinner being the strongest advocate of environment's influence. However, humanistic theorists do believe that people have the innate ability to become self-actualized. Trait theorists vary in their emphasis on heredity and environment; Eysenck stressed the biological basis of personality, while Allport weighted biology and environment more equally.

2. *Conscious versus unconscious.* Is personality due more to conscious factors or unconscious factors? How aware are individuals that they are conceited and self-centered? How aware are they of the reasons they became conceited and self-centered? Freud and Jung were the strongest advocates of the unconscious mind's role in personality. Freud stressed that our deeply repressed experiences in infancy and early childhood determine what our personalities are like as adults, for example. Most psychoanalytic theorists argue that we are largely unaware of how our individual personalities developed. Skinner argues that neither unconscious nor conscious thoughts are important in determining personality, although social cognitive theorists Bandura and Mischel stress that cognitive factors mediate the environment's influence on personality. The humanists, such as Rogers and Maslow, stress the conscious aspects of personality, especially in the form of self-perception. Trait theorists pay little attention to the conscious/unconscious issue.

3. *Internal versus external determinants.* Is personality due more to an inner disposition or more to outer situations? Are individuals conceited and self-centered because of something inside themselves, a characteristic they have and carry around with them, or are they conceited and self-centered because of the situations they are in and the way they are influenced by people around them? Psychoanalytic theorists emphasize the internal dimensions of personality (Freud's internal structures of id, ego, and superego, for example). Trait theorists also stress internal determinants through

| | PERSONALITY THEORY | | | |
ISSUE	Psychoanalytic Perspectives	Behavioral and Social Cognitive Perspectives	Humanistic Perspectives	Trait Perspectives
Innate versus learned	Strong emphasis on biological foundations by Freud. Adler, Sullivan, and Erikson gave social experiences and culture more importance than Freud.	Skinner said personality is behavior that is environmentally determined. Social cognitive theorists also emphasize environmental experiences.	Humanistic theorists emphasize that personality is influenced by experience and can be changed.	Eysenck stresses personality's biological basis; Allport gave attention to both heredity and environment.
Conscious versus unconscious	Strong emphasis on unconscious thought, especially Freud and Jung	Skinner didn't think conscious or unconscious thought was important in personality. Bandura and Mischel emphasize cognitive process.	Stress conscious aspects of personality, especially self-concept, self-perception	Pay little attention to this issue
Internal versus external determinants	Emphasize internal determinants, personality structures	Emphasize external situational determinants of personality. Bandura and Mischel emphasize internal and external determinants, especially self-control.	Emphasize internal determinants of self-concept and self-determination	Stress internal, person variables
Personality measurement	Clinical interviews, unstructured personality tests, and psychohistorical analysis of lives	Observation, especially laboratory observation	Self-report measures and interviews. Clinical judgment more important than scientific measurement is view of many humanists.	Self-report tests such as MMPI–2

Sigmund Freud   B.F. Skinner   Carl Rogers   Gordon Allport

*F*igure 12.15
Comparing Perspectives on Personality

SUMMARY TABLE 12.4
Personality Assessment and Comparing Perspectives on Personality

Concept	Processes/ Related Ideas	Characteristics/Description
Personality Assessment	Some Themes	Psychologists use a wide variety of tests and measures to assess personality. These measures are often tied to psychologists' theoretical orientations. Personality tests were basically designed to measure stable, enduring aspects of personality.
	Projective Tests	A projective test involves presenting individuals with an ambiguous stimulus and then asking them to describe it or tell a story about it. Projective tests are based on the assumption that the ambiguity of the stimulus allows individuals to project their personality into it. Projective tests are designed to assess the unconscious aspects of personality. The Rorschach inkblot test is a widely used projective test; its effectiveness is controversial. The Thematic Apperception Test (TAT) is another projective test.
	Self-Report Tests	Self-report tests assess your personality traits by asking you what they are. In constructing self-report tests, we discussed face validity and the problem of socially desirable responses. Empirically keyed tests rely on their items to predict some criterion. The Minnesota Multiphasic Personality Inventory (MMPI) is the most widely used and researched self-report personality test. The MMPI-2 (a revision that appeared in 1989) has a number of new items but preserves the 10 clinical scales and some validity scales. Some items were deleted from the original MMPI and some new content scales were added. Two tests that have been created to assess the big five personality factors are the NEO-PI-R and the HPI. Self-report tests mesh with the trait theoretical approach to personality. As with other types of personality assessment, some criticisms of the self-report tests have been made.
	Behavioral and Cognitive Assessment	Behavioral assessment tries to obtain more objective information about personality through observation of behavior and its environmental ties. Cognitive assessment is increasingly being used.
Comparing Perspectives on Personality	Some Issues and Measures	Three important issues addressed by perspectives on personality are the degree to which personality is innate versus learned, conscious versus unconscious, and internally versus externally determined. Different perspectives on personality advocate the use of particular assessment strategies. We examined how psychoanalytic, behavioral/social cognitive, humanistic, and trait perspectives address these issues and which assessment strategies they support.

Society for Personality and Social Psychology

their belief in the importance of self-concept and self-determination. By contrast, behaviorists emphasize personality's external, situational determinants, although social cognitive theorists examine both external and internal determinants.

A summary of comparisons of personality perspectives on these three important issues—innate versus learned, conscious versus unconscious, and internal versus external determination—is presented in figure 12.15, along with a comparison of the methods advocated by theorists.

At this point we have discussed a number of ideas about personality assessment and comparing personality perspectives. An overview of these ideas is presented in summary table 12.4. In this chapter we discussed the normal aspects of personality. In the next chapter, we will explore abnormal psychology, including some personality disorders.

Overview

Overview

WE BEGAN THIS CHAPTER by exploring what personality is. Our coverage of perspectives included many ideas about psychoanalytic perspectives, behavioral and social cognitive perspectives, humanistic perspectives, and trait perspectives. We examined these dimensions of personality assessment: its themes, projective tests, and self-report tests, as well as behavioral and cognitive assessment. And we compared the main perspectives on personality on some important issues and described the types of methods they use to assess personality.

Remember that you can obtain a more detailed overview of the chapter by again studying the four summary tables on pages 422, 430, 434, and 442.

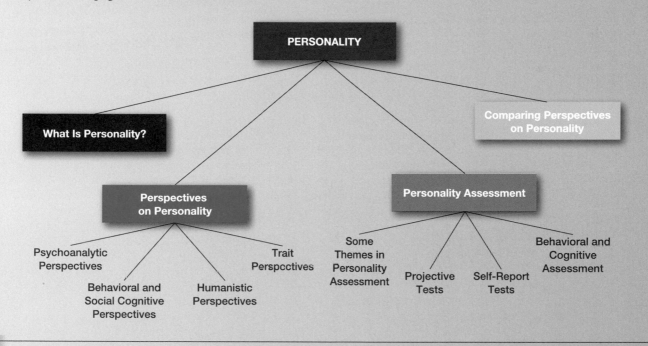

Key Terms

Key Terms

personality 412
psychoanalytic perspectives 413
id 415
pleasure principle 415
ego 415
reality principle 415
superego 415
defense mechanisms 415
repression 416
erogenous zones 417
fixation 417
oral stage 417
anal stage 417
phallic stage 418

Oedipus complex 418
latency stage 418
genital stage 419
collective unconscious 420
archetype 420
individual psychology 420
striving for superiority 420
compensation 421
overcompensation 421
inferiority complex 421
superiority complex 421
behavioral and social cognitive perspectives 423
social cognitive theory 424
humanistic perspectives 425

conditional positive regard 426
self-concept 426
unconditional positive regard 426
hierarchy of motives 427
self-actualization 427
self-esteem 427
trait theories 429
cardinal traits 431
central traits 431
secondary traits 431
big five factors of personality 431
situationism 432

Barnum effect 434
projective test 435
Rorschach inkblot test 435
Thematic Apperception Test (TAT) 435
graphology 436
self-report tests 436
face validity 436
social desirability 436
empirically keyed test 436
Minnesota Multiphasic Personality Inventory (MMPI) 437

Key People

Sigmund Freud 413
Karen Horney 419
Carl Jung 420
Alfred Adler 420
B. F. Skinner 423

Albert Bandura 424
Walter Mischel 424
Carl Rogers 425
Abraham Maslow 427
Jerry Wiggins 429

Gordon Allport 430
Hans Eysenck 431
Sampo Paunonen 433
Hermann Rorschach 435

Henry Murray and
 Christina Morgan 435
Paul Costa and Robert McRae
 438
Douglas Jackson 438

Psychology Checklist
PERSONALITY

How much have you learned since the beginning of the chapter? Use the following statements to help you review your knowledge and understanding of the chapter material. First, read the statement and mentally or briefly on paper demonstrate that you can discuss the relevant information.

_____ I know what personality is.
_____ I can describe the psychoanalytic perspective, including Freud's theory, as well as the psychoanalytic dissenters and revisionists.
_____ I can discuss the behavioral and social cognitive perspectives.
_____ I can evaluate the humanistic perspectives, including Rogers' and Maslow's views.
_____ I can describe what self-esteem is and how it can be increased.

_____ I know what trait theory is and am aware of Allport's and Eysenck's views.
_____ I can describe the big five personality factors.
_____ I am aware of what trait-situation interaction is.
_____ I can evaluate personality assessment, including some themes of assessment, projective tests, self-report tests, and behavioral/cognitive assessment.
_____ I can compare the main personality perspectives on issue and the methods they use.

For any items that you did not check off, go back and locate the relevant material in the chapter. Review the material until you feel you can check off the item. You also may want to use this checklist later in preparing for an exam.

Taking It to the Net

1. Imagine a boy who has extreme anger, rage, and fantasies of violence. He generally keeps his emotions to himself and rarely shows how angry he is. Moreover, he is embarrassed by his violent fantasies and hasn't told anyone about them. Instead, he plays football and focuses all of his emotions into the sport. Fortunately, he winds up being very good at football, and ends up playing professionally. Describe the defense mechanisms that he has used to reduce his anxiety about his emotions. Is this an effective strategy?

2. Consider a famous experiment by Albert Bandura. Three groups of children watched an adult in a playroom behave aggressively (e.g., hit, kick, yell) toward a large plastic doll. The film had three different endings. One group of children saw the adult praised for his or her behavior; a second group saw the adult being told that he or she must go sit down in a corner and not play with the toys; a third group (the control group) saw a film with the adult simply walking out of the room. The children were then left in the room to play with the plastic doll in any way they chose. What do you think happened? Do you think there were differences between boys and girls? Explain.

3. Personality tests are often a good way to learn more about yourself. They are also used to predict how people will act in a given situation. For example, a personality assessment might show that you are very introverted (i.e., reserved, sober, unsociable). It is therefore reasonable to predict that in a party atmosphere, you would not want all of the attention directed at you. Because of this predictive value, some employers have used personality tests in their hiring process. What do you think of this practice? How would you feel if you were not accepted for a job on the basis of a personality assessment? Consider also the benefits of learning what jobs suit your personality.

Connect to http://www.mcgrawhill.ca/college/santrock to find the answers!

Resources for Psychology and Life

Gentle Roads to Survival (1991)
    by Andre Auw
    Lower Lake, CA: Aslan

In *Gentle Roads to Survival,* Auw presents a guide to making self-healing choices in difficult circumstances. Auw, a psychologist who was a close associate of Carl Rogers, tells you how to become a survivor.

Handbook of Personality Psychology (1997)
    by Robert Hogan, John Johnson, and Stephen Briggs (eds.)
    San Diego: Academic Press

This book includes articles by leading experts on personality on a wide variety of topics ranging from theory to research to assessment.

Journal of Personality Assessment

This research journal publishes articles on many aspects of personality assessment, including empirically keyed tests, such as the MMPI, and projective techniques, such as the Rorschach.

Journal of Personality and Social Psychology

This prestigious journal publishes research articles in the following areas: attitudes and cognition, interpersonal relations and group processes, and personality processes and individual differences.

Man and His Symbols (1964)
    by Carl Jung
    Garden City, NY: Doubleday

This book includes the writings of Jung and four of his disciples; Jung's ideas are applied to anthropology, literature, art, and dreams.

Man, the Manipulator (1972)
    by Everett Shostrum
    New York: Bantam

This paperback presents humanistic ideas about the route from manipulation to self-actualization. Many case studies are included.

Mental Measurements Yearbook (1992, 11th ed.)
    edited by Jack Kramer and Jane Conoley
    Lincoln: University of Nebraska Press

This voluminous resource provides details about a wide range of personality tests.

Personality Research, Methods, and Theory (1995)
    by Patrick Shrout and Susan Fiske (eds.)
    Hillsdale, NJ.: Erlbaum

This volume examines current thinking about what can be known about personality, how concepts related to personality can best be measured, and how to approach research problems in specific areas of personality. Topics include the big-five trait factors, cultural dimensions, and conceptualizing and measuring self-esteem.

The Five-Factor Model of Personality: Theoretical Perspectives (1996)
    by Jerry Wiggins (ed.)
    New York: Guilford Press

This book includes articles by leading experts on the big five factors.

Chapter 13

CHAPTER OUTLINE

UNDERSTANDING ABNORMAL BEHAVIOR

Defining Abnormal Behavior

Legal Aspects of Mental Disorders

The Causes of Abnormal Behavior

Rates of Disorders

Classifying Abnormal Behavior

CATEGORIES OF MENTAL DISORDERS

Anxiety Disorders

Somatoform Disorders

Dissociative Disorders

Mood Disorders

Schizophrenia

Personality Disorders

Images of Psychology and Life
The World of Jenny Z.

AT THIRTY-TWO, worried about blank spells Jenny came to Collin Ross for help one day in 1985, (Ross, 1994). She had just flown back to Winnipeg from Vancouver but remembered nothing of the trip. She was inexplicably in trouble with the law in both Vancouver and Winnipeg for forging her boyfriend's name on, and cashing, several checks. Under hypnosis, she vividly relived her brutal rape and beating, at the hands of her father. Jenny was just twelve years old at the time. Subsequently, again under hypnosis, Sally emerged. It was Sally, not Jenny, who had gone to Vancouver and passed the bad checks. Sally did not feel that Jenny's body was hers; she had never been repeatedly raped and Jenny's father was not hers.

Jenny suffered from dissociative identity disorder. As her father raped her, she retreated out of her body to escape the humiliation and pain. As she was repeatedly abused, she got better at escaping. The resulting identity, Sally, got stronger and established an amnesiac barrier with Jenny, who didn't even know she was there. Unwittingly, Jenny had lost her center. She became depressed and nightmare-prone. She was left drifting though life while Sally was bright, enthusiastic and outgoing.

Later therapy uncovered more dissociated identities: Margaret, Liz, Sheila, Roseanne and Samantha. Jenny had learned her early grisly lesson only too well; she had learned to dissociate under stress. Therapy eventually helped her reintegrate her seven identities, but not before she had paid for her father's crime by losing contact with her own children, spending time in jail, and becoming involved in prostitution and alcohol abuse.

In contrast to Jenny, thirty-year-old Ruth felt contaminated and compelled to carry out many cleansing activities daily (Leon, 1990). She washed her hands at least three or four times an hour, showered six to seven times a day, and thoroughly cleaned her apartment at least twice a day.

Thirty-year-old Janet's mood became depressed when her husband divorced her because he loved a younger woman. Janet was raising her three children and completing her college education on a part-time basis (Oltmanns, Neale, & Davison,

Preview

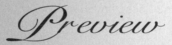

MENTAL DISORDERS know no social and economic boundaries. They find their way into the lives of the rich and famous and the poor and unknown. These are some of the questions we will explore in this chapter:
• How can you tell if someone has a mental disorder?
• What is involved in the insanity defense in courtrooms?
• What causes abnormal behavior?
• How many people have mental disorders?
• How are mental disorders classified?
• What are some of the main types of mental disorders?

447

1986). She had bouts of crying, in some cases for long periods of time. From her point of view, the future looked bleak.

Twenty-seven-year-old Jim was an unemployed, single man who said that what really bothered him was that he had a special power (Gorenstein, 1997). He said he could influence other people, even endanger them, with the way he breathed. He believed he had to go to great lengths to avoid people so that he wouldn't put them in jeopardy.

Each of these three individuals had a mental disorder. Ruth had an obsessive-compulsive disorder, Janet had a depressive disorder, and Jim had schizophrenia. We will discuss these and many other disorders in this chapter's coverage of the fascinating landscape of abnormal psychology.

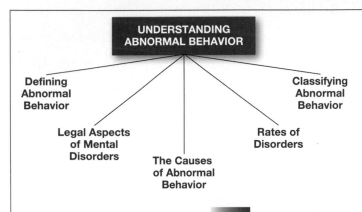

Understanding Abnormal Behavior

Many people live their lives in mental suffering and desperation. Abnormal psychology is concerned with these problems of adaptation.

Defining Abnormal Behavior

In thinking about how to define abnormal behavior, consider the individuals you just read about: Jenny, who had blank spells during which she engaged in criminal behavior; Ruth, who compulsively cleaned herself and her surroundings; Janet, who had severe feelings of depression; and Jim, who has isolated himself from the world because he believes his breath can influence, even endanger, others. Would you agree that their behavior is abnormal? If so, what do you base your judgment on?

Abnormal behavior is one of those concepts that is not easy to define. The line between what is normal and what is abnormal is not always clear-cut and easy to specify. Nonetheless, the following definition specifies several criteria that can help us think about what abnormal behavior is. **Abnormal behavior** *is behavior that is deviant, maladaptive, or personally distressful.*

There are three criteria in our definition of abnormal behavior: (1) deviance, (2) maladaptiveness, and (3) personal distress. Only one of these criteria needs to be met for the classification of abnormal behavior, but two or three may be present.

Abnormal behavior is *deviant.* Let's consider Ruth's compulsive behavior again. Is it deviant? One way that abnormal behavior has been described is to refer to it as *atypical.* People like Mordecai Richler, Albert Einstein and Shania Twain are atypical, but we don't usually categorize them as abnormal because of their extraordinary storytelling ability, intellectual power, and entertaining skills, respectively. However, when atypical behavior deviates from what is acceptable in a culture, it is often considered abnormal. Ruth's compulsive behavior deviates from acceptable norms. Normal people don't wash their hands three to four times an hour, take seven showers a day, and clean their apartment at least twice a day.

Abnormal behavior is *maladaptive.* Maladaptive behavior interferes with a person's ability to function effectively in the world. Jenny's criminal activities marginalize her, while Jim's belief that his breath has powerful, even harmful, effects on others prevents him from functioning in the everyday world.

Abnormal behavior involves *personal distress.* Jenny battles alcohol abuse and struggles to remain integrated. Janet is also distressed about her life and sees the future as extremely bleak.

A number of myths and misconceptions about abnormal behavior exist. Figure 13.1 describes some of these myths and misconceptions.

Legal Aspects of Mental Disorders

The legal status of the mentally disordered raises a number of controversial issues, including these: What is involved in committing disordered and dangerous individuals to mental institutions? What is the status of using the insanity defense for capital crimes?

The behavior of some mentally disordered individuals is so severe and extreme that they are a threat to themselves and/or others, and they may need protective confinement. Determining whether a mentally disordered individual is dangerous and should be formally committed to a mental institution is not easy, even for mental health professionals. Nonetheless, sometimes professionals have to make "dangerousness" judgments (Slobogin, 1996). Unlike the United States, there is currently no statutory law in Canada imposing a duty on mental health professionals to warn others about threats against them made by unconfined clients. This, however, does not automatically protect a mental health professional from a lawsuit charging that he or she failed to properly warn a victim of an aggressive client. In this light, the Canadian Psychiatric Association code of ethics does permit a breach of confidentiality in cases where a mental health professional worries about serious threat of physical harm to others (Evans, 1997).

Insanity is a legal term, not a psychological term. The **insanity defense** *requires that the defendant be wholly or partially irrational when the crime took place, and that the irrationality affected his or her behavior.* When the insanity defense is successful, the defendant is said to be "not guilty by reason of insanity." The insanity defense in the Canadian Criminal Code dates to 1892 and requires only establishing that the defendant was unable to appreciate the nature and quality or wrongfulness of his or her acts. Someone found not guilty by reason of insanity, or declared unfit to stand trial for the same reason, was not imprisoned but was placed under a Lieutenant-Governor's Warrant to be held in custody for a possibly indeterminate term.

Warrants could be abused, however. For example, in 1964, Emmerson Bonnar, a New Brunswick teenager, was charged with attempted purse-snatching. In court, he pleaded guilty and declined counsel. With no criminal record, he was remanded for a pre-sentence report in which a psychiatrist casually noted that he was mentally retarded. The presiding judge declared Bonnar unfit for trial and placed him under a Warrant. He remained in custody at the provincial hospital for the criminally insane in Campbellton for sixteen years, all for an offence which would likely have netted a "normal" offender a suspended sentence.

Under the impact of the 1982 Canadian Charter of Rights and Freedoms, Canadian law began to change. Since 1991 the correct designation is *not criminally responsible on account of mental disorder,* and those suspected of mental disorder are more likely to be formally evaluated, receive appropriate treatment and have their cases reviewed periodically (Savage & McKague 1987). To read further about the "insanity" defense, see Explorations in Psychology.

Myth/ Misconception	Fact
Abnormal behavior is always bizarre.	The behavior of many people who are diagnosed as having a mental disorder often cannot be distinguished from that of "normal" people. In some cases, like Jim's belief in the power of his breath, abnormal behavior is bizarre. However, in the case of Janet's depression, her behavior would not be considered bizarre.
Normal and abnormal behavior are different in kind.	Few, if any, types of behavior displayed by individuals with a mental disorder are unique to them. Abnormal behavior often consists of a poor fit between the behavior and the situation in which it is enacted.
People with a mental disorder are dangerous.	With the exception of a few people, such as those with an antisocial personality disorder (which we will discuss later in the chapter), most people with a mental disorder are not dangerous.
Once people have a mental disorder, they will never get rid of it.	Most people can be successfully treated for a mental disorder.

ℱigure 13.1
Some Myths and Misconceptions About Abnormal Behavior

Legal Aspects of Mental Disorders
The Insanity Defense

EXPLORATIONS IN PSYCHOLOGY
Some Famous Insanity Plea Cases

FOLLOWING ARE some famous cases in which the insanity plea failed, and some in which it succeeded (Wrightsman, Nietzel, & Fortune, 1998).

Famous Cases in Which the Insanity Defense Plea Failed

A gruesome example of a murder defendant who pleaded insanity as a defense but was convicted anyway is Jeffrey Dahmer. In 1991, a man in handcuffs dashed out of Dahmer's Milwaukee apartment and called the police, stammering that someone had tried to kill him. At least 17 other victims had not gotten away. Dahmer killed his first victim in 1978 with a barbell. He dismembered the victims' bodies, hoarded them, and ate the parts he "liked" the most. Dahmer's lawyers said, "This is not an evil man, this is a mentally sick man." The prosecution argued that Dahmer knew what he was doing all the time. The jury ruled 10–2 that Dahmer was sane. He was sentenced to life in prison and while there was beaten to death by a fellow prisoner.

In Canada, in 1984, Helmuth Buxbaum was found guilty of hiring people to kill his wife, Hanna. While he did not plead insanity, he tried to explain away his bizarre lifestyle by arguing that a stroke he had suffered some years previous to the murder had interfered with his ability to control himself. This argument did not sway the jury's deliberations and they found him guilty of murder.

Famous Cases in Which the Insanity Defense Plea Succeeded

Ed Gein, another serial killer from Wisconsin, was acquitted by reason of insanity on charges involving the murder of two women in the 1950s in the Plainfield, Wisconsin area. Gein admitted to other heinous crimes, including robbing bodies from graves. He later made the corpse parts into ornaments and clothes that he wore to reenact the image of his dead mother. Gein was the real-life inspiration for several Hollywood films, including *Psycho* and *Silence of the Lambs.* Gein was committed to a mental institution, where he remained until his death in 1984.

John Hinckley, Jr's case stimulated tremendous public debate in the United States and Canada. As seen live on television, Hinckley shot President Ronald Reagan in 1981. Hinckley's attorneys argued that Hinckley was insane, and the jury agreed. Hinckley was sent to a mental institution, where he resides today. On several occasions, he has requested to be released from the institution but the requests have been denied.

In 1994, Lorena Bobbitt waited for her husband to go to sleep and then she cut off his penis, drove away from the house, and threw it out the car window. Her attorneys claimed that she had suffered years of physical and mental abuse from her husband, John. Bobbitt was ruled "guilty but insane." She spent several weeks at a mental hospital, then was released.

The Causes of Abnormal Behavior

What causes people to become abnormal—to behave in deviant, maladaptive, and personally distressful ways? The causes include biological, psychological, and sociocultural factors, as well as a possible combination of these factors.

Biological Factors   In the biological approach to mental disorders, it is believed that a malfunctioning of the person's body is responsible for the disorders. Today, scientists who adopt a biological approach to mental disorders often focus on brain processes, such as neurotransmitters, and genetic factors as the causes of abnormal behavior ◀||||| P. 75. In the biological approach, drug therapy is frequently used to treat abnormal behavior (Hales & Yudofsky, 1999).

The biological approach is evident in the **medical model,** *which describes mental disorders as medical diseases with a biological origin.* From the perspective of the medical model, abnormalities are called mental *illnesses,* the individuals afflicted are *patients in mental hospitals,* and they are treated by *doctors.*

Psychological Factors   Among the psychological factors that have been proposed as contributors to abnormal behavior are distorted thoughts, emotional turmoil, inappropriate learning, and troubled relationships. When we examine some of the main mental disorders later in the chapter, such as the mood disorders and schizophrenic disorders, we will further explore these psychological factors.

Many of the theories of personality we discussed in chapter 12 address abnormal as well as normal aspects of behavior. Recall that psychoanalytic theorists often attribute psychological problems to stressful early experiences with parents. Remember that social learning theorists believe that behavior, whether normal or abnormal, is learned through social experiences with others. And recall that humanistic theorists believe that inadequate emotional support from others and low self-esteem are especially implicated in people's problems.

In the next chapter, "Therapies," we will extensively examine the theories of personality—psychoanalytic, behavioral/social learning, and humanistic—in terms of how to help people with a mental disorder.

Sociocultural Factors   Most experts on abnormal behavior agree that many psychological disorders are universal, appearing in most cultures (Al-Issa, 1982). However, the frequency and intensity of abnormal behavior varies across cultures with variations related to social, economic, technological, and religious aspects of cultures (Draguns, 1990). Some disorders, though, are culture-related, as indicated in figure 13.2.

Sociocultural factors that influence mental disorders include socioeconomic status and neighborhood quality (Brown & Adler, 1998). People from low-income, minority neighborhoods have the highest rates of mental disorders. When socioeconomic status and ethnicity are examined for their roles in mental disorders, socioeconomic status plays a much stronger role. Thus, the living conditions of poverty create stressful circumstances that can contribute to whether a person has a mental disorder (Grizenko, 1998).

Gender is another sociocultural factor that is associated with the presence of certain mental disorders (Greenglass, 1998; Paludi, 1998). Women tend to be diagnosed as having internalized disorders. In particular, women are more likely than men to suffer from anxiety disorders and depression, which have symptoms that are turned inward (internalized). Conversely, men are socialized to direct their energy toward

In July of 1995, 14-year-old Sandy Charles of La Ronge, Saskatchewan, and an eight-year-old accomplice, brutally murdered seven-year old Johnathan Thimpsen. Charles then cut sections of flesh from Thimsen's body and boiled them down to fat. He was mimicking a scene in the movie Warlock, *in which the protagonist drank the rendered fat of a young male virgin in order to fly. While in detention awaiting trial, he claimed that he needed to drink blood because his teeth were becoming vampire's teeth. A Saskatoon judge ruled that Charles was aware of his actions but not criminally responsible because he suffered from schizophrenia. He was remanded for treatment and a case review every six months until he is able to return to society.*

Disorder	Culture	Description/Characteristics
Amok	Malaysia, Philippines, Africa	This disorder involves sudden, uncontrolled outbursts of anger in which the person may injure or kill someone. Amok is often found in males who are emotionally withdrawn before the onset of the disorder. After the attack on someone, the individual feels exhausted and depressed, and does not remember the rage and attack.
Anorexia Nervosa	Western cultures, especially North America	This eating disorder involves a relentless pursuit of thinness through starvation, and can eventually lead to death.
Windigo	Algonquin Indian hunters	This disorder involves a fear of being bewitched. The hunter becomes anxious and agitated, worrying he will be turned into a cannibal with a craving for human flesh.

Figure 13.2
Some Culture-Related Disorders

the external world (that is, to externalize their feelings). They more often have externalized disorders that involve aggression and substance abuse. We will have more to say about gender differences shortly in our discussion of rates of mental disorders and later in the chapter when we study depression.

An Interactionist Approach: Biopsychosocial   When considering an individual's behavior, whether normal or abnormal, biological as well as psychological/sociocultural factors may be involved. Abnormal behavior can be influenced by biological factors (such as brain processes and heredity), psychological factors (such as emotional turmoil and distorted thoughts), and sociocultural factors (such as poverty). These factors can interact to produce abnormal behavior. Sometimes this interactionist approach is called "biopsychosocial" (Evans and others, 1999).

Rates of Disorders

How prevalent are mental disorders in North America? Nearly 20,000 individuals were randomly selected from five U.S. regions and asked whether they had ever experienced a mental disorder and whether they were currently suffering from one (Robins & Regier, 1991). One-third said they had experienced one or more disorders in their lifetime, and 20 percent said they currently had an active disorder. In a comparable Edmonton study, about 17 percent of respondents said they had experienced a mental disorder in the preceding six months (Bland, Newman & Orn, 1988).

You might be surprised that so many people have had, or currently have, a mental disorder. However, the figures include individuals in institutions and in the community. They also include individuals who have a substance abuse disorder (alcohol or drugs). As we describe a number of mental disorders we will list the percentage of individuals in these studies who reported experiencing the particular disorder.

Surprisingly, only one-third of the individuals in the U.S. study who said they currently had a mental disorder had been treated for it in the previous six months.

Classifying Abnormal Behavior

Ever since human history began, people have suffered from diseases, sadness, and bizarre behavior. And for almost as long, healers have tried to treat and cure them. The classification of mental disorders goes back to the ancient Egyptians and Greeks, and has its roots in biology and medicine.

The first classification of mental disorders in the United States, based on the census data of 1840, used one category for all mental disorders. This one category included both the mentally retarded and the insane.

In the twentieth century, the American Psychiatric Association (APA) developed the first major classification of mental disorders in the United States. The *Diagnostic and Statistical Manual of Mental Disorders (DSM),* first published in 1952, included better definitions of mental disorders than previous classification efforts. A revised edition, the *DSM-II,* with more systematic assistance from expert diagnosticians, appeared in 1968. The APA published a third edition, the *DSM-III,* in 1980, and a revision of that manual, the *DSM-III-R,* in 1987. Published in 1994, the current *DSM-IV* emphasizes refined empirical support of diagnostic categories.

The revisions of the *DSM* underscore that (1) classifying mental disorders is not an easy task and (2) clinicians are making an ongoing, conscientious effort to achieve a clearer, more accurate categorization of mental disorders.

Before we discuss the system most widely used to classify mental disorders, we will explore the benefits of classifying mental disorders. First, a classification system gives professionals a shorthand system for communicating with each other. For example, if one psychologist says in a case review that her client has a panic disorder and another psychologist says that his client has schizophrenia, the two psychologists understand which disorders these clients have been diagnosed as having. Second, a classification system can help clinicians make predictions about disorders; it provides information about the likelihood that a disorder will occur, which individuals are most susceptible to the disorder, progress of the disorder once it appears, and the prognosis for effective treatment (Meehl, 1986).

Continuing changes in the *DSM* reflect advancements in knowledge about the classification of mental disorders (Hales & others, 1999). On the basis of research and clinical experience, the *DSM-IV* added, dropped, or revised categories, sometimes generating controversy among the diagnosticians who rely on the classification system.

For example, the *DSM-III* dropped two important categories that have some historical importance: the categories of neurosis and psychosis. The term **neurotic** *referred to conditions that are personally distressful but the individual has not lost contact with reality.* Individuals who are extremely anxious, troubled, and unhappy may still be able to carry out their everyday functions and have a clear perception of reality; these individuals would be referred to by some people as "neurotic."

The term **psychotic** *referred to severe mental disorders in which the individual has lost contact with reality.* The thinking and perception of psychotic individuals are so distorted that they live in a world far removed from others. Psychotic individuals might hear voices that are not present or think they are famous individuals, such as Jesus Christ or Napoleon. Although the *DSM* classification system still mentions the terms *neurotic* and *psychotic,* most psychologists believe they are too broad and ill-defined to be used as effective diagnostic labels.

The *DSM-IV* (Diagnostic and Statistical Manual of Mental Disorders, Fourth Edition) *is the most recent major classification of mental disorders; it contains eighteen major classifications and describes more than 200 specific disorders.*

One feature of the *DSM-IV* is its **multiaxial system,** *which classifies individuals on the basis of five dimensions, or "axes," that include the individual's history and highest level of functioning in the last year.* This system ensures that the individual will not merely be assigned to a mental disorder category, but instead will be characterized in terms of a number of clinical factors (Gelder, Mayou, & Geddes, 1999). Figure 13.3 describes the multiaxial system.

What are some of the changes in the *DSM-IV*? The more than 200 mental health professionals who contributed to the development of the *DSM-IV* were a much more diverse group than their predecessors, who were mainly White male psychiatrists. More women, ethnic minorities, and nonpsychiatrists, such as clinical psychologists, were involved in the construction of the *DSM-IV,* and greater attention was given to gender- and ethnicity-related diagnosis. For example, the *DSM-IV* contains an appendix entitled "Guidelines for Cultural Formation and Glossary of Culture-Related Syndromes" (Nathan, 1994). Also, the *DSM-IV* is accompanied by a number of sourcebooks that present the empirical base of the *DSM-IV* (Frances & Ross, 1996). In previous versions of the *DSM,* the reasons for diagnostic changes were not always explicit, so the evidence that led to their formulation was never available for public evaluation.

The most controversial aspect of the *DSM-IV* continues to be an issue that has been present since the publication of the *DSM-I* in 1952. Although more nonpsychiatrists than in previous editions were responsible for drafting the *DSM-IV,* it still reflects a medical, or disease, model (Clark, Watson, & Reynolds, 1995; Nathan & Langenbucher, 1999). Classifying individuals based on their symptoms and using medical terminology continues the dominance of the psychiatric tradition of thinking

Axis	Description
I	The primary classification or diagnosis of the disorder (for example, fear of people). This axis includes all disorders except the personality disorders and mental retardation.
II	Personality disorders, long-standing problems in relating to others (for example, a person with long-standing antisocial personality disorder) and mental retardation.
III	General medical conditions that might be relevant in understanding the mental disorder (for example, an individual's history of disease, such as a cardiovascular problem)
IV	Psychosocial stressors in the individual's recent past that might have contributed to the mental problem (for example, divorce, death of a parent, or loss of job)
V	The individual's current level of functioning and highest level of functioning in the last year. For example, does the individual have a history of poor work and relationship patterns, or have there been times in the recent past when the individual performed effectively at work and enjoyed positive interpersonal relationships? If functioning has been high at some point in the past, prognosis for recovery is improved.

*F*igure 13.3
The *DSM-IV* Multiaxial System
These are brief descriptions of the five axes in the *DSM-IV* classification of mental disorders.

DSM-IV

SUMMARY TABLE 13.1
Understanding Abnormal Behavior

Concept	Processes/ Related Ideas	Characteristics/Discussions
Defining Abnormal Behavior	Its Nature	Abnormal behavior is behavior that is deviant, maladaptive, or personally distressful. Only one of these criteria needs to be present for the classification of abnormal behavior, but two or all three can be present. We described some myths and misconceptions about abnormal behavior, and we indicated that there is often a thin line between what is normal and what is abnormal.
Legal Aspects of Mental Disorders		Individuals with a mental disorder must be dangerous either to themselves or to others for formal commitment to a mental institution. *Insanity* is a legal term, not a psychological term. The insanity defense requires that the defendant be wholly or partially irrational when the crime took place, and that the irrationality affected his or her behavior. Controversy swirls about the insanity defense.
The Causes of Abnormal Behavior	Biological Factors	In the biological approach, the malfunctioning of the person's body is responsible for abnormal behavior. Today, the biological factors of brain processes and heredity are emphasized. In the biological approach, drug therapy is often used to treat abnormal behavior. The biological approach is evident in the medical model, which describes mental disorders as medical diseases with biological origins.
	Psychological Factors	Psychological factors include emotional turmoil, inappropriate learning, distorted thoughts, and inadequate relationships as determinants of abnormal behavior. Theories of personality—psychoanalytic, behavioral/social learning, and humanistic—specify psychological factors in abnormal behavior.
	Sociocultural Factors	Sociocultural factors in abnormal behavior include cultural bias, poverty and low socioeconomic conditions, as well as gender.
	An Interactionist Approach	This proposes that abnormal behavior might result from an interaction of biological, psychological, and sociocultural factors. Sometimes this approach is called "biopsychosocial."
Rates of Disorders	Their Nature	In North American studies, almost one-third of the individuals interviewed reported that they had experienced a mental disorder in their lifetime and 17 percent said they were currently suffering from one. These figures might seem surprisingly high, but they include people in institutions and the community, and they include individuals with a substance-abuse disorder.
Classifying Abnormal Behavior	Its Nature	*DSM* stands for *Diagnostic and Statistical Manual of Mental Disorders.* The *DSM-II* included the categories of *neurotic* and *psychotic* behavior, although most psychologists today believe the terms are too broad and ill-defined to be effective diagnostic categories. Mental disorder classification systems have advantages and disadvantages. The most recent version of the *DSM—DSM IV*—was published in 1994. One of its features is a multiaxial system. *DSM-IV* continues to be controversial, with one of the main criticisms by psychologists being its perpetuation of the medical model of mental disorders.

about mental disorders in terms of illness and disease. This strategy implies an internal cause that is more or less independent of external or environmental factors (Adams & Cassidy, 1993). Thus, even though researchers have begun to illuminate the complex interaction of genetic, neurobiological, cognitive, and environmental factors in the *DSM* disorders, the *DSM-IV* continues to espouse the medical/disease model of mental disorders (Sarbin & Keen, 1998).

The *DSM-IV* is also controversial because it continues to label as mental disorders what are often thought of as everyday problems. For example, under learning or academic skills disorders, the *DSM-IV* includes reading disorder, mathematics disorder, and disorder of written expression. Under substance-related disorders, it includes caffeine-use disorders. We don't usually think of these problems as mental disorders, but including them implies that such "normal behavior" should be treated as a mental disorder. Similarly, Hacking (1998) worries about the rapidity with which classifications have changed and wonders why some disorders become "currently fashionable." The developers of the *DSM* argue that mental health providers have been treating many problems not included in earlier editions and that comprehensiveness is important. One practical reason for including everyday problems is to help more people get treatment since most American health insurance companies only reimburse clients for disorders listed in the *DSM-IV*. In contrast, mental health care in Canada does not depend so heavily on the *DSM-IV* system.

Another criticism of the *DSM-IV*, and indeed of this type of classification system in general, is that the system focuses strictly on pathology and problems, with a bias toward finding something wrong with anyone who becomes the object of diagnostic study (Allen, 1998).

Because labels can become self-fulfilling prophecies, emphasizing strengths as well as weaknesses might help to destigmatize labels such as *paranoid schizophrenic* or *ex-mental patient*. It would also help to provide clues to treatment that promote mental competence rather than working only to reduce mental distress.

Although psychologists usually go along with the *DSM-IV*, psychiatrists are more satisfied with it. Even though the *DSM-IV* has its critics, it is still the most comprehensive classification system available.

At this point, we have discussed a number of ideas about what abnormal behavior is, what causes abnormal behavior, and how abnormal behavior can be classified. A summary of these ideas is presented in summary table 13.1. Now we turn our attention to the specific diagnostic categories of mental disorders.

National Institute of Mental Health
Mental Health Net
Mental Health Disorders
Mental Health Web

Categories of Mental Disorders

This cognitive map gives you a picture of the topics we will be discussing before we get to the next summary table. It outlines the first three of six main categories of diagnosis in the *DSM-IV* that we will explore in this chapter. Figure 13.4 gives you an overall picture of eight prominent categories of mental disorders—the six we will evaluate in this chapter, plus two that we have examined in previous chapters—substance-related disorders (chapter 5) and eating disorders (chapter 11). Let's now begin our coverage of categories of mental disorders with anxiety disorders.

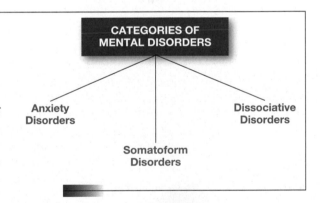

Anxiety Disorders

To explore the anxiety disorders, we will describe their general characteristics, then turn to five main types of anxiety disorders. Anxiety is a diffuse, vague, highly unpleasant feeling of fear and apprehension. People with high levels of anxiety worry a lot. **Anxiety disorders** *are psychological disorders that include the following main features: motor tension (jumpiness, trembling, inability to relax); hyperactivity (dizziness, a racing heart, or, possibly, perspiration); and apprehensive expectations and thoughts.*

Anxiety Disorders

Generalized Anxiety Disorder   Evita, who is 27 years old, had just arrived for her visit with the psychologist. She seemed very nervous and was wringing her hands, crossing and uncrossing her legs, and playing nervously with strands of her hair. She said her stomach felt like it was in knots, that her hands were cold, and that her neck muscles were so tight they hurt. She said that lately arguments with her husband had escalated. In recent weeks, Evita indicated, she felt more and more nervous throughout the day, as if something bad were about to happen. If the doorbell sounded or the phone rang, her heart beat rapidly and her breathing quickened.

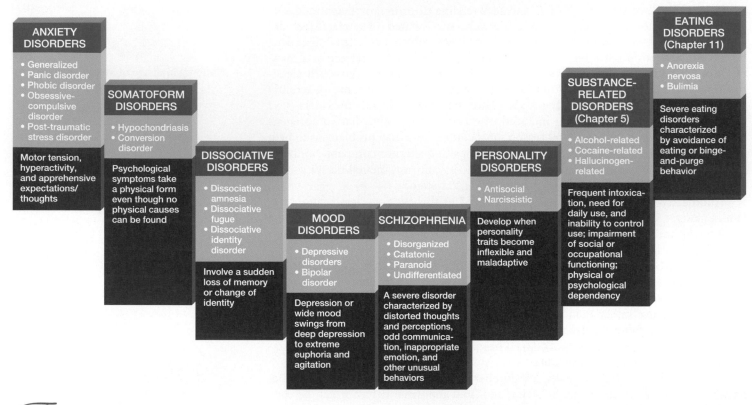

*F*igure 13.4
Some Prominent Categories of Mental Disorders in the *DSM-IV*

When she was around people she had a difficult time speaking. She began to isolate herself. Her husband became impatient with Evita, so she decided to see a psychologist (Goodstein & Calhoun, 1982).

Evita has a **generalized anxiety disorder,** *an anxiety disorder that consists of persistent anxiety for at least a month; the individual with a generalized anxiety disorder is unable to specify the reasons for the anxiety.* People with generalized anxiety disorder are nervous most of the time. In the Edmonton study of the prevalence of mental disorders, about 6.5 percent of the individuals interviewed said they had experienced an anxiety disorder in the preceding six months (Bland, Newman & Orn, 1988).

Panic Disorder

Panic Disorder   Panic disorder *is an anxiety disorder marked by the recurrent sudden onset of intense apprehension or terror.* The individual often has a feeling of impending doom but may not feel anxious all the time. Anxiety attacks often strike without warning and produce severe palpitations, extreme shortness of breath, chest pains, trembling, sweating, dizziness, and a feeling of helplessness (Cox & others, 1994). Victims are seized by fear that they will die, go crazy, or do something they cannot control (Asnis & van Praag, 1995).

What are some psychosocial and biological factors involved in panic disorder? In many instances, a stressful life event has occurred in the last six months, most often a threatened or actual separation from a loved one or a change in job. Biological factors in panic disorder have also been explored (McNally, 1998). For example, in a panic attack an overreaction to lactic acid (which is produced by the body when it is under stress) occurs.

Mrs. Reiss is a 48-year-old woman who is afraid to go out alone, a fear she has had for six years but which has intensified in the last two years (Greenberg, Szmulker, & Tantum, 1986). The first signs of her fear appeared after an argument with her husband. After the argument, she went to the mailbox to get the mail and began to feel very anxious and dizzy. It was a struggle to get back to the house. Her fear lessened for several years, but reappeared even more intensely after she learned that her sister had cancer. Her fear continued to escalate after arguments with her husband. She became increasingly apprehensive about going outside alone. When she did try to leave, her heart would pound, she would perspire, and she would begin to tremble. After being outside only briefly, she would quickly go back into her house.

Mrs. Reiss had developed **agoraphobia,** *an anxiety disorder characterized by an intense fear of entering crowded, public places, of traveling away from home, especially by public transportation, of feeling confined or trapped, and of being separated from a place or person associated with safety.* In the *DSM-IV,* a panic attack can be classified as with or without agoraphobia (Thorpe, 1998). Agoraphobia causes some people to remain housebound (Cox, Endler & Swinson, 1995). It usually first appears in early adulthood, with 2.5 percent of individuals in the United States classified as having the disorder. Females are more likely than males to have the disorder.

Edvard Munch's The Scream. *Many experts interpret Munch's painting as an expression of the terror brought on by a panic attack.*

Agoraphobia

Phobic Disorders

Agnes is an unmarried 30-year-old woman who had been unable to go higher than the second floor of any building for more than a year. When she tried to overcome her fear of heights by going up to the third, fourth, or fifth floor, she became overwhelmed by anxiety. She remembers how it all began. One evening she was working alone and was seized by an urge to jump out of an eighth-story window. She was so frightened by her impulse that she hid behind a file cabinet for more than two hours until she calmed down enough to gather her belongings and go home. As she reached the first floor of the building, her heart was pounding and she was perspiring heavily. After several months she gave up her position and became a lower-paid salesperson so she could work on the bottom floor of the store (Cameron, 1963).

A **phobic disorder,** *commonly called phobia, is an anxiety disorder in which the individual has an irrational, overwhelming, persistent fear of a particular object or situation.* Individuals with generalized anxiety disorder cannot pinpoint the cause of their nervous feelings; individuals with phobias can. A fear becomes a phobia when a situation is so dreaded that an individual goes to almost any length to avoid it. For example, Agnes quit her job to avoid being in high places. Some phobias are more debilitating than others. An individual with a fear of automobiles has a more difficult time functioning in our society than a person with a fear of snakes, for example. Wayne Gretzky's hockey career was threatened by a phobia of flying, until a friendly pilot invited him into the cockpit and showed him how all the controls worked.

Phobias come in many forms. Some of the most common phobias involve social situations, dogs, height, dirt, flying, and snakes. Figure 13.5 labels and describes a number of phobias.

Social phobia is an intense fear of being humiliated or embarrassed in social situations. Individuals with this phobia are afraid that they will say or do the wrong thing. As a consequence, they might avoid speaking up in a conversation, giving a speech, going out to eat, or attending a party. Their intense fear of such contexts can severely restrict their social life and increase their loneliness (Schneider & others, 1992).

Why do people develop phobias? Different theoretical perspectives provide different explanations. Psychoanalytic theorists, for example, say phobias develop as defense mechanisms to ward off threatening or unacceptable impulses—Agnes hid behind a file cabinet because she feared she would jump out of an eighth-story window. Learning theorists, however,

Acrophobia	Fear of high places
Aerophobia	Fear of flying
Ailurophobia	Fear of cats
Algophobia	Fear of pain
Amaxophobia	Fear of vehicles, driving
Arachnophobia	Fear of spiders
Astrapophobia	Fear of lightning
Cynophobia	Fear of dogs
Gamophobia	Fear of marriage
Hydrophobia	Fear of water
Melissophobia	Fear of bees
Mysophobia	Fear of dirt
Nyctophobia	Fear of darkness
Ophidiophobia	Fear of nonpoisonous snakes
Thanatophobia	Fear of death
Xenophobia	Fear of strangers

*F*igure 13.5
Phobias
This is only a partial listing of phobias.

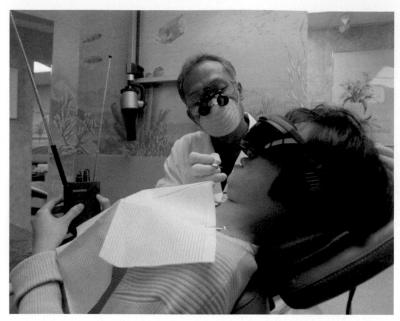

As Dr. Howard Lim works in his Toronto office, his patients can wear goggles containing a tiny TV monitor. Dental phobia is usually rooted in childhood experiences and dentists are going to great lengths to put patients at ease.

Obsessive-Compulsive Disorder
Post-Traumatic Stress Disorder

explain phobias differently; they say phobias are learned fears. In Agnes' case, she may have fallen from a high place when she was a little girl. As a result, she associates falling with pain and now fears high places. Or she may have heard about or seen other people who were afraid of high places. These last two examples are classical conditioning and observational learning explanations for Agnes' phobia.

Neuroscientists are finding that biological factors, such as greater blood flow and metabolism in the right side of the brain than in the left hemisphere, may also be involved in phobias. First-generation relatives of individuals suffering from agoraphobia and panic attacks have high rates of these disorders themselves, suggesting a possible genetic predisposition for phobias (d'Ansia, 1989). Others have found that identical twins reared apart sometimes develop the same phobias; one pair independently became claustrophobic, for example (Eckert, Heston, & Bouchard, 1981).

Obsessive-Compulsive Disorder

At the beginning of this chapter you read about 30-year-old Ruth who has an obsessive-compulsive disorder. Twenty-seven-year-old Bob also has this disorder. As a young adult, he found himself ensnared in an exacting ritual in which he would remove his clothes in a prearranged sequence, then scrub every inch of his body from head to toe. He dresses himself in an order precisely the opposite to that in which he takes off his clothes. If he deviates from this order, he feels compelled to start the sequence all over again. Sometimes Bob performs the cleansing ritual four or five times a day, and even though he is aware the ritual is absurd, he simply can't stop performing it (Meyer & Osborne, 1982).

Obsessive-compulsive disorder (OCD) *is an anxiety disorder in which the individual has anxiety-provoking thoughts that will not go away (obsession) and/or urges to perform repetitive, ritualistic behaviors to prevent or produce some future situation (compulsion).* Individuals with OCD repeat and rehearse normal doubts and daily routines, sometimes hundreds of times a day (Frost & Steketee, 1998). In the U.S. study of the prevalence of mental disorders, almost 3 percent of individuals said they had experienced an obsessive-compulsive disorder some time in their lives (Robins & Regier, 1991).

The most common compulsions are excessive checking, cleansing, and counting. For example, a young man feels he has to check his apartment for gas leaks and make sure the windows are locked. His behavior is normal if he does this once, but if he checks five or six times and then constantly worries that he might not have checked carefully enough, his behavior is compulsive. Most individuals do not enjoy their ritualistic behavior but feel anxious when they do not carry it out (Bouchard, Rhéaume & Ladouceur, 1999).

Positron emission tomography (PET) and other new brain-imaging techniques indicate a neurological basis for OCD. Irregularities in neurotransmitter systems, especially serotonin and dopamine, seem to be involved. And there may be a genetic basis for the disorder since OCD runs in families.

Post-Traumatic Stress Disorder

Post-traumatic stress disorder *is a mental disorder that develops through exposure to a traumatic event, such as war; severely oppressive*

Jack Nicholson portrayed an individual with obsessive-compulsive disorder in the movie, As Good As It Gets.

situations, such as the Holocaust; severe abuse, as in rape; natural disasters, such as floods and tornados; and accidental disasters, such as plane crashes. The disorder is characterized by anxiety symptoms that may immediately follow the trauma or be delayed by months or even years until onset (Ford, 1999; Ursano & others, 1999). The symptoms vary, but can include the following:

"*He always times '60 Minutes.*'"

- "Flashbacks" in which the individual relives the event
- Constricted ability to feel emotions, often reported as feeling numb, resulting in an inability to experience happiness, sexual desire, or enjoyable interpersonal relationships
- Excessive arousal, resulting in an exaggerated startle response, or inability to sleep
- Difficulties with memory and concentration
- Feelings of apprehension, including nervous tremors
- Impulsive outbursts of behavior such as aggressiveness, or sudden changes in lifestyle

About 15 to 20 percent of Vietnam veterans experienced post-traumatic stress disorder (PTSD). Even "peacekeeping" is stressful, with 10 percent of Canadian peacekeepers similarly affected (Carbonneau, 1994). PTSD can also strike closer to home. Shootings like those at l'École Polytechnique in Montréal turn bystanders into victims. Further, some experts consider sexual abuse and assault victims to be the single largest group of PTSD sufferers (Koss & Boeschen, 1998). Recently, Ottawa researchers have explored the transmission of PTSD from survivors to their offspring (Baranowsky & others, 1998). Not every individual exposed to the same disaster develops PTSD, which overloads the individual's usual coping abilities (Brewin & others, 1999; Jaycox & Foa, 1998). Soldiers with decision-making authority are less likely to develop PTSD than soldiers who have no option but to follow orders. Also, preparation for a trauma reduces the likelihood an individual will develop PTSD.

Somatoform Disorders

"Look, I am having trouble breathing. You don't believe me. Nobody believes me. There are times when I can't stop coughing. I'm losing weight. I know I have cancer. My father died of cancer when I was twelve." Herb has been to six cancer specialists in the last two years; none can find anything wrong with him. Each doctor has taken X-rays and conducted excessive laboratory tests, but Herb's test results do not indicate any illnesses. Might some psychological factors be responsible for Herb's sense that he is physically ailing?

Somatoform disorders *are mental disorders in which psychological symptoms take a physical, or somatic, form even though no physical causes can be found.* Although these symptoms are not caused physically, they are highly distressing for the individual; the symptoms are real or believed, not faked. Two examples of somatoform disorders are hypochondriasis and conversion disorder.

Hypochondriasis   Individuals with hypochondriasis overreact to a missed heartbeat, shortness of breath, or a slight chest pain, fearing that something is wrong with them. **Hypochondriasis** *is a somatoform disorder in which the individual has a pervasive fear of illness and disease.* At the first indication of something amiss in their bodies, individuals with hypochondriasis call a doctor. When a physical examination reveals no problems, hypochondriacs usually do not believe the doctor. They often change doctors, moving from one to another searching for a diagnosis that matches their own. Most individuals with hypochondriasis are pill enthusiasts whose medicine chests spill over with bottles of drugs that they hope will cure their imagined maladies (Lautenbacher & Rollman, 1999).

Hypochondriasis is a difficult category to diagnose accurately. It is quite rare for it to occur without other mental disorders, such as depression.

Hypochondriasis

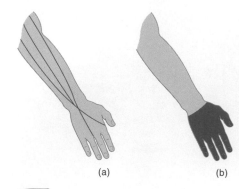

(a)   (b)

Figure 13.6
Glove Anesthesia

A patient who complains of numbness in the hand might be diagnosed as suffering from conversion disorder if the area of the hand affected showed that a disorder of the nervous system was not responsible. The skin areas served by nerves in the arm are shown in *(a)*. The glove anesthesia shown in *(b)* could not result from damage to these nerves.

Dissociative Disorders

Conversion Disorder   **Conversion disorder** *is a somatoform disorder in which the individual experiences specific physical symptoms even though no physiological problems can be found.* Conversion disorder received its name from psychoanalytic theory, which stressed that anxiety was "converted" into a specific physical symptom. The individual with hypochondriasis has no physical disability; the individual with a conversion disorder does have some loss of motor or sensory ability. Individuals with a conversion disorder might be unable to speak, might faint, or they even might be deaf or blind.

Conversion disorder was more common in Freud's time than today. Freud was especially interested in this disorder, in which physical symptoms made no neurological sense. For example, with *glove anesthesia* individuals report that their entire hand is numb from the tip of their fingers to a cutoff point at the wrist. As shown in figure 13.6, if these individuals were experiencing true physiological numbness, their symptoms would be very different. Like hypochondriasis, conversion disorder often appears in conjunction with other mental disorders. During long-term evaluation, conversion disorder turns out to be another mental or physical disorder.

Dissociative Disorders

Our exploration of dissociative disorders focuses on their basic nature and then turns to some specific dissociative disorders.

Dissociative disorders *are psychological disorders that involve a sudden loss of memory or change in identity.* Under extreme stress or shock, the individual's conscious awareness becomes dissociated (separated or split) from previous memories and thoughts. Three kinds of dissociative disorders are dissociative amnesia, dissociative fugue, and dissociative identity (Klein & Doane, 1994).

Dissociative Amnesia and Fugue   Amnesia is the inability to recall important events ◀‖‖ P. 244. Amnesia can be caused by an injury to the head, for example. But **dissociative amnesia** *is a dissociative disorder involving memory loss caused by extensive psychological stress.* For example, an individual showed up at a hospital and said he did not know who he was. After several days in the hospital, he awoke one morning and demanded to be released. Eventually he remembered that he had been involved in an automobile accident in which a pedestrian had been killed. The extreme stress of the accident and the fear that he might be held responsible triggered the amnesia.

Dissociative fugue *("fugue" means flight) is a dissociative disorder in which the individual not only develops amnesia, but also unexpectedly travels away from home and assumes a new identity.* For example, one day a woman named Barbara vanished without a trace. Two weeks later, looking more like a teenager—with her hair in a ponytail and wearing bobby socks—than a 31-year-old woman, Barbara was picked up by police in a nearby city. When her husband came to see her, Barbara asked, "Who are you?" She could not remember anything about the last two weeks of her life. During psychotherapy, she gradually began to recall her past. She had left home with enough money to buy a bus ticket to the town where she grew up as a child. She spent days walking the streets and standing near a building where her father had worked. Later she went to a motel with a man; according to the motel manager, she entertained a series of men over a three-day period (Goldstein & Palmer, 1975).

Dissociative Identity Disorder   **Dissociative identity disorder (DID)**, *formerly called multiple personality disorder, is the most dramatic but least common dissociative disorder; individuals suffering from this disorder have two or more distinct personalities or selves, like the fictional Dr. Jekyll and Mr. Hyde of Robert Louis Stevenson's novel.* Each personality has its own memories, behaviors, and relationships; one personality dominates the individual at one point, another personality will take over at another time. The shift from one personality to the other usually occurs under distress.

Figure 13.7
The Three Faces of Eve
Chris Sizemore, the subject of the book and film *The Three Faces of Eve,* is shown here with a work she painted, entitled *Three Faces in One.*

Jenny Z., whom you read about at the beginning of this chapter, suffered from DID (Ross, 1994). One of the most famous cases of DID involves the "three faces of Eve" (Thigpen & Cleckley, 1957). Eve White was the original dominant personality. She had no knowledge of her second personality, Eve Black, who had been alternating with Eve White for years. Eve White was bland, quiet, and serious—a rather dull personality. By contrast, Eve Black was carefree, mischievous, and uninhibited. She would "come out" at the most inappropriate times, leaving Eve White with hangovers, bills, and a reputation in local bars that she could not explain. During treatment, a third personality, Jane, emerged. More mature than the other two, Jane seemed to have developed as a result of therapy. Figure 13.7 provides a portrayal of the three faces of Eve.

In some cases, therapists have been blamed for creating a second or third personality. At one point, Eve said that her therapist had created one of her personalities.

A summary of research on dissociative identity disorder suggests that the disorder is characterized by an inordinately high rate of sexual or physical abuse during early childhood (Ludolph, 1982). Sexual abuse occurred in 56 percent of the reported cases, for example. Note, though, that the majority of individuals who have been sexually abused do not develop this disorder. Mothers tend to be rejecting and depressed; fathers distant, alcoholic, and abusive. Remember that, while fascinating, dissociative identity disorder is rare. Until the 1980s only approximately 300 cases had ever been reported (Suinn, 1984). In the last decade, hundreds more have been labeled "dissociative identity disorder," although some argue that the increase represents a diagnostic fad. Others believe that it is not so rare, but has been frequently misdiagnosed as schizophrenia. Improved techniques for assessing the physiological changes that occur when individuals change personalities increase the likelihood that more accurate rates can be determined.

At this point, we have considered three major types of mental disorders—anxiety, somatoform, and dissociative. An overview of the main ideas about these disorders is presented in summary table 13.2. Next, we turn to the final three main categories of mental disorders we will discuss in this chapter (mood, schizophrenic, and personality), beginning with the mood disorders.

SUMMARY TABLE 13.2
The Anxiety, Somatoform, and Dissociative Disorders

Concept	Processes/ Related Ideas	Characteristics/Description
Anxiety Disorders	Their Nature	Anxiety is a diffuse, vague, highly unpleasant feeling of fear and apprehension. The main features of anxiety disorders are motor tension, hyperactivity, and apprehensive expectations and thoughts.
	Generalized Anxiety Disorder	This disorder consists of persistent anxiety for at least one month without being able to specify the reason for the anxiety.
	Panic Disorder	Recurrent panic attacks marked by the sudden onset of intense apprehension or terror characterize a panic disorder. Panic disorder can occur with or without agoraphobia.
	Phobic Disorders	Commonly called phobias, they involve an irrational, overwhelming, persistent fear of a particular object or situation. Phobias come in many forms. Psychoanalytic and learning explanations of phobias have been given. Biological factors have also been implicated, with individuals possibly having a genetic predisposition to develop a phobia.
	Obsessive-Compulsive Disorder	Recurrent obsessions or compulsions characterize these disorders. Obsessions are anxiety-provoking thoughts that won't go away. Compulsions are urges to perform repetitive, ritualistic behaviors that usually occur to prevent or produce a future situation.
	Post-Traumatic Stress Disorder	This disorder develops through exposure to a traumatic event, such as war; severely oppressive situations, such as the Holocaust; severe abuse, such as rape; natural disasters; and accidental disasters. Anxiety symptoms may immediately follow the trauma, or be delayed months or even years until onset. PTSD can be transmitted from survivors to offspring.
Somatoform Disorders	Their Nature	Psychological symptoms take a physical, or somatic, form, even though no physical cause can be found.
	Hypochondriasis	This disorder involves a pervasive fear of illness and disease. It rarely occurs alone; depression often accompanies hypochondriasis.
	Conversion Disorder	This disorder occurs when an individual experiences specific symptoms even though no physiological problems can be found. Conversion disorder received its name from psychoanalytic theory, which stressed that anxiety was "converted" into a specific physical symptom. Some loss of motor or sensory ability occurs. The disorder was more common in Freud's time than today.
Dissociative Disorders	Their Nature	Dissociative disorders occur when a person has a sudden loss of memory or change in identity. Under extreme stress or shock, conscious awareness becomes dissociated (separated or split) from previous memories and thoughts.
	Dissociative Amnesia and Fugue	Dissociative amnesia involves memory loss caused by extensive psychological stress. Dissociative fugue also involves a loss of memory, but individuals unexpectedly travel away from home or work, assume a new identity, and do not remember their old one.
	Dissociative Identity Disorder	Formerly called multiple personality disorder, this disorder involves the presence of two or more distinct personalities in the same individual. The disorder is rare.

Mood Disorders

Our coverage of the mood disorders focuses on their basic nature, depressive disorders, bipolar disorder, and causes of mood disorders. The **mood disorders** *are psychological disorders characterized by wide emotional swings, ranging from deep depression to extreme euphoria and agitation.* Depression can occur alone, as in the depressive disorders, or it can alternate with mania (an overexcited, unrealistically optimistic state), as in bipolar disorder. In the U.S. study of the prevalence of mental disorders, almost eight percent of the individuals reported that they had ever experienced a mood disorder (Robins & Regier, 1991).

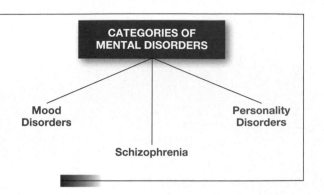

The Depressive Disorders
Major Depressive Disorder

Depressive Disorders   The **depressive disorders** *are mood disorders in which the individual suffers depression without ever experiencing mania.* The severity of the depressive disorders varies, with some individuals experiencing what is classified as major depressive disorder while others are given the diagnosis of dysthymic disorder (more chronic depression with fewer symptoms than major depression).

In **major depressive disorder** *the individual experiences a major depressive episode and depressed characteristics, such as lethargy and hopelessness, for at least two weeks or longer.* The individual's daily functioning becomes impaired. Nine symptoms define a major depressive episode (and of the nine, at least five must be present during a two-week period):

1. Depressed mood most of the day
2. Reduced interest or pleasure in all or most activities
3. Significant weight loss or gain, or significant decrease or interest in appetite
4. Trouble sleeping or sleeping too much
5. Psychomotor agitation or retardation
6. Fatigue or loss of energy
7. Feeling worthless or guilty in an excessive or inappropriate manner
8. Problems in thinking, concentrating, or making decisions
9. Recurrent thoughts of death and suicide

Consider Peter, who had been depressed for several months. Nothing cheered him up. His depression began when the girl he wanted to marry decided marriage was not for her, at least not with Peter. Peter's emotional state deteriorated to the point where he didn't leave his room for days at a time, he kept the shades drawn and the room dark, and he could hardly get out of bed in the morning. When he managed to leave his room, he had trouble maintaining a conversation and he felt exhausted most of the time. By the time Peter finally contacted his university counseling center, he had gone from being mildly depressed to being in the grip of major depression.

Dysthymic disorder *is generally more chronic and has fewer symptoms than major depressive disorder.* The individual has a depressed mood for most days for at least two years as an adult or at least one year as a child or adolescent. To be classified as having dysthymic disorder, a major depressive episode must not have occurred and the two-year period of depression must not have been broken by a normal mood lasting more than two months. Two or more of these six symptoms must be present: poor appetite or overeating, sleep problems, low energy or fatigue, low self-esteem, poor concentration or difficulty making decisions, and feelings of hopelessness (Munoz, 1998).

Although most people don't spiral into major depression as Peter did, everyone feels "blue" sometimes (Flett, Vredenburg & Krames, 1997). In our stress-filled world, people often use the term *depression* to describe brief bouts of normal sadness or discontent over life's problems. Perhaps you haven't done well in a class or things aren't working out in your love life. You feel down in the dumps and say you are depressed. In most instances, though, your depression won't last as long or be as intense as

This painting by Vincent Van Gogh, Portrait of Dr. Gatchet, *reflects the extreme melancholy that characterizes the depressive disorders.*

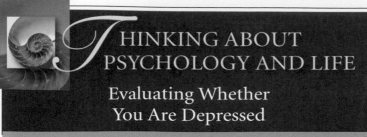

THINKING ABOUT PSYCHOLOGY AND LIFE

Evaluating Whether You Are Depressed

BELOW IS A LIST of the ways that you might have felt or behaved in the last week. Indicate what you felt by putting an X in the appropriate box for each item.

During the past week:	Rarely or None of the Time (Less Than 1 Day)	Some or a Little of the Time (1–2 Days)	Occasion-ally or a Moderate Amount of the Time (3–4 Days)	Most or All of the Time (5–7 Days)
1. I was bothered by things that usually don't bother me.	☐	☐	☐	☐
2. I did not feel like eating; my appetite was poor.	☐	☐	☐	☐
3. I felt that I could not shake off the blues even with help from my family and friends.	☐	☐	☐	☐
4. I felt that I was just as good as other people.	☐	☐	☐	☐
5. I had trouble keeping my mind on what I was doing.	☐	☐	☐	☐
6. I felt depressed.	☐	☐	☐	☐
7. I felt that everything I did was an effort.	☐	☐	☐	☐
8. I felt hopeful about the future.	☐	☐	☐	☐
9. I thought my life had been a failure.	☐	☐	☐	☐
10. I felt fearful.	☐	☐	☐	☐
11. My sleep was restless.	☐	☐	☐	☐
12. I was happy.	☐	☐	☐	☐
13. I talked less than usual.	☐	☐	☐	☐
14. I felt lonely.	☐	☐	☐	☐
15. People were unfriendly.	☐	☐	☐	☐
16. I enjoyed life.	☐	☐	☐	☐
17. I had crying spells.	☐	☐	☐	☐
18. I felt sad.	☐	☐	☐	☐
19. I felt that people disliked me.	☐	☐	☐	☐
20. I could not get going.	☐	☐	☐	☐

For items 4, 8, 12, and 16, give yourself a 3 each time you checked rarely or none, 2 each time you checked some or little, 1 each time you checked occasionally or moderate, and a 0 each time you checked most or all of the time. For the remaining items, give yourself a 0 each time you checked rarely or none, 1 each time you checked some or a little, 2 each time you checked occasionally or moderate, and 3 each time you checked most or all of the time. Total up your score for all 20 items.

If your score is around 7, then you are like the average male in terms of how much depression you have experienced in the last week. If your score is around 8 or 9 your score is similar to the average female. Scores less than the average for either males or females indicate that depression has probably not been a problem for you during the past week. If your score is 16 or more and you are bothered by your feelings, you might benefit from professional help.

Keep in mind, though, that self-diagnosis is not always accurate and to adequately diagnose anyone, the professional judgment of a qualified clinician is required.

Peter's; after a few hours, days, or weeks, you snap out of your gloomy state and begin to cope more effectively with your problems. Nonetheless, depression is so widespread that it has been called the "common cold" of mental disorders; more than 250,000 individuals are hospitalized every year for the disorder. Students, professors, corporate executives, laborers—no one is immune to depression, not even F. Scott Fitzgerald, Ernest Hemingway, Virginia Woolf, Leonard Cohen, or Winston Churchill—each of whom experienced depression.

After years of depression, Hemingway eventually took his own life. To read about suicide, including some helpful strategies for communicating with someone who is considering suicide, see Explorations in Psychology.

The inadequate care that results from a lack of understanding or a misunderstanding of depression is tragic. Given the existing range of psychological and pharmacological treatments available today, those individuals who go untreated suffer needlessly.

Bipolar Disorder   At 33, shortly before the birth of her first child, Mrs. M. became very depressed. One month after the baby was born she became agitated and euphoric. Mrs. M. signed a year's lease on an apartment, bought furniture, and piled up debts. Several years later other manic and depressive mood swings occurred. In one of her excitatory moods, Mrs. M. swore loudly and created a disturbance at a club where she was not a member. Several days later she began divorce proceedings. On the day prior to her admission to a mental hospital, she went on a spending spree and bought 57 hats. Several weeks later, she became despondent, saying "I have no energy. My brain doesn't work right. I have let my family down. I don't have anything to live for." (Kolb, 1973). York University psychologist Norman Endler (1990a) courageously described his own encounter with bipolar disorder both from his own personal point of view and from his perspective as an eminent clinical psychologist.

Bipolar disorder *is a mood disorder that is characterized by extreme mood swings that include one or more episodes of mania (an overexcited, unrealistically optimistic state)* (Coryell & others, 1999). *Bipolar* means that the person may experience depression and mania. Most bipolar individuals experience multiple cycles of depression interspersed with mania. Less than 10 percent of bipolar individuals tend to experience manic-type episodes and not depression.

A manic episode is like the flip side of a depressive episode (DeBattista, Solvason, & Schatzberg, 1998). Instead of feeling depressed, the person feels euphoric and on top of the world. However, as the manic episode unfolds the person can experience panic and eventually depression. Instead of feeling fatigued as many depressed individuals do, when individuals experience mania they have tremendous energy and might sleep very little. When individuals are in a manic state there is often an impulsivity that can get them in trouble in business and legal transactions. For example, they might spend their life

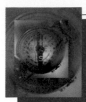

EXPLORATIONS IN PSYCHOLOGY
Suicide

EACH YEAR ABOUT 4,000 Canadians (Sakinofsky, 1998) and 25,000 Americans (Weissman & others, 1999) take their own lives. Suicide accounts for 12 percent of the mortality in the adolescent and young adult age group. Suicide rates among Canada's aboriginal peoples are 2 to 4 times the national average. Men are about 3 to 4 times more likely than women to succeed at committing suicide. This may be due to their choice of method—shooting themselves, for example. By contrast, females more often select methods, such as sleeping pills, which do not immediately cause death. Although males commit suicide more frequently, females attempt it more often (Maris, 1998).

Estimates indicate that 6 to 10 suicide attempts occur for every successful suicide in the general population. For adolescents, the figure is as high as 50 attempts for every life taken. As many as 2 in every 3 college students have thought about suicide on at least one occasion.

There is no simple answer to why people commit suicide. Biological factors appear to be involved. Suicide, as with major depressive disorder, tends to run in families. In aboriginal groups, the abandonment of traditional values is often cited as a factor (Sakinofsky, 1998). Immediate and highly stressful circumstances, such as the loss of a spouse or a job, flunking out of school, or an unwanted pregnancy, can lead people, especially those who are genetically predisposed, to attempt suicide.

However, earlier experiences, such as a long-standing history of family instability and unhappiness, can also play a role in attempted suicides. Studies of gifted men and women found several predictors of suicide, such as anxiety, conspicuous instability in work and relationships, depression, and alcoholism (Shneidman, 1971; Tomlinson-Keasey, Warren, & Elliot, 1986).

Substance abuse and having a terminal illness are related to suicidal thoughts and behavior. Also, in high-pressure cultures, such as Japan, Canada, and the United States, suicide rates are much higher than in less achievement-oriented cultures.

TABLE 13.A
What To Do and What Not To Do When Someone is Threatening Suicide

What To Do	What Not To Do
1. Ask direct, straightforward questions in a calm manner. For example: "Are you thinking about hurting yourself?" Be a good listener.	1. Don't ignore the warning signs.
2. Take the suicide threat very seriously. Ask questions about the person's feelings, relationships, and thoughts about the type of method to be used. If a gun, pills, rope, or other means is mentioned and a specific plan has been developed, the situation is dangerous. Stay with the person until help arrives.	2. Don't refuse to talk about suicide if the person wants to talk about it. 3. Don't react with horror, disapproval, or repulsion. 4. Don't offer false reassurances ("Everything will be all right") or make judgments ("You should be thankful for . . .").
3. Listen and be supportive. Emphasize that unbearable pain can be survived.	5. Don't abandon the person after the crisis seems to have passed or after professional counseling has begun.
4. Encourage the person to get professional help and assist him or her in getting this help. If the person is willing, take the person to a mental health facility or hospital.	

Suicide

Bipolar Disorder

Bipolar Disorder Resources

savings on a foolish business venture. By definition in the *DSM-IV* classification, manic episodes must last one week. They average 8 to 16 weeks. Individuals with bipolar disorder can have manic and depressive episodes that occur four or more times a year, but they usually are separated by six months to a year.

Causes of Mood Disorders

Causes of mood disorders, such as Peter's depression and Mrs. M.'s bipolar disorder, are biological as well as psychosocial.

Biological Causes Biological explanations of mood disorders involve heredity and brain processes, especially neurotransmitters (DeBattista, Solvason, & Schatzberg, 1998). Depressive and bipolar disorders tend to run in families, although the family link is stronger for bipolar disorder than depressive disorders. One of the greatest risks for developing a mood disorder is having a biological parent who suffers from a mood disorder. For example, in bipolar disorder, the rate of the disorder in first degree relatives is 10 to 20 times higher than in the general population.

Abnormalities in what are called monoamine neurotransmitters, such as serotonin, norepinephrine, and dopamine, have been implicated in mood disorders (Meyers & others, 1999) ◀▥ P. 76. Mood disorders are also associated with neuroendocrine abnormalities, such as higher levels of the stress hormone cortisol ◀▥ P. 95.

Psychosocial Causes Psychosocial factors that may be involved in the mood disorders have been proposed by psychoanalytic theorists such as Freud ◀▥ P. 413. Cognitive and sociocultural explanations have also been proposed.

Freud (1917) believed that depression was a turning inward of aggressive instincts. He theorized that the child's early attachment to a love object (usually the mother) contains a mixture of love and hate. When the child loses the love object or her dependency needs are frustrated, feelings of loss coexist with anger. Since the child cannot openly accept such angry feelings toward the individual she loves, the hostility is turned inward and experienced as depression. The unresolved mixture of anger and love is carried forward to adolescence and adulthood, where loss can bring back these early feelings of abandonment.

The British psychiatrist John Bowlby (1989) agrees with Freud that childhood experiences are an important determinant of depression in adulthood ◀▥ P. 340. He believes a combination of an insecure attachment to the mother, a lack of love and affection as a child, and the actual loss of a parent during childhood gives rise to a negative cognitive set, or schema. The schema built up during childhood causes the individual to interpret later losses as yet other failures in one's effort to establish enduring and close positive relationships.

The cognitive approach provides another perspective on mood disorders. Individuals who are depressed rarely think positive thoughts, although the *depressive realism hypothesis* suggests that depressed persons may be more accurate in their perceptions of various situations than are nondepressed persons (Dobson & Franche, 1989). Depressed people interpret their lives in self-defeating ways and have negative expectations about the future (Bradley, 1996). Beck (1967) believed that such negative thoughts reflect schemas that shape the depressed individual's experiences. These habitual negative thoughts magnify and expand a depressed person's negative experiences (Teasdale & others, 1995). A person might be given a slightly negative work evaluation and might, through catastrophic thinking, expect to be fired and to be unable to find another job. Canadian researchers have conducted much useful research on negative self-schemas in depression (Rector, Segal & Gemar, 1998). For example, Tripp, Catano & Sullivan (1997) have explored the relationship of attributional style, expectancies and self-esteem in depression.

Learned helplessness *occurs when individuals are exposed to aversive stimulation, such as prolonged stress or pain, over which they have no control.* The inability to avoid such aversive stimulation produces an apathetic state of

𝒯hrough the Eyes of Psychologists

Norman Endler, *York University*

"One of the major problems is the attitude of society toward the affective disorders and their treatment"

helplessness. Martin Seligman (1975) argued that learned helplessness is one reason some individuals become depressed. When individuals encounter stress and pain over which they have no control, they eventually feel helpless and depressed. Some researchers believe that the hopelessness characteristic of learned helplessness is often the result of a person's extremely negative, self-blaming attributions (Metalsky & others, 1993).

Seligman (1989) believes the reason so many North Americans face depression is our society's emphasis on self, independence, and individualism, along with an erosion of connectedness to others, family, and religion, which has led to widespread hopelessness. To make matters worse, depressed people also face stigma (Endler, 1990b). Depressive disorders are found virtually worldwide, but their incidence, intensity, and components vary across cultures. A major difference in depression between Western and many non-Western cultures is the absence of guilt and self-deprecation in the non-Western cultures (Draguns, 1990).

Earlier we mentioned that women suffer depression more frequently than men. Janet Stoppard (1999) of the University of New Brunswick Fredericton has stressed the need to understand women's depression in a sociocultural context. For example, Leadbeater, Bishop & Raver (1996) found that young women are more vulnerable to depression through interpersonal relations; being, for example, more reactive to stressful events involving others. Further, depression is especially high among single women who are heads of households and among young married women who work at unsatisfying, dead-end jobs (Russo, 1990). Sexual abuse, sexual harassment, unwanted pregnancy, and powerlessness all also disproportionately affect women. These sociocultural factors can interact with biological and cognitive factors to increase women's rate of depression.

Schizophrenia

Bob began to miss work. He spent his time watching his house from a rental car parked inconspicuously down the street and following his fellow employees as they left work to see where they went and what they did. He kept a little black book in which he scribbled cryptic notes. When he went to the water cooler at work, he pretended to drink but instead looked carefully around the room to observe if anyone looked guilty or frightened.

Schizophrenia

Bob's world seemed to be closing in on him. After an explosive scene at the office one day, he became very agitated. He left and never returned. By the time Bob arrived at home, he was in a rage. He could not sleep that night and the next day he kept his children home from school; all day he kept the shades pulled on every window. The next night he maintained his vigil. At 4 A.M., he armed himself and burst out of the house, firing shots in the air while daring his enemies to come out (McNeil, 1967).

Bob, like Jim who was described at the beginning of the chapter (recall that he believed his breath possessed a special power), has a schizophrenic disorder. Schizophrenia produces a bizarre set of symptoms and wreaks havoc on the individual's personality. **Schizophrenia** *is a severe psychological disorder characterized by distorted thoughts and perceptions, odd communication, inappropriate emotion, abnormal motor behavior, and social withdrawal.* The term *schizophrenia* comes from the Latin words *schizo*, meaning "split," and *phrenia*, meaning "mind." The individual's mind is split from reality, and personality loses its unity. Schizophrenia is not the same as multiple personality, which is sometimes called a "split personality." Schizophrenia involves the split of an individual's personality from reality, not the coexistence of several personalities within one individual.

In U.S. studies of the prevalence of psychological disorders, between 1 and 1.5 percent reported that they had ever experienced schizophrenia (Gottesman, 1989; Robins & Regier, 1991). In the Edmonton study, about 1 percent reported they had experienced schizophrenia in the preceding six months (Bland, Newman & Orn,

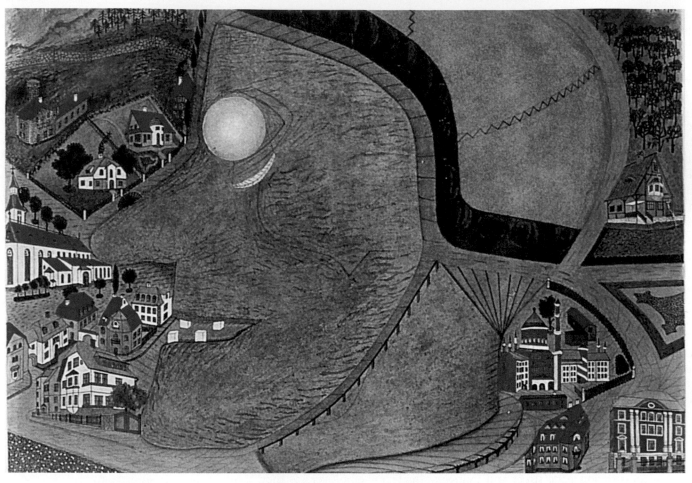

This painting is named Landscape *and it is by August Neter, a successful nineteenth-century electrical engineer until he developed schizophrenia in 1907. He lost interest in his work as an engineer as his mind became disorganized.*

1988). Schizophrenia is a serious, debilitating mental disorder. Drug therapy has helped more individuals with schizophrenia stay out of hospital. About one-third of individuals who develop schizophrenia get better, about one-third get worse, and about one-third stay the same.

What are the symptoms of schizophrenia? First and foremost, schizophrenics suffer from profound neurocognitive deficits. Heinrichs & Zakzanis (1998) surveyed 204 studies and found that schizophrenics showed poorer perfomance in 22 different tasks ranging from selective verbal memory and general intelligence to visual and auditory attention and language. Neurocognitive deficits include *delusions,* or false beliefs. One individual might think he is Jesus Christ, another Napoleon, for example. The delusions are utterly implausible. One individual might think her thoughts are being broadcast over the radio, another might think that a double agent is controlling her every move. Individuals with schizophrenia might also hear, see, feel, smell, and taste things not there. These *hallucinations* often take the form of voices. An individual with schizophrenia might think that he hears two people talking about him. Or he might say, "Hear that rumbling noise in the pipe? That is one of my men watching out for me."

Often individuals with schizophrenia do not make sense when they talk or write. For example, one individual with schizophrenia might say, "Well, Rocky, babe, help is out, happening, but where, when, up, top, side, over, you know, out of the way, that's it. Sign off." Such speech has no meaning. These incoherent, loose word associations are called *word salad.*

The motor behavior of the individual with schizophrenia can be bizarre, sometimes taking the form of an odd appearance, pacing, statue-like postures, or strange mannerisms. Some individuals with schizophrenia withdraw from their social world. They become so insulated from others they seem totally absorbed in their interior thoughts.

Types of Schizophrenia

There are four main types of schizophrenia: disorganized, catatonic, paranoid, and undifferentiated.

Disorganized schizophrenia *is a type of schizophrenia in which an individual has delusions and hallucinations that have little or no recognizable meaning—hence, the label disorganized.* An individual with disorganized schizophrenia may withdraw from human contact and may regress to silly, childlike gestures and behavior. Many of these individuals were isolated or maladjusted during adolescence.

Catatonic schizophrenia *is a type of schizophrenia characterized by bizarre motor behavior, which sometimes takes the form of a completely immobile stupor* (see figure 13.8). Even in this stupor, individuals with catatonic schizophrenia are completely conscious of what is happening around them. In a catatonic state, the individual sometimes shows *waxy flexibility;* for example, if the person's arm is raised and then allowed to fall, the arm stays in the new position.

Paranoid schizophrenia *is a type of schizophrenia characterized by delusions of reference, grandeur, and persecution.* The delusions usually form a complex, elaborate system based on a complete misinterpretation of actual events. It is not unusual for the individual with paranoid schizophrenia to develop all three delusions in the following order. First, they sense they are special and have been singled out for attention (delusions of reference). Individuals with delusions of reference misinterpret chance events as being directly relevant to their own lives—a thunderstorm, for example, might be perceived as a personal message from God. Second, they believe that this special attention is the result of their admirable and special characteristics (delusions of grandeur). Individuals with delusions of grandeur think of themselves as exalted beings—the pope or the president, for example. Third, they think that others are so jealous and threatened by these characteristics that they spy and plot against them (delusions of persecution). Individuals with delusions of persecution often feel they are the target of a conspiracy—for example, recall Bob's situation described earlier.

Undifferentiated schizophrenia *is a type of schizophrenia characterized by disorganized behavior, hallucinations, delusions, and incoherence.* This category of schizophrenia is used when an individual's symptoms either don't meet the criteria for the other types or they meet the criteria for more than one of the other types.

Causes of Schizophrenia

As with mood disorders, possible causes of schizophrenia are found in biological and psychosocial factors.

Biological Factors   Biological factors that have been proposed to explain schizophrenia involve heredity and neurobiological factors. If you have a relative with schizophrenia, what are the chances you will develop schizophrenia? It depends on how closely you are related. As genetic similarity increases, so does a person's risk of becoming schizophrenic (Pritchard, 1996). As shown in figure 13.9, an identical twin of an individual with schizophrenia has a 46 percent chance of developing the disorder, a fraternal twin 14 percent, a sibling 10 percent, a nephew or niece 3 percent, and an unrelated individual in the general population 1 percent (Gottesman & Shields, 1982). Such data strongly suggest that genetic factors are involved in schizophrenia, although the precise nature of the genetic influence is unknown. More about genetic and genetic-environmental influences on schizophrenia appears in Explorations in Psychology, which tells the fascinating story of quadruplets with schizophrenia.

Many neuroscientists believe imbalances in brain chemistry, including deficits in brain metabolism, a malfunctioning dopamine system, and distorted cerebral

Figure 13.8
A Person with Catatonic Schizophrenia
Unusual motor behaviors are prominent symptoms in catatonic schizophrenia. Individuals may cease to move altogether, sometimes taking on bizarre postures.

On November 5, 1995, 34-year-old André
Dallaire entered the grounds of the Prime
Minister's residence at 24 Sussex Drive. Entering
the house carrying a three-inch-long knife, he
encountered Aline Chrétien, Jean Chrétien's
wife, who locked the couple in their bedroom
and called for help.

Dallaire was found guilty of break-and-enter,
possession of a dangerous weapon and attempted
murder, but was deemed not criminally
responsible because he was suffering a paranoid
crisis at the time and had been diagnosed as a
paranoid schizophrenic at the age of 14. He
hallucinated voices telling him to kill Jean
Chrétien and thought he was a secret agent
whose mission was to avenge the No side's
victory in that year's Québec referendum on
independence. He also had delusions of grandeur
and thought he would be glorified for ridding
Canada of the Prime Minister.

Only a small percentage of individuals
with schizophrenia are violent toward others.
Individuals with schizophrenia who get no
treatment are much more likely to harm
themselves than others. About 15 percent of
individuals with schizophrenia commit suicide.
Some mental health experts fear that high-
profile cases like André Dallaire's will stigmatize
all individuals with schizophrenia, even those
who have never committed a crime. Others
hope it will bring attention to the problems of
individuals with schizophrenia and help people
to better understand them. They also hope it will
encourage people who know individuals with
schizophrenia to help them get treatment and
medication, and stay on the medication.

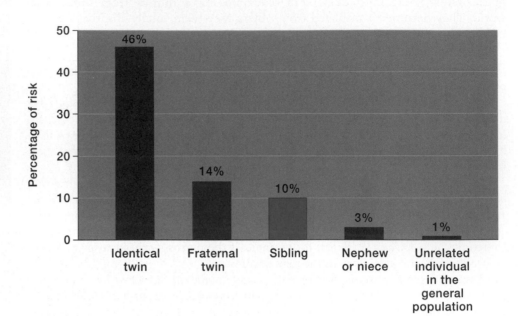

*F*igure 13.9
Lifetime Risk of Developing Schizophrenia, According to Genetic Relatedness
As your genetic relatedness to an individual with schizophrenia
increases, so does your risk of becoming schizophrenic.

blood flow, cause schizophrenia (Bertolino & others, 1999; Byrne & Davis, 1999;
Goldberg, Berman, & Weinberger, 1995). Imaging techniques, such as the PET scan,
clearly show deficits in brain metabolism ◀║║║ P. 94. Do these deficits cause the disorder, or are they simply symptoms of a disorder whose true origin lies deeper in the
brain, in the genes, or in the environment? Whether cause or effect, information
about neurobiological factors improves our knowledge of schizophrenia's nature. We
do know that individuals with schizophrenia produce higher than normal levels of
the neurotransmitter dopamine. They also have a reduced blood flow in the prefrontal cortex (Poole & others, 1999). For example, when scientists monitored the
brains of individuals with schizophrenia as they performed a card-sorting task, blood
did not adequately flow into the prefrontal region, where much of our advanced
thinking takes place (Weinberger, Berman, & Zec, 1986).

Psychosocial Factors   Although contemporary theorists don't propose psychosocial factors as stand-alone causes of schizophrenia, stress is the psychosocial
factor that is given the most attention in understanding schizophrenia. The
diathesis–stress view *argues that a combination of biogenetic disposition and stress
causes schizophrenia* (Meehl, 1962). The term *diathesis* means physical vulnerability
or predisposition to a particular disorder. A defective gene makeup might produce
schizophrenia only when the individual lives in a stressful environment. Advocates of
the diathesis–stress view emphasize the importance of stress reduction and family
support in treating schizophrenia.

Disorders of thought and emotion are common to schizophrenia in all cultures,
but the type and incidence of schizophrenic disorders may vary from culture to culture. Individuals in poverty are more likely to have schizophrenia than people at
higher socioeconomic levels. The link between schizophrenia and poverty is correlational, though contemporary theorists do not believe that poverty causes schizophrenia (Schiffman & Walker, 1998).

EXPLORATIONS IN PSYCHOLOGY
NIMH—Nora, Iris, Myra, and Hester, the Schizophrenic Genain Quadruplets

THE STORY OF the Genain quadruplets began more than 50 years ago. Henry Genain had forgotten to buy his wife a birthday present, so she suggested he give her a child for their third wedding anniversary instead. The wish came true, but there were four presents instead of one (see figure 13.A). The names given to the quadruplets by scientists—Nora, Iris, Myra, and Hester—come from the acronym for the National Institute of Mental Health (NIMH), where the quadruplets have been extensively studied.

Their birth was a celebrated occasion; one paper ran a contest to name the girls and received 12,000 entries. The city found a rent-free house for the unemployed father, a dairy company donated milk, and a baby carriage for four was given to the family. Newspaper stories appeared from time to time about the quadruplets, portraying their similarities, especially their drama talent and a song-and-dance routine they had developed.

However, a darker side to the quadruplets' story had emerged by the time they reached high school. It became clear that the girls had serious mental problems. By the time they were in their twenties, each had been diagnosed with schizophrenia. A perceptive doctor recognized their symptoms and contacted NIMH. A research team led by David Rosenthal began extensive evaluation of the schizophrenic quadruplets (Rosenthal, 1963).

About 20 years later, psychologist Alan Mirksy invited the quadruplets back to NIMH to determine how they might have changed. The scientists also wanted to know if recently developed techniques could discover something special about their biological makeup. PET scans revealed an unusually high rate of energy use in the rear portion of the quadruplets' brains (see figure 13.B). Their brains also showed much less alpha-wave activity than the brains of normal individuals. Remember that alpha-wave activity appears in individuals in a relaxed state; scientists speculate that the onset of hallucinations might possibly block alpha-wave activity.

Some environmental experiences may have contributed to the Genain quadruplets' schizophrenia as well. Their father placed strict demands on his daughters, delighted in watching them undress, and would not let them play with friends or participate in school or church activities. He refused to let the quadruplets participate in social activities even as adults, and he followed them to their jobs and opened their mail.

What makes the Genain quadruplets such fascinating cases is their uniqueness—identical quadruplets occur once in every 16 million births and only half survive to adulthood; only 1 in 100 develop schizophrenia, and the chances of all of them developing schizophrenia happens only once in tens of billions of births, a figure much greater than the current world population.

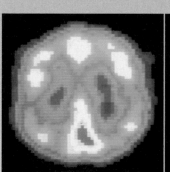
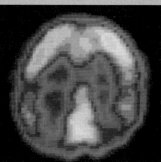

Figure 13.A
The Genain Quadruplets as Children
All of the quadruplets had been diagnosed with schizophrenia by the time they were in their twenties.

Figure 13.B
PET Scans of the Genain Quadruplets
In a normal brain (right photo), the areas of high energy use are at the top (frontal lobes). The quadruplets all showed energy use in the visual areas at the bottom of their PET scan brain slices. Are these hallucinations? (Note: The other three sisters showed PET scans much more similar to Nora's than to a normal individual's.)

Odd/Eccentric Cluster	
Paranoid	Lack of trust in others, suspicious. See themselves as morally correct yet vulnerable and envied.
Schizoid	Inability to form adequate social relationships. Shy, withdrawn behavior, difficulty expressing anger. Most are considered "cold" people.
Schizotypal	Many of the same features of the schizoid category also apply here. Some differences with the schizoid disorder are that the schizotypal disorder involves odd thinking patterns likely to have developed because of eccentric beliefs, more overt suspicion, and more overt hostility.

Dramatic/Emotionally Problematic Cluster	
Histrionic	Seek attention and are over reactive. Responses are expressed more dramatically and intensely than is appropriate, hence the term *histrionic*. The disorder is much more common in women than in men.
Narcissistic	Unrealistic sense of self-importance, exhibitionistic attention seeking, inability to take criticism, interpersonal manipulation, and lack of empathy. These characteristics lead to substantial problems in interpersonal relationships.
Antisocial	Guiltless, law-breaking, exploitive, irresponsible, self-indulgent, and interpersonally intrusive. These individuals often resort to a life of crime and violence. The disorder is considerably more common in men than in women.
Borderline	Similar to schizotypal but borderline disorder does not involve behavior that is as consistently withdrawn and thinking that is as bizarre. These individuals are often emotionally unstable, impulsive, unpredictable in their behavior, irritable, and anxious. They are also prone to boredom.

Chronic Fearfulness/Avoidant Cluster	
Avoidant	These individuals are shy and inhibited yet desire interpersonal relationships, which distinguishes them from the schizotypal or schizoid disorders. They often have low self-esteem and are extremely sensitive to rejection. This disorder is close to being an anxiety disorder but is not characterized by as much personal distress.
Dependent	These individuals lack self-confidence and don't express their own personality. They have a pervasive need to cling to stronger personalities, whom they allow to make a wide range of decisions for them. The disorder is far more common in women than in men.
Obsessive-compulsive	This disorder is often confused with the obsessive-compulsive disorder (which is an anxiety disorder), but there are significant differences between them. The obsessive-compulsive personality seldom becomes obsessed about issues. Obsessive-compulsive personality involves a lifestyle in which compulsive features are chronic and pervasive, but it does not involve a specific behavior such as persistent hand-washing. And the obsessive-compulsive personality does not become upset or distressed about his/her lifestyle. Individuals with obsessive-compulsive personality disorder are preoccupied with rules and duties, rarely express warmth or caring, are emotionally insensitive, and oriented toward a lifestyle of productivity and efficiency.
Passive-aggressive	Pouting, procrastination, stubbornness, or intentional inefficiency designed to frustrate other people. A typical thought pattern is "I don't have to get there. Nobody can tell me what to do."

Figure 13.10
Three Clusters of Personality Disorders

Personality Disorders

Personality Disorders

We will explore the nature of personality disorders, in general, then examine antisocial personality disorder.

Personality disorders *are chronic, maladaptive cognitive-behavioral patterns that are thoroughly integrated into the individual's personality.* The patterns are often recognizable by adolescence or earlier. Personality disorders are usually not as bizarre as schizophrenia and they don't have the intense, diffuse feelings of fear and apprehension that characterize the anxiety disorders (Meyer, 1998).

In the *DSM-IV*, the personality disorders fall into three clusters (see figure 13.10). The odd/eccentric cluster includes the paranoid, schizoid, and schizotypal disorders. The dramatic and emotionally problematic cluster consists of the histrionic, narcissistic, antisocial, and borderline disorders. The chronic fearfulness/avoidant cluster is made up of the avoidant, dependent, obsessive-compulsive, and passive-aggressive personality disorders. Some of the personality disorders have names that are similar to other disorders we described earlier in other categories, such as schizotypal personality disorder and schizophrenic disorders, as well as obsessive-compulsive personality disorder and obsessive-compulsive anxiety disorder. The schizotypal disorder is not as clearly bizarre as schizophrenia. Figure 13.10 lists a number of differences between obsessive-compulsive personality disorder and obsessive-compulsive anxiety disorder.

Antisocial personality disorder *is in the dramatic/emotionally problematic cluster. It is the most problematic disorder for society, because these individuals often resort to a life of crime and violence.* They are guiltless, exploitive, irresponsible, self-indulgent, and interpersonally intrusive (Carson, Butcher, & Mineka, 1998). In the Edmonton study of the prevalence of psychological disorders, 2.5 percent of male respondents reported experiencing antisocial personality disorder in the preceding six months (Bland, Newman & Orn, 1988).

People with antisocial personality disorder used to be called psychopaths or sociopaths. They regularly violate other people's rights. The disorder begins before the age of 15 and continues into adulthood. It is much more common in males than in females. These individuals represent a small percentage of the population but commit a disproportionately large percentage of violent and property crimes (Meyer, Wolverton, & Deitsch, 1998). The disorder is very difficult to treat (Wong, in press).

Both biological and psychosocial explanations of antisocial personality disorder have been given. A genetic predisposition for the disorder may be present. For example, the disorder is more likely to appear in identical twins than in fraternal twins (Gottesman & Goldsmith, 1994).

Preferring the older designation of psychopath, Robert Hare of the University of British Columbia has explored brain abnormalities underlying antisocial personality disorder. Hare and his colleagues (Williamson, Harpur & Hare, 1991) compared the brain waves of a group of normal subjects with those of psychopaths while they recognized words. They found that normal subjects spent more time processing emotion-laden words than psychopaths. Normal subjects took longer recognizing emotionally-laden words like "cancer," but for psychopaths, words like "cancer" were recognized as quickly as words like "table," suggesting that psychopaths did not have many emotional connotations for any words. Hare and his colleagues (Intrator & others, 1997) showed that normal subjects process emotionally-laden words in the areas around the ventromedial frontal cortex and amygdala, whereas psychopaths show brain activity only in cortex and not the amygdala, "the seat of emotion." These results suggest that psychopaths do not experience the integration of cognition and emotion that normal people do.

At this point we have discussed a number of ideas about the mood disorders, schizophrenic disorders, and personality disorders. An overview of these ideas is presented in summary table 13.3. In the next chapter, we continue our exploration of abnormal psychology by examining the therapies used to treat people's mental disorders.

Paul Bernardo is a classic case of a personality disorder. By the time he attended the University of Toronto, he was beating up the women he dated and preferred forceful anal sex. As the Scarborough rapist, he sexually assaulted at least 14 young women in southern Ontario between 1987 and 1991. On December 24, 1990, Bernardo and his former wife Karla Homolka, now serving 12 years for manslaughter, drugged and raped her 15-year-old sister Tammy, who choked to death on her own vomit. In June, 1991, they repeatedly raped Leslie Mahaffy in their Port Dalhousie home for nearly 24 hours, then strangled her, dismembered the body and disposed of the parts in Lake Gibson. In April, 1992, they held Kristen French hostage for almost 72 hours, brutally raping her before strangling her to death. Bernardo, who was officially declared a dangerous offender, will likely spend the rest of his life in prison, ineligible for parole.

Antisocial Personality Disorder
The Psychopath's Brain

SUMMARY TABLE 13.3
Mood Disorders, Schizophrenia, and Personality Disorders

Concept	Processes/ Related Ideas	Characteristics/Description
Mood Disorders	Their Nature	Mood disorders are psychological disorders characterized by wide emotional mood swings, ranging from deep depression to extreme euphoria and agitation. Depression can occur alone, as in the depressive disorders, or it can alternate with mania, as in bipolar disorder.
	Depressive Disorders	These are mood disorders in which the individual suffers depression without ever experiencing mania. In major depressive disorder, the individual experiences a major depressive episode and depressed characteristics, such as lethargy and hopelessness, for two weeks or longer. Dysthymic disorder is generally more chronic and has fewer symptoms than major depressive disorder.
	Bipolar Disorder	This is a mood disorder characterized by extreme mood swings that include one of more episodes of mania (an overexcited, unrealistic, optimistic state). "Bipolar" means the person may experience depression and mania. Less than 10 percent of bipolar individuals experience mania and not depression.
	Causes of Mood Disorders	Biological explanations include heredity and brain processes, especially the monoamine neurotransmitters. Psychosocial factors include those proposed by psychoanalytic theorists such as Freud, cognitive explanations such as Beck's emphasis on cognitive distortions, and Seligman's focus on the negative expectations of learned helplessness, as well as sociocultural factors such as gender (with women diagnosed with depression about twice as often as men).
Schizophrenia	Its Nature	This is a severe psychological disorder characterized by distorted thoughts and perceptions, odd communication, inappropriate emotion, abnormal motor behavior, and social withdrawal. The individual's mind is split from reality and personality loses its unity. About 1 in 100 Americans develops schizophrenia.
	Types of Schizophrenia	There are four main types of schizophrenia: disorganized, catatonic, paranoid, and differentiated.
	Causes of Schizophrenia	Biological factors include heredity and such neurobiological factors as too much of the neurotransmitter dopamine. Possible psychosocial factors include stress.
Personality Disorders	Their Nature	Personality disorders are chronic, maladaptive cognitive-behavioral patterns that are thoroughly integrated into the individual's personality. They are often recognizable by adolescence or earlier. In the *DSM-IV*, they are divided into three clusters: odd/eccentric, dramatic/emotionally problematic, and chronic fearfulness/avoidant.
	Antisocial Personality Disorder	This is in the dramatic/emotionally problematic cluster and is the most problematic personality disorder for society because these individuals often resort to a life of crime and violence. They are guiltless, exploitive, irresponsible, self-indulgent, and interpersonally intrusive.

Overview

OUR COVERAGE OF ABNORMAL PSYCHOLOGY began by examining a number of ideas about understanding abnormal behavior. These ideas focused on defining abnormal behavior, legal aspects of mental disorders, the causes of abnormal behavior, rates of disorders, and classifying abnormal behavior. Our extensive discussion of categories of mental disorders emphasized six prominent categories: anxiety disorders, somatoform disorders, dissociative disorders, mood disorders, schizophrenia, and personality disorders.

Remember that you can obtain a more detailed overview of the chapter by again studying the three summary tables on pages 454, 462, and 474.

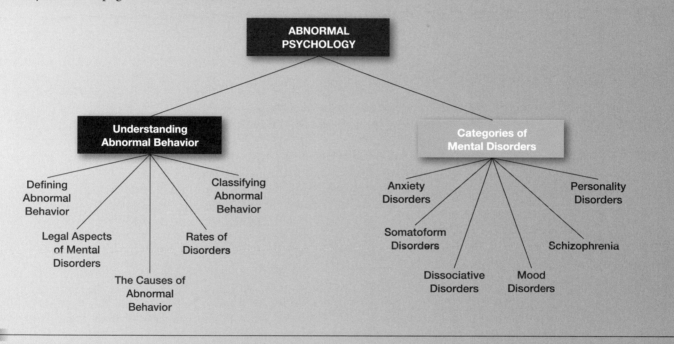

Key Terms

abnormal behavior 448
insanity defense 449
medical model 450
neurotic 453
psychotic 453
DSM-IV 453
multiaxial system 453
anxiety disorders 455
generalized anxiety disorder 456
panic disorder 456

agoraphobia 457
phobic disorder 457
obsessive-compulsive disorder (OCD) 458
post-traumatic stress disorder 458
somatoform disorders 459
hypochondriasis 459
conversion disorder 460
dissociative disorders 460
dissociative amnesia 460

dissociative fugue 460
dissociative identity disorder (DID) 460
mood disorders 463
depressive disorders 463
major depressive disorder 463
dysthymic disorder 463
bipolar disorder 464
learned helplessness 466
schizophrenia 467

disorganized schizophrenia 469
catatonic schizophrenia 469
paranoid schizophrenia 469
undifferentiated schizophrenia 469
diathesis–stress view 470
personality disorders 472
antisocial personality disorder 473

Key People

Sigmund Freud 466
John Bowlby 466

Norman Endler 466

Martin Seligman 467

Robert Hare 473

Psychology Checklist
ABNORMAL PSYCHOLOGY

How much have you learned since the beginning of the chapter? Place a check mark beside any item for which you now feel you have a good understanding.

_____ I know how to define abnormal behavior.
_____ I can describe the legal aspects of mental disorders.
_____ I can discuss the causes of mental disorders.
_____ I am aware of the rates of abnormal behavior.
_____ I know how abnormal behavior is classified.
_____ I can describe the anxiety disorders, including generalized anxiety disorder, panic disorder, phobic disorders, obsessive-compulsive disorder, and post-traumatic stress disorder.
_____ I can discuss the somatoform disorders, including hypochondriasis and conversion disorder.

_____ I am aware of the nature of the dissociative disorders, including dissociative amnesia, dissociative fugue, and dissociative identity disorder.
_____ I can describe the mood disorders, including the depressive disorders and bipolar disorder.
_____ I am aware of the causes of the mood disorders.
_____ I can discuss schizophrenia and evaluate its cause.
_____ I know about the personality disorders, including the three main clusters of these disorders and antisocial personality disorder.

For any items that you did not check off, go back and study the related material in the chapter again until you have a good command of the ideas.

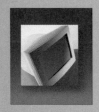

Taking It to the Net

1. Imagine you are sitting in a movie theater enjoying a film when all of the sudden your heart starts to race. You begin to tremble, sweat, and feel very dizzy. Because there are no explanations for this event, you think you are either having a heart attack or going crazy. In fact, you have just experienced a panic attack, the hallmark of panic disorder. What are the causes of panic disorder and what can be done about it? Can people with panic disorder lead normal lives? Explain.

2. Have you ever felt depressed? Chances are that you answered yes, but this might be because you are using a different meaning of the word. Where do you think the line is drawn between feeling "the blues" and clinical depression? To be clinically depressed, there are strict criteria that must be met. What are those criteria? How are they different from merely feeling "the blues"? What are some of the effective treatments for depression?

3. Seasonal affective disorder (SAD) is a disorder in which mood and behavior are affected by time of year. Therefore, during winter seasons, some people become very depressed, eat more, have trouble sleeping, and feel lethargic. Interestingly, researchers have discovered that the symptoms can be alleviated by exposure to bright light for extended periods of time. So, people with SAD sit in front of a special bright light every day, and although the light is otherwise completely normal, their symptoms are alleviated. Why do you suppose that bright light helps these people? Would moving to a location with more sunlight also improve their moods? Explain.

Connect to http://www.mcgrawhill.ca/college/santrock to find the answers!

Resources for Psychology and Life

The Law, Standards of Practice, and Ethics in the Practice Of Psychology (1997)
> by David Evans (Ed.)
> Toronto: Emond Montgomery Publications.

This current book covers the legal and ethical issues which a practitioner of psychology in Canada might face.

Mental Health Law in Canada (1987).
> by Harvey Savage & Carla McKague
> Toronto: Butterworths

Although a bit dated now, this book still gives excellent coverage to Canadian mental health legal issues.

Abnormal Psychology: Perspectives (1999)
> by William Marshall and Philip Firestone
> Scarborough, ON: Prentice Hall Allyn and Bacon Canada

The book gives a thoroughly Canadian treatment of the topic of abnormal psychology.

Mad Travelers: Reflections on the Reality of Transient Mental Illness (1998)
> by Ian Hacking
> Charlottesville, VA: University Press of Virginia

This book explores how it is possible for some psychological disorders to come into fashion, like dissociative identity disorder, or to go out of fashion, like dissociative fugue, which was common at the turn of the century but rare today.

The Osiris Complex: Case Studies in Multiple Personality Disorder (1994)
> by Collin Ross
> Toronto: University of Toronto Press

Collin Ross spent several years as a psychologist at the University of Manitoba. He has presented a number of fascinating case studies of multiple personality disorder (dissociative identity disorder), including the case of Jenny Z. with which this chapter began.

Holiday of Darkness (Revised Ed.) (1990)
> by Norman Endler
> Toronto: Wall & Thompson Publishers

This unique, courageous book combines Norman Endler's considerable expertise as a clinical psyhcologist with his personal experience facing bipolar disorder.

Suicide in Canada (1998)
> by Antoon Leenaars, Susanne Wenckstern, Isaac Sakinofsky, Ronald Dyck, Michael Kral and Roger Bland (Eds.)
> Toronto: University of Toronto Press

This book gives current coverage to the problem of suicide in Canada, with a special focus on our indigenous peoples.

Feeling Good (1980)
> by David Burns
> New York: Avon

Feeling Good is a cognitive therapy approach to coping with depression.

Journal of Abnormal Psychology

This long-standing journal publishes articles on many different topics in abnormal psychology, including depression, schizophrenia, anxiety disorders, and the nature of abnormal behavior.

Without Conscience: The Disturbing World of the Psychopaths Among Us (1998)
> by Robert Hare
> New York: Simon & Schuster

This book is a fascinating journey into the minds of these dangerous individuals. Are they born unable to feel empathy, or are they created by circumstance?

Chapter 14

CHAPTER OUTLINE

THE NATURE AND HISTORY OF PSYCHOTHERAPY

What Is Psychotherapy?

The History of Psychotherapy

Mental Health Professionals

Connections with Personality Theories

APPROACHES TO PSYCHOTHERAPY

Psychodynamic Therapies

Humanistic Therapies

Behavior Therapies

Cognitive Therapies

Group Therapies

Is Psychotherapy Effective?

BIOMEDICAL THERAPIES

Drug Therapy

Electroconvulsive Therapy

Psychosurgery

THERAPY INTEGRATIONS

Therapies

> *"Nothing can be changed until it is faced."*
>
> James Baldwin
> *American Novelist, 20th Century*

Images of Psychology and Life
Our Native Peoples Heal Themselves

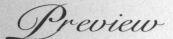

Preview

MANY PEOPLE seek therapy. Some, like our Native peoples, whom you will read about shortly, need help healing from past cultural mistreatment. Others may need help overcoming trauma, such as physical or sexual abuse in childhood. And others may be in the throes of conflict with a partner, in the immobilizing grip of fears such as agoraphobia, or immersed in the delusions of schizophrenia. Whatever the reason people seek therapy, there are many different approaches to help them—at last count more than 400. These are some of the questions that we will explore in this chapter:

- How were individuals with a mental disorder dealt with at different points in history?
- What are some approaches to psychotherapy?
- What is it like to go to a therapist with a particular approach?
- How effective is psychotherapy? Are some types of psychotherapy more effective with some mental disorders than others?
- What are biomedical therapies like? Which drugs are most effective in treating particular mental disorders?
- What is meant by "therapy integrations"?

IN 1995, SUSAN AGLUKARK released a CD entitled *This Child*, which catapulted her onto the world stage. Born on Hudson Bay and often singing in her native language, Inuktitut, she has come a long way. But she has never forgotten her past. Her songs often deal with the many ills that tear at the social fabric of our Native peoples. She was sexually abused by a family friend at age nine and was finally able to confront her abuser 13 years later, when she learned he was still abusing other girls. Her 1989 testimony in a Rankin Inlet courtroom helped convict the man.

Susan Aglukark's family has also been touched by the tidal wave of suicide that washes over many Native communities. *In Kathy I,* a heartbreaking song on *This Child,* Aglukark laments the loss of Kathy, her good friend and cousin, who killed herself: "Kathy, I set you free/On your journey to find your peace/In my heart you'll always be/Kathy, I set you free." Despite all she has experienced, Susan Aglukark is one of the lucky ones. Her music has given her a way to express her experiences and share them with other Canadians.

C. Murray Sinclair, a First Nations member from Winnipeg, also shared his experiences with other Canadians when he delivered a moving keynote address to the 1992 annual conference of the Canadian Association for Suicide Prevention (Sinclair, 1998). For him, growing up Native in Canada was a "difficult and sometimes traumatic experience." Although mainly carried out by well-meaning people, according to Sinclair, the treatment of Native peoples by Canadian governments was a form of cultural genocide. The belief was that Native societies were inferior and must be destroyed to save Native peoples.

Under the Indian Act, traditional chiefs could be removed from office and Natives could be prevented from competing economically with Whites, leaving their reservations without permission, or benefiting from natural resources on their lands. Subsequent amendments made it an offence for Natives to participate in tribal ceremonies or wear traditional costumes, and legally required Native children to attend residential schools, where they were often abused.

According to Sinclair, this policy destroyed traditional leadership and tribal institutions without replacing them with appropriate Canadian alternatives, resulting in social chaos and an inevitable toll of depression, alcoholism, abuse, and suicide.

What can be done? The usual image of an individual therapist healing an individual patient must, in this case, be augmented by tribal and national healing. Sinclair advocates that Native peoples must take control of who they are to be and look to their own cultural heritage as well as to the future to heal. Chandler & Lalonde (1998) have presented compelling evidence that Sinclair is right. They first showed that suicide rates vary widely across British Columbia's nearly 200 Native groups: some communities show rates 800 times the national average, while in others suicide is rare. They also showed that lower suicide rates were associated with Native bands that are actively working to preserve and rehabilitate their own cultures.

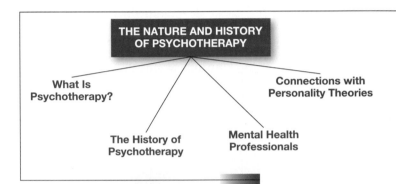

The Nature and History of Psychotherapy

To begin, we will explore what psychotherapy is, then turn to psychotherapy's intriguing history, which includes early efforts to cure people's psychological problems by cutting holes in their skulls. Then we will discuss the range of mental health professionals and describe the ties of different psychotherapy approaches to personality theories.

What Is Psychotherapy?

Psychotherapy

Psychotherapy *is the process used by mental health professionals to help individuals recognize, define, and overcome their psychological and interpersonal difficulties and improve their adjustment.* Psychotherapists use a number of strategies to accomplish these goals: talking, interpreting, listening, rewarding, and modeling, for example.

The History of Psychotherapy

To begin our exploration of therapies, let's trace the evolution of views and treatments from ancient times to the twentieth century. In this journey, you will see how views have changed from a focus on supernatural causes to natural causes.

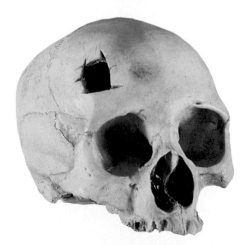

Figure 14.1
Trephining

The technique of trephining involved chipping a hole in the skull through which an evil spirit, believed to be the source of the person's abnormal behavior, might escape. The fact that some people actually survived the operation is shown by this skull. The bone had had time to heal considerably before the individual died.

Early History   In primitive societies, abnormal behavior was thought to be caused by evil spirits residing within the afflicted person. *Trephining,* which involved chipping a hole in the skull, was one early method of letting the evil spirit escape (see figure 14.1). The Greek physician Hippocrates, however, believed that mental problems and abnormal behavior were the result of brain damage or an imbalance of body fluids. In the fourth century B.C., Hippocrates prescribed rest, exercise, a bland diet, and abstinence from sex and alcohol as cures for depression.

Over time, Hippocrates' ideas were lost. In the Middle Ages, theories of "possession" by evil spirits or the devil again became popular. People who were simply "different" or who suffered from neurological disorders such as Tourette's syndrome or epilepsy were thought to be possessed or witches. *Exorcism,* a religious rite that involved prayer, starvation, beatings, and various forms of torture, was used to cast out evil spirits. The notion behind exorcism was to make the mentally disordered people so physically uncomfortable that no devil would want to stay in their bodies. If that didn't work, the only "cure" left was to get rid of the body altogether. Between the fourteenth and seventeenth centuries, 200,000 to 500,000 people thought to be witches were either hanged or burned at the stake.

During the Renaissance, *asylums* (*asylum* means "sanctuary") were built to house the mentally disordered. Mentally disordered people were placed in an asylum to protect them from the exploitation they experienced on the streets. But the asylums were not much better; the mentally disordered were often chained to walls, caged, or fed sparingly.

Fortunately, Philippe Pinel (1745–1826), the head physician at a large asylum in Paris, initiated a significant change in the treatment of the mentally disordered. Pinel described them as ordinary people who could not reason well because of their serious personal problems. He believed that treating the mentally disordered like animals was not only inhumane but also hindered their recovery. Pinel convinced the French government to unchain large numbers of patients, some of whom had not been outside of the asylum for 30 to 40 years (see figure 14.2). He replaced the dungeons with bright rooms and spent long hours talking with patients, listening to their problems and giving advice.

Although Pinel's efforts led to reform, it was slow. As late as the 19th century in the U.S., the mentally disordered were kept alongside criminals in prisons. Dorothea Dix, a nurse working at a prison in the middle of the 19th century, was instrumental in getting the mentally disordered separated from criminals. State governments began building large asylums because of Dix's efforts, although the conditions were often no better than in the prisons. The National Committee for Mental Hygiene was founded in the early 1900s, due to the efforts of Clifford Beers. In 1918, Clarence Hincks, a Canadian doctor influenced by Beers, founded what is currently known as the Canadian Mental Health Association.

Mental Hospitals and Deinstitutionalization

In the first half of the 20th century, severely mentally disordered individuals were usually institutionalized for life in large government mental hospitals (Lamb, 1998). Between 1955, when the numbers of people in state hospitals reached their peak, and the mid-1990s, the U.S. figures had dropped from 500,000 to 70,000 even though the U.S. population had gone up by 85 million. In Canada, 78 percent of the in-patient beds were closed, also despite a rapidly increasing population (Freeman, 1994).

Deinstitutionalization *is the movement to transfer the treatment of mental disorders from inpatient mental hospitals to community-based facilities that stress outpatient care.* Why was deinstitutionalization possible? New drugs for treating the severely mentally disordered, especially individuals with schizophrenia, meant that large numbers of people could be released from mental institutions and treated in community-based facilities. As indicated in Figure 14.3, controversy still characterizes the release of severely mentally disordered individuals from mental hospitals.

In 1963, The Canadian Mental Health Association published *More for the Mind,* the charter document for deinstitutionalization in Canada (Tyhurst, 1963). As envisaged there, community mental health centers were intended to meet two basic goals: (1) to provide community-based mental health services, and (2) to commit resources to help prevent, as well as treat, mental disorders. Outpatient care is an important community health center service. Individuals can attend therapy sessions at the center and still keep their jobs and live with their families. Community mental health centers have successfully helped large numbers of people with psychological problems (Seidman & French, 1998). They have been especially important in reaching low-income people who have mental health problems, many of whom otherwise would never have received psychological help.

*F*igure 14.2
Pinel Unchaining Mentally Disordered Individuals

In this painting, Philippe Pinel is shown unchaining the inmates at La Bicêtre Hospital. Pinel's efforts led to widespread reform and more humane treatment of mentally disordered individuals.

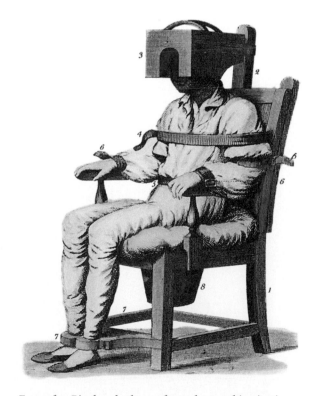

Even after Pinel and others reformed mental institutions, some rather strange techniques were invented to control the most difficult mentally disordered individuals. This tranquilizing chair was used to calm mentally disordered individuals at the beginning of the 19th century. Fortunately, its use was soon abandoned.

$\mathscr{F}$igure 14.3

Deinstitutionalization: Ongoing Controversy

The increased use of drug therapy in mental institutions facilitated the transfer of many mental patients back to the community. The architects of deinstitutionalization believed that these individuals could be given medication to keep them stabilized until they could find continuing care. However, many residents of mental health institutions have no families or homes to go to and community mental health facilities are not adequately equipped to deal with severe cases. Many who are discharged from provincial mental hospitals join the ranks of "the homeless." Of course, though, not all homeless people are former mental patients. Controversy continues about whether individuals should be discharged so readily from provincial mental institutions, which usually struggle with underfunding and staff shortages.

Recent Developments   The need to control rising health-care costs in Canada led governments to restructure the delivery of health care, including mental health care. In response, the Canadian Mental Health Association developed an influential framework for mental health policy (Trainor, Pomeroy & Pape, 1999). The framework is structured around the Community Resource Base, which assumes the perspective of the person living at the center—the person with a mental health problem. Surrounding that person are four key components:

- The traditional mental health services, which continue to have a role to play in psychosocial rehabilitation.
- Family and friends, which are the largest and most influential group of caregivers.
- Consumer groups and organizations, which constitute a new and growing body of stakeholders with the capacity to develop self-help services.
- Generic community services and groups, such as welfare and family services, as well as religious organizations and service clubs, which must be integrated into an overall support plan.

Managed Care
Mental Health Advocacy

In the United States, rising costs led to the development of private managed care. **Managed care** *consists of strategies for controlling health care costs, including mental health treatment, and demands for accountability of treatment success.* Emerging in the 1980s (Hoge, 1998), managed care providers attempt to offer services at lower costs by limiting traditional services, using stringent review procedures, and using lower-cost brief treatment options (Villani & Sharfstein, 1999). Criticisms of managed care include providing fewer therapy sessions per patient, eliminating longer-term therapy, and using less well-trained, less expensive therapists (Butcher, 1997; Giles & Marafiote, 1998; Lazarus, 1996; Roback & others, 1999).

Mental Health Professionals

In Canada, psychotherapy is practiced by a variety of mental health professionals, including clinical psychologists, psychiatrists, and counselors. You might recall from chapter 1 that psychiatrists have a medical degree. Clinical psychologists, by contrast, are trained in graduate programs in psychology. Figure 14.4 lists the main types of mental health professionals, their degrees, the years of education required, and the nature of their training.

Professional Type	Degree	Education Beyond Bachelor's Degree	Nature of Training
Clinical psychologist	Ph.D.	5–7 years	Includes both clinical and research training. Involves a 1-year internship in a psychiatric hospital or mental health facility. Some American universities offer Psy.D. programs which lead to a professional degree with a stronger emphasis on clinical work rather than research. Under some circumstances it is possible to complete a Psy.D. degree in the United States and go on into clinical practice in Canada.
Psychiatrist	M.D.	7–9 years	Four years of medical school, plus an internship and residency in psychiatry are required. A psychiatry residency involves supervision in therapies, including psychotherapy and biomedical therapy.
Counseling psychologist	M.A., Ph.D., or Ed.D.	3–7 years	Similar to clinical psychologist with emphasis on counseling and therapy. Some counseling psychologists specialize in vocational counseling. Some counselors complete master's degree training, others Ph.D. or Ed.D training, in graduate schools of psychology or education.
School psychologist	M.A., Ph.D., or Ed.D.	3–7 years	Training in graduate programs of education or psychology. Emphasis on psychological assessment and counseling practices involving students' school-related problems. Training is at the master's or doctoral level.
Social worker	M.S.W./D.S.W. or Ph.D.	2–5 years	Graduate work in a school of social work that includes specialized clinical training in mental health facilities.
Psychiatric nurse	R.N., M.A., or Ph.D.	0–5 years	Graduate work in a school of nursing with special emphasis on care of mentally disturbed individuals in hospital settings and mental health facilities.
Occupational therapist	B.S., M.A., or Ph.D.	0–5 years	Emphasis on occupational training with focus on physically or psychologically handicapped individuals. Stresses getting individuals back into the mainstream of work.
Pastoral counselor	None to Ph.D. or D.D. (Doctor of Divinity)	0–5 years	Requires ministerial background and training in psychology. An internship in a mental health facility as a chaplain is recommended.
Counselor	M.A. or M.Ed.	2 years	Graduate work in a department of psychology or department of education with specialized training in counseling techniques.

Figure 14.4
Main Types of Mental Health Professionals

Licensing and certification are two ways that society retains control over individuals who practice psychotherapy (Evans, 1997; Harmatz, 1997). Laws at the provincial level are used to license or certify such professionals. The requirements vary but generally they consist of advanced academic qualifications, supervised clinical experience, and some form of competency examination. Once psychologists become licensed to practice they must maintain high standards of competence as specified by the Canadian Psychological Association's Canadian Code of Ethics for Psychologists (Evans, 1997).

Licensing and certification also require mental health practitioners to engage in ethical practices. Laws typically address the importance of doing no harm to clients, protecting the privacy of clients, and avoiding inappropriate relationships with clients. Violations of ethical codes can result in a loss of the license to practice psychotherapy (Evans, 1997; Wierzbicki, 1999).

Connections with Personality Theories

Many of the theories of personality we discussed in chapter 12 are foundations for some important approaches to psychotherapy. The psychoanalytic theories of Freud and his dissenters and revisionists underlie the psychodynamic therapies ◀▥ P. 413. The humanistic theories of Rogers and Maslow provide an important foundation for the humanistic therapies ◀▥ P. 425. The term **insight therapy** *characterizes both psychodynamic and humanistic therapies because their goal is to encourage insight and self-awareness.*

The behavioral and social learning theories of Skinner and Bandura, as well as Pavlov's classical conditioning (Chapter 6, "Learning"), stimulated the development of the behavior therapies ◀▥ P. 186. We will discuss other important approaches to psychotherapy, including cognitive therapy and group therapy.

At this point we have discussed many ideas about the nature and history of psychotherapy. An overview of these ideas is presented in summary table 14.1. Next, we will begin our evaluation of psychotherapies with the insight therapies, first examining psychodynamic therapies, and then turning to humanistic therapies.

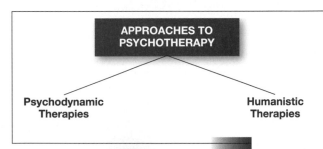

APPROACHES TO PSYCHOTHERAPY

Psychodynamic Therapies   **Humanistic Therapies**

Exploring Psychotherapies

Approaches to Psychotherapy

Our coverage of psychotherapies will focus on these main approaches: psychodynamic, humanistic, behavioral, cognitive, and group. Figure 14.5 provides an overview of these approaches. The cognitive map outlines the two main approaches that we will discuss before the next summary table. We begin our discussion of psychotherapies with the psychodynamic approaches because they are the oldest of the approaches.

Psychodynamic Therapies

Our study of psychodynamic therapies focuses on their basic nature, Freud's psychoanalysis, and contemporary psychodynamic therapies.

The **psychodynamic therapies** *stress the importance of the unconscious mind, extensive interpretation by the therapist, and the role of experiences in early childhood.* Many psychodynamic approaches have grown out of Freud's psychoanalytic theory of personality. Today some therapists with a psychodynamic perspective show allegiance to Freud, others do not (Watkins & Guarnaccia, 1999).

Freud's Psychoanalysis   Freud once said that if you give psychoanalysis your little finger, it will soon have your whole hand. As you read about the basic philosophy of psychoanalysis and its therapy techniques, you will see that Freud believed the therapist acts like a psychological detective, sometimes taking the smallest clue and using it as a springboard for understanding the individual's major problems. Let's see how one analyst approached an individual's problems.

SUMMARY TABLE 14.1
The Nature and History of Psychotherapy

Concept	Processes/Related Ideas	Characteristics/Description
What Is Psychotherapy?	Its Nature	Psychotherapy is the process used by mental health professionals to help individuals recognize, define, and overcome their psychological difficulties and improve their adjustment.
The History of Psychotherapy	Early History	Many early treatments of mental disorders were inhumane. Asylums were built during the Renaissance. Pinel's efforts led to extensive reform. Dix's efforts helped to separate mentally disordered individuals from prisoners.
	Mental Hospitals and Deinstitu-tionalization	In 1955, the mental hospital population in North America reached a peak. In the last half of the twentieth century this population dropped dramatically. Deinstitutionalization is the movement to transfer the treatment of mental disorders from inpatient mental hospitals to community-based facilities that stress outpatient care. Deinstitutionalization was possible because of advances made in drug therapy. Community mental health centers have successfully reached many people who otherwise might not have received help for their mental problems, especially individuals in low-income neighborhoods.
	Recent Developments	Rising costs have forced changes in mental health care delivery in recent years. In Canada, the Community Resource Base framework has received considerable attention. In the United States, managed care has evolved, consisting of strategies for controlling health care costs, including mental health treatment, and demands for accountability of treatment success. Numerous criticisms of managed care have been made.
Mental Health Professionals	Who Are They?	They include clinical and counseling psychologists, psychiatrists, school psychologists, social workers, psychiatric nurses, occupational therapists, pastoral counselors, and counselors. These mental health professionals have different degrees, education, and training. Licensing and certification are two ways society retains control over individuals who practice psychotherapy.
Connections with Personality Theories	Their Nature	Many of the theories of personality—psychoanalytic, humanistic, and behavioral—serve as foundations for main approaches to psychotherapy. The term *insight therapy* characterizes both psychodynamic and humanistic therapies because their goal is to encourage insight and self-awareness.

A 50-year-old business executive came to therapy because he felt depressed and anxious and these feelings wouldn't go away. Although he was perceived as being very successful by his family and business associates, he perceived himself to be weak and incompetent. Through many sessions, the psychoanalyst had begun to suspect that the man's feelings of failure stemmed from his childhood experiences with a punitive and critical father, who was even more successful than his son. The father never seemed to be satisfied with the son's efforts. Following is an exchange between the analyst and the businessman that occurred about one year into therapy (Davison & Neale, 1994, p. 533):

Client: "I don't really feel like talking today."
Analyst: Remains silent for several minutes, then says "Perhaps you would like to talk about why you don't feel like talking."
Client: "There you go again, making demands on me, insisting I do what I just don't feel up to doing. (Pause) Do I always have to talk here, when I don't feel like it? (Voice becomes angry and petulant) Can't you just get off my back? You don't really care how I feel."

Psychoanalysis

PSYCHODYNAMIC	HUMANISTIC	BEHAVIOR	COGNITIVE	GROUP
• Freud's psychoanalysis • Contemporary psychodynamic therapies	• Person-centered therapy • Gestalt therapy	• Classical conditioning • Operant conditioning	• Cognitive-behavior • Rational-emotive • Beck's cognitive	• Family/couple • Self-help
Emphasize the unconscious mind, extensive interpretation by the therapist, and early child experiences	Emphasize self-understanding, personal growth, conscious thoughts, the present rather than past, and fulfillment	Emphasize principles of learning to reduce or eliminate maladaptive behavior	Emphasize that the individual's cognition or thoughts are the main source of abnormal behavior and mood; attempt to change the person's feelings and behaviors by changing cognitions	Emphasize solving people's mental problems through experiences in a group rather than an individual therapy session; focus is on interpersonal relationships

ℱigure 14.5
Overview of Main Psychotherapy Approaches

We will be discussing these five main psychotherapy approaches. For each, this figure lists several representatives of the approach and gives a brief description of the approach.

Analyst: "I wonder why you feel I don't care?"
Client: "Because you're always pressuring me to do what I feel I can't do."

This exchange was interpreted by the analyst as an expression of resentment by the client of his *father's* pressures that were put on him and had little to do with the analyst himself. The transfer of the client's feelings from the father to the analyst was regarded as significant by the analyst and was used in subsequent sessions to help the client overcome his fear of expressing anger toward his father.

Psychoanalysis *is Freud's therapeutic technique for analyzing an individual's unconscious thoughts.* Freud believed that clients' current problems could be traced to childhood experiences, many of which involved conflicts about sexuality. He also recognized that the early experiences were not readily available to the individual's conscious mind. Only through extensive questioning, probing, and analyzing was Freud able to put the pieces of the person's personality together and help the individual become aware of how these early experiences were affecting present adult behavior.

To reach the shadowy world of the unconscious, psychoanalytic therapists often use the following therapeutic techniques: free association, catharsis, interpretation, dream analysis, analysis of transference, and analysis of resistance, each of which we discuss in turn.

One technique used by psychoanalysts is **free association,** *which consists of encouraging individuals to say aloud whatever comes to mind no matter how trivial or embarrassing.* When Freud detected a person resisting the spontaneous flow of thoughts, he probed further. He believed that the crux of the person's emotional problem probably lurked below this point of resistance. By encouraging people to talk freely, Freud thought, emotional feelings would emerge. **Catharsis** *is the psychoanalytic term for people's release of emotional tension when they relive an emotionally charged and conflicted experience.*

Interpretation plays an important role in psychoanalysis. As the therapist interprets free association and dreams, the person's statements and behavior are not taken at face value. To understand what is truly causing the person's conflicts, the therapist constantly

To encourage his patients to relax, Freud had them recline on the couch while he sat in the chair on the right, out of their view.

searches for symbolic, hidden meanings in what the individual says and does. From time to time the therapist suggests possible meanings of the person's statements and behavior. Explorations in Psychology provides an example of how a psychoanalyst used interpretation to improve a woman's understanding of her problems.

Dream analysis *is the psychotherapeutic technique used by psychoanalysts to interpret a person's dream.* Psychoanalysts believe dreams contain information about the individual's unconscious thoughts and conflicts ◀▥▥▥ P. 164. Freud distinguished between the dream's manifest and latent content. **Manifest content** *is the psychoanalytic term for the conscious, remembered aspects of a dream.* **Latent content** *is the psychoanalytic term for the unconscious, unremembered, symbolic aspects of a dream.* The psychoanalyst interprets the dream by analyzing the manifest content for disguised unconscious wishes and needs, especially those that are sexual and aggressive in nature. For some examples of the sexual symbols psychoanalysts use to interpret dreams, see figure 14.6. But even Freud cautioned against overinterpreting. As he once quipped, "Sometimes a cigar is just a cigar."

Freud believed transference was an inevitable and essential aspect of the analyst-patient relationship. **Transference** *is the psychoanalytic term for the person's relating to the analyst in ways that reproduce or relive important relationships in the individual's life.* A person might interact with an analyst as if the analyst were a parent or lover, for example. When transference dominates therapy, the person's comments may become directed toward the analyst's personal life. Transference is often difficult to overcome in psychotherapy. However, transference can be used therapeutically as a model of how individuals relate to important people in their lives (Boyer, 1999; Gelso & others, 1999).

Resistance *is the psychoanalytic term for the person's unconscious defense strategies that prevent the analyst from understanding the person's problems.* Resistance occurs because it is painful to bring conflicts into conscious awareness. By resisting therapy, individuals do not have to face their problems. Showing up late or missing sessions, arguing with the psychoanalyst, or faking free associations are examples of resistance. Some people go on endlessly about a trivial matter to avoid facing their conflicts. A major goal of the analyst is to break through this resistance (Strean, 1996).

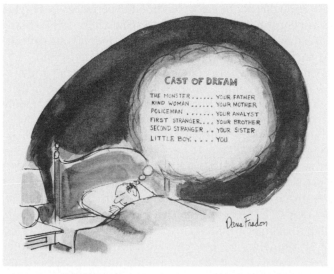

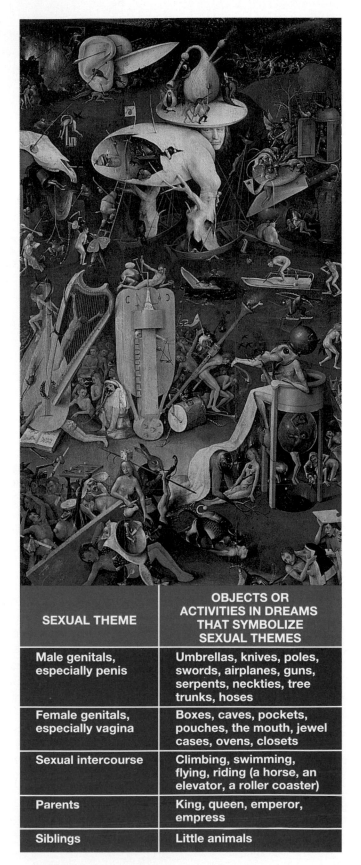

SEXUAL THEME	OBJECTS OR ACTIVITIES IN DREAMS THAT SYMBOLIZE SEXUAL THEMES
Male genitals, especially penis	Umbrellas, knives, poles, swords, airplanes, guns, serpents, neckties, tree trunks, hoses
Female genitals, especially vagina	Boxes, caves, pockets, pouches, the mouth, jewel cases, ovens, closets
Sexual intercourse	Climbing, swimming, flying, riding (a horse, an elevator, a roller coaster)
Parents	King, queen, emperor, empress
Siblings	Little animals

Figure 14.6
Freudian Interpretation of Sexual Symbolism in Dreams

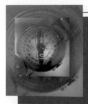

*E*XPLORATIONS IN *P*SYCHOLOGY
Penetrating Mrs. A. H.'s Thoughts

MRS. A. H. BEGAN her session with a psychoanalyst by describing how her husband, a businessman, had been caught in a financial squeeze and had anxiously gone to the bank to raise additional funds. She was in a state of panic, even though there was a good probability her husband would be able to obtain a loan from the bank. The previous night she had had diarrhea and had dreamed that her two sisters were discussing her mother, saying that she seldom did all that she had promised to others. Mrs. A. H. then commented that her mother had been wealthy and could have provided all the money her husband needed. Her father could have too, she said, but he was hard to deal with. She went on to recall her mother's involvement with another man and the illness her mother had had when Mrs. A. H. was an infant. Her sisters, who were considerably older, had taken care of their mother, but Mrs. A. H. wondered why they criticized their mother, who had been briefly hospitalized. They tended to blame poor health habits for her illness. Mrs. A. H. also reviewed her adolescent years, during which her mother denied the impact of her absence. She thought her mother's attitude was rather bizarre.

The psychoanalytic session seemed to be prompted by the husband's financial crisis and the repercussions it had for Mrs. A. H.'s longings for her mother, who would rescue her and her husband; her rage at her mother for her absence and possible unfaithfulness; and some im-

plied concerns regarding her husband's ability to handle the business situation. There was little in the session to suggest what unconscious thoughts were evoking the gastrointestinal symptoms.

However, this session is intriguing in the light of the next session that took place. In that session, Mrs. A. H. revealed she had inadvertently not mentioned an incident that had occurred prior to the previous session. One of her girlfriends had seen her husband having a drink with an attractive woman at a local restaurant. In this context, the psychoanalyst was able to gain more insight into what Mrs. A. H. had said in the previous session. In fact, she had used the past to conceal the present. She had used her mother as a screen to hide her most active and meaningful conflicts and unconscious fantasies about her husband. In the second session, her free associations related to fears of finding out that her husband was having an affair, to her dread of confronting him, and to her anxiety that others would be talking about his having an affair. The associations revealed her rage, her wishes to publicly humiliate him, and her death wishes toward him. The sister in the dream had also been suspected of having an affair. The bowel symptoms actually related to fantasies of defecating on and soiling her husband in an uncontrolled release of aggression, according to the analyst (Langs, 1978).

"Looking good!"

Contemporary Psychodynamic Therapies   Although the face of psychodynamic therapy has changed extensively since its inception almost a century ago, many contemporary psychodynamic therapists still probe a person's unconscious thoughts about early childhood experiences to provide clues to the person's current problems (Comarow & Chescheir, 1999). Many contemporary psychodynamic therapists also try to help individuals gain insight into their emotionally laden, repressed conflicts (Horowitz, 1998).

However, only a small percentage of contemporary psychodynamic therapists rigorously follow Freud's guidelines. Although many psychodynamic therapists still emphasize the importance of unconscious thought and early family experiences, they also accord more power to the conscious mind, current relationships, and emotions (Greenberg & Paivio, 1997) in understanding a person's problems. Therapy is often short-term, involving a few months rather than many years, even in dramatic cases (De Luca, Grayston & Romano, 1999).

Contemporary psychodynamic approaches emphasize the development of the self in social contexts (Erikson, 1968; Horowitz, 1998; Kohut, 1977; St. Clair, 1996; Summers, 1999). In Heinz Kohut's view, early relationships with attachment figures, such as one's parents, are critical. As we develop we do not relinquish these attachments; we continue to need them. Kohut's prescription for therapy involves getting the person to identify and seek out appropriate relationships with others. He also wants individuals to develop more realistic appraisals of relationships. Kohut believes therapists need to interact with individuals in ways that are empathic and understanding. As we will see next, empathy and understanding are absolute cornerstones for humanistic therapists as they encourage individuals to further their sense of self.

Humanistic Therapies

To understand the humanistic therapies we will describe their basic nature, then turn to two representatives of this approach: person-centered therapy and Gestalt therapy.

The underlying philosophy of humanistic therapies is captured by the metaphor of how an acorn, if provided with appropriate conditions, will grow in positive ways, pushing naturally toward its actualization as an oak (Corey, 1996). In the **humanistic therapies,** *people are encouraged to understand themselves and to grow personally.* In contrast to the psychoanalytic therapies, the humanistic therapies emphasize conscious rather than unconscious thoughts, the present rather than the past, and growth and self-fulfillment rather than illness ◀▥▥ P. 425.

Person-Centered Therapy

Person-Centered Therapy

Therapist: "Everything's lousy, huh? You feel lousy. (Silence of 39 seconds). Want to come in Friday at 12 at the usual time?"

Client: (Yawns and mutters something unintelligible). (Silence of 48 seconds).

Therapist: "Just kind of feel sunk way down deep in those lousy, lousy feelings, hm? Is that something like it?"

Client: "No."

Therapist: "No?" (Silence of 20 seconds).

Client: "No. I'm just no good to anybody, never was, and never will be."

Therapist: "Feeling that now, hm? That you're no good to yourself, no good to anybody. Just that you're completely worthless, huh? Those are really lousy feelings. Just feel that you're no good at all, hm?"

This is an excerpt from a therapy session conducted by a person-centered therapist with a young man who was depressed. The therapist was Carl Rogers (Meador & Rogers, 1979). Notice how Rogers unconditionally accepted the client's feelings. **Person-centered therapy** *is a form of humanistic therapy developed by Carl Rogers (1961, 1980) in which the therapist provides a warm, supportive atmosphere to improve the client's self-concept and encourage the client to gain insight about problems.* Rogers' therapy was initially called client-centered therapy, but he rechristened it person-centered therapy to underscore his deep belief that every person has the ability to grow. The relationship between the therapist and the person is an important aspect of Rogers' therapy. The therapist must enter into an intensely personal relationship with the client, not as a physician diagnosing a disease, but as one human being to another. Notice that Rogers referred to the "client" and then the "person" rather than the "patient."

You might recall from chapter 12, "Personality," that Rogers believed each of us grows up in a world filled with *conditions of worth,* the positive regard we received from others that has strings attached. We do not usually receive love and praise unless we conform to the standards and demands of others. This causes us to be unhappy and have low self-esteem. Rarely do we feel that we measure up to such standards or that we are as good as others expect us to be.

To free the person from worry about society's demands, the therapist engages in **unconditional positive regard** *in which the therapist creates a warm and caring environment, never disapproving of the client.* Rogers believed this unconditional positive regard improves the person's self-esteem. The therapist's role is "nondirective," that is, he or she does not lead the client to any particular revelation. The therapist is there to listen sympathetically to the client's

*T*hrough the Eyes of Psychologists

Carl Rogers *(1902–1987)*

"People who enter psychotherapy are often asking: How can I discover my real self? How can I become what I deeply wish to become?"

problems and to encourage positive self-regard, independent self-appraisal, and decision-making. Though person-centered therapists give approval of the person, they do not always approve of the person's behavior.

In addition to unconditional positive regard, Rogers also advocated the use of these techniques in person-centered therapy:

- *Genuineness,* which involves letting a client know the therapist's feelings and not hiding behind a facade.
- *Accurate empathy,* which focuses on the therapist's identification with the client. Rogers believed that therapists must sense what it is like to be the client at any moment in the client-therapist relationship.
- *Active listening,* which consists of giving total attention to what the person says and means. One way therapists improve active listening is to restate and support what the client has said and done.

Gestalt Therapy

Gestalt Therapy *Gestalt therapy is a humanistic therapy developed by Fritz Perls (1893–1970) in which the therapist questions and challenges clients to help clients become more aware of their feelings and face their problems.* Perls was trained in Europe as a Freudian psychoanalyst, but as his career developed, his ideas became different from Freud's. Perls (1969) agreed with Freud that psychological problems originate in unresolved past conflicts and that these conflicts need to be acknowl-

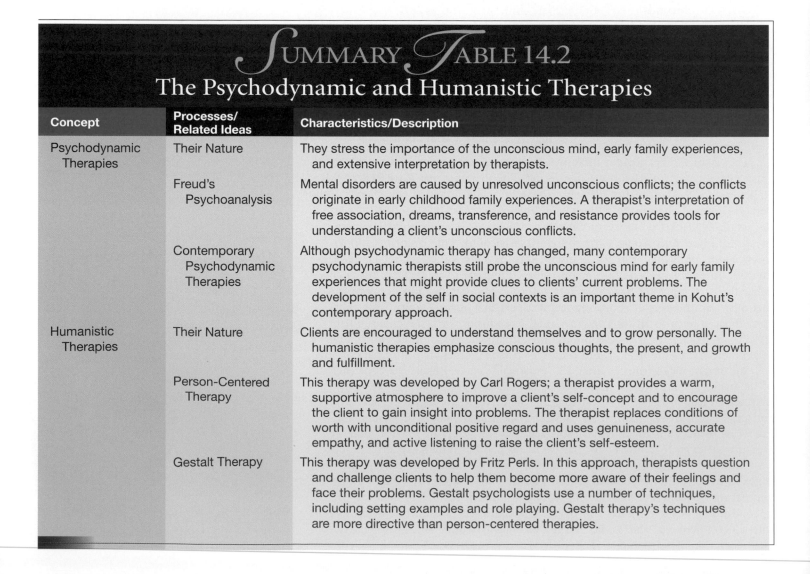

SUMMARY TABLE 14.2
The Psychodynamic and Humanistic Therapies

Concept	Processes/ Related Ideas	Characteristics/Description
Psychodynamic Therapies	Their Nature	They stress the importance of the unconscious mind, early family experiences, and extensive interpretation by therapists.
	Freud's Psychoanalysis	Mental disorders are caused by unresolved unconscious conflicts; the conflicts originate in early childhood family experiences. A therapist's interpretation of free association, dreams, transference, and resistance provides tools for understanding a client's unconscious conflicts.
	Contemporary Psychodynamic Therapies	Although psychodynamic therapy has changed, many contemporary psychodynamic therapists still probe the unconscious mind for early family experiences that might provide clues to clients' current problems. The development of the self in social contexts is an important theme in Kohut's contemporary approach.
Humanistic Therapies	Their Nature	Clients are encouraged to understand themselves and to grow personally. The humanistic therapies emphasize conscious thoughts, the present, and growth and fulfillment.
	Person-Centered Therapy	This therapy was developed by Carl Rogers; a therapist provides a warm, supportive atmosphere to improve a client's self-concept and to encourage the client to gain insight into problems. The therapist replaces conditions of worth with unconditional positive regard and uses genuineness, accurate empathy, and active listening to raise the client's self-esteem.
	Gestalt Therapy	This therapy was developed by Fritz Perls. In this approach, therapists question and challenge clients to help them become more aware of their feelings and face their problems. Gestalt psychologists use a number of techniques, including setting examples and role playing. Gestalt therapy's techniques are more directive than person-centered therapies.

edged and worked through. Also like Freud, Perls stressed that interpretation of dreams is an important aspect of therapy.

But in other ways, Perls and Freud were miles apart. Perls believed that unresolved conflicts should be brought to bear on the here and now of the individual's life. The therapist *pushes* clients into deciding whether they will continue to allow the past to control their future or whether they will choose *right now* what they want to be in the future. To this end, Perls *confronted* individuals and encouraged them to actively control their lives and be open about their feelings.

Gestalt therapists use a number of techniques to encourage individuals to be open about their feelings, to develop self-awareness, and to actively control their lives. The therapist sets examples, encourages congruence between verbal and nonverbal behavior, and uses role playing. To demonstrate an important point to a client, the Gestalt therapist might exaggerate a client's characteristic. To stimulate change, the therapist will often openly confront the client.

Another technique used in Gestalt therapy is role playing, either by the client, the therapist, or both. For example, if an individual is bothered by conflict with her mother, the therapist might play the role of the mother and reopen the quarrel. The therapist might encourage the individual to act out her hostile feelings toward her mother by yelling, swearing, or kicking the couch, for example. In this way, Gestalt therapists hope to help individuals better manage their feelings instead of letting their feelings control them.

As you probably noticed, the Gestalt therapist is much more directive than the nondirective, person-centered therapist. By being more directive, the Gestalt therapist provides more interpretation and feedback. Nonetheless, both of these humanistic therapies encourage individuals to take responsibility for their feelings and actions, to truly be themselves, to understand themselves, to develop a sense of freedom, and to look at what they are doing with their lives.

At this point we have studied a number of ideas about the insight therapies—psychodynamic and humanistic. An overview of these ideas is presented in summary table 14.2. Now that we have explored the insight therapies, we turn our attention to therapies that take a very different approach to working with individuals to reduce their problems and improve their adjustment—the behavior therapies.

Frederick (Fritz) Perls was the founder of Gestalt therapy.

Behavior Therapies

Behavior therapies offer action-oriented strategies to help people change what they are doing. We will describe their basic nature, then turn to two main approaches: classical conditioning and operant conditioning.

Behavior therapies *use principles of learning to reduce or eliminate maladaptive behavior.* Behavior therapies are based on the behavioral and social cognitive theories of learning and personality ◀▥ P. 433. Behavior therapists do not search for unconscious conflicts like psychodynamic therapists or encourage individuals to develop accurate perceptions of their feelings and self like humanistic therapists. Insight and self-awareness are not the keys to helping individuals develop more adaptive behavior patterns, say the behavior therapists.

Behavior therapists assume that the overt maladaptive symptoms are the problem (Sloan & Mizes, 1999). Individuals can become aware of why they are depressed and still be depressed, say the behavior therapists. The behavior therapist tries to eliminate the depressed symptoms or behaviors themselves rather than trying to get individuals to gain insight or awareness of why they are depressed (Lazarus, 1996).

The behavior therapies were initially based almost exclusively on the learning principles of classical and operant conditioning. As social cognitive theory grew in popularity, however, behavior therapists increasingly included observational learning, cognitive factors, and self-instruction in their efforts to help people with their problems (Meichenbaum, 1977, 1991; Maultsby & Wirga, 1998; Tracy, Sherry, & Albright, 1999). In self-instruction, therapists try to get people to change what they say to

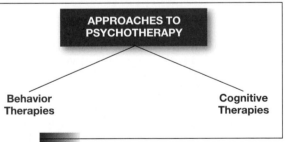

APPROACHES TO PSYCHOTHERAPY

Behavior Therapies

Cognitive Therapies

1. On the way to the university on the day of an examination
2. In the process of answering an examination paper
3. Before the unopened doors of the examination room
4. Awaiting the distribution of examination papers
5. The examination paper lies face down before her
6. The night before an examination
7. One day before an examination
8. Two days before an examination
9. Three days before an examination
10. Four days before an examination
11. Five days before an examination
12. A week before an examination
13. Two weeks before an examination
14. A month before an examination

ℱigure 14.7
A Desensitization Hierarchy Involving Test Anxiety

In the above hierarchy, the individual begins with the least feared circumstance (a month before the exam) and moves through each of the circumstances until reaching the most feared circumstance (being on the way to the university the day of the examination). At each step of the way, the person replaces fear with deep relaxation and successful visualizations.

themselves. We will have more to say about these self-instructional strategies later in this section and in the next chapter when we discuss coping with stress. For now, though, let's focus on classical conditioning and operant conditioning.

Classical Conditioning Approaches   Some behaviors, especially fears, can be acquired or learned through classical conditioning ◀▥ P. 192. If such fears can be learned, possibly they can be unlearned as well. If an individual has learned to fear snakes or heights through classical conditioning, perhaps the individual can unlearn the fear.

The two main therapy techniques based on classical conditioning are systematic desensitization and aversive conditioning. **Systematic desensitization** is a *method of behavior therapy based on classical conditioning that treats anxiety by getting the person to associate deep relaxation with increasingly intense anxiety-producing situations* (Wolpe, 1963). Consider the common fear of giving a speech. Using systematic desensitization, the behavior therapist first asks the person which aspects of the feared situation—in this case, giving a speech—are the most and least frightening. Then, the behavior therapist arranges these circumstances in order from most to least frightening. An example of this type of desensitization hierarchy is shown in figure 14.7.

The next step is to teach individuals to relax. Clients are taught to recognize the presence of muscular contractions or tensions in various parts of their bodies and then how to contract and relax different muscles. Once individuals are relaxed, the therapist asks them to imagine the least fearful stimulus in the hierarchy. Subsequently, the therapist moves up the list of items from least to most fearful while clients remain relaxed. Eventually, individuals are able to imagine the most fearsome circumstance without being afraid—in our example, on the way to the university the day of the oral exam. In this manner, individuals learn to relax while thinking about the speech instead of feeling anxious.

Researchers have found that systematic desensitization is often an effective treatment for a number of phobias, such as fear of giving a speech, fear of heights, fear of flying, fear of dogs, and fear of snakes. If you were afraid of snakes, for instance, the therapist might initially have you watch someone handle a snake. Then the therapist would ask you to engage in increasingly more feared behaviors—you might first just go into the same room with the snake, next you would approach the snake, subsequently you'd touch the snake, and eventually you would play with the snake (Bandura, Blanchard, & Ritter, 1969). Figure 14.8 shows a desensitization treatment with individuals who were afraid of snakes.

The second main therapy technique that involves classical conditioning is **aversive conditioning**, *which consists of repeated pairings of the undesirable behavior with aversive stimuli to decrease the behavior's rewards.* Aversive conditioning is used to teach people to avoid such behaviors as smoking, eating, and drinking. Electric shocks, nausea-inducing substances, and verbal insults are some of the noxious stimuli used in aversive conditioning.

How could aversive conditioning be used to reduce a person's alcohol consumption? Every time a person drank an alcoholic beverage, he or she would also consume a mixture that induced nausea. In classical conditioning terminology, the alcoholic beverage is the conditioned stimulus and the nausea-inducing agent is the unconditioned stimulus. By repeatedly pairing alcohol with the nausea-inducing agent, alcohol becomes the conditioned stimulus that elicits nausea, the conditioned response. As a consequence, alcohol is no longer associated with something pleasant, but rather something highly unpleasant. Figure 14.9 illustrates how classical conditioning is the backbone of aversive conditioning.

Operant Conditioning Approaches   The basic philosophy of using operant conditioning as a therapy approach is that because maladaptive behavior patterns are learned, they can be unlearned. Therapy involves conducting a careful analysis of the person's environment to determine what factors need to be modified. Especially important is changing the consequences of the person's behavior to ensure that behavioral responses are followed by positive reinforcement.

Operant therapy's techniques focus on **behavior modification,** *the application of operant conditioning principles to change human behavior; its main goal is to replace unacceptable, maladaptive responses with acceptable, adaptive ones* ◀||||| P. 203. Consequences for behavior are established to ensure that acceptable actions are reinforced and unacceptable ones are not. Advocates of behavior modification believe that many emotional and behavioral problems are caused by inadequate (or inappropriate) response consequences (Stanley & Turner, 1995). Consider the serious crisis between Barbara and her parents that brings them all to see a clinical psychologist. The psychologist, who has a behavioral orientation, talks with each family member, trying to get them to pinpoint the problem. The psychologist gets the family to sign a behavioral contract that spells out what everyone needs to do to reduce the conflict. Barbara agrees to (1) be home before 11 P.M. weeknights; (2) look for a part-time job so she can pay for some of her activities; and (3) refrain from calling her parents insulting names. Her parents agree to (1) talk to Barbara in a low tone rather than yell if they are angry; (2) refrain from criticizing Barbara's friends; and (3) give Barbara a weekly allowance until she has found a job.

A **token economy** *is a behavior modification system in which behaviors are reinforced with tokens (such as poker chips) that later can be exchanged for desired rewards (such as candy, money, or going to a movie).* Token economies have been established in a number of classrooms, institutions for the mentally retarded, homes for delinquents, and mental hospitals with schizophrenics.

Donald Meichenbaum, of the University of Waterloo, is one of the founders of cognitive behavior modification, an approach which integrates the behavior therapy techniques you just read about with the cognitive therapy techniques you will be reading about in the next section (Meichenbaum, 1977, 1991). While Meichenbaum stresses behavior modification techniques, he also uses self-instruction, asking people to change what they say to themselves. The key idea is that if people reorganize their verbal statements about themselves and the surrounding world, the result can be a corresponding reorganization of their behavior. In other words, Meichenbaum holds that how individuals control their minds shapes their behavior (Meichenbaum, & Fong, 1993).

ℱigure 14.8
Systematic Desensitization

Systematic desensitization is often used to help eliminate phobias. In this systematic desensitization treatment, individuals have progressed from handling rubber snakes *(top),* to peering at snakes in an aquarium *(second from top),* to handling snakes with rubber gloves *(second from bottom),* to handling live but harmless snakes *(bottom).*

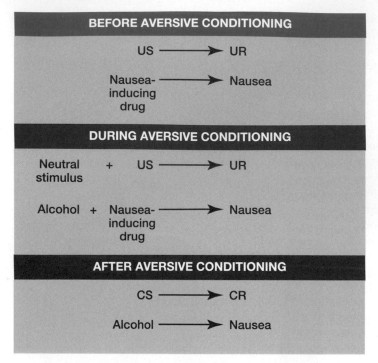

Figure 14.9
Classical Conditioning: The Backbone of Aversive Conditioning

The above illustrations reveal how classical conditioning can provide a conditional aversion to alcohol. After the association of the drug with alcohol, the alcohol becomes a conditioned stimulus for nausea. Remember these abbreviations from chapter 6, "Learning": US (unconditioned stimulus), UR (unconditioned response), CS (conditioned stimulus), and CR (conditioned response).

Rational-Emotive Behavior Therapy
Beck's Cognitive Therapy

The behavior therapies have been used to treat a wide variety of problems. To read about the use of this approach in treating depression, see Explorations in Psychology.

Cognitive Therapies

To understand the cognitive therapies, we will discuss their basic nature and then turn to two main cognitive therapy approaches: (1) rational-emotive behavior therapy and (2) Beck's cognitive therapy.

Rahul, an undergraduate, thinks he is a failure in school and to his parents. He is preoccupied with negative thoughts, dwells on his problems, and exaggerates his faults. The cognitive therapies stress that such individual cognitions are the main source of abnormal behavior. They attempt to change the individual's feelings and behaviors by changing cognitions. Cognitive therapies differ from psychoanalytic therapies by focusing on overt symptoms instead of unconscious thoughts, by structuring the individual's thoughts, and by being less concerned about the origin of the problem (Dobson, Backs-Dermott, & Dozois, in press). Cognitive therapies have been applied to depression (Hurst & Genest, 1995), panic disorder (Néron, Lacroix & Chaput, 1995), pathological gambling (Ladouceur & others, 1998) and obsessive-compulsive disorder (Ladouceur, Freeston & Gagnon, 1996).

Rational-Emotive Behavior Therapy   *Rational-emotive behavior therapy is based on Albert Ellis' assertion that individuals become psychologically disordered because of their beliefs, especially those that are irrational and self-defeating.* Ellis (1962, 1996) says that we usually talk to ourselves when we experience stress; too often the statements are irrational, making them more harmful than helpful.

Ellis abbreviated the therapy process into the letters *A, B, C, D, E* (see fig. 14.10). Therapy usually starts at C, the individual's upsetting emotional *C*onsequence; this might involve depression, anxiety, or a feeling of worthlessness. The individual often says that C was caused by A, the *A*ctivating Experience, such as a blowup in marital relations, loss of job, or failure in school. The therapist works with the individual to show that an intervening factor, B, the individual's *B*elief System, is actually responsible for why he moved from A to C. Then the therapist goes on to D, which stands for *D*isputation; at this point, the individual's irrational beliefs are disputed or contested by the therapist. Finally, E is reached, which stands for *E*ffects or outcomes of the rational-emotive behavior therapy, as when individuals put their changed beliefs to work. To learn more about Ellis' rational-emotive behavior therapy, read Explorations in Psychology.

Beck's Cognitive Therapy   Aaron Beck (1976, 1993) developed a form of cognitive therapy to treat psychological problems, especially depression. A basic assumption in Beck's therapy is that psychological problems like depression result when people think illogically about themselves, the world they live in, and the future. Beck's approach shares with Ellis' approach the idea that the goal of therapy should be to help people recognize and discard self-defeating cognitions.

In the initial phases of therapy, individuals are taught to make connections between their patterns of thinking and their emotional responses. The therapist helps them to identify their own automatic thoughts and to keep records of their thought content and emotional reactions. With the therapist's assistance, they learn about logical errors in their thinking and to challenge the accuracy of these automatic

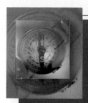

EXPLORATIONS IN PSYCHOLOGY
Contemporary Behavior Therapy and the Treatment of Depression—the Lewinsohn Approach

HENRY GREENE IS a 36-year-old lawyer who wrestled with depression for months before finally seeking psychotherapy. His initial complaints were physical—fitful sleep, often ending at 3 A.M., lack of appetite, weight loss of 15 pounds, and a lack of interest in sex. Henry began to move more slowly and his voice became monotonous. He reached the point where he could barely cope with life. Henry finally let his guard down and confessed that, although he looked successful on the outside, he felt like a failure on the inside. He said he was actually a third-rate lawyer, husband, lover, and father—he felt he was bound to remain that way. Henry perceived life as a treadmill of duty and guilt; he felt exhausted and saw no reason to continue (Rosenfeld, 1985).

How would a contemporary behaviorist treat someone like Henry Greene? Peter Lewinsohn and his colleagues developed the "Coping with Depression Course" (Lewinsohn & others, 1984). A basic principle of the program is that feelings are caused by behavior. Therapists encourage people to increase the ratio of positive life events to negative life events to improve mood. To accomplish the desired ratio, most individuals require a variety of skill training exercises.

Someone like Henry Greene would first be asked to monitor his moods. This would force him to pay attention to his daily mood changes. This information is used to determine which events are associated with which moods. Relaxation training would follow, because relaxation skills improve an individual's sense of well-being. Along with direct benefits of relaxation, clients experience an en-

hanced sense of self-efficacy by mastering a new skill.

The next step for Henry Greene would be to determine how his moods are associated with pleasant and unpleasant events in his life. Henry would be asked to fill out a "Pleasant Events Schedule" and an "Unpleasant Events Schedule." Each week, Henry would complete a graph showing the number of pleasant and unpleasant events, as well as his mood, for each day. Henry would probably see a close relation between unpleasant events and negative moods, and between pleasant events and positive moods. The therapist would encourage Henry to increase the time he spends in pleasant activities with the hope that more positive moods will follow. The outcome should be that Henry gains control over his moods.

Some people require individually tailored approaches. For example, some people need training in social skills to improve their social relationships. Others need more work in changing their thoughts. In Lewinsohn's approach, for example, thoughts are treated as behaviors to be modified, positive thoughts are reinforced or a specified period is set aside for "worry time."

The final stage in this approach is maintenance planning. Henry would be asked to identify the components of the behavioral therapy that were the most successful in changing his maladaptive behavior, once they have been identified, Henry would be encouraged to continue their use. He would also be required to develop emergency plans for those times when stress overwhelms him. Henry would continue to go to follow-up sessions for six months after his treatment.

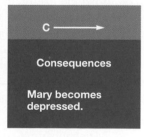
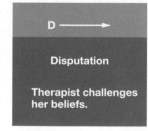
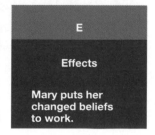

A → **Activating experience** — Mary loses her job.

B → **Belief system** — "I'm a failure!"

C → **Consequences** — Mary becomes depressed.

D → **Disputation** — Therapist challenges her beliefs.

E — **Effects** — Mary puts her changed beliefs to work.

Figure 14.10
A–E Steps in Ellis' Rational-Emotive Behavior Therapy

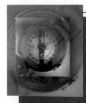

EXPLORATIONS IN PSYCHOLOGY
"My Work Is Boring and I Resent It"

THE FOLLOWING CASE illustrates the nature of rational emotive behavior therapy. You will notice that this type of therapy is a forceful type of therapeutic persuasion.

Client: I know that I should do the inventory before it piles up to enormous proportions, but I just keep putting it off. To be honest, I guess it's because I resent it so much.

Therapist: But why do you resent it so much?

Client: It's boring; I just don't like it.

Therapist: So it's boring. That's a good reason for disliking this work, but is it an equally good reason for resenting it?

Client: Aren't the two the same thing?

Therapist: By no means. Dislike equals the sentence, "I don't enjoy this thing; therefore, I don't want to do it." That's a perfectly sane sentence in most instances, but resentment is the sentence, "*Because* I dislike doing this thing, I shouldn't *have* to do it," and that's invariably a very crazy sentence.

Client: Why is it so crazy to resent something that you don't like to do?

Therapist: There are several reasons. First of all, from a purely logical standpoint, it just makes no sense at all to say to yourself, "Because I dislike doing this thing, I shouldn't *have* to do it." The second part of this sentence just doesn't follow in any way from the first part. Your reasoning goes something like this: "Because I dislike doing this thing, *other people* and the *universe* should be so considerate of me that they should never make me do what I dislike," but, of course, this doesn't make any sense. Why *should* other people and the universe be that considerate of you? It might be nice if they were, but why the devil *should* they be? In order for your reasoning to be true, the entire universe, and all the people in it, would really have to revolve around and be uniquely considerate of you. (Ellis, 1962)

The therapist has directly attacked the client's belief and forcefully told him that his thoughts are irrational. This represents an important distinction between cognitive therapists, such as Ellis, and behavioral or psychodynamic therapists. Behavioral and psychodynamic therapists might describe this client's behavior and attitudes as maladaptive and self-defeating, but Ellis points out that they are irrational and illogical as well.

---

thoughts. Their logical errors in thinking lead them to do the following (Carson, Butcher, & Mineka, 1996):

- Perceive the world as harmful while ignoring evidence to the contrary, such as still feeling worthless even though a friend has just told them how much other people like them
- Overgeneralize on the basis of limited examples, such as seeing themselves as worthless because one individual stopped dating them
- Magnify the importance of undesirable events, such as seeing the loss of a dating partner as the end of the world
- Engage in absolutistic thinking, such as exaggerating the importance of someone's mildly critical comment and perceiving it as proof of their inadequacy

Meichenbaum's cognitive behavioral therapy and Beck's and Ellis' cognitive therapies are similar since they all stress that cognition mediates behavior. However, there are also some differences between them. Cognitive behavioral therapy relies on behavior modification techniques more than do the two cognitive therapies. Rational-emotive behavior therapy is very directive, persuasive, and confrontational. It also focuses on the therapist's teaching role. In contrast, Beck's cognitive therapy involves more of an open-ended dialogue between the therapist and the individual. The aim of this dialogue in Beck's approach is to get individuals to reflect on personal issues and discover their own misconceptions.

Through the Eyes of Psychologists

Donald Meichenbaum,
University of Waterloo

"*What a person says to himself, that is, how he evaluates and interprets events, is explicitly modifiable by many of the behavior therapy techniques that have been used to modify maladaptive overt behaviors.*"

SUMMARY TABLE 14.3
The Behavior and Cognitive Therapies

Concept	Processes/Related Ideas	Characteristics/Description
Behavior Therapies	Their Nature	They use principles of learning to reduce or eliminate maladaptive behavior. They are based on the behavioral and social cognitive theories of personality. Behavior therapies try to eliminate the symptoms of behaviors rather than getting individuals to gain insight into their problems. Behavior therapists have increasingly used observational learning, cognitive factors, and self-instruction in their efforts to help people with their problems.
	Classical Conditioning Approaches	The two main therapy techniques are systematic desensitization and aversive conditioning. In systematic desensitization, anxiety is treated by getting the person to associate deep relaxation with increasingly intense anxiety-producing situations. In aversive conditioning, repeated pairings of the undesirable behavior with aversive stimuli decrease the behavior's rewards.
	Operant Conditioning Approaches	In operant conditioning approaches to therapy, a careful analysis of the person's environment is conducted to determine which factors need to be modified. Behavior modification is the application of operant conditioning to change human behavior; its main goal is to replace unacceptable, maladaptive responses with acceptable, adaptive ones. A token economy is a behavior modification system in which behaviors are reinforced with tokens that later can be exchanged for desired rewards.
	Cognitive Behavior Modification	Meichenbaum's approach is based on self-instruction, using behavior modification techniques to help people change what they say to themselves in order to change their behavior.
Cognitive Therapies	Their Nature	They emphasize that the individual's cognitions or thoughts are the main source of abnormal behavior. Cognitive therapies attempt to change the person's feelings and behaviors by changing cognitions.
	Rational-Emotive Behavior Therapy	Ellis' approach is based on the assertion that individuals become psychologically disordered because of their beliefs, especially those that are irrational and self-defeating.
	Beck's Cognitive Therapy	Especially used for depression, this involves initially getting people to make connections between their patterns of behavior and emotional responses. With the therapist's assistance, they learn about logical errors in their thinking, then how to challenge these mistakes in thinking.

At this point we have discussed a number of ideas about the behavior therapies and the cognitive therapies. An overview of these ideas is presented in summary table 14.3. Next, we will consider yet another set of therapies—the group therapies.

Group Therapies

A major issue in therapy is how it can be structured to reach more people and at less cost. One way to address this problem is for the therapist to see clients in a group.

Nine people make their way into a room, each looking tentatively at the others. Although each person has met the therapist during a diagnostic

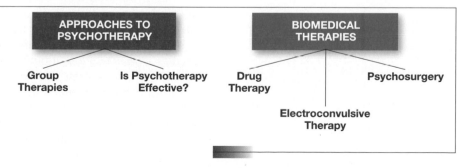

Because many psychological problems develop in the context of interpersonal relationships and group experiences—within one's family, marriage, or peer group—group therapy can be an important context for learning how to cope more effectively with these problems.

Group Therapies
Exploring Group Psychotherapy

interview, no one knows any of the other clients. Some of the people seem reluctant, others enthusiastic. All are willing to follow the therapist's recommendation that group therapy might help each of them learn to cope better with their problems. As they sit down and wait for the session to begin, one thinks, "Will they really understand me?" Another thinks, "Do the others have problems like mine?" Yet another thinks, "How can I stick my neck out with these people?"

Individual therapy is often expensive and time consuming. Freud believed that therapy is a long process and saw clients as often as three to five times a week for a number of years. Advocates of group therapy stress that individual therapy is limited because the client is seen outside the normal context of relationships, relationships that may hold the key to successful therapy (Gladding, 1995, 1999). Many psychological problems develop in the context of interpersonal relationships—within one's family, marriage, or peer group, for example. By seeing individuals in the context of these important groups, therapy may be more successful (Fuhriman & Burlingame, 1995; Morgan & Cummings, 1999).

Group therapy is diversified. Psychodynamic, humanistic, behavior, or cognitive therapy is practiced by some therapists. Others use group approaches that are not based on the major psychotherapeutic perspectives. Six features make group therapy an attractive format (Yalom, 1975, 1995):

1. *Information.* The individual receives information about his problem from either the group leader or other group members.
2. *Universality.* Many individuals develop the sense that they are the only person who has such frightening and unacceptable impulses. In the group, individuals observe that others feel anguish and suffering as well.
3. *Altruism.* Group members support one another with advice and sympathy and learn that they have something to offer others.
4. *Corrective recapitulation of the family group.* A therapy group often resembles a family (and in family therapy the group *is* a family), with the leaders representing parents and the other members siblings. In this "new" family, old wounds may be healed and new, more positive "family" ties made.
5. *Development of social skills.* Corrective feedback from peers may correct flaws in the individual's interpersonal skills. A self-centered individual may see that he is self-centered if five other group members inform him about his self-centeredness; in individual therapy he may not believe the therapist.
6. *Interpersonal learning.* The group can serve as a training ground for practicing new behaviors and relationships. A hostile woman may learn that she can get along better with others by not behaving so aggressively, for example.

Family/Couple Therapy   "A friend loves you for your intelligence, a mistress for your charm, but your family's love is unreasoning; you were born into it and are of its flesh and blood. Nevertheless, it can irritate you more than any group of people in the world," commented the French biographer André Maurois. His statement suggests that the family may be the source of the individual's problems.

Family therapy *is group therapy with family members.* **Couple therapy** *is group therapy with married or unmarried couples whose major problem is their relationship.* These approaches stress that while one person may have some abnormal symptoms, the symptoms are a function of family or couple relationships (Capuzzi & Gross, 1999; Christensen & Heavy, 1999; Davis, 1996). Psychodynamic, humanistic, or behavior therapies may be used in family or couple therapy, but the main form of family therapy is family systems therapy.

Four of the most widely used family therapy techniques
are these:

1. *Validation.* The therapist expresses an understanding and
   acceptance of each family member's feelings and beliefs,
   and thus validates the person. When the therapist talks
   with each family member, she finds something positive
   to say.
2. *Reframing.* The therapist teaches families to reframe
   problems; problems are cast as a family problem, not an
   individual's problem. A delinquent adolescent boy's
   problems are reframed in terms of how each family
   member contributed to the situation. The father's lack of
   attention to his son and marital conflict may be involved,
   for example.
3. *Structural change.* The family systems therapist tries to
   restructure the coalitions in a family. In a mother-son
   coalition, the therapist might suggest that the father take a
   stronger disciplinarian role to relieve some of the burden
   from the mother. Restructuring might be as simple as
   suggesting that parents explore satisfying ways to be
   together; the therapist may recommend that once a week
   the parents go out for a quiet dinner together, for example.
4. *Detriangulation.* In some families, one member is the scapegoat for two other
   members who are in conflict but pretend not to be. For example, in the triangle
   of two parents and one child, the parents may insist that their marriage is fine
   but find themselves in subtle conflict over how to handle the child. The therapist
   tries to disentangle, or *detriangulate,* this situation by shifting attention away
   from the child to the conflict between the parents.

*Family therapy has become increasingly popular in recent years. In family
therapy, the assumption is that psychological adjustment is related to
patterns of interaction within the family unit.*

Family Therapy and Culture

Couples therapy proceeds in much the same way as family therapy. Conflict in marriages and in relationships between unmarried individuals frequently involves poor
communication. In some instances, communication has broken down entirely. The
therapist tries to improve the communication between the partners. In some cases, she
will focus on the roles partners play: one may be "strong," the other "weak"; one may
be "responsible," the other "spoiled," for example. Couples therapy addresses diverse
problems such as jealousy, sexual messages, delayed childbearing, infidelity, gender
roles, two-career families, divorce, and remarriage (Sullivan & Christensen, 1998).

Self-Help Support Groups

Self-help support groups *are voluntary or-
ganizations of individuals who get together on a regular basis to discuss topics of common interest.* The groups are not conducted by a professional therapist but rather by
a paraprofessional or a member of the common interest group. A paraprofessional is
someone who is taught by a professional to provide some mental health services, but
who does not have formal mental health training. The group leader and members
provide support to help individuals with their problems. Self-help support groups
play an important role in Canada's mental health, with millions of people participating in such groups each year.

In addition to reaching so many people in need of help, these groups are important because they use community resources and are relatively inexpensive. They
also serve people who are less likely to receive help otherwise, such as less-educated
adults, individuals living in low-income circumstances, and homemakers.

Founded in 1930 by a reformed alcoholic, Alcoholics Anonymous (AA) is one of
the best-known self-help groups. Mental health professionals often recommend AA
for their alcoholic clients. Weight Watchers and TOPS (Take Off Pounds Sensibly) are
also self-help groups. There are myriad self-help groups such as Parents Without Partners, lesbian and gay support groups, cocaine-abuse support groups, and child-abuse

Social Concerns

Gamblers Anonymous
Hope for Youth Foundation
Kids Help Phone
Victim Services
St. John's Rape Crisis and Information
  Centre

Canadian Association of Retired
  Persons (North East Avalon Chapter)
St. John's Native Friendship Centre
  Association
CHANNAL—Adult Survivors of Child
  Sexual Abuse (C.A.S.C.S.A.)

Bereavement

Adolescent Grief Group
Bereavement Group

Janeway Bereaved Parents Support
  Group
Survivors of Suicide Group (S.O.S.)

Alcohol/Substance Abuse

Addictions Services
Alcoholics Anonymous (A.A.)

Coping Without Smoking (C.W.S.)
Narcotics Anonymous

Parenting

St. John's Parents Rights Group
  Newfoundland and Labrador
Association for Gifted Children
Single Parent Association of
  Newfoundland (S.P.A.N.)
Breastfeeding Support Group
  Program (BFSGP)

Autism Society—Parent Support Group
Parents of Children With a Disability
Newfoundland and Labrador Association
  for Spina Bifida and Hydrocephalus
Support for Parents of Adolescents (SPA)
Foster Families Association—
  Newfoundland and Labrador

Health

Lupus Society of Newfoundland
Epilepsy Newfoundland and Labrador
Chronic Pain Support Group
Thyroid Foundation of Canada

St. John's Stroke Survivors Support Group
Schizophrenia Society of Newfoundland
  and Labrador Support Group
Canadian Hard of Hearing Association

$\mathcal{F}$igure 14.11
Examples of Self-Help Groups

A partial listing of self-help groups in Newfoundland and Labrador from the website of the Canadian Mental Health Association, Newfoundland and Labrador Division.

support groups. Figure 14.11 lists a sampling of the variety of self-help groups available in one province.

Self-help support groups also provide members with a sympathetic audience for confession, sharing, and emotional release. The social support, role modeling, and sharing of concrete strategies for solving problems that unfolds in self-help groups adds to their effectiveness. A woman who has been raped might not believe a male therapist who tells her that, with time, she will be able to put back together the pieces of her shattered life and work through much of the psychological pain. But the same message from another rape survivor—someone who has had to work through the same feelings of rage, fear, and violation—might be more believable.

Self-help support groups have broad, though not universal, appeal (Gottlieb, 1998). For people who tend to cope by seeking information and affiliation with similar peers, such groups can reduce stress and promote adjustment. However, as with any group therapy, there is the possibility that negative emotions will spread through the group, especially if the members face circumstances that deteriorate over time, such as terminal cancer patients. Group leaders who are sensitive to the spread of negative emotions can minimize such effects.

Is Psychotherapy Effective?

Do individuals who go through therapy get better? Are some approaches more effective than others? Or is the situation similar to that of the Dodo in *Alice's Adventures in Wonderland*? The Dodo was asked to judge the winner of a race; he decided, "Everybody has won and all must have prizes." And how would we evaluate the effectiveness of psychotherapy? Would we take the client's word? The therapist's word? What would be our criteria for effectiveness? Would it be "feeling good," "adaptive behavior," "improved interpersonal relationships," "autonomous decision making," or "more positive self-concept," for example? During the last several decades an extensive amount of thought and research has addressed these questions.

**Society of Clinical Psychology
The Effectiveness of Psychotherapy**

Research on the Effectiveness of Psychotherapy Four decades ago, Hans Eysenck (1952) came to the shocking conclusion that psychotherapy is ineffective. Eysenck analyzed 24 studies of psychotherapy and found that approximately two-thirds of the individuals with neurotic symptoms improved. Sounds impressive so far. But Eysenck also found that a similar percentage of neurotic individuals on waiting lists to see a psychotherapist also showed marked improvement even though they were not given any psychotherapy at all.

Eysenck's pronouncement prompted a flurry of research on psychotherapy's effectiveness (Kopta & others, 1999; Pilkonis, 1999; Pilkonis & Krause, 1999). Hundreds of studies on the outcome of psychotherapy have now been conducted (Dawes, 1998; Wampold & others, 1997). One strategy for analyzing these diverse studies is called **meta-analysis,** *in which the researcher statistically combines the results of many different studies.* In one meta-analysis of psychotherapy research, 475 studies were statistically combined (Smith, Glass, & Miller, 1980). Only those studies in which a therapy group had been compared with an untreated control group were compared. The results showed greater psychotherapy effectiveness than Eysenck's earlier results: On 88 percent of the measures, individuals who received therapy improved more than those who did not. This meta-analysis and others (Lipsey & Wilson, 1993) document that psychotherapy is effective in general, but they do not inform us about the specific ways in which different therapies might be effective.

People who are thinking about seeing a psychotherapist not only want to know whether psychotherapy in general is effective, but they also especially want to know which form of psychotherapy is most effective for their particular problem. Mary Lee Smith and her colleagues (Smith, Glass, & Miller, 1980) conducted a meta-analysis to compare types of psychotherapy. For example, behavior therapies were compared with insight therapies (psychodynamic, humanistic). Behavior and insight therapies were found to be superior to no treatment at all, but they did not differ from each other in effectiveness.

Research that evaluates the effectiveness of a psychotherapy usually includes a comparison group—either a control group of individuals who do not experience the therapy or a group that receives a different type of psychotherapy (Alloy, Jacobson, & Acocella, 1999) P. 46. When a control group is included, it often consists of individuals waiting to see a psychotherapist but who as yet have not been given therapy (this is called a *wait-list control group*). Why is it so important for psychotherapy research to include a control or comparison group? Because it gives us some idea of how many people in the study who experienced the targeted psychotherapy (such as cognitive therapy for depression) would have gotten better without the psychotherapy.

Let's examine one study that illustrates how control and comparison groups are used in psychotherapy research. The National Institute of Mental Health conducted an evaluation

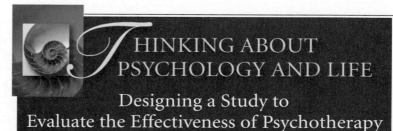

THINKING ABOUT PSYCHOLOGY AND LIFE

Designing a Study to Evaluate the Effectiveness of Psychotherapy

THERE IS A GREAT deal of interest among therapists in finding out the effectiveness of various psychotherapies. Based on what you have read about psychotherapy and psychotherapy research in this chapter, and what you learned in chapter 2, "Psychology's Scientific Methods," design a study to measure the effectiveness of psychotherapy. Describe which approach(es) of psychotherapy you will be evaluating, what you might use as a control group(s), how you would measure successful treatment, and how long the study would last (including follow-up data collection) (Zakrajsek, 1999).

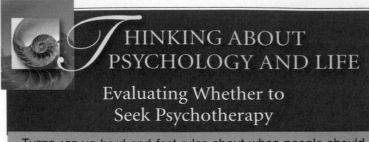

THINKING ABOUT PSYCHOLOGY AND LIFE

Evaluating Whether to Seek Psychotherapy

THERE ARE NO hard-and-fast rules about when people should go to a psychotherapist for help with their personal problems. However, to get a sense of whether you should see a psychotherapist evaluate whether you have recently experienced the following:

• I feel sad or blue a lot.
• My self-esteem is really low.
• I feel like other people are always out to get me.
• I feel so anxious that it is hard for me to function.
• I have trouble concentrating on my academic work.
• I don't do anything social and spend much of my spare time alone.
• I have a tendency to alienate people when I don't really want to.
• I'm frightened by things that I know should not be fear-provoking.
• I hear voices that tell me what I should do.
• I know I have problems, but I just don't feel I can talk with anyone about them.

If any of the above statements describe your life, consider talking over your concerns with a qualified therapist. Most universities have counseling or mental health services that are covered by your student fees. This is a good place to start in seeking mental health consultation.

of three types of treatment for depression (cognitive therapy; interpersonal therapy, which emphasized improving the individual's social relationships; and drug therapy) (Mervis, 1986). Two hundred and forty individuals who were depressed were randomly assigned to the three psychotherapy conditions or a control group (who received a placebo medication along with supportive advice). A placebo is a medically inactive substance that mimics the appearance of the active drug. After 16 weeks in treatment, just over 50 percent of the individuals in each of the three psychotherapy groups were not depressed anymore. How did the people in the control group fare? Twenty-nine percent of them were no longer depressed after 16 weeks, a significantly lower percentage than in the psychotherapy groups.

Although no particular therapy was found to be best in this study, some therapies have been found to be more effective than others in treating some disorders (DeRubeis & Crits-Christoph, 1998). Behavior therapies have been most successful in treating specific behavioral problems, such as phobias and sexual dysfunctions (Bowers & Clum, 1988; Sanderson, 1995). Cognitive therapies have been most successful in treating depression and anxiety (Butler & others, 1991; Clark & others, 1994). Relaxation therapy, which we will discuss in the next chapter, has also been successful in treating anxiety disorders (Arnitz & van den Hout, 1996).

Common Themes in Psychotherapy

After carefully studying the nature of psychotherapy for more than 25 years, Jerome Frank (1982) concluded that effective psychotherapies have the common elements of expectations, mastery, and emotional arousal. By inspiring an expectation of help, the therapist motivates the client to continue coming to therapy (Jennings & Skovholt, 1999). These expectations are powerful morale builders and symptom relievers in themselves. The therapist also increases the client's sense of mastery and competence (Brammer & MacDonald, 1999; Hill & O'Brien, 1999). For example, clients begin to feel that they can cope effectively with their world. Therapy also arouses the individual's emotions, essential to motivating behavioral change, according to Frank.

The therapeutic relationship is another important ingredient in successful psychotherapy (Strupp, 1989, 1995). Confidence and trust in the therapist is essential to effective psychotherapy. In one study, the most common ingredient in the success of different psychotherapies was the therapist's supportiveness (Wallerstein, 1989). The client and therapist engage in a "healing ritual," which requires the active participation of both the client and the therapist. In a supportive therapeutic relationship, the client can constructively retell his or her life narrative (Angus & Hardtke, 1994). To read about guidelines for seeking professional help, turn to Explorations in Psychology.

Gender and Ethnicity

In the last several decades, psychologists have become sensitive to the concerns of gender and ethnicity in psychotherapy (Helms & Cook, 1999; Wisch & Mahalik, 1999). Let's explore the roles of gender and ethnicity in psychotherapy.

Gender One of the by-products of changing gender roles for women and men is evaluation of the goals of psychotherapy 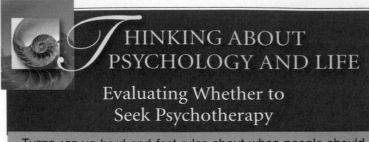 P. 13. Women have argued that the traditional goal of psychotherapy, autonomy, is often more central in the lives of men than women, for whom relatedness and connection with others may be more central (Worrell &

MARCIA FELT ANXIOUS most of the time. But what caused her the greatest difficulty was that she became so anxious during exams in her classes that she would nearly freeze. Her mind would go blank and she would begin to sweat and shake all over. It was such a problem that she was failing her classes. She told one of her professors that this was the problem with her grades. He told her that it sounded like she had a serious case of test anxiety, and that she should get some help. Marcia decided that she had better take his advice and wanted to find a psychotherapist. How would she go about finding a therapist? Are certain professionals more qualified than others? How could she know that she was going to see someone who could help her, as opposed to a professional who would not be helpful, or perhaps even make things worse? These are only a few of the questions people commonly have when they seek to find a therapist.

When trying to find a therapist, Marcia could consider a psychologist, psychiatrist, social worker, counselor, or any number of other helping professionals. Each of these mental health professionals is qualified to provide psychotherapeutic services. They all practice from any one or combination of the therapeutic orientations discussed in this chapter. They may also see people on an individual, one to one basis, or in small groups, as in group therapy. The critical question is, of course, how does someone go about selecting a therapist to help them? This is not as easy a question as it may appear at first glance. We may face many of the same problems when we try to find a "good" medical doctor, accountant, or dentist; however, the way that most people go about finding these other professional services may not be the best way of selecting a therapist. Asking a friend for a good therapist ignores the fact that some approaches to therapy work better with some problems than others. Also, every therapeutic relationship is different, so one person's experience in therapy is not translatable to another person's. Below, we offer some general suggestions when looking for a therapist.

Identify the Professional's Credentials

Although all different types of mental health professionals may be competent, psychologists, psychiatrists, and social workers all differ in their approach to therapy based on differences in training: psychologists tend to be focused on the person's emotions and behaviors; psychiatrists are trained as medical doctors so their perspective is likely to involve physical aspects of psychological problems; and social workers will be inclined to take a person's entire family and social situation into account. Regardless of the exact profession, some minimal credentials should be considered important. All provinces have licensing regulations for professionals who provide public services. Thus, a therapist should be licensed or certified by a province in order to practice (Evans, 1997). In addition, in some cases it may be important for a professional to have some advanced, specialized training in a certain area. For example, if a person is seeking help with a specific problem, like drug abuse, alcohol abuse, or a sexual problem, the therapist should have some training in that area. You should ask about the professional's credentials either before or during a first visit.

When Starting Therapy, Give It Some Time Before Judging Its Usefulness

Making changes is very difficult. Expecting too much too soon can result in premature dissatisfaction and disappointment. Because a large part of therapy involves the development of a relationship with the therapist, it may take several meetings to really know if things are going well. One suggestion is to give it between four and six weekly meetings. If it does not seem like things are going the way you would like, it is a good idea to discuss your progress with the therapist and ask what you should expect with regard to making progress. Setting specific goals with specific time expectations can be helpful. If your goals are not being met, you should consider a new therapist.

Be a Thoughtful and Careful Consumer of Mental Health Services

Just as when you seek any services, the more informed you are about the services provided, the better decision you can make about whether or not they are the right services for you. Calling around and asking specific questions about approaches and specializations is one way to become informed about the services offered by therapists. Consider how important it may be that the therapist is of your same or opposite sex, whether it is important that they have experience with your specific difficulty, as well as other specific characteristics. You may also want to learn more about their theoretical orientation to therapy as described in this chapter. Another way to find out more about the therapist is to ask these kinds of questions during your first visit. Most professionals are quite comfortable talking about their background and training. Your confidence and trust in the professional is an important part of how well therapy will work for you.

These general guidelines should be used when first looking for a therapist. Remember that people should continually evaluate their own progress throughout therapy and when they feel dissatisfied with how it is going, they should discuss this with their therapist. Remember that therapy is like other services: When dissatisfied, you can always look for another therapist. Don't think that just because one therapist has not been helpful none will be. All therapists and therapeutic relationships are different. Finding the right therapist is one of the most important factors in therapy success.

Greater attention has been paid to the roles of gender and ethnicity in psychotherapy in recent decades. Among the issues raised by this increased attention are these: (1) What should the appropriate goals of psychotherapy be? (2) Does psychotherapy work best when there is an ethnic match between the therapist and the client?

**Psychotherapeutic Drugs
Drug Therapy**

Robinson, 1993). For example, Janet Stoppard of the University of New Brunswick Fredericton questions viewing depression as an individual pathology (Stoppard, 1999) to be treated medically (Gammell & Stoppard, 1999) in favor of a sociocultural view. Similarly, Hurst & Genest (1995) argued in favor of cognitive-behavior therapy approaches more sensitive to women's perspectives.

Ethnicity   Many ethnic minority individuals prefer discussing problems with parents, friends, and relatives rather than with mental health professionals (Atkinson, Morten, & Sue, 1998; Gibson & Mitchell, 1999). Might therapy progress best when the therapist and the client are from the same ethnic background? Researchers have found that when there is an ethnic match between the therapist and client and when ethnic-specific services are provided, clients are less likely to drop out of therapy early and in many cases have better treatment outcomes (Orlinksy, Grawe, & Parks, 1994; Sue, 1977). Ethnic-specific services include culturally appropriate greetings and arrangements (for example, serving tea rather than coffee to Chinese-Canadian clients), providing flexible hours for treatment, and employing a bicultural/bilingual staff (Nystul, 1999).

Nonetheless, therapy can be effective when the therapist and client are from different ethnic backgrounds if the therapist has excellent clinical skills and is culturally sensitive (Atkinson, Morten, & Sue, 1998; Fischer, Jome, & Atkinson, 1998). Culturally skilled psychotherapists have good knowledge of the cultural groups they work with, understand sociopolitical influences, and have skills in working with culturally diverse groups (Toukmanian & Brouwers, 1998).

So far we have discussed a variety of psychotherapies that can help individuals cope more effectively with stress and develop more adaptive behavior. In recent years considerable progress has also been made in biomedical therapies, which we now discuss.

Biomedical Therapies

Biomedical therapies *are treatments to reduce or eliminate the symptoms of psychological disorders by altering the way an individual's body functions.* Drug therapy is the most common form of biomedical therapy. Much less widely used biomedical therapies are electroconvulsive therapy and psychosurgery. Psychologists and other mental health professionals may provide psychotherapy in conjunction with the biomedical therapy administered by psychiatrists and medical doctors. Indeed, in many instances a combination of psychotherapy and medication is a desirable course of treatment.

Drug Therapy

Although medicine and herbs have long been used to alleviate symptoms of emotional distress, it was not until the twentieth century that drug treatments began to revolutionize mental health care. Psychotherapeutic drugs are used mainly in three diagnostic categories: anxiety, mood, and schizophrenia. Let's explore the effectiveness of drugs in these areas, beginning with drugs to treat anxiety.

Antianxiety Drugs   **Antianxiety drugs** *are commonly known as tranquilizers* ◀‖‖ P. 173. These drugs reduce anxiety by making individuals less excitable and more calm ◀‖‖ P. 455. Benzodiazepines are the antianxiety drugs that offer the greatest relief for anxiety symptoms. They work by binding to the receptor sites of neurotransmitters that become overactive during anxiety. The most frequently prescribed benzodiazepines include Xanax, Valium, and Librium.

While antianxiety drugs may bring relief from high levels of anxiety and stress, they may not always be helpful. Cox & others (1992) found that antianxiety drugs may be helpful for panic and anxiety but not for phobia, which is better dealt with via systematic desensitization. In general, the anxiety disorders may be better dealt with by combining biological and psychological interventions (Gauthier, 1999).

Antianxiety medications are controlled drugs that should be used only temporarily for symptomatic relief. They can be overused and become addictive.

Antidepressant Drugs

Antidepressant drugs *regulate mood* ◀|||| P. 463. The three main classes of antidepressant drugs are tricyclics, such as Elavil; MAO inhibitors, such as Nardil; and SSRI drugs, such as Prozac (Gorman & Kent, 1999). The *tricyclics,* so called because of their three-ringed molecular structure, are believed to work by increasing the level of certain neurotransmitters, especially norepinephrine and serotonin (Evans, 1999; Feighner, 1999). The tricyclics reduce the symptoms of depression in approximately 60 to 70 percent of cases. The tricyclics usually take two to four weeks to improve mood. They sometimes have adverse side effects, such as restlessness, faintness, and trembling.

The MAO (monamine oxidase) inhibitors are not as widely used as the tricyclics because they are more toxic. However, some individuals who do not respond to the tricyclics do respond to the MAO inhibitors.

The most prominent of the SSRI (selective serotonin reuptake inhibiting) antidepressant drugs is Prozac. SSRI drugs work mainly by interfering with the reabsorption of serotonin in the brain. Prozac is most frequently prescribed for dysthymic disorder. Zoloft and Paxil are other drugs in the SSRI category. The SSRI drugs are not only being used to treat mood disorders but they are also often effective for individuals with obsessive-compulsive disorder.

Lithium *is a drug that is widely used to treat bipolar disorder* (recall that this disorder involves wide mood swings of depression and mania). The amount of lithium that circulates in the bloodstream needs to be carefully monitored because its effective dosage is precariously close to toxic levels.

Antipsychotic Drugs

Antipsychotic drugs *are powerful drugs that diminish agitated behavior, reduce tension, decrease hallucinations and delusions, improve social behavior, and produce better sleep patterns in individuals who have a severe mental disorder, especially schizophrenia* ◀|||| P. 467. Before antipsychotic drugs were developed in the 1950s, few, if any, interventions brought relief from the torment of psychotic symptoms. Once the effectiveness of these medications was apparent, the medical community significantly reduced more intrusive interventions, such as brain surgery and electroconvulsive shock for schizophrenia (Grunberg, Klein, & Brown, 1998).

The *neuroleptics* are the most widely used class of antipsychotic drugs. The most widely accepted explanation for the effectiveness of the neuroleptics is their ability to block the dopamine system's action in the brain (Rebec, 1996). Schizophrenics have too much of the neurochemical messenger dopamine. Numerous well-controlled investigations reveal that when used in sufficient doses, the neuroleptics reduce a variety of schizophrenic symptoms, at least in the short term (Friedman, Temporini, & Davis, 1999; Holcomb & others, 1996).

The neuroleptics do not cure schizophrenia, and they can have severe side effects. The neuroleptics treat the symptoms of schizophrenia, not its causes. If an individual with schizophrenia stops taking the drug, the symptoms return. Neuroleptic drugs have substantially reduced the length of hospital stays for individuals with schizophrenia. However, although these individuals are able to return to the community because drug therapy keeps their symptoms from reappearing, most have difficulty coping with the demands of society and most are chronically unemployed.

Tardive dyskinesia *is a major side effect of the neuroleptic drugs; it is a neurological disorder characterized by grotesque, involuntary movements of the facial muscles and*

Drug Treatment of Schizophrenia

mouth as well as extensive twitching of the neck, arms, and legs. As many as 20 percent of individuals with schizophrenia taking neuroleptics develop this disorder. Elderly women are especially vulnerable. Long-term neuroleptic therapy is also associated with increased depression and anxiety. Nonetheless, for the majority of schizophrenics, the benefits of neuroleptic treatment outweigh its risk and discomforts.

A new group of medications called "atypical antipsychotic medications" was introduced in the 1990s. The most widely used drug in this group is Clozaril, which shows promise for reducing schizophrenia's symptoms without the side effects of neuroleptics (Rosenheck & others, 1999). Clozaril produces its effects by blocking the reuptake of the neurotransmitter serotonin. However, for a small portion of individuals with schizophrenia, Clozaril has a toxic effect on white blood cells, which requires regular blood testing.

Strategies to increase the effectiveness of the antipsychotic drugs involve administering lower dosages over time, rather than a large initial dose, and combining drug therapy with psychotherapy. The small percentage of schizophrenics who are able to hold jobs suggests that drugs alone will not make them contributing members of society. They also need training in vocational, family, and social skills.

We have discussed a number of drugs that can be used for various mental disorders. A summary of these drugs, the disorders for which they are used, their effectiveness, and side effects is shown in figure 14.12. Notice that for some types of anxiety disorders, such as agoraphobia, MAO inhibitors (which are antidepressant drugs) might be used rather than antianxiety drugs.

At this point we have discussed not only drug therapy but a number of psychotherapy approaches to help people with mental disorders. This is a good time to reflect on all of these different therapies and compare their strategies. To help you do this, see figure 14.13.

The use of psychotherapeutic drugs is the most widely practiced biomedical therapy. However, as we see next, in extreme circumstances, electroconvulsive therapy and even psychosurgery might be used.

Electroconvulsive Therapy

Electroconvulsive Therapy

Electroconvulsive therapy (ECT), *commonly called "shock treatment," is used mainly to treat severely depressed individuals. The goal of ECT is to cause a seizure in the brain much like what happens spontaneously in some forms of epilepsy.* A small electric current lasting for one second or less passes through two electrodes placed on the individual's head. The current excites neural tissue, stimulating a seizure that lasts for approximately one minute.

ECT has been used for more than 40 years. In earlier years it was often used indiscriminately, sometimes even as a punishment for patients. ECT is still used with as many as 60,000 individuals a year, mainly to treat major depressive disorder. Adverse side effects can include memory loss and other cognitive impairment. Today ECT is given mainly to individuals who have not responded to drug therapy or psychotherapy. ECT sounds as if it would entail intolerable pain, but the manner in which it is administered today involves little discomfort. The patient is given anesthesia and muscle relaxants before the current is applied; this allows the individual to sleep through the procedure, minimizes convulsions, and reduces the risk of physical injury. The individual awakens shortly afterward with no conscious memory of the treatment.

How effective is electroconvulsive therapy? In one analysis of studies, its effectiveness in treating depression was compared with cognitive therapy and antidepressant drugs (Seligman, 1994). ECT was as effective as cognitive therapy or drug therapy, with about four of five individuals showing marked improvement in all three therapies. However, as with the other therapies, the relapse rate for ECT is moderate to high. The side effects for ECT are more severe than for drugs. Cognitive therapy shows no side effects. A positive aspect of ECT is that its effects appear in a matter of days, whereas the effects of antidepressant drugs can take weeks, and those for cognitive therapy months, to appear.

Mental Disorder	Drug	Effectiveness	Side Effects
EVERYDAY ANXIETY AND ANXIETY DISORDERS			
Everyday anxiety	Anti-anxiety drugs (tranquilizers); most frequently prescribed are the benzodiazepines (Xanax, Valium, and Lithium)	Substantial improvement short-term	Less powerful the longer people take them; may be addictive
Generalized anxiety disorder	Anti-anxiety drugs	Not very effective	Less powerful the longer people take them; may be addictive
Panic disorder	Anti-anxiety drugs	About half show improvement	Less powerful the longer people take them; may be addictive
Agoraphobia	Tricyclic drugs and MAO inhibitors	Majority show improvement	For tricyclics, restlessness, fainting, and trembling; for MAO inhibitors, toxicity
Specific phobias	Anti-anxiety drugs	Not very effective	Less powerful the longer people take them; can be addictive
MOOD DISORDERS			
Depressive disorders	Tricyclic drugs, MAO inhibitors, and SSRI drugs (Prozac)	Majority show moderate improvement	For tricylics, cardiac problems, mania, confusion, memory loss, fatigue; for MAO inhibitors, toxicity; for SSRI drugs, nausea, nervousness, insomnia, and in a few cases possible suicidal thoughts
Bipolar disorder	Lithium	Large majority show substantial improvement	Toxicity
SCHIZOPHRENIC DISORDERS			
Schizophrenia	Neuroleptics; atypical antipsychotic medications (Clozaril)	Majority show partial improvement	For neuroleptics, irregular heartbeat, low blood pressure, uncontrolled fidgeting, tardive dyskinesia, and immobility of face in neuroleptics. These side effects are less extensive with Clozaril but Clozaril can have a toxic effect on white blood cells.

𝓕igure 14.12
Drug Therapy for Mental Disorders

Psychosurgery

Psychosurgery *is a biomedical therapy that involves removal or destruction of brain tissue to improve the individual's psychological adjustment.* The effects of psychosurgery are irreversible. In the 1930s, Portuguese physician Egas Moniz developed a procedure known as a *prefrontal lobotomy.* In this procedure, a surgical instrument is inserted into the brain and rotated, severing fibers that connect the frontal lobe, important in higher thought processes, and the thalamus, important in emotion.

Psychosurgery

Topic	Psychodynamic Therapies	Humanistic Therapies	Behavior Therapies	Cognitive Therapies	Group Therapies	Drug Therapies
Cause of problem	Client's problems are symptoms of deep-seated, unresolved unconscious conflicts.	Client is not functioning at an optimal level of development.	Client has learned maladaptive behavior patterns.	Client has developed inappropriate thoughts.	Diverse causes depending on type of group therapy.	Problems have a biological origin.
Therapy emphasis	Discover underlying unconscious conflicts and work with client to develop insight.	Develop awareness of inherent potential for growth.	Learn adaptive behavior patterns through changes in the environment or cognitive processes.	Change feelings and behaviors by changing cognitions.	Diverse depending on type of therapy but emphasis on group's role in changing person's behavior.	Change behaviors, thoughts, and feelings by administering psychotherapeutic drugs.
Nature of therapy and techniques	Psychoanalysis, including free association, dream analysis, resistance, and transference: therapist interprets heavily.	Person-centered therapy, including unconditional positive regard, genuineness, accurate empathy, and active listening; Gestalt therapy including confrontation to encourage honest expression of feelings; self-appreciation emphasized.	Observation of behavior and its controlling conditions; specific advice given about what should be done; therapies based on classical conditioning, operant conditioning.	Conversation with client designed to get him or her to change irrational and self-deflating beliefs.	Interaction with other people who have psychological problems. In family therapy, emphasis on changing patterns of interaction among family members.	Often used in conjunction with psychotherapy but emphasis is on the drug's ability to improve the person's symptoms.

Figure 14.13
Therapy Comparisons

Moniz theorized that by severing the connections between these brain structures the symptoms of severe mental disorders could be alleviated. Prefrontal lobotomies were conducted on thousands of patients from the 1930s through the 1950s. Moniz was even awarded the Nobel Prize for his work. However, while some patients may have benefited from the lobotomies, many were left in vegetable-like states because of the massive assaults on their brains.

These crude lobotomies are no longer performed. Since the 1960s, psychosurgery has become more precise. When psychosurgery is now performed, a small lesion is made in the amygdala or another part of the limbic system. Today, in North America, only several hundred patients, who have severely debilitating conditions, undergo psychosurgery per year. It is used only as a last resort and with extreme caution.

Therapy Integrations

Approximately 30 to 50 percent of practicing therapists do not identify themselves as adhering to one particular approach, but rather refer to themselves as "integrative" or "eclectic" (Garfield & Kurtz, 1976; Norcross & Prochaska, 1983, 1988).

Just what is meant by "integrative therapy"? In the single-therapy approach, the therapist believes that one particular kind of therapy works best. Integrative therapy looks beyond a single-therapy approach to see what can be learned from other therapies. It is characterized by an openness to various ways of integrating diverse therapies. For example, a therapist might use a behavior approach to treat an individual with panic disorder and a cognitive therapy approach to treat an individual with major depressive disorder. There is no single well-defined integrative therapy that ties all of the therapy approaches together. For that reason, the term *therapy integrations* probably best captures what is taking place in this field (Arkowitz, 1997).

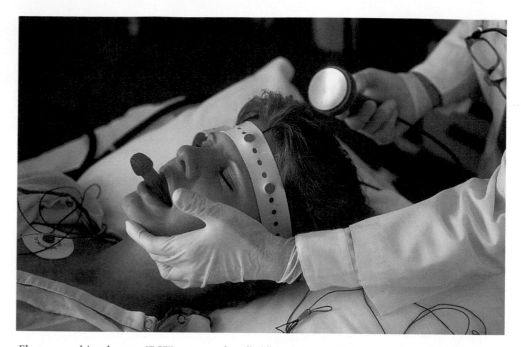

Electroconvulsive therapy (ECT), commonly called "shock therapy," causes a seizure in the brain. ECT is still given to as many as 60,000 people a year, mainly to treat major depression disorder.

In the last two decades, therapy integration has grown dramatically (Arkowitz, 1997). What has fostered the movement toward integrative therapy? The motivating factors include the proliferation of therapies, the inadequacy of a single therapy to be relevant to all clients and all problems, a lack of evidence that one therapy is better than others, and recognition that therapy commonalities play an important role in therapy outcomes (Norcross & Newman, 1992).

One worry about therapy integrations is that their increased use will result in an unsystematic, haphazard eclecticism, which some therapists say would be no better than a narrow, dogmatic approach to therapy (Lazarus, Beutler, & Norcross, 1992). At their best, therapy integrations are effective, systematic uses of a variety of therapy approaches (Corey, 1996).

With the increased diversity of client problems and populations, future therapy integration is likely to include more attention to ethnic and cultural factors in treating clients (Sue, Ivey, & Pedersen, 1996). This increased ethnic and cultural diversity also will require therapists to integrate spiritual concerns into their therapy approach (Pate & Bondi, 1992).

Therapy integration is also at work when individuals are treated with both psychotherapy and drug therapy. For example, cognitive therapy and drug therapy might be combined to treat an individual with major depressive disorder. This integrative approach might be conducted by a mental health team that included a psychiatrist and a clinical psychologist.

Therapy integrations are conceptually compatible with the biopsychosocial model of abnormal behavior we described in chapter 13. That is, many therapists believe that abnormal behavior can involve biological, psychological, and social factors. Many single-therapy approaches focus on one aspect of the person more than others; for instance, drug therapies focus on biological factors, and cognitive therapies focus on psychological factors. Therapy integrations often take a broader look at individuals' problems.

At this point we have discussed many ideas about group therapies, the effectiveness of psychotherapy, biomedical therapies, and integrative therapies. An overview of these ideas is presented in summary table 14.4. In the next chapter, we will continue our exploration of how people can live more mentally healthy lives.

SUMMARY TABLE 14.4

Group Therapies; Effectiveness of Psychotherapies; and Biomedical Therapies

Concept	Processes/ Related Ideas	Characteristics/Description
Group Therapies	Their Nature	Group therapies emphasize that relationships can hold the key to successful therapy. Group therapy is diversified.
	Family/Couple Therapy	Family therapy is group therapy with family members. Couple therapy is group therapy with married or unmarried couples whose major problem is their relationship. Four widely used family therapy techniques are validation, reframing, structural change, and detriangulation.
	Self-Help Support Groups	These are voluntary organizations of individuals who get together on a regular basis to discuss topics of common interest. They are conducted without a professional therapist.
Is Psychotherapy Effective?	Research on Psychotherapy Effectiveness	Psychotherapy in general is effective. Behavior therapies are often most successful in treating specific behavior problems, such as phobias. Cognitive therapy is often effective in treating depression and anxiety.
	Common Themes	Common themes in successful therapies include positive expectations of help, increasing the client's sense of mastery, arousing the person's emotions, and developing confidence and trust in the therapist.
	Gender and Ethnicity	In recent years, psychologists have become more sensitive to gender and ethnicity issues in therapy. The issues raised include these: (1) What should be the appropriate goals of therapy (e.g., autonomy or relatedness, or both)? and (2) Does psychotherapy work best when there is a gender and/or ethnic match between the therapist and the client? In conducting therapy with people of a different ethnicity or gender, it is important to be a culturally sensitive therapist.
Biomedical Therapies	Their Nature	They are treatments to reduce or eliminate the symptoms of psychological disorders by altering the way the person's body functions. Drug therapy is the most common form. Much less used are electroconvulsive therapy and psychosurgery.
	Drug Therapy	Three major classes of psychotherapeutic drugs are (1) antianxiety drugs, (2) antidepressant drugs, and (3) antipsychotic drugs. Antianxiety drugs are commonly known as tranquilizers. Benzodiazepines are the most commonly used antianxiety drugs. Antidepressant drugs regulate mood. The three main classes are tricyclics, MAO inhibitors, and SSRI drugs. Lithium is often successfully used in the treatment of bipolar disorder. Antipsychotic drugs are powerful drugs that are used to treat people with severe mental disorders, especially schizophrenia. We described the effectiveness and side effects of various drug therapies.
	Electroconvulsive Therapy	This is commonly called "shock therapy" and is used mainly to treat severe depression when other strategies have not worked.
	Psychosurgery	This is an irreversible procedure in which brain tissue is destroyed in an attempt to improve adjustment. Today's psychosurgery, although rarely used, is more precise than the early prefrontal lobotomies.
Therapy Integrations	Their Nature	Approximately 30 to 50 percent of practicing therapists refer to themselves as "integrative" or "eclectic." Therapy integrations are characterized by an openness to various ways of integrating diverse therapies.

Overview

Overview

WE BEGAN THIS CHAPTER by examining these aspects of the nature and history of psychotherapy: the nature of psychotherapy, the history of psychotherapy, mental health professionals, and connections with personality theories. Our coverage of psychotherapies focused on psychodynamic therapies, humanistic therapies, behavior therapies, cognitive therapies, and group therapies, as well as how effective psychotherapy is. We explored these aspects of biomedical therapies: drug therapy, electroconvulsive therapy, and psychosurgery. And we evaluated therapy integrations.

Remember that you can obtain a more detailed overview of the chapter by again studying the four summary tables on pages 485, 490, 497, and 510.

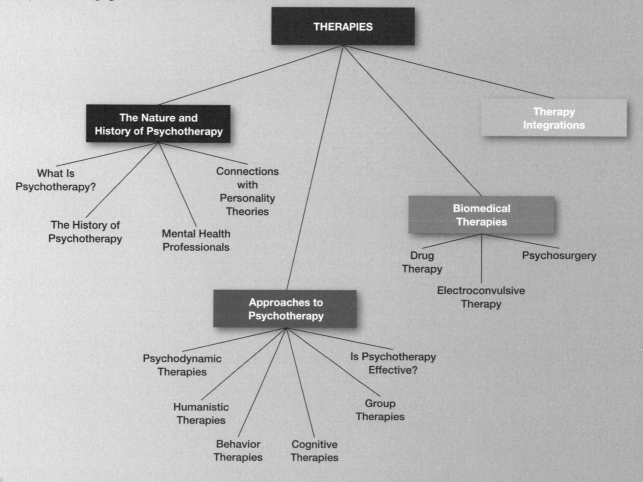

Key Terms

psychotherapy 480
deinstitutionalization 481
managed care 482
insight therapy 484
psychodynamic therapies 484
psychoanalysis 486
free association 486
catharsis 486
dream analysis 487
manifest content 487

latent content 487
transference 487
resistance 487
humanistic therapies 489
person-centered therapy 489
unconditional positive regard 489
gestalt therapy 490
behavior therapies 491
systematic desensitization 492

aversive conditioning 492
behavior modification 493
token economy 493
cognitive therapies 494
rational-emotive behavior therapy 494
family therapy 498
couple therapy 498
self-help support groups 499
meta-analysis 501

biomedical therapies 504
antianxiety drugs 504
antidepressant drugs 505
lithium 505
antipsychotic drugs 505
tardive dyskinesia 505
electroconvulsive therapy (ECT) 506
psychosurgery 507

Key People

Philippe Pinel 481
Dorothea Dix 481
Sigmund Freud 484

Carl Rogers 489
Frederick (Fritz) Perls 490

Donald Meichenbaum 493
Albert Ellis 494

Aaron Beck 494
Egas Moniz 507

Psychology Checklist
THERAPIES

How much have you learned since the beginning of the chapter? Use the following statements to help you review your knowledge and understanding of the chapter material. First, read the statement and mentally or briefly on paper demonstrate that you can discuss the relevant information.

_____ I know what psychotherapy is.
_____ I can discuss psychotherapy's history, including its early history, mental hospitals and deinstitutionalization, and some recent developments.
_____ I am aware of the different types of mental health professionals.
_____ I can describe the connections of psychotherapies with different personality theories.
_____ I can discuss the psychodynamic therapies, including Freud's psychoanalysis and some contemporary psychodynamic therapies.
_____ I know about the humanistic therapies, including person-centered therapy and gestalt therapy.

_____ I am aware of the behavior therapies, including classical conditioning, operant conditioning approaches, and cognitive behavior modification.
_____ I can describe the cognitive therapies, including rational-emotive behavior therapy and Beck's cognitive therapy
_____ I can discuss group therapies, including their nature, family/couple therapy, and self-help support groups.
_____ I can evaluate the effectiveness of psychotherapy, including research on the topic, common themes in psychotherapy, and gender/ethnicity issues.
_____ I can describe the biomedical therapies, including drug therapy, electroconvulsive therapy, and psychosurgery.
_____ I can discuss therapy integrations.

For any items you did not check off, go back and locate the relevant material in the chapter. Review the material until you feel that you can check off the item. You may also want to use this checklist later in preparing for an exam.

Taking It to the Net

1. "Battacca bats" are padded sticks that are used to hit chairs or sofas in psychotherapy. They are often used in couples therapy or therapy involving adolescents. The client is instructed to use the bats to safely express their anger. Clients often feel a sense of purging their anger after effectively using the battacca bats. Which type of psychotherapy uses battacca bats? What other tools are employed by this type of therapy?

2. Prefrontal lobotomies were prescribed for a variety of disorders. The lobotomy could be performed in the physician's office, without the need to be hospitalized. The physician simply jammed a sharp instrument behind the eye of the patient and severed the nearby neural fibers. The procedure was usually effective in reducing symptoms, but the side effects were devastating. In time, the procedure became very unpopular, and few are performed today. Some types of psychosurgery are still performed, however, in spite of their drastic nature. What psychosurgery procedures are still being done? What disorders are treated by psychosurgery?

3. Freud's psychoanalysis is a therapeutic technique for analyzing an individual's unconscious thought. Freud used several techniques to uncover people's thoughts, including free association and dream analysis. Free association consists of encouraging people to say whatever comes to their mind, no matter what. Dream analysis involves interpreting a person's dreams to uncover any hidden fantasies or conflicts. We've all heard the term Freudian slip. Have you ever made a Freudian slip? What is it, and does it really tell people what you are unconsciously thinking? Explain.

Connect to http://www.mcgrawhill.ca/college/santrock to find the answers!

Resources for Psychology and Life

Building a Framework for Support: A Community Development Approach to Mental Health Policy (1999)
>   by John Trainor, Edward Pomeroy and Bonnie Pape (Eds.)
>   Toronto, ON: Canadian Mental Health Association

This publication of the Canadian Mental Health Association lays out a framework meant to bring Canada's mental health policy into the 21st century.

Journal of Clinical and Consulting Psychology
This excellent journal publishes articles on many different topics in clinical psychology. Special sections feature a series of articles on a particular topic.

Canadian Journal of Community Mental Health
>   c/o Ed Pomeroy
>   Department of Psychology
>   Brock University
>   St. Catharines, ON L2S 3A1
>   http://www.psyc.brocku.ca/cjcmh/index.html

This journal is an interdisciplinary publication devoted to the sharing of information and valid knowledge about phenomena pertinent to the mental well-being of Canadians and their communities.

The Consumer's Guide to Psychotherapy (1992)
>   by Jack Engler and Daniel Goleman
>   New York: Simon & Schuster

This is a comprehensive manual on psychotherapy for consumers. Among the questions the authors ask and evaluate are these:

• How do I decide if I need therapy?
• Which therapy approach is best for me?
• How do I find the right therapist?
• What questions should I ask during the first session?
• How can I afford therapy?
• How can I tell if therapy is really working?
• How do I know when to end therapy?

The book is based on the clinical opinions of almost 1,000 therapists across the U.S. Included are case studies and listings of mental health organizations, as well as therapist referral sources.

Case Approach to Counseling and Psychotherapy (1996, 4th ed.)
>   by Gerald Corey
>   Pacific Grove, CA: Brooks/Cole

A central client, Ruth, becomes the focus for the application of nine different therapies, including psychoanalytic, Adlerian, person-centered, Gestalt, cognitive-behavior, and family systems.

Behavior Therapy
This journal publishes a wide-ranging set of behavior therapy strategies and a number of fascinating case studies. Look through recent issues to learn how behavior therapy is conducted.

Canadian Mental Health Association
>   2160 Yonge Street, 3rd Floor
>   Toronto, ON, M4S 2Z3
>   416-484-7750
>   http://www.cmha.ca/

The Canadian Mental Health Association, founded in 1918, is one of the oldest voluntary organizations in Canada and the only one to deal with all aspects of mental health and mental illness.

Chapter 15

CHAPTER OUTLINE

THE SCOPE OF HEALTH PSYCHOLOGY

STRESS

Biological Factors
Personality Factors
Cognitive Factors
Environmental Factors
Sociocultural Factors

COPING

Problem-Focused Coping and Emotion-Focused Coping
Optimism and Positive Thinking
Self-Efficacy
Social Support
Assertive Behavior
Stress Management
Multiple Coping Strategies

PROMOTING HEALTH

Regular Exercise
Proper Nutrition
Not Smoking
Sound Sexual Decision-Making

Health Psychology

Health Psychology

Images of Psychology and Life
Mort, Overwhelmed with Stress

MORT, AGE 52, has worked as an air traffic controller for the past 15 years. An excitable person, he compares the job to being in a cage. During peak air traffic, the tension is almost unbearable. In these frenzied moments, Mort's emotions are a mixture of rage, fear, and anxiety. Unfortunately, the tension also spills over into his family life. In his own words, "When I go home, my nerves are hopping. I take it out on the nearest person." Two years ago, Mort's wife, Sally, told him that if he could not calm his emotions and handle stress more effectively, she would leave him. She suggested that he change to a less upsetting job, but he ignored her advice. His intense emotional behavior continued, and she left him. Last week the roof fell in on Mort. That Sunday evening, the computer that monitors air traffic temporarily went down and Mort had a heart attack. Quadruple bypass surgery saved his life.

Yesterday his doctor talked with him about the stress in his life and what could be done to reduce it. Mort rarely gets enough sleep, weighs too much but frequently skips meals, never exercises, smokes two packs of cigarettes a day, and drinks two or three scotches every evening (more on weekends). He professes no religious interests. He rarely dates since his divorce and has no relatives living within 50 miles. He has only one friend and does not feel very close to him. Mort says that he never has enough time to do the things he wants to do and rarely has quiet time to himself during the day. He has fun only about once every two weeks.

The doctor gave Mort a test, shown in figure 15. 1, to reveal his vulnerability to stress. Mort scored 68 on the stress test, indicating he is seriously vulnerable to stress and close to the extremely vulnerable range. Stress is inevitable in our lives, so it is important to understand what factors are involved in managing stress and in maintaining a healthy lifestyle. How do *you* fare on the stress test?

"*Look* to your health and if you have it value it next to a good conscience. . . . Health is a blessing we mortals can achieve."

Izaak Walton
English Writer, 17th Century

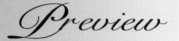

IN THE "IMAGES OF PSYCHOLOGY" section you will read about Mort, who has figured out how to live a healthy lifestyle. This chapter places a special emphasis on psychology's role in understanding stress, coping, and health. You will see that many illnesses are no longer explained solely in biological terms; psychological and social factors can also be involved. The main theme of this chapter is how these factors influence our health, determine how we experience stress, and influence how we cope with it. These are among the questions we will explore in the chapter:

- What are the relatively new fields of health psychology and behavioral medicine?
- What are the biological pathways that are activated when we experience stress?
- Are some personality traits linked to whether people are healthy or develop illnesses?
- What are the best ways to cope with stress?
- What are the best strategies for promoting health?

Rate yourself on each item, using a scale of 1–5:

1 = almost always   2 = often   3 = sometimes   4 = seldom   5 = never

1. I eat at least one hot, balanced meal a day.

2. I get 7 to 8 hours of sleep at least four nights a week.

3. I give and receive affection regularly.

4. I have at least one relative within 50 miles whom I can rely on.

5. I exercise to the point of perspiration at least twice a week.

6. I smoke less than half a pack of cigarettes a day.

7. I take fewer than five alcoholic drinks a week.

8. I am the appropriate weight for my height.

9. I have an income adequate to meet my basic expenses.

10. I get strength from my religious beliefs.

11. I regularly attend church.

12. I have a network of friends and acquaintances.

13. I have one or more friends to confide in about personal matters.

14. I am in good health (including eyesight, hearing, teeth).

15. I am able to speak openly about my feelings when angry or worried.

16. I have regular conversations with the people I live with about domestic problems (e.g., chores, money, and daily living issues).

17. I do something for fun at least once a week.

18. I am able to organize my time effectively.

19. I drink fewer than three cups of coffee (or tea or cola drinks) a day.

20. I take quiet time for myself during the day.

Total:

To get your total score, add up the figures and subtract 20. Any number over 30 indicates a vulnerability to stress. You are seriously vulnerable if your score is between 50 and 75 and extremely vulnerable if it is over 75.

$\mathcal{F}$igure 15.1
Stress Test

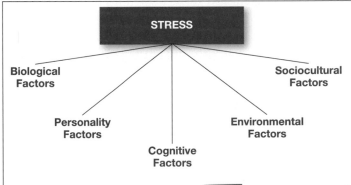

The Scope of Health Psychology

Around 2600 B.C., Asian physicians and later, around 500 B.C., Greek physicians recognized that good habits were essential for good health. They did not blame the gods for illness and think that magic would cure the illness. They realized that people have some control over their health. The physician's role was as a guide, assisting the patient in restoring a natural and emotional balance. Today, we are returning to the ancient view that the ultimate responsibility for influencing health rests with individuals themselves.

Except for the ancient Asian and Greek physicians, throughout most of history physical illness has been viewed purely in biological terms. That is, health involves bodily factors, not mental factors. The contemporary view is that body *and* mind can exert important influences on health. Indeed, a combination of biological, psychological, and social factors may be explored as possible causes of health or illness. Thus, the *biopsychosocial model* that we discussed in Chapter 13, "Abnormal Psychology," applies to health psychology as well ◀▥ P. 452.

Two relatively new fields reflect the belief that lifestyles and psychological states can play important roles in health: health psychology and behavioral medicine. **Health psychology** *emphasizes psychology's role in promoting and maintaining health and preventing and treating illness.* In 1980 the Canadian Psychological Association added a new section, Health Psychology, thus recognizing the increasing interest in psychology's role in health. That interest continues to grow today. **Behavioral medicine** *is an interdisciplinary field that focuses on developing and integrating behavioral and biomedical knowledge to promote health and reduce illness.*

Behavioral medicine and health psychology are overlapping fields that are sometimes indistinguishable. When distinctions are made, behavioral medicine is viewed

Health Psychology
European Health Psychology Society

as a broader field that focuses on both behavioral and biomedical factors, whereas health psychology is more likely to focus on behavioral factors. The interests of health psychologists and behavioral medicine researchers are broad (Kaplan & Kerner, 1998). They include examining how stress affects an individual's immune functioning, why we do or do not comply with medical advice, how effective media campaigns are in reducing smoking, psychological factors in losing weight, and the role of exercise in reducing stress (Salovey, Rothman, & Rodin, 1998).

Changing patterns of illness have fueled the increased interest in health psychology and behavioral medicine. Just a century ago, the leading causes of death were diseases such as influenza, polio, typhoid fever, rubella, and small pox. Today, none of these diseases are among the major causes of death. Rather, 7 of the 10 leading causes of death in the United States today are due to the *absence* of health behaviors. In Canada the various forms of cardiovascular disease (stroke, heart attack) and cancer alone accounted for 63% of all deaths in 1996 (Health Canada, 1999). Personal habits and lifestyles often play key roles in these diseases (Taylor, 1999).

Chronic diseases—such as heart disease, cancer, and diabetes—are the main contributors to disability and death today. This contrasts with acute disorders (such as tuberculosis, pneumonia, and other infectious diseases), which were the main contributors to disability and death prior to the twentieth century. Psychological and social factors are often involved in chronic diseases, and the fields of health psychology and behavioral medicine evolved partly to examine these factors and to find ways to help people cope more effectively (Baum & Posluszny, 1999).

In 1993, total health-care costs—from doctor to druggist and from work absence to lost productivity—amounted to $5,450 for every man, woman, and child in Canada (Statistics Canada, 1999). America's health-care costs are even higher and are moving toward the $1 trillion mark annually. Health experts hope to make a dent in these costs by encouraging people to live healthier lives. Many corporations now recognize that health promotion for their employees is cost-effective.

One of the main areas of research in health psychology and behavioral medicine is the link between stress and illness. Our psychological and physical well-being are related to stress and how we cope with it. Because stress is an inevitable part of our lives, we need to understand it better and learn how to handle it more effectively.

Behavioral Medicine
American Psychosomatic Society
Men's and Women's Health

Stress

We live in a stressful world. In 1994-95 over 25 percent of Canadians reported high stress levels. Many of the 1.1 million Canadians who reported experiencing major depression also reported high stress levels (Statistics Canada, 1999). Stress is a major contributor to coronary heart disease, cancer, lung disease, accidental injuries, cirrhosis of the liver, and suicide—six of the leading causes of death in North America. Antianxiety drugs and ulcer medications are among the best-selling prescription drugs in North America today.

Stress is a sign of the times. Everywhere you look, people are jogging, going to health clubs, and following diets designed to reduce tension. Even corporations have developed elaborate stress management programs. No one really knows whether we experience more stress than our parents or grandparents, but it seems as if we do.

How can we define stress? Stress is one of those terms that is not easy to define. Initially, the word *stress* was loosely borrowed from physics. Humans, it was thought, are in some ways similar to physical objects, such as metals that resist moderate outside forces but lose their resiliency at some point of greater pressure. But unlike metal, human beings can think and reason,

Members of the Masai tribe in Kenya, Africa, can stay on a treadmill for a long time because of their very active life. Heart disease is extremely low in the Masai tribe, which can also be attributed to their energetic lifestyle. (inset) North Americans are increasingly recognizing the health benefits of exercise and an active lifestyle. The role of exercise in health is one of health psychology's many interests.

BIOLOGICAL FACTORS	PERSONALITY FACTORS	COGNITIVE FACTORS	ENVIRONMENTAL FACTORS	SOCIOCULTURAL FACTORS
Example: The body's response to stress	Example: How a person handles anger	Example: Whether a person perceives an event as threatening or challenging	Example: Frustrating stressors in the environment, such as being blocked from reaching a goal	Example: Living in poverty

ℱigure 15.2
Factors Involved in Stress

Stress

and experience a myriad of social, environmental circumstances that make defining stress more complex in psychology than in physics (Hobfoll, 1989).

Although psychologists debate whether stress is the threatening events in our world or whether it is our response to those demands, we will define stress broadly. **Stress** *is the response of individuals to the circumstances and events, called stressors, that threaten them and tax their coping abilities.* To understand stress, we need to know about the following factors: physical and biological, emotional, personality, cognitive, environmental, sociocultural, and coping skills (see figure 15.2).

Biological Factors

When you are under stress, what happens to your body? As it readies itself to handle the assault of stress, a number of physiological changes take place.

The General Adaptation Syndrome   According to the Austrian-born founder of stress research, the late Hans Selye (1974, 1983), stress is simply the wear and tear on the body due to the demands placed on it. Any number of environmental events or stimuli will produce the same stress response in the body. Selye, who spent his research career at the Université de Montréal, observed patients with different problems: the death of someone close, loss of income, arrest for embezzlement. Regardless of which problem the patient had, similar symptoms appeared: loss of appetite, muscular weakness, and decreased interest in the world.

General adaptation syndrome (GAS) *is Selye's term for the common effects on the body when demands are placed on it. The GAS consists of three stages: alarm, resistance, and exhaustion.* First, in the *alarm stage,* the body enters a temporary state of shock, a time when resistance to illness and stress fall below normal limits. In trying to cope with the initial effects of stress, the body quickly releases hormones, which, in a short time, adversely affect the immune system's functioning. It is during this time that the individual is prone to infections from illness and injury. Fortunately, the alarm stage passes rather quickly as the body begins to build up its resistance. In the *resistance stage,* a number of glands throughout the body begin to manufacture different hormones that protect the individual in many ways. During this

Normal level of resistance to stress

ℱigure 15.3
Selye's General Adaptation Syndrome

The general adaptation syndrome (GAS) describes an individual's general response to stress in terms of three stages: (1) alarm, in which the body mobilizes its resources; (2) resistance, in which resistance levels off; and (3) exhaustion, in which resistance becomes depleted.

stage, the body's immune system can fight off infection with remarkable efficiency. Similarly, hormones that reduce inflammation normally associated with injury are present at high levels. If the all-out effort to combat stress fails and the stress persists, the individual moves into the *exhaustion stage.* Now the wear and tear on the body takes its toll—the person might collapse in a state of exhaustion and vulnerability to disease increases. Figure 15.3 provides an illustration of Selye's general adaptation syndrome.

Not all stress is bad, though. **Eustress** *is Selye's term for the positive features of stress.* Competing in an athletic event, writing an essay, or pursuing someone who is attractive requires the body to expend energy. Selye does not say we should avoid these fulfilling experiences in life, but he does emphasize that we should minimize the wear and tear on our bodies.

One of the main criticisms of Selye's view is that human beings do not always react to stress in the uniform way he proposed (Seffge-Krenke, 1995). There is much more to understanding stress in humans than knowing their physical reactions to it. We also need to know about their personality, their physical makeup, their perceptions, and the context in which the stressor occurred.

Two Biological Pathways to Stress   Though Selye's general adaptation syndrome described some general biological stages people go through, scientists today are zeroing in on some more-precise biological changes in the stress-body linkage. Many scientists now agree that there are two main biological pathways that connect the brain and the endocrine system in response to stress (Anderson, 1998; Anderson, Kiecolt-Glaser, & Glaser, 1994; Sternberg & Gold, 1996): (1) the neuroendocrine-immune pathway, and (2) the sympathetic nervous system pathway (see figure 15.4).

As shown in figure 15.4, the neuroendocrine-immune pathway goes through the hypothalamus and pituitary gland to the adrenal glands, where cortisol is released ◀▥ P. 95. Cortisol is a steroid that is good for the body over the short term because it causes cellular fuel—glucose—to move to muscles. But over the long term, high levels of cortisol can be bad for the body, suppressing the immune system and straining the brain's cellular functioning. Too much cortisol also increases appetite and can cause weight gain.

In the second biological pathway, the route is through the hypothalamus and then the sympathetic nervous (rather than the pituitary gland) before reaching the adrenal glands, where epinephrine and norepinephrine (but not cortisol) are released ◀▥ P. 71. Recall from chapter 3, "Biological Foundations and Neuroscience," and chapter 11, "Motivation and Emotion," that the sympathetic nervous system is a subsystem of the autonomic nervous system that is responsible for the body's arousal. It produces a quick response to a stressor (often referred to as the "fight-or-flight" response). The release of the hormones epinephrine and norepinephrine causes a number of physiological changes, including elevation of blood pressure. Over time, this can lead to increased risk of illness and disease, such as cardiovascular disease.

Psychoneuroimmunology   *Psychoneuroimmunology* *is the field that explores connections among psychological factors (such as attitudes and emotions), the nervous system, and the immune system.* The immune system keeps us healthy by recognizing foreign materials such as bacteria, viruses, and tumors, and then destroying them. Its machinery consists of billions of white blood cells located in the lymph system. The number of white blood cells and their effectiveness in killing foreign viruses or bacteria are related to stress levels. When in the alarm or exhaustion stage, for example, the immune system functions poorly. During these stages, viruses and bacteria are more likely to multiply and cause disease.

The immune system and the central nervous system at first glance appear to be organized in different ways. The brain is usually regarded as a central command center, sending and receiving electronic signals along fixed pathways, much like a telephone network. By contrast, the immune system is decentralized, with its organs (spleen, lymph nodes, thymus, and bone marrow) located throughout the body. The classical view is that the immune system communicates by releasing immune cells into the bloodstream that float, like boats, to new locations as they deliver their messages to perform other functions.

However, scientists are increasingly recognizing that the central nervous system and immune system are in fact more similar than different in their modes of receiving, recognizing, and integrating signals from the external environment (Sternberg & Gold, 1996). The central nervous system and the immune system both possess "sensory" elements, which receive information from the environment and other parts of the body, and "motor" elements, which carry out an appropriate response. Both systems also rely

Psychoneuroimmunology

Psychoneuroimmunology Research

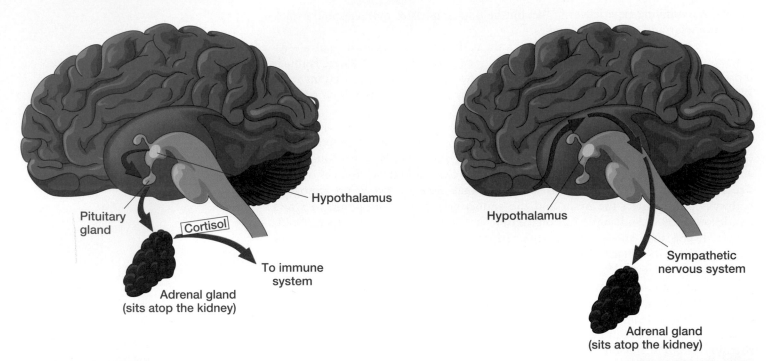

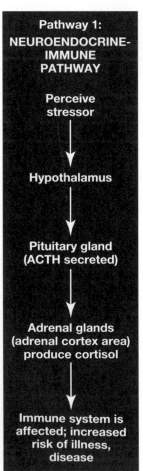

Pathway 1:
NEUROENDOCRINE-
IMMUNE
PATHWAY

Perceive
stressor

↓

Hypothalamus

↓

Pituitary gland
(ACTH secreted)

↓

Adrenal glands
(adrenal cortex area)
produce cortisol

↓

Immune system is
affected; increased
risk of illness,
disease

on chemical mediators for communication. A key hormone shared by the central nervous system and immune system is corticotropin-releasing hormone (CRH), which is produced in the hypothalamus and unites the stress and immune responses.

Currently, there is considerable research interest in links between the immune system and stress (Olff, 1999). Three lines of research provide support for this connection (Anderson, 1998; Anderson, Kiecolt-Glaser, & Glaser, 1994).

First, acute stressors can produce immunological changes in healthy individuals. For example, in relatively healthy HIV-infected individuals, as well as individuals with cancer, the onset of acute stressors was associated with poorer immune system functioning (Roberts, Anderson, & Lubaroff, 1994; Vedhara & others, 1999).

Second, chronic stressors are associated with an increasing downturn in immune system responsiveness, rather than adaptation. This effect has been documented in a number of contexts, including living next to a damaged nuclear reactor, failures in close relationships (divorce, separation, and marital distress), and burdensome caregiving for a family member with a progressive illness (Kiecolt-Glaser & others, 1991).

Third, research with cancer patients links quality of life with immunity. Social adjustment often predicts higher NK-cell levels (*NK* stands for "natural killer"), while negative-distress indicators often predict lower NK-cell levels (Levy & others, 1990). NK cells can attack tumor cells (see figure 15.5).

The scientific study of psychoneuroimmunology is relatively young. Much of what we know needs to be clarified, explained, and verified further. Researchers hope to clarify the precise links among psychological factors, the brain, and the immune system (Redd, 1995; Schleifer, 1999). Some preliminary hypotheses about the interaction

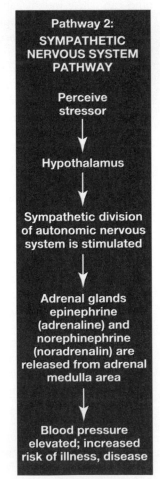

Pathway 2:
SYMPATHETIC
NERVOUS SYSTEM
PATHWAY

Perceive
stressor

↓

Hypothalamus

↓

Sympathetic division
of autonomic nervous
system is stimulated

↓

Adrenal glands
epinephrine
(adrenaline) and
norephinephrine
(noradrenalin) are
released from adrenal
medulla area

↓

Blood pressure
elevated; increased
risk of illness, disease

Figure 15.4
Two Biological Pathways
in Stress

that causes vulnerability to disease include the following: (1) Stressful experiences lower the efficiency of immune systems, making individuals more susceptible to disease; (2) stress directly promotes disease-producing processes; and (3) stressful experiences may cause the activation of dormant viruses that diminish the individual's ability to cope with disease. These hypotheses may lead to clues for more successful treatments for some of the most baffling diseases—cancer and AIDS among them (Servaes & others, 1999).

In an example of research on psychoneuroimmunology recently conducted by Sheldon Cohen and his colleagues (1998), adults who faced interpersonal or work-related stress for at least a month were more likely than people who were less stressed to catch a cold after exposure to viruses. In the study, 276 adults were exposed to viruses, then quarantined for 5 days. The longer people experienced major stress, the more likely they were to catch a cold. Individuals who reported high stress for the past two years tripled their risk of catching a cold. Those who experienced work-related stress for a month or longer were nearly five times more likely to develop colds than individuals without chronic stress. Interpersonal stress for a month or more doubled their chances of catching a cold. Cohen concluded that stress-triggered changes in the immune system and hormones might create greater vulnerability to infection. The findings suggest that when we know we are under stress, we need to take better care of ourselves than usual, although often we do just the opposite. Cohen and his colleagues (1997) also found that positive social ties with friends and family provide a protective buffer that helps to prevent people from catching a cold when they are exposed to cold viruses.

Personality Factors

Do you have certain personality characteristics that help you cope more effectively with stress? Do other characteristics make you more vulnerable to stress?

Type A/Type B Behavioral Patterns
In the late 1950s a secretary for two California cardiologists, Meyer Friedman and Ray Rosenman, observed that the chairs in their waiting rooms were tattered and worn, but only on the front edges. The cardiologists had noticed the impatience of their cardiac patients, who often arrived exactly on time for an appointment and were in a great hurry to leave. Subsequently they conducted a study of 3,000 healthy men between the ages of 35 and 59 over a period of eight years (Friedman & Rosenman, 1974). During the eight years, one group of men had twice as many heart attacks or other forms of heart disease as anyone else. And autopsies of the men who died revealed that this same group had coronary arteries that were more obstructed than those of other men. Friedman and Rosenman described the coronary disease group as characterized by **Type A behavior pattern**, *a cluster of characteristics—being excessively competitive, hard-driven, impatient, and hostile—thought to be related to the incidence of heart disease.* Rosenman and Friedman labeled the behavior of the other group, who were relaxed and easygoing, **Type B behavioral pattern.**

Further research on the link between Type A behavior and coronary disease reveals greater complexity than Friedman and Rosenman believed (Suls & Swain, 1998; Williams, 1995). Researchers have examined components of Type A behavior, such as hostility, competitiveness, goal orientation, and impatience, to determine a more precise link with coronary risk, and have found that hostility is most consistently associated with coronary problems (Allan & Scheidt, 1996; Faber & Burns, 1996; Räikkönen & others, 1999). Further research has shown that hostility is itself a complex construct. For example, Greenglass (1996) has shown that Canadian managers who suppress their anger and show cynical distrust are more vulnerable to coronary problems. Miller & others (1996) found that outwardly hostile people may be especially vulnerable. On the other hand, anger-defensive individuals also show elevated cardiovascular responses in response to some stressors (Miller, 1993). Regardless, Williams (1995) believes that hostile people have the ability to control their anger and develop more trust in others, which he thinks can reduce their risk for heart disease.

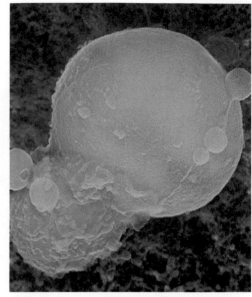
(a)

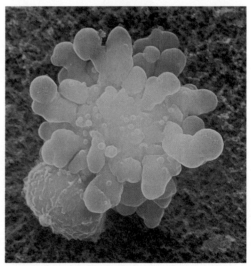
(b)

Figure 15.5
NK Cells and Cancer
David vs. Goliath: *(a)* a small white blood cell (lymphocyte) takes on a large cancer cell (the one with the smoother surface); *(b)* a small natural killer (NK) cell attacks a larger tumor cell, which defends itself by forming blisters on its surface.

TYPE Z BEHAVIOR

© The New Yorker Collection 1987 *Donald Reilly from cartoonbank.com. All Rights Reserved.*

Anger and Heart Disease

Hardiness   Hardiness *is a personality style characterized by a sense of commitment (rather than alienation), control (rather than powerlessness), and a perception of problems as challenges (rather than threats).* Dion, Dion & Pak (1992) studied the hardiness of members of Toronto's Chinese community and found that the relationship between experienced discrimination and psychological symptoms was stronger among respondents low in hardiness than in those high in hardiness. In the Chicago Stress Project, male business managers were studied over a five-year period during which most of them experienced stressful events, such as divorce, job transfers, the death of a close friend, and working with an unpleasant boss. In one study, managers who developed an illness (ranging from the flu to a heart attack) were compared with those who did not (Kobasa, Maddi, & Kahn, 1982). The latter group was more likely to have a hardy personality. In another study, when hardiness was combined with exercise and social support, the level of illness dropped dramatically (Kobasa & others, 1985). This suggests the power of multiple buffers of stress in maintaining health (Maddi, 1998).

Cognitive Factors

Most of us think of stress as environmental events that place demands on our lives, such as losing one's notes from a class, being yelled at by a friend, failing a test, or being in a car wreck. While there are some common ways we all experience stress, not everyone perceives the same events as stressful. For example, one person may perceive an upcoming job interview as threatening, while another person may perceive it as challenging. One person may perceive a D grade on a paper as threatening, another person may perceive the same grade as challenging. To some degree, then, what is stressful depends on how people cognitively appraise and interpret events. This view has been most clearly presented by Richard Lazarus (1993). **Cognitive appraisal** *is Lazarus' term for individuals' interpretation of events in their lives as harmful, threatening, or challenging, and their determination of whether they have the resources to effectively cope with the events.*

In Lazarus' view, events are appraised in two steps: primary appraisal and secondary appraisal. In *primary appraisal,* individuals interpret whether an event involves *harm* or loss that has already occurred, a *threat* of some future danger, or a *challenge* to be overcome. Lazarus' view that it is a good strategy to evaluate stress as a challenge to overcome fits with the challenge component of hardiness we just discussed. To understand Lazarus' concept of primary appraisal, consider two students, both of whom have a failing grade in their psychology class at midterm. Student A is almost frozen by the stress of the low grade and looks to the rest of the term as a threatening circumstance. In contrast, student B does not become overwhelmed by the harm already done and the threat of more future failures. She looks at the low midterm grade as a challenge to do something about and a stressful situation to overcome.

In the second cognitive appraisal step, *secondary appraisal,* individuals evaluate their resources and determine how effectively they can be used to cope with the event. This appraisal is called *secondary* because it comes after primary appraisal and depends on the degree to which the event is appraised as harmful, threatening, and challenging. For example, student A might have some helpful resources for coping but view the stressful circumstance as so harmful and threatening that she doesn't use them. Student B, who perceives the stressful situation of a low midterm grade as challenging, then evaluates the resources she can call on to improve her grade during the second half of the term. These include asking the instructors for suggestions about how to study better for the tests in the course, setting up a time management program to include more study hours, and asking several students who are doing well in the class about their strategies.

*T*hrough the Eyes of Psychologists

Richard Lazarus, *University of California, Berkeley*

"Cognitive appraisal involves judgments of how we are doing in an encounter with the environment and in our lives overall, and how to deal with potential harms and benefits."

In many instances, viewing stress as a challenge in step 1 (primary appraisal) paves the way for examining the availability of effective coping resources in step 2 (secondary appraisal). Of course, some individuals might examine their resources for coping and not have adequate ones. For example, if student B is extremely shy, she might lack the courage and skills to go talk to the instructor or to ask several students in the class about their strategies for doing well in course. Later in the chapter, we will explore a number of coping strategies, including assertiveness training, that could help the shy student in this stressful circumstance. Figure 15.6 illustrates Lazarus' cognitive appraisal view of stress.

Environmental Factors

Many circumstances, large and small, can produce stress in our lives. In some instances, cataclysmic events such as war, an automobile accident, a fire, or the death of a loved one produce stress. In others, the everyday pounding of being overloaded with work, of being frustrated in an unhappy relationship, or of living in poverty produce stress. What makes some situations stressful and others less so?

Figure 15.6
Lazarus' Cognitive Appraisal View of Stress
Perceiving stress as harmful and/or threatening in step 1, and having few or no coping resources available in step 2, yields high stress. Perceiving stress as a challenge in step 1, and having good coping resources available in step 2, reduces stress.

Overload, Conflict, and Frustration   Sometimes stimuli become so intense that we can no longer cope with them. For example, persistent high levels of noise overload our adaptability. *Overload* can occur with work as well. How often have you said to yourself, "There are not enough hours in the day to do all I have to do." In today's computer age especially, we are faced with information overload. It is easy to develop the stressful feeling that we don't know as much about a topic as we should, even if we are a so-called "expert."

Overload can lead to **burnout,** *a hopeless, helpless feeling brought about by relentless work-related stress.* Burnout leaves its sufferers in a state of physical and emotional exhaustion that includes chronic fatigue and low energy. According to Michael Leiter of Acadia University, burnout usually occurs because of a gradual accumulation of work-related stress (Leiter & Maslach, 1998). Burnout is most likely among individuals who deal with others in highly emotional situations (such as nurses and social workers), but have only limited control over their clients' or patients' outcomes (Leiter, 1991). Greenglass, Burke & Konarski (1998) have shown that co-worker support is an important buffer against burnout among teachers. In women, co-worker support leads to lower emotional exhaustion, while in men it leads to higher personal accomplishment. Greenglass (1991) also found gender differences in precursors of burnout. While work sources are the main precursors of burnout in men, in women both work and family variables, such as marital satisfaction, can precede burnout.

It is now more common for university students to leave school before earning their degrees, due to burnout. Dropping out for a term or two is now sometimes called "stopping out" because the student fully intends to return. Before recommending stopping out, most counselors suggest that the student examine ways to reduce overload and possible coping strategies. The simple strategy of taking a reduced or better-balanced class load sometimes works, for example.

Stimuli not only overload us, but they also can be a source of conflict. Conflict occurs when we must decide between two or more incompatible stimuli. Three major types of conflict are approach/approach, avoidance/avoidance, and approach/avoidance. The **approach/approach conflict** *is a conflict in which the individual must choose between two attractive stimuli or circumstances.* Should you go out with the attractive blonde or with the attractive brunette? Do you buy a Ford Escort or a Saturn? The approach/approach conflict is the least stressful of the three types of conflict because either choice leads to a positive result.

The **avoidance/avoidance conflict** *is a conflict in which the individual must choose between two unattractive stimuli or circumstances.* Do you go through the stress of

"I THINK WE CAN RULE OUT STRESS."

© Sidney Harris

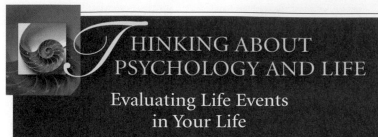

THINKING ABOUT PSYCHOLOGY AND LIFE

Evaluating Life Events in Your Life

THE EVENTS LISTED BELOW commonly occur in the lives of college students. Check the space provided for the events that have occurred in your life during the last 12 months. When you have finished checking off all of events that have happened in your life in the last 12 months, total the point values in parentheses for each checked item.

(100)	_____	Death of a close family member
(80)	_____	Jail term
(63)	_____	Final year or first year in college
(60)	_____	Pregnancy (yours or caused by you)
(53)	_____	Severe personal illness or injury
(50)	_____	Marriage
(45)	_____	Any interpersonal problems
(40)	_____	Financial difficulties
(40)	_____	Death of a close friend
(40)	_____	Arguments with your roommate (more than every other day)
(40)	_____	Major disagreements with your family
(30)	_____	Major change in personal habits
(30)	_____	Change in living environment
(30)	_____	Beginning or ending a job
(25)	_____	Problems with your boss or professor
(25)	_____	Outstanding personal achievement
(25)	_____	Failure in some course
(20)	_____	Final exams
(20)	_____	Increased or decreased dating
(20)	_____	Change in working conditions
(20)	_____	Change in your major
(18)	_____	Change in your sleeping habits
(15)	_____	Several-day vacation
(15)	_____	Change in eating habits
(15)	_____	Family reunion
(15)	_____	Change in recreational activities
(15)	_____	Minor illness or injury
(11)	_____	Minor violations of the law

_____ Total Life Events Score

The total number that you added up may predict the frequency of serious illness you will experience in the coming year. If your life events score totals 300 points or more, you have an 80 percent chance of having a significant illness in the coming year. If your total score is 299 to 150, you have a 50 percent chance of having a major illness. If your total score is 149 points or less, your risk of significant illness decreases to 30 percent.

Keep in mind, in interpreting your life events total score, that such event checklists don't take into account how you cope with such events. Some people who experience stressful life events cope and adjust well to them, others do not.

Source: Girdano, D., & Everly, G. S. (1979). Controlling your stress and tension, pp. 56–57.

giving an oral presentation in class or not show up and get a zero? You want to avoid both, but in each case, you must choose one. Obviously these conflicts are more stressful than having the luxury of having two enticing choices. In many instances, we delay our decision about the avoidance/avoidance conflict until the last possible moment.

The **approach/avoidance conflict** *is a conflict involving a single stimulus or circumstance that has both positive and negative characteristics.* Let's say you really like the person you are going with and are thinking about getting married. On the one hand you are attracted by the steady affection and love that marriage might bring, but on the other hand, marriage is a commitment you might not feel ready to make. You look at a menu and face a dilemma—the double chocolate delight would be sumptuous, but is it worth the extra pound of weight? Our world is full of approach/avoidance conflicts and they can be highly stressful. In these circumstances, we often vacillate before deciding (Miller, 1959).

Frustration is another circumstance that produces stress. **Frustration** *refers to any situation in which a person cannot reach a desired goal.* If we want something and cannot have it, we feel frustrated. Our world is full of frustrations that build up to make our life more stressful—not having enough money to buy the car we want, not getting promoted at work, not getting an A average, being delayed for an important appointment by traffic, and being rejected by a friend. Failures and losses are especially frustrating—not getting grades that are high enough to get into medical school or losing someone we are closely attached to through death, for example. Sometimes the frustrations we experience are major life events, as in the case of divorce and death. At other times, the accumulation of daily hassles may make us feel as though we're being nibbled to death by ducks.

Life Events and Daily Hassles

Think about your life. What events have created the most stress for you? A change in financial status, getting fired at work, a divorce, the death of someone you loved, a personal injury? And what about the everyday circumstances of your life? What hassles you the most? Not having enough time to study, arguing with your girlfriend or boyfriend, not getting enough credit for the work you do at your job?

Researchers have proposed that significant life events are a major source of stress and have loosely linked such life events with illnesses ◀⁣⁣⁣ P. 359. The effects of individual life events, such as a tornado or volcanic eruption, can be evaluated, or the effects of *clusters* of events can be studied. Thomas Holmes and Richard Rahe (1967) devised a scale to measure clusters of life events and their possible impact on illness. Their widely used Social Readjustment Rating Scale includes events ranging from the death of a spouse (100 stress points) to minor violations of the law (11 stress points).

People who experience clusters of life events, such as divorce, being fired from a job, and sexual difficulties, are more likely to become ill (Maddi, 1996). However, the ability to predict illness from life events alone is modest. Total scores of life events scales such as the Social Readjustment Rating Scale are frequently ineffective at predicting future health problems. A life-events checklist tells us nothing about a person's physiological makeup, constitutional strengths and weaknesses, ability to cope with stressful circumstances, support systems, or the nature of the social relationships involved—all of which are important in understanding how stress is related to illness. A divorce, for example, might be less stressful than a marriage filled with day-to-day tension. In addition, the Holmes-Rahe scale includes positive events, such as marital reconciliation and gaining a new family member, which can also create stressors that must be faced. However, the changes that result from positive events are not as difficult to cope with as the changes that result from negative events.

"You take all the time you need, Larry—this certainly is a big decision."

Drawing by Eric Teitelbaum; © *1990* The New Yorker Magazine, Inc.

Psychologists increasingly consider the nature of daily hassles and daily uplifts to gain better insight about the nature of stress (Pillow, Zautra, & Sandler, 1996). It might be our daily experiences, and not life's major events, that are the primary sources of stress (Kohn & MacDonald, 1992). Enduring a boring but tense job or marriage and living in poverty do not show up on scales of major life events. Yet the everyday tension involved in these living conditions adds up to a highly stressful life and in some cases psychological disorder or illness. In one study, people who experienced the most daily hassles had the most negative self-images (Tolan, Miller, & Thomas, 1988).

How about your own life? What are the biggest hassles? One study showed that the most frequent daily hassles of college students were wasting time, being lonely, and worrying about meeting high achievement standards (Kanner & others, 1981). In fact, the fear of failing in our success-oriented world often plays a role in college students' depression. College students also found that the small things in life—having fun, laughing, going to movies, getting along well with friends, and completing a task—were their main sources of feeling uplifted.

Critics of the daily hassles approach argue that some of the same problems with life events scales occur when assessing daily hassles (Dohrenwend & Shrout, 1985). For example, knowing about a person's daily hassles tell us nothing about the body's resilience to stress, coping ability or strategies, or how that person perceives stress. Further, the hassles scale has not been consistently related to objective measures of health and illness. Yet another criticism is that hassles can be conceived of as dependent measures rather than causes. People who complain about things, who report being anxious and unhappy, and who see the bad side of everything see more hassles in their daily lives. From this perspective, hassles don't predict bad moods; bad moods predict hassles. Supporters of the daily hassles concept contend that information about daily hassles can be used in concert with information about physiological reactions, coping, and how stress is perceived to provide a more complete picture of the causes and consequences of stress.

Sociocultural Factors

Sociocultural factors influence the stressors individuals are likely to encounter, whether events are perceived as stressful or not, and the expectations individuals have about how stressors should be confronted (Chang, 1996). Sociocultural factors involved in stress include acculturative stress and poverty.

Acculturative Stress   **Acculturative stress** *refers to the negative consequences that result from contact between two distinctive cultural groups.* Many immigrants to North America have experienced acculturative stress. Florida teacher Daniel Arnoux (1998) called out a student's name in class and asked if she was Haitian. She became so embarrassed that she slid under her seat and disappeared from view. Arnoux realized how stressful school was for many immigrant students, some of whom were beaten and harassed for being Haitian, and began developing lessons to help students gain empathy and tolerance for people from different ethnic and cultural backgrounds.

Queen's University cross-cultural psychologist John Berry (1980) believes that when people like the student above experience cultural change, they can adapt in one of four main ways: (1) assimilation, (2) integration, (3) separation, or (4) marginalization.

Assimilation *occurs when individuals relinquish their cultural identity and move into the larger society.* The nondominant group may be absorbed into an established "mainstream," or many groups may merge to form a new society (what is often called a "melting pot"). By contrast, **integration** *implies the maintenance of cultural integrity as well as the movement to become an integral part of the larger culture.* In this circumstance, a number of ethnic groups all cooperate within a large social system ("a mosaic"). **Separation** *refers to self-imposed withdrawal from the larger culture.* If imposed by the larger society, separation becomes *segregation.* People might maintain a traditional way of life because they desire an independent existence (as in "separatist" movements) or the dominant culture may exclude the other culture (as in slavery and apartheid). Finally, **marginalization** *refers to the process in which groups are put out of cultural and psychological contact with both their traditional society and the larger, dominant society.* Marginalization often involves feelings of alienation and a loss of identity. Marginalization does not mean that a group has no culture but indicates that this culture may be disorganized and unsupportive of the acculturating individual.

Separation and marginalization are the least adaptive responses to acculturation. While separation can sometimes have benefits, it may be especially stressful for individuals who seek separation while most members of their group seek assimilation. Integration and assimilation are healthier adaptations to acculturative pressures. But assimilation means some cultural loss, so it may be more stressful than integration.

While Canadians generally hold positive attitudes about the idea of a multicultural society, they have variable attitudes toward ethnocultural groups (Berry, 1993). Schwean and others (1999) find that the vulnerability of cultural minority people to negative psychosocial outcomes lies not with cultural differences but rather with acculturative stress, especially in the case of the Native peoples of Canada. For example, Canadians still hold negative social stereotypes of the Innu, based mainly upon information derived from television and newspapers (Claxton-Oldfield & Keefe, 1999).

Poverty   Poverty can cause considerable stress for individuals and families (Huston, 1995; McLoyd, 1999). Chronic conditions such as inadequate housing, dangerous neighborhoods, burdensome responsibilities, and economic uncertainties are potent stressors in the lives of the poor (Chase-Lansdale & Brooks-Gunn, 1996). Ethnic minority families are disproportionately among the poor. So too, are families headed by a single mother (Statistics Canada, 1999). The U.S. National Advisory Council on Economic Opportunity (1980) reported that families headed by African American women are ten times more likely to live in poverty than are families headed by White men. Many people who become poor during their lives remain so for only one or two years. However, ethnic minority groups and female heads of household are especially at risk for persistent poverty.

Poverty is also related to threatening and uncontrollable life events (Russo, 1990). Poor women are more likely to experience crime and violence than middle-class women are. And poverty undermines sources of social support that play a role in buffering the effects of stress. Poverty is related to marital unhappiness and with having spouses who are unlikely to serve as confidants (Brown, Bhrolchain, & Harris, 1975). Children growing up in poverty are more likely to have a depressed parent and to have their own emotional difficulties (Statistics Canada, 1999). Further, poverty means having to depend on many overburdened and unresponsive bureaucratic systems for financial, housing, and health assistance. To read about welfare poverty in Canada, see Explorations in Psychology.

At this point we have discussed many ideas about the nature of health psychology and stress. An overview of these ideas is presented in summary table 15.1. Next we turn our attention to an extremely important aspect of stress—how to cope effectively with it.

*T*hrough the Eyes of Psychologists

Vonnie McLoyd, *Duke University*

"Poverty and stress are common in the lives of many ethnic minority women who are single parents, and too often this translates into stressful lives for their children."

EXPLORATIONS IN PSYCHOLOGY
Jen and Nick:
Faces of Welfare Poverty in Canada

JEN (NOT HER REAL NAME) is a single mother living on welfare with three children. Living in British Columbia, she receives welfare only because she has virtually no other cash assets. Jen receives $1436 a month, including income assistance, child support, the BC Family Bonus, the Canada Child Tax Credit, and the GST Credit. She keeps her monthly rent down to $650 by living in a two-bedroom basement apartment of a family member's home. Her three boys are growing so, for Jen, food is an important priority, costing $500 each month. Her three boys are enrolled in their school lunch program, which costs an additional $105 per month. Jen's overall expense for groceries and the lunch program is still lower than that recommended by federal nutrition guidelines.

After these major costs are covered, Jen has $181 left over every month. Expenses still to be covered include laundry, bus fares, phone, utilities, dental care, haircuts, extracurricular activities for children, cable, clothing, and emergencies. Like other stories of growing up in poverty (Kotlowitz, 1991), Jen's is a true story, which she shared with members of the BC Campaign 2000.

Nick (not his real name) also told his story to the BC Campaign 2000. The unavailability of jobs means that a disproportionately high number of youths like Nick must rely on welfare. Each month he receives $500. He is lucky to be able to share an apartment and pays $340 per month as his share. He also shares a phone and hydro, costing him another $30 per month. Nick relies on public transit and purchases a bus pass each month. He cannot afford a three-zone pass so he buys a one-zone bus pass for $54 and prays that he won't get caught with the wrong pass. After these expenses are paid, what's left over is $76. With many other monthly expenses, such as food, Nick relies as much as possible on food banks and on those around him for food so that he can cover other monthly expenses. Some of his other expenses include laundry, clothing, household products, food and litter for his cats, and emergencies.

How might the stress of poverty affect children's development? How might it affect the parent-child relationship? Although these kinds of circumstances are often harmful to children, might some children be resilient to such stressors and have positive outcomes in life?

Some children triumph over life's adversities (Wilson & Gottman, 1996). Norman Garmezy (1985, 1993) has studied resilience amid disadvantage for many years. He concluded that three factors help children become resilient to stress and disadvantage: (1) good cognitive skills, especially attention (which helps children focus on tasks, such as school work); (2) a family, even if enveloped in poverty, characterized by warmth, cohesion, and a caring adult (such as a grandparent who takes responsibility in the absence of responsive parents or in the presence of intense marital conflict); and (3) external support, such as a teacher, a neighbor, a mentor, a caring agency, or a church. In one longitudinal study of resilient individuals from birth to 32 years of age, these three factors were present in their lives (Werner, 1989).

Coping

Coping *involves managing taxing circumstances, expending effort to solve life's problems, and seeking to master or reduce stress.* A stressful circumstance is rendered considerably less stressful when a person successfully copes with it (Endler, 1997). Let's explore some of the different ways that people can effectively cope with stress.

Problem-Focused Coping and Emotion-Focused Coping

In our discussion of stress earlier in this chapter, we described Richard Lazarus' (1993) view that cognitive appraisal—interpreting events as harmful, threatening, or

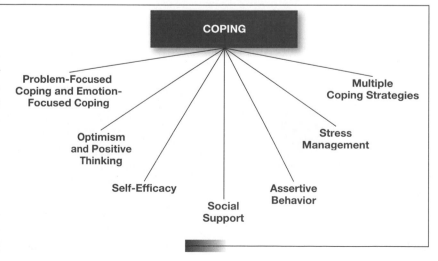

SUMMARY TABLE 15.1
Health Psychology and Stress

Concept	Processes/Related Ideas	Characteristics/Description
Health Psychology	Its Nature	Health psychology is a multidimensional approach to health that emphasizes psychological factors, lifestyle, and the nature of the health-care delivery system. Closely aligned with health psychology is behavioral medicine, which combines medical and behavioral knowledge to craft ways to reduce illness and promote health.
Stress	Its Nature	Stress is the way we respond to circumstances that threaten us and tax our coping abilities. Biological, personality, cognitive, environmental, and sociocultural factors are all involved in stress.
	Biological Factors	Selye proposed the general adaptation syndrome, which consists of three stages: alarm, resistance, and exhaustion. Not all stress is bad stress. Selye calls good stress "eustress." Many scientists now agree that there are two main biological pathways in stress: the neuroendocrine-immune pathway, and the sympathetic nervous system pathway. Currently there is considerable interest in links between stress and the immune system. The term *psychoneuroimmunology* refers to the field that explores connections among psychological factors, the nervous system, and the immune system.
	Personality Factors	Personality factors involved in stress include Type A/Type B behavioral patterns and hardiness. The Type A behavioral pattern includes a cluster of characteristics—such as being hostile, excessively competitive, impatient, and hard driven—that are said to be related to cardiovascular disease. Type B behavioral pattern involves being relaxed and easygoing. The dimension of the Type A cluster that is most consistently related to heart disease is hostility. Hardiness, which involves a sense of commitment, control, and perceptions of problems as challenges rather than threats, is a stress buffer and is related to reduced illness.
	Cognitive Factors	Lazarus believes that stress depends on how people cognitively appraise and interpret events. Cognitive appraisal involves two steps: primary appraisal (Is the stressful event harmful, threatening, or challenging?) and secondary appraisal (What resources do I have available to cope with the stressful event?).
	Environmental Factors	Environmental factors involved in stress include overload, conflict, frustration, and life events and daily hassles. Three types of conflict are approach/approach, avoidance/avoidance, and approach/avoidance. Frustration occurs when we cannot reach a goal.
	Sociocultural Factors	Sociocultural factors in stress include acculturative stress and poverty.

Coping Strategies

challenging, and determining whether one has the resources to cope effectively with the event—is critical to coping. Remember that Lazarus believes that events are appraised in two stages—primary appraisal (when individuals interpret whether an event involves harm or loss that has already occurred, a threat of some future danger, or a challenge to be overcome) and secondary appraisal (evaluation of one's resources and determining how effectively they can be used to cope with the stressful event).

Lazarus also believes that two general types of coping efforts can be distinguished. **Problem-focused coping** *is Lazarus' term for the cognitive strategy of squarely facing one's troubles and trying to solve them.* For example, if you are having trouble with a class, you might go to the study skills center at your university and enter a training program to learn how to study more effectively. You have faced your problem and attempted to do something about it. **Emotion-focused coping** *is Lazarus' term for responding to stress in an emotional manner, especially using defensive appraisal.* Norman Endler of York University and James Parker of Trent University developed the Coping Inventory for Stressful Situations, which measures both problem- and emotion-focused coping as well as a third coping style, avoidance coping (Endler & Parker, 1993).

Emotion-focused and avoidance coping involve defense mechanisms. In emotion-focused coping we might rationalize what has happened to us, joke about it, or say it doesn't matter. In avoidance coping we might deny what happened, distract ourselves with other people, or avoid going to the class. In one study, depressed individuals used these coping strategies to avoid facing problems more than individuals who were not depressed (Ebata & Moos, 1989).

Sometimes emotion-focused or avoidance coping is adaptive. Denial is one of the main protective mechanisms enabling people to cope with the flood of feelings that occur when the reality of death or dying becomes too great. At other times, emotion-focused or avoidance coping is maladaptive (Zeidner & Saklofske, 1996). Denying that the person you were dating doesn't love you any more when that person is engaged to someone else is not adaptive. Denial can be used to avoid the destructive impact of shock, however, by postponing the time when you have to deal with stress. Over the long term, though, we want to use problem-focused more than emotion-focused or avoidance coping. Many individuals use more than one coping style at a time. Folkman & Lazarus (1980) found that individuals said they used both problem-focused and emotion-focused coping strategies in 98 percent of the stressful encounters they faced.

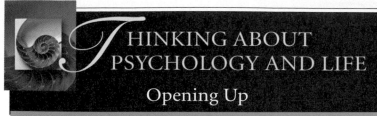

THINKING ABOUT PSYCHOLOGY AND LIFE
Opening Up

JAMES PENNEBAKER (1990) found that university students who wrote in a journal about their stressful experiences coped more effectively and were healthier the day after their writing ended (as well as six weeks later). The individuals who benefited the most by writing about their stressful experiences were the ones who had been the most inhibited in talking about their problems. Pennebaker believes that many people tend to suppress problems and that we can cope more effectively with them not only by talking with others about them but also by writing about them. In the course of writing about our stressful experiences, we tend to get them out in the open and think about ways to cope with them.

To do what the students in Pennebaker's study did, write for 20 minutes a day for four consecutive days about your deepest thoughts and feelings concerning the most stressful aspects of your life. If what you write about becomes very troubling to you, talk further about the stress with someone you can confide in or contact the counseling services at your university.

Optimism and Positive Thinking

Thinking positively and avoiding negative thoughts is generally a good coping strategy when trying to handle stress more effectively. A positive mood improves our ability to process information more efficiently, makes us more altruistic, and gives us higher self-esteem. In most cases, an optimistic attitude is superior to a pessimistic one. It gives us a sense that we are controlling our environment, much like what Bandura talks about when he describes the importance of self-efficacy in coping. For example, sports psychologist Jim Loehr (1989) pieced together videotaped segments of 17-year-old Michael Chang's most outstanding tennis points in the past year. Chang periodically watched the videotape—he always saw himself winning, he never saw himself make mistakes, and he always saw himself in a positive mood. Several months later Chang became the youngest male ever to win the French Open tennis championship.

Optimism

Cognitive Restructuring and Positive Self-Talk   Many cognitive therapists believe the process of **cognitive restructuring**—*modifying the thoughts, ideas, and beliefs that maintain an individual's problems*—can be used to get people to think more positively and optimistically. **Self-talk** (also called **self-statements**)—*the soundless mental speech we use when we think about something, plan, or solve problems*—is often very helpful in cognitive restructuring. Positive self-talk can do a lot to give you the confidence that frees you to use your talents to the fullest. Because self-talk has a way of becoming a self-fulfilling prophecy, uncountered negative thinking can spell trouble. That's why it's so important to monitor your self-talk.

Several strategies can help you to monitor your self-talk. First, at random times during the day, ask yourself, "What am I saying to myself right now?" Then, if you can, write down your thoughts along with a few notes about the situation you are in

Rod Martin, *University of Western Ontario*

"I am interested in the relationship between psychosocial stress and health, and in personality variables that moderate this relationship. Sense of humour is of interest as a personality variable that has a potentially stress-buffering effect."

and how you're feeling. Your goal is to fine-tune your self-talk to make it as accurate as possible. Before you begin, it is important to record your self-talk without any censorship.

You can also use uncomfortable emotions or moods—such as stress, depression, and anxiety—as cues for listening to your self-talk. When this happens, identify the feeling as accurately as possible. Then ask yourself, "What was I saying to myself right before I started feeling this way?" or "What have I been saying to myself since I've been feeling this way?"

Situations that you anticipate might be difficult for you are also excellent times to access your self-talk. Write down a description of the coming event. Then ask yourself, "What am I saying to myself about this event?" If your thoughts are negative, think how you can use your strengths to turn these disruptive feelings into more positive ones and help turn a potentially difficult experience into a success.

It is also useful to compare your self-talk predictions (what you thought would or should happen in a given situation) with what actually took place. If the reality conflicts with your predictions—as it often does when your self-talk is in error—pinpoint where your self-talk needs adjustment to fit reality.

You are likely to have a subjective view of your own thoughts. So it is helpful to enlist the assistance of a sympathetic but objective friend, partner, or therapist who is willing to listen, discuss your self-assessment with you, and help you to identify ways your self-talk is distorted and might be improved. Some examples of how positive self-statements can be used to replace negative self-statements in coping with various stressful situations is presented in figure 15.7.

Positive Self-Illusion   For a number of years, mental health professionals believed that seeing reality as accurately as possible was the best path to health. Recently though, researchers have found increasing evidence that maintaining some positive illusions about oneself and the world is healthy. Happy people often have falsely high opinions of themselves, give self-serving explanations for events, and have exaggerated beliefs about their ability to control the world around them (Taylor, 1988; Taylor & Brown, 1994).

Illusions, whether positive or negative, are related to one's sense of self-esteem. Having too grandiose an idea of yourself or thinking too negatively about yourself both have negative consequences. Instead, the ideal overall orientation may be to have mildly-inflated illusions or a reality orientation (Baumeister, 1989) (see Figure 15.8).

A negative outlook can increase our chances of getting angry, feeling guilty, and magnifying our mistakes. And for some people, seeing things too accurately can lead to depression. Seeing one's suffering as meaningless and random does not help a person cope and move forward, even if the suffering is random and meaningless. An absence of illusions may also thwart individuals from undertaking the risky and ambitious projects that may yield the greatest rewards (Baumeister, 1993). In some cases, though, a strategy of defensive pessimism may actually work best in handling stress. By imagining negative outcomes, people can prepare for stressful circumstances (Norem & Cantor, 1986; Showers, 1986). The honors student who is worried that she will flunk the next test may not be paralyzed but instead may be motivated to do everything necessary to ensure that things go smoothly.

Among other qualities, people with more positive outlooks often have a good sense of humor. Rod Martin and his colleagues at The University of Western Ontario have extensively investigated the impact of humor on self-concept and well-being (Martin & others, 1993). They found that a greater level of humor in a person is associated with a more positive self-concept, more positivity in the face of stress (see also Martin, 1996), and greater positive affect in response to both positive and negative life events (see also Kuiper & Martin, 1998).

Situation	Negative self-statement	Positive self-statement
Having a long, difficult assignment due the next day	"I'll never get this work done by tomorrow."	"If I work real hard I may be able to get it all done for tomorrow." "This is going to be tough but it is still possible to do it." "Finishing this assignment for tomorrow will be a real challenge." "If I don't get it finished, I'll just have to ask the teacher for an extension."
Losing one's job	"I'll never get another job."	"I'll just have to look harder for another job." "There will be rough times ahead, but I've dealt with rough times before." "Hey, maybe my next job will be a better deal altogether." "There are agencies that can probably help me get some kind of job."
Moving away from friends and family	"My whole life is left behind."	"I'll miss everyone, but it doesn't mean we can't stay in touch." "Just think of all the new people I'm going to meet." "I guess it will be kind of exciting moving to a new home." "Now I'll have two places to call home."
Breaking up with a person you love	"I have nothing to live for. He/she was all I had."	"I really thought our relationship would work, but it's not the end of the world." "Maybe we can try again in the future." "I'll just have to try to keep myself busy and not let it bother me." "If I met him (her), there is no reason why I won't meet someone else someday."
Not getting into graduate school	"I guess I'm really dumb. I don't know what I'll do."	"I'll just have to reapply next year." "There are things I can do with my life other than going to grad school." "I guess a lot of good students get turned down. It's just so unbelievably competitive." "Perhaps there are a few other programs that I could apply to."
Having to participate in a class discussion	"Everyone else knows more than I do, so what's the use of saying anything."	"I have as much to say as anyone else in the class." "My ideas may be different, but they're still valid." "It's OK to be a bit nervous; I'll relax as I start talking." "I might as well say something; how bad could it sound?"

Figure 15.7
Replacing Negative Self-Statements with Positive Ones

Developing an Optimistic Outlook Although some individuals at times use a strategy of defensive pessimism to improve their ability to cope with stress, overall a positive feeling of optimism is the best strategy.

How can you develop a more optimistic outlook? As mentioned in the previous section, developing your sense of humor may help (Lefcourt & Thomas, 1998). Martin Seligman (1990) believes the best tools for overcoming chronic pessimism lie in cognitive therapy, which we discussed in Chapter 14. Cognitive therapy involves emphasizing positive thinking to challenge self-defeating attitudes in an optimistic style that limits self-blame and negative generalizations.

An optimistic outlook might also help individuals resist disease, as evidenced in a series of studies conducted by Christopher Peterson and his colleagues (Peterson & Seligman, 1984; Peterson, Seligman, & Vaillant, 1986). For example, university students were given the Attributional Style Questionnaire, which evaluates an individual's optimistic and pessimistic tendencies. Then their health was monitored over the next year. The pessimists had twice as many infections and doctor's visits as the optimists. Also, in one recent study, optimistic individuals had lower blood pressure than pessimistic individuals (Räikkönen & others, 1999). To read further about the benefits of optimism, see Explorations in Psychology.

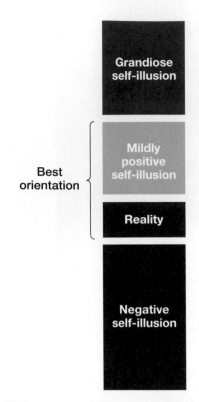

𝒻igure 15.8
Reality and Self-Illusion

Individuals often have self-illusions that are slightly above average. Having too grandiose an opinion of yourself or thinking negatively about yourself can have negative consequences. For some individuals, seeing things too accurately can be depressing. Overall, in most contexts, a reality orientation or a mildly inflated self-illusion might be most effective.

Self-Efficacy

Self-Efficacy

Self-efficacy—*the belief that one can master a situation and produce positive outcomes*—can be an effective strategy in coping with stress and challenging circumstances. Albert Bandura (1997, 1998) and others have shown that people's self-efficacy affects their behavior in a variety of circumstances, ranging from solving personal problems to going on diets. Self-efficacy influences whether people even try to develop healthy habits, how much effort they expend in coping with stress, how long they persist in the face of obstacles, and how much stress they experience (Allison, Dwyer, & Makin, 1999; Clark & Dodge, 1999).

Researchers have found that self-efficacy can improve individuals' ability to cope and be mentally healthy (Bandura, 1997, 1998). In one study, clients' self-efficacy was strongly linked to their motivation to come to psychotherapy sessions and overcome setbacks in the course of psychotherapy (Longo, Lent, & Brown, 1992). In another study, researchers examined a number of cognitive therapy techniques to determine their link to therapy outcomes (Kavanaugh & Wilson, 1989). Perceived self-efficacy to control dejecting thoughts emerged as the best predictor of positive cognitive therapy outcomes.

Let's examine how self-efficacy might work in several other domains of coping. Overweight individuals will likely have more success with their diets if they believe they have the self-control to restrict their eating. Smokers who believe they will not be able to break their habit probably won't try to quit smoking, even though they know that smoking is likely to cause poor health and shorten their life.

How can you increase your self-efficacy beliefs? The following steps can help (Watson & Tharp, 1989). First, select something you expect to be able to do, not something you expect to fail at. As you develop a stronger sense of self-efficacy, you can tackle projects that you previously might not have thought possible. Second, distinguish between your past performance and your present project. You might have learned from past failures that you cannot do certain things. However, remind yourself that past failures are just that, in the past, and that you now have a new sense of confidence and accomplishment. Third, keep good records so you can be concretely aware of your successes. A person who sticks to a study schedule for four days and then fails to adhere to the schedule on the fifth day should not think, "I'm a failure. I can't do it." This statement ignores the student's 80 percent success rate of keeping to schedule on four of five days. Fourth, pay close attention to your successes. Some individuals have a tendency to remember their failures but not their successes. Fifth, make a list of the specific kinds of situations in which you expect to have the most difficulty and the least difficulty. Then, begin with the easier tasks and cope with the harder ones after you have experienced success and improved your coping skills.

Social Support

Our crowded, polluted, noisy, and achievement-oriented world can make us feel overwhelmed and isolated. Now more than ever, we may need support systems such as family members, friends, and co-workers to buffer stress. **Social support** *is information and feedback from others that one is loved and cared for, esteemed and valued, and included in a network of communication and mutual obligation.*

The benefits of social support can be grouped into three categories: tangible assistance, information, and emotional support (Taylor, 1999). Family and friends can provide *tangible assistance* by giving individuals actual goods and services in stressful circumstances. For example, gifts of food are often given after a death in the family occurs, meaning that bereaved family members won't have to cook for themselves and for visiting relatives at a time when their energy and motivation is low. Individuals who provide support can also give *information* by recommending specific actions and plans to help the person under stress cope more effectively. Friends may notice that a co-worker is overloaded with work and suggest ways for him or her to manage time more efficiently or delegate tasks more effectively. In stressful situations, individuals often suffer emotionally and may develop depression, anxiety, and loss of

EXPLORATIONS IN PSYCHOLOGY
Using Optimistic Thinking to Go from
Sausage Stuffer to Supersalesman

FORTY-FIVE YEAR OLD Bob Dell had a wife, two children, and a mortgage. After working 25 years in a meat-packing plant, he suddenly was fired from his job and had no immediate job prospects. With only a high school education, his situation looked grim. However, he was approached by an insurance agent who wanted to sell him a policy. He informed the agent that he was unemployed and could not afford anything. The agent told Bob that his insurance company currently was hiring new sales representatives and suggested that he apply for a position. Bob had never sold anything but being an optimist he decided to give it a try.

Psychologist Martin Seligman, a consultant for the in-surance company, had persuaded the company to hire salespeople who did not meet all of the qualifications but were high in optimism. Dell was one of 130 applicants identified as "optimists" on a measure Seligman had developed, which was included in the measures that job applicants had to complete.

In less that a year, Bob went from sausage-stuffer to supersalesman, earning twice what he had made at the meat-packing plant. When he learned from a magazine article about the experimental program that he had participated in, with characteristic optimism he called Martin Seligman, introduced himself, and sold him a retirement policy!

self-esteem. Friends and family can provide *emotional support* by reassuring the person under stress that he or she is a valuable individual who is loved by others. Knowing that others care allows a person to approach stress and cope with stress with greater assurance.

Researchers have consistently found that social support helps individuals cope with stress (Rodriquez & Cohen, 1998; Wellman, 1998). For example, in one study depressed persons had fewer and less supportive relationships with family members, friends, and co-workers than people who were not depressed (Billings, Cronkite, & Moos, 1983). In another study, the prognosticators of cancer, mental illness, and suicide included a lack of closeness to one's parents and a negative attitude toward one's family (Thomas, 1983). Widows die at a rate that is three to thirteen times higher than married women for every known cause of death.

Having diverse social ties may be especially important in coping with stress. People who participate in more diverse social networks—for example, have a close relationship with a partner, interact with family members, friends, neighbors, and fellow workers, and belong to social and religious groups—live longer than people with fewer types of social relationships (Berkman & Syme, 1979; Vogt & others, 1992). One recent study investigated the effects of diverse social ties on susceptibility to getting a common cold (Cohen & others, 1997). Individuals reported the extent of their participation in twelve types of social ties like those described earlier. Then they were given nasal drops containing a cold virus and monitored for the appearance of a common cold. Individuals with more diverse social ties were less likely to get a cold than their counterparts with less diverse social networks.

The studies we have cited in our discussion of social support are correlational in nature. Why does that mean we should be cautious about interpreting their meaning?

Assertive Behavior

We have just seen that social ties, especially diverse ones, play important roles in helping people cope more effectively with stress in their lives. Another aspect of social relationships that can affect coping is how we deal with conflict in these relationships. Assertive expression has become a communication ideal. However, not everyone acts assertively, and when they don't it can harm their coping. We can deal with conflict in our lives in four main ways: aggressively, manipulatively, passively, and assertively.

Assertive Behavior

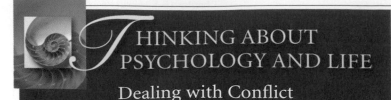

THINK ABOUT the following situations one at a time. Check which response is most typical of the way you would behave in that situation.

	Assertive	Aggressive	Manipulative	Passive
You are being kept on the phone by a salesperson trying to sell you something you don't want.	____	____	____	____
You want to break off a relationship that is no longer working for you.	____	____	____	____
You are sitting in a movie and the people behind you are talking.	____	____	____	____
Your doctor keeps you waiting more than 20 minutes.	____	____	____	____
You are standing in line and someone moves in front of you.	____	____	____	____
Your friend has owed you money for a long time and it is money you could use.	____	____	____	____
You receive food at a restaurant that is over- or undercooked.	____	____	____	____
You want to ask a major favor of your friend, romantic partner, or roommate.	____	____	____	____
Your friends ask you to do something that you don't feel like doing.	____	____	____	____
You are at a large lecture. The instructor is speaking too softly and you know other students are having trouble hearing what is being said.	____	____	____	____
You want to start a conversation at a gathering, but you don't know anyone there.	____	____	____	____
You are sitting next to someone who is smoking, and the smoke bothers you.	____	____	____	____
You are talking to someone about something that is important to you, but they don't seem to be listening.	____	____	____	____
You are speaking and someone interrupts you.	____	____	____	____
You receive an unjust criticism from someone.	____	____	____	____

In most circumstances, being assertive is the best strategy. However, there can be some situations in which a different style of interaction is needed. Look at each of the situations again and determine if the assertive style is always the best strategy and whether there is any circumstance in which the other styles might work best.

Source: Adapted from Bourne, 1995.

That is, when faced with conflict you can blow up, get down and dirty, cave in, or speak up.

- *Acting Aggressively.* People who respond aggressively to conflict run roughshod over others. They are demanding, abrasive, and hostile. Aggressive people are often insensitive to the rights of others.
- *Acting Manipulatively.* Manipulative people try to get what they want by making other people feel sorry for them or feel guilty. They don't take responsibility for meeting their own needs. Instead, manipulative people play the role of the victim or martyr to get others to do things for them. They work indirectly to get their needs met.
- *Acting Passively.* Passive people act in nonassertive, submissive ways. They let others run roughshod over them. Passive people don't express their feelings. They don't let others know what they want or need.
- *Acting Assertively.* Assertive individuals express their feelings, ask for what they want, and say "no" to something they don't want. When individuals act assertively, they act in their own best interests and stand up for their legitimate rights. In the view of assertiveness experts Robert Alberti and Michael Emmons (1995), assertiveness builds equal relationships.

Following are some strategies for becoming more assertive (Bourne, 1995):

Set up a time for discussing what you want to discuss. Talk with the other person to establish a mutually convenient time to talk. This step is omitted when you need to be assertive on the spot.

State the problem in terms of its consequences for you. Outline your point of view clearly. This gives the other person a better sense of your position. Describe the problem as objectively as you can without blaming or judging the other person. For example, you might tell a roommate or family member, "I'm having a problem with the loud music you are playing. I'm studying for a test tomorrow and the music is so loud I can't concentrate."

Express your feelings. Go ahead and express your feelings (openly but noncombatively.) It lets the other person know how important the issue is to you. Suppressing your feelings prolongs the problem.

Make your request. This is an important part of being assertive. Ask for what you want in a straightforward, direct way.

Stress Management

Because many people have difficulty in managing stress themselves, psychologists have developed a variety of stress management programs that can be taught to individuals (Auerbach & Gramling, 1998). We will study the nature of these stress management programs and evaluate some of the techniques that are used in them, such as meditation, relaxation, and biofeedback.

Stress management programs *teach individuals how to appraise stressful events, how to develop skills for coping with stress, and how to put these skills into use in their everyday lives.* Stress management programs are often taught through workshops, which are increasingly offered in the workplace (Taylor, 1999). Aware of the high cost of lost productivity to stress-related disorders, many organizations have become increasingly motivated to help their workers identify and cope with stressful circumstances in their lives. Some stress management programs are broad in scope, teaching a variety of techniques to handle stress; others are more narrow, teaching a specific technique, such as relaxation or assertiveness training.

Some stress management programs are also taught to individuals who are experiencing similar kinds of problems—such as migraine headache sufferers or individuals with chronically high blood pressure. Universities are increasingly developing stress management programs for students. If you are finding the experience of university extremely stressful and are having difficulty coping with taxing circumstances in your life, you might want to consider enrolling in a stress management program at your university or in your community. Let's now examine some of the techniques used in stress management programs.

Meditation and Relaxation At one time, meditation was believed to have more in common with mysticism than science. While meditation has become popular in North America only in recent years, it has been an important part of life in Asia for centuries.

Meditation *is the practice and system of thought that incorporates exercises to attain bodily or mental control and well-being, as well as enlightenment.* The strategies of meditation vary but usually take one of two forms: either cleansing the mind to have new experiences or increasing concentration. **Transcendental meditation** (TM) *is the most popular form of meditation in North America; it is derived from an ancient Indian technique and involves a mantra, which is a resonant sound or phrase that is repeated mentally or aloud to focus attention.* One widely used TM mantra is the phrase *Om mani padme hum.* By concentrating on this phrase, the individual replaces other thoughts with the syllables *Om mani padme hum.* In transcendental meditation the individual learns to associate a mantra with a special meaning, such as beauty, peace, or tranquility. Meditation groups that practice TM or other techniques meet on many campuses.

As a physiological state, meditation shows qualities of both sleep and wakefulness, yet it is distinct from them. It resembles the hypnagogic state, which is the transition from wakefulness to sleep, but at the very least it is the prolongation of that state (Friedman, Myers, & Benson, 1998).

In early research on meditation's effects on the body, oxygen consumption was lowered, heart rate slowed down, blood flow increased in the arms and forehead, and EEG patterns were predominantly of the alpha variety—regular and rhythmic (Wallace & Benson, 1972). Other researchers have found support for the positive physiological changes that result from meditation and believe that meditation is superior to relaxation in reducing body arousal and anxiety (Eppley, Abrams, & Shear, 1989). Yet other researchers acknowledge meditation's positive physiological effects but believe relaxation is just as effective (Holmes, 1988).

Would you like to feel more tranquil and peaceful? If so, you can probably reach that feeling state by following some simple instructions. First, you need to find a quiet place to sit. Get a comfortable chair and sit quietly and upright in it. Let your chin rest comfortably on your chest, your arms in your lap. Close your eyes. Then, pay

THINKING ABOUT PSYCHOLOGY AND LIFE
Coping with Failure

AN UNDERGRADUATE STUDENT whose ambition was to go to medical school and become a doctor received rejection letters from all the medical schools he applied to (Carson, Butcher, & Mineka, 1998). This unexpected result left him feeling very depressed and empty. He felt frustrated about his failure and conflict over what his next steps should be. His family and peers were encouraging him to try again, but his fear of failing was overwhelming. He felt bitter about all of this and began contemplating dropping everything and becoming a beach bum or a blackjack dealer in Las Vegas. At this point in his life, he had no realistic backup plans and little interest in pursuing meaningful alternative careers.

Based on what you read in chapter 14, "Therapies," and in this chapter about coping with stress, what would the student's best course of action be? Is there a particular therapy you think might work best to help him? What aspects of coping with stress do you believe would help him the most?

Stress Management

Meditation has been an important dimension of Asians' lives for centuries.

Biofeedback

attention to your breathing. Every time you inhale and every time you exhale, notice it and pay attention to the sensations of air flowing through your body, the feeling of your lungs filling and emptying. After you have done this for several breaths, begin to repeat silently to yourself a single word every time you breathe out. The word you choose does not have to mean anything. You can make the word up, you could use the word *one,* or you could try a word that is associated with the emotion you want to produce, such as *trust, love, patience,* or *happy.* Try several different words to see which one works for you. At first, you will find that thoughts intrude and you are no longer attending to your breathing. Just return to your breathing and say the word each time you exhale. After you have practiced this exercise for 10 to 15 minutes, twice a day, every day for 2 weeks, you will be ready for a shortened version. If you notice stressful thoughts or circumstances appearing, simply engage in the relaxation response on the spot for several minutes. If you are in public, you don't have to close your eyes, just fix your gaze on some nearby object, attend to your breathing and say your word silently every time you exhale.

Audiotapes that induce the relaxation response are available in most bookstores. They usually include soothing background music along with instructions for how to do the relaxation response. These audiotapes can especially help induce a more relaxed state before you go to bed at night.

Biofeedback   For many years operant conditioning was believed to be the only effective means to deal with voluntary behaviors such as aggression, shyness, and achievement ◀▥ P. 196. Behavior modification helped people to reduce their aggression, to be more assertive and outgoing, and to get better grades, for example. Involuntary behaviors such as blood pressure, muscle tension, and pulse rate were thought to be outside the boundaries of operant conditioning and more appropriate for classical conditioning. Beginning in the 1960s, though, psychologist Neal Miller (1969) and others began to demonstrate that people can control internal behaviors. **Biofeedback** *is the process in which individuals' muscular or visceral activities are monitored by instruments, and information from the instruments is given (fed back) to the individuals so they can learn to voluntarily control their physiological activities.*

How does biofeedback work? Let's consider the problem of reducing an individual's muscle tension. The individual's muscle tension is monitored and the level of tension is fed back to him. Often the feedback is in the form of an audible tone. As muscle tension rises, the tone becomes louder; as it drops, the tone becomes softer. The reinforcement in biofeedback is the raising and lowering of the tone (or in some cases, seeing a dot move up or down on a television screen) as the individual learns to control muscle tension (Labbe, 1998).

Researchers have found that biofeedback can help people reduce the intensity of migraine headaches and chronic pain (Qualls & Sheehan, 1981). But is biofeedback more effective than less expensive, simpler methods of relaxation? This issue has not been completely resolved, but several large-scale studies have found no distinct advantage of biofeedback over meditation and relaxation techniques (Labbe, 1998). Indeed, relaxation is believed to be a key aspect of how biofeedback works.

Multiple Coping Strategies

An important idea to keep in mind when coping with stress is that multiple strategies often work better than a single strategy alone. As we have already seen, individuals who face stressful

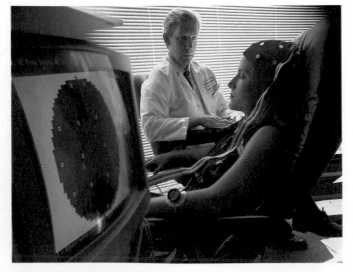

In biofeedback, instruments monitor physiological activities and give individuals information about them so they can learn to voluntarily control the activities.

circumstances have many different strategies to choose from. For example, people who have experienced a stressful life event or a cluster of life events (such as the death of a parent, a divorce, and a significant reduction in income) might adopt the following multiple-strategy plan for coping:

- Engage in problem-focused coping
- Use positive self-talk
- Seek social support
- Practice relaxation

In addition, the individual might also engage in a regular exercise program. As you will soon see in our discussion of promoting health, exercise not only has substantial physical health benefits, but mental health ones as well.

At this point we have discussed a number of ideas about coping. An overview of these ideas is presented in summary table 15.2.

Promoting Health

We can do a great deal to promote better health by establishing healthy habits and evaluating and changing our behaviors that interfere with good health. Regular exercise and good nutrition are essential ingredients to a healthier lifestyle. Not overeating and not smoking are important in improving the quality of a person's health, as is sound sexual decision-making.

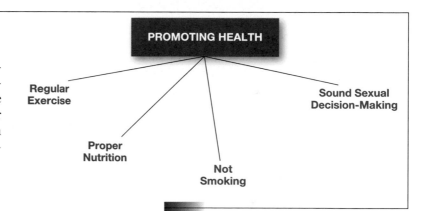

Regular Exercise

Exercise

Canadians have recently begun to recognize that they need to get more exercise. In the 1996-97 National Population Health Survey, almost half of all Canadians had changed some health-related behavior, such as exercise, in the previous year (Health Canada, 1999). Without question, people are jogging, cycling, and acrobically exercising more today than in the past, but far too many of us are still couch potatoes. **Aerobic exercise** *is sustained exercise—jogging, swimming, or cycling, for example—that stimulates heart and lung activity.*

The main focus of exercise's effects on health has involved preventing heart disease. Most health experts recommend that you should try to raise your heart rate to 60 percent of your maximum heart rate. Your maximum heart rate is calculated as 220 minus your age multiplied by 0.6, so if you are 20, you should aim for an exercise heart rate of 120 (220 − 20 = 200 × 0.6 = 120). If you are 45, you should aim for an exercise heart rate of 105 (220 − 45 = 175 × 0.6 = 105).

People in some occupations get more vigorous exercise than those in others. For example, longshoremen have about half the risk of fatal heart attacks as co-workers like crane drivers and clerks who have physically less demanding jobs. Further, elaborate studies of 17,000 male alumni of Harvard University found that those who exercised strenuously on a regular basis had a lower risk of heart disease and were more likely to still be alive in their middle adulthood years than their more sedentary counterparts (Lee, Hsieh, & Paffenbarger, 1995; Paffenbarger & others, 1986). Based on such findings, some health experts conclude that, regardless of other risk factors (smoking, high blood pressure, being overweight, heredity), if you exercise enough to burn more than 2,000 calories a week, you can cut your risk of heart attack by an impressive two-thirds (Sherwood, Light, & Blumenthal, 1989). Burning up 2,000 calories a week through exercise requires a lot of effort, far more than most of us are willing to expend. To burn 300 calories a day, through exercise, you would have to do one of the following: swim or run for about 25 minutes, walk for 45 minutes at about 4 miles an hour, or participate in aerobic dancing for 30 minutes.

SUMMARY TABLE 15.2
Coping

Concept	Processes/ Related Ideas	Characteristics/Description
What Is Coping?	Its Nature	Coping involves managing taxing circumstances, expending effort to solve life's problems, and seeking to master or reduce stress. A stressful circumstance can be rendered considerably less stressful by successfully coping with it.
	Problem-Focused Coping and Emotion-Focused Coping	Lazarus distinguished between problem-focused coping, which involves squarely facing one's troubles and trying to solve them, and emotion-focused coping, which consists of responding to stress in an emotional manner, especially using defensive appraisal. Endler & Parker also studied avoidance coping. Problem-focused coping is usually the better coping strategy.
	Optimism and Positive Thinking	Many cognitive therapists believe cognitive restructuring can be used to get people to think more positively and optimistically. Positive self-talk is often helpful in cognitive restructuring. Individuals' coping often benefits from mildly positive self-illusion, although some people cope best by facing reality. Grandiose self-illusion and negative self-illusion are generally not good coping strategies, although some successful individuals use a defensive pessimism strategy to motivate themselves. An optimistic outlook can help people resist disease. Humor is also very important.
	Self-Efficacy	Self-efficacy is the belief that one can master a situation and produce positive outcomes. Bandura has shown that self-efficacy is an effective strategy in many domains of coping.
	Social Support	Social support is information and feedback from others that one is loved and cared for, esteemed and valued, and included in a network of communication and mutual obligation. Three important benefits of social support are tangible assistance, information, and emotional support. Researchers have consistently shown that social support, especially diverse social ties, helps people cope with stress and live healthier lives.
	Assertive Behavior	Four ways individuals can deal with conflict are assertively, manipulatively, passively, or assertively. Assertive expression has become the communication ideal.
	Stress Management	Stress management programs teach people how to appraise stressful events, develop skills for coping with stress, and put these skills into use in their everyday lives. These programs are often taught through workshops. Meditation, relaxation, and biofeedback are among the techniques used in these workshops. Meditation is a system of thought that incorporates exercises to attain bodily or mental control and well-being, as well as enlightenment. Transcendental meditation is the most popular form of meditation in the United States. Researchers have found that meditation reduces bodily arousal and anxiety, but whether it is more effective than relaxation is debated. The "relaxation response" can be especially helpful in reducing arousal and calming a person. Biofeedback has been successful in reducing muscle tension and blood pressure.
	Multiple Coping Strategies	Multiple coping strategies often work better than a single coping strategy.

Many experts recommend that adults engage in 30 minutes or more of moderate-intensity physical activity on most, preferably all, days of the week. However, only about one-fifth of adults are active at these recommended levels of physical activity. Examples of the physical activities that qualify as moderate or vigorous are listed in figure 15.9.

Researchers have found that exercise benefits not only physical health, but mental health as well (Leith, 1998). In particular, exercise improves self-concept and reduces anxiety and depression. In one study, 109 nonexercising volunteers were randomly assigned to one of four conditions: high-intensity aerobic training, moderate-intensity aerobic training, low-intensity nonaerobic training, and waiting list (Moses & others, 1989). In the high-intensity aerobic group, participants engaged in a continuous walk-jog program that elevated their heart rate to between 70 and 75 percent of maximum. In the moderate-intensity aerobic group, participants engaged in walking or jogging that elevated their heart rate to 60

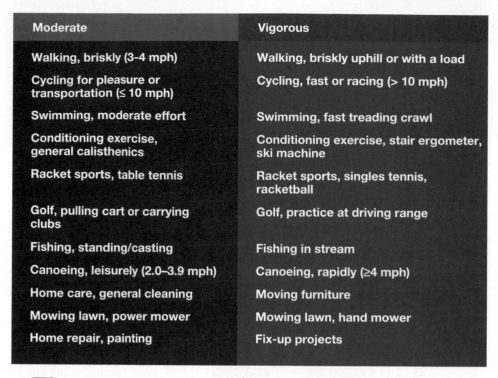

Moderate	Vigorous
Walking, briskly (3-4 mph)	Walking, briskly uphill or with a load
Cycling for pleasure or transportation (≤ 10 mph)	Cycling, fast or racing (> 10 mph)
Swimming, moderate effort	Swimming, fast treading crawl
Conditioning exercise, general calisthenics	Conditioning exercise, stair ergometer, ski machine
Racket sports, table tennis	Racket sports, singles tennis, racketball
Golf, pulling cart or carrying clubs	Golf, practice at driving range
Fishing, standing/casting	Fishing in stream
Canoeing, leisurely (2.0–3.9 mph)	Canoeing, rapidly (≥4 mph)
Home care, general cleaning	Moving furniture
Mowing lawn, power mower	Mowing lawn, hand mower
Home repair, painting	Fix-up projects

$\mathcal{F}$igure 15.9
Moderate and Vigorous Physical Activities

percent of maximum. In the low-intensity nonaerobic group, participants engaged in strength, mobility, and flexibility exercises in a slow, discontinuous manner for approximately 30 minutes. Those who were assigned to exercise programs worked out three to five times a week. Those who were on the waiting list did not exercise. The programs lasted for 10 weeks. As expected, the group assigned to the high-intensity aerobic program showed the greatest aerobic fitness on a 12-minute walk-run. Fitness also improved for those assigned to moderate- and low-exercise programs. However, only the people assigned to the moderate-intensity aerobic training programs showed psychological benefits. These benefits appeared immediately in the form of reduced tension and anxiety, and, after three months, in the form of improved ability to cope with stress.

Why were the psychological benefits superior in the moderate-intensity aerobic condition? Perhaps the participants in the high-intensity program found the training too demanding, not so surprising since these individuals were nonexercisers prior to the study. The superiority of the moderate-intensity aerobic training program over the nonaerobic low-intensity exercise program suggests that a minimum level of aerobic conditioning may be required to obtain important psychological benefits.

Research on the benefits of exercise suggests that both moderate and intense activities produce important physical and psychological gains (Thayer & others, 1996). Some people enjoy rigorous, intense exercise. Others enjoy more moderate exercise routines. The enjoyment and pleasure we derive from exercise added to its aerobic benefits make exercise one of life's most important activities.

Proper Nutrition

In chapter 11, "Motivation and Emotion," we discussed many aspects of eating and weight. We concluded that obesity is a serious and pervasive health problem, with about one-third of the North American population overweight enough to be at increased health risk. We now fill up on empty calories instead of the vitamin-packed natural fruits our ancient ancestors once relied on. We also concluded that most diets

Nutrition

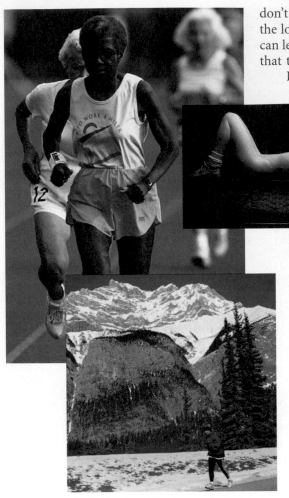

Moderate or intense exercise benefits physical and mental health.

Smoking/Tobacco Control
Smoking and Cancer

don't work, although some people do lose weight when they diet and do maintain the loss. Many women face a special challenge in our culture. The pressure to be thin can lead to harmful effects for people who are not overweight. Researchers have found that the most effective component of weight loss programs is regular exercise.

Despite the growing variety of choices North Americans can make in the grocery store, many of us are unhealthy eaters. We take in too much sugar and not enough foods that are high in vitamins, minerals, and fiber. We eat too much fast food and too few well-balanced meals. These choices increase our fat and cholesterol intake, both of which are implicated in long-term health concerns.

Evidence for the negative effects of poor nutritional choices comes from both animal and cross-cultural research. For example, mice fed a high-fat diet are more likely to develop breast cancer than mice fed on a low-fat diet. And a cross-cultural study of women found a strong positive correlation between fat consumption and death rates from breast cancer (Cohen, 1987) (see figure 15.10).

One telling comparison linking fat intake and cancer is between Canada, the United States and Japan. These three countries have similar levels of industrialization and education, as well as high medical standards. Although the overall cancer rates of the three countries are similar, cancers of the breast, colon, and prostate are common in Canada and the United States but rare in Japan. Within two generations, descendants of Japanese immigrants to Hawaii, California and British Columbia have developed breast cancer rates that are significantly higher than those in Japan and that approach those of North Americans. Many researchers believe that the high fat intake of North Americans and the low fat intake of the Japanese are implicated in the countries' different cancer rates.

Canadian nutritional standards have changed over time, and this has added to our confusion about which foods we should eat. Only a few decades ago, eggs and dairy foods were promoted as virtually ideal food sources. Now we know that some dairy products, such as whole milk, eggs, and butter should generally be avoided and replaced with low-fat substitutes. Today, nutritionists believe that proper nutrition involves more than merely taking in an appropriate number of calories. It involves carefully selecting foods that provide appropriate nutrients with their calories. A sound nutritional plan provides the right amounts of the nutrients we need—fat, carbohydrates, proteins, vitamins, minerals, and water.

Several health goals can be accomplished through a sound nutritional plan. Not only does a well-balanced diet provide more energy; it can also lower blood pressure and lessen our risk of cancer and even tooth decay.

Not Smoking

Shifts toward promoting health are most obvious in the area of smoking prevention. Governments in Canada and the United States have developed public anti-smoking campaigns and even undertaken massive litigation against tobacco companies. Tobacco companies are finally accepting some responsibility and are negotiating to limit their liability for health-related damages.

Converging evidence from a number of studies underscores the dangers of smoking or being around those who do (Millis, 1998). Smoking is linked to 30 percent of cancer deaths, 21 percent of heart disease deaths, and 82 percent of chronic pulmonary disease deaths. In Canada it has been estimated that smoking leads to nearly one in five deaths—more than deaths from suicide, vehicle crashes, AIDS and murder combined (Statistics Canada, 1999). Secondhand smoke is implicated in as many as 9,000 lung cancer deaths a year in the United States (Sandler & others, 1989). Children of smokers are at special risk for respiratory and middle-ear diseases.

Fewer people smoke today than in the past, and almost half of all living adults who ever smoked have quit. The prevalence of smoking in men has dropped from

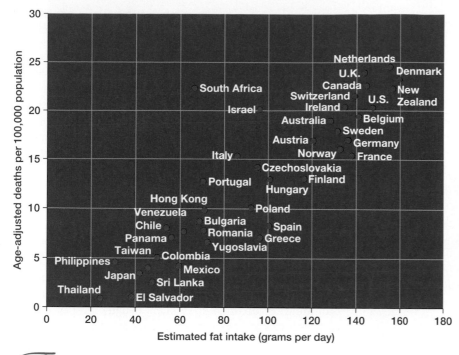

$\mathcal{F}$igure 15.10
Cross-Cultural Comparisons of Diet and Breast Cancer Rates

In countries in which individuals have a low daily intake of fat, the rate of breast cancer is low (in Thailand, for example). In countries in which individuals have a high daily intake of fat, the rate of breast cancer is high (the Netherlands, for example).

over 50 percent in 1965 to about 25 percent today. However, more than 7 million Canadians and 50 million Americans still smoke cigarettes today. And recently cigar smoking, with risks similar to those of cigarette smoking, has increased.

Strategies for Quitting Smoking   Most adult smokers would like to quit, but their addiction to nicotine often turns their efforts into dismal failure. Nicotine, the active drug in cigarettes, is a stimulant that increases the smoker's energy and alertness, a pleasurable and reinforcing experience (Payne & others, 1996; Seidman, Rosecan, & Role, 1999). Nicotine also stimulates neurotransmitters that have a calming or pain-reducing effect. However, smoking not only works as a positive reinforcer, it also works as a negative reinforcer by ending a smoker's painful craving for nicotine. A smoker gets relief from this painful aversive state simply by smoking another cigarette. The immediate gratification of smoking is extremely hard to overcome even for adults who recognize that smoking is "suicide in slow motion."

How can smokers quit? Four methods can be effective in helping smokers abandon their habit: nicotine substitution, stimulus control, aversive conditioning, and going "cold turkey."

Nicotine Substitutes   Nicotine gum and the nicotine patch work on the principle of supplying small amounts of nicotine to diminish the intensity of withdrawal (Eissenberg, Stitzer, & Henningfield, 1999). Nicotine gum, now available without a prescription, is a drug that smokers can take orally when they get the urge to smoke. The nicotine patch is a nonprescription adhesive pad that delivers a steady dose of nicotine to the individual. The dose is gradually reduced over an 8- to 12-week period. Success rates for the nicotine patch have been encouraging.

Stimulus Control   This behavior modification technique sensitizes the smoker to social cues associated with smoking ◀▥ P. 203. For example, the individual might associate a morning cup of coffee or a social drink with smoking. Stimulus control

Smoking Cessation

THINKING ABOUT PSYCHOLOGY AND LIFE

Sexual Myths and Realities

READ EACH of the following statements and check whether you think it is true or false:

	True	False
1. There is a right way and a wrong way to have sexual intercourse.		
2. It is important for couples to have simultaneous orgasms.		
3. Individuals should not have sexual intercourse at any time during pregnancy.		
4. Once individuals are sterilized, their interest in sex diminishes.		
5. You can tell the size of a man's penis by the size of his hands and feet.		
6. If you contract a sexually transmitted disease and treat it effectively, you can't get it again.		
7. You can tell immediately if you have a sexually transmitted disease.		
8. Gonorrhea, syphilis, and AIDS can be contracted from toilet seats.		
9. Masturbation can cause mental disorders.		
10. Females rarely masturbate.		
11. Only homosexual males and intravenous drug abusers are at risk for contracting AIDS.		
12. Most sexual dysfunctions are due to physical problems.		

Most people mark one or more of the above items true. However, according to experts on human sexuality, all of the above statements are myths (Crooks & Bauer, 1999; Greenberg, Bruess, & Mullen, 1992). Thus, although sexuality is an integral part of life, many people have misconceptions about it.

Reproductive Health Research

strategies help the smoker to avoid these cues or learn to substitute other behaviors for smoking. This approach has met with mixed results.

Aversive Conditioning   In chapter 14, "Therapies," we discussed the behavioral therapy technique of aversive conditioning, which involves repeated pairings of an undesirable behavior with aversive stimuli to decrease the behavior's rewards ◄▦ P. 492. Imagine smoking as many cigarettes as possible until the ashtray overflows and the smell of stale cigarettes feels like it is permanently embedded in your fingertips. The concept behind aversive conditioning is to smoke until you feel nauseated, with the hope that this feeling will condition you to the point that you won't want to smoke anymore. Sometimes this works, sometimes it doesn't.

Going "Cold Turkey"   Some people have success by simply stopping smoking without making any major changes in their lifestyle. They decide they are going to quit and they do. Lighter smokers usually have more success with this approach than heavier smokers.

Sound Sexual Decision-Making

In chapter 11, "Motivation and Emotion," we discussed heterosexual and homosexual attitudes and behavior ◄▦ P. 384. Here we focus on the importance of making healthy decisions in your sex life. To begin, let's examine how sexually knowledgeable North Americans are.

Sexual Knowledge   According to June Reinisch (1990), director of the Kinsey Institute, the United States is a nation whose citizens know more about how their automobiles function than about how their bodies function sexually. In an assessment of 2,000 adults' sexual knowledge, almost two-thirds did not know that most erection problems begin with physical, not psychological, problems. Fifty percent did not know that oil-based lubricants should not be used with condoms or diaphragms because some can produce holes in them in less than a minute.

One conclusion we can draw is that there is a great deal we do not know. Even more problematic are the unfounded sexual myths we believe. According to Barrett and colleagues (1997), young Canadians get most of their information about sex from television and from their friends. North American adolescents believe a distressing amount of misinformation and myths about sex. In one study, a majority of adolescents believed that pregnancy risk is greatest during menstruation (Zelnick & Kanter, 1977). These examples underscore the need to improve our sexual awareness and knowledge, which can help reduce unwanted pregnancies and promote sexual self-awareness.

Contraception   Most couples in North America want to control whether and when they will conceive a child. For them it is important to have accurate knowledge about contraception.

Inadequate knowledge about contraception and inconsistent use of effective contraceptive methods has resulted in the U.S. having the highest adolescent pregnancy rate in the industrialized world (Colemen, 1995) and Canadian rates rising again (Statistics Canada, 1999). Although the rate of use among teenagers is improving, many still do not use contraception. Moreover, a majority of adolescents do not use contraception during their first sexual intercourse experience (Hofferth, 1990). Seventy percent of females who become sexually active before the age of 15 have unprotected first intercourse; the percentage drops to about 50 percent for those who become active around the age of 18 or 19.

Age also influences the choice of contraceptive method. Older adolescents and young adults are more likely to rely on the pill or diaphragm; younger adolescents are more likely to use a condom or withdrawal (Hofferth, 1990). Even adults in stable relationships sometimes do not use adequate contraception, perhaps feeling that some contraceptives, such as condoms, interrupt the spontaneity of sex, or they might overestimate the effectiveness of some of the unreliable methods.

No method of contraception is best for everyone. When choosing a method of contraception, couples need to consider such factors as their physical and emotional concerns, the method's effectiveness, the nature of their relationship, their values and beliefs, and the method's convenience. Calculations of the effectiveness of a contraceptive method are often based on the failure rates during the first year of use. It is estimated that if no contraceptive method were used, about 90 percent of women would become pregnant in their first year of being (heterosexually) sexually active (Hatcher & others, 1988).

Sexually Transmitted Diseases   Sexually transmitted diseases (STDs) *are diseases that are contracted primarily through sex—intercourse as well as oral-genital and anal-genital sex.* No single STD has had a greater impact on sexual behavior, or created more fear in the last decade, than AIDS. **AIDS** *is a sexually transmitted disease that is caused by the human immunodeficiency virus (HIV), which destroys the body's immune system* ◀▥ P. 519. A person who has contracted HIV is vulnerable to germs that a normal immune system could destroy.

Although 90 percent of Canadian and U.S. AIDS cases continue to occur among homosexual males and intravenous drug users, a disproportionate increase among female sexual partners of bisexual males or intravenous drug users has recently been noted (Statistics Canada, 1999). In 1997, 25 percent of AIDS patients were female (Centers for Disease Control and Prevention, 1998). This increase suggests that the risk of AIDS is increasing among heterosexuals who have multiple sex partners.

Experts say that AIDS can be transmitted only by (Kalichman, 1996):

- sexual contact
- sharing hypodermic needles
- blood transfusion (which in the last few years has been tightly monitored)
- other direct contact of cuts or mucous membranes with blood and sexual fluids

AIDS and HIV
HIV/AIDS Prevention

Remember that it is not who you are, but what you do, that puts you at risk for getting HIV. *Anyone* who is sexually active or uses intravenous drugs is at risk. *No one* is immune (Hynie, 1998). Once an individual is infected, the prognosis is likely illness and death. The only safe behavior is abstinence from sex, which is not perceived as an option by most individuals. Beyond abstinence, there is only safer behavior, such as sexual behavior without exchange of semen, vaginal fluids, or blood, and sexual intercourse with a condom.

Just asking a date about his or her sexual behavior does not guarantee protection from AIDS and other sexually transmitted diseases. For example, in one investigation, 655 university students were asked to answer questions about lying and sexual behavior (Cochran & Mays, 1990). Of the 422 respondents who said they were sexually active, 34 percent of the men and 10 percent of the women said they had lied so their partner would have sex with them. Much higher percentages—47 percent of the men and 60 percent of the women—said they had been lied to by a potential sexual partner. When asked what aspects of their past they would be most likely to lie about, more than 40 percent of the men and women said they would understate the number of their sexual partners. Twenty percent of the men, but only 4 percent of the women, said they would lie about their results from an AIDS blood test.

SUMMARY TABLE 15.3
Promoting Health

Concept	Processes/ Related Ideas	Characteristics/Description
Regular Exercise	Its Nature	Both moderate and intense exercise produce important physical and psychological gains, such as lowered risk of heart disease and reduced anxiety.
Proper Nutrition	Its Nature	Too many people are unhealthy eaters, taking in too much sugar and not eating balanced meals. Healthy food selections can lower blood pressure and lower our risk of cancer and even tooth decay.
Not Smoking	Health Effects	Smoking is linked to 30 percent of cancer deaths, 21 percent of heart disease deaths, and 82 percent of chronic pulmonary disease deaths. Secondhand smoke is implicated in as many as 9,000 lung cancer deaths a year.
	Strategies for Quitting Smoking	These include nicotine substitutes, such as a nicotine patch or nicotine gum, stimulus control, aversive conditioning, and "going cold turkey." These strategies have met with mixed results.
Sound Sexual Decision-Making	Sexual Knowledge	Overall, North Americans are not very knowledgeable about sex.
	Contraception	Inadequate knowledge about contraception, coupled with inconsistent use of effective methods, has resulted in the United States having the highest adolescent pregnancy rate in the industrialized world and rising Canadian rates.
	Sexually Transmitted Diseases	STDs are contracted primarily through sex—intercourse as well as oral-genital and anal-genital sex. AIDS is a sexually transmitted disease that is caused by the human immunodeficiency virus (HIV), which destroys the body's immune system. Some good strategies for protecting against AIDS and other STDs are to (1) know your and your partner's risk status, (2) obtain medical examinations, (3) have protected, not unprotected, sex, and (4) not have sex with multiple partners.

What are some good strategies for protecting against AIDS and other sexually transmitted diseases (Fisher & Fisher, 1992)? They include these:

- *Know Your and Your Partner's Risk Status.* Anyone who has had previous sexual activity with another person might have contracted an STD without being aware of it. Spend time getting to know a prospective partner before you have sex. Use this time to inform the other person of your STD status and inquire about your partner's. Remember that many people lie about their STD status.
- *Obtain Medical Examinations.* Many experts recommend that couples who want to begin a sexual relationship should have a medical checkup to rule out STDs before they engage in sex. If cost is an issue, contact your campus health service or a public health clinic.
- *Have Protected, Not Unprotected, Sex.* When correctly used, latex condoms help to prevent many STDs from being transmitted. Condoms are most effective in preventing gonorrhea, syphilis, chlamydia, and AIDS. They are less effective against the spread of herpes.
- *Don't Have Sex with Multiple Partners.* One of the best predictors of getting an STD is having sex with multiple partners. Having more than one sex partner elevates the likelihood that you will encounter an infected partner.

At this point we have discussed many ideas about promoting health. An overview of those ideas is presented in summary table 15.3. In this chapter we explored how important social relationships are in coping with stress. In the next chapter, "Social Psychology," we will continue our exploration of social relationships.

Overview *Overview*

WE BEGAN THIS CHAPTER by exploring the scope of health psychology. Then we studied stress, including its biological factors, personality factors, cognitive factors, environmental factors, and sociocultural factors. Our coverage of coping focused on problem-focused coping and emotion-focused coping, optimism and positive thinking, self-efficacy, social support, assertive behavior, stress management, and multiple coping strategies. We also read that promoting health involves regular exercise, proper nutrition, not smoking, and sound sexual decision-making.

Don't forget that you can obtain a more detailed overview of the chapter's contents by again studying the three summary tables on pages 528, 538, and 544.

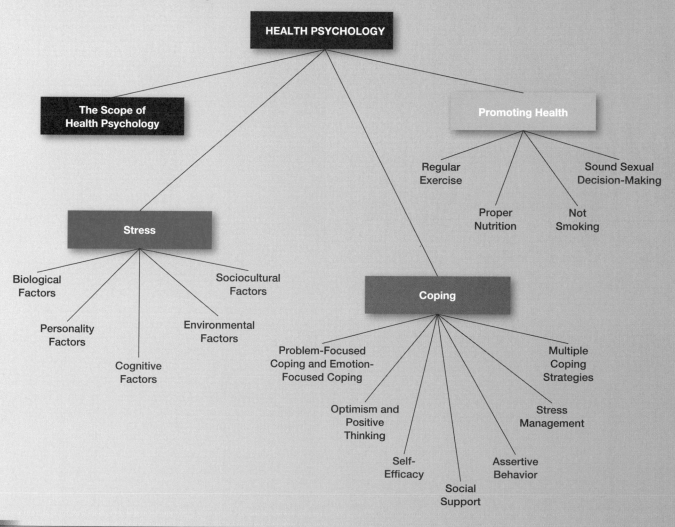

Key Terms

health psychology 516
behavioral medicine 516
stress 518
general adaptation syndrome
  (GAS) 518
eustress 518
psychoneuroimmunology 519
Type A behavior pattern 521
Type B behavior pattern 521
hardiness 522
cognitive appraisal 522

burnout 523
approach/approach conflict
  523
avoidance/avoidance conflict
  523
approach/avoidance conflict
  524
frustration 524
acculturative stress 525
assimilation 526
integration 526

separation 526
marginalization 526
coping 527
problem-focused coping 528
emotion-focused coping 529
cognitive restructuring 529
self-talk (self-statements) 529
self-efficacy 532
social support 532
stress management programs
  535

meditation 535
transcendental meditation
  (TM) 535
biofeedback 536
aerobic exercise 537
sexually transmitted diseases
  (STDs) 543
AIDS 543

Key People

Hans Selye 518
Sheldon Cohen 521
Meyer Friedman and Ray
  Rosenman 521

Richard Lazarus 522
John Berry 526

Norman Endler and James
  Parker 529
Rod Martin 530

Martin Seligman 531
Albert Bandura 532
Neal Miller 536

Psychology Checklist
HEALTH PSYCHOLOGY

How much have you learned since the beginning of the chapter? Use the following statements to help you review your knowledge and understanding of the chapter material. First, read the statement and mentally or briefly on paper demonstrate that you can discuss the relevant information.

_____ I know about the scope of health psychology.
_____ I can define stress.
_____ I can discuss biological factors in stress.
_____ I am aware of personality factors involved in stress.
_____ I can describe cognitive factors in stress.
_____ I know about the environmental and sociocultural factors in stress.
_____ I can define coping.
_____ I know what problem-focused coping is.
_____ I can discuss the roles of optimism, positive thinking, and self-efficacy in coping.

_____ I can evaluate the importance of social support in coping.
_____ I know what assertive behavior is.
_____ I can discuss stress management, as well as the importance of multiple coping strategies.
_____ I can describe the role of exercise in physical and mental health.
_____ I know what proper nutrition is and how it affects health.
_____ I am aware of the health effects of smoking as well as strategies for quitting smoking.
_____ I can discuss sexual knowledge, contraception, and sexually transmitted diseases.

For any items that you did not check off, go back and locate the relevant material in the chapter. Review the material until you feel that you can check off the item. You also may want to use this checklist later in preparing for an exam.

Taking It to the Net

1. University students quickly realize what the effects of stress are. According to psychologists, stress is the response of individuals to the circumstances and events, called stressors, that threaten them and tax their coping abilities. During exam periods, how are you affected? Do you catch a cold or get no sleep? What other side effects accompany stress? Describe some of the ways you can reduce your stress and help others do the same.

2. Some psychologists believe that health is directly related to personality characteristics. In particular, people with Type A behavior pattern are excessively competitive, hard-driven, impatient, and hostile. It seems that there is an association between Type A behavior and coronary risk. In contrast, people with Type B behavioral pattern are relaxed and easygoing. Not surprisingly, these people are thought to be healthier. Using your Internet skills, find five famous people and describe whether they are Type A or Type B personalities. How do you think this has affected their overall health?

3. Nutrition is a clear contributor to both mental and physical health. Unfortunately, many university students do not realize the importance of healthy diets, instead relying on too much fast food and too few well-balanced meals. Researchers now believe that some diets (those high in fat and cholesterol) may be directly linked to cancer and coronary disease. A diet that is too high in carbohydrates has significant effects on the brain. Describe your diet. How is it unhealthy and what can you do to improve it? What effects do you think this will have on your overall health?

Connect to http://www.mcgrawhill.ca/college/santrock to find the answers!

Resources for Psychology and Life

AIDS Foundation of Canada
Suite 1000 - 885 Dunsmuir St.
Vancouver, BC V6C 2T6
604-688-7294
http://www.aidsfoundation.ca
The AIDS Foundation of Canada is committed to working towards the prevention and management of HIV disease in Canada.

Division of STD/HIV Prevention
National Center for Prevention Services
Centers for Disease Control and Prevention
Atlanta, GA 30333
404-639-2564
This organization offers very up-to-date information about preventing sexually transmitted diseases. This division administers a number of government programs for the prevention of STDs and HIV infection.

The Relaxation and Stress Workbook (1995, 4th ed.)
by Martha Davis, Elizabeth Eshelman, and Matthew McKay
Oakland, CA: New Harbinger
This book describes many different exercises to help you learn relaxation techniques and improve your ability to cope with stress.

Exercise Psychology: The Influence of Physical Exercise upon Psychological Processes (1993)
by Peter Seraganian
New York: John Wiley & Sons
This book provides an overall look at the relationship between exercise and psychological well-being.

Your Perfect Right (1995, 7th ed.)
by Robert Alberti and Michael Emmons
San Luis Obispo, CA: Impact

The most widely recommended assertiveness training book. Takes you step by step through ways to improve your self-expression. Many examples and exercises.

Health Psychology (1999, 4th ed.)
by Shelley Taylor
New York: McGraw-Hill
This text, written by a leading researcher, provides a broad, up-to-date look at the field of health psychology.

The Psychology of Women's Health (1995)
by Annette Stanton and Sherly Gallant (eds.)
Washington, DC: American Psychological Association
This book explores the roles of biological, psychological, and social factors that frame conceptions and assessments of women's health. Among the issues discussed are AIDS, smoking, exercise, eating disorders, heart disease, and alcohol use.

Handbook of coping: theory, research, applications (1996)
by Moshe Zeidner and Norman Endler (Eds.)
New York: John Wiley & Sons.
This edited volume gives excellent contemporary coverage of the study of coping.

First Call: BC Child and Youth Advocacy Coalition
L-408 4480 Oak Street
Vancouver, BC V6H 3V4
604-875-3629
http://www.firstcallbc.org/
First Call is a movement for people who believe that children and youth should have "first call" on resources. BC Campaign 2000 information can also be accessed through First Call.

Chapter 16

CHAPTER OUTLINE

SOCIAL THINKING
Attribution
Social Perception
Attitudes
SOCIAL INFLUENCE
Conformity and Obedience
Group Influence
Cultural and Ethnic Influences
SOCIAL INTERACTION AND RELATIONSHIPS
Aggression
Altruism
Attraction, Love, and Relationships

Social Psychology

> "*M*an is a knot, a web, a mesh into which relationships are tied."
>
> Antoine de St. Exupéry,
> *French Novelist, 20th Century*

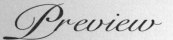

Images of Psychology and Life
The Reverend James Jones' Dark Side

WITH THE NOBLE INTENT of eliminating social injustice and improving interracial harmony, James W. Jones established a small church in Indiana in 1953. His congregation included a number of African Americans. He and his wife adopted seven children, including an African American, a Chinese, and a Korean. As a missionary for two years, Jones lived in Brazil, where he founded an orphanage and a mission. When he returned to the United States he changed the name of his church to the People's Temple Full Gospel.

Jones moved his church to northern California, where he increased his money-making efforts and community work. By the early 1970s, Jones had developed churches in the African American areas of San Francisco and Los Angeles. He was showered with accolades; and his social programs were rated among the best in the country.

But Reverend Jones' dark side began to surface. As he stepped up fund-raising, he at first asked his congregation to make modest donations in the name of universal brotherhood and peace. Eventually he induced people to sell their homes and turn over all their money as a testament to their faith and loyalty. Rumors leaked that physical abuse, death threats, and attempts to gain the guardianship of children were meted out to members who were disobedient or tried to leave Jones' church. Jones was able to deflect public investigations through his tight reign on information and his respectability in the community.

By the early 1970s, Jones increasingly saw parallels between himself and Christ. He portrayed himself as a

The Jonestown massacre, elaborately planned by People's Temple leader James Jones, reveals the macabre side of social thinking and influence.

Preview

IN THE FOURTH CENTURY B.C., the Greek philosopher Aristotle once commented that humans are by nature social animals. The subfield of social psychology studies people's social thinking, influence, and relationships. Social psychology differs from the field of sociology in that social psychology focuses more on the individual as a social being while sociology places more emphasis on society at large. In our coverage of social psychology, these are among some of the questions we will explore:

- How do people think about their social world?
- Do people's attitudes predict their behavior?
- How much do people conform to what others are doing?
- Why do people join groups?
- Why are prejudice, stereotyping, and ethnocentrism so pervasive? How can interethnic relations be improved?
- Why are people aggressive? altruistic?
- What attracts us to others?

Cults

On-line Articles about Cults

Cults and University Campuses

Order of the Solar Temple

Heaven's Gate

messiah and required his congregation to call him "Father." Jones declared that everything he said was law. Jones was a charismatic leader and a master at getting members to conform to his wishes.

In 1977, shortly before an article exposing Jones' megalomania and repressive cruelty appeared in *New West* magazine, Jones' "flock" migrated en masse to Jonestown, Guyana. In Jonestown, the members of the People's Temple were isolated from their families and the world. They had been stripped of their possessions and individuality, and they were utterly obedient.

On November 17, 1978, United States Representative Leo Ryan and four of his aides, who were in Guyana to evaluate charges of abuse in the People's Temple, were gunned down by Jones' henchmen as they boarded a plane to leave the country. Jones convinced his congregation that hostile intruders were on their way to exterminate them in retaliation for the deaths at the airstrip.

The next day, Jones gathered before him more than 900 members of the People's Temple. It was time, he said, for them to die. Their death, the "martyr" Jones claimed, would be a revolutionary and positive act. Amidst few protests or acts of resistance, parents gave their children cyanide-laced Kool-Aid, drank it themselves, then lay down and waited to die.

The Jonestown massacre is but one of North America's many experiences with cults (Galanter, 1999). With founder Luc Jouret leading the way, 74 members of the Order of the Solar Temple "departed" for the star Sirius in the early 1990s. Their suicides, including those in St. Casimir and Morin Heights, Quebec, were intended as a triumphant escape from a "planet of fools." Similarly, in 1997, Marshall Applewhite and members of his Heaven's Gate cult committed suicide to journey to the Hale-Bopp comet and ascend to a "level above human." Luc Jouret and Marshall Applewhite were also charismatic leaders who gained enormous influence over others.

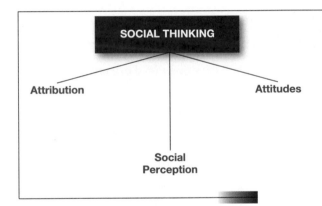

SOCIAL THINKING

Attribution   Attitudes

Social
Perception

Social Psychology

Social Thinking

Social psychologists are intrigued by how people think about the social world. Our exploration of social thinking focuses on attribution, social perception, and attitudes.

Attribution

You might remember that in chapter 11, "Motivation and Emotion," we introduced attribution theory in the context of achievement ◀||| P. 389. We revisit attribution here and expand on its important contributions to understanding the ways people think about their social world.

Human beings are curious, seeking answers to all sorts of questions about their social world. We often ask and explore why something has happened or is happening. We might be curious about why someone is yelling at another person, why someone is in love with a particular person, or why someone got into a sorority or fraternity. Finding causal explanations for these and many other social circumstances is complex. We can observe people's behavior and listen to what they say, but to determine the cause of their behavior we have to make inferences from these observations.

Attribution theorists argue that we want to know why people do the things they do because the knowledge will enable us to cope more effectively with the situations that confront us (Alderman, 1999). Recall from chapter 11 that **attribution theory** *views people as motivated to discover the underlying causes of behavior as part of their effort to make sense of the behavior.* Thus, attributions are thoughts about why people behave the way they do. In a way, attribution theorists say people are a lot like detectives or scientists, seeking the reasons for human actions.

The Dimensions of Causality   Social psychologists have proposed a number of dimensions to describe the types of attributions people make (Jones,

1998). These dimensions reflect whether the cause is internal or external, stable or unstable, controllable or uncontrollable.

Internal/External Causes   In our discussion of achievement in chapter 11, we indicated that an important attribution people make is whether the cause of achievement is due to external causes or internal causes ◀‖‖ P. 389. Fritz Heider (1958) argued that this internal/external explanation is the central issue in attribution. *Internal attributions* include all causes internal to the person, such as personality traits, intelligence, models, attitudes, and health. *External attributions* include all causes external to the person, such as social pressure, aspects of the social situation, money, the weather, and luck.

To think about how internal and external causes are involved in the attributions we make, consider this situation: Jason and Ashley have been dating for several months when Ashley breaks off the relationship. Jason wants to know why. Ashley says she is ending the relationship because of pressure from her parents, who want her to tone down her social life and study more (external attribution). But is that the true reason she is breaking off the relationship? Possibly Ashley is dumping Jason because she has grown tired of his introverted personality (internal cause).

Stable/Unstable Causes   In addition to internal and external causes, a second dimension involved in making attributions focuses on whether the cause is stable or unstable. This refers to whether an internal or external cause is relatively enduring and permanent or whether it is temporary. If Ashley infers that Jason's introverted personality is not going to change and that he is always going to be this way, a stable cause is present. On the other hand, if Ashley perceives that Jason just isn't putting enough effort forth but has the capability of being more outgoing, an unstable cause is involved. These are both examples of internal causes. What are some examples of stable and unstable external causes? If Ashley's parents never like anybody she dates, an external stable cause is present, but if they don't like Jason and approve of someone else Ashley dates, an external unstable cause is at work.

Controllable/Uncontrollable Causes   A third dimension of causality consists of whether a cause is controllable or uncontrollable (Weiner, 1986). We perceive that we can control some causes but that others are beyond our control. This dimension can coexist with any combination of internal/external and stable/unstable dimensions. We won't go through all of the combinations of these dimensions, but consider these to illustrate the nature of causes we can control and causes we can't control. An internal unstable cause like effort or mood is usually thought of as controllable. An external unstable cause like luck is generally seen as uncontrollable.

According to Weiner (1986), successful outcomes that we attribute to ourselves increase our self-esteem more than outcomes attributed to external causes like luck. Attributions regarding controllability are of particular importance because personal responsibility is involved. Attributions of controllability for personal failure are linked to guilt, shame, and humiliation. We also hold others responsible for failures attributed to controllable causes and may feel angry toward them. On the other hand, we might feel sympathy toward people whose failures are beyond their control. For example, consider the situation in which a vase is accidentally knocked off a table and broken, in one instance by a child with a disability, in another by a drunken adult. The child with the disability is likely to elicit sympathy, the drunk, anger. One interesting aspect of attribution theory is the degree to which we believe in a just world (Hafer & Olson, 1998). Someone who strongly believes the world is a just place is more likely to accept his or her own personal deprivation as just but is also more likely to respond negatively to innocent victims.

Attributional Errors and Biases   So far what we have said about attribution suggests it is a logical, rational process. However, some common errors and biases infiltrate our attributions.

Actor	Observer
More likely to give external, situational explanations of own behavior	More likely to give internal, trait explanations of actor's behavior

ℱigure 16.1
The Fundamental Attribution Error

In this situation, the female supervisor is the observer and the male employee is the actor. If the employee has made an error in his work, how are the employee and his supervisor likely to differ in their explanations of his behavior, based on your knowledge of actor/observer differences and the fundamental attribution error?

Social Cognition

The Fundamental Attribution Error   In attribution, the person who acts, or the actor, produces the behavior to be explained. Then the onlooker, or the observer, offers a causal explanation of the actor's behavior or experience. Actors often explain their own behavior in terms of external causes. In contrast, observers frequently explain the actor's behavior in terms of internal causes. The **fundamental attribution error** *is that observers overestimate the importance of traits and underestimate the importance of situations when they seek explanations of an actor's behavior* (see figure 16.1).

The fundamental attribution error suggests that when most people encounter examples of social behavior, they have a tendency to explain the behavior in terms of the personalities of the people involved rather than the situation they are in (Aronson, Wilson, & Akert, 1997). For example, when we try to explain why people do repugnant or bizarre things, such as the people in Jonestown, St. Casimir, or the Heaven's Gate cult who took their own lives and the lives of their children, the tendency is to describe them as flawed human beings. This emphasis on traits of victims without considering how they may have been overpowered by the social forces of the situation reflects the fundamental attribution error.

Because actors and observers often have different ideas about what causes behavior, many attributions are biased. Behavior is determined by a number of factors, so it is not surprising that our lives are full of squabbling and arguing about the causes of behavior (Harvey, 1995).

Self-Serving Bias   We tend to be self-enhancing (Sedikides & others, 1998). We often believe that we are more trustworthy, moral, and physically attractive than other people are. We also tend to believe that we are above-average teachers, managers, and leaders. One mechanism through which individuals maintain such exaggerated positive beliefs about themselves involves self-serving bias (Pittman, 1998).

When our self-esteem is threatened, we may depart from the fundamental attribution error and infuse our attributions with a different type of bias. **Self-serving bias** *involves attributing explanations for one's successes to internal factors and explanations for one's failures to external factors.* That is, we tend to take credit for our successes and blame our failures on others or the situation. In the case of Ashley breaking up with Jason, Jason might go along with Ashley's external explanation that she is doing it because of her parents. That's a lot easier for Jason to take than the internal attribution that he is basically a "hermit-like" introvert. As we indicated earlier, self-serving bias tends to rear its head when our self-esteem is threatened.

Social Perception

When we think about our social world and try to make sense of it, we not only make attributions but also engage in these social perceptions: We develop social impressions of others, gain self-knowledge by engaging in social comparison, and present ourselves to others in an attempt to influence their social perceptions of us.

Developing Impressions of Others   Our evaluations of people often fall into broad categories—good or bad, happy or sad, introvert or extravert, for example. If someone asked for your impression of your psychology professor, you might respond, "She is great." Then you might go on to describe your perception of her characteristics, for example, "She is charming, intelligent, witty, and sociable." From this description we can infer that you have a positive impression of her.

As we form impressions of others, we cognitively organize the information in two important ways. First, our impressions are *unified,* and second, our impressions are *integrated.* Traits, actions, appearance, and all of the other information we obtain about a person are closely connected in memory even though the information may have been obtained in an interrupted or random fashion. We might obtain some information today, more next week, some more in two months. During those two months, we interacted with many other people and developed impressions of them as well. Nonetheless, we usually perceive the information about a particular person as unified, as a continuous block of information (Brown, 1986).

Impressions are integrated, in the sense that we reach beyond the information we have, adding, manipulating, and modifying the information to form a whole impression (Asch, 1946). When we do not have much information about an individual, we stretch it to form a complete impression of that person. In Solomon Asch's original work (1946), participants were asked to think of a short list of traits for an individual. Asch then asked the participants to write character sketches based on a brief list of traits. The sketches included many different combinations of the traits and went far beyond the original list. **Implicit personality theory** *is the term given to the public's or a layperson's conception of how personality traits go together in an individual* (Bruner & Tagiuri, 1954). Implicit personality theory is reflected in this person's perception: "Because most of my friends who are extraverted are also optimistic, I assume all extraverted people are optimistic."

When we integrate information about people, we follow certain rules. We use some evaluative dimensions more than others. Norman Anderson (1974, 1989) thinks we use three dimensions more than any others to categorize people. The most common dimension is good/bad. Think for a moment about the people you know. Chances are you categorize each of them as either good or bad. Our tendency to categorize people as good or bad is so strong that Anderson calls this *the* evaluation dimension. Potency (strong/weak) and activity (active/passive) are two other dimensions we often use to categorize people (see figure 16.2).

You might recall our discussion of schemas from chapter 7, "Memory" ◀ᴵᴵᴵᴵ P. 230. A *schema* is a category we use to organize information. When we read a book, we do not remember every paragraph word for word; rather, we get the gist of what the author says and fit the

*F*igure 16.2
Developing Impressions of Others: Three Dimensions We Use to Categorize People
Look at the individual running. What is your impression of her? You probably will categorize her as good or bad, possibly as strong or weak, or as active or passive.

What is the prototype for a business executive? How well do these men fit the prototype?

information into existing categories in our mind. We "read" people in a similar way. We don't remember everything about what they are like and what they do, but we get the gist of their personality and behavior, and we fit the information about them into existing categories of memory. One set of categories has been given special attention: **prototypes** *are abstract categorizations of traits that describe a particular personality type.* Prototypes act as standards against which we match the individuals we evaluate. For example, a prototype for extraversion is being outgoing, talkative, and assertive.

We tend to simplify the task of understanding people by classifying them as members of groups or categories with which we are familiar. It takes more mental effort to consider a person's individual characteristics than it does to label her as a member of a particular group or category. Thus, when we categorize an individual, the categorization is often based on stereotypes.

We do not always respond to others on the basis of categories, however. Imagine that you meet a salesman. Based on the category-classification system, you would develop an impression of him based on the "salesman" category. Without seeking any additional information, you might perceive that person as pushy, self-serving, and materialistic; however, as you interact with him, you discover that he is actually interesting, modest, bright, and altruistic. You would then have to revise your impression and perceive him differently. When impressions are formed in this manner, a more individualized, or *individuated,* orientation in impression formation occurs.

The information available largely determines whether a category-based or an individuated-based impression formation will occur. When we discover information that is inconsistent with a category or when we simply become more personally involved with someone, we are more likely to take an individuated approach.

Our first encounter with someone also contributes to the impression we form. First impressions are often enduring. **Primacy effect** *is the term used to describe the enduring quality of initial impressions.* One reason for the primacy effect is that we pay less attention to subsequent information about the individual (Anderson, 1965). The next time you want to impress someone, a wise strategy is to make sure that you put your best foot forward in your first encounter.

Gaining Self-Knowledge from Our Perceptions of Others: Social Comparison

How many times have you asked yourself questions such as "Am I as smart as Jill?" "Is Sergei better looking than I am?" or "Is my taste as good as Carmen's?" We gain self-knowledge from our own behavior; we also gain it from others through **social comparison,** *the process in which individuals evaluate their thoughts, feelings, behaviors, and abilities in relation to other people.* Social comparison helps individuals to evaluate themselves, tells them what their distinctive characteristics are, and aids them in building an identity.

Some years ago Leon Festinger (1954) proposed a theory of social comparison. He stressed that when no objective means is available to evaluate our opinions and abilities, we compare ourselves with others. Festinger believed that we are more likely to compare ourselves with others who are similar to us than dissimilar to us. He reasoned that if we compare ourselves with someone who is very different from us, we will not be able to obtain an accurate appraisal of our own behavior and thoughts. This means that we will develop more accurate self-perceptions if we compare ourselves with people in communities similar to where we grew up and live, with people who have similar family backgrounds, and with people of the same sex, for example. Social comparison theory has been extended and modified over the years and continues to provide an important rationale for why we affiliate with others and how we come to know ourselves (Gibbons, Benbow, & Gerrard, 1994; Gibbons & Buunk, 1999).

In contrast to Festinger's emphasis on the role of social comparison in evaluating one's abilities, recently researchers have focused more on the self-enhancing properties of downward comparisons (Wood, 1989). Individuals under threat (from negative feedback, low self-esteem, depression, and illness, for example) try to im-

"Randall, my old college nemesis, I was hoping I'd find you here."

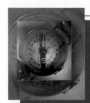

EXPLORATIONS IN PSYCHOLOGY
Impression Management and Job Interviewing

MOST OF US WANT to make a good impression the first time we meet someone. We especially want to make a good impression if the other person is interviewing us for a job. What nonverbal cues might we use to improve the likelihood that an interviewer will develop a favorable impression of us? People who are successful at impression management recognize that certain facial expressions, patterns of eye contact, and body postures or movements are part of the reason we are liked or disliked. For example, to improve the likelihood that an interviewer will have a favorable impression of you, you might smile often, lean forward, maintain a high degree of eye contact, and frequently nod your head in agreement with what the interviewer says.

Some people smile frequently, maintain good eye contact, and show a strong interest in what someone else is saying more naturally than others. Even if you don't normally behave this way when you are interacting with someone, you can make a conscious effort to control your nonverbal behavior. In general, researchers have found that individuals who use these impression management techniques receive more favorable ratings than individuals who do not (Riggio, 1986). These nonverbal cues, along with other impression management strategies such as behavioral matching, conforming to situational norms, and showing appreciation of others, apply to a number of social encounters in addition to interviews, including first dates and salesperson-customer situations. In one investigation, it was observed that individuals who were selected for engineering apprenticeships had smiled more, had maintained greater eye contact with the interviewer, and had nodded their heads affirmatively more often during their interviews than had rejected applicants (Forbes & Jackson, 1980).

Is there a point, though, at which there can be too much of a good thing and we can overuse impression management? You *can* overdo it, using so many positive nonverbal cues that the other individual perceives you negatively and labels you as insincere. In one research investigation, the frequent use of positive nonverbal cues had favorable outcomes in a job interview situation only when the applicants also had competent qualifications (Rasmussen, 1984).

In sum, using positive nonverbal cues can improve the way other people perceive you, but don't overdo it (Reece & Brandt, 1990).

prove their well-being by comparing themselves with someone less fortunate (Gibbons & McCoy, 1991).

Presenting Ourselves to Others to Influence Their Social Perceptions

How do you present yourself to others? Do you try to act naturally and be yourself, or do you deliberately change your behavior to get other people to have a more favorable impression of you? Let's explore two dimensions of presenting ourselves to others to influence their social perceptions: impression management and self-monitoring.

Impression Management Impression management (also called **self-presentation**) *involves acting in a way to present an image of oneself as a certain sort of person, which might or might not be who one really is.* In most instances, we try to present ourselves to look better than we really are. We spend billions of dollars rearranging our faces, bodies, minds, and social skills, usually to make a favorable impression on others. We especially use self-presentational motives with people we are not familiar with and with people in whom we have a sexual interest (Leary & others, 1994).

Nonverbal cues can often be used in successful impression management. To read about how nonverbal cues can get other people to perceive you positively, especially in a job interview, turn to Explorations in Psychology.

Keep in mind, though, that impression management techniques that work in one cultural setting may not work in another. In particular, appreciation and flattery are often culture bound. For example, in some Eastern European countries, if one person expresses great admiration for another's watch, courtesy dictates that the watch should be given to the admirer! In the Native American culture of the

THINKING ABOUT PSYCHOLOGY AND LIFE

Self-Monitoring

THESE STATEMENTS CONCERN personal reactions to a number of situations. No two statements are exactly alike, so consider each statement carefully before answering. If a statement is true or mostly true as applied to you, check the T. If a statement is false or not usually true as applied to you, check the F.

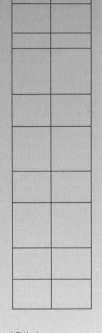

	True	False
1. I find it hard to imitate the behavior of other people.		
2. I guess I put on a show to impress or entertain people.		
3. I would probably make a good actor.		
4. I sometimes appear to others to be experiencing deeper emotions than I actually am.		
5. In a group of people, I am rarely the center of attention.		
6. In different situations and with different people, I often act like very different persons.		
7. I can only argue for ideas I already believe.		
8. In order to get along and be liked, I tend to be what people expect me to be.		
9. I may deceive people by being friendly when I really dislike them.		
10. I'm not always the person I appear to be.		

Scoring: Give yourself one point for each of questions, 1, 5, and 7 that you answered F. Give yourself one point for each of the remaining questions that you answered T. Add up your points. If you are a good judge of yourself and scored 7 or above, you are probably a high-self-monitoring individual; 3 or below, you are probably a low-self-monitoring individual.

Attitudes

Sioux, it's considered courteous to open a conversation with a compliment.

Self-Monitoring Some people are more concerned about and aware of the impressions they make than others are (Snyder & Stukas, 1999). **Self-monitoring** *is individuals' attention to the impressions they make on others and the degree to which they fine-tune their performance accordingly.* Lawyers and actors are among the best self-monitors; salespeople, con artists, and politicians are not far behind. A former mayor of New York City, Fiorello LaGuardia, was so good at self-monitoring that, by watching silent films of his campaign speeches, it was possible to tell which ethnic group he was courting for votes.

Individuals who are very skilled at self-monitoring seek information about appropriate ways to present themselves and invest considerable time in trying to "read" and understand others (Simpson, 1995). In thinking about self-monitoring, keep in mind that overall it is neither good nor bad.

Attitudes

Social thinking involves not only attributions and social perceptions but also attitudes.

Attitudes *are beliefs or opinions about people, objects, and ideas.* We have attitudes about all sorts of things, such as "Most people are out for themselves," "Money is evil," and "Television has caused families to talk less with each other." We also live in a world where people try to influence others' attitudes, as when politicians try to get your vote and advertisers try to convince you that their product is the best (Petty, Wegener & Fabrigar, 1997).

Many strategies have been devised to change people's attitudes. Two such strategies are foot-in-the-door and door-in-the-face. In the **foot-in-the-door strategy,** *an individual presents a weaker point or makes a small request with which the listeners will probably comply in the beginning, saving the strongest point until the end.* In the words of social psychologist Robert Cialdini (1993), "Start small and build." For example, a sales pitch for a health spa might offer you four weeks' use of the facility for $10 and hope that, after the four weeks, you will pay $200 for a one-year membership. In contrast, in the **door-in-the-face strategy,** *a communicator makes the strongest point or demand in the beginning, which the listeners will probably reject, then presents a weaker point or moderate "concessionary" demand toward the end.* For example, the salesperson for the health spa might initially offer you the one-year membership for $200, which you turn down, then offer you a "bargain" four-weeks-for-$10 package.

Do Attitudes Predict Behavior? Strategies such as the foot-in-the-door technique imply that changing people's attitudes will lead to changes in their behavior. However, in some cases individuals will say one thing and do another. For example, they might respond in a poll that they are going to vote for one candidate and then actually vote for another. In others, what they say is what they do. Studies over the course of the last half century indicate that under some conditions attitudes guide actions (Eagly & Chalkin, 1998).

Predicting behavior from attitudes is more reliable when the person's attitudes are strong (Petty & Krosnick, 1995). For example, people whose attitudes toward gambling are "highly favorable" are more likely to buy lottery tickets or visit a casino than their counterparts who have only "moderately favorable" attitudes toward gambling. Predicting behavior from attitudes is also more reliable when the person shows a strong awareness of his or her attitudes and when the person rehearses and practices them (Fazio & others, 1982). Furthermore, predicting behavior from attitudes is more reliable when the attitudes are relevant to the behavior. In many instances, the more specifically relevant the attitude is to the behavior, the better it will predict the behavior. For example, in one study, general attitudes toward birth control were virtually unrelated to the use of birth control pills in the next two years, but a more specific attitude toward taking birth control pills in the next two years showed a much higher correlation with actual use (Davidson & Jacard, 1979).

Can Behavior Predict Attitudes?

In examining attitudes, social psychologists have studied behavior's influence on attitudes, the role that cognitive dissonance plays in the connection between attitudes and behavior, and how perceiving our behavior influences our attitudes.

Behavior's Influence on Attitudes

"The actions of men are the best interpreters of their thoughts," asserted the seventeenth-century English philosopher John Locke. Does doing change your believing? If you quit drinking, will you have a more negative attitude toward drinking? If you take up an exercise program, are you more likely to praise cardiovascular fitness when someone asks your attitude about exercise?

Ample evidence exists that changes in behavior can precede changes in attitudes (Bandura, 1989). Merely repeatedly expressing attitudes increases their importance to us (Roese & Olson, 1994). Two main explanations of why behavior influences attitudes have been offered. The first view is that we have a strong need for cognitive consistency; consequently, we change our attitudes to make them more consistent with our behavior (Carkenord & Bullington, 1995). The second view is that our attitudes are not completely clear, so we observe our behavior and make inferences about it to determine what our attitudes should be. Let's consider these two views in more detail.

Cognitive Dissonance

Cognitive dissonance, *a concept developed by social psychologist Leon Festinger (1957), refers to an individual's motivation to reduce the discomfort (dissonance) caused by two inconsistent thoughts.* We may feel uneasy about a discrepancy between our attitudes and behavior. Without internal justification for the difference between what we believe and what we do, we experience dissonance (Harmon-Jones & Mills, 1999). We engage in a variety of actions to reduce dissonance. Most smokers believe it is unhealthy to smoke, yet can't resist lighting up. This discrepancy between attitude and behavior creates discomfort. To reduce the dissonance, the smoker must either stop smoking or change attitudes. "No one has proven smoking kills people" and "I'll have to die from something" are dissonance-reducing attitudes.

We often justify our behavior, as George Bernard Shaw did with his father's alcoholism: "If you cannot get rid of the family skeleton, you may as well make it dance." Shaw's justification helped him reduce the tension between his attitude about his father's drinking problems and its actual occurrence. Cognitive dissonance is about trying to reduce tension by cognitively justifying unpleasant things (Aronson, 1995). Interestingly, if we are simultaneously aware of cognitively inconsistent elements, our degree of discomfort is reduced (McGregor, Newby-Clark & Zanna, 1999).

We justify the negative things we do in life. We need to convince ourselves that we are decent, reasonable human beings. For example, when we have had a bad argument with someone, we often develop a negative attitude toward that person, which justifies the nasty things we said. We also have a strong need to justify the effort we put forth in life. We positively evaluate goals that require

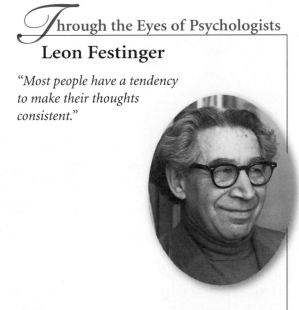

*T*hrough the Eyes of Psychologists

Leon Festinger

"Most people have a tendency to make their thoughts consistent."

considerable effort. Whether we reach the goals or not, we engage in the process of *effort justification*. The reasoning goes like this: if we work hard to attain a goal but then evaluate that goal in a negative way, dissonance would occur. If we put forth considerable effort, yet still do not reach the goal, how could we reduce the dissonance? We could convince ourselves that we did not work as hard as we actually did, or we could say that the goal was not all that important in the first place.

Our most intense justifications of our actions take place when our self-esteem is involved (Aronson, 1999; Aronson, Cohen, & Nails, 1999). If you do something cruel, then it follows that you have to perform some mental gymnastics to keep yourself from thinking you are a cruel person. The clearest results in the hundreds of research studies on cognitive dissonance occur when self-esteem is involved, and it is when individuals with the highest self-esteem act in cruel ways that the most dissonance results. What about individuals with low self-esteem? They probably experience less dissonance because acting in a cruel way is consistent with their attitudes toward themselves—attitudes that might entail such labels as *loser, jerk, zero,* or *bad guy.* Put another way, individuals who think of themselves as bad might do bad things because it keeps dissonance at a minimum.

Not all of our thoughts and behaviors are aimed at reducing dissonance, however. Some of us learn from our mistakes. There are times when we need to catch ourselves, look in the mirror, and say, "You blew it. Now what can you do to prevent that from happening again?" Eliot Aronson (1995) offers three suggestions that can keep our lives from being a treadmill of dissonance reduction:

1. Know your defensive and dissonance-reducing tendencies. Be able to sense them before you get in over your head.
2. Realize that behaving in stupid and cruel ways does not necessarily mean that you are a stupid and cruel person.
3. Develop enough strengths and competencies to be able to tolerate your mistakes without having to spend a lifetime rationalizing them away.

Self-Perception Theory   Not all social psychologists, however, are satisfied with cognitive dissonance as an explanation for the influence of behavior on attitudes. Daryl Bem (1967), for example, believes that the cognitive dissonance view relies too heavily on internal factors, which are difficult to measure. Bem argues that we should move away from such fuzzy and nebulous concepts as "cognitions" and "psychological discomfort" and replace them with more behavioral terminology. **Self-perception theory** *is Bem's theory about the connection between attitudes and behavior; it stresses that individuals make inferences about their attitudes by perceiving their behavior.* For example, consider the remark, "I am spending all of my time thinking about the test I have next week. I must be anxious." Or, "This is the third time I have gone to the student union in two days. I must be lonely." Bem believes we look to our own behavior when our attitudes are not completely clear. This means that when we have clear ideas about something, we are less likely to look to our behavior for clues about our attitudes; but if we feel more ambivalent about something or someone, our behavior is a good place to look to determine our attitude. Figure 16.3 provides a comparison of cognitive dissonance theories and self-perception theories.

Theory	Cognitive dissonance theory	Self-perception theory
Theorist	Festinger	Bem
Nature of theory	We are motivated toward consistency between attitude and behavior and away from inconsistency.	We make inferences about our attitudes by perceiving and examining our behavior and the context in which it occurs, which might involve inducements to behave in certain ways.
Example	"I hate my job. I need to develop a better attitude toward it, or I could quit and be a beach bum."	"I am spending all of my time thinking about how much I hate my job. I really must not like it."

Figure 16.3
Two Theories of the Connections Between Attitudes and Behavior

Which theory is right: the theory of cognitive dissonance or self-perception? Bem's self-perception theory is most compelling when people are not strongly committed to attitudinal positions before taking actions relevant to them (Aronson, Wilson, & Akert, 1997). Self-perception theory has also been more useful in understanding what happens to people's attitudes when they are offered an inducement to do something they would want to do anyway. The pattern of research on cognitive dissonance suggests that the heart of dissonance has to do with not wanting to feel cheap or stupid or guilty. Dissonance theory argues that individuals should avoid information inconsistent with their views. Early attempts to document this selective exposure failed, although more recently researchers have found that people will avoid unpleasant information only if (1) they think they cannot refute the uncomfortable argument, and (2) they are irrevocably committed to their way of thinking or behaving. In sum, cognitive dissonance theory and self-perception theory both have merit in explaining different dimensions of the connection between attitudes and behavior (Sabini, 1995).

At this point we have studied many ideas about social thinking. An overview of these ideas is presented in summary table 16.1. In our discussion of social thinking, we touched on the topic of social influence, such as how we present ourselves to others to influence their perception of us. Next, we will further explore many other aspects of social influence.

Social Influence

Social psychologists are interested in how our behavior is influenced by other people and groups. In this section, we will explore these aspects of social influence: conformity and obedience, group influence, and cultural and ethnic influences.

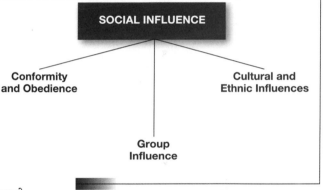

Conformity and Obedience

How extensively do people change their behavior so it will coincide more with what others are doing? How readily do people obey someone in authority? What factors influence whether people will resist such social influences?

Social Influence

Conformity   **Conformity** *involves a change in a person's behavior to coincide more with a group standard.* Conformity comes in many forms and affects many aspects of people's lives. Conformity is at work when a person takes up jogging because everyone else is doing it. Conformity is also present when an individual lets his hair grow short one year because it's fashionable and long next year because long hair has become vogue.

Conformity to rules and regulations results in people's engaging in a number of behaviors that make society run more smoothly. For example, consider what would happen if most people did not conform to rules such as these: stopping at red lights, driving on the correct side of the road, not punching others in the face, and going to school regularly. However, in the following experiments, researchers reveal how conformity pressures can sometimes make us act against our better judgment, which can lead to dramatic, unfortunate consequences.

Asch's Conformity Experiment   Put yourself in this situation: You are taken into a room where you see six other people seated around a table. A person in a white lab coat enters the room and announces that you are about to participate in an experiment on perceptual accuracy. The group is shown two cards, the first having only a single vertical line on it, the second card three vertical lines of varying length. You are told that the task is to determine which of the three lines on the second card is the same length as the line of the first card. You look at the cards and think, "What a snap. It's so obvious which is longest" (see figure 16.4).

SUMMARY TABLE 16.1
Social Thinking

Concept	Processes/Related Ideas	Characteristics/Description
Attribution	What Are Attributions?	Attributions are our thoughts about why people behave the way they do and about who or what is responsible for the outcome of the events. Attribution theory views people as motivated to discover the causes of behavior as part of their effort to make sense of the behavior.
	The Dimensions of Causality	These include internal/external, stable/unstable, and controllable/uncontrollable. There are motivational and emotional implications of differing attributions.
	Attributional Errors and Biases	The fundamental attribution error states that observers overestimate the importance of traits and underestimate the importance of situations when they seek explanations of an actor's behavior. When our self-esteem is threatened, we might depart from the fundamental attribution error and engage in a self-serving bias, which involves attributing explanations for one's success to internal causes and explanations for one's failures to external causes.
Social Perception	Developing Impressions of Others	Our impressions are unified and integrated. An individual's notion of how traits go together is called implicit personality theory. We have social schemas, or prototypes, that we use to evaluate others. We simplify our impressions by categorizing others. In some instances, though, we develop a more individuated approach to impressions. First impressions are important and influence impressions at a later point.
	Gaining Self-Knowledge from Our Perceptions of Others: Social Comparison	We evaluate ourselves by comparison with others. Festinger stresses that social comparison provides an important source of self-knowledge, especially when no other objective means is available. We are more likely to compare ourselves with similar others.
	Presenting Ourselves to Others to Influence Their Social Perceptions	Two dimensions of presenting ourselves to others to influence their social perceptions are impression management (self-presentation) and self-monitoring. Impression management involves acting in a way to present an image of oneself, which might or might not be who one is. Self-monitoring involves individuals' awareness of the impressions they make on others and the degree to which they fine-tune their performance accordingly.
Attitudes	What Are Attitudes?	Attitudes are beliefs or opinions about people, objects, and ideas. Two strategies for changing people's attitudes are foot-in-the-door and door-in-the-face.
	Do Attitudes Predict Behavior?	Under these conditions, predicting behavior from attitudes is likely to be more reliable: when the person's attitudes are strong, when the person is very aware of his or her attitudes and rehearses, and practices them, and when attitudes are specifically relevant to the behavior.
	Can Behavior Predict Attitudes?	Evidence exists that sometimes changes in behavior precede changes in attitude. Cognitive dissonance theory, developed by Festinger, argues that we have a strong need for cognitive consistency. We change our attitudes to make them more consistent with our behavior in order to reduce dissonance. In many cases, this involves justification of our actions. Justification is most intense when our self-esteem is involved. Not all of our thoughts are dissonance reducing. Bem developed a more behavioral approach called self-perception theory. It stresses the importance of making inferences about our own behavior, especially when our attitudes are not clear.

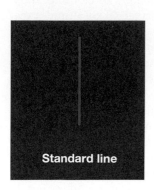

$\mathscr{F}$igure 16.4
Asch's Conformity Experiment

The figures on the left show the stimulus materials for the Asch conformity experiment on group influence. The photograph shows the dilemma for one subject after five confederates of the experimenter chose the incorrect line.

The other people in the room are actually in league with the experimenter; they've been hired to perform in ways the experimenter dictates (of course, you are not aware of this). On the first several trials everyone agrees about which line matches the standard. Then on the fourth trial each of the others picks an incorrect line; you have a puzzled look on your face. As the last person to make a choice, you're in the dilemma of responding as your eyes tell you or conforming to what the others before you said. How do you think you would answer?

Solomon Asch conducted this classic experiment on conformity in 1951. He believed there would be little yielding to group pressure. To find out if this was so, Asch instructed the hired accomplices to give incorrect responses on 12 of the 18 trials. To his surprise, Asch found that the volunteer participants conformed to the incorrect answers 35 percent of the time. (Figure 16.4 shows the actual participants in Asch's experiment on conformity.) The pressure to conform is strong. Even in a clear-cut situation, such as the Asch experiment, we often conform to what others say and do. We don't want to be laughed at or have others be angry with us.

In a more recent test of group pressure and conformity, American university students watched the third Bush-Clinton presidential debate and then rated the candidates' performances (Fein & others, 1993). Students were randomly assigned to one of three groups: (1) a 30-student group that included 10 confederates of the experimenter who openly supported Bush and criticized Clinton, (2) a 30-student group that included 10 confederates who cheered Clinton and put down Bush, and (3) a 30-student group with no confederates of the experimenter. The effects of the group pressure exerted by the confederates were powerful; even Bush supporters rated Clinton's performance more favorably when their group included pro-Clinton confederates of the experimenter.

Factors that Contribute to Conformity   Many factors influence whether an individual will conform or not (Cialdini & Trost, 1998). When people do conform, they usually do so because of either normative social influence or informational social influence. **Normative social influence** *is the influence that other people* *have on us because we seek their approval or avoid their disapproval.* When normative social influence is at work, we conform in order to be liked and accepted by others. So if a group is important to us, we might wear a particular kind of clothing, adopt a particular hairstyle, use some slang words, and show a certain set of attitudes that characterize the group's members.

Informational social influence *is the influence other people have on us because we want to be right.* Thus, while normative social influence causes people to conform because they want to be liked, informational social influence causes people to conform because they want to be right (Taylor, Peplau, & Sears, 1997). The tendency to conform based on informational social influence especially depends on two factors: how confident we are in our own independent judgment and how well-informed we perceive the group to be. Thus, if you don't know much about computers and three of your acquaintances who work in the computer industry say not to buy a particular brand of computer, you are likely to conform to their recommendation.

Let's explore some other factors involved in conforming or not conforming. In Asch's study with lines on cards, the group opinion was unanimous. When unanimity is broken, the group's power is lessened and individuals feel less pressure to conform. Also, if you do not have a prior commitment to an idea or action, you are more likely to be influenced by others. If you publicly commit to a course of action, conformity to another point of view is less likely.

Three other factors that contribute to conformity involve an individual's characteristics, the characteristics of the group members, and the culture in which people live. People with low self-esteem and doubts about their abilities are more likely to conform (Campbell, Tesser, & Fairey, 1986), and you are more likely to conform if the group members are experts, attractive to you, or similar to you in any way. In experiments conducted in fourteen countries, conformity rates were lower in individualistic cultures (like that of Canada and the United States) and higher in collectivistic cultures (like that of China) (Bond & Smith, 1996).

Obedience

Obedience   **Obedience** *is behavior that complies with the explicit demands of the individual in authority.* That is, we are obedient when someone demands that we do something and we do it. How is obedience different from conformity? In conformity, people change their thinking or behavior so that it will be more like others'. Explicit demands are not made to conform. However, such demands are present in obedience.

Obedient behavior can sometimes be destructive. The mass suicides at Jonestown described at the beginning of the chapter, the massacre of Vietnamese civilians at My Lai, and the Nazi crimes against Jews in World War II are other examples of destructive obedience. Karl Adolf Eichmann, for example, has been described as an ambitious functionary who believed that it was his duty to obey Hitler's orders. An average middle-class man with no identifiable criminal tendencies, Eichmann ordered the killing of six million Jews. The following experiment by Stanley Milgram provides insight into such obedience.

As part of an experiment in psychology, you are asked to deliver a series of painful electric shocks to another person. You are told that the purpose of the study is to determine the effects of punishment on memory. Your role is to be the "teacher" and punish the mistakes made by the "learner." Each time the learner makes a mistake your job is to increase the intensity of the shock by a certain amount.

You are introduced to the "learner," a nice 50-year-old man who mumbles something about having a heart condition. He is strapped to a chair in the next room; he communicates with you through an intercom. As the trials proceed, the "learner" quickly runs into trouble and is unable to give the correct answers. Should you shock him? The apparatus in front of you has thirty switches, ranging from 15 volts (light) to 450 volts (marked as dangerous, "severe shock XXX"). Before this part of the experiment began, you had been given a 75-volt shock to see how it feels. As you raise the intensity of the shock, the "learner" says he's in pain. At 150 volts, he demands to have the experiment stopped. At 180 volts, he cries out that he can't stand it any-

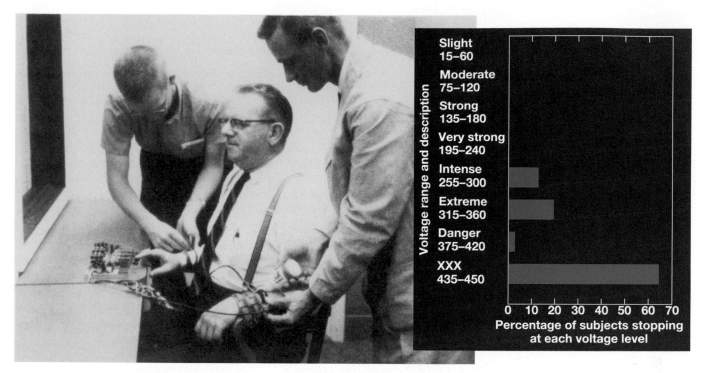

Figure 16.5
Milgram Obedience Study

A 50-year-old man ("learner") is strapped into a chair. The experimenter makes it look as if a shock generator is being connected to his body through several electrodes. The chart at the right shows the percentage of subjects ("teachers") who stopped shocking the experimenter at each voltage level.

more. At 300 volts, he yells about his heart condition and pleads to be released. But if you hesitate in shocking the learner, the experimenter tells you that you have no choice, the experiment must continue.

The experiment just described is a classic one devised by Stanley Milgram (1963, 1974) to study obedience. As you might imagine, the "teachers" were uneasy about shocking the "learner." At 240 volts, one "teacher" responded, "240 volts delivered; Aw, no. You mean I've got to keep going with that scale? No sir, I'm not going to kill that man—I'm not going to give him 450 volts!" (Milgram, 1965). At the very high voltage, the "learner" quit responding. When the "teacher" asked the experimenter what to do, he simply instructed the "teacher" to continue the experiment and told him that it was his obligation to complete the job. Figure 16.5 shows the results of the study and what the situation in the Milgram experiment was like. By the way, the 50-year-old man was in league with the experimenter. He was not being shocked at all. Of course, the "teachers" were completely unaware of this.

Forty psychiatrists were asked how they thought individuals would respond to this situation. The psychiatrists predicted that most would go no further than 150 volts, that less than 1 in 25 would go as far as 300 volts, and that only 1 in 1,000 would deliver the full 450 volts. The psychiatrists, it turns out, were way off the mark. The majority of the individuals obeyed the experimenter. In fact, almost two of every three delivered the full 450 volts.

In subsequent studies, Milgram set up a storefront in Bridgeport, Connecticut, and recruited volunteers through newspaper ads. Milgram wanted to create a more natural environment for the experiment and to use a wider cross section of volunteers. In these additional studies, close to two-thirds of the individuals still selected the highest level of shock for the "learner." In variations

Through the Eyes of Psychologists
Stanley Milgram (1933–1984)

"Most people do what they are told to do as long as they perceive that the command comes from a legitimate authority."

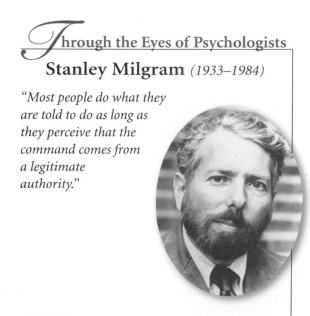

of the experiment, Milgram discovered some factors that encouraged disobedience: When an opportunity was given to see others disobey, when the authority figure was not perceived to be legitimate and was not close by, and when the victim was made to seem more human.

We're going to sidetrack for a moment and raise an important point about the Milgram experiments: How *ethical* were they? The volunteers in Milgram's experiment clearly felt anguish and some were very disturbed about "harming" another individual. After the experiment was completed, they were told that the "learner" was not actually shocked. Even though they were debriefed and told that they had really not shocked or harmed anyone, was the anguish imposed on them ethical?

Milgram argues that we have learned a great deal about human nature from the experiments. He claims that they tell us how far individuals will go in their obedience, even if it means being cruel to someone. The volunteers were interviewed later and more than four of every five said that they were glad they had participated in the study; none said they were sorry they participated. When Milgram conducted his studies on obedience, the ethical guidelines for research were not as stringent as they are today. The current ethical guidelines of the Canadian Psychological Association stress that researchers should obtain informed consent from their volunteers. Deception should be used only for very important purposes. Individuals are supposed to feel as good about themselves when the experiment is over as they did when it began. Under today's guidelines, it is unlikely that the Milgram experiment would be conducted.

Resisting Social Influence   "If a man does not keep pace with his companions, perhaps it is because he hears a different drummer. Let him step to the music which he hears, however measured or far away." Thoreau's words suggest that some of us resist social influence. Most of us would prefer to think of ourselves as stepping to our own music, maybe even setting the rhythms for others, rather than trying to keep apace with our companions. However, a certain degree of conformity is required if society is to function at all. As we go through our lives we are both conformists and nonconformists. Sometimes we are overwhelmed by the persuasion and influence of others; in other circumstances we resist and gain personal control over our lives. It is important to remember that our relation to the social world is recip-

In 1989, Chinese students led a massive demonstration against the Chinese government in Beijing. The students resisted the government's social influence by putting together resources to challenge the Chinese authorities; however, the government eventually eliminated the protests, massacring hundreds.

rocal. Individuals may be trying to control us, but we can exert personal control over our actions and influence others in turn (Bandura, 1986).

If you believe someone in a position of authority is making an unjust request or asking you to do something wrong, what choice of action do you have?

- You can comply.
- You can also give the appearance of complying but secretly do otherwise.
- You can publicly dissent by showing doubts and disenchantment but still follow directives.
- You can openly disregard the orders and refuse to comply.
- You can challenge or confront the authority.
- You might get higher authorities to intervene or organize a group of people who agree with you to show the strength of your view.

Group Influence

A student joining a fraternity, a jury making a decision about a criminal case, a president of a company delegating authority, a prejudiced remark against a minority group, conflict among nations, and attempts to reach peace—all of these circumstances reflect our lives as members of groups. The smallest group (called a "dyad") consists of two people. Each of us belongs to many different groups. Some we choose, others we do not. We choose to belong to a club, but we are all born into a particular ethnic group, for example. Some of the important questions about group relations are these: Why do we join groups? What is the structure of groups? How do we perform and make decisions in groups? Why are some people leaders and others followers? How do groups deal with each other, especially ethnic groups?

**Group Dynamics
Group Processes**

Motivation for Group Behavior and the Structure of Groups   Why does one student join a study group? A church? An athletic team? A company? Groups satisfy our personal needs, reward us, provide information, raise our self-esteem, and give us an identity. We might join a group because we think it will be enjoyable and exciting and satisfy our need for affiliation and companionship. We might join a group because we will receive rewards, either material or psychological. By taking a job with a company we get paid to work for a group, but we also reap prestige and recognition. Groups are an important source of information. For example, as we listen to other members talk in a Weight Watchers group we learn about their strategies for losing weight. As we sit in the audience at a real estate seminar we learn how to buy property with no money down. The groups in which you are a member—your family, university, a club, a team—make you feel good, raise your self-esteem, and provide you with an identity.

Any group to which you belong has certain things in common with all other groups. **Norms** *are rules that apply to all members of a group.* A sorority may require each of its members to maintain a 3.00 grade point average. This is a norm. The city government requires each of its workers to wear socks. Mensa requires individuals to have a high IQ. The Polar Bear club says its members must complete a 15-minute swim in below-freezing temperatures. These, too, are norms.

Roles *are rules and expectations that govern certain positions in the group.* Roles define how people should behave in a particular position in the group. In a family, parents have certain roles, siblings have other roles, and a grandparent has yet another role. On a football team, many different roles must be fulfilled: center, guard, tackle, end, quarterback, running back, and wide receiver, for example, and that only covers the offense. Roles and norms, then, tell us what is expected of a particular group.

Group Performance   Do we perform better in a group or when alone? The very first experiment in social psychology examined this question. Norman Triplett (1898) found that bicyclists performed better when they raced against each other than when they raced alone against the clock. Triplett also built a "competition

Do you perform better as a member of a group or as an individual?

(a)

(b)

(c)

We can become deindividuated in groups. Examples of situations in which people can lose their individual identity include (a) at Mardi Gras, (b) at Ku Klux Klan rallies, and (c) in national patriotism crowds.

machine" made out of fishing reels. The machine allowed two individuals to turn the reels side by side. Observing 40 children, he discovered that those who reeled next to another child worked faster than those who reeled alone.

Since Triplett's work a century ago, many investigations of group versus individual performance have been conducted. Some studies reveal that we do better in groups, others that we are more productive when we work alone (Paulus, 1989). Is there any way we can make sense out of these contradictory findings?

Social facilitation *is the phenomenon that occurs when an individual's performance improves because of the presence of others.* Social facilitation occurs with well-learned tasks but not with new or difficult tasks. Robert Zajonc (1965) argued that the presence of other individuals arouses us. The arousal produces energy and facilitates our performance in groups. If our arousal is too high, however, we won't be able to learn new or difficult tasks efficiently. Social facilitation, then, improves our performance on well-learned tasks. In 1954, Toronto's Rich Ferguson ran the race of his life at the Vancouver Commonwealth Games. He placed third behind Britain's Roger Bannister and Australia's John Landy in the "miracle mile." How much did social facilitation contribute to the first race in which two runners broke the four-minute barrier? For new or difficult tasks, we might be best advised to work things out on our own before trying them in a group. In one investigation, expert and poor pool players were observed (Michaels & others, 1982). When they were observed unobtrusively, the experts hit 71 percent of their shots, the poor players 36 percent; when four individuals walked up to observe their play, however, the experts improved, making 80 percent of their shots, whereas the poor players got worse, making only 25 percent of their shots.

Another factor in group performance is how closely our behavior is monitored. **Social loafing** *is each person's tendency to exert less effort in a group because of reduced monitoring.* The effect of social loafing is lowered group performance (Latané, 1981). Social loafing is common when a group of students is assigned a school project. The larger the group, the more likely a person can loaf without being detected. One way to decrease social loafing is for people to develop a sense of personal responsibility (Brickner, Harkins, & Ostrom, 1986). Another way is to provide a standard that allows the group to evaluate its performance.

Our behavior in groups also can become deindividuated (Dodd, 1995). **Deindividuation** *occurs when the presence of a group results in the loss of personal identity and a decrease in responsibility.* As early as 1895, Gustav LeBon observed that a group can foster uninhibited behavior, ranging from wild celebrations to mob activity. Ku Klux Klan violence, Mardi Gras wild times, and a mob rolling a car on spring break in Fort Lauderdale might be due to deindividuated behavior. One explanation of deindividuation is that groups give us anonymity. We may act in a disinhibited way because we believe that authority figures and victims are less likely to discover that we are the culprits.

Group Interaction and Decision Making

Many of the decisions we make take place in a group—juries, teams, families, clubs, school boards, the Senate, a class vote, for example (Davis, 1996; Levine & Moreland, 1998). What happens when people put their minds to the task of making a group decision? How do they decide whether a criminal is guilty, a country should attack another, a family should stay home or go on vacation, or sex education should be part of a school curriculum? Three aspects of group decision making bear special mention: the risky shift and group polarization, groupthink, and majority-minority influence.

The Risky Shift and Group Polarization   When we make decisions in a group, do we take risks and stick our necks out or do we compromise our opinions and move toward the center? The **risky shift** *is the tendency for a group decision to be riskier than the average decision made by individual group members.* In one investigation, fictitious dilemmas were presented, and subjects were asked how much risk the characters in the dilemmas were willing to take (Stoner, 1961). When the individuals discussed the dilemmas as a group, they were more willing to say the characters would make risky decisions than when they were queried alone. Many studies have been conducted on this topic with similar results (Goethals & Demorest, 1995).

We do not always make riskier decisions in a group than when alone; however, hundreds of research studies show that being in a group does move us even more strongly in the direction of the position we initially held (Moscovici, 1985). The **group polarization effect** *is the solidification and further strengthening of a position as a consequence of group discussion.* An environmentalist concerned about logging old-growth forest in B.C. may listen to hours of discussion about sustainable logging; a representative of the logging industry hears the same words. After, each is more strongly committed to her position than before the deliberation began. Initially held views often become even more polarized because of group discussion.

Why does group polarization occur? It may take place because people hear more persuasive arguments as group members than they knew about previously; such arguments strengthen their position. It might also occur because of social comparison. We may find that our position is not as extreme as others, which may motivate us to take a stand at least as strong as the most extreme advocate of the position.

Groupthink   Sometimes groups make rational decisions and come up with the best solution to a problem. But not always. Group members, especially leaders, often seek to develop or maintain unanimity among group members. **Groupthink** *involves impaired decision making and avoidance of realistic appraisal to maintain group harmony.* Groupthink evolves because members boost each other's ego and increase each other's self-esteem by seeking conformity, especially in the face of stress (Janis, 1972). Groupthink involves many heads, but only one group mind. This motivation for harmony and unanimity can result in disastrous decisions and policy recommendations. On October 30, 1995, Canada almost came apart. The "No" side in the Quebec referendum on separation had won by the slim majority of 50.56 percent. The inactivity of "No" side leaders may have been due to groupthink. Early polls showing the "No" side far ahead convinced them victory was inevitable. As decision day approached, the "No" side advantage collapsed, especially when Lucien Bouchard became leader of the "Yes" side. Yet the "No" side leaders did nothing until just before the referendum. Thousands of non-Quebeckers traveled to Quebec to make personal appeals to Quebeckers to stay in Canada. While it will never be known for certain, it is possible that without this populist action, groupthink might have torn Canada apart.

In groupthink, leaders typically have a favored solution and promote it within the group. Members of the group also tend to be cohesive and isolate themselves from qualified outsiders who could influence their decisions (as the "No" side leaders isolated themselves from those who urged more definitive action and from polls showing the "No" side lead slipping away). Leaders can avoid groupthink by encouraging dissident opinions, by not presenting a favored plan at the outset, and by having several independent groups working on the same problem.

Leadership   "I am certainly not one of those who needs to be prodded. In fact, if anything, I am the prod," the British Prime Minister Winston Churchill once

Groupthink

© The New Yorker Collection 1979 Henry Martin from cartoonbank.com. All Rights Reserved.

(a)   **(b)**

Certain individuals in the minority have played important roles in history. (a) Martin Luther King, Jr., helped African Americans gain important rights. (b) Corazon Aquino, who became president of the Philippines after defeating Ferdinand Marcos, toppled a corrupt political regime and reduced the suffering of many Philippine citizens.

Leadership

said of himself. What made Churchill a great leader? Was it a set of personality traits, the situation into which he was thrust, or some combination of the two?

The **great-person theory** *says that some individuals have certain traits that are best suited for leadership positions.* Leaders are commonly thought to be assertive, cooperative, decisive, dominant, energetic, self-confident, tolerant of stress, willing to assume responsibility, diplomatic and tactful, and persuasive. While we can list traits and skills possessed by leaders, a large number of research studies conclude that we cannot predict who will become a leader solely from the individual's personality characteristics.

Is it the situation, then, that produces leaders? The situational view of leadership argues that the needs of a group change from time to time. The individual who emerges as the leader in one particular circumstance will not necessarily be the individual who becomes the leader in another circumstance.

The **contingency model of leadership** *states that both personality characteristics and situational influences determine who will become a leader.* Leadership is viewed as a complex undertaking in which leaders influence their followers and followers influence their leaders (Fielder, 1978). In the contingency model, leaders follow one of two styles: They direct leadership either toward getting a task completed or toward members' relationships (helping members get along). Is one of these two styles superior? The contingency model emphasizes that the appropriate style of leadership depends on the situation. If a group is working under very favorable or very unfavorable conditions, a task-oriented leader is better, but if group conditions are more moderate, a relationship-oriented leader is better. Full tests of these ideas have not been made, but the concept that leadership is a function of both personality characteristics and situational influences is an important one.

Majority and Minority Influence   Think about the groups in which you have been a member. Who had the most influence, the majority or the minority? In most groups—whether a jury, family, or corporate meeting—the majority holds sway over the minority. The majority exerts both normative and informational pressure on the group. Its adherents set the group's norm; those who do not go along may be rejected or even given the boot. The majority also has a greater opportunity to provide information that will influence decision making.

In most cases the majority wins, but there are occasions when the minority has its day (Latané, 1996). How can the minority swing the majority? The minority cannot win through normative influence because it is outnumbered. It must do its work through *informational pressure*. If the minority presents its view consistently and confidently, then the majority is more likely to listen to the minority's views.

In group situations, some individuals are able to command the attention of others and thus have a better opportunity to shape and direct subsequent social outcomes. To achieve such a high social impact, they have to distinguish themselves in various ways from the rest of the group. They have to make themselves noticed by others—by the opinions they express, the jokes they tell, or their nonverbal style. They might be the first ones to raise a new idea, to disagree with a prevailing point of view, or to propose a creative alternative solution to a problem. People who have a strong social impact are often willing to be different.

(a)

(b)

Conflicts among ethnic and cultural groups are common in today's world. They include conflicts between (a) Israelis and Palestinians in the Middle East and (b) Native Canadians and security forces in Canada, exemplified by standoffs such as those at Oka, Quebec (above), Gustafsen Lake, BC, and Ipperwash, Ontario.

Certain individuals in a minority may play a crucial role. Individuals with a history of taking minority stands may trigger others to dissent, showing them that disagreement is possible and that it may be the best course. Such is the ground of some of history's greatest moments—when Lincoln spoke out against slavery, racism dominated and tore at the country; when Corazon Aquino became a candidate for president of the Philippines, few people thought Ferdinand Marcos could be beaten.

Cultural and Ethnic Influences

Membership in some groups, such as cultural and ethnic groups, can be especially intense. This intensity can generate conflicts and produce clashes between the groups. In chapter 1 ("What is Psychology?") we described the nature of sociocultural diversity ◀ P. 12. Here we focus on the prejudice, stereotyping, and ethnocentrism that often characterize cultural and ethnic groups, as well as ways to improve interethnic relations.

Conflicts among ethnic and cultural groups are rampant around the world today. Serbs and Croats act on centuries-old hatred related to geographic, familial, and political loyalties in the former Yugoslavia. Israelis and Palestinians fight over territory in the Middle East, each claiming religious rights to disputed land. In Africa, the countries of Rwanda and Burundi are experiencing civil turmoil as new tribal chiefs try to craft a new social order favorable to their own rule. In Northern Ireland, clashes between Catholics and Protestants break out with almost clockwork regularity. While we have experienced conflict in Canada between Native Canadians and security forces and between English and French, we have been lucky that the clashes here have been nowhere near as violent as in the other parts of the world just mentioned. Prejudice, stereotyping, and ethnocentrism can help us understand the intensity of such cultural and ethnic conflicts.

Prejudice, Stereotyping, and Ethnocentrism   Understanding the antagonism that develops between groups requires knowledge about prejudice, stereotyping, and ethnocentrism. These factors are involved in discrimination against groups.

Prejudice   Like most people, you probably know what prejudice means and don't think of yourself as being prejudiced. In fact, each of us has prejudices and stereotypes. **Prejudice** *is an unjustified negative attitude toward an individual based*

PeaceNet

Racism

THINKING ABOUT PSYCHOLOGY AND LIFE

Prejudice and Reconstructive Memory

IN CHAPTER 7, "MEMORY," you read about the pioneering work of Sir Frederick Bartlett on reconstructive memory. Since Bartlett's research in the 1930s, hundreds of studies have shown that memory is reconstructive and that people often distort information to fit their assumptions and cultural expectations (Task Force on Diversity Issues, 1998). Our schemas influence what we recall about members of particular groups. In one early study on rumors, an initial description of a razor being held by a White workman was changed to the point at which the razor was being held by a well-dressed African American man (Allport & Postman, 1947).

How might people's prejudices influence what they remember about people? How might they influence what we see or hear about? How might this tendency to remember or forget things systematically help or hinder our encounters with others?

Through the Eyes of Psychologists

Mark Zanna, *University of Waterloo*

"Prejudicial attitudes are not merely a function of stereotypes."

on the individual's membership in a group. The group against which the individual is prejudiced can be made up of people of a particular race, sex, age, religion, nation, or can have some other detectable difference (Jones, 1997). Prejudice is a worldwide phenomenon. Its dark side has appeared on many occasions in human history, from the extermination of millions of Native North Americans by invading Europeans to the murder of millions of Jews by the Nazis. The slavery of blacks and the persecution of homosexuals are two other examples. In fact, virtually every social group has been the victim of prejudice at one time or another.

Stereotyping A **stereotype** *is a generalization about a group's characteristics that does not consider any variation from one individual to the next.* Characterizing all accountants as boring or all Italians as excitable is clearly stereotyping. We are less likely to detect variations among individuals who belong to "outgroups" than those who belong to our "ingroup." For example, Whites are more likely to stereotype African Americans than other Whites during eyewitness identification (Brigham, 1986). Stereotypes are often described as cognitive categories that people use when thinking about groups and group members (Fiske, 1998; Steele, 1996). In this perspective, the perceiver's beliefs about groups are biased, sometimes unconsciously (Greenwald & Banaji, 1995).

The simplest approach holds that prejudice stems from stereotypes: a person who stereotypes all outgroup members as lazy will experience prejudice toward that outgroup. However, Mark Zanna and his colleagues at the University of Waterloo have shown that prejudice is based on more than stereotypes (Zanna, 1994; Haddock, Zanna & Esses, 1994; Haddock & Zanna, 1998). For example, Gardner (1994) showed that English Canadian prejudice toward French Canadians has little relationship to stereotypes of French Canadians. In Zanna's theory, prejudice arises from four interrelated factors: stereotypes, symbolic beliefs, emotions, and past experience. Symbolic beliefs are beliefs about whether a group helps or hinders the reaching of important values. For example, a negative symbolic belief that an outgroup prevents a person from getting a job can also lead to prejudice. In addition, emotions experienced about outgroups and past experiences of outgroups can also lead to prejudice.

Zanna (1994) asked Canadian university students their opinions of four Canadian outgroups: French Canadians, Native Canadians, Pakistanis and homosexuals. The students' degree of prejudice was better predicted by combining stereotype, symbolic belief and emotion factors. For example, these students stereotyped Native Canadians as alcoholic and lazy, giving rise to feelings of anger and uneasiness, and symbolic beliefs of Native Canadians violating peace. The students stereotyped homosexuals as effeminate, normal and friendly, giving rise to feelings of disgust, confusion and discomfort, and symbolic beliefs of promoting freedom, blocking the traditional family and promoting peace. Zanna (1994) also showed that authoritarian personalities (Altemeyer,1996) were more likely to be prejudiced. In subsequent work, the fourth factor, quality of past experience, was also shown to improve the prediction of degree of prejudice toward Native Canadians (Haddock, Zanna & Esses, 1994).

Ethnocentrism   **Ethnocentrism** *is the tendency to favor one's own group over other groups.* Ethnocentrism's positive side is that it fosters a sense of pride that fulfills the human urge toward a positive self-image. As we approach the end of the twentieth century, group pride has mushroomed. There's Black Pride and Gay Pride. The Scots grow more Scottish, the Irish more Irish. There is something paradoxical about such pride. Most members of a group will attest that the group does not discriminate against others. As African American Stokley Carmichael said, "I'm for the Negro. I'm not against anything." Too often members of groups stress differences with others rather than emphasizing pride in their own group.

However, in-group pride does not always reflect ethnocentrism. What might be occurring in some in-group/out-group considerations is in-group/out-group bias, the tendency to view members of one's own group as having heterogeneous and desirable qualities and to view the members of other groups as having homogeneous and undesirable qualities. Members of socioeconomical and/or sociopolitical minority groups often assert in-group pride as a necessary counter to the many overt and covert messages transmitted by society that denigrate them simply by virtue of their group membership (Crocker, Major, & Steele, 1998; Gaines & Reed, 1995).

Henry Tajfel (1978) proposed **social identity theory,** *which states that when individuals are assigned to a group, they invariably think of the group as an in-group for them.* This occurs because individuals want to have a positive self-image. Social

Group members often show considerable pride in their group identity, as reflected in (a) Caribbean Canadians' celebration of Caribana, (b) Gay and Lesbians' celebration of Gay Pride Day, (c) Native Canadians' celebration of their heritage, and (d) Polish Canadians' celebration of their cultural background.

identity theory helps explain prejudice and conflict between groups. Tajfel is one of a shrinking group of European Jews who survived World War II. His goal was to explain the extreme violence and prejudice his group experienced.

Self-image consists of both a personal identity and many different social identities. Tajfel argues that individuals can improve their self-image by enhancing either their personal or their social identity. Tajfel believes our social identity is especially important. When we compare the social identity of our group with the social identity of another group, we often maximize the distinctiveness of the two groups. Think about your social identity with your home town. Or imagine two fans of pro football teams. One lives in Red Deer, Alberta and is a Calgary Stampeders fan; the other lives in Dundas, Ontario and is a Hamilton Tiger Cats fan. When the Tiger Cats won the 1999 Grey Cup, the Tiger Cats fan's self-image was enhanced.

As these fans argue, they reinforce their distinct social identities. Soon they intersperse proud, self-congratulatory remarks with nasty comments about the opponents: "My team is good and I am good. Your team is bad and you are bad." And so it goes with the sexes, ethnic groups, nations, social classes, religions, sororities, fraternities, etc. These comparisons lead to competition and even to "legitimizing" discrimination. Curiously, people perceive discrimination against their group as more severe than discrimination against themselves personally (Taylor, Ruggiero & Louis, 1996). Dion & Kawakami (1996) studied six minorities in Toronto (Blacks, Chinese, South Asians, Italians, Jews, and Portuguese) and found that all of them experienced *a personal/group discrimination discrepancy.*

Tajfel showed that it doesn't take much for us to think in terms of "we" and "they." For example, he assigned one person to a particular group because she overestimated the number of dots on a screen. He assigned another person to a different group because he underestimated the number. Once assigned to the two groups, the members were asked to award money to other participants. Those eligible to receive the money were distinguished only by their membership in one of the two groups just described. Invariably, an individual acted favorably (awarded money) toward a member of his or her own group. It is no wonder, then, that if we favor our own group based on such trivial criteria that we will show intense in-group favoritism when differences are not so trivial (Hogg, 1996).

Improving Interethnic Relations

Diversity

Martin Luther King once said, "I have a dream that my four little children will one day live in a nation where they will not be judged by the color of their skin but by the content of their character." How might we possibly reach the world Martin Luther King envisioned—a world without prejudice and racism? Researchers have consistently found that contact itself does not improve relations with people from other ethnic backgrounds (Brewer & Brown, 1998). What does improve interethnic relations?

Superordinate Goals   Years ago social psychologist Muzafer Sherif and his colleagues (1961) fueled "we/they" competition between two groups of 11-year-old boys at a summer camp called Robbers Cave in Oklahoma. In the first week one group hardly knew the other group existed. One group became known as the Rattlers (a tough and cussing group) and the other was known as the Eagles.

Near the end of the first week each group learned of the other's existence. It took little time for "we/they" talk to surface ("They had better not be on our ball field." "Did you see the way one of them was sneaking around?"). Sherif, who disguised himself as a janitor so he could unobtrusively observe the Rattlers and Eagles, arranged for the two groups to compete in baseball, touch football, and tug-of-war. Counselors manipulated and judged events so the teams were close. Each team perceived the other to be unfair. Raids, burning the other group's flag, and fights resulted. The Rattlers and Eagles further derided one another, as they held their noses in the air as they passed each other. Rattlers described all Rattlers as brave, tough, and friendly, and called all Eagles sneaky and smart alecks. The Eagles reciprocated by labeling the Rattlers crybabies.

Eliot Aronson developed the concept of the jigsaw classroom to reduce ethnic conflict. How does the jigsaw classroom work?

After we/they competition transformed the Rattlers and Eagles into opposing "armies," Sherif devised ways to reduce hatred between the groups. He tried noncompetitive contact but that didn't work. Only when both groups were required to work cooperatively to solve a problem did the Rattlers and Eagles develop a positive relationship. Sherif created superordinate tasks that required the efforts of both groups: working together to repair the only water supply to the camp, pooling their money to rent a movie, and cooperating to pull the camp truck out of a ditch.

Might Sherif's idea—that of creating cooperation between groups rather than competition—be applied to ethnic groups? When the schools of Austin, Texas, were desegregated through extensive busing, increased racial tension among African Americans, Mexican Americans, and Whites resulted in violence in the schools. The superintendent consulted Eliot Aronson, a prominent social psychologist, who was at the University of Texas in Austin at the time. Aronson (1986) thought it was more important to prevent ethnic hostility than to control it. He observed a number of elementary school classrooms in Austin and saw how fierce the competition was between children of unequal status.

Aronson stressed that the reward structure of the classrooms needed to be changed from a setting of unequal competition to one of cooperation among equals, without making any curriculum changes. To accomplish this, he put together the *jigsaw classroom*. The jigsaw classroom works by creating a situation where all of the students have to pull together to get the "big picture." Let's say we have a class of 30 students, some White, some Caribbean and some Native Canadian. The academic goal is to learn about the Canadian Prairies. The class might be broken up into five study groups of six students each, with the groups being as equal as possible in terms of ethnic composition and academic achievement level. Learning about the Canadian Prairies becomes a class project divided into six parts, with one part given to each member of the six-person group. The components might be early immigration to the prairies, animals and plants of the Prairies, Prairie crops, cities on the Prairies, and so on. The parts are like the pieces of a jigsaw puzzle. They have to be put together to form the complete puzzle.

Each student has an allotted time to study her or his part. Then the group meets and each member tries to teach her or his part to the group. After an hour or so each student is tested on the Canadian Prairies. Each student must learn the entire lesson; learning depends on the cooperation and effort of other members. Aronson believes

THINKING ABOUT PSYCHOLOGY AND LIFE
Seeking Common Ground

IDENTIFY SOMEONE WHO comes from a different cultural and ethnic background from you. It might be a classmate, someone who lives in your neighborhood, or someone in an interest group you attend. Ask him or her to sit down and talk with you for 15 minutes. Tell them this involves a requirement for a university class you are taking. Your conversation objective: Establish how similar you are in as many ways as you can.

that this type of learning increases students' interdependence through cooperatively teaching a common goal.

The strategy of emphasizing cooperation rather than competition and the jigsaw approach have been widely used in classrooms in North America (Johnson & Johnson, 1999). A number of studies reveal that this type of cooperative learning is associated with increased self-esteem, better academic performance, friendships among classmates, and improved interethnic perceptions (Slavin, 1989).

It is not easy to get groups who do not like each other to cooperate. The air of distrust and hostility is hard to overcome. Creating superordinate goals that require cooperation of both groups is one viable strategy, as evidenced in Sherif's and Aronson's work. Other strategies involve disseminating positive information about the "other" and reducing the potential threat of each group.

Intimate Contact   We indicated earlier that contact by itself does not improve interethnic relations. However, one form of contact—intimate contact—can (Brislin, 1993). Intimate contact in this context does not mean sexual relations; rather it involves sharing one's personal worries, troubles, successes, failures, personal ambitions, and coping strategies. When people reveal personal information about themselves, they are more likely to be perceived as an individual rather than as a member of a category. And the sharing of personal information often produces the discovery that others previously considered as "them" or the out-group have many of the same feelings, hopes, and concerns, which can help to break down in-group/out-group, we/they barriers. Intimate contact may be more effective when the individuals involved are of relatively equal status (Devine, Evett, & Vasquez-Suson, 1996).

In one of the initial investigations of extensive interethnic contact, African American and White residents in an integrated housing project were studied (Deutsch & Collins, 1951). Initially any conversations focused on such nonintimate matters as washing machines. Over time the Whites and African Americans discovered that they shared a number of similar concerns, such as jobs and work, the quality of schools for their children, taxes, and so on. This revelation helped to diminish in-group/out-group thoughts and feelings. Sharing intimate information and becoming friendly with someone from another ethnic group helps to make people more tolerant and less prejudiced toward the other ethnic group. Richard Clément and his colleagues at the University of Ottawa have explored shared language, one of the important variables mediating intimate contact. Intimate contact is virtually impossible between people who cannot speak to each other (Clément & Bourhis, 1996). In a study of Chinese undergraduates in Canada, Noels, Pon & Clément (1996) found that self-confidence in using Chinese and English was an important part of the student's adjustment. Noels & Clément (1996) studied French Canadians and English Canadians, and found that linguistic self-confidence mediated interethnic contact. These sorts of findings underscore the value of bilingual education in Canada (Noels & Clément, 1998).

At this point we have studied many ideas about social influence. An overview of these ideas is presented in summary table 16.2. Next, we continue our exploration of social psychology by examining some important aspects of social interaction and relationships.

Intimate personal contact that involves sharing doubts, hopes, problems, ambitions, and much more is one way to improve interethnic relations.

SUMMARY TABLE 16.2
Social Influence

Concept	Processes/ Related Ideas	Characteristics/Description
Conformity and Obedience	Conformity	Conformity involves a change in a person's behavior to coincide more with a group standard. Asch's classic study on judgments of line length illustrated the power of conformity. Many factors influence whether we conform, including normative social influence and informational social influence.
	Obedience	Obedience is behavior that complies with the explicit demands of an individual in authority. Milgram's classic experiment demonstrated the power of obedience. Participants obeyed the experimenter's directions even though they thought they were hurting someone. Milgram's work raises the question of ethics in psychological experimentation.
	Resisting Social Influence	As we go through our lives we are both conformist and nonconformist, obedient and not obedient. Sometimes we are overwhelmed by persuasion. At other times, we exert personal control and resist such influence.
Group Influence	Motivation for Group Behavior and Structure	Groups satisfy our personal needs, reward us, provide us with information, raise our self-esteem, and enhance our identity. Every group has norms and roles.
	Group Performance	Our performance in groups can be improved through social facilitation and lowered because of social loafing. In a group we can also experience deindividuation—a loss of personal identity and a decrease in responsibility.
	Group Interaction and Decision Making	The risky shift is the tendency for a group decision to be riskier than the average decision made by individual group members. The group polarization effect is the solidification and further strengthening of a position as a consequence of group discussion. Groupthink involves impaired decision making and avoidance of realistic appraisal to maintain group harmony. The majority usually gets its way in group influence, but occasionally the minority has its day.
	Leadership	Theories of group leadership include the great-person theory, the situational approach, and the person-situation view, known as the contingency model of leadership.
Cultural and Ethnic Influences	Prejudice, Stereotyping, and Ethnocentrism	Prejudice is an unjustified negative attitude toward an individual based on the individual's membership in a group. A stereotype is a generalization about a group's characteristics that does not consider any variation from one individual to the next. Zanna's theory states that prejudice arises from four interrelated factors: stereotypes, symbolic beliefs, emotions and past experience. Ethnocentrism is the tendency to favor one's own group over other groups. A theory to explain prejudice and conflict is Tajfel's social identity theory, which states that when individuals are assigned to a group they invariably think of the group as an in-group for them. This occurs because they want to have a positive self-image.
	Improving Interethnic Relations	Contact between ethnic groups, by itself, does not decrease conflict or improve relations. One effective strategy is to develop a superordinate goal requiring the cooperation of both groups. Sherif found support for the superordinate goal strategy in his study of boys at a summer camp. Aronson showed its effectiveness in the jigsaw classroom. Another effective way to improve interethnic relations is for members of different ethnic groups to share intimate information. Clément states that a shared language is helpful to share intimate information.

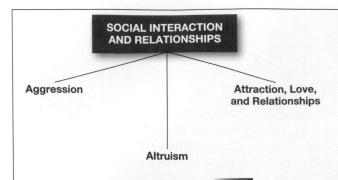

Violence

Social Interaction and Relationships

Our social interactions and relationships bring us warm and cherished moments. They can also bring us experiences we would rather forget, moments that are charged with conflict and harm. Our exploration of social interactions and relationships focuses on aggression, altruism, attraction, love, and relationships.

Aggression

The strength of aggression was captured vividly by Yoda in the movie *The Empire Strikes Back*: "Beware of the dark side. Anger, fear, aggression. Easily they flow. Once you start down the dark path, it will forever dominate your destiny and consume your will." Is this dark side biologically based or is it learned?

Biological Influences   The ancient Assyrian king Ashurbanipal delighted in beheading his enemies and blinding and mutilating his prisoners. Russian Czar Ivan the Terrible bludgeoned his own son and destroyed Novgorod, the second largest city in his empire, in the sixteenth century. In the twentieth century, 80 to 100 million people have been violently killed. In the 1970s, 4 million Cambodians were killed by their fellow Cambodians; murders in the United States take place at the rate of 20,000 per year, assaults at 700,000 per year. Rape and domestic abuse have increased dramatically (Walker, 1999); there are at least 200,000 reports of rape per year in North America. Asked Shakespeare, "Is there any cause in nature that makes these hard hearts?"

Ethologists say that aggression is biologically based; certain stimuli act as *innate* releasers of an organism's responses (Lorenz, 1965; Tinbergen, 1969). For example, a male robin will attack another male when it sees a red patch of the other bird's breast. When the patch is removed, however, no attack takes place. Severe fighting and some intraspecies killing does occur in the animal kingdom, but most hostile encounters do not escalate to killing or even severe harm. Much of the fighting is ritualistic and involves threat displays. For example, elephant seals show approximately 65 threat displays for every fight that actually takes place (LeBoeuf & Peterson, 1969). The type of threat display varies from one species to the next: a cat arches its back, bares its teeth, and hisses; a chimpanzee stares, stomps the ground, and screams.

Evolutionary theory stresses survival of the fittest P. 68. Early in human evolution, the more aggressive individuals were likely the survivors. Hunters and food gatherers had to kill animals and compete for the best food territories to survive. There may even be an evolutionary underpinning for homicide (Daly & Wilson, 1988).

Freud argued that aggression is instinctive. He said we have a self-destructive urge he called *thanatos*, the death instinct. He believed that the self-destructive nature of humans comes in conflict with *eros*, their self-preserving life instinct; thus, the death instinct is redirected and aimed at others in the form of aggression. However, humans do not have an instinct to be killers or murderers. Most psychologists feel uneasy about the concept of instinct. For example, the instinct theorists would support their belief that humans have an instinct for aggression by referring to the behaviors to which it is related, such as the 80 to 100 million people killed in the twentieth century. However, to give a behavior such as aggression the label *instinct* is not to explain it. Rather than an instinct for aggression, what may have evolved is an aggressive capability wired into the human neuromuscular system. For example, children born deaf and blind still show aggressive patterns—foot stomping, teeth clenching, and fist-making—even though they have had no opportunity to observe these behaviors (Eibl-Eibesfeldt, 1977).

Genes are important in understanding the biological basis of aggression P. 66. The selective breeding of animals provides evidence for the genetic basis of

(a)   (b)

Aggression is pervasive, both in today's world and in the past. (a) Russian Czar Ivan the Terrible bludgeoned his own son. (b) In the 1970s, 4 million Cambodians were killed by their fellow Cambodians.

aggression. After a number of breedings of aggressive animals with each other and docile animals with each other, vicious and timid strains of animals emerge. The vicious strains attack virtually anything in sight; the timid strains rarely fight, even when attacked. The genetic basis for aggression is more difficult to demonstrate with humans (Brennan, Mednick, & Kandel, 1991). Nonetheless, in one investigation of 573 sets of adult twins, identical twins had more similar aggressive tendencies than did fraternal twins (Rushton & others, 1986).

The brain is also involved in the biological processes of aggression (Niehoff, 1999). In 1966 Charles Whitman climbed to the top of the campus tower at the University of Texas at Austin. As he looked down on students walking to and from class, he pulled the trigger of a high-powered rifle and killed fifteen people. Then he took his own life. An autopsy revealed a tumor in the limbic system of Whitman's brain. In another instance, an electrode was implanted in the amygdala portion of a meek female mental patient's brain (which is part of the limbic system)  P. 81. Immediately after electric current stimulated the amygdala, this mild-mannered woman became vicious. She yelled, snarled, and flailed around the room (King, 1961). We do not have a specific aggression center in the brain, but, when the lower, more primitive areas of the brain (such as the limbic system) are stimulated by fine electric currents, aggressive behavior often results (Herbert, 1988).

Alcohol is a drug that acts on the brain to cause a disinhibiting effect on many of our behaviors, especially those we might otherwise resist, such as violent aggression P. 172. Something said or done may provoke an individual under the influence of alcohol to unleash harsh words, throw a punch, or pull the trigger of a gun (Dougherty, Cherek, & Bennett, 1996). If not under the influence, the individual might not respond so violently to such words or actions. Aggression-prone individuals are more likely to drink and to become violent when they become intoxicated (Seto & Barbaree, 1995). People under the influence of alcohol commit almost one-half of all rapes and other violent crimes (Abbey, Ross, & McDuffie, 1993).

Hormones also play a part in aggression (Susman & others, 1996) P. 95. For example, Sam, a bull, was a terror. With hooves scratching, eyes glazed, and nostrils snorting, he roared across a field at an intruder. Barely escaping with his life, the intruder (who turned out to be a tractor salesman) filed a complaint against the bull's owner. The local sheriff convinced the owner it was time to do something about Sam. What was Sam's fate? He was castrated, which changed him from a simmering volcano into a docile ox. The castration reduced Sam's motivation to terrorize by acting on his male hormone system. Although humans are less sensitive to hormonal changes than animals are, violent criminals tend to be muscular young males with higher than average testosterone levels (Dabbs, 1992).

Environmental and Psychological Influences   In our exploration of environmental and psychological influences on aggression, we will discuss culture, frustrating and aversive circumstances, and reducing aggression.

Culture   In the past, hunters and food gatherers had to kill animals and compete for the best food territories to survive. However, as anthropologist Loren Eiseley commented, "The need is now for a gentler, a more tolerant people than those who won for us against the ice, the tiger, and the bear."

Some cultures are more violence prone than others (Bellesiles, 1999; Geen, 1998; Staub, 1996). The homicide rate in Canada ranks 32nd among 65 countries surveyed. The rate for the United States is much higher than in many other countries—about four times as high as for Canadians and six times as high as for Europeans (United Nations, 1992). Crime rates are higher in countries where there is a considerable gap between the rich and the poor and where fathers do not participate in child care (Triandis, 1994).

What in a culture promotes aggression in its members? Imagine yourself on a barren mountainside away from civilization in the country of Uganda. For about 2,000 years, your ancestors lived as nomadic hunters, but, early in this century, the government of Uganda turned your hunting grounds into a national park. Hunting is forbidden in the park, so you are now forced to farm its steep, barren mountain areas. Famine, crowding, and drought have led to tremendous upheaval in families and moral values. You were sent out on your own at the age of six with no life supports; you fight and maim others to obtain food and water. Love does not seem to exist at all in your culture (Turnbull, 1972). If you were placed in this circumstance of the Ik culture, would you be this callous and aggressive?

Frustrating and Aversive Circumstances   The world of the Ik involved many frustrating and aversive circumstances that produced pain and hunger. Frustration is the blocking of motivated behavior, as in situations in which an individual's attempt to reach a goal is prevented from taking place. Some years ago, John Dollard and his colleagues (1939) proposed that frustration triggers aggression. The **frustration-aggression hypothesis** *states that frustration always leads to aggression.* Not much later, psychologists acknowledged that, although aggression is one outcome of frustration, other responses are possible. Some individuals who experience frustration become passive, for example (Miller, 1941). Psychologists also later recognized that a broad range of aversive experiences can cause aggression; frustration is just one such experience. Others include physical pain, personal insults, and unpleasant events such as divorce. An individual's cognitive interpretation of an aversive circumstance influences whether the individual will respond aggressively (Baumeister, 1999; Berkowitz, 1990; Novaco, 1998).

Aversive circumstances can also involve the physical environment. For example, environmental psychologists have demonstrated how such factors as noise, weather, and crowding can stimulate aggression. Murder, rape, and assault increase when temperatures are the hottest (during the third quarter of the year), as well as in the hottest years and in the hottest cities (Anderson, 1989).

Our everyday encounters with other people also produce aversive experiences that can trigger aggressive responses (Schwartz, 1999). For example, when someone cuts into a line in front of us (such as at a ticket booth), we may respond aggressively toward that person (Milgram & others, 1986).

Whether we respond aggressively to aversive situations is determined by such psychological factors as expectations, equity, intentions, and responsibility (Berkowitz, 1990). With regard to *expectations,* you expect to be jostled on a crowded bus, but don't expect someone to run into you when there are only five or six people on the bus; thus, you might respond more aggressively. With regard to *equity*, if you perceive that an aversive experience is not equitable, or justified, you might also respond aggressively. For example, if you deserve a D in a class, you are less likely to say nasty things about the professor than if you perceive the grade to be unfair. With regard to *intentions*, if you think someone has intentionally tripped you, you are more likely to respond aggressively than if you think the individual's feet accidentally became tangled with yours. With regard to *responsibility*, when you perceive that other people are responsible for their aggressive actions, you are more likely to behave aggressively toward them. For example, when are you more likely to respond aggressively: when an eight-year-old child hits you with her shopping cart in a store, or when her assertive, healthy, 30-year-old mother does the same thing? You are likely to perceive that the mother is more responsible for her behavior, so you would probably respond more aggressively toward her.

Observational Learning and Reinforcement   Social learning theorists also believe that aggression is learned through the processes of reinforcement and observational learning ◀‖‖‖ P. 207. Aggression is reinforced when it helps individuals attain money, attention, sex, power, or status. Aggression can also be learned by watching others behave aggressively (Bandura, 1989). One of the most frequent opportunities people have to observe aggression in our culture is to watch violence on television.

Violence is pictured as a way of life on many television shows. Evildoers kill and get killed; police and detectives violently uphold society's laws. Violence on television is portrayed unrealistically; viewers rarely see its lasting effects. In real life, an injured person may not recover for weeks, for months, or perhaps at all, but on television recovery takes only 30 to 60 minutes.

The amount of aggression on television is a special problem for children. In 1996, Canadian children watched an average of almost 18 hours of television each week (Statistics Canada, 1999). Almost every day of their lives, children watch someone being stabbed, maimed, or slaughtered. Does television violence merely stimulate a child to go out and buy a Star Wars ray gun, or can it trigger an attack on a playmate and increase the likelihood that, when the child grows up, he will violently attack or murder someone? (McCreary, 1997)

Although some critics have argued we cannot conclude that TV violence causes aggression (Freedman, 1984), many experts argue that TV violence can induce aggressive or antisocial behavior in children (Huston, Watson, & Kunkel, 1989; Singer & Singer, 1998). In recent years, violent video games have also begun to elicit concern, although not so much yet in the case of girls (de Castell & Bryson, 1998). Video games have been blamed for contributing to actual violence, as in the case of the Columbine massacre. Of course, media violence is not the *only* cause of aggression. There is no *one* cause of any social behavior. Aggression, like all other social behaviors, has multiple determinants. The link between media and aggression in children is influenced by children's aggressive tendencies and parental monitoring.

Many of the studies of television violence and aggression have been correlational in nature. As we have mentioned frequently, cause cannot be determined from correlational studies. However, as indicated in our discussion of research methods in chapter 2, some experimental studies have shown that watching television violence causes increased aggression, but mainly in children who are the most aggressive before they watch the violence (Friedrich & Stein, 1973; Steur, Applefield, & Smith, 1971).

Reducing Aggression   You might recall that in chapter 11, "Motivation and Emotion," we explored the negative emotion of anger, a powerful emotion that can generate aggression ◀‖‖‖ P. 404. We explored several strategies for reducing anger that apply to our evaluation of aggression here. Both psychoanalytic and ethological theorists believe that catharsis helps to reduce aggression. **Catharsis** *is the release of*

Calvin and Hobbes

GRAPHIC VIOLENCE IN THE MEDIA.

DOES IT GLAMORIZE VIOLENCE? SURE. DOES IT DESENSITIZE US TO VIOLENCE? OF COURSE. DOES IT HELP US TOLERATE VIOLENCE? YOU BET. DOES IT STUNT OUR EMPATHY FOR OUR FELLOW BEINGS? HECK YES.

DOES IT *CAUSE* VIOLENCE? ...WELL, THAT'S HARD TO PROVE.

THE TRICK IS TO ASK THE RIGHT QUESTION.

CALVIN AND HOBBES © 1995 Watterson. Reprinted with permission of UNIVERSAL PRESS SYNDICATE. All rights reserved.

Television and Aggression
Conflict and Violence
Prevention of Youth Violence

anger or aggressive energy by directly engaging in anger or aggression. The catharsis hypothesis states that behaving angrily or watching others behave angrily reduces subsequent anger or aggression.

Social learning theorists argue strongly against catharsis as a strategy for reducing aggression. They believe that by acting aggressively people are often rewarded for their aggression and that by watching others behave aggressively, people learn to be aggressive themselves. Researchers have found more support for the social learning view than for the psychoanalytic and ethological views on reducing aggression (Bandura, 1986, 1997). That is, decreasing rewards for aggression and observing fewer incidences of aggression are good candidates for reducing aggression. Parents' roles in children's lives have also been targeted for reducing aggression. Recommended parenting strategies include encouraging young children to develop empathy toward others and better monitoring of adolescents. For example, Gerald Patterson and his colleagues (1989) have consistently found that a lack of parental monitoring is related to juvenile delinquency. Another strategy that is being tried in many schools is to teach youths conflict management skills and have them serve as peer counselors.

Aggression and Gender   In a classic meta-analysis of research studies, the following conclusions were reached about aggression and gender (Maccoby & Jacklin, 1974): (1) Males are more aggressive than females in all cultures; (2) males are more aggressive than females from early in life, with differences consistently appearing as early as two years of age; and (3) more aggression by males than females is found in animals as well as humans. These findings have often been interpreted as supporting the view that gender differences in aggression are biologically based.

What are some examples of gender differences in aggression? As children, boys are more likely to engage in rough-and-tumble play and get in more fights in which they are physically aggressive toward each other. As adolescents, males are more likely to be members of gangs and commit violent acts. As adults, males are more likely to murder or rape.

As we mentioned earlier, these gender differences in aggression have often been interpreted as having a biological basis. However, environment and culture also contribute to gender differences in aggression (Geen, 1998). In one cross-cultural study, both biological and cultural factors were at work in gender differences in aggression (Archer & McDaniel, 1995). Individuals in twelve different countries were asked to write stories in response to conflicts presented to them. In all twelve countries, males wrote stories with more violent themes than females did, suggesting a biological interpretation of gender differences in aggression. However, the degree of violence described varied considerably across the cultures, suggesting an environmental/cultural interpretation.

An important point needs to be made about gender differences in aggression, as well as other areas. When we say that males are more aggressive than females, it does not mean that all males are more aggressive than all females. In any given culture, some females will be more aggressive than some males.

Another important point about gender and aggression focuses on the type of aggression. Differences in aggression are much stronger for physical aggression than for verbal aggression (Eagly & Steffen, 1986). In one longitudinal study, no gender differences in verbal aggression were found in eight-year-old children (Björkqvist, Österman, & Lagerspetz, 1994). However, at age 18, females displayed more verbal aggression than males.

Altruism

Our exploration of altruism focuses on what altruism is, biological influences, environmental and psychological influences, and gender. **Altruism** *is an unselfish interest in helping someone else.* We often hear or read about acts of generosity and courage,

Helping Others

(a)   (b)

Examples of altruism: (a) Shown here is an example of animal altruism—a baboon plucking bugs from another baboon. Most acts of animal altruism involve kin. (b) A young woman assists a handicapped child.

such as rock concerts and fund raisers to help AIDS victims, the taxi driver who risks his life to save a woman in a dark alley, and volunteers who pull a baby from an abandoned well. You may have placed some of your hard-earned cash in the palm of a homeless person or perhaps cared for a wounded cat (Brehony, 1999). How do psychologists account for such acts of human altruism?

The Biological Basis of Altruism   Evolutionary psychologists emphasize that some types of altruism help to perpetuate our genes (Buss, 1995, 1999; Buss & Kendrick, 1998). An act in the biological realm is altruistic if it increases another's prospects for survival and having the opportunity to reproduce (Sober & Wilson, 1998).

Evolutionary psychologists believe that tremendous benefits can accrue to individuals who form cooperative reciprocal relationships (Trivers, 1971). By being good to someone now, individuals increase the likelihood that they will receive a benefit from the other person in the future. Through this reciprocal process, both gain something beyond what they could have by acting alone.

Evolutionary psychologists also stress that those who carry our genes—our children—have a special place in the domain of altruism ◀▥ P. 68. Natural selection favors parents who care for their children and improve their probability of surviving. A parent feeding its young is performing a biological altruistic act because the young's chance of survival is increased. So is a mother bird who performs a distraction ritual to lure predators away from the eggs in her nest. She is willing to sacrifice herself so that three or four of her young offspring will have the change to survive, thus preserving her genes. Individuals also often show more empathy toward other relatives in relation to their genetic closeness. In the case of a natural disaster, people's uppermost concern is their family (Cunningham, 1986). In one study involving a hypothetical decision to help in life-or-death situations, university students chose to aid close kin over distant kin, the young over the old, the healthy over the sick, the wealthy over the poor, and the

Evolutionary Psychology

"All I'm saying is, giving a little something to the arts might help our image."

How strongly are today's university students interested in self-fulfillment versus helping others?

premenopausal woman over the postmenopausal woman (Burnstein, Crandall, & Kitayama, 1994). In this same study, when an everyday favor rather than a life-or-death situation was involved, the university students gave less weight to kinship and chose to help either the very young or the very old over those of intermediate age, the sick over the healthy, and the poor over the wealthy.

Environmental and Psychological Influences

Reciprocity and exchange are important aspects of altruism. Reciprocity, which encourages us to do unto others as we would have them do unto us, is present in every widely practiced religion in the world—Judaism, Christianity, Buddhism, and Islam, for example. Certain human sentiments are involved in reciprocity: Trust is probably the most important principle over the long run, guilt occurs if we do not reciprocate, and anger results if someone else does not reciprocate.

Not all altruism is motivated by reciprocity but this view alerts us to the importance of considering interactions between oneself and others to understand altruism. And not all seemingly altruistic behavior is unselfish. Some psychologists even argue that true altruism has never been demonstrated, while others argue that a distinction between altruism and egoism is possible (Cialdini & others, 1987). **Egoism** *involves giving to another person to ensure reciprocity; to gain self-esteem; to present oneself as powerful, competent, or caring; or to avoid social and self-censure for failing to live up to normative expectations.* By contrast, altruism occurs when someone gives to another person with the ultimate goal of benefiting that other person. Any benefits that come to the giver are unintended.

Describing individuals as having altruistic or egoistic motives implies that person variables are important in understanding altruistic behavior. Altruistic behavior is determined by both person and situational variables. A person's ability to empathize with the needy or to feel a sense of responsibility for another's welfare affects altruistic motivations. The stronger these personality dispositions, the less we would expect situational variables to influence whether giving, kindness, or helping occurs.

But as with any human behavior, characteristics of the situation influence the strength of altruistic motivation. Some of these characteristics include the degree of need shown by the other individual, the needy person's responsibility for his plight, the cost of assisting the needy person, and the extent to which reciprocity is expected (Batson, 1998).

One of the most widely studied aspects of altruism is bystander intervention. Why does one person help a stranger in distress while another won't lift a finger? It often depends on the circumstances. More than 30 years ago a young woman named Kitty Genovese cried out repeatedly as she was brutally murdered. She was attacked at about 3 A.M. in a respectable area of New York City. The murderer left and returned three times; he finally put an end to Kitty's life as she crawled to her apartment and screamed for help. It took the slayer about 30 minutes to kill Kitty. Thirty-eight neighbors watched the gory scene and heard Kitty Genovese's screams. No one helped or even called the police.

The **bystander effect** happens when *individuals who observe an emergency help less when someone else is present than when they are alone.* The bystander effect helps to explain the apparent cold-blooded indifference to Kitty Genovese's murder. Social psychologists John Darley and Bibb Latané (1968) documented the bystander effect in a number of simulated criminal and medical emergencies. Most of the bystander intervention studies show that when alone, a person will help 75 percent of the time, but when another bystander is present, the figure drops to 50 percent. Apparently the difference is due to the *diffusion of responsibility* among witnesses and our tendency to look to the behavior of others for clues about what to do. People may think that someone else will call the police or that since no one else is helping, possibly the person does not need help.

Many other aspects of the situation influence whether the individual will intervene and come to the aid of the person in distress. Bystander intervention is less likely to occur in the following situations (Shotland, 1985): a situation is not clear; the in-

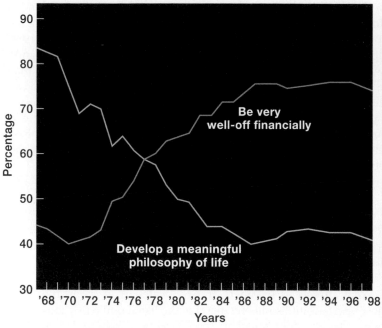

$\mathscr{F}$igure 16.6
Changing First-Year Student Life Goals, 1968–1998

In the last three decades, a significant change has occurred in first-year university students' life goals. A far greater percentage of today's first-year university students state that a "very important" life goal is to be well off financially, and far fewer state that developing a meaningful philosophy of life is a "very important" life goal.

dividuals struggling or fighting are married or related; a victim is perceived to be intoxicated; the person is thought to be from a different ethnic group; the intervention might lead to personal harm, or retaliation by the criminal. Also, helping requires considerable time, such as days in court testifying. When bystanders have no prior history of victimization themselves, have seen few crimes and intervention efforts, or have not had training in first aid, rescue, or police tactics, intervention is less likely to occur.

How altruistic are university students? Are they less altruistic than several decades ago? Over the past two decades, university students have shown an increased concern for personal well-being and a decreased concern for the well-being of others, especially the disadvantaged (Sax & others, 1998). As shown in figure 16.6, today's first-year university students are more strongly motivated to be well-off financially and less motivated to develop a meaningful philosophy of life than were their counterparts of 20 or 30 years ago.

However, there are some signs that today's university students are shifting toward a stronger interest in the welfare of our society. For example, between 1986 and 1995, there was a small increase in the percentage of first-year university students who said they were strongly interested in participating in community action programs (19 percent in 1998 compared to 18 percent in 1986) and helping promote racial understanding (40 percent in 1998 compared to 27 percent in 1986) (Sax & others, 1998). For successful adjustment in adult life, it is important to seek self-fulfillment *and* have a strong commitment to others.

Altruism and Gender   The main areas in which gender and altruism have been investigated are helping and caring. Who is more helping and caring, females or males? You likely responded: females. However, as with most domains, it is a good idea to think about gender in context. Females are more likely to help when

Values of University Students
Volunteerism

the context involves nurturing, as when volunteering time to help a child with a personal problem. However, males are more likely to help in situations in which a perceived danger is present and they feel competent to help (Eagly & Crowley, 1986). For example, males are more likely than females to help a person who is stranded by the roadside with a flat tire. An automobile problem is an area in which many males feel a sense of competence. Males are also more likely than females to give a ride to a hitchhiker, because of the perceived danger in this situation.

In terms of caring, females have a stronger orientation than males toward caregiving. However, in the few cultures where boys and girls are placed in charge of caring for their younger siblings on a regular basis, girls and boys are similar in their tendencies to nurture (Whiting, 1989).

Attraction, Love, and Relationships

Social relationships involve more than aggression and altruism. Attraction, love, and close relationships are also important dimensions of our social relationships (Baumeister & Bratslavsky, 1999).

Relationships

Attraction   What attracts us to others and motivates us to spend more time with them? Does just being around someone increase the likelihood a relationship will develop? Do birds of a feather flock together; that is, are we likely to associate with those who are similar to us? How important is physical attraction in a relationship?

Familiarity and Similarity   Physical proximity does not guarantee that we will develop a positive relationship with another person. Familiarity can breed contempt, but familiarity is a condition that is necessary for a close relationship to develop. For the most part, friends and lovers have been around each other for a long time; they may have grown up together, gone to high school or university together, worked together, or gone to the same social events. Once we have been exposed to someone for a period of time, what is it that makes the relationship breed friendship and even love?

Birds of a feather do indeed flock together. One of the most powerful lessons generated by the study of close relationships is that we like to associate with people who are similar to us. Our friends, as well as our lovers, are much more like us than unlike us. We have similar attitudes, behavior, and characteristics, as well as clothes, intelligence, personality, other friends, values, lifestyle, physical attractiveness, and so on. In some limited cases and on some isolated characteristics, opposites may attract. An introvert may wish to be with an extravert, or someone with little money may wish to associate with someone who has a lot of money, for example. But overall we are attracted to individuals with similar rather than opposite characteristics. In one study, for example, the old adage "Misery loves company" was supported as depressed university students preferred to meet unhappy others while nondepressed university students preferred to meet happy others (Wenzlaff & Prohaska, 1989). The fact that individuals are attracted to each other on the basis of similar characteristics and attitudes is reflected in the questions that computer dating services ask their clients.

Consensual validation *provides an explanation of why people are attracted to others who are similar to them.* Our own attitudes and behavior are supported when someone else's attitudes and behavior are similar to ours—they validate us. People tend to shy away from the unknown. We might tend, instead, to prefer people whose attitudes and behavior we can predict. And similarity implies that we will enjoy doing things with the other person, which often requires a partner who likes the same things and has similar attitudes. In one study, self-verifying evaluations were especially important in marriage (Swann, De La Ronde, & Hixon, 1994).

Physical Attraction   How important is *physical attraction* in a relationship? Advertising shows it as the most important factor in establishing and maintaining a relationship. Perhaps in guilty agreement, people intentionally underreport the impact of physical attractiveness on their dating preferences (Hadjistavropoulos & Genest,

1994). However, people differ on the importance they place on looks when they seek an intimate partner (Dion & Dion, 1995). For example, heterosexual women tend to value considerateness, honesty, dependability, kindness, and understanding; heterosexual men prefer good looks, cooking skills, and frugality (Buss & Barnes, 1986).

Complicating research conclusions about the role of physical attraction in relationships is changing standards of what is deemed attractive. The criteria for beauty can differ, not just *across* cultures, but over time *within* cultures as well (Lamb & others, 1993). In the 1950s, the ideal female beauty in North America was typified by the well-rounded figure of Marilyn Monroe. As a result of the current preoccupation with health, Monroe's 135 pound, 5-foot-5-inch physique is regarded as overweight by today's standards. In the 1980s and 1990s, the ideal physique for both men and women is neither pleasingly plump nor extremely slender.

The force of similarity also operates at a physical level. We usually seek out someone at our own level of attractiveness in both physical characteristics and social attributes. Most of us come away with a reasonably good chance of finding a "good match." Research indicates that this **matching hypothesis**—*that while we may prefer a more attractive person in the abstract, in the real world we end up choosing someone who is close to our own level of attractiveness*—holds up (Kalick & Hamilton, 1986).

Several additional points help to clarify the role of physical beauty and attraction in our close relationships. Much of the research has focused on initial or short-term encounters; researchers have not often evaluated attraction over the course of months and years. As relationships endure, physical attraction assumes less importance. Rocky Dennis, as portrayed in the movie *Mask,* is a case in point. His peers and even his mother initially wanted to avoid Rocky, whose face was severely distorted, but over the course of his childhood and adolescent years, the avoidance turned into attraction and love as people got to know him. As Rocky's story shows, familiarity can overcome even severe initial negative reactions to a person.

Once attraction initiates a relationship, other opportunities exist to deepen the relationship to friendship and love.

Romantic Love   **Romantic love** *is also called passionate love or Eros; it has strong components of sexuality and infatuation, and it often predominates in the early part of a love relationship.* According to Ellen Berscheid (1988), we mean romantic love when we say that we are "in love." Berscheid believes that sexual desire is the most important ingredient of romantic love. In 1967, men maintained that they would not get married if they were not "in love," whereas women said they might (Kephart, 1967). By the 1980s, women and men agreed they would not get married unless they were "in love." Today, half of men and women say that not being "in love" is enough to dissolve a marriage (Bersheid, Snyder, & Omoto, 1989).

Romantic love is especially important among university students. One study of unattached university men and women found that over half identified a romantic partner, rather than a parent, sibling, or friend, as their closest relationship (Berscheid, Snyder, & Omoto, 1989). Another study found that romantic loves were more likely than friends to be the cause of depression (Berscheid & Fei, 1977).

University of Toronto psychologists Kenneth and Karen Dion found that people with an individual (as opposed to collective) value orientation were less likely to have experienced romantic love. When individualistic people did experience romantic love, they experienced less affective involvement with their partners (Dion & Dion, 1991).

Paradoxically, in societies with an individual value orientation (such as Canada and the U.S.), greater stress is placed on romantic love and personal fulfillment in marriage than in societies with a collective value orientation (such as China and India). This may be because psychological individualism makes achieving romantic love more difficult (and hence desirable) whereas in

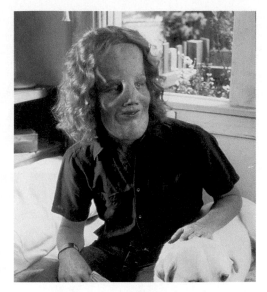

Eric Stoltz's portrayal of Rocky Dennis in the movie Mask. *Rocky was unloved and unwanted as a young child because of his grotesque features. As his mother and peers got to know him, they became much more attracted to him.*

Love

*T*hrough the Eyes of Psychologists

Ellen Berscheid, *University of Minnesota*

"To discuss romantic love without also prominently mentioning the role that sexual arousal and desire plays in it is very much like printing a recipe for tiger soup that leaves out the main ingredient."

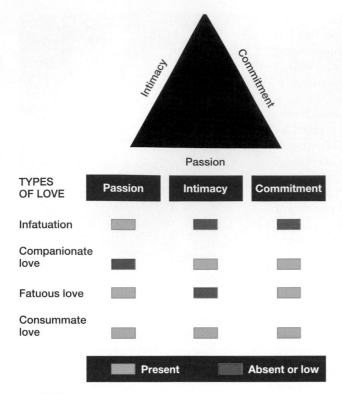

$\mathcal{F}$igure 16.7
Sternberg's Triangle of Love
Sternberg identified three dimensions that shape the experience we call love: passion, intimacy, and commitment. Various combinations of the three dimensions produce particular types of love.

Gender

societies with a collective value orientation intimacy is likely to be diffused across a network of family relationships (Dion & Dion, 1993).

Affectionate Love
Love is more than just passion. **Affectionate love,** *also called companionate love, is the type of love that occurs when individuals desire to have the other person near and have a deep, caring affection for the person.*

There is a growing belief that the early stages of love have more romantic ingredients, but as love matures, passion tends to give way to affection (Berscheid & Reis, 1998). Phillip Shaver (1986) describes the initial phase of romantic love as a time that is fueled by a mixture of sexual attraction and gratification, a reduced sense of loneliness, uncertainty about the security of developing another attachment, and excitement from exploring the novelty of another human being. With time, he says, sexual attraction wanes, attachment anxieties either lessen or produce conflict and withdrawal, novelty is replaced with familiarity, and lovers either find themselves securely attached in a deeply caring relationship or distressed—feeling bored, disappointed, lonely, or hostile, for example. In the latter case, one or both partners may eventually seek another close relationship.

When two lovers go beyond their preoccupation with novelty, unpredictability, and the urgency of sexual attraction, they are more likely to detect deficiencies in each other's caring. This may be the point in a relationship when women, who are often better caregivers than men, sense that the relationship has problems. Wives are almost twice as likely as husbands to initiate a divorce, for example (National Center for Health Statistics, 1989).

So far we have discussed two forms of love: romantic (or passionate) and affectionate (or companionate). Robert J. Sternberg (1988) described a third form of love, consummate love, which he said is the strongest, fullest type of love. Sternberg proposed the **triangular theory of love:** *that love includes three dimensions—passion, intimacy, and commitment* (see figure 16.7). Couples must share all three dimensions to experience consummate love.

Passion, as described earlier, is physical and sexual attraction to another. Intimacy is the emotional feelings of warmth, closeness, and sharing in a relationship. Commitment is our cognitive appraisal of the relationship and our intent to maintain the relationship even in the face of problems. If passion is the only ingredient (with intimacy and commitment low or absent), we are merely *infatuated.* This might happen in an affair or a fling in which there is little intimacy and even less commitment. A relationship marked by intimacy and commitment but low or lacking in passion is called *affectionate love,* a pattern often found among couples who have been married for many years. If passion and commitment are present but intimacy is not, Sternberg calls the relationship *fatuous love,* as when one person worships another from a distance.

A current interest in close relationships is the role that environmental changes play in them (Berscheid, in press). It is not enough to know a partner's vulnerabilities or strengths in a vacuum in predicting the relationship's future. We also need to know the nature of environments the relationship will face as it moves through time (Berscheid & Lopez, 1997). Some fragile relationships survive forever because they never encounter a relationship-toxic environment, but some strong relationships dissolve because of external forces they encounter, such as economic strains, job stress, and disapproval by others (Berscheid, 1999).

Relationships and Gender
Earlier we indicated that women are more strongly motivated caregivers than men and often are quicker to sense that a relationship has problems. As children, boys often define themselves apart from their

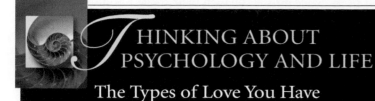

THINKING ABOUT PSYCHOLOGY AND LIFE

The Types of Love You Have

IMAGINE THE BLANK SPACES filled in with the name of one person you love or care about deeply. Then rate each of the items from 1–9 with 1 = not at all, 5 = moderately, and 9 = extremely.

_____ 1. I actively support _____'s well-being.
_____ 2. I have a warm relationship with _____.
_____ 3. I can count on _____ in times of need.
_____ 4. _____ is able to count on me in times of need.
_____ 5. I am willing to share myself and my possessions with _____.
_____ 6. I receive considerable emotional support from _____.
_____ 7. I give considerable emotional support to _____.
_____ 8. I communicate well with _____.
_____ 9. I value _____ greatly in my life.
_____ 10. I feel close to _____.
_____ 11. I have a comfortable relationship with _____.
_____ 12. I feel that I really understand _____.
_____ 13. I feel that _____ really understands me.
_____ 14. I feel that I can really trust _____.
_____ 15. I share deeply personal information about myself with _____.
_____ 16. Just seeing _____ excites me.
_____ 17. I find myself thinking about _____ frequently during the day.
_____ 18. My relationship with _____ is very romantic.
_____ 19. I find _____ to be very personally attractive.
_____ 20. I idealize _____.
_____ 21. I cannot imagine another person making me as happy as _____.
_____ 22. I would rather be with _____ than anyone.
_____ 23. There is nothing more important to me than my relationship with _____.
_____ 24. I especially like physical contact with _____.
_____ 25. There is something special about my relationship with _____.
_____ 26. I adore _____.
_____ 27. I cannot imagine my life without _____.
_____ 28. My relationship with _____ is passionate.
_____ 29. When I see romantic movies and read romantic books I think of _____.
_____ 30. I fantasize about _____.
_____ 31. I know that I care about _____.

_____ 32. I am committed to maintaining my relationship with _____.
_____ 33. Because of my commitment to _____, I would not let other people come between us.
_____ 34. I have confidence in the stability of my relationship with _____.
_____ 35. I could not let anything get in the way of my commitment to _____.
_____ 36. I expect my love for _____ to last for the rest of my life.
_____ 37. I will always feel a strong responsibility for _____.
_____ 38. I view my commitment to _____ as a solid one.
_____ 39. I cannot imagine ending my relationship with _____.
_____ 40. I am certain of my love for _____.
_____ 41. I view my relationship with _____ as permanent.
_____ 42. I view my relationship with _____ as a good decision.
_____ 43. I feel a sense of responsibility toward _____.
_____ 44. I plan to continue my relationship with _____.
_____ 45. Even when _____ is hard to deal with, I remain committed to our relationship.

The first 15 items reflect intimacy, 16–30 measure passion, and 31–45 evaluate commitment. Add up your total score for each of the three areas: 1–15 (intimacy), 16–30 (passion), and 31–45 (commitment). You can compare your scores with the average scores of a group of women and men (average age = 31) who were either married or in a close relationship:

Intimacy	Passion	Commitment	Percentile
93	73	85	15
102	85	96	30
111	98	108	50
120	110	120	70
129	123	131	85

The fourth column (percentile) shows the percentage of adults who scored at that level or above. Thus, if your intimacy score is 122, your intimacy is greater than 70 percent of the adults whose scores are averaged here.

Source: Sternberg, R. (1988). The Triangle of Love.

Many females show a stronger interest in relationships than many males do. What has been your experience with the gender differences in relationship orientation that we have discussed? If you are a female, do you have a strong interest in relationships? If you are a male, do you have less interest in relationships than most females you know?

caregivers and peers, while girls emphasize their social ties. You might recall our discussion of Carol Gilligan's care perspective in chapter 10, "Human Development." Gilligan believes that social relationships are more important to females than they are to males and that females are more sensitive in these social relationships ◀ ▥ P. 349. By contrast, she argues that males have a stronger individualistic, self orientation. Researchers have found that adult females are often caring, supporting, and empathic, while adult males are independent, self-reliant, and unexpressive (Brannon, 1999; Paludi, 1998).

Deborah Tannen (1990) analyzed the talk of women and men. She reported that a common complaint women have about their husbands is, "He doesn't listen to me anymore." Another is, "He doesn't talk to me anymore." Lack of communication, while high on women's list of reasons for divorce, is much less often mentioned by men.

Tannen distinguishes between rapport talk and report talk. **Rapport talk** *is the language of conversation. It is a way of establishing connections and negotiating relationships.* Women prefer to engage in rapport talk. Women enjoy private conversations more than men do, and it is men's lack of interest in rapport talk that bothers many women. By contrast, **report talk** *is talk designed to give information, which includes public speaking.* Men prefer to engage in report talk. Men hold center stage through such verbal performances as telling stories and jokes. They learn to use talk as a way of getting and keeping attention. Tannen and others (Nadien & Denmark, 1999; Snarey, 1998) argue that these gender differences are the result of girls and boys being socialized differently as they grow up. Mothers have participated far more in rearing children than fathers have and have modeled a stronger interest in relationships when interacting with their daughters than when interacting with their sons.

Tannen and others (Levant, 1995; Levant & Brooks, 1997) recommended that men develop a stronger interest in relationships and make women feel more comfortable in public speaking contexts. Tannen also recommends that women seek more report-talk opportunities, including speaking up in groups.

Not all of us have close relationships, and not all of us have experienced the passion, intimacy, and commitment of love. We have all heard that it is better to have loved and lost than never to have loved at all. However, as we see next, over many lives hangs the dark cloud of loneliness, something few people want to feel.

Loneliness   Some of us are lonely. We might feel that no one knows us very well. We might feel isolated and sense that we do not have anyone we can turn to in times of need or stress. Our society's emphasis on self-fulfillment and achievement, the importance we attach to commitment in relationships, and a decline in stable close relationships are among the reasons loneliness is common today (de Jong-Gierveld, 1987). Researchers have found that married individuals are less lonely than their nonmarried counterparts (never married, divorced, or widowed) in studies conducted in more than twenty countries (Perlman & Peplau, 1998).

Loneliness is interwoven with how people pass through life transitions. One of those transitions is the first year of university. When students leave the familiar world of their hometown and family to enter university, they can feel especially lonely. Many first-year students feel anxious about meeting new people and developing a new social life. As one student commented:

My first year here at the university has been pretty lonely. I wasn't lonely at all in high school. I lived in a fairly small town—I knew everybody and everyone knew me. I was a member of several clubs and played on the basketball team. It's not that way at the university. It is a big place and I've felt like a stranger on so many occasions. I'm starting to get used to my life here and the last few months I've been making myself meet people and get to know them, but it has not been easy.

As this comment illustrates, first-year students rarely bring their popularity and social standing from high school into the university environment. There may be a dozen high school basketball stars, Canadian Millennium scholars, and former student council presidents in a single dormitory wing. Especially if students attend university away from home, they face the task of forming completely new social relationships.

One study found that two weeks after the school year began, 75 percent of 354 first-year students felt lonely at least part of the time since arriving on campus (Cutrona, 1982). More than 40 percent said their loneliness was moderate to severe in intensity. Students who were the most optimistic and had the highest self-esteem were more likely to overcome their loneliness by the end of their first year. Loneliness is not reserved only for first-year students, though. Senior students are often lonely as well.

Lonely males and females attribute their loneliness to different sources, with men more likely to blame themselves, women more likely to blame external factors. Men are socialized to initiate relationships, whereas women are traditionally socialized to wait, then respond. Perhaps men blame themselves because they feel they should do something about their loneliness, while women wonder why no one calls.

How do you determine if you are lonely? Scales of loneliness ask you to respond to items like "I don't feel in tune with the people around me" and "I can find companionship when I want it." If you consistently respond that you never or rarely feel in tune with people around you and rarely or never can find companionship when you want it, you are likely to fall into the category of people who are described as moderately or intensely lonely (Russell, 1996).

If you are lonely, how can you become better connected with others? Following are some strategies:

- *Participate in activities that you can do with others.* Join organizations or volunteer your time for a cause you believe in. You will likely get to know others whose views are similar to yours. Going to just one social gathering can help you develop social contacts. When you go, introduce yourself to others and start a conversation. Another strategy is to sit next to new people in your classes or find someone to study with.
- *Be aware of the early warning signs of loneliness.* People often feel bored or alienated before loneliness becomes pervasive. Head off loneliness by becoming involved in new social activities.
- *Draw a diagram of your social network.* List whether the people in the diagram meet your social needs. If not, pencil in the people you would like to get to know.
- *Engage in positive behaviors when you meet new people.* You will improve your chances of developing enduring relationships if, when you meet new people, you are nice, considerate, honest, trustworthy, and cooperative. Have a positive attitude, be supportive of the other person, and make positive comments about him or her.
- *See a counselor or read a book on loneliness.* If you can't get rid of your loneliness on your own, you might want to contact the counseling services at your university. The counselor can talk with you about strategies for reducing your loneliness. You also might want to read a good book on loneliness. A good one is *Intimate Connections* by David Burns (1985), which is described at the end of this chapter in the "Resources" section.

At this point we have studied many ideas about social relationships. An overview of these ideas is presented in summary table 16.3.

You have arrived at the end of this book. You should be able to look back and say you learned a lot about human beings, both others and yourself. Many unanswered questions about human behavior remain, but psychology's quest to understand human behavior produces information we can use to make our life more enjoyable and humane. What could be more intriguing and important to all of us than psychology's mission of describing, explaining, and predicting the behavior of the human species?

SUMMARY TABLE 16.3
Social Interaction and Relationships

Concept	Processes/ Related Ideas	Characteristics/Discussion
Aggression	Biological Influences	We do not have an instinct for aggression, but biological factors are at work in aggression through genes, the brain, and hormones.
	Environmental and Psychological Influences	Aggression is more prevalent in some cultures than in others. Frustration is one of many aversive experiences that can cause aggression. An individual's cognitive interpretation of aversive circumstances determines whether the individual will respond aggressively. Aggression can be learned through reinforcement and observational learning. There is little support for the catharsis hypothesis. Various strategies have been proposed for reducing aggression, including increased parental involvement and monitoring of children and adolescents. Poverty and a sense of powerlessness can especially be involved in youth violence.
	Aggression and Gender	Males are more physically aggressive than females, and this difference has often been explained as biologically based. However, there are cultural variations in aggression. Gender differences in verbal aggression are less consistent than for physical aggression.
Altruism	What Is Altruism?	Altruism is an unselfish interest in helping someone else.
	Biological Basis	Evolutionary psychologists stress that altruism increases the prospects of survival as well as reproduction. Examples involve kin as well as when a parent cares for its young.
	Environmental and Psychological Influences	Reciprocity is often involved in altruism. The motivation can be altruistic or egoistic. Psychologists have studied both the person and situation variables in altruism. Extensive research has been conducted on bystander intervention.
	Altruism and Gender	In considering altruism and other areas of behavior, it is important to consider gender in context. Females are more likely to help in situations that are not dangerous and that involve caregiving. Males are more likely to help in situations where danger is perceived or where they feel competent.
Attraction, Love, and Relationships	Attraction	Familiarity precedes a close relationship. We like to associate with people who are similar to us. The principles of consensual validation and matching can explain this. Physical attraction is usually more important in the early part of a relationship, and criteria of physical attractiveness vary across cultures and historical time.
	Romantic Love	Also called passionate love, this love is involved when we say we are "in love." It includes passion, sexuality, and a mixture of emotions, not all of which are positive. Individualists do not experience romantic love as strongly.
	Affectionate Love	Also called companionate love, this type of love usually becomes more important as relationships mature. Shaver proposed a developmental model of love and Sternberg a triarchic model of love (passion, intimacy, and commitment).
	Relationships and Gender	Females have a stronger interest in relationships than males do. Tannen distinguishes between rapport talk (females) and report talk (males).
	Loneliness	Loneliness often emerges when people make life transitions, so it is not surprising that loneliness is common among first-year university students. A number of strategies were described to help lonely individuals become more socially connected.

Overview

WE BEGAN THIS CHAPTER on social psychology by examining these dimensions of social thinking: attribution, social perception, and attitudes. Our coverage of social influence focused on conformity and obedience, group influence, and cultural and ethnic influences. We also read about these aspects of social interaction and relationships: aggression, altruism, and attraction, love, and relationships.

Don't forget that you can obtain a more detailed overview of the chapter by again studying the summary tables on pages 560, 575, and 590.

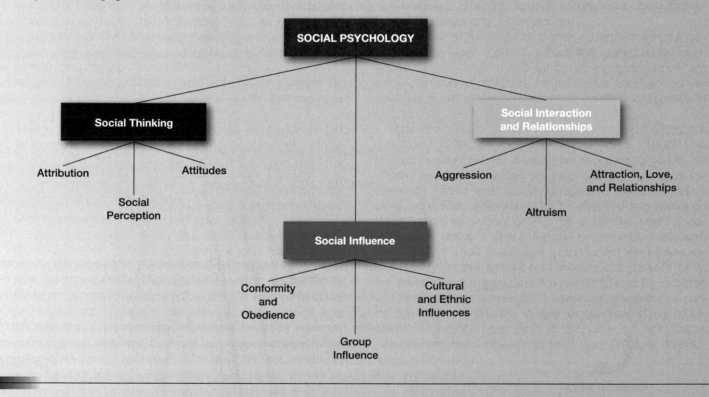

Key Terms

attribution theory 550
fundamental attribution error 552
self-serving bias 552
implicit personality theory 553
prototypes 554
primacy effect 554
social comparison 554
impression management (self-presentation) 555
self-monitoring 556
attitudes 556

foot-in-the-door strategy 556
door-in-the-face strategy 556
cognitive dissonance 557
self-perception theory 558
conformity 559
normative social influence 561
informational social influence 562
obedience 562
norms 565
roles 565
social facilitation 566
social loafing 566

deindividuation 566
risky shift 567
group polarization effect 567
groupthink 567
great-person theory 568
contingency model of leadership 568
prejudice 569
stereotype 570
ethnocentrism 571
social identity theory 571
frustration-aggression hypothesis 578

catharsis 579
altruism 580
egoism 582
bystander effect 582
consensual validation 584
matching hypothesis 585
romantic love 585
affectionate love 586
triangular theory of love 586
rapport talk 588
report talk 588

Key People

Key People

Fritz Heider 551
Bernard Weiner 551
Norman Anderson 553
Leon Festinger 554
Daryl Bem 558
Solomon Asch 561

Stanley Milgram 563
Norman Triplett 565
Robert Zajonc 566
Mark Zanna 570
Henry Tajfel 571

Muzafer Sherif 572
Eliot Aronson 573
Richard Clément 574
John Darley and Bibb Latané 582

Ellen Berscheid 585
Kenneth and Karen Dion 585
Phillip Shaver 586
Deborah Tannen 588

Psychology Checklist

SOCIAL PSYCHOLOGY

Checklist

How much have you learned since the beginning of the chapter? Place a checkmark beside any item for which you now feel that you have a good understanding.

_____ I know what attribution theory is and can describe the dimensions of causality as well as attributional errors and biases.

_____ I can discuss these aspects of social perception: developing impressions of others, gaining self-knowledge from our perceptions of others, and presenting ourselves to others to influence their social perceptions.

_____ I can describe the nature of attitudes, including various aspects of connections between attitudes and behavior.

_____ I can evaluate these dimensions of conformity: what contributes to it, Asch's and Zimbardo's studies, and resisting social influence.

_____ I am aware of various aspects of group influence.

_____ I know about these aspects of cultural and ethnic influences: prejudice, stereotyping, and ethnocentrism; improving interethnic relations.

_____ I can describe Zanna's theory of prejudice.

_____ I can describe the biological and environmental/psychological influences on aggression, as well as gender aspects of aggression.

_____ I can discuss these dimensions of altruism: what it is, biological influences, and environmental/psychological influences, as well as aspects of altruism.

_____ I know about these aspects of attraction, love, and relationships: why we are attracted to others, passionate love, affectionate love, relationships and gender, as well as loneliness.

For any items that you did not check off, go back and study the related material in the chapter again until you have a good command of the ideas.

Taking It to the Net

1. In the early 1990s, an incident involving a child arsonist received tremendous press. Although children light fires all the time, this case was different. After careful questioning, the boy revealed that he was a regular viewer of MTV's *Beavis and Butthead,* a popular (and often violent) cartoon. Moreover, he told police that he had seen Beavis and Butthead light fires and burn down buildings. The boy merely imitated the behavior he saw on TV. Unfortunately, this event is not isolated. Between the local news and *Cops,* we are exposed to violence on television on a daily basis. Does viewing television violence necessarily lead people to become violent? What evidence supports this?

2. Imagine an old woman walking down the street in a small town on her way to the grocery store. Suddenly, a masked man grabs her purse and hits her, knocking her to the ground. Horrified, the old woman cries out for help. A young man runs to her aid and helps her to safety. Now, imagine the same scenario in downtown Toronto. Would anyone come to her aid? Who is more likely to offer assistance: people in small towns, people in suburbs, or people in the inner city? Why do you think this is so?

3. Have you ever noticed that you don't usually laugh out loud at a funny movie when you see it on video alone, even though you are always laughing when you see a funny movie with your friends? Conversely, do you tend to cry more when you see a movie alone than with your friends? Do music groups sound better if the audience is more lively? Why do you think this is? Chances are that you are influenced by people around you, whether you realize it or not. Why do we experience things differently depending on who we are with? Explain the process of social influence and how you might be affected by it.

Connect to http://www.mcgrawhill.ca/college/santrock to find the answers!

Resources for Psychology and Life

A Textbook of Social Psychology, 4th Ed. (1998)
   by James Alcock, William Carment and
   Stanley Sadava
   Scarborough, ON: Prentice-Hall
This social psychology textbook features research by Canadian psychologists and special chapters addressing Canadian issues.

Applied Social Psychology (1997)
   by Stanley Sadava and Donald McCreary, (Eds.)
   Upper Saddle River, NJ: Prentice-Hall
This book offers an in-depth understanding of how social psychology has been applied in the real world.

The Authoritarian Specter (1996)
   by Robert Altemeyer
   Cambridge, MA: Harvard University Press
This book shows that many ordinary people today are highly susceptible to hate literature and are psychologically disposed to embrace antidemocratic, fascist policies.

The Psychology of Prejudice: The Ontario Symposium, Vol. 7. (1994)
   by Mark Zanna (Ed.)
   Hillsdale, NJ: Lawrence Erlbaum
This book offers excellent coverage of issues involving prejudice.

Influence (1993, rev. ed.)
   by Robert Cialdini
   New York: Quill
This highly acclaimed book by a well-known social psychologist explores how influence works in today's marketplace. Cialdini provides valuable suggestions for persuading other people and understanding how others try to persuade us. He also covers how power works, the role of reciprocity in influence, the importance of commitment and consistency, how to say no, scarcity, relationships with others, advertising, sales techniques, and instant influence.

You Just Don't Understand (1990)
   by Deborah Tannen
   New York: Ballantine
A national best-seller, this book is full of valuable suggestions for better understanding how males and females communicate.

Getting the Love You Want (1988)
   by Harvill Hendrix
   New York: Henry Holt
Getting the Love You Want is a guide that helps couples improve their relationships.

Intimate Connections (1985)
   by David Burns
   New York: William Morrow
This book describes how to overcome loneliness. Burns believes lonely individuals need to change their patterns of perception. He tells you how to make social connections and develop closer relationships with others. Checklists, daily mood logs, and self-assessments are found throughout the book.

Analyzing the Data: Statistics in Psychology and Everyday Life

APPENDIX OUTLINE

THE NATURE OF STATISTICS

DESCRIPTIVE STATISTICS

Descriptive Statistics for One Variable

Descriptive Statistics for Two Variables

INFERENTIAL STATISTICS

"What would life be without math?"

—Sydney Smith, 1835

Preview

IN THIS APPENDIX, we will explore the nature of statistics, which psychologists use to analyze data. The main sections of this appendix focus on the nature of statistics, descriptive statistics, and inferential statistics.

Images of Psychology and Life
Everyday Exposure to Statistics

WHETHER OR NOT YOU realize it, you are exposed to statistics every day. For example, the federal government releases reports showing the number of homeless people per 1,000 province by province, the dramatic increase in the number of women in prisons, and so on. Advertisers use statistics to try to persuade you to buy their products by showing you how consumers prefer their products over the competition by five to one. High schools, colleges, and universities use statistics to track student demographics such as the number of students attending, the number of students in particular programs, and student grade point averages. Statistics are also widely used in sports such as football, baseball, and basketball. Statistics also are used in psychology and the other sciences to analyze data that have been collected. In short, statistics are so much a part of our lives that an understanding of basic statistics is essential if you want to be an informed member of society (Hastings, 1995). Thus, the purpose of this appendix is to help you make sense out of some basic statistical concepts that are used in everyday life as well as in scientific research.

The Nature of Statistics

Statistics *are mathematical methods used to describe, summarize, and draw conclusions about data.* There are two basic categories of statistics: (1) descriptive and (2) inferential.

Descriptive Statistics

Descriptive statistics *are mathematical procedures used to describe and summarize samples of data in a meaningful fashion.* More specifically, descriptive statistics can be used to describe the characteristics of either a single variable or an interaction between two variables. This is important in most psychological studies because, if we simply reported all the individual scores, it would be virtually impossible to summarize the results. Descriptive statistics allow us to avoid this situation by providing numerous measures that reveal the overall characteristics of the data. Let's look at some of those measures.

Descriptive Statistics for One Variable

The descriptive statistics for one variable include frequency distributions, histograms, and frequency polygons; measures of central tendency; measures of variability; and normal distribution.

Frequency Distributions, Histograms, and Frequency Polygons
Recently some researchers found a connection between how many siblings a student has and her academic performance. Let's assume your introductory psychology class is dubious about this finding, but your classmates want to see if a connection between number of siblings and academic performance applies to them. All 20 students in your psychology class answer a short questionnaire, indicating the number of brothers and sisters they have, if any, and their cumulative high school grade point average. For now let's focus on the variable of number of siblings. Following are the number of siblings each member of your class indicated:

6	4	3	8
6	2	0	2
1	2	3	0
2	3	2	1
3	2	2	8

It is difficult to draw any general conclusions about the overall tendencies of the group just by looking at the raw data (that is, the number of brothers and sisters each person reported). It would be even more difficult if our sample size were 500 or 1,000 students instead of just 20. In any case, the first thing we need to do is to organize the data in a more meaningful way, such as in a frequency distribution. A **frequency distribution** *is simply a listing of scores from lowest to highest with the number of times each score appears in a sample.* Figure A.1a shows the frequency distribution for our data on number of siblings. The column on the left lists the possible responses (number of siblings) and the column on the right shows how often that response was given.

Another way to present the data is visually through the use of either a histogram or a frequency polygon. A **histogram** *is a frequency distribution in graphic form, in which vertical bars represent the frequency of scores per category or class.* Figure A.1b shows a histogram for our data on the category of number of siblings. A histogram is often called a *bar graph* or, occasionally, a *block diagram.*

A **frequency polygon** *is basically the same as a histogram except that the data are represented with lines rather than bars.* Figure A.1c shows a frequency polygon for the data on number of siblings. Notice that, in both the histogram and the frequency

Score	Frequency
8	2
7	0
6	2
5	0
4	1
3	4
2	7
1	2
0	2

(a) Frequency distribution

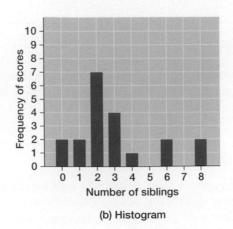

(b) Histogram

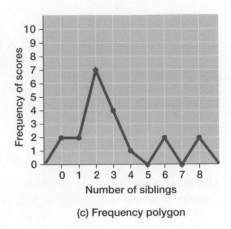

(c) Frequency polygon

Figure A.1
Frequency Distribution, Histogram, and Frequency Polygon

These data are from a hypothetical survey on number of siblings reported by 20 students in your psychology class.
(*a*) A frequency distribution lists the scores from lowest to highest, with the number of times each score appears.
(*b*) A histogram depicts the frequency distribution in graphic form, with vertical bars representing the frequency of scores. (*c*) A frequency polygon is basically the same as a histogram except that the data are represented with lines rather than bars. *Which of these formats do you find easiest to interpret?*

Mean

| 6 |
| 6 |
| 1 |
| 2 |
| 3 |
| 4 |
| 2 |
| 2 |
| 3 |
| 2 |
| 3 |
| 0 |
| 3 |
| 2 |
| 2 |
| 8 |
| 2 |
| 0 |
| 1 |
| 8 |

$60 \overline{)20} = 3$

Median

Ranking	Scores in order	
1	0	
2	0	
3	1	
4	1	
5	2	
6	2	
7	2	
8	2	
9	2	Middle of rankings
10	2	
11	2	
12	3	
13	3	
14	3	
15	3	
16	4	
17	6	
18	6	
19	8	
20	8	

Because there is an even set of scores, median equals middle, two scores added together, then divided by 2. Thus, $\dfrac{2 + 2}{2} = 2$

Mode

Score	Frequency	
8	2	
7	0	
6	2	
5	0	
4	1	
3	4	
2	7	← Most frequent score
1	2	
0	2	

Mode = 2

0 1 2 3 4 5 6 7 8

Figure A.2
Mean, Median, and Mode

These data are from a hypothetical survey on number of siblings reported by 20 students in your psychology class. The mean is the numerical average for a group of scores; it is calculated by adding all the scores and then dividing by the number of scores. The median is the score that falls exactly in the middle of a distribution of scores after they have been ranked from highest to lowest. When there is an even number of scores, as there is here, you add the middle two scores and divide by 2 to calculate the median. The mode is the score that appears most often.

polygon, the horizontal axis (the *y*-axis) indicates the possible scores and the vertical axis (the *x*-axis) indicates how often each score occurs in the set of data points.

Although frequency distributions, histograms, and frequency polygons can help *graphically* represent a group of scores, you may want to represent a group of scores *numerically* by providing a measure of central tendency, a measure of variability, or both. Let's look at these two measures.

Measures of Central Tendency   If you want to describe an "average" value for a set of scores, you would use one of the measures of central tendency. In essence, a **measure of central tendency** *is a single number that tells you the overall characteristics of a set of data.* There are three measures of central tendency: the mean, the median, and the mode.

The **mean** *is the numerical average for a group of scores or values.* The mean is calculated by adding all the scores and then dividing by the number of scores. To compute the mean for the data collected on number of siblings, we add all the scores, equalling 60, then divide by the total number of scores, 20. This gives us a mean of 3 siblings. This procedure is shown on the left side of figure A.2.

In general the mean is a good indicator of the central tendency for a group of scores; it is the measure of central tendency that is used most often. One exception to this general rule is when a group of scores contains a few extreme scores. For example, consider the annual earnings for the two groups of five people in the table that follows. Group 1 lists the earnings of five relatively average people. Group 2 is composed of the earnings of four average people plus the approximate earnings of movie director Steven Spielberg. The vast difference between the mean earnings for the two groups is due to the one extreme score. In such a situation, one of the other two measures of central tendency would more accurately describe the data's overall characteristics.

Group 1	Group 2
$17,000	$17,000
21,000	21,000
23,000	23,000
24,000	24,000
25,000	45,000,000
Mean = $22,000	Mean = $9,017,000
Median = $23,000	Median = $23,000
Mode = N/A	Mode = N/A

The **median** *is the score that falls exactly in the middle of a distribution of scores after they have been arranged (or ranked) from highest to lowest.* When you have an odd number of scores (say, 5 or 7 scores), the median is the score with the same number of scores above it as below it after they have been ranked. Thus, in our example comparing earnings, each group had a median income of $23,000. When you have an even number of scores (8, 10, or 20 scores, for example), you simply add the middle 2 scores and divide by 2 to arrive at the median. In our example using number of siblings, we have an even number of scores (20), so the median is the 10th and 11th scores added together and divided by 2, or (2 + 2)/2. Thus, the median number of siblings for our set of 20 responses is 2, as shown in the middle panel of figure 2.

Notice that, unlike the mean, the median is unaffected by one or a few extreme scores. Look again at the earnings of the two groups. The medians are the same for both groups ($23,000), but their means are extremely different ($22,000 versus $9,017,000).

The **mode** *is the score that occurs most often.* The mode can be determined very easily by looking at a frequency distribution, histogram, or frequency polygon. In our present example, the mode is 2, which is the number of siblings indicated most often by the members of your psychology class. Although the mode is the least used measure of central tendency, it has descriptive value because, unlike the mean and the median, there can be two or more modes. Consider the following 15 scores on a 10-point surprise quiz: 9, 3, 8, 5, 9, 3, 6, 9, 4, 10, 2, 3, 3, 9, 7. The quiz scores 9 and 3 each appear four times. No other score in this example appears as often or more often. Thus, this set of scores has two modes, or a *bimodal distribution*. It is, in fact, possible to have several modes, or a *multimodal distribution*. It also is possible to have no mode at all, which was the case when we compared the earnings of the two groups of five people. Depending on the research question being investigated, the mode may actually provide more meaningful information than either the mean or the median. For example, developers of a program to help people stop smoking would benefit more from knowing that the "modal" age of the greatest number of people who smoke is either 22 *or* 58 than from knowing that the mean age of smokers is 37. By knowing that smoking behavior is distributed bimodally in the population, they can more appropriately target their program to young adults and older adults rather than to middle-aged adults.

Selecting the right measure of central tendency can be challenging. In general, the mean is a good indicator of the central tendency for a group of scores; it is the measure of central tendency that researchers use most often. One exception to this rule is when a group of scores contains extreme scores.

Annual earnings represent a single variable that will illustrate the importance of selecting the right measure of central tendency to communicate about the data.

Suppose we have collected annual earnings data on group 1, consisting of seven people. The frequency distribution is as follows:

Group 1	
$17,000	1
$21,000	2
$23,000	1
$24,000	1
$25,000	1
$28,000	1

Test yourself on the differences in concepts. What is the mode? What would be the median score? Calculate the mean by adding up the raw scores and dividing by the number of scores.

The mode is easy to determine from the frequency distribution. The value $21,000 occurs twice and stands out in the distribution as the only repeated value. We determine the median score by identifying the score that occupies the middle (or 4th) position in this frequency distribution: $24,000. In calculating the mean, the sum of all the earnings adds up to $159,000. When you divide that by 7, you discover that the mean is about $22,700. In this example the median, mode, and mean are all relatively close.

Suppose we examine another group in which all of the scores are identical except for the last one. In this case, we are including as the 7th score Steven Spielberg's approximate annual earnings as a highly successful movie director. The data for group 2 are as follows:

Group 2	
$17,000	1
$21,000	2
$23,000	1
$24,000	1
$25,000	1
$45,000,000	1

Which measures of central tendency would change? Which ones would *not* be influenced by the inclusion of an extreme score? As you have probably guessed, the median would stay the same. The fourth score in the distribution is still $24,000. The mode remains the same. The value of $21,000 still occurs twice. The mean is the measure that is dramatically influenced. In this case, the average salary is now over $6 million. This example illustrates how important it is to find out what kind of "average" figure is being presented to communicate the characteristics of any group of data. These insights may also help you develop appropriate skepticism when evaluating statistical claims. For example, radio humorist Garrison Keillor jokes that in his fictionalized hometown of Lake Woebegone, "all the women are strong, all the men are good-looking, and all the children are *above average*."

Measures of Variability   Consider the following example. You are the owner of three clothing stores that all have the same mean annual earnings of $1,000,000. These three stores fluctuate widely in their monthly earnings, however. Store 1 consistently produces a monthly income of about $100,000. Store 2 generates no income some months but produces $250,000 of income other months. Store 3 loses money the first 9 months of every year but makes enormous profits during October, November, and December. It would be to your advantage to be able to represent the individual fluctuations of your three stores. Measures of variability can be very useful in this regard.

Along with obtaining the overall or central characteristics for a sample, *we can also ask how much the scores in a sample vary from one another. These measures are called* **measures of variability** *or* **measures of dispersion.** The two measures of variability are called the range and the standard deviation.

The **range** *is the distance between the highest and the lowest scores.* The range for our data on number of siblings would be 8 (high score) minus 0 (low score), for a range of 8. Generally speaking, the range is a rather simplistic estimate of variability, or dispersion, for a group of scores. More importantly, because the range involves only two scores, it can produce a misleading index of variability; thus, the range is rarely used as a measure of variability. The most commonly used measure of variability is the standard deviation.

The **standard deviation** *is a measure of how much the scores vary on the average around the mean of a sample.* Put another way, it indicates how closely scores are clustered around the mean. The smaller the standard deviation, the less variability from the mean and vice versa. A simple example will illustrate how this measure of variability works. Consider the following four race scores for each of three joggers:

	Jogger 1	Jogger 2	Jogger 3
Race 1	44 minutes	40 minutes	32 minutes
Race 2	36 minutes	40 minutes	48 minutes
Race 3	44 minutes	40 minutes	32 minutes
Race 4	36 minutes	40 minutes	48 minutes
Mean time	40 minutes	40 minutes	40 minutes
Standard deviation	4 minutes	0 minutes	8 minutes

Notice that all three joggers had the same mean race time of 40 minutes, but jogger 1 and jogger 3 each had race times that varied from race to race, whereas jogger 2 had exactly the same time for each of the four races. This variability from race to race, or the lack of it, is expressed by the three different standard deviations. Because jogger 2 had no variability from race to race, that person's standard deviation is 0. Jogger 1's race time varied 4 minutes on the average from his mean of 40 minutes. In other words, jogger 1 had a standard deviation of 4 minutes for his race times. Jogger 3's race times varied 8 minutes on the average from her mean time of 40 minutes. Thus, jogger 3 had a standard deviation of 8 minutes for her race times. The different standard deviations tell you that jogger 2 had no variability among his race scores, jogger 1 had some variability among his race scores, and jogger 3 had even more variability among her race scores.

Calculating a standard deviation is really not very difficult if you use a calculator capable of doing square roots. To compute a standard deviation, follow these four steps:

1. Calculate the mean of the scores.
2. From each score, subtract the mean and then square that difference. (Squaring the scores will eliminate any negative signs that result from subtracting the mean.)
3. Add the squares and then divide by the number of scores.
4. Calculate the square root of the value obtained in Step 3. This is the standard deviation.

The formula for these four steps is

$$\textbf{Standard deviation} = \sqrt{\frac{\Sigma x^2}{N}}$$

where x = the individual score minus the mean, N = the number of scores, and Σ = the sum of. The application of these four steps to our example of number of

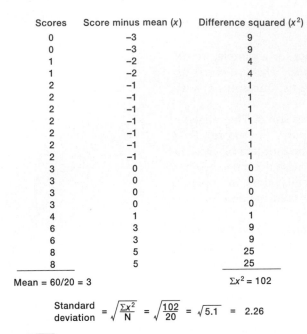

Scores	Score minus mean (x)	Difference squared (x²)
0	−3	9
0	−3	9
1	−2	4
1	−2	4
2	−1	1
2	−1	1
2	−1	1
2	−1	1
2	−1	1
2	−1	1
2	−1	1
3	0	0
3	0	0
3	0	0
3	0	0
4	1	1
6	3	9
6	3	9
8	5	25
8	5	25

Mean = 60/20 = 3 $\Sigma x^2 = 102$

$$\text{Standard deviation} = \sqrt{\frac{\Sigma x^2}{N}} = \sqrt{\frac{102}{20}} = \sqrt{5.1} = 2.26$$

Figure A.3
Computing the Standard Deviation

The standard deviation is a measure of how much the scores vary on the average around the mean of a sample. In this figure, you can see how the standard deviation was calculated for the data gathered from a hypothetical survey on number of siblings reported by 20 students in your psychology class.

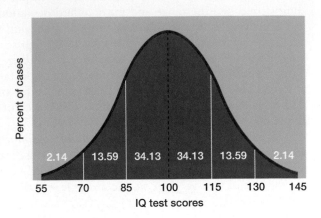

Figure A.4
Normal Distribution, or Bell-Shaped Curve

This graph shows the normal distribution of IQ scores as measured by the Wechsler Adult Intelligence Scale. The normal distribution is a type of frequency polygon in which most of the scores are clustered around the mean. The scores become less frequent the farther they appear above or below the mean.

siblings is illustrated in figure A.3. As you can see, when all the calculations are completed, the standard deviation equals 2.26.

The Normal Distribution   As we saw earlier, the scores for any distribution can be plotted on a frequency polygon, and can take a variety of shapes. One shape in particular has been of considerable interest to psychologists—the **normal distribution,** or **bell-shaped curve.** *In this type of frequency polygon, most of the scores cluster around the mean. The farther above or below the mean a score appears, the less frequently it occurs.* Many naturally occurring phenomena, such as human intelligence, height, weight, and athletic abilities, follow or closely approximate a normal distribution. For example, the normal distribution of IQ scores as measured by the Wechsler Adult Intelligence Scale is shown in figure A.4. Notice that the mean IQ is 100 and the standard deviation is 15 IQ points. We will come back to these numbers in a moment.

Figure A.5 illustrates several important characteristics of the normal distribution. First, it is perfectly symmetrical. There is the same number of scores above the mean as below it. Because of this perfect symmetry, the mean, median, and mode are identical in a normal distribution. Second, its bell shape illustrates that the most common scores are near the middle. The scores become less frequent and more extreme the farther away from the middle they appear. Third, the normal distribution incorporates information about both the mean and the standard deviation, as shown in figure A.5. The area on the normal curve that is one standard deviation above the mean and one standard deviation below the mean represents 68.26 percent of the scores. At two standard deviations above and below the mean, 95.42 percent of the scores are represented. Finally, at three standard deviations above and below the mean, 99.74 percent of the scores are contained. If we apply this information to figure A.4, which shows the normal distribution of IQ scores in the population, you can readily see that 68 percent of the population has an IQ between 85 and 115, 95 percent of the population has an IQ between 70 and 130, and 99 percent of the population has an IQ between 55 and 145.

Descriptive Statistics for Two Variables

Descriptive statistics for two variables include scatter plots and the correlation coefficient.

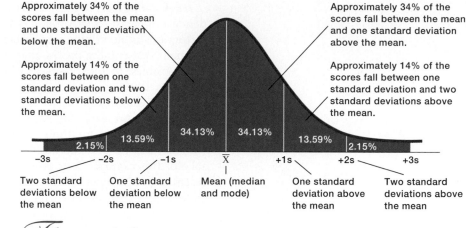

Figure A.5
The Normal Distribution

Scatter Plots Up to this point, we've focused on descriptive statistics used to describe only one variable. Often the goal of research is to describe the relationship between two variables. In our example, we collected information from the 20 members of your psychology class on their number of siblings and their high school grade point average. The raw data we collected are shown on the left side of figure A.6. Also shown is a scatter plot of those scores. A **scatter plot** *is a graph on which pairs of scores are represented.* In this case, we are looking at the possible relationship between number of siblings and academic performance. The possible scores for one variable—number of siblings—are indicated on the *x*-axis, and the scores for the second variable—grade point average—are indicated on the *y*-axis. Each dot on the scatter plot represents one pair of scores as reported by each member of your class. As you can see, there seems to be a distinct pattern to our scatter plot—that is, as the number of siblings increases, high school GPA decreases. Tentatively, at least, there appears to be an association between these two variables. Just how related are these two factors? It's difficult to go beyond a broad generalization from simply viewing a scatter plot.

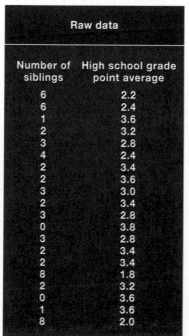

Number of siblings	High school grade point average
6	2.2
6	2.4
1	3.6
2	3.2
3	2.8
4	2.4
2	3.4
2	3.6
3	3.0
2	3.4
3	2.8
0	3.8
3	2.8
2	3.4
2	3.4
8	1.8
2	3.2
0	3.6
1	3.6
8	2.0

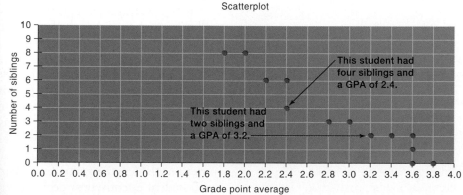

Figure A.6
Descriptive Measures for Two Variables

This scatter plot depicts the possible relationship between number of siblings and grade point average. Each dot on the scatter plot represents one pair of scores as reported by each member of your class in a hypothetical survey. The raw data from that survey are shown on the left.

The Correlation Coefficient

Just as we found measures of central tendency and measures of variability to be more precise than frequency distributions or histograms in describing one variable, it would be helpful if we had a type of measurement that is more precise than a scatter plot to describe the relationship between two variables. In such cases, we could compute a correlation coefficient (Toothaker & Miller, 1996).

A **correlation coefficient** *is a numerical value that expresses the degree of relationship between two variables.* For example, let's assume that we have calculated the correlation coefficient for the relationship between how long your instructor lectures (the *X* variable) and the number of times students yawn (the *Y* variable). For the sake of this example, let's assume these data produce a correlation coefficient (represented by the letter *r*) of +.70. Remember this number, as we will use it to illustrate what a correlation coefficient tells you.

The numeric value of a correlation coefficient falls within the range from +1.00 to −1.00. This is simply an arbitrary range that does *not* parallel an integer number line (for example, . . . −3, −2, −1, 0, 1, 2, 3, . . .). In other words, negative numbers are *not* less than positive numbers. A correlation of +.65 is just as strong as a correlation of −.65. The plus or minus sign has a different meaning when applied to correlation coefficients, which we will discuss in a moment. Also, avoid the temptation to attach value judgments to correlational signs. A positive correlation is not "good" or "desirable" and a negative correlation is not "bad" or "undesirable."

There are two parts to a correlation coefficient: the number and the sign. The number tells you the strength of the relationship between the two factors. The rule is simple: regardless of the sign, the closer the number is to 1.00, the stronger the correlation; conversely, the closer the number is to .00, the weaker the correlation. Remember that the plus or minus sign tells you nothing about the strength of the correlation; thus, a correlation of −.87 is stronger than a correlation of +.45. Table A.1 offers guidelines for interpreting correlational numbers.

The plus or minus sign tells you the direction of the relationship between the two variables. A **positive correlation** *is a relationship in which the two factors vary in the same direction.* Both factors tend to go up together or both factors tend to go down together. Either relationship represents a positive correlation. A **negative correlation** *is a relationship in which the two factors vary in opposite directions.* As one factor increases, the other factor decreases. Thus, a correlation of +.15 would indicate a weak positive correlation, and a −.74 would indicate a strong negative correlation. Examples of scatter plots showing positive and negative correlations appear in figure A.7.

Let's return to our example about how long your professor lectures and the number of times students yawn. Those two variables produced a correlation coefficient of +.70. The number .70 tells us that these two factors happen together frequently. We also know from the preceding discussion that the positive sign indicates the two factors vary in the same direction. As the amount of time your professor lectures increases, the number of yawns increases. An example of a negative correlation in this situation might be the relationship between how long your instructor lectures and the level of student attentiveness. As the length of time your instructor lectures increases, the level of student attentiveness decreases—these two factors vary in opposite directions.

The following formula is used to calculate a correlation coefficient:

$$r = \frac{\Sigma xy}{\sqrt{\Sigma x^2 \Xi \, \Sigma y^2}}$$

where *x* is the difference between each *X* variable minus the mean; *y* is the difference between each *Y* variable minus the mean; Σxy is the sum of the cross products (each *x* score multiplied by its corresponding

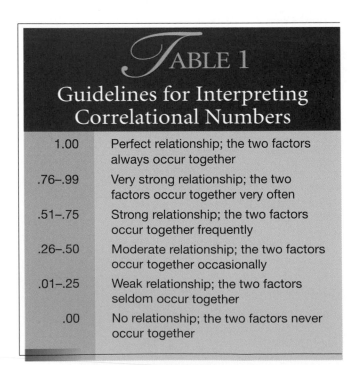

TABLE 1

Guidelines for Interpreting Correlational Numbers

1.00	Perfect relationship; the two factors always occur together
.76–.99	Very strong relationship; the two factors occur together very often
.51–.75	Strong relationship; the two factors occur together frequently
.26–.50	Moderate relationship; the two factors occur together occasionally
.01–.25	Weak relationship; the two factors seldom occur together
.00	No relationship; the two factors never occur together

y score); $\sum x^2$ is the sum of the squares of the x scores; and $\sum y^2$ is the sum of the squares of the y scores.

Let's return to our original example examining the relationship between number of siblings and high school grade point average. Figure A.8 contains the calculation of the correlation coefficient of −.95. From our previous discussion, we know that this is a very strong association indicating that, as number of siblings increases, grade point average decreases. What exactly does this mean? How are we supposed to interpret this hypothetical finding? Does this mean that, if you are an only child, you will have a 4.0 GPA? Does this mean that, if you grew up in a large family, you are destined to make poor grades?

Although correlation coefficients are frequently used by researchers to analyze the relationship between two variables, they are almost as frequently misinterpreted by the general public. The problem is that *correlation does not necessarily indicate causality.* Causality means that one factor makes, produces, or creates change in a second factor. Correlation means that two factors *seem* to be related, associated, or connected such that, as one factor changes, the other factor seems to change. Correlation implies potential causality that may or may not actually be there. Even though two factors are strongly or even perfectly correlated, in reality a third factor may be responsible for the changes observed. Thus, in our hypothetical example showing a very strong negative correlation between number of siblings and GPA, the changes observed in these two variables could be due to a third factor. For example, perhaps children who grow up in larger families have a greater tendency to hold part-time jobs after school, thereby limiting the amount of time they can study, or children who grow up in small families may be more likely to have their own room, with a desk, thereby allowing them more uninterrupted study time. In any case, the point remains the same: correlation only potentially indicates a causal relationship.

Look at the terms in bold type in the following headlines:

Researchers **Link** Coffee Consumption to Cancer of Pancreas
Scientists Find **Connection** Between Ear Hair and Heart Attacks
Psychologists Discover **Relationship** Between Marital Status and Health
Researchers Identify **Association** Between Loneliness and Social Skills
Parental Discipline **Tied** to Personality Disorders in Children

All of the words in bold type are synonymous with correlation, not causality. The general public, however, tends to equate such terms as *connection* or *association* with causality. As you read about the findings of psychological studies, or findings in other sciences, guard against making the same interpretation. Remember, correlation means only that two factors seem to occur together (Cohen, 1996).

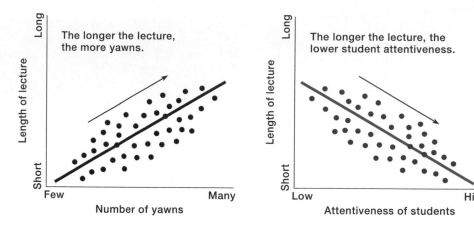

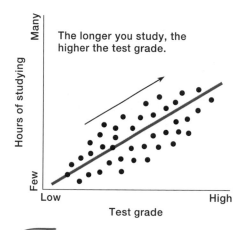

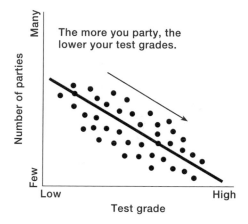

𝒻igure A.7
Scatter Plots Showing Positive and Negative Correlations
A positive correlation is a relationship in which two factors vary in the same direction, as shown in the two scatter plots on the left. A negative correlation is a relationship in which two factors vary in opposite directions, as shown in the two scatter plots on the right.

Student number	Number of siblings (X variable)	Score minus mean (3.0)	Difference squared	High school GPA (Y variable)	Score minus mean (3.0)	Difference squared	x multiplied by y
N	X	x	x^2	Y	y	y^2	xy
1	6	3	9	2.2	−.8	.64	−2.4
2	6	3	9	2.4	−.6	.36	−1.8
3	1	−2	4	3.6	.6	.36	−1.2
4	2	−1	1	3.2	.2	.04	−0.2
5	3	0	0	2.8	−.2	.04	0.0
6	4	1	1	2.4	−.6	.36	−0.6
7	2	−1	1	3.4	.4	.16	−0.4
8	2	−1	1	3.6	.6	.36	−0.6
9	3	0	0	3.0	0.0	.00	0.0
10	2	−1	1	3.4	.4	.16	−0.4
11	3	0	0	2.8	−.2	.04	0.0
12	0	−3	9	3.8	.8	.64	−2.4
13	3	0	0	2.8	−.2	.04	0.0
14	2	−1	1	3.4	.4	.16	−0.4
15	2	−1	1	3.4	.4	.16	−0.4
16	8	5	25	1.8	−1.2	1.44	−6.0
17	2	−1	1	3.2	.2	.04	−0.2
18	0	−3	9	3.6	.6	.36	−1.8
19	1	−2	4	3.6	.6	.36	−1.2
20	8	5	25	2.0	−1.0	1.00	−5.0

N = 20   Mean = 3.0 $\Sigma x^2 = 102$ Mean = 3.0 $\Sigma y^2 = 6.72$ $\Sigma xy = -25.00$

$$r = \frac{\Sigma xy}{\sqrt{\Sigma x^2 \times \Sigma y^2}} = \frac{-25.00}{\sqrt{(102)\,(6.72)}} = \frac{-25.00}{\sqrt{685.44}} = \frac{-25.00}{26.18} = -.95$$

Figure A.8
Computation of a Correlation Coefficient

These data are from a hypothetical survey on number of siblings and high school GPA reported by 20 students in your psychology class. The correlation coefficient of −.95 indicates a very strong negative relationship between number of siblings and high school GPA.

How, then, can a researcher provide compelling evidence of a causal relationship between two variables? In the experimental method, researchers try to hold all variables constant, then systematically manipulate the factor that they think produces change (the independent variable); finally, they measure the variable believed to be affected by these manipulations (the dependent variable). If the researchers have held all factors constant except for their manipulation of the independent variable, then any changes observed in the dependent variable can be attributed to the independent variable; changes in the independent variable *caused* changes to occur in the dependent variable. This is the most compelling evidence of causality that science can provide, assuming that the experiment was carefully designed and controlled to avoid such experimental pitfalls as experimenter bias, subject bias, situational bias, or invalid scores. Furthermore, experimental evidence of causality is even more compelling if the research can be *replicated*, or repeated by other researchers using different subjects.

Why do researchers even bother doing correlational studies if they only potentially indicate causality? Why don't researchers simply conduct experiments all the time, since experiments provide the most compelling evidence of causality? There are several reasons. One, it is not always ethically possible to conduct an experiment on the research question at hand. It may be unethical to conduct an experiment because it poses either physical or psychological danger to the subjects. For instance, it would be unethical to carry out an experiment in which expectant mothers are directed to smoke varying numbers of cigarettes (the independent variable) to see how cigarette smoke affects birth weight and fetal activity level (the dependent variable). Two, the issue under investigation may be post hoc (after the fact) or historical, such as studying the childhood backgrounds of people who are abusive parents. Three, sometimes the factors simply cannot be manipulated experimentally, such as the effects of the October 17, 1989, earthquake on the residents of San Francisco. Fourth, experiments can be incredibly costly to conduct. Correlational studies, on the other hand, are often less expensive. These are some of the limitations associated with the experimental method.

What do researchers do in the situations in which formal experiments are inappropriate or impossible? They use the correlational method and collect data based on *systematic observation* of subjects rather than *systematic manipulation* of the subjects. Systematic observation techniques include case studies, naturalistic observation, interviews, questionnaires, and standardized tests.

Thus, the correlation coefficient is a very useful and important statistical tool for psychological as well as for other kinds of research. By understanding how to interpret the number and sign of a correlation coefficient, you can judge how closely two factors are related and in what direction they vary. By understanding the difference between "correlation" and "causation," you are more likely to interpret correctly the research findings described in newspapers, magazines, and journals. Every time the words *association, link, tie, connection,* and *relationship* are used to explain research findings, a correlational study is being described, because all of those words imply correlation, not causation.

Although descriptive statistics can help us summarize and characterize a sample of data, they have limitations. For instance, descriptive statistics cannot tell us whether data are meaningful or significant. A different category of statistics is necessary to accomplish this—inferential statistics (Evans, 1996).

Correlation methods permit research in situations that cannot be experimentally manipulated, such as natural disasters like the 1996 flood in the Saguenay region of Quebec.

Inferential Statistics

Assume you have conducted a naturalistic observation investigating whether boys play more aggressively than girls. Assume further that you have followed all the procedures for a good research design to eliminate or minimize any bias or other factors that might distort the data you have collected. When you calculate the descriptive statistics comparing the aggressive behavior of boys with that of girls, it appears that there are large differences between the two groups. How large do those differences have to be before you are willing to conclude confidently that the differences are significant? Inferential statistics can help answer that question.

Inferential statistics *are complex mathematical methods used to draw conclusions about data that have been collected.* More specifically, inferential statistics are used to indicate whether or not data sufficiently support or confirm a research hypothesis. To accomplish this, inferential statistics rely on statements of probability and statistical significance, two important concepts that we will examine briefly.

There are many kinds of inferential statistics. Depending on the characteristics of the data and the number of groups being compared, different tests are applied. Some examples of inferential statistical measures include the *t*-test, the chi-square, analysis of variance, and the Mann-Whitney *U* Test. Although it's beyond the scope of this Appendix to look at these different measures of inferential statistics in detail, the logic behind inferential statistics is relatively simple. Measures of inferential statistics yield a statement of probability about the differences observed between two or more groups; this probability statement tells what the odds are that the observed differences were due simply to chance. If an inferential statistical measure tells you that the odds are less than 5 out of 100 (or .05) that the differences are due to chance, the results are considered statistically significant. In statistical jargon, this is referred to as the *.05 level of statistical significance,* or the *.05 confidence level.* Put another way, **statistical significance** *means that the differences observed between two groups are so large that it is highly unlikely those differences are due merely to chance.*

The .05 level of statistical significance is considered the minimum level of probability that scientists will accept for concluding that the differences observed are real, thereby supporting a hypothesis. Some researchers prefer to use more rigorous levels of statistical significance, such as the .01 level of statistical significance (1 out of 100) or the .001 level of statistical significance (1 out of 1,000). Regardless of which level of statistical significance is used, by knowing that a research result is statistically significant, you can be reasonably confident that the finding is not due simply to chance. Of course, replication of the study, with similar significant results, can increase your confidence in the finding even further.

However, a statistically significant difference does not always translate into a difference that has meaning in everyday life. Before assuming that a finding is significant both statistically and in everyday terms, it's wise to look at the actual differences involved. Sometimes the differences are so small as to be inconsequential. For example, in comparisons of average scores for males and females on the math section of the Scholastic Aptitude Test, the difference is statistically significant, with males performing better than females (Benbow & Stanley, 1983). In reality, however, the average difference is only a few points. Caution, therefore, should be exercised in the practical interpretation of statistically significant findings.

At this point we have studied a number of ideas about the nature of statistics, descriptive statistics, and inferential statistics. An overview of these ideas is presented in summary table 1.

SUMMARY TABLE 1
The Nature of Statistics, Descriptive Statistics, and Inferential Statistics

Concept	Processes/Related Ideas	Characteristics/Description
Nature of Statistics	Basic ideas	Statistics are a part of our everyday life. Therefore, an understanding of statistics helps us to be informed participants in today's society. Statistics are mathematical methods that are used to describe, summarize, and infer conclusions about data. The two basic categories of statistics are (1) descriptive and (2) inferential.
Descriptive Statistics	Descriptive statistics for one variable	Descriptive statistics used to describe the characteristics of one variable include frequency distributions, histograms, frequency polygons, measures of central tendency, and measures of variability. The most commonly used descriptive statistics are measures of central tendency and measures of variability. Measures of central tendency describe the overall or average characteristics of a group of scores. Measures of central tendency include the mean, median, and mode. Measures of variability describe how much scores differ from one another. The standard deviation is the most commonly used measure of variability. The normal distribution, or bell-shaped curve, is a frequency polygon of special interest to psychologists. A perfect normal distribution is completely symmetrical; thus, the mean, median, and mode are identical. By knowing the mean and the standard deviation for a normally distributed variable, you can determine what percentage of the population has a particular score.
	Descriptive statistics for two variables	Descriptive statistics examining the relationship between two variables include the scatter plot and the correlation coefficient. Whereas a scatter plot provides a graphic illustration of the relationship between two variables, correlation coefficients provide a numeric summary of the association between two variables. Although correlational research is widely used, many people confuse correlation and causality. Correlation simply means that two variables seem to occur together in a systematic fashion. Correlation, however, does not necessarily indicate causality. Causality means that one factor makes, produces, or creates change in a second factor. The most compelling evidence to demonstrate that one variable causes change to occur in a second variable comes from experiments. Formal experiments, however, cannot always be conducted for a variety of reasons; thus, scientists frequently rely on correlational research to demonstrate a potential relationship between two variables.
Inferential Statistics	Their nature	Inferential statistics are complex mathematical methods used to draw conclusions based on data. Inferential statistical measures yield a statement of probability about the differences observed between two or more groups. This probability statement tells you what the odds are that the observed differences were due simply to chance. If an inferential statistical measure tells you that the odds are less than 5 out of 100 (or .05) that the observed differences are due to chance, the results are considered statistically significant. Although research results may be statistically significant, they may actually have little or no implication in everyday terms. Thus, caution should be exercised in the practical interpretation of statistically significant findings.

Overview

IN THIS APPENDIX we explored the basic nature of statistics, descriptive statistics, and inferential statistics. Don't forget that you can obtain a more detailed review of the appendix by studying the summary table on page A16.

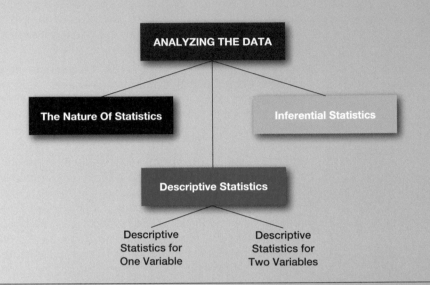

ANALYZING THE DATA

The Nature Of Statistics

Inferential Statistics

Descriptive Statistics

Descriptive Statistics for One Variable

Descriptive Statistics for Two Variables

Key Terms

statistics A1
descriptive statistics A1
frequency distribution A1
histogram A1
frequency polygon A1
measure of central tendency A2

mean A2
median A3
mode A3
measures of variability (measures of dispersion) A5
range A5
standard deviation A5

normal distribution (bell-shaped curve) A6
scatter plot A7
correlation coefficient A8

positive correlation A8
negative correlation A8
inferential statistics A12
statistical significance A12

Resources for Psychology and Life

Elementary Statistics (1989, 2nd ed.)
    by A. Comrey, P. Bott, and H. Lee
    New York: McGraw-Hill
This excellent introductory statistics text uses a step-by-step problem-solving approach to understanding statistics.

How to Lie with Statistics (1954)
    by D. Huff
    New York: W.W. Norton
This delightful book is the classic primer on how statistics are frequently used to mislead or deceive people. Originally published in 1954, the examples are not only humorous and effective, but they also provide a wonderful glimpse of everyday life in North America over four decades ago. Currently in its thirty-seventh printing, this book is must reading for every college student.

Glossary

abnormal behavior   Behavior that is deviant, maladaptive, or personally distressful. Only one of these criteria needs to be present for the classification of abnormal behavior, but two or all three can be present.   448

absolute threshold   The minimum amount of energy that we can detect.   102

accommodation   Adjustment of the eye lens to change its curvature.   108

accommodation   An individual's adjustment to new information.   331

acculturative stress   The negative consequences of cultural change that result from contact between two distinctive cultural groups.   525

acetylcholine (ACh)   A neurotransmitter that usually stimulates the firing of neurons and is involved in the action of muscles, learning, and memory.   76

achievement tests   Tests that measure what a person has learned or the skills the person has mastered.   295

action potential   The brief wave of electrical charge that sweeps down the axon.   75

activation-synthesis view   The view that dreams have no inherent meaning but, rather, reflect the brain's efforts to make sense out of or find meaning in the neural activity that takes place during REM sleep. In this view, the brain has considerable random activity during REM sleep, and dreams are an attempt to synthesize the chaos.   166

activity theory   The theory that the more active and involved older people are, the more satisfied they will be with their lives and the more likely they will stay healthy.   359

acupuncture   A technique in which thin needles are inserted at specific points in the body to produce various effects, such as local anesthesia.   122

addiction   A pattern of behavior characterized by an overwhelming involvement with using a drug and securing its supply.   178

adolescence   The transition from childhood to adulthood, which involves physical, cognitive, and socioemotional changes. In most cultures adolescence begins at about 10 to 13 years of age and ends at about 18 to 21 years of age.   321

adolescent egocentrism   The adolescent's belief that others are as preoccupied with the adolescent as she is herself, that she is unique, and that she is indestructible.   347

adrenal glands   Glands that play an important role in our moods, energy level, and ability to cope with stress; each adrenal gland secretes epinephrine (also called adrenaline) and norepinephrine (also called noradrenaline).   96

aerobic exercise   Sustained exercise (such as jogging, swimming, or cycling) that stimulates heart and lung activity.   537

affectionate love   Also called companionate love, this type of love occurs when individuals desire to have each other near and have a deep, caring affection for each other.   586

afferent nerves   Sensory nerves that carry information to the brain.   72

afterimages   Sensations that remain after a stimulus is removed.   113

agonist   A drug that mimics or increases a neurotransmitter's effects.   78

agoraphobia   An anxiety disorder characterized by an intense fear of entering crowded, public places, of traveling away from home, especially by public transportation, of feeling confined or trapped, and of being separated from a place or person associated with safety.   457

AIDS   A sexually transmitted disease that is caused by the human immunodeficiency virus (HIV), which destroys the body's immune system.   543

alcoholism   A disorder that involves long-term, repeated, uncontrolled, compulsive, and excessive use of alcoholic beverages, impairing the drinker's health and interpersonal relationships.   172

algorithms   Strategies that guarantee a solution to a problem.   260

all-or-none principle   The principle that once the electrical impulse reaches a certain level of intensity, it fires and moves all the way down the axon, remaining at the same strength throughout its travel.   75

alpha waves   Brain waves that make up the EEG pattern of a person who is awake but relaxed.   157

altered states of consciousness   Mental states that noticeably differ from normal awareness. Drugs, meditation, fatigue, hypnosis, and sensory deprivation can produce altered states of consciousness.   151

alternate forms reliability   Giving alternate forms of the same test on two different occasions.   288

altruism   An unselfish interest in helping someone else.   581

Alzheimer's disease   A progressive, irreversible brain disorder that is characterized by gradual deterioration of memory, reasoning, language, and eventually physical functioning.   354

amnesia   Loss of memory.   244

amplitude   The amount of pressure produced by a sound wave relative to a standard, measured in decibels (dB).   116

amygdala   A limbic system structure located within the base of the temporal lobe; involved in the discrimination of objects and emotion.   81

anal stage   Freud's second stage of development, occurring between 1½ and 3 years of age, in which the child's greatest pleasure involves the anus or the eliminative functions associated with it.   417

analogy   A type of formal reasoning that involves four parts, relationship between the first two parts being the same as the relationship between the last two.   263

androgen   A class of sex hormones, the most important of which is testosterone, that promotes the development of male genitals and male secondary sex characteristics. Androgens influence sexual motivation in both sexes and are produced by the adrenal glands in males and females, and in the testes in males.   380

anorexia nervosa   An eating disorder that involves the relentless pursuit of thinness through starvation.   378

antagonist   A drug that can block a neurotransmitter's effects.   78

anterograde amnesia   A memory disorder that affects the retention of new information or events. What was learned before the onset of the condition is not affected.   244

antianxiety drugs   Drugs that reduce anxiety by making the individual less excitable and more calm. Commonly known as tranquilizers.   504

antidepressant drugs   Drugs that regulate mood. The three main classes of antidepressant drugs are tricyclics, such as Elavil; MAO inhibitors, such as Nardil; and SSRI drugs, such as Prozac.   505

antipsychotic drugs   Powerful drugs that diminish agitated behavior, reduce tension, decrease hallucinations and delusions, improve social behavior, and produce better sleep patterns in individuals who have a severe mental disorder, especially schizophrenia.   505

antisocial personality disorder   A disorder in the dramatic/emotionally problematic cluster of personality disorders. It is the most problematic because these individuals often resort to a life of crime and violence. They are guiltless, exploitive, irresponsible, self-indulgent, and interpersonally intrusive.   473

anxiety disorders   Psychological disorders that include these main features: motor tension, hyperactivity, and apprehensive expectations and thoughts.   455

aphrodisiacs   Substances that supposedly arouse a person's sexual desire and increase the capacity for sexual activity.   381

apparent movement   Our perception of a stationary object as being in motion.   136

applied behavior analysis (behavior modification)   The application of operant conditioning principles to change human behavior.   203

approach/approach conflict   A conflict in which the individual must choose between two attractive stimuli or circumstances.   523

approach/avoidance conflict   A conflict involving a single stimulus or circumstance that has both positive and negative characteristics.   524

aptitude tests   Tests that predict an individual's ability to learn a skill or what the individual can accomplish with training.   294

archetype   The primordial influences in every individual's collective unconscious; Jung's psychoanalytic theory is often referred to as "depth psychology" because archetypes rest deep within the unconscious mind, far deeper than the Freudian personal unconscious.   420

artificial intelligence (AI)   The science of creating machines capable of performing activities that require intelligence when they are done by people.   256

assimilation   The incorporation of new information into one's existing knowledge; Piagetian concept.   331

assimilation   Individuals' relinquishing of their cultural identity and moving into the larger society.   526

association cortex (association areas)   The region of the neocortex involved in the highest intellectual functions, such as problem solving and thinking.   86

associative learning   Learning that two events are related or linked.   188

Atkinson-Shiffrin theory   The theory that memory involves a sequence of three stages: sensory memory, short-term (working) memory, and long-term memory.   224

attachment   A close emotional bond between the infant and its caregiver.   339

attitudes   Beliefs or opinions about people, objects, and ideas.   556

attribution theory   The theory that individuals are motivated to discover the underlying causes of behavior as part of an effort to make sense out of the behavior.   389

attribution theory   The theory that individuals are motivated to discover the underlying causes of behavior as part of their interest in making sense out of the behavior.   550

auditory nerve   The nerve that carries neural impulses to the brain's auditory areas.   120

authoritarian parenting   A restrictive, punitive style in which the parent exhorts the child to follow the parent's directions and to respect work and effort. The authoritarian parent places firm limits and controls on the child and allows little verbal exchange. Authoritarian parenting is associated with children's social incompetence.   341

authoritative parenting   A style in which parents encourage children to be independent but still places limits and controls on their actions. Extensive verbal give-and-take is allowed, and parents are warm and nurturant toward the child. Authoritative parenting is associated with children's social competence.   341

autobiographical memory   A person's recollection of her or his life experiences.   239

automatic processes   Forms of consciousness that require minimal attention and do not interfere with other ongoing activities.   151

autonomic nervous system   The system of nerves that takes messages to and from the body's internal organs, monitoring such processes as breathing, heart rate, and digestion.   72, 393

autonomy versus shame and doubt   Erikson's second stage, occurring from 1 to 3 years of age. The positive side of the stage involves developing a sense of independence and autonomy, the negative side a sense of shame and doubt.   337

availability heuristic   Judging the probability of an event by recalling the frequency of the event's past occurrences.   266

aversive conditioning   A behavior therapy based on classical conditioning in which there are repeated pairings of the undesirable behavior with aversive stimuli to decrease the behavior's rewards.   492

avoidance/avoidance conflict   A conflict in which the individual must choose between two unattractive stimuli or circumstances.   523

axon   The part of the neuron that carries information away from the cell body to other cells.   73

barbiturates   Depressant drugs, such as Nembutal and Seconal, that induce sleep or reduce anxiety.   173

Barnum effect   If you make your predictions broad enough, any person can fit the description.   434

basal ganglia   Forebrain structures essential to starting and stopping voluntary movements.   82

basal metabolism rate (BMR)   The minimal amount of energy a person uses in a resting state.   377

basic-skills-and-phonetics approach   The view that reading instruction should stress phonetics and its basic rules for translating written symbols into sounds.   275

basilar membrane   A membrane housed inside the cochlea that runs its entire length.   118

behavior   Everything we do that can be directly observed.   5

behavior modification   The application of operant conditioning techniques to change human behavior. Its main goal is to replace unacceptable, maladaptive responses with acceptable, adaptive ones.   493

behavior therapies   Therapies that use principles of learning to reduce or eliminate maladaptive behavior.   491

behavioral and social cognitive perspectives   Perspectives that emphasize the importance of studying environmental experiences and peoples' observable behavior to understand personality. The contemporary version of social cognitive theory stresses the importance of person/cognitive factors in personality.   423

behavioral approach   An emphasis on the scientific study of observable behavioral responses and their environmental determinants.   8

behavioral medicine   An interdisciplinary field that focuses on developing and integrating behavioral and biomedical knowledge to promote health and reduce illness.   516

behaviorial neuroscience and comparative psychology   This area focuses on biological processes, especially the brain's role in behavior.   25

behavioral neuroscience approach   An approach that emphasizes the importance of understanding the brain and nervous system if we are to understand behavior, thought, and emotion.   11

belief perseverance   The tendency to hold on to a belief in the face of contradictory evidence.   265

big five factors of personality   Emotional stability (neuroticism), extraversion, openness to experience, agreeableness, and conscientiousness.   431

binocular cues   Depth cues that are based on both eyes working together.   130

biofeedback   The process in which individuals' muscular or visceral activities are monitored by instruments and information is given (fed back) to the individuals so they can learn to voluntarily control their physiological activities.   536

biological processes   Processes that involve changes in an individual's physical nature.   320

biomedical therapies   Treatments to reduce or eliminate the symptoms of psychological disorders by altering the way an individual's body functions. Drug therapy is the most common form; less common are electroconvulsive therapy and psychosurgery.   504

bipolar disorder   A mood disorder characterized by extreme mood swings that include one or more episodes of mania (an overexcited, unrealistically optimistic state). *Bipolar* means that the person may experience depression and mania.   464

bisexual   Being sexually attracted to people of both sexes.   385

blind spot   The area of the retina where the optic nerve leaves the eye on its way to the brain.   109

brain graft   The transplantation of healthy tissue into a damaged brain.   91

brainstorming   A technique in which members of a group are encouraged to come up with as many ideas as possible, play off others' ideas, and say practically whatever comes to mind.   312

brightness   A characteristic of color based on its intensity.   112

brightness constancy   Recognition that an object retains the same degree of brightness even when different amounts of light fall on it.   136

bulimia   An eating disorder in which the individual consistently follows a binge-and-purge eating pattern.   378

burnout   A hopeless, helpless feeling brought about by relentless work-related stress. Burnout leaves its sufferers in a state of physical and emotional exhaustion that includes chronic fatigue and low energy.   523

bystander effect   Individuals who observe an emergency help less when someone else is present than when they are alone.   582

Cannon-Bard theory   The theory that emotions and physiological reactions occur simultaneously.   396

cardinal traits   In Allport's view, the most powerful and pervasive traits.   431

care perspective   In Carol Gilligan's theory of moral development, the care perspective focuses on people in terms of their connectedness with others, interpersonal communication, relationships with others, and concern for others.   349

carpentered-world hypothesis   The hypothesis that people who live in cultures in which straight lines, right angles, and rectangles predominate (for instance, in which most rooms and buildings are rectangular and many things, such as city streets, have right-angled corners) should be more susceptible to illusions involving straight lines, right angles, and rectangles (such as the Müller-Lyer illusion) than are people who live in noncarpentered cultures.   141

case study   An in-depth look at a single individual, used mainly by clinical psychologists when, for ethical or practical reasons, the unique aspects of an individual's life cannot be duplicated.   43

catatonic schizophrenia   A type of schizophrenia characterized by bizarre motor behavior, which sometimes takes the form of a completely immobile stupor.   469

catharsis   The release of anger or aggressive energy by directly or vicariously engaging in anger or aggression; the catharsis hypothesis states that behaving angrily or agressively reduces subsequent anger.   405, 486, 580

cell body   The part of the neuron that contains the nucleus, which directs the manufacture of the substances the neuron uses for its growth and maintenance.   73

cellular clock theory   Hayflick's view that cells can divide, at maximum, about 100 times, and that as we age, our cells become increasingly less capable of dividing.   353

central nervous system (CNS)   The brain and spinal cord.   71

central traits   In Allport's view, a limited number of traits that are adequate to describe most people's personalities. Most people have 6 to 12 of these traits.   431

cerebellum   A part of the brain that extends from the rear of the hindbrain, above the medulla. It consists of two rounded structures thought to play important roles in motor control.   80

chromosomes   Threadlike structures that come in 23 pairs, one member of each pair coming from each parent; chromosomes contain DNA.   66

chunking   A beneficial organizational strategy for memory that involves grouping or "packing" information into higher-order units that can be remembered as single units.   222

circadian rhythm   A daily behavioral or physiological cycle, an example being the 24-hour sleep/wake cycle.   154

clairvoyance   The ability to perceive remote events that are out of view.   142

classical conditioning   A form of learning in which a neutral stimulus becomes associated with a meaningful stimulus and acquires the capacity to elicit a similar response.   187

clinical and counseling psychology   The most widely practiced specialization in psychology; clinical and counseling psychologists diagnose and treat people with psychological problems.   24

cochlea   A long tubular fluid-filled structure in the inner ear that is coiled up like a snail.   118

cognitive appraisal   Lazarus' term for individuals' interpretation of events in their lives as harmful, threatening, or challenging, and their determination of whether they have the resources to effectively cope with the events.   522

cognitive approach   An emphasis on the mental processes involved in knowing: How we direct our attention, perceive, remember, think, and solve problems.   11

cognitive dissonance   A concept developed by social psychologist Leon Festinger that refers to an individual's motivation toward consistency and away from inconsistency.   557

cognitive map   An organism's mental representation of the structure of physical space.   208

cognitive monitoring   Taking stock of your progress in an activity such as reading or studying.   247

cognitive processes   Processes that involve changes in an individual's thought, intelligence, and language.   320

cognitive restructuring   Modifying the thoughts, ideas, and beliefs that maintain an individual's problems.   529

cognitive theory of dreaming   The theory that dreaming can be best understood by relying on the same cognitive concepts that are used in studying the waking mind. That is, dreaming involves processing information, memories, and possible problem solving.   165

cognitive therapies   Therapies that emphasize the individual's cognitions or thoughts as the main source of abnormal behavior. Cognitive therapists attempt to change the individual's feelings and behaviors by changing cognitions.   494

cohorts   Groups of individuals born in the same year or time period.   359

collective unconscious   According to Jung, the impersonal, deepest layer of the unconscious mind, which is shared by all human beings because of their common ancestral past.   420

community psychology   A branch of psychology that focuses on providing accessible care for people with psychological problems. Community-based mental health centers are one means of providing such services as outreach programs to people in need, especially those who traditionally have been underserved by mental health professionals.   25

compensation   Adler's term for the individual's attempt to overcome imagined or real inferiorities or weaknesses by developing one's abilities.   421

complex sounds   Sounds in which sound waves of numerous frequencies blend together.   117

computer-assisted axial tomography (CAT scan)   Three-dimensional imaging obtained from X rays of the head that are assembled into a composite image by computer.   94

conception   The penetration of an ovum (egg) by a sperm cell; also called fertilization.   325

concepts   Mental categories used to group similar objects, events, and characteristics.   256

concrete operational stage   Piaget's third cognitive stage, which lasts from about 7 to 11 years of age. This stage involves using operations, and operational thought replaces intuitive thought, but only in concrete situations. It is characterized by a lack of abstract thinking, but classification skills are present.   334

concurrent validity   A form of criterion validity that assesses the relation of a test's scores to a criterion that is presently available (concurrent).   289

conditional positive regard   Rogers' term for love and praise being withheld if the individual does not conform to parental or social standards.   426

conditioned response (CR)   The learned response to the conditioned stimulus that occurs after CS-US association.   188

conditioned stimulus (CS)   A previously neutral stimulus that elicits the conditioned response after being paired with the unconditioned stimulus.   188

cones   Receptors in the retina for color perception.   108

confidentiality   Researchers are responsible for keeping all of the data they collect completely confidential and, when possible, completely anonymous.   52

confirmation bias   The tendency to search for and use information that supports our ideas rather than refutes them.   264

conformity   Changing one's behavior to make it coincide more with a group standard.   559

consciousness   Awareness of both external and internal stimuli or events.   150

consensual validation   An explanation of why people are attracted to others who are similar to them: Our own attitudes and behavior are supported when someone else's attitudes and behavior are similar to ours—their attitudes and behavior validate ours.   584

conservation   A belief in the permanence of certain attributes of objects or situations in spite of superficial changes.   333

content validity   A test's ability to test a broad range of the content that is to be measured.   289

contingency (in classical conditioning)   The predictability of the occurrence of one stimulus from the presence of another.   188

contingency model of leadership   The view that both personality characteristics and situational influences determine who will become a leader; leadership is viewed as a complex undertaking in which leaders influence their followers and followers influence their leaders.   568

continuity of development   The view that development involves gradual, cumulative change from conception to death.   324

continuous reinforcement   Reinforcement of a response every time it occurs.   199

contour   A location on a surface at which a sudden change of brightness occurs.   129

control group   A comparison group that is treated in every way like the experimental group except for the manipulated factor.   46

controlled processes   The most alert states of consciousness, in which individuals actively focus their efforts toward a goal.   150

conventional level   Kohlberg's second level of moral thinking, in which an individual shows an intermediate level of internalization. The individual abides by certain standards (internal), but they are the standards of others (external), such as parents' standards (stage 3) or society's laws (stage 4).   347

convergent thinking   Thinking that produces one correct answer; characteristic of the kind of thinking required on conventional intelligence tests.   310

conversion disorder   A somatoform disorder in which the individual experiences specific physical symptoms even though no physiological problems can be found. Conversion disorder received its name from psychoanalytic theory, which stressed that anxiety was "converted" into a specific physical symptom.   460

coping   The process of managing taxing circumstances, expending effort to solve personal and interpersonal problems, and seeking to master, minimize, reduce, or tolerate stress and conflict.   527

cornea   A clear membrane on the front surface of the eye. Its function is to bend the light falling on the surface of the eye just enough to focus it at the back of the eye.   107

corpus callosum   A large bundle of axons that connects the brain's two hemispheres.   87

correlational research   Research with the goal of describing the strength of the relation between two or more events or characteristics.   45

counterconditioning   A classical conditioning procedure for weakening a conditioned response of fear by associating the fear-provoking stimulus with a new response that is incompatible with the fear.   192

couple therapy   Group therapy with married or unmarried couples whose major problem is their relationship.   498

crack   An intensified form of cocaine; chips of pure cocaine that are usually smoked.   174

creativity   The ability to think about something in novel and unusual ways and come up with unique solutions to problems.   310

criterion validity   The test's ability to predict an individual's performance when assessed by other measures, or criteria, of an attribute.   289

critical period   A period when there is learning readiness; beyond this period learning is difficult or impossible.   273

critical thinking   Thinking reflectively and productively, and evaluating the evidence.   22, 262

cross-cultural psychology   An area of psychology that examines the role of culture in understanding behavior, thought, and emotion.   27

cultural-familial retardation   A mental deficit in which no evidence of organic brain damage can be found; individuals' IQs range from 55 to 70.   308

culture   The behavior patterns, beliefs, and other products of a particular group of people, such as the values, work patterns, music, dress, diet, and ceremonies that are passed on from generation to generation.   12

culture-fair tests   Intelligence tests that are intended to not be culturally biased.   305

daydreaming   A form of consciousness that involves a low level of conscious effort.   151

debriefing   Informing participants of the purpose and methods used in a study after the study has been completed.   53

decay theory   The theory that a neurochemical "memory trace" is formed when something new is learned, but that this trace tends to disintegrate.   244

decision making   Evaluating alternatives and making choices among them.   264

declarative memory   The conscious recollection of information, such as specific facts or events, and at least in humans, information that can be verbally communicated. Because of its conscious and verbalizable nature, declarative memory has been called "explicit memory."   227

deductive reasoning   Reasoning from the general to the specific.   264

defense mechanisms   The ego's protective methods for reducing anxiety by unconsciously distorting reality.   415

deindividuation   The loss of personal identity and a decrease in responsibility in the presence of a group.   566

deinstitutionalization   The movement to transfer the treatment of mental disorders from inpatient mental hospitals to community-based facilities that stress outpatient care.   481

delta waves   Large, slow brain waves associated with deep sleep.   157

dendrite   The receiving part of the neuron, serving the important function of collecting information and orienting it toward the cell body.   73

deoxyribonucleic acid (DNA)   A complex molecule that contains genetic information.   66

dependent variable   The factor that is measured in an experiment. It can change as the independent variable is manipulated. The label "dependent" is used because this variable depends on what happens to the participants in the experiment.   46

depressants   Psychoactive drugs that slow down mental and physical activity.   172

depressive disorders   Mood disorders in which the individual suffers depression without ever experiencing mania. The severity varies; some individuals experience a major depressive disorder others dysthymic disorder.   463

depth perception   The ability to perceive objects three-dimensionally.   130

development   The pattern of movement or change that begins at conception and continues through the life span.   320

developmental psychology   A branch of psychology concerned with how we become who we are, from conception to death.   27

diathesis-stress view   The view that a combination of biogenetic disposition and stress causes schizophrenia.   470

dichromats   People with only two kinds of cones.   113

difference threshold   The smallest difference in stimulation required to discriminate one stimulus from another 50 percent of the time. Also called the just noticeable difference (jnd).   105

discontinuity of development   The view that development involves distinct stages in the life span.   324

discrimination (in classical conditioning)   The process of learning to respond to certain stimuli and not to respond to others.   190

discrimination (in operant conditioning)   The tendency to respond only to those stimuli that are correlated with reinforcement.   201

disease model of addiction   The view that addictions are biologically based, lifelong diseases that involve a loss of control over behavior and require medical and/or spiritual treatment for recovery.   178

disorganized schizophrenia   A type of schizophrenia in which an individual has delusions and hallucinations with little or no recognizable meaning.   469

disparity   The difference between the images from the left and right eye that the brain uses as a binocular cue to determine the depth or distance of an object.   131

display rules   Sociocultural standards that determine when, where, and how emotions should be expressed.   400

dissociative amnesia   A dissociative disorder involving memory loss caused by extensive psychological stress.   460

dissociative disorders   Psychological disorders that involve a sudden loss of memory or change in identity. Under extreme stress or shock, the individual's conscious awareness becomes dissociated (separated or split) from previous memories and thoughts.   460

dissociative fugue   A dissociative disorder in which the individual not only develops amnesia but also unexpectedly travels away from home and assumes a new identity. *Fugue* means "flight."   460

dissociative identity disorder (DID)   The most dramatic but least common dissociative disorder. In this disorder, individuals have two or more distinct personalities or selves. Formerly called multiple personality disorder.   460

divergent thinking   Thinking that produces many answers to the same question and is more characteristic of creativity.   310

dominant-recessive genes principle   The principle that if one gene of a pair is dominant and the other is recessive, the dominant gene exerts its effect, overriding the potential influence of the recessive gene. A recessive gene exerts its influence only if both genes in the pair are recessive.   66

door-in-the-face strategy   The technique in which a communicator makes the strongest point or demand in the beginning, which listeners will probably reject, then presents a weaker point or moderate, "concessionary" demand toward the end.   556

dopamine   A neurotransmitter that usually is inhibitory and is involved in the control of voluntary movement. Low levels are found in Parkinson's disease, high levels in schizophrenia.   76

double-blind experiment   An experiment in which neither the experimenter nor the research participants are aware of which participants are in the experimental group and which are in the placebo control group until after the results are calculated.   49

dream analysis   A technique used by psychoanalysts to interpret a person's dream. Psychoanalysts believe dreams contain information about the unconscious mind's thoughts and contents.   487

drive   An aroused state that occurs because of a physiological need.   369

DSM-IV   *Diagnostic and Statistical Manual of Mental Disorders,* fourth edition. The most recent major classification of mental disorders, containing 18 major classifications and describing more than 200 specific disorders.   453

dysthymic disorder   A depressive disorder that generally is more chronic and has fewer symptoms than major depressive disorder. The individual has a depressed mood for most days for at least 2 years as an adult or at least 1 year as a child or adolescent.   463

E

early adulthood   The developmental period that begins in the late teens or early twenties and ends in the thirties. It is a time when individuals establish personal and economic independence, intensely pursue a career, and seek intimacy with one or more individuals.   321

early childhood   The developmental period that extends from the end of infancy to about 5 or 6 years; sometimes the period is called the preschool years.   321

echoic memory   Auditory sensory memory in which information is retained for up to several seconds.   225

eclectic approach   An approach that follows no one particular conceptual perspective; rather, it uses whatever is considered best in each approach.   14

ecological approach   A view of perception that stresses an active perceiver exploring and moving about the environment.   139

ecological theory   The relatively recent view that sleep is evolution based. This theory argues that the main purpose of sleep is to prevent animals from wasting their energy and harming themselves during the parts of the day or night to which they have not adapted.   154

efferent nerves   Motor nerves that carry the brain's output.   72

ego   The Freudian structure of personality that deals with the demands of reality; the ego is called the executive branch of personality because it makes decisions based on rationality.   415

egocentrism   A salient feature of preoperational thought; the inability to distinguish between one's own perspective and someone else's perspective.   333

egoism   Giving to another to ensure reciprocity; to gain self-esteem; to appear powerful, competent, or caring; or to avoid social and self-censure for failing to live up to normative expectations.   582

elaboration   The extensiveness of processing at any given depth of memory.   220

electroconvulsive therapy (ECT)   This therapy used mainly to treat severely depressed individuals. The goal of ECT is to cause a seizure in the brain much like what happens spontaneously in some forms of epilepsy. Commonly called "shock treatment."   506

electroencephalograph (EEG)   A machine that records the electrical activity of the brain. Electrodes placed on an individual's scalp record brain-wave activity, which is reproduced on a chart known as an electroencephalogram.   93

embryonic period   The period of prenatal development that occurs from 3 to 8 weeks after conception. During the embryonic period, the rate of cell differentiation intensifies, support systems for the cells form, and the beginnings of organs appear.   325

emotion   Feeling or affect, that can involve physiological arousal (a fast heartbeat, for example), conscious experience (thinking about being in love with someone, for example), and behavioral expression (a smile or grimace, for example).   393

emotion-focused coping   Lazarus' term for responding to stress in an emotional manner, especially using defensive appraisal.   529

empirically keyed test   A test that relies on its items to predict a particular criterion; unlike tests based on face validity, empirically keyed tests make no assumptions about the nature of the items.   436

encoding   How information gets into memory.   219

encoding specificity principle   The principle that associations formed at the time of encoding or learning tend to be effective retrieval cues.   238

endocrine glands   Glands that release their chemical products, called hormones, directly into the bloodstream.   95

endorphins   Neurotransmitters that function as natural opiates which usually stimulate the firing of neurons; involved in pleasure and pain.   76

environment   All of the surrounding conditions and influences that affect the development of living things.   69

episodic memory   The retention of information about the where and when of life's happenings.   228

erogenous zones   According to Freud, parts of the body that have especially strong pleasure-giving qualities at particular stages of development.   417

estradiol   A hormone associated in girls with breast, uterine, and skeletal development.   346

estrogens   A class of sex hormones, the most important of which is estradiol, that influences the development of female physical characteristics and helps to regulate the menstrual cycle. Estrogens are produced by the ovaries.   380

ethnic gloss   Using an ethnic label, such as "Aboriginal peoples" or "Chinese," in a superficial way that portrays an ethnic group as being more homogeneous than it actually is.   56

ethnicity   A person's heritage based on cultural heritage, nationality characteristics, race, religion, and language.   13

ethnocentrism   The tendency to favor one's own group over other groups.   570

ethology   The study of the biological basis of behavior in natural habitats.   370

eustress   Selye's term for the positive features of stress.   518

evolutionary psychology approach   Emphasizes the importance of adaptation, reproduction, and "survival of the fittest" in explaining behavior.   68

evolutionary psychology approach   Psychology's newest approach, emphasizing the importance of adaptation, reproduction, and "survival of the fittest" in explaining behavior.   12

experiment   A carefully regulated procedure in which one or more factors believed to influence the behavior being studied are manipulated and all other factors are held constant.   46

experimental group   A group whose experience is manipulated.   46

experimental psychology   Areas of psychology in which psychologists often conduct basic research and use an experimental strategy. These areas include sensation and perception, cognitive processes (such as memory), learning, motivation, and emotion.   25

experimental research   Research that allows psychologists to discover behavior's causes.   46

experimenter bias   The influence of the experimenter's own expectations on the outcome of the research.   48

extinction (in classical conditioning)   The weakening of the conditioned response in the absence of the unconditioned stimulus.   188

extinction (in operant conditioning)   A decrease in the tendency to perform a behavior that no longer receives either positive or negative reinforcement.   201

extrasensory perception (ESP)   Perception that occurs without the use of any known sensory process.   141

F

face validity   An assumption that the content of the test items is a good indicator of an individual's personality.   436

facial feedback hypothesis   The hypothesis that facial expressions can influence emotions as well as reflect them. In this view, facial muscles send signals to the brain, which helps individuals recognize the emotion they are experiencing.   399

family therapy   Group therapy with family members.   498

feature detectors   Neurons in the brain's visual system that respond to particular lines or other features of a stimulus.   110

fetal alcohol syndrome (FAS)   A cluster of abnormalities that appear in the offspring of mothers who drink alcohol heavily during pregnancy.   326

fetal period   The prenatal period of development that begins 2 months after conception and lasts for 7 months, on the average.   325

figure-ground relationship   The principle by which we organize the perceptual field into stimuli that stand out (figure) and those that are left over (ground).   129

fixation   Focusing only on a prior strategy and failing to look at a problem from a fresh, new perspective.   261

fixation   The psychoanalytic defense mechanism that occurs when the individual remains locked in an earlier developmental stage because needs are under- or overgratified.   417

fixed-interval schedule   Reinforcement of the first appropriate response after a fixed amount of time has elapsed.   199

fixed-ratio schedule   Reinforcement of a behavior after a set number of responses.   199

flashbulb memories   Memories of emotionally significant events that people often recall with more accuracy and vivid imagery than everyday events.   240

foot-in-the-door strategy   A strategy in which an individual presents a weaker point or makes a small request with which the listeners will probably comply in the beginning, saving the strongest point until the end.   556

forebrain   The highest and evolutionarily newest region of the human brain. Among its most important structures are the limbic system, amygdala, hippocampus, thalamus, basal ganglia, hypothalamus, and neocortex.   80

forensic psychology   The field of psychology that applies psychological concepts to the legal system.   27

formal operational stage   Piaget's fourth and final cognitive stage, which is entered at about 11 to 15 years of age and continues through adulthood. It involves abstract, idealistic, and logical thinking.   335

fovea   A minute area in the center of the retina where vision is at its best.   109

free association   The psychoanalytic technique of encouraging individuals to say aloud whatever comes to mind, no matter how trivial or embarrassing.   486

free-radical theory   The theory that people age because inside their cells unstable oxygen molecules known as free radicals are produced. These ricochet around the cells, damaging DNA and other cellular structures.   354

frequency   The number of cycles (or full wavelengths) that pass through a point in a given time.   116

frequency theory   The theory that the perception of a sound's frequency is due to how often the auditory nerve fires.   120

frontal lobe   A portion of the cerebral cortex that is behind the forehead and is involved in the control of voluntary muscles and in intelligence.   84

frustration   Any situation in which a person cannot reach a desired goal.   524

frustration-aggression hypothesis   The hypothesis that frustration always leads to aggression.   578

functional fixedness   A type of fixation in which individuals fail to solve a problem because they are fixated on a thing's usual functions.   261

functionalism   William James's theory that psychology's role is to study the functions of the mind and behavior in adapting to the environment.   7

fundamental attribution error   Observers' tendency to overestimate the importance of traits and underestimate the importance of situations when they seek explanations of an actor's behavior.   552

GABA   Gamma aminobutyric acid, a neurotransmitter that inhibits the firing of neurons and is found throughout the central nervous system.   76

gate-control theory   The theory that the spinal column contains a neural gate that can be opened (allowing the perception of pain) or closed (blocking the perception of pain).   122

gender   The sociocultural dimension of being female or male, especially how we learn to think and behave as females and males.   13

general adaptation syndrome (GAS)   Selye's term for common effects on the body when demands are placed on it. The GAS consists of three stages: alarm, resistance, and exhaustion.   518

generalization (in classical conditioning)   The tendency of a new stimulus that is similar to the original conditioned stimulus to elicit a response that is similar to the conditioned response.   190

generalization (in operant conditioning)   Giving the same response to similar stimuli.   201

generalized anxiety disorder   An anxiety disorder that consists of persistent anxiety for at least a month; the individual is unable to specify the reasons for the anxiety.   456

generativity versus stagnation   Erikson's seventh stage, which occurs in middle adulthood. A chief concern is to assist the younger generation in developing and leading useful lives. The feeling of having done little or nothing for the next generation is what is meant by stagnation.   338

genes   Short segments of chromosomes that are the units of hereditary information and are composed of DNA.   66

genital stage   The fifth Freudian stage of development, occurring from puberty on; the genital stage is the time of sexual reawakening and the source of sexual pleasure now becomes someone outside of the family.   419

genotype   The person's genetic heritage, the actual genetic material.   67

germinal period   The period of prenatal development that takes place in the first 2 weeks after conception. It includes the creation of the zygote, continued cell division, and the attachment of the zygote to the uterine wall.   325

Gestalt psychology   An approach that states that people naturally organize their perceptions according to certain patterns. *Gestalt* is a German word that means "configuration" or "form." One of Gestalt psychology's main principles is that the whole is not equal to the sum of its parts.   129

Gestalt therapy   The humanistic therapy developed by Fritz Perls in which the therapist questions and challenges clients to help them become more aware of their feelings and face their problems.   490

giftedness   Having above-average intelligence (an IQ of 120 or higher) and/or superior talent for something.   309

glial cells   Non-neuron cells that provide supportive and nutritive functions.   78

graphology   The use of handwriting analysis to determine an individual's personality.   436

great-person theory   The theory that some individuals have certain traits that are best suited for leadership positions.   568

group polarization effect   The solidification and further strengthening of a position as a consequence of group discussion.   567

groupthink   Impaired decision making and avoidance of realistic appraisal in order to maintain group harmony.   567

hallucinogens   Psychoactive drugs that modify a person's perceptual experiences and produce hallucinatory visual images; hallucinogens are called psychedelic ("mind altering") drugs.   175

hardiness   A personality style characterized by a sense of commitment (rather than alienation), control (rather than powerlessness), and a perception of problems as challenges (rather than threats).   522

health psychology   A multidimensional approach to health that emphasizes psychological factors, lifestyle, and the nature of the health care delivery system.   27, 516

heuristics   Strategies or rules of thumb that can suggest a solution to a problem but do not guarantee a solution.   260

hierarchy of motives   Maslow's view that we need to satisfy our main needs in this sequence: physiological, safety, love and belongingness, esteem, and self-actualization.   371, 427

hindbrain   Located at the skull's rear, is the lowest and evolutionarily oldest portion of the brain. The three main parts of the hindbrain are the medulla, cerebellum, and pons.   80

hindsight bias   Our tendency to falsely report, after the fact, that we accurately predicted an event.   266

hippocampus   A limbic system structure that has a special role in the storage of memories.   82

homeostasis   The body's tendency to maintain an equilibrium, or steady state.   369

hue   A characteristic of color based on its wavelength content.   111

human sexual response cycle   Consists of four phases: excitement, plateau, orgasm, and resolution. Identified by Masters and Johnson.   382

humanistic approach   An emphasis on a person's capacity for personal growth, freedom to choose his or her own destiny, and positive qualities.   10

humanistic perspectives   Perspectives that stress personal growth, choosing one's own destiny, and positive qualities.   425

humanistic therapies   Therapies that encourage people to understand themselves and to grow personally. In contrast to the psychoanalytic therapies, the humanistic therapies emphasize conscious rather than unconscious thoughts, the present rather than the past, and growth and self-fulfillment rather than illness.   489

hypnosis   A psychological state of altered attention and awareness in which the individual is unusually receptive to suggestions.   167

hypochondriasis   A somatoform disorder in which the individual has a pervasive fear of illness and disease.   459

hypothalamus   Located just below the thalamus, the hypothalamus monitors three enjoyable activities—eating, drinking, and sex. It also helps to direct the endocrine system through the pituitary gland, and is involved in emotion, stress, and reward.   82

hypotheses   Specific assumptions or predictions that can be tested to determine their accuracy.   36

hypothetical-deductive reasoning   Piaget's name for adolescents' cognitive ability to develop hypotheses, or best guesses, about how to solve problems, such as algebraic equations.   335

iconic memory   Visual sensory memory in which information is retained for about 1/4 second.   225

id   The Freudian structure of personality that consists of instincts, which are the individual's reservoir of psychic energy.   415

identity versus identity confusion   Erikson's fifth stage, which occurs during adolescence. At this time, individuals are faced with finding out who they are, what they are all about, and where they are going in life. If they don't adequately explore their identity, they emerge from this stage with a sense of identity confusion.   338

implicit personality theory   The public's conception of how personality traits go together in an individual.   553

impression management (also called self-presentation)   Presenting an image of oneself as a certain sort of person, which might or might not be who one really is.   555

imprinting   The tendency of an infant animal to form an attachment to the first moving object it sees or hears.   339

incentives   Positive or negative stimuli that motivate an individual's behavior.   371

independent variable   The manipulated, influential, experimental factor in an experiment. The label "independent" is used because this variable can be changed independent of other factors to determine its effect on the dependent variable.   46

individual differences   The stable, consistent ways in which people are different from each other.   286

individual psychology   The name Adler gave to his theory of psychology to emphasize the uniqueness of every individual.   420

inductive reasoning   Reasoning from the specific to the general. That is, drawing conclusions about all members of a category based on observing only some members.   263

indulgent parenting   A style of parenting in which parents are very involved with their children but place few demands or controls on them; it is associated with children's social incompetence, especially a lack of self-control.   342

industrial/organizational psychology   A branch of psychology that deals with the workplace, focusing on both the workers and the organizations that employ them.   27

industry versus inferiority   Erikson's fourth stage, which occurs from 6 years to puberty. Industry is achieved by mastering knowledge and intellectual skills. When children don't attain this mastery, they can feel inferior.   338

infancy   The developmental period that extends from birth to 18 or 24 months of age.   321

inferiority complex   Adler's name for exaggerated feelings of inadequacy.   421

infinite generativity   The ability to produce an endless number of meaningful sentences using a finite set of words and rules.   268

information theory   The contemporary explanation of how classical conditioning works: The key to understanding classical conditioning is the information the organism obtains from the situation.   191

informational social influence   The influence other people have on us because we want to be right.   562

information-processing approach   The most widely adopted cognitive approach. Information-processing psychologists study how individuals process information—how they attend to information, how they perceive it, how they store it, how they think about it, and how they retrieve it for further use.   11, 139

informed consent   Participants' consent based on knowing what their participation will involve and any risks that might develop.   52

initiative versus guilt   Erikson's third stage, which occurs from 3 to 5 years of age. Asked to assume more responsibility for themselves, children develop initiative. If children are irresponsible or made to feel anxious, they may develop guilt.   338

inner ear   The oval window, cochlea, and the organ of Corti.   118

insanity defense   A defense that requires that the defendant have been wholly or partially irrational when the crime took place, and that the irrationality affected his or her behavior.   449

insight learning   A form of problem solving in which an organism develops a sudden understanding of a problem's solution.   209

insight therapy   A term for psychodynamic and humanistic therapies because their goal is to encourage insight and self-awareness.   484

insomnia   A common sleep problem; the inability to sleep.   161

instinct   An innate (unlearned), biological pattern of behavior that is assumed to be universal throughout the species.   368

instinctive drift   The tendency of animals to revert to instinctive behavior that interferes with learning.   210

integration   Maintenance of cultural integrity as well as the movement to become an integral part of the larger culture.   526

integrity versus despair   Erikson's eighth and final stage, which occurs in late adulthood. At this point people review their lives. If their retrospective glances are positive, integrity results; if they are negative, despair is the outcome.   338

intelligence   Verbal ability, problem-solving skills, and the ability to adapt to and learn from life's everyday experiences.   286

interference theory   The theory that we forget, not because memories are actually lost from storage, but because other information gets in the way of what we want to remember.   243

internalization   The developmental change from behavior that is externally controlled to behavior that is controlled by internal, self-generated standards and principles.   347

interneurons   Central nervous system neurons that go between sensory input and motor output. Interneurons make up most of the brain.   73

interview   Asking questions to find out about a person's experiences and attitudes.   43

intimacy versus isolation   Erikson's sixth stage, which occurs in early adulthood. At this time, individuals face the developmental task of forming intimate relationships with others. If they don't find intimacy in relationships with a partner and/or friends, they may develop a sense of social isolation.   338

ions   Electrically charged particles, including sodium (Na) chloride (Cl) and potassium (K). The neuron creates electrical signals by moving these charged ions back and forth through its membrane; the waves of electricity that are created sweep along the membrane.   75

iris   The colored part of the eye, which can range from light blue to dark brown.   107

James-Lange theory   The theory that emotion results from physiological changes triggered by stimuli in the environment: Emotion follows a physiological reaction.   396

justice perspective   A theory of moral development that focuses on the rights of the individual; individuals independently make moral decisions. Kohlberg's theory is a justice perspective.   349

K

keyword method A mnemonic strategy in which vivid imagery is attached to important words.   246

kinesthetic sense The sense that provides information about movement, posture, and orientation.   125

L

laboratory A controlled setting with many of the complex factors of the "real world" removed.   41

language A form of communication, whether spoken, written, or signed, that is based on a system of symbols.   268

late adulthood The developmental stage that begins around 60 to 70 years of age and ends when an individual dies. It is a time of adjustment to decreased strength and health, retirement, reduced income, new social roles, and learning how to age successfully.   321

latency stage The fourth Freudian stage of development, occurring approximately between 6 years of age and puberty; the child represses all interest in sexuality and develops social and intellectual skills.   418

latent content A dream's hidden content, its unconscious meaning.   164, 487

law of effect Developed by Robert Thorndike, this law states that behaviors followed by positive outcomes are strengthened, whereas behaviors followed by negative outcomes are weakened.   196

learned helplessness A condition that occurs in individuals who are exposed to aversive stimulation over which they have no control. The inability to avoid such aversive stimulation produces an apathetic state of helplessness.   466

learning A relatively permanent change in behavior that occurs through experience.   186

lens of the eye A transparent and somewhat flexible ball-like entity at the front of the pupil, filled with a gelatinous material; its function is to bend the light falling on the surface of the eye just enough to focus it at the back of the eye.   107

levels of processing theory The theory that memory is processed on a continuum from shallow to deep, with deeper processing producing better memory.   220

life expectancy The number of years that will probably be lived by the average person born in a particular year.   353

life span The upper boundary of life for a species, the maximum number of years an individual of that species can live.   353

life-process model of addiction The view that addiction is not a disease but rather a habitual response and a source of gratification and security that can be understood only in the context of social relationships and experiences.   178

light A form of electromagnetic energy that can be described in terms of wavelengths.   106

limbic system A loosely connected network of structures under the cerebral cortex that plays an important role in both memory and emotion.   81

linguistic relativity hypothesis The hypothesis that language determines the structure of thinking and shapes our basic ideas.   277

lithium A drug that is widely used in treating bipolar disorder.   505

long-term memory A relatively permanent type of memory that holds huge amounts of information for a long period of time.   226

loudness The perception of a sound wave's amplitude.   117

M

magnetic resonance imaging (MRI) A technology in which a magnetic field is created around a person's body and radio waves are used to construct images of the person's brain tissues and biochemical activity.   93

major depressive disorder A depressive disorder in which the individual experiences a major depressive episode and depressed characteristics, such as lethargy and hopelessness, for at least 2 weeks. Daily functioning becomes impaired.   463

managed care Strategies for controlling health care costs, including mental health treatments.   482

manifest content A dream's surface content, which contains dream symbols that distort and disguise the dream's true meaning.   164, 487

marginalization The process in which groups are put out of cultural and psychological contact with both their traditional society and the larger, dominant society.   526

matching hypothesis The hypothesis that while we may prefer a more attractive person in the abstract, in the real world we end up choosing someone who is close to our own level of attractiveness.   585

medical model A model that describes mental disorders as mental diseases with a biological origin.   450

meditation The practice and system of thought that incorporates exercises to attain bodily or mental control and well-being, as well as enlightenment.   535

medulla The portion of the brain located where the spinal cord enters the skull. It helps control breathing and regulates a portion of the reflexes that allow us to maintain an upright posture.   80

memory The retention of information over time. Psychologists study how information is initially encoded into memory, how it is retained or stored, and how it is found or retrieved for a certain purpose later.   218

memory span The number of digits an individual can report back in order after a single presentation of them.   226

menopause The time in middle age, usually in the late forties or early fifties, when a woman's menstrual periods cease completely.   352

mental age (MA) An individual's level of mental development relative to others.   291

mental processes The thoughts, feelings, and motives that each of us experiences privately but that cannot be observed directly.   5

mental retardation A condition of limited mental ability in which an individual has a low IQ (usually below 70 on a traditional intelligence test), has difficulty adapting to everyday life, and has an onset of these characteristics in the so-called developmental period—by age 18.   308

mental set A type of fixation in which an individual tries to solve a problem in a particular way that has worked in the past.   261

meta-analysis A research technique that involves statistically combining the results of many different studies.   501

method of loci A mnemonic strategy in which you develop an image of items to be remembered and store them in familiar locations *(loci)*.   246

midbrain Located between the hindbrain and forebrain, this is an area where many nerve-fiber systems ascend and descend to connect lower and higher portions of the brain; in particular, the midbrain relays information between the brain and the eyes and ears.   80

middle adulthood The developmental period that begins at about 35 to 45 years of age and ends at about 55 to 65 years of age. It is a time of expanding personal and social involvement, increased responsibility, adjustment to physical decline, and attainment and maintenance of career satisfaction.   321

middle and late childhood The developmental period that extends from about 6 to 11 years of age, approximately corresponding to the elementary school years; sometimes the period is called the elementary school years.   321

middle ear The section of the ear consisting primarily of the eardrum, hammer, anvil, and stirrup.   118

Minnesota Multiphasic Personality Inventory (MMPI) The self-report personality test most widely used in clinical and research settings.   437

mnemonics Specific memory aids for remembering information.   246

monochromats People with only one kind of cone.   112

monocular cues Depth cues based on each eye working independently.   130

mood disorders Psychological disorders characterized by wide mood swings, ranging from deep depression to extreme euphoria and agitation. Depression can occur alone, as in the depressive disorders, or it can alternate with mania, as in bipolar disorder.   463

mood-congruent memory Memory is better when mood is similar during encoding and retrieval.   243

morphology The rules for word formation.   268

motivation Why people behave, think, and feel the way they do. Motivated behavior is energized, directed, and sustained.   368

movement aftereffects An illusion of movement that occurs when people watch continuous movement and then look at another surface, which then appears to move in the opposite direction.   136

multiaxial system   A feature of the DSM-IV system that classifies individuals on the basis of five dimensions, or "axes," that include the individual's history and highest level of functioning in the last year.   453

multiple-factor theory   L. L. Thurstone's theory that intelligence consists of seven primary mental abilities: verbal comprehension, number ability, word fluency, spatial visualization, associative memory, reasoning, and perceptual speed.   295

myelin sheath   A layer of fat cells that encases most axons; this sheath not only insulates the axon but also helps the nerve impulse travel faster.   73

N

narcolepsy   The overpowering urge to fall asleep.   162

natural selection   The evolutionary principle that the organisms that are best adapted to their environment are the most likely to survive, reproduce, and pass on their genes to their offspring.   6, 68

naturalistic observation   Observations of behavior in real-world settings with no effort made to manipulate or control the situation.   42

nature   An organism's biological inheritance.   69

need for achievement   The desire to accomplish something, to reach a standard of excellence, and to expend effort to excel.   388

need   A deprivation that energizes the drive to eliminate or reduce the deprivation.   369

negative punishment   The removal of a positive stimulus after a behavior, decreasing the likelihood that the behavior will occur again.   202

negative reinforcement   The frequency of a response increases because it is followed by the removal of an aversive (unpleasant) stimulus.   197

neglectful parenting   A style of parenting in which parents are very uninvolved in the child's life; it is associated with children's social incompetence, especially a lack of self-control.   342

neocortex   The most recently evolved part of the brain; covering the rest of the brain almost like a cap, it is the largest part of the brain and makes up about 80 percent of its volume.   84

nervous system   The body's electrochemical communication circuitry, made up of billions of neurons.   70

neurons   Nerve cells, the basic units of the nervous system.   71

neuroscience   The umbrella term for the multidisciplinary study of the nervous system.   71

neurotic   A term for mental disorders that are personally distressful but in which the individual does not lose contact with reality; the term is largely out of use because it is vague.   453

neurotransmitters   Chemical substances that carry information across the synaptic gap to the next neuron.   76

night terror   Sudden arousal from sleep, with intense fear, usually accompanied by a number of physiological reactions.   162

nightmare   A frightening dream that awakens the sleeper from REM sleep.   162

noise   Irrelevant and competing stimuli.   103

nondeclarative memory   Memory that is affected by prior experience without that experience being consciously recollected. Because nondeclarative memory cannot be verbalized or consciously recollected, at least not in the form of specific events or facts, it also is called "implicit memory."   227

nonstate theory   The theory that individuals who become hypnotized are under the social influence of the hypnotist, that they are carrying out the social role of being a good hypnotic subject and letting the hypnotist direct their imaginative thinking.   170

norepinephrine   A neurotransmitter that usually is inhibitory but excites the heart muscles, intestines, and urogenital tract; is involved in the control of alertness and wakefulness.   76

normal distribution   A symmetrical distribution with a majority of the cases falling in the middle of the possible range of scores and few scores appearing toward the extremes of the range.   291

normative social influence   The influence that other people have on us because we seek their approval or avoid their disapproval.   561

norms   Established standards of performance for a test. Norms are established by giving the test to a large group of individuals who are representative of the population for whom the test is intended. Norms allow the test constructor to determine the distribution of test scores, informing us which scores are considered high, low, or average.   290

norms   Rules that apply to the members of a group.   565

nucleus (pl. nuclei)   A group of specialized nerve cells in the brain or spinal cord.   80

nurture   An organism's environmental experiences.   69

O

obedience   Behavior that complies with the explicit demands of the individual in authority.   562

object permanence   The Piagetian term for one of an infant's most important accomplishments: understanding that objects and events continue to exist even when they cannot directly be seen, heard, or touched.   332

observational learning   Learning that occurs when a person observes and imitates someone else's behavior; also called imitation or modeling.   207

obsessive-compulsive disorder (OCD)   An anxiety disorder in which the individual has anxiety-provoking thoughts that will not go away (obsession) and/or urges to perform repetitive, ritualistic behaviors to prevent or produce some future situation (compulsion).   458

occipital lobe   The portion of the cerebral cortex at the back of the head that is involved in vision.   84

Oedipus complex   Freud's idea that the young child develops an intense desire to replace the parent of the same sex and enjoy the affections of the opposite-sex parent.   418

olfactory epithelium   Tissue located at the top of the nasal cavity that contains a sheet of receptor cells for smell.   124

operant conditioning (instrumental conditioning)   A form of learning in which the consequences of behavior produce changes in the probability of the behavior's occurrence.   195

operational definition   A description that is as precise as possible about the aspects of problem and how it is to be studied in terms of observable events that can be measured.   35

operations   In Piaget's theory, mental representations that are reversible; internalized sets of actions that allow the child to do mentally what was done physically before.   333

opiates   Opium and its derivatives; these depress the central nervous system's activity.   173

opponent-process theory   The theory that cells in the visual system respond to red-green and blue-yellow colors; a given cell might be excited by red and inhibited by green, while another cell might be excited by yellow and inhibited by blue.   114

oral stage   The term Freud used to describe development during the first 18 months of life, in which the infant's pleasure centers on the mouth.   417

organ of Corti   A tissue that runs the length of the cochlea and sits on the basilar membrane. It contains the ear's sensory receptors, which change the energy of sound waves into nerve impulses that can be processed by the brain.   118

organic retardation   Mental retardation caused by a genetic disorder or by brain damage; *organic* refers to the tissue or organs of the body, so there is some physical damage in organic retardation.   308

outer ear   The pinna and the external auditory canal.   118

overcompensation   Adler's term for the individual's attempt to deny rather than acknowledge a real situation or the individual's exaggerated effort to conceal a weakness.   421

overconfidence bias   The tendency to have more confidence in our judgments and decisions than we should based on the relative frequency of our correct answers.   265

P

pain   The sensation that warns us that damage is occurring to our bodies.   121

panic disorder   An anxiety disorder marked by the recurrent sudden onset of intense apprehension or terror.   456

papillae   Bumps on the surface of the tongue that contain taste buds, the receptors for taste.   122

paranoid schizophrenia   A type of schizophrenia characterized by delusions of reference, grandeur, and persecution.   469

parasympathetic nervous system   The division of the autonomic nervous system that calms the body.   72, 394

parietal lobe   A portion of the cerebral cortex at the top of the head, and toward the rear, that is involved in processing bodily sensations.   84

partial reinforcement   Reinforcement of responses only a portion of the time they occur.   199

perception   The brain's process of organizing and interpreting sensory information to give it meaning.   102

peripheral nervous system   A network of nerves that connects the brain and spinal cord to other parts of the body. The peripheral nervous system takes information to and from the brain and spinal cord and carries out the commands of the CNS to execute various muscular and glandular activities.   71

personality disorders   Chronic, maladaptive cognitive-behavioral patterns that are thoroughly integrated into the individual's personality.   472

personality psychology   An area that focuses on relatively enduring traits and characteristics of individuals.   27

personality   The enduring, distinctive thoughts, emotions, and behaviors that characterize the way an individual adapts to the world.   412

person-centered therapy   A form of humanistic therapy developed by Carl Rogers in which the therapist provides a warm, supportive atmosphere to improve the client's self-concept and encourage the client to gain insight about problems.   489

phallic stage   Freud's third stage of development, which occurs between the ages of 3 and 6. Its name comes from the Latin word phallus, which means "penis." During the phallic stage, pleasure focuses on the genitals as the child discovers that self-stimulation is enjoyable.   418

phenotype   The way an individual's genotype is expressed in observable, measurable characteristics.   67

pheromones   Odorous substances released by animals that are powerful attractants in the lower animals but much less so in humans.   381

phobias   Irrational fears.   192

phobic disorder   An anxiety disorder in which the individual has an irrational, overwhelming, persistent fear of a particular object or situation; commonly called phobia.   457

phonology   A language's sound system.   268

physical dependence   The physical need for a drug that is accompanied by unpleasant withdrawal symptoms when the drug is discontinued.   172

pitch   The perceptual interpretation of a sound's frequency.   116

pituitary gland   An important endocrine gland that sits at the base of the skull and is about the size of a pea; it controls growth and regulates other glands.   95

place theory   The theory that each frequency of sound waves produces vibrations at a particular spot on the basilar membrane.   118

placebo effect   Production of the desired experimental outcome by participants' expectations rather than the experimental treatment.   49

plasticity   The brain's capacity to modify and reorganize itself following damage.   91

pleasure principle   The Freudian concept that the id always seeks pleasure and avoids pain.   415

polygraph   A machine used by examiners to determine if someone is lying; it monitors changes in the body—heart rate, breathing, and electrodermal response (an index that detects skin resistance to passage of a weak electric current)—thought to be influenced by emotional states.   394

pons   A bridge in the hindbrain that contains several clusters of fibers involved in sleep and arousal.   80

population   The entire group about which the investigator wants to draw conclusions.   38

positive punishment   An unpleasant stimulus following a behavior which decreases the likelihood that that behavior will occur again.   202

positive reinforcement   The frequency of a response increases because it is followed by a rewarding stimulus.   196

positron-emission tomography (PET scan)   A technology in which the amount of specially treated glucose in various areas of the brain is measured and then analyzed by computer.   94

postconventional level   Kohlberg's highest level of moral thinking; moral development is completely internalized and not based on others' standards. An individual recognizes alternative moral courses, explores the options, and then develops a personal moral code. The code is among the principles generally accepted by the community (stage 5) or it is more individualized (stage 6).   348

post-traumatic stress disorder   A mental disorder that develops through exposure to a traumatic event, such as war; severely oppressive situations, such as the holocaust; severe abuse, as in rape; natural disasters, such as floods and tornados; and accidental disasters, such as plane crashes. Characterized by anxiety symptoms that might immediately follow the trauma or be delayed in onset by months or even years.   458

PQ4R   A study system that involves Preview, Question, Read, Reflect, Recite, and Review.   248

precognition   "Knowing" events before they occur.   142

preconventional level   Kohlberg's lowest level of moral thinking, in which an individual shows no internalization of moral values—moral thinking is based on punishments (stage 1) or rewards (stage 2) that come from the external world.   347

predictive validity   A form of criterion validity that assesses the relation of a test's scores to an individual's performance at a point in the future.   289

prejudice   An unjustified negative attitude toward an individual based on the individual's membership in a group.   569

prenatal period   The time from conception to birth.   321

preoperational stage   Piaget's second stage of cognitive development, which lasts from about 2 to 7 years of age. This stage is more symbolic than sensorimotor thought, does not involve operational thought, is egocentric, and is intuitive rather than logical.   333

preparedness   The species-specific biological predisposition to learn in certain ways but not in others.   210

preterm infant   An infant who is born prior to 38 weeks into the prenatal period; also called a premature infant.   327

primacy effect   Superior recall for items at the beginning of a list.   237

primacy effect   The enduring quality of initial impressions.   554

primary prevention   Prevention that attempts to stop people from taking drugs by helping them to not start.   178

primary reinforcement   The use of reinforcers that are innately satisfying (that is, they do not require any learning on the organism's part to make them pleasurable).   198

priming   Activating particular connections or associations in memory. These associations often are unconscious.   238

proactive interference   Material that was learned earlier disrupts the recall of material learned later.   243

problem solving   An attempt to find an appropriate way of attaining a goal when the goal is not readily available.   259

problem-focused coping   Lazarus' term for the cognitive strategy of squarely facing one's own troubles and trying to solve them.   528

projective test   A test that presents individuals with an ambiguous stimulus and then asks them to describe it or tell a story about it. Projective tests are based on the assumption that the ambiguity of the stimulus allows individuals to project into it their feelings, desires, needs, and attitudes.   435

prototype matching   Deciding whether an item is a member of a category by comparing it with the most typical item(s) of the category.   258

prototypes   Abstract categorizations of traits that describe a particular personality type. Prototypes act as standards against which we match the individuals we evaluate.   554

psychiatry   A branch of medicine practiced by physicians with a doctor of medicine (M.D.) degree who subsequently specialize in abnormal behavior and psychotherapy.   25

psychoactive drugs   Drugs that act on the nervous system to alter states of consciousness, modify perceptions, and change moods.   170

psychoanalysis   Freud's therapeutic technique for analyzing an individual's unconscious thought.   486

psychoanalytic approach   An emphasis on the unconscious aspects of the mind, conflict between biological instincts and society's demands, and early family experiences.   10

psychoanalytic perspectives   Perspectives that view personality as primarily unconscious and as occurring in stages. Most psychoanalytic perspectives emphasize the role of early experiences in sculpting personality.   413

psychodynamic therapies   Therapies that stress the importance of the unconscious mind, extensive interpretation by the therapist, and the role of experiences in early childhood.   484

psychokinesis   Closely associated with ESP, the mind-over-matter phenomenon of being able to move objects without touching them, such as mentally getting a chair to rise off the floor or shattering a glass merely by staring at it.   142

psychological dependence   The strong craving to repeat the use of a drug in order to obtain its emotional effects, such as a feeling of well-being and a reduction of stress.   172

psychology   The scientific study of behavior and mental processes.   5

psychology of women   An area of psychology that emphasizes the importance of promoting the research and study of women, integrating this information about women with current psychological knowledge and beliefs, and applying the information to society and its institutions.   27

psychoneuroimmunology   The field that explores the connections among psychological factors (such as attitudes and emotions), the nervous system, and the immune system.   519

psychophysics   The field that studies links between the physical properties of stimuli and a person's experience of them.   102

psychosexual dysfunctions   Disorders that involve impairments in the sexual response pattern, either in the desire for gratification or in the ability to achieve it.   383

psychosurgery   A biomedical therapy that involves removal or destruction of brain tissue to improve the individual's psychological adjustment.   507

psychotherapy   The process used by mental health professionals to help individuals recognize, define, and overcome their psychological and interpersonal difficulties and improve their adjustment.   480

psychotic   A term for severe mental disorders in which the individual has lost contact with reality; the term is generally out of use because it is vague.   453

puberty   A period of rapid skeletal and sexual maturation that occurs in early adolescence.   346

punishment   A consequence that decreases the likelihood a behavior will occur.   202

pupil   The opening in the center of the iris; it appears black. The iris contains muscles that control the size of the pupil and, hence, the amount of light that enters the eye.   107

questionnaires (surveys)   A data collection method similar to structured interviews except that the respondents read the questions and mark their answers on paper rather than verbally responding to an interviewer.   43

random assignment   Assignment of participants to experimental and control groups by chance. This practice reduces the likelihood that the experiment's results will be due to any preexisting differences between groups.   46

random sample   A sample in which every member of the population has an equal chance of being selected.   38

rapport talk   The language of conversation. A way of establishing connections and negotiating relationships. Preferred by women.   588

rational-emotive behavior therapy   A cognitive therapy based on Albert Ellis' assertion that individuals invariably become psychologically disordered because of their beliefs, especially those that are irrational and self-defeating.   494

reality principle   The Freudian principle that the ego tries to bring the individual pleasure within the norms of society.   415

reasoning   The mental activity of transforming information to reach conclusions.   263

recall   A memory measure in which the individual must retrieve previously learned information, as on an essay test.   238

recency effect   Superior recall for items at the end of a list.   237

reciprocal socialization   Bidirectional socialization, in which children socialize their parents just as parents socialize their children.   342

recognition   A memory measure in which the individual only has to identify ("recognize") learned items, as on a multiple-choice test.   238

reflexes   Automatic stimulus-response connections that are "hardwired" into the brain.   187

rehearsal   The conscious repetition of information that increases the length of time that information stays in memory.   219

reliability   The extent to which a test yields a consistent, reproducible measure of performance.   288

REM sleep   A periodic, active stage of sleep during which dreaming occurs.   157

repair theory   The theory that sleep restores, replenishes, and rebuilds our brains and bodies, which are somehow worn out by the day's waking activities.   154

report talk   Talk designed to give information, as in public speaking. Preferred by men.   588

representativeness heuristic   Making decisions based on how well something matches a prototype—that is, the most common or representative example.   266

repression   The most powerful and pervasive defense mechanism, according to Freud; it works to push unacceptable id impulses out of awareness and back into the unconscious mind.   416

research participant bias   The influence of research participants' beliefs about how they are expected to behave.   49

resistance   The psychoanalytic term for the person's unconscious defense strategies that prevent the analyst from understanding the person's problems.   487

resting potential   The stable, negative charge of an inactive neuron.   75

restrained eaters   Individuals who chronically restrict their food intake to control their weight. Restrained eaters are often on diets, are very conscious of what they eat, and tend to feel guilty after splurging on sweets.   377

reticular formation   A diffuse collection of neurons involved in stereotyped patterns of behavior such as walking, sleeping, or turning to attend to a sudden noise.   80

retina   The light-sensitive surface at the back of the eye that houses light receptors called rods and cones.   108

retrieval   Bringing information out of memory storage.   219

retroactive interference   Material learned later disrupts retrieval of information learned earlier.   243

retrograde amnesia   Memory loss for a segment of the past but not for new events.   244

risky shift   The tendency for a group decision to be riskier, on the average, than decisions made by individual group members.   567

rods   The receptors in the retina that are exquisitely sensitive to light but are not very useful for color vision.   108

roles   Rules and expectations that govern certain positions in the group. Roles define how people should behave in a particular position in the group.   565

romantic love   Also called passionate love or eros, this type of love has strong components of sexuality and infatuation; it often predominates in the early part of a love relationship.   585

romantic script   Sex is synonymous with love. If we develop a relationship with someone and fall in love, it is acceptable to have sex with the person whether we are married or not.   382

Rorschach inkblot test   The most well known projective test, developed in 1921 by the Swiss psychiatrist Hermann Rorschach. It uses individuals' perceptions of inkblots to determine their personality.   435

sample   The subset of the population chosen by the investigator for study.   38

saturation   A characteristic of color based on its purity.   111

schedules of reinforcement   Timetables that determine when a response will be reinforced.   199

schema   A concept or framework that already exists in a person's mind and that organizes and interprets information.   230, 331

schizophrenia   A severe psychological disorder characterized by distorted thoughts and perceptions, odd communication, inappropriate emotion, abnormal motor behavior, and social withdrawal. The individual's mind is split from reality and personality loses its unity.   467

school and educational psychology   An area of psychology that is concerned with children's learning and adjustment in school.   27

science   In psychology, the use of systematic methods to observe, describe, explain, and predict behavior.   5

scientific method   An approach used to discover accurate information about phenomena, including mind and behavior. It includes these steps: Identify a problem, collect information (data), draw conclusions, and revise theory.   35

scientific research   Research that is objective, systematic, and testable.   34

sclera   The white outer part of the eye that helps maintain the shape of the eye and protect it from injury.   107

script   A schema for an event.   233

secondary prevention   Prevention that attempts to minimize the harm caused by drug use with a high-risk population or with a group that is involved in experimental or occasional use.   178

secondary reinforcement   Reinforcement that acquires its positive value through experience; secondary reinforcers are learned, or conditioned, reinforcers.   198

secondary traits   In Allport's view, traits that are limited in frequency and least important in describing an individual's personality.   431

secure attachment   Securely attached infants use the caregiver, usually the mother, as a secure base from which to explore the environment. Ainsworth believes that secure attachment in the first year of life provides an important foundation for psychological development later in life.   340

selective attention   Focusing on a specific aspect of experience while ignoring others.   128

self-actualization   The highest and most elusive human need, according to Maslow; the motivation to develop one's full potential as a human being.   372

self-actualization   The highest and most elusive of Maslow's needs; the motivation to develop one's full potential as a human being.   427

self-concept   A central theme in the views of Rogers and other humanists; individuals' overall perceptions of their abilities, behavior, and personality.   426

self-efficacy   The belief that one can master a situation and produce positive outcomes; an effective coping strategy.   532

self-esteem   The evaluative and affective dimension of self-concept. Self-esteem is also referred to as self-worth.   427

self-help support groups   Voluntary organization of individuals who get together on a regular basis to discuss topics of common interest. The groups are not conducted by a professional therapist but rather by a paraprofessional or a member of the common interest group.   499

self-monitoring   Individuals' attention to the impressions they make on others and the degree to which they fine-tune their performance accordingly.   556

self-perception theory   Bem's theory of attitude-behavior connection; it stresses that individuals make inferences about their attitudes by perceiving their behavior.   558

self-report tests   Tests that involve directly asking people whether items (usually true-false or agree-disagree) describe their personality traits or not; also called objective tests or inventories.   436

self-serving bias   Attributing explanations for one's successes to internal factors and explanations for one's failures to external factors.   552

self-talk (self-statements)   The soundless, mental speech people use when they think about something, plan, or solve problems; often helpful in cognitive restructuring.   529

semantic memory   A person's knowledge about the world. This includes a person's field of expertise, general academic knowledge of the sort learned in school, and everyday knowledge about meanings of words, famous individuals, important places, and common things.   228

semantics   The meanings of words and sentences.   268

semicircular canals   Canals in the inner ear that contain the sensory receptors that detect head motion caused by tilting the head or other bodily motion.   126

sensation   The process of detecting and encoding stimulus energy in the world.   102

sensorimotor stage   The first Piagetian stage, which lasts from birth until about 2 years of age. In this stage, infants construct an understanding of the world by coordinating sensory experiences with physical motoric actions. This stage is nonsymbolic through much of its duration, and object permanence is an important accomplishment.   332

sensory adaptation   A change in the responsiveness of the sensory system based on the average level of surrounding stimulation.   110

sensory memory   A form of memory storage that holds information from the world in its original sensory form for only an instant, not much longer than the brief time it is exposed to the visual, auditory, and other senses.   224

separation   Self-imposed withdrawal from the larger culture.   526

serial position effect   Recall is superior for the items at the beginning of a list and the end of a list.   237

serotonin   A neurotransmitter that is mainly inhibitory and is involved in the regulation of sleep and depression.   76

set point   The weight maintained when no effort is made to gain or lose weight.   376

sex   The biological dimension of being female or male.   13

sexual scripts   Stereotyped patterns of expectancies for how people should sexually behave.   382

sexually transmitted diseases (STDs)   Diseases that are contracted primarily through sex—intercourse as well as oral-genital and anal-genital sex.   543

shape constancy   Recognition that an object remains the same shape even though its orientation to us changes.   136

shaping   The process of rewarding approximations of desired behavior.   198

signal detection theory   The theory that sensitivity to sensory stimuli depends on a variety of factors besides the physical intensity of the stimulus and the sensory abilities of the observer.   105

situationism   Mischel's view that personality often varies from one context to another.   432

size constancy   Recognition that an object remains the same size even though the retinal image of the object changes.   136

sleep apnea   A sleep disorder in which the sleeper stops breathing because the windpipe fails to open or brain processes involved in respiration fail to work properly.   162

sleep spindles   Brief bursts of higher-frequency waves that periodically occur during stage 2 sleep.   157

social cognitive theory   The theory that behavior is determined not only by environmental conditions, but also by how thought processes modify these experiences.   8, 424

social comparison   The process in which individuals evaluate their thoughts, feelings, behaviors, and abilities in relation to other people.   554

social desirability   The tendency of participants to tell the interviewer what they think is socially acceptable or desirable rather than what they truly feel or think.   43, 436

social facilitation   The phenomenon that occurs when an individual's performance improves because of the presence of others; occurs with well-learned tasks not with new or difficult tasks.   566

social identity theory   The theory that when individuals are assigned to a group, they invariably think of the group as an in-group for them. This occurs because individuals want to have a positive self-image. Social identity theory helps to explain prejudice and conflict between groups.   571

social loafing   Each person's tendency to exert less effort in a group because of reduced monitoring. The result is lowered group performance.   566

social psychology   An area that deals with people's social interactions, relationships, perceptions, and attitudes.   27

social support   Information and feedback from others that one is loved and cared for, esteemed and valued, and included in a network of communication and mutual obligation.   532

sociocultural approach   An approach that emphasizes the influences of culture, ethnicity, and gender, among other sociocultural factors, on behavior, thought, and emotion.   12

socioemotional processes   Processes that involve changes in an individual's relationships with other people, changes in emotions, and changes in personality.   320

somatic nervous system   The sensory nerves, which convey information from the skin and muscle to the CNS about such matters as pain and temperature, and the motor nerves, which tell muscles when to act.   71

somatoform disorders   Mental disorders in which psychological symptoms take a physical, or somatic, form even though no physical causes can be found.   459

somnambulism   The formal term for sleepwalking; somnambulism occurs during the deepest stages of sleep.   161

sounds   Vibrations of air that are processed by the auditory (hearing) system; also called sound waves.   116

special process theory   The theory that hypnotic behavior is different from nonhypnotic behavior, and that hypnotic responses are elicited by suggestion rather than being voluntary reactions.   168

split-half reliability   Dividing the items into two halves, such as the first half of the test and the second half of the test. Individuals' scores on the two halves are compared to determine how consistently they performed.   288

spontaneous recovery   The process in classical conditioning by which a conditioned response can appear again after a time delay without further conditioning.   188

sport psychology   The field of psychology that applies psychology's principles to improving sport performance and enjoying sport participation.   28

standardization   Developing uniform procedures for administering and scoring a test, as well as creating norms for the test.   290

standardized tests   Tests that require people to answer a series of written and/or oral questions. Standardized tests have two distinct features: (1) An individual's score is totaled to yield a single score, or set of scores, and (2) the individual's score is compared with the scores of a large group of similar people to determine how the individual responded relative to others.   44

stereotype   A generalization about a group's characteristics that does not consider any variation from one individual to another.   570

stimulants   Psychoactive drugs that increase the central nervous system's activity.   174

stimulus substitution   Pavlov's theory of how classical conditioning works: The nervous system is structured in such a way that the CS and US bond together and eventually the CS substitutes for the US.   191

storage   The retention of information over time.   219

storm-and-stress view   G. Stanley Hall's view that adolescence is a turbulent time charged with conflict and mood swings.   345

stream of consciousness   A continuous flow of changing sensations, images, thoughts, and feelings.   150

stress   The response of individuals to the circumstances and events, called stressors, that threaten them and tax their coping abilities.   518

stress management programs   Programs that teach individuals how to appraise stressful events, how to develop skills for coping with stress, and how to put these skills into use.   535

striving for superiority   According to Jung, the human motivation to adapt, improve, and master the environment.   420

stroboscopic motion   The illusion of movement created by a rapid stimulation of different parts of the retina.   136

Stroop effect   An example of automatic perception in which it is difficult to name the colors that words are printed in when the actual words refer to different colors.   129

structuralism   The early theory of psychology developed by Titchener that emphasized the importance of conscious thought and classification of the mind's structures.   7

subgoaling   Setting intermediate goals that put you in a better position to reach a final goal or solution.   259

superego   The Freudian structure of personality that is the moral branch of personality. The superego takes into account whether something is right or wrong.   415

superiority complex   Adler's concept of exaggerated self-importance designed to mask feelings of inferiority.   421

sympathetic nervous system   The division of the autonomic nervous system that arouses the body.   72

sympathetic nervous system   The subdivision of the autonomic nervous system that is involved in the body's arousal, being responsible for quick responses to a stressor, which sometimes is referred to as the "fight-or-flight" response.   393

synapses   Tiny gaps between neurons. Most synapses are between the axon of one neuron and the dendrites or cell body of another neuron.   75

syntax   Rules for the ways words are combined to form acceptable phrases and sentences.   268

systematic desensitization   A method of behavior therapy based on classical conditioning that treats anxiety by getting the person to associate deep relaxation with increasingly intense anxiety-producing situations.   492

T

tardive dyskinesia   A major side effect of the neuroleptic drugs; a neurological disorder characterized by grotesque, involuntary movements of the facial muscles and mouth as well as extensive twitching of the neck, arms, and legs.   505

telegraphic speech   The use of short and precise words to communicate; it is characteristic of young children's two- and three-word combinations.   272

telepathy   The extrasensory transfer of thought from one person to another.   142

temperament   An individual's behavioral style and characteristic way of responding.   341

temporal lobe   A portion of the neocortex that is just above the ears and is involved in hearing.   84

teratogen   (The word comes from the Greek word *tera*, meaning "monster.") Any agent that causes a birth defect. The field of study that investigates the causes of birth defects is called teratology.   326

tertiary prevention   Treatment for people who abuse drugs.   179

testosterone   A hormone associated in boys with development of the genitals, an increase in height, and a change of voice.   346

test-retest reliability   The extent to which a test yields the same measure of performance when an individual is given the test on two different occasions.   288

thalamus   A portion of the brain that sits at the top of the brain stem in the central core of the brain. It serves as an important relay station, functioning much like a telephone switchboard between the diverse areas of the cortex and the reticular formation.   82

Thematic Apperception Test (TAT)   A projective test designed to elicit stories that reveal something about an individual's personality; developed by Henry Murray and Christina Morgan in the 1930s.   435

theory   A coherent set of interrelated ideas that helps to make predictions and explain data.   36

thermoreceptors   Receptors located under the skin that respond to changes in temperature.   121

thinking   Mentally manipulating information, as when we form concepts, solve problems, reason, and make decisions.   256

timbre   The tone color or perceptual quality of a sound.   117

time-out   A form of negative punishment in which a child is removed from a positive reinforcement.   202

tip-of-the-tongue (TOT) phenomenon   A type of "effortful retrieval" that occurs when people are confident they know something but just can't quite seem to pull it out of memory.   235

token economy   A behavior modification system in which behaviors are reinforced with tokens (such as poker chips) that later can be exchanged for desired rewards (such as candy, money, or going to a movie).   493

tolerance   The need for a greater amount of a drug to produce the same effect.   172

traditional religious script   Sex is accepted only within marriage. Extramarital sex is taboo, especially for women. Sex means reproduction and sometimes affection.   382

trait theories   Theories that propose that people have broad dispositions (traits) that are reflected in the basic ways they behave, such as whether they are outgoing and friendly or whether they are dominant and assertive.   429

tranquilizers   Depressant drugs, such as Valium and Xanax, that reduce anxiety and induce relaxation.   173

transcendental meditation (TM)   The most popular form of meditation in North America, TM is derived from an ancient Indian technique and involves a mantra, which is a resonant sound or phrase that is repeated mentally or aloud to focus attention.   535

transduction   The conversion of one form of energy into another. In sensation, this consists of converting stimulus energy into neural impulses.   108

transference   The psychoanalytic term for the person's relating to the analyst in ways that reproduce or relive important relationships in that person's life.   487

triangular theory of love　Sternberg's view that love comes in three main dimensions: passion, intimacy, and commitment.　586

triarchic theory　Sternberg's theory that intelligence consists of componental intelligence, experiential intelligence, and contextual intelligence.　298

trichromatic theory　The theory that color perception is based on the existence of three types of receptors that are maximally sensitive to different, but overlapping, ranges of wavelengths.　112

trichromats　People with normal color vision—they have three kinds of cone receptors.　113

trust versus mistrust　Erikson's first psychosocial stage, which occurs in the first year of life. Trust is built when a baby's basic needs—such as comfort, food, and warmth—are met. If infants' needs are not met by responsive, sensitive caregivers, the result is mistrust.　337

two-factor theory　Spearman's theory that individuals have both a general intelligence (*g*) and a number of specific intelligences (*s*).　295

two-factor theory of emotion　Schachter and Singer's theory that emotion is determined by physiological arousal and cognitive labeling.　397

Type A behavior pattern　A cluster of characteristics—being excessively competitive, hard-driven, impatient, and hostile—thought to be related to the incidence of heart disease.　521

Type B behavior pattern　Being primarily calm and easy-going.　521

U

unconditional positive regard　Rogers' term for accepting, valuing, and being positive toward another person regardless of the person's behavior.　426, 489

unconditioned response (UR)　An unlearned response that is automatically associated with the unconditioned stimulus.　187

unconditioned stimulus (US)　A stimulus that produces a response without prior learning.　187

unconscious thought　According to Freud, a reservoir of unacceptable wishes, feelings, and thoughts that we are not consciously aware of.　150

undifferentiated schizophrenia　A type of schizophrenia characterized by disorganized behavior, hallucinations, delusions, and incoherence.　469

V

validity　The extent to which a test measures what it is intended to measure.　289

variable-interval schedule　Reinforcement of a response after a variable amount of time has elapsed.　201

variable-ratio schedule　A timetable in which responses are rewarded an average number of times, but on an unpredictable basis.　199

vestibular sense　The sense that provides information about balance and movement.　125

visual illusion　Illusion that occurs when two objects produce exactly the same retinal image but are perceived as different images.　137

volley principle　The principle that neural cells can fire neural impulses in rapid succession, producing a volley of impulses. This alternate rapid neural firing attains a combined frequency above 1,000 firings per second.　120

W

wavelength　The distance from the peak of one wave to the peak of the next.　106

Weber's law　This law states that the difference threshold is a constant percentage of the magnitude of the comparison stimulus rather than a constant amount. Weber's law generally holds true.　105

whole language approach　The view that reading instruction should be parallel to children's natural language learning. Reading materials should be whole and meaningful.　275

wisdom　Expert knowledge about the practical aspects of life.　356

wish fulfillment　In Freud's theory, the reason we dream. For Freud, dreaming is an unconscious attempt to fulfill needs (especially sex and aggression) that cannot be expressed or go ungratified during the waking hours.　164

working memory　Also sometimes called short-term memory, working memory is a limited-capacity storage system in which information is retained for as long as 30 seconds, unless it is rehearsed, in which case it can be retained longer.　225

Y

Yerkes-Dodson law　The law that performance is best under conditions of moderate rather than low or high arousal.　394

Z

zygote　A single cell formed through fertilization.　325

References

* denotes Canadian research

A

Abbey, A., Ross, L.T., & McDuffie, D. (1993). Alcohol's role in sexual assault. In R.R. Watson (Eds.), *Drug and alcohol abuse reviews. Vol. 5: Addictive behaviors in women.* Totowa, NJ: Humana Press.

Abel, E.L. (1984). *Fetal alcohol syndrome and fetal alcohol effects.* New York: Plenum.

Ackerman, P.L., Kyllonen, P.C., & Roberts, R.D. (Eds.) (1999). *Learning and individual differences: Process, trait, and content determinants.* Washington, DC: American Psychological Association.

Adams, H.E., & Cassidy, J.F. (1993). The classification of abnormal behavior: An overview. In P.B. Sutker & H.E. Adams (Eds.), *Comprehensive textbook of psychopathology* (2nd ed.). New York: Plenum Press.

Adams, R. (1998). *The abuses of punishment.* New York: St. Martin's Press.

Adler, A. (1927). *The theory and practice of individual psychology.* Fort Worth: Harcourt Brace.

Adler, T. (1991, January). Seeing double? Controversial twins study is widely reported, debated. *APA Monitor, 22,* 1, 8.

Agnew, N. McK., & Pyke, S.W. (1993). *The science game: An introduction to research in the social sciences.* Upper Saddle River, NJ: Prentice Hall.*

Aiken, L.R. (1996). *Assessment of intellectual functioning* (2nd ed.). New York: Plenum.

Ainsworth, M.D.S. (1979). Infant-mother attachment. *American Psychologists, 34,* 932–937.

Alberti, R. & Emmons, M. (1995). *Your perfect right* (7th ed.). San Luis Obispo, CA: Impact.

Alberto, P., & Troutman, A.C. (1999). *Applied behavior analysis for teachers.* Upper Saddle River, NJ: Merrill.

Alcock, J.E. (1981). *Parapsychology: Science or magic?* London: Pergamon.*

Alcock, J.E. (1987). The status of parapsychology in the world of science. *Behavior and Brain Sciences, 10,* 553-564.*

Alcock, J.E. (1998). Science, pseudoscience and anomaly. *Behavior and Brain Sciences, 21,* 303.*

Alderman, M.K. (1999). *Motivation for achievement.* Mahwah, NJ: Erlbaum.

Aldrich, M.S. (1999). *Sleep medicine.* New York: Oxford University Press.

Al-Issa, I. (1982). Does culture make a difference in psychopathology? In I. Al-Issa (Ed.), *Culture and psychopathology.* Baltimore: University Park Press.*

Allan, R., & Scheidt, S. (Eds.). (1996). *Heart and mind.* Washington, DC: American Psychological Association.

Allen, J.J.B. (1998). DSM-IV. In H.S. Friedman (Ed.), *Encyclopedia of mental health* (Vol. 2). San Diego: Academic Press.

Allison, K.R., Dwyer, J.J., & Mankin, S. (1999). Self-efficacy and participation in vigorous physical activity by high school students. *Health Education & Behavior, 26,* 12–24.*

Alloy, L.B., Jacobson, N.S., & Acocella, J. (1999). *Abnormal psychology* (8th ed.). New York: McGraw-Hill.

Allport, G. H., & Postman, L. (1947). *The psychology of rumor.* New York: Holt.

Allport, G.W. (1937). *Personality: A psychological interpretation.* New York: Holt.

Almagor, M., Tellegen, A., & Waller, N.G. (1995). The big seven model: A cross-cultural replication and further exploration of the basic dimensions of natural language trait descriptors. *Journal of Personality and Social Psychology, 69,* 300–307.

Alsaker, F.D, & Flammer, A. (Eds.). (1999). *The adolescent experience.* Mahwah, NJ: Erlbaum.

Altemeyer, B. (1996). *The authoritarian specter.* Cambridge, MA: Harvard University Press.*

Anastasi, A., & Urbina, S. (1996). *Psychological testing* (7th ed.). Upper Saddle River, NJ: Prentice Hall.

Anderson, B.L. (1983). Primary orgasmic dysfunction: Diagnostic considerations and a review of treatment. *Psychological Bulletin, 93,* 105–136.

Anderson, B.L. (1998). Cancer. In H.S. Friedman (Ed.), *Encyclopedia of mental health* (Vol. 1). San Diego: Academic Press.

Anderson, B.L., Kiecolt-Glaser, J.K., & Glaser. R. (1994). A biobehavioral model of cancer stress and disease course. *American Psychologist, 49,* 389–404.

Anderson, C.A. (1989). Temperature and aggression. *Journal of Personality and Social Psychology, 106,* 74–96.

Anderson, N.H. (1965). Primacy effects in personality impression formation using a generalized order effect paradigm. *Journal of Personality and Social Psychology, 2,* 1–9.

Anderson, N.H. (1974). Cognitive algebra: Integration theory applied to social attribution. In L. Berkowitz (Ed.), *Advances in experimental social psychology* (Vol. 7). New York: Academic Press.

Anderson, N.H. (1989). Functional memory and on-line attribution. In J.N. Bassili (Ed.), *On-line cognition in person perception.* Mahwah, NJ: Erlbaum.

Angus, L., & Hardtke, K. (1994). Narrative processes in psychotherapy. *Canadian Psychology, 35(2),* 190-203.*

Anselmi, D.L. (1998). *Questions of gender.* New York: McGraw-Hill.

Applebaum, M.I., Booth, C.L., Bradley, R.H., Burchinal, M.R., Campbell, S.B., Cox, M., Friedman, S.L., Hirsh-Pasek, K., Kelly, J.F., Marshall, N.L., McCartney, K.A., O'Brien, M., Owen, M.T., Pianta, R.C., Robeson, W.W., Vandell, D., Wallner-Allen, K.E., & Weintraub, M. (1999, April). *Effect sizes from the NICHD study of early child care.* Paper presented at the meeting of the Society for Research in Child Development, Albuquerque.

Archer, D., & Gartner, R. (1976). Violent acts and violent times: A comparative approach in postwar homicide. *American Sociological Review, 41,* 937–963.

Archer, D., & McDaniel, P. (1995). Violence and gender: Differences and similarities across societies. In R.B. Ruback & N.A. Weiner (Eds.), *Interpersonal violent behaviors: Social and cultural aspects.* New York: Springer.

Arkowitz, H. (1997). Integrative theories of therapy. In P.L. Wachtel & S.B. Messer (Eds.), *Theories of psychotherapy.* Washington, DC: American Psychological Association.

Armstrong, D.L., & Rossie, S. (Eds.)(1999). *Advances in second messenger and phosphoprotein research: Ion channel regulation.* San Diego: Academic Press.

Arnitz, A., & van den Hout, M.A. (1996). Psychological treatment of panic disorder without agoraphobia: Cognitive therapy versus applied relaxation. *Behaviour Research and Therapy, 34,* 113–121.

Arnoux, D. (1998, September). Description of teaching experiences prepared for John Santrock's text, *Educational Psychology.* New York: McGraw-Hill.

Aronson, E. (1986, August). *Teaching students things they think they already know all about: The case of prejudice and desegregation.* Paper presented at the meeting of the American Psychological Association, Washington, DC.

Aronson, E. (1995). *The social animal* (7th ed.). New York: W.H. Freeman.

Aronson, E. (1999). Self-affirmation theory. In E. Harmon-Jones & J. Mills (Eds.), *Cognitive dissonance.* Washington, DC: American Psychological Association.

Aronson, E., Wilson, T.D., & Akert, R.M. (1997). *Social psychology* (2nd ed.). New York: Longman.

Aronson, J., Cohen, G., & Nails, P.R. (1999). Unwanted consequences and the self: In search of the motivation for dissonance reduction. In E. Harmon-Jones & J. Mills (Eds.), *Cognitive dissonance.* Washington, DC: American Psychological Association.

Artz, S. (1998). *Sex, power, & the violent school girl.* Toronto: Trifolium Books.*

Arvanitogiannis, A., & Amir, S. (1999). Circadian clock resetting by ultra-short light flashes. *Neuroscience Letters, 261,* 159-162.*

Asch, S.E. (1946). Forming impressions of personality. *Journal of Personality and Social Psychology, 41,* 248–290.

Asch, S.E. (1951). Effects of group pressure on the modification and distortion of judgments. In H.S. Guetzkow (Ed.), *Groups, leadership, and men.* Pittsburgh: Carnegie University Press.

Asher, J., & Garcia. R. (1969). The optimal age to learn a foreign language. *Modern Language Journal, 53,* 334–341.

Ashton, M. C., Jackson, D. N., Helmes, E., & Paunonen, S. V. (1998). Joint factor analysis of the Personality Research Form and the Jackson Personality Inventory: Comparisons with the Big Five. *Journal of Research in Personality, 32,* 243-250.*

Ashton, M. C., Paunonen, S. V., Helmes, E., & Jackson, D. N. (1998). Kin altruism, reciprocal altruism, and the Big Five personality factors. *Evolution and Human Behavior, 19,* 243-255.*

Asnis, G.M., & van Praag, H.M. (1995). *Panic disorder.* New York: Wiley.

Atkin, J.M., & Black, P. (1997, September). Policy perils of international comparisons. *Phi Delta Kappan, 79,* 22–28.

Atkinson, D., Morten, G., & Sue, D. (1998). *Counseling American minorities* (5th ed.). New York: McGraw-Hill.

Atkinson, J.W., & Raynor, I.O. (1974). *Motivation and achievement.* Washington, DC: Winston.

Atkinson, R.C., & Shiffrin, R.M. (1968). Human memory: A proposed system and its control processes. In K.W. Spence & J.T. Spence (Eds.), *The psychology of learning and motivation* (Vol. 2). San Diego: Academic Press.

Auerbach, J.S. (1999). Psychoanalysis and projective testing: A review of *The interpretation of psychological tests. Journal of Personality Assessment, 72,* 147–163.

Auerbach, S.M., & Gramling, S.E. (1998). *Stress management.* Upper Saddle River, NJ: Prentice-Hall.

Averill, J.R. (1983). Studies on anger and aggression: Implications for theories of emotion. *American Psychologist, 38,* 1145–1160.

Avis, M.H. (1999). *Drugs and life* (4th ed.). New York: McGraw-Hill.

Azar, B. (1996, January). Damaged area of brain can reorganize itself. *APA Monitor,* p. 19.

B

Baars, B. (1999). Psychology in a world of sentimental, self-knowing beings: A modest utopian fantasy. In R.L. Solso (Ed.), *Mind and brain sciences in the 21st century.* Cambridge, MA: MIT Press.

Baddeley, A. (1990). *Human memory.* Boston: Allyn & Bacon.

Baddeley, A. (1992). Working memory. *Science, 255,* 556–560.

Baddeley, A. (1993). Working memory and conscious awareness. In A.F. Collins, S.E. Gatherhole, M.A. Conway, & P.E. Morris (Eds.), *Theories of memory.* Mahwah, NJ: Erlbaum.

Baddeley, A. (1995). Applying the psychology of memory to clinical problems. In D. Hermann, C. McEvoy, C. Hertzog, P. Hertel, & M. Johnson (Eds.), *Basic and applied memory research* (Vol. 1). Mahwah, NJ: Erlbaum.

Baddeley, A. (1998). *Human memory* (Rev. ed.). Boston: Allyn & Bacon.

Bahrick, H.P., Bahrick, P.O., & Whitlinger, R.P. (1975). Fifty years of memory for names and faces: A cross-sectional approach. *Journal of Experimental Psychology: General, 104,* 54–75.

Baillargeon, R. (1997). The object concept revisited. In C.E. Granrud (Ed.), *Visual perception and cognition in infancy.* Mahwah, NJ: Erlbaum.

Baity, M.R., & Hilsenroth, M.J. (1999). Rorschach aggression variables: A study of reliability and validity. *Journal of Personality and Assessment, 72,* 93–110.

Balch, W.R., Myers, D.M., & Papotto, C. (1999). Dimensions of mood in mood-congruent memory. *Journal of Experimental Psychology: Learning, Memory, and Condition, 25,* 70–83.

Baldwin, J.D., & Baldwin, J.I. (1998). Sexual behavior. In H.S. Friedman (Ed.), *Encyclopedia of mental health* (Vol. 3). San Diego: Academic Press.

Baldwin, J.D., & Baldwin, J.I. (1999). *Behavior principles in everyday life* (3rd ed.). Upper Saddle River, NJ: Prentice-Hall.

Bales, J. (1988, December). Vincennes: Findings could have averted tragedy, scientists tell Hill panel. *APA Monitor,* pp. 10–11.

Ball, W. & Tronick, E. (1971). Infant responses to impending collision: Optical and real. *Science, 171,* 818–820.

Baltes, P.B. (1993). The aging mind: Potentials and limits. *Gerontologist, 33,* 580–594.

Baltes, P.B., Lindenberger, U., & Staudinger, U.M. (1998). Life-span theory in developmental psychology. In W. Damon (Ed.), *Handbook of child psychology* (5th ed., Vol. 1), New York: Wiley.

Bandura, A. (1965). Influences of models' reinforcement contingencies on the acquisition of imitative responses. *Journal of Personality and Social Psychology, 1,* 589–596.

Bandura, A. (1977). *Social learning theory.* Upper Saddle River, NJ: Prentice Hall.

Bandura, A. (1986). *Social foundations of thought and action.* Englewood Cliffs, NJ: Prentice Hall.

Bandura, A. (1989). Social cognitive theory. In R. Vasta (Ed.), *Six theories of child development.* Greenwich, CT: JAI Press.

Bandura, A. (1994). Social cognitive theory of mass communication. In J. Bryant & D. Zillman (Eds.), *Media effects.* Mahwah, NJ: Erlbaum.

Bandura, A. (1997). *Self-efficacy.* New York: W.H. Freeman.

Bandura, A. (1998). Self-efficacy. In H.S. Friedman (Ed.), *Encyclopedia of mental health* (Vol. 3). San Diego: Academic Press.

Bandura, A. (1998, August). *Exercise of agency in accenting the positive.* Paper presented at the meeting of the American Psychological Association, San Francisco.

Bandura, A., Blanchard, E.B., & Ritter, B. (1969). Relative efficacy of desensitization and modeling approaches for inducing behavioral, affective, and attitudinal changes. *Journal of Personality and Social Psychology, 13,* 173–199.

Baranowsky, A.B., Young, M., Johnson-Douglas, S., Williams-Keeler, J. & McCarrey, M. (1998). PTSD transmission: A review of secondary traumatization in Holocaust survivor families. *Canadian Psychology, 39(4),* 247-256.*

Bard, P. (1934). Emotion. In C. Murchison (Ed.), *Handbook of general psychology.* Worcester, MA: Clark University Press.

Barker, P. (1998). Family therapy. In H.S. Friedman (Ed.), *Encyclopedia of mental health* (Vol. 2). San Diego: Academic Press.*

Barman, J. (1996). Aboriginal education at the crossroads: The legacy of residential schools and the way ahead. In D.A. Long & O.P. Dickason (Eds.), *Visions of the heart : Canadian aboriginal issues.* Toronto: Harcourt Brace Canada.*

Baron, N. (1992). *Growing up with language.* Reading, MA: Addison-Wesley.

Barrera, M.E. & Maurer, D. (1981). Discrimination of strangers by the three-month-old. *Child Development, 52(2),* 558-563.*

Barrett, M.C., King, A., Lévy, J., Maticka-Tyndale, E., & McKay, A. (1997). Canada. In R.T. Francoeur (Ed.), *The International encyclopedia of sexuality (Vol 1): Argentina to Greece.* New York: Continuum.*

Barron, R.W. (1994). The sound-to-spelling connection: Orthographic activation in auditory word recognition and its implications for the acquisition of phonological awareness and literacy skills. In V.W. Berninger (Ed.), *The varieties of othographic knowledge I: Theoretical and developmental issues.* Dordrecht, the Netherlands: Kluwer.*

Barry, H., Child, I.L., & Bacon, M.K. (1959). Relation of child training to subsistence economy. *American Anthropologist, 61,* 51–63.

Bartlett, F.C. (1932). *Remembering.* Cambridge: Cambridge University Press.

Bartlett, J.C. (1998, March). *Personal communication.* Richardson, TX: University of Texas at Dallas, Program in Psychology.

Bartoshuk, L.M., & Beauchamp, G.K. (1994). Chemical senses. *Annual Review of Psychology* (Vol. 45). Palo Alto, CA: Annual Reviews.

Bates, J.A. (1995). Teaching hypothesis testing by debunking a demonstration of telepathy. In M.E. Ware & D.E. Johnson (Eds.), *Handbook of demonstrations and activities in the teaching of psychology* (Vol. 1). Washington, DC: American Psychological Association.

Batson, C.D. (1998). Altruism and prosocial behavior. In D.T. Gilbert, S.T. Fiske, & G. Lindzey (Eds.), *Handbook of social psychology* (4th ed., Vol. 2). New York: McGraw-Hill.

Baum, A., & Posluszny, D.M. (1999). Health psychology. *Annual Review of Psychology, 50.* Palo Alto, CA: Annual Reviews.

Baumeister, R.F. (1989). The optimal margin of illusion. *Journal of Social and Clinical Psychology, 8,* 176–189.

Baumeister, R.F. (1991). *Meanings of life.* New York: Guilford.

Baumeister, R.F. (1993). *Self-esteem: The puzzle of low self-regard.* New York: Plenum Press.

Baumeister, R.F. (1997). Identity, self-concept, and self-esteem. In R. Hogan, J. Johnson, & S. Briggs (Eds.), *Handbook of personality psychology.* San Diego: Academic Press.

Baumeister, R.F. (1999). *Evil: Inside human violence and cruelty.* New York: W.H. Freeman.

Baumeister, R.F., & Bratslavsky, E. (1999). Passion, intimacy, and time: Passionate love as a function of change in intimacy. *Personality and Social Psychology Review, 3,* 2–22.

Baumrind, D. (1971). Current patterns of parental authority. *Developmental Psychology Monographs, 4,* (1, Pt. 2).

Baumrind, D. (1991). Parenting styles and adolescent development. In J. Brooks-Gunn, R. Lerner, & A.C. Petersen (Eds.), *The encyclopedia of adolescence* (Vol. 2). New York: Garland.

Beattie, G., & Couglan, J. (1999). An experimental investigation of the role of iconic gestures in lexical access using the tip-of-the-tongue phenomenon. *British Journal of Psychology, 90,* 35–56.

Beatty, J. (1995). *Principles of neuroscience.* New York: McGraw-Hill.

Beck, A.T. (1967). *Depression.* New York: Harper & Row.

Beck, A.T. (1976). *Cognitive therapies and the emotional disorders.* New York: International Universities Press.

Beck, A.T. (1993). Cognitive therapy: Past, present, and future. *Journal of Consulting and Clinical Psychology, 61,* 194–198.

Bednar, R.L., Wells, M.G., & Peterson, S.R. (1995). *Self-esteem* (2nd ed.). Washington, DC: American Psychological Association.

Begg, I. (1983). Imagery instruction and the organization of memory. In J.C. Yuille (Ed.), *Imagery, memory and cognition.* Mahwah, NJ: Erlbaum.*

Begg, I.M., Needham, D.R., & Bookbinder, M. (1993). Do backward messages unconsciously affect listeners? No. *Canadian Journal of Experimental Psychology, 47(1),* 1-14.*

Belicki, K., & Cuddy, M. (1996). Identifying a history of sexual trauma from patterns of dream and sleep experience. In D. Barrett (Ed.), *Trauma and dreams.* Boston: Harvard University Press.*

Belicki, K., Chambers, E., & Ogilvie, R. (1997). Nightmares and sleep quality. *Sleep Research, 26,* 637.*

Belicki, K., Correy, B., Cuddy, M., Dunlop, A., & Boucock, A. (1993). Examining the authenticity of reports of sexual abuse. *Canadian Psychology, 34,* 284.*Benjafield, J. (1996). A history of psychology. Boston: Allyn & Bacon.*

Bell, A.P., Weinberg, M.S., & Mamersmith, S.K. (1981). *Sexual preference.* New York: Simon & Schuster.

Bellesiles, M.A. (1999). *Lethal imagination.* New York: New York University Press.

Belsky, J.K. (1999). *The psychology of aging* (3rd ed.). Belmont, CA: Wadsworth.

Belson, W. (1978). *Television violence and the adolescent boy.* London: Saxon House.

Bem, D. (1967). Self-perception: An alternative explanation of cognitive dissonance phenomena. *Psychological Review, 74,* 183–200.

Benet, V., & Waller, N.G. (1995). The big seven factor model of personality description: Evidence for its cross-cultural generality in a Spanish sample. *Journal of Personality and Social Psychology, 69,* 701–718.

Benjafield, J.G. (1997). **Cognition** (2nd Ed). Upper Saddle River, NJ: Prentice Hall.*

Benjamin, L.T. (1999). Psychology's portrait gallery: Part III. *Contemporary Psychology, 44,* 27–28.

Bennett, M.E., McGrady, B.S., Frankenstein, W., Laitman, L., Van Horn, D.H.A., & Keller, D.S. (1993). Identifying young adult substance abusers: The Rutgers Collegiate substance abuse screening test. *Journal of Studies on Alcohol, 54,* 522-527.

Bennett, W.I., & Gurin, J. (1982). *The dieter's dilemma: Eating less and weighing more.* New York: Basic Books.

Ben-Shakhar, G., Bar-Hillel, M., Yoram, B., Ben-Abba, E., & Flug, A. (1986). Can graphology predict occupational success? Two empirical studies and some methodological ruminations. *Journal of Applied Psychology, 71,* 645–653.

Bereiter, C., & Scardamalia, M. (1993). *Surpassing ourselves: An inquiry into the nature and implications of expertise.* Chicago: Open Court.*

Berkman, L.F., & Syme, L.L. (1979). Social networks, host resistance, and mortality. *American Journal of Epidemiology, 109,* 186–204.

Berko, J. (1958). The child's learning of English morphology. *World, 14,* 150–157.

Berkowitz, L. (1990). On the formation and regulation of anger and aggression: A cognitive neoassociationistic analysis. *American Psychologist, 45,* 494–503.

Bernstein, D., & Belicki, K. (1996). The reliability and validity of retrospective measures of dream content. *Imagination, Cognition and Personality, 15,* 349-362.*

Berry, J.W. (1969). On cross-cultural comparability. *International Journal of Psychology, 4,* 119-128.*

Berry, J.W. (1976). *Human ecology and cognitive style.* Newbury Park, CA: Sage.*

Berry, J.W. (1980). Acculturation as varieties of adaptation. In A. Padilla (Ed.), *Acculturation: Theory, model, and some new findings.* Washington, DC: American Association for the Advancement of Science.*

Berry, J.W. (1993). Psychology in and of Canada: One small step toward a universal psychology. In U. Kim & J.W. Berry (Eds.), *Indigenous psychologies: Research and experience in cultural context.* Newbury Park, CA: Sage.*

Berry, J.W. (1999). Intercultural relations in plural societies. *Canadian Psychology, 40(1),* 12-21.*

Berry, J.W., Poortinga, Y.H., Segall, M.H., & Dasen, P.R. (1992). *Cross-cultural psychology: Research and applications.* New York: Cambridge University Press.*

Berscheid, E. (1988). Some comments on love's anatomy: Or, whatever happened to old-fashioned lust? In R.J. Sternberg (Ed.), *Anatomy of love.* New Haven, CT: Yale University Press.

Berscheid, E. (1999). Integrating relationship knowledge. In W.A. Collins & B. Laursen (Eds.), *Relationships as developmental contexts.* Mahwah, NJ: Erlbaum.

Berscheid, E. (in press). The greening of relationship science. *American Psychologist.*

Berscheid, E., & Fei, J. (1977). Sexual jealousy and romantic love. In G. Clinton & G. Smith (Eds.), *Sexual jealousy.* Englewood Cliffs, NJ: Prentice Hall.

Berscheid, E., & Lopez, J. (1997). A temporal model of relationship satisfaction and stability. In R.J. Sternberg (Ed.), *Satisfaction in close relationships.* New York: Guilford.

Berscheid, E., & Reis, H.T. (1998). Attraction and close relationships. In D.T. Gilbert, S.T. Fiske, & G. Lindzey (Eds.), *Handbook of social psychology* (4th ed., Vol. 2). New York: McGraw-Hill.

Berscheid, E., Snyder, M., & Omato, A.M. (1989). Issues in studying close relationships. In C. Hendrick (Ed.), *Close relationships.* Newbury Park, CA: Sage.

Bertolino, A., Knable, M.B., Saunders, R.C., Callicott, J.H., Kolachana, B., Mattay, V.S., Bachevalier, J., Frank, J.A., Egan, M., & Weinberger, D.R. (1999). The relationship between dorsolateral prefrontal *N*-Acetylasparate measures and striatal dopamine activity in schizo-phrenia. *Biological Psychiatry, 45,* 660–667.

Besner, D., & Humphreys, G.W. (Eds.). (1990). *Basic processes in reading visual word recognition.* Mahwah, NJ: Erlbaum.*

Besner, D., & Stolz, J.A. (1999). What kind of attention modulates the Stroop effect? *Psychonomic Bulletin & Review, 6,* 99–105.*

Best, J. (1999). *Cognitive psychology.* Belmont, CA: Wadsworth.

Bexton, W.H., Heron, W., & Scott, T.H. (1954). Effects of decreased variation in the sensory environment. *Canadian Journal of Psychology, 8,* 70–76.*

Bhugra, D., & de Silva, P. (1998). Sexual dysfunction therapy. In H.S. Friedman (Ed.), *Encyclopedia of mental health* (Vol. 3). San Diego: Academic Press.

Bialystok, E. (1997). Effects of bilingualism and biliteracy on children's emerging concepts of print. *Developmental Psychology, 33,* 429-440.*

Bialystok, E. (Ed.). (1991). *Language processing in bilingual children.* London: Cambridge University Press.*

Bialystok, E. (in press). Towards a definition of metalinguistic awareness. In H. Dechert (Ed.), *Metacognition and second language acquisition.* Clevedon, England: Multilingual Matters.*

Bialystok, E., & Herman, J. (1999). Does bilingualism matter for early literacy? *Bilingualism: Language and Cognition, 2,* 35-44.*

Bialystok, E., & Mitterer, J. (1987). Metalinguistic differences among three kinds of readers. *Journal of Educational Psychology, 79(2),* 147-153.*

Bidikov, I., & Meier, D.E. (1997). Clinical decision-making with the woman after menopause. *Geriatrics, 52,* (3), 28–35.

Biller, H. (1993). *Fathers and families.* Westport, CT: Auburn House.

Billings, A.G., Cronkite, R.C., & Moos, R.H. (1983). Social-environment factors in unipolar depression. *Journal of Abnormal Psychology, 92* 119–133.

Birdsong, D. (Ed.) (1999). *Second language acquisition and the critical period hypothesis.* Mahwah, NJ: Erlbaum.

Bisanz, J., Bisanz, G. L., & Korpan, C. A. (1994). Inductive reasoning. In R. J. Sternberg (Ed.), *Handbook of perception and cognition: Vol. 12. Thinking and problem solving.* Orlando, FL: Academic Press.*

Björkqvist, K., Österman, K., & Lagerspetz, K.M.J. (1994). Sex differences in covert aggression among adults. *Aggressive Behavior, 20,* 27–33.

Black, I.B. (1999). Plasticity. In M.S. Gazzaniga (Ed.), *The new cognitive neurosciences* (2nd ed.). Cambridge, MA: MIT Press.

Blackmore, S. (1987). A report of a visit to Carl Sargent's laboratory. *Journal of the Society for Psychical Research, 54,* 186–198.

Blackwell, J.C., Thurston, W.E., & Graham, K.M. (1996). Canadian women and substance use: overview and policy implications. In M. Adrian, C. Lundy, & M. Eliany (Eds.), *Women's use of alcohol and other drugs in Canada.* Toronto: Addiction Research Foundation.*

Blair, C., & Ramey, C. (1996). Early intervention with low-birthweight infants: The path to second generation research. In M.J. Guralnick (Ed.), *The effectiveness of early interventions.* Baltimore: Paul H. Brookes.

Blake, J., Quartaro, G., & Onorati, S. (1993). Evaluating quantitative measures of grammatical complexity in spontaneous speech samples. *Journal of Child Language, 20,* 139-152.*

Bland, R.C., Newman, S.C., & Orn, H. (1988). Period prevalence of psychiatric disorders in Edmonton. *Acta Psychiatrica Scandanvica, 77(S388),* 33-42.*

Blundell, J.E. (1984). Systems and interactions: An approach to the pharmacology of feeding. In A.J. Stunkdard & E. Stellar (Eds.), *Eating and its disorders.* New York: Raven Press.

Bond, R., & Smith, P.B. (1996). Culture and conformity: A meta-analysis of studies using the Asch-type perceptual judgment task. *Psychological Bulletin,119 (I),* 111-137.

Bonebakker, A. E., Bonke, B., Klein, M. D., Wolters, G., Stijnen, Th., Passchier, J., & Merikle, P. M. (1996). Information processing during general anesthesia: Evidence for unconscious memory. *Memory and Cognition, 24,* 766-776.*

Bonvillain, N. (1998). *Women and men: Cultural constructs of gender* (2nd ed.). Upper Saddle River, NJ: Erlbaum.

Booth, A., Johnson, D.R., & Granger, D.A. (1999). Testosterone and men's health. *Journal of Behavioral Medicine, 22,* 1–12.

Boring, E.G. (1950). *A history of experimental psychology* (2nd ed.). New York: Appleton-Century-Crofts.

Bouchard, C., Rhéaume, J., & Ladouceur, R. (1999). Responsibility and perfectionism in OCD: An experimental study. *Behavior Research and Therapy, 37,* 239-248.*

Bouchard, T.J., Heston, L., Eckert, E., Keyes, M., & Resnick, S. (1981). The Minnesota Study of Twins Reared Apart: Project description and sample results in the developmental domain. *Twin Research, 3,* 227–233.

Bouchard, T.J., Lykken, D.T., Tellegen, A., & McGue, M. (1996). Genes, drives, environment, and experience. In D. Lubinski & C. Benbow (Eds.), *Psychometrics and social issues concerning intellectual talent.* Baltimore: Johns Hopkins University Press.

Boudewyns, P.A. (1996). Post-traumatic stress syndrome. In M. Herson & P.M. Miller (Eds.), *Progress in behavior modification* (Vol. 30). Pacific Grove, CA: Brooks/Cole.

Bourne, E.J. (1995). *The anxiety and phobia workbook* (2nd ed.). Oakland, CA: New Harbinger.

Bower, G.H., Clark, M., Winzenz, D., & Lesgold, A. (1969). Hierarchical retrieval schemes in recall of categorized word lists. *Journal of Verbal Learning and Verbal Behavior, 3,* 323–343.

Bowers, T.G., & Clum, G.A. (1988). Relative contribution of specific and nonspecific treatment effects: Meta-analysis of placebo-controlled behavior therapy research. *Psychological Bulletin, 103,* 315–323.

Bowlby, J. (1969). *Attachment and loss* (Vol. 1). London: Hogarth Press.

Bowlby, J. (1989). *Secure and insecure attachment.* New York: Basic Books.

Boyer, L.B. (1999). *Countertransference and agression.* Mahwah, NJ: Erlbaum.

Bradley, M. T., & Rettinger, J. (1992). Awareness of crime relevant information and the guilty knowledge test. *Journal of Applied Psychology, 77(1),* 55-59.*

Bradley, M.M. (1996). Gonna change my way of thinking. *Contemporary Psychology, 41,* 258–259.

Brammer, L.M., & MacDonald, G. (1999). *The helping relationship* (7th ed.). Boston: Allyn & Bacon.

Brannon, L. (1999). *Gender: Psychological perspectives* (2nd Ed.). Boston: Allyn & Bacon.

Bransford, J.D., & Stein, B.S. (1993). *The IDEAL problem solver.* New York: W.H. Freeman.

Brazelton, T.B. (1998, September 7). Commentary. *Dallas Morning News,* p. C2.

Bregman, A.S. (1990). *Auditory scene analysis.* Cambridge, MA: Bradford/MIT Press.*

Brehm, J.W. (1999). The intensity of emotion. *Personality and Social Psychology Review, 3,* 2–22.

Brehony, K.A. (1999). *Ordinary grace.* New York: Riverhead Books.

Breland, K., & Breland, M. (1961). The misbehavior of organisms. *American Psychologist, 16,* 681–684.

Brennan, P., Mednick, S., & Kandel, E. (1991). Congenital determinants of violent and property offencing. In D. Pepler & K. Rubin (Eds.), *The development and treatment of childhood aggression.* Mahwah, NJ: Erlbaum.

Brewer, J.B., Zuo, Z., Desmond, J.E., Glover, G.H., & Gabrieli, J.D.E. (1998). Making memories: Brain activity that predicts how well visual experience will be remembered. *Science, 281,* 1185–1187.

Brewer, M.B., & Brown, R.J. (1998). Intergroup relations In D.T. Gilbert, S.T. Fiske, & G. Lindzey (Eds.), *Handbook of social psychology* (4th ed., Vol. 2). New York: McGraw-Hill.

Brewin, C.R., Andrews, B., Rose, S., & Kirk, M. (1999). Acute stress disorder and posttraumatic stress disorder in victims of violent crime. *The American Journal of Psychiatry, 156,* 360–366.

Brickman, P., Coates, D., & Janoff-Bulman, R.J. (1978). Lottery winners and accident victims: Is happiness relative? *Journal of Personality and Social Psychology, 36,* 917–927.

Brickner, M.A., Harkins, S.G., & Ostrom, T.M. (1986). Effects of personal involvement: Thought-provoking implications for social loafing. *Journal of Personality and Social Psychology, 51,* 763–769.

Brigham, J.C. (1986). Race and eyewitness identifications. In S. Worschel & W.G. Austin (Eds.), *Psychology of intergroup relations.* Chicago: Nelson-Hall.

Brigham, J.C., Maas, A., Snyder, L.D., & Spaulding, K. (1982). Accuracy of eyewitness identification in a field setting. *Journal of Personality and Social Psychology, 41,* 683–691.

Brim, O., & others (1999). *Midlife development in the United States.* New York: The McArthur Foundation.

Brislin, R. (1993). *Understanding culture's influence on behavior.* Fort Worth, TX: Harcourt Brace.

Brislin, R.W. (Ed.). (1990). *Applied cross-cultural psychology.* Newbury Park, CA: Sage.

Brodbeck, D.R., and Shettleworth, S.J. (1995). Memory for the location and color of a compound stimulus: Comparison of a food-storing and a non-storing bird species. *Journal of Experimental Psychology: Animal Behavior Processes, 21,* 64-77.*

Brook, J.S., Brook, D.W., Gordon, A.S., Whiteman, M., & Cohen, P. (1990). The psychosocial etiology of adolescent drug use: A family interactional approach. *Genetic Psychology Monographs, 116,* no. 2.

Brooks, J.G., & Brooks, M.G. (1993). *The case for constructivist classrooms.* Alexandria, VA: Association for Supervision and Curriculum Development.

Brooks, L.R. (1978). Nonanalytic concept formation and memory for instances. In E. Rosch & B.B. Lloyd (Eds.), *Cognition and categorization.* Mahwah, NJ: Erlbaum.*

Brooks-Gunn, J. (1996, April). *The uniqueness of the early adolescent transition.* Paper presented at the meeting of the Society for Research on Adolescence, Boston.

Broughton, R. & Shimisu, T. (1995). Sleep-related violence: a medical and forensic challenge. *Sleep, 18,* 727-730.*

Broughton, R., Billings, R., Cartwright, R., Doucette, D., Edmeads, J., Edwardh, M., Ervin, F., Orchard, B., Hill, R., & Turrell, G. (1994). Homicidal somnambulism: a case report. *Sleep, 17(3),* 253-64.*

Broughton, R.J. & Ogilvie, R.D. (Eds.). (1992). *Sleep, arousal and performance: Problems and promises.* Boston, MA: Birkhauser.*

Broughton, W.A., & Broughton, R.J. (1994). Psychosocial impact of narcolepsy. *Sleep, 17(8 Suppl),* 45-9.*

Brown, A.L. (1997). Transforming schools into communities of thinking and learning about serious matters. *American Psychologist, 52,* 399–413.

Brown, A.L., & Campione, J.C. (1996). Psychological theory and the design of innovative learning environments. In L. Schauble & R. Glaser (Eds.), *Innovations in learning.* Mahwah, NJ: Erlbaum.

Brown, A.S., & Nix, L.A. (1996). Age-related changes in the tip-of-the-tongue experiences. *American Journal of Psychology, 109,* 79–92.

Brown, G., Bhrolchain, M., & Harris, T. (1975). Social class and psychiatric disturbance among women in an urban population. *Sociology, 9,* 225–254.

Brown, G.D. (1995). *Human evolution.* New York: McGraw-Hill.

Brown, H.D., & Adler, N.E. (1998). Socioeconomic status. In H.S. Friedman (Ed.), *Encyclopedia of mental health* (Vol. 3). San Diego: Academic Press.

Brown, L.S. (1989). New voices, new visions: Toward a lesbian/gay paradigm for psychology. *Psychology of Women Quarterly, 13,* 445–458.

Brown, R. (1973). *A first language: The early stages.* Cambridge, MA: Harvard University Press.

Brown, R. (1986). *Social psychology* (2nd ed.). New York: Free Press.

Brownell, K.A., & Rodin, J. (1994). The dieting maelstrom: Is it possible and advisable to lose weight? *American Psychologist, 9,* 781–791.

Brownell, K.D., & Cohen, L.R. (1995). Adherence to dietary regimens. *Behavioral Medicine, 20,* 226–242.

Brownlee, S. (1997, January 13). The senses. *US News & World Report,* pp. 51–59.

Bruck, M., & Ceci, S.J. (1999). The suggestibility of children's memory. *Annual Reviews of Psychology.* Palo Alto, CA: Annual Reviews, Inc.*

Bruner, J. (1964). The concept of cognitive growth. *American Psychologist, 19,* 1–15.

Bruner, J.S., & Tagiuri, R. (1954). The perception of people. In G. Lindzey (Ed.), *Handbook of social psychology* (Vol. 2). Boston: Addison-Wesley.

Bruning, R.H., Schraw, G.J., & Ronning, R.R. (1999). *Cognitive psychology and instruction* (3rd ed.). Upper Saddle River, NJ: Erlbaum.

Bryden, M.P. (1986). The nature of complementary specialization. In F. Lepore, M. Ptito, & H.H. Jasper (Eds.), *Two hemispheres – One brain: Functions of the corpus callosum.* New York: Alan R. Liss.*

Buchanan, L., & Besner, D. (1993) Reading aloud: Evidence for the use of a whole word nonsemantic pathway. *Canadian Journal of Experimental Psychology, 47(2),* 133-152.*

Buree, B.U., Papageorgis, D., & Hare, R.D. (1990). Eating in anorexia nervosa and bulimia nervosa: An application of the tripartite model of anxiety. *Canadian Journal of Behavioral Science, 22(2),* 207-218.*

Burns, D. (1985). *Intimate connections.* New York: William Morrow.

Burnstein, E., Crandall, C., & Kitayama, S. (1994). Some neo-Darwinian decision rules for altruism: Weighing cues for inclusive fitness as a function of the biological importance of the decision. *Journal of Personality and Social Psychology, 67,* 773–789.

Buss, A.H., & Plomin, R. (1987). Commentary. In H.H. Goldsmith, A.H. Buss, R. Plomin, M.K. Rothbart, A. Thomas, A. Chess, R.R. Hinde, & R.B. McCall (Eds.). Roundtable: What is temperament? Four approaches. *Child Development, 58,* 505–529.

Buss, D. (1995). Evolutionary psychology: A new paradigm for psychological science. *Psychological Inquiry, 6,* 1–30.

Buss, D.M. (1995). Psychological sex differences: Origins through sexual selection. *American Psychologist, 50,* 164–168.

Buss, D.M. (1999). *Evolutionary psychology: The new science of the mind.* Boston: Allyn & Bacon.

Buss, D.M., & Barnes, M. (1986). Preferences in human mate selection. *Journal of Personality and Social Psychology, 50,* 559–570.

Buss, D.M., & Greiling, H. (1999). Adaptive individual differences. *Journal of Personality, 67,* 209–244.

Buss, D.M., & Kendrick, D.T. (1998). Evolutionary social psychology. In D.T. Gilbert, S.T. Fiske, & G. Lindzey (Eds.), *Handbook of social psychology* (4th ed., Vol. 2). New York: McGraw-Hill.

Buss, D.M., (1999). Adaptive individual differences revisited. *Journal of Personality, 67,* 259–264.

Butcher, J.N. (1997, August). *Psychological assessment, therapy, and managed care.* Paper presented at the meeting of the American Psychological Association, Chicago.

Butcher, J.N. (1999). *A beginner's guide to the MMPI-2.* Washington, DC: American Psychological Association.

Butcher, J.N., Lim, J., & Nezami, E. (1998). Objective study of abnormal personality in cross-cultural settings: The Minnesota Multiphasic Personality Inventory (MMPI-2). *Journal of Cross-Cultural Psychology, 29,* 189–211.

Butler, G., Fennell, M., Robson, P., & Gelder, M. (1991). Comparison of behavior therapy and cognitive behavior therapy in the treatment of generalized anxiety disorder. *Journal of Consulting and Clinical Psychology, 59,* 167–175.

Butler, R.A. (1953). Discrimination learning by rhesus monkeys to visual-exploration motivation. *Journal of Comparative and Physiological Psychology, 46,* 95–98.

Byne, W., & Davis, K.L. (1999). The role of the prefrontal cortex in the dopaminergic dysregulation of schizophrenia. *Biological Psychiatry, 45,* 657–659.

Cacioppo, J.T., & Gardner, W.L. (1999). Emotions. *Annual Reviews of Psychology.* Palo Alto: Annual Reviews.

Cairns, R.B. (1998). The making of developmental psychology. In W. Damon (Ed.), *Handbook of child psychology* (5th ed., Vol. 1), New York: Wiley.

Cameron, N. (1963). *Personality development and psychopathology.* Boston: Houghton Mifflin.

Campbell, F.A., & Ramey, C.T. (1993, March). *Mid-adolescent outcomes for high risk students: An examination of the continuing effects of early intervention.* Paper presented at the biennial meeting of the Society for Research in Child Development, New Orleans.

Campbell, J.D., Tesser, A., & Fairey, P.J. (1986). Conformity and attention to the stimulus: Some temporal and contextual dynamics. *Journal of Personality and Social Psychology, 51,* 315–324.*

Campbell, L., Campbell, B., & Dickinson, D. (1999). *Teaching and learning through multiple intelligences* (2nd ed.). Boston: Allyn & Bacon.

Cannon, W.B. (1927). The James-Lange theory of emotions: A critical examination and an alternative theory. *American Journal of Psychology, 39,* 106–124.

Cannon, W.B., & Washburn, A.L. (1912). An explanation of hunger. *American Journal of Physiology, 29,* 444–454.

Cantor, N., & Langston, C.A. (1989). Ups and downs of life tasks in a life transition. In L.A. Pervin (Ed.), *Goal concepts in personality and social psychology.* Mahwah, NJ: Erlbaum.

Capuzzi, D., & Gross, D.R. (1999). *Counseling and psychotherapy* (2nd ed.). Upper Saddle River, NJ: Prentice-Hall.

Carbonneau, L. (1994). When bullets have ceased: Critical incident stress is the biggest source of morbidity in Canada's peacekeepers. *Medical Post, 30,* 9.*

Carkenord, D.M., & Bullington, J. (1995). Bringing cognitive dissonance to the classroom. In M.E. Ware & D.E. Johnson (Eds.), *Demonstrations and activities in teaching of psychology* (Vol. 3). Mahwah, NJ: Erlbaum.

Carlson, N. (1999). *Foundations of physiological psychology* (4th ed.). Boston: Allyn & Bacon.

Caron, S.L. (1998). *Cross-cultural perspectives on human sexuality.* Boston: Allyn & Bacon.

Carr, T.H., & Levy, B.A. (Eds.). (1990). *Reading and its development: Component skills approaches.* San Diego: Academic Press.*

Carroll, D.W. (1999). *Psychology of language* (3rd Ed.). Belmont, CA: Wadsworth.

Carson, R.C., Butcher, J.N., & Mineka, S. (1998). *Abnormal psychology and life.* (10th ed.). New York: HarperCollins.

Carswell, R.S. (1992). Graphology: Canadian legal implications. In B. Bayerstein & G. Bayerstein (Eds.), *The write stuff.* Buffalo, NY: Prometheus.*

Case, R. (1991). *The mind's staircase: Exploring the conceptual underpinnings of children's thought and knowledge.* Mahwah, NJ: Erlbaum.*

Ceci, S. (1996). Unpublished review of *Child Development* (8th ed.) by J.W. Santrock. New York: McGraw-Hill.

Centers for Disease Control and Prevention (1998, June). *Combating complacency in HIV prevention.* Atlanta: Centers for Disease Control and Prevention.

Cermak, L.S., Verfaellie, M., Sweeney, M., & Jacoby, L.L. (1992). Fluency versus conscious recollection in the word-completion performance of amnesic patients. *Brain and Cognition, 20,* 367-377.*

Chaikelson, J.S., Arbuckle, T., Lapidus, S., & Gold, D. (1994). Measurement of lifetime alcohol consumption. *Journal of Studies on Alcohol, 55,* 133-140.*

Chance, P. (1979). *Learning and behavior.* Belmont, CA: Wadsworth.

Chance, P. (1999). *Learning and behavior* (4th ed.). Belmont, CA: Wadsworth.

Chandler, M.J., & Lalonde, C.E. (1998). Cultural continuity as a hedge against suicide in Canada's First Nations. *Transcultural Psychiatry, 35(2),* 193-211.*

Chang, E.C. (1996). Cultural differences in optimism, pessimism, and coping. *Journal of Counseling Psychology, 43,* 113–123.

Changeux, J., & Chavillion, J. (1995). *Origins of the human brain.* New York: Oxford University Press.

Chase-Landsdale, P.L., & Brooks-Gunn, J. (Eds.). (1996). *Escape from poverty.* New York: Cambridge University Press.

Chastain, G., & Landrum, R.E. (1999). *Protecting human subjects.* Washington, DC: American Psychological Association.

Chen, C., & Stevenson, H.W. (1989). Homework: A cross-cultural comparison. *Child Development, 60,* 551–561.

Chess, S., & Thomas, A. (1977). Temperamental individuality from childhood to adolescence. *Journal of Child Psychiatry, 16,* 218–226.

Chodorow, N. (1978). *The reproduction of mothering.* Berkeley: University of California Press.

Chodorow, N. (1989). *Feminism and psychoanalytic theory.* New Haven, CT: Yale University Press.

Chomsky, N. (1975). *Reflections on language.* New York: Pantheon.

Christensen, L. (1996). *Diet-behavior relationships.* Washington, DC: American Psychological Association.

Christiansen, A. & Heavey, C.L. (1999). Intervention for couples. *Annual Review of Psychology, 50.* Palo Alto: CA. Annual Reviews.

Cialdini, R.B. (1993). *Influence: Science and practice* (3rd ed.). New York: HarperCollins.

Cialdini, R.B., & Trost, M.R. (1998). Social influence: Social norms, conformity, and compliance. In D.T. Gilbert, S.T. Fiske, & G. Lindzey (Eds.), *Handbook of social psychology* (4th ed., Vol. 2). New York: McGraw-Hill.

Cialdini, R.B., Schaller, M., Houlihan, D., Arps, K., Fultz, J., & Beaman, A.L. (1987). Empathy-based helping: Is it selflessly of selfishly motivated? *Journal of Personality and Social Psychology, 52,* 749–758.

Cicchetti, D., & Toth, S. (1998). Perspectives on research and practice in developmental psychopathology. In I.E. Sigel & K.A. Renninger (Eds.), *Handbook of child psychology* (5th ed., Vol. IV). New York: Wiley.

Clark, D.M., Salkovskis, P.M., Hackmann, A., Middelton, H., Anastasiades, P., & Gelder, M. (1994). A comparison of cognitive therapy, applied relaxation, and imipramine in the treatment of panic disorder. *British Journal of Psychiatry, 164,* 759–769.

Clark, E.V. (1983). Meanings and concepts. In P.H. Mussen (Ed.), *Handbook of child psychology* (4th ed., Vol. 2). New York: Wiley.

Clark, L.A., Watson, D., & Reynolds, S. (1995). Diagnosis and classification in psychopathology. *Annual Review of Psychology, 46.* Palo Alto, CA: Annual Reviews.

Clark, N.M., & Dodge, J.A. (1999). Exploring self-efficacy as a predictor of disease management. *Health Education & Behavior, 26,* 72–89.

Claxton-Oldfield, S & Keefe, S.M. (1999). Assessing stereotypes about the Innu of Davis Inlet, Labrador. *Canadian Journal of Behavioural Science, 31(2),* 86-89.*

Clayton, L. (1999). *Alcohol drug dangers.* New York: Enslow Publications.

Clément, R. & Bourhis, R.Y. (1996). Bilingualism and intergroup communication. *International Journal of Psycholinguistics, 12(2),* 171-191.*

Clifford, R. M., Harms, T., Pepper, S., & Stuart, B. (1992). Assessing quality in family day care. In D. R. Peters & A.R. Pence (Eds.), *Family day care: Current research for informed public policy.* New York: Teachers College Press.*

Cloninger, S.C. (1996). *Theories of personality* (2nd ed.). Upper Saddle River, NJ: Prentice Hall.

Cochran, S.D., & Mays, V.M. (1990). Sex, lies, and HIV. *New England Journal of Medicine, 322,* 774–775.

Cohen, J.D., & Schooler, J.W. (Eds.) (1996). *Scientific approaches to consciousness.* Mahwah, NJ: Erlbaum.

Cohen, L.A. (1987, November). Diet and cancer. *Scientific American,* pp. 128–137.

Cohen, R.J., Swerdlik, M.E., & Phillips, S.M. (1996). *Psychological testing and assessment* (3rd ed.). Mountain View, CA: Mayfield.

Cohen, R.L., & Borsoi, D. (1996). The role of gestures in description-communication: A cross-sectional study of aging. *Journal of Nonverbal Behavior, 20,* 45–64.*

Cohen, S., Doyle, W.J., Skoner, D.P., Rabin, B.S., & Gawaltney, J.M. (1997). Social ties and susceptibility to the common cold. *Journal of the American Medical Association, 277,* 1940–1944.

Cohen, S., Frank, E., Doyle, W., Skoner, D.P., Rabin, B.S., & Gwaltney, J.M. (1998). Types of stressors that increase susceptibility to the common cold in healthy adults. *Health Psychology, 17,* 214–223.

Coie, J.D., & Dodge, K. (1998). Aggression and anti-social behavior. In W. Damon (Ed.), *Handbook of child psychology* (5th ed., Vol. 3). New York: Wiley.

Colby, A., Kohlberg, L. Gibbs, J., & Lieberman, M. (1983). A longitudinal study of moral judgment. *Monographs of the Society for Research in Child Development* (Serial No. 201).

Cole, M. (1999). Culture in development. In M.H. Bornstein & M.E. Lamb (Eds.), *Developmental psychology: An advanced textbook* (4th ed.). Mahwah, NJ: Erlbaum.

Cole, M., & Cole, S.R. (1996). *The development of children* (3rd ed.). New York: W.H. Freeman.

Cole, M., & Cole, S.R. (2000). *The development of children* (4th ed.). New York: W.H. Freeman.

Coleman, J. (1995, March). *Adolescent sexual knowledge: Implications for health and health risks.* Paper presented at the meeting of the Society for Research in Child Development, Indianapolis.

Collins, M. (1996, Winter). The job outlook for '96 grads. *Journal of Career Planning.* 51–54.

Collins, W.A., & Laursen, B. (Eds.)(1999). *Relationships as developmental contexts.* Mahwah, NJ: Erlbaum.

Comarow, D.D., & Chescheir, M.W. (1999). *Talking about therapy.* Westport, CT: Greenwood.

Committee on Pediatric AIDS (1998). Surveillance of pediatric HIV infection. *Pediatrics, 101,* 315–319.

Condry, J.C. (1989). *The psychology of television.* Mahwah, NJ: Erlbaum.

Conlan, R., Hobson, J.A., Hyman, S., Kagan, J., & Conlan, R. (1999). *States of mind.* New York: Wiley.

Conway, M.A., & Rubin, D.C. (1993). The structure of autobiographical memory. In A.F. Collins, S.E. Gathercole, M.A. Conway, & P.E. Morris (Eds.), *Theories of memory.* Mahwah, NJ: Erlbaum.

Coren, S., & Girgus, J.S. (1972). Illusion decrement in intersecting figures. *Psychonomic Science, 26,* 108–110.*

Coren, S., & Hewitt, P.L. (1998). Is anorexia nervosa associated with elevated rates of suicide? *American Journal of Public Health, 88,* 1206-1207.*

Coren, S., Ward, L.M., & Enns, J.T. (1999). *Sensation and perception (5th Ed).* Fort Worth, TX: Harcourt Brace.*

Corey, G. (1996). *Theory and practice of counseling and psychotherapy* (5th ed.). Pacific Grove, CA: Brooks/Cole.

Cornelius, R.R. (1996). *The science of emotion.* Upper Saddle River, NJ: Prentice Hall.

Cornell, D. (1998, April 6). Commentary. *Newsweek,* p. 24

Coryell, W.H., Turvey, C., Coryell, W.H., Arndt, S., Solomon, D.A., Leon, A.C., Endicott, J., Mueller, T., Keller, M., & Akiskal, H. (1999). Polarity sequence, depression, and chronicity in bipolar I disorder. *The Journal of Nervous and Mental Disease, 187(3),* 181–187.*

Costa, P.T., & McCrae, R.R. (1995). Solid ground on the wetlands of personality: A reply to Black. *Psychological Bulletin, 117,* 216–220.

Costa, P.T., & McCrae, R.R. (1998). Personality assessment. In H.S. Friedman (Ed.), *Encyclopedia of mental health* (Vol. 3). San Diego: Academic Press.

Costa, P.T., & McRae, R.R. (1992). *Revised NEO personality inventory.* Odessa, FL: Psychological Assessment Resources.

Cowley, G. (1988, May 23). The wisdom of animals. *Newsweek,* pp. 52–58.

Cowley, G. (1998, April 6). Why children turn violent. *Newsweek,* pp. 24–25.

Cox, B. J., Endler, N. S., & Swinson, R. P. (1995). An examination of levels of agoraphobic severity in panic disorder. *Behaviour Research and Therapy, 33,* 57-62.*

Cox, B. J., Swinson, R. P., Endler, N. S., & Norton, G. R. (1994). The symptom structure of panic attacks. *Comprehensive Psychiatry, 35,* 349-353.*

Cox, B.J., Endler, N.S., Lee, P.S., & Swinson, R.P. (1992). A meta-analysis of treatments for panic disorder with agoraphobia: imipramine, alprazolam, and in vivoexposure. *Journal of Behavior Therapy and Experimental Psychiatry, 23,* 175-182.*

Cozby, F. (1991). *Juggling.* New York: Macmillan.

Craik, F.I.M., & Jacoby, L.L. (1996). Aging and memory: Implications for skilled performance. In W.A. Rogers, A.D. Fisk, & N. Walker (Eds.), *Aging and skilled performance: Advances in theory and applications.* Mahwah, NJ: Erlbaum.*

Craik, F.I.M., & Lockhart, R.S. (1972). Levels of processing; A framework for memory research. *Journal of Verbal Learning and Verbal Behavior, 11,* 671–684.*

Craik, F.I.M., & Tulving, E. (1975). Depth of processing and retention of words in episodic memory. *Journal of Experimental Psychology: General, 104,* 268–294.*

Cramer, P. (1999). Future directions for the Thematic Apperception Test. *Journal of Personality Assessment, 72,* 74–92.

Crasilneck, H.B. (1995). The use of the Crasilneck bombardment technique in problems of intractible organic pain. *American Journal of Clinical Hypnosis, 37,* 255–266.

Crocker, J., Major, B., & Steele, C. (1998). Social stigma. In D.T. Gilbert, S.T. Fiske, & G. Lindzey (Eds.), *Handbook of social psychology* (4th ed., Vol. 2). New York: McGraw-Hill.

Crooks R., & Bauer, K. (1999). *Our sexuality* (7th ed.). Belmont, CA: Wadsworth.

Crouter, A.C., Helms-Erikson, H., Updegraff, K., & McHale, S.M. (1999). Conditions underlying parents' knowledge about children's daily lives in middle childhood: Between- and within-family comparisons. *Child Development, 70,* 246–259.

Csikszentmihalyi, M. (1996). *Creativity.* New York: HarperCollins.

Cuddy, L.L. (1993). Melody comprehension and tonal structure. In T. Tighe & W.J. Dowling (Eds.), *Psychology and music: The understanding of melody and rhythm.* Mahwah, NJ: Erlbaum.*

Culebras, A. (1996). *Clinical handbook of sleep disorders.* Boston: Butterworth-Heinemann.

Cunningham, M.R. (1986). Measuring the physical in physical attractiveness. *Journal of Personality and Social Psychology, 50,* 925–935.

Curtiss, S. (1977). *Genie.* New York: Academic Press.

Cushner, K., & Brislin, R.W. (1995). *Intercultural interactions* (2nd ed.). Newbury Park, CA: Sage.

Cutler, B.L., & Penrod, S.D. (1995). *Mistaken identities: The eyewitness, psychology, and the law*. New York: Cambridge University Press.

Cutrona, C.E. (1982). Transition to college: Loneliness and the process of social adjustment. In L.A. Peplau & D. Perlman (Eds.), *Loneliness*. New York: Wiley.

Czeisler, C.A., Johnson, M.P., Duffy, J.F., Brown, E.N., Ronda, J.M., & Kronauer, R.E. (1990). Exposure to bright light and darkness to treat physiologic maladaption to night work. *New England Journal of Medicine, 322*, 1253–1259.

d'Ansia, G.I.D. (1989). Familial analysis of panic disorder and agoraphobia. *Journal of Affective Disorders, 17*, 1–8.

Dabbs, J.M. (1992). Testosterone measurements in social and clinical psychology. *Journal of Social and Clinical Psychology, 11*, 302–321.

Daly, M., & Wilson, M. (1988). *Homicide*. New York: Aldine De Gruyte.*

Daly, M., & Wilson, M. (1983). *Sex, evolution, and behavior*. Boston: Willard Grant Press.*

Daly, M., & Wilson, M. (1998). *The truth about Cinderella: A Darwinian view of parental love*. London: Weidenfeld & Nicolson.*

Daneman, M. (1991). Working memory as a predictor of verbal fluency. *Journal of Psycholinguistic Research, 20*, 445-464.*

Daneman, M., & Merikle, P.M. (1996). Working memory and comprehension: A meta-analysis. *Psychonomic Bulletin and Review, 3*, 422-433.*

Darley, J.M., & Latané, B. (1968). Bystander intervention in emergencies: Diffusion of responsibility. *Journal of Personality and Social Psychology, 8*, 377–383.

Darou, W.S. (1992). Native Canadians and intelligence testing. *Canadian Journal of Counselling, 26(2)*, 96-99.*

Darwin, C. (1859). *On the origin of species*. London: John Murray.

Darwin, C. (1872/1965). *The expression of the emotions in man and animals*. Chicago: University of Chicago Press.

Das, J. P., & Naglieri, J. A. (1996). Mental retardation and assessment of cognitive processes. In J. Jacobson (Ed.), *APA manual on mental retardation*. Washington, DC: American Psychological Association.*

David, J.P., & Suls, J. (1999). Coping efforts in daily life: Role of big-five traits and problem appraisals. *Journal of Personality, 67*, 265–294.

Davidson, A.R., & Jacard, J.J. (1979). Variables that moderate the attitude-behavior relation: Results of a longitudinal survey. *Journal of Personality and Social Psychology, 37*, 1364–1376.

Davies, D. (1999). *Insomnia*. New York: Bantam.

Davis, J.H. (1996). Group decision making and quantitative judgments: A consensus model. In E.H. Witte & J.H. Davis (Eds.), *Understanding group behavior* (Vol. 1). Mahwah, NJ: Erlbaum.

Davis, K. (1996). *Families*. Pacific Grove, CA: Brooks/Cole.

Davis, K.L. (1999). Alzheimer's disease: Seeking new ways to preserve brain function. *Geriatrics, 54*, 42–47.

Davison, G. C., & Neale, J.M. (1994). *Abnormal psychology* (6th ed.). New York: Wiley.

Dawes, R.M. (1998). Standards for psychotherapy. In H.S. Friedman (Ed.), *Encyclopedia of mental health* (Vol. 3). San Diego: Academic Press.

Dawson, M.R.W. (1998). *Understanding cognitive science*. Malden, MA: Blackwell.*

de Castell, S., & Bryson, M. (1998). Retooling play: Dystopia, dysphoria, and difference. In J. Cassell & H. Jenkins (Eds.), *From Barbie to Mortal Kombat: Gender and computer games*. Cambridge, MA: MIT Press.*

de Jong-Gierveld, J. (1987). Developing and testing a model of loneliness. *Journal of Personality and Social Psychology, 53*, 119–128.

De Luca, R. V., Grayston, A. G., & Romano, E. (1999). Time-limited group therapy for sexually abused boys. In C. Schaefer (Ed.), *Short-term psychotherapy groups for children*. New York: Jason Aronson.*

Dean, G.A., Kelly, I.W., Saklofske, D.H., & Furnham, A. (1992). Graphology and human judgment. In B. Bayerstein & G. Bayerstein (Eds.). *The write stuff*. Buffalo, NY: Prometheus.*

DeBattista, C., Solvason, H.B., & Schatzberg, A.F. (1998). Mood disorders. In H.S. Friedman (Ed.), *Encyclopedia of mental health* (Vol. 2). San Diego: Academic Press.

deCatanzaro, D. (1999). *Motivation and emotion: Evolutionary, physiological, developmental, and social perspectives*. Upper Saddle River, NJ: Prentice Hall.*

Deci, E., & Ryan, R. (1994). Promoting self-determined education. *Scandinavian Journal of Educational Research, 38*, 3–14.

DeCola, J.P., & Fanselow, M.S. (1995). Differential inflation with short and long CS-US intervals: Evidence of a nonassociative process in long delay taste avoidance. *Animal Learning & Behavior, 23*, 154–163.

DeCourville, N., & Sadava, S.W. (1997). The structure of problem drinking in adulthood: A confirmatory approach. *Journal of Studies on Alcohol, 58*, 146-154.*

Dement, W.C. (1978). *Some must watch while some must sleep*. New York: Norton.

Dement, W.C. (1999). *The promise of sleep*. New York: Delacourte Press.

Denmark, F.L., Russo, N.F., Frieze, I.H., & Sechzer, J. (1988). Guidelines for avoiding sexism in psychological research: A report of the ad hoc committee on nonsexist research. *American Psychologist, 43*, 582–585.

DeRubeis, R.J., & Crits-Cristoph, P. (1998). Empirically supported individual and group psychological treatments for adult mental disorders. *Journal of Consulting and Clinical Psychology, 66*, 37–52.

DeSpelder, L.A., & Strickland, A.L. (1999). *The last dance* (5th ed.). Mountain View, CA: Mayfield.

Deutsch, M., & Collins, M. (1951). *Interracial housing: A psychological evaluation of a social experiment*. Minneapolis: University of Minnesota Press.

deVilliers, J.G., & deVilliers, P.A. (1999). Language development. In M.H. Bornstein & M.E. Lamb (Eds.), *Developmental psychology: An advanced textbook*. Mahwah, NJ: Erlbaum.

Devine, P.G., Evett, S.R., & Vasquez-Suson, K.A. (1996). Exploring the interpersonal dynamics of intergroup contact. In R.M. Sorrentino & E.T. Higgins (Eds.), *Handbook of motivation and cognition: The interpersonal context* (Vol. 3). New York: Guilford Press.

Devries, L.K. (1998). *Insomnia: Finding the help you need: Don't lose sleep over it*. New York: Harold Shaw.

Dewey, J. (1993). *How we think*. Lexington, MA: D.C. Heath.

Dibbell, J. (1996, March 25). Technology. *Time*, pp. 57–58.

Dickson, G.L. (1990). A feminist post-structuralist analysis of the knowledge of menopause. *Advances in Nursing Science, 12*, 15–31.

Dickson, K.L., & Harris, S.D. (1999). *Instructor's manual for Santrock life-span development*, 7th Ed. New York: McGraw-Hill.

Diener, E. (1984). Subjective well-being. *Psychological Bulletin, 109*, 542–575.

Diener, E., & Diener, M.B. (1998). Happiness. In H.S. Friedman (Ed.), *Encyclopedia of mental health* (Vol. 2). San Diego: Academic Press.

Diener, E., Suh, E.M., Lucas, R.E., & Smith, H.L. (1999). Subjective well-being: Three decades of progress. *Psychological Bulletin, 125*, 276–301.

Dimeff, L.A. (Ed.)(1999). *Brief alcohol screening and intervention for college students*. New York: Guilford.

Dion, K. L., & Kawakami, K. (1996). Ethnicity and perceived discrimination in Toronto: Another look at the personal/group discrimination discrepancy. *Canadian Journal of Behavioural Science, 28(3)*, 203-213.

Dion, K.K., & Dion, K.L. (1991). Psychological individualism and romantic love. *Journal of Social Behavior and Personality, 6(1)*, 17-33.*

Dion, K.K., & Dion, K.L. (1993). Individualistic and collectivistic perspectives on gender and the cultural context of love and intimacy. *Journal of Social Issues, 49(3)*, 53-69.*

Dion, K.K., & Dion, K.L. (1995). On the love of beauty and the beauty of love: Two psychologists study attraction. In G.G. Brannigan & M.R. Merrens (Eds.), *The social psychologists: Research adventures*. New York: McGraw-Hill.*

Dion, K.L., Dion, K.K., & Pak, A.W. (1992). Personality-based hardiness as a buffer for discrimination-related stress in members of Toronto's Chinese community. *Canadian Journal of Behavioural Science, 24(4)*, 517-536.*

Dobson, K. & Franche, R.-L. (1989). A conceptual and empirical review of the depressive realism hypothesis. *Canadian Journal of Behavioural Science, 21(4)*, 419-433.*

Dobson, K. S., Backs-Dermott, G. J., & Dozois, D. J. (in press). Cognitive and cognitive-behavioral therapies. In R. E. Ingram & C. R. Snyder (Eds.), *Handbook of psychological change: Psychotherapy processes and practices for the 21st Century*. New York: Wiley.*

Dobson, K., & Breault, L. (1998). The Canadian code of ethics and the regulation of psychology. *Canadian Psychology, 39(3),* 212-218.*

Dobson, K.S. (1995). Psychology in Canada: The future is not the past. *Canadian Psychology, 36(1),* 1-11.*

Dodd, D.K. (1995). Robbers in the classroom: A deindividuation exercise. In M.E. Ware & D.E. Johnson (Eds.), *Demonstrations and activities in teaching of psychology* (Vol. 3). Mahwah, NJ: Erlbaum.

Dohrenwend, B.P., & Shrout, P.E. (1985). "Hassles" in the conceptualization and measurement of life event stress variables. *American Psychologist, 40,* 780–785.

Dollard, J., Doob, L.W., Miller, N.E., Mowrer, O.H., & Sears, R.R. (1939). *Frustration and aggression.* New Haven, CT: Yale University Press.

Domhoff, G.W., & Schneider, A. (1997). New rationales and methods for quantitative dream research outside of the laboratory. *Sleep, 21,* 398–404.

Domjan, M.P. (1996). *Essentials of conditioning and learning.* Pacific Grove: CA: Brooks/Cole.

Dorn, L.D., & Chrousos, G.P. (1996, March). *Behavioral predictors of stress hormone responses.* Paper presented at the meeting of the Society for Research on Adolescence, Boston.

Doty, R.L., & Muller-Schwarze, S.D. (1992). *Chemical signals in vertebrates.* New York: Plenum.

Dougherty, D.M., Cherek, D.R., & Bennett, R.H. (1996). The effects of alcohol on the aggressive responding of women. *Journal of Alcohol Studies, 57,* 178–186.

Doyle, J., & Paludi, M. (1998). *Sex and gender* (4th ed.). New York: McGraw-Hill.

Draguns, J.G. (1990). Applications of cross-cultural psychology in the field of mental health. In R.W. Brislin (Ed.), *Applied cross-cultural psychology.* Newbury Park, CA: Sage.

Druckman, D., & Bjork, R.A. (Eds.) (1994). *Learning, remembering, and believing.* Washington, DC: National Academy Press.

Dryfoos, J.G. (1990). *Adolescents at risk.* New York:Oxford University Press.

Dunnett, S.B. (1989). Neural transplantation: Normal brain function and repair after damage. *Psychologist, 1,* 4–8.

Durrant, J. E. (1996). Public attitudes toward corporal punishment in Canada. In D. Frehsee, W. Horn, & K.-D. Bussman (Eds.), *Family violence against children: A challenge for society.* Berlin: de Gruyter.*

Durrant, J.E., Broberg, A.G., & Rose-Krasnor, L. (in press). Predicting use of physical punishment during mother-child conflicts in Sweden and Canada. In P. Hastings and C. Piotrowski (Eds.), *New directions for child development.* San Francisco, CA: Jossey-Bass.*

Dutton, D., & Aron, A. (1974). Some evidence for heightened sexual attraction under conditions of high anxiety. *Journal of Personality and Social Psychology, 30,* 510–517.*

Dywan, J., & Murphy, W.E. (1996). Aging and inhibitory control in text comprehension. *Psychology and Aging, 11(2),* 199-206.*

Eagly, A.H., & Chalken, S. (1998). Attitude structure and function. In D.T. Gilbert, S.T. Fiske, & G. Lindzey (Eds.), *Handbook of social psychology* (4th ed., Vol. 2). New York: McGraw-Hill.

Eagly, A.H., & Crowley, M. (1986). Gender and helping: A meta-analytic review of the social psychological literature. *Psychological Bulletin, 108,* 233–256.

Eagly, A.H., & Steffen, V.J. (1986). Gender and aggressive behavior: A meta-analytic review of the social psychological literature. *Psychological Bulletin, 111,* 3–22.

Ebata, A.T., & Moos, R.H. (1989, April). *Coping and adjustment in four groups of adolescents.* Paper presented at the meeting of the Society for Research in Child Development, Kansas City.

Eccles, J.S., Wigfield, A., & Schiefele, U. (1998). Motivation to succeed. In W. Damon (Ed.), *Handbook of child psychology* (Vol. 3). New York: Wiley.

Eckert, E.D., Heston, L.L., & Bouchard, T.J. (1981). MZ twins reared apart. In L. Gedda, P. Paris, & W.D. Nance (Eds.), *Twin research* (Vol. 1). New York: Alan Liss.

Educational Testing Service (1992, February). *Cross-national comparisons of 9–13 year-olds' science and math achievement.* Princeton, NJ: Educational Testing Service.

Edwards, B. (1979). *Drawing on the right side of the brain.* Los Angeles: Tarcher.

Edwards, C.D. (1999). *How to handle a hard-to-handle kid.* Los Angeles: Free Spirit Pub.

Edwards, J.R., & Rothbard, N.P. (1999). Work and family stress and well-being: An examination of person-environment fit in the work and family domains. *Organizational Behavior and Human Decision Processes, 77,* 85–129.

Eibl-Eibesfeldt, I. (1977). Evolution of destructive aggression. *Aggressive Behavior, 3,* 127–144.

Eissenberg, T., Stitzer, M.L., & Henningfield, J.E. (1999). Current issues in nicotine replacement. In D.F. Seidman & L.S. Covey (Eds.), *Helping the hard-core smoker.* Mahwah, NJ: Erlbaum.

Ekman, P. (1980). *The face of man.* New York: Garland.

Ekman, P. (1996). Lying and deception. In N.L. Stein, C. Brainerd, P.A. Ornstein, & B. Tversky (Eds.), *Memory for everyday emotional events.* Mahwah, NJ: Erlbaum.

Ekman, P., & Friesen, W.V. (1968). The repertoire of nonverbal behavior—Categories, origins, usage, and coding. *Semiotica, 1,* 49–98.

Ekman, P., & Friesen, W.V. (1971). Constants across cultures in the face and emotion. *Journal of Personality and Social Psychology, 17,* 124–129.

Ekman, P., & Friesen, W.V. (1984). *Unmasking the face.* Palo Alto, CA: Consulting Psychology Press.

Ekman, P., & O'Sullivan, M. (1991). Facial expressions: Methods, means, and moues. In R.S. Feldman & B. Rime (Eds.), *Fundamentals of nonverbal behavior.* Cambridge: Cambridge University Press.

Ekman, P., Levenson, R.W., & Friesen, W.V. (1983, September 16). Autonomic nervous system

activity distinguishes among emotions. *Science, 223,* 1208–1210.

Elder, J.H., & Zucker, S.W. (1993). The effect of contour closure on the rapid discrimination of two-dimensional shapes. *Vision Research, 33(7),* 981-991.*

Elder, J.H., & Zucker, S.W. (1998). Evidence for boundary-specific grouping. *Vision Research, 38(1),* 143-152.*

Elkind, D. (1978). Understanding the young adolescent. *Adolescence, 13,* 127–134.

Ellis, A. (1962). *Reason and emotion in psychotherapy.* New York: Lyle Stuart.

Ellis, A. (1996). A rational-emotive behavior therapist's perspective on Ruth. In G. Corey (Ed.), *Case approach to counseling and psychotherapy.* Pacific Grove, CA: Brooks/Cole.

Ellis, H.C. (1987). Recent developments in human memory. In V.P. Makosky (Ed.), *The G. Stanley Hall Lecture Series.* Washington, DC: American Psychological Association.

Ellis, L., & Ames, M.A. (1987). Neurohormonal functioning and sexual orientation. *Psychological Bulletin, 101,* 233–258.

Ellis, R., & Humphreys, G.W. (Eds.). (1999). *Connectionist psychology.* Philadelphia: Psychology Press.

Embretson, S.E. (1999). Issues in the measurement of cognitive abilities. In S.E. Embretson & S.L. Hershberger (Eds.), *The new rules of measurement.* Mahwah, NJ: Erlbaum.

Emmons, R.A. (In Press). Religion in the psychology of personality: An introduction. *Journal of Personality.*

Empson, J.A.C., & Clarke, P.R.F. (1970). Rapid eye movements and remembering. *Nature, 227,* 287–288.

Emrick, D.C. (1982). Evaluation of alcoholism therapy methods. In E.M. Pattison & E. Kaufman (eds.), *Encyclopedic handbook of alcoholism.* New York: Gardner.

Endler, N. S. (1990a). *Holiday of darkness.* Toronto: Wall & Thompson.*

Endler, N. S. (1990b). Sociopolitical factors and stigma in depression. In C. D. McCann & N. S. Endler (Eds.), *Depression: New directions in theory, research and practice.* Toronto: Wall & Emerson.*

Endler, N. S. (1993). Personality: An interactional perspective. In P. J. Hettema & I. J. Deary (Eds.), *Foundations of personality.* Dordrecht, Netherlands: Kluwer.*

Endler, N. S. (1997). Stress, anxiety and coping: The multidimensional interaction model. *Canadian Psychology, 38,* 136-153.*

Endler, N. S., & Parker, J.D. (1991). Personality research: Theories, issues and methods. In M. Hersen, A. E. Kazdin, & A. S. Bellack (Eds.), *The clinical psychology handbook (2nd Ed.).* New York: Pergamon.*

Endler, N.S. (1995). *Personality theories* (4th ed.). Fort Worth: Harcourt Brace.

Endler, N.S., & Parker, J.D. (1993). The multidimensional assessment of coping: Concepts, issues, and measurement. In G.L. Van Heck & P. Bonaiuto (Eds), *Personality psychology in Europe* (Vol. 4). Tilburg, Netherlands: Tilburg University Press.*

Enzle, M.E, Roggeveen, J., & Look, S.C. (1991). Self-versus other-reward administration and intrinsic motivation. *Journal of Experimental Social Psychology, 27*, 468-479.*

Enzle, M.E., & Anderson, S.C. (1993). Surveillant intentions and intrinsic motivation. *Journal of Personality and Social Psychology, 64(2)*, 257-266.*

Eppley, K.R., Abrams, A.I., & Shear, J. (1989). Differential effects of relaxation effects on trait anxiety. *Journal of Clinical Psychology, 45*, 957–974.

Erikson, E. (1968). *Identity: Youth and crisis*. New York: W.W. Norton.

Evans, D.L. (1999). Introduction: Assessing antidepressant effectiveness. *Journal of Clinical Psychology, 60, Supplement 4*, 3.

Evans, D.L., Evans, D.L., Staab, J.P., Petitto, J.M., Morrison, M.F., Szuba, M.P., Ward, H.E., Wingate, B., Luber, P., & O'Reardon, J.P. (1999). Depression in the medical setting: Biopsychosocial interactions and treatment considerations. *Journal of Clinical Psychology, 60, Supplement 4*, 40–56.

Evans, D.R. (1997). *The law, standards of practice, and ethics in the practice of psychology*. Toronto: Emond Montgomery.*

Eysenck, H.J. (1952). The effects of psychotherapy: An evaluation. *Journal of Consulting Psychology, 16*, 319–324.

Eysenck, H.J. (1967). *The biological basis of personality*. Springfield, IL: Charles C Thomas.

F

Faber, D., & Burns, J.W. (1996). Anger management style, degree of expressed anger, and gender influence on cardiovascular recovery from interpersonal harassment. *Journal of Behavioral Medicine, 19*, 55–72.

Fairburn, C.G. (1995). *Overcoming binge eating*. New York: Guilford.

Fancher, R. (1996). *Pioneers of psychology* (3rd ed.). New York: W.W. Norton.*

Fancher, R.E. (1998). Alfred Binet: General psychologist. In G. Kimble & M. Wertheimer (Eds.), *Portraits of pioneers in psychology (Vol. 3)*. Washington DC: American Psychological Association.*

Fanselow, M.S., DeCola, J.P., & Young, S.L. (1993). Mechanisms responsible for reduced contextual conditioning with massed unsignaled unconditioned stimuli. *Journal of Experimental Psychology: Animal Processes, 19*, 121–127.

Farah, M.J. (1999). *The cognitive neuroscience of vision*. Philadelphia: Blackwell.

Fazio, R.H., Chen, J., McDonel, E.C., & Sherman, S.J. (1982). Attitude accessibility, attitude-behavior consistency, and the strength of the object-evaluation association. *Journal of Experimental Social Psychology, 18*, 339–357.

Feehan, G.G., & Enzle, M.E. (1991). Subjective control over rewards: Effects of perceived choice of reward schedule on intrinsic motivation and behavior maintenance. *Perceptual and Motor Skills, 72(3)*, 995-1006.*

Feighner, J.P. (1999). Mechanisms of action of antidepressant medications. *Journal of Clinical Psychology, 60, Supplement 4*, 4–13.

Fein, S., Goethals, G.R., Kassin, S.M., & Cross, J. (1993, August). *Social influence and presidential debates*. Paper presented at the meeting of the American Psychological Association, Toronto.

Feist, J., & Feist, G.J. (1998). *Personality* (4th ed.). New York: McGraw-Hill.

Feldhusen, J. (1999). Giftedness and creativity. In M.A. Runco & S. Pritzker (Eds.), *Encyclopedia of creativity*. San Diego: Academic Press.

Feldman, D.H. (1997, August). *Hitting middle C: Toward a more comprehensive domain for creativity research*. Paper presented at the meeting of the American Psychological Association, Chicago.

Feldman, M.A., & Case, L. (1997). Effectiveness of self-instructional audiovisual materials in teaching child-care skills to parents with intellectual disabilities. *Journal of Behavioral Education, 7*, 235-257.*

Fentress, J.C. (1999) The *Organization of Behavior* revisited. *Canadian Journal of Experimental Psychology, 53(1)*, 8-19.*

Feshbach, S., & Weiner, B. (1996). *Personality* (4th ed.). Lexington, MA: Heath.

Festinger, L. (1954). A theory of social comparison processes. *Human Relations, 7*, 117–140.

Festinger, L. (1957). *A theory of cognitive dissonance*. Evanston, IL: Row Peterson.

Field, T.M. (1992, September). Stroking babies helps growth. *Brown University Child and Adolescent Behavior Letter*, pp. 1,6.

Field, T.M. (Ed.) (1995). *Touch in early development*. Mahwah, NJ: Erlbaum.

Field, T.M., Scafidi, F., & Schanberg, S. (1987). Massage of preterm newborns to improve growth and development. *Pediatric Nursing, 13*, 386–388.

Fielder, F.E. (1978). Contingency model and the leadership process. In L. Berkowitz (Ed.), *Advances in experimental social psychology* (Vol. 11). New York: Academic Press.

Fiez, J.A., Raife, E.A., Balota, D.A., Schwarz, J.P., Raichle, M.E., & Petersen, S.E. (1996). A positron emission tomography study of the short-term maintenance of verbal information. *The Journal of Neuroscience, 16*, 808–822.

Finger, M.S., & Ones, D.S. (1999). Psychosomatic equivalence of the computer and booklet forms of the MMPI: A meta-analysis. *Psychological Assessment, 11*, 58–66.

Fischer, A.R., Jome, L.R., & Atkinson, D.R. (1998). Reconceptualizing multicultural counseling: Universal healing conditions in a culturally specific context. *Counseling Psychologist, 26*, 525–588.

Fischer, J., & Gochros, H.L. (1975). *Planned behavior change*. New York: Free Press.

Fisher, J. D., & Fisher, W. A. (1992). Changing AIDS risk behavior. *Psychological Bulletin, 111*, 455-474.*

Fiske, S.T. (1998). Stereotyping, prejudice, and discrimination. In D.T. Gilbert, S.T. Fiske, & G. Lindzey (Eds.), *The handbook of social psychology* (4th ed., Vol. 2). New York: McGraw-Hill.

Fleming, J.S., & Courtney, B.E. (1984). The dimensionality of self-esteem. *Journal of Personality and Social Psychology, 46*, 404–421.

Flett, G. L., Vredenburg, K., & Krames, L. (1997). The continuity of depression in clinical and nonclinical samples. *Psychological Bulletin, 121*, 395-416.*

Flynn, J.R. (1999). Searching for justice: The discovery of IQ gains over time. *American Psychologist, 54*, 5–20.

Fogarty, R., & Bellanca, J. (1998). *Multiple intelligences*. Boston: Allyn & Bacon.

Folkman, S., & Lazarus, R.S. (1980). An analysis of coping in a middle-aged community sample. *Journal of Health and Social behavior, 21*, 219–239.

Forbes, R.J., & Jackson, P.R. (1980). Non-verbal behavior and the outcome of selection interviews. *Journal of Occupational Psychology, 53*, 65–72.

Ford, J.D. (1999). Disorders of extreme stress following war-zone military trauma: Associated features of posttraumatic stress disorder or comorbid but distinct syndromes? *Journal of Consulting and Clinical Psychology, 67*, 3–12.

Foulkes, D. (1993). Cognitive dream theory. In M.A. Carskadon (Ed.), *Encyclopedia of sleep and dreams*. New York: Macmillan.

Foulkes, D. (1999). *Children's dreaming and the development of consciousness*. Cambridge, MA: Harvard University Press.

Fowler, C.A., Wolford, G., Slade, R., & Tassinary, L. (1981). Lexical access without awareness. *Journal of Experimental Psychology: General, 110*, 341–362.

Fox, J.L. (1984). The brain's dynamic way of keeping in touch. *Science, 225*, 820–821.

Fox, S.I. (1996). *Human physiology* (5th ed.). New York: McGraw-Hill.

Frances, A., & Ross, R. (1996). *DSM-IV case studies*. Washington, DC: American Psychiatric Association.

Frank, J.D. (1982). Therapeutic components shared by all psychotherapies. In J.H. Harvey & M.M. Parks (Eds.), *Psychotherapy research and behavior change*. Washington, DC: American Psychological Association.

Fraser, S. (Ed.). (1995). *The bell curve wars: Race, intelligence, and the future of America*. New York: Basic Books.

Freeman, S.J. (1994). An overview of Canada's mental health system. In L.L. Bachrach, P. Goering, & D. Wasylenki (Eds.), *Mental health care in Canada. New directions for mental health services*. San Francisco, CA: Jossey-Bass.*

Freud, S. (1900/1953). The interpretation of dreams. In J. Strachey (Ed.), *The standard edition of the complete psychological works of Sigmund Freud*. New York: Washington Square Press.

Freud, S. (1908). Creative writers and day-dreaming. In *Collected Works* (Vol. 9).

Freud, S. (1917) *A general introduction to psychoanalysis*. New York: Washington Square Press.

Fried, P.A., & Watkinson, B. (1990). 36- and 48-month neurobehavioral follow-up of children prenatally exposed to marijuana, cigarettes, and alcohol. *Developmental and Behavioral Pediatrics, 11*, 49–58.*

Friedman, H.S., & Schustack, M.W. (1999). *Personality: Classic theories and modern research*. Boston: Allyn & Bacon.

Friedman, J.I., Temporini, H., & Davis, K.L. (1999). Pharmacologic strategies for augmenting cognitive performance in schizophrenia. *Biological Psychiatry, 45*, 1–16.

Friedman, M., & Rosenman, R. (1974). *Type A behavior and your heart.* New York: Knopf.

Friedman, M.A., & Brownell, K.A. (1998). Obesity. In H.S. Friedman (Ed.), *Encyclopedia of mental health* (Vol. 3). San Diego: Academic Press.

Friedman, R., Myers, P., & Benson, H. (1998). Meditation and the relaxation response. In H.S. Friedman (Ed.), *Encyclopedia of mental health* (Vol. 2). San Diego: Academic Press.

Friedrich, L.K., & Stein, A.H. (1973). Aggressive and prosocial TV programs and the natural behavior of preschool children. *Monographs of the Society for Research in Child Development, 38,* (4, Serial No. 151).

Frischoltz, E.Z. (1995, August.). *Discriminating hypnotic and nonhypnotic influences on human memory.* Paper presented at the meeting of the American Psychological Association, New York City.

Fromm, E. (1947). *Man for himself.* New York: Holt, Rinehart & Winston

Frost, R.O., & Steketee, G. (1998). Obsessive-compulsive disorder. In H.S. Friedman (Ed.), *Encyclopedia of mental health* (Vol. 3). San Diego: Academic Press.

Fuhriman, A., & Burlingame, G.M. (1995). *Handbook of group psychotherapy.* New York: Wiley.

Furnham, A. (1988). Write and wrong: The validity of graphological analysis. *Skeptical Inquirer, 13,* 64–69.

Furth, H. (1971). Linguistic deficiency and thinking: Research with deaf subjects. *Psychological Bulletin, 75,* 52–58.

Furth, H.G., & Wachs, H. (1975). *Thinking goes to school.* New York: Oxford University Press.

Gage, F.H., & Bjorklund, A. (1986). Cholinergic septal grafts into the hippocampal formation improve spatial learning and memory in aged rats by an atropine-sensitive mechanism. *Journal of Neuroscience, 6,* 2837–2847.

Gaines, S.O., & Reed, E.S. (1995). Prejudice: From Allport to Dubois. *American Psychologist, 50,* 96–103.

Galanter, E. (1962). Contemporary psychophysics. In R. Brown (Ed.), *New directions in psychology.* New York: Holt, Rinehart, & Winston.

Galanter, M. (1999). *Cults.* New York: Oxford University Press.

Gammell, D.J., & Stoppard, J.M. (1999). Women's experiences of treatment of depression: Medicalization or empowerment? *Canadian Psychology, 40(2),* 112-128.*

Garbarino, J. (1999). *Lost boys: Why our sons turn violent and what we can do to save them.* New York: Free Press.

Garcia, J. (1989). Food for Tolman: Cognition and cathexis in concert. In T. Archer & L. Nilsson (Eds.), *Aversion, avoidance, and anxiety.* Mahwah, NJ: Erlbaum.

Garcia, J., Ervin, F.E., & Koelling, R.A. (1966). Learning with prolonged delay of reinforcement. *Psychonomic Science, 5,* 121–122.

Gardner, B.T., & Gardner, R.A. (1971). Two-way communication with an infant chimpanzee. In A. Schreir & F. Stollnitz (Eds.), *Behavior of non-human primates* (Vol. 4). New York: Academic Press.

Gardner, H. (1983). *Frames of mind.* New York: Basic Books.

Gardner, H. (1985). *The mind's new science.* New York: Basic Books.

Gardner, H. (1993). *Multiple intelligences.* New York: Basic Books.

Gardner, H. (1999). *The disciplined mind.* New York: Simon & Schuster.

Gardner, R. C. (1994). Stereotypes as consensual beliefs. In M.P. Zanna & J.M. Olson (Eds.), *The psychology of prejudice: The Ontario symposium (Vol. 7).* Mahwah, NJ: Erlbaum.*

Gardner, R. C., & Tremblay, P. F. (1995). On motivation: Measurement and conceptual considerations. *Modern Language Journal, 78,* 524-527.*

Garelik, G. (1985, October). Are the progeny progenies? *Discoverer, 6,* 45–47, 78–84.

Garfield, S.L., & Kurtz, R. (1976). Clinical psychologists in the 70s. *American Psychologist, 31,* 1-9.

Garmezy, N. (1985). Stress resistant children: The search for protective factors. In J.E. Stevenson (Ed.). Recent research in developmental psychopathology. *Journal of Child Psychology and Psychiatry Book Supplement, 4,* 213–233.

Garmezy, N. (1993). Children in poverty: Resilience despite risk. *Psychiatry, 56,* 127–136.

Garraghty, P.E. (1996, June). *Neuroplasticity: From mechanisms to behavior.* Paper presented at the meeting of the American Psychological Association, San Francisco.

Garrod, S., & Pickering, M. (Eds.) (1999). *Language processing.* Philadelphia: Psychology Press.

Gauthier, J.G. (1999). Bridging the gap between biological and psychological perspectives in the treatment of anxiety disorders. *Canadian Psychology, 40(1),* 1-11.*

Gazzaniga, M.S., Ivry, R.B., & Mangun, G.R. (1998). *Cognitive neuroscience.* New York: Norton.

Geen, R.G. (1998). Aggression and antisocial behavior. In D.T. Gilbert, S.T. Fiske, & G. Lindzey (Eds.), *Handbook of social psychology* (4th ed., Vol. 2). New York: McGraw-Hill.

Gelder, M.G., Mayou, R., & Geddes, J. (1999). *Psychiatry* (2nd ed.). New York: Oxford University Press.

Gelso, C.J., Hill, C.E., Mohr, J.J., Rochlen, A.B., & Zack, J. (1999). Describing the face of transference. *Journal of Counseling Psychology, 46,* 257–267.

Geschwind, N., & Galaburda, A.M. (1987). *Cerebral lateralization.* Cambridge, MA: MIT Press.

Gevins, A.S. (1999). What to do with your own personal brain scanner. In R.L. Solso (Ed.), *Mind and brain sciences in the 21st century.* Cambridge, MA: MIT Press.

Gibbons, F.X., & Buunk, B.P. (1999). Individual differences in social comparison: Development of a scale of social comparison orientation. *Journal of Personality and Social Psychology 76,* 129–142.

Gibbons, F.X., & McCoy, S.B. (1991). Self-esteem, similarity, and reactions to active versus passive downward comparison. *Journal of Personality and Social Psychology, 60,* 414–424.

Gibbons, F.X., Benbow, C.P., & Gerrard, M. (1994). From top dog to bottom half: Social comparison strategies in response to poor performance. *Journal of Personality and Social Psychology, 67,* 638–652.

Gibbs, J.T., & Huang, L.N. (1989). A conceptual framework for assessing and treating minority youth. In J.T. Gibbs & L.N. Huang (Eds.), *Children of color.* San Francisco: Jossey-Bass.

Gibbs, J.T., & Huang, L.N. (Eds.). (1989). *Children of color.* San Francisco: Jossey-Bass.

Gibson, E.J., & Walk, R.D. (1960). The visual cliff. *Scientific American, 202,* 64–71.

Gibson, J.J. (1966). *The senses considered as perceptual system.* Boston: Houghton Mifflin.

Gibson, R.L., & Mitchell, M.H. (1999). *Introduction to counseling and guidance* (5th ed.). Upper Saddle River, NJ: Prentice-Hall.

Gick, M.L., & Lockhart, R.S. (1995). Cognitive and affective components of insight. In R.J. Sternberg & J.E. Davidson (Eds.), *The nature of insight.* Cambridge, MA: Bradford.*

Giles, T.R., & Marafiote, R.A. (1998). Managed care and the practitioner. *Clinical Psychology and Practice, 5,* 41–50.

Gilligan, C. (1982). *In a different voice.* Cambridge, MA: Harvard University Press.

Gilligan, C. (1996). The centrality of relationships in psychological development. In G. Noam & K.W. Fischer (Eds.), *Development and vulnerability in close relationships.* Mahwah, NJ: Erlbaum.

Gilligan, C. (1998). *Minding women: Reshaping the educational realm.* Cambridge, MA: Harvard University Press.

Gladding, S.T. (1995). *Group work* (2nd ed.). Upper Saddle River, NJ: Prentice Hall.

Gladding, S.T. (1999). *Family therapy* (2nd ed.). Upper Saddle River, NJ: Prentice-Hall.

Gladding, S.T. (1999). *Group work: A counseling specialty* (3rd ed.). Upper Saddle River, NJ: Prentice-Hall.

Gladue, B.A. (1994). The biopsychology of sexual orientation. *Current Directions in Psychological Science, 3,* 150–154.

Goddard. M.J. (1997). Spontaneous recovery in US extinction. *Learning and Motivation, 28,* 118-128.*

Goel, V. (1995). *Sketches of thought.* Cambridge, MA: MIT Press.*

Goel, V., Gold, B., Kapur, S., & Houle, S. (1997). The seats of reason: A localization study of deductive & inductive reasoning using PET (O15) blood flow technique. *NeuroReport, 8(5),* 1305-1310.*

Goethals, G.R., & Demorest, A.P. (1995). The risky shift is a sure bet. In M.E. Ware & D.E. Johnson (Eds.), *Demonstrations and activities in teaching of psychology* (Vol. 3). Mahwah, NJ: Erlbaum.

Goldberg, R. (2000). *Clashing views on controversial issues in drugs and society* (4th ed.). New York: McGraw-Hill.

Goldberg, T.E., Berman, K.F., & Weinberger, D.R. (1995). Neuropsychology and neurophysiology of schizophrenia. *Current Opinions in Psychiatry, 8,* 34–40.

Goldenberg, I. (1996). *Family therapy* (4th ed.). Pacific Grove, CA: Brooks/Cole.

Goldstein, E.B. (1999). *Sensation and perception* (5th ed.). Pacific Grove, CA: Brooks/Cole.

Goldstein, M.J., & Palmer, J.O. (1975). *The experience of anxiety.* New York: Oxford University Press.

Goleman, D., Kaufman, P., & Ray, M. (1993). *The creative mind.* New York: Plume.

Goleman, D., Kaufman, P., & Ray, M. (1993). *The creative spirit.* New York: Plume.

Goodstein. I.K., & Calhoun, J.F. (1982). *Understanding abnormal behavior.* Reading, MA: Addison-Wesley.

Goodwin, D.W. (1988). Alcoholism: Who gets better and who does not. In R.M. Rose & J. Barrett (eds.), *Alcoholism.* New York: Raven Press.

Gorenstein, E.E. (1997). *Case studies in abnormal psychology.* New York: Longman.

Gorman, J.M., & Kent, J. M. (1999). SSRIs and SNRIs: Broad spectrum of efficacy beyond major depression. *Journal of Clinical Psychology, 60,* Supplement 4, 33–39.

Gottesman, I.I. (1989). Vital statistics, demography, and schizophrenia. *Schizophrenia Bulletin, 15,* 5–8.

Gottesman, I.I., & Goldsmith, H.H. (1994). Developmental psychopathology of antisocial behavior. In C.A. Nelson (Ed.), *Threats to optimal development.* Mahwah, NJ: Erlbaum.

Gottesman, I.I., & Shields, J. (1982). *The schizophrenic puzzle.* New York: Cambridge University Press.

Gottlieb, B.H. (1998). Support groups. In H.S. Friedman (Ed.), *Encyclopedia of mental health* (Vol. 3). San Diego: Academic Press.*

Gottlieb, G., Wahlsten, D., & Lickliter, R. (1998). The significance of biology for human development: A developmental psychobiological systems view. In W. Damon (Ed.), *Handbook of child psychology* (5th ed.). New York: Wiley.*

Gottman, J.M., Coan, J., Carrere, S., & Swanson, C. (1998). Predicting marital happiness and stability from newlywed interactions. *Journal of Marriage and the Family, 60,* 5–22.

Graber, R., Garber, R., & Gouin, P. (1998). *How to get a good night sleep.* New York: Wiley.

Grabowski, J. (1999, January). Addicted to addictions? *APA Monitor,* p. 8.

Graf, P., & Schacter, D.L. (1985). Implicit and explicit memory for new associations in normal and amnesiac subjects. *Journal of Experimental Psychology: Learning, Memory and Cognition, 11,* 501-518.*

Graham, S. (1986, August). *Can attribution theory tell us something about motivation in Blacks?* Paper presented at the meeting of the American Psychological Association, Washington, DC.

Graham, S. (1992). Most of the subjects were white and middle class. *American Psychologist, 47,* 629–637.

Gray, C.R., & Gummerman, K. (1975). The enigmatic eidetic image: A critical examination of methods, data, and theories. *Psychological Bulletin, 82,* 383–407.

Graziano, W.J. (1995). Evolutionary psychology: Old music, but now on CDs? *Psychological Inquiry, 6,* 41–44.

Greenberg, J.S., Bruess, C.E., & Mullen, K.D. (1992). *Sexuality* (3rd ed.). New York: McGraw-Hill.

Greenberg, L., & Paivio, S. (1997). *Working with emotion in psychotherapy.* New York Guilford Press.*

Greenberg, M., Szmukler, G., & Tantam, D. (1986). *Making sense of psychiatric cases.* New York: Oxford University Press.

Greene, R.L. (1999). Applied memory research: How far from bankruptcy? *Contemporary Psychology, 44,* 29–31.

Greenglass, E.R. (1991). Burnout and gender: Theoretical and organizational implications. *Canadian Psychology, 32(4),* 562-574.*

Greenglass, E.R. (1996). Anger suppression, cynical distrust, and hostility: Implications for coronary heart disease. In C.D. Spielberger & I.G. Sarason (Eds.), *Stress and emotion: Anxiety, anger, and curiosity (Vol 16).* Washington, DC: Taylor & Francis.*

Greenglass, E.R. (1998). Gender differences in mental health. In H.S. Friedman (Ed.), *Encyclopedia of mental health* (Vol. 2). San Diego: Academic Press.*

Greenglass, E.R., Burke, R.J., & Konarski, R. (1998). Components of burnout, resources, and gender-related differences. *Journal of Applied Social Psychology, 28(12),* 1088-1106.*

Greenough, W. (1999, April). *Experience, brain development, and links to mental retardation.* Paper presented at the meeting of the Society for Research in Child Development, Albuquerque.

Greenwald, A.G., & Banaji, M.R. (1995). Implicit social cognition: Attitudes, self-esteem, and stereotypes. *Psychological Review, 102,* 4–27.

Greenwald, A.G., Draine, S.C., & Abrams, R.L. (1996). Three cognitive markers of unconscious semantic activation. *Science, 273,* 1699–1702.

Gregory, R.L. (1978). *Eye and brain: The psychology of seeing* (3rd ed.). New York: McGraw-Hill.

Grizenko, N. (1998). Protective factors in development of psychopathology. In H.S. Friedman (Ed.), *Encyclopedia of mental health* (Vol. 3). San Diego: Academic Press.*

Grossenbacher, P.G. (1999). *Finding consciousness in the brain.* New York: John Benjamins Pub.

Grunberg, N.E., Klein, L.C., & Brown, K.J. (1998). Psychopharmacology. In H.S. Friedman (Ed.), *Encyclopedia of mental health* (Vol. 3). San Diego: Academic Press.

Guilford, J.P. (1967). *The structure of intellect.* New York: McGraw-Hill.

Gupta, P., & Dell, G.S. (1999). The emergence of language from serial order and procedural memory. In B. MacWhinney (Ed.), *The emergence of language.* Mahwah, NJ: Erlbaum.

Guttman, N., & Kalish, H.I. (1956). Discriminability and stimulus generalization *Journal of Experimental Psychology, 51,* 79–88.

H

Haberlandt, K. (1999). *Human memory.* Boston: Allyn & Bacon.

Hacking, I. (1998). *Mad travelers: Reflections on the reality of transient mental illness.* Charlottesville, VA: University Press of Virginia.*

Haddock, G., & Zanna, M. P. (1998). Assessing the structure of anti-gay attitudes: The impact of right-wing authoritarianism and values on anti-gay prejudice and discrimination. In G. M. Herek (Ed.), *Stigma and sexual orientation: Understanding prejudice against lesbians, gay men, and bisexuals.* Newbury Park, CA: Sage.*

Haddock, G., Zanna, M.P., & Esses, V.M. (1994). The (limited) role of trait-laden stereotypes in predicting attitudes toward Native Peoples. *British Journal of Social Psychology, 33,* 83-106.*

Hadjistavropoulos, T., & Genest, M. (1994). The underestimation of the role of physical attractiveness in dating preferences: Ignorance or taboo? *Canadian Journal of Behavioural Science, 26(2),* 298-318.*

Hafer, C.L., & Olson, J.M. (1998). Individual differences in the belief in a just world and responses to personal misfortune. In L. Montada & M.J. Lerner (Eds.), *Responses to victimizations and belief in a just world: Critical issues in social justice.* New York: Plenum.*

Hakuta, K. (1999). The debate on bilingual education. *Developmental and Behavioral Pediatrics, 20,* 36–37.

Hakuta, K., & Garcia, E.E. (1989). Bilingualism and education. *American Psychologist, 44,* 374–379.

Hales, D. (1999). *Invitation to health* (8th ed.). New York: McGraw-Hill.

Hales, R.E., Yudofsky, S.C. (Eds.) (1999). *Essentials of clinical psychiatry.* Washington, DC: American Psychiatric Pub.

Hales, R.E., Yudofsky, S.C., Talbott, J.A., & Pardes, H. (Eds.) (1999). *Textbook of psychiatry* (3rd ed.). Washington, DC: American Psychiatric Pub.

Hall, W. (1998, February 24). IQ scores are up, and psychologists wonder why. *Wall Street Journal,* pp. B11–12.

Hallahan, D.P., & Kaufmann, J.M. (2000). *Exceptional learners* (8th ed.). Boston: Allyn & Bacon.

Halliday, T. (Ed.) (1998). *The senses and communication.* New York: Springer Verlag.

Halonen, J.A., & Santrock, J.W. (1999). *Psychology* (3rd ed.). New York: McGraw-Hill.

Halpern, D.F. (1996). *Thinking critically about critical thinking.* Mahwah, NJ: Erlbaum.

Halpern, D.F. (in press). Teaching and learning critical thinking: Lessons from cognitive psychology. *American Psychologist.*

Hampton, R.R., & Shettleworth, S.J. (1996). Hippocampal lesions impair memory for location but not color in passerine birds. *Behavioral Neuroscience, 110,* 831-835.*

Hancock, P.A. (Ed.). (1999). *Human performance and ergonomics.* San Diego: Academic Press.

Handler, L. (1999). Introduction to the special series on personality assessment: Classics in contemporary perspective. *Journal of Personality Assessment, 72,* 144–146.

Hannigan, J.H., Spear, L.P., Spear, N.E., & Goodlet, C.R. (Eds.)(1999). *Alcohol and alcoholism.* Mahwah, NJ: Erlbaum.

Harackiewicz, J.M. (1998). Intrinsic motivation and goals. In H.S. Friedman (Ed.), *Encyclopedia of mental health* (Vol. 2). San Diego: Academic Press.

Harkness, S., & Super, E.M. (1995). Culture and parenting. In M.H. Bornstein (Ed.), *Handbook of parenting* (Vol. 3). Hillsdale, NJ: Erlbaum.

Harlow, H.F., & Zimmerman, R.R. (1959). Affectional responses in the infant monkey. *Science, 130,* 421–432.

Harmatz, M. (1997). Introduction to clinical psychology. In Santrock, J.W. *Psychology* (5th ed.). New York: McGraw-Hill.

Harmon-Jones, E., & Mills, J. (Eds.) (1999). *Cognitive dissonance.* Washington, DC: American Psychological Association.

Harris, A.S. (1996). *Living with paradox: An introduction to Jungian Psychology.* Pacific Grove, CA: Brooks/Cole.

Harris, J.R. (1998). *The nurture assumption.* New York: Free Press.

Harris, L.R. & Jenkin M.R. (Eds.). (1998). *Vision and action.* New York: Cambridge University Press.*

Harris, L.R., Jenkin, M., & Zikovitz, D.C. (1999). Vestibular cues and virtual environments: choosing the magnitude of the vestibular cue. *IEEE International Conference on Virtual Reality,* 229-236.*

Harris, R.F., Wolf, N.M., & Baer, D.M. (1964). Effects of adult social reinforcement on child behavior. *Young Children, 20,* 8–17.

Harrison, Y. (1999). *Sleep talking.* New York: Blanford.

Hart, B., & Risley, T.R. (1995). *Meaningful differences.* Baltimore: Paul H. Brookes.

Harter, S. (1998). The development of serf-representations. In W. Damon (Ed.), *Handbook of child psychology* (5th ed., Vol. 3). New York: Wiley.

Hartmann, E. (1993). Nightmares. In M.A. Carskadon (Ed.), *Encyclopedia of sleep and dreams.* New York: Macmillan.

Hartwell, L., Hood, L., Goldberg, M.L., Silver, L.M., Veres, R.C., & Reynolds, A. (2000). *Genetics: From genes to genomes.* New York: McGraw-Hill.

Harvey, J.H. (1995). *Odyssey of the heart.* New York: W.H. Freeman.

Hatcher, R.A., Guest, F., Stewart, F., Stewart, G.K., Trussel, J., Cerel, S., & Cates, W. (1988). *Contraceptive technology, 1988–1989* (14th ed.). New York: Irvington.

Hauser, S.T. (1999). Understanding resilient outcomes: Adolescent lives across time and generations. *Journal of Research on Adolescence, 9,* 1–24.

Hayes, N. (1997, July). The distinctive skills of a psychology graduate. *APA Monitor,* p. 33.

Hayflick, L. (1997). The cellular basis for biological aging. In C.E. Finch & L. Hayflick (Eds.), *Handbook of the biology of aging.* New York: Van Nostrand.

Health Canada (1998). *Canada's drug strategy.* Available from Health Canada (online at http://www.hc-sc.gc.ca/). Current URL http://www.hc-sc.gc.ca/hppb/alcohol-other-drugs/publications.htm.*

Health Canada (1999). *Statistical report on the health of Canadians.* Available from Health Canada (online at http://www.hc-sc.gc.ca/). Current URL: http://www.hc-sc.gc.ca/hppb/phdd/report/stat/eng/index.html.*

Heatherton, T.F., & Polivy, J. (1992). Chronic dieting and eating disorders: a spiral model. In J.H. Crowther, S.E. Hobfall, M.A.P. Stephens, & D.L. Tennenbaum (Eds.), *The etiology of bulimia: the individual and familial context.* Washington, DC: Hemisphere Publishers.*

Hebb, D. O. (1961). *The organization of behavior: An neuro-psychological theory.* New York: Wiley.*

Heider, F. (1958). Attitudes and cognitive organization. *Journal of Psychology, 21,* 107–122.

Heider, F. (1958). *The psychology of interpersonal relations.* New York: Wiley.

Heiman, G.W. (1995). *Research methods.* Boston: Houghton Mifflin.

Heinrichs, R.W., & Zakzanis, K.K. (1998). Neurocognitive deficit in schizophrenia: A quantitative review of the evidence. *Neuropsychology, 12,* 426-445.*

Helms, J.E., & Cook, D.A. (1999). *Using race and culture in counseling and psychotherapy.* Boston: Allyn & Bacon.

Herbert, J. (1988). The physiology of aggression. In J. Groebel & R. Hinde (Eds.), *Aggression and war: The biological and social bases.* New York: Cambridge University Press.

Herbert, W. (1997, April 21). Politics of biology. *U.S. News & World Report,* pp. 72–79.

Hernandez, D.J. (1988). Demographic trends and the living arrangements of children. In E.M. Hetherington & J.D. Arasteh (Eds.), *Impact of divorce, single-parenting, and stepparenting on children.* Mahwah, NJ: Erlbaum.

Herrnstein, R.J., & Murray, C. (1994). *The bell curve: Intelligence and class structure in American life.* New York: Macmillan.

Hersen, M., & Miller, P.M. (Eds.) (1996). *Progress in behavior modification* (Vol. 30). Pacific Grove: CA: Brooks/Cole.

Herzog, H.A. (1995). Discussing animal rights and animal research in the classroom. In M.E. Ware & D.E. Johnson (Eds.), *Demonstrations and activities in teaching of psychology* (Vol. 1). Mahwah, NJ: Erlbaum.

Heyes, C.M., & Galef, Jr. B.G. (Eds.). (1996). *Social learning in animals: The roots of culture.* San Diego: Academic Press.*

Hilgard, E.R. (1965). *Hypnotic suggestibility.* Ft. Worth, TX: Harcourt Brace.

Hilgard, E.R. (1977). *Divided consciousness: Multiple controls in human thought and action.* New York: Wiley.

Hill, C.E., & O'Brien, K.M. (1999). *Helping skills.* Washington, DC: American Psychological Association.

Hilleras, P., Jorm, A.F., Herlitz, A., & Winblad, B. (1999). Activity patterns in very old people. *Age and Aging, 28,* 147–152.

Hines, T. (1988). *Pseudoscience and the paranormal.* Buffalo, NY: Promethus Books.

Hoagwood, K., Jensen, P., & Fischer, C. (Eds.). (1996). *Ethical issues in mental health research with children.* Mahwah, NJ: Erlbaum.

Hobfoll, S.E. (1989). Conversation of resources: A new attempt at conceptualizing stress. *American Psychologist, 44,* 513–524.

Hobson, J.A. (1999). Dreams. In R. Conlan (Ed.), *States of mind.* New York: Wiley.

Hobson, J.A., & McCarley, R.W. (1977). The brain as a dream state generator: An activation-synthesis hypothesis of the dream process. *American Journal of Psychiatry, 134,* 1335–1348.

Hochberg, J. (Ed.). (in press). *Perception and cognition at century's end.* San Diego: Academic Press.

Hofferth, S.L. (1990). Trends in adolescent sexual activity, contraception, and pregnancy in the United States. In J. Bancroft & J.M. Reinisch (Eds.), *Adolescence and puberty.* New York: Oxford University Press.

Hoffman, D.D. (1998). *Visual intelligence.* New York: Norton.

Hoffnung, M. (1984). Motherhood. In J. Freeman (Ed.), *Women* (3rd ed.). Palo Alto, CA: Mayfield.

Hogan, J. (1986). *Hogan Personality Inventory manual.* Minneapolis: National Computer Systems.

Hogan, R.T. (1987, August). *Conceptions of personality and the prediction of job performance.* Paper presented at the meeting of the American Psychological Association, New York City.

Hoge, M.A. (1998). Managed care. In H.S. Friedman (Ed.), *Encyclopedia of mental health* (Vol. 2). San Diego: Academic Press.

Hogg, M.A. (1996). Social identity, self-categorization, and the small group. In E.H. Witte & J.H. Davis (Eds.), *Understanding group behavior* (Vol. 2). Mahwah, NJ: Erlbaum.

Holcomb, H.H., Cascella, N.G., Thaker, G.K., Medoff, D.R., Dannals, R.F., & Tamminga, C.A. (1996). Functional sites of neuroleptic drug action in the human brain. *American Journal of Psychiatry, 153,* 41–49.

Holden, R.R., & Kroner, D.G. (1992). Relative efficacy of differential response latencies for detecting faking on a self-report measure of | psychopathology. *Psychological Assessment: A Journal of Consulting and Clinical Psychology, 4,* 170-173.*

Holland, P.C. (1996). The effects of intertrial and feature-target intervals on operant serial feature-positive discrimination learning. *Animal Learning & Behavior, 24,* 411–428.

Holmes, D.S. (1988). The influence of meditation versus rest on physiological considerations In M. West (Ed.), *The psychology of meditation.* New York: Oxford University Press.

Holmes, T.H., & Rahe, R.H. (1967). The social readjustment rating scale. *Journal of Psychosomatic Research, 11,* 213–218.

Holtzmann, W. (1982). Cross-cultural comparisons of personality development in Mexico and the United States. In D. Wagner & H.W. Stevenson (Eds.), *Cultural perspectives on child development.* San Francisco: Jossey-Bass.

Honts, C. (1998, June). Commentary. *APA Monitor,* p. 30.

Hood, R.W. (1995). *Handbook of religious experience.* Birmingham, AL: Religious Education Press.

Hooper, J., & Teresi, D. (1993). *The 3-Pound Universe.* New York: Tarcher/Putnam.

Hopkins, K.D. (1998). *Educational and psychological measurement and evaluation* (8th Ed.). Boston: Allyn & Bacon.

Hoptman, M.J., & Davidson, R.J. (1994). How and why do the two cerebral hemispheres interact? *Psychological Bulletin, 116,* 195–219.

Horney, K. (1945). *Our inner conflicts.* New York: W.W. Norton.

Horowitz, M.J. (1998). Psychoanalysis. In H.S. Friedman (Ed.), *Encyclopedia of mental health* (Vol. 3). San Diego: Academic Press.

Howard, I.P., & Rogers, B.J. (1995). Binocular vision and stereopsis. New York: Oxford University Press.*

Howe, M.L. (March, 1995). *Early memory development and the emergence of autobiographical memory.* Paper presented at the meeting of the Society for Research in Child Development, Indianapolis.*

Hoyer, W.J., Rybash, J.M., & Roodin, P.A. (1999). *Adult development and aging* (4th ed.). New York: McGraw-Hill.

Hubel, D.H., & Wiesel, T.N. (1965). Receptive fields and functional architecture in two nonstriate areas (18 and 19) of the cat. *Journal of Neurophysiology, 28,* 229–289.

Hultsch, D.F., & Plemons, J.K. (1979). Life events and life-span development. In P.B. Baltes & O.G. Brim (Eds.), *Life-span development and behavior.* San Diego: Academic Press.

Hunsberger, B. (1991) Empirical work in the psychology of religion. *Canadian Psychology, 32(3),* 497-504.*

Hunt, H.T. (1995). *On the nature of consciousness: Cognitive, phenomenological, and transpersonal perspectives.* New Haven, CT: Yale University Press.*

Hunt, M. (1974). *Sexual behavior in the 1970s.* Chicago: Playboy.

Hunt, M.M. (1982). *The universe within.* New York: Simon & Schuster.

Hunt, R.R., & Kelly, R.E.S. (1996). Accessing the particular from the general: The power of distinctiveness in the context of organization. *Memory and Cognition, 24,* 217–225.

Hurst, S.A., & Genest, M. (1995). Cognitive-behavioural therapy with a feminist orientation: A perspective for therapy with depressed women. *Canadian Psychology, 36(3),* 236-257.*

Hurvich, L.M., & Jameson, D. (1969). Human color perception. *American Scientist, 57,* 143–166.

Huston, A.C. (1995, August). *Children in poverty.* Paper presented at the meeting of the American Psychological Association, New York City.

Huston, A.C., Watkins, B.A., & Kunkel, D. (1989). Public policy and children's television. *American Psychologist, 44,* 424–433.

Hy, L., & Loevinger, J. (1996). *Measuring ego development.* Mahwah, NJ: Erlbaum.

Hyde, J.S., & Plant, E.A. (1995). Magnitude of psychological gender differences: Another side of the story. *American Psychologist, 50,* 159–161.

Hynie, M. (1998). The AIDS/ HIV pandemic. In F. Aboud (Ed.), *Health psychology in global perspective.* Newbury Park, CA: Sage.*

Iacono, W.G., & Lykken, D.T. (1997). The validity of the lie detector: Two surveys of scientific opinion. *Journal of Applied Psychology, 82,* 426–433.

Intrator, J., Hare, R., Strizke, P., Brichtswein, K., Dorfman, D., Harpur, T., Bernstein, D., Handelsman, L., Schaefer, C., Keilp, J., Rosen, J., & Machac, J. (1997). Brain imaging (SPECT) study of semantic and affective processing in psychopaths. *Biological Psychiatry, 42,* 96-103.*

Iverson, G.L., & Barton, E. (1999). Interscorer reliability of the MMPI-2: Should TRIN and VRIN be computer scored? *Journal of Clinical Psychology, 55,* 65–70.*

Izard, C.E., Schultz, D., & Levinson, K.L. (1998). Emotions and mental health. In H.S. Friedman (Ed.), *Encyclopedia of mental health* (Vol. 2). San Diego: Academic Press.

Jackson, D.N. (1991). Computer-assisted personality test interpretation: The dawn of discovery. In T.B. Gutkin & S.L. Wise (Eds), *The computer and the decision-making process. Buros-Nebraska Symposium on Measurement & Testing, (Vol 4).* Mahwah, NJ: Erlbaum.*

Jacobsen, N., & Gottman, J.M. (1998). *When men batter women.* New York: Simon & Schuster.

Jacoby, L.L. (1998). Invariance in automatic influences of memory: Toward a user's guide for the process-dissociation procedure. *Journal of Experimental Psychology: Learning, Memory, and Cognition, 24,* 3-26.*

Jacoby, L.L., Jennings, J.M., & Hay, J.F. (1996). Dissociating automatic and consciously controlled processes: Implications for diagnosis and rehabilitation of memory deficits. In D.J. Herrmann, C.L. McEvoy, C. Hertzog, P. Hertel, & M.K. Johnson (Eds.), *Basic and applied memory research: Theory in context (Vol.1).* Mahwah, NJ: Erlbaum.*

Jalbert, N.L. (1996, Summer). What can I do with a psychology major? *Psi Chi Newsletter, 22* (No. 3, pp. 1, 6.

James, W. (1890/1950). *Principles of psychology.* New York: Dover.

Jameson, D., & Hurvich, L.M. (1989). Essay concerning color constancy. *Annual Review of Psychology* (Vol. 40). Palo Alto, CA: Annual Reviews.

Janis, I. (1972). *Victims of groupthink: A psychological study of foreign-policy decisions and fiascos.* Boston: Houghton Mifflin.

Jausovec, N. (1999). Brain biology and brain functioning. In M.A. Runco & S. Pritzker (Eds.), *Encyclopedia of creativity.* San Diego: Academic Press.

Jaycox, L.H., & Foa, E.B. (1998). Post traumatic stress. In H.S. Friedman (Ed.), *Encyclopedia of mental health* (Vol. 2). San Diego: Academic Press.

Jenkins, H.M., & Sainsbury, R.S. (1969). The development of stimulus control through differential reinforcement. In N.J. Mackintosh & W.K. Honig (Eds.), *Fundamental issues in associative learning.* Halifax, NS: Dalhousie University Press.*

Jenkins, J.J. (1969). Language and thought. In J.F. Voss (Ed.), *Approaches to thought.* Columbus, OH: Merrill.

Jennings, L., & Skovholt, T.M. (1999). The cognitive, emotional, and relational characteristics of master therapists. *Journal of Counseling Psychology, 46,* 3–11.

Jensen, A.R. (1969). How much can we boost IQ and scholastic achievement? *Harvard Educational Review, 39,* 1–123.

Jensen, A.R. (1998). *The g factor: The science of mental ability.* Westport, CT: Praeger.

Johnson, D.W., & Johnson, R.T. (1999). *Learning together and alone* (5th ed.). Boston: Allyn & Bacon.

Johnson, G.B. (2000). *The living world* (2nd ed.). New York: McGraw-Hill.

Johnson, J.S., & Newport, E.L. (1989). Critical period effects in second language learning. *Cognitive Psychology, 21,* 60–69.

Johnson, L.D., Bachman, J.G., & O'Malley, P.M. (1989, February 24). *Teenage drug use continues decline* [News release]. Ann Arbor: University of Michigan, Institute for Social Research.

Johnston, L.D., O'Malley, P.M., & Bachman, J.G. (1997). *National survey results on drug use from The Monitoring the Future Study: Vol. II College Students.* Ann Arbor, MI: University of Michigan, Institute for Social Research.

Johnston, L.D., O'Malley, P.M., & Bachman, J.G. (1998, December). *Report of the Monitoring the Future Project.* Ann Arbor, MI: University of Michigan, Institute for Social Research.

Jones, E.E. (1998). Major developments in five decades of social psychology. In D.T. Gilbert, S.T. Fiske, & G. Lindzey (Eds.), *Handbook of social psychology* (4th ed., Vol. 1). New York: McGraw-Hill.

Jones, J.H. (1997). *Prejudice and racism* (2nd ed.). New York: McGraw-Hill.

Jones, M.C. (1924). A laboratory study of fear: The case of Peter. *Journal of Genetic Psychology, 31,* 308–315.

Jou, J., Shanteau, J., & Harris, R.J. (1996). An information processing view of framing effects: The role of causal schemas in decision making. *Memory and Cognition, 24,* 1–15.

Jung, C. (1917). *Analytic psychology.* New York: Moffat, Yard.

Kagan, J. (1992). Yesterday's premises, tomorrow's promises. *Developmental Psychology, 28,* 990–997.

Kagan, J. (1998). Biology and the child. In W. Damon (Ed.), *Handbook of child psychology* (5th ed., Vol. 3), New York: Wiley.

Kagan, S., & Madsen, M.C. (1972). Experimental analysis of cooperation and competition of Anglo-American and Mexican children. *Developmental Psychology, 6,* 49–59.

Kagitcibasi, C. (1995). Is psychology relevant to global human development issues? Experiences from Turkey. *American Psychologist, 50,* 293–300.

Kahneman, D., & Tversky, A. (1995). Conflict resolution: A cognitive perspective. In K. Arrow, R.H. Mnookin, L. Ross, A. Tversky, & R. Wilson (Eds.), *Barriers to conflict resolution.* New York: Norton.

Kail, R., & Pellegrino, J.W. (1985). *Human intelligence.* New York: W.H. Freeman.

Kaiser, P.K., & Boynton, R.M. (1996). *Human color vision, (2nd Ed).* Washington, DC: Optical Society of America.*

Kales, A., Tan, T.L., Kolar, E.J., Naitoh, P., Preston, T.A., & Malmstrom, E.J. (1970). Sleep patterns following 205 hours of sleep deprivation. *Psychosomatic Medicine, 32,* 189–200.

Kalichman, S. (1996). *Answering your questions about AIDS.* Washington, DC: American Psychological Association.

Kalick, S.M., & Hamilton, T.E. (1986). The matching hypothesis reexamined. *Journal of Personality and Social Psychology, 51*, 673–682.

Kamin, L.J. (1968). Attention-like processes in classical conditioning. In M.R. Jones (Ed.), *Miami Symposium on the prediction of behavior: Aversive stimuli.* Coral Gables, FL: University of Miami Press.*

Kandel, E. R., & Schwartz, J.H. (1982). Molecular biology of learning: Modulation of transmitter release. *Science, 218*, 433–443.

Kanner, A.D., Coyne, J.C., Schaefer, C., & Lazarus, R.S. (1981). Comparisons of two modes of stress measurement: Daily hassles and uplifts versus major life events. *Journal of Behavioral Medicine, 4*, 1–39.

Kaplan, R.M., & Kerner, D.N. (1998). Behavioral medicine. In H.S. Friedman (Ed.), *Encyclopedia of mental health* (Vol. 1). San Diego: Academic Press.

Kapur, S., Craik, F.I.M., Tulving, E., Wilson, A.A., Houle, S., & Brown, G.M. (1994). Neuroanatomical correlates of encoding in episodic memory: Levels of processing effect. *Proceedings of the National Academy of Science of the United States, 91*, 2008–2111.*

Karni, A., Tanne, D., Rubenstein, B.S., Askensay, J.J.M., & Sagi, D. (1994). Overnight improvement in a perceptual skill. *Science, 265*, 679–681.

Katigbak, M.S., Church, A.T., & Akamine, T.X. (1996). Cross-cultural generalizability of personality dimensions. *Journal of Personality and Social Psychology, 70*, 99–114.

Katz, A.N. (1984). Creative styles: Relating tests of creativity to the work patterns of scientists. *Personality and Individual Differences, 5*, 281-292.*

Kavanaugh, D.J., & Wilson, P.H. (1989). Prediction of outcome with a group version of cognitive therapy for depression. *Behaviour Research and Therapy, 27*, 333–347.

Keenan, T., Olson, D., & Marini, Z.A. (1998). Working memory and children's developing understanding of mind. *Australian Journal of Psychology, 50*, 76-82.*

Kelley, C.M., & Jacoby, L.L. (1996). Memory attributions: Remembering, knowing and feeling of knowing. In L.M. Reder (Ed.). *Implicit memory and metacognition.* Mahwah, NJ: Erlbaum.*

Kennedy, P.G.E., & Folk-Seang, J.F. (1986). Studies on the development, antigenic phenotype and function of human glial cells in tissue culture. *Brain, 109*, 1261–1277.

Kephart, W.M. (1967). Some correlates of romantic love. *Journal of Marriage and the Family, 29*, 470–474.

Kiecolt-Glaser, J.K., Dura, J.R., Specher, C.E., Trask, O.J., & Glaser, R. (1991). Spousal caregivers of dementia victims. *Psychosomatic Medicine, 53*, 345–362.

Kihlstrom, J.F., & McConkey, K.M. (1990). William James and hypnosis: A centennial reflection. *Psychological Science, 1*, 174–177.

Kimble, G.A. (1989). Psychology from the standpoint of a generalist. *American Psychologist, 44*, 491–499.

Kimmel, A. (1996). *Ethical issues in behavioral research.* Cambridge, MA: Blackwell.

Kimura, D. (1987). Are men's and women's brains really different? *Canadian Psychology, 28*, 133-47.*

Kimura, D. (1999). *Sex and cognition.* Cambridge, Mass: Bradford.*

King, H.E. (1961). Psychological effects of excitement of the limbic system. In D.E. Sheer (Ed.), *Electrical stimulation of the brain.* Austin: University of Texas Press.

King, L.A., & Pennebaker, J. (1998). *Unpublished manuscript, subjective well-being.* Dept. of Psychology, Southern Methodist U., Dallas, TX.

Kinsey, A.C., Pomeroy, W.B., & Martin, E.E. (1948). *Sexual behavior in the human male.* Philadelphia: W.B. Saunders.

Kirlik, A., & Bisantz, A.M. (1999). Cognition in human-machine systems. In P.A. Hancock (Ed.), *Human performance and ergonomics.* San Diego: Academic Press.

Kirsch, I., & Lynn, S.J. (1998). Dissociation theories of hypnosis. *Psychological Bulletin, 123*, 100–115.

Kirsner, K., Speelman, C., Maybery, M., O'Brien-Malone, A., Anderson, M., & McLeod, C. (Eds.) (1998), *Implicit and explicit memory processes.* Mahwah, NJ: Erlbaum.

Kisilevsky, B. S., Muir, D. W., & Low, J. A. (1992). Maturation of human fetal responses to vibroacoustic stimulation. *Child Development, 63*, 1497-1508.*

Klatsky, R.L. (1984). *Memory and awareness.* New York: W.H. Freeman.

Klein, B. (1997). *Slow dance: A story of love, stroke, and disability.* Toronto: Random House Canada.*

Klein, R.M., & Doane, B.K. (Eds.). (1994). *Psychological concepts and dissociative disorders.* Mahwah, NJ: Erlbaum.*

Knussmann, R., Christiansen, K., & Couwenbergs, C. (1986). Relations between sex hormone level and sexual behavior in men. *Archives of Sexual Behavior, 15*, 429–445.

Kobasa, S., Maddi, S., & Kahn, S. (1982). Hardiness and health: A prospective study. *Journal of Personality and Social Psychology, 42*, 168–177.

Kobasa, S., Maddi, S., Puccetti, M., & Zola, M. (1985). Relative effectiveness of hardiness, exercise, and social support as resources against illness. *Journal of Psychosomatic Research, 29*, 525–533.

Kohlberg, L. (1969). Stage and sequence: The cognitive-developmental approach to socialization. In D. Goslind (Ed.), *Handbook of socialization theory and research.* Chicago: Rand McNally.

Kohlberg, L. (1976). Moral stages and moralization: The cognitive-developmental approach. In T. Lickona (Ed.), *Moral development and behavior.* New York: Holt, Rinehart, & Winston.

Kohlberg, L. (1986). A current statement on some theoretical issues. In S. Modgil & C. Modgil (Eds.), *Lawrence Kohlberg.* Philadelphia: Falmer.

Kohlenberg, R.J., Tsai, M., & Kohlenberg, G.S. (1996). Functional analysis in behavioral therapy. In M. Hersen & P.M. Miller (Eds.), *Progress in behavior modification* (Vol. 30). Pacific Grove: CA: Brooks/Cole.

Kohler, W. (1925). *The mentality of apes.* New York: Harcourt Brace Jovanovich.

Kohn, A., & Kalat, J.W. (1995). Preparing for an important event: Demonstrating the modern view of classical conditioning. In M.E. Ware & D.E. Johnson (Eds.), *Demonstrations and activities in teaching psychology* (Vol. 2). Mahwah, NJ: Erlbaum.

Kohn, P.M., & Macdonald, J.E. (1992). Hassles, anxiety, and negative well-being. *Anxiety, Stress, and Coping, 5*, 151-163.*

Kohut, H. (1977). *Restoration of the self.* New York: International Universities Press.

Kolb, B. (1989). Brain development, plasticity, and behavior. *American Psychologist, 44*, 1203–1212.*

Kolb, B. (1990). Recovery from occipital stroke: A self-report and an inquiry into visual processes. *Canadian Journal of Psychology, 44(2)*, 130-147.*

Kolb, B., & Whishaw, I.Q. (1999). *Human neuropsychology* (4th ed.). New York: W.H. Freeman.*

Kolb, B., Forgie, M., Gibb, R. , Gorny, G., & Rowntree, S. (1998). Age, experience, and the changing brain. *Neuroscience and Biobehavioral Reviews, 22*, 143-159.*

Kolb, L. (1973). *Modern clinical psychiatry* (8th ed.). Philadelphia: W.B. Saunders.

Konner, M. (1991). *Childhood: A multicultural view.* Boston: Little, Brown.

Kopp, C. (1984). *Baby steps.* New York: W.H. Freeman.

Kopta, S.M., Lueger, R.J., Saunders, S.M., & Howard, K.I. (1999). Individual psychotherapy outcome and process research. *Annual Reviews of Psychology.* Palo Alto: Annual Reviews, Inc.

Koss, M., & Boeschen, L. (1998). Rape. In H.S. Friedman (Ed.), *Encyclopedia of mental health* (Vol. 3). San Diego: Academic Press.

Kotlowitz, A. (1991). *There are no children here.* New York: Anchor Books.

Kozma, A., & Stones, M.J. (1980). The measurement of happiness: Development of the Memorial University of Newfoundland Scale of Happiness (MUNSH*). Journal of Gerontology, 35*, 906-912.*

Kozma, A., Stones, M.J., & McNeil, K.V. (1991). *Psychological well-being in later life.* Toronto: Butterworths.*

Krosnick, J.A. (1999). Survey research. *Annual Reviews of Psychology.* Palo Alto, CA: Annual Reviews, Inc.

Kübler-Ross, E. (1974). *Questions and answers on death and dying.* New York: Macmillan.

Kuhn, D. (1998). Afterword to Volume 2. In W. Damon (Ed.), *Handbook of child psychology* (5th ed., Vol. 2). New York: Wiley.

Kuhn, D., Weinstock, M., & Flaton, R. (1994). How well do jurors reason? Competence dimensions of individual variation in a juror reasoning task. *Psychological Science, 5*, 289–296.

Kuiper, N. A., & Martin, R. A. (1998). Laughter and stress in daily life: Relation to positive and negative affect. *Motivation and Emotion, 22(2)*, 133-153.*

Kulik, J.A., Bangert-Drowns, R.L., & Kulik, C.C. (1984). The effectiveness of coaching for aptitude tests. *Psychological Bulletin, 95*, 179–188.

Kulik, J.A., Kulik, C.C., & Bangert-Drowns, R.L. (1985). Effectiveness of computer-based education in elementary schools. *Computers in Human Behavior, 1*, 59–74.

Kutchinsky, B. (1992). The child sexual abuse panic. *Norsisk Sexoligi, 10,* 30–42.

L

Labbe, E.E. (1998). Biofeedback. In H.S. Friedman (Ed.), *Encyclopedia of mental health* (Vol. 1). San Diego: Academic Press.

Labouvie-Vief, G. (1986, August). *Modes of knowing and life-span cognition.* Paper presented at the meeting of the American Psychological Association, Washington, DC.

Labov, W. (1973). The boundaries of words and their meanings. In C.N. Bailey & R.W. Shuy (Eds.), *New ways of analyzing variations in English.* Washington, DC: Georgetown University Press.

Ladouceur, R. (1996). Prevalence of pathological gamblers in Canada and related issues. *Journal of Gambling Studies, 12,* 129-142.*

Ladouceur, R., Boisvert, J.-M., Pépin, M., Loranger, M., & Sylvain, C. (1994). Social costs of pathological gambling. *Journal of Gambling Studies, 10,* 399-409.*

Ladouceur, R., Freeston, M. & Gagnon, F. (1996). Cognitive and behavioral treatment of obsessive-compulsive disorder. *Canadian Family Medicine, 42,* 1169-1178.*

Ladouceur, R., Sylvain, C., Letarte, H., Giroux, I., & Jacques, C. (1998). Cognitive treatment of pathological gamblers. *Behaviour Research and Therapy, 36,* 1111-1120.*

Lahari, A. (1999). On phonology and phonetics. In L.R. Wheeldon (Ed.), *Aspects of language production.* Philadelphia: Psychology Press.

Lamb, C.S., Jackson, L.A., Cassiday, P.B., & Priest, D.J. (1993). Body figure preferences of men and women: A comparison of two generations. *Sex Roles, 28,* 345–358.

Lamb, H.R. (1998). Mental hospitals and deinstitutionalization. In H.S. Friedman (Ed.), *Encyclopedia of mental health* (Vol. 2). San Diego: Academic Press.

Lamb, M. (1998). Nonparental child care. In W. Damon (Ed.), *Handbook of child psychology* (5th ed., Vol. 4). New York: Wiley.

Lamb, M.E., Hwang, C.P., Ketterlinus, R.D., & Fracasso, M.P. (1999). Parent-child relationships: Development in the context of the family. In M.H. Bornstein & M.E. Lamb (Eds.), *Developmental psychology: An advanced textbook* (4th ed.). Mahwah, NJ: Erlbaum.

Lambert, W.E., & Anisfeld, E. (1969). A note on the relationship of bilingualism and intelligence. *Canadian Journal of Behavioural Science, 1,* 123-128.*

Lambert, W.E., & Tucker, R. (1972). *Bilingual education of children: The St. Lambert study.* Rowley, MA: Newburg House.*

Lambert, W.E., Genesee, F., Holobow, N., & Chartrand, L. (1993). Bilingual education for majority English-speaking children. *European Journal of Psychology of Education, 8,* 3–22.*

Lane, H. (1976). *The wild boy of Aveyron.* Cambridge, MA: Harvard University Press.

Lange, C.G. (1922). *The emotions.* Baltimore: Williams & Wilkins.

Langer, E. (1989). *Mindfulness.* Reading, MA: Addison-Wesley.

Langer, E. (1997). *The power of mindful learning.* Reading, MA: Addison-Wesley.

Langer, L.L. (1991). *Holocaust testimonies: The ruins of memory.* New Haven: Yale University Press.

Langs, R. (1978). *Technique in transition.* New York: Jason Aronson.

Lashley, K. (1950). In search of the engram. In *Symposium of the Society for Experimental Biology* (Vol. 4). New York: Cambridge University Press.

Latané, B. (1981). The psychology of social impact. *American Psychologist, 36,* 343–356.

Latané, B. (1996). Strength from weakness: The fate of opinion minorities in spatially distributed groups. In E.H. Witte & J.H. Davis (Eds.), *Understanding group behavior* (Vol. 1). Mahwah, NJ: Erlbaum.

Lautenbacher, S., & Rollman, G. B. (1999). Hypochondriasis, somatoform pain disorder, and related conditions. In: A. R. Block, E. F. Kremer, & E. Fernandez (Eds.), *Handbook of pain syndromes: Biopsychosocial perspectives.* Mahwah, NJ: Erlbaum.*

Lazarus, A.A. (1996). A multimodal behavior therapist's perspective on the truth. In G. Corey (Ed.), *Case approach to counseling and psychotherapy* (4th ed.). Pacific Grove, CA: Brooks/Cole.

Lazarus, A.A., Beutler, L.E., & Norcross, J.C. (1992). The future of technical eclecticism. *Psychotherapy, 29,* 11–20.

Lazarus, R.S. (1991). On the primacy of cognition. *American Psychologist, 39,* 124–129.

Lazarus, R.S. (1993). Coping theory and research: Past, present, and future. *Psychosomatic Medicine, 55,* 234–247.

Leadbeater, B.J., Bishop, S., & Raver, C. (1996). Quality of mother-toddler interactions, maternal depressive symptoms and behavior problems in preschoolers of adolescent mothers. *Developmental Psychology, 32,* 280 288.*

Leahey, T.H. (1997). *A history of psychology.* Upper Saddle River, NJ: Prentice Hall.

Leary, M.R., Nezlek, J.B., Downs, D., Radford-Davenport, J., Martin, J., & McMullen, A. (1994). Self-presentation in everyday interactions. *Journal of Personality and Social Psychology, 67,* 664–673.

LeBoeuf, B.J., & Peterson, R.S. (1969). Social status and mating activity in elephant seals. *Science, 163,* 91–93.

Lebow, J.L., & Gurman, A.S. (1995). Research assessing couple and family therapy. *Annual Review of Psychology, 46,* Palo Alto, CA: Annual Reviews.

Lee, I., Hsieh, C., & Paffenbarger, O. (1995). Exercise intensity and longevity in men. *Journal of the American Medical Association, 273,* 1179–1184.

Lefcourt, H.M., & Thomas, S. (1998). Humor and stress revisited. In W. Ruch (Ed.), *The sense of humor.* Berlin: Mouton de Gruyter.*

Lefebvre, L., & Giraldeau, L.-A. (1996). Is social learning an adaptive specialization? In C.M. Heyes & B.G. Galef, Jr. (Eds.), *Social learning in animals: The roots of culture.* San Diego: Academic Press.*

Leiter, M. (1991). The dream denied: Professional burnout and the constraints of human service organizations. *Canadian Psychology, 32(4),* 547-558.*

Leiter, M.P., & Maslach, C. (1998). Burnout. In H.S. Friedman (Ed.), *Encyclopedia of mental health* (Vol. 1). San Diego: Academic Press.*

Leith, L.M. (1998). Exercise and mental health. In H.S. Friedman (Ed.), *Encyclopedia of mental health* (Vol. 2). San Diego: Academic Press.*

Lemme, B.H. (1999). *Development in adulthood* (2nd ed.). Boston: Allyn & Bacon.

Lenneberg, E. (1967). *The biological foundations of language.* New York: Wiley.

Lenneberg, E.H., Rebelsky, F.G., & Nichols, I.A. (1965). The vocalization of infants born to deaf and hearing parents. *Human Development, 8,* 23–37.

Leon, G.R. (1990). *Case histories of psychopathology* (4th ed.). Boston: Allyn & Bacon.

Lepper, M., Greene, D., & Nisbett, R.E. (1973). Undermining children's intrinsic interest with extrinsic rewards. *Journal of Personality and Social Psychology, 28,* 129–137.

Lerner, R.M. (1989). Theories of human development: Contemporary perspectives. In W. Damon (Ed.), *Handbook of child psychology* (5th ed., Vol. 1), New York: Wiley.

Levant, R.F. (1995). *Masculinity Reconstructed: Changing rules of manhood.* New York: Dutton.

Levant, R.F., & Brooks, G.R. (1997). *Men and sex: New psychological perspectives.* New York: Wiley.

LeVay, S. (1991). A difference in the hypothalamic structure between heterosexual and homosexual men. *Science, 253,* 1034–1037.

Leventhal, H., & Tomarken, A.J. (1986). Emotion: Today's problems. *Annual Review of Psychology, 37,* 565–610.

Levine, B., Cabeza, R., Black, S., Sinden, M., Toth, J.B., Tulving, E., & Stuss, D.T. (1997). Functional and structural neuroimaging correlates of selective retrograde amnesia: A case study with MRI and PET. *Brain and Cognition, 35,* 372-376.*

Levine, J.M., & Moreland, R.L. (1998). Small groups. In D.T. Gilbert, S.T. Fiske, & G. Lindzey (Eds.), *Handbook of social psychology* (4th ed., Vol. 2). New York: McGraw-Hill.

Levinson, D. (1978). *The seasons of a man's life.* New York: Knopf.

Levy, J. (1974). Psychobiological implications of bilateral asymmetry. In S. Dimond & J.B. Beaumont (Eds.), *Hemisphere functions in the human brain.* London: Paul Elek.

Levy, L. (1979). Handwriting and hiring. *Dun's Review, 113,* 72–79.

Levy, S.M., Herberman, R.B., Lee, J., Whiteside, T., Kirckwood, J., & McFreeley, S. (1990). Estrogen receptor concentration and social factors as predictors of natural killer cell activity in early-stage breast cancer patients. *Natural Immunity and Cell Growth Regulation, 9,* 313–324.

Levy, T.M. (Ed.) (1999). *Handbook of attachment interventions.* San Diego: Academic Press.

Lewin, R. (1988). Brain graft puzzles. *Science, 240,* 879.

Lewinsohn, P. (1987). The Coping with Depression course. In R.F. Munoz (Ed.), *Depression prevention.* New York: Hemisphere.

Lewinsohn, P.M., Antonuccio, D.O., Steinmetz, J., & Teri, L. (1984). *The coping with depression course: A psychoeducational intervention for unipolar depression.* Eugene, OR: Castalia.

Lewis, J.R. (1999). *Cults in America.* New York: Abc-Clio.

Lewis, M. (1997). *Altering fate.* New York: Guilford.

Lewis, R. (1999). *Human genetics* (3rd ed.). New York: McGraw-Hill.

Lipsey, M.W., & Wilson, D.B. (1993). The efficacy of psychological, educational, and behavioral treatment: Confirmation from meta-analysis. *American Psychologist, 48,* 1181–1209.

Lister, P. (1992, July). A skeptic's guide to psychics. *Redbook,* pp. 103–105, 112–113.

Locke, J.L. (1993). *The child's path to spoken language.* Cambridge, MA: Harvard University Press.

Locke, J.L. (1999). Towards a biological science of language development. In M. Barrett (Ed.), *The development of language.* Philadelphia: Psychology Press.

Loehr, J. (1989, May). (Personal Communication). United States Tennis Association Training Camp, Saddlebrook, FL.

Loftus, E.F. (1975). Spreading activation within semantic categories. *Journal of Experimental Psychology, 104,* 234–240.

Loftus, E.F. (1980). *Memory.* Reading, MA: Addison-Wesley.

Loftus, E.F. (1993a). Psychologists in the eyewitness world. *American Psychologist, 48,* 550–552.

Loftus, E.F. (1993b). The reality of repressed memories. *American Psychologist, 48,* 518–537.

Logue, A.W. (1995). *Self-control.* Upper Saddle River, NJ: Prentice Hall.

Longo, D.A., Lent, R.W., & Brown, S.D. (1992). Social cognitive variables in the prediction of client motivation and attribution. *Journal of Counseling Psychology, 39,* 447–452.

Lorenz, K.Z. (1965). *Evolution and modification of behavior.* Chicago: University of Chicago Press.

Ludolph, P. (1982, August). *A reanalysis of the literature on multiple personality.* Paper presented at the meeting of the American Psychological Association, Washington, DC.

Luiselli, J.K., & Cameron, M.J. (1998). *Antecedent control: Approaches to behavioral support.* Baltimore: Paul H. Brookes.

Luszcz, M.A., & Bryan, J. (1999). Toward understanding age-related memory loss in late adulthood. *Gerontology, 45,* 2–9.

Lutz, D.J., & Sternberg, R.J. (1999). Cognitive development. In M.H. Bornstein & M.E. Lamb (Eds.), *Developmental psychology: An advanced textbook* (4th ed.). Mahwah, NJ: Erlbaum.

Lycan, W. (Ed.). (1999). *Mind and cognition.* Malden, MA: Blackwell.

Lykken, D.T. (1987). The probity of the polygraph. In S.M. Kassin & L.S. Wrightsman (Eds.), *The psychology of evidence and trial procedures.* Newbury Park, CA: Sage.

Lynch, G. (1990, June). *The many shapes of memory and the several forms of synaptic plasticity.* Paper presented at the meeting of the American Psychological Society, Dallas.

Lynn, R. (1996). Racial and ethnic differences in intelligence in the U.S. on the Differential Ability Scale. *Personality and Individual Differences, 20,* 271–273.

Lynn, S.J., Rhue, J.W., & Spanos, N.P. (1994). Hypnosis. In *Encyclopedia of human behavior.* New York: Academic Press.

Maas, J. (1998). *Power sleep.* New York: Villard.

Maccoby, E.E., & Jacklin, C.N. (1974). *The psychology of sex differences.* Palo Alto, CA: Stanford University Press.

MacLeod, C.M. (1992). The Stroop task: The "gold standard" of attentional measures. *Journal of Experimental Psychology: General, 121,* 12-14.*

MacWhinney, B. (Ed.) (1999). *The emergence of language.* Mahwah, NJ: Erlbaum.

Maddi, S. (1996). *Personality theories* (6th ed.). Pacific Grove, CA: Brooks/Cole.

Maddi, S. (1998). Hardiness. In H.S. Friedman (Ed.), *Encyclopedia of mental health* (Vol. 3). San Diego: Academic Press.

Mader, S. (1999). *Biology* (6th ed.). New York: McGraw-Hill.

Mader, S.S. (2000). *Inquiry into life* (9th ed.). New York: McGraw-Hill.

Mager, R.F. (1972). *Goals analysis.* Belmont, CA: Fearon.

Mahoney, G.J. (1995, March). *The maternal behavior rating scale.* Paper presented at the meeting of the Society for Research in Child Development, Indianapolis.

Maier, N.R.F. (1931). Reasoning in humans. *Journal of Comparative Psychology, 12,* 181–194.

Malinowski, B. (1927). *Sex and repression in savage society.* New York: Humanities Press.

Mandler, G. (1980). Recognizing: The judgment of previous occurrence. *Psychological Review, 87,* 252–271.

Mandler, G. (1996). The situation of psychology: Landmarks and choice points. *American Journal of Psychology, 109,* 1–35.

Mandler, J.M. (1998). Representation. In W. Damon (Ed.), *Handbook of child psychology* (5th ed., Vol. 2), New York: Wiley.

Manning, A. (1989). The genetic basis of aggression. In J. Groebel & R.A. Hinde (Eds.), *Aggression and war: Their biological and social bases.* New York: Cambridge University Press.

Maratsos, M. (1999). Some aspects of innateness and complexity in grammar acquisition. In M. Barrett (Ed.), *The development of language.* Philadelphia: Psychology Press.

Marcia, J.E. (1999). Representational thought in ego identity, psychotherapy, and psychosocial developmental theory. In I.E. Sigel (Ed.), *Development of mental representation.* Mahwah, NJ: Erlbaum.*

Maris, R.W. (1998). Suicide. In H.S. Friedman (Ed.), *Encyclopedia of mental health* (Vol. 3). San Diego: Academic Press.

Marr, D. (1982). *Vision.* New York: W.H. Freeman.

Marshall, G.N., Wortman, C.B., Vickers, R.R., Kusulas, J.W., & Hervig, L.K. (1994). The five-factor model of personality as a framework for personality-health research. *Journal of Personality and Social Psychology, 67,* 278–286.

Martin, G., & Pear, J. (1999). *Behavior modification* (6th ed.). Upper Saddle River, NJ: Prentice-Hall.*

Martin, R. A. (1996). Humour as therapeutic play: Stress-moderating effects of humor. *Journal of Leisurability, 23(4),* 8-15.*

Martin, R. A., Kuiper, N. A., Olinger, L. J., & Dance, K. A. (1993). Humor, coping with stress, self-concept, and psychological well-being. *Humor: International Journal of Humor Research, 6,* 89-104.*

Martins, Y., & Pliner, P. (1999). Restrained eating among vegetarians: Does a vegetarian eating style mask concerns about weight? *Appetite, 32(1),* 145-154.*

Maslow, A. (1971). *The farther reaches of human nature.* New York: Viking.

Maslow, A.H. (1954). *Motivation and personality.* New York: Harper & Row.

Masson, M. E. J., & MacLeod, C. M. (1997). Episodic enhancement of processing fluency. In D. L. Medin (Ed.), *The psychology of learning and motivation (Vol. 37).* San Diego: Academic Press.*

Masters, W.H., & Johnson, V.E. (1966). *Human sexual response.* Boston: Little, Brown.

Matas, L., Arend, R.A., & Sroufe, L.A. (1978). Continuity in adaptation: Quality of attachment and later competence. *Child Development, 49,* 547–556.

Matlin, M. (1993). *The psychology of women* (2nd ed.). Fort Worth: Harcourt Brace.

Matlin, M.W. (1998). *Cognition* (4th ed.). Fort Worth: Harcourt Brace.

Matsumoto, D. (1996). *Culture and psychology.* Pacific Grove, CA: Brooks/Cole.

Matthews, G., & Dreary, I.J. (1998). *Personality traits.* Cambridge, Eng: Cambridge U. Press.

Maultsby, M.C., & Wirga, M. (1998). Behavior therapy. In H.S. Friedman (Ed.), *Encyclopedia of mental health* (Vol. 1). San Diego: Academic Press.

Maurer, D., & Maurer, C. (1988). *The world of the newborn.* New York: Basic Books.*

Mawhinney, T.A. (1983). A picture vocabulary test for the Eastern James Bay Cree. In S.H. Irvine & J.W. Berry (Eds.), *Human assessment and cultural factors.* New York: Plenum.*

Mayer, R. (1999). Problem solving. In M.A. Runco & S. Pritzker (Eds.), *Encyclopedia of psychology.* San Diego: Academic Press.

McAdams, D.P. (1993). *The stories we live by.* New York: Morrow.

McCarley, R.W. (1989). The biology of dreaming sleep. In M.H. Drager, T. Roth, & W.C. Dement (Eds.), *Principles and practices of sleep medicine.* Ft. Worth, TX: Harcourt Brace.

McClelland, D.C. (1955). Some social consequences of achievement motivation. In M.R. Jones (Ed.), *Nebraska Symposium of Motivation.* Lincoln: University of Nebraska Press.

McClelland, D.C. (1978). Managing motivation to expand human freedom. *American Psychologist, 33,* 201–210.

McClelland, D.C., Atkinson, J.W., Clark, R., & Lowell, E.L. (1953). *The achievement motive.* New York: Appleton-Century-Crofts.

McConaghy, N. (1993). *Sexual behavior: Problems and management.* New York: Plenum Press.

McCormick, C.M., & Witelson, S.F. (1994). Functional cerebral asymmetry and sexual orientation in men and women. *Behavioral Neuroscience, 108(3)*, 525-31.*

McCormick, C.M., Witelson, S.F., & Kingstone, E. (1990). Left-handedness in homosexual men and women: neuroendocrine implications. *Psychoneuroendocrinology, 15(1)*, 69-76.*

McCreary, D.R. (1997). Media influences. In S.W. Sadava & D.R. McCreary (Eds.), *Applied social psychology.* Upper Saddle River, NJ: Prentice Hall.*

McDonnell, P.M., Corkum, V.L., & Wilson, D.L. (1989). Patterns of movement in the first 6 months of life: New directions. *Canadian Journal of Psychology, 43(2)*, 320-339.*

McDougall, W. (1908). *Social psychology.* New York: G. Putnam & Sons.

McFarlane, T., Polivy, J., & Herman, C.P. (1998). Dieting. In H.S. Friedman (Ed.), *Encyclopedia of mental health* (Vol. 1). San Diego: Academic Press.*

McFarlane, T., Polivy, J., & McCabe, R. (1999). Help, not harm: Psychological foundation for a nondieting approach toward health. *Journal of Social Issues, 55*, 261-276.*

McGregor, I., Newby-Clark, I. R., & Zanna, M. P. (1999). Remembering" dissonance: Simultaneous accessibility of inconsistent cognitive elements moderates epistemic discomfort. In E. Harmon-Jones & J. Mills (Eds.), *Cognitive dissonance: Progress on a pivotal theory in social psychology.* Washington, DC: American Psychological Association.*

McIver, T. (1988). Backward masking and other backward thoughts about music. *Skeptical Inquirer, 13*, 50-63.

McKim, M.K., Cramer, K.M., Stuart, B., & O'Connor, D.H. (1999). Infant care decisions and attachment security: The Canadian *Transition to Child Care Study. Canadian Journal of Behavioral Science, 31(2)*, 92-106.*

McKinlay, J.B. (1999, March). *Erectile dysfunction: The most overlooked biobehavioral marker of disease.* Paper presented at the meeting of the American Psychosomatic Association, Vancouver.

McKinlay, S.M., & McKinlay, J.B. (1984). *Health status and health care utilization by menopausal women.* Unpublished manuscript, Cambridge Research Center, American Institutes for Research, Cambridge, MA.

McKnight, C.C., Crosshite, F.J., Dossey, J.A., Kifer, E., Swafford, J.O., Travers, K.J., & Cooney, T.J. (1987). *The underachieving curriculum.* Champaign, IL: Stipes.

McLoyd, V.C. (1998). Children in poverty. In W. Damon (Ed.), *Handbook of child psychology* (5th ed., Vol. 4). New York: Wiley.

McLoyd, V.C. (1999). Cultural influences in a multicultural society. In A.S. Masten (Ed.), *Cultural processes in child development.* Mahwah, NJ: Erlbaum.

McMillan, J.H. (2000). *Educational research* (3rd ed.). New York: Pearson.

McMurray, G.A. (1950). Experimental study of a case of insensitivity to pain. *Archives of Neurological Psychiatry, 64*, 650.*

McNally, D. (1990). *Even eagles need a push.* New York: Dell.

McNally, R.J. (1998). Panic attacks. In H.S. Friedman (Ed.), *Encyclopedia of mental health* (Vol. 3). San Diego: Academic Press.

McNeil, E.B. (1967). *The quiet furies.* Englewood Cliffs, NJ: Prentice Hall.

McShane, D.A., & Plas, J.M. (1984). The cognitive functioning of American Indian school children: Moving from the WISC to the WISC-R. *School Psychology Review, 13*, 61-73.

Meador, B.D., & Rogers, C.R. (1979). Person-centered therapy. In R.J. Corsini, *Current psychotherapies* (2nd ed.). Itasca, IL: Peacock.

Meehl, P. (1962). Schizotonia, schizotypy, schizophrenia. *American Psychologist, 17*, 827-838.

Meehl, P.E. (1986). Diagnostic taxa as open concepts. In T. Millon & G.I. Klerman (Eds.), *Contemporary directions in psychopathology.* New York: Guilford.

Meichenbaum, D. (1977). *Cognitive-behavior modification: An integrative approach.* New York: Plenum.*

Meichenbaum, D. (1991). Evolution of cognitive behavior therapy: Origins, tenets and clinical examples. In J. Zeig (Ed.), *The evolution of psychotherapy, II.* New York: Brunner/Mazel.*

Meichenbaum, D., & Fong, G.T. (1993). How individuals control their own minds: A constructive narrative perspective. In D. Wagner & J. Pennebaker (Eds.), *Handbook of mental control.* Upper Saddle River, NJ: Prentice Hall.*

Melzack, R. (1973). *The puzzle of pain.* New York: Basic Books.*

Melzack, R. (1989). Phantom limbs, the self, and the brain. *Canadian Psychology, 30(1)*, 1-16.*

Melzack, R. (1993). Pain: Past, present and future. *Canadian Journal of Experimental Psychology, 47(4)*, 615-629.*

Melzack, R., & Wall, P.D. (1965). Pain mechanisms: A new theory. *Science, 150*, 971-979.*

Melzack, R., & Wall, P.D. (1988) *The challenge of pain (2nd Ed.).* New York: Basic Books.*

Mercer, J.R., & Lewis, J.F. (1978). *System of multicultural pluralistic assessment.* New York: Psychological Corporation.

Merikle, P. M., & Daneman, M. (1996). Memory for unconsciously perceived events: Evidence from anesthetized patients. *Consciousness and Cognition, 5*, 525-541.*

Merikle, P. M., & Daneman, M. (1998). Psychological investigations of unconscious perception. *Journal of Consciousness Studies, 5*, 5-18.*

Mervis, J. (1996, July). NIMH data point way to effective treatment. *APA Monitor*, pp. 1, 13.

Messer, W.S., & Griggs, R.A. (1989). Student belief and involvement in the paranormal and performance in introductory psychology. *Teaching of Psychology, 16*, 187-191.

Messinger, J.C. (1971). Sex and repression in an Irish folk community. In D.S. Marshall & R.C. Suggs (Eds.), *Human sexual behavior.* New York: Basic Books.

Metalsky, G.I., Joiner, T.E., Hardin, T.S., & Abramson, L.Y. (1993). Depressive reactions to failure in a naturalistic setting. *Journal of Abnormal Psychology, 102*, 101-109.

Metcalfe, J., & Mischel, W. (1999). A hot/cool system analysis of delay of gratification: Dynamics of will power. *Psychological Review, 106*, 3-19.

Meyer, R.G. (1998). Personality disorders. In H.S. Friedman (Ed.), *Encyclopedia of mental health* (Vol. 2). San Diego: Academic Press.

Meyer, R.G., & Osborne, Y.V.H. (1982). *Case studies in abnormal behavior.* Boston: Allyn & Bacon.

Meyer, R.G., Wolverton, D., & Deitsch, S.E. (1998). Antisocial personality disorder. In H.S. Friedman (Ed.), *Encyclopedia of mental health* (Vol. 2). San Diego: Academic Press.

Meyers, B.S., Alexopoulos, G.S., Kukuma, T., Tirumalasetti, F., Gabriele, M., Alpert, S., Bowden, C., & Meltzer, H.Y. (1999). Depression dopamine beta-hydroxylase activity in unipolar geriatric delusional depression. *Biological Psychiatry, 45*, 448-456.

Michael, R.T., Gagnon, J.H., Laumann, E.O., & Kolata, G. (1994). *Sex in America.* Boston, Little, Brown.

Michael, W. (1999). Guilford's view. In M.A. Runco & S. Pritzker (Eds.), *Encyclopedia of creativity.* San Diego: Academic Press.

Michaels, J.W., Bloomel, J.M., Brocato, R.M., Linkous, R.A., & Rowe, J.S. (1982). Social facilitation and inhibition in a natural setting. *Replications in Social Psychology, 2*, 21-24.

Milgram, S. (1963). Behavioral study of obedience. *Journal of Abnormal and Social Psychology, 67*, 171-178.

Milgram, S. (1965). Some conditions of obedience and disobedience to authority. *Human Relations, 18*, 56-76.

Milgram, S. (1974). *Obedience to authority.* New York: Harper & Row.

Milgram, S., Liberty, H.J., Toledo, R., & Wackenhut, J. (1986). Response to intrusion in waiting lines. *Journal of Personality and Social Psychology, 51*, 683-689.

Miller, G.A. (1956). The magical number seven, plus or minus two: Some limits on our capacity for information processing. *Psychological Review, 48*, 337-442.

Miller, L. T., & Vernon, P. A. (1996). Intelligence, reaction time, and working memory in 4- to 6-year-old children. *Intelligence, 22*, 155-190.*

Miller, N.E. (1941). The frustration-aggression hypothesis. *Psychological Review, 48*, 337-442.

Miller, N.E. (1959). Liberalization of basic S-R concepts: Extension to conflict behavior, motivation, and social learning. In S. Koch (Ed.), *Psychology: A study of science.* New York: McGraw-Hill.

Miller, N.E. (1969). Learning of visceral glandular responses. *Science, 163*, 434-445.

Miller, N.E. (1985). The value of behavioral research on animals. *American Psychologist, 40*, 432-440.

Miller, S.B. (1993). Cardiovascular reactivity in anger-defensive individuals: The influence of task demands. *Psychosomatic Medicine, 55(1)*, 79-85.*

Miller, S.B., Dolgoy L., Friese M., & Sita, A. (1996). Dimensions of hostility and cardiovascular response to interpersonal stress. *Journal of Psychosomatic Research, 41(1)*, 81-95.*

Miller-Jones, D. (1989). Culture and testing. *American Psychologist, 44*, 360–366.

Millis, R.M. (1998). Smoking. In H.S. Friedman (Ed.), *Encyclopedia of mental health* (Vol. 3). San Diego: Academic Press.

Mills, J.A. (1998). *Control: A history of behavioral psychology*. New York: New York University Press.*

Milner, A. D., & Goodale, M. A. (1995). *The visual brain in action*. Oxford: Oxford University Press.*

Milner, B. , Corkin, S., & Teuber, H.L. (1968). Further analysis of the hippocampal amnesic syndrome: 14-year follow-up study of H.M. *Neuropsychologia, 6*, 215-234.*

Milner, P.M. (1991). Brain-stimulation reward: A review. *Canadian Journal of Psychology, 45(1)*, 1-36.*

Mindell, J.A. (1996). Children and sleep. In M.R. Pressman & W.C. Orr (eds.), *Understanding sleep*. Washington, DC: American Psychological Association.

Mineka, S., & Nugent, K. (1995). Mood-congruent memory biases in anxiety and depression. In D.L. Schacter, J.T. Coyle, G.D. Fischbach, M.M. Mesulam, & L.E. Sullivan (Eds.), *Memory distortion: How minds, brains, and societies reconstruct the past*. Cambridge, MA: Harvard University Press.

Minnes, P.M. (in press). Mental retardation: The impact upon the family. In J.A. Burack, R.M. Hodapp, &. E. Zigler (Eds.), *Handbook of mental retardation and development*. New York: Cambridge University Press.*

Mischel, W. (1968). *Personality and assessment.* New York: Wiley.

Mischel, W. (1973). Toward a cognitive social learning theory reformulation of personality. *Psychological Review, 80*, 252–283

Mischel, W. (1995, August). *Cognitive-affective theory of person-environment psychology*. Paper presented at the meeting of the American Psychological Association, New York City.

Mishkin, M., & Appenzellar, T. (1987). The anatomy of memory. *Scientific American, 256*, 80–89.

Mitchell, D.E. (1989). Normal and abnormal development visual development in kittens: Insights into the mechanisms that underlie visual development in humans. *Canadian Journal of Psychology, 43(2)*, 141-164.*

Mitterer, J. (1982). There are at least two kinds of poor reader: Whole-word poor readers and recoding poor readers. *Canadian Journal of Psychology, 36*, 445-461.*

Mitterer, J., & Begg, I. (1979). Can meaning be extracted from meaningless stimuli? *Canadian Journal of Psychology, 33*, 193-198.*

Moldoveanu, M.C., & Langer, E. (1999). Mindfulness. In M.A. Runco & S. Pritzker (Eds.), *Encyclopedia of creativity*. San Diego: Academic Press.

Money, J. (1986). *Lovemaps: Clinical concepts of sexual/erotic health and pathology, paraphilia, and gender transposition in childhood, adolescence, and maturity*. New York: Irvington.

Monk, T.H. (1993). Shiftwork. In M.A. Carskadon (Ed.), *Encyclopedia of sleep and dreaming*. New York: Macmillan.

Moore, B.R. (1996). The evolution of imitative behavior. In C.M. Heyes & B.G. Galef, Jr. (Eds.), *Social learning in animals: The roots of culture*. San Diego: Academic Press.*

Moore, T.E. (1995). Subliminal self-help auditory tapes: An empirical test of perceptual consequences. *Canadian Journal of Behavioural Science, 27*, 9–20.*

Moore-Ede, M.C., Sulzman, F.M., & Fuller, C.A. (1982). *The clocks that time us*. Cambridge, MA: Harvard University Press.

Morgan, T., & Cummings, A.L. (1999). Change experienced during group therapy of female survivors of childhood sexual abuse. *Journal of Consulting and Clinical Psychology, 67*, 28–36.*

Moscovici, S. (1985). Social influence and conformity. In G. Lindzey & E. Aronson (Eds.), *Handbook of social psychology* (3rd ed., Vol. 2). New York: Random House.

Moses, J., Steptoe, A., Mathews, A., & Edwards, S. (1989). The effects of exercise training on mental well-being in a normal population: A controlled trial. *Journal of Psychosomatic Research, 33*, 47–61.

Mountcastle, V.B. (1986). *The parietal visual system and optic flow*. Paper presented at the meeting of the American Psychological Association, Washington, DC.

Mountcastle, V.B. (1998). *Perceptual neuroscience*. Cambridge, MA: Harvard University Press.

Muir, D.W., Clifton, R.K., & Clarkson, M.C. (1989). The development of a human auditory localization response: A U-shaped function. *Canadian Journal of Psychology, 43(2)*, 199-216.*

Mumford, M., & Porter, P.P. (1999). Analogies. In M.A. Runco & S. Pritzker (Eds.), *Encyclopedia of creativity*. San Diego: Academic Press.

Munoz, R.F. (1998). Depression—applied aspects. In H.S. Friedman (Ed.), *Encyclopedia of mental health* (Vol. 1). San Diego: Academic Press.

Murdock, B.B. (1999). The buffer 30 years later: Working memory in a theory of distributed associative model (TODAM). In C. Izawa (Ed.), *On human memory*. Mahwah, NJ: Erlbaum.*

Murray, H.A. (1938). *Explorations in personality*. Cambridge, MA: Harvard University Press.

Murstein, B.I., & Mathes, S. (1996). Projection on projective techniques 5 pathology: The problem that is not being addressed. *Journal of Personality Assessment, 66*, 337–351.

Murtha, S., Fitch, T., DelCarpio, R., Bergman, H., Chertkow, H. (1998). Does atrophy of the temporal lobes predict decline to dementia. *Journal of Canadian Congress of Neurological Sciences*, Supple 1, S28.*

Mussell, M.P., & Mitchell, J.E. (1998). Anorexia nervosa and bulimia nervosa. In H.S. Friedman (Ed.), *Encyclopedia of mental health* (Vol. 1). San Diego: Academic Press.

Nadien, M.B., & Denmark, F.L. (1999). *Females and autonomy: A life-span perspective*. Boston: Allyn & Bacon.

Nakamizo, S., Ono, H., & Ujuke, H. (1999). Subjective staircase: A multiple wallpaper illusion. *Perception & Psychophysics, 61*, 13–22.

Narvaez, D., Getz, I., Rest, J.R., & Thoma, S.J. (1999). Individual moral judgment and cultural ideologies. *Developmental Psychology, 3*, 478–488.

Nash, J.M. (1997, February 3). Fertile minds. *Time*, pp. 50–54.

Nathan, P.E. (1994). DSM-IV. *Journal of Clinical Psychology, 50*, 103–109.

Nathan, P.E., & Langenbucher, J.W. (1999). Psychopathology: Description and classification. *Annual Reviews of Psychology*. Palo Alto: Annual Reviews, Inc.

National Advisory Council on Economic Opportunity. (1980). *Critical choices for the 80s.* Washington, DC: U.S. Government Printing Office.

National Association for the Education of Young Children. (1996). NAEYC position statement: Responding to linguistic and cultural diversity. *Young Children, 51*, 4–12.

National Center for Health Statistics. (1989, June). *Statistics on marriage and divorce.* Washington, DC: U.S. Government Printing Office.

National Commission on Sleep Disorders Research. (1993, January). *Report of the National Commission on Sleep Disorders Research*. Report submitted to the United States Congress and to the Secretary of the U.S. Department of Health and Human Services.

Neergaard, L. (1998, August 21). Scientists get insight on memory by watching brain activity. *Philadelphia Inquirer*, p. A9.

Neisser, U., Boodoo, G., Bouchard, T.J., Boykin, A.W., Brody, N., Ceci, S.J., Halpern, D.F., Loehlin, J.C., Perloff, R., Sternberg, R.J., & Urbina, S. (1996). Intelligence: Knowns & unknowns. *American Psychologist, 51*, 77–101.

Nelson, T.O. (1996). Consciousness and metacognition. *American Psychologist, 51*, 102–116.

Néron, S., Lacroix, D., & Chaput, Y. (1995). Group vs individual cognitive behaviour therapy in panic disorder: An open clinical trial with a six month follow-up. *Canadian Journal of Behavioural Science. 27(4)*, 379-392.*

Neufeldt, A.H. (1989). Applying psychology: Some real-world possibilties for scientists and practitioners. *Canadian Psychology, 30(4)*, 681-691.*

Neugarten, B.L. (1980). Must everything be a midlife crisis? *Annual Editions Human Development 80/81*. Guilford, CT: Dushkin.

Nevo, B. (1986). *Scientific aspects of graphology*. Springfield, IL: Charles C Thomas.

NICHD Early Child Care Research Network. (1997). Infant child care and attachment security. *Child Development, 68*, 860–879.

NICHD Early Child Care Research Network. (in press). Relations between family predictors and child outcomes: Are they weaker for children in child care? *Developmental Psychology*.

Nicholls, J.G. (1979). Development of perception of own attainment and causal attribution for success and failure in reading. *Journal of Educational Psychology, 71*, 94–99.

Nicholls, J.G., Cobb, P., Wood, T., Yackel, E., & Patashnick, M. (1990). Assessing students' theories of success in mathematics: Individual and classroom differences. *Journal for Research in Mathematics Education, 21,* 109–122.

Nickerson, R.S. (1999). Engineering psychology. In P.A. Hancock (Ed.), *Human performance and ergonomics.* San Diego: Academic Press.

Niehoff, D. (1999). *The biology of violence.* New York: The Free Press.

Nisbett, R.E., & Ross, L. (1980). *Human inference.* Upper Saddle River, NJ: Prentice Hall.

Noels, K. A., & Clément, R. (1998). Language in education: Bridging educational policy and social psychological research. In J. Edwards (Ed.), *Language in Canada.* Cambridge: Cambridge University Press.*

Noels, K.A., & Clément, R. (1996). Communicating across cultures: Social determinants and acculturative consequences. *Canadian Journal of Behavioural Science, 28(3),* 214-228.*

Noels, K.A., Pon, G., & Clément, R. (1996). Language, identity, and adjustment: The role of linguistic self-confidence in the acculturation process. *Journal of Language and Social Psychology, 15(3),* 246-264.*

Norcross, J.C., & Kobayashi, M. (1999). Treating anger in psychotherapy: Introduction and cases. *Journal of Clinical Psychology in Session, 55,* 275–282.

Norcross, J.C., & Newman, C.F. (1992). Psychotherapy integration: Setting the context. In J.C. Norcross & M.R. Gottfried (Eds.), *Handbook of psychotherapy integration.* New York: Basic Books.

Norcross, J.C., & Prochaska, J.O. (1983). Clinicians' theoretical orientations. *Professional Psychology: Research and Practice, 14,* 197–208.

Norcross, J.C., & Prochaska, J.O. (1988). A study of eclectic (and integrative) views revisited. *Professional Psychology: Research and Practice, 19,* 170–174.

Norem, J.K., & Cantor, N. (1986). Anticipatory and post-hoc cushioning strategies: Optimism and defensive pessimism in risk "situations." *Cognitive Therapy Research, 10,* 347–362.

Notarius, C.I. (1996). Marriage: Will I be happy or sad? In N. Vanzetti & S. Duck (Eds.), *A lifetime of relationships.* Pacific Grove: CA: Brooks/Cole.

Nottelmann, E.D., Susman, E.J., Blue, J.H., Inoff-Germain, G., Dorn, L.D., Loriaux, D.L., Cutler, G.B., & Chrousos, G.P. (1987). Gonadal and adrenal hormone correlates of adjustment in early adolescence. In R.M. Lerner & T.T. Foch (Eds.), *Biological-psychological interactions in early adolescence.* Hillsdale, NJ: Erlbaum.

Novaco, R.W. (1998). Aggression. In H.S. Friedman (Ed.), *Encyclopedia of mental health* (Vol. 1). San Diego: Academic Press.

Novak, C.A. (1977). Does youthfulness equal attractiveness? In L.E. Troll, J. Israel, & D. Israel (Eds.), *Looking ahead: A woman's guide to the problems and joys of growing older.* Upper Saddle River, NJ: Prentice Hall.

Nystul, M.S. (1999). *Introduction to counseling.* Boston: Allyn & Bacon.

O'Donnell, L., Stueve, A., San-Doval, A., Duran, R., Atnafou, R., Haber, D., Johnson, N., Murray, H.,

Grant, U., Juhn, G., Tang, J., Bass, J., & Piessens, P. (1999). Violence prevention and young adolescents' participation in community service. *Journal of Adolescent Health, 24,* 28–37.

O'Rahilly, R., & Muller, F. (1999). *The embryonic human brain.* New York: Wiley.

Occupational Outlook Handbook. (1998–1999). Washington, DC: U.S. Dept. of Labor, Bureau of Labor Statistics.

Ogilvie, R.D, & Harsh, J.R. (Eds). (1994). *Sleep onset: Normal and abnormal processes.* Washington DC: American Psychological Association.*

Ogilvie, R.D. (1993). Sleep onset. In: M. Carskadon, A. Rechtschaffen, G. Richardson, T. Roth, & J. Siegel (Eds.), *Encyclopedia of sleep and dreaming.* New York: Macmillan.*

Olds, J.M. (1958). Self-stimulation experiments and differential reward systems. In H.H. Jasper, L.D. Proctor, R.S. Knighton, W.C. Noshay, & R.T. Costello (Eds.), *Reticular formation of the brain.* Boston: Little, Brown.*

Olds, J.M., & Milner, P.M. (1954). Positive reinforcement produced by electrical stimulation of the septal area and other areas of the rat brain. *Journal of Comparative and Physiological Psychology, 47,* 419–427.*

Olff, M. (1999). Stress, depression, and immunity. *Psychiatry Research, 85,* 7–16.

Olthof, A., Iden, C. M., & Roberts, W. A. (1997). Judgment of ordinality and summation of number symbols by squirrel monkeys (Saimiri sciureus). *Journal of Experimental Psychology: Animal Behavior Processes, 32,* 325-339.*

Oltmanns, T.F., Neale, J.M., & Davison, G.C. (1986). *Case studies in abnormal psychology* (2nd ed.). New York: Wiley.

Orlinsky, D.E., Grawe, K., & Parks, B.K. (1994). Process and outcome in psychotherapy. In A.E. Bergin & S.L. Garfield (Eds.), *Handbook of psychotherapy and behavior change* (4th ed.). New York: Wiley.

Ozer, D.J., & Riese, S.P. (1994). Personality assessment. *Annual Review of Psychology, 45,* 357–388.

Padma-Nathan, H. (1999, March). *Oral drug therapy for erectile dysfunction: What have we learned from the Viagra experience?* Paper presented at the meeting of the American Psychosomatic Association, Vancouver.

Paffenbarger, R.S., Hyde, R.T., Wing, A.L., & Hsieh, C. (1986). Physical activity, all-cause mortality, and longevity of college alumni. *New England Journal of Medicine, 324,* 605–612.

Paivio, A. (1971). *Imagery and verbal processes.* New York: Holt, Rinehart & Winston.*

Paivio, A. (1986). *Mental representations: A dual coding approach.* New York: Oxford University Press.*

Paloutzian, R. (1996). *The psychology of religion* (2nd ed.). Boston: Allyn & Bacon.

Paloutzian, R. (2000). *Invitation to the psychology of religion* (3rd ed.). Boston: Allyn & Bacon.

Paludi, M.A. (1998). *The psychology of women.* Upper Saddle River, NJ: Prentice Hall.

Pan, B.A., & Snow, C.E. (1999). The development of conversational and discourse skills. In M. Barrett (Ed.), *The development of language.* Philadelphia: Psychology Press.

Panskepp, J. (1993). Neurochemical control of moods and emotions: Amino acids to neuropeptides. In M. Lewis & J.M. Haviland (Eds.), *Handbook of emotion.* New York: Guilford Press.

Parducci, A. (1996). *Happiness, pleasure, and judgment.* Hillsdale, NJ: Erlbaum.

Park, D.C., Nisbett, R., & Hedden, T. (1999). Aging, culture, and cognition. *Journal of Gerontology, 54B,* P75–P84.

Parke, R.D., & Buriel, R. (1998). Socialization in the family. In W. Damon (Ed.), *Handbook of child psychology* (5th ed., Vol. 3). New York: Wiley.

Pascual-Leone, J., & Johnson, J. (1999). A dialectical constructivist view of representation. In I.E. Sigel (Ed.), *Development of mental representation.* Mahwah, NJ: Erlbaum.*

Passuth, P.M., Maines, D.R., & Neugarten, B.L. (1984). *Age norms and age constraints twenty years later.* Paper presented at the meeting of the Midwest Sociological Society, Chicago.

Pate, R.H., & Bondi, A.M. (1992). Religious beliefs and practice: An integral aspect of multicultural awareness. *Counselor Education and Supervision, 32,* 108–115.

Patterson, C. (1995). Lesbian and gay parenthood. In M.H. Bornstein (Ed.), *Handbook of parenting* (Vol. 3). Mahwah, NJ: Erlbaum.

Patterson, G.R., DeBaryshe, B.D., & Ramsey, E. (1989). A developmental perspective on antisocial behavior. *American Psychologist, 44,* 329–335.

Paulus, P.B. (1989). An overview and evaluation of group influence. In P.B. Paulus (Ed.), *Psychology of group influence.* Mahwah, NJ: Erlbaum.

Paunonen, S. V., & Ashton, M. C. (1998). The structured assessment of personality across cultures. *Journal of Cross-Cultural Psychology, 29,* 150-170.*

Paunonen, S. V., & Jackson, D. N. (1996). The Jackson Personality Inventory and the Five-Factor Model of personality. *Journal of Research in Personality, 30,* 42-59.*

Paunonen, S. V., Zeidner, M., Engvik, H., Oosterveld, P., & Maliphant, R. (in press). The nonverbal assessment of personality in five cultures. *Journal of Cross-Cultural Psychology.*

Paunonen, S., Jackson, D., Trzebinski, J., & Forserling, F. (1992). Personality structures across cultures: A multimethod evaluation. *Journal of Personality and Social Psychology, 62,* 447–456.*

Pavlov, I.P. (1927). *Conditioned reflexes* (G.V. Anrep, Trans.). New York: Dover.

Payne, L.R., Smith, P.O., Sturges, L.V., & Holleran, S.A. (1996). Reactivity to smoking cues: Mediating roles of nicotine and duration of deprivation. *Addictive Behaviors, 21,* 139–154.

Payne, M.A. (1989). Use and abuse of corporal punishment: A Caribbean view. *Child Abuse and Neglect, 13(13),* 389-401.

Peckford, T., Templer, D.I., & Ruff, C.F. (1975). American bias of WAIS administered to Canadian patients. *Canadian Journal of Behavioural Science, 7,* 446-448.*

Pederson, D.R., Gleason, K.E., Moran, G., & Bento, S. (1998) Maternal attachment representations, maternal sensitivity, and infant-mother attachment. *Developmental Psychology, 34,* 925-933.*

Peele, S., & Brodsky, A. (1991). *The truth about addiction and recovery.* New York: Simon & Schuster.

Pellegrini, A.D. (1996). *Observing children in their natural worlds.* Mahwah, NJ: Erlbaum.

Pence, A.R. (1989). In the shadow of mother-care: Contexts for an understanding of child day care in North America. *Canadian Psychology, 30(2),* 140-147.*

Pence, A.R. (Ed.). (1988). *Ecological research with children and families: From concepts to methodology.* New York: Teachers College Press.*

Penfield, W. (1947). Some observations in the cerebral cortex of man. *Proceedings of the Royal Society, 134,* 349.*

Penfield, W., & Rasmussen, T. (1950). *The cortex of man.* New York: Macmillan.*

Pennebaker, J. (1990). *Opening up.* New York: Avon.

Pentz, M.A. (1993). Comparative effects of community-based drug abuse prevention. In J.S. Baer, G.A. Marlatt, & R.J. McMahon (Eds.), *Addicitve behaviors across the life span.* Newbury Park, CA: Sage.

Perkins, D. (1994, September). Creativity by design. *Educational Leadership,* pp. 18–25.

Perlman, D., & Peplau, L.A. (1998). Loneliness. In H.S. Friedman (Ed.), *Encyclopedia of mental health* (Vol. 2). San Diego: Academic Press.*

Perls, F.S. (1969). *Gestalt therapy verbatim,* Lafayette, CA: Real People Press.

Pert, A.B., & Snyder, S.H. (1973). Opiate receptor: Demonstration in a nervous tissue. *Science, 179,* 1011.

Pert, C.B. (1999). *Molecules of emotion.* New York: Simon & Schuster.

Pervin, L.A. (1993). *Personality* (6th ed.). New York: Wiley.

Petersen, A. (1979, January). Can puberty come any faster? *Psychology Today,* pp. 45–56.

Peterson, C. (1988). *Personality.* Fort Worth: Harcourt Brace.

Peterson, C., & Seligman, M.E.P. (1984). Casual explanations as a risk factor for depression. *Psychological Review, 91,* 347–374.

Peterson, C., & Seligman, M.E.P., & Vaillant, G.E. (1986). *Explanatory style as a risk factor for physical illness.* Unpublished manuscript, Dept. of Psychology, University of Michigan, Ann Arbor.

Peterson, J.B. (1999). *Maps of meaning: The architecture of belief.* Routledge.*

Peth-Pierce, R. (1998). *The NICHD Study of early child care.* Washington, DC: National Institute of Child Health Development.

Petri, H.L. (1996). *Motivation.* Pacific Grove: CA: Brooks/Cole.

Petrinovich, L. (1996). *Living and dying well.* New York: Plenum.

Pettifor, J.L. (1998). The Canadian code of ethics for psychologists: A moral context for ethical decision-making in emerging areas of practice. *Canadian Psychology, 39(3),* 231-238.*

Petty, R. E., Wegener, D. T., & Fabrigar, L. R. (1997). Attitudes and attitude change. *Annual Review of Psychology, 48,* 609-647.*

Petty, R.E., & Krosnick, J.A. (Eds.). *Attitude strength: Antecedents and consequents.* Mahwah, NJ: Erlbaum.

Phares, E.J. (1984). *Personality.* Columbus, OH: Merrill.

Philips, H.C., & Rachman, S. (1996). *The psychological management of chronic pain* (2nd ed.). New York: Springer.*

Piaget, J. (1952). *The origins of intelligence in children.* New York: Oxford University Press.

Piaget, J., & Inhelder, B. (1969). *The child's conception of space* (F.J. Langdon & J.L. Lunzer, Trans.). New York: W.W. Norton.

Pierce, W.D., & Epling, W.F. (1999). *Behavior analysis and learning* (2nd ed.). Upper Saddle River, NJ: Prentice-Hall.*

Pilkonis, P.A. (1999). Introduction: Paradigms for psychotherapy outcome research. *Journal of Clinical Psychology, 55,* 145–146.

Pilkonis, P.A., & Krause, M.S. (1999). Summary: Paradigms for psychotherapy outcome research. *Journal of Clinical Psychology, 55,* 201–206.

Pillow, D.R., Zautra, A.J., & Sandler, I. (1996). Major life events and minor stressors. *Journal of Personality and Social Psychology, 70,* 381–394.

Pinger, R.R., Payne, W.A., Hahn, D.B., & Hahn, E.J. (1998). *Drugs* (3rd ed.). New York: McGraw-Hill.

Pinker, S. (1994). *The language instinct.* New York: HarperCollins.

Pinker, S. (1997). *How the mind works.* New York: Norton.

Pinker, S. (1999). *How the mind works.* New York: Norton.

Pipes, R.B., & Davenport, D.S. (1999). *Introduction to psychotherapy* (2nd ed.) Boston: Allyn & Bacon.

Pittman, T.S. (1998). Motivation. In D.T. Gilbert, S.T. Fiske, & G. Lindzey (Eds.), *Handbook of social psychology* (4th ed., Vol. 1). New York: McGraw-Hill.

Plunkett, J. & Schafer, G. (1999). Early speech perception and word learning. In M. Barrett (Ed.), *The development of language.* Philadelphia: Psychology Press.

Plutchik, R. (1980). *Emotion: A psychoevolutionary synthesis.* New York: Harper & Row.

Polivy, J., & Herman, C.P. (1985). Dieting and bingeing: A causal analysis. *American Psychologist, 40,* 193-201.*

Pollock, V.E., Schneider, L.S., Gabrielli, W.F., & Goodwin, D.W. (1987). Sex of parent and sex of offspring in the transmission of alcoholism: A meta-analysis. *Journal of Nervous and Mental Disease, 173,* 668–673.

Poole, J.H., Ober, B.A. , Shenaut, G.K., & Vinogradov, S. (1999). Independent frontal-system deficits in schizophrenia. *Psychiatry Research, 85,* 161–176.

Popham, W.J. (1999). *Classroom assessment.* Boston: Allyn & Bacon.

Premack, D. (1986). *Gavagi! The future history of the ape language controversy.* Cambridge, MA: MIT Press.

Preston, J.M. (1998). From mediated environments to the development of consciousness. In J. Gackenbach (Ed.), *Psychology and the Internet: Intrapersonal, interpersonal, and transpersonal implications.* San Diego: Academic Press.*

Preuger, V.J., & Rogers, T.B. (1993) Development of a scale to measure cross-cultural sensitivity in the Canadian context. *Canadian Journal of Behavioral Science, 25(4),* 615-621.*

Pritchard, D.J. (1996). Genetic analysis of schizophrenia. *Annual of Human Genetics, 60,* 105–123.

Proctor, R.A. (1999). Artificial intelligence. In M.A. Runco & S. Pritzker (Eds.), *Encyclopedia of creativity.* San Diego: Academic Press.

Pugh, G.M., & Boer, D.G. (1989). An examination of culturally appropriate items for the WAIS-R Information subtest with Canadian subjects. *Journal of Psychoeducational Assessment, 7* 131-140.*

Pugh, G.M., & Boer, D.G. (1991). Normative data on the validity of Canadian subtest items for the WAIS-R Information subtest. *Canadian Journal of Behavioral Science, 23(2),* 149-158.*

Pyke, S.W. (1997) Education and the "woman question". *Canadian Psychology, 38(3),* 154-163.*

Pylyshyn, Z.W. (1981). The imagery debate: Analogue media versus tacit knowledge. *Psychological Review, 88,* 16-45.*

Qualls, P.J., & Sheehan, P.W. (1981). Electromyograph biofeedback as a relaxation technique: A critical appraisal and reassessment. *Psychological Bulletin, 90,* 21–42.

Räikkönen, K.A., Matthews, K.A., Flory, J.D., & Owens, J.F. (1999). Effects of hostility on ambulatory blood pressure and mood during daily living in healthy adults. *Health Psychology, 18,* 44–53.

Räikkönen, K.A., Matthews, K.A., Flory, J.D., Owens, J.F., & Gump, B.B. (1999). Effects of optimism, pessimism, and trait anxiety on ambulatory blood pressure and mood during everyday life. *Journal of Personality and Social Psychology, 76,* 104–113.

Randi, J. (1980). *Flim-flam!* New York: Lippincott.

Randi, J. (1997). *An encyclopedia of claims, frauds, and hoaxes of the occult and supernatural.* New York: St. Martin's Press.

Rapaport, D. (1967). On the psychoanalytic theory of thinking. In M.M. Gill (Ed.), *The collected papers of David Rapaport.* New York: Basic Books.

Raskin, D.C., & Yuille, J.C. (1989), Problems in evaluating interviews of children in sexual abuse cases. In S.J. Ceci, D.F. Ross, & M.P. Toglia (Eds.), *Perspectives on children's testimony.* New York: Springer-Verlag.*

Rasmussen, K.G. (1984). Nonverbal behavior, verbal behavior, resume credentials, and selection interview outcomes. *Journal of Applied Psychology, 69,* 551–556.

Ratner, N.B. (1993). Learning to speak. *Science, 262,* 260.

Raven, P.H., & Johnson, G.B. (1999). *Biology* (5th ed.). New York: McGraw-Hill.

Ray, O.S., & Ksir, C. (1999). *Drugs, society, and human behavior* (8th ed.). New York: McGraw-Hill.

Rebec, G.V. (1996, June). *Neurochemical and behavioral insights into mechanisms of action of stimulant drugs.* Paper presented at the meeting of the American Psychological Society, San Francisco.

Rector, N.A., Segal, Z.V., & Gemar, M. (1998). Schema research in depression: A Canadian perspective. *Canadian Journal of Behavioural Science, 30(4)*, 213-224.*

Redd, W.H. (1995). Behavioral research in cancer as a model for health psychology. *Health Psychology, 14*, 99–100.

Reece, B.L., & Brandt, R. (1990). *Effective human relations in organizations* (4th ed.). Boston: Houghton Mifflin.

Reed, E.S., Turiel, E., & Brown, T. (1995). *Values and knowledge.* Mahwah, NJ: Erlbaum.

Regan, D. (Ed.). (1991). *Binocular vision.* New York: Macmillan.*

Reinisch, J.M. (1990). *The Kinsey Institute new report on sex: What you must know to be sexually literate.* New York: St. Martin's Press.

Rescorla, R.A. (1966). Predictability and number of pairings in Pavlovian fear conditioning. *Psychonomic Science, 4*, 383–384.

Rescorla, R.A. (1988). Pavlovian conditioning: It's not what you think it is. *American Psychologist, 43*, 151–160.

Rescorla, R.A. (1996). Spontaneous recovery after training with multiple outcomes. *Animal Learning & Behavior, 24*, 11–18.

Restak, R.M. (1988). *The mind.* New York: Bantam.

Revitch, E., & Schlesinger, L.B. (1978). Murder: Evaluation, classification, and prediction. In I.L. Kutash, S.B. Kutash, & O.B. Schlesinger (Eds.), *Violence.* San Francisco: Jossey-Bass.

Rickabaugh, C. (1998). *Sex and gender.* New York: McGraw-Hill.

Riggio, R.E. (1986). Assessment of basic social skills. *Journal of Personality and Social Psychology, 51*, 649–660.

Rijsdijk, F. V., Boomsma, D. I., & Vernon, P. A. (1995). Genetic analyses of peripheral nerve conduction velocity in men and its relation with IQ. *Behavior Genetics, 25*, 341-348.*

Rinkenauer, G., Mattes, S., & Ulrich, R. (1999). The surface-weight illusion. *Perception & Psychophysics, 61*, 23–30.

Roback, H.W., Barton, D., Castelnuovo-Tedesco, P., Gay, V., Havens, L., & Nash, J. (1999). A symposium on psychotherapy in the age of managed care. *American Journal of Psychotherapy, 53*, 1–16.

Roberts, D., Anderson, B.L., & Lubaroff, A. (1994). *Stress and immunity at cancer diagnosis.* Unpublished manuscript, Dept. of Psychology, Ohio State University, Columbus.

Roberts, W. A. (1998). *Principles of animal cognition.* Boston: McGraw-Hill.*

Robins, L. & Regier, D. (Eds.). (1991). *Psychiatric disorders in America.* New York: Free Press.

Robson, A.L. (1997). Low birthweight and parenting stress during early childhood. *Journal of Pediatric Psychology, 22*, 297-311.*

Rodin, J. (1984, December). Interview: A sense of control. *Psychology Today*, pp. 38–45.

Rodrigues, M.S., & Cohen, S. (1998). Social support. In H.S. Friedman (Ed.), *Encyclopedia of mental health* (Vol. 3). San Diego: Academic Press.

Roehrs, T., & Roth, T. (1998). Reported in Maas, J. (1998). *Power sleep.* New York: Villard, p. 44.

Roese, N.J., & Olson, J.M. (1994). Attitude importance as a function of repeated attitude expression. *Journal of Experimental Social Psychology, 30(1)*, 39-51.*

Roffwarg, H.P., Muzio, J.N., & Dement, W.C. (1966). Ontogenetic development of human sleep-dream cycle. *Science, 152*, 604–609.

Rogers, C.R. (1961). *On becoming a person.* Boston: Houghton Mifflin.

Rogers, C.R. (1974). In retrospect: Forty-six years. *American Psychologist, 29*, 115–123.

Rogers, C.R. (1980). *A way of being.* Boston: Houghton Mifflin.

Rogoff, B. (1990). *Apprenticeship in thinking.* New York: Oxford University Press.

Rogoff, B. (1998). Cognition as a collaborative process. In W. Damon (Ed.), *Handbook of child psychology* (5th ed., Vol. 2), New York: Wiley.

Rogosch, F.A., Cicchetti, D., Shields, A., & Toth, S.L. (1995). Parenting dysfunction in child maltreatment. In M.H. Bornstein (Ed.), *Handbook of parenting* (Vol. 4). Hillsdale, NJ: Erlbaum.

Rollman, G. B. (1998). Culture and pain. In: S. S. Kazarian & D. R. Evans (Eds.), *Cultural clinical psychology: Theory, research, and practice.* New York: Oxford University Press.*

Romaine, S. (1999). Bilingual language development. In M. Barrett (Ed.), *The development of language.* Philadelphia: Psychology Press.

Rosch, E. (1973). On the internal structure of perceptual and semantic categories. In T.E. Mooer (Ed.), *Cognition and the acquisition of language.* San Diego: Academic Press.

Rose, S. (Ed.). (1999). *From brains to consciousness?* Princeton, NJ: Princeton University Press.

Rose-Krasnor, L., Rubin, K.H., Booth, C.L., & Coplan, R. (1996). The relation of maternal directiveness and child attachment security to social competence in preschoolers. *International Journal of Behavioral Development, 19*, 309-325.*

Rosenfeld, A.H. (1985, June). Depression: Dispelling despair. *Psychology Today*, pp. 28–34.

Rosenheck, R., Dunn, L., Peszke, M., Cramer, J., Xu, W., Thomas, J., & Charney, D. (1999). Impact of Clozapine on negative symptoms and on the deficit syndrome in refractory schizophrenia. *The American Journal of Psychiatry, 156*, 88–96.

Rosenthal, D. (1963). *The Germain quadruplets.* New York: Basic Books.

Rosenthal, R. (1966). *Experimenter effects in behavioral research.* New York: Appleton-Century-Crofts.

Rosenthal, R. (1994). Interpersonal expectancy effects: A 30-year-perspective. *Current Dimensions in Psychological Science, 3*, 176–179.

Rosenthal, R., & Jacobsen, L. (1968). *Pygmalion in the classroom.* Fort Worth: Harcourt Brace.

Rosenzweig, M. (1969). Effects of heredity and environment on brain chemistry, brain anatomy, and learning ability in the rat. In M. Monosevitz, G. Lindzey, & D.D. Theissen (Eds.), *Behavioral genetics.* New York: Appleton-Century-Crofts.

Rosnow, R.L. (1995). Teaching research ethics through role-playing and discussion. In M.E. Ware & D.E. Johnson (Eds.), *Demonstrations and activities in teaching psychology* (Vol. 1). Mahwah, NJ: Erlbaum.

Rosnow, R.L., & Rosenthal, R. (1996). *Beginning behavioral research* (2nd ed.). Upper Saddle River, NJ: Prentice Hall.

Ross, C.A. (1994). *The Osiris complex: Case-studies in multiple personality disorder.* Toronto: University of Toronto Press.*

Rothbart, M.K., & Bates, J.E. (1988). Temperament. In W. Damon (Ed.), *Handbook of child psychology* (5th ed., Vol. 3). New York: Wiley.

Rothstein, R. (1998, May). Bilingual education: The controversy. *Phi Delta Kappan*, 672–678.

Rubin, D.C., & Kozin, M. (1984). Vivid memories. *Cognition, 16*, 81–95.

Rubin, Z., & Mitchell, C. (1976). Couples research as couples counseling. *American Psychologist, 31*, 17–25.

Runco, M. (1999). Critical thinking. In M.A. Runco & S. Pritzker (Eds.), *Encyclopedia of creativity.* San Diego: Academic Press.

Runko, M.A., & Pritzker, S. (Eds.) (1999). *Encyclopedia of creativity.* San Diego: Academic Press.

Rushton, J.P., Fulker, D.W., Neal, M.C., Nias, D.K.B., & Eysenck, H.J. (1986). Altruism and aggression: The heritability of individual differences. *Journal of Personality and Social Psychology, 50*, 1192–1198.*

Russell, D.W. (1996). UCLA Loneliness Scale (Version 3): Reliability, validity, and factor structure. *Journal of Personality, Assessment, 66*, 20–43.

Russell, J.A. (1999). Emotion communicates. *Contemporary Psychology, 44*, 26–27.*

Russell, J.A., & Fernandez-Dols, J.-M. (Eds.). (in press). *The psychology of facial expression.* New York: Cambridge University Press.*

Russo, N.F. (1990). Overview: Forging research priorities for women's health. *American Psychologist, 45*, 373–386.

Ryan-Finn, K.D., Cause, A.M., & Grove, K. (1995, March). *Children and adolescents of color: Where are you? Selection, recruitment, and retention in developmental research.* Paper presented at the meeting of the Society for Research in Child Development, Indianapolis.

Ryff, C.D., & Singer, B. (1998). Middle age and well-being. In H.S. Friedman (Ed.), *Encyclopedia of mental health* (Vol. 2). San Diego: Academic Press.

Rymer, R. (1993). *Genie.* New York: HarperCollins.

S

Sabini, J. (1995). *Social psychology* (2nd ed.). New York: Norton.

Sacks, O. (1985). *The man who mistook his wife for a hat.* New York: Summit Books.

Sadava, S.W. (1987). Interactional theory. In H.T. Blane & K.E. Leonard (Eds.), *Psychological theories of drinking and alcoholism.* New York: Guilford.*

Sagan, C. (1980). *Cosmos.* New York: Random House.

Sakinofsky, I. (1998). The epidemiology of suicide in Canada. In A.A. Leenaars, S. Wenckstern, I. Sakinofsky, R.J. Dyck, M.J. Kral, & R.C. Bland, R. (Eds.), *Suicide in Canada.* Toronto: University of Toronto Press.*

Saklofske, D.H. (1996). Using the WISC-III Canadian Study results in academic research. In D. Wechsler: *WISC-III manual Canadian supplement*. Toronto: The Psychological Corporation.*

Saklofske, D.H., & Eysenck, H.J. (1994). Extraversion-introversion. In V.S. Ramachandran (Ed.), *Encyclopedia of human behavior (Vol.2)*. San Diego: Academic Press.*

Saklofske, D.H., Hildebrand, D.K., Reynolds, C.R., & Wilson, V.L. (1998). Substituting symbol search for coding on the WISC-III; Canadian normative tables for Performance and Full Scale IQ scores. *Canadian Journal of Behavioural Science, 20*, 57-68.*

Sales, P. (1999). *Alcohol abuse*. New York: Ixia Publications.

Salovey, P., Rotman, A.J., & Rodin, J. (1998). Health behavior. In D.T. Gilbert, S.T. Fiske, & G. Lindzey (Eds.), *The handbook of social psychology* (Vol. 2). New York: McGraw-Hill.

Salthouse, T. (1994). The nature of influence of speed on adult differences in cognition. *Developmental Psychology, 30*, 240–259.

Samson, J.-M., Levy, J.J., Dupras, A., & Tessier, D. (1993). Active oral-genital sex among married or cohabiting heterosexual adults. *Sexological Review, 1(1)*, 143-156.*

Sanderson, W.C. (1995, March). Which therapies are proven effective? *APA Monitor*, p. 4.

Sandler, D.P., Comstock, G.W., Helsing, K.J., & Shore, D.L. (1989). Deaths from all causes in nonsmokers who lived with smokers. *American Journal of Public Health, 79*, 163–167.

Sanson, A., & Rothbart, M.K. (1995). Child temperament and parenting. In M.H. Bornstein (Ed.), *Handbook of parenting* (Vol. 4). Hillsdale, NJ: Erlbaum.

Santrock, J.W. (1998). *Adolescence* (7th ed.). New York: McGraw-Hill.

Santrock, J.W. (1999). *Life-span development* (7th ed.). New York: McGraw-Hill.

Santrock, J.W., & Halonen, J.S. (1999). *Your guide to college success*. Belmont, CA: Wadsworth.

Sapon-Shevin, M. (1999). *Because we can change the world*. Boston: Allyn & Bacon.

Saravi, R.D. (1993). The right hemisphere: An esoteric closet? *Skeptical Inquirer, 17*, 380–387.

Sarbin, T.R., & Keen, E. (1998). Classifying mental disorders. In H.S. Friedman (Ed.), *Encyclopedia of mental health* (Vol. 1). San Diego: Academic Press.

Sargent, C. (1987). Skeptical fairytales from Bristol. *Journal of the Society for Psychical Research, 54*, 166–185.

Saucier, G., & Ostendorf, F. (1999). Hierarchical subcomponents of the big five personality factors: A cross-language replication. *Journal of Personality and Social Psychology, 76*, 613–627.

Savage, H., & McKague, C. (1987). *Mental health law in Canada*. Toronto: Butterworths.*

Savage-Rumbaugh, E.S., Murphy, J., Sevcik, R.A., Brakke, K.E., Williams, S.L., & Rumbaugh, D.M. (1993). Language comprehension in ape and child. *Monographs of the Society for Research in Child Development*, Serial No. 233 (Vol. 58, Nos. 3–4).

Savage-Rumbaugh, S., Shanker, S., & Taylor, T. (1998). *Apes, language, and mind*. New York: Oxford U. Press.*

Sax, G. (1997). *Principles of educational and psychology measurement* (4th ed.). Belmont, CA: Wadsworth.

Sax, L.J., Astin, A.W., Korn, W.S., & Mahoney, K. M. (1998). *The American freshman: National norms for fall 1998*. Los Angeles: American Council on Education, UCLA.

Sax, L.J., Astin, A.W., Korn, W.S., & Mahoney, K.M. (1995). *The American college freshman: National norms for fall, 1995*. Los Angeles: UCLA, Higher Education Research Institute.

Saxe, L. (1998, June). Commentary. *APA Monitor*, p. 30.

Saxe, L., Dougherty, D., & Cross, T. (1985). The validity of polygraph testing. *American Psychologist, 40*, 355–366.

Scarr, S. (1984, May). Interview. *Psychology Today*, pp. 59–63.

Scarr, S., & Weinberg, R.A. (1980). Calling all camps! The war is over. *American Sociological Review, 45*, 859–865.

Scarr, S., & Weinberg, R.A. (1983). The Minnesota adoption studies: Genetic differences and malleability. *Child Development, 54*, 182–203.

Schachter, S. (1971). Some extraordinary facts about obese humans and rats. *American Psychologist, 26*, 129–144.

Schachter, S., & Singer, J.E. (1962). Cognitive, social, and physiological determinants of emotional state. *Psychological Review, 69*, 379–399.

Schacter, D.L. (1995). Memory distortion. In D.L. Schacter, J.T. Coyle, G.D. Gisbach, M.M. Mesulam, & L.E. Sullivan (Eds.), *Memory distortion*. Cambridge, MA: Harvard University Press.

Schacter, D.L. (1996). *Searching for memory*. New York: Basic Books.

Schacter, D.L. (1999). Consciousness. In M.S. Gazzaniga (Ed.), *The new cognitive neurosciences* (2nd ed.). Cambridge, MA: MIT Press.

Schacter, D.L. (1999). The seven sins of memory: Insights from psychology and cognitive neuroscience. *American Psychologist, 54*, 182–203.

Schaeffer, H.R., & Emerson, P.E. (1964). The development of social attachments in infancy. *Monographs of the Society for Research in Child Development, 29*, (3, Serial No. 94).

Schank, R., & Abelson, R. (1977). *Scripts, plans, goals, and understanding*. Mahwah, NJ: Erlbaum.

Schiffman, J., & Walker, E. (1998). Schizophrenia. In H.S. Friedman (Ed.), *Encyclopedia of mental health* (Vol. 2). San Diego: Academic Press.

Schleifer, S.J. (1999). Psychoneuroimmunology. *Psychiatry Research, 85*, 3–6

Schliecker, E., White, D.R., & Jacobs, E. (1991). The role of daycare quality in the prediction of children's vocabulary. *Canadian Journal of Behavioral Science, 23(1)*, 12-24.*

Schneider, B.A., Moraglia, G., & Speranza, F. (in press). Binocular vision enhances phase discrimination by filtering the background. *Perception & Psychophysics*.*

Schneider, F.R., Johnson, J., Hornig, C.D., Olibowitz, M.R., & Weissman, M.M. (1992). Social phobia: Comorbidity and morbidity in an epidemiologic sample. *Archives of General Psychiatry, 49*, 288–288.

Schneider-Rosen, K., & Burke, P.B. (1999). Multiple attachment relationships within families. *Developmental Psychology, 35*, 436–441.

Scholnick, E.K. (1999). Piaget's legacy: Heirs to the house that Jean built. In E.K. Scholnick, K. Nelson, S.A. Gelman, & Miller, P.H. (Eds.), *Conceptual development: Piaget's legacy*. Mahwah, NJ: Erlbaum.

Scholnick, E.K., Nelson, K., Gelman, S.A., & Miller, P.H. (Eds.). (1999). *Conceptual development: Piaget's legacy*. Mahwah, NJ: Erlbaum.

Schultheiss, O.C., & Brunstein, J.C. (1999). Goal imagery: Bridging the gap between implicit motives and explicit goals. *Journal of Personality, 67*, 1–38.

Schunk, D.H. (1996). *Learning theories* (2nd ed.). Upper Saddle River, NJ: Prentice Hall.

Schwartz, T. (1999). *Kids and guns*. New York: Franklin Watts.

Schwean, V.L., Mykota, D., Robert, L., & Saklofske, D.H. (1999). Determinants of psychosocial disorders in cultural minority children. In V.L. Schwean & D.H. Saklofske (Eds), *Handbook of psychosocial characteristics of exceptional children*. New York: Kluwer.*

Sedikides, C., Campbell, W.K., Reeder, G.D., & Elliot, A.J. (1998). The self-serving bias in relational context. *Journal of Personality and Social Psychology, 74*, 378–386.

Seffge-Krenke, I. (1995). *Stress, coping, and relationships in adolescence*. Mahwah, NJ: Erlbaum.

Segall, M.H., Campbell, D.T., & Herskovits, M.J. (1963). Cultural differences in the perception of geometric illusions. *Science, 193*, 769–771.

Segall, M.H., Dasen, P.R., Berry, J.W., & Poortinga, Y.H. (1990). *Human behavior in global perspective*. New York: Pergamon.*

Segalowitz, N. (1997). Individual differences in second language acquisition. In A. de Groot & J. Kroll (Eds.), *Tutorials in bilingualism*. Mahwah, NJ: Erlbaum.*

Segalowitz, S.J. (1983). *Two sides of the brain: Brain lateralization explored*. Upper Saddle River, NJ: Prentice Hall.*

Seidemann, E., Meilijson, I., Abeles, M., Bergman, H., & Vaadia, E. (1996). Simultaneously recorded single units in the frontal cortex go through sequences of discrete and stable states in monkeys performing a delayed localization task. *The Journal of Neuroscience, 16*, 752–768.

Seidman, D.F., Rosecan, J., & Role, L. (1999). Biological and clinical perspectives on nicotine addiction. In D. F. Seidman & L.S. Covey (Eds.), *Helping the hard-core smoker*. Mahwah, NJ: Erlbaum.

Seidman, E., & French, S.E. (1998). Community mental health. In H.S. Friedman (Ed.), *Encyclopedia of mental health* (Vol. 1). San Diego: Academic Press.

Seligman, C., Olson, J.M., & Zanna, M.P. (Eds.). (1996). *The psychology of values*. Mahwah, NJ: Erlbaum.*

Seligman, M.E.P. (1970). On the generality of the laws of learning. *Psychological Review, 77*, 406–418.

Seligman, M.E.P. (1975). *Helplessness: On depression, development, and death*. San Francisco: W.H. Freeman.

Seligman, M.E.P. (1990). *Learned optimism*. New York: Knopf.

Seligman, M.E.P. (1993). *What you can change and what you can't.* New York: Knopf.

Seligman, M.E.P. Why is there so much depression today? In *The G. Stanley Hall Lecture Series.* Washington, DC: American Psychological Association.

Seligman, M.E.P., & Rosenhan, D.L. (1998). *Abnormality.* New York: Norton.

Seligman, M.E.P. (1994). *What you can change and what you can't.* New York: Knopf.

Selye, H. (1974). *Stress without distress.* Philadelphia: W.B. Saunders.*

Selye, H. (1983). The stress concept: Past, present, and future. In C.I. Cooper (Ed.), *Stress research.* New York: Wiley.*

Servaes, P., Vignerhoets, A., Vreugdenhil, G., Keuning, J.J., & Broekhuijsen, A.M. (1999). Inhibition of emotional expression in breast cancer patients. *Behavioral Medicine, 25,* 26–34.

Seto, M.C., & Barbaree, H.E. (1995). The role of alcohol in sexual aggression. *Clinical Psychology Review, 15,* 545–566.*

Shanks, D.R. (1991). Categorization by a connectionist network. *Journal of Experimental Psychology: Learning, Memory, and Cognition, 17,* 433–443.

Shaver, P. (1986, August). *Being lonely, falling in love: Perspectives from attachment theory.* Paper presented at the meeting of the American Psychological Association, Washington, DC.

Shepard, R.N. (1967). Recognition memory for words, sentences, and pictures. *Journal of Verbal Learning and Verbal Behavior, 6,* 156–163.

Shepard, R.N. (1996, August). *The eye's mind and the mind's eye.* Paper presented at the meeting of the American Psychological Association, Toronto.

Sher, K.J. (1991). *Children of alcoholics: A critical appraisal of theory and research.* Chicago: University of Chicago Press.

Sher, K.J. (1993). Children of alcoholics and the intergenerational transmission of alcoholism: A biopsychological perspective. In J.S. Baer, G.A. Marlatt, & R.J. McMahon (Eds.), *Addicitve behaviors across the life span.* Newbury Park, CA: Sage.

Sher, K.J., & Trull, J.J. (1994). Personality and disinhibitory psychopathology: Alcoholism and antisocial personality disorder. *Journal of Abnormal Psychology, 103,* 92–102.

Sherif, M., Harvey, O.J., White, B.J., Hood, W.R., & Sherif, C.W. (1961). *Intergroup cooperation and competition: The Robbers Cave experiment.* Norman: University of Oklahoma Press.

Sherwood, A., Light, K.C., & Blumenthal, J.A. (1989). Effects of aerobic exercise training on hemodynamic responses during psychosocial stress in normotensive and borderline hypertensive Type A men: A preliminary report. *Psychosomatic Medicine, 51,* 123–136.

Shettleworth, S.J. (1998). *Cognition, evolution, and behavior.* New York: Oxford University Press.*

Shettleworth, S.J., & Hampton, R.R. (1998). Adaptive specializations of spatial cognition in food-storing birds? Approaches to testing a comparative hypothesis. In: R.P. Balda, I.M. Pepperberg, & A.C. Kamil (Eds.), *Animal cognition in nature: The convergence of psychology and biology in laboratory and field.* San Diego: Academic Press.*

Shields, S.A. (1991). Gender in the psychology of emotion. In K.T. Strongman (Ed.), *International Review of Studies of Emotion* (Vol. 1). New York: Wiley.

Shier, D., Butler, J., & Lewis, R. (1999). *Human anatomy and physiology* (8th ed.). New York: McGraw-Hill.

Shneidman, E.S. (1971). Suicide among the gifted. *Suicide and Life-Threatening Behavior, 1,* 23–45.

Shotland, R.L. (1985, June). When bystanders just stand by. *Psychology Today.* pp. 50–55.

Showers, C. (1986). *The motivational consequences of negative thinking.* Paper presented at the meeting of the American Psychological Association, Washington, DC.

Siegel, S. (1979). The role of conditioning in drug tolerance and addiction. In Keehn, J.D. (Ed.), *Psychopathology in animals.* New York: Academic Press.*

Siegel, S. (1983). Classical conditioning, drug tolerance, and drug dependency. In Y. Israel, F.B. Slower, H. Kalant, R.E. Popham, W. Schmidt, & R.G. Smart (Eds.), *Research advances in alcohol and drug abuse (Vol. 7).* New York: Plenum.*

Siegel, S. (1999). Drug anticipation and drug addiction. The 1998 H. David Archibald Lecture. *Addiction, 94(8),* 1113–1124.*

Siegel, S., Hinson, R.E., Krank, M.D., & McCully, J. (1982). Heroin "overdose" death: Contribution of drug-associated environmental cues. *Science, 216,* 436–7.*

Siegfried, T. (1994, August 1). Ability to learn while asleep not just in a scientist's dreams. *Dallas Morning News,* p. 7D.

Siegler, R.S. (1998). *Children's thinking* (3rd ed.). Upper Saddle River, NJ: Erlbaum.

Siffre, M. (1975). Six months alone in a cave. *National Geographic, 147,* 426–435.

Silverman, N.N., & Corsini, R.J. (1984). Is it true what they say about Adler's individual psychology? *Teaching of Psychology, 11,* 188–189.

Simon, H.A. (1969). *The sciences of the artificial.* Cambridge, MA: MIT Press.

Simon, H.A. (1996). Putting the story together. *Contemporary Psychology, 41,* 12–14.

Simpson, J.A. (1995). Self-monitoring and commitment to dating relationships: A classroom demonstration. In M.E. Ware & D.E. Johnson (Eds.), *Demonstrations and activities in teaching of introductory psychology.* Mahwah, NJ: Erlbaum.

Sinclair, C. (1998). Nine unique features of the Canadian code of ethics for psychologists. *Canadian Psychology, 39(3),*167–176.*

Sinclair, C.M. (1998). Suicide in First Nations People. In A.A. Leenaars, S. Wenckstern, I. Sakinofsky, R.J. Dyck, M.J. Kral, & R.C. Bland, R. (Eds.), *Suicide in Canada.* Toronto: University of Toronto Press.*

Singer, D.G., & Singer, J.L. (1998). Television viewing. In H.S. Friedman (Ed.), *Encyclopedia of mental health* (Vol. 3). San Diego: Academic Press.

Skinner, B.F. (1938). *The behavior of organisms: An experimental analysis.* New York: Appelton-Century-Crofts.

Skinner, B.F. (1948). *Walden Two.* New York: Macmillan.

Skinner, B.F. (1957). *Verbal behavior.* New York: Appleton-Century-Crofts.

Skinner, E.A., Wellborn, J.G., & Connell, J.P. (1990). What it takes to do well in school and whether I've got it. *Journal of Educational Psychology, 82,* 22–32.

Slavin, R. (1989). Cooperative learning and student achievement. In R. Slavin (Ed.), *School and classroom organization.* Mahwah, NJ: Erlbaum.

Sloan, D.M., & Mizes, J.S. (1999). Foundations of behavior therapy in the contemporary health-care context. *Clinical Psychology Review, 19,* 255–274.

Sloan, P., Arsenault, L., Hilsenroth, M., & Harvill, L. (1996). Rorschach measures of post-traumatic stress in Persian Gulf War veterans: A three-year follow-up study. *Journal of Personality Assessment, 66,* 54–64.

Slobin, D. (1972, July). Children and language: They learn the same way around the world. *Psychology Today,* 71–76.

Slobogin, C. (1996). A jurisprudence of dangerousness as a criterion in the criminal process. In B.D. Sales & D.W. Shuman (Eds.), *Law, mental health, and mental disorder.* Pacific Grove, CA: Brooks/Cole.

Smith, J., & Baltes, P.B. (1999). Life-span perspectives on development. In M.H. Bornstein & M.E. Lamb (Eds.), *Developmental psychology: An advanced textbook* (4th ed.). Mahwah, NJ: Erlbaum.

Smith, K.H., & Rogers, M. (1994). Effectiveness of subliminal messages in television commercials. *Journal of Applied Psychology, 79,* 866–874.

Smith, M.L., Glass, G.N., & Miller, R.L. (1980). *The benefit of psychotherapy.* Baltimore: Johns Hopkins University Press.

Smock, T.K. (1999). *Physiological psychology: A neuroscience approach.* Upper Saddle River, NJ: Prentice-Hall.

Smyth, M.M., Collins, A.F., Morris, P.E., & Levy, P. (1994). *Cognition in action* (2nd ed.). Hove, Great Britain: Erlbaum.

Snarey, J. (1998). Fathers. In H.S. Friedman (Ed.), *Encyclopedia of mental health* (Vol. 2). San Diego: Academic Press.

Snow, C.E. (1998). *Preventing reading difficulties in young children.* Washington, DC: U.S. Department of Education.

Snow, C.E. (1999). Social perspectives on the emergence of language. In B. MacWhinney (Ed.), *The emergence of language.* Mahwah, NJ: Erlbaum.

Snowden, D.A. (1995). *An epidemiological study of aging in a select population and its relationship to Alzheimer's disease.* Unpublished manuscript, Sanders Brown Center on Aging, Lexington, KY.

Snyder, M., & Stukas, A.A. (1999). Interpersonal processes: The interplay of cognitive, motivational, and behavioral activities in social interaction. Palo Alto: Annual Reviews, Inc.

Sobell, M.B., & Sobell, M. (1993). Treatment for problem drinkers: A public health priority. In J.S. Baer, G.A. Marlatt, & R.J. McMahon (Eds.), *Addicitve behaviors across the life span.* Newbury Park, CA: Sage.*

Sober, E., & Wilson, D.S. (1998). *Unto others: The evolution of unselfish behavior.* Cambridge, MA: Harvard University Press.

Solomon, B., Powell, K., & Gardner, H. (1999). Multiple intelligences. In M.A. Runco & S. Pritzker (Eds.), *Encyclopedia of creativity.* San Diego: Academic Press.

Sorrentino, R. M., and Roney, C. J. (1999). *The uncertain mind: Individual differences in facing the unknown.* New York: Psychology Press.*

Spanos, N. P., & Chaves, J.F. (1991) History and historiography of hypnosis. In S.J. Lynn & J.W. Rhue (Eds.), *Theories of hypnosis: Current models and perspectives.* New York: Guilford Press.*

Spanos, N.P. (1991) A sociocognitive approach to hypnosis. In S.J. Lynn & J.W. Rhue (Eds.), *Theories of hypnosis: Current models and perspectives.* New York: Guilford Press.*

Spanos, N.P. (1996). *Multiple identities and false memories: A social cognitive perspective.* Washington, DC: American Psychological Association.*

Spearman, C.E. (1927). *The abilities of man.* New York: Macmillan.

Sperling, G. (1960). The information available in brief presentations. *Psychological Monographs, 74* (Whole No. 11).

Sperry, R.W. (1964). The great cerebral commissure. *Scientific American, 210,* 42–52.

Sperry, R.W. (1968). Hemisphere deconnection and unity in conscious awareness. *American Psychologist, 23,* 723–733.

Sperry, R.W. (1974). Lateral specialization in surgically separated hemispheres. In F.O. Schmitt & F.G. Worden (Eds.), *The neurosciences: Third study program.* Cambridge, MA: MIT Press.

Squire, L. (1990, June). *Memory and brain systems.* Paper presented at the meeting of the American Psychological Society, Dallas.

St. Clair, M. (1996). *Object relations and self psychology.* Pacific Grove, CA: Brooks/Cole.

Stack, D.M., & Tsonis, M. (in press). Seven-month-old infants' haptic perception of texture in the presence and absence of visual cues. *British Journal of Developmental Psychology.*

Stanley, M.A., & Turner, S.M. (1995). Current status of pharmacological and behavioral treatment of obsessive-compulsive disorder. *Behavior Therapy, 26,* 163–177.

Stanovich, K.E. (1998). *How to think straight about psychology* (5th ed.). New York: Longman.*

Stanovich, K.E. (1999). *Who is rational? Individual differences in reasoning.* Mahwah, NJ: Erlbaum.*

Staples, S.L. (1996). Human response to environmental noise. *American Psychologist, 51,* 143–150.

Stark-Adamec, C. (1992). Sexism in research: The limits of academic freedom. *Women and Therapy, 12(4),* 103-111.*

Stark-Adamec, C., & Kimball, M. (1983). *Science free of sexism: A psychologist's guide to the conduct of nonsexist research.* Ottawa: Canadian Psychological Association.*

Stark-Adamec, C., & Kimball, M. (1984). Science free of sexism: A psychologist's guide to the conduct of nonsexist research. *Canadian Psychology, 25(1),* 23-34.*

Statistics Canada (1999). *Canada yearbook 1999.* Ottawa: Statistics Canada.*

Staub, E. (1996). Cultural-societal roots of violence. *American Psychologist, 51,* 117–132.

Staudinger, U.M. (1996). Psychologische prodktivitat und selbstentfaltung im alter. In M.M. Baltes & L. Montada (Eds.), *Produktives leben im alter.* Berlin: Campus.

Steele, C.M. (1996, August). *A burden of suspicion: The role of stereotypes in shaping intellectual identity.* Paper presented at the meeting of the American Psychological Association, Toronto.

Stefanick, M.L. (1999). Estrogen, progesterons, and cardiovascular risk. *Journal of Reproductive Medicine, 44,* 221–226.

Stengel, R. (1996, April 22). Fly till I die. *Time,* pp. 34–40.

Sternberg, E.M., & Gold, P.W. (1996). The mind-body interaction in disease. *Mysteries of the mind.* New York: Scientific American.

Sternberg, R.J. (1986). *Intelligence applied.* Fort Worth: Harcourt Brace.

Sternberg, R.J. (1988). *The triangle of love.* New York: Basic Books.

Sternberg, R.J. (1994, December). Commentary. *APA Monitor,* p. 22.

Sternberg, R.J. (1997b). *Successful intelligence.* New York: Simon & Schuster.

Sternberg, R.J. (1999). Intelligence. In M.A. Runco & S. Pritzker (Eds.), *Encyclopedia of creativity.* San Diego: Academic Press.

Sternberg, R.J. (Ed) (1997a). *Career paths in psychology.* Washington, DC: American Psychological Association.

Sternberg, R.J., & Grigorenko, E. (Eds.). (1997). *Intelligence, heredity, and environment.* New York: Cambridge University Press.

Sternberg, R.J., & Spear-Swirling, P. (1996). *Teaching for thinking.* Washington, DC: American Psychological Association.

Steuer, F.B., Applefield, J.M., & Smith, R. (1971). Televised aggression and interpersonal aggression of preschool children. *Journal of Experimental Child Psychology, 11,* 442–447.

Stevenson, H.G. (1995, March). *Missing data: On the forgotten substance of race, ethnicity, and socioeconomic classifications.* Paper presented at the meeting of the Society for Research in Child Development, Indianapolis.

Stevenson, H.W. (1992, December). Learning from Asian school. *Scientific American,* pp. 6, 70–76.

Stevenson, H.W. (1995). Mathematics achievement of American students: First in the world in 2000? In C.A. Nelson (Ed.), *Basic and applied perspectives on learning, cognition and development. Minneapolis: University of Minnesota Press.*

Stevenson, H.W. (1997, August). *Bronfenbrenner award address.* Paper presented at the meeting of the American Psychological Association, Chicago.

Stigler, J.W., & Hiebert, J. (1997, September). Understanding and improving classroom mathematics instruction. *Phi Delta Kappan, 79,* 14–21.

Stoler, D.R., & Hill, B.A. (1998). *Coping with mild brain injury.* New York: Avery.

Stoner, J. (1961). *A comparison of individual and group decisions, including risk.* Unpublished master's thesis, School of Industrial Management, MIT.

Stones, M.J., & Kozma, A.K. (1989). Happiness and activities in later life: A propensity formulation. *Canadian Psychology, 30(3),* 526-537.*

Stoppard, J.M. (1999). Why new perspectives are needed for understanding depression in women. *Canadian Psychology, 40(2),* 79-90.*

Strauss, M.A., Sugarman, D.B., & Giles-Sims, J. (1997). Spanking by parents and subsequent antisocial behavior in children. *Archives of Pediatric and Adolescent Medicine, 151,* 761–767.

Strean, H.S. (1996). Resistance viewed from different perspectives. *American Journal of Psychotherapy, 50,* 29–31.

Streissguth, A. (1997). *Fetal alcohol syndrome: A guide for families and communities.* Baltimore, Paul H. Brookes.

Striefel, S. (1998). *How to teach through modeling and imitation.* Austin, TX: ProEd.

Strupp, H.H. (1989). Psychotherapy. *American Psychologist, 44,* 717–724.

Strupp, H.H. (1995). The psychotherapist's skills revised. *Clinical Psychology: Science and Practice, 2,* 70–74.

Sue, D.W., Ivey, A.E. & Pedersen, P. (1996). Research, practice, and training implications of multicultural counseling theory. In D.W. Sue (Ed.), *Theory of multicultural counseling and therapy.* Pacific Grove, CA: Brooks/Cole.

Sue, D.W., Ivey, A.E., & Pedersen, P. (1996). *A theory of multicultural counseling and therapy.* Pacific Grove, CA: Brooks/Cole.

Sue, S. (1977). Community mental health services to minority groups: Some optimism, some pessimism. *American Psychologist, 32,* 616–624.

Sue, S. (1997, August). *Insearch of cultural competence in psychotherapy and counseling.* Paper presented at the meeting of the American Psychological Association, Chicago.

Suinn, R.M. (1984). *Fundamentals of abnormal psychology.* Chicago: Nelson-Hall.

Sullivan, H.S. (1953). *The interpersonal theory of psychiatry.* New York: W.W. Norton.

Sullivan, K.T., & Christensen, A. (1998). Couples therapy. In H.S. Friedman (Ed.), *Encyclopedia of mental health* (Vol. 1). San Diego: Academic Press.

Suls, J., & Swain, A. (1998). Type A–Type B personalities. In H.S. Friedman (Ed.), *Encyclopedia of mental health* (Vol. 3). San Diego: Academic Press.

Summers, F.L. (1999). *Transcending the self.* Hillsdale, NJ: The Analytic Press.

Susman, E.J., Worrall, B.K., Murowchick, E., Frobose, C.A., & Schwab, J.E. (1996). Experience and neuroendocrine parameters of development: Aggressive behaviors and competencies. In D.M. Stoff & R.B. Cairns (Eds.), *Aggression and violence.* Mahwah, NJ: Erlbaum.

Sutker, P.B., & Allain, A.N. (1993). Behavior and personality assessment in men labeled adaptive sociopaths. *Journal of Behavioral Assessment, 5,* 65–79.

Swann, W.B., De La Ronde, C., & Hixon, J.G. (1994). Authenticity and positive strivings in marriage and courtship. *Journal of Personality and Social Psychology, 66,* 857–869.

Swanson, J. (Ed.)(1999). *Sleep disorders sourcebook.* New York: Omnigraphics, Inc.

Sylvain, C., Ladouceur, R., & Boisvert, J.-M. (1997). Cognitive and behavioral treatment of pathological gambling: A controlled study. *Journal of Consulting and Clinical Psychology, 65,* 727-732.*

T

Tager-Flusberg, H. (1999). Language development in atypical children. In M. Barrett (Ed.), *The development of language*. Philadelphia: Psychology Press.

Tager-Flusberg, H. (Ed.). (1994). *Constraints on language acquisition*. Mahwah, NJ: Erlbaum.

Tajfel, H. (1978). The achievement of group differentiation. In H. Tajfel (Ed.), *Differentiation between social groups*. London: Academic Press.

Tam, E.M, Lam, R.W, & Levitt A.J. (1995). Treatment of seasonal affective disorder: A review. *Canadian Journal of Psychiatry, 40(8)*, 457-66.*

Tamarin, R.H. (1999). *Principles of genetics* (6th ed.). New York: McGraw-Hill.

Tannen, D. (1990). *You just don't understand!* New York: Ballantine.

Task force on diversity issues. (1998, January). Talking about prejudice can be a powerful teaching tool. *APA Monitor*, p. 32.

Tavris, C. (1989). *Anger: The misunderstood emotion* (2nd ed.). New York: Touchstone.

Tavris, C., & Wade, C. (1984). *The longest war: Sex differences in perspective* (2nd ed.). Fort Worth: Harcourt Brace.

Taylor, D.M., Ruggiero, K.M., & Louis, W.R. (1996). Personal/group discrimination discrepancy: Towards a two-factor explanation. *Canadian Journal of Behavioural Science, 28(3)*, 193-202.*

Taylor, S.E. (1998). Positive illusions. In H.S. Friedman (Ed.), *Encyclopedia of mental health* (Vol. 3). San Diego: Academic Press.

Taylor, S.E. (1999). *Health psychology* (4th ed.). New York: McGraw-Hill.

Taylor, S.E., & Brown, J.D. (1994). Positive illusions and well-being revisited: Separating fact from fiction. *Psychological Bulletin, 116*, 21–27.

Taylor, S.E., Peplau, L.A., & Sears, D.O. (1997). *Social psychology* (8th ed.). Upper Saddle River, NJ: Prentice Hall.

Teachman, J.D., & Polonko, K.A. (1990). Cohabitation and marital stability in the United States. *Social Forces, 69*, 207–220.

Teasdale, J.D., Taylor, M.J., Cooper, Z., Hayhurst, H., & Paykel, E.S. (1995). Depressive thinking. *Journal of Abnormal Psychology, 104*, 500–507.

Temoshok, L. (1998). HIV/AIDS. In H.S. Friedman (Ed.), *Encyclopedia of mental health* (Vol. 2). San Diego: Academic Press.

Terman, L. (1925). *Genetic studies of genius* (Vol. 1.) Stanford, CA: Stanford University Press.

Terr, L.C. (1988). What happens to early memories of trauma? *Journal of the American Academy of Child and Adolescent Psychiatry, 27*, 96–104.

Tetreault, M.K.T. (1997). Classrooms for diversity: Rethinking curriculum and pedagogy. In J.A. Banks & C.A. Banks (Eds.), *Multicultural education* (3rd ed.). Boston: Allyn & Bacon.

Thalman, R.H. (1999). *Basic concepts in neuroscience*. New York: McGraw-Hill.

Thayer, J.F., Rossy, I., Sollers, J., Friedman, B. H., & Allen, M.T. (1996, March). *Relationships among heart period variability and cardiodynamic measures vary as a function of fitness*. Paper presented at the meeting of the American Psychosomatic Society, Williamsburg, VA.

Thigpen, C.H., & Cleckley, H.M. (1957). *Three faces of Eve*. New York: McGraw-Hill.

Thoma, S.J., & Rest, J.R. (1999). The relationship between moral decision making and patterns of consolidation and transition in moral judgment development. *Developmental Psychology, 35*, 323–334.

Thomas, C.B. (1983). *Stress and coping*. Unpublished manuscript, Johns Hopkins University, Baltimore.

Thompson, C.P., Hermann, D.J., Read, D., Bruce, D., Payne, D.G., & Toglia, M.P. (1998). *Autobiographical memory*. Mahwah, NJ: Erlbaum.

Thompson, C.P., Hermann, D.J., Read, D., Bruce, D., Payne, D.G., & Toglia, M.P. (1998). *Eyewitness memory*. Mahwah, NJ: Erlbaum.

Thompson, R.A. (1991). Emotional regulation and emotional development. *Educational Psychology Review, 3*, 269–307.

Thompson, R.A. (1998). Early social development. In W. Damon (Ed.), *Handbook of child psychology* (5th ed., Vol. 3), New York: Wiley.

Thompson, R.A. (1999). The individual child: Temperament, emotion, self, and personality. In M.H. Bornstein & M.E. Lamb (Eds.), *Developmental psychology: An advanced textbook* (4th ed.). Mahwah, NJ: Erlbaum.

Thompson, V. A. (1996). Reasoning from false premises: The role of soundness in making logical deductions. *Canadian Journal of Experimental Psychology, 50(3)*, 315-319.*

Thornton, A., & Camburn, D. (1989). Religious participation and sexual behavior and attitudes. *Journal of Marriage and the Family, 49*, 17–128.

Thorpe, G.L. (1998). Agoraphobia. In H.S. Friedman (Ed.), *Encyclopedia of mental health* (Vol. 1). San Diego: Academic Press.

Thurstone, L.L. (1938). *Primary mental abilities*. Chicago: University of Chicago Press.

Tinbergen, N. (1969). *The study of instinct*. New York: Oxford University Press.

Toga, A.W. (Ed.)(1998). *Brain warping*. San Diego: Academic Press.

Toga, A.W., & Mazziota, J.C. (Eds.). *Brain mapping*. New York: Morgan Kaufman.

Tolan, P., Miller, L., & Thomas, P. (1988). Perception and experience of two types of social stress and self-image among adolescents. *Journal of Youth and Adolescence, 17*, 147–163.

Tolman, E.C. (1932). *Purposive behavior in animals and man*. New York: Appleton-Century-Crofts.

Tolman, E.C. (1948). Cognitive maps in rats and men. *Psychological Review, 55*, 189–208.

Tomlinson-Keasey, C., Warren, L.W., & Elliott, J.F. (1986). Suicide among gifted women. *Journal of Abnormal Psychology, 95*, 123–130.

Toth, S.K., Connor, P.D., & Streissguth, A.P. (1999, April). *Psychiatric/behavioral and learning and memory problems in young adults with fetal alcohol syndrome and fetal alcohol effects*. Paper presented at the meeting of the Society for Research in Child Development, Albuquerque.

Toukmanian, S.G., & Brouwers, M.C. (1998). Cultural aspects of psychotherapy and self-disclosure. In S. Kazarian & D.R. Evans (Eds.), *Cultural clinical psychology: Theory, research, and practice*. Toronto: Oxford University Press.*

Tracey, T.J., Sherry, P., & Albright, J.M. (1999). The interpersonal process of cognitive-behavioral therapy. *Journal of Counseling Psychology, 46*, 80–91.

Tracy, K. (Ed.). (in press). Language and social interaction at the turn of the century. *Research on Language and Social Interaction*.

Trainor, J., Pomeroy, E., & Pape, B. (1999). A new framework for support. In J. Trainor, E. Pomeroy, & B. Pape (Eds.), *Building a framework for support: A community development approach to mental health policy*. Toronto: Canadian Mental Health Association.*

Trehub, S.E., & Thorpe, L.A. (1989). Infant's perception of rhythm: Categorization of auditory sequences by temporal structure. *Canadian Journal of Psychology, 43(2)*, 217-229.*

Tremblay, R.E., & Schaal, B. (1995, March). *Testosterone levels of physically active boys*. Paper presented at the meeting of the Society for Research in Child Development, Indianapolis.*

Triandis, H.C. (1994). *Culture and social behavior*. New York: McGraw-Hill.

Trimble, J.E. (1998, August). *The enculturation of contemporary psychology*. Paper presented at the meeting of the American Psychological Association, New Orleans.

Triplett, N. (1898). The dynamogenic factors in peacemaking and competition. *American Journal of Psychology, 9*, 507–533.

Tripp, D.A., Catano, V., & Sullivan, M.J. (1997). The contributions of attributional style, expectancies, depression, and self-esteem in a cognition-based depression model. *Canadian Journal of Behavioural Science, 29(2)*, 101-111.*

Trivers, R. (1971). The evolution of reciprocal altruism. *Quarterly Review of Biology, 46*, 35–57.

Tulving, E. (1972). Episodic and semantic memory. In E. Tulving & W. Donaldson (Eds.), *Origins of memory*. San Diego: Academic Press.*

Tulving, E. (1983). *Elements of episodic memory*. New York: Oxford University Press.*

Tulving, E. (1985). Memory and consciousness. *Canadian Psychology, 26*, 1-12.*

Tulving, E. (1989). Remembering and knowing the past. *American Scientist, 77*, 361–367.*

Tulving, E. (2000). Concepts of memory. In E. Tulving & F.I.M. Craik (Eds.), *The Oxford handbook of memory*. New York: Oxford University Press.*

Tulving, E. (in press). On the uniqueness of episodic memory. In L.-G. Nilsson & H.J. Markowitsch (Eds), *Cognitive neuroscience of memory*. Göttingen: Hogrefe & Huber Publishers.*

Tulving, E., & Markowitsch, H.J. (1998). Episodic and declarative memory: Role of the hippocampus. *Hippocampus, 8*, 198-204.*

Turnbull, C. (1972). *The mountain people*. New York: Simon & Schuster.

Tversky, A., & Fox, C.R. (1995). Weighing risk and uncertainty. *Psychological Review, 102*, 269–283.

Tyhurst, J. (Ed.). (1963). *More for the mind*. Toronto: Canadian Mental Health Association.*

Tyler, C. (1983). Sensory processing of binocular disparity. In C.M. Schor & K.J. Ciuffreda (Eds.), *Vergence eye movements*. Boston: Butterworth.

Udry, R., Billy, J., Morris, N., Groff, T., & Raj, M. (1985). Serum androgenic hormones motivate sexual behavior in adolescent boys. *Fertility and Sterility, 43,* 90–94.

United Nations. (1992). *1991 demographic yearbook.* New York: United Nations.

Ursano, R.J., Fullerton, C.S., Epstein, R.S., Crowley, B., Kao, K.C., Vance, K., Craig, K.J., Dougall, A.L., & Baum,A. (1999). Acute and chronic post-traumatic stress disorder in motor vehicle accident victims. *The American Journal of Psychiatry, 156,* 589–595.

Vadum, A.E., & Rankin, N.O. (1998). *Psychological research.* New York: McGraw-Hill.

Vaillant, G.E. (1977). *Adaptation to life.* Boston: Little, Brown.

Vaillant, G.E. (1983). *The natural history of alcoholism.* Cambridge, MA: Harvard University Press.

Vaillant, G.E. (1992). Is there a natural history of addiction? In C.P. O'Brien & J.H. Jaffe (eds.), *Addictive states.* Cambridge, MA: Harvard University Press.

Vallone, R.P., Griffin, D.W., Lin, S., & Ross, L. (1990). Overconfident prediction of future actions and outcomes by self and others. *Journal of Personality and Social Psychology, 58,* 582–592.

Van Deventer, W. (1983, November). Graphoanalysis as a management tool. *United States Banker,* pp. 74–76.

Vedhara, K., Schifitto, G., McDermott, M., and the Dana Consortium on Therapy for HIV Dementia and Related Disorders (1999). Disease progression in HIV-positive women with moderate to severe immunosuppression: The role of depression. *Behavioral Medicine, 25,* 53–61.

Vernoy, M.W. (1995). Demonstrating classical conditioning in introductory psychology: Needles do not always make balloons pop! In M.E. Ware & D.E. Johnson (Eds.), *Demonstrations and activities in teaching psychology* (Vol. 2). Mahwah, NJ: Erlbaum.

Villani, S., & Sharfstein, S.S. (1999). Evaluating and treating violent adolescents in the managed care era. *The American Journal of Psychiatry, 156,* 458–464.

Vogt, T.M., Mullooly, J.P., Ernst, D., Pople, C.R., & Hollis, J.F. (1992). Social networks as predictors of ischemic heart disease, cancer, stroke, and hypertension. *Journal of Clinical Epidemiology, 45,* 659–666.

Vokey, J.R., & Read, J.D. (1985). Subliminal messages: Between the devil and the media. *American Psychologist, 40,* 1231–1239.*

Volpe, E.P., & Rosenbaum, P.A. (2000). *Understanding evolution* (6th ed.). New York: McGraw-Hill.

Von Békésy, G. (1960). Vibratory patterns of the basilar membrane. In E.G. Wever (Ed.), *Experiments in hearing.* New York: McGraw-Hill.

Vygotsky, L.S. (1962). *Thought and language.* Cambridge, MA: MIT Press.

Wadden, T.A., Foster, G.D., Stunkard, A.J., & Conill, A.M. (1996). Effects of weight cycling on the resting energy expenditure and body composition of obese women. *Eating Disorders, 19,* 5–12.

Wagner, A.D., Schacter, D.L., Rotte, M., Koutstaal, B., Maril, A., Dale, A.M., Rosen, B.R., & Buckner, R.L. (1998). Building memories: Remembering and forgetting of verbal experiences as predicted by brain activity. *Science, 281,* 1185–1187.

Wahlsten, D. (1997). The malleability of intelligence is not constrained by heritability. In B. Devlin, S.E. Fienburg, D.P. Resnick, & K. Roeder (Eds.), *Intelligence, genes, and success: Scientists respond to the Bell Curve.* New York: Copernicus (Springer Verlag).*

Wahlsten, D. (1994). The intelligence of heritability. *Canadian Psychology, 35,* 244-258.*

Wahlsten, D. (1996). Advances in genetic analysis of IQ await a better understanding of environment. In D. K. Detterman (Ed.), *Current topics in human intelligence, (Vol. 5).* Norwood, NJ: Ablex.*

Wahlsten, D., & Gottlieb, G. (1997). The invalid separation of effects of nature and nurture: Lessons from animal experimentation. In R. J. Sternberg & E. L. Grigorenko (Eds.), *Intelligence, heredity and environment.* Cambridge: Cambridge University Press.*

Waits, C., & Shors, D. (1999). *Unabomber.* New York: American World Geographic Publishing.

Walker, L.E. (1999). Psychology and domestic violence around the world. *American Psychologist, 54,* 6–20.

Wallace, R.K., & Benson, H. (1972). The physiology of meditation. *Scientific American, 226,* 83–90.

Wallerstein, R.S. (1989). The psychotherapy research project of the Menninger Foundation: An overview. *Journal of Consulting and Clinical Psychology, 57,* 195–205.

Walsh, W.B. (1995, August). *Person-environment psychology: Contemporary models and perspectives.* Paper presented at the meeting of the American Psychological Association, New York City.

Walsh, W.B., & Betz, N.E. (1995). *Tests and assessment* (3rd ed.). Upper Saddle River, NJ: Prentice Hall.

Wampold, B.E., Mondin, G.W., Moody, M., Stich, F., Benson, K., & Ahn, H. (1997). A meta-analysis of outcome studies comparing bona fide psychotherapies: Empirically, "All must have prizes." *Psychological Bulletin, 122,* 203–215.

Ward, R.A., & Grashial, A.F. (1995). Using astrology to teach research methods to introductory psychology students. In M.E. Ware & D.E. Johnson (Eds.), *Demonstrations and activities in teaching of psychology* (Vol. 1). Mahwah, NJ: Erlbaum.

Warren, R.M. (1999). *Auditory perception.* New York: Cambridge University Press.

Waters, E., Merrick, S.K., Albersheim, L.J., & Treboux, E. (1995, March.). *Attachment security from infancy to early adulthood.* Paper presented at the meeting of the Society for Research on Adolescence, Boston.

Watkins, C.E., & Guarnaccia, C.A. (1999). Introduction: The future of psychotherapy training: Psychodynamic, experimental, and eclectic perspectives. *Journal of Clinical Psychology, 55* 381–383.

Watson, D.L., & Tharp, R.G. (1989). *Self-directed behavior* (5th ed.). Pacific Grove, CA: Brooks/Cole.

Watson, J.B. (1913). Psychology as the behaviorist views it. *Psychological Review, 20,* 158–177.

Watson, J.B. (1928). *Psychological care of the infant and child.* Philadelphia: Lippincott.

Watson, J.B., & Raynor, R. (1920). Emotional reactions. *Journal of Experimental Psychology, 3,* 1–14.

Webb, W.B. (1993). Functions of sleep. In M.A. Carskadon (Ed.), *Encyclopedia of sleep and dreaming.* New York: Macmillan.

Wechsler, D. (1972). "Hold" and "Don't Hold" test. In S.M. Chown (Ed.), *Human aging.* New York: Penguin.

Wechsler, H., Davenport, A., Dowdall, G., Moeykens, B., & Castillo, S. (1994). Health and behavioral consequences of binge drinking in college. *Journal of the American Medical Association, 272,* 1672–1677.

Weidemann, G., Georgilas, A., & Kehoe, E.J. (1999). Temporal specificity in patterning of the rabbit nictitating membrane response. *Animal Learning & Behavior, 27,* 99–109.

Weinberger, D.R., Berman, K.F., & Zec, R.F. (1986). Physiological dysfunction of the dorsalateral prefrontal cortex in schizophrenia. *Archives of General Psychiatry, 43,* 114–124.

Weiner, B. (1986). *An attributional theory of motivation and emotion.* New York: Springer-Verlag.

Weiner, I.B., Exner, J.E., & Sciara, A. (1996). Is the Rorschach welcome in the courtroom? *Journal of Personality Assessment, 67,* 422–424.

Weissman, M.M., Bland, R.C., Canino, G.J., Greenwald, S., Hwu, H.G., Joyce, P.R., Karam, E.G., Lee, C.K., Lellouch, J., Lepine, J.P., Newman, S.C., Rubio-Stipec, M., Wells, J.E., Wickramaratne, P.J., Wittchen, H.U. & Yeh, E.K. (1999). Prevalence of suicide ideation and suicide attempts in nine countries. *Psychological Medicine, 29,* 9–18.

Wellman, B. (1998). Social networks. In H.S. Friedman (Ed.), *Encyclopedia of mental health* (Vol. 3). San Diego: Academic Press.*

Wenzlaff, R.M., & Prohaska, M.L. (1989). When misery loves company: Depression, attributions, and responses to others' moods. *Journal of Experimental Social Psychology, 25,* 220–223.

Werner, E.E. (1989). High risk children in young adulthood: A longitudinal study from birth to 32 years. *American Journal of Orthopsychiatry, 59,* 72–81.

Whipple, B., Ogden, G., & Komisaruk, B. (1992). Analgesia produced in women by genital self-stimulation. *Archives of Sexual Behavior, 9,* 87–99.

White, N.M., & Milner, P.M. (1992). The psychobiology of reinforcers. *Annual Review of Psychology, 43,* 443–471.*

Whiting, B.B. (1989). *Culture and interpersonal behavior.* Paper presented at the meeting of the Society for Research in Child Development, Kansas City.

Whitley, B.E. (1996). *Principles of research in behavioral science.* Mountain View, CA: Mayfield.

Whorf, B.L. (1956). *Language, thought, and creativity.* New York: Wiley.

Wicks, S. R., & Rankin, C. H. (1997). The effects of tap withdrawal response habituation on other withdrawal behaviors: The localization of habituation in the nematode Caenorhabditis elegans. *Behavioral Neuroscience, 111,* 342-353.*

Wicks, S. R., Roehrig, C. J., & Rankin, C. H. (1996). A dynamic network simulation of the nematode tap withdrawal circuit: Predictions concerning synaptic function using behavioral criteria. *Journal of Neuroscience, 16,* 4017-4031.*

Wierzbicki, M. (1999). *Introduction to clinical psychology.* Boston: Allyn & Bacon.

Wiggins, J. S. (1997). In defense of traits. In R. Hogan, J. A. Johnson, & S. R. Briggs (Eds.), *Handbook of personality psychology.* San Diego: Academic Press.*

Wiggins, J. S. (Ed.). (1996). *The five-factor model of personality: Theoretical perspectives.* New York: Guilford Press.*

Wiggins, J. S., & Pincus, A. L. (1992). Personality: Structure and assessment. In M. R. Rosenzweig & L. W. Porter (Eds.), *Annual review of psychology, (vol. 43).* Palo Alto: Annual Reviews Inc.*

Wiggins, J.S., & Trapnell, P.D. (1997). Personality structure: The return of the big five. In R. Hogan, J. Johnson, & Briggs (Eds.), *Handbook of personality research.* San Diego: Academic Press.*

Williams, R.B. (1995). Coronary prone behaviors, hostility, and cardiovascular health. In K. Orth-Gomer & N. Schneiderman (Eds.), *Behavioral medicine approaches to cardiovascular disease prevention.* Mahwah, NJ: Erlbaum.

Williamson, S. E., Harpur, T. J., & Hare, R. D. (1991). Abnormal processing of affective words by psychopaths. *Psychophysiology, 28(3),* 260-273.*

Willis, S.L., & Schaie, K.W. (1994). Assessing everyday competence in the elderly. In C. Fisher & R. Lerner (Eds.), *Applied developmental psychology.* Mahwah, NJ: Erlbaum.

Wilson, B.J., & Gottman, J.M. (1996). Attention—The shuttle between emotion and cognition: Risk, resiliency, and physiological bases. In E.M. Hetherington & E.A. Blechman (Eds.), *Stress, coping, and resilience in children and families.* Mahwah, NJ: Erlbaum.

Wilson, M.A., & McNaughton, B.L. (1994). Reactivation of hippocampal ensemble memories during sleep. *Science, 265,* 676-678.

Winner, E. (1996). *Gifted children: Myths and realities.* New York: Basic Books.

Wisch, A.F., & Mahalik, J.R. (1999). Male therapists' clinical bias: Influence of client gender roles and therapist gender role conflict. *Journal of Counseling Psychology, 46,* 51-61.

Witelson, S. F. (1985). The brain connection: The corpus callosum is larger in left handers. *Science, 229,* 665-668.*

Witelson, S.F., & Kigar, D.L. (1992). Sylvian fissure morphology and asymmetry in men and women: Bilateral differences in relation to handedness in men. *Journal of Comparative Neurology, 323,* 326-340.*

Witelson, S.F., Kigar, D.L., & Harvey, T. (1999). The exceptional brain of Albert Einstein. *Lancet, 353,* 2149-2153.*

Wober, M. (1966). Sensotypes. *Journal of Social Psychology, 70,* 181–189.

Wolpe, J. (1963). Behavior therapy in complex neurotic states. *British Journal of Psychiatry, 110,* 28–34.

Wong, P.T.P. (1989). Personal meaning and successful aging. *Canadian Psychology, 30(3),* 516-525.*

Wong, S. (in press). Treatment of criminal psychopaths. In S. Hodgins & R. Miller-Isberner (Eds.), *Violence, crime and mentally disordered offenders: Concepts and methods for effective treatment and prevention.* New York: Wiley.*

Wood, J.V. (1989). Theory and research concerning social comparisons of personal attributes. *Psychological Bulletin, 106,* 231–248.*

Woodruff-Pak, D.S. (1999). New directions for a classical paradigm: Human eyeblink conditioning. *Psychological Science, 10,* 1–3.

Wooley, S.C., & Garner, D.M. (1991). Obesity treatment: The high cost of false hope. *Journal of the American Dietetic Association, 91,* 1248–1251.

Worell, J., & Robinson, D. (1993). Feminist counseling therapy for the 21st century. *Counseling Psychologist, 21,* 92–96.

Wright, B.D. (1999). Fundamental measurement for psychology. In S.E. Embretson & S.L. Hershberger (Eds.), *The new rules of measurement.* Mahwah, NJ: Erlbaum.

Wright, J.C. (1995, March). *Effects of viewing Sesame Street: The longitudinal study of media and time use.* Paper presented at the meeting of the Society for Research in Child Development, Indianapolis.

Wright, R. (1996, March 25). Can machines think? *Time,* pp. 50–56.

Wrightsman, L.S., Nietzel, M.T., & Fortune, W.H. (1998). *Psychology and the legal system* (4th ed.). Pacific Grove, CA: Brooks/Cole.

Yalom, I.D. (1975). *The therapy and practice of group psychotherapy.* New York: Basic Books.

Yalom, I.D. (1995). *The theory and practice of group psychotherapy* (4th ed.). New York: Basic Books.

Yarmey, A.D. (1973). I recognize your face but I can't remember your name: Further evidence for the tip-of-the-tongue phenomenon. *Memory and Cognition, 1,* 287–290.*

Yoder, J.D. (1999). *Women and gender: Transforming psychology.* Upper Saddle River, NJ: Prentice-Hall.

Yuille, J.C. (1997). Interviewing children is a complex task. *Contemporary Psychology, 42(9),* 803-804.*

Yuille, J.C., & McEwan, N.H. (1985). Use of hypnosis as an aid to eyewitness memory. *Journal of Applied Psychology, 70(2),* 389-400.*

Yuille, J.C., & Wells, G.L. (1991) Concerns about the applications of research findings: The issue of ecological validity. In Doris, J. (Ed.), *The suggestibility of children's recollections: Implications for eyewitness testimony.* Washington, DC: American Psychological Association.*

Zajonc, R.B. (1965). Social facilitation. *Science, 149,* 269–274.

Zajonc, R.B. (1984). On the primacy of affect. *American Psychologist, 39,* 117–123.

Zakrajsek, T. (1999). *Instructor's manual for Psychology* (3rd ed.). by J. Halonen and J.S. Santrock. New York: McGraw-Hill.

Zanna, M.P. (1994). On the nature of prejudice. *Canadian Psychology, 35,* 11-23.*

Zeidner, M., & Saklofske, D.H. (1996). Adaptive and maladaptive coping. In M. Zeidner & N.S. Endler (Eds.), *Handbook of coping: Theory, research, applications.* New York: Wiley.*

Zelnik, M., & Kantner, J.F. (1977). Sexual and contraceptive experiences of young unmarried women in the United States, 1976 and 1971. *Family Planning Perspectives, 9,* 55–71.

Zepelin, H., & Rechtschaffen, A. (1974). Mammalian sleep, longevity, and energy metabolism. *Brain, Behavior, and Evolution, 10,* 425–470.

Zeren, A.S., & Makosky, V.P. (1995). Teaching observational methods. In M.E. Ware & D.E. Johnson (Eds.), *Demonstrations and activities in teaching of psychology* (Vol. 1). Mahwah, NJ: Erlbaum.

Ziegert, K.A. (1983). The Swedish prohibition of corporal punishment: A preliminary report. *Journal of Marriage and the Family, 45,* 917-926.

Zikovit,z, D.C. & Harris, L.R. (1999). Head tilt during driving. *Ergonomics, 42,* 740-746.*

Zilbergeld, B. (1992). *The new male sexuality.* New York: Bantam Books.

Zillman, D. (1998). Anger. In H.S. Friedman (Ed.), *Encyclopedia of mental health* (Vol. 1). San Diego: Academic Press.

Zimmerman, B.J., Bonner, S., & Lovach, R. (1996). *Developing self-regulated learners.* Washington, DC: American Psychological Association.

Zimmerman, C., Bisanz, G. L., &, Bisanz, J. (1998). Everyday scientific literacy: Do students use knowledge about the social context and methods of research to evaluate news briefs about science? *Alberta Journal of Educational Research, 44,* 188-207.*

Zola, S. (1996, June). *The medial temporal lobe memory system: Findings from human and non-human primates.* Paper presented at the meeting of the American Psychological Society, San Francisco.

Zuckerman, M. (1979). *Sensation seeking.* Hillsdale, NJ: Erlbaum.

Credits

Figure 16.9: From *The Triangle of Love* by Robert J. Sternberg. Copyright ©1988 by Basic Books, Inc. Reprinted by permission of Basic Books, a division of HarperCollins Publishers, Inc.

APPENDIX

Figure A.1: *Psychology: Themes and Variations,* 4th edition, by W. Weiten, © 1998. Reprinted with permission of Wadsworth Publishing, a division of International Thomson Publishing. Fax 800-730-2215.

PHOTOGRAPHS

CHAPTER 1

Opener: © Michael Tcherevkoff/The Image Bank; **p. 3** (left): AP/Wide World Photos; **p. 3** (right): © Mike Ridewood/Canadian Press; **p. 6:** © The Bettman Archive; **p. 7 & p. 8:** Psychology Archives-University of Akron; **p. 9:** © The Bettman Archive; **p. 10:** © Corbis; **p. 11:** © Tom McHugh/Photo Researchers; **p. 12:** Llavenil Subbiah; **p. 13** (left): © Jay Dickman; **p. 13** (right): © V. Pietropaolo **1.2:** Wendt, James, Binet, Pavlov: © The Bettmann Archive; Murray: Reprinted by permission of the McCord Museum; Skinner: Courtesy of Jane Reed, Howard University News Office.; Erikson: © UPI/Bettmann Newsphotos; Maslow: © The Bettmann Archive; Rogers: Centers for the Study of the Person; Bandura: Courtesy of Albert Bandura; Bem: Courtesy of Sandra Bem; Hebb: Courtesey of the McGill Archives Calkins: Courtesy of Archives of the History of American Psychology, University of Akron; Hall and Washburn: Courtesy of Archives of the History of American Psychology, University of Akron; Watson: © The Bettmann Archive; Baldwin: Courtesy of the Department of Psychology, University of Toronto; Horney, Allport, Freud: © The Bettmann Archive; Sperry: Courtesy of Roger Sperry; Berry: Courtesy of John Berry; photo credit Monica Hurt; Pyke: Courtesy of Sandra Pyke; Simon: © UPI/Bettman News Photos; **p. 15** (top): AP/Wide World Photos; **p. 15** (bottom): J. D. Francolon/The Gamma Liaison Network; **p. 18:** Courtesy of Mark R. Rosenzweig; **p. 19:** © Tim Krochak/Canadian Press; **p. 20:** © Carol Stone/Tony Stone; **p. 22:** Courtesy of Sandra Pyke; **p. 23** (Tiger): © Blos (M. Gunter)/Peter Arnold, Inc.; **p. 23** (Chart): © The Bettman Archive

CHAPTER 2

Opener: © Ray Stott/The Image Works; **p. 34:** (All): © PhotoDisc; **2.1** (left & right): Courtesy of Albert Bandura; **p. 40:** © Sharon Beals/Insight; **p. 42:** © Ken Regan Pictures; **p. 44:** © John Madere/Psychology Today/Sussex Publishers; **p. 45:** © John Amos/Photo Researchers; **2.5:** © Doug Martin/Photo Researchers; **p. 55:** Courtesy of Cannie Stark; **p. 56** (top): Courtesy of Sandra Graham; (bottom): © John Mitterer; **p. 58:** Photo by Paula Stanovich

CHAPTER 3

Opener : © Scott Camazine/Photo Researchers; **p. 65:** © Enrico Ferorelli; **3.1:** © Will and Deni McIntyre/Photo Researchers; **p. 67:** © Ted Thai/Time/Magazine; **p. 68:** Courtesy of David M. Buss; **p. 69:** Courtesy of Martin Daly & Margo Wilson; **3.4 & 3.9:** © Lennart Nilsson/ Albert Bonniers Forlag AB; **3.10:** © Hank Morgan/Photo Researchers; **p. 82:** Courtesy of Jackson Beatty; **3.13:** © John Wiley, California Institute of Technology, estate of James Olds; **3.14:** © A. Glauberman/Photo Researchers; **3.16:** From H. Damasio, T. Grabowski, R. Frank, A. M. Galaburda, and A. R. Damasio, "The Return of Phineas

Gage: Clues about the brain from a famous patient" in *Science*, 264:1102–1105, 1994. Department of Neurology and Image Analysis Facility, University of Iowa. Copyright © 1994 American Association for the Advancement of *Science*.; **3.17:** © Wilder Penfield Papers/ Montreal Neurological Institute; **p. 89** (top): Courtesy of Sandra Witelson; (bottom): Courtesy of Steven and Cindi Binder; **p. 91:** Courtesy of Bryan Kolb; **3.B** (left & right): © James Balog/Tony Stone Images; **3.21:** © Charles Gupton/Picturesque; **3.22:** © Steven Peterson; **3.24:** Lennart Nilsson/Albert Bonniers Forlag AB

CHAPTER 4

Opener: © Dennis Lisl/The Image Bank-Texas; **p. 104:** © H. Werb/Shooting Star; **p. 105:** Courtesy of Ronald Melzack; **4.5:** © Morris Karol; **4.6:** © Burrton McNeely/ The Image Bank-Texas; **4.7:** Fritz Gorol/Life Magazine © Time; **4.8:** Courtesy of MacBeth, Division of Kollmorgen, Inc.; **4.14** (top): © Chuck Kuhn/The Image Bank-Chicago; (right): © Martin Chamberland/Canadian Press; **4.18 a:** © J. P. Laffont/Sygma; **b:** Courtesy Peabody Museum of Salem, Salem, Mass. Photograph by Mark Sexton; **p. 124:** © Chip Simons 1996; **4.20 a:** © Lennart Nilsson/Albert Bonniers Forlag AB; **b:** © Lou Jones/The Image Bank-Chicago; **4.23:** M. C. Escher's "Relativity" © 1999 © Cordon Art B. V.-Baarn-Holland. All rights reserved.; **4.25:** © 1994 Jun Oi; **4.26:** Reprinted by permission of The Art Gallery of Ontario and Mrs. James Knox; **4.A:** Van Gogh, Vincent. *The Starry Night* (1889). Oil on canvas, 29 × 36 1/4" (73.7 × 92.1 cm). The Museum of Modern Art, New York. Acquired through the Lillie P. Bliss Bequest. Photograph © 1996 The Museum of Modern Art, New York.; **4.B:** © Scala/Art Resource, NY; **4.C:** Emily Carr, *Old Time Coastal Village,* Reproduced by permission of The Vancouver Art Gallery/Trevor Mills; **4.D:** Picasso, Pablo. *Nude Woman,* Alisa Mellon Bruce Fund. Photograph © 1996 Board of Trustees, National Gallery of Art, Washington.; **4.29:** © Lawrence Migdale; **4.34** (left): © Herman Eisenbeiss/Photo Researchers; (right): © Emilio Mercado/Jeroboam; **4.36:** © Dr. Peter Thompson; **4.38:** © Enrico Ferorelli; **p. 141:** Courtesy of James Alcock; **p. 143:** © Dana Fineman/Sygma; **4.40:** © R. Joedecke/ The Image Bank-Chicago; **4.41:** © Don Peterson/Psychology Today/Sussex Publishers

CHAPTER 5

Opener: © David Hiser/Photographers Aspen; **5.1** (top to bottom): © Steve Dunwell Photography/The Image Bank-Texas; © David Young-Wolff/Photo Edit; © David R. Frazier Photolibrary, Inc.; © Randy Duchaine/The Stock Market; © Luis Castaneda/The Image Bank-Chicago; © Cesar Paredes/The Stock Market; © Barry Christensen/Stock Boston; **p. 153** (a) inset: © Joel Gordon 1991; (b): © Dean Press Images/The Image Works; **5.2** (top): © Stephen Dalton/Photo Researchers; (bottom): © J. Stephens/Superstock; **p. 155** (top): Courtesy of San Diego Historical Society Union Tribune Collection; (bottom): © Michel Siffre/NGS Image Collection; **p. 157** (top): Courtesy of Roger Broughton; **5.3** (left): © Will and Dean McIntyre/Photo Researchers; **5.4:** © J. Allan Hobson & Hoffman-LaRouche, Inc.; **p. 158:** Courtesy of Mary Carskadon; **5.8** (top left): THE NIGHTMARE by Henry Fuseli. Oil on canvas, 101.6 x 127.0. Founders Society Purchase with funds Mr. and Mrs. Bert L. Smokler and Mr. and Mrs. Lawrence A. Fleischman. Photograph © 1996 The Detroit Institute of Arts.; (top right): Scala/ Art Resource, NY; (bottom right): Chagall, Marc. I AND THE VILLAGE. 1911. Oil on canvas 6´ 3 5/8" × 59 5/8" (192.1 × 151.4 cm) The Museum of Modern Art, New York. Mrs. Simon

Guggenheim Fund. Photograph © 1999 The Museum of Modern Art, New York.; **p. 168** (top): © Jane Steig Parsons/Prints Charming Photography; (bottom): © James Wilson/Woodfin Camp; **p. 169:** © Billy E. Barnes/PhotoEdit; **5.9:** © Photodisc; **p. 170:** © David Parker/Photo Researchers; **5.10 p. 176** (top): © Derik Allen Murray/The Image Bank-Chicago; (middle & bottom): Courtesy of Drug Enforcement Administration; **5.10 p. 177** (All): Courtesy of Drug Enforcement Administration

CHAPTER 6

Opener: © Photodisc; **p. 185:** © Canadian Press/Toronto Sun; **p. 187** (top): © Whitney Lane/The Image Bank-Texas; (bottom): © The Granger Collection, New York; **p. 191:** Courtesy of Robert Rescorla; **6.3:** © Photodisc; **p. 198:** © Rita Nammin/Photo Researchers; **6.8:** Nina Leen, Life Magazine © Time, Inc.; **p. 199** (bottom): © Bob Krist/Leo de Wys; **p. 204:** © Chris Johnson/Stock Boston; **6.15:** Courtesy of Animal Behavior Enterprises, Inc.

CHAPTER 7

Opener: © Grant V. Faint/The Image Bank; **7.6:** © Photodisc; **p. 226:** Courtesy of Mike Pugh; **p. 230:** Courtesy of Endel Tulving; **p. 232** (top): AP/Wide World Photos; (bottom): © Heather Spears/Canadian Press; **p. 233:** Courtesy of Elizabeth Loftus; **7.16** (left): AP/Wide World Photos; (right): © Reuters/Rick Wilking/Archive Photos; **p. 240** (left): © Eric Gay/Associated Press; (right): © Bassignac-Deville-Merillon-Turpin/The Gamma Liaison Network; **p. 242:** AP/Wide World Photos; **p 243:** Courtesy of The Wellcome Institute Library, London; **p. 244:** Courtesy of Endel Tulving;

CHAPTER 8

Opener: © The Purcell team/CORBIS; **p. 253** (left): AP/Wide World Photos; (right): Ted Thai/Time Magazine; **p. 255:** Courtesy of Herbert Simon; **p. 256:** © Peter Menzel/Stock Boston; **8.2** (top left): Scala/Art Resource, NY; (top right): Palazzo da Mula, Venice, Chester Dale Collection, © 1998 Board of Trustees, National Gallery of Art, Washington, 1908, oil on canvas, .620 × .811 (24½ × 31⅞); framed: .863 × 1.054 × .107 (34 × 41½ × 4 ¼); (bottom): Paul Klee, DANCE YOU MONSTER TO MY SOFT SONG!, 1972. Gift, Solomon R. Guggenheim, 1938. Photograph by Lee B. Ewing © The Solomon R. Guggenheim Foundation, New York. (FN 38.508); **p. 260** (All): © John W. Thoeming; **p. 264:** Courtesy of Ellen J. Langer; **8.7** (left & right): © Everett Collection, Inc.; **p. 269** (top): © 1999 James Balog; (bottom): Courtesy of Noam Chomsky; **p. 270:** © John Carter/Photo Researchers; **p. 272:** © Anthony Bannister/Animals Animals/Earth Scenes; **p. 274:** From Curtiss, *Genie: A Psycholinguitic Study of a Modern Day "Wild Child,"* Copyright © 1977 Academic Press, Orlando, FL.; **8.9:** © Enrico Ferorelli; **8.A** (top left inset): © Superstock; (top right): © Holton/Superstock; (bottom): Courtesy of Ellen Bialystok; **p. 283** (All): © John W. Thoeming

CHAPTER 9

Opener: © John Riley/Tony Stone Images; **p. 287:** © Rita Mass/The Image Bank-Texas; **p. 290** (top): © Stephen Collins/Photo Researchers; **9.2:** © Monkmeyer Press/Merrim; **p. 291:** Courtesy of the National Library of Medicine; **p. 295:** © Jay Gardner, 1998; **9.5:** (top left): © Photodisc; (top middle left): © Charles Place/The Image Bank-Chicago; (top middle right): © Bill Varies/The Image Bank-Chicago; (top right): © John P. Kelly/The Image Bank-Chicago; (bottom

Name Index

A

Abbey, A., 577
Abel, E. L., 326
Abeles, M., 93
Abelson, R., 233
Abrams, A. I., 535
Abrams, R. L., 104
Abramson, L. Y., 467
Ackerman, P. L., 432
Acocella, J., 501
Adams, H. E., 454
Adler, A., 419
Adler, N. E., 451
Adler, T., 66
Agnew, N. McK., 22
Ahn, H., 501
Aiken, L. R., 317
Ainsworth, M. D. S., 338, 339, 340
Akamine, T. X., 433
Akert, R. M., 552, 559
Akiskal, H., 464
Al-Issa, I., 451
Albersheim, L. J., 340
Alberti, R., 534, 547
Alberto, P., 203
Albright, J. M., 491
Alcock, J. E., 141, 143
Alderman, M. K., 550
Aldrich, M. S., 159
Alexopoulos, G. S., 466
Allan, R., 521
Allen, J. J. B., 521
Allen, M. T., 539
Allison, K. R., 532
Alloy, L. B., 501
Allport, G. W., 430, 431, 570
Almagor, M., 432
Alpert, S., 466
Alsaker, F. D., 346
Altemeyer, B., 570
American Sleep Disorders
        Association, 160
Ames, M. A., 385
Amir, S., 155
Anastasi, A., 306
Anastasiades, P., 502
Anderson, B. L., 383, 519, 520
Anderson, M., 238
Anderson, N. H., 553, 554, 578
Anderson, S. C., 389
Andrews, B., 459
Angus, L., 502
Anisfeld, E., 274
Anselmi, D. L., 54
Antonuccio, D. O., 495
Appenzellar, T., 234
Applebaum, M. I., 343
Applefield, J. M., 46, 579
Arbuckle, T., 172
Archer, D., 405, 580
Arkowitz, H., 509
Arndt, S., 464
Arnitz, A., 502
Arnoux, D., 525
Aron, A., 398
Aronson, E., 552, 557, 558, 559, 573

Aronson, J., 558
Arps, K., 582
Arsenault, L., 435
Artz, S., 4
Arvanitogiannis, A., 155
Asch, S. E., 553, 561
Asher, J., 275
Ashton, M. C., 433, 438, 439
Askensay, J. J. M., 160
Asnis, G. M., 456
Astin, A. W., 161, 583
Atkin, J. M., 391
Atkinson, D. R., 504, 513
Atkinson, J. W., 388
Atkinson, R. C., 224, 237
Atnafou, R., 351
Auerbach, J. S., 435
Auerbach, S. M., 534
Averill, J. R., 404
Avis, M. H., 172, 175
Azar, B., 91

B

Baars, B., 150
Bachevalier, J., 470
Bachman, J. G., 172, 175, 352
Backs-Dermott, G. J., 494
Bacon, M. K., 390
Baddeley, A., 224, 226, 243, 251
Baer, D. M., 204
Bahrick, H. P., 227
Bahrick, P. O., 227
Baillargeon, R., 336
Baity, M. R., 435
Baldwin, J. D., 203, 386
Baldwin, J. I., 203, 386
Baldwin, J.M., 7
Bales, J., 266
Ball, W., 140
Balota, D. A., 94
Baltes, P. B., 324, 356, 360
Banaji, M. R., 570
Bandura, A., 8, 36, 41, 49, 207, 215, 269, 389, 424, 492, 532, 557, 565, 579, 580
Bangert-Drowns, R. L., 204, 294
Bar-Hillel, M., 437
Baranowsky, A. B., 459
Barbaree, H. E., 577
Bard, P., 396
Barman, J., 392
Barnes, M., 585
Baron, N., 270, 283
Barrera, M. E., 329
Barrett, M. C., 384, 542
Barron, R. W., 275
Barry, H., 390
Bartlett, F. C., 230, 231, 570
Bartlett, J. C., 224
Barton, D., 482
Barton, E., 438
Bartoshuk, L. M., 122
Bass, J., 351
Bates, J. A., 122
Bates, J. E., 341

Batson, C. D., 122
Bauer, K., 380, 383, 542
Baum, A., 459
Baumeister, R. F., 427, 530, 578, 584
Baumrind, D., 341
Beaman, A. L., 582
Beattie, G., 235
Beatty, J., 71, 121
Beauchamp, G. K., 122
Beck, A. T., 466, 494
Bednar, R. L., 428
Begg, I., 220, 221
Begg, I. M., 104
Belicki, K., 162, 166, 242
Bell, A. P., 385
Bellanca, J., 297
Bellesiles, M. A., 578
Belsky, J. K., 356
Belson, W., 45
Bem, D., 558
Ben-Abba, E., 437
Ben-Shakhar, G., 437
Benbow, C. P., 554
Benet, V., 432
Benjafield, J.G., 6, 7, 11, 38, 254, 255
Benjamin, L. T., 6
Bennett, R. H., 577
Bennett, W. I., 378
Benson, H., 535
Benson, K., 501
Bento, S., 340
Bereiter, C., 261
Bergman, H., 93, 234
Berkman, L. F., 533
Berko, J., 273
Berkowitz, L., 578
Berman, K. F., 470
Bernstein, D., 166, 473
Berry, J., 13
Berry, J. W., 141, 304, 578
Berscheid, E., 585, 586, 587
Bertolino, A., 470
Besner, D., 275
Best, J., 254
Betz, N. E., 434
Beutler, L. E., 509
Bexton, W. H., 370
Bhrolchain, M., 526
Bhugra, D., 383
Bialystok, E., 274, 275
Bidikov, I., 353
Biller, H., 345
Billings, A. G., 533
Billings, R., 161
Billy, J., 380
Birdsong, D., 275
Bisantz, A. M., 255
Bisanz, G. L., 263
Bisanz, J., 263
Bishop, S., 467
Bjork, R. A., 160, 170
Bjorklund, A., 93
Björkqvist, K., 580
Black, P., 391
Black, S., 236
Blackmore, S., 142
Blackwell, J. C., 179
Blair, C., 303

Blake, J., 272
Blanchard, E. B., 492
Bland, R. C., 452, 456, 465, 467, 473
Bloomel, J. M., 566
Blue, J. H., 346
Blumenthal, J. A., 537
Blundell, J. E., 376
Boer, D. G., 304
Boeschen, L., 459
Boisvert, J.-M., 199, 494
Bond, R., 562
Bondi, A. M., 509
Bonebakker, A. F., 104
Bonke, B., 104
Bonner, S., 390
Bonvillain, N., 14
Boodoo, G., 303, 304, 317
Bookbinder, M., 104
Boomsma, D. I., 288
Booth, A., 380
Booth, C. L., 342, 343
Boring, E. G., 287
Borsoi, D., 401
Bouchard, C., 458
Bouchard, T. J., 65, 66, 303, 304, 317, 458
Boucock, A., 242
Bourhis, R. Y., 574
Bourne, E. J., 534
Bowden, C., 466
Bower, G. H., 222
Bowers, T. G., 502
Bowlby, J., 324, 339, 466
Boyer, L. B., 487
Boykin, A. W., 303, 304, 317
Boynton, R. M., 112
Bradley, M. M., 466
Bradley, M. T., 395
Bradley, R. H., 343
Brakke, K. E., 276
Brammer, L. M., 502
Brandt, R., 555
Brannon, L., 401, 588
Bransford, J. D., 258, 283
Bratslavsky, E., 584
Brazelton, T. B., 342
Breault, L., 52
Bregman, A. S., 116
Brehm, J. W., 393
Brehony, K. A., 581
Breland, K., 210
Breland, M., 210
Brennan, P., 577
Brewer, J. B., 235
Brewer, M. B., 572
Brewin, C. R., 459
Brichtswein, K., 473
Brickman, P., 404
Brickner, M. A., 566
Brigham, J. C., 232, 570
Brim, O., 358
Brislin, R. W., 13, 44, 574
Broberg, A. G., 202, 211–212
Brocato, R. M., 566
Brodbeck, D. R., 208, 209
Brodsky, A., 178
Brody, N., 303, 304, 317
Broekhuijsen, A. M., 521
Brook, D. W., 179

Brook, J. S., 179
Brooks, G. R., 588
Brooks, J. G., 22, 263
Brooks, L. R., 257, 258
Brooks, M. G., 22, 263
Brooks-Gunn, J., 346, 526
Broughton, R., 161
Broughton, R. J., 154, 156, 162
Broughton, W. A., 162
Brouwers, M. C., 504
Brown, A. S., 235
Brown, E. N., 155
Brown, G., 526
Brown, G. D., 69
Brown, G. M., 234
Brown, H. D., 451
Brown, J. D., 530
Brown, K. J., 505
Brown, L. S., 386
Brown, R., 269, 553
Brown, R. J., 572
Brown, S. D., 532
Brown, T., 54
Brownell, K. A., 376, 377, 378
Brownell, K. D., 378
Brownlee, S., 110
Bruce, D., 231, 239
Bruck, M., 242
Bruess, C. E., 542
Bruner, J. S., 279, 553
Bruning, R. H., 222, 263
Brunstein, J. C., 389
Bryan, J., 356
Bryden, M. P., 89
Bryson, M., 579
Buchanon, L., 275
Buckner, R. L., 235
Bullington, J., 557
Burchinal, M. R., 343
Buree, B. U., 378
Buriel, R., 343
Burke, P. B., 340
Burke, R. J., 523
Burlingame, G. M., 498
Burns, D., 589, 593
Burns, J. W., 521
Burnstein, E., 582
Buss, A. H., 341
Buss, D. M., 12, 68, 370, 380, 581, 585
Butcher, J. N., 438, 473, 482, 496, 535
Butler, G., 502
Butler, J., 78, 80
Butler, R. A., 369
Buunk, B. P., 554
Byne, W., 470

C

Cabeza, R., 236
Cacioppo, J. T., 393
Cairns, R. B., 324
Calhoun, J. F., 456
Callicott, J. H., 470
Camburn, D., 20
Cameron, N., 457

Campbell, B., 297
Campbell, D. T., 141
Campbell, F. A., 301
Campbell, J. D., 562
Campbell, L., 297
Campbell, S. B., 343
Campbell, W. K., 552
Canino, G. J., 465
Cannon, W. B., 373, 396
Cantor, N., 389, 530
Capuzzi, D., 498
Carbonneau, L., 459
Carkenord, D. M., 557
Carlson, N., 87, 91
Caron, S. L., 382
Carr, T.H., 275
Carrere, S., 20
Carroll, D. W., 178, 268
Carson, R. C., 473, 496, 535
Carswell, R. S., 437
Cartwright, R., 161
Cascella, N. G., 505
Case, L., 309
Case, R., 336
Cassiday, P. B., 585
Cassidy, J. F., 454
Castelnuovo-Tedesco, P., 482
Castillo, S., 172
Catano, V., 466
Cates, W., 543
Cause, A. M., 56
Ceci, S. J., 242, 301, 303,
    304, 317
Centers for Disease Control
    and Prevention, 543
Cerel, S., 543
Cermak, L. S., 227
Chaikelson, J. S., 172
Chaiken, S., 556
Chambers, E., 162
Chance, P., 193, 199
Chandler, M. J., 480
Chang, E. C., 525
Changeux, J., 12
Chaput, Y., 494
Charney, D., 506
Chartrand, L., 274
Chase-Landsdale, P. L., 526
Chastain, G., 53
Chaves, J. F., 167
Chavillion, J., 12
Chen, C., 391
Chen, J., 557
Cherek, D. R., 577
Chertkow, H., 234
Chescheir, M. W., 488
Chess, S., 341
Chichetti, D., 342
Child, I. L., 390
Chodorow, N., 420
Chomsky, N., 269
Christensen, A., 498, 499
Christensen, L., 378
Christiansen, K., 380
Chrousos, G. P., 346
Church, A. T., 433
Cialdini, R. B., 556, 561,
    582, 593
Cicchetti, D., 342
Clark, D. M., 502
Clark, E. V., 272
Clark, L. A., 453
Clark, M., 222
Clark, N. M., 532
Clarke, P. R. F., 158
Clarkson, M. C., 329

Claxton-Oldfield, S., 526
Clayton, L., 172
Cleckley, H. M., 461
Clément, R., 274, 574
Clifford, R. M., 343
Clifton, R. K., 329
Cloninger, S. C., 430
Clum, G. A., 502
Coan, J., 20
Coates, D., 404
Cobb, P., 390
Cochran, S. D., 543
Cohen, G., 558
Cohen, J. D., 150
Cohen, L. A., 540
Cohen, L. R., 378
Cohen, P., 179
Cohen, R. L., 401
Cohen, S., 521, 533
Coie, J. D., 37
Colby, A., 348
Cole, M., 212, 336
Cole, S. R., 212, 336
Coleman, J., 542
Collins, M., 356, 357, 574
Comarow, D. D., 488
Committee on Pediatric
    AIDS, 326
Comstock, G. W., 540
Conill, A. M., 378
Connell, J. P., 389
Connor, P. D., 326
Conway, M. A., 239
Cook, D. A., 502
Cooney, T. J., 391
Cooper, Z., 466
Coplan, R., 342
Coren, S., 112, 116, 138, 378
Corey, G., 138, 509
Corkin, S., 244
Cornelius, R. R., 397
Cornell, D., 3
Correy, B., 242
Corsini, R. J., 420
Coryell, W. H., 464
Costa, P. T., 431, 438
Couglan, J., 235
Courtney, B. E., 428
Couwenbergs, C., 380
Cowley, G., 4, 276
Cox, B. J., 457, 505
Cox, M., 343
Coyne, J. C., 525
Cozby, F., 5
Craig, K.J., 459
Craik, F. I. M., 219, 220,
    234, 355
Cramer, J., 506
Cramer, K. M., 343
Cramer, P., 436
Crandall, C., 582
Crasilneck, H. B., 170
Crits-Cristoph, P., 502
Crocker, J., 572
Cronkite, R. C., 533
Crooks, R., 380, 383, 542
Cross, J., 561
Cross, T., 395
Crosshite, F. J., 391
Crouter, A. C., 342
Crowley, B., 459
Crowley, M., 584
Csikszentmihalyi, M., 311,
    312, 313, 317
Cuddy, L. L., 118
Cuddy, M., 242

Culebras, A., 162
Cummings, A. L., 498
Cunningham, M. R., 581
Curtiss, S., 273
Cushner, K., 44
Cutler, B. L., 232
Cutler, G. B., 346
Cutrona, C. E., 589
Czeisler, C. A., 155

Dabbs, J. M., 578
Dale, A. M., 235
Daly, M., 12, 68, 69, 576
Dance, K. A., 530
Daneman, M., 104, 226
Dannals, R. F., 505
d'Ansia, G. I. D., 458
Darley, J. M., 582
Darou, W. S., 304
Darwin, C., 68, 400
Das, J. P., 308
Dasen, P. R., 141
Davenport, A., 172
David, J. P., 431
Davidson, R. J., 89
Davies, D., 161
Davis, J. H., 566
Davis, K. L., 354, 470, 498, 505
Davison, A. R., 557
Davison, G. C., 354, 448
Dawes, R. M., 501
Dawson, M. R. W., 256
de Castell, S., 579
de Jong-Gierveld, J., 588
De La Ronde, C., 584
De Luca, R. V., 488
de Silva, P., 383
Debaryshe, B. D., 580
DeBattista, C., 464, 466
deCatanzaro, D., 68, 370
Deci, E., 389
DeCola, J. P., 188, 191
DeCourville, N., 172
Deitsch, S. E., 473
DelCarpio, R., 234
Dell, G. S., 279
Dement, W. C., 154, 156
Demorest, A. P., 567
Denmark, F. L., 55, 588
DeRubeis, R. J., 502
Desmond, J. E., 235
DeSpelder, L. A., 361
Deutsch, M., 574
deVilliers, J. G., 273
deVilliers, P. A., 273
Devine, P. G., 574
Devries, L. K., 161
Dewey, J., 263
Dibbell, J., 254
Dickinson, D., 297
Dickson, G. L., 352
Diener, E., 402, 404
Diener, M. B., 402
Dimeff, L. A., 172
Dion, K. K., 522, 585, 586
Dion, K. L., 522, 572, 585, 586
Doane, B. K., 460
Dobson, K., 52, 466
Dobson, K. S., 6, 494
Dodd, D. K., 566
Dodge, J. A., 532

Dodge, K., 37
Dohrenwend, B. P., 525
Dolgoy, L., 521
Dollard, J., 578
Domhoff, G. W., 166
Domjan, M. P., 191
Doob, L. W., 578
Dorfman, D., 473
Dorn, L. D., 346
Dossey, J. A., 391
Doty, R. L., 124
Doucette, D., 161
Dougall, A. L., 459
Dougherty, D. M., 395, 577
Dowdall, G., 172
Downs, D., 555
Doyle, J., 14
Doyle, W. J., 521, 533
Dozois, D. J., 494
Draguns, J. G., 451, 467
Draine, S. C., 104
Dreary, I. J., 430
Druckman, D., 160, 170
Dryfoos, J., 179, 350
Duffy, J. F., 155
Dunlop, A., 242
Dunn. L., 506
Dunnett, S. B., 93
Dupras, A., 384
Dura, J. R., 520
Duran, R., 351
Durrant, J. E., 202, 211
Dutton, D., 398
Dwyer, J. J., 532
Dywan, J., 355

Eagly, A. H., 556, 580, 584
Ebata, A. T., 529
Eccles, J. S., 390
Eckert, E. D., 66, 458
Edmeads, J., 161
Educational Testing Service,
    391
Edwardh, M., 161
Edwards, B., 89
Edwards, C. D., 203
Edwards, J. R., 432
Edwards, S., 539
Egan, M., 470
Eibl-Eibesfeldt, I., 576
Eissenberg, T., 541
Ekman, P., 398, 399, 400, 409
Elder, J. H., 129
Elkind, D., 347
Elliot, A. J., 552
Elliott, J. F., 465
Ellis, A., 221, 494, 496
Ellis, L., 385
Ellis, R., 256
Embretson, S. E., 289
Emerson, P. E., 340
Emmons, M., 534, 547
Empson, J. A. C., 158
Emrick, D. C., 179
Endicott, J., 464
Endler, N. S., 412, 427, 457,
    464, 467, 505, 529
Engvik, H., 433
Enns, J. T., 116
Enzle, M. E., 389
Epling, W. F., 203

Eppley, K. R., 535
Epstein, R. S., 459
Erikson, E. H., 10, 337, 339,
    419, 488
Ernst, D., 533
Ervin, F., 161
Ervin, F. E., 210
Esses, V. M., 570
Evans, D. L., 452, 505
Evans, D. R., 54, 449, 484
Everly, G. S., 524
Evett, S. R., 574
Exner, J. E., 435
Eysenck, H. J., 431, 501, 577

Faber, D., 521
Fabrigar, L. R., 556
Fairburn, C. G., 378
Fairey, P. J., 562
Fancher, R., 286
Fancher, R. E., 291
Fanselow, M. S., 188, 191
Farah, M. J., 110
Fazio, R. H., 557
Feehan, G. G., 389
Fei, J., 585
Feighner, J. P., 505
Fein, S., 561
Feist, G. J., 412
Feist, J., 412
Feldhusen, J., 309
Feldman, D. H., 309
Feldman, M. A., 309
Fennell, M., 502
Fentress, J.C., 11
Fernandez-Dols, J.-M., 398
Feshbach, S., 435
Festinger, L., 554, 557
Fiedler, F. E., 568
Field, T. M., 327
Fiez, J. A., 94
Finger, M. S., 438
Fischer, A. R., 504
Fischer, C., 51
Fischer, J., 198
Fisher, J. D., 544
Fisher, W. A., 544
Fiske, S. T., 570
Fitch, T., 234
Flammer, A., 346
Flaton, R., 265
Fleming, J. S., 428
Flett, G. L., 463
Flory, J. D., 521, 531
Flug, A., 437
Flynn, J. R., 303
Foa, E. B., 459
Fogarty, R., 297
Folk-Seang, J. F., 78
Folman, S., 529
Fong, G. T., 493
Forbes, R. J., 555
Ford, J. D., 459
Forgie, M., 91
Forserling, F., 431, 433
Fortune, W. H., 450, 471
Foser, G. D., 378
Foulkes, D., 165
Fowler, C. A., 104
Fox, C. R., 264
Fox, S. I., 85

Fracasso, M. P., 342
Frances, A., 453
Franche, R. -L., 466
Frank, E., 521
Frank, J. A., 470
Frank, J. D., 502
Fraser, S., 301
Freeman, S. J., 481
Freeston, M., 494
French, S. E., 481
Freud, S., 9, 150, 164, 368, 414, 415, 466
Fried, P. A., 326
Friedman, B. H., 539
Friedman, H. S., 412
Friedman, J. I., 505
Friedman, M. A., 376, 521
Friedman, R., 535
Friedman, S. L., 343
Friedrich, L. K., 579
Friese, M., 521
Friesen, W. V., 399, 400
Frieze, I. H., 55
Frischoltz, E. Z., 169
Frobose, C. A., 577
Fromm, E., 419
Frost, R. O., 458
Fuhriman, A., 498
Fulker, D. W., 577
Fuller, C. A., 155
Fullerton, C.S., 459
Fultz, J., 582
Furnham, A., 437
Furth, H., 279

Gabriele, M., 466
Gabrielli, W. F., 173
Gage, F. H., 93
Gagnon, F., 494
Gagnon, J. H., 384, 385, 409
Gaines, S. O., 572
Galaburda, A. M., 87
Galanter, M., 550
Galef, Jr. B. G., 207
Gammell, D. J., 504
Garbarino, J., 4
Garcia, E. E., 274
Garcia, J., 210
Garcia, R., 275
Gardner, B. T., 276
Gardner, H., 20, 254, 262, 283, 285, 295, 296, 297, 317
Gardner, R. A., 276
Gardner, R. C., 368, 570
Gardner, W. L., 393
Garelik, G., 302
Garfield, S. L., 509
Garmezy, N., 527
Garner, D. M., 378
Garraghty, P. E., 91
Garrod, S., 268
Gartner, R., 405
Gauthier, J. G., 505
Gawaltney, J. M., 521, 533
Gay, V., 482
Gazzaniga, M. S., 235
Geddes, J., 453
Geen, R. G., 578, 580
Gelder, M. G., 453, 502
Gelman, S. A., 336
Gelso, C. J., 487

Gemar, M., 466
Genesee, F., 274
Genest, M., 494, 504, 584
Gerrard, M., 554
Geschwind, N., 87
Getz, I., 349
Gibb, R., 91
Gibbons, F. X., 554, 555
Gibbs, J. T., 304, 348, 392
Gibson, E. J., 139, 140
Gibson, J. J., 139
Gibson, R. L., 504
Gick, M. L., 311
Giles, T. R., 482
Giles-Sims, J., 203
Gilligan, C., 55, 349
Giordano, D., 524
Giraldeau, L.-A., 207
Girgus, J. S., 138
Giroux, I., 494
Gladding, S. T., 498
Gladue, B. A., 385
Glaser, R., 519, 520
Glass, G. N., 264, 501
Gleason, K. E., 340
Glover, G. H., 235
Gochros, H. L., 198
Goddard, M. J., 190
Goel, V., 94, 264
Goethals, G. R., 561, 567
Gold, B., 94, 264
Gold, D., 172
Gold, P. W., 519
Goldberg, R., 171
Goldberg, T. E., 470
Goldsmith, H. H., 473
Goldstein, E. B., 102
Goldstein, M. J., 460
Goleman, D., 259, 285, 312
Goodale, M. A., 84, 110
Goodlet, C. R., 173
Goodstein, I. K., 456
Goodwin, D. W., 173, 179
Gordon, A. S., 179
Gorenstein, E. E., 448
Gorman, J. M., 505
Gorny, G., 91
Gottesman, I. I., 467, 469, 473
Gottlieb, G., 301
Gottliev, B. H., 60, 500
Gottman, J. M., 20, 45, 49, 527
Gouin, P., 161
Graber, R., 161
Graf, P., 227
Graham, K. M., 179
Graham, S., 55, 392
Gramling, S. E., 534
Granger, D. A., 380
Grant, U., 351
Grashial, A. F., 23
Grawe, K., 504
Gray, C. R., 226
Grayston, A. G., 488
Graziano, W. J., 69
Greenberg, J. S., 542
Greenberg, L., 488
Greenberg, M., 456
Greene, D., 389
Greenglass, E. R., 451, 521, 523
Greenwald, A. G., 104, 570
Greenwald, S., 465
Gregory, R. L., 141
Greiling, H., 12
Griffin, D. W., 266
Griggs, R. A., 23
Grigorenko, E., 303

Grizenko, N., 451
Grobowski, J., 178
Groff, T., 380
Gross, D. R., 498
Grossenbacher, P. G., 150
Grove, K., 56
Grunberg, N. E., 505
Guarnaccia, C. A., 484
Guest, F., 543
Guildord, J. P., 310
Gummerman, K., 226
Gump, B. B., 521, 531
Gunn, R., 242
Gupta, P., 279
Gurin, J., 378
Guttman, N., 201, 202

H

Haber, D., 351
Hacking, I., 455
Hackmann, A., 502
Haddock, G., 570
Hadjistavropoulos, T., 584
Hafer, C. L., 551
Hahn, D. B., 178
Hahn, E. J., 178
Hakuta, K., 274
Hales, C., 171
Hales, R. E., 450
Hall, W., 303
Hallahan, D. P., 308
Halliday, T., 102
Halonen, J. A., 247
Halonen, J. S., 350
Halpern, D. F., 22, 23, 238, 283, 303, 304, 317
Hamilton, T. E., 585
Hampton, R. R., 208, 209
Hancock, P. A., 256
Handelsman, L., 473
Handler, L., 435
Hannigan, J. H., 173
Harackiewicz, J. M., 389
Hardin, T. S., 467
Hardtke, K., 502
Hare, R. D., 378, 473
Harkins, S. G., 566
Harkness, S., 340
Harlow, H. F., 339
Harmatz, M., 479, 480, 484
Harmon-Jones, E., 557
Harms, T., 343
Harper, T. J., 473
Harpur, T. J., 473
Harris, A. S., 420
Harris, J. R., 342
Harris, L. R., 126
Harris, R. F., 204
Harris, R. J., 230
Harris, T., 526
Harsh, J. R., 156
Hart, B., 270, 303
Harter, S., 428
Hartmann, E., 162
Harvey, J. H., 552
Harvey, O. J., 572
Harvey, T., 89
Harvill, L., 435
Hatcher, R. A., 543
Hauser, S. T., 345
Havens, L., 482
Hay, J. F., 227

Hayes, N., 24
Hayflick, L., 353
Hayhurst, H., 466
Health Canada, 161, 172, 174, 179, 326, 353, 517, 537
Heatherton, T. F., 378
Hebb, D.O., 11, 69, 301
Hedden, T., 356
Heider, F., 389, 551
Heiman, G. W., 38, 385
Heinrichs, R. W., 468
Helmes, E., 438, 439
Helms, J. E., 502
Helms-Erikson, H., 342
Helsing, K. J., 540
Henningfield, J. E., 541
Herberman, R. B., 520
Herbert, J., 577
Herbert, W., 69
Herlitz, A., 359
Herman, C. P., 377, 378
Herman, J., 275
Hermann, D. J., 231, 239
Hernandez, D. J., 357
Heron, W., 370
Herrnstein, R. J., 299, 300, 301
Hersen, M., 203
Herskovits, M. H., 141
Hervig, L. K., 432
Herzog, H. A., 54
Heston, L. L., 66, 458
Hewitt, P. L., 378
Heyes, C. M., 207
Hiebert, J., 391
Hildebrand, D. K., 304
Hilgard, E. R., 168
Hill, C. E., 487, 502
Hill, R., 161
Hilleras, P., 359
Hilsenroth, M. J., 435
Hines, T., 143, 437
Hinson, R. E., 186
Hirsh-Pasek, K., 343
Hixon, J. G., 584
Hoagwood, K., 51
Hobfoll, S. E., 518
Hobson, J. A., 159
Hochberg, J., 255
Hofferth, S. L., 543
Hoffnung, M., 343
Hogan, J., 438
Hogan, R. T., 431
Hogg, M. A., 572
Holcomb, H. H., 505
Holden, R. R., 438
Holland, P. C., 198
Holleran, S. A., 541
Hollis, J. F., 533
Holmes, D. S., 535
Holmes, T. H., 359, 524
Holobow, N., 274
Holtzmann, W., 392
Honts, C., 395
Hood, R. W., 153
Hood, W. R., 572
Hooper, J., 166
Hopkins, K. D., 290
Hoptman, M. J., 89
Horney, K., 419
Hornig, C. D., 457
Horowitz, M. J., 488
Houle, S., 94, 234, 264
Houlihan, D., 582
Howard, I. P., 131
Howard, K. I., 501

Howe, M. J., 231
Hoyer, W. J., 356
Hsieh, C., 537
Huang, L. N., 304, 392
Hubel, D. H., 110
Hultsch, D. F., 359
Humphreys, G. W., 256, 275
Hunt, H. T., 150, 153
Hunt, M., 384
Hunt, M. M., 18
Hunt, R. R., 221
Hurst, S. A., 494, 504
Hurvich, L. M., 114
Huston, A. C., 526, 579
Hwang, C. P., 342
Hwu, H.G., 465
Hy, L., 434
Hyde, J. S., 55
Hyde, R. T., 537
Hynie, M., 543

I

Iacono, W. G., 395
Iden, C. M., 208
Inhelder, B., 333
Inoff-Germain, G., 346
Intrator, J., 473
Iverson, G. L., 438
Ivey, A., 509
Ivry, R. B., 235
Izard, C. E., 397

J

Jacard, J. J., 557
Jacklin, C. N., 580
Jackson, D., 431, 433
Jackson, D. N., 434, 438, 439
Jackson, L. A., 585
Jackson, P. R., 555
Jacobs, E., 343
Jacobsen, L., 306
Jacobsen, N., 45, 49
Jacobson, N. S., 501
Jacoby, L. L., 150, 151, 219, 227, 355
Jacques, C., 494
Jalbert, N. L., 25
James, W., 6, 7, 150, 241, 396
Jameson, D., 114
Janis, I., 567
Janoff-Bulman, R. J., 404
Jausovec, N., 11
Jaycox, L. H., 459
Jenkin, M. R., 126
Jenkins, H. M., 201
Jenkins, J. J., 279
Jennings, J. M., 227
Jennings, L., 502
Jensen, A. R., 299, 301
Jensen, P., 51
Johnson, D. R., 380
Johnson, D. W., 574
Johnson, G. B., 69, 76, 96
Johnson, J., 336, 457
Johnson, J. S., 275
Johnson, M. P., 155
Johnson, N., 351
Johnson, R. T., 574

Johnson, V. E., 382
Johnson-Douglas, S., 459
Johnston, L. D., 172, 175, 352
Joiner, T. E., 467
Jome, L. R., 504
Jones, E. E., 550
Jones, J. H., 570, 593
Jones, M. C., 192
Jorm, A. F., 359
Jou, J., 230
Joyce, P.R., 465
Juhn, G., 351
Jung, C., 419

K

Kagan, J., 324, 340, 341
Kagan, S., 390
Kagitcibasi, C., 141
Kahn, S., 522
Kahneman, D., 266
Kail, R., 268
Kaiser, P. K., 112
Kalat, J. W., 191
Kales, A., 155
Kalichman, S., 543
Kalick, S. M., 585
Kalish, H. I., 201, 202
Kamin, L. J., 191
Kandel, E., 577
Kandel, E. R., 12, 233
Kanner, A. D., 525
Kantner, J. F., 542
Kao, K.C., 459
Kaplan, R. M., 517
Kapur, S., 94, 234, 264
Karam, E.G., 465
Karni, A., 160
Kassin, S. M., 561
Katigbak, M. S., 433
Kaufman, P., 259, 285, 312
Kaufmann, J. M., 308
Kavanaugh, D. J., 532
Kawakami, K., 572
Keefe, S. M., 526
Keen, E., 454
Keenan, T., 336
Keilp, J., 473
Keller, M., 464
Kelley, C. M., 150
Kelly, J. F., 343
Kelly, R. E. S., 221
Kendrick, D. T., 581
Kennedy, P. G. E., 78
Kent, J. M., 505
Kephart, W. M., 587
Kerner, D. N., 517
Ketterlinus, R. D., 342
Keuning, J. J., 521
Keyes, M., 66
Kiecolt-Glaser, J. K. 519, 520
Kifer, E., 391
Kigar, D. L., 89
Kihlstrom, J. F., 170
Kimball, M., 54, 55
Kimble, G. A., 53, 54, 188
Kimmel, A., 51
Kimura, D., 86
King, A., 384, 542
King, H. E., 577
King, L. A., 404
Kingstone, E., 386
Kinsey, A. C., 384, 385

Kirchwood, J., 520
Kirk, M., 459
Kirlik, A., 255
Kirsch, I., 167
Kirsner, K., 238
Kisilevsky, B. S., 329
Kitayama, S., 582
Klatsky, R. L., 226
Klein, B., 91
Klein, L. C., 505
Klein, M. D., 104
Klein, R. M., 11, 460
Knable, M. B., 470
Knussmann, R., 380
Kobasa, S., 522
Kobayashi, M., 404
Koelling, R. A., 210
Kohlberg, L., 55, 347, 348
Kohlenberg, G. S., 203
Kohlenberg, R. J., 203
Kohler, W., 209
Kohn, A., 191
Kohn, P. M., 525
Kohut, H., 419, 488
Kolachana, B., 470
Kolar, E. J., 155
Kolata, G., 384, 385, 409
Kolb, B., 11, 91
Kolb, L., 464
Komisaruk, B., 380
Konarski, R., 523
Konner, M., 19
Kopp, C., 326, 327
Kopta, S. M., 501
Korkum, V. L., 329
Korn, W. S., 161, 583
Korpan, C. A., 263
Kosin, M., 240
Koss, M., 459
Kotlowitz, A., 527
Koutstaal, B., 235
Kozma, A., 404
Kozma, A. K., 359
Krames, L., 463
Krank, M. D., 186
Krause, M. S., 501
Kronauer, R. E., 155
Kroner, D. G., 438
Krosnick, J. A., 43, 557
Kübler-Ross, E. 361
Kuhn, D., 21, 265
Kuiper, N. A., 530
Kukuma, T., 466
Kulik, C. C., 204, 294
Kulik, J. A., 204, 294
Kunkel, D., 579
Kurtz, R., 509
Kusulas, J. W., 432
Kutchinsky, B., 242
Kyllonen, P. C., 432

L

Labbee, E. E., 536
LaBoeuf, B. J., 576
Labouvie-Vief, G., 355
Labov, W., 258
Lacroix, D., 494
Ladouceur, R., 199, 458, 494
Lagerspetz, K. M. J., 580
Lahiri, A., 268
Lalonde, C. E., 480

Lam, R. W., 155
Lamb, C. S., 585
Lamb, H. R., 481
Lamb, M., 345
Lamb, M. E., 342
Lambert, W. E., 274
Landrum, R. E., 53
Lane, H., 268
Lange, C. G., 396
Langenbucher, J. W., 453
Langer, E., 263
Langer, L. L., 241
Langs, R., 488
Langston, C. A., 389
Lapidus, S., 172
Lashley, K., 233
Latané, B., 566, 568, 582
Laumann, E. O., 384, 385, 409
Lautenbacher, S., 459
Lazarus, A. A., 482, 491, 509
Lazarus, R. S., 398, 522, 525, 527, 529
Leadbeater, B. J., 467
Leahy, T. H., 6, 7
Leary, M. R., 555
Lee, C.K., 465
Lee, I., 537
Lee, J., 520
Lee, P. S., 505
Lefcourt, H. M., 530
Lefebvre, L., 207
Leiter, M. P., 523
Leith, L. M., 539
Lellouch, J., 465
Lemme, B. H., 353
Lenneberg, E., 272, 273
Lent, R. W., 532
Leon, A.C., 464
Leon, G. R., 447
Lepine, J.P., 465
Lepper, M., 389
Lerner, R. M., 324
Lesgold, A., 222
Letarte, H., 494
Levant, R. F., 588
LeVay, S., 386
Levenson, R. W., 399
Leventhal, H., 398
Levine, B., 236
Levine, J. H., 566
Levinson, D., 358
Levinson, K. L., 397
Levitt, A. J., 155
Levy, B.A., 275
Levy, J., 87
Lévy, J., 384, 542
Levy, J. J., 384
Levy, L., 437
Levy, S. M., 520
Levy, T. M., 340
Lewin, R., 93
Lewinsohn, P. M., 204, 495
Lewis, J. F., 305
Lewis, J. R., 69
Lewis, M., 324
Lewis, R., 78, 80
Liberty, H. J., 578
Lickliter, R., 69, 301
Lieberman, M., 348
Light, K. C., 537
Lim, J., 438
Lin, S., 266
Linden, R., 242
Lindenberger, U., 324, 356
Linkous, R. A., 566
Lipsey, M. W., 501

Lister, P., 23
Locke, J. L., 269, 272
Lockhart, R. S., 219, 220, 221, 311
Loehlin, J. C., 303, 304, 317
Loehr, J., 529
Loevinger, J., 434
Loftus, E., 218
Loftus, E. F., 232, 233, 238, 242
Logue, A. W., 204, 215
Longo, D. A., 532
Look, S. C., 389
Lopez, J., 586
Loranger, M., 494
Lorenz, K. Z., 339, 370, 575
Loriaux, D. L., 346
Louis, W. R., 572
Lovach, R., 390
Low, J. A., 329
Lowe, D. G., 129
Lubaroff, A., 520
Luber, P., 452
Lucas, R. E., 402
Ludolph, P., 461
Lueger, R. J., 501
Luszcz, M. A., 356
Lutz, D. J., 336
Lycan, W., 278
Lykken, D. T., 65, 395
Lynch, G., 233
Lynn, R., 304
Lynn, S. J., 167, 169

M

Maas, A., 232
Maas, J., 156, 160, 161
Maccoby, E. E., 580
MacDonald, G., 502
Macdonald, J. E., 525
Machac, J., 473
MacLeod, C. M., 129, 275
MacWhinney, B., 273
Maddi, S., 412, 522, 524
Mader, S., 95
Madsen, M. C., 390
Mager, R. S., 205
Mahalik, J. R., 502
Mahoney, G. J., 42
Mahoney, K. M., 161, 583
Maier, N. R. F., 261
Maines, D. R., 359
Major, B., 572
Makosky, V. P., 40
Malinowski, B., 418
Maliphant, R., 433
Malmstrom, E. J., 155
Mamersmith, S. K., 385
Mandler, G., 11, 222
Mandler, J. M., 336
Mangum, G. R., 235
Mankin, S., 532
Manning, A., 45
Marafiote, R. A., 482
Maratsos, M., 269
Marcia, J. E., 338
Maril, A., 235
Marini, Z. A., 336
Markowitsch, H. J., 160, 234
Marr, D., 139
Marshall, G. N., 432
Marshall, N. L., 343

Martin, E. E., 384, 385
Martin, G., 200, 205, 215
Martin, J., 555
Martin, R. A., 530
Martins, Y., 377
Maslach, C., 523
Maslow, A. H., 10, 371, 427
Masson, M. E. J., 275
Masters, W. H., 382
Mathes, S., 435
Mathews, A., 539
Maticka-Tyndale, E., 384, 542
Matlin, M. W., 264, 266, 343
Matsumoto, D., 13
Mattay, V.S., 470
Matthews, G., 430
Matthews, K. A., 521, 531
Maultsby, M. C., 491
Maurer, C., 328, 330
Maurer, D., 328, 329, 330
Mawhinney, T. A., 305
Maybery, M., 238
Mayer, R., 259
Mayou, R., 453
Mays, V. M., 543
Mazziota, J. C., 94
McAdams, D. P., 240
McCabe, R., 377
McCarley, R. W., 159, 166
McCarrey, M., 459
McCartney, K. A., 343
McClelland, D. C., 388
McConaghy, N., 383
McConkey, K. M., 170
McCormick, C. M., 89, 385
McCoy, S. B., 555
McCrae, R. R., 431, 438
McCreary, D. R., 579
McCully, J., 186
McDaniel, P., 580
McDermott, M., 520
McDonel, E. C., 557
McDonnell, P. M., 329
McDougall, W., 368
McDuffie, D., 577
McEwan, N. H., 169
McFarlane, T., 377
McFreeley, S., 520
McGregor, I., 557
McGue, M., 65
McHale, S. M., 342
McIver, T., 104
McKague, C., 449
McKay, A., 384, 542
McKim, M. K., 343
McKinlay, J. B., 353, 383
McKinlay, S. M., 353
McKnight, C. C., 391
McLeod, D., 238
McLoyd, V. C., 13, 303, 526
McMillan, J. H., 20, 34
McMullen, A., 555
McMurray, G. A., 101
McNally, D., 390, 409
McNally, R. J., 456
McNaughton, B. L., 160
McNeil, E. B., 467
McNeil, K. V., 404
Meador, D. B., 489
Mednick, S., 577
Medoff, D. R., 505
Meehl, P. E., 453, 470
Meichenbaum, D., 491, 493
Meier, D. E., 353
Meilijson, I., 93
Meltzer, H.Y., 466

Melzack, R., 17, 101, 122
Mercer, J. R., 305
Merikle, P. M., 104, 226
Merrick, S. K., 340
Mervis, J., 502
Messer, W. S., 23
Messinger, J. C., 382
Metalsky, G. I., 467
Metcalfe, J., 424
Meyer, R. G., 458, 473
Meyers, B. S., 466
Michael, R. T., 384, 385, 409
Michael, W., 310
Michaels, J. W., 566
Middelton, H., 502
Milgram, S., 563, 578
Miller, G. A., 224, 226
Miller, L., 525
Miller, L. T., 288
Miller, N. E., 53, 524, 536, 578
Miller, P. H., 336
Miller, P. M., 203
Miller, R. L., 264, 501
Miller, S. B., 521
Miller-Jones, D., 304
Millis, R. M., 540
Mills, J., 557
Mills, J.A., 8
Milner, A. D., 84, 110
Milner, B., 244
Milner, P. M., 83, 397
Mindell, J. A., 161
Mineka, S., 243, 473, 496, 535
Minnes, P. M., 308
Mischel, W., 424, 432, 433, 434
Mishkin, M., 234
Mitchell, C., 52
Mitchell, D. E., 17
Mitchell, J. E., 378
Mitchell, M. H., 504
Mitterer, J., 129, 220, 275
Mizes, J. S., 491
Moeykens, B., 172
Mohr, J. J., 487
Moldoveanu, M. C., 263
Mondin, G. W., 501
Money, J., 381
Monk, T. H., 155
Moody, M., 501
Moore, B. R., 207
Moore, T. E., 104
Moore-Ede, M. C., 155
Moos, R. H., 529, 533
Moran, G., 340
Moreland, R. L., 566
Morgan, T., 498
Morris, N., 380
Morrison, M. F., 452
Morten, G., 504, 513
Moscovici, S., 567
Moses, J., 539
Mountcastle, V. B., 110
Mowrer, O. H., 578
Mueller, T., 464
Muir, D. W., 329
Mullen, K. D., 542
Muller, F., 80, 356
Muller-Schwarze, S. D., 124
Mullooly, J. P., 533
Mumford, M., 264
Munoz, R. F., 463
Murdock, B. B., 224
Murowchick, E., 577
Murphy, J., 276
Murphy, W. E., 355
Murray, C., 299, 300, 301

Murray, H., 351
Murray, H. A, 388, 436
Murstein, B. I., 435
Murtha, S., 234
Mussell, M. P., 378
Myers, P., 535
Mykota, D., 526

Nadien, M. B., 588
Naglieri, J. A., 308
Nail, P. R., 558
Naitoh, P., 155
Narvaez, D., 349
Nash, J. M., 17, 89, 482
Nathan, P. E., 453
National Advisory Council
   on Economic
   Opportunity, 526
National Association for the
   Education of Young
   Children, 275, 365
National Center for Health
   Statistics, 586
National Committee on Sleep
   Disorders Research,
   156, 159
Neal, M. C., 577
Neale, J. M., 354, 448
Needham, D. R., 104
Neegaard, L., 235
Neisser, U., 303, 304, 317
Nelson, K., 336
Nelson, T. O., 150
Néron, S., 494
Neufeldt, A. H., 53
Neugarten, B. L., 323, 359
Nevo, B., 437
Newby-Clark, I. R., 557
Newman, C. F., 509
Newman, S. C., 452, 456, 465,
   467, 473
Newport, E. L., 275
Nezami, E., 438
Nezlek, J. B., 555
Nias, D. K. B., 577
NICHD Early Child Care
   Research Network, 343
Nicholls, J. G., 390
Nichols, L. A., 272
Nickerson, R. S., 256
Niehoff, D., 577
Nietzel, M. T., 450, 471
Nisbett, D., 264
Nisbett, R. E., 356, 389
Nix, L. A., 235
Noels, K. A., 274, 574
Norcross, J. C., 404, 509
Norem, J. K., 530
Notarius, C. I., 357
Nottelmann, E. D., 346
Novaco, R.W., 578
Novak, C. A., 352
Nugent, K., 243
Nystul, M. S., 504

Ober, B. A., 470
O'Brien, K. M., 502

O'Brien, M., 343
O'Brien-Malone, A., 238
O'Connor, D. H., 343
O'Donnell, L., 351
Ogden, G., 380
Ogilvie, R., 162
Ogilvie, R. D., 154, 156
Olds, J. M., 83
Olff, M., 520
Olibowitz, M. R., 457
Olinger, L. J., 530
Olson, D., 336
Olson, J. M., 54, 551, 557
Olthof, A., 208
Oltmanns, T. F., 448
O'Malley, P. M., 172, 175
Omato, A. M., 585
Ones, D. S., 438
Onorati, S., 272
Oosterveld, P., 433
O'Rahilly, R., 80, 356
Orchard, B., 161
O'Reardon, J. P., 452
Orlinsky, D. E., 504
Orn, H., 452, 456, 467, 473
Orne, M., 169
Osborne, Y. V. H., 458
Ostendorf, F., 431
Osterman, K., 580
Ostrom, T. M., 566
O'Sullivan, M., 399
Owen, M. T., 343
Owens, J. F., 521, 531
Ozer, D. J., 431

Padma-Nathan, H., 383
Paffenbarger, R. S., 537
Paivio, A., 221
Paivio, S., 488
Pak, A. W., 522
Palmer, J. O., 460
Paloutzian, R., 19
Paludi, M. A., 14, 69, 451, 588
Pan, B. A., 271
Panskepp, J., 397
Papageorgis, D., 378
Pape, B., 482
Parducci, A., 402
Park, D. C., 356
Parke, R. D., 343
Parker, J. D., 412, 529
Parks, B. K., 504
Pascual-Leone, J., 336
Passchier, J., 104
Passuth, P. M., 359
Patashnick, M., 390
Pate, R. H., 509
Patterson, C., 386
Patterson, G. R., 580
Paulus, P. B., 580
Paunonen, S. V., 431, 433,
   438, 439
Pavlov, I. P., 188
Paykel, E. S., 466
Payne, D. G., 231, 239
Payne, I. R., 541
Payne, M. A., 211
Payne, W. A., 178
Pear, J., 200, 205, 215
Peckford, T., 304
Pedersen, P., 509

Pederson, D. R., 340
Peele, S., 178
Pellegrini, A. D., 42
Pellegrino, J. W., 268
Pence, A. R., 42, 343
Penfield, W., 84, 85, 121
Pennebaker, J., 404, 529
Penrod, S. D., 232
Pentz, M. A., 178, 179
Pépin, M., 494
Peplau, L. A., 562, 588
Pepper, S., 343
Perkins, D., 311
Perlman, D., 588
Perloff, R., 303, 304, 317
Perls, F. S., 490
Pert, A. B., 76
Pert, C. B., 76
Pervin, L. A., 433
Peszke, M., 506
Petersen, A., 346
Petersen, S. E., 94
Peterson, C., 411, 414, 420, 531
Peterson, J. B., 20
Peterson, R. S., 576
Peterson, S. R., 428
Peth-Pierce, R., 343
Petitto, J. M., 452
Petri, H. L., 370
Petrinovich, L., 361
Pettifor, J. L., 53
Petty, R. E., 556, 557
Phares, E. J., 423
Phillips, H. C., 121
Piaget, J., 331, 333
Pianta, R. C., 343
Pickering, M., 268
Pierce, W. D., 203
Piessens, J., 351
Pilkonis, P. A., 501
Pillow, D. R., 525
Pincus, A. L., 429
Pinger, R. R., 178
Pinker, S., 12, 17, 269, 397
Pittman, T. S., 552
Plant, E. A., 55
Plemons, J. K., 359
Pliner, P., 377
Plomin, R., 341
Plunkett, J., 272
Plutchik, R., 402
Polivy, J., 377, 378
Pollok, V. E., 173
Polonko, K. A., 5
Pomeroy, E., 482
Pomeroy, W. B., 384, 385
Pon, G., 574
Poole, J. H., 470
Poortinga, Y. H., 141
Popham, W .J., 290
Pople, C. R., 533
Porter, P. P., 264
Postman, L., 570
Powell, K., 296
Premack, D., 276
Preston, J. M., 151
Preston, T.A., 155
Prichard, D. J., 469
Priest, D. J., 585
Pritzker, S., 18
Prochaska, J. O., 509
Proctor, R. A., 256
Prohaska, M. L., 584
Prueger, V. J., 13
Puccetti, M., 522
Pugh, G. M., 304

Pyke, S. W., 14, 22
Pylyshyn, Z. W., 221

Qualls, P. J., 536
Quartaro, G., 272

Rabin, B. S., 521, 533
Rachman, S., 121
Radford-Davenport, J., 555
Rahe, R. H., 359, 524
Raichle, M. E., 94
Raife, E. A., 94
Räikkönen, K. A., 521, 531
Raj, M., 380
Ramey, C. T., 301, 303
Ramsey, E., 580
Randi, J., 142, 143
Rankin, C.H., 12, 233
Rankin, N. O., 48
Rapaport, D., 419
Raskin, D. C., 232
Rasmussen, K. G., 555
Rasmussen, T., 85, 121
Ratner, N. B., 271
Raven, P. H., 96
Raver, C., 467
Ray, M., 259, 285, 312
Ray, O. S., 178
Raynor, I. O., 388
Raynor, R., 192
Read, D., 231, 239
Read, J. D., 104
Rebec, G. V., 505
Rebelsky, F. G., 272
Rector, N. A., 466
Redd, W. H., 520
Reece, B. L., 555
Reed, E. S., 54, 572
Reeder, G. D., 552
Regan, D., 130
Regier, D., 452, 458, 463,
   467, 473
Reinisch, J. M., 542
Reis, H. T., 586
Rescorla, R. A., 188, 191
Resnick, S., 66
Rest, J. R., 349
Restak, R. M., 84, 149, 255
Rettinger, J., 395
Revitch, E., 43
Reynolds, C. R., 304
Reynolds, S., 453
Rhéaume, J., 458
Rhue, J. W., 169
Rickabaugh, C., 54
Riese, S. P., 431
Riggio, R. E., 555
Rijsdijk, F. V., 288
Risley, T. R., 270, 303
Ritter, B., 492
Roback, H. W., 482
Robert, L., 526
Roberts, D., 520
Roberts, R. D., 432
Roberts, W. A., 208

Robeson, W. W., 343
Robins, L., 452, 458, 463, 467, 473
Robinson, D., 504
Robson, A. L., 327
Robson, P., 502
Rochlen, A. B., 487
Rodin, J., 374, 376, 517
Rodriques, M. S., 533
Roehrig, C.J., 12
Roehrs, T., 156
Roese, N. J., 557
Rogers, B. J., 131
Rogers, C. R., 10, 425, 426, 489
Rogers, M., 104
Rogers, T. B., 13
Roggeveen, J., 389
Rogoff, B., 304, 336
Rogosch, F. A., 342
Role, L., 541
Rollman, G. B., 121, 459
Romaine, S., 274
Romano, E., 488
Ronda, J. M., 155
Roney, C. J., 259
Ronning, R. R., 222, 263
Roodin, P. A., 356
Rosch, E., 258, 277
Rose, S., 151, 459
Rose-Krasnor, L., 202, 211–212, 342
Rosecan, J., 541
Rosen, B. R., 235
Rosen, J., 473
Rosenbaum, P. A., 68
Rosenfeld, A. H., 495
Rosenhan, D. L., 179
Rosenheck, R., 506
Rosenman, R., 521
Rosenthal, D., 471
Rosenthal, N. E., 155
Rosenthal, R., 48, 306
Rosenzweig, M., 17
Rosnow, R. L., 52, 306
Ross, C. A., 447, 461
Ross, L. T., 264, 266, 577
Ross, R., 453
Rossy, I., 539
Roth, T., 156
Rothbard, N. P., 432
Rothbart, M. K., 341
Rothstein, R., 274
Rotman, A. J., 517
Rotte, M., 235
Rowe, J. S., 566
Rowntree, S., 91
Rubenstein, B. S., 160
Rubin, D. C., 239, 240
Rubin, K. H., 342
Rubin, Z., 52
Rubio-Stipec, M., 465
Ruff, C. F., 304
Ruggiero, K. M., 572
Rumbaugh, D. M., 276
Runco, M. A., 18, 217, 262
Rushton, J. P., 577
Russell, D. W., 589
Russell, J. A., 398, 401
Russo, N. F., 55, 467, 526
Ryan, R., 389
Ryan-Finn, K. D., 56
Rybash, J. M., 356
Ryff, C. D., 404
Rymer, R., 273, 283

Sabini, J., 550
Sacks, O., 101
Sadava, S. W., 172, 173
Sagan, C., 68
Sagi, D., 160
Sainsbury, R. S., 201
Sakinofsky, I., 465
Saklofske, D. H., 304, 431, 526, 529
Sales, P., 179
Salkovskis, P. M., 502
Salovey, P., 517
Salthouse, T., 355
Samson, J.-M., 384
San-Doval, A., 351
Sanderson, W. C., 502
Sandler, D. P., 540
Sandler, I., 525
Sanson, A., 341
Santrock, J. W., 203, 247, 324, 345, 350
Saravi, R. D., 88
Sarbin, T. R., 454
Sargent, C., 142
Saucier, G., 431
Saunders, R. C., 470
Saunders, S. M., 501
Savage, H., 449
Savage-Rumbaugh, E. S., 276
Sax, G., 288, 306
Sax, L. J., 161, 583
Saxe, L., 395
Scafidi, F., 327
Scardamalia, M., 261
Scarr, S., 69, 304
Schaal, B., 44
Schachter, S., 375, 397, 398
Schacter, D. L., 150, 218, 227, 232, 235, 237, 238, 239, 241, 251
Schaefer, C., 473, 525
Schaeffer, H. R., 340
Schafer, G., 272
Schaie, K. W., 356
Schaller, M., 582
Schanberg, S., 327
Schank, R., 233
Schatzberg, A. F., 464, 466
Scheidt, S., 521
Schiefele, U., 390
Schiffman, J., 470
Schiffrin, R. M., 224, 237
Schifitto, G., 520
Schlesinger, L. B., 43
Schliecker, E., 343
Schleifer, S. J., 520
Schlonick, E. K., 335, 336
Schneider, A., 166
Schneider, F. R., 457
Schneider, L. S., 173
Schneider-Rosen, K. S., 340
Schooler, J. W., 150
Schraw, G. J., 222, 263
Schultheiss, O. C., 389
Schultz, D., 397
Schunk, D. H., 389
Schustack, M. W., 412
Schwab, J. E., 577
Schwartz, J. H., 12, 233
Schwartz, T., 578

Schwarz, J. P., 94
Schwean, V. L., 526
Sciara, A., 435
Scott, T. H., 370
Sears, D. O., 562
Sears, R. R., 578
Sechzer, J., 55
Sedikides, C., 552
Seffge-Krenke, I., 519
Segal, Z. V., 466
Segall, M. H., 141
Segalowitz, S. J., 89, 274
Seidemann, E., 93
Seidman, D. F., 541
Seidman, E., 481
Seligman, C., 54
Seligman, M. E. P., 179, 210, 463, 467, 506, 531
Selye, H., 518
Servaes, P., 521
Seto, M. C., 577
Sevcik, R. A., 276
Shanker, S., 276
Shanks, D. R., 229
Shanteau, J., 230
Sharfstein, S. S., 482
Shaver, P., 586
Shear, J., 535
Sheehan, P. W., 536
Shenaut, G. K., 470
Shepard, R. N., 221, 232
Sher, K. J., 173
Sherif, C. W., 572
Sherif, M., 572
Sherman, S. J., 557
Sherry, P., 491
Sherwood, A., 537
Shettleworth, S. J., 68, 208, 209
Shields, A., 342
Shields, J., 469
Shields, S. A., 401
Shier, D., 78, 80
Shore, D. L., 540
Shotland, R. L., 582
Showers, C., 530
Shrout, P. E., 525
Siegel, S., 185, 186
Siegfried, T., 160
Siegler, R. S., 336
Siffre, M., 155
Silverman, N. N., 420
Simon, H. A., 11
Simpson, J. A., 556
Sinclair, C., 52
Sinclair, C. M., 479–480
Sinden, M., 236
Singer, B., 404
Singer, D. G., 579
Singer, J. E., 397, 398
Singer, J. L., 579
Sita, A., 521
Skinner, B. F., 8, 150, 195, 198, 215, 269
Skinner, E. A., 389
Skoner, D. P., 521, 533
Skovholt, T. M., 502
Slade, R., 104
Slavin, R., 574
Sloan, D. M., 491
Sloan, P., 435
Slobin, D., 272
Slobogin, C., 449
Smith, H. L., 402
Smith, J., 360
Smith, K. H., 104

Smith, M. L., 264, 501
Smith, P. B., 562
Smith, P. O., 541
Smith, R., 46, 579
Smock, T. K., 79
Snarey, J., 345, 588
Snow, C. E., 269, 271
Snow, D. E., 275
Snowden, D. A., 92
Snyder, L. D., 232
Snyder, M., 556, 585
Snyder, S. H., 76
Sobell, M. B., 173
Sober, E., 581
Sollers, J., 539
Solomon, B., 296
Solomon, D. A., 464
Solvason, H. B., 464, 466
Sorrentino, R. M., 259
Spanos, N. P., 167, 169, 170
Spaulding, K., 232
Spear, L. P., 173
Spear, N. E., 173
Spear-Swirling, P., 261
Spearman, C. E., 295
Specher, C. E., 520
Speelman, C., 238
Sperling, G., 225
Sperry, R. W., 12, 87, 89
Squire, L., 233
St. Clair, M., 488
Staab, J. P., 452
Stack, D. M., 329
Stanley, M. A., 493
Stanovich, K. E., 20, 36, 47, 49, 63, 264
Staples, S. L., 117
Stark-Adamec, C., 54, 55
Statistics Canada, 13, 172, 175, 274, 295, 357, 376, 517, 526, 540, 542, 543, 579
Statistics Sweden, 211
Staub, E., 578
Staudinger, U. M., 324, 356, 360
Steele, C. M., 570, 572
Stefanick, M. L., 353
Steffen, V. J., 580
Stein, A. H., 579
Stein, B. S., 258, 283
Steinmetz, J., 495
Steketee, G., 458
Stengel, R., 320
Steptoe, A., 539
Sternberg, E. M., 519
Sternberg, R. J., 24, 261, 288, 298, 299, 301, 303, 317, 336, 586, 587
Steuer, F. B., 46, 579
Stevenson, H. G., 56
Stevenson, H. W., 391
Stewart, F., 543
Stewart, G. K., 543
Stich, F., 501
Stigler, J. W., 391
Stijnen, T., 104
Stitzer, M. L., 541
Stoner, J., 567
Stones, M. J., 359, 404
Stoppard, J. M., 467, 504
Strauss, M. A., 203
Strean, H. S., 487

Streissguth, A. P., 326
Strickland, A. L., 361
Strizke, P., 473
Strupp, H. H., 502
Stuart, B., 343
Stueve, A., 351
Stukas, A. A., 556
Stunkard, A. J., 378
Sturges, L. V., 541
Stuss, D. T., 236
Sue, D. W., 504, 509, 513
Sue, S., 504
Sugarman, D. B., 203
Suh, E. M., 402
Suinn, R. M., 461
Sullivan, H. S., 419
Sullivan, K. T., 499
Sullivan, M. J., 466
Suls, J., 431, 521
Sulzman, F.M., 155
Summers, F. L., 488
Super, E. M., 340
Susman, E. J., 346, 577
Swafford, J. O., 391
Swain, A., 521
Swann, W. B., 584
Swanson, C., 20
Swanson, J., 161
Sweeney, M., 227
Swinson, R. P., 457, 505
Sylvain, C., 199, 494
Syme, L. L., 533
Szmukler, G., 456
Szuba, M. P., 452

Tager-Flusberg, H., 273
Tagiuri, R., 553
Taifel, H., 572
Tam, E. M., 155
Tamarin, R. H., 69
Tamminga, C. A., 505
Tan, T. L., 155
Tang, J., 351
Tannen, D., 160, 588, 593
Tantam, D., 456
Task Force on Diversity Issues, 570
Tassinary, L., 104
Tavris, C., 401, 405
Taylor, D. M., 572
Taylor, M. J., 466
Taylor, S. E., 517, 530, 532, 535, 547, 562
Taylor, T., 276
Teachman, J. D., 5
Teasdale, J. D., 466
Tellegen, A., 65, 432
Temoshok, L., 326
Templer, D. I., 304
Temporini, H., 505
Teresi, D., 166
Teri, L., 495
Terman, L., 309
Terr, L. C., 241
Tesser, A., 562
Tessier, D., 384
Tetreault, M. K. T., 55
Teuber, H. L., 244
Thaker, G. K., 505
Thalman, R. H., 71

Tharp, R. G., 532
Thayer, J. F., 539
Thigpen, C. H., 461
Thoma, S. J., 349
Thomas, A., 341
Thomas, C. B., 533
Thomas, J., 506
Thomas, P., 525
Thomas, S., 530
Thompson, C. P., 231, 239
Thompson, R. A., 340, 341
Thompson, V. A., 264
Thorpe, G. L., 457
Thorpe, L. A., 329
Thornton, A., 20
Thurston, W. E., 179
Thurstone, L. L., 295
Tinbergen, N., 576
Tirumalasetti, F., 466
Toga, A. W., 94
Toglia, M. P., 231, 239
Tolan, P., 525
Toledo, R., 578
Tolman, E. C., 191, 208
Tomarken, A. J., 398
Tomlinson-Keasy, C., 465
Toth, J. B., 236
Toth, S. K., 326, 342
Toth, S. L., 342
Toukmanian, S. G., 504
Tracey, T. J., 491
Tracy, K., 269
Trainor, J., 482
Trapness, P. D., 438
Trask, O. J., 520
Travers, K. J., 391
Treboux, E., 340
Trehub, S. E., 329
Tremblay, P. F., 368
Tremblay, R. E., 44
Triandis, H. C., 13, 578
Trimble, J. E., 56
Triplett, N., 565
Tripp, D. A., 466
Trivers, R., 581
Tronick, E., 140
Trost, M. R., 561
Troutman, A. C., 203
Trussel, J., 543
Trzebinski, J., 431, 433
Tsai, M., 203
Tsonis, M., 329
Tucker, R., 274
Tulving, E., 160, 220, 227,
    228, 234, 236, 244
Turiel, E., 54
Turnbull, C., 578
Turner, S. M., 493
Turrell, G., 161
Turvey, C., 464
Tversky, A., 264, 266
Tyhurst, J., 481
Tyler, C., 131

Udry, R., 380
United Nations, 578
Updegraff, K., 342
Urbina, S., 303, 304, 306,
    317
Ursano, R. J., 459

Vaadia, E., 93
Vadum, A. E., 48
Vaillant, G. E., 179, 358, 531
Vallone, R. P., 266
van den Hout, M. A., 502
Van Deventer, W., 437
van Praag, H. M., 456
Vance, K., 459
Vandell, D., 343
Vasquez, Suson, K. A., 574
Vedhara, K., 520
Verfaellie, M., 227
Vernon, P. A., 288
Vernoy, M. W., 191
Vickers, R. R., 432
Vignerhoets, A., 521
Villani, S., 482
Vinogradov, S., 470
Vogt, T. M., 533
Vokey, J. R., 104
Volpe, E. P., 68
Von Békésy, G., 119
Vredenburg, K., 463
Vreugdenhil, G., 521
Vygotsky, L. S., 336

Wackenhut, J., 578
Wadden, T.A., 378
Wade, C., 401
Wagner, A. D., 235
Wahlsten, D., 69, 301
Walk, R. D., 139, 140
Walker, E., 470
Walker, L. E., 576
Wall, P. D., 122
Wallace, R. K., 535
Waller, N. G., 432
Wallerstein, R. S., 502
Wallner-Allen, K. E., 343
Walsh, W.B., 433, 434
Wampold, B. E., 501
Ward, H. E., 452
Ward, L. M., 116
Ward, R. A., 23
Warren, L. W., 465
Warren, R. M., 118
Washburn, A. L., 373
Waters, E., 340
Watkins, B. A., 579
Watkins, C. E., 484
Watkinson, B., 326
Watson, D. L., 453, 532
Watson, J. B., 7, 150, 192, 211
Webb, W. B., 154
Wechsler, D., 355
Wechsler, H., 172
Wegener, D. T., 556
Wehr, T. A., 155
Weinberg, M. S., 385
Weinberg, P. R., 69, 304
Weinberger, D. R., 470
Weiner, B., 435, 551
Weiner, I. B., 435
Weinstock, M., 265
Weintraub, M., 343
Weissman, M. M., 465

Wellborn, J. G., 389
Wellman, B., 533
Wells, G. L., 232
Wells, J. E., 465
Wells, M. G., 428
Wenzlaff, R. M., 584
Werner, E. E., 527
Whipple, B., 380
Whishaw, I. Q., 11
White, B. J., 572
White, D. R., 343
White, N. M., 397
Whiteman, M., 179
Whiteside, T., 520
Whiting, B. B., 584
Whitley, B. E., 53
Whitlinger, R. P., 227
Whorf, B. L., 277
Wickramaratne, P. J., 465
Wicks, S.R., 12, 233
Wiesel, T. N., 110
Wiezbicki, M., 484
Wigfield, A., 390
Wiggins, J. S., 429, 431,
    432, 438
Williams, R. B., 438
Williams, S. L., 276
Williams-Keeler, J., 459
Williamson, S. E., 473
Willis, S. L., 356
Wilson, A. A., 234
Wilson, B. J., 527
Wilson, D. B., 501
Wilson, D. L., 329
Wilson, D. S., 581
Wilson, M., 12, 68, 69,
    576
Wilson, M. A., 160
Wilson, P. H., 532
Wilson, T. D., 552, 559
Wilson, V. L., 304
Winblad, B., 359
Wing, A. L., 537
Wingate, B., 452
Winner, E., 309, 317
Winzenz, D., 222
Wirga, M., 491
Wisch, A. F., 502
Witelson, S. F., 89, 386
Wittchen, H. U., 465
Wolf, N. M., 204
Wolford, G., 104
Wolpe, J., 492
Wolters, G., 104
Wolverton, D., 473
Wong, P. T. P., 360
Wong, S., 473
Wood, J. V., 554
Wood, T., 390
Woodruff-Pak, D. S., 191
Wooley, S. C., 378
Worrall, B. K., 577
Worrell, J., 502
Wortman, C. B., 432
Wright, B. D., 288
Wright, R., 253
Wrightsman, L. S., 450,
    471

Xu, W., 506

Yackel, E., 390
Yalom, I. D., 498
Yarmey, A. D., 235
Yeh, E. K., 465
Yoram, B., 437
Young, M., 459
Young, S. L., 191
Yudofsky, S. C., 450
Yuille, J. C., 169, 232

Zack, J., 487
Zajonc, R. B., 398, 566
Zakrajsek, T., 139, 501
Zakzanis, K. K., 468
Zanna, M. P., 54, 557, 570
Zautra, A. J., 525
Zec, R. F., 470
Zeidner, M., 433, 529
Zelnik, M., 542
Zeren, A. S., 40
Ziegert, K. A., 211
Zikovitz, D. C., 126
Zilbergeld, B., 385, 386
Zillman, D., 404
Zimmerman, B. J., 390
Zimmerman, C., 263
Zimmerman, R. R., 339
Zola, M., 522
Zola, S., 234
Zucker, S. W., 129
Zuckerman, M., 369
Zuo, Z., 235

Subject Index

A

Abnormal behavior
 anxiety disorders, 455–459
 biological factors, 450
 cultural influences, 451
 definition of, 448
 dissociative disorders, 460–461
 DSM-IV classification, 452–455
 elements of, 448
 gender differences, 451–452
 insanity defense, 449, 450
 medical model, 450
 mood disorders, 463–467
 myths/facts about, 449
 personality disorders, 472–474
 prevalence of, 452
 psychological factors, 450–451
 schizophrenia, 467–472
 somatoform disorders, 459–460
Aboriginal peoples
 acculturative stress, 525
 achievement, 392
 and assimilation, 392
 conflict, 569
 culturally biased IQ test questions, 304
 and invading Europeans, 570
 standardized intelligence tests, 304
 stereotypes of, 570
 suicide, 465, 479
 tribal healing, 480
Absolute threshold, 102–103
Abstract thinking, formal operational stage, 335
Accommodation
 Piaget's theory, 331
 visual, 108
Acculturative stress, 525–526
Acetylcholine (ACh), 76, 78
Achievement motivation, 387–392
 attribution theory, 389
 cultural influences, 390–392
 and goal-setting, 389–390
 and intrinsic/extrinsic motivation, 388–389
 need for achievement, 388
 and planning, 390
 and socioeconomic status, 392
Achievement tests, 295
Acronyms, memory strategy, 246
Action potential, 75
Activation-synthesis theory, dreams, 166
Activity theory, aging, 359–360
Acupuncture, 122, 123
Adaptation, sensory, 110–111
Addiction
 definition of, 178
 disease model, 178
 life-process model, 178
 and withdrawal, 178
Adler's theory, 420–421
 compensation and overcompensation, 421
 inferiority and superiority complex, 421
 striving for superiority, 420–421

Adolescence, 345–351
 at-risk youth, 350–351
 cognitive development, 335, 346–347
 identity development, 349–350
 moral development, 347–349
 physical development, 346
 socioemotional development, 338
 storm-and-stress view, 345
 time span of, 321, 322
 use of contraception in, 542–543
Adrenal glands, 96
Adrenaline. See Epinephrine
Adulthood
 see also Early adulthood; Late adulthood; Middle adulthood
 cohort effects, 359
 and life events, 359
 social clocks, 359
 stage theories of, 358–359
 time span of periods in, 321, 322
Aerobic exercise, 537
Affectionate love, 586
Afferent nerves, 72–73
African Americans
 achievement motivation, 392
 intelligence test issue, 304
 intimate contact with whites, effects of, 574
 and societal prejudice, 569–570
 stereotyping of, 570
Afterimages, 113–114
Aggression, 576–580
 vs. assertive behavior, 534
 biological influences, 576–578
 and brain, 577
 cultural influences, 578
 Freudian view, 9, 576
 frustration-aggression hypothesis, 578–579
 genetic factors, 576–577
 and hormones, 577–578
 and observational learning, 579
 observational learning of, 36–37, 208
 physiological research on, 44–45
 reduction of, 579–580
 and TV viewing, 45–47, 579
Aging
 activity theory, 359–360
 and Alzheimer's disease, 354
 cellular clock theory, 353–354
 death and dying, 361–362
 free-radical theory, 354
 life expectancy, 353
 life span, 353
 and memory loss, 355
 successful aging, 360
 and wisdom, 356
Agonists, 78
AIDS, 543–544
 heroin addiction, 174
 and heroin addiction, 174
 in newborns, 326
 prevention guidelines, 543–544
 transmission of, 543
Albert, classical conditioning of phobia, 192
Alcohol, 172

Alcoholics Anonymous (AA), 499
Alcoholism, 172–173
 binge drinking, 172
 cultural influences, 173
 definition of, 172–173
 environmental factors, 173
 genetic factors, 173
 recovery, criteria for, 179
 and violent behavior, 577
Algorithms, problem solving, 260
All-or-none principle, 75
Alpha waves, 157
Altered states of consciousness
 causes of, 151
 definition of, 151
 hypnosis, 167–170
 psychoactive drugs, 170–180
Altered states of consciousness and religion, 153
Altruism, 580–584
 biological influences, 581–582
 bystander intervention, 582–583
 definition of, 580–581
 and egoism, 582
 environmental influences, 582–583
 gender differences, 583–584
Alzheimer's disease
 brain graft treatment, 93
 theories of cause, 354
 treatment of, 354
 working memory deficits, 226
American Psychological Association (APA), 52
Amnesia, 228, 244
 anterograde amnesia, 244
 dissociative amnesia, 460
 implicit vs. explicit memory, 227
 and magnetic resonance imaging, 236
 retrograde amnesia, 244
Amok, 451
Amphetamines, 174
Amplitude, 116, 118
Amygdala, 81–82
 and aggression, 577
 and emotion, 396–397
Anal stage, 417
Analogy, and problem solving, 263–264
Androgens, 380
Anger, 404–405
 and catharsis, 405
 causes of, 404
 self-control tips, 405
Anima and animus archetypes, 420
Animal research
 ethical issues, 53–54
 examples of, 53
 physiological research, 44–45
Animals
 attachment behavior, 339
 and cognition, 208
 cognitive maps, 208–209
 dreams of, 166
 hormones and aggression, 577–578
 imprinting and attachment, 339
 instinctive drift, 210
 language learning, 275–276, 278
 observational learning in, 207

 sexuality of, 380, 381
 taste aversion, 210
Anorexia nervosa, 378, 451
Antagonists, 78
Anterograde amnesia, 244
Anti-smoking campaigns, 540
Anti-spanking laws, 211
Antianxiety drugs, 504–505
Antidepressant drugs, 505
Antipsychotic drugs, 505–506
 atypical types of, 506
 tardive dyskinesia, 505–506
Antisocial personality disorder, 472, 473–474
Anxiety disorders, 455–459
 antianxiety drugs, 504–505
 biological intervention, 505
 generalized anxiety disorder, 455–456
 obsessive-compulsive disorder, 458
 panic disorder, 456–457
 phobic disorder, 457–458
 post-traumatic stress disorder, 458–459
 psychological intervention, 505
Aphasia, 87
Aphrodisiacs, 381
Apparent movement, 136
Applied behavior analysis, 203
 see also Behavior modification
Approach/approach conflict, 523
Approach/avoidance conflict, 524
Aptitude tests, 294–295
Archetypes, Jung's theory, 420
Arousal
 and autonomic nervous system, 393–394
 and emotion, 393–394
 and performance, 394
 Yerkes-Dodson law, 394
Art
 and depth perception, 131, 133, 134–135
 Freudian symbols in, 414
Artificial intelligence (AI), 256
Assertive behavior, 533–534
Assimilation
 to cultural change, 526
 in Piaget's theory, 331
Association cortex, 86
Associative learning, 188
Astrology, 24
Asylums, 481
At-risk youth, 350–351
Atkinson-Shiffrin theory, 224
Attachment, 339–340
 critical period, 339
 definition of, 339
 evaluation of theory, 340
 and later life competency, 340
 and later life depression, 466
 secure attachment, 340
Attachment imprinting studies, 339
Attention, 128–129
 and memory, 246
 and observational learning, 207
 selective attention, 128–129
 Stroop effect, 128, 129
Attitude change, 556

Attitudes, 556–559
  behavioral influence on, 557
  cognitive dissonance, 557–558
  definition of, 556
  and prediction of behavior, 556–557
  self-perception theory, 558–559
Attraction, 584–585
  and consensual validation, 584
  matching hypothesis, 585
  physical attraction, 584–585
  and similarity, 584
Attribution, 550–552
  and achievement motivation, 389
  basis of, 389
  and controllable/uncontrollable events, 551
  definition of, 550
  fundamental attribution error, 552
  internal and external attributions, 551
  self-serving bias, 552
Auditory nerve, 84, 120
Auditory system, 116–120
  and brain, 120
  and ear, 118
  frequency theory of hearing, 120
  place theory of hearing, 118–120
  and sound, 116–118
  volley principle, 120
Authoritarian parenting, 341
Authoritative parenting, 341–342
Autobiographical memory, 239–240
Automatic processes, consciousness, 151
Autonomic nervous system
  and arousal, 393–394
  divisions of, 72
  functions of, 72
Autonomy vs. shame and doubt, 337
Availability heuristic, 266
Aversive conditioning
  method in, 492
  smoking cessation method, 542
Avoidance/avoidance conflict, 523–524
Avoidance coping, 529
Avoidant personality disorder, 472
Awareness. See Consciousness
Axon, 73–74

Babbling, 272
Barbiturates, 173
Basal ganglia, 82
Basal metabolism rate (BMR), 377
Basic-skills-and-phonetics approach, 275
Basilar membrane, 118
Beck's cognitive therapy, 494, 496
Behavior
  biological aspects of, 17
  cultural influences, 19–20
  environmental aspects of, 17–18
  influence on attitudes, 557–559
  meaning of, 5
  and mental processes, 18–19
  prediction from attitudes of person, 556–557
  social factors in, 19
Behavior modification, 202–205, 493
  case examples, 204, 493
  self-control training, 200, 205

smoking cessation methods, 541–542
  time-out, 202–203
Behavior therapies, 491–493
  aversive conditioning, 492
  behavior modification, 202–205, 493
  systematic desensitization, 492
  token economy, 493
Behavioral approach
  applications. See Behavior therapies
  behavior modification, 202–205
  child care, 211
  classical conditioning, 186–193
  emotion, 398–400
  evaluation of, 425
  historical view, 8
  language learning, 269
  operant conditioning, 194–205
  personality theories, 423–424
Behavioral medicine, 516
Behavioral neuroscience approach
  basis of, 11
  historical view, 11–12
  study of, 25
Belief perseverance, 265
Benzodiazepines, 504–505
Bias, 47–48, 264–265
Bilingualism, 274–275
  bilingual education issue, 274
  and critical period, 274–275
  and intelligence measures, 274
Binet tests, 291–292
  intelligence quotient (IQ), 291
  mental age (MA), 291
  normal distribution, 291
  revisions of, 291–292
Binocular cues, 130–131
Binocular vision, 131
Biofeedback, for stress management, 536
Biological influences
  see also Genetic influences
  abnormal behavior, 450
  aggression, 576–578
  altruism, 581–582
  on behavior, 17
  brain, 80–94
  in development, 320
  emotion, 393–397, 400
  endocrine system, 95–96
  evolutionary theory, 68–69
  heredity, 66–67
  homosexuality, 385–386
  hunger, 373–375
  instinctive drift, 210
  language development, 269
  learning, 209–210
  mood disorders, 466
  motivation, 368–370
  nature and nurture, 69–70
  nervous system, 70–72
  neurons, 72–78
  preparedness, 210
  schizophrenia, 469–470
  sex drive, 380
  stress response, 518–519
Biomedical therapy
  drug therapy, 504–506
  electroconvulsive therapy (ECT), 506
  psychosurgery, 507–508
Bipolar disorder, 464, 466
  lithium for, 505
  manic episodes, 464, 466

Birth defects, 326
Bisexuality, 385
Blind spot, 109
Blindness, recovery from, 140–141
Blood sugar, and hunger, 374
Body weight, 376–378
Borderline personality disorder, 472
Brain, 80–94
  and aggression, 577
  basal ganglia, 82
  capacity to self-repair, 91
  complementary specialization, 89
  and emotion, 396–397
  and endocrine system, 95–96
  forebrain, 80
  gender differences, 86
  grafts, 91, 93
  and hearing, 84, 120
  hemispheres of, 87–89
  hindbrain, 80
  hormones, 86
  and hunger, 374–375
  hypothalamus, 82–84
  and infant development, 329–330
  integration of brain function, 88, 90
  limbic system, 81–82
  lobes of, 84
  and memory, 233–235
  midbrain, 80
  neocortex, 84–87
  plasticity, 91
  and schizophrenia, 469–471
  and sexual activity, 380
  and sleep, 159
  and stress response, 519–520
  thalamus, 82
  visual cortex, 84, 110
Brain imaging, 93–94
  computer-assisted axial tomography (CAT scan), 94
  electroencephalograph (EEG), 93–94
  magnetic resonance imaging (MRI), 94
  memory studies, 234–235
  positron-emission tomography (PET scan), 94
  single-unit recording, 93
  sleep research, 156–157
Brainstorming, 312
Brightness, 112
Brightness constancy, 136
Broca's area, 87
Bulimia, 378
Burnout, 523
Bystander intervention, 582–583

Caffeine, 174
Canada Child Care Act, 343
Canadian Achievement Tests (CAT), 294, 295
Canadian Association for Suicide Prevention, 479
Canadian Code of Ethics for Psychologists, 484
Canadian Criminal Code, 449
Canadian Mental Health Association, 481, 482
Canadian Psychological Association, 5, 27, 52

breach of confidentiality, exceptions, 449
Canadian Code of Ethics for Psychologists, 484
  ethical guidelines, 192
  health psychology, 516
  informed consent, 564
  nonsexist research policy, 55
Canadian Test of Cognitive Skills (CTCS), 294, 295
Canadian Transition to Child Care Study, 343
Cancer, and nutrition, 540, 541
Cannon-Bard theory, 396
Cardinal personality traits, 431
Care perspective of moral development, 349
Careers
  and adult development, 356
  in psychology, 24
Carpentered-world hypothesis, 141, 142
Case studies, 43–44
Catatonic schizophrenia, 469
Catharsis
  and aggression reduction, 579–580
  of angry feelings, 405
  in psychotherapy, 486
Causality. See Attribution
Cellular clock theory, 353–354
Central nervous system (CNS), components of, 71
Central personality traits, 431
Cerebellum, 80
Certification, 484
Charter of Rights and Freedoms, 449
Chemical senses, 122–125
Chicago Stress Project, 522
Child abuse
  and dissociative identity disorder, 461
  repressed memory, 241–242
Child care, 343
Child development. See Early childhood; Infancy; Middle/late childhood
Child poverty, 526, 527
Child rearing, 211
Child witnesses, 232
Chunking, 222
Cigarette smoking
  cessation strategies, 541–542
  dangers of, 540
  and prenatal development, 326
Circadian rhythms, 154–156
Clairvoyance, 142
Classical conditioning, 186–193
  acquisition, 188
  advertising and, 192
  application. See Classical conditioning methods
  as associative learning, 188
  conditioned response (CR), 188, 189, 191
  conditioned stimulus (CS), 188, 189, 191, 193
  contemporary perspective of, 191
  contingency in, 188
  counterconditioning, 192
  discrimination in, 190–191
  and drug overdoses, 185–186
  evaluation of, 193
  extinction, 188
  generalization, 190
  and health problems, 192
  information theory of, 191

Pavlov's experiment, 187–188, 189
of phobia, 192
spontaneous recovery, 188, 190
stimulus substitution in, 191
temporal contiguity in, 188
unconditioned response (UR), 187–188, 189
unconditioned stimulus (US), 187, 189, 190, 191, 193
Classical conditioning methods, 492
Classroom, jigsaw, 573–574
Clinical psychology
specialties of field, 26
study of, 24
training of therapists, 483
Closure, 130, 131
Clozaril, 506
Cocaine, 174
Cochlea, 118
Cognition
cognitive maps, 208–209
frontal lobes, 264
insight learning, 209
and learning, 208–209
spatial cognition, 208
Cognitive appraisal, 522–523
Cognitive development, 331–336
adolescence, 346–347
early adulthood, 354–355
late adulthood, 355–256
middle/late adulthood, 355
Piaget's theory, 331–336
Cognitive dissonance, 557–558
Cognitive influences
dreams, 165
emotion, 397–398
impression formation, 553
language development, 278–279
mood disorders, 466
motivation, 370
sexuality, 380–381
stress, 522–523
Cognitive maps, 208–209
Cognitive monitoring, 247
Cognitive processes, 320
Cognitive restructuring, 529–530
Cognitive theory
basis of, 11
and development of computers, 254–255
historical view, 11
Cognitive therapies, 494–497
Beck's cognitive therapy, 494, 496
cognitive restructuring in, 529–530
Ellis' cognitive therapy, 496
rational-emotive behavior therapy, 494
Cohort effects, 359
Cohorts, 359
Collective unconscious, 420
Collective value orientation, 585–586
Color
characteristics of, 111–112
color wheel, 114
opponent pairs, 113
Color blind, 112
Color deficient, 112–113
Color vision, 111–114
afterimages, 113–114
dichromats, 113
monochromats, 113
opponent-process theory, 113–114
trichromatic theory, 112
trichromats, 113
Columbine High School, 3
Communication, 588
Community mental health centers, 481

Community psychology, 25
Community-wide programs
at-risk youth, 350–351
drug treatment, 179
Compensation, 421
Complementary specialization, 89
Complex sounds, 117
Compulsions, 458
Computer-assisted axial tomography (CAT scan), 94
Computers
artificial intelligence (AI), 256
and cognitive revolution, 254–255
Concept maps, 248
Conception, 325
Concepts, 256–258
definition of, 256
formation of, 257–258
importance of, 256–257
prototype matching, 258
Concrete operational stage, 334–335
Concurrent validity, 289
Conditional positive regard, 426
Conditioned response (CR), 188, 189, 191
Conditioned stimulus (CS), 188, 189, 191, 193
Cones of eye, 108–110
Confidentiality, 52
Confirmation bias, 264–265
Conflict, 523–524
approach/approach conflict, 523
approach/avoidance conflict, 524
avoidance/avoidance conflict, 523–524
Conformity, 559, 561–562
Asch experiment, 559, 561
definition of, 559
influencing factors, 561–562
and obedience, 562–585
Consciousness, 150–153
automatic processes, 151
controlled processes, 150
daydreaming, 151
definition of, 150
stream of consciousness, 150
unconscious thought, 150
Wundt's study, 7
Consciousness, states of
see also Altered states of consciousness
consciousness, 150–153
sleep, 154–159
Consensual validation, 584
Conservation, 333
Consumers of psychological information, 56–59
Content validity, 289
Contingency, 188
Contingency model, 568
Continuity, 323–324
Continuous reinforcement, 199
Contraception, 542–543
Control group, 46
Controlled processes, 150
Controlled processing of information, 355
Conventional level, 347
Convergent thinking, 309
Conversion disorder, 460
Coping
and assertive behavior, 533–534
avoidance, 529
and denial, 529
emotion-focused, 529
and optimism, 531
and positive self-illusion, 530

and positive self-talk, 529–530
problem-focused, 528
and self-efficacy, 532
and social support, 532–533
stress management methods, 534–536
Cornea, 107
Cornell Method, 248
Corpus callosum, 87–88
Correlational research, 45–46
Cortisol, 519
Counseling psychology
specialties of field, 24
study of, 24
training of psychologists, 483
Counterconditioning, 192
Couple therapy, 498, 499
Crack cocaine, 174
Creativity, 310–313
characteristics of creative thinkers, 311–312
creative process, steps in, 311
definition of, 309
and divergent thinking, 309
and intelligence, 309
nurturing, guidelines for, 313
Criterion validity, 289
Critical period
attachment, 339
language development, 273–274
second language learning, 274–275
Critical thinking, 262–263
see also Cultural influences
about psychological information, 58–59
compared to mindfulness, 263
definition of, 262–263
guidelines for, 22
importance of, 23
Cross-cultural psychology, 27
Cues
and hunger, 375–376
memory retrieval, 237–238
Cultural bias
intelligence tests, 304–305
and psychological research, 55–56
Cultural-familial retardation, 308–309
Cultural influences
abnormal behavior, 451
achievement motivation, 390–392
aggression, 578
alcoholism, 173
on behavior, 19–20
conflicts between cultures. See Interethnic relations
death and dying, 361
depression, 467
emotion, 400–401
language development, 277
motivation, 371
on perception, 141
sexuality, 382
stress, 525–526
Cultural pluralism, 13
Culture, 12–13
Culture-fair tests, 305–306

Daily hassles, 525
Darwin, Charles
evolutionary theory, 6, 68
and history of psychology, 6

Data collection, 36
Daydreaming, 151
Death and dying, 361–362
cultural differences, 361
death of partner, effects of, 361–362
drug overdoses, 185–186
stages of, 361
Debriefing, 53
Decay theory, 244
Decision making, 264–267
availability heuristic, 266
belief perseverance, 265
confirmation bias, 264–265
definition of, 264
group decision making, 566–567
hindsight bias, 266
overconfidence bias, 265–266
representativeness heuristic, 266–267
Declarative memory, 227
Deductive reasoning, 264
Defense mechanisms, 415–417
denial, 416
displacement, 416
functions of, 415–416
projection, 416
rationalization, 416
reaction formation, 416
regression, 416
repression, 416
sublimation, 416
Deindividuation, as group influence, 566
Deinstitutionalization, 481–482
Delta waves, 157
Delusions, 468, 469
Dendrite, 73–74
Denial, 416, 529
Dependence and drugs, 172
Dependent personality disorder, 472
Dependent variable, 46
Depressants, 172–174
alcohol, 172–173
barbiturates, 173
dependence, risk of, 177
effects of, 176
medical uses, 176
opiates, 173–174
overdose, signs of, 177
tranquilizers, 173
Depression
antidepressant drugs, 505
behavior therapy for, 495
and cognitive therapy, 494
depressive realism hypothesis, 466
dysthymic disorder, 463
electroconvulsive therapy (ECT) for, 506
Freud's theory, 466
and high stress levels, 517
and learned helplessness, 466–467
major depressive disorder, 463
and self-esteem, 428
self-test, 464
sociocultural view, 504
and suicide, 464, 465
Depressive disorders, 463–464
Depressive realism hypothesis, 466
Depth perception, 130–131, 130–133
binocular cues, 130–131
and art, 131, 133, 134–135
definition of, 130
monocular cues, 130–131, 133
stereogram, 132
visual cliff, 139–140
and visual disparity, 131

Development
    see also specific developmental
        stages
    biological processes in, 320
    cognitive development, 331–336
    cognitive processes in, 320
    definition of, 320
    physical development, 328–330
    socioemotional development,
        336–345
    socioemotional processes in,
        320–321
    time periods/stages in, 321–323
Developmental issues
    continuity and discontinuity,
        323–324
    early-later experience, 324
    nature and nurture, 323
Developmental psychology, 27
Diagnostic and Statistical Manual of
    Mental Disorders (DSM)-IV,
    452–455
    medical model of, 453–454
    multiaxial system, 453
    terms dropped from, 453
    versions of, 452
Diathesis-stress model, 470
Dichromats, 113
Dieting, 377–378
Difference threshold, 103, 105
Difficult child, 341
Discontinuity, 323–324
Discrimination
    classical conditioning, 190–191
    operant conditioning, 201
Disease model. See Medical model
Disorganized schizophrenia, 469
Displacement, 416
Display rules, 400
Dissociative disorders, 460–461
    and childhood experiences, 461
    dissociative amnesia, 460
    dissociative fugue, 460
    dissociative identity disorder,
        460–461
    Eve White case, 461
Dissociative identity disorder, 460–461
Divergent thinking, 309
DNA (deoxyribonucleic acid), 66
Dominant genes, 66
Dominant-recessive genes principle, 66
Door-in-the-face strategy, 556
Dopamine
    functions of, 76, 78, 397
    and mood disorders, 466
    and Parkinson's disease, 93
Double-blind experiments, 49
Down syndrome, 308
Drawing conclusions, 36–37
Dream analysis, 164, 413, 487
    latent content, 164, 487
    manifest content, 164, 487
    symbolism in, 487
Dreams, 164–166
    activation-synthesis theory, 166
    cognitive theory of, 165
    colors in, 166
    gender differences, 166
    memory of dreams, 157, 166
    and REM sleep, 157
Drives, 369
Drug abuse
    addiction, 178
    and brain, 83–84
    conditioned compensatory
        response, 186

overdose, 185–186
    prevention, levels of, 178–179
    self-test, 173
    treatment, long term effects, 179
Drug overdose, 185–186
Drug therapy, 504–506
    antianxiety drugs, 504–505
    antidepressant drugs, 505
    antipsychotic drugs, 505–506
Drug tolerance, 185
Dual-code hypothesis, 221
Dysthymic disorder, 463–464

E

Ear
    anatomy of, 118, 119
    hearing, theories of, 118–120
    and vestibular sense, 126
Eardrum, 118
Early adulthood
    careers and work, 356
    cognitive development, 354–355
    lifestyles, 356–358
    physical development, 352
    socioemotional development, 338,
        356, 358
    time span of, 321, 322
Early childhood
    cognitive development, 333–334
    physical development, 330
    senses, development of, 330
    socioemotional development,
        337–338
    time span of, 321, 322
Early-later experience, 324
Easy child, 341
Eating behavior
    dieting, 377–378
    hunger, 372–376
Eating disorders
    anorexia nervosa, 378
    bulimia, 378
Echoic memory, 225
Eclectic approach, 14
Ecological approach, 139
Efferent nerves, 72–73
Effort, 389
Ego, 415
Egocentrism
    adolescents, 347
    preoperational stage, 333–334
Egoism
    and altruism, 582
    definition of, 582
Elaboration, 220–221
Elavil, 505
Elderly, REM sleep of, 157–158
Electra complex, 418
Electroconvulsive therapy (ECT), 506
Electroencephalograph (EEG), 93–94,
    156–157
Ellis' cognitive therapy, 496
Embryonic period, 325
Emotion-focused coping, 529
Emotional trauma, 241–243
Emotions
    anger, 404–405
    and arousal, 393–394
    behavioral approach, 398–400
    biological influences, 393–397, 400
    and brain, 396–397
    Cannon-Bard theory, 396

cognitive influences, 397–398
    cultural influences, 400–401
    definition of, 393
    display rules, 400
    facial feedback hypothesis,
        399–400
    gender differences, 401–402
    happiness, 402, 404
    and hypothalamus, 83
    James-Lange theory, 396
    and limbic system, 81–82
    love, 585–586
    memory of, 240–243
    and motivation, 393
    nonverbal communication, 401
    primacy issue, 398
    two-factor theory, 397–398
    wheel model, 402, 403
Empathy, 426
Empirically keyed test, 436
Encoding, 219–223
Encoding specificity principle, 238
Endocrine glands, 95
Endocrine system, 95–96
    see also Hormones
    adrenal glands, 96
    endocrine glands, 95
    pituitary gland, 95–96
    and stress response, 519–521
Endorphins, 76–77, 78, 397
Environment, 69
Environmental influences
    alcoholism, 173
    altruism, 582–583
    effects on behavior, 17–18
    intelligence issue, 299, 301–303
    language development, 269–271
    love relationships, 586
    motivation, 370–371
    nature and nurture, 69–70
    obesity, 377
    stress, 523–525
Epilepsy, 84–85, 87
Epinephrine, 96
Episodic memory, 228
Erikson's theory, 336–339
    autonomy vs. shame and doubt,
        337
    basis of, 10
    evaluation of, 338
    generativity vs. stagnation, 338, 358
    identity vs. identity confusion,
        338, 350
    industry vs. inferiority, 338
    initiative vs. guilt, 338
    integrity vs. despair, 338
    intimacy vs. isolation, 338
    trust vs. mistrust, 337
Erogenous zones, 417
Eros, 576
Estradiol, 346
Estrogen replacement therapy, 353
Estrogens, 380
Ethics, 51–54
    animal research, 53–54
    APA guidelines, 52–53
    Canadian Code of Ethics for
        Psychologists, 484
    confidentiality, 52
    cultural bias, 55–56
    debriefing, 53
    gender bias, 54–55
    importance of, 51–52
    informed consent, 52
    values of psychologist, 53, 54
Ethnic diversity, 13

Ethnic gloss, 56
Ethnicity
    see also Cultural influences
    acculturative stress, 525
    adjustment to cultural change,
        525–526
    conflicts. See Interethnic relations
    definition of, 13
    and psychotherapy, 504
Ethnocentrism, 571–572
    definition of, 571
    and social identity theory, 571–572
Ethology, 370
Eustress, 518–519
Evolutionary psychology approach
    basis of, 12, 68–69
    emotion, 400
    historical view, 12
    motivation, 370
Evolutionary theory, 6, 68–69
Excessive sleepiness, 155
Excitement phase, 382
Exercise, 378, 537, 539
Exorcism, 480
Experiment, 46
Experimental group, 46
Experimental psychology, 25
Experimental research, 46–49
    bias in, 47–48
    double-blind experiment, 49
    experimental and control
        groups, 46
    variables in, 46
Experimenter bias, 48–49
External attributions, 551
External cues of hunger, 375–376
Extinction
    classical conditioning, 188
    operant conditioning, 201
Extrasensory perception, 141, 142–143
Extraversion
    personality trait, 431
    self-test, 432
Extrinsic motivation, 388–389
Eye, 107–110
    see also Visual system
    accommodation, 108
    anatomy of, 107–108
    blind spot, 109
    iodopsin, 109
    presbyopia, 108
    rhodopsin, 109
    rods and cones, 108–110
    transduction, 108
Eyewitness testimony, 232

F

Face validity, 436
Facial feedback hypothesis, 399–400
Family influences
    see also Mother-child interaction
    father, effects on development, 345
    language development, 270–271
    parenting styles, 341–342
Family therapy, 498–499
Fathers' role, 345
Fear, 397
Feature detectors, 110
Feminist theory, 419–420
Fetal alcohol syndrome (FAS), 326
Fetal period, 325–326
Fight-or-flight response, 519

Figure-ground relationship, 129
First Call BC Child and Youth
    Advocacy Movement, 527
Fixation
    Freud's theory, 417
    mental set, 261
    obstacle to problem solving, 261
Fixed-interval reinforcement schedule,
    199–200
Fixed-ratio reinforcement schedule, 199
Flashbulb memories, 240–241
Follicle-stimulating hormone
    (FSH), 96
Foot-in-the-door strategy, 556
Forebrain, 80
Forensic psychology, 27
Forgetting, 243–244
Formal operational stage, 335, 346
Fovea, 109
Free association, 486
Free-radical theory, 354
Free-running cycle, 156
French Canadians, 567, 570
French immersion, 4, 274
Frequency
    cps (cycles per second), 116
    Hertz (Hz), 116
    measurement of, 116
    of sound, 116, 118
    theory of hearing, 120
Freudian slip, 413
Freud's theory, 413–419
    of aggression, 9, 576
    anal stage, 417
    basis of, 10
    criticisms of, 419
    defense mechanisms, 415–417
    depression, 466
    dream analysis, 164, 413, 487
    ego, 415
    Electra complex, 418
    erogenous zones, 417
    fixation, 417
    Freudian symbols in art, 414
    genital stage, 419
    historical view, 9–10, 413
    id, 415
    latency stage, 418
    limitations of, 10
    Oedipus complex, 418
    oral stage, 417
    penis envy, 418
    phallic stage, 418
    pleasure principle, 415
    psychoanalysis, 484–487
    reality principle, 415
    repression, 242
    superego, 415
    unconscious in, 150, 413
Frontal lobe, 84
Frustration, 524
Frustration-aggression hypothesis,
    578–579
Fugue, 460
Fully functioning person, 426–427
Functional fixedness, 261
Functionalism, 7
Fundamental attribution error, 552

GABA (gamma aminobutyric acid),
    76, 78

Gate-control theory, 122, 123
Genain quadruplets, 471
Gender, 13
Gender bias
    and psychological research, 53
    SAT test, 294
Gender differences
    abnormal behavior, 451–452
    altruism, 583–584
    brain, 86
    communication, 588
    dreams, 166
    emotion, 401–402
    life expectancy, 353
    moral development, 349
    relationships, 586, 588
General adaptation syndrome (GAS),
    518–519
Generalization
    classical conditioning, 190
    operant conditioning, 201
    overgeneralization problem,
        58–59
    in scientific method, 38–39
Generalized anxiety disorder,
    455–456
Generativity vs. stagnation, 338
Genes, 66–67
    dominant-recessive genes
        principle, 66
    functions of, 66
    genotype and phenotype, 67
Genetic engineering, 67
Genetic influences
    aggression, 576–577
    alcoholism, 173
    intelligence issue, 299, 301–303
    mood disorders, 466
    nature and nurture, 69–70
    obesity, 376
    obsessive-compulsive disorder, 458
    schizophrenia, 469
Genital stage, 419
Genotype, 67
Germinal period, prenatal, 325
Gestalt psychology, 129–130
Gestalt therapy, 490–491
Giftedness, 309
Gilligan's theory of moral
    development, 349
Glial cells, 78
Glucose level, 374
Goal-setting
    and achievement motivation,
        389–390
    benefits of, 389–390
Great-person theory, 568
Group decision making, 566–567
Group influence, 565–569
    deindividuation, 566
    group performance, 565–566
    and leadership, 567–569
    norms and roles, 565
    social facilitation, 566
    social loafing, 566
Group intelligence tests, 293–294
Group polarization effect, 567
Group therapies, 497–500
    couple therapy, 498, 499
    family therapy, 498–499
    features of, 498
    self-help support groups,
        499–500
Groupthink, 567
Growth hormone (GH), 96
Guilty Knowledge Test, 395

Hallucinations, and schizophrenia,
    468
Hallucinogens
    definition of, 175
    dependence, risk of, 177
    effects of, 175, 176
    LSD (lysergic acid diethyl-amide),
        175
    marijuana, 175
    medical uses, 176
    overdose, signs of, 177
Handwriting analysis, 437
Happiness, 402, 404
Hardiness, 522
Health care costs, 517
Health promotion, 537–544
    cigarette smoking cessation,
        540–542
    exercise, 537, 539
    sexual decision-making, 542–544
Health psychology
    definition of, 516
    health promotion activities,
        537–544
    stress, 517–527
    study of, 27
Hearing, 84, 120
    see also Auditory system
Hemispheres of brain, 87–88
    corpus callosum, 87–88
    misconceptions about right/left
        brain, 89
    specialization of, 87–88
Heredity, 66–67
    see also Genetic influences
    chromosomes, 66–67
    genes, 66–67
    and intelligence, 301
Heroin addiction, 173–174
Heterosexuality, 384–385
Heuristics, 266–267
Hierarchy of motives, 371–372, 427
Hindbrain, 80
Hindsight bias, 266
Hippocampus, 82
Hippocrates, 480
History of psychology
    behavioral approach, 8
    behavioral neuroscience approach,
        11–12
    cognitive approach, 11
    Darwin's influence, 6
    eclectic approach, 14
    evolutionary psychology approach,
        12
    functionalism, 7
    humanistic approach, 10
    information-processing approach,
        11
    mental health treatment, 480–482
    psychoanalytic theory, 9–10
    sociocultural approach, 12–14
    structuralism, 7
    time line of theories/pioneers, 15
    Wundt's laboratory, 6–7
Histrionic personality disorder, 472
Hogan Personality Inventory (HPI),
    438
Homeostasis, 369
Homosexuality, 385–387
    identity development, 386–387
    theories of cause, 385–386

Hormones
    of adrenal glands, 96
    and aggression, 577–578
    of pituitary gland, 95–96
    and puberty, 346
    sex hormones, 380
Horney's theory, 419–420
Hostility, 521
Hue, 111
Human Genome Project, 67
Humanistic approach
    basis of, 10, 425
    evaluation of, 429
    historical view, 10
    Maslow's theory, 10, 427
    Roger's theory, 10, 425–427
    self-esteem in, 427–429
Humanistic therapies, 489–491
    Gestalt therapy, 490–491
    person-centered therapy, 489–490
Hunger, 372–376
    biological factors, 373–375
    and brain, 374–375
    external cues, 375–376
    and self-control, 376
Hypersomnia, 155
Hypnosis, 167–170
    criteria for success, 168
    definition of, 167
    history of, 168
    nonstate theory, 170
    and remembering, 169
    special process theory, 168–169
    therapeutic uses of, 170
Hypochondriasis, 459
Hypothalamus, 82–84
    homosexual males, 386
    and hunger, 374–375
    and psychological states, 83–84
    and sexual activity, 380
Hypotheses, 36
Hypothetical-deductive reasoning,
    335, 346

Iconic memory, 225
Id, 415
Identity, 350
    vs. identity confusion, 338, 350
    development, 349–350
    Erikson's theory, 338, 350
    homosexuals, 386–387
Illusion
    positive self-illusion, 530
    and self-esteem, 530
Illusions, 137–139
Imagery, 221
Imitation. See Observational learning
Immune system
    and optimism, 531
    response to stress, 519–521
    study of, 520–521
Implicit memory, 227
Implicit personality theory, 553
Impression formation, 553–554
    cognitive influences, 553
    implicit personality theory, 553
    primacy effect, 554
    and prototypes, 554
    social comparison, 554
Impression management, 555–556
Imprinting, 339

Incentives, 370–371
Independent variable, 46
Indian Act, 479
Individual differences
  definition of, 286
  importance in field of
    psychology, 20
  standardized test information, 44
Individual psychology. *See* Adler's
  theory
Individual value orientation, 585
Inductive reasoning, 263
Indulgent parenting, 342
Industrial/organizational psychology,
  26, 27
Industry *vs.* inferiority, 338
Infancy, 328–329
  attachment, 339–340
  cognitive development, 331–333
  language development, 270,
    272–274
  physical development, 328–329
  REM sleep, 158
  senses, development of, 329
  socioemotional development, 337
  time span of, 321, 322
Infant Care (Watson), 211
Infant massage, 327
Inferiority complex, 421
Information-processing approach
  basis of, 11
  historical view, 11
  perception, 139
Information theory, 191
Informational social influence, 562
Informed consent, 52, 564
Initiative *vs.* guilt, 338
Inner ear, 118
Insanity defense, 449, 450
Insight learning, 209
Insomnia, 161, 162
Instability, 431
Instinctive drift, 210
Instincts
  definition of, 368
  Freudian view, 9, 576
  vs. learned behavior, 210
  and motivation, 368–369
Instrumental conditioning. *See*
  Operant conditioning
Integration, 526
Integrative therapy, 509
Integrity *vs.* despair, 338
Intellectual functions, 86
Intelligence
  and bilingualism, 274
  creativity, 310–313
  definition of, 286
  and environment, 301
  giftedness, 309
  and heredity, 301
  mental retardation, 308–309
  multiple-factor theory, 295
  nature and nurture issue, 299,
    301–303
  seven-intelligences theory,
    295–297
  triarchic theory, 298–299
  two-factor theory, 295
Intelligence quotient (IQ), elements
  of, 291
Intelligence tests
  achievement tests, 295
  aptitude tests, 294–295
  Binet tests, 291–292
  Canadians *vs.* Americans, 304

cultural bias, 304–305
culture-fair tests, 305–306
group tests, 293–294
history of, 286–288
minority groups, 301, 304
reliability, 288–289
standardization, 290
use and misuse of, 306–307
validity, 289
Wechsler scales, 292
Interethnic relations, 569–576
  ethnocentrism, 571–572
  improvement guidelines, 572–574
  intimate contact, value of, 574
  prejudice, 569–570
  Robbers Cave experiment,
    572–573
  stereotyping, 570
Interference theory, 243
Internal attributions, 551
Interneurons, 73
Interpretation, 486–487
Interviews for research, 43
Intimacy *vs.* isolation, 338
Intimate contact and interethnic
  relations, 574
Intrinsic motivation, 388–389
Introversion
  personality trait, 431
  self-test, 432
Ion channels, 75

J

Jackson Personality Inventory (JPI),
  434, 438
James, William, 7
James-Lange theory, 396
Jet lag, 154–155
Jigsaw classroom, 573–574
Jung's theory, 420
Justice perspective, 349

K

Keyword method, 246
Kinesthetic senses, 125–126
Kohlberg's theory, 347–349
Kohut's therapy, 488–489

L

Laboratory observation, 41–42
Language, 268–269
  definition of, 268
  metalinguistic awareness, 274
  morphology, 268
  phonology, 268
  semantics, 268–269
  syntax, 268
Language development
  animals, 275–276
  babbling, 272
  bilingualism, 274–275
  biological factors, 269
  and cognition, 278–279
  critical period, 273–274

cultural influences, 277
environmental influences, 269–271
first words, 272
guidelines for parents, 270
linguistic relativity hypothesis, 277
reading, 275
telegraphic speech, 272–273
Late adulthood
  see also Aging
  aging, 353–354
  cognitive development, 355–256
  socioemotional development, 338,
    359–360
  time span of, 321, 322
Latency stage, 418
Latent content, 164, 487
Law of effect, 195–196
Leadership, 567–569
Learned helplessness, 466–467
Learning
  biological factors, 209–210
  classical conditioning, 186–193
  cognition and learning, 208–209
  cultural factors, 211–212
  definition of, 186
  insight learning, 209
  observational learning, 207–208
  operant conditioning, 194–205
  during sleep, 160
Lens of eye, 107
Levels of processing theory, 220
Librium, 505
Licensing, 484
Lie detector, 394, 395
Life events
  autobiographical memory,
    239–240
  effects on adult development, 359
  and stress, 524–525
  stress scale, 524–525
Life expectancy, 353
Life-process model, 178
Life span, 353
Lifestyles, 356–358
Light, 106–107
Limbic system, 81–82
Linguistic relativity hypothesis, 277
Lithium, 505
Loneliness, 588–589
  and life transitions, 588–589
  reduction guidelines, 589
Long-term memory, 226–227
Loudness, 117
Love, 585–586
  affectionate love, 586
  environmental influences, 586
  romantic love, 585
  triangular theory of, 586
LSD (lysergic acid diethylamide),
  effects of, 175

M

Magnetic resonance imaging (MRI),
  94, 236
Maier String Problem, 261
Maintenance rehearsal, 219–220
Major depressive disorder, 463
Manic episodes, 464, 466, 487
Manifest content, 164
Manipulation, *vs.* assertion, 534
Mankato nuns, 92
Marginalization, 526

Marijuana, 175
Marriage, 357
Maslow's theory
  basis of, 10
  hierarchy of motives, 371–372, 427
  self-actualization, 372, 427
Massage, 327
Matching hypothesis, 585
Media
  presentation of psychological
    information, 57–58
  violence, 579
Medical model
  abnormal behavior, 450
  addiction, 178
  of DSM-IV, 453–454
Meditation, 535–536
  steps in, 535–536
  transcendental meditation (TM),
    535
Medulla, 80
Melatonin, 161
Memorial University of
  Newfoundland Scale of
  Happiness (MUNSH), 404
Memory
  see also Forgetting
  and aging, 355
  Atkinson-Shiffrin theory, 224
  autobiographical memory,
    239–240
  child witnesses, 232
  controlled processing of
    information, 355
  declarative memory, 227
  definition of, 218
  dissociation, 227
  of dreams, 157, 166
  dual-code hypothesis, 221
  echoic memory, 225
  elaboration, 220–221
  encoding, 219–223
  episodic memory, 228
  eyewitness testimony issue, 232
  flashbulb memories, 240–241
  and hypnosis, 169
  iconic memory, 225
  and imagery, 221
  imperfections of, 218
  implicit, 227
  levels of processing theory, 220
  limbic system, 81–82
  long-term memory, 226–227
  memory span, 226
  mood-congruent memory, 243
  network theory, 220–230
  neurobiological basis, 233–235
  nondeclarative memory, 227
  organization in, 222
  procedural, 227
  rehearsal, 219–220, 226
  and REM sleep, 158
  repressed memory, 241–242
  schema theory, 230–231, 233
  semantic memory, 228
  sensory memory, 224–225
  time-frames in, 223–227
  traumatic memory, 241
  working memory, 225–226
Memory retrieval
  cues, 237–238
  encoding specificity principle, 238
  primacy and recency effect, 237
  priming, 238
  recall, 238
  recognition, 238

serial position effect, 237
tip-of-the-tongue phenomenon, 235, 237
Memory strategies
acronyms, 246
attention, 246
chunking, 222
cognitive monitoring, 247
keyword method, 246
method of loci, 246
note-taking, 247–248
PQ4R method, 248
time management, 247
understanding *vs.* memorization, 246
Menarche, 346
Menopause, 352–353
Menstruation, 346
Mental age (MA), 291
Mental disorders. *See* Abnormal behavior
Mental health care
Community Resource Base, 482
framework for mental health policy, 482
Mental health professionals
licensing/certification of, 484
specialties of, 483
Mental health treatment
see also Psychotherapy
historical view, 480–482
and managed care, 482
Mental hospitals, 481–482
Mental processes
and behavior, 18–19
nature of, 5–6
Mental retardation, 308–309
classifications of, 308
cultural-familial retardation, 308–309
definition of, 308
organic retardation, 308
Mental set, 261
Meta-analysis, 501
Metalinguistic awareness, 274
Method of loci, 246
Midbrain, 80
Middle adulthood
careers and work, 356
cognitive development, 355
crisis *vs.* consciousness, 359
physical development, 352–353
socioemotional development, 338, 356–359
stage theory of, 358
time span of, 321, 322
Middle ear, 118
Middle/late childhood
cognitive development, 334–335
physical development, 330
socioemotional development, 338
time span of, 321, 322
Midnight Cave experiment, 155–156
Milgram experiment, 562–564
Mindfulness, 263
Minnesota Multiphasic Personality Inventory (MMPI), 44, 437–438
Minnesota Study of Twins Reared Apart, 65–66
Mnemonics, 246
Modeling. *See* Observational learning
Monoamine oxidase (MAO) inhibitors, 505
Monochromats, 113

Monocular cues
and art, 131–133
depth perception, 130–131, 133
Mood-congruent memory, 243
Mood disorders, 463–467
biological influences, 466
bipolar disorder, 464, 466
cognitive approach, 466
depressive disorders, 463–464
dysthymic disorder, 463–464
genetic factors, 466
psychosocial factors, 466–467
Moon illusion, 138
Moral development, 347–349
care *vs.* justice perspective, 349
Gilligan's theory, 349
Kohlberg's theory, 347–349
More for the Mind, 481
Morphine, 173
Morphology, language, 268
Mother-child interaction
attachment, 339–340
and language development, 270–271
parenting styles, 341–342
and working mothers, 343
Motion perception, 136
apparent movement, 136
movement aftereffects, 136
stroboscopic motion, 136
Motivation
achievement motivation, 387–392
biological factors, 368–370
cognitive influences, 370
of creative persons, 312
cultural influences, 371
definition of, 368
and emotion, 393
environmental influences, 370–371
evolutionary psychology approach, 370
extrinsic motivation, 388–389
hierarchy of motives, 371–372
and incentives, 370–371
and instincts, 368–369
intrinsic motivation, 388–389
issues in study of, 372
needs and drives, 369
and problem solving, 261–262
Motor development
childhood, 330
infant, 328–329
Motor functions, 84–85
Movement aftereffects, 136
Müller-Lyer illusion, 137
Multiaxial system, DSM-IV, 453
Multiple-factor theory, 295
Myelin sheath, 73, 78

Narcissistic personality disorder, 472
Narcolepsy, 162
Nardil, 505
National Committee for Mental Hygiene, 481
National Population Health Survey (1996-7), 537
Natural selection
meaning of, 6
process of, 68
Naturalistic observation, 42–43

Nature and nurture, 69–70
as developmental issue, 323
influences of parenting, 342
intelligence issue, 299, 301–303
perception, 139–141
The Nature of Things, 19
Need for achievement, definition of, 388
Needs
definition of, 369
in hierarchy of motives, 371
hunger, 372–376
and motivation, 369
sexuality, 379–384
Negative punishment, 202
Negative reinforcement, 197
Negative thoughts, 466
Neglectful parenting, 342
Neocortex, 84–87
association cortex, 86
lobes of, 84
mapping of, 85, 86
sensory and motor functions, 84–85
and sexual activity, 380
Nervous system, 70–72
autonomic nervous system, 72
central nervous system (CNS), 71
functions of, 70–71
parasympathetic nervous system, 72
peripheral nervous system, 71
somatic nervous system, 71–72
sympathetic nervous system, 72
Network theory, 220–230
Neurocognitive deficits, 468
Neuroleptic drugs, 505
Neurons, 72–78
action potential, 75
afferent and efferent nerves, 72–73
dendrites, 329
electrical charge of, 75
functions of, 71
and glial cells, 78
interneurons, 73
and memory, 233–234
neurotransmitters, 76–78
repair mechanisms of, 91, 92
resting potential, 75
structure of, 73–74
synapses, 75, 77
Neuroscience, 86–87, 236
Neurotic, 453
Neuroticism Extraversion Openness Personality Inventory, Revised (NEO-PI-R), 438
Neurotransmitters, 76–78
acetylcholine (ACh), 76, 78
agonist and antagonists of, 78
dopamine, 76, 78
endorphins, 76–77, 78
functions of, 76
GABA (gamma aminobutyric acid), 76, 78
and mood disorders, 466
norepinephrine, 76, 78
serotonin, 76, 78
Newborn preterm infants, 327
Nicotine substitutes, 541
Night terrors, 149, 162
Nightmares, 162
Nobel Prize sperm bank, 301, 302
Noise, 103
Nondeclarative memory, 227
Nonstate theory, 170

Nonverbal communication of emotions, 401
Norepinephrine
functions of, 96, 397
and mood disorders, 466
Normal distribution, 291
Normative social influence, 561–562
Norms
group behavior, 565
standardized tests, 290
Nose, 124
Not criminally responsible on account of mental disorder, 449
Note-taking, 247–248
Nucleus, 80
Nurture, 69
Nutrition, 540

Obedience, 562–565, 562–585
definition of, 562
Milgram experiment, 562–564
negative aspects of, 562
resisting social influence, 564–565
Obesity, 376–377
and basal metabolism rate (BMR), 377
costs related to, 376
environmental influences, 377
genetic factors, 376
and set point, 376–377
Object permanence, 332–333
Observation, 40–43
Observation systematic approach, 40
Observational learning, 207–208
of aggression, 36–37, 208, 579
in animals, 207
as basis of learning, 8–9
definition of, 207
process of, 207–208
Obsessive-compulsive disorder, 458, 472, 494
Occipital lobe, 84, 110
Occupational therapist, 483
Oedipus complex, 418
Olfactory epithelium, 124
Operant, 195
Operant conditioning, 194–205
applications. *See* Operant conditioning methods
definition of, 195
discrimination, 201
extinction, 201
generalization, 201
intraspecies view, 197–198
law of effect, 195–196
punishment, 201–203
reinforcement, 196–197, 198–199
schedules of reinforcement, 199–201
shaping, 198
Skinner's experiment, 196, 197–198
time interval in, 198
Operant conditioning methods
behaviour modification, 202–205, 493
self-control program, 200, 205
time-out, 202–203
token economy, 493
Operational definition, 35–36
Operations, 333

Opiates, 173–174
Opium, 76–77
Opponent pairs, 113
Opponent-process theory, 113–114
Optimism, 531
Oral stage, 417
Organ implantation, 91, 93
Organ of Corti, 118
Organic retardation, 308
Organization of Behaviour, 11
Orgasm, 383
Outer ear, 118
Outlining, 248
Overcompensation, 421
Overconfidence bias, 265–266
Overload, 523

P

Pain, 121–122
   and acupuncture, 122
   gate-control theory, 122, 123
   phantom limb, 122
   sensation of, 121–122, 123
Panic disorder, 456–457, 494
Papillae, 122–123
Paranoid personality disorder, 472
Paranoid schizophrenia, 469
Parapsychology, 141–143
Parasympathetic nervous system
   and arousal, 394
   functions of, 72
Parenting, 341–345
   father's role, 345
   mother's role, 342–343
   nature and nurture, 342
   reciprocal socialization, 342
Parenting styles, 341–342
   authoritarian parenting, 341
   authoritative parenting, 341–342
   indulgent parenting, 342
   neglectful parenting, 342
Parietal lobe, 84
Parkinson's disease, 93
Partial reinforcement, 199
Passive-aggressive personality disorder, 472
Pastoral counselor, 483
Pathological gambling, 494
Pavlov, Ivan, 8
Pavlov's experiment, 187–188, 189
   see also Classical conditioning
Paxil, 505
Penis envy, 418–419
Perception
   attention, 128–129
   cross-cultural factors, 141
   definition of, 102
   depth perception, 130–133
   ecological approach, 139
   extrasensory perception, 141, 142–143
   and illusions, 137–139
   information-processing approach, 139
   motion perception, 136
   nature and nurture, 139–141
   perceptual constancy, 136
   shape perception, 129–130
Perceptual constancy, 136
   brightness constancy, 136
   shape constancy, 136, 137
   size constancy, 136, 137

Performance
   achievement-oriented. *See* Achievement motivation
   and arousal, 394
Peripheral nervous system, 71–72
Person-centered therapy, 489–490
Personal/group discrimination discrepancy, 572
Personality, 412
Personality assessment
   cognitive assessment in, 439
   Hogan Personality Inventory, 438
   Minnesota Multiphasic Personality Inventory (MMPI), 437–438
   Neuroticism Extraversion Openness Personality Inventory, 438
   Rorschach Inkblot Test, 435
   Thematic Apperception Test (TAT), 435–436
   themes in, 434
Personality disorders, 472–474
   antisocial, 472, 473–474
   avoidant, 472
   borderline, 472
   clusters of, 472
   dependent, 472
   histrionic, 472
   narcissistic, 472
   obsessive-compulsive, 472
   paranoid, 472
   passive-aggressive, 472
   schizoid, 472
   schizotypal, 472
Personality psychology, 27
Personality Research Form (PRF), 434, 438
Personality theories
   Adler's theory, 420–421
   comparison of theories, 439–442
   Freud's theory, 413–419
   Horney's theory, 419–420
   Jung's theory, 420
   self-esteem concept, 427–429
   Skinner's theory, 423–424
   social cognitive theory, 424–425
   trait-situation interaction, 432–433
   trait theories, 429–432
Personality traits
   big five traits, 431
   cardinal traits, 431
   central traits, 431
   of hardy personality, 522
   introversion-extraversion dimension, 431
   psychoticism, 431
   secondary traits, 431
   stable-unstable dimension, 431
   of Type A behavior pattern, 521
   of Type B behavior pattern, 521
Pessimism, 530
Phallic stage, 418
Phantom limb pain, 122
Phenotype, 67
Pheromones, 381
Philosophy, 6
Phobia
   and antianxiety drugs, 505
   classical conditioning of, 192
   definition of, 192
   systematic desensitization treatment, 492, 505
Phobic disorder, 457–458
Phonology, 268
Physical attraction, 584–585

Physical dependence to psychoactive drugs, 172
Physical development, 328–330
   adolescence, 346
   early adulthood, 352
   early childhood, 330
   infancy, 328–329
   late adulthood, 353–354
   middle/late adulthood, 352–353
   middle/late childhood, 330
Physiological research, 44–45
Piaget's theory, 331–336
   accommodation in, 331
   assimilation in, 331
   concrete operational stage, 334–335
   evaluation of, 335–336
   formal operational stage, 335, 346
   preoperational stage, 333–334
   schema in, 331
   sensorimotor stage, 332–333
Pitch, 116–117
Pituitary gland, 95–96
Place theory of hearing, 118–120
Placebo effect, 49
Plasticity, 91–92
Plateau phase, 382–383
Play, 330
Pleasure principle, 415
Polygraph, 394, 395
Pons, 80
Ponzo illusion, 137, 138
Population, 38
Positive outlook, 530
Positive punishment, 202
Positive reinforcement
   process of, 196
   vs. punishment, 203
Positron-emission tomography (PET scan), 94
Post-traumatic stress disorder, 458–459
   symptoms of, 241, 459
   vulnerability to, 459
Postconventional development, 348
Poverty
   and schizophrenia, 470
   stress from, 526
PQ4R method, 248
Precognition, 142
Preconventional level, 347
Predictive validity, 289
Prefrontal lobotomy, 507–508
Prejudice, 569–570
Prenatal period, 325–328
   stages of, 325–326
   teratogens, effects on fetus, 326
   time span of, 321, 322
Preoperational stage, 333–334
   conservation, 333
   egocentrism, 333–334
   operations in, 333
Preparedness, 210
Presbyopia, 108
Preterm infants
   gestational age of, 327
   massage/touch for, 327
Prevention levels, 178–179
Primacy effect
   impression formation, 554
   memory retrieval, 237
Primary appraisal, 522–523
Primary prevention, 178
Primary reinforcement, 198
Priming, 238
Proactive interference, 243

Problem-focused coping, 528
Problem solving, 258–262
Procedural memory, 227
Project Spectrum, 297
Projection, 416
Projective tests
   Rorschach Inkblot Test, 435
   Thematic Apperception Test (TAT), 435–436
Prototype
   impression formation, 554
   matching, 258
Proximity, 130, 131
Prozac, 505
Psychiatric nurses, 483
Psychiatry
   study of, 25
   training of psychiatrists, 483
Psychoactive drugs, 170–180
   see also Drug abuse
   actions of, 170–171
   attraction of, 171
   dangers of, 171–172
   depressant drugs, 172–174
   hallucinogens, 175
   physical dependence on, 172
   psychological dependence, 172
   stimulant drugs, 174–175
   tolerance to, 172
Psychoanalysis, 484–487
   catharsis, 486
   dream analysis, 164, 413, 487
   free association, 486
   interpretation, 486–487
   resistance, 487
   transference, 487
Psychoanalytic theories
   Adler's theory, 420–421
   basis of, 413
   Erikson's theory, 10
   evaluation of, 421–422
   Freud's theory, 10–11, 413–419
   Horney's theory, 419–420
   Jung's theory, 420
Psychodynamic therapies, 484–489
   Freud's psychoanalysis, 484–487
   modern therapies, 488–489
   short-term nature of, 488
Psychokinesis, 142
Psychological dependence to psychoactive drugs, 172
Psychological information
   evaluation of information, factors in, 58–59
   media presentation of, 57–58
   research journals, 56–57
Psychologists, 4
Psychology
   behavioral neuroscience, 25
   careers in, 24
   clinical/counseling psychology, 24–25, 26
   community psychology, 25
   controversial topics in, 21
   cross-cultural psychology, 27
   definition of, 5
   developmental psychology, 27
   forensic psychology, 27
   health psychology, 27
   history of. *See* History of psychology
   industrial/organizational psychology, 26, 27
   personality psychology, 27
   school/educational psychology, 27
   science of, 5, 20–21

social psychology, 27
sports psychology, 28
women, study of, 27
Psychology experimental psychology, 25
Psychoneuroimmunology, 519–521
Psychopaths, 473
Psychophysics, 102
Psychosexual stages. *See* Freud's theory
Psychosocial stages. *See* Erikson's theory
Psychosurgery, 507–508
Psychotherapy
behavior therapies, 491–493
effectiveness, research on, 501–502
and ethnic minorities, 504
finding professional help, guidelines for, 503
gender issues, 502, 504
group therapies, 497–500
historical view, 480–481
humanistic therapies, 489–491
psychodynamic therapies, 484–489
therapeutic relationship, 502
therapy integrations, 509
Psychotherapy cognitive therapies, 494–497
Psychotic, 453
Psychoticism, 431
Puberty, 346
Punishment, 201–203
aversive stimuli, avoiding, 203
positive and negative, 202
vs. reinforcement, 202
time-out, 202–203
Pupil of eye, 107

Questionnaires for research, 43

Random assignment, 46
Random sample, 38
Rapport talk, 588
Rational-emotive behavior therapy, 494
Rationalization, 416
Raven Progressive Matrices Test, 305
Reaction formation, 416
Reading
basic-skills-and-phonetics approach, 275
whole language approach, 275
Reality principle, 415
Reasoning, 263–264
analogy, 263–264
deductive reasoning, 264
definition of, 263
inductive reasoning, 263
Recall, 238
Recency effect, 237
Recessive genes, 66
Reciprocal socialization, 342
Recognition, 238
Reflexes
and classical conditioning, 187–188
infant, 328–329
nature of, 187

Regression, 416
Rehearsal, 219–220, 226
Reinforcement, 196–197, 198–199
negative reinforcement, 197
and observational learning, 207–208
positive reinforcement, 196
primary reinforcement, 198
secondary reinforcement, 198–199
time factors. *See* Schedules of reinforcement
token reinforcer, 199
Relationships
attraction, 584–585
gender differences, 586, 588
love, 585–586
Reliability of tests, 288–289
definition of, 288
split-half reliability, 288–289
test-retest reliability, 288
Religion
and altered states of consciousness, 153
and behavior, 19–20
REM sleep, 157–158
Report talk, 588
Repository for Germinal Choice, 302
Representativeness heuristic, decision making, 266–267
Repression
defense mechanism, 416
repressed memory, 241–242
Research journals, 56–57
Research methods
case studies, 43–44
correlational research, 45–46
ethics and values. *See* Ethics
experimental research, 46–49
interviews, 43
observation, 40–43
physiological research, 44–45
questionnaires, 43
standardized tests, 44
Research participation bias, 49
Resistance, 487
Respository for Germinal Choice, 301, 302
Resting potential, 75
Restrained eating, 377
Retention, 207
Reticular formation, 80
Retina, 107–109
Retroactive interference, 243
Retrograde amnesia, 244
Risk-taking, 312
Rods of eye, 108–110
Roger's theory, 425–427
basis of, 10
fully functioning person, 426–427
person-centered therapy, 489–490
self-concept, 426
unconditional and conditional positive regard, 426
Role-playing, 491
Roles, 565
Romantic love, 585
Rorschach Inkblot Test, 435
Rote rehearsal, 219–220

Sample, 38
Saturation, 111

Schedules of reinforcement, 199–201
continuous reinforcement, 199
fixed-interval schedule, 199–200
fixed-ratio schedule, 199
partial reinforcement, 199
variable-ratio schedule, 199, 201
Schema
definition of, 230
and impression formation, 553–554
in Piaget's theory, 331
schema theory of memory, 230–231, 233
Schizoid personality disorder, 472
Schizophrenia, 467–472
antipsychotic drugs, 505–506
and brain, 469–471
catatonic schizophrenia, 469
cultural factors, 470
definition of, 467
diathesis-stress model, 470
disorganized schizophrenia, 469
genetic factors, 469
neurocognitive deficits, 468
paranoid schizophrenia, 469
symptoms of, 468–469
undifferentiated schizophrenia, 469
Schizotypal personality disorder, 472
Scholastic Aptitude Test (SAT), 294
School/educational psychology, 27, 483
School violence, 3–4
Science of psychology, 5, 20–21
Scientific method
conception of problem in, 35–36
data collection, 36
definition of, 35
drawing conclusions, 36–37
population in, 38
random sample, 38
sample in, 38
Scientific method theory, 36
Scientific research, 34
Sclera of eye, 107
Scripts
memory, 233
sexual scripts, 382
Seasonal affective disorder (SAD), 155
Secondary appraisal, 522–523
Secondary personality traits, 431
Secondary prevention, 178–179
Secondary reinforcement, 198–199
Secure attachment, 340
Selective attention, 128–129
Selective serotonin reuptake inhibitors (SSRI), 505
Self-actualization
characteristics of self-actualizers, 428
definition of, 372, 427
Maslow's theory, 372, 427
Roger's theory, 426–427
Self-concept, 426
Self-control
and anger, 405
behavior modification program, 205
and hunger, 376
immediate/delayed consequences, effects of, 200
Self-efficacy
and coping, 532
definition of, 532
increasing, 532
meaning of, 424

Self-esteem, 427–428
definition of, 427
and illusion, 530
improvement of, 428–429
research issues, 427–428
Self-help support groups, 499–500
Self-image, 572
Self-instruction techniques, 491–492, 493
Self-monitoring
and impression management, 556
self-test, 556
Self-perception theory, 558–559
Self-reports, 436–439
construction of, 436
evaluation of, 439
Hogan Personality Inventory, 438
Minnesota Multiphasic Personality Inventory (MMPI), 437–438
Neuroticism Extraversion Openness Personality Inventory, 438
Self-serving bias, 552
Self-statements, 529–530
Semantic memory, 228
Semantics, 268–269
Semicircular canals, and kinesthesia, 126
Sensation
absolute threshold, 102–103
auditory system, 116–120
chemical senses, 122–125
definition of, 102
difference threshold, 103, 105
kinesthetic senses, 125–126
and neocortex, 84–85
and noise, 103
sensory adaptation, 110–111
signal detection theory, 105
skin senses, 120–122
study of, 102
vestibular senses, 125–126
visual system, 106–115
Weber's law, 105
Sensation seeking, 369
Sensorimotor stage, 332–333
Sensory adaptation, 110–111
Sensory factors, 381
Sensory memory, 224–225
Separation, 526
Serial position effect, 237
Serotonin
functions of, 68, 76
and mood disorders, 466
Set point, 376–377
Seven-intelligences theory, 295–297
Sex, 13–14
Sex hormones, 380
Sexual dysfunction, 383–384
Sexual orientation
bisexuality, 385
heterosexuality, 384–385
homosexuality, 385–387
Sexual response, 382–384
dysfunction of, 383–384
phases of, 382–383
Sexual scripts, 382
Sexuality, 379–384
biological influences, 380
cognitive influences, 380–381
contraception, 542–543
cultural influences, 382
sensory factors, 381
sexual knowledge, 542
sexual scripts, 382

Sexually transmitted disease (STD), 543–544
    AIDS, 543–544
    prevention guidelines, 544
    sexuality, myths/realities about, 542
Shadow archetype, 420
Shape constancy, 136, 137
Shape perception, 129–130
    figure-ground relationship, 129
    Gestalt psychology, 129–130
Shaping, 198
Shift workers, 155
Sign language, 276
Signal detection theory, 105
Similarity
    and attraction, 584
    Gestalt principle, 130, 131
Single-parent mother-headed households, 343, 526
Singlehood, 357–358
Situationism, 432–433
Size constancy, 136, 137
Skin senses, 120–122
    pain, 121–122
    temperature, 121
    touch, 121
Skinner, B.F.
    see also Operant conditioning
    behaviorism of, 8
    personality development, 423–424
    Skinner's experiment, 196, 197–198
Sleep, 154–159
    alpha waves, 157
    and brain, 159
    changes over life span, 158
    and circadian rhythms, 154–156
    delta waves, 157
    deprivation effects, 156
    dreams, 164–167
    and learning, 160
    REM sleep, 157–158
    sleep needs, 156
    stages of, 156–159
Sleep apnea, 162–163
Sleep disorders, 159–163
    insomnia, 161
    narcolepsy, 162
    night terrors, 149, 162
    nightmares, 162
    sleep apnea, 162–163
    sleep talking, 162
    sleepwalking, 161
Sleep research, 156–157
Sleep talking, 162
Sleep/Wake Disorders Canada, 159
Sleepwalking, 161
Slow-to-warm-up child, 341
Smell, 124–125
Social clocks, 359
Social cognitive theory
    aggression reduction, 580
    basis of, 8
    evaluation of, 425
    personality development, 424–425
Social comparison, 554–555
Social desirability
    definition of, 43
    and research interviewees, 43
    self-reports, 436
Social facilitation, 566
Social identity theory, 571–572
Social influences
    on behavior, 19
    conformity, 559, 561–562

on conformity, 561–562
    ethnic and cultural conflict. See Interethnic relations
    group influence, 565–569
    obedience, 562–565
    resistance to, 564–565
Social interaction
    aggression, 576–580
    altruism, 580–584
    attraction, 584–585
    loneliness, 588–589
    love, 585–586
Social loafing, 566
Social psychology, 27
Social Readjustment Rating Scale, 524–525
Social support, 532–533
Social thinking, 550–559
    attitudes, 556–559
    attribution, 550–552
    impression formation, 553–554
    impression management, 555–556
    social comparison, 554–555
Social workers, 483
Sociocultural approach
    elements of, 12–14
    Horney's theory, 419–420
Socioeconomic status
    and achievement motivation, 392
    poverty and stress, 526
Socioemotional development, 336–345
    attachment, 339–340
    early adulthood, 338, 356, 358
    Erikson's theory, 336–339
    late adulthood, 359–360
    middle/late adulthood, 356–359
    and parenting, 341–345
    temperament, 341
Socioemotional processes, in development, 320–321
Sociopaths, 473
Somatic nervous system, 71–72
Somatoform disorders, 459–460
    conversion disorder, 460
    hypochondriasis, 459
Somnambulism, 161
SOMPA (System of Mulitcultural Pluralistic Assessment), 305–306
Sound, 116–118
Spanking, 203, 211–212
Spatial cognition, 208
Special process theory, 168–169
Split-half reliability, 288–289
Spontaneous recovery, 188, 190
Sports psychology, 28
Stability, 431
Standardized tests
    features of, 44
    intelligence tests, 290
    norms, 290
    pros/cons of, 44
Stanford-Binet intelligence test, 44
Stereogram, 132
Stereopsis, 131
Stereotypes, 570
Stimulants, 174–175
    amphetamines, 174
    caffeine, 174
    cocaine, 174
    definition of, 174
    dependence, risk factors, 177
    effects of, 176
    medical uses, 176
    overdose, signs of, 177

Stimulus
    control, smoking cessation method, 541–542
    response criterion, 105
    sensitivity to, 105
    substitution, in classical conditioning, 191
Stomach contractions, 373–374
Storm-and-stress view, 345
Stream of consciousness, 150
Stress, 517–527
    see also Coping
    assessment scale for, 524–525
    and burnout, 523
    cognitive influences, 522–523
    and conflicts, 523–524
    cultural influences, 525–526
    and daily hassles, 525
    definition of, 517–518
    and depression, 517
    environmental influences, 523–525
    eustress, 518–519
    and frustration, 524
    general adaptation syndrome (GAS), 518–519
    hardiness, 522
    hormonal response to, 96
    and hypothalamus, 83
    and life events, 524–525
    and personality type, 521–522
    physiological response to, 518–519
    psychoneuroimmunology, 519–521
    and socioeconomic factors, 526
Stress management methods, 534–536
    biofeedback, 536
    goals of, 535
    meditation, 535–536
Stroboscopic motion, 136
Stroop effect, 128, 129
Structuralism, 7
Study strategies. See Memory strategies
Sublimation, 416
Subliminal perception, 104
Suicide, 464, 465
Superego, 415
Superior colliculus, 80
Superiority, 420–421
Superiority complex, 421
Supernatural, 23
Supreme Court of Canada, 395
Symbolic beliefs, 570
Sympathetic nervous system
    and arousal, 393–394
    functions of, 72
Synapses, 75, 77
Syntax, 268
Systematic desensitization, 492

T

Tardive dyskinesia, 505–506
Taste, 122, 124
Taste aversion, 210
Telegraphic speech, 272–273
Telepathy, 142
Television viewing, 45–47, 579
Temperament, 341
Temperature
    sensation of, 121
    sensitivity to, 82–83
Temporal contiguity, 188

Temporal lobe, 84
Teratogens, 326
Tertiary prevention, 179
Test-retest reliability, 288
Testosterone, 346
Thalamus, 82
Thanatos, 576
Thatcher illusion, 139
Thematic Apperception Test (TAT), 435–436
Theory, 36
Therapeutic relationship, 502
Therapy integrations, 509
Thinking, 256–267
    concepts, 256–258
    critical thinking, 262–263
    decision making, 264–267
    definition of, 256
    problem solving, 258–262
    reasoning, 263–264
Third force, 10, 427
Third International Mathematics and Science Study, 391
Thorndike's experiment, 195–196
Timbre, 117–118
Time frames, 223–227
Time management, 247
Time-out, 202–203
Tip-of-the-tongue phenomenon, 235, 237
Toddlers, 270, 272
Token economy, 493
Token reinforcer, 199
Tolerance to drugs, 172
Tongue, 122–124
Touch, 121
Trait-situation interaction, 432–433
Trait theories, 429–432
    see also Personality traits
    Allport's theory, 430–431
    basis of, 429
    big five factors of personality concept, 431–432
    criticism of, 432
    Eysenck's theory, 431
Tranquilizers, 173
Transcendental meditation (TM), 535
Transduction, 108
Transference, 487
Traumatic memory, 241
Trephining, 480
Triangular theory of love, 586
Triarchic theory, 298–299
Trichromatic theory, 112
Trichromats, 113
Tricyclic antidepressants, 505
Trust vs. mistrust, 337
Twin studies, 65–66
Two-factor theory
    emotion, 397–398
    intelligence, 295
Type A behavior pattern, 521
Type B behavior pattern, 521

U

Uncertainty orientation, 259
Unconditional positive regard, 426, 490
Unconditioned response (UR), 187–188, 189
Unconditioned stimulus (US), 187, 189, 190, 191, 193

Unconscious
 Freud's view, 150, 413, 486–487
 Jung's theory, 420
Undifferentiated schizophrenia, 469
University students
 altruism of, 583
 romantic love and, 585

Validity of tests, 289
 concurrent validity, 289
 content validity, 289
 criterion validity, 289
 definition of, 289
 predictive validity, 289
Valium, 505
Values of psychologist, 53, 54
Variable-ratio reinforcement schedule,
 199, 201
Variables, 46
Vestibular senses, 125–126
Viagra, 383–384
Video games, 579
Violence
 see also Aggression
 and alcohol use, 577

media, 579
 predictors of, 4
 school violence, 3–4
 television viewing, 45–47, 579
 video games, 579
Virtual environments, 126
Visual attention, 80
Visual cliff, 139–140
Visual cortex, 110
Visual disparity, 131
Visual system, 106–115
 see also Eye
 adaptation of, 110–111
 and brain, 84, 110
 color vision, 111–114
 dark adapt, 110
 and eye, 107–110
 and light, 106–107
 light adapt, 111
 opponent pairs, 113
Volley principle, 120

Walden Two (Skinner), 198
Wavelength, 106–107, 116
Weber's law, 105

Wechsler scales
 intelligence tests, 292
 subscales, 293
 Wechsler Adult Intelligence
  Scale - Revised (WAIS-R),
  44, 292
 Wechsler Intelligence Scale
  for Children-III (WISC-III),
  292
 Wechsler Preschool and
  Primary Scale of Intelligence
  (WPPSI), 292
Wernicke-Geschwind model, 87
Wernicke's area, 87
Wheel model, 402, 403
Whole language approach, 275
Widows and widowers, 361–362
Wild child, 273–274
Windigo, 451
Wisdom and aging, 356
Wish fulfillment, 164
Withdrawal, 178
Women
 see also Gender differences
 psychology of, 27
 and psychotherapy, 504
Women in Psychology (SWAP),
 27
Working memory, 225–226
Wundt, Wilhelm, 6–7

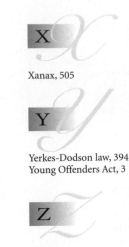

Xanax, 505

Yerkes-Dodson law, 394
Young Offenders Act, 3

Zeitgebers, 155
Zoloft, 505
Zygote, 325